IMPORTANT

HERE IS YOUR REGISTRATION CODE TO ACCESS MCGRAW-HILL PREMIUM CONTENT AND MCGRAW-HILL ONLINE RESOURCES

For key premium online resources you need THIS CODE to gain access. Once the code is entered, you will be able to use the web resources for the length of your course.

Access is provided only if you have purchased a new book.

If the registration code is missing from this book, the registration screen on our website, and within your WebCT or Blackboard course will tell you how to obtain your new code. Your registration code can be used only once to establish access. It is not transferable

To gain access to these online resources

1. **USE** your web browser to go to: **www.mhhe.com/brown11e**

2. **CLICK** on "First Time User"

3. **ENTER** the Registration Code printed on the tear-off bookmark on the right

4. After you have entered your registration code, click on "Register"

5. **FOLLOW** the instructions to setup your personal UserID and Password

6. **WRITE** your UserID and Password down for future reference. Keep it in a safe place.

If your course is using WebCT or Blackboard, you'll be able to use this code to access the McGraw-Hill content within your instructor's online course.

To gain access to the McGraw-Hill content in your instructor's WebCT or Blackboard course simply log into the course with the user ID and Password provided by your instructor. Enter the registration code exactly as it appears to the right when prompted by the system. You will only need to use this code the first time you click on McGraw-Hill content.

These instructions are specifically for student access. Instructors are not required to register via the above instructions.

Thank you, and welcome to your McGraw-Hill/Irwin Online Resources.

Brown/Sukys
Business Law with UCC Applications, 11E
0-07-296066-3

REGISTRATION CODE

2JX7-SUV6-6S00-I6L0-39M2

Business Law

With UCC Applications

ELEVENTH EDITION

Gordon W. Brown

PROFESSOR EMERITUS
NORTH SHORE COMMUNITY COLLEGE
DANVERS, MASSACHUSETTS

Paul A. Sukys

PROFESSOR OF LAW AND LEGAL STUDIES
NORTH CENTRAL STATE COLLEGE
MANSFIELD, OHIO

McGraw-Hill Irwin

Boston   Burr Ridge, IL   Dubuque, IA   Madison, WI   New York   San Francisco   St. Louis
Bangkok   Bogotá   Caracas   Kuala Lumpur   Lisbon   London   Madrid   Mexico City
Milan   Montreal   New Delhi   Santiago   Seoul   Singapore   Sydney   Taipei   Toronto

Answer Key

Part 1 Ethics, Law, and the Judicial System

Chapter 1 Ethics

Questions for Analysis Page 19

1. The question of whether a corporation should pursue short-range profits or long-term gains based on risk taking is open to various answers. Accept all well-reasoned responses.

2. The question of whether a corporation should trade the interests of the shareholders for the best interests of the country is open to various answers. Accept all well-reasoned responses.

3. The question of whether a corporation should be compelled by legislation to focus on national issues rather than corporate goals is open to various answers. Accept all well-reasoned responses.

4. The question of whether politicians should build election campaigns based on a change in corporate responsibility is open to various answers. Accept all well-reasoned responses.

5. The question of whether America's immigration regulations should promote an influx of international students or protect American students is open to various answers. Accept all well-reasoned responses.

Questions for Review and Discussion Page 21

1. The law consists of rules of conduct established by the government of a society to maintain harmony, stability, and justice. Morality involves the values that govern a society's attitude toward right and wrong.

2. Values form the basic foundation for moral judgments. Ethics, in contrast, attempts to develop a means for determining what those values ought to be and for formulating and applying rules in line with those values.

3. Ethical relativism holds that there are no fixed or stable standards of right and wrong.

4. Social contract theory holds that right and wrong are measured by the obligations imposed on each individual by an implied social agreement.

5. The steps in applying utilitarianism follow: (1) The action to be evaluated should be stated in nonemotional, general terms; (2) every person or class of people who will be affected by the action must be identified; (3) good and bad consequences in the relation to those people affected must be considered; (4) all alternatives to the action stated in step 1 must be considered; and (5) a conclusion must be reached.

6. The first principle of rational ethics is the Golden Rule. The second principle states that as rational beings people realize that it is logical to establish rules that support the continued existence of society. A rule that destroys a society which tries to follow it would be an illogical rule.

7. The ethical character traits generally reflected in role model ethics are honesty, compassion, fairness, and integrity.

8. Corporations owe society a level of responsibility because the government has granted certain legal advantages to corporations. Another reason for expecting socially responsible decisions from corporate executives is that corporations have a great deal of power in the economic structure and with power comes responsibility. Finally, corporations should act responsibly because it is in their own best interest to do so.

9. Our society needs law and the legal system to give it structure, harmony, predictability, and justice.

10. Harmony is established between law and ethics when laws are based on ethical principles.

Cases for Analysis Page 21

Special Directions to the Instructor: It is virtually impossible to predict the wide variety of answers that students will provide for the ethical cases outlined at the end of Chapter 1. Therefore, the instructor should not be looking for "right" and "wrong" answers in the conventional sense. Instead the instructor should look to see that the ethical character traits theories are applied correctly and consistently.

Chapter 2 Sources of the Law

Questions for Analysis Page 40

1. The author indicates that Americans believe in the ideal of democracy but dislike politicians and politics.

2. According to the author the primary factor that shapes American politics is money.

3. The author says that America is not "strictly speaking" a democracy because the U.S. Constitution is designed to prevent the uncontrolled exercise of the will of the people.

4. The wave of discontentment with politics has been with the American system since it first started.

5. Specifically, by the doctrine of "minority rule," the author is referring to the fact that the smallest states in the Union can control a majority of votes in the Senate.

Questions for Review and Discussion Page 42

1. The law consists of rules of conduct established by the government to maintain harmony, stability, and justice

within a society. Ideally, the two primary objectives of the law are to promote justice and harmony.

2. The law, or more properly, the entire legal framework, is a complex adaptive system exhibiting each of the five attributes of such systems. First, the law functions as a complex adaptive system because of the interaction of a variety of agents within the legal system; second, as in all complex adaptive systems, in the law there is no central controlling agent; third, the law is an intricate network of interactive organizational levels, each of which depends on the others for the smooth operation of the entire network; fourth, the more proficient the law becomes, the more easily it adapts to changing social, political, and economic influences; and fifth, the legal system includes embedded niches each of which is populated by experts upon whom others, outside those niches, depend and who, in turn, depend on others for knowledge and guidance outside their own embedded niche.

3. The articles establish the organization of the national government. The first three of the seven articles distribute the power of the government among the legislative, executive, and judicial branches. Article I establishes Congress as the legislative (statute-making) branch of the government. Article II gives the executive power to the President, and Article III gives judicial power to the Supreme Court and other courts established by Congress. Article IV explains the relationships among the states, while Article V outlines the methods for amending the Constitution. Article VI establishes the U.S. Constitution, federal laws, and treaties as the supreme law of the land. Finally, Article VII outlines how the original thirteen states would go about ratifying the new Constitution. The amendments change provisions in the original articles and add ideas that the founding fathers did not include in those articles.

   The amendments to the Constitution establish the rights that belong to the people, change some of the provisions in the original articles, and add ideas that the Founding Fathers did not include in those articles. Thus, the amendments are attempts to "fine-tune" the Constitution and to update its provisions to meet the demands of a changing socioeconomic structure. The U.S. Constitution has twenty-six amendments. The first ten make up the Bill of Rights and were added soon after the ratification of the Constitution by the original thirteen states. Other amendments that secure the rights of the people include the Thirteenth, which abolished slavery; the Fourteenth which guaranteed equal protection of the law and due process; the Fifteenth, which guaranteed voting rights; the Nineteenth, which extended voting rights to women; the Twenty-fourth, which outlawed poll taxes, and the Twenty-sixth, which extended the right to vote to eighteen-year-old citizens.

4. The laws passed by a legislature are known as statutes. At the federal level these are the laws made by Congress and signed by the President. At the state level, statutes are enacted by state legislatures such as the Ohio General Assembly or the Oregon Legislative Assembly. Many statutes prohibit certain activities. Most criminal statutes are prohibitive statutes. Other statutes demand the performance of some action. Some statutes, such as those which create governmental holidays or which name the state flower, simply declare something.

5. Because many different statutes are passed each year by the fifty state legislatures, there are important differences in state statutory law throughout the nation. This lack of similarity can cause problems when people from different states must deal with one another. One solution to the problem is the creation of uniform state laws. The National Conference of Commissioners on Uniform State Laws (NCCUSL) was founded to write these uniform laws.

6. The Uniform Computer Information Transaction Act and the Uniform Electronic Transaction Act are two cyberlaw statutes recently approved by the commissioners for adoption by state legislatures.

7. The term common law comes from the attempts of the early English kings to establish a body of law that all the courts in the kingdom would hold in common. At that time judges were sent out to the towns and villages of the kingdom with instructions to settle all disputes in as consistent a manner as possible. The judges maintained this consistency by relying on previous legal decisions whenever they faced a similar set of circumstances. In this way they began to establish this body of common law. As the process continued, judges began to write down their decisions and to share their decisions with other judges. This body of recorded decisions became known as the common law.

8. The process of relying on these previous decisions is known as *stare decisis* ("let the decision stand"). The past decisions themselves are called precedents. Although today's judges do not ride around on horseback, they do make decisions in the same way as their counterparts from the Middle Ages. They rely on precedent according to the principle of *stare decisis*. A precedent is a model case that a court can follow when facing a similar situation. There are two types of precedent, binding and persuasive. Binding precedent is a previous case that a certain court must follow. Persuasive precedent is precedent that a court is free to follow or to ignore. Generally, whether a precedent is binding or persuasive is determined by the court's location. For instance, decisions made by the Ohio Supreme Court would be binding on all Ohio state courts but persuasive for courts in all other states' courts.

9. A second way that court decisions operate to make law is in the interpretation of statutes. When legislators enact a new statute, they cannot predict how people will react to the new law. Nor can they foresee all the ramifications and implications of that new statute. Thus, when two or more parties have a dispute that

impacts on a statute, they may differ as to what the legislature had in mind when it wrote the statute. Also, legislators may leave gaps in the language of a statute. Those gaps must be filled by someone. The job of reacting to unforeseen circumstances and filling in the gaps falls to the courts. As a result a judge may be called upon to determine how a certain statute should be interpreted. A third way that courts make law is through judicial review. Judicial review is the process of determining the constitutionality of various legislative statutes, administrative regulations, or executive actions. In exercising the power of judicial review, a court will look at the statute, regulation, or action and will compare it with the Constitution. If the two are compatible, no problem exists. However, if they are not compatible, one of the two must be declared void. Since the Constitution is the supreme law of the land, the Constitution always rules, and the statute, regulation, or action must be ruled unconstitutional.

10. Neither legislators nor judges can deal with all aspects of today's society. Moreover, legislators are generalists. They know a little about a lot, but are rarely experts in all areas over which they have power. Since legislators are generalists, and because today's problems are so complex, statutory law created by the legislators is very limited in what it can do. To broaden the power of statutory law, legislators delegate their power to others. They do this when they create administrative agencies.

Cases for Analysis Page 43

1. The Fourteenth Amendment to the United States Constitution guarantees equal protection of the law and due process. This means that the state government must provide the same protections for its citizens that the federal government guarantees. The First Amendment, therefore, applies to the state government as much as it applies to the federal government. In this case, by calling upon the First Amendment, the school board opened an issue which permitted the court to rule that the school board, as an arm of the state government, could not interfere with the teachers' right to religious observance.

2. In this case, the court chose to protect the social order and to preserve stability, rather than press the free speech rights of a small group of people. The court said it this way, "While the First Amendment protects the rights of citizens to express their viewpoints, however unpopular, it does not guarantee ideal conditions for doing so, since the individual's right to speech must always be balanced against the state's interest in safety, and its right to regulate conduct that it legitimately considers potentially dangerous."

3. Chadha was correct in his argument. While the fact that the Senate did not have to participate in the legislative veto does not violate the separation of powers doctrine, the fact that the President did not have to participate does violate that principle.

4. In reading through the Constitution, students should be able to see that the Equal Protection Clause of the Fourteenth Amendment would guarantee Hogan's right to be admitted to a state-supported educational institution.

5. In interpreting a statute, courts look to a variety of sources. These sources include the legislative history of the statute and the old statute that the new statute replaced, if any. The court must also review any binding precedent that interprets that statute, because the court must rely upon previous cases when engaged in statutory interpretation, just as it does when deciding questions of common law.

6. The lower federal courts do have the authority to determine the constitutionality of federal statutes. This authority would extend to an interpretation of the Civil Rights Act. The United States Supreme Court has ultimate authority in determining the constitutionality of any state or federal statute, including the Civil Rights Act. The United States Supreme Court upheld the constitutionality of the statute. Since so many of the hotel's guests came from out of state, the hotel was engaged in interstate commerce and, thus, was under the regulatory power of Congress, as granted in Article I, Section 8, Clause 3 of the Constitution.

Chapter 3   The Judicial Process

Questions for Analysis Page 51

1. Subject matter jurisdiction is based established in federal district court because the law under scrutiny is a federal statute.

2. It is best to have cases brought in American courts because, compared to foreign systems, American courts are more effective and more efficient.

3. The downside to the influx of foreign-based cases is that American courts will become overburdened and that the U.S. court system may become a world court.

4. The argument stated that subject matter jurisdiction would have been appropriate in federal district court because American antitrust statutes are very powerful. The U.S. Supreme Court ultimately rejected claims that the U.S. courts had jurisdiction.

5. Class action cases must meet a set of requirements detailed in Chapter 2. Have students review these factors and respond accordingly.

Questions for Review and Discussion Page 65

1. A court of original jurisdiction has the authority to hear a case when it is first brought to court. Courts having the power to review a case for errors of law are courts of appellate jurisdiction. Courts having the power to hear any type of case are said to exercise general jurisdiction. Those with the power to hear only certain types of cases have special jurisdiction. Examples of courts with special jurisdiction are probate courts and courts of claims. Courts also exercise subject matter jurisdiction and personal jurisdiction.

2. Each state and territory in the United States has at least one federal district court. Federal district courts are also known as U.S. district courts. The district courts are the courts of general jurisdiction in the federal system. Usually, most federal cases begin in the federal district court. Presently, thirteen U.S. courts of appeals exist within the federal court system. Eleven of these appellate courts cover geographical groupings of states. For example, the Sixth Circuit Court of Appeals includes Michigan, Ohio, Kentucky, and Tennessee, whereas the Fifth Circuit includes Texas, Louisiana, and Mississippi. There is also a special appellate court for the District of Columbia called the U.S. Court of Appeals for the District of Columbia. In addition to these twelve appellate courts, organized on a geographical basis, there is a thirteenth appellate court which has special jurisdiction over certain types of cases. This court is known as the U.S. Court of Appeals for the Federal Circuit. This court hears cases appealed from the Court of International Trade, the U.S. Claims Court, and the International Trade Commission, among others. This court can also hear certain types of appeals from the district courts. Established by the Constitution, the U.S. Supreme Court is the court of final jurisdiction in all cases appealed from the lower federal courts and in cases coming from state supreme courts. It has original jurisdiction in cases affecting ambassadors or other public ministers and consuls, and in cases in which a state is a party. The Supreme Court is composed of a nine justices, one chief justice, and eight associate justices. They are appointed by the President with the consent of the Senate and hold office during good behavior. The federal courts have subject matter jurisdiction over cases involving federal law and cases involving diversity. Federal district courts have subject matter jurisdiction over cases involving a federal question. A federal question could involve the U.S. Constitution, a federal statute or statutes, or a treaty. A state law issue can be included in a suit involving a federal question if the state claim involves the same situation that created the federal question. If the federal claim is thrown out by the federal court, the state law issue usually cannot stand by itself. The people bringing the lawsuit would have to take their case to state court. Subject matter jurisdiction in federal court also arises in cases of diversity, even when no federal law is involved. Diversity cases include lawsuits that are (1) between citizens of different states, (2) between citizens of a state or different states and citizens of a foreign nation, and (3) between citizens of a state and a foreign government as the plaintiff. For legal purposes corporations are considered citizens of the state in which they are incorporated and the state where they have their principal place of business. Diversity cases must involve an amount over $50,000.

3. In many situations, a case will reach the U.S. Supreme Court only if the court agrees to issue a *writ of certiorari*.

A *writ of certiorari* is an order from the Supreme Court to a lower court to deliver its records to the U.S. Supreme Court for review. The Court will issue a *writ of certiorari* if several lower courts have dealt with an issue, but cannot agree on how it should be handled. Often the Court will also hear a case if it involves a constitutional issue. Finally, if the case involves an issue that affects a large segment of society, the Court is likely to grant a writ.

4. Cyberspace jurisdiction falls on a spectrum that includes three types of transactions. On one end of the spectrum are those cybertransactions that clearly involve minimum contacts. These would include cybertransactions carried out from beginning to end on the Internet. On the other end of the spectrum are those cases that can establish that the defendant did nothing more than post a passive advertisement on the Web. Such passive advertisements will usually not establish jurisdiction. The final type of case falls in that vast expanse on the spectrum between the two extremes. These cases concern cybertransactions that involve more than simple passive advertising on the Internet. The courts have not established any single normative approach to such transactions and so the matter is still open to debate. This means that each situation must be handled on a case-by-case basis. Therefore, it is best to check the status of this legal problem on a regular basis.

5. Each state has an arrangement of inferior, or lower, courts that serve as limited jurisdiction courts. Higher-level trial courts with broader jurisdiction are also provided. In addition, each state has appellate courts to which questions of law (not questions of fact) may be appealed. The general jurisdiction trial courts have the power to hear any type of case. It is often called the superior court, the circuit court, or the court of common pleas. These are usually organized around the counties of the state so that each county has its own trial court of general jurisdiction. Most states also have other trial courts that are lower than these general jurisdiction courts. These limited jurisdiction courts usually hear only certain types of cases. For instance, a municipal court may be empowered to hear only those cases that involve municipal ordinances, criminal cases involving crimes within the city limits, and other cases that involve monetary claims of less than $10,000. Many localities have small claims courts that hear civil cases involving small dollar amounts, ranging from $500 to $5,000 depending on state law. State court systems provide for a variety of appellate court structures. Still, the purpose of the appellate courts remains the same; that is to hear appeals on questions of law from the lower courts. Usually, appeals are heard by a three-judge panel. The panel will examine the records of the lower court, read the written arguments submitted by the attorneys, study the law on their own and listen to the oral arguments of the attorneys. If the panel agrees with the lower court it will affirm the decision of that court. However, if the panel

disagrees with the lower court's decision it can set aside or modify the decision of that court. Twenty-seven states rely on their supreme court as their only appellate court. These states have no intermediate appellate courts. The other twenty-three have both the intermediate appellate courts and the state supreme court. Most supreme courts consist of a panel of from three to nine judges. As is true at the intermediate appellate level, the panel of judges will examine the records of the lower court, read the written arguments submitted by the attorneys, study the law on their own, and listen to the oral arguments of the attorneys. The decisions of a state supreme court are final unless a federal issue or a constitutional right is involved.

6. The steps in a lawsuit are as follows: commencement of the action, serving the defendant, the preanswer stage, the answer, the pretrial stage, the trial, the appeal, appellate procedure, and the execution of the judgment.

7. Depositions are oral statements made out of court under oath by witnesses or parties to the action in response to questions from the opposing attorneys. The answers are later recorded by a court stenographer and can be used for later reference. Interrogatories are written questions that must be answered in writing under oath by the opposite party. Interrogatories cannot be given to witnesses. Only plaintiffs and defendants can be required to answer interrogatories.

8. Some law firms today make it a conventional practice to conduct depositions using the Internet. The Internet has also become a tool for videoconferencing about discovery procedures and problems. Some enterprising attorneys and paralegals have also found that the Internet can be used to send and to respond to interrogatories. The use of mobile phones, PDAs, fax machines, and e-mail have all helped make discovery less costly and more effective than it has ever been before. The widespread use of computers in business, government, and education has altered the way that information can be retrieved during discovery. Law firms must, therefore, be ready to change the way that they conduct discovery to ensure that important cyberevidence does not remain hidden because it is produced and stored in cyberspace. This inevitably includes e-mail files, calendering programs, databases, and all other types of cyberrecords. Lawyers must also warn clients to preserve such cyberrecords so that cyberrecords that should have been preserved are not destroyed. Many law firms have decided to employ their own cyberexperts to help them navigate the complex world of cyberspace, cyberrecords, and cyberevidence.

9. An appeal is the referral of a case to a higher court for review. For an appeal to be successful, it must be shown that some legal error occurred. A party could argue that some of the evidence that was admitted should have been excluded or that evidence that was not allowed should have been allowed. A party could also argue that the judge's instructions were erroneous or were

stated in an inappropriate manner. However, it is also possible that the party which prevailed at trial may wish to file an appeal. This is referred to as a cross appeal.

10. The steps in a criminal prosecution include the arrest and initial appearance, the preliminary hearing, the formal charges, the arraignment, and the trial.

Cases for Analysis   Page 65

1. Although the court in the Martha Stewart case ruled to restrict the access that the press had to *voir dire,* it is still an open question. Accept all reasonable answers.

2. The court ruled that the juror's misunderstanding of the question is what prompted her negative answer and that her conduct and the jury's conduct in general revealed no bias against the defendant. Therefore, the jury's verdict stood.

3. This is the type of issue that belongs in U.S. Supreme Court because it involves a constitutional issue. The Supreme Court should uphold the decision of the lower court because the reapportionment plan violates the Equal Protection Clause of the Fourteenth Amendment of the Constitution and the Due Process Clause of the Fifth Amendment of the Constitution.

4. A case involving a dispute over whether computer software can be copyrighted might be heard by the Supreme Court because it would affect a large segment of society; a case involving an appeal of a zoning board's decision to limit the number of adult book stores on any single city block might be heard by the Supreme Court because it would affect First Amendment rights of free speech and freedom of the press; a case involving the constitutionality of an abortion statute might be heard by the Supreme Court because it would affect the constitutional right to privacy; a case involving an antitrust suit based on a violation of a federal antitrust statute between the National Football League and the United States Football League might be heard by the Supreme Court because it would involve an interpretation of an important federal statute; a libel case against a small town newspaper involving allegations of the mayor's dishonesty might be heard by the Supreme Court because it would affect First Amendment rights of freedom of the press; a case involving the placement of a religious scene on city property might be heard by the Supreme Court because it would affect the First Amendment right of freedom of the religion; a case brought by a steel company to enjoin employees from going on strike might be heard by the Supreme Court because it would involve an interpretation of an important federal statute; a case involving the distribution of antiwar flyers at a private shopping mall might be heard by the Supreme Court because it would affect First Amendment rights of free speech and freedom of assembly; a case involving the search of a high school student's locker without her permission might be heard by the Supreme Court because

it would involve the Fourth Amendment protection against unreasonable search and seizure and the Fourteenth Amendment right of equal protection of the law.

5. Yes. The defendants had to submit to the jurisdiction of Ohio under provisions of the state long-arm statute. The court stated, "The complementary provisions of Ohio's 'long-arm' statute . . . authorize the court to exercise personal jurisdiction over a nonresident defendant and provides for service of process to effectuate that jurisdiction when the cause of action arises from the nonresident defendant's '[t]ransacting any business in the state.'" Later the court added, "The term 'transact' as utilized in the phrase '[t]ransacting any business' encompasses '"to carry on business"' and '"to have dealings."'"

6. The U.S. Supreme Court should overturn the decision of the lower court. The right to an attorney is a fundamental right that should be guaranteed by the states. The Sixth Amendment of the Constitution guarantees the right to representation by an attorney. The U.S. Supreme Court has ruled that the Fourteenth Amendment to the Constitution requires that the right to representation by counsel must also be protected by state governments.

7. This is the type of issue that belongs in U.S. Supreme Court because it involves a constitutional issue. The Supreme Court should overturn the conviction in the lower court because Miranda was not informed of his rights, was not assisted by counsel, and was apparently compelled to testify against himself in the allegedly voluntary confession. The Fifth Amendment of the Constitution prohibits self-incrimination in a criminal case and thus guarantees the right to remain silent. The U.S. Supreme Court has ruled that the Fourteenth Amendment to the Constitution requires that the right to remain silent must also be protected by state governments.

Chapter 4   Criminal Law

Questions for Analysis Page 77

1. The case involves an alleged violation of a federal income tax laws.
2. Extortion involves taking property by coercing consent. Larceny involves taking and carrying away property without the right to do so. This case involves embezzlement.
3. It is not clear whether the crimes in this article are felonies or misdemeanors.
4. The defendant's motive does not matter in this case.
5. The intent to return the funds would not be an adequate defense here.

Questions for Analysis Page 84

1. The Sixth Amendment is at the heart of the Supreme Court's ruling in the Blakely case.
2. The ruling will affect all federal cases.
3. The question of the constitutional significance of the quotation is open to various answers. Accept all well-reasoned responses.

4. In the Blakely case the Supreme Court used its power of judicial review to strike down a federal statute.
5. Most judges issue rulings within the recommended sentencing guidelines because by doing so they can be relatively certain that their decisions will not be overruled by a higher court.

Questions for Review and Discussion Page 88

1. The purpose of criminal law is to protect the public at large, to preserve order and stability within society, and to discourage future disruptive conduct.
2. Under common law, crimes were dealt with in the order of their seriousness: treason, felonies, and misdemeanors. Most states now divide offenses into felonies and misdemeanors. A felony is a crime punishable by death or imprisonment in a federal or state prison for a term exceeding one year. A misdemeanor is a less serious crime that is generally punishable by a prison sentence for not more than one year.
3. A crime cannot be committed unless some overt act has occurred. An individual cannot be accused of a crime for merely "thinking" of the criminal act in question. Sometimes the failure to act, an omission, or the outright refusal to act may be considered criminal. Generally, however, an omission must be coupled with a legally imposed duty. Many states specifically exclude involuntary movement and behavior from their general definition of a criminal act. Convulsions, reflexes, movements during sleep or unconsciousness, or behavior during a seizure are all considered involuntary movement or behavior falling outside the limits of criminal liability. However, the mere fact that someone is unconscious during a seizure may not absolve that individual of criminal liability if that person knew that he might suffer the seizure yet took no precautions to avoid harming people or property.
4. The four mental states that can be found in the criminal code are purpose or intent, knowledge, recklessness, and negligence. Purpose or intent means that a person acts with the intention to cause the result that does in fact occur. Knowledge means that a person acted knowing that a particular result would probably occur. Recklessness means that a person acted with a perverse disregard of a known risk of negative consequences. Negligence means that a person acted failing to see the possible negative consequences of his or her actions.
5. Motive in criminal law is the wrongdoer's reason for committing the crime. One common misconception about criminal law, which is promoted and perpetuated by countless novels, plays, television programs, and theatrical motion pictures, is that motive is an element of criminal liability. Such is not the case. Establishing motive may help the prosecution convince the jury that the accused is guilty, but proving an evil motive is not necessary for a criminal conviction.

6. Crimes against the people, most often referred to as felonies, include homicide, assault, battery, kidnapping, and hate speech. Homicide is any killing of one human by another. Criminal homicide is either murder or manslaughter. Battery is the unlawful touching of another person. Assault is an attempt to commit a battery. Kidnapping is the unlawful abduction of an individual against that person's will. Hate speech is the use of certain symbols, writings, and speech intended to provoke outrage or fear in others on the basis of race, religion, color, or gender.

7. Embezzlement is the act of wrongfully taking property that has been entrusted to person's care. Larceny by false pretenses is the taking of someone's money or property by intentionally deceiving that person.

8. One approach to this task of defining cybercrime is to state that cybercrimes involve any criminal transgression that includes or impacts upon a computer. This approach is often referred to as computer trespass or simply as cybertrespass. Another way to classify cybercrimes is to distinguish between crimes committed with a computer and crimes committed against computers. Crimes committed with a computer include cyberextortion, cyberstalking, and cyberspoofing. Crimes committed against computers include cyberterrorism, identity theft, cybervandalism, and cybergerm warfare. Another way to fight cybercrime is through the creation of federal anticybercrime statutes.

9. The oldest test of insanity is the M'Naughten Rule. Under this rule, defendants can be found NGRI, if at the time the criminal act was committed they were suffering from a mental disease that was so serious that they did not know the nature of the act or did not know that act was wrong. Another test of insanity is the irresistible impulse test. This test holds that criminal defendants can be found NGRI, if at the time of the offense, they were stricken with a mental disease which prevented them from knowing right from wrong or compelled them to commit the crime. A more modern insanity test has been developed by the American Law Institute (ALI). Under the ALI test, a person is not responsible if "as a result of mental disease or defect he lacks substantial capacity either to appreciate the criminality of his conduct or to conform his conduct to the requirements of law."

10. If a law enforcement officer induces a law-abiding citizen to commit a crime, entrapment may be used as a defense. The person using the defense must show that the crime would not have been committed had it not been for the inducement of the officer. The defense of entrapment is not available to a defendant who would have committed the crime even without the involvement of the officer.

Cases for Analysis Page 88

1. The two boys can be charged with murder because, in most jurisdictions, first-degree murder results in three circumstances: (1) killing someone with premeditation; (2) killing someone in a cruel way; and (3) killing someone while committing a major crime such as robbery. Here the three boys were attempting to rob the victim. This qualifies as first-degree murder under the third definition. The intended victim can use self-defense in this case. He will probably succeed as long as he believed that he was in danger of severe bodily harm or death and tried to or could not retreat, and used only necessary force.

2. The provisions of RICO can give rise not only to criminal charges but also to civil liability. Thus, it is not uncommon for individuals to seek damages in lawsuits filed against corporations which have violated RICO.

3. Yes. The appellate court felt that it was clear that Scott had acted under the mistaken belief that his life and the life of the President were in danger. The court said, "When a person commits an act based on mistake of fact, his guilt or innocence is determined as if the facts were as he perceived them. If the defendant were a government agent and his life or the life of the President were in danger and the defendant attempted to commandeer vehicles for the purpose of saving his life or the life of the President, his actions would be legally justified."

4. No. The defendant's motive is irrelevant. All that matters is that he acted intentionally when he placed the poison within his wife's reach.

5. No. The St. Paul ordinance outlawing "hate speech" is not constitutional. Such an ordinance would be constitutional only if it were not content specific. While it would have been acceptable for the city to draft an ordinance that outlawed any speech designed to rouse fear or outrage regardless of the content of that speech, it was impermissible to outlaw speech aimed at inciting outrage or fear based solely on race, religion, color, gender, or any similar category.

6. Reese has committed robbery. This is because robbery is the act of taking personal property, including money, from the possession of another against that person's will and under threat to do great bodily harm or damage.

7. No. The trial court was incorrect. Since Cuttiford was in his own apartment he did not have the duty to retreat any further before attempting to repel the attack from Banks. The appellate court pointed out that Cuttiford did not have to retreat to the furthest part of his apartment. Nor did he have to remain in the bedroom, to which he had run to retrieve the guns, but could return to the kitchen.

8. No. Entrapment will not succeed as a defense if the defendant is induced to commit a crime by a private party, even when that private party later becomes a government informer. In this case, during the original Cowen-Busby agreement, Cowen was not operating for the government. The police knew nothing of Cowen's activities at the time. The simple request to keep the police informed did not give the police any power over Cowen. Nor did it make Cowen legally responsible to the police.

Chapter 5   Tort Law

Questions for Analysis Page 98

1. The plaintiff in the case is Jerome Zamos; the defendants are Patricia Brookes and her attorney James Stroud.

2. The case preceding the malicious prosecution case was a fraud case.

3. The two negative consequences that the California Supreme Court tried to avoid are (a) *bringing* a case without probable cause and (b) *continuing* a case without probable cause.

4. The California Supreme Court said that malicious prosecution cases could involve both bringing a case without probable cause and continuing a case without probable cause.

5. The plaintiff offered a statement made by the judge in the first case that the defendant could not have had a better lawyer than the plaintiff.

Questions for Analysis Page 106

1. Most of the concerns related to the widespread use of RFID technology involves invasion of privacy matters. One concern is that RFID tags identifying individual items purchased by consumers will connect those purchasers to certain databases that the consumers would just as well like to avoid. A second concern is that RFID tags may be used to create "automatic audit tails of commercial transactions." Another concern involves the fact that many workers may be displaced by the use of RFID technology.

2. One possible application of RFID technology in the legal arena involves using the logs created by RFID tags as evidence.

3. The European Data Protection Act provides limits on the legal availability of RFID tag records.

4. Some firms have promised not to use RFID tags outside of their own stores. Some corporations promised to place RFID tags in packaging only, not on the actual merchandise.

5. One requirement that has been suggested is that all RFID tags contain a "kill switch" that permits the tag to be deactivated after a transaction has been concluded. Another is that consumers must be notified when an item contains an RFID tag. Another is that all RFID tags be deactivated at the checkout counter. Another is that all RFID tags be visible and detachable. A final suggested requirement is that all RFID tags should be placed in the package rather than on the actual merchandise.

Questions for Review and Discussion Page 114

1. The primary purpose of tort law is to compensate the innocent party by making up for any loss suffered by that victim. Another objective is to protect potential victims by deterring future torts. In contrast, criminal law involves a public wrong rather than a private wrong, that is, a wrong that affects the entire society. Since criminal law is concerned with protecting the public, its focus differs from that of tort law. When a crime is committed, government authorities begin legal actions designed to remove the offender from society. It is possible, however, for a single act to be both a tort and a crime.

2. Duty is best understood in relation to rights. Legal duties arise because one of the objectives of the law is to promote justice. Justice demands that people be allowed to enjoy their health, their property, their reputation, their business relationships, and their privacy without the unjust interference of others. Since another object of the law is to promote harmony, a duty corresponding to each right also rises within each member of our society. For instance, because each member of society has a right to engage in business without unjust interference, everyone else has the duty not to wrongfully interfere with that right. Some rights and their corresponding duties are universal. For example, all persons have the right to enjoy their property without the unwarranted intrusion of others. Those who take or destroy property violate that right. In contrast, some special rights arise because of changing circumstances. When patients enter a health care facility, they have the right to expect professional care that meets the appropriate standard of competence. Therefore, all health care providers who treat patients in health care facilities have a duty to perform according to a professional standard of care.

3. Under American tort law, the principal intentional torts include assault, battery, false imprisonment, defamation, disparagement, fraud, invasion of privacy, invasion of the right to publicity, intentional infliction of emotional distress, and malicious prosecution.

4. The elements of negligence are duty, breach of duty, proximate cause, and actual harm.

5. Contributory negligence and comparative negligence both measure the plaintiff's relative negligence in relation to the harm suffered by that plaintiff and reduces his or her damage award accordingly. Under contributory negligence, the damage award is eliminated entirely. Under comparative negligence, it is reduced by a percentage determined by the jury. Assumption of risk is a defense to negligence which says that the plaintiff entered the situation in question realizing that there was a possibility that he or she mighty suffer harm.

6. Strict liability, or liability without fault, arises when the defendant was engaged in an ultrahazardous activity like keeping wild animals or using explosives.

7. A cybertort involves the invasion, distortion, theft, falsification, misuse, destruction, or financial exploitation of information stored in or related to an electronic device including but not limited to desktop PCs, laptops, mobile phones, mainframes, phonecams, personal digital assistants (PDAs), and home computers that stand alone or are part of a network.

8. The remedies available in tort law are damages and injunctive relief.

9. A damage cap is a limit on the amount of damages that a plaintiff can be awarded by the court.

10. Suggestions for reform at the state level include statutory adjustments in tort law that include appeal bond reform, expert evidence reform, forum shopping reform, jury reform, and product liability reform.

Cases for Analysis Page 115

1. Yes. In this landmark case, the U.S. Supreme Court created the actual malice test. In doing so the Court stated, "Constitutional guarantees require, we think, a federal rule that prohibits a public official from recovering damages for a defamatory falsehood relating to his official conduct unless he proves that the statement was made with 'actual malice'—that is, with knowledge that it was false or with reckless disregard of whether it was false or not."

2. Under British libel law, the presumption is that the publication is false. The defendant then has the burden of proof to show that the allegedly libelous information was true. Under American libel law, the presumption is that the publication is true. The plaintiff then has a burden to show that the publication was false. When the plaintiff in the case is a public official (such as the President) or a public figure (such as a member of the Saudi Royal Family), those plaintiffs must also prove actual malice, that is, that the defendant had knowledge of its falsity or printed the matter with reckless disregard for its truth or falsity.

3. No. Duty is measured by foreseeability. In this case, the police officers had no reason to believe that Ralph would drive. In fact, they had been assured by Ralph's brother, Eddie, that Eddie would drive and that he would drive Ralph straight home. This can be distinguished from a situation in which the police release the intoxicated driver who later injures someone while driving. In the latter situation, it is reasonable to foresee that the drunk driver who is allowed to drive may hit someone. In the case presented, the police officers received assurances that the intoxicated driver would not drive.

4. Yes. The drugstore in this case owed a duty to Booker and other customers to maintain a safe environment. In this case, the heavy doors and the hazardous nature of the exposed coil represented a danger that placed a duty on the store owners. According to the court, "Revco had a duty to reduce the tension on the door and remove the coil, or warn business invitees about the hazard." Booker's lawsuit is based upon allegations that the store owners were negligent. The reasonable person test would be used to judge whether the drugstore owners should be held liable for Booker's injuries. This test compares the actions of the tortfeasor with those of the reasonable person in a similar situation. If the reasonable person would not have done what the tortfeasor actually did, then the tortfeasor is liable.

5. No. There can be no recovery in tort under product liability when the only damage caused by a defect is damage to the product itself.

6. No. Forest City was not negligent in this case. The court concluded that the "appellee (Forest City) could not constantly police the area and that ice could have built up even though appellee was not negligent in its attempt to maintain the property," To determine if the alleged tortfeasor has met the standard of care, the court uses the reasonable person test. This test compares the actions of the tortfeasor with those of the reasonable person in a similar situation. If the reasonable person would not have done what the tortfeasor actually did, then the tortfeasor is liable.

7. No. This is a case of comparative negligence. The jury found that the plaintiff had been 40 percent negligent and the railroad company 60 percent negligent. Therefore, the plaintiff could recover damages here.

Part 1 Case Study Page 119

1. Whether or not judges should use their own personal code of ethics to guide the creation of law is an open-ended question with no "right" answer. Nevertheless, the question should generate a lot of discussion in the classroom. The instructor should accept any answer that seems to be well thought out and supported by well-formed arguments.

2. The justices seem to be promoting the ethical trait of fairness. A fair person is one who treats people with justice and equality. A person who is fair minded can also be trusted to deal evenhandedly not only with friends and family but also with his or her enemies. Since everyone wants to be treated fairly it stands to reason that they would admire a person who has the ability to exercise fairness. That is what the justices appear to be attempting to do here. They may also be exercising compassion. Compassion means being sympathetic to the needs and desires of others. Moreover, a compassionate person respects other individuals and their right to make their own decisions regarding what is best for them. Individuals who have compassion also try to preserve individual freedom and liberty. The justices are certainly concerned with promoting the liberty of women to make their own choices in regard to reproductive decisions. In contrast, it could be argued that the justices are sacrificing their integrity by not following their own moral codes in the shaping of this rule of law.

3. It does not appear that the justices are submitting to subjective ethics. They seem to be looking for an objective standard that can be applied in most every case.

4. Planned Parenthood probably brought this case in federal court to avoid any prejudice for Pennsylvania law that might be found in a Pennsylvania courtroom. Since constitutional rights are involved, subject matter jurisdiction in federal court is established by federal question. The governor is a defendant because, as the chief executive officer of the state, he is charged with carrying out the allegedly unconstitutional law.

5. The strength of an independent judiciary is demonstrated in several ways. First, Sandra Day O'Connor,

Anthony M. Kennedy, and David H. Souter had all been appointed by conservative Presidents for their conservative legal philosophies. Nevertheless, each of them lent their support to *Roe v. Wade,* a development that was decidedly unexpected in most legal circles and which demonstrated that the federal judiciary is a very independent body. The court also faced down an attempt by the executive branch to compel the court to reevaluate the law as stated in *Roe v. Wade.* According to the majority opinion, the Justice Department had in five separate cases asked the Court to overturn *Roe v. Wade.* Despite this, the court refused, once again demonstrating its independence.

6. The Supreme Court might have agreed to hear the case because it represented an opportunity for the Court to clarify some of the doubts, uncertainties, and controversy surrounding *Roe v. Wade.* The Court also felt that it needed to address what the justices had begun to perceive as an attempt by the executive branch to compel the court to reevaluate the law as stated in *Roe v. Wade.*

7. The judges can ask a series of questions as they contemplate whether or not to overturn a rule of law established in an earlier case. These questions include the following: (1) Has the old rule become impractical? (2) Have so few people relied upon the old rule that overturning it would cause neither difficulty nor injustice? (3) Has the rule become merely a relic of an outdated and deserted legal doctrine? (4) Has the old rule become obsolete because of changes in society? Only if judges can answer these questions satisfactorily should they consider overturning an established precedent like *Roe v. Wade.* The court did indeed apply these factors in *Planned Parenthood of Pennsylvania v. Casey.* The Court said, "Although *Roe* has engendered opposition, it has in no sense proven 'unworkable,' representing as it does a simple limitation beyond which a state law is enforceable. . . . But to do this (i.e., overrule *Roe*) would simply refuse to face the fact that for two decades of economic and social developments people have organized intimate relationships and made choices that define their views of themselves and their places in society, in reliance on the availability of abortion in the event that contraception would fail. . . . No evolution of legal principle has left *Roe*'s doctrinal footing weaker than they were in 1973. No development of constitutional law since the case was decided has implicitly or explicitly left *Roe* behind as a mere survivor of obsolete constitutional thinking. . . . We have seen how time has overtaken some of *Roe*'s factual assumptions: advances in maternal health care allow for abortions safe to the mother in later pregnancy than was true in 1973, and advances in neonatal care have advanced viability to a point somewhat earlier. But these facts go only to the scheme of time limitis on the realization of competing interests, and the divergences from factual premises of 1973 have no bearing on the validity of *Roe*'s central holding, that viability marks the earliest point at which the state's interest in fetal life is constitutionally adequate to justify a legislative ban on nontherapeutic abortions."

8. The Court clearly upheld the central ruling of *Roe v. Wade.* On several occasions the Court said, "Within the bounds of normal *stare decisis* analysis, then, and subject to considerations on which it customarily turns, the stronger argument is for affirming *Roe*'s central holding, with whatever degree of personal reluctance any of us may have, not for overruling it."

9. The competing rights that the Court attempted to balance in this case are the woman's right to make the ultimate decision regarding health matters that affect her own body and the right of the state to protect potential life.

10. The case may have displeased both sides of the controversy because the court set out to and did in fact affect a compromise. *Roe v. Wade* was not overturned. Rather, the essential central holding preserving a woman's right to control her own body was affirmed. This pleased the Pro-Choice faction, but displeased the Pro-Life faction. On the other hand, a woman's rights were limited by the informed consent provision and the parental notification provision of the Pennsylvania law. This pleased the Pro-Life faction, but displeased the Pro-Choice faction.

Part 2   Contract Law

Chapter 6   The Nature, Characteristics, and Status of Contracts

Questions for Analysis   Page 129

1. The plaintiff is Neil Gaiman, a writer of *Spawn* comics; the defendant is Todd McFarlane, the creator of *Spawn* comics. The subject matter involved the question of copyright ownership.

2. One argument is that McFarlane and Gaiman never entered a contract. Another argument is that the characters created by Gaiman were stereotypical characters that could not be copyrighted. However, the question of what legal defense to bring is open to various answers. Accept all well-reasoned responses.

3. The question of what legal argument the plaintiff should bring is open to various answers. Accept all well-reasoned responses.

4. The second writer sought a declaratory judgment indicating that he was an owner of the *Spawn* comic.

5. The plaintiff, Gaiman, won the case. The court ruled that the characters created by Gaiman were not stock characters and were, therefore, subject to copyright laws.

Questions for Review and Discussion   Page 132

1. In the will theory the court looks to see whether both parties freely entered the agreement understanding the

obligations that they have assumed and the benefits due to them. Under the formalist theory of contract law, the courts look to see if certain elements exist. Those elements are offer, acceptance, mutual assent, capacity, consideration, and legality. If each element is present, then a contract exists, regardless of what the parties may argue after the fact.

2. These six elements include offer, acceptance, mutual assent, capacity, consideration, and legality. An offer is a proposal made by one party to another indicating a willingness to enter into a contract. The person who makes an offer is called the offeror. The person to whom the offer is made is the offeree. Acceptance means that the offeree agrees to be bound by the terms set up by the offeror in the offer. If a valid offer has been made by the offeror and a valid acceptance has been made by the offeree, then the parties have agreed to the terms and mutual assent exists between them. Mutual assent is sometimes called a "meeting of the minds." It means that both parties know what the terms are and have readily agreed to be bound by those terms. Capacity is the legal ability to enter into a contractual relationship. The law has established a general presumption that anyone entering a contractual relationship has the legal capacity to do so. The fifth element to any complete contract is the mutual exchange of benefits and sacrifices. This exchange is called consideration. Consideration is the thing of value promised to the other party in exchange for something else of value promised by the other party. It is this exchange of valued items or services that binds the parties together. The final element of a binding contract is legality. Parties cannot be allowed to enforce a contract that involves doing something that is illegal. Some illegal contracts involve agreements to perform a crime or a tort. However, activities that are neither crimes nor torts have been made illegal by specific statutes. Among these activities are usurious agreements, wagering agreements, unlicensed agreements, and unconscionable agreements.

3. Article 2 of the UCC covers sale of goods contracts.

4. All contracts contain agreements, but not all agreements are contracts. An agreement may or may not be legally enforceable. To be enforceable, an agreement must conform to the law of contracts. The courts have never been agreeable to the enforcement of social agreements: dates, dinner engagements, or the like.

5. Privity means that both parties to a contract have a legally recognized interest in the subject matter of the agreement.

6. A valid contract is one which is legally binding and fully enforceable by the court. This means that both parties are obligated to perform all terms and conditions mutually agreed upon. A voidable contract is one that may be avoided or canceled by one of the parties. Contracts made by minors and contracts that are induced by fraud or misrepresentation are examples of voidable contracts. A void contract is one that has no legal effect

whatsoever. A contract to perform an illegal act would be void. An unenforceable contract is one which, because of some rule of law, cannot be upheld by a court of law. An unenforceable contract may have all the elements of a complete contract and still be unenforceable.

7. A unilateral contract is an agreement in which one party makes a promise to do something in return for an act of some sort. The classic example of a unilateral contract is a reward contract. A person who promises to pay the finder of his wristwatch $10 does not expect a promise in return. Rather, the person expects the return of the watch. When the watch is returned, the contract arises and the promisor owes the finder $10. In contrast, a bilateral contract is one in which both parties make promises. Bilateral contracts come into existence at the moment the two promises are made. A breach of contract occurs when one of the two parties fails to keep the promise.

8. Implied contracts are created by the actions or gestures of the parties involved in the transaction. An express contract requires some sort of written or spoken expression indicating the desire to enter the contractual relationship.

9. Contracts implied by the direct or indirect acts of the parties are known as implied-in-fact contracts. Courts follow the objective concept rule in interpreting the acts and gestures of a party. Under this concept, the meaning of one's acts is determined by the impression they would make upon any reasonable person who might have witnessed them, not by a party's self-serving claim of what was meant or intended. An implied-in-law contract can be imposed by a court when someone in unjustly enriched. It is used when a contract cannot be enforced or when there is no actual written, oral, or implied-in-fact agreement. Applying reasons of justice and fairness, a court may obligate one who has unfairly benefited at the innocent expense of another. An implied-in-law contract is also called a quasi-contract.

10. When a contract that has not yet been fully performed by the parties is called an executory contract. Such a contract may be completely executory, in which case nothing has been done, or it may be partly executory, in which case the contract is partially complete. An example of an executory contract is an agreement to paint a house, payment to be made upon completion. When a contract's terms have been completely and satisfactorily carried out by both parties it is an executed contract. Such contracts are no longer active agreements and are valuable only if a dispute about the agreement occurs. An example of an executed contract is one whereby a house has been painted and the work paid for.

Cases for Analysis Page 132

1. The United States Supreme Court decided that the Contracts Clause of the Constitution meant that the state government, including the courts, could not impair the rights under a contract that the parties had freely agreed to. In this case, the first bridge-building contract

contained no clause that stated that there would be only one bridge built over the Charles River. Under the second bridge-building contract, the state had agreed to permit the second bridge to be built and the court could not now impair that right.

2. The appeals court should reverse the ruling of the lower court. The clause is ambiguous enough to require the trial court to look at factual evidence to determine the actual intent of the parties. If the case goes to trial, the court can make a factual determination of intent by looking at evidence beyond the terms in the writing.

3. No. The contract in this case is between Stewart's corporate employer and the bank. The bank breached the contract with the corporate employer. Since Stewart was not in privity with the bank, he could not hold it liable for the nonpayment. Instead, Stewart was in privity with his client. His action was against his client, not the bank.

4. Yes. Vokes was induced to enter the contract by the statements that she had great talent and would be a professional dancer. Since these turned out to be untrue, the contract was voidable by her.

5. Yes. The court agreed with Copeland and required that Anderson pay for the use of the tractor for eleven days. The court stated that under the circumstances, the law would imply the existence of a quasi-contract, since otherwise Anderson would be unjustly enriched at Copeland's expense.

6. Yes. A contract to perform an illegal act is void. This contract was void because the city made no provision for raising the money that it needed to pay Nelson. Such provisions for payment were required by the state constitution.

7. (a) The agreement to "take over all executory contracts" would itself be executed at the time these contracts were taken over.

   (b) This part of the contract would be executory until such time as payment was made and the tools were actually accepted by Peters.

   (c) Peters's obligations to those holding the warranties would be executory, but as to Dowling they would be part of Peters's executed agreements.

   (d) Dowling's agreement to remain would be executory for the five-year period agreed to by him and Peters.

Chapter 7   Offer and Acceptance

Questions for Analysis Page 143

1. Jonesheirs, Inc. controls the right to use the Bobby Jones name.

2. Generally, the offeror would be the merchandiser and the offeree would be Jonesheirs, Inc.

3. It is important to control the roles of offeror and offeree because the offeree can reject the terms presented in the offer.

4. The question calls for speculation by the students. Accept all-reasoned answers here.

5. The two laws here would be the E-Sign Act and the Uniform Computer Transactions Act.

Questions for Review and Discussion Page 149

1. As the courts attempted to use the will theory, they could see how challenging it was to establish whether the parties actually agreed to the terms of a contract. Because the actual intent of each party was out of reach, the courts had to examine behavior to determine that intent. This problem led the courts to establish a formalist approach. According to formalism, if certain requirements are met, the court concludes that the parties intended to make and accept an offer.

2. An offer is valid only if it has (1) serious intent, (2) clear and reasonably definite terms, and (3) communication to the offeree.

3. A public offer is one made through the public media but which is intended for only one person whose identity or address is unknown to the offeror. The classic example of a public offer is an advertisement in a lost-and-found column in a newspaper. By contrast, invitations to trade are not offers. An invitation to trade is an announcement published to reach many persons for the purpose of creating interest and attracting responses. Newspaper and magazine advertisements, radio and television commercials, store window displays, price tags on merchandise, and prices in catalogs come within this definition. In the case of an invitation to trade, no binding agreement develops until a responding party makes an offer which the advertiser accepts.

4. Unilateral contracts do not usually require communication of expressed acceptance. When the offeror makes a promise in a unilateral contract, the offeror expects an action, not another promise in return. Performance of the action requested within the time allowed by the offeror and with the offeror's knowledge creates the contract. In bilateral contracts, unlike unilateral ones, the offeree must communicate acceptance to the offeror. Bilateral contracts consist of a promise by one party in return for a promise by the other. Until the offeree communicates a willingness to be bound by a promise, there is no valid acceptance.

5. The Uniform Commercial Code was written by the National Conference of Commissioners on Uniform State Laws. The UCC is written in a form that can be directly enacted into law by the various state legislatures. Article 2 of the UCC covers the rules involving sale of goods contracts.

6. Under the mirror image rule, the terms as stated in the acceptance must exactly "mirror" the terms in the offer. If the acceptance changes or qualifies the terms in the offer, it is not an acceptance. Instead, a qualified acceptance is actually a counteroffer. A counteroffer is a response to an offer in which the terms of the original offer are changed. No agreement is reached unless the counteroffer is accepted by the original offeror.

7. The UCC has altered the mirror image rule when contract negotiations are being carried on. In contracts for the sale of goods, as long as there is a definite expression of acceptance, a contract will come into existence even though an acceptance has different or additional terms. If the parties are not both merchants, the different or additional terms are treated as proposals for additions to the contract. If the parties are both merchants, however, the different or additional terms become part of the contract unless (1) they make an important difference, (2) the offeror objects, or (3) the offer limits acceptance to its terms. This exception is discussed further in Chapter 15. What is the mirror image rule? How has the UCC altered the mirror image rule?

8. Offers may be revoked by (1) communication, (2) automatic revocation, (3) passage of time, (4) death or insanity of the offeror, (5) destruction of the subject matter, or (6) the subsequent illegality of the contract.

9. An option contract is both a contract and an offer. It differs from a simple offer because the offeree contracts to have the offer remain open by offering consideration to the offeror. By agreement and for consideration, the offeror waives the right to revoke for the time limit set by the mutual agreement of the parties. A special rule has been developed under the UCC which holds that no consideration is necessary when a merchant agrees in writing to hold an offer open. This is called a firm offer.

10. The rules concerning the interpretation and the enforcement of cybercontracts are found in the federal Electronic Signatures in Global and National Commerce Act (the E-Sign Act), the Uniform Electronic Transactions Act (UETA), and the Uniform Computer Information Transactions Act (UCITA).

Cases for Analysis Page 150

1. No. This ad was not an offer. Rather, it was an invitation to trade. In this case, the ad did not limit the sale of the Volvo to one particular person. Rather, the offer was open to anyone who appeared at any time. As a general rule, a newspaper ad that contains an erroneous price through no fault of the advertiser and that contains no other terms is not an offer.

2. Yes. The offer is definite enough to allow Leftkowitz to tender an acceptance. The ad contained a very specific promise to deliver the one stole to the first customer who appeared. Since the number of items and the number of people who could accept were both very limited, the ad was an offer.

3. Yes. Since Thoelke had used the same agent (the U.S. mail) to accept as Morrison had used to make the offer, the acceptance was valid when the letter was mailed, not when the acceptance was received.

4. No. The acceptance was not in accord with the offer; therefore, there was a qualified acceptance. Guyan's qualified acceptance made a material alteration in the offer. As such, it became a counteroffer. However, when Wholesale Coal accepted the seven carloads, it was accepting Guyan's counteroffer, making a valid binding contract for those seven carloads.

5. Yes. The communication of the acceptance had not been made within the time period set by the offeror. The offer was therefore automatically revoked. Although Rothenbeucher delivered the signed agreement to his own agent, such delivery did not constitute acceptance or delivery to Tockstein.

6. No. As a general rule, the offeror, in this case Greenhouse and Dollar-or-Less, cannot force the offeree, Bolick, into a contract by saying that silence will mean acceptance. However, the offeree can force the offeror into a contract if the offeror set up the silence condition.

Chapter 8   Mutual Assent and Defective Agreement

Questions for Analysis Page 162

1. A team could not claim economic duress in that type of situation. Economic duress requires that the other party cause the victimized party's financial difficulty wrongfully. If two parties enter a contract voluntarily, as is the case when a ballclub signs a ballplayer, then there is no wrongful conduct and neither party will be able to claim economic duress, should that party later suffer economic problems as a result of that contract.

2. Undue influence involves a fiduciary or confidential relationship between an independent and a dependent party. This situation does not exist here.

3. No. Mistake in value is not a valid argument.

4. It is possible that the courts might allow a team to rescind a contract with a player based on the misrepresentation of the player's health.

5. No. Poor performance would not constitute mistake as to description.

Questions for Review and Discussion Page 165

1. A contract consists of six elements. The first element is the offer. An offer is a proposal made by one party, the offeror, to another party, the offeree. The proposal indicates the offeror's willingness to enter into a contract with the offeree. If the offer is seriously intended, clear and definite, and communicated to the offeree, then the offeree may accept or reject it. The second element of a contract is the acceptance. If the offeree accepts the offer, then there is mutual assent between the parties. Mutual assent means that the parties have had a "meeting of the minds." In other words, both parties know what the terms are and both have voluntarily agreed to be bound by those terms.

2. Mutual assent can be destroyed as a result of fraud, misrepresentation, mutual mistake, duress, or undue influence.

3. To destroy mutual assent on a claim of fraud, the complaining or innocent party must prove the existence of five elements. First, the complaining party will have to show that the other party made a false representation about some material fact (i.e., an important fact, a fact of substance) involved in the contract. A material fact is one that is very crucial to the terms of the contract. Second, it must be shown that the other party made the representation knowing of its falsity. Third, it must be shown that the false representations were made with the intent that they be relied upon by the innocent party. Fourth, the complaining party must demonstrate that there was a reasonable reliance on the false representations. Finally, it must be shown that the innocent party actually suffered some loss by relying on the false representation after entering the contract. A case involving either active or passive fraud must be based on these five elements. To be fraudulent, statements must involve facts. Opinions and sales puffery consist of the persuasive words and exaggerated claims made by salespeople to induce a customer to buy their product. As long as the comments are reserved to opinion and do not misstate facts, they cannot be considered fraud in a lawsuit even if they turn out to be grossly wrong.

4. The existence of hidden problems and fiduciary relationships give rise to a duty not to conceal certain material facts when entering a contract.

5. Misrepresentation is a false statement made innocently with no intent to deceive. Innocent misrepresentation makes an existing agreement voidable and the complaining party may demand rescission. Rescission means that both parties are returned to their original positions, before the contract was entered into. Unlike cases based on fraud which allow rescission and damages, cases based on innocent misrepresentation allow only rescission and not money damages.

6. A mistake made by only one of the contracting parties is a unilateral mistake and does not offer sufficient grounds for rescission or renegotiation. When both parties are mistaken, it is a bilateral or mutual mistake. A bilateral or mutual mistake allows a rescission by either the offeror or the offeree.

7. A party can get out of a contract if he or she can demonstrate (1) mistake as to description, (2) mistake as to existence, (3) mistakes through failure to read conditions in fine print or conditions not included in the body of the written contract, (4) mistake as to the law of another state.

8. Physical duress involves either violence or the threat of violence against an individual or against that person's family, household, or property. If only threats are used, they must be so intense and serious that a person of ordinary prudence would be forced into the contract without any real consent. Emotional duress arises from acts or threats that would create emotional distress in the one on whom they are inflicted. Exposure to public ridicule, threatened attacks on one's reputation, or efforts to prevent employment might constitute emotional duress.

9. In order to establish economic duress, the complaining party must demonstrate the existence of three elements. (1) The complaining party must first show that the other party was responsible for placing the complainant in a precarious economic situation and that the other party acted wrongfully in doing so. (2) The complainant must also show that there was no alternative other than to submit to the contractual demands of the wrongful party. (3) Finally, the innocent party must also show that he or she acted reasonably in entering the contract. If the plaintiff can prove the existence of these three elements, the court will rule the contract voidable on grounds of economic duress.

10. A confidential relationship involves the existence of trust and dependence between the two parties. Examples of confidential relationships include the relationships of parent to child, guardian to ward, husband to wife, attorney to client, physician to patient, pastor to parishioner, and so forth. In most cases involving undue influence, one party, with strength and leadership, dominates the other, who is obviously weaker and dependent.

Cases for Analysis Page 165

1. Yes. Since Walker knew the land had considerably less than 80,000 cubic yards of gravel, he had deliberately misled Cousineau. This amounted to fraud allowing Cousineau to get out of the contract.

2. No. The fact that the lot had been filled was a hidden problem that could not be discovered upon ordinary inspection. Therefore, Young had an obligation to reveal this fact to Sorrell. When this revelation was not made, Young was liable for intentional concealment.

3. Yes. The bilateral mistake here would allow for rescission of the contract.

4. Duress. Any agreement to grant immunity or amnesty that is produced by unlawful threats of harm is void. Promises extorted through threats of violence are the result of duress and will not be upheld by the court.

5. Yes. This situation clearly involves economic duress. The court ruled that the price increase was "voidable on the grounds of duress when it was established that the party making the claim was forced to agree to it by means of wrongful threat predicating the exercise of free will."

6. No. Vargas was mentally alert and physically strong and no false representations had been made to him. He had been handed the contract, and he knew it was a contract that specified the terms of his employment, but he had chosen not to read it.

Chapter 9   Contractual Capacity

Questions for Analysis Page 177

1. At the time the article was written the actress Lindsay Lohan was 17.

2. No. Ms. Lohan's age would not prevent her from entering a contract.

3. Targeting a market whose members have not reached the age of majority means that those individuals still have the power to void their contracts.

4. The court would not protect a minor who sits through an entire movie and then demands a refund.

5. The teen boy market might be safer because the same films that appeal to teenaged boys often also appeal to many adult men.

Questions for Review and Discussion Page 180

1. The law has established a general presumption that anyone entering into a contractual relationship has the legal capacity to do so. This means that someone enforcing an agreement does not have to prove that the other party had contractual capacity when the contract was entered into. However, this is a rebuttable presumption; that is, a defending party (a minor, mental incompetent, or drunk) has the right to attack the presumption in order to rescind a contract.

2. The courts allow minors this privilege to protect them from adults who might take advantage of young people who might not fully understand their obligations. In effect, the privilege allows minors to get out of contracts they have entered before reaching adulthood.

3. Minority, under common law, was a term that described persons who had not yet reached the age of twenty-one. Today, in most states, minority describes a person who has not reached eighteen years of age. Upon reaching that age, a person is said to have reached majority.

4. Ratification and adoption of Amendment 26 to the U.S. Constitution in 1971 lowered the voting age in federal elections from twenty-one to eighteen. To avoid the confusion that would result from having two voting ages, the states started to enact new laws that enabled eighteen-year-olds to vote in state and local elections. Then states began to lower the age of majority to eighteen years for certain types of contracts. However, differences still exist within and between states as to the age requirements for achieving majority; this is particularly apparent in matters related to the use of alcoholic beverages, marriage, and the operation of motor vehicles. Recently, in response to outside influences from a variety of social organizations and governmental institutions, many states have raised the drinking age to twenty-one.

5. Minors are said to be emancipated when they are no longer under the control of their parents. Emancipated minors are responsible for their contracts. Emancipated minors include those who are married as well as those who leave home and give up all right to parental support. They are said to have abandoned the usual protective shield given them.

6. Most states will allow the minor who lies about his or her age to disaffirm the contract. Some jurisdictions do not permit the minor to get away with the lie. Some jurisdictions require the minor to place the adult in the same situation that he or she was in before the contract. Others allow the adult to use tort law rather than contract law to sue the minor for fraud. Some states have also enacted statutes which allow recovery against a minor when the minor is engaged in business and misrepresents his or her age in a commercial contract. A number of states, for example, have statutes that deny disaffirmance if the minor has signed a written statement falsely asserting adult status. Without such a statute the minor will be allowed to get out of the contract despite her or his signature.

7. Necessaries are those goods and services that are essential to a minor's health and welfare. Thus, necessaries can include clothing, food, shelter, medical and dental services, tools and equipment needed for the minor to carry out his or her business, and even, in some cases, educational expenses. If a minor makes a contract for necessaries he or she will be liable for the fair value of those necessaries. Still, if the necessaries have already been provided to the minor by parents or others, the rule does not apply. Also, technically, a minor's contract covering necessaries is not enforceable against the minor in the truest sense of the term. Instead, the minor is required to pay the fair value of the necessaries that have been provided by the adult. The fair value is determined by the court. This approach to the law is an extension of the concept of quasi-contract. Another rule related to necessaries states that the rules related to necessaries apply only to executed contracts. An executed contract is one whose terms have been completely and satisfactorily carried out by both parties. In contrast, an executory contract is one that has not yet been fully performed by the parties. Wholly executory contracts calling for a future delivery or rendering of services may be repudiated by the minor.

8. Minors may not disaffirm a valid marriage or repudiate an enlistment contract in the armed forces based on a claim of incapacity to contract. Neither may a minor repudiate a contract for goods and services required by law; for example, minors may not repudiate payments for inoculations and vaccinations required for attendance at a university or college or required in securing a visa for travel in certain foreign lands. They may also be prevented from terminating contracts with banks and other financial institutions for educational loans. Some states also bar minors from repudiating agency contracts and insurance contracts. Others prevent minors from voiding contracts for psychological care, pregnancy care, the transfer of stocks and bonds, and contracts involving child support. This is a state-by-state issue, so it is wise to check your own state statutes to determine which of these contracts are not voidable by minors in your jurisdiction.

9. A contract made by a person who is mentally infirm or who suffers from mental illness may be valid, if the person's infirmity or illness is not severe enough to rob that

person of the ability to understand the nature, purpose, and effect of that contract. Thus mental impairment alone does not necessarily reduce a person's ability to enter into contracts. The question will always be whether the mental problem was so serious that the person did not understand the nature of the contract. If that is the case, the mentally infirm or mentally ill person may disaffirm any contract except one for necessaries. The incompetent must return all consideration received, if he or she still has it. A second rule is also recognized by the Restatement of Contracts and by some states. That rule says that a person's contractual obligations may be voidable if that person suffers from a mental impairment that prevents him or her from acting in a reasonable manner. This rule goes beyond the orthodox rule which requires that a person with an impairment be unable to comprehend the nature of the agreement. Under this version of the rule, a person may understand the nature of the contract but may, because of his or her impairment, be unable to stop himself or herself from entering the contract. In such a situation, as long as the contract has yet to be executed or, if executed, can be shown to be very unjust, the impaired person may void the contract. If the contract is executed or fair, the impaired party may still void the contract but must also return the other party to the place he or she was in before the contract was entered. If returning the other party to his or her precontract condition cannot be done the court will decide on a fair alternative. Finally, persons declared to be insane by competent legal authority are denied the right to enter contracts. Any contractual relationship with others results in nothing more than a void agreement.

10. Contracts agreed to by persons under the influence of alcohol or drugs may be voidable. Incompetence related to either alcohol or drugs must be of such degree that a contracting party would have lost the ability to comprehend or be aware of obligations being accepted under the contract. One who contracts while in this condition may either affirm or disaffirm the agreement at a later time.

Cases for Analysis Page 180

1. This is an interesting case. In most states Mrs. Mitchell would *not* be correct and she would *not* be able to void the release with State Farm, based on her minority. This is because in most states married minors are seen as emancipated and, therefore, capable of making contracts on their own. They are also seen as responsible for living up to the terms agreed upon in those contracts. Kentucky, however, holds to the opposite rule (at least in this case). Accordingly, the court said that Mrs. Mitchell was correct. The mere fact that she was married did not remove the essential reason for protecting minors, that is, their immaturity and inexperience.

2. No. The court ruled that dullness of intellect does not necessarily reduce one's competence to contract. The question before the court was whether Galloway had

the ability to comprehend the nature of the agreement. There is a presumption that one is capable when there is not sufficient evidence to prove otherwise. At issue was not whether he understood the agreement, but whether he was capable of understanding it. The court felt that Galloway was capable but failed to take the effort and time to really study the agreement and how it affected his rights with the employer.

3. No. Skidmore is incorrect. While minors can void contracts, this privilege is not available to an adult who contracts with a minor. Minors are generally excused from contractual liability. This means that their contracts are voidable. The courts allow minors this privilege to protect them from adults who might take advantage of young people who might not fully understand their obligations.

4. No. Winston will not be required to honor Graham's rescission demand. While individuals who buy goods from minors have voidable ownership rights, under the UCC those same individuals can transfer valid ownership rights to an innocent third-party purchaser of those goods. Thus, disaffirmance by a minor will not require the innocent purchaser to return the goods.

5. No. Bowling was a minor, and as a minor he retained the right to disaffirm any contract that he entered during minority.

6. No. Hays was a minor, and as a minor he could disaffirm the contract. The sale to the adult was simply a ruse concocted by Quality. Since Quality knew who was actually buying the car, it could not deny that knowledge simply to avoid Hays's legal right as a minor to disaffirm the contract.

7. No. While housing is generally a necessity, this does not mean that adding vinyl siding to a house falls into the same category.

8. No. Voluntary enlistment in the armed forces is an exception to the rule that minors may void their agreements. The court ruled that Lonchyna had continued to receive valuable benefits under his contract for a period of eleven years after his enlistment. In any case, the time between the enlistment and the suit to void the agreement was more than was reasonable, and even without the exception allowed in enlistment agreements, the time period was too long.

9. No. The court ruled that dullness of intellect does not necessarily reduce one's competence to contract. The question before the court was whether Kruse had the ability to comprehend the nature of the agreement. There is a presumption that one is capable when there is not sufficient evidence to prove otherwise. At issue was not whether he understood the agreement, but whether he was capable of understanding it. The court felt that Kruse was capable but failed to take the effort and time to really study the agreement and how it affected his rights with the employer.

10. Yes. Contracts made by people lacking mental competence are voidable. Evidence in this case indicated not

only that Berk was mentally incompetent at the time of the renegotiation but also that he was unable to understand the nature of the agreement.

Chapter 10   Consideration

Questions for Analysis   Page 192

1. The consideration paid by the college is providing a service for the student, that is, an education.
2. The student provides money in return for the education.
3. Answers will vary here. Accept all well-reasoned responses.
4. The bank cannot label the tax break as consideration because it undergoes no detriment. The tax break comes from the government not the bank.
5. Students should recognize that there is not enough information in the story to formulate a definite answer here. Therefore, the instructor should accept all well-reasoned responses.

Questions for Review and Discussion   Page 197

1. The promise to exchange things of value is called consideration. It is the thing of value promised to the other party in exchange for something else of value promised by that other party. It is this promise to exchange valued items or services that binds the parties together. If an agreement has no consideration, it is not a binding contract.
2. A legal detriment can be any of the following: (1) doing something (or promising to do something) that one has a legal right not to do; (2) giving up something (or promising to give up something) that one has a legal right to keep; and (3) refraining from doing something (or promising not to do something) that one has a legal right to do.
3. Consideration has three characteristics: (1) The agreement must involve a bargained-for exchange; (2) the contract must involve adequate consideration; (3) the benefits and detriments promised must themselves be legal.
4. A court may refuse to enforce a contract or any clause of that contract if it considers the contract or clause to be unconscionable, that is, where the consideration is ridiculously inadequate as to shock the court's conscience.
5. Yes, a promise not to sue can be consideration. This type of consideration is generally referred to as a release.
6. There are three ways that the courts can seek to uphold charitable pledges. The first way involves actual consideration. This occurs when charitable contributions are made on the condition that the promisor be remembered for the gift by having his or her name inscribed in some way on a memorial associated with the project. Some courts see this promise to install a memorial to the pledgor as consideration. A more contemporary approach is to use either promissory estoppel or public policy to support the claim. Promissory estoppel

involves the detrimental reliance on a promise made by another party. If in reliance on a pledge or a series of pledges, a charity goes forward with a project, the courts will see the commencement of the project as evidence that the charity relied on the promises, and will stop the promisors from denying the effects of the promise. When there is no promise to carry out a specific project, the courts have held that each pledge made is supported by the pledges of all others who have made similar pledges. This concept of consideration is used in support of all promises of money for undefined causes. The ultimate argument in this situation is that it would violate public policy to allow one pledgor to get away with denying his or her pledge when the other promisors relied on each other in making their individual pledges.

7. A disputed amount is one on which the parties never reached mutual agreement. If a creditor accepts as full payment an amount that is less than the amount due, then the dispute has been settled by accord and satisfaction. Accord is the implied or expressed acceptance of less than what has been billed the debtor. Satisfaction is the agreed-to settlement as contained in the accord. Only if the dispute is honest, made in good faith, and not superficial or trivial will the courts entertain arguments based on accord and satisfaction. An undisputed amount is one on which the parties have mutually agreed. Although a party may have second thoughts about the amount promised for goods or services rendered, the amount that was agreed to by the parties when they made their contract remains an undisputed amount. A part payment in lieu of full payment when accepted by a creditor will not cancel an undisputed debt.

8. The most common agreements that are enforceable without proof of consideration are promises bearing a seal, promises after discharge in bankruptcy, debts barred by the statute of limitations, promises enforced by promissory estoppel, and options governed by the UCC.

9. Promissory estoppel is the legal doctrine that restricts an offeror from revoking an offer, under certain conditions, even though consideration has not been promised to bind an agreement. To be effective, promissory estoppel requires that the offeror know, or be presumed to know, that the offeree might otherwise make a definite and decided change of position in contemplation of promises contained in the offer. Courts, in reaching this doctrine, have accepted the principles of justice and fairness in protecting the offeree from otherwise unrecoverable losses.

10. There are certain promises, however, which the courts will not enforce because they lack even the rudimentary qualities of valid consideration. Included in this category are promises based on preexisting duties, promises based on past consideration, illusory promises, and promises of future gifts and legacies.

Cases for Analysis Page 197

1. Aviation has not transferred anything to the Institute that it did not already owe the Institute under the original contract. Therefore, under the doctrine of preexisting duties, Aviation cannot make its obligation to deliver the component parts consideration under a new contract.

2. The small claims referee will rule in favor of Wilma. Even though there are probably some health benefits to Wilma by giving up meat, pastries, and caffeine, she suffered a legal detriment by giving up several things that she had the legal right to do.

3. Evans left her job to take the job offered to her by Davidson. Davidson knew that Evans was going to change her position in reliance on the promises that he made to her. Consequently, the doctrine of promissory estoppel applies here. Davidson had to pay Evans the wages that she lost when she was not employed for six months.

4. Mers can use the doctrine of promissory estoppel. Promissory estoppel is the legal doctrine that restricts an offeror from revoking an offer, under certain conditions, even though consideration has not been promised to bind the agreement. To be effective, promissory estoppel requires that the offeror know, or be presumed to know, that the offeree might make a definite and decided change of position in contemplation of promises contained in the offer. Courts, in reaching this doctrine, have accepted the principles of justice and fairness in protecting the offeree from otherwise unrecoverable losses. Although Mers had received no consideration supporting the promise of reemployment, he had accepted the promise and had placed himself in a very different and difficult position through his reliance upon the promise. Had Dispatch Printing not made such a promise, Mers would have looked for another job.

5. No. This is an illusory promise that does not obligate Kennelsworth in any way. An illusory promise is one that does not obligate the promissor to anything. A party who makes an illusory promise is the only one with any right to determine whether the other party will be benefited in any way. Illusory promises fail to provide the mutuality of promises required in establishing consideration. The benefits that Kennelsworth were to derive from the schedule of discounts is not supported by an enforceable promise on Kennelsworth's part. Consequently, a lawsuit brought in this situation would not succeed.

6. No. Tippon's promise to O'Hanlon is not enforceable. A promise to give another something of value in return for goods or services rendered and delivered in the past, without expectation or reward, is past consideration. Only when goods or services are provided as the result of bargained-for present or future promises is an agreement enforceable.

7. No. Vanoni cannot make the delivery of the remaining 12,000 specimens consideration in a new agreement with the Institute. A promise to do something that one is already obligated to do by law or by some other promise or agreement cannot be made consideration in a new contract. Such obligations are called preexisting duties.

8. No. As a general rule, courts do not try to determine the value of consideration. Rather, they allow the parties to enter their own agreements, setting the value of the consideration on their own.

9. Yes. The court ruled that the agreement not to sue was enforceable and supported by consideration. The decision not to sue benefited Koedding in that he received a new and substantial guarantee. West benefited through Koedding's promise to drop the suit.

10. No. In this situation there was no genuine dispute as to the value of the amount owed by Evans to Rosen. Evans used the card to make the purchase knowing the prices involved. In fact, Evans never denied that he owed that amount to Rosen. Consequently, the doctrine of accord and satisfaction does not apply in this case.

11. Yes. To succeed in this case Anderson will have to show that there was a genuine dispute over the amount she owed to the Dawsons. A disputed amount is one on which the parties never reached mutual agreement. The court agreed that in this case such a genuine dispute existed. Consequently, when the Dawsons accepted as full payment an amount that was less than the amount they thought was due, the dispute was settled by accord and satisfaction.

12. The court ruled in favor of Aspen Labs. Inc. The court stated that "a past consideration which imposed no legal obligations at the time it was furnished will not support a subsequent promise to confer a benefit." The agreement to compensate old Aspen Dealers was in consideration of their loyalty and business given in the past.

13. Yes. Vignola had a preexisting duty to deliver an undamaged love seat to Trisko. Consequently, this duty could not be valid consideration in the new agreement in which Trisko promised not to sue. That agreement, therefore, is void.

Chapter 11 Legality

Questions for Analysis Page 202

1. The illegal action involves receiving stolen goods.
2. A contract that obligates an "order verification specialist" to check incoming packages would be void, if the incoming packages contain stolen goods.
3. The contract is not *in pari delicto.*
4. The court will not enforce this contract.
5. The list of suggestions is detailed on page 202 of the text.

Questions for Review and Discussion Page 217

1. Parties cannot be allowed to enforce agreements that are contrary to the law. If the courts enforced illegal

contracts, those contracts would have more power than the law itself. If such logic were the rule, then anyone could avoid the law simply by entering into a contract.

2. Statutory law outlaws the following agreements: usurious agreements, wagering agreements, unlicensed agreements, unconscionable agreements, and Sunday (Sabbath) agreements.

3. Most states have usury laws to regulate the interest rate that may be charged in consumer transactions in order to protect borrowers from excessive interest charges.

4. States make exceptions when bets are placed in accordance with laws that permit horse racing, state-run lotteries, church-related or charitable games of bingo, and gambling casinos regulated by state authority.

5. The legal effect of a transaction entered by a party who should have a license but does not, depends on the type of license involved. Courts distinguish between licenses purely for revenue and licenses for protection of the public. If a license is required simply to raise revenue, the lack of a license will not necessarily make a contract void. In contrast, if a licensing requirement is designed to protect the public, it is likely that unlicensed people will not be able to enforce their contracts.

6. An agreement is considered unconscionable if its terms are so grossly unfair that they shock the court's conscience. The party seeking to uphold the contract is allowed to present evidence that would show that the agreement is not as unfair as it may, at first, appear. The court would look at the commercial setting as well as the purpose and the effect of the agreement to determine its overall fairness.

7. Statutes that are nicknamed "blue laws" make Sunday (Sabbath) contracts illegal. Geographical differences, differences in social attitudes, and the influence brought to the legislative bodies by religious groups all influence any state's position in its attitude toward Sunday agreements and their enforcement. Legislative reaction to the attitudes of the population usually determines whether laws permitting Sunday agreements will be continued, outlawed, or simply not enforced.

8. Public policy is that general legal principle that says no one should be allowed to do anything that tends to injure the public at large. The courts normally find agreements that violate public policy void.

9. Agreements most commonly invalidated as contrary to public policy are agreements to obstruct justice, agreements interfering with public service, agreements to defraud creditors, agreements to escape liability, and agreements in restraint of trade.

10. In a divisible contract, a court may void that part of the contract that is illegal and enforce the other parts that are not illegal. With an entire contract, an opposite view is taken. The entire agreement may be voided if one of the integral parts is found to be illegal.

Cases for Analysis   Page 217

1. No. The court held that the release was too general. It would insulate Melton from liability for injuries inflicted by the animals only if he had not been negligent. Audley could recover from Melton if she could prove that Melton was negligent.

2. Yes. The court held that the undisclosed, exorbitant filing fee requirement was unconscionable.

3. Yes. The court would uphold the agreement if B/F could show that any information revealed by Kennedy was actually a trade secret, that the secret information was crucial to the running of B/F, that B/F had the right to use the trade secret, that Kennedy came into possession of the trade secret while in a position of trust and confidence at B/F and in such a way that it would be unfair for Kennedy to disclose that trade secret in a way that would hurt B/F. Of course, it is also necessary to show that the employee actually revealed confidential information to the competitor. Unfortunately, for B/F in this case, the court ruled that B/F had merely stated that it had "reason to believe" that Kennedy had revealed confidential trade secrets to Hankook, but had not convinced the court that there were any underlaying facts to support that supposition.

4. No. The purpose of the licensing law is to guard the public against the consequences of incompetent workmanship and deception. The purpose is not furthered by strict enforcement when the party seeking to escape the obligation has received the full protection contemplated by the law. Asdourian substantially complied with the law by obtaining a license, although in a different name. In essence, Asdourian and Artko were the same.

5. Yes. The court held that the agreement between the men was a "death gamble" and came within the prohibitions of gambling and wagering agreements. The agreement was struck down and the property was placed under the jurisdiction of the trial court to dispose of according to the rights of heirs of all former members of the club.

6. Yes. Illinois statute indicates that it is a misdemeanor to place job applicants in this type of position without first obtaining a license. A statute that declares an act illegal and imposes a penalty for its violation renders a contract void for the performance of such an act. Also, no party can obtain recovery if the performance of the contract involves the violation of existing law.

7. Yes. The court stated that the test to be applied is whether the clause is "so extreme as to appear unconscionable according to the mores and business practices of the time and place." (Note: In this case, the court did not decide that the clause was unconscionable. Rather, it sent the case back to the trial court because the trial court had not considered the question of unconscionability which the appeals court thought was at the heart of the case.)

8. Yes. The clause is clearly an exculpatory clause because, as written, it allows Detroit to escape its legal responsibilities. Such clauses are void as a violation of public policy.

9. Yes. The clause held that the Topps agreement "cannot be said to restrain trade unreasonably." The court said that Fleer could have competed with Topps by seeking a license with players in the minor leagues.

10. No. Restrictive employment covenants that tend to prevent an employee from pursuing a similar vocation after leaving a previous employer must be reasonable in type of work, time, and geographic area. The court, in this case, thought that the covenant was unreasonable.

Chapter 12   Written Contracts

Questions for Analysis   Page 238

1. The new law was named The Electronic Notary Journal of Official Acts (ENJOA).

2. Accept all well-reasoned answers here.

3. Acceptance of digital signatures has been slowed because people still like the time-honored ritual of signing paper documents.

4. The author predicts that digital signatures will ultimately prevail.

5. The use of electronic signatures will prevent forgeries.

Questions for Review and Discussion   Page 240

1. In British law, the parties in a breach of contract lawsuit could not testify in court about the promises they had made. Consequently, witnesses as to the nature of a contract had to be brought in to testify. Problems arose because many of the witnesses brought to a trial took bribes to lie in support of one or the other party in a case. The Statute of Frauds was introduced to help eliminate this problem.

2. The six types of contracts that must be in writing under the Statute of Frauds are (1) contracts that cannot be completed within one year; (2) contracts transferring real property rights; (3) contracts for the sale of goods of $500 or more; (4) certain contracts entered by executors and administrators; (5) contracts by one party to pay a debt incurred by another party; and (6) contracts in consideration of marriage.

3. The following information must be in a written contract: the terms of the agreement, an identification of the subject matter, a statement of the consideration promised, the names and identities of the parties obligated under the contract, and the signature of the party sought to be bound to the agreement.

4. The parol evidence rule states that evidence as to oral statements made before a contract is reduced to writing cannot be offered as evidence in court to contradict the written terms.

5. The exceptions under the parol evidence rule include (1) evidence of conditions precedent; (2) evidence to add

missing terms or to correct obvious or small clerical errors; (3) evidence of alterations in the contracts or evidence of rescission of the agreement after the contract is reduced to writing; (4) and evidence to show that the agreement was never genuine in the first place because of fraud, duress, mistake, undue influence, misrepresentation, lack of capacity, and so on.

6. The best evidence rule is the rule that states that a court would prefer to have an original of a written contract rather than a copy introduced as evidence.

7. The equal dignities rule states that if a contract that is to be negotiated by an agent must be in writing, then the contract that appoints the agent must also be in writing.

8. Certain formalities are followed in the formation of contracts. Written agreements need not be signed by both parties. However, any agreement signed by only one party would obligate only that party. Facsimile signatures are allowed on a contract if the contract states that such signatures are valid. Some states have statutes allowing facsimile signatures. Persons who are illiterate usually sign written contracts with an X.

9. If an individual is illiterate and must sign a contract with an X then a witness is required. Otherwise, witnesses are not required when parties enter written agreements. However, to avoid misunderstanding, the use of witnesses is still advisable. Some official documents, such as the certificate of title to a motor vehicle and a deed to land, require the owner's signature and an acknowledgment by a notary public that the signature was the person's free act and deed. Some states still make use of the seal when a party enters a contract. Most, however, have disposed of the custom. The law provides that some documents must be recorded in a public office for inspection by the public.

10. Three modern laws involving cybercommerce include: the E-Sign Act, the Uniform Electronic Transaction Act (UETA), and the Uniform Computer Information Transaction Act (UCITA).

Cases for Analysis   Page 240

1. In Case 1, Perdue is correct and Paynter is wrong. Since Johnson Construction could have finished the office within one month, or less for that matter, the contract *could* have been performed within one year. If Johnson Construction actually did move out within the first month, Paynter would have begun work one month later. Paynter's term of employment from that point would have run nine months. Therefore, the entire contract could have been performed within eleven months. Recall that the operative words in the statute state that contracts "not to be performed" within one year must be in writing. If it is possible to perform a contract within one year, then it falls outside the statute and no writing is required. That was the case here.

2. No. The contract alleged by Meng was one that could not be fully performed in one year because it called for

payments of salary and benefits over a fourteen month period.

3. Bazzy's company successfully argued that an option to buy stock comes within the meaning of the phrase "contract for the sale of securities." Such a contract must be in writing under section 8-319 of the Uniform Commercial Code.

4. No. The oral contract was enforceable. It did not fall within the Statute of Frauds, which requires certain contracts to be in writing.

5. No. The oral contract was enforceable. It did not fall within the Statute of Frauds, which requires certain contracts to be in writing.

6. The agreement to spend one week at each of eighty-seven different boutiques would clearly take more than one year to complete. Contracts taking more than a year to perform must be in writing under the Statutes of Frauds.

7. No. The court ruled that the Statute of Frauds does not require that the written agreement be included in one writing alone. The court stated that a combination of letters, documents, and the like was sufficient as long as it contained the information and signatures required of a memorandum.

8. No. The court ruled that there was no enforceable promise because Ray's agreement to take care of any problems with the mobile home was not contained with other conditions in the written sales agreement. The parol evidence rule will not allow evidence of the oral promise to be presented in court.

9. No. The court ruled that whether a contract is under seal depends on the intent of the parties. As the word *seal* was so far separated from their signatures, it became apparent that there was no intention that it be adopted as their seal for the purposes of the contract.

Chapter 13   Third Parties in Contract Law

Questions for Analysis   Page 253

1. Movie advertisements must attract as many first weekenders as possible because the next film in the schedule may replace a movie that does not do well during the first weekend.

2. The movie industry has realized that many of the members of a first weekend audience pay more attention to the Web than to television and other traditional advertising vehicles.

3. Accept all well-reasoned answers to this question.

4. No. A network cannot bring suit as a third party beneficiary to recover a loss due to a film company's choice to use another approach to advertise its movie.

5. No. A pizza place cannot bring suit as a third party beneficiary to recover a loss due to a film company's choice to pull a movie from a local theater.

Questions for Review and Discussion   Page 254

1. A beneficiary in whose favor a contract is made is an intended beneficiary. Intended beneficiaries can enforce the contract made by those in privity of contract. Those who are most frequently recognized to be intended beneficiaries and have the right to demand and enforce the benefits promised are creditor beneficiaries, donee beneficiaries, and insurance beneficiaries.

2. An incidental beneficiary is an outside party for whose benefit a contract was not made but who would substantially benefit if the agreement were performed according to its terms and benefits.

3. An assignment is a transfer of a contract right, so that the assignee has the same rights that the original party, the assignor, had under the contract.

4. A delegation is a transfer of a contract duty, so that the assignee has the same duties that the original party, the assignor, had under the contract.

5. The three parties in an assignment are the party who assigns the contract rights (or duties), known as the assignor; the party to whom the assignment is made, known as the assignee, and the remaining party to the original agreement, known as the obligor.

6. The assignee is responsible for giving notice of an assignment.

7. The rights and duties of the assignee under the assignment are the same as those previously held by the assignor under the original contract.

8. Contracts for personal services or professional services cannot be assigned. It is also possible for the parties to a contract to agree that the duties and/or rights cannot be assigned.

9. A novation occurs when two contracting parties agree to replace one of the parties with a new party. The new party (the assignee) agrees to enter to contract with the remaining original party (the obligor), causing a privity of contract between them.

10. A novation is a new contract that severs one of the original parties as if that party had never been a part of the contract in the first place.

Cases for Analysis   Page 255

1. Ordinarily Jolas would be right in that duties may be delegated if there is no agreement not to do so. However, this job was based on Jolas's professional reputation, Mrs. Prendergast, therefore, had the right to expect that he would personally do the work. The fact that he did not and that he delegated the duty to another artist put him in breach of contract.

2. Despite the privity rule, it is possible for two or more parties to provide benefits to a third party. However, the law still makes a distinction between third parties who are intended beneficiaries and third parties who are incidental beneficiaries. In this case the restaurants and hotels are incidental beneficiaries. The court should

grant the team's summary judgment motion and dismiss the second case.

3. Yes. The attorney was a creditor beneficiary, a type of intended beneficiary, under the contract between Leslie and Roland. An intended beneficiary may recover on a contract to which it is not a party.

4. Although the giving of notice is the obligation of the assignee, either party may give notice. Once notice is received, the obligor (Blackston) should deal with the assignee (Department of Human Resources). In this case, notice was given to Blackston by the assignor, the clerk of court.

5. Yes. Once the obligor has notice of the assignment, the obligor cannot lawfully pay the amount to the assignor, but must pay it to the assignee. When the assignor is paid, as in this example, the assignee may sue the obligor directly.

6. Yes. The contract in this case was to furnish comic strips as items of commerce. If this had been a contract with the artist for personal service, the result might have been different.

7. No. Employees are intended beneficiaries of a collective bargaining agreement between the corporation and the union. As such, they can bring suit to enforce the agreement. As their assignee, Springer also has this right.

8. Yes. The court held that Copeland's abilities and skills were not of a routine nature but were unique, owing to Copeland's personal qualifications. His contract with McDonald's Systems, Inc., therefore, implied a restriction against assignment.

9. No. The Murphys knew of no problems with the house when the sale took place. Consequently, they had no claim against Timbercrest either at the time of the sale or at the time of the assignment. Since they had no right to bring a claim against Timbercrest, they could not assign this nonexistent right.

10. No. It was not necessary for Sam Fox to obtain Nolan's permission before assigning the publishing contract to Williamson. The court held that the agreement between Nolan and Sam Fox did not contain the type of personal trust that would require Nolan's consent before an assignment could be made.

Chapter 14   Discharge and Remedies

Questions for Review and Discussion Page 273

1. In the performance of a contract, reasonable time means the time that can be justly, suitably, and feasibly required to do the job specified in the contract, in the face of the existing situation.

2. The satisfactory performance of a contract occurs when either personal taste, if specified as the criterion under which performance will be judged, or an objective standard determines that the parties to the contract have done the job they promised to do based on contractual terms.

3. Complete performance occurs when all of the parties to the contract fully accomplish every term, condition, and promise that they agreed to. Substantial performance occurs when a party, in good faith, executes all promised terms and conditions with the exception of minor details that have little effect on the actual intent of the contract.

4. When a condition precedent is added to a contract, the contract does not go into effect until that condition is fulfilled. When a condition concurrent is part of a contract both parties are required to perform at the same time. A condition subsequent is one that happens after the contract has been entered and which will terminate the contract should it occur (or not occur).

5. Tender of performance means that a party has offered to do what he or she has agreed to do under the contract.

6. A contract can be discharged by nonperformance in the following ways: agreement, impossibility, operation of law, and breach of contract.

7. Anticipatory repudiation occurs when a party to a contract expresses or clearly implies an intent not to perform before the date of performance has arrived.

8. In the event of a breach of contract the complaining party has the following options for damages available: actual or compensatory damages, incidental damages, consequential damages, punitive damages, and nominal damages.

9. The principle of the mitigation of damages requires the injured party to keep the damages as low as possible.

10. Specific performance requires a party to perform a contract while injunctive relief orders a party to refrain from an action.

Cases for Analysis Page 273

1. The court ruled that the contractor was correct. While there were minor deviations from certain specified parts of the agreement concerning the plumbing fixtures, the contractor had, nevertheless, substantially performed the contract.

2. The court decided the case in favor of Morin Building Products. The court concluded that, using an objective standard to judge the work, the siding that the company had installed fit in quite well with the utilitarian function of the business.

3. The court awarded Grafio $1,845 less $50 under the legal theory that Grafio had substantially performed his contract to paint the house.

4. Great American successfully argued that the liquidated damage clause was not reasonable in view of the fact that Kvassay would collect $1.45 per case or about 41 percent of projected profits if the contract were breached.

5. No. The judgment was for Parker. The court held that, due to the circumstances, the doctrine of impossibility

of performance would overshadow the other agreements included in the contracts. The court further stated that it would be unreasonable to believe that Parker anticipated such an accident in his future and that he did not, therefore, sign away his rights under the circumstances that did develop.

6. Yes. The condition requiring a minimum payment of $470 per month was a condition concurrent with Mobil's agreement to deliver at least 33,572 gallons per month. Mobil's failure to do so was a breach of contract releasing Shaw from his obligations.

7. Yes. Bob Pagan Ford was permitted to seek injunctive relief restraining Smith from continuing to work for a competing auto dealership in Galveston County. Money damages would not be sufficient to stop Smith from damaging Bob Pagan's business. The court, however, felt that the three-year time limit was too severe and reduced it to six months.

8. No. When land or any interest therein is the subject matter of a contract, the power of a court of equity to grant specific performance is beyond question. Real estate is assumed to possess the characteristic of uniqueness. An imprudent or bad bargain in and of itself is not an excuse for nonperformance of a contract.

9. Yes. Under the doctrine of substantial performance, the general rule regarding building contracts is that a builder is not required to perform perfectly, but rather is held to a duty of substantial performance in a workerlike manner. A purchaser who receives substantial performance of the building contract must pay the price agreed to less an offset for defects in what he or she received as compared to what strict performance would have given. A contractor whose work amounts to less than substantial performance may not recover on the contract. Such a contractor may recover under a quasi-contractual theory for the reasonable value of the services the contractor rendered less any damages suffered by the purchaser. In this example, the cracks did not affect the operation of the structure as a water slide. In addition, the owner received and enjoyed the benefits from the work. The court held that there was substantial performance.

10. The frustration-of-purpose doctrine was used by the court to excuse Paonessa from completing the contract with Chase. The court quoted s. 265 of the Restatement (Second) of Contracts: "Where, after a contract is made, a party's principle purpose is substantially frustrated without his fault by the occurrence of an event the non-occurrence of which was a basic assumption on which the contract was made, his remaining duties to render performance are discharged, unless the language or the circumstances indicate the contrary."

Part 2   Case Study   Page 278

1. If the agreement was made in consideration that the parties should cohabit, the court's early decision

precluded the enforcement of an agreement between unmarried parties.

2. Illicit sexual relations must not be an inherent aspect of the agreement or a serious and not merely an incidental part of the performance of the agreement.

3. With the prevalence of nonmarital relationships today, a considerable number of people live together without benefit of the rules of law that govern property, financial, and other matters in a marital relationship.

4. The theory of these cases is that while cohabitation without marriage does not give rise to the property and financial rights which normally attend the marital relation, neither does cohabitation disable the parties from making an agreement within the normal rules of contract law.

5. The court adopts the view that unmarried cohabitants may lawfully contract concerning property, financial, and other matters relevant to their relationship. Such a contract is subject to the rules of contract law and is valid even if expressly made in contemplation of a common living arrangement, except to the extent that sexual services constitutes they only, or dominant, consideration for the agreement, or that enforcement should be denied on some other public policy ground.

Part 3   Sales and Consumer Protection

Chapter 15   Sales and Leases of Goods

Questions for Analysis   Page 293

1. It is important to identify dealers in the crowd at an auction to be able to watch how they are bidding. They will pay a price only up to the point at which their markups are still large enough.

2. At a live auction, people can view everything before a sale. They can touch the items and ask specialists on the floor questions.

3. It is easier to make a mistake when buying on eBay because you can't see anything in person.

4. In addition to specialists on hand to assist buyers during previews and sales, most auction houses put their catalogs as well as tutorials that walk buyers through the auction process on their websites.

5. The hammer price may not be the final cost at an auction because auction houses tack on a buyer's premium of anywhere from 5 percent to 20 percent of the winning bid as well as taxes and shipping.

Questions for Review and Discussion   Page 294

1. The law of sales applies to contracts for the sale and lease of goods. The law applies to transactions between

private parties as well as transactions by business people or merchants.

2. Any items of personal property that are movable are acceptable answers to the first part of the question. For examples, see text page 281. Future goods include fish in the sea, minerals in the ground, crops not yet planted, and goods not yet manufactured.

3. When a contract includes both goods and services, the dominant element of the contract determines whether it is a contract for goods or a contract for services.

4. A contract for sale includes both a present sale of goods and a contract to sell goods at a future time.

5. Students may choose any three of the following special rules: (1) Prior dealings and usage of trade may be used to supplement or qualify the terms of a sales contract. (2) A sales contract may be made in any manner that shows that the parties reached an agreement. (3) A contract may come about even though some terms are not agreed upon. (4) Unless otherwise specified, an offeree may accept an offer in any way that is reasonable, including a prompt shipment of the goods. (5) A written promise by a merchant to hold an offer open needs no consideration to be binding. (6) A sales contract may be made even though the price is not settled. If the parties cannot agree on a price, it will be a reasonable price at the time of delivery. (7) Output and requirement contracts are allowed in a sales contract as long as the parties deal in good faith and according to reasonable expectations. (8) A sales contract will result even when an offeree adds terms that are different from or additional to those offered or agreed upon. The different terms do not become part of the contract unless the parties are both merchants and no objection is made to them within a reasonable time. (9) No consideration is necessary to modify a contract for the sale of goods.

6. An option contract is a binding promise to hold an offer open. Consideration is required to make an option contract binding on the parties. No consideration is necessary, on the other hand, if a *merchant* promises in writing to hold an offer open for the sale of goods. The offer is called a firm offer and is limited to a period of three months.

7. A contract for the sale of goods for the price of $500 or more must be in writing to be enforceable. A lease of goods for $1,000 or more must be in writing to be enforceable.

8. A sales contract need not be in writing under the following four conditions: Between merchants, if either merchant receives a written confirmation of the oral agreement from the other within a reasonable length of time and if the receiver does not object within ten days, the oral agreement is enforceable.

If the goods are to be specially manufactured for the buyer and are not suitable for sale to others in the ordinary course of the seller's business and if the seller has already made either a substantial beginning in manufacturing the goods or has made commitments to buy them, the oral agreement is enforceable.

If the party against whom enforcement is sought admits in court that an oral contract for the sale of goods was made, the contract will be enforceable up to the quantity of goods admitted.

Executed contracts need not be in writing. If there has been a part payment or a part delivery, the law will enforce that portion of the agreement that has been performed.

9. The writing that is required to satisfy the UCC must indicate that a contract for sale has been made between the parties and must mention the quantity of goods being sold.

10. In an auction with reserve, the auctioneer may withdraw the goods at any time until he or she announces completion of the sale. In an auction without reserve, after the auctioneer calls for bids on an article or lot that article or lot cannot be withdrawn unless no bid is made within a reasonable time. An auction sale is with reserve unless the goods are explicitly put up for auction without reserve.

Cases for Analysis   Page 295

1. Under the UCC, goods that are not yet in existence are called *future goods,* and contracts to sell them in the future are legally enforceable.

2. No. A lease of goods, under the UCC, must be in writing if the total payments to be made under the lease are $1,000 or more.

3. No. The court held that the dominant element of the contract was services rather than goods; therefore, the UCC did not apply to the case. MFA lost its case against McBee for services rendered.

4. No. An agreement modifying a contract for the sale of goods needs no consideration to be binding. Any such modification may be oral unless the original agreement is in writing and provides that it may not be modified except by a signed writing.

5. Yes. Although the auction was one with reserve, because nothing was said about its being without reserve, the owner's right to reject a bid must be exercised before the auctioneer accepts the bid. The auctioneer is the seller's agent, whose act of accepting a bid is binding on the seller.

6. No. This is an output contract for the sale of all of the farmer's cotton that was produced during the year, and it is sufficient to satisfy the requirements of the UCC.

7. No. Under the UCC, if the party against whom enforcement is sought admits in court that an oral contract for the sale of goods was made, the contract will be enforceable even though it is over $500.

8. Yes. The contract came within the exception to the Statute of Frauds, which states that a contract for the sale of goods is enforceable with respect to goods that have been received and accepted.

9. Yes. The contract was unenforceable. It is necessary to put the quantity of goods to be bought and sold in the written agreement. When the writing relied upon to form the contract of sale does not specify quantity, parol (oral) evidence cannot be used to supply the missing amount.

Chapter 16   Title and Risk of Loss in Sales of Goods

Questions for Review and Discussion   Page 307

1. Void title is no title at all. Voidable title means that title may be voided if one of the parties elects to do so.

2. An innocent purchaser of stolen goods has no rights of title when property is claimed by the real owner. The innocent purchasers may bring suit against the person from whom stolen goods were purchased for breach of warranty of title.

3. Examples of people who have voidable title to goods are people who buy goods from minors or the mentally ill, and people who obtain property as a result of another's fraud, misrepresentation, mutual mistake, undue influence, or duress.

4. When goods are entrusted to a merchant who sells them in the ordinary course of business to a third party, the third party receives good title to them. The original owner who entrusted them to the merchant loses title to the goods altogether. His or her remedy is against the merchant for money damages caused by the loss.

5. In a shipment contract, title and risk of loss pass to the buyer when the goods are given to the carrier.

6. In a destination contract, title and risk of loss pass to the buyer when the seller tenders the goods at the place of destination.

7. When the contract calls for the buyer to pick up the goods, title passes to the buyer when the contract is made. Risk of loss, on the other hand, passes at different times depending on whether the seller is a merchant. If the seller is a merchant, the risk of loss passes when the buyer receives the goods. If the seller is not a merchant, the risk of loss passes to the buyer when the seller tenders the goods to the buyer.

8. When a document of title is used, both title and risk of loss pass to the buyer when the document is delivered to the buyer.

9. Sales that allow goods to be returned even though they conform to the contract are sales on approval when the goods are primarily for the buyer's use and sales or returns when the goods are delivered primarily for resale. On a sale on approval, title and risk of loss do not pass until the buyer gives approval of the goods on trial. On a sale or return, title passes at the time of the sale. Also, the goods must be returned at the buyer's risk and expense.

10. Buyers may place insurance on goods the moment a contract is made and the goods are identified to the contract. It is then that buyers receive an insurable interest in the goods that they buy.

Cases for Analysis   Page 308

1. The seller, Wheel Sports Center, must suffer the loss. Under Section 2-509(3) of the Uniform Commercial Code, the risk of loss passes to the buyer on the receipt of the goods if the seller is a merchant. In this case, the buyer did not receive the goods.

2. No. Regardless of the number of transactions, one cannot remove oneself from the rule that a purchaser can take only those rights that his or her transferor has in the goods. A thief has neither title nor the power to convey such.

3. Martin owned the fuel in the tanks. Parties to a sale contract may, if they wish, enter into an agreement stating when and where title will pass from the seller to the buyer. In such a case, title will pass at the time and place agreed, and Brown agreed to buy the stored motor fuel when it was removed from the tanks through and by means of computing pumps. Title passed to Brown when the fuel was pumped, Prior to that, it belonged to Martin.

4. No. Although Gerard had voidable title to the bicycle because she purchased it from a minor, anyone with voidable title to goods is able to transfer good title to others. According to the UCC, "A person with voidable title has power to transfer a good title to a good faith purchaser for value."

5. Heiselman had title to the boat. When anyone entrusts goods to a merchant and the merchant sells them in the ordinary course of business to a third party, the third party receives good title to them.

6. No. The sale of the cattle did not occur in October, as Weisbart claimed. A sale is defined as "the passing of title from the seller to the buyer for a price. "Unless otherwise agreed, title passes to the buyer at the time and place at which the seller completes his or her performance with reference to the physical delivery of the goods. Since the contract called for delivery at destination (Weisbart's ranch), title could not pass until the delivery was made there. A sale did not occur.

7. No. Automobile certificates of title have not generally been accorded the legal status of documents of title. Therefore, unless otherwise agreed, title to the property passes to the buyer at the time physical possession is transferred. Mann received title to the car when he received possession of it even though he did not receive the correct certificate of title.

8. Brown suffered the loss. A contract that contains neither an f.o.b. term nor any other term explicitly allocating loss is a shipment contract. A shipment contract is regarded as the normal one, and the destination contract is viewed as the variant type. A seller is not obligated to

deliver to a named destination and bear the risk of loss to that point unless he or she has specifically agreed to do so.

9. No. Buyers receive an insurable interest in goods the moment the contract is made and the goods are identified to the contract. The sugar falls into the definition of fungible goods, that is, "goods of which any unit is, by nature or usage of trade, the equivalent of any like unit." An undivided share of an identified bulk of fungible goods is sufficiently identified to be sold even if the quantity of the bulk is not determined.

Chapter 17   Performance and Breach of the Sales Contract

Questions for Analysis   Page 311

1. The crux of Hays's argument is that a ruinous arrogance crept in over the decades, causing the company to cease dealing in good faith with a number of key constituents, including its bottlers and regulators.

2. As growth began to slow, Coke increasingly tried to make its numbers through debilitating price hikes on the concentrate it sells to bottlers.

3. Answers should relate generally to the issue of dealing in good faith with the company's key constituents.

Questions for Review and Discussion   Page 322

1. The seller is obligated to turn over the goods to the buyer, and the buyer is obligated to accept and to pay for them, each in accordance with the terms of the contract. In addition, all parties must act in good faith, which means that they must act honestly. The court will not enforce a contract or part of a contract that it finds to be unconscionable.

2. Tender of performance is necessary in order to test the other party's ability and willingness to perform his or her part of the bargain. If tender is not made and the other party fails to perform, the one not making tender cannot bring suit.

3. Tender of delivery requires the seller to put and hold conforming goods at the buyer's disposition. In addition the seller must give the buyer notice that the goods are being tendered. Tender of delivery must be at a reasonable hour of the day to allow the buyer to take possession of the goods. When the contract for sale is a shipment contract, the seller must put the goods in the possession of a carrier and contract with the carrier for their transportation. Any necessary documents must be sent to the buyer, and he or she must be promptly notified of the shipment. When the goods are in the possession of a warehouse and are to be delivered without being shipped, the seller must either tender a negotiable document of title covering the goods or obtain an acknowledgment by the warehouse of the buyer's right to possession of them.

Tender of payment may be made by the buyer by any means or in any manner that is commonly used in the ordinary course of business. The seller, however, may demand payment in legal tender if he or she gives the buyer a reasonable time to obtain it.

4. Except when goods are shipped c.o.d., or when the contract provides for payment against a document of title, the buyer has the right to inspect the goods before accepting them or paying for them. The inspection may take place after the goods have arrived at their destination, when shipped by the seller.

5. When defective or nonconforming goods are delivered, the buyer may elect to reject all of them, accept all of them, or accept any commercial unit or units and reject the rest.

6. A rejection of goods must be done within a reasonable time after their delivery or tender to the buyer. After a rejection, the buyer may not claim ownership of the goods. In addition, he or she must notify the seller of the particular defect in the goods so as to give the seller an opportunity to cure the defect. If the goods are in the buyer's possession, he or she must hold them with reasonable care long enough for the seller to remove them. If the seller gives no instructions within a reasonable time after being notified of the rejection, the buyer may store the goods for the seller's account, reship them to the seller, or resell them for the seller's account. Merchant buyers are under a special duty after the rejection of goods in their possession or control to follow any reasonable instructions received from the seller with respect to the goods. If there are no instructions, they must make reasonable efforts to sell the goods for the seller's account if they are perishable or threaten to decline quickly in value.

7. When the time for performance has not yet expired, the seller has the right to cure the defect and make a proper tender within the contract time.

8. Under older contractual law, when one party notified the other party before the time for performance that he or she was not going to perform the contract, the injured party would have to wait for the actual time for performance before bringing suit. Under the UCC, when either party repudiates the contract before the time for performance, the injured party may take action immediately if it would be unjust or cause a material inconvenience to wait longer.

9. When a buyer breaches a contract for sale, the seller may withhold delivery of any goods not yet delivered; stop any goods that are in transit if the buyer is insolvent or stop delivery of a carload, truckload, planeload, or larger shipments of express or freight when the buyer repudiates or fails to make a payment that is due before delivery or otherwise breaches the contract; resell the goods or the undelivered balance of them—in the case of unfinished manufactured goods, a seller may either complete the manufacture and resell the

finished goods or cease manufacture and resell the un-finished goods for scrap or salvage value; retain the merchandise and sue the buyer for either the difference between the contract price and the market price at the time the buyer breached the agreement or the profit that the seller would have made had the contract been performed; sue the buyer for the price of any goods that the buyer has accepted; or cancel the contract.

10. When a seller breaches a contract for sale, the buyer may cover the sale, that is, buy similar goods from someone else and sue the seller for the difference between the agreed price and the cost of the purchase; deduct all or any part of the damages resulting from breach of contract from any price still due and, in addition, sue the seller for damages for nondelivery—damages sought would be the difference between the contract price and the price of the same goods in the marketplace on the date of the breach; when the goods are unique, ask the court to order the seller to turn the goods over to the buyer in an action for specific performance of the contract: or bring an action to replevy goods that have been identified to the contract if, after a reasonable effort, the buyer is unable to buy the goods elsewhere.

Cases for Analysis Page 323

1. If a buyer has accepted goods on the assumption that their nonconformity would be corrected by the seller and the seller does not do so, the buyer may revoke the acceptance. The court held in this case that the buyer could revoke the acceptance.

2. Friend Lumber successfully argued that it was not notified of the nonconformity within a reasonable time. When the buyer accepts goods and later discovers something wrong with them, the buyer must notify the seller within a reasonable time after the discovery. Although the door units arrived on the job individually wrapped in clear plastic, they were susceptible to inspection, including a check of measurements. The court held that three-and-one-half months was beyond a reasonable time to notify the seller of the defect.

3. Young recovered $132,902 which was the profit he would have made had the contract been performed.

4. No. Schleimer cannot recover from Googe because she did not make tender of delivery. The court held that Googe had the right to cancel the contract because tender was not made. Although the buyer is obligated to accept and pay for the goods after a contract for sale has been made, this obligation is conditioned upon the seller's making tender of delivery. Failure of the seller to do this is an excuse for the buyer to cancel the contract [see UCC Sections 2-507(1) and 2-711(1)].

5. No. The buyers did not reject the goods within a reasonable time. Two years and 14,000 miles after purchasing a vehicle is too late to reject it. The court said,

"One who exercises dominion over or alters goods in their possession thereby accepts the goods."

6. No. The removal of the equipment to Innes's field constituted a tender of delivery of the equipment.

7. Yes. Since the delivered goods did not conform to the contract, Formetal was permitted to "reject the whole." To meet the requirements of an effective rejection, the company had to reject within a reasonable time and notify Presto to that effect. Formetal did all it needed to do. It was not required to return the goods even though it promised to do so. After a rejection, the buyer's only duty is to "hold them with reasonable care at the seller's disposition for a time sufficient to permit the seller to remove them. The buyer has no further obligation with regard to goods rightfully rejected" (see UCC Section 2-602)

8. The bank neither tendered a delivery nor delivered the forms to Goosic. For a delivery or tender to be effective, it must enable the buyer or his or her agent to take possession of the goods in a peaceful manner and without interference. Goosic recovered $1,320.45, which was the difference between the contract price and the fair market value plus court costs.

9. No. There can be no question that Pace accepted the goods. The UCC defines acceptance as occurring when, among other things, the buyer does any act inconsistent with the seller's ownership. Here, Pace took possession of the goods, put them into inventory in his yard, and offered them for sale to the public. Moreover, he failed to express dissatisfaction effectively, made a partial payment on the goods, and never attempted to return or tender the shipment back to Sagebrush.

10. No. McQueen did not have the right to revoke her acceptance. The right to revoke an acceptance of the car arises only if the buyer accepted the goods on the assumption that its nonconformity would be corrected by the seller, and the seller does not do so. It also may be done in cases in which the nonconformity is difficult to detect. There was no evidence that the car was accepted with any knowledge of a nonconformity. Similarly, there was no evidence that the mileage as shown on the odometer was not the actual mileage or that discovery was prevented by the seller. The fact that the fan belt broke two days after the sale is insufficient to show such nonconformity as would allow McQueen to revoke her acceptance. In addition, there was nothing to show that she did not discover the mileage of the car due to the difficulty of discovery.

Chapter 18   Warranties and Product Liability

Questions for Analysis Page 328

1. The Big Three were late making the move toward small, fuel-efficient cars. Later, U.S. auto brands

compounded their error, offering horrible styling and quality to newly affluent baby boomers.

2. U.S. and foreign automakers devote much attention to generation Y because many of the sixteen- to twenty-four-year-olds shifted their loyalties to such automakers as Mercedes-Benz and BMW, and the group buys 850,000 cars a year.

3. The selling points that car makers are discovering for kids are the same as thirty years ago: price and value.

4. Hyundai's biggest attraction to young buyers is its long warranties. The company guarantees its cars for five years and 60,000 miles. Engines and transmissions carry a 10-year, 100,000-mile warranty.

Questions for Analysis Page 340

1. The U.S. Supreme Court held that the Due Process Clause of the Fourteenth Amendment "prohibits the imposition of grossly excessive or arbitrary punishments on defendants in tort cases."

2. It is not always possible for victims to detect careless medical practices, dangerous goods, and other behavior. Moreover, some victims may be unwilling to file lawsuits because of the sizable expense in time and money, the discomfort of having to testify, and the uncertainty that they will win even legitimate cases.

3. Justice Scalia argued that the determination of punitive damages should continue to be left to individual judges and juries because the Supreme Court cannot devise a "principal application" that determines what these damages should be in different circumstances.

4. Punitive damages amounted to 145 times compensatory damages in the State Farm case.

5. Companies pass the costs on to consumers via higher prices and large punitive damages encourage expensive class action law firms, driven by big contingency fees, to pursue unwarranted suits.

6. Examples are loss of life in automobile accidents caused by drunk drivers, or wrong statements by producers of drugs that cause severe harm or death to inappropriate users or damage victims and their heirs in ways that go far beyond the loss of future earnings.

Questions for Review and Discussion Page 341

1. Express warranties may arise by an affirmation of fact or promise, by a description of the goods, and by a sample or model.

2. When a written warranty is given to a consumer under the Magnuson-Moss Warranty Act, the written warranty must be made available before the consumer decides to buy the product, the writing must express the terms and conditions of the warranty in simple and readily understood language, and the warranty must disclose whether it is a full or a limited warranty.

3. A full warranty is one in which a defective product will be repaired or replaced without charge within a reasonable time after a complaint has been made about it. A

limited warranty is any written warranty that does not meet all of the requirements for a full warranty. Under a limited warranty, the consumer is not given the absolute, free of charge repair or replacement of a defective product, as is given in a full warranty.

4. The implied warranty of fitness for a particular purpose arises whenever a seller knows the particular purpose for which the buyer will use the goods and knows that the buyer is relying on the seller's skill and judgment to select the product. The implied warranty of merchantability is given whenever a merchant sells goods, unless the warranty is specifically excluded by the merchant.

5. Whenever goods are sold, the seller warrants that the title being conveyed is good and that the transfer is rightful.

6. To exclude the implied warranty of merchantability, the word *merchantability* must be used in the disclaimer. If the exclusion is in writing, it must be in large, bold type so that it is conspicuous. To exclude the implied warranty of fitness for a particular purpose, the exclusion must be in writing and be conspicuous also. The use of such expression as *as is, with all faults,* and the like is another way to exclude implied warranties. Implied warranties may also be excluded under the UCC by having buyers examine the goods. When the buyer has examined the goods or the sample or model as fully as he or she desires (or has refused to examine them when given the opportunity), there is no implied warranty as to defects that an examination would have revealed.

7. To recover damages for breach of warranty, buyers of defective goods must notify the seller of the defect within a reasonable time after the discovery or after the defect should have been discovered. Failure to do so will prevent them from recovering damages for breach of warranty.

8. The UCC provides three alternatives from which a state may choose. In all of the alternatives, warranties extend to people who would normally be expected to use the goods as well as to those who actually use them. Most states have adopted one of the alternatives. A few states have written their own version of the law.

9. It is difficult for injured parties to obtain actual evidence of a negligent act on the part of the manufacturer, since they were not present when the goods were made and normally they have very little information about the manufacturing process.

10. An injured party must prove that the manufacturer or seller sold the product in a defective condition, that the manufacturer or seller was engaged in the business of selling the product, that the product was unreasonably dangerous to the user or consumer, that the defective condition was the proximate cause of the injury or damage, that the defective condition existed at the time the product left the hands of the manufacturer or seller, and that the consumer sustained physical harm or property damage by use or consumption of the product.

Cases for Analysis Page 342

1. Kile would have a cause of action against the manufacturer. The UCC has abolished the requirement of privity. Instead, it provides three alternatives from which a state may choose. In all of the alternatives, warranties extend to people who would normally be expected to use the goods as well as to those who actually buy them.

2. No. Under the UCC, goods must be adequately contained and packaged to be merchantable. In addition, the serving for value of food or drink to be consumed either on or off the premises is a sale for the purposes of the warranty of merchantability. The wine could not be served as a drink nor could it be consumed without an adequate container. The drink that was sold included the wine and the container, both of which must be fit for the ordinary purposes for which they were to be used.

3. McCoy has a remedy against the trading post for breach of warranty title. In a sales contract under Section 2-312 of the UCC, there is a warranty by the seller that the title conveyed shall be good and its transfer rightful. Since the Old Ford Trading Post had no title to the gun, the warranty was breached.

4. Yes. Werner has a cause of action against Montana on the grounds of breach of express warranty. In general, statements of fact made by a seller about the goods being sold are considered a part of the description of the goods and are regarded as forming a part of the sales agreement. There was evidence that during the course of negotiations the parties had discussed the ship's watertightness and that Montana had told Werner that the sloop would become watertight once placed in water and allowed sufficient time to "make up." These assurances were part of the basis of the bargain and amounted to an express warranty under the UCC.

5. No. Romedy failed to comply with the requirement of the UCC, which states that "the buyer must within a reasonable time after he discovers or should have discovered any breach notify the seller of the breach or be barred from any remedy." Romedy waited more than a reasonable time to notify the seller that the car did not contain the equipment he had said it would contain.

6. Yes. In addition to having a cause of action against the manufacturer for breach of its express warranty that the mobile home was sheathed with the plywood, the Benfers have a cause of action against the retailer, Thomas, for two reasons: The statement by Thomas that the type of mobile home he carried has a one-quarter-inch sheathing on the siding created an express warranty because it was an affirmation of fact. The showing of the model home, which was part of the basis of the bargain, created an express warranty that the mobile home that was delivered would conform to the model that was shown to them.

7. Yes. When the seller is a merchant, unless excluded, it is implied that the goods will be merchantable, or fit for the ordinary purposes for which the goods are to be used. This implied warranty of merchantability was breached when Hensley received the car in unworkable condition. The language on the reverse side of the purchase agreement was not sufficient to exclude the implied warranty of merchantability because it was not conspicuously printed and did not contain the word *merchantability.*

8. Yes. An injured party can recover on a theory of strict liability in tort if there is sufficient evidence that an unreasonably dangerous product design proximately caused the injuries. In this case, the manufacturer produced a vehicle that was capable of off-the-road use. It was advertised for such use. The only protection provided the user in the case of rollovers or pitchovers proved wholly inadequate. The product was unreasonably dangerous.

9. No. There is no evidence that the El Toro's design proximately caused the injury or that the product failed to perform as expected when used with the recommended pad. In addition, the manufacturer had no reason to believe that the product would be used in a bar.

Chapter 19   Consumer Protection

Questions for Analysis Page 350

1. More than 25 percent of the junk e-mail sent around the globe now originates from servers in China and South Korea.

2. It is important that Asia act fast to curtail the use of spam because it could endanger the security of the global Net. Junk e-mail dangerously clogs the cyberways, and executives worry that spammers, using China as a base, will team up with hackers and virus writers and be very destructive.

3. Spam artists are moving operations to Asia because South Korea has the world's most advanced broadband infrastructure, allowing spammers to take advantage of its high-speed connections. Also, China is a safe harbor for spammers.

Questions for Review and Discussion Page 359

1. Consumer protection laws apply to transactions between someone conducting a business and a consumer.

2. The FTC Act states that "unfair or deceptive acts or practices in or affecting commerce are hereby declared unlawful."

3. It is unfair or deceptive for a seller to make a fraudulent misrepresentation, that is, a statement that has the effect of deceiving the buyer. Making false statements about the construction, durability, reliability, safety, strength, condition, or life expectancy of a product is a deceptive practice. It is also deceptive to fail to disclose to a buyer any fact that would cause the buyer not to enter into the contract. People who receive unordered

merchandise through the mail may treat it as a gift. They may keep the merchandise or dispose of it in any manner they see fit without any obligation whatsoever to the sender. An FTC rule prohibits bait-and-switch advertising schemes. The schemes are an alluring but insincere offer to sell a product or service that the advertiser in truth does not intend or want to sell. Its purpose is to switch customers from buying the advertised merchandise to buying something else, usually at a higher price or on a basis more advantageous to the advertiser. The Federal Odometer Law prohibits people from disconnecting, resetting, or altering the odometer of a motor vehicle to register any mileage other than the true mileage driven. Anyone who sells a car or even gives it away, unless it is over twenty-five years old, must provide the new owner with a written statement disclosing the odometer reading at the time of the transfer. If the seller has reason to believe that the mileage reading on the odometer is incorrect, the disclosure statement must indicate that the actual mileage traveled is unknown.

4. The Used Car Rule requires dealers to place a window sticker, called a Buyer's Guide, in the window of each used car they offer for sale. The Buyer's Guide gives the following information: a statement that the car is sold "as is" if it is sold with no warranties, a statement that the car is sold with implied warranties only if that is the case, and a statement telling whether the warranty is "full" or "limited" and the length of the warranty period if the car is sold with an express warranty. In addition, the guide must list the specific systems that are covered by the warranty and state the percentage of the repair costs that the buyer will be required to pay. The guide also includes a statement that tells consumers not to rely on spoken promises, a suggestion that consumers ask whether they may have the vehicle inspected by their own mechanic either on or off the premises, and a list of the fourteen major systems of an automobile and some of the principal defects that may occur in these systems.

Under the Cooling-Off Rule, sales of consumer goods or services over $25 that are made away from the seller's regular place of business, such as at a customer's home, may be canceled within three business days after the sale occurs. The rule requires the seller to give the buyer two copies of a cancellation form, one of which the buyer may send to the seller any time before midnight of the third business day after the contract was signed, canceling the contract.

Under the Mail, Telephone, Internet, or Fax Rule, sellers of mail-order goods must ship orders within the time promised in their advertisement. If no time period is promised, sellers must either ship the order within thirty days after they receive it or send the consumer an option notice. The option notice tells the consumer of a shipping delay and gives the consumer the option of agreeing to the delay or canceling the order and

receiving a prompt refund. Instructions on how to cancel the order must be included in the notice. In addition, the seller must provide a free way for the consumer to reply.

5. The Telemarketing Sales Rule gives consumers the power to stop unwanted telemarketing calls by placing their telephone numbers on the national Do Not Call registry. Many restrictions are placed on telemarketing practices. Regulations require that people who dial 900-prefix numbers be warned of the cost of the calls and be given a chance to hang up before being charged. In addition, telephone companies must block service to 900-prefix numbers if requested by the customer. Telephone companies cannot disconnect phone service to customers who refuse to pay for 900-number calls, and rules have been established for resolving billing disputes. The Negative Option Rule protects consumers when they subscribe to magazines, CD clubs, or other plans that send products on an ongoing basis. Under the Negative Option Rule, sellers must tell subscribers how many selections they must buy, if any; how and when they can cancel the membership; how to notify the seller when they do not want the selection; when to return the "negative option" form to cancel shipment of a selection; when they can get credit for the return of a selection; how postage and handling costs are charged; and how often they will receive announcements and forms.

Under the antispam law, unsolicited commercial e-mail messages must be truthful and must not use misleading subject lines or incorrect return addresses. E-mail containing pornography must be specifically labeled in the subject line. In addition, spammers cannot harvest e-mail addresses from chat rooms and other sites without permission. The law authorizes the FTC to establish a "Do-Not-E-mail registry," and provides for fines of $250 for each e-mail violation. The antislam law removes the profit out of slamming thereby protecting consumers from illegal telephone charges.

6. The Consumer Product Safety Act protects consumers from unreasonable risk of injury from hazardous products that are American-made or imported and manufactured or distributed for personal use, consumption, or enjoyment. The Consumer Product Safety Commission has powers to devise standards, safety rules, and sanctions; obtain injunctions in any federal court; ban hazardous products that are in the chain of distribution and on the retailer's shelf; and impose civil fines.

7. Consumers can use the information required to be disclosed by the Consumer Leasing Act to compare one lease with another or to compare the cost of leasing with the cost of buying the same property.

8. The Truth-in-Lending Act requires creditors to disclose the finance charge and the annual percentage rate (APR), before consumers enter into credit transactions. The Equal Credit Opportunity Act prohibits any creditor

from denying credit to a consumer on the basis of sex, marital status, color, race, religion, national origin, age, or receipt of public assistance.

9. Under the Truth-in-Lending Act, credit card holders are not responsible for any unauthorized charges made after the card issuer has been notified of the loss, theft, or possible unauthorized use of the card. Even then, credit card holders are responsible only for the first $50 of any unauthorized charges. The Fair Credit Billing Act establishes procedures for resolving mistakes on credit card accounts.

10. The Fair Debt Collection Practices Act prohibits debt collectors from engaging in unfair, deceptive, or abusive practices, including overcharging, harassment, and disclosing consumers' debts to third parties.

Cases for Analysis Page 360

1. Emerson should notify the credit card issuer of the dispute immediately by telephone. She should fill out the form sent to her by the credit card issuer and return it together with a copy of the sales slip and any other documentary evidence that she has. The chances are that the amount of the purchase will be deducted from her credit card bill by the credit card issuer.

2. No. Consumer protection laws apply to transactions entered into between someone conducting a business activity and a consumer. A consumer is someone who buys or leases real estate, goods, or services for personal, family, or household purposes. Barrett was not a consumer as that term is defined. He did not live in any of the apartments served by the propane-tank storage system, and the apartment buildings were commercial enterprises owned and operated by him for business purposes.

3. Yes. A debt collector may not communicate with the consumer at any unusual or inconvenient time, including before 8 A.M. or after 9 P.M. In addition, the use or threatened use of violence or other criminal means to harm a consumer and the use of profane language are not allowed.

4. Yes. Under the Used Car Rule, used car dealers who sell more than five used vehicles in a twelve-month period must place a window sticker, called a Buyer's Guide, in the window of each used car that they offer for sale. The Buyer's Guide must state that the car is sold "as is" if it is sold with no warranties.

5. Yes. Under the Equal Credit Opportunity Act, applicants may apply for credit in their name given at birth, their married name, or a combination of both.

6. Yes. The federal Odometer Law prohibits people from disconnecting, resetting, or altering the odometer of a motor vehicle to register any mileage other than the true mileage driven. Anyone who sells a car or even gives it away, unless it is over twenty-five years old, must provide the new owner with a written statement disclosing the odometer reading at the time of the transfer.

7. No. Under the Truth-in-Lending Act, Carboni is responsible only for the first $50 of unauthorized charges.

8. Yes. Consumer protection laws apply to transactions entered into between someone conducting a business activity and a consumer. A consumer is someone who buys or leases real estate, goods, or services for personal, family, or household purposes. The court said that Bierlein was "obviously" a consumer in this transaction.

9. No. Sales of consumer goods or services made away from the seller's regular place of business may be canceled within three business days after the sale occurs. Under New York law, the three-day right to cancel formally did not begin until the seller gave the buyer written notice of the right to cancel. Until that time, cancellation was permitted by any means; thus, the telephone cancellation and following attorney's letter were effective to cancel the contract.

10. No. The court said that even though the consumer protection law does not exclude services performed by physicians, it is clear that it is intended to prohibit unlawful practices relating to trade or commerce and of the type associated with business enterprises. It is equally clear that the legislature did not intend the law to apply to physicians rendering medical services. The liability of a physician, the court said, is premised upon either fault, lack of informed consent, or a specific contract warranting certain results. There is no indication that the consumer protection law was intended to create a cause of action for every statement made by a physician regarding a patient's condition, the likelihood for success of a given procedure, or the recommended course of treatment.

Part 3 Case Study Page 362

1. Section 2-401(2) provides that "unless otherwise explicitly agreed, title passes to the buyer at the time and place at which the seller completes his performance with reference to the physical delivery of the goods."

2. Circuit City claims that the testimony indicates an understanding between the parties that the transaction that takes place in Massachusetts constitutes, not a concluded sale, but only an order for merchandise.

3. The sales receipt represents proof of the customer's right to the purchased merchandise. The fact that the sale is credited to the Massachusetts store is indicative of an intent on Circuit City's part that more than an order for merchandise takes place in Massachusetts.

4. The vendor has done that which makes the whole consideration payable when the goods have been appropriated and set apart.

5. Circuit City performed its obligations with respect to delivery when the sale was entered as an alternative location sale into Circuit City's DPS system and the purchased merchandise was "reserved" for the customer at the designated location.

6. The court said that the reserve notation marked on the customer sales receipt for the purchased merchandise

sufficiently reflects its status of being set aside for, or identified to, that particular transaction.

7. The court held that the sales were taxable in Massachusetts.

Part 4   Property

Chapter 20   Personal Property

Questions for Analysis   Page 377

1. Until recently, file swappers have been targeted in an attempt to stop illegal copying.

2. Companies such as Intel, eBay, and Google are opposed to the passage of the Inducing Infringement of Copyright Act because they believe the bill could let content owners use law suits to kill off nascent technologies they find threatening. They believe the law will "freeze investment in technology."

3. The Supreme Court's 1984 Betamax decision declared that makers of VCRs couldn't be held liable if people used the machines to tape TV programs. If this were changed, VCR makers might be held liable whenever their machines were used for illegal taping.

4. According to this article, the real foe of the movie, music, and software industries is technology.

Questions for Review and Discussion   Page 381

1. Community property is property (except a gift or inheritance) that is acquired by the personal efforts of either spouse during marriage and which, by law, belongs to both spouses equally. Nine states (Arizona, California, Idaho, Louisiana, Nevada, New Mexico, Texas, Washington, and Wisconsin) are community property states.

2. Someone who finds lost property may claim ownership of it after a reasonable effort is made to find the owner without success.

3. If an abandoned shipwreck is found in the submerged land of any state of the United States, the Abandoned Shipwreck Act of 1987 applies rather than the law of finds or the law of salvage.

4. For a gift to be completed, the donor must intend to make a gift, the gift must be delivered to the donee, and the donee must accept the gift.

5. Minors are assured that gifts to them will be either used for their benefit or made available to them when they become adults. In addition, the income from gifts that are given to minors over the age of fourteen is taxable to the minor rather than to the person who made the gift.

6. A thief acquires no title to goods that are stolen and, therefore, cannot convey a good title to anyone, even an innocent person.

7. Patents give protective coverage to inventors for the exclusive rights to processes, machines, chemical formulas, and articles of manufacture.

8. Copyrights protect the writings of authors; the works of artists, painters, and sculptors; and the musical scores of composers and computer software from unauthorized reproduction, republication, and sale.

9. The registration of a trademark gives protective coverage to the owner for the exclusive use of the trademark.

10. Companies can lose their trademark protection if the marks are used as a generic term by a large segment of the public for a long period of time. Cornflakes, cube steak, dry ice, escalator, high octane, kerosene, lanolin, linoleum, mimeograph, nylon, raisin bran, shredded wheat, trampoline, and yo yo are some products that have lost trademark protection in this way.

Cases for Analysis   Page 381

1. No. A thief acquires no title to goods that are stolen and, therefore, cannot convey a good title to anyone, even an innocent person.

2. No. Originality is a requirement for something to be copyrighted. Mere facts, standing alone, cannot be copyrighted because they are not original. Selecting raw data from the white pages of a phone book is not a copyright infringement because the directory was devoid of even the slightest trace of originality or creativity.

3. No. The duplication of copyrighted materials for profit by a copyshop is not a "fair use" because it adversely affects the potential market for the copyrighted work.

4. No. A finder does not get title to another's lost property. An effort must be made to find or identify the real owner. State laws provide, however, that if a reasonable effort is made to locate the owner without success, the finder may claim ownership of the goods. Different states have different time limits beyond which the finder will be recognized as the actual owner.

5. Lane was the legal owner. For a gift to be completed, the property must be delivered to the donee. Since Hartwell's uncle kept the book collection in his possession instead of delivering it to Hartwell, the gift was not delivered, and the books became the property of the uncle's sole heir.

6. No. Copying items for such purposes as criticism, comment, news reporting, teaching, scholarship, and research may be done without permission under the doctrine of fair use.

7. Yes and no. The nineteen thoroughbred horses were tangible personal property, as the judge correctly ruled. They were susceptible to the sense of touch, capable of ownership, and endowed with intrinsic value. However, the cashier's check was not tangible personal property. It was intangible property. The holder of the check did not own any specific $33,000 of the bank's assets. Rather, he or she had a right to $33,000 of the bank's money. Caroline received only the nineteen thoroughbred horses, not the $33,000.

Chapter 21   Bailments

Questions for Analysis Page 398

1. Answers will vary.
2. Answers will vary.

Questions for Review and Discussion Page 402

1. A bailment for the sole benefit of the bailor results when possession of personal property is transferred to another for purposes that will benefit only the bailor. An example of this type of bailment is asking a friend to take your clothes to the cleaners for you as a favor.

    A bailment for the sole benefit of the bailee occurs when possession of personal property is transferred to the bailee for purposes that will benefit only the bailee. Borrowing a neighbor's lawn mower to mow one's lawn is an example of this type of bailment. When personal property is transferred to a bailee with the intent that both parties will benefit, a mutual-benefit bailment results. Delivering a television set to a service center for repairs is an example of a mutual-benefit bailment.

2. Former law required the bailee to use great care in a bailment for the sole benefit of the bailee, slight care in a bailment for the sole benefit of the bailor, and ordinary care in a mutual-benefit bailment. The standard of care adopted by many courts today does away with the degrees of care. Instead, all bailees are required to use reasonable care.

3. Under today's law, when items in the possession of a bailee are damaged, the burden of proof is shifted to the one who is in the best position to know what happened; that is, the bailee. The burden is on the bailee to prove that it was not negligent.

4. An innkeeper has an obligation to accept all guests. People may be turned away when all rooms are occupied or reserved. In addition, innkeepers may refuse to accommodate people whose presence might imperil the health, welfare, or safety of other guests.

5. Common carriers of goods are insurers of all goods accepted for shipment. With certain exceptions, they are liable as insurers regardless of whether they have or have not been negligent.

6. The TSA's approach to security includes thorough screening of baggage and passengers by highly trained screeners, fortified cockpit doors in all airliners, thousands of federal air marshals aboard a record number of flights, and armed federal flight deck officers.

7. Under CAPPS II, airlines would have asked passengers for a slightly expanded amount of reservation information, including full name, date of birth, home address, and home telephone number. The system would verify the identity of passengers and conduct a risk assessment using commercially available data and current intelligence information. It would then assign one of the following risk scores: unknown risk, no risk, elevated risk, and high risk. Once the system had computed a traveler's risk score, it would have sent an encoded message to be printed on the boarding pass indicating the appropriate level of screening and be sent to screeners at security checkpoints.

8. A public warehouser is one who owns a warehouse where any member of the public who is willing to pay the regular charge may store goods. A warehouser whose warehouse is not for general public use is a private warehouser.

9. A warehouser must use that amount of care that a reasonably careful person would use under similar circumstances. Failure to use such care is negligence and makes the warehouser liable for losses or damages to the goods.

10. A warehouser's lien is the right to retain possession of the goods until the satisfaction of the charges imposed upon them. The lien is for the amount of money owed for storage charges, transportation charges, insurance, and expenses necessary for the preservation of the goods. The lien is a possessory one. It is lost when the warehouser voluntarily delivers the goods or unjustifiably refuses to deliver them.

Cases for Analysis Page 402

1. Yes. Carriers may refuse passengers when they "are or might be inimical to safety."

2. No. Rather than the burden being on Scott, the bailor, to prove negligence on the part of the bailee, the burden is on Purser, the bailee, to prove that he was not negligent. The trial court applied incorrect legal standards when it found that no evidence was submitted that demonstrated any negligence on Purser's part.

3. Yes. Although the bailee is not an insurer of the property, it owes a duty to exercise reasonable care and to take precautions against reasonably foreseeable damages to the property. The burden was on Noel, the bailee, to prove that it was not negligent. Noel produced no evidence to prove that the cause of the loss was other than its failure as a bailee to safeguard the aircraft.

4. No. A bailor-bailee relationship did not exist. Their relationship was that of a master and servant (see Chapter 32). While a bailee has possession and control of the property, a servant has only custody. Further, a servant, unlike a bailee, is under the orders and control of the owner of the property.

5. No. In this case, F-M Potatoes had complete control of the potatoes. If the person leaving the property relinquishes exclusive possession, control, and dominion over the property to another, it is a bailment. If there is no such delivery and relinquishment of exclusive possession and control, it is a lease.

6. Yes. While innkeepers are not insurers of their guests' safety, they do owe a duty to take steps to protect their guests against unreasonable risk of physical harm. This includes risks arising from possible acts of an arsonist.

By failing to provide adequate lighting and a clear and obvious exit path from the building in the event of fire, the inn failed to perform its duty of protecting the guests against an unreasonable risk of injury.

7. No. There was no basis for concluding that the parties entered into a tenancy that gave Poroznoff a legal status other than that of a transient guest residing on a week-to-week basis. Innkeepers may refuse to accommodate people whose presence might imperil the health, welfare, or safety of other guests.

8. Yes. The dormitories were within the definition of the term *hotel* as defined in the hotel and motel dwelling law of that state, and the state agency could inspect them.

9. Yes. In addition to giving notice to all persons known to claim an interest in the goods, the sale must be advertised in a local newspaper. Anyone claiming a right to the goods may pay the money due before the sale and have the lien discharged.

10. If the airline can arrange alternate transportation that is scheduled to arrive at Fairchild's destination within one hour of the original arrival time, there is no compensation. However, if the alternate flight gets to the destination between one and two hours late, she is entitled to a cash payment equal to the price of one fare up to $200. This amount is doubled if Fairchild is more than two hours late.

Chapter 22   Real Property

Questions for Analysis   Page 423

1. Since Wal-Mart took over vacant space in a struggling neighborhood in South Central Los Angeles, it has lured black and Latino shoppers with low prices. People stay in the neighborhood for bargains and are stopping at other local stores, too.

2. Some reasons for the fierce opposition Wal-Mart faces sometimes when it attempts to open a store in a poor neighborhood are low wages and benefits, change of zoning laws, land use, and design issues.

3. The study by Emek Basker of the University of Missouri in 2003 found that five years after the opening of Wal-Marts in most markets, there is a small net gain in retail employment in counties where they are located with a drop of only about 1 percent in the number of small local businesses. Also, retail prices for many goods fall 5 percent to 10 percent.

4. Some suggestions offered to Wal-Mart by the authors of this article are: (1) develop a well-thought-out plan to ease its entry into cities, (2) revise its wage scale, (3) consider more flexibility in its floor design, and (4) talk early and often with the communities it wants to be in.

Questions for Review and Discussion   Page 426

1. Trees, shrubs, vineyards, and field crops that are harvested each year without replanting (perennials) are considered to be real property. Crops or garden plantings that produce vegetables or other harvests only for the year in which they are planted (annuals) are treated as personal property.

2. Landowners own the airspace above their land to as high as they can effectively possess or reasonably control.

3. In deciding whether or not an item is a fixture, the courts ask the following questions: Has there been a temporary or permanent installation of the personal property? Has the personal property been adapted to the intended use of the real property? What was the intent of the party at the time the personal property was attached to the real property?

4. An easement may be created by grant, by reservation, and by prescription.

5. In a freehold estate, the holder owns the land for life or forever. In a leasehold estate, an interest in real estate is held under a lease and is less than a freehold estate.

6. Years ago, in England, dower was the right that a widow had to a life estate in one-third of the real property owned by the husband during the marriage. Curtesy was the right that a widower had, if children of the marriage were born alive, to a life estate in all real property owned by the wife during the marriage.

7. In the case of a tenancy in common, the heirs succeed to the deceased's title interest. In the case of a joint tenancy, the co-owners succeed. In the case of a tenancy by the entirety, the surviving spouse succeeds.

8. Title to real property may be acquired by sale or gift, will or descent, or occupancy.

9. A nonconforming use of real property is a use of land that was in existence before a zoning law made such use illegal. Variances may be issued by boards of appeals to people who suffer undue hardship from zoning laws.

10. Eminent domain is the right of federal, state, and local governments, or other public bodies, to take private lands, with compensation to their owners, for public use.

Cases for Analysis   Page 426

1. The court should hold in favor of Bell. Once an easement is created and properly recorded, it runs with the land. This means that future owners will have the right to use the easement unless one of them gives it up by a deed or by not using it for a long period of time.

2. At her death in 1981, Maria owned the property subject to Annie's life estate in one half of the property. Annie's life estate ended when she died in 1985, at which time the property became fully owned by Maria's heirs.

3. Yes. Trade fixtures are those items of personal property that are brought upon the premises by the tenant and that are necessary to carry on the trade or business to which the said premises will be devoted. Contrary to the general rule, trade fixtures remain the personal

property of the tenant or occupier of the property and are removable at the expiration of the term of occupancy.

4. Dudley has the legal right to cut off the branches that are trespassing into the airspace over his property.

5. Yes. To resume their supply of water, the surrounding landowners would have to dig deeper wells. The landowners were entitled to recover the costs of the digging from the Eisenmanns. Under modern laws, property owners may draw only the water that is reasonably required to satisfy their needs. Other property owners damaged by unreasonable and excess use may seek an injunction against such use and also recover money damages to compensate them for their losses.

6. No. A deed is valid and operative between the parties whether or not it is founded upon consideration. The deed that was used by Jean Russell in this case was not a bargain-and-sale deed, which would have required consideration to be valid.

7. Yes. A tenancy by the entirety cannot be severed by the unilateral action of one tenant. Husband and wife have no separate interest in entireties property. A conveyance by one tenant only is ineffective to pass legal title. Both parties must agree to any sale or conveyance of the property.

8. The Misners could continue to use the ten campsites with facilities and the three primitive campsites because they were in existence when the new zoning law was passed and were nonconforming uses. They could not, however, expand the campsite any further.

9. Yes. With exceptions in some states, since the husband has the exclusive right to possession, he can sell the property or give a mortgage on it without the wife's consent. However, anyone buying the property or receiving a mortgage on it would lose all ownership interest should the wife survive the husband. Some states require both spouses to consent to a valid mortgage on property owned as tenants by the entirety.

10. No. A joint tenant with the right of survivorship may deed away his or her interest to a new owner without permission of the other joint tenants. The new owner, in such a case, becomes a tenant in common with the remaining joint tenants. In this case, Wheeler would own a one-half undivided interest in the property as a tenant in common with Chandler Clements.

Chapter 23   Landlord and Tenant

Questions for Analysis Page 435

1. Beginning in 1899, New York's 42nd Street created the greatest concentration of playhouses America has ever seen.

2. Starting in the 1930s, 42nd Street's fame gradually soured into infamy as the musicals were supplanted by burlesque reviews and B movies.

3. XXX fare descended on the area in the late 1960s when peep show machines were adapted to pornographic movies.

4. Disney CEO Michael D. Eisner, a native New Yorker, was motivated by his nostalgic memories of 42nd Street to restore the New Amsterdam Theater. Disney was able to acquire a forty-nine-year lease in the theater.

5. The cost of enhancing the area's tourist appeal alienated many New Yorkers.

6. Disney restored the theater to a condition approximating its original splendor. In 1997, the company opened the theater with a live adaptation of *The Lion King* which continues to play to full houses on the new 42nd Street.

Questions for Review and Discussion Page 443

1. The five elements that are necessary for the creation of the landlord-tenant relationship are consent of the landlord to the occupancy by the tenant, transfer of possession and control of the property to the tenant in an inferior position to the rights of the landlord, the right of the landlord to the return of the property, the creation of an estate in the tenant known as a leasehold estate, and either an express or implied contract between the parties.

2. A lease differs from a license in that a lease conveys an interest in real property and transfers possession, whereas a license gives no property right or ownership interest in the property but merely allows the licensee to do certain acts that would otherwise be a trespass. A lodger is one who has the use of property without actual or exclusive possession of it.

3. A tenancy for years is an estate for a definite or fixed period of time, no matter how long or how short; a periodic tenancy is a fixed-period tenancy that continues for successive periods until one of the parties terminates it by giving notice to the other party; a tenancy at will is a tenancy under which no specific term of lease is agreed upon; and a tenancy at sufferance arises when a tenant wrongfully remains in possession of the premises after his or her tenancy has expired.

4. The essential requirements of a lease are a definite agreement as to the extent and bounds of the leased property, a definite and agreed term, and a definite and agreed price of rental and manner of payment.

5. An assignment of a lease occurs when the interest in the leased premises is transferred to another person for the balance of the term of the lease. A sublease occurs when the transfer is for a part of the term but not for the remainder of it.

6. When real property is rented for dwelling purposes, there is an implied warranty in most states that the premises are fit for human habitation. This statement

means that the landlord warrants that no defects prohibit the use of the premises for residential purposes.

7. A landlord's duties under a lease include the duty to refrain from discrimination, the duty to maintain the premises, and the duty to deliver peaceful possession. The landlord may not commingle security deposits and must return the balance of any security deposits to the tenant at the end of the lease.

8. A tenant's duties under a lease include the duty to pay rent, the duty to observe the valid restrictions in the lease, the duty to turn all fixtures over to the landlord upon termination of the lease, and the duty to refrain from committing waste.

9. If they are negligent, landlords are responsible for injuries to others caused by defects in the common areas and tenants are responsible for injuries caused by defects in the portion of the premises over which tenants have control.

10. Peaceful entry of the premises by the landlord is allowed in some states, if it can be done without force and violence. Ejectment is the common law name given to the lawsuit brought by the landlord to have the tenant evicted from the premises. This older remedy is still available in many states; however, it is time-consuming, expensive, and subject to long delays. Unlawful detainer is the most commonly used method to evict tenants in modern times. This remedy provides landlords with a quick method of regaining possession of their property and protects tenants from being ousted by force and violence.

Cases for Analysis Page 444

1. No. Strict notice requirements must be followed by the landlord. The state's thirty-day notice requirement was necessary to terminate Cuevas's tenancy.

2. No. One of the essential requirements of a lease is a definite and agreed term. The court held that "the option document fails to define the time period over which the rental was to extend."

3. No. A tenancy at will may be terminated at the will of either party by giving proper notice.

4. No. The evidence clearly showed a lease of the apartment with a transfer of possession, control, and care to the lessees, who were tenants and not lodgers. A lodger is one who has the use of property without actual or exclusive possession of it. He or she is a type of licensee, with a mere right to use the property. The agreement to rent the one larger apartment until each of the single apartments was completed still gave Brown and Soverow the exclusive control of the larger apartment.

5. Yes. The lease to Alabama Outdoor Advertising Co. did not contain a term of years; however, it did create a tenancy at will. When the end of the term is indefinite and uncertain, there is no valid lease for a term of years, but a tenancy at will is thereby created. The rule generally followed in this country is that a tenancy at will is ended by a conveyance of the premises by the landlord to another person.

6. Nash. Tenants cannot be ousted by force and violence. If a forcible eviction becomes necessary, it is done by the sheriff under the supervision of the court.

7. Yes. The landlord should have returned the deposit on or before July 30 to comply with the statute. Friedman was entitled to recover three times the amount of the security deposit, plus 5 percent interest, plus court costs and reasonable attorney's fees.

8. Yes. An assignment or sublease will be held valid if the landlord accepts rent over a period of time from either an assignee or subtenant. By receiving the rent for five years, the Cummingses waived their right to object to the assignment without their consent.

9. No. The implied warranty of habitability applies to leases of single-family as well as multiple-family dwellings. A tenant will legitimately have the same expectation that a single-family dwelling will be fit to live in as he or she would have in the case of a structure with multiple dwelling units.

10. The landlord was responsible. When a person is injured on leased property, the one who is in control of that part of the premises where the injury occurs is generally responsible if the injury was caused by that person's negligence. The landlord owed the guest of the tenant a duty to maintain the outside of the premises.

Chapter 24   Wills, Trusts, and Estates

Questions for Analysis Page 460

1. The estates of some wealthy taxpayers could wind up paying thousands of dollars in taxes because eighteen states plus the District of Columbia have opted to retain the estate tax within their borders.

2. In the past, Uncle Sam shared its estate tax revenue with the states; however, in 2002 the federal government began reducing the states' allocation, which fell to zero in 2005.

3. Some states, including New York and New Jersey, are freezing estate tax exclusions much lower than the federal exclusion. Other states, such as Vermont, are conforming to the federal government's exclusion but are taxing at a high rate along with the federal government on estates that exceed the exclusion. Still other states, such as Massachusetts, shield a certain amount from the estate tax, but the amount increases each year. Illinois follows the federal limits.

4. In 2005, the IRS allowed estates to deduct state taxes from their federal returns, reducing the total tax bite for those in the top state estate tax bracket.

5. Some defensive steps that taxpayers can take to lower the federal estate tax are (1) relocate to a state with no

estate tax such as Florida or California; (2) have spouses change their wills to give their children or other relatives the maximum they can protect from state estate tax when the first spouse dies; (3) put any expected taxable amount into a contingency trust allowing the executor to pay or defer state estate taxes, depending on the survivor's needs and the outlook for tax rates at the time.

Questions for Review and Discussion Page 464

1. Any person who has reached the age of adulthood (eighteen) and is of sound mind may make a will.
2. When making the will, did the testator know, in a general way, the nature and extent of the property he or she owned? Did the testator know who would be the most natural recipients of his or her estate? Was the testator free from delusions that might influence the disposition of the property? Did the testator know that he or she was making a will?
3. A will must be in writing, signed by the testator, and attested to in the testator's presence by the number of witnesses established by state law.
4. Some devices that are designed to give protection to family members when a spouse dies are a family allowance, the homestead exemption, exempt property, dower and curtesy, and the right of a surviving spouse to choose an elective share of the estate.
5. Children must prove that they were mistakenly (rather than intentionally) left out of a parent's will. A testator who wishes to disinherit a child should name the child in the will and state that he or she has intentionally omitted to provide for that child.
6. Adopted children, under modern laws, are given the same legal rights as natural children.
7. A will may be revoked by burning, tearing, canceling, or obliterating the will with the intent to revoke it; executing a new will; and subsequent marriage of the testator. In addition, the divorce or annulment of a marriage automatically revokes all gifts made under a will to the former spouse.
8. The spouse will inherit $30,000; each child will inherit $15,000. (If the deceased is survived by one or more issue, the surviving spouse is entitled to one half, and the children are entitled to the other half in equal shares.)

The spouse will inherit $300,000; the father and mother will each inherit $100,000. (If the deceased is survived by no issue but blood relatives, the surviving spouse is entitled to $200,000 plus one-half of the remainder of the estate. The remainder of the estate is $200,000 after $200,000 is deducted. One-half of that is $100,000; $200,000 plus $100,000 equals $300,000, the amount inherited by the surviving spouse. The balance of $100,000 is divided equally between the father and mother.)

The spouse will inherit the entire $90,000. (If the deceased is survived by no issue and no blood relatives, the surviving spouse is entitled to the entire estate.)

Each child will inherit $30,000. (If the deceased is survived by issue and no surviving spouse, his or her children inherit the estate in equal shares.)

The brother will inherit $45,000; each child will inherit $22,500. (If the deceased is survived by no issue and no father or mother, the property passes to his or her brothers and sisters, the issue of any deceased brother or sister taking his or her parent's share. The surviving brother inherits one-half, or $45,000, as the deceased had only one brother and sister. Since the sister is deceased, her $45,000 share is divided equally between her two children.)

The $90,000 will escheat to the state. (If the deceased is survived by no blood relatives and no surviving spouse, the estate escheats to the state.)

The spouse will inherit $350,000; the 90-year-old aunt will inherit $150,000. (If the deceased is survived by no issue but blood relatives, the surviving spouse is entitled to $200,000 plus one-half of the remainder of the estate. The remainder of the estate is $300,000 after $200,000 is deducted. One-half of that is $150,000; $200,000 plus $150,000 equals $350,000, the amount inherited by the surviving spouse. The balance of $150,000 is inherited by the aunt.)

9. When people die owning assets, their estates must be probated. Heirs are notified and an executor or administrator is appointed by the probate court. The fiduciary gathers the assets, pays the debts and taxes, and distributes the remainder in accordance with the will or the law of intestate succession.
10. When a trust is established, title is split between the trustee, who holds legal title, and the beneficiary, who holds equitable or beneficial title. This holding allows the trustee to manage the trust property for the benefit of the beneficiary.

Cases for Analysis Page 464

1. Yes. A surviving spouse who does not like the provisions of a deceased spouse's will may waive the will and take an amount set by state statute.
2. Yes. A signature on a will made by an X is valid, but the circumstances necessitating such a signature, like all of the other circumstances of making a will, may be considered in determining the question of competence.
3. Under the Uniform Simultaneous Death Act, half of each item of jointly-owned property will pass to James's two children; the other half will pass to Wanda's child. James's car and Lucent stock will pass to his two children. Wanda's car and certificate of deposit will pass to her child.
4. No. The law does not require a witness to a will to be a legal adult. He or she must be of sufficient understanding and competent to testify in court as to the facts relating to the execution of the will.
5. Yes. Any person who has reached the age of adulthood (eighteen) and is of sound mind may make a will.

Lazer had not reached adulthood when he made the will.

6. No. Parents are not obligated to leave children anything in a will. The gift of one dollar to Carlos indicates that his father did not forget him, but made the gift intentionally.

7. Yes. A child lawfully adopted is deemed a descendant of the adopting parent for purposes of inheritance and has the same rights as a natural child.

8. No. There was no evidence that the decedent did not understand the ordinary affairs of life or the nature and extent of the property that she was disposing of or that she didn't know the persons who were the natural objects of her bounty or her natural obligations to those persons.

9. The trust was a valid *inter vivos* trust, not an invalid testamentary disposition. It was created by the settlor while he was alive by a proper declaration of trust.

10. No. The testator clearly stated that Lucy should be his heir to the exclusion of all others, and then explained why that was to be so. His language removed any question that the omission of specific mention of Caroline was other than intentional or that it was occasioned by accident or mistake.

Part 4   Case Study   Page 468

1. A prescriptive easement requires use of land that is open and notorious, hostile to the true owner, and continuous for five years under California law.

2. A prescriptive easement is not an ownership right, but a right to a specific use of another's property.

3. The court held that because Kapner enclosed and possessed the land in question, his claim to a prescriptive easement is without merit.

4. The declaration of protective covenants and restrictions places the duty on the MRA to maintain the roadway. The imposition of the duty necessarily carries with it the power to carry it out. One cannot maintain a roadway by allowing obstructions on it.

5. All tenants in common have the right to share equally in the possession of the entire property.

6. Shortly after a survey disclosed that thirty-five of fifty-four landowners had encroachments on the roadway, the MRA sent letters requiring the offending landowners to either remove them or sign an encroachment agreement. That does not indicate waiver or abandonment.

7. Laches is the equitable doctrine that a delay or failure to assert a right or claim at the proper time, which causes a disadvantage to the adverse party, is a bar to recovery. The trial court was not required to find delay because a former MRA board member testified that prior to the survey, nobody really knew where the boundary lines were.

Part 5   Negotiable Instruments

Chapter 25   Purpose and Types of Negotiable Instruments

Questions for Analysis   Page 476

1. Wal-Mart scans paper checks for pertinent information such as the bank and account number and then gives them back to customers in the checkout line.

2. Handling an online payment costs 10 cents, roughly one-third that of processing a paper check.

3. AirNet Systems, Inc., is an unforeseen victim of the rapid change in the processing of paper checks because it gets nearly 70 percent of its revenues from flying checks between cities in Learjets.

4. Besides cost savings, customers are more likely to stay with a bank if they pay bills online there.

5. With digital check processing, proximity no longer matters. Merchants can choose banks that offer quick and secure processing for the lowest price—wherever that happens to be located.

Questions for Review and Discussion   Page 484

1. Throughout history people have had a need to transact business without carrying around large sums of money. There also developed a need to borrow money in order to buy things now and to pay for them later. The law of negotiable instruments was developed to meet both of these needs.

2. The two kinds of negotiable instruments that contain a promise to pay money are notes and certificates of deposit.

3. The two kinds of negotiable instruments that contain an order to pay money are drafts and checks.

4. The parties to a note are the maker and the payee. The parties to a draft are the drawer, the drawee, and the payee.

5. A demand note is payable whenever the payee demands payment. A time note, on the other hand, is payable at some future time, on a definite date named in the instrument. In an installment note, the principal together with interest on the unpaid balance is payable in installments at specified times.

6. Drawees are liable on drafts only when they *accept* them; that is, agree to become liable on them.

7. Any writing, no matter how crude, may be used as a check if it is a draft drawn on a bank and is payable on demand. The use of a printed form to write a check is not required.

8. A bank draft is a check drawn by one bank on another bank in which it has funds on deposit. A cashier's check is a check drawn by the bank upon itself.

9. The UCC places no obligation on a bank to certify a check.

10. A bearer is a person who is in possession of a negotiable instrument that is payable to "bearer" or to "cash." A person who is in possession of an instrument that has been indorsed in blank is also a bearer. In contrast, a holder is a person who is in possession of a negotiable instrument that is issued or indorsed to his or her order or to bearer.

Cases for Analysis   Page 484

1. The court held that the negotiability of the check was not affected by the fact that it was postdated fifteen years. In addition, the court said that the indorsement modified the check by providing for acceleration (advancement) of the time for payment. The court, therefore, ordered that the son be paid $20,000.

2. Yes. When a draft is presented for payment, the drawee is not required to pay it unless it has been accepted. Since this draft was not accepted by Nichols, he has no liability to pay it.

3. No. Postdating a check does not affect its negotiability. The fact that a check is postdated does not make the promise qualified or conditional.

4. No. To accept a draft, the drawee writes *Accepted* across the face of the instrument and dates and signs it. An acceptance must be written on the draft. It has no effect when written in a separate letter.

5. No. The draft was not a check because it was not drawn on the drawee's account in the bank. Instead, it was drawn by the drawer on itself as drawee payable through the bank. It merely designated the bank as a collecting bank to present the draft to the drawer-drawee for payment.

6. No. A check may be postdated when the drawer has insufficient funds in the bank at the time the check is drawn but expects to have sufficient funds to cover the amount of the check at a future date.

7. Yes. The bank must pay the check. A cashier's check is a draft drawn by a bank upon itself. The bank, in effect, lends its credit to the purchaser of the check. It is the equivalent of a promissory note of the bank. The court held that since John Deere Company was a holder in due course, it was not subject to the personal defense of lack of delivery.

Chapter 26   Transferring Negotiable Instruments

Questions for Analysis   Page 489

1. Eastman Chemical Co. got the $244 million to buy a rival's resin business by issuing commercial paper–thirty-day, renewable notes with a mere 2.5 percent interest rate.

2. Eastman's chief financial officer traded $400 million of Eastern's short-term borrowing for longer-term notes because "The short-term markets are not as stable as they used to be."

3. The sudden rush to bonds illustrates how many companies let their balance sheets get out of whack in the 1990s. Many companies quietly used commercial paper to slash borrowing costs and bolster sagging profits.

4. With short maturities—from 1 to 270 days—commercial paper was originally intended to help cover short-term funding needs such as payrolls. But when the interest costs for commercial paper fell as low as 1.75 percent in the late 1990s, many companies began using it to finance longer-term projects such as constructing new factories.

5. Commercial paper is an inherently risky form of borrowing because if questions of financial health arise, a company may find itself unable to roll over short-term notes. This is because money market funds—the main buyers of commercial paper—must keep at least 95 percent of their assets in the highest-grade commercial paper.

Questions for Review and Discussion   Page 499

1. A negotiable instrument is assigned when a person whose indorsement is required on an instrument transfers it without indorsing it or when it is transferred to another person and does not meet the requirements of negotiability. A negotiation, on the other hand, is the transfer of an instrument in such form that the transferee becomes a holder.

2. The concept of negotiability says, when an instrument is transferred by negotiation, the person receiving the instrument is provided with more protection than was available to the person from whom it was received. The person receiving the instrument is able, in many instances, to recover money on the instrument even when the person from whom the instrument was received could not have done so.

3. A blank indorsement consists of the signature alone written on the instrument. A special indorsement is made by writing the words *Pay to the order of* or *Pay to* followed by the name of the person to whom it is to be transferred (the indorsee) and the signature of the indorser.

4. If the instrument containing a blank indorsement is lost or stolen and gets into the hands of another holder, the new holder can recover its face value by delivery alone.

5. A restrictive indorsement limits the subsequent use of an instrument. In contrast, a qualified indorsement limits the liability of the indorser.

6. An indorser who receives consideration warrants that he or she has good title to the instrument, that all signatures are genuine or authorized, that the instrument has not been materially altered, that no defense of any party is good against him or her (a qualified indorser only

warrants that he or she has no knowledge of such a defense), and that he or she has no knowledge of any bankruptcy of the maker, acceptor, or drawer of an unaccepted instrument.

7. Unless the indorsement otherwise specifies (as by words such as *without recourse*), every indorser agrees to pay any subsequent holder the face amount of the instrument.

8. If an instrument is payable to one person *and* another person, the indorsement of both of the payees is necessary to negotiate it. On the other hand, if an instrument is payable to one person *or* another person, only the indorsement of one of the payees is necessary for a proper negotiation.

9. With three exceptions, and unless ratified, an unauthorized forged signature does not serve as the signature of the person whose name is signed. In addition, the tort of conversion is committed when an instrument is paid on a forged indorsement.

10. The three exceptions to the general rule that any unauthorized indorsement is not effective are as follows:

When an instrument is issued to an imposter in the false belief that the imposter is the payee, the indorsement by any person in the name of the payee is effective; when the maker or drawer of an instrument intends the payee to have no interest in the instrument, the indorsement by any person in the name of the payee is effective; and when an agent or employee of the maker or drawer pads the payroll by supplying the employer with fictitious names, an indorsement by any person in the name of each fictitious payee is effective.

Cases for Analysis Page 500

1. The legal term that describes the transfer of the note from Gaff to Lai is assignment. It was not a negotiation because to be negotiable, an instrument must be for a fixed amount of money, which is a medium of exchange adopted by a domestic or foreign government as part of its currency. Silver is not money.

2. Yes. The indorsement was valid. When an instrument is made payable to a person under a misspelled name or a name other than that person's own, he or she may indorse in the incorrect name, in the correct name, or both. Signatures in both names may be required by a person paying or giving value for the instrument.

3. Yes. An indorsement can be written anywhere on the instrument. For convenience, an indorsement is usually placed on the back of the instrument. However, the UCC does not require indorsements to be on any particular side of the paper.

4. No. Although a qualified indorsement absolves the indorser from liability on the contract that nonqualified indorsers make, it does not insulate the indorser from liability on the warranties made by an indorser. A qualified indorser warrants that the instrument has not been

materially altered. Reynolds was liable for breach of this warranty.

5. No. A holder is a person who is in possession of an instrument issued or indorsed to that person, to his or her order, to bearer, or in blank. Here, the note was payable to the order of James Waskow. It would have to be indorsed by him for the landlord to become a holder.

6. No. A restrictive indorsement uses the words *for deposit only.* When a restrictive indorsement is used, the indorser is assured that the amount of the instrument will be credited to his or her account before it is negotiated further. This example described blank indorsements, as they consisted of the signature alone written on the instrument.

7. Yes. Indorsements may be written on a separate paper (rider, or *allonge*) as long as the separate paper is so firmly affixed to the instrument that it becomes part of it.

8. No. A forged signature does not serve as the signature of the person whose name is signed. The forged signature of the payee in this case was inoperative to make the bank a holder. The second indorsement, although valid, did not make the check payable to bearer.

9. Since the check was not payable in the alternative (to Floors, Inc., or American Fidelity), it could not have been negotiated by fewer than both of the payees. Therefore, it was not properly negotiated. The Peoples National Bank committed the tort of conversion because payment upon a missing indorsement was equivalent to payment over a forged indorsement.

10. No. The Kentucky court held that under section 3-111 of the UCC, an instrument is payable to bearer when by its terms it is payable to: (a) bearer or the order of bearer; or (b) a specified person or bearer; or (c) "cash" or the order of "cash," or any other indication which does not purport to designate a specific payee. The note is not a bearer instrument under any of the above statutory definitions. Note: In states that have adopted the revised version of Article 3 of the UCC, the answer would be yes. UCC Revised (1990) 3-109 (a) states that an instrument is payable to bearer when it does not state a payee.

Chapter 27   Holders in Due Course, Defenses, and Liabilities

Questions for Review and Discussion Page 513

1. A holder in due course is a holder who takes the instrument for value, in good faith, and without notice that it is overdue or has been dishonored or notice of any defenses against or claim to it on the part of any person.

2. The shelter provision is designed to permit holders in due course to transfer all of the rights they have in an instrument to others. The provisions will not apply should the transferee be a party to fraud or other illegal

acts that affect the instrument. In that event, the transferee would not have the rights of a holder in due course.

3. Personal defenses are sometimes called limited defenses because they cannot be used against a holder in due course—their use is limited. When a negotiable instrument is negotiated to a holder in due course, all personal defenses are not permissible. The most common personal defenses are breach of contract, lack or failure of consideration, fraud in the inducement, lack of delivery, and payment.

4. When sellers of consumer products have arrangements with financial institutions to finance their customers' purchases, the financial institutions are subject to the customers' personal defenses. They lose their protection as holders in due course.

5. Real defenses may be used against everyone, including a holder in due course. Real defenses are infancy and mental incompetence, illegality and duress, fraud as to the essential nature of the transaction, bankruptcy, unauthorized signature, and alteration.

6. Makers of notes and acceptors of drafts are obligated to pay an instrument without reservation. Indorsers must pay instruments only if the following happen: an instrument is presented properly for payment, the instrument is dishonored, and proper notice of dishonor is given to the drawee or party obliged to pay the instrument.

7. Presentment may be made by any commercially reasonable means, including an oral, written, or electronic communication.

8. An instrument is dishonored when proper presentment is made and acceptance or payment is refused. Dishonor also occurs when presentment is excused and the instrument is past due and unpaid.

9. Notice of dishonor may be given by any reasonable means including an oral, written, or electronic communication.

10. Nonbank holders must give notice of the dishonor to the drawer and indorsers within thirty days following the day of dishonor.

Cases for Analysis Page 514

1. No. Unless ratified, an unauthorized signature (a forgery) does not operate as a signature of the person whose name is signed. It is a real defense and can be used against a holder in due course.

2. No. The bank was not a holder in due course, because without a valid indorsement of Refrigerated Transport Co., Inc., it was not a holder. One must first be a holder to be a holder in due course.

3. Yes. To be negotiable, an instrument must contain the words of negotiability *Pay to the order of* or *Pay to bearer.* This instrument lacked the words of negotiability. Since it was not negotiable, the transfer by Great Lake Nursery Corporation to First Investment Company was an assignment rather than a negotiation, and

the assignee stood in the shoes of the assignor and was subject to all defenses. First Investment Company did not have the rights of a holder in due course because the instrument was nonnegotiable.

4. Yes. A holder in due course takes an instrument free from all defenses of any party to the instrument *with whom the holder has not dealt.* Since Bucci dealt with Paulick, Bucci took the instrument subject to the defense of failure of consideration.

5. Yes. Fraudulent misrepresentation that induces the execution of an otherwise valid contract renders it voidable but not void. It is a personal defense and, consequently, does not constitute a defense against a holder in due course.

6. When this case was decided, the UCC said that a telephone call is not a proper presentment. UCC Revised (1990) 3-501 now says that presentment may be made by any commercially reasonable means, including an oral, written, or electronic communication.

7. No. To hold an indorser liable on an instrument, presentment must be made to the maker on the due date and timely notice of dishonor must be given to the indorser. Since neither was done in this case, the indorser was not liable on the instrument.

8. No. The waiver provision of the notes eliminated the prior conditions of presentment and notice, and bound the indorser to pay the notes.

9. No. The purchaser of a note with knowledge that it is in default does not qualify as a holder in due course. Craig was subject to any defenses that Rutherford had against Stokes.

10. No. Joyce was not a holder in due course because she did not acquire the check for value. She received it as a gift.

Chapter 28 Bank Deposits, Collections, and Depositor Relationships

Questions for Analysis Page 521

1. Visa no longer calls itself a credit card company because debit cards now account for over half its business.

2. Consumers save time, feel more secure carrying fewer dollars, and track their spending better. Also, banks quickly replace lost or stolen cards. Merchants avoid credit risks and the costs of late payments, postage, employee theft, and check-clearing fees. More important, customers are more loyal.

3. Answers will vary.

Questions for Review and Discussion Page 531

1. A *depository bank* is the first bank to which an item is transferred for collection even though it is also the

payor bank. A *payor bank* is a bank by which an item is payable as drawn or accepted. It includes a drawee bank.

2. The depository bank acts as its customer's agent to collect the money from the payor bank. The check is sent (sometimes through an intermediary bank) to a collecting bank that presents the check to the payor bank for payment. If it is honored by the payor bank, the amount will be deducted from the drawer's account, and the check will be returned to the drawer with the next bank statement. If the check is dishonored for any reason, it will be returned to the payee via the same route that it was sent, and all credits given for the item will be revoked.

3. The principal feature of the Check 21 Act is the use of a *substitute check*—a paper reproduction of both sides of an original check that can be processed just like the original check. Bank customers no longer have an absolute right to see their original canceled check. Instead, they have the right only to the return of a substitute check.

4. Consumers who use ATMs are entitled to receive a written receipt whenever they use a machine. In addition, the transaction must appear on the periodic statement sent to the consumer. Banks must promptly investigate errors pointed out by consumers. A consumer's liability for the unauthorized use of an ATM card is limited to $50 if notice of the loss or theft of a card is given the issuer within two business days. The consumer's liability increases to $500 when notice is withheld beyond two business days. It becomes unlimited when notice is not given within sixty days.

5. Businesses that deal with large sums of money need to be able to make quick transfers to avoid a loss of interest, among other reasons. EFTs help to meet this need.

6. If a bank fails to honor an uncertified check because of a mistake on its part, the bank is liable to the customer for any actual damages that the customer suffers, the bank is not liable to a holder of the check for dishonoring the instrument, and the bank is under no obligation to a customer to pay a stale check (over six months old) unless it is certified.

7. The bank is not liable for the payment of a check before it has notice of the death or incompetence of the drawer. In any event, a bank may pay or certify checks for ten days after the death of the drawer.

   If a bank pays an altered amount of a check to a holder, it may deduct from the drawer's account only the amount of the check as it was originally written. The bank is liable to the depositor if it pays any check on which the depositor's signature has been forged.

8. Funds from checks drawn on the U.S. Treasury, or any state or local government, and any bank draft, cashier's check, or postal money order must be made available on the next business day following the banking day of deposit; funds from checks drawn on banks within the same Federal Reserve district must be made available within two business days following the banking day of deposit; funds from checks drawn on banks outside the bank's Federal Reserve district must be made available within five business days following the banking day of deposit.

9. Most states have statutes making it larceny or attempted larceny for a person to issue a check drawn on a bank in which the person knows he or she has insufficient funds. Also, it is important for depositors to examine their bank statements promptly because, if they do not do so, they cannot hold the bank responsible for losses due to the bank's payment of a forged or altered instrument.

10. An oral stop payment order is binding upon the bank for fourteen calendar days only. A written order is effective for only six months, unless renewed in writing.

11. A husband, wife, and one child may have insured accounts totaling $600,000 by having individual accounts of $100,000 for each of them and joint $100,000 accounts for the husband and wife, the husband and child, and the wife and child.

Cases for Analysis   Page 532

1. No. The absolute time for notifying a bank of a forged or altered check is one year from the time the depositor receives the bank statement (UCC Section 4-406). The court held that the statement was "made available" to Woods when it was sent to her attorney.

2. No. Courts have held that payment cannot be stopped on a cashier's check because the bank, by issuing it, accepts the check in advance.

3. No. A written stop-payment order is effective for only six months unless renewed in writing. A bank is under no obligation to pay a check, other than a certified check, that is presented more than six months after its date, but it may charge its customer's accounts for payments made thereafter in good faith (UCC Section 4-404). In the absence of any facts that could justify a finding of dishonesty, bad faith, recklessness, or lack of ordinary care, the bank was not liable to Granite Equipment Leasing for payment of its check drawn to Overseas Equipment.

4. Yes. A bank may continue to pay checks for ten days after the date of death of the drawer even though it has notice (UCC Section 4-405). This rule permits holders of checks that are drawn shortly before the drawer's death to cash them without the necessity of filing a claim with the probate court.

5. Yes. The bank became accountable for the amount of the item when it retained it beyond midnight of June 23, its midnight deadline. Section 4-302 of the UCC makes a bank strictly liable for undue retention of an item presented for payment.

6. No. A drawee bank owes no duty to the holder of an uncertified check. Stewart's remedy was against the

drawer and indorser of the check for the dishonor, not the drawee.

7. No. When a dishonor occurs by mistake, liability is limited to actual damages proved. Since Fitting was unable to prove that she suffered damages, she could not recover compensation from the bank.

8. Roberta's deposit is considered to have been received on Monday. The first $100 must be available to her the next business day, Tuesday. Because the check is nonlocal, the remaining amount must be available by the fifth business day, which is the following Monday.

Part 5   Case Study   Page 533

1. To be a negotiable instrument, any writing must (1) be signed by the maker or drawer; (2) contain an unconditional promise or order to pay a sum certain in money and no other promise, order, obligation, or power given by the maker or drawer except as authorized by this division; (3) be payable on demand or at a definite time; and (4) be payable to order or to bearer. (Note footnote on page 534 where the court mentioned that although the UCC had been revised since the transactions in this case occurred, its basic provisions survived the amendments. UCC 3-104 contains the 1990 revised version of the requirements of a negotiable instrument.)

2. The signature by the drawer or maker includes any symbol executed or adopted by a party with present intention to authenticate a writing. Authentication may be printed, stamped or written; it may be by initials or by thumbprint.

3. The alleged conditions on the back of the money orders are nothing more than a restatement of American Express's statutory defenses against payment because of alteration, absence of signature, and forgery. Expressing these statutory defenses on an instrument does not elevate them to a condition. It is simply a warning that American Express has reserved its statutory defenses.

4. Authorized completion and delivery are not listed as requisites to negotiability. Moreover the UCC specifically permits the enforcement of incomplete and undelivered instruments.

5. Triffin could not become a holder in due course because he had notice of American Express's defenses when he took the money orders from Chuckie's.

6. Triffin could acquire the status of a holder in due course because he received the money orders from Chuckie's who was a holder in due course. A transferee acquires whatever rights the transferor has, even if the transferee is aware of the defenses to enforcement.

7. Mr. Justice Castille argued that the language in the money orders created express conditions that the money orders not be altered or stolen and the indorsements not be missing or forged.

8. Answers will vary.

Part 6   Insurance, Secured Transactions, and Bankruptcy

Chapter 29   The Nature of the Insurance Contract

Questions for Analysis   Page 552

1. The legal loophole allows health insurers to buy another company and then dump the costliest individual policyholders and keep the healthiest, most profitable ones.

2. To increase profits in a three-year period, health insurers culled, or attempted to cull, as many as 28,700 people from their rolls—or forced them to pay steep premium hikes to keep their coverage—after a merger or acquisition.

3. The Missouri Department of Insurance saw "movement across the industry to privatize the good risk and socialize the bad risk."

Questions for Review and Discussion   Page 557

1. Insurance policies require offer, acceptance, mutual assent, capable parties, consideration, and valid subject matter.

2. The principal types of life insurance are straight life, limited-payment life, term, and endowment insurance. Straight life insurance (also known as *ordinary life insurance,* or *whole life insurance,* is a kind of insurance that requires the payment of premiums throughout the life of the insured and which pays the beneficiary the face value of the policy upon the insured's death. Limited-payment life insurance is a kind of insurance that provides that the payment of premiums will stop after a stated length of time—usually ten, twenty, or thirty years. The amount of the policy will be paid to the beneficiary upon the death of the insured, whether the death occurs during the payment period or after. Term insurance is insurance that is issued for a particular period, usually 5 or 10 years and provides protection only, having no cash value. Endowment insurance is a type of protection that combines life insurance and investment so that if the insured outlives the time-period of the policy, the face value is paid to the insured. If the insured does not outlive the time-period of the policy, the face value is paid to the beneficiary.

3. Four situations that may eliminate the coverage provided by life insurance are the legal execution of the insured, causing the death of the insured, the suicide of the insured, and war activities.

4. The waiver-of-premium option excuses the insured from paying premiums if he or she becomes disabled. A guaranteed-insurability option allows the insured to

pay an extra premium initially in exchange for a guaranteed option to buy more insurance at certain specified times later, without a new medical examination. These options are popular because they provide protection in the event of future illness or disability.

5. A person is said to have an insurable interest in a given subject matter if he or she might suffer financial loss or liability through its damage, destruction, or loss. In property insurance, there must be a continuing insurable interest in the property that is to be insured, from the time of application for the insurance up until the time of a claim. In life insurance, the insurable interest must exist only when the policy is issued.

6. Under most fire insurance policies, claims may also be made for losses from water used to fight the fire; scorching; smoke damage to goods; deliberate destruction of property as a means of controlling a spreading fire; lightning, even if there is no resultant fire; riot or explosion, if a fire does result; and losses through theft or exposure of goods removed from a burning building. A homeowner's policy gives protection for losses from fire, windstorm, burglary, vandalism, and injuries suffered by other persons while on the property.

7. Seven types of automobile insurance are bodily injury liability, property damage liability, collision, comprehensive coverage, medical payments, uninsured motorist, and no-fault. Bodily injury liability insurance covers the liability of the insured for bodily injury to pedestrians and other motorists. Property damage liability insurance covers damage to the property of others. Collision insurance provides against loss arising from damage to the insured's automobile caused by accidental collision with another object, any part of the roadbed, or by an upset. Comprehensive insurance provides protection against loss or damage to the motor vehicle insured if caused by fire, lightning, flood, hail, windstorm, riots, breakage of glass, theft, or pilferage. Medical payments insurance pays for medical expenses resulting from bodily injuries to anyone occupying the policyholder's car at the time of an accident. Uninsured-motorist insurance provides protection when the insured is injured in an automobile accident caused by another driver who has no bodily injury liability insurance to cover the loss to the injured party. No-fault insurance provides that car owners may collect damages and medical expenses from their own insurance carriers regardless of responsibility.

8. Health insurance policies often include the following benefits: physician care, prescription drugs, inpatient and outpatient hospital care, surgery, dental and vision care, and long-term care for the elderly. Medicare is a federally funded health insurance program for people sixty-five and over who are covered by Social Security. Medicaid is a health care plan for low-income people. State governments administer Medicaid, which is funded by both state and federal funds.

9. The first step in obtaining an insurance policy is filling in an application. A binder provides temporary insurance coverage between the time of the application and the time the policy goes into effect.

10. Premiums differ from one person to another because the amount is determined by the nature and character of the risk involved and by its likelihood of occurring. The premium increases as the chance of loss increases. When the insured stops paying premiums, an insurance policy is said to lapse. This does not mean an automatic termination, as most policies allow a grace period of thirty or thirty-one days during which the insured can save the policy by making a premium payment.

11. A warranty is an insured's promise to follow certain restrictions included in the policy. If the insured breaches (breaks) the warranty, the insurance company can cancel the policy or refuse payment of loss. Concealment is any intentional withholding of a material fact that should be provided to the insurer. Misrepresentation is giving false answers to direct questions from the insurer. In both situations the insurance company has issued the policy on false information and, for this reason, has the right to cancel.

Cases for Analysis   Page 557

1. The Ramos's have no recourse against the insurance company. Most homeowner's policies do not cover flood damage. To obtain such coverage, special flood insurance must be obtained from an insurance agent.

2. Yes. A corporation has an insurable interest in the lives of its officers, key employees, and principal stockholders. In addition, if the insurable interest requirement is satisfied at the time the policy is issued, the proceeds of the policy must be paid upon the death of the insured without regard to whether the beneficiary has an insurable interest at the time of death.

3. No. This was a warranty violation. The policy requirements concerning pilot experience were intended to be conditions precedent to the existence of coverage. The insurer is entitled to rely on a policy provision that unambiguously makes coverage dependent on the pilot of the aircraft meeting particular experience standards.

4. No. Victory does not own the Warrensburg property. Since Victory has no ownership, it has no insurable interest. The fact that the brothers own both properties was irrelevant. Victory had the same relationship to Warrensburg as any outside third party would have had.

5. Yes. To establish the existence of an insurable interest, the insurer must demonstrate that he or she has a monetary interest in the property. This monetary interest means that the insured may suffer a loss if the property is damaged and destroyed. Avrit and Schuring demonstrated their monetary interest in the property when they paid the $1,000 as a down payment.

6. In a majority of states, Allstate would prevail. The majority rule states that sanity clauses negate any issue as to the mental facilities of the deceased. In a minority of states, Alice Searle would prevail. The minority rule holds that mental state remains an issue despite the sanity clause. Moreover, if the deceased was so mentally incapacitated at the time of the suicide that he or she did not realize the consequences of the action, then the insurance company would be liable. *Note:* California follows the minority rule. Thus, the issue of Martin Searle's mental capacity remained open. The ruling did not mean that Alice Searle won the case, however. It merely opened the issue of mental incapacity. The ruling was, nevertheless, an important victory for Mrs. Searle, since Allstate had the burden of proving that Martin Searle understood the consequences of his actions when he committed suicide.

7. No. Whitaker's insurance covered his vehicles only. Uninsured-motorist coverage is meant to protect an insured motorist, his or her family, and permitted users of his or her vehicle against the peril of injury by an uninsured wrongdoer. Bayer's vehicle was not an insured automobile, and Bayer was not insured under the policy.

8. Yes. Binders are deemed to include all the usual terms of the policy that will eventually be issued. The key word here is *usual.* The issue was whether the exclusion of liquor from an all-risk policy was a usual term. The court found that it was not a usual term. While the insurance company and Riggins had different interpretations of the phrase *all-risk,* the court found it reasonable to believe that the term meant that the parties intended to cover all the property Riggins would haul. Moreover, a holding to the contrary would negate the effect of any binder. To avoid a loss during the binder period, an insurance company would simply have to produce a final policy exempting the loss that occurred during the binder period. Such a situation would place complete control over the risk of loss in the hands of the insurance company. The court felt such a result would be extremely unfair.

9. No. The fact that Mr. Henry died of cancer and not a disease he was questioned about is irrelevant. A representation is material if it involves facts that influence the insurer's decision to insure the policy. Here, a positive response to any of the health questions Mr. Henry was asked about would have prompted an investigation and would have affected State Farm's decision to insure Mr. Henry.

10. Yes. A waiver occurs when the insurer agrees to rescind one of its customary rules for the benefit of the insured. A waiver need not be expressed but can be implied from the conduct of the insurer. In this case, State Farm knew of the loss and the lapse and still cashed the check. This conduct implied a waiver of its right to cancel the policy for nonpayment.

Chapter 30   Mortgages and other Security Devices

Questions for Analysis Page 567

1. Cano was unable to buy a house when he first moved to Houston from Mexico even though he earned a large salary because he had no credit history.

2. GMAC considered Cano's rent- and utility-payment history and accepted a smaller down payment than normal to allow him to obtain a mortgage.

3. To allow some families to qualify for a loan, Wells Fargo allows the incomes of a spouse and an unlimited number of aunts, uncles, and cousins to count for up to 30 percent of the income that is needed to qualify for a loan. It will also accept as much as 30 percent of qualifying income to be in cash. GMC's program allows borrowers to put down as little as $1,000 and use cash gifts from family members. Bank of America allows up to four family members on an application.

4. Undocumented Hispanic immigrants, mostly from Mexico, apply for an Internal Revenue Service ID number, which, in conjunction with a Mexican consular ID enables them to obtain mortgage loans.

5. Lending to immigrants can be risky because cash-based incomes are hard to verify and many immigrant mortgages cannot be packaged for resale as mortgage-backed securities, which banks use to spread some of their lending risks.

6. (1) 1.15 percent; (2) 0.59 percent; (3) 2.78 percent.

Questions for Review and Discussion Page 574

1. Since very few people have enough money in cash to pay for large purchases such as real estate, automobiles, and the like, most must borrow the money to make those purchases. Institutions and individuals that act as lenders need some assurance that their money, plus interest, will be returned. Security devices provide that necessary assurance.

2. A conventional mortgage is one that has no government backing, either by way of insurance or guarantee. The loan that such a mortgage secures is made by private lenders, and the risks of loss are borne exclusively by them. FHA and VA mortgages are backed by federal agencies. The FHA and the VA are responsible to the lending institution in the event of a mortgagor's default and foreclosure on an FHA or VA mortgage. The U.S. Government, through these agencies, reimburses the mortgage for any loss and takes over the property.

3. A variable-rate mortgage has a rate of interest that changes according to fluctuations in the index to which it is tied. A graduated payment mortgage contains a fixed-interest rate during the life of the mortgage; however, the monthly payments made by the mortgagor increase over the term of the loan. A balloon-payment mortgage has relatively low fixed payments during the

life of the mortgage followed by one large final (balloon) payment.

4. If the mortgage is not recorded, the mortgagee may lose his or her rights under the mortgage to another party who may have recorded the mortgage in a public office in the county in which the property is located. This loss of rights occurs because the holder of an unrecorded deed to real property is estopped from denying the superior title of a subsequent purchaser whose deed is recorded. However, this estoppel occurs only when the second purchaser has taken his or her deed in good faith, for consideration, and with no knowledge of the previous unrecorded sale.

5. First, under the rule followed by a majority of the states, the mortgagor has the right to possess the property. Second, the mortgagor has the right to any income produced by the property and can assign that income to another party. Third, the mortgagor has the right to use the property for a second or third mortgage. Fourth, the mortgagor has the right to pay off the mortgage in full. The last right is the right of redemption.

   The mortgagee has the unrestricted right to sell, assign, or transfer the bond and mortgage to a third party. Second, the mortgagee has the right to receive installment payments on time and in the amount designated in the agreement. Third, the mortgagee has the right to accelerate the debt and foreclose on default of the mortgagor. Fourth, under the Fourteenth Amendment to the Constitution, the mortgagee cannot lose his or her interest in the property without due process of law.

6. When buyers assume the mortgage, they agree to pay it. When buyers take the property subject to the mortgage, the seller agrees to continue paying the debt.

7. A security agreement must be in writing, it must be signed by the debtor, and it must describe the collateral used for security.

8. A security interest is effective only between the debtor and creditor when it attaches. To be effective as to others who might claim the collateral, such as other creditors or people who buy the collateral from the debtor, the security interest must be perfected. There are three ways to perfect a security interest: by attachment only (in limited situations), by possession of the collateral (called a pledge), and by filing a financing statement in a public office.

9. The UCC follows these rules to determine who prevails over whom when secured and unsecured parties lay claim to the same collateral: (*a*) A perfected *purchase money security interest* in inventory has priority over a conflicting security interest in the same inventory. (*b*) A *purchase money security interest* in collateral other than inventory has priority over a conflicting security interest in the same collateral if it is perfected within ten days after the debtor receives possession of the collateral. (*c*) Buyers of goods in the ordinary course of business (except farm products) prevail over security interests in the seller's inventory. (*d*) Buyers of farm products in the ordinary course of business, to the extent that they pay for and receive collateral without knowledge of the security interest, take precedence over nonperfected security interests. (*e*) Buyers of *consumer goods* take free of perfected security interests of which they have no knowledge. (*f*) In all other cases, a perfected security interest prevails over an unperfected security interest. (*g*) Conflicting security interests rank according to priority in time of filing or perfection. (*h*) When two or more parties have unperfected security interests in the same collateral, the first to attach prevails over the other parties.

10. If a debtor defaults by failing to make payments when due, the secured party may satisfy the debt by taking possession of the collateral. After repossessing the goods, the secured party must sell the collateral and use the money received in the sale to pay himself or herself and the other creditors. If money is left over after all creditors are paid, the secured party must give the extra money to the debtor. If the sale doesn't produce enough money to pay all creditors, the debtor must pay them back out of his or her own funds. If there is a sale, it may be public (an auction) or private, as long as the terms of the sale are reasonable. If the goods are consumer goods and the debtor has paid 60 percent of the cash price or more of a purchase money security interest, the secured party cannot keep the goods. They must be sold. The debtor must be told about any sale and has the right to buy the goods personally.

Cases for Analysis   Page 575

1. Yes. Homeowners can request cancellation of private mortgage insurance when their equity position reaches 20 percent of the original value of the property. Since Sanchez has an excellent credit rating and always paid her mortgage payments when they were due, she should qualify for this benefit.

2. No. The second mortgage is paid out of the remaining proceeds. Once First Colonial Bank foreclosed its first mortgage, it became the trustee of the surplus funds for the benefit of the junior mortgagee, Ford Motor Credit Company.

3. Yes. Variable-rate mortgages are not in themselves unenforceable as long as their terms are certain and definite. A mortgage agreement that places no limit on the amount of interest that can be charged is uncertain. To be enforceable, such an agreement would have to be definite enough that the parties could easily figure out the extent of their obligation. With no ceiling on the interest rate, it was impossible for the Prestons to ascertain the extent of their obligation.

4. No. The Woolseys were not entitled to a jury trial. The mortgage held by the bank was a lien on the property. The bank had no legal right to possess the property. Its only recourse was the equitable action of foreclosure. Therefore, the Woolseys had no right to a jury trial. The burden of proving bad faith on the part of the bank fell to the Woolseys. They would have to demonstrate that the bank did not really believe that its security interest was impaired, but, instead, that it acted from some ulterior motive. Since the Woolseys were insolvent and had defaulted on their obligations, they could not sustain this burden.

5. Northridge had first rights to the property. Recording a mortgage protects a creditor or subsequent purchaser, without notice, who duly records a deed, mortgage, or other instrument, while penalizing a party who does not duly record his or her instrument. Bloom's mortgage in favor of Lakeshore was executed on September 16 but was not recorded until 3:07 P.M. on October 25. In the interim, another mortgage was executed by Bloom in favor of Northridge on October 4, which was recorded at 9:28 A.M. on October 25. Thus, Lakeshore was a prior purchaser that failed to duly record its instrument. Northridge, the subsequent purchaser, was completely without constructive notice that was due entirely to Lakeshore's failure to record promptly. In addition, Northridge duly recorded its mortgage.

6. Yes. By refusing to pay money in escrow, Cramer failed to perform a covenant, which was a condition of the mortgage. The bank had the right to foreclose.

7. No. Matthew Motors had sold the Buick to Jenkins. Since Jenkins owned the car, Matthew Motors had no power to pledge it as security for the loan from Owensboro National Bank. To be effective, a security interest must attach. Attachment occurs when the collateral comes into possession of the secured party by agreement or when the debtor signs a security agreement. In addition, the secured party must give value and the debtor must have rights in the collateral. In this case, despite the security agreement and the value given by the secured party, the interest did not attach because the debtor had no rights in the collateral.

8. No. A financing statement does not have to be filed to perfect a security interest if the property used as collateral is in the possession of the secured party.

9. Yes. Since the filing statement was filed in the wrong country, the bank had an unperfected security interest in the property. An unperfected security interest is subordinate to the rights of a person who becomes a lien creditor before the security interest is perfected.

10. No. Under the Uniform Commercial Code, the debtor must be given notice of the *time and place* of any public sale so that he or she may bid on the goods personally. Because the bank failed to give proper notice of the public sale, it lost the case against Lallana for the balance due on the loan.

Chapter 31   Bankruptcy and Debt Adjustment

Questions for Analysis Page 588

1. According to the director of investor education and assistance at the Securities and Exchange Commission, if you purchase stock in a bankrupt company, it is highly likely that your investment will not rise in value, but that you'll be holding worthless shares.

2. One reason that people buy stock in bankrupt companies is the temptation of a quick buck. Because these stocks often are highly volatile, investors can score with well-timed buys. Also, many investors believe that the companies can turn themselves around.

3. According to Dethy, "To make money, things have to get substantially better, and that doesn't usually happen. The vast majority of these do not work out."

Questions for Review and Discussion Page 593

1. In Article 1, Section 8, Clause 4, the U.S. Constitution grants Congress the authority to create statutory law dealing with bankruptcy. The clause states "Congress shall have the Power . . . To establish . . . uniform laws on the subject of Bankruptcies throughout the United States."

2. To institute a voluntary bankruptcy proceeding a debtor would go to the nearest federal district court and file a bankruptcy petition. The debtor would then fill in a form that asks him or her to name all creditors and to indicate how much money is owed to each. The form also requires a listing of the debtor's property, a statement of income and expenses, and an identification of exempt property. Involuntary bankruptcy proceedings can be started if the debtor continuously fails to pay bills as they become due. Also, three creditors must file if the debtor has twelve or more creditors, and the combined debt owed the three must exceed $10,000. One creditor owed a debt of more than $10,000 can file if the debtor has less than twelve creditors.

3. After a petition for bankruptcy is filed, the automatic stay goes into effect. This means that the debtor's creditors can make no further move to collect debts or file a lawsuit against the debtor. Automatic stay protects creditors by placing them on equal footing, thus preventing one creditor from taking advantage of the others. It is fair to debtors because it gives them more control over their situation.

4. A debtor's possible exemptions under Bankruptcy Code provisions fall into three categories: exemptions for homestead and for household items, exemptions for necessities, and exemptions for benefits and support payments.

5. Once a debtor's property has been sold and reduced to cash, creditors are paid off in the following order: secured creditors; expenses of administering the

bankruptcy process: unsecured debts incurred after the petition was filed but before the relief order was issued; wages and benefit plans; fishermen and farmers, when the debtor owns or operates a fish storage and processing plant or a grain storage plant; deposits and advances; paternity, alimony, maintenance and support; and taxes and other unsecured debts.

6. Debts that cannot be discharged under a bankruptcy proceeding belong in three categories; debts created by misconduct (including debts that arise by fraud or by willful, malicious conduct, and those that the debtor did not reveal at the outset of the proceeding); government-enforced debts (including back taxes, student loans, fines, penalties, court-enforced debts such as alimony, support payments, and debts that were not discharged under a previous bankruptcy); and debts created by excessive spending (including debts for luxury items that top $500 if purchased within ninety days of the relief order and a cash advance beyond $1,000 if obtained within twenty days of the relief order).

7. Chapter 11 provisions allow debtors to free themselves from a devastating financial situation without having to sell most of their property. Instead, debtors draw up reorganization plans to alter repayment schedules.

8. A reorganization plan under Chapter 11 must be approved by one-half of the creditors in each class before it will go into effect. The one exception involves creditors whose standard legal rights have not been altered. These creditors, called unimpaired creditors or members of an unimpaired class, have no approval power, since their collection rights are the same as they would have been without the plan.

9. Only individuals can file under Chapter 13. Neither corporations nor partnerships can file under its provisions. A debtor wishing to file under Chapter 13 must have unsecured debts under $250,000 or secured debts under $750,000. Also, the debtor must have an already established steady income.

10. Chapter 12 debt adjustment procedures are open only to family farmers. Family farmers are farmers who receive more than one-half of their income from the farm. In addition, the complete debt owed under Chapter 12 can be as high as $1.5 million, while Chapter 13 has a ceiling of $250,000 in unsecured debts and $750,000 in secured debts. Also, Chapter 12 is open to partnerships and corporations involved in family farming, whereas Chapter 13 is limited to individuals.

Cases for Analysis   Page 594

1. A personal bankruptcy filing remains on a debtor's credit report for ten years and has a detrimental effect on the ability to establish a line of credit. However, most debtors who file bankruptcy have already established a poor credit rating anyway, and filing bankruptcy gives them an opportunity to begin anew. A good number of their debts become discharged, which

improves their debt-to-income ratio—a factor that potential creditors look at carefully. The more time that elapses after the bankruptcy filing, the easier it is to re-establish credit. People who are able to make a down payment and have steady income may be eligible for a mortgage loan as soon as two years following a discharge in bankruptcy.

2. No. Student loans that do not impose a hardship on the debtor cannot be discharged by bankruptcy.

3. No. Since the California case violated the Florida court's twelve-month prohibition against further Bankruptcy Code filings by Cortez, it was ineffective to trigger the automatic stay provisions of the Bankruptcy Code.

4. No. Landrin's debt to the bank is not discharged by the bankruptcy petition because her conduct was willful and malicious. Debts that have fallen into the debtor's lap because of misconduct cannot be discharged in bankruptcy.

5. No. The issue before the court was not whether the debtor *could* pay the bills as they came due. The issue that faced the court was whether the debtor was actually paying its bills as they came due. Since it was not, the court granted the order for relief.

6. Yes. Automatic suspension prohibits creditors from attempting to collect any money owed by the debtor. The provision extends to actions brought against the debtor by creditors in a court other than the court handling the bankruptcy. One of the sanctions available to the court for a violation of the suspension is a contempt ruling.

7. No. The court looked first for a definition of *item*. Since it was not defined in the Bankruptcy Code, the court turned to *Webster's Third New International Dictionary,* which defined *item* as "an individual thing (as an article of household goods, an article of apparel, an object in an art collection, a book in a library) singled out from an aggregate of individual things. . . ." After looking at several other similar definitions, the court concluded that "each particular knife, fork, or spoon is a separate item, although the items are of the same pattern and constitute a 'set' of silverware. Therefore, each particular item that does not exceed $200 in value is exempt under the . . . Bankruptcy Code." (Since this case, the exemption has been increased to $925).

8. Yes. Under the Bankruptcy Code debtors cannot discharge debts that result from the debtor's own fraudulent conduct.

9. Yes. The Bankruptcy Code only requires that the plan be feasible, which means that it must have a good chance of success. The code does not require an absolute guarantee of success. A plan may be difficult to implement yet still may be feasible. The labor problems facing U.S. Truck may be difficult to overcome. However, there were enough indications that the problems could be overcome to satisfy the court that the plan was feasible.

Part 6   Case Study Page 598

1. To be excepted from the rule that a student loan obligation cannot be discharged in bankruptcy, a debtor must prove that the discharge will cause an undue hardship.

2. To determine whether an exception exists, the court has adopted the "totality of the circumstances test."

3. To meet the test, debtors must prove (1) their past, present, and reasonably reliable future financial resources; (2) theirs' and their dependent's reasonably necessary living expenses; and (3) that other relevant facts or circumstances particular to the debtor's case are such that excepting the student loans from discharge will prevent the debtor from maintaining a minimal standard of living, even with the advantage of a discharge of other prepetition debts.

4. (1) The court believes that the debtor could significantly enhance her future income by exploiting her educational credentials and the job skills she has acquired in past employment, and that she could do more to maximize her income by increasing the length of her work week. (2) The court likewise finds the debtor has not done all she can to minimize her reasonably necessary living expenses, such as by taking a more affordable apartment or by taking in a roommate in her present home. (3) The debtor has failed to present evidence of any facts or circumstances that would lead this court to conclude that excepting her student loans from discharge would impose an undue hardship.

5. The court held that it could find no compelling reason to grant this Debtor a discharge of her student loans and found in favor of the defendant, ECMC.

Part 7   Agency and Employment

Chapter 32   The Principal and Agent Relationship

Questions for Review and Discussion Page 616

1. Agency is a legal relationship between two persons. In an agency relationship one person is the agent of the other. The agent is empowered to act for and under the control of the principal. The agent's job is generally to negotiate and make contracts for the principal with a third party. An agency relationship is always consensual because the agent must agree to act on behalf of and subject to the control of the principal. The agency relationship is fiduciary because the agent acts in trust for the benefit of the principal. The relationship is always consensual. It may or may not be contractual. If an agency relationship does not result from a contract, it is said to be a gratuitous agency.

2. Vicarious liability is the legal theory that is used to hold the master liable for the torts of his or her servant. To establish vicarious liability two elements are needed: (1) a master-servant relationship, generally shown by demonstrating that the alleged master had control over or the right to exercise control over the alleged servant; and (2) that the servant was acting within the scope of his or her employment at the time of the alleged tort. Generally, vicarious liability is used in negligence cases. However, it can sometimes be used to hold the master liable for the intentional torts of the servant if the servant's employment relates to the activity or if the master had reason to foresee that the servant would engage in such activity. The law has also developed special rules for dealing with two torts in particular. These two torts are misrepresentation and defamation. First, the rule for misrepresentation states that if an agent with actual or apparent authority makes a false statement which a third party relies on to his or her detriment then the principal is liable. Similarly, with defamation, if an agent with actual or apparent authority communicates a falsehood to someone other than the victim and the victim is harmed, then the principal is liable. Perhaps the most interesting aspect about the rules regarding misrepresentation and defamation is that they apply whether the statements are uttered by servants, agents, or independent contractors.

3. The different types of principals include disclosed, undisclosed, and partially disclosed principals. In the case of a disclosed principal, the third party knows both the existence of the agency and the identity of the principal. In the case of a partially disclosed principal, the third party knows that the agency relationship exists but does not know the identity of the principal. In the case of an undisclosed principal, the third party does not know that an agency exists and, therefore, believes he or she is dealing directly with the other party.

4. The different types of agents include general agents and special agents. A general agent is a person who is given broad authority to conduct business on behalf of the principal. A special agent is a person authorized to conduct a particular transaction, to conduct a series of transactions, or to perform only a specified act for the principal.

5. When an agent is not known to be an agent and is acting as a principal, the agent can be held liable as a principal. When a person is known to be an agent, but it is not known for whom the agent acts, the third party can also hold the agent liable. Also, when an agent exceeds his or her authority the agent can be made personally liable.

6. Principals are liable on all contracts that a general or a special agent may enter into with third parties, as long as the agent acts within his or her authority. An undisclosed principal can be held liable for the acts of the agent once the identity of the principal is made known.

Once the principal's identity is revealed, a third party may sue either the principal or the agent.

7. Almost every executive of a corporation acts as an agent of the corporation. Partners act as agents of the partnership for business purposes of that partnership.

8. Agency relationships can be created by appointment, by implication, by necessity, by law, by estoppel, and by ratification.

9. The Uniform Computer Informations Transactions Act (UCITA) establishes a cyberagent as a computer program that acts without human intervention to begin an activity, to answer cybermessages, to deliver or accept cybermail, or to enter cybercontracts, as a representative of an individual who does not intervene in the action taken by the cyberagent at the actual time of the cyberagent's activity.

10. The Uniform Electronic Transactions Act (UETA) has certified that contracts made by cyberagents have the same binding effect as contracts created by human agents.

Cases for Analysis Page 617

1. No. In this case the court held that vicarious liability did not apply. The court held that, although the driver a servant of the *Evening Star,* he was not operating within the scope of employment when he chased a traffic violator. The court noted that the job of the newspaper truck driver was to deliver papers, not chase criminals.

2. Yes on both counts. The power to grant contracts to employees can be implied from the president's power to preside over the union's administrative matters. Also, the past acceptance by the union of the president's hiring practices could reasonably lead a person in Young's position to the belief that he had the power to enter employment contracts on behalf of the union.

3. The New Jersey Court found that the record revealed evidence of active wrongdoing on the part of Mularchuk in the wounding of McAndrew. It concluded that the Borough of Keansburg was responsible for that shooting, having authorized Mularchuk when on duty to carry a revolver without training. The court further concluded that the borough may be found liable under the doctrine of respondeat superior for the negligent act of Mularchuk of his wrongful intentional act in shooting McAndrew, committed during the course and within the scope of his police duties.

4. The decision was for Chicken Delight, Inc. Although Carfiro's act of delivering food under the Chicken Delight name did enhance the financial interests, reputation, and good will of the company, such was not sufficient reason to establish an agency relationship. The court reasoned that an essential factor in an agency relationship is the right of the principal to control the performance of the work of the agent. Since Chicken Delight had no right to control the activities of Carfiro, he was not an agent of Chicken Delight.

5. No. The actions of the prison guard in striking the inmate were within the scope of his employment. The court said, to take an action outside the scope of employment it must, "be so divergent that it serves the employer-employee relationship no longer." Such was not the case here.

6. The judgment was for Nielson. The court reasoned that although an agent is generally personally liable to third parties for actions in excess of the agent's authority, this is not true when the third party knows the agent has exceeded his or her authority.

7. The only argument that makes sense here is agency by estoppel. An agency by estoppel is created when one person is falsely represented to be an agent when no such agency relationship exists. The conduct of the agent alone cannot create an agency by estoppel. The principal must willfully or negligently or by silence give the false impression that another is the principal's agent. Further, having dealt with the alleged agent in reliance on the false impression, the third party must be damaged by the fact that an actual agency relationship did not exist.

Chapter 33   Agency Operation

Questions for Review and Discussion Page 633

1. There are two kinds of actual agency authority: express actual agency authority and implied actual agency authority. Express authority is the authority that the principal voluntarily and specifically sets forth as oral and written instructions to the agent. Implied authority is the agent's authority to perform those acts needed or customary to carrying out express authority.

2. Apparent authority is an accountability doctrine whereby the principal, by virtue of words or actions, leads a third party to believe that a nonagent is an agent or that an agent has authority that he or she really does not have.

3. If an agent delegates authority without being authorized to do so, the acts of the subagent do not impose any liability on the principal to third parties.

4. An agent can legally appoint a subagent if given express authority to do so or if the intention can be implied from the nature of the employment or from custom and usage.

5. An agent has the duty to obey all instructions, to be loyal to the principal; to exercise reasonable judgment, prudence, and skill; to account for all money and property belonging to the principal; to perform work personally; and to communicate fully all facts affecting the subject matter of the agency.

6. The remedies available to a principal include: terminate the agent's contract, withhold compensation, recover a profit made by the agent in violation of the agency agreement, recover money or property gained

or held by the agent to which the principal is entitled, restrain the agent from continuing to breach the agency agreement, recover damages for breach of contract, and rescind a contract entered by the agent that the agent should not have entered.

7. The duties that a principal has in relation to an agent include: compensation, reimbursement, indemnification, and cooperation.

8. The remedies of an agent include: leave the principal's employ, recover damages for breach of contract, recover the value of services, obtain reimbursement, and secure indemnity for personal liabilities.

9. An agency relationship can be terminated by an act of the parties (fulfillment of the purpose of the agency agreement, mutual agreement, revocation, and renunciation) or by operation of law (death, insanity, bankruptcy, and impossibility).

10. Actual notice is required when the third party has extended credit to the principal through the agent; a public notice in a newspaper of general circulation is sufficient for third parties who have never given credit but who have had cash transactions with the agent.

Cases for Analysis Page 633

1. The executor was correct that the death of Sturgill automatically terminated the agency and that the bank, therefore, had no right to continue to cash the checks. The bank, however, would have a cause of action against the agent for breach of the implied warranty that she had the authority to cash the check.

2. The court held that there was substantial evidence that the actions and nonactions of Buckeye Parking, Inc., could have clothed the imposter attendant with apparent authority.

3. Jackson has violated his duty of loyalty to Ozan.

4. The court will rule in favor of Pierce and Global. Since Global extended credit to Super through Savant in the past, they are entitled to actual notice of Savant's discharge. The newspaper notice is insufficient.

5. Decision for LaPage. The court relied upon the doctrine of apparent authority involving the accountability of an agent when the principal conveys to a third party that the agent may act on the principal's behalf, and the third party believes that such authority exists. In this case, the facts did not warrant a finding that apparent authority had been created because LaPage did clarify the situation.

6. The judgment was for Fortune Furniture. The court held the sending of the memo was chargeable to Castle Fabrics, Inc., under the doctrine of apparent authority. Having clothed the agent with the semblance of authority, a principal will not be permitted, after third parties have been led to act in reliance on the appearance thus produced, to deny to the damage to such others what the principal theretofore affirmed as to the agent's power.

7. As an agent, Lloyd had the duty to keep a separate account of each principal's funds. Whatever money Lloyd received during and as a result of the principal relationships could have been held in trust for each of the principals. An accounting should have been given to the principals within a reasonable period of time after the money was received. The money collected by Lloyd should have been held separate from his own funds. When Lloyd deposited the checks in the bank, he should have made the deposit in separate trust accounts. The failure to keep such funds separate is known as commingling, and Lloyd would be held personally liable for any resulting losses.

8. The judgment was for Clifton. The court held that Clifton had been authorized to act for Ross as special agent, to purchase the grinding mill on his behalf. Having done so, Clifton was entitled to compensation for the loss he incurred in so doing.

Chapter 34   Employment Law

Questions for Analysis Page 644

1. No. Couch would be considered a contractual employee under his original contract with the Cleveland Browns.

2. No. The Cleveland Browns committed no breach of contract violation when Couch was released. The question of whether there was an ethical breach is a matter of opinion. Accept all well-reasoned responses.

3. Couch filed a grievance with the Cleveland Browns for not permitting him to use the Browns' training facilities for workout purposes.

4. Accept all well-reasoned arguments here.

5. No. Couch would be considered a contractual employee under his contract with the Green Bay Packers.

Questions for Analysis Page 648

1. The "sue-your-boss" bill permits employees to sue an employer over alleged labor code violations that have not been handled by the state labor commissioner.

2. The bill was created because the number of employees working for state labor agencies has dropped in recent years.

3. Under the statute, employers can be fined $100 per employee pay period and $200 for each subsequent violation as well as for attorney fees and court costs. The employees winning the case receive 25 percent of the penalties. Half then goes to the general fund of the state, and the remaining 25 percent to the state Labor and Workforce Development Agency.

4. The statute covers wage-and-hour obligations, employee classification issues, drug and alcohol rehabilitation programs, the state layoff requirements, public works requirements, and occupational safety and health requirements.

5. Accept all well-reasoned answers to this question.

Questions for Review and Discussion Page 659

1. Employment-at-will is that legal doctrine that says that an employer can discharge an employee at any time for any reason or for no reason with or without notice.

2. Those employment situations in which an employee is not subject to employment-at-will include those employees covered by a collective bargaining agreement, those employees with individual employment contracts, those employees discharged for reason that are discriminatory, and those employees protected by the notification standards of the WARN Act.

3. The theories of wrongful discharge include implied contract, promissory estoppel, public policy tort, and implied covenant.

4. The after acquired evidence rule is applied when an employer uncovers evidence, usually during discovery, that reveals that the employer could have legitimately fired the employee even if the employee's claims of wrongful discharge prove to be true.

5. The Occupational Health and Safety Act establishes and enforces occupational safety and health standards that employers must follow.

6. The Fair Labor Standards Act provides that workers in interstate commerce must be paid the minimum wage, must work no more than forty hours per week (unless they are paid time and a half for overtime). It also forbids employment of children under fourteen.

7. Unemployment insurance is available to individuals who are unemployed through no fault of their own and who earned sufficient credits from prior employment. Workers' compensation statutes compensate covered workers or their dependents for injuries, disease, or death resulting from their job.

8. Under the Family Medical Leave Act, employers who have fifty or more employees must give those employees up to twelve weeks of leave time for child, spousal, or parental care. This leave time may be unpaid but must not jeopardize the job of the employee.

9. Under disparate treatment, the employer intentionally discriminates against the employee (or potential employee) who belongs to a protected class (race, color, creed, gender, national origin). Discrimination through disparate impact involves an employment requirement which appears to be neutral on its face, but which has a disproportionate impact on a protected class.

10. A defense of business necessity arises when a particular employment requirement is needed for a job. A *bona fide* occupational qualification is an employment requirement that in good faith requires a member of a protected class to perform the job in question. However, the law does state that race can never be a BFOQ.

Cases for Analysis Page 659

1. No. Discrimination based on single status is not illegal under the Civil Rights Act. Status as a single person is not a protected category under the Civil Rights Act. Since there is no discrimination it can be neither disparate treatment nor disparate impact.

2. No. Juergens was incorrect. The overtime clause and the oral representations made did not amount to an implied contract between the staff accountant and the accounting firm.

3. Henderson used the public policy exception to employment-at-will. The public policy exception prevents employers from discharging an employee for reasons that violate public policy. Here Henderson was fired for refusing to violate the law and for reporting the company's illegal actions. Since the court must encourage people to obey the law, it cannot support an employer who fires an employee for refusing to break the law.

4. Yes. The court held that the injury to Bennerson, who was on his lunch hour at the time of the accident and performing no duties for the employer, did not arise out of the course of his employment. In so holding, the court reversed the ruling of the state workers' compensation board.

5. Yes. The court affirmed the decision of the Board of Review that Barillaro and Fotia were ineligible to receive unemployment compensation benefits because they refused offers of suitable work without good cause. The court explained that good cause for refusing suitable work must be real and not imaginary, substantial not trivial, and reasonable not whimsical. With regard to the claimants arguments, the court held the following: a desire to avoid a cut in pay was not sufficiently compelling to constitute good cause to refuse an employer's offer to return to work in reasonably similar positions after the layoff; loss of seniority was not sufficient to constitute good cause where claimants would have retained partial seniority rights; and claimants were without good cause for refusing employer's offer because of unfamiliarity with the operation of the machine and the feeling of being too short for the machine.

6. No. The court ruled that a BFOQ defense will fail if the defendant does demonstrate that there is a reasonable need for the BFOQ. Moreover that reasonable need must be connected to the everyday tasks of the business. To allow the local customs of a foreign country to determine the existence of a BFOQ would be to permit such customs to determine the limits of Title VII's jurisdiction. The court found this to be unsatisfactory. Moreover, the court characterized the company's desire for a male sales executive as a business convenience rather than a business necessity.

7. No. Since it was possible to mask Tylo's pregnancy with various techniques including body doubles, creative camera angles, face shots, and altered shooting schedules, the need for a non-pregnant actress may have been convenient for the business but it was not an absolute necessity.

8. No. The court held that although mere possession of a college degree did not qualify a person to be employed in the public health program, it did not follow that the lack of a degree was irrelevant or that the degree requirement was not based on program necessity or was not job-related. The court reasoned that the representatives were called upon to participate in difficult and taxing tasks. They were required to have the ability to communicate with others, frequently in a highly emotion-charged atmosphere, and to have the ability to speak and write intelligibly.

9. Yes. The court of appeals agreed with the trial court that the height and weight requirements that eliminated 98 percent of the female applicants from eligibility were improper inasmuch as the Commonwealth of Virginia did not demonstrate the need for the physical requirements. It was also held that the written tests used by the state police to fill certain positions with the state police and for trooper positions were not fair measures of qualities needed to do the job.

10. Yes. The plaintiff has stated sufficient grounds for her wrongful discharge suit. The courts said, "an exception to the employment-at-will doctrine is justified where an employer has discharged his employee in contravention of 'sufficiently clear public policy.' The existence of such a public policy may be discerned by the Ohio judiciary based on sources such as the Constitutions of Ohio and the United States, legislation, administrative rules and regulations, and the common law." (Note: Ultimately, the court in this case decided that the plaintiff was not entitled to a judgment. The decision was based on the court's interpretation of the state constitution. Thus, although the court ruled that the plaintiff could bring a wrongful discharge lawsuit based on a constitutional issue, in this case the constitution did not give her the rights that she believed that it did.)

Chapter 35   Labor-Management Relations Law

Questions for Analysis   Page 671

1. The union leader was accused of using union business agents to perform actions for his personal benefit. He was also accused of embezzlement.

2. The union leader could be expelled from his position of authority.

3. The union involved in this suit is the International Brotherhood of Teamsters.

4. The federal law that could be involved here is the Landrum-Griffin Act (also known as the Labor Management Reporting and Disclosure Act of 1959).

5. Accept all well-reasoned answers here.

Questions for Review and Discussion   Page 675

1. One of the first successful union organizing efforts took place in 1886 in Columbus, Ohio, when Samuel Gompers organized the American Federation of Labor (AFL). The AFL, however, limited its membership to skilled workers such as tailors and coppersmiths. It was not until 1935 when John L. Lewis created the Congress of Industrial Workers (CIO) that semiskilled and unskilled workers had a union that gave them the opportunity for membership and the protection afforded by union solidarity. These two unions joined forces in 1955 to form the AFL-CIO, one of the most powerful union organizations in operation today.

2. The legal tug-of-war between Congress and the federal courts began with the Sherman Antitrust Act in 1890. The act was also used by big business with the support of the courts to outlaw union activities in a way that had not been intended. One tool the courts used against strikes was the injunction. Big business argued that the net effect of a strike was to hurt a company's ability to compete with rival companies. As such, it was an illegal restraint of trade under the Sherman Act. The courts agreed and willingly issued injunctions even when a union simply threatened to strike against a company as a bargaining tactic. Congress reacted to this by passing the Clayton Act in 1914 which was designed to eliminate the federal courts' ability to issue injunctions to stop union activities. The federal judicial system, however, effectively destroyed the Clayton Act when the Supreme Court created two criteria that allowed the courts to freely issue injunctions to stop labor activities. The first test was the objectives test. Under this test a court could issue an injunction if it determined that the goal or the objective of a strike was unlawful. Under the second test, the means test, the courts could stop a strike if it was conducted in an unlawful manner. Congress reacted to this subterfuge by passing the Norris-LaGuardia Act in 1932. The net effect of the Norris-LaGuardia Act was to completely prohibit the federal courts from issuing injunctions against union organized activities.

3. The basic aims of labor unions are: (1) to create a seniority system to protect workers' jobs from arbitrary layoffs and replacement with cheaper wage earners; (2) to upgrade worker status through wage and fringe benefit increases; and (3) to sponsor laws that improve social, economic, and political conditions for workers.

4. The major provision of the Norris-LaGuardia Act involved limiting the power of the federal courts to issue injunctions to stop labor disputes.

5. The Wagner Act, created the National Labor Relations Board, authorized the NLRB to conduct representative elections and to determine the bargaining unit; outlawed certain conduct as unfair labor practices; and authorized the NLRB to hold hearings on unfair labor practices.

6. The Taft-Hartley Act outlawed certain practices by unions as unfair labor practices, allowed states to legislate right-to-work laws, provided an eighty-day

cooling off period in strikes that endangered national health or safety, and created a mediation and conciliation service to assist in settlement of labor disputes.

7. The Landrum-Griffin Act established a bill of rights for union members; required unions to adopt constitutions and bylaws; required unions to submit annual reports detailing assets, liabilities, payments, and loans; and added further provisions to the list of unfair labor practices.

8. The National Labor Relations Board has exclusive jurisdiction to enforce the Taft-Hartley Act and related laws. It has the authority to act when cases are brought before it, but only in cases in which the employer's operation or the labor dispute affects commerce.

9. A complaint filed with the NLRB can result in a cease and desist order restoring the parties to the state that existed before the unfair labor practice began.

10. In the states, the public sector does not have the right to strike unless that right is authorized by a state statute. The public sector at the federal level does not have the right to strike.

Cases for Analysis   Page 675

1. The provision suggested by Franco and Allanson on behalf of the union amounts to what is called a closed shop. The concept of the closed shop was outlawed by federal labor law. In contrast, the provision suggested by the company involves establishing what is known as a union shop. Union shops are permitted under federal law. However, it would be necessary to check state law because some states have established right-to-work laws that outlaw both the closed shop and the union shop. The company's proposal to set up a company run union clearly runs counter to federal law.

2. The judgment was for the NLRB. The Court explained that the Wagner Act does not prevent an employer from making and enforcing reasonable rules covering the conduct of employees on company time. It is, therefore, the right of an employer to make and enforce a rule prohibiting the solicitation of union members during working hours, absent evidence that it was adopted for discriminatory purposes. It is no less true, however, that time outside working hours, whether before or after work, during lunch or rest periods, is the employee's time to use as he or she wishes without unreasonable restraint, although the employee is on company property. Therefore, since the employee was soliciting outside of working hours but on company property, the rule must be presumed to be an unreasonable hindrance to self-organization and discriminatory, unless it can be shown that the rule is necessary to maintain production or discipline.

3. The judgment was for the NLRB. The Court ruled that conferring benefits while a representation election was pending was an unfair labor practice. The Court explained that the practice induced the employees to vote

against the union and interfered with the employees' protected right to organize. The Court noted that the well-timed benefits carried with them an inherent suggestion of a "fist within a velvet glove." This was because employees could infer that the source of benefits given is also the source from which future benefits must flow and which may dry up if the employer is not obliged.

4. The judgment was for the NLRB. The Court set aside the judgment of the court of appeals. The Court agreed that so far as the Wagner Act is concerned, an employee has the absolute right to terminate the entire business for any reason. Notwithstanding, a partial closing is an unfair labor practice under the Wagner Act if the purpose is to chill unionism in any of the remaining plants of a single employer.

5. Yes. The U.S. Supreme Court found that the practice of the union prevented the fair and free choice of a bargaining representative contemplated by the Wagner Act. The Court complained that the union was buying indorsements. That is, some employees might sign cards merely to hedge against possible payments of the initiation fee; others would infer that their fellow workers actually supported the union and vote in a manner consistent with the judgment of their fellow workers. While employees were not obliged in the secret ballot election to vote yes if they signed a recognition slip, there might be some who would feel obliged to carry through their stated intention. The Court also recognized that the failure to sign a recognition slip might seem ominous to nonunion employees, who might fear that if they did not sign, they would face the wrathful union should the union win. The Court reasoned that this influence may well have had a decisive impact in this case, where a change of one vote would have changed the outcome of the election.

Part 7   Case Study   Page 677

1. A summary judgment motion asks the court for an immediate judgment for the party filing the motion because there are no material issues in dispute and the moving party is entitled to a judgment as a matter of law.

2. Under the doctrine of employment-at-will, employment agreements that have no term of duration are terminable at the will of either party for any reason not contrary to law.

3. An employee who can prove that his or her discharge somehow violated public policy, may recover damages in tort. Upholding public policy is the broad legal principle that says that the courts will not allow anyone to do anything that tends to injure the public at large. For example, in many jurisdictions if an employee is fired for refusing to violate the law, such a discharge would violate public policy. Public policy encourages people to obey the law. Firing someone who wants to obey the

law would clearly violate public policy. Similarly, if the firing itself violates the law, public policy will provide a remedy for the employee.

4. In this case the court interpreted the public policy exception to employment-at-will to include any firing that somehow violates public policy, rather than just those firings that are expressly forbidden by statute. The court was, of course, quite specific in its explanation of what constitutes public policy because it does not believe that judges should use the public policy label to create policies, doctrines, and legal rules that simply reflect a judge's personal social or legal philosophy. To support this point, the court said, "We understand and share the Supreme Court's concern that the conclave of judges should not be allowed to pull public policy out of thin air to make the law conform to their individual conceptions of what the law ought to be. A public policy ought to be objectively discernable [sic] from sources outside the judge's individual social or legal philosophy before being permitted to override the settled doctrine of employment-at-will."

In this situation the court was convinced that the state's policy of attempting to protect the public at large from the serious dangers caused by drunk drivers is clearly a statemade policy that must be enforced by the courts. The court said, "The public policy of this state in favor of keeping drunk drivers off of the streets appears to be both strong and clear. It is not a matter of a conclave of judges announcing to the world a 'public policy' invented by them for the purpose of subjecting the citizens of this state to a rule of law that has little or no support outside the minds of the judges. Recent, sweeping enactments by the General Assembly designed to discourage drunk driving are an objective manifestation of the public policy of this state in favor of taking all reasonable steps to eliminate drunk driving.

"The police drunk driving hotline . . . has been well publicized. It is consistent with the reasonable efforts to get drunk drivers off the roads of our state, and manifests an intent to rely upon citizen informants to assist the police in detecting drunk driving."

The final conclusion of the court was that this policy was crucial enough to make it clear that its preservation can override the doctrine of employment-at-will. The court concluded, "We hold that the public policy in favor of removing drunk drivers from the roads of our state is sufficiently clear, and sufficiently compelling, to override the doctrine of employment-at-will when an employee is discharged because, having a reasonable basis for her suspicions, she has informed the police of the likelihood that her superior at work is going to be driving while intoxicated."

5. It is clear in this case that King is a servant rather than an independent contractor. Whether Litton Systems can be held liable should King injure someone while driving

under the influence of alcohol under the doctrine of *respondeat superior* is problematical. The question that would have to be answered in that situation is whether, at the time of the accident, King was acting within the scope of his employment. If, on the one extreme, he was on his own time and, while returning from lunch or while driving home injured someone, then he would not have been within the scope of his employment. If, on the other hand, he left lunch and ran an errand for his employer, he would be operating within the scope of his employment. Also, even if he is simply returning from lunch and his employer knew of his habit of becoming intoxicated and then driving back from lunch, it is conceivable that the court might rule that such a "condoned" activity would fall within the scope of King's employment.

6. Yes. The court must not determine the exclusive bargaining rights of the union. To do so would fragment the bargaining unit, thereby creating the type of friction which the bargaining process is supposed to prevent.

Part 8   Business Organization and Regulation

Chapter 36   Sole Proprietorships and Partnerships

Questions for Analysis Page 686

1. If no partnership agreement was drawn up in this case, the court could be convinced that a partnership existed if counsel could prove that there was a sharing of profits. This would create a *prima facie* case for the existence of a partnership.

2. The Buttercup Bake Shop appears to be a sole proprietorship.

3. Accept all well-reasoned answers to this question.

4. The elements that should be included in the partnership agreement include the name and duration of the partnership; the amount of capital put in by each partner; the reserve funds to be held by the partnership; the location and withdrawal procedure for all partnership funds; the location and accessibility of partnership transaction records; the time and amounts each partner is permitted to withdraw from partnership earnings; provisions for the preparation of an annual balance sheet and income sheet; limitations on all partners; and termination notice procedures.

5. Accept all well-reasoned answers to this question.

Questions for Review and Discussion Page 694

1. The most common forms of business associations include the sole proprietorship, the general partnership,

the registered limited liability partnership, the limited partnership, the corporation, and the limited liability company.

2. The greatest advantage to a sole proprietorship is that the owner has complete control over the business. The major disadvantage is that the sole proprietor is subject to unlimited liability.

3. The two model acts that govern partnership law are the Uniform Partnership Act and the Revised Uniform Partnership Act.

4. Under the entity theory a partnership exists as an individual person with its own separate identity. This unique, individual entity is separate from the identities of the partners. In contrast, under the aggregate theory, the partnership is seen simply as an assembly or a collection of the partners who do business together.

5. RUPA is quite specific about the nature of a partnership agreement. In fact, it defines such an agreement as "the agreement, whether written, oral, or implied, among the partners concerning the partnership, including amendments to the partnership agreement."

6. RUPA says that certain types of profit sharing, while real enough, will not rise to the level needed to create a partnership. These profit-sharing activities include the following: (1) the repayment of a debt; (2) wages to an employee; (3) payments to an independent contractor; (4) rent payments to a landlord; (5) annuity payments or health benefit payments to a beneficiary, to a representative, or to a designee of a retired or deceased partner; (6) interest payments on a loan, even if the level of payments is tied to profit fluctuations; or (7) consideration for the sale of goodwill or for the sale of other property even if the payments are made in installments.

7. The term "person" can refer to a flesh and blood individual, a corporation, other partnerships, joint ventures, trusts, estates, and other commercial or legal institutions.

8. Under UPA, the rule was that each partner had a property interest in all specific items of partnership property. Each partner was, therefore, a co-owner of that property. This form of ownership was known as tenancy in partnership. Under UPA, a tenancy in partnership had the following characteristics:

   a. A partner had an equal right with all other partners to possess and use specific partnership property for partnership purposes, but not for that partner's personal use.

   b. A partner's interest in partnership property could not be assigned (i.e., transferred by sale, mortgage, pledge, or otherwise) to a nonpartner, unless the other partners agreed to the transfer.

   c. A partner's rights in partnership property was not subject to attachment (i.e., taking a person's property and bringing it into the custody of the law) for personal debts or claims against the partners themselves.

   d. A deceased partner's interest in real property held by the partnership passed to the surviving partners.

   e. Partner's rights in specific partnership property was not subject to any allowances or rights to widows, heirs, or next of kin.

   Under RUPA all of this has changed. RUPA states that "A partner is not co-owner of partnership property and has no interest in partnership property which can be transferred, either voluntarily or involuntarily."

9. Under RUPA, a dissociation takes place whenever a partner is no longer associated with the running of the firm. Partners can leave a partnership firm whenever they want. A partner leaves a firm wrongfully if he or she does not have the legal right to do so. The dissolution of a partnership occurs when a partner ceases to be associated with the partnership and the partnership ends. The dissolution of a partnership can occur in one of three ways: (1) by an action committed the partners, (2) by operation of law, or (3) by the decree of a court of law.

10. A registered limited liability partnership is a general partnership in all respects except one—liability. A limited partnership has at least one general partner and one limited partner.

Cases for Analysis Page 695

1. No. Taylor will not succeed in her claim against Roberts and Hull. The share of profits she received each month was a fixed rent installment paid to her according to the lease agreement she negotiated with Roberts and Hull when they first opened their restaurant in the warehouse. It was, therefore, not a sharing of profits within the meaning of the statute.

2. The court decided that no partnership existed. The money that went from Stephen to Lois was in the form of rent. The court concluded that "there is also no indication that the parties shared net profits. Both the appellant and Linda testified that Stephen operated and maintained the farm, but also sold crops and deposited the proceeds into an account that the appellant did not have access to. Linda Nuss acknowledged that the appellant did not receive any additional income from the sale of crops beyond payment of property taxes, utilities, and other expenditures associated with maintaining the farm."

3. Yes. Under a Nebraska state statute a partnership is an entity. Therefore, a plaintiff who wishes to recover against an individual partner must first show that the partnership property is insufficient to satisfy his or her claim.

4. No. Sharing of profits is prima facie evidence of the existence of a partnership. There are, however, several exceptions to the rule. One exception exists if the sharing of profits is paid in the form of wages. That is what happened in this case.

5. Yes. The Idaho Supreme Court ruled that Summers was not entitled to reimbursement. The court explained that the business was a two-person partnership, with each partner having an equal say. Dooley made it clear that he opposed the decision to hire a third worker. The court explained that when partners are equally divided, those against the proposed course of action must get their way. Thus, Summers did not have authority to incur the expense for the partnership. Since the expense was incurred only by Summers, the court denied his claim for reimbursement from his partner.

Chapter 37   The Corporate Entity

Questions for Review and Discussion   Page 711

1. Capitalism prospered in America in the nineteenth century because the economic system provided the perfect engine for capitalistic progress. Much of this was because there was a lot of land to be developed and an influx of energetic immigrants who were willing to improve that land. The corporation grew in response, because the capitalistic system needed an efficient way to raise capital in order to finance these land development projects. The process of doing business as a self-governing business association, that is, as a corporation, is called associative corporativism, or simply, corporativism.

2. A corporation is a legal entity (also referred to as a legal person) the creation of which is empowered by a state or a federal statute authorizing individuals to operate an enterprise.

3. A corporation is a legal person and, therefore, has certain constitutional rights such as the right to equal protection of the law and the right not to be deprived of property without due process. Corporations also have dual citizenship. They are citizens of the state in which they are incorporated and in which they have their principal place of business.

4. A close corporation is a corporation in which the outstanding shares of stock and managerial control are closely held by a few people (hence the term "close" corporation) or held by one person. An S corporation is one in which the shareholders have agreed to have their profits and losses taxed directly to them rather than to the corporation, thus escaping the penalty of double taxation generally associated with corporations.

5. A private corporation is one formed by private persons to accomplish a task best undertaken by an entity that can raise large amounts of capital quickly and which offers limited liability. A public corporation is one created for governmental purposes. A quasi-public corporation is one organized for profit but which performs a public function, such as providing public utilities, The gas company and the electric company are quasi-public corporations.

6. Typically, the articles of incorporation of a corporation should include such things as the name of the corporation, the duration of the corporation, the purpose of the corporation, the number and classes of shares, the shareholders' rights, the name and address of the statutory agent, the number of directors, and each incorporator's name and address.

7. The articles of organization are the written application to form a limited liability company. The operating agreement of a limited liability company outlines the structure and the operation of the LLC. The operating agreement sets up the bylaws or regulations that the LLC will follow.

8. A *de jure* corporation is a corporation in law, that is, one that has been lawfully created; a *de facto* corporation is a corporation in fact, that is, one that, while not legally formed, nevertheless acts like a corporation. To prove the existence of a *de facto* corporation a party must show that there has been a good faith attempt to create a corporation under an existing incorporation statute, and that there has been an exercise of corporate power, that is, the "owners" have acted as if there were a corporation, even though in law the "corporation" does not really exist.

9. The objective of corporate veil piercing is to cut through a corporate façade to reach the true owner or owners of the corporation who are literally hiding behind a fake corporate "veil." Generally, the corporation exists in law, but has not been permitted to become a true entity, separate from the incorporators, the shareholders, or the parent corporation. Such a corporation is sometimes referred to as a dummy corporation or a corporate shell.

10. Common stock carries with it all of the risks of the business, inasmuch as it does not guarantee its holders the right to receive profits. Preferred stock involves classes of stock with special privileges, such as receiving a payment of dividends before other shareholders.

Cases for Analysis   Page 712

1. Aerenthal is correct. The corporation is a separate legal entity that has certain constitutional rights. One of these rights under the U.S. Constitution is the right not to be deprived of property without due process of law.

2. Yes. The two names were similar enough that, along with the damage that had been caused to General Housing Assistance's reputation and the resulting loss in funding, the court ordered General Mutual to cease and desist in the use of the name.

3. No. Balderson was incorrect. He was a promoter when he entered the preincorporation agreement. Since there was no evidence that the corporation formally adopted the contract, and since Balderson was not specifically released from liability on that agreement, he remained

personally liable on that contract. The court said, "mere adoption of the contract by the corporation will not relieve promoters from liability in the absence of a subsequent novation [citations omitted]. This view is founded upon 'the well-settled principle of the law of contracts that a party to a contract cannot relieve himself from its obligations by the substitution of another person, without the consent of [the] other party' [citations omitted]. Consequently, the promoters of a corporation who execute a contract on its behalf are personally liable for the breach thereof irrespective of the later adoption of the contract by the corporation unless the contract provides that the performance thereunder is solely the responsibility of the corporation.

Applying these principles to the facts of the present case, we find that the promoters remain personally liable on the pre-incorporation agreement. While the corporation was subsequently formed as envisioned in the contract, the agreement does not state that the parties intended that the corporate entity was to be exclusively liable for any breach. Even if the agreement did so provide, there is no evidence that the corporation, once formed, formally adopted it."

4. No. The due process clause of the Fourteenth Amendment of the U.S. Constitution allows a state court to exercise jurisdiction over a noncitizen corporation only so long as there exists an appropriate contact between the defendant corporation and the state where the lawsuit started. The relationship between the defendant corporation and the state must be such that it is reasonable to require the corporation to defend in the forum state. In this case, there was a total absence of those circumstances that are a necessary link to the exercise of state court jurisdiction over a foreign corporation. WWV was incorporated in New York and did business there. It was therefore a citizen of New York not a citizen of Oklahoma. WWV performed no services, owned no property, and closed no sales in Oklahoma. It solicited no business in Oklahoma either through salespersons or through advertising. It also did not indirectly through others serve or seek to serve the Oklahoma market.

5. No. Spence is a promoter. As a promoter, he is liable for all contracts he makes for the corporation before it is formed. Since there was no evidence of adoption, novation, or release, Spence was personally liable.

6. No. A *de facto* corporation existed at the time the contract was made between MBI and the Department of Administration. MBI had made a good faith attempt to incorporate under Montana's existing incorporation statute. It had also exercised corporate power. The only problem in the incorporation process involved the name. A small technical error like this one would not prevent the existence of a de facto corporation.

7. Yes. Under the corporation by estoppel doctrine, Baldwin could not deny that he had dealt with Lamas as a corporation. Baldwin's payments to Lamas were enough to indicate that Baldwin knew that he was dealing with a corporation.

8. Yes. The court could not disregard the corporate entity because it could find no fraud, no attempt to conceal a crime, and no intent to evade contractual or tort liability. In addition, there was some separation maintained, since the hospital handled its own daily accounts, and had the power to make its own contracts.

9. Yes. Alaskan Chemical Disposal had no business other than providing waste disposal services to NCIT. Alaskan Chemical Disposal was listed as a division of NCIT, was financed by NCIT, and shared the same board of directors and officers as NCIT. Alaskan Chemical Disposal was also badly undercapitalized. All decisions in the running of Alaskan Chemical Disposal were made by NCIT. Consequently, it is easy to conclude that Alaskan Chemical Disposal was probably formed to allow NCIT to escape liability in just this type of situation. As a result, the court had no difficulty piercing the corporate veil and holding NCIT liable.

Chapter 38   Corporate Governance

Questions for Analysis   Page 723

1. Many corporate lawsuits happen in Delaware because state statutes dominate corporate law and more than half of all publicly-traded companies are incorporated in Delaware.

2. Traditionally the state courts in Delaware have given a very liberal interpretation to the Business Judgment Rule. This interpretation has made it difficult for people to challenge decisions made by corporate directors. Recently the scope of the rule has been *narrowed*.

3. The courts are reacting to an increase in corporate crime.

4. This has not lured corporations away from Delaware because Delaware still has an enormous amount of case law on corporate decisions.

5. The fact that Delaware's economy depends on the corporate law industry means that the law in Delaware will not become too radical.

Questions for Review and Discussion   Page 733

1. Associative corporativism prospers when innovative people take risks. Risk takers employ one of three positions. The risk taker may be an inventor or entrepreneur with a new idea, an original product, or an innovative business technique. A second risk taker is the investor who is willing to put his or her capital into a

venture that may or may not reap dividends. The final risk takers are the managers themselves, that is, those individuals who are willing to take a chance as the directors and officers of a corporation. In order to be effective, corporate risk takers must avoid the central pitfall of associate corporativism, that is, the tendency of a corporate system to move from a simple and direct hands-on operation to one that is filled with bureaucratic red tape. The more successful a corporation is, the bigger and more complex it becomes which leads to a layered bureaucracy that promotes the status quo rather than innovation and risk taking. In this bureaucratic environment, the innovator is stifled and the bureaucrat rewarded. Two consequences occur from the inclination of associative corporativism to move from simplicity to bureaucracy. One is the almost unstoppable predisposition of the corporate giant to destroy smaller, less powerful corporate competitors. The second is the bureaucracy's inclination to eliminate any voices of dissent from the board and the officer corps.

2. The directors of a corporation create the broad policies of a corporation, while the officers run the day-to-day activities of the corporation. The shareholders are the ultimate owners of the corporation. Their primary governance role is to elect the directors.

3. The five theories of associative corporativism are special interest group control, government control, independent director control, managerial control, and shareholder control.

4. In cumulative voting, the minority shareholders are given the chance to elect one or more directors to the board of a corporation. Cumulative voting permits the shareholders to multiply their shares by the number of directors to be elected. These votes can be cast for one director or distributed among several candidates. A proxy is the authority given to one shareholder or to management to cast a shareholder's votes. Proxy solicitation is the process by which one shareholder (or the management of the corporation) asks another shareholder for the right to cast the votes of that shareholder.

5. A voting trust is an agreement among shareholders to transfer their voting rights to a trustee. A trustee is a person who is given the management and control of another's property and/or the rights associated with that property. In a voting trust, the trustee actually votes the shareholders' shares. A pooling agreement is a situation in which several shareholders agree to pool their shares and vote in a certain way that is agreed to before the election. The difference between a pooling agreement and a voting trust is that, in a trust, the shareholders give up actual control of their votes, while in a pooling agreement the shareholders still retain control over and actually cast their own votes.

6. A shareholder proposal is a suggestion about a board policy or procedure that is submitted by a shareholder. The proposal cannot be about the ordinary day-to-day operation of the business. It must concern something that affects all shareholders. To qualify as a valid shareholder proposal, under SEC rules, the proposal must be no more than 500 words long, and must be submitted to management at least 120 days before a shareholders' meeting.

7. A shareholder direct suit is brought by shareholders to vindicate a right that belongs to them directly by virtue of their position as shareholders, such as the right to vote or to receive dividends. A shareholder derivative suit is a suit brought by a shareholder to vindicate the rights of the corporation itself. The right to sue is derived from the injury to the corporation, of which the shareholder is a partial owner.

8. The business judgment rule states that a manager's decision will stand as long as it was legal, was made with due care and in good faith, and as long as the decision was made in the best interests of the corporation. The fairness rule says that a decision made by a manager will stand if it is fair to the corporation. The business judgment rule is used by the courts when the manager is disinterested, that is, he or she is not personally gaining from the decision. When the manager is interested, that is, when he or she is gaining from the decision, the fairness rule is used.

9. The rights that belong to shareholders include the right to receive dividends, the right to vote (as explained above), the right to sue (as explained above), the right to examine corporate records, the right to transfer stock, and certain preemptive rights.

10. If the members choose to run the LLC, they become agents of the LLC. As agents they can enter contracts on behalf of the LLC in most matters involving the ordinary operation of the LLC. However, there are some provisions that require the agreement of all the members of the LLC. These matters include, but are not limited to, disposing of the firm's goodwill and submitting a claim of the LLC to arbitration. Otherwise, the members of the LLC share their management powers in proportion to each member's interest in the firm. The operating agreement can make changes in these provisions. If the members choose to hire outside managers, the managers become the agents of the LLC. It would be within their power to enter contracts for the LLC. However, these contracts would be limited to the ordinary affairs of the LLC. They would not include any of the transactions that would require the consent of all of the members of the firm. Regardless of whether the members or the managers run the LLC, both groups have a fiduciary duty to the LLC and to the members of the LLC. Still, it would be wise to outline specific management duties in the operating agreement.

Cases for Analysis Page 734

1. The church members in this case had failed to exhaust internal remedies. They had made no parliamentary moves to stop the election and had used their own absentee ballots in the voting that they had complained about. Since they had not exhausted their internal remedies, and since the same rules that apply to profit corporations also apply to nonprofit corporations, the court concluded that the litigants were not entitled to attorney's fees.

2. Yes. Weinberger was correct on two counts. First, since the meeting was defined as a special meeting, the bylaws required that Weinberger be notified of the meeting. The fact that he was not notified made every piece of business carried out at the meeting void. This included the change in the bylaws as well as the vote to remove Weinberger. Similarly, the fact that only six directors showed up meant that a quorum had not been reached and no business could transpire.

3. No. The business judgment rule also calls for due care in making business decisions in the best interests of the corporation. In this case, the directors had not taken the time, or the effort, to investigate the merger. Instead, they had accepted a hastily delivered explanation from the CEO and had done no investigative work on their own.

4. The fairness rule should be used when evaluating the decisions made by the directors of S.L.&E., and LGT. The court said, "the business judgment rule presupposes that the directors have no conflict of interest. When a shareholder attacks a decision in which the directors have an interest other than as directors of the corporation, the directors may not escape review of the merits of the transaction. . . . [A] contract between a corporation and an entity in which its directors are interested may be set aside unless the proponent of the contract 'shall establish affirmatively that the contract or transaction was fair and reasonable to the corporation.'"

5. Yes. The trust created by Jackson was not a voting trust. In a voting trust, only voting rights are transferred to the trustee. In the Jackson trust, all rights, including the right to sell the shares, were held by the trustee. Because it was not a voting trust, the ten-year limit did not apply. The trust was therefore valid and remained in effect.

6. The suit was a derivative suit because it involved injury to the corporation, in this case Berlinair, Inc., rather than an injury to the shareholder's rights. The fairness rule should be used to judge Lundgren's conduct because he was self-dealing in the transaction between BFR and ABC. Klinicki won the suit because Lundgren violated the corporate opportunity doctrine, which was a breach of his fiduciary duty of loyalty to Berlinair.

7. No. Naquin's request to see the corporate records had to be honored by Dubois and Hoffpauir. He had a legitimate reason for wanting to inspect the records, and he made the request under reasonable circumstances. The court issued an order forcing Dubois and Hoffpauir to open the records to Naquin.

8. Snodgrass could increase her voting power by purchasing more shares. She could use cumulative voting if that was permitted by the bylaws of the corporation. She could seek out other shareholders to obtain their proxies, form a voting trust, or enter a pooling agreement. Finally, she might be eligible to file a shareholder proposal with the directors.

9. After exhausting internal remedies and making the required security deposit, Harris could bring a derivative suit, asking the court to compel Fleure to transfer all profits made from the real estate deal back to Fastway.

Chapter 39   Government Regulation of Corporate Business

Questions for Review and Discussion Page 754

1. The federal power to regulate business comes from the Commerce Clause of the Constitution, that is, Article I, Section 8, Clause 3. The Commerce Clause has expanded the ability of the federal government to regulate almost every aspect of business as long as the activity has an impact on interstate commerce.

2. The source of state power to regulate business is the state's police power, that is, the state's power to regulate the health, safety, welfare, and morals of the people. This power is inherent in the state government simply by virtue of the fact that it is, in fact, a legitimate government.

3. The Securities and Exchange Commission prevents unfair practices by regulating the issuance of new securities by requiring the filing of a registration statement and prospectus before the new securities can be sold by a corporation. It also requires periodic reports of financial information concerning registered securities. The SEC also prohibits manipulative and deceptive actions in the sale and purchase of securities. It also prohibits insiders, including corporate directors and officers, among others, from realizing any profit from the purchase or sale of securities based on inside information. Finally, the SEC also regulates the proxy solicitation process.

4. A *per se* antitrust violation is one that is so contrary to antitrust policy matters, that the harm is presumed and the practice is prohibited, without the need for proving any harm as a result. Price-fixing is an example of a *per se* violation. The rule of reason standard will stop certain practices only if they are an unreasonable restriction on competition.

5. The techniques of corporate expansion include mergers, consolidations, asset acquisitions, and stock acquisitions. A merger involves the joining of two companies one of which is absorbed into the other. A consolidation involves the joining of two companies both of which disappear and from which a new company emerges. An asset acquisition occurs when one company buys all the property of another company. A stock acquisition occurs when one company buys a controlling interest in the stock of another corporation. This is also called a takeover or a takeover bid.

6. The SEC is interested in regulating the expansion itself, while the FTC is interested in the effects of the expansion.

7. The Environmental Protection Agency is empowered to conduct research on all aspects of pollution, set and enforce pollution control standards, monitor programs to determine whether pollution abatement standards are being met, and administer grants to assist states in controlling pollution. The Federal Energy Regulatory Commission is responsible for regulating the transportation and the wholesale price of natural gas and electricity sold for use in interstate commerce.

8. Under the Employee Retirement Income Security Act an employer is responsible for putting pension contributions into a pension trust on behalf of employees, independent of that employer. If the sale of a business involves a plant closing or a mass layoff, the provisions of the Worker Adjustment and Retraining Notification Act require employers (with at least 100 full-time workers) to give employees sixty-days' notice.

9. A corporation may undergo dissolution by voluntary or involuntary means.

10. A limited liability company may undergo dissolution by the unanimous agreement of all its members. A dissolution may also be triggered by the expulsion, bankruptcy, or withdrawal of a member. The articles of organization or the operating agreement can also specify events that trigger a dissolution.

Cases for Analysis   Page 754

1. No. The United States Supreme Court ruled that Filburn was incorrect. Even though Filburn's wheat was not sold at market, it still had an effect on interstate commerce. Because he was using his own wheat, he was not buying wheat on the open market. Thus, the wheat grown for home use was competing with wheat on the open market in interstate commerce. This was enough of an impact on interstate commerce to allow federal regulation via the Commerce Clause.

2. Yes. A security is defined as money investment that expects a return solely because of another person's efforts. These land and service contracts were purchased by out-of-state residents who had no intention and no

ability to cultivate the crops. All that the buyers expected was a share of the profits based on the amount of acreage that they owned. Such an arrangement qualifies as an investment that expects a return solely because of another person's efforts.

3. No. Certain practices have been interpreted by the courts as constituting per se violations of the Sherman Antitrust Act. These practices will always be found to violate the act. An agreement between competitors at the same level of the market structure to allocate territories among themselves in order to minimize competition is one example of a per se violation.

4. Yes. Debts and liabilities do not, in general, flow from the selling corporation to the acquiring corporation in an asset acquisition.

5. No. Federal pollution laws regulate the discharge of pollution whether or not the pollution activity was intentional. The court pointed out that the law would be severely weakened if only intentional acts were interpreted as prohibited.

6. Yes. In this case the complaining shareholder was allowed absolutely no input into the operation of the business. In addition, he received no salary, dividends, or other money from the corporation. Under such circumstances, the appeals court had no trouble finding that the trial court had been correct in concluding that the rights of the complaining shareholder had been violated. The dissolution was, thus, necessary to protect those rights.

Part 8   Case Study   Page 756

1. The plaintiffs-appellants, that is Gries Sports Enterprises, Inc. and Robert Gries, had the burden of proof in this case.

2. According to the court in this case, a director or directors will be interested if he or she "appears on both sides of the transaction" or if he or she "has or expects to derive a personal financial benefit not equally received by the stockholders."

3. According to the court in this case, a director will be independent if his or her "decision is based on the corporate merits of the subject before the board rather than extraneous considerations or influences." Moreover, a director will lose that independence if he or she "is dominated by or beholden to another person through personal or other relationship."

4. The court says that a director will be considered informed if he or she "makes a reasonable effort to become familiar with the relevant and reasonably available facts prior to making a business judgment."

5. When the business judgment rule is not applied, as occurred in this case, the fairness rule is used to judge a decision made by directors that has been challenged by a shareholder.

6. No. The court did not believe that the purchase of Cleveland Stadium Corporation was fair to the Cleveland Browns or to minority shareholders. The court said "no arms length negotiations as to price, terms, the elements to be included (or not to be included), or any other aspect of the proposed acquisition ever took place between the Browns and CSC. The $6,000,000 price was arrived at by Messrs. AMA (Modell), Bailey and Poplar . . . prior to any disclosure to plaintiffs of the possibility of such an acquisition, and never changed despite plaintiff's objections and despite the valuations furnished the defendants by plaintiffs. The manner in which the subject transaction was initiated, structured, and disclosed to plaintiffs therefore did not satisfy the reasonable concept of fair dealing."

7. There is sufficient evidence of the existence of a tying agreement to allow the case to go to trial.

Part 9   Emerging Trends

Chapter 40   Professional Liability

Questions for Analysis   Page 766

1. The good news is that compliance with the Sarbanes-Oxley Act has not been as difficult as many experts predicted it would be. Also, most companies have already complied with the act or will do so soon. The bad news is that problems involving compliance will continue.

2. A *material weakness* is a very severe problem that means that the management of a company cannot affirm that their organization has effective internal controls. A *significant weakness* is a situation that might lead to a material deficiency.

3. In attempting to comply rapidly with Sarbanes-Oxley, some firms have taken ill-advised "short-cuts."

4. The author suggests that companies should take advantage of the expertise offered by their IT departments and use that expertise to "automate the testing and documentation processes." The hope is that such electronic procedures will allow companies to stay ahead of the process and figure out how to comply with the law.

5. It is likely that auditors will be lenient during the first round after Sarbanes-Oxley. However, this will change as time passes. Whether this trend is good, bad, or neutral is a judgment call. Accept all reasonable, well-thought-out answers.

Questions for Review and Discussion   Page 780

1. A certified public accountant is an accountant who has met certain age, experience, and testing requirements imposed by the state. Public accountants are accountants who work for a variety of clients but who are not certified by the state.

2. An audit is an examination of the financial records of an organization to determine whether those records represent an accurate and fair representation of the financial health of the organization. When auditors are satisfied that the financial records accurately reflect the company's financial status, they will issue an *unqualified opinion*. When auditors issue a *qualified opinion* they are saying that the books represent the company's financial health as of a given date. However, the auditors may qualify the opinion in one of two ways. They may issue an opinion that is *subject to* some factor. Or they may issue an opinion that says the books are accurate *except for* some minor deviations. An *adverse opinion* is rendered when the deviations from accepted principles are so serious that an unqualified opinion is impossible and a qualified opinion is just not justified. A *disclaimer* declares that the auditor cannot give any opinion at all on the company's financial records.

3. Generally accepted accounting principles are procedures that accountants must use in accumulating financial data and in preparing financial statements. Generally accepted auditing standards explain how an auditor can determine whether proper accounting procedures have been used.

4. Accountants owe their clients the duty of due care. This means that the accountant must perform the job with the same skill and competence that a reasonable accounting professional would use in the same situation. Accountants must also perform their duties with the best interests of their clients in mind.

5. The state will generally impose age, character, education, experience, and testing requirements on architects.

6. Architects owe a duty to exercise due care and skill in carrying out professional duties. The standard does not demand that the architect design perfect or faultless structures. Architects can make mistakes as long those mistakes do not result from a failure to use appropriate skill and good judgment according to accepted professional standards.

7. An attorney has the duty to represent clients with good faith, loyalty, and due care.

8. The health care professional must act with the same skill, care, and level of knowledge that a reasonable health care provider would display in a similar situation.

9. Under the locality rule, similar health care professionals are compared in relation to their level of skill, while under the national standard all health care professionals are expected to have the same level of skill.

10. Ostensible authority has been used by plaintiffs to hold a hospital liable for the torts of its independent contractor physicians. Ostensible authority is created when a hospital presents itself to the public as a provider of health care services and in some way leads the patient to believe that an independent contractor physician with staff privileges is an employee of the hospital.

Cases for Analysis   Page 781

1. Applying the actually named third parties test, the accounting firm would not be liable because under that test only parties that the accounting firm knows will see the report can sue the firm if they are financially damaged as a result of any misinformation in that report. This was the test that was actually applied in the case at the appellate level by Judge Benjamin Cardoza. Under both of the other two tests, the accounting firm would be liable to the loan company. The specifically foreseen test requires only that the accounting firm know that the plaintiff was in the class of persons who *might* see the report. In this case Touche knew that possible creditors would see the report and Ultramares would clearly be in that class. Under the reasonably foreseeable third parties test, the loan company was a reasonably foreseeable third party.

2. No. Alexander Grant violated its duty of loyalty to CDS by revealing confidential information. The court will refer to the AICPA Code of Professional Ethics to make its decision.

3. No. The SEC was incorrect. Arthur Young and Company was required to follow GAAS. Having done so, it met its standard of care. In addition, while auditors are required to look for fraud and illegal acts, they cannot be held liable for not detecting extremely complex and clever fraud. As long as the auditor exercised due diligence, that is, as long as the auditor is able to show some evidence of a search following accepted standards, he or she will be protected.

4. No. The accountants were incorrect. Third parties damaged by negligence or fraud of an accountant can bring suit against that accountant. Whether the third party will succeed in that suit will depend upon the facts and the law of the state. Protection from negligently prepared financial statements will always extend to actually named third parties. Most states also extend protection to limited classes of specifically foreseen third parties. A few states extend protection to reasonably foreseeable classes of third parties. Also, if fraud is alleged, as it is in this case, the accountant may be liable to anyone who can be reasonably foreseen as relying on that fraudulently prepared statement.

5. No. The measure of damages in a suit against architects for failing to fulfill the terms of a contract does not depend on a drop in the market value of the structure. The appropriate measure of damages, when the value of the structure has not been altered, is the amount of money spent to correct the error, known as the cost of repair rule. In this case the cost of repair was $112,532. The court should award this amount to Bainbridge.

6. The attorneys violated their duty of loyalty to Craybaugh. The mother was not a proper party in this lawsuit. Attorneys are generally not liable to third parties who are not their clients unless they acted with the malicious intent to harm that third party. No malicious intent was indicated in these facts.

7. Probably not. The court may use two standards that might hold the physician in this case liable. The court might judge performance by determining how the same procedure is performed at another hospital located in a similar locality. Under the similar locality rule, rural hospitals are compared to other rural hospitals, urban hospitals to urban hospitals, and suburban hospitals to suburban hospitals. However, courts today often use a national standard. Under the national standard, a nurse in metropolitan New York can be held to the same standard of care as one who practices in suburban St. Louis or rural Kansas. Courts who adhere to the national standard feel that mass communication and mass transportation have made it possible for health care providers to keep up-to-date with the latest trends regardless of where they practice.

Chapter 41   Substantive and Procedural Cyberlaw

Questions for Analysis   Page 790

1. The situations include one in which an employer used an employee's work records to run up bills, another in which a father used his son's social security number to obtain a credit card, another in which a son used his father's identification numbers, and one in which a man posted his ex-wife's social security number on the Web.

2. What is especially insidious about a family member or a friend being involved in identity theft is that the victim usually does not proceed with a case.

3. Identity theft can also be considered as fraud.

4. First, victims of identity theft should proceed with the case against the perpetrator. Otherwise, the victim can be seen as enabling the perpetrator. Also, victims should place passwords on all accounts to prevent future identity theft.

5. The Identity Theft Center is a clearinghouse that provides information on how a person can recover from an identity theft incident.

Questions for Analysis   Page 805

1. At the heart of the *Times v. Tasini* case is the question of whether *The New York Times* could post the work of freelance writers on its website.

2. The Supreme Court was concerned that certain "holes in history" might appear if a newspaper like *The New York Times* had to secure permission from all of its freelance writers before posting all stories on its website. The Court ruled that a newspaper could post all stories on its website, but would have to pay the freelance writer under a theory called *compulsory contract*.

3. The *Napster* case involved the publication of copyrighted musical pieces on the Internet without permission from the writers, artists, and record companies. Music-based lawsuits are more difficult than literary suits because in music-based suits the record companies have little interest in permitting the works they own to be posted on the Internet. The court in the *Napster* case ordered Napster to get permission before posting songs on the Internet.

4. The Supreme Court's concept of compulsory contract might help Napster, because Napster could argue that certain "holes in history" might appear if certain songs are not posted on the Web. This would mean that Napster might be able to enforce compulsory contracts with the artists who produced those songs.

5. Songwriters, music publishers, and the record companies benefit. The public also benefits.

Questions for Review and Discussion Page 809

1. The key terms involved in cyberlaw include the following: intellectual property, computer hardware, computer program, algorithm, computer software, computer package, computer firmware, source code, object code, screen display, and database. Intellectual property is intangible personal property that is sheltered from infringement by copyright protection, patent protection, trade secret protection, or trademark protection, Computer hardware is the actual device that includes the computer and its component parts such as the monitor, the hard drive, the printer, the scanner, the keyboard, the mouse, and so on. Computer programs involve the instructions that tell the hardware what to do and when to do it. An algorithm is a series of steps that, if followed properly, will reach a desired goal. A computer package involves computer hardware and software sold together. Computer firmware is software implanted into the computer hardware. A source code is a set of instructions that tells the computer what to do or how to perform a particular task. An object code is the program after it has been translated by the computer into a language only the computer can comprehend. The screen display is the audiovisual configuration that appears on the screen of the computer monitor. A database is the compilation of information in a form that can be understood and used by a computer.

2. Cybertrespass is defined as gaining access to a computer with the intent to commit a crime. In effect, in one swipe of the pen, this technique incorporates the entire criminal code of a jurisdiction into cyberlaw.

3. The cybercrimes that can be committed with a computer include the following: cyberextortion or cyberblackmail, cyberstalking, and cyberspoofing. The cybercrimes that can be committed against a computer include cyberterrorism, identity theft, cybervandalism, and cybergerm warfare.

4. A cybertort involves the invasion, distortion, theft, falsification, misuse, destruction, or financial exploitation of information stored in or related to an electronic device, including but not limited to laptops, desktop PCs, mobile phones, mainframes, fax machines, phonecams, personal digital assistants (PDAs), and home computers that stand alone or are part of a network.

5. Cyberdefamation is the communication of false and destructive information about an individual through the use of an electronic device including but not limited to laptops, desktop PCs, mobile phones, mainframes, fax machines, phonecams, personal digital assistants (PDAs), and home computers that stand alone or are part of a network; cyberinvasion of privacy is the unwelcome intrusion into private matters initiated or maintained by an electronic device.

6. The primary statutes that are involved in cybercontract law include the following: the Federal Electronic Signatures Act; the Uniform Electronic Transactions Act; and the Uniform Computer Information Transactions Act.

7. The cybercourt network is a computerized set of connections that will send elements of data to a central computerized depository which will create a master database so that attorneys, judges, paralegals, law clerks, law professors, law students, and others can access the Web to see how the criminal and civil cases of a single (or multiple) jurisdiction(s) is (are) related to one another throughout that single (or multiple) jurisdiction(s).

8. Cybermanagement software can improve the practice of law by combining the various record-keeping tasks of a law firm into a central computerized database that allows the attorneys and paralegals in that firm to coordinate their activities effectively, economically, and efficiently.

9. A trade secret is a plan, process, or device that is used in a business and known only to the employees of that business who need to know that secret to carry on their jobs. Trade secret status is available to firms that distribute their software on a limited, highly secretive basis.

10. In order for an invention to be patentable it must display three characteristics. These characteristics are usefulness, novelty, and nonobviousness.

Cases for Analysis Page 810

1. The appeals court should rule that no trade secrets were involved in this case. Semco clearly made no attempt to protect the alleged secrets from vendors and from the public in general. Employees were not required to sign secrecy agreements.

2. No. J&K Computer Systems, Inc., did its best to keep the accounts receivable program a secret. The company did so by telling Parrish, Chlarson, and all other J&K employees that the program was a secret. The program was labeled J&K's property and it was not actually sold to the customers. Instead, customers were allowed to use the program under strict licensing agreements. The accounts receivable program was not a software package sold on the open market, but a tightly controlled secret released only under strictly controlled conditions.

3. Yes. If a computer program is part of a large, more conventional process, the process itself will not be unpatentable simply because of the program. In this case, the program simply figured the exact curing time and ordered the opening of the mold. It was, therefore, part of the larger, more conventional process and was patentable. The court did not address the issue of whether the process met the novelty and nonobviousness test.

4. No. A patent cannot be rejected based solely on the position that the invention involves an algorithm. The Court of Appeals for the Federal Circuit concluded that, "Since (the statute) expressly includes processes as a category of inventions which may be patented and . . . further defines the word 'processes' as meaning 'process, art, or method, and includes a new use of a known process, machine, manufacture, composition of matter, or material,' it follows that it is no ground for holding a claim is directed to nonstatutory subject matter to say it includes or is directed to an algorithm. This is why the proscription against patenting has been limited to mathematical algorithms and abstract formulae which, like the laws of nature are not patentable subject matter." It is true that this invention includes an algorithm. However, that is not the end of the test. "Once a mathematical algorithm has been found, the claim *as a whole* must be further analyzed. If it appears that the mathematical algorithm is implemented in a specific manner to define structural relationships between the physical elements of the claim (in apparatus claims) or to re-define or limit claim step (in process claims), the claim being otherwise statutory, the claim passes muster under (the statute.)"

5. No. The Copyright Act does protect motion pictures and other audiovisual displays. The courts have extended this protection to include computer-generated audiovisual displays. Although the display does change with each player, certain elements (such as the spaceships, missile bases, fuel depots, and the terrain) remain fixed. This was enough to persuade the court that a computer-generated audiovisual display for a video game is protected as an original work fixed in a tangible medium.

Chapter 42   Alternative Dispute Resolution

Questions for Analysis   Page 818

1. Instead of being shorter than a conventional lawsuit, arbitration sometimes ends up taking more time.

2. If motion practice works properly it "defines and crystallizes the issues." Discovery is designed to "provide a window into the opposition's case and prevent surprises."

3. When motion practice and discovery are eliminated, an attorney, in the process of preparing a case, must be ready for every eventuality. This takes time and costs money.

4. No. Arbitration sometimes results in very, very high damage awards.

5. Parties who enter arbitration often give up some of the basic protections offered by the law in civil procedure.

Questions for Review and Discussion   Page 826

1. One major shortcoming of litigation is that it is expensive. Another major shortcoming is that it is time consuming.

2. ADR can provide an economical and efficient alternative to litigation. Depending on the ADR technique employed, the time involved in settling a dispute can be shortened considerably and the expenses lowered significantly.

3. Mediation is advantageous if the parties stay involved in the compromises that result from the process. The mediator can be of great help because he or she can serve as an intermediary who attempts to understand what created the dispute. The mediator may also be able to get at the center of a disagreement in ways that the parties themselves cannot.

4. Arbitration hearings can be set up by the parties themselves. The parties create the ground rules for choosing the arbitrators, for carrying out discovery, for presenting evidence, for determining the outcome, and for enforcing the reward, if any. The parties must also set details such as the time and the place of the hearing, filling vacancies on the arbitration panel, recording the proceedings, handling objections, granting extensions, and so on. Because of the details involved, many parties use professional arbitration organizations like the American Arbitration Association to set up their arbitration hearings.

5. In a med-arb procedure, the individuals first submit their disagreement to mediation. If mediation succeeds, the case is over. If, however, some issues are not resolved via mediation, the parties can go to arbitration. During arbitration, the undecided issues are placed before the arbitrators for a final decision.

6. An early neutral evaluator, after examining the details of a case, renders an objective assessment of the legal

rights of each party and a determination of the award (if any) that should be rendered.

7. During a summary jury trial, strict time limits are imposed upon the parties. Opening statements should last no more than twenty minutes. The presentation of each side's case should take no more than one hour for the case in chief and thirty minutes for the rebuttal. The closing arguments are limited to twenty minutes. A posttrial conference is also held during which the parties have a chance to discuss settling the case.

8. Private civil trials are usually held as scheduled. Private civil trials are not postponed nor are they interrupted because the court has other business to attend to. Private civil trials are also less expensive.

9. The private ADR techniques include, but are not limited to partnering and ADR contract clauses.

10. The governmental alternatives within ADR include settlement week, negotiated rule making, and the science court.

Cases for Analysis   Page 827

1. No. Most states that have been faced with this question have disagreed with these arguments as long as the arbitration requirement does not replace the jury trial and as long as the motives for establishing mandatory arbitration are reasonable.

2. Yes. The failure of the arbitrator to make findings of fact and findings of law as required by the ADR clause in the settlement of a dispute would be grounds for the court to revoke the arbitrator's ruling.

3. No. The appellate court should not overrule the trial court's decision rejecting the requirement that the parties arbitrate the trade secret dispute. This is because the language in the ADR contract clause was not specific enough to extend arbitration to the trade secret dispute.

4. This is the type of situation that would be appropriate for a reg-neg approach. Rules made in this area would certainly affect a wide range of individuals and institutions; they would be both complex and controversial; they would meet with resistance if those affected did not have a hand in shaping the rules, and they would involve details that might be outside the expertise of the agency. A science court could also handle this type of situation. This is because a panel of objective judges with scientific backgrounds would provide a neutral body capable of making unbiased, but well-informed decisions about such experiments.

5. Kerensky could ask that the dispute be submitted to an arbitration panel, one member of which is an expert in electronics. Kerensky could also ask that the dispute be submitted to mediation as long as the mediator is an expert in electronics.

Chapter 43   International Law

Questions for Analysis   Page 839

1. The Fourth Geneva Convention was used to justify the argument that certain Iraqi prisoners were not entitled to the full protection of the Geneva Conventions. While hostilities continue, the Fifth Article of the Fourth Convention, which is designed to protect civilian detainees, permits the military to withhold the full protection of the Geneva Conventions from those detainees who have been labeled as security risks.

2. At the time of the news story, the American administration's position was that all Iraqi prisoners were entitled to the full protection of the Geneva Conventions. This put the administration at odds with the position stated in the December letter.

3. While it is difficult to know for certain whether the interpretation of the Geneva Conventions as outlined by the military in the December letter follows the rules established by the U.S. Courts, a plausible argument can be made that the interpretation is not in line with the Courts' rules. For instance, the first and second interpretive rules say that the U.S. Courts will first look at the literal language of the Conventions and then at any Red Cross commentaries on the Conventions. The literal language of Article 5 of the Fourth Convention says that the rules of the conventions cannot be suspended unless required by "absolute military security." The situation in this case does not seem to involve "absolute military security." However, even if absolute military security were involved, according to the Red Cross such determinations must be made on a selective basis rather than as the result of a blanket policy dictating how to deal with an entire class of prisoners. Specifically, the Red Cross has said that "Article 5 can only be applied in individual cases of an exceptional nature." A situation in which it becomes an automatic policy to treat all Iraqi prisoners as security risks cannot be considered an individual, exceptional situation.

4. Whether the interpretation offered by the December letter is actually in line with the objectives of the Geneva Convention is unclear. Accept all reasonable answers here. However, the dangers associated with an acceptance of the military's interpretation are outlined by the Red Cross. The Red Cross's standing commentary says, "What is most feared is that widespread application of the Article may eventually lead to the existence of a category of civilian internees who do not receive the normal treatment laid down by the Conventions but are detained under conditions which are impossible to check. It must be emphasized most strongly, therefore, that Article 5 can only be applied in individual cases of an exceptional nature."

5. The authors of the Conventions included Article 5 to give military officials a way to deal with insurgents

who represent a "continuing threat to the occupying force." Whether it was a good idea to include Article 5 is open to interpretation. Accept all reasonable answers here.

Questions for Review and Discussion Page 849

1. Many countries in the international community do not share the same view of the law as the United States. Two areas of disagreement are the belief that the adversarial system is the best procedure for the courts to follow and the position that the Rule of Law is absolutely inviolable.

2. The criteria for a just war are as follow: (1) the war must be waged for a just cause, (2) the war must be fought with a just intention, (3) the war must be declared by competent authority, (4) there must be a reasonable chance that the war will be successful, (5) the good advanced by the war must exceed the negative consequences, and (6) the war must be waged as a last resort.

3. Only sovereign nations have standing to bring a case to the International Court of Justice. Included in this category are nations that are member states of the United Nations. Nations that are not member states, however, may also have cases heard before the court. Questions on the legal standing of nonmember states are left up to the determination of the General Assembly and the Security Council. Subject matter jurisdiction of the ICJ is outlined within the United Nations charter. This jurisdiction includes legal questions specifically referred to in the charter as well as any legal questions raised by a member nation. Such legal questions may involve the interpretation of treaties and international conventions. Unlike the federal courts of the United States, which can render opinions only in an actual case, the ICJ is permitted to issue advisory opinions when requested by the United Nations General Assembly, the Security Council, or other authorized agencies within the structure of the United Nations.

4. In order to deal with crimes against humanity, an official International Criminal Court (ICC) was established by the United Nations in 1998. The objective of the new court is to preside over trials involving genocide, war crimes, and other human rights violations.

5. UNICATRAL consists of thirty-six nations chosen to represent the primary social, economic, legal, and geographical areas of the globe. The goal of the commission is to cultivate the organization and integration of international law in relation to international trade. To this end, the commission coordinates the activities of institutions involved in international trade, encourages continued commitment to current treaties and conventions, and constructs new agreements for the community of international trade.

6. The differences between the UCC and the CISG are, first, the UCC applies to contracts between merchants and also to those that involve nonmerchants. The CISG involves only contracts between merchants. Second, the UCC involves not only sale of goods contracts, but also other commercial agreements, such as leases. The CISG is limited to sale of goods contracts. Third, the UCC has modified the traditional mirror image rule to overcome problems caused by the battle of the forms. The CISG still applies the mirror image rule to the acceptance of a contractual offer. Finally, the UCC has a provision that says that any contract for sale of goods valued at over $500 must be in writing to be enforceable. Then CISG has no such provision.

7. The World Trade Organization involves three levels: the Ministerial Conference, the General Council, and the Secretariat. The power to make key determinations under the authority of multinational trade agreements falls under the Ministerial Conference, which meets every two years. The responsibilities of the Ministerial Conference pass to the General Council whenever the Ministerial Conference is not in session. Finally, the Secretariat is responsible for the administration of the WTO. It is headed by a Director General.

8. The objectives of the Dispute Settlement Understanding are to implement a number of measures designed to improve the way trading quarrels are handled. For example, the DSU has set up a series of precise time limits for the stages in a trade conflict. The DSU ensures that a network of comprehensive guidelines is consistently followed in all such controversies. The DSU also allows effective retaliatory measures that can be implemented by one nation against another if the offending nation refuses to adhere to a decision rendered by the DSU.

9. The major purpose of NAFTA is to establish a trading market in North America free of the burdens imposed by internal tariff barriers. Thus, each country within the agreement can take advantage of this free market by importing those goods that it cannot produce itself in exchange for the tariff-free exportation of the goods that it can produce.

10. The European Union is a coalition of European nations. The EU was created to formulate a common European economic policy, and to introduce a common currency for most of Europe. The goal is to help transform Europe into a major player in the global marketplace.

Cases for Analysis Page 849

1. The trial system planned for Saddam Hussein does not resemble the American adversarial process as much as it resembles a continental system. The American adversarial system would begin with the presumption of the defendant's innocence and allow the two attorneys, acting as advocates for each side, to present the facts to the judge and jury. In contrast, in the continental system, the trial is based on a fact-finding approach. Thus, a system which permits (requires?) the judges to

fact-find before the trial begins is very much like a continental system.

2. At one point during questioning, Saddam Hussein is alleged to have said, at a time when he was not represented by an attorney, that he had decided to invade Kuwait to forestall a rebellion among his own troops. Such an admission would not be admissible as evidence in an American court during a criminal trial because it was made without legal representation. Such an admission would be permitted as evidence in a continental-style court.

3. Taking into account the spirit of the Geneva Conventions as well as the United States courts' intent to liberally construe the Geneva Conventions, the conclusions in this memo do not appear to be in line with those conventions.

4. Taking the definitions of armed conflict outlined within the Geneva Conventions together with the United States courts' intent to liberally construe the Geneva Conventions, the court should declare Noriega a POW.

5. No. Arkansas was incorrect. The federal district court does have extra territorial power to mediate this international trade dispute. The court said, "[C]ertain factors are relevant in determining whether the contracts and interests of the United States are sufficient to support the exercise of extra territorial jurisdiction. These include the citizenship of the defendant, the effect on United States commerce, and the existence of a conflict with foreign law." In this case, Arkansas, the defendant, is a U.S. corporation. Second, there was no conflict with foreign law because Arkansas had no registration privileges within Saudi Arabia. Finally, the court found an impact upon American commerce despite the fact that none of the products were actually a part of the American marketplace. In this regard, the court said, "Each of Riceland's [Arkansas'] activities from the processing and packaging of the rice to the transportation and distribution of it, are activities within commerce. And by unlawfully selling its products under the infringing marks in Saudi Arabia, Riceland diverted sales from ARI [American Rice, Inc.], whose rice products are also processed, packaged, transported, and distributed in commerce regulated by Congress. Merely because the consummation of the unlawful activity occurred on foreign soil is of no assistance to the defendant."

6. Yes, the American court did have jurisdiction over an exclusively American contract affected by the 1973 oil embargo. The court also agreed that Gulf had breached its contract with Eastern Airlines. The court said, "With regard to the contention that the contract has become 'commercially impracticable,' . . . because of the increase in the market price of foreign crude oil and certain domestic crude oils, the court finds that the tendered defense has not been proved." Moreover, the court believed that Gulf Oil could have foreseen the coming energy crisis and should have made allowances for the precipitation of that crisis in any contracts that it entered. The court said, "[E]ven if Gulf had established great hardship, . . . which it has not, Gulf would not prevail because the events associated with the so-called energy crisis were reasonably foreseeable at the time the contract was executed."

7. No. Armstrong is not correct. The Lanham Act is a United States statute which seeks to protect trademark owners from infringement and counterfeit copying in foreign market places. The court decided that Armstrong's activities violated the Lanham Act because his actions affected United States commerce even though the computers were sold only in Bolivia. This resulted because the component parts were purchased within the United States, because Armstrong was an American citizen, and because many of the counterfeit computers eventually found their way into the United States marketplace.

8. No. The WTO cannot directly sanction Japan. Instead, it can permit France to impose tariffs on certain specified items imported from Japan to France. This form of sanction is known as retaliation.

9. Godel's purchase of the silverware would be protected by the Directive on the Protection of Consumers in Respect of Distance Contracts (ECD) and she would be permitted to cancel the transaction without penalty within seven business days. However, when she attempts to return unsealed software, she will find that she has not been granted this cancellation privilege. This is because it is very easy to make unauthorized copies of items such as software.

Part 9   Case Study   Page 852

1. In this case, the Court was attempting to balance the rights of the freelance writers of certain newspaper and magazine articles with the rights of the publishers of those articles. The Court took the case to determine whether duplicating the authors' articles in the databases was protected under section 201[3] of the Copyright Act.

2. In the provisions of Section 201[3] of the Copyright Act, Congress attempted to balance a publisher's right to republish a revised version of a published work that includes articles written by freelance writers with the rights of the authors who wrote the articles in the first place.

3. The Court rejected the publishers' microform analogy because in microfilm or microfiche the articles appear in the context in which they were originally published. On the databases this is not the case.

4. The publishers predicted that the ruling would "punch gaping holes in the electronic record of history" because the publishers would be unable to seek permission for all the articles written by freelance writers.

5.   To escape the predictions of the publishers, the Court suggested that the writers and the publishers add a clause to their original contract, passing the right to publish individual articles in databases to the publisher. The Court further suggested, using an analogy with eminent domain that the writers could be compelled to enter to such an arrangement for the public good. This ruling could affect the results of the Napster case because it could permit the publishers of songs to have the writers and artists enter agreements transferring to those publishers the right to have the music transferred to a database. This would allow Napster and Napster clones to purchase the rights from a central party at a reasonable rate.

Business Law

With UCC Applications

ELEVENTH EDITION

Gordon W. Brown

PROFESSOR EMERITUS

NORTH SHORE COMMUNITY COLLEGE

DANVERS, MASSACHUSETTS

Paul A. Sukys

PROFESSOR OF LAW AND LEGAL STUDIES

NORTH CENTRAL STATE COLLEGE

MANSFIELD, OHIO

McGraw-Hill Irwin

Boston   Burr Ridge, IL   Dubuque, IA   Madison, WI   New York   San Francisco   St. Louis
Bangkok   Bogotá   Caracas   Kuala Lumpur   Lisbon   London   Madrid   Mexico City
Milan   Montreal   New Delhi   Santiago   Seoul   Singapore   Sydney   Taipei   Toronto

McGraw-Hill
Irwin

BUSINESS LAW WITH UCC APPLICATIONS
Published by McGraw-Hill/Irwin, a business unit of The McGraw-Hill Companies, Inc., 1221 Avenue of the Americas, New York, NY, 10020. Copyright © 2006, 2001, 1997, 1993, 1989, 1983, 1978, 1972, 1966, 1961, 1953 by The McGraw-Hill Companies, Inc. All rights reserved. No part of this publication may be reproduced or distributed in any form or by any means, or stored in a database or retrieval system, without the prior written consent of The McGraw-Hill Companies, Inc., including, but not limited to, in any network or other electronic storage or transmission, or broadcast for distance learning.

Some ancillaries, including electronic and print components, may not be available to customers outside the United States.

This book is printed on acid-free paper.

1 2 3 4 5 6 7 8 9 0 DOW/DOW 0 9 8 7 6 5

ISBN 0-07-296057-4 (student edition)

ISBN 0-07-296059-0 (instructor's edition)

Editorial director: *John E. Biernat*
Publisher: *Andy Winston*
Senior sponsoring editor: *Kelly H. Lowery*
Developmental editor: *Natalie J. Ruffatto*
Senior marketing manager: *Lisa Nicks*
Producer, Media technology: *Mark Molsky*
Project manager: *Jim Labeots*
Senior production supervisor: *Sesha Bolisetty*
Lead designer: *Pam Verros*
Photo research coordinator: *Lori Kramer*
Photo researcher: *Kelly Mountain*
Media project manager: *Lynn M. Bluhm*
Supplement producer: *Gina F. DiMartino*
Developer, Media technology: *Brian Nacik*
Cover design: *Kiera Pohl*
Interior design: *Kiera Pohl*
Typeface: *10/12 Times Roman*
Compositor: *GTS–York, PA Campus*
Printer: *R. R. Donnelley*

Library of Congress Cataloging-in-Publication Data

Brown, Gordon W., 1928-
    Business law : with UCC applications / Gordon W. Brown, Paul A. Sukys.
      p. cm.
    Includes index.
    ISBN 0-07-296057-4 (alk. paper)
    1. Commercial law—United States. I. Sukys, Paul. II. Title.
  KF889.3.B76 2006
  346.7307—dc22   2004061118

Contents in Brief

Contents

Part Three
Sales and Consumer Protection   279

Part Four
Property   365

Part Five
Negotiable Instruments 469

Part Six
Insurance, Secured Transactions, and Bankruptcy 539

Part Seven
Agency and Employment 599

Part Eight
Business Organization and Regulation 679

Part Nine
Emerging Trends and Issues 759

Preface

The eleventh edition of *Business Law with UCC Applications* reflects the many changes that have taken place in the law over the past four years. As in previous editions, we've taken care to present business law concepts in the most coherent and accessible way, and to provide up-to-date coverage of business law topics that are essential to today's students.

All of the chapters for this edition have been updated, and we have continued to enhance our coverage of the important topics of e-commerce, limited liability companies (LLC), ethics, and Alternative Dispute Resolution.

The popular format of the tenth edition has been enhanced with a new and accessible design. Each chapter begins with an outline followed by The Opening Case and Chapter Outcomes. Major headings and chapter summaries continue to be numbered following the chapter outline. The popular case illustrations, presenting either hypothetical or actual situations based on well-founded court decisions, have been retained and updated. Our QuickQuiz feature appears in each chapter and allows students to test their knowledge of the chapter topics while they are actively studying the text. We also retained case studies pertaining to each of the nine parts of the book, which summarize an actual litigated case, present a lengthy extract from the judge's decision, and provide follow-up questions that are pertinent to the cases and which are appropriate as a review of the legal concepts involved. Activities at the end of each chapter, including Key Terms, Questions for Review and Discussion, Investigating the Internet, and Cases for Analysis, help students self-check their understanding of the terms and concepts presented in the chapter.

The U.S. Constitution is given in Appendix A. Included in Appendix B are four articles of the Uniform Commercial Code. Marginal references within the student chapters tie these specific documents to the content.

We are happy to introduce a new feature called Business Law in the News, which takes excerpts from current news stories from a variety of sources and ties them directly to chapter material. Discussion questions for each article are also included.

The eleventh edition of *Business Law with UCC Applications* offers a comprehensive package of materials to meet both instructor and student needs.

A Guided Tour

Business Law with UCC Applications, 11/e, is full of useful chapter features to make studying productive and hassle-free. The following pages show the kind of engaging, helpful pedagogical features which complement the accessible, easy-to-understand approach to teaching business law.

Chapter Outline

Each chapter features an outline that allows students to recognize the organization of the chapter at a glance. For reinforcement, the outline's numbering system is used throughout the body of the chapter and is repeated in the end-of-chapter Summary.

Chapter 2 — Sources of the Law

2-1 The Purpose and Operation of the Law
Complex Adaptive Systems • The Law as a Complex Adaptive System • Complex Adaptation and Cyberlaw

2-2 Constitutional Law
The Articles of Confederation • The Principles of the United States Constitution • The Structure of the United States Constitution • The Question of Democracy • State Constitutions

The Opening Case
"The 9-11 Commission"

Shortly after the horrific attacks by Al Qaeda on Center and the Pentagon on September 11, 200 requesting the appointment of an independent b events leading to that fateful day. The independe determine not only whether the tragedy could ha but also how to deter similar attacks in the future. Bush responded by stating that no investigative formed by the government. He added that no pu be conducted and that none of his staff member

Complex Adaptive Systems

The law acts as a constantly changing complex adaptive system. A **complex adaptive system** is a network of interacting conditions which reinforce one another while, at the same time, adjusting to changes from agents both outside and inside the system. The entire

The Opening Case Revisited
"The 9-11 Commission"

When the 9-11 Commission issued its findings in the summer of 2004, many government officials found that they could no longer conduct business as usual. Their professional and personal lives were disrupted by the commission's recommendations for reform in the executive branch, especially as those proposals affected the intelligence-gathering agencies of the government. The recommendations had the potential to cause disorder within those agencies, thus leading to a period of instability within the government. Nevertheless, any other ruling would have been unfair to the people of the United States who depend on these agencies for their safety and security and for the overall stability of the entire nation. This situation reveals the balancing act that the law and the government must engage in on a daily basis. In this case, the orderly lives of certain gove officials had to be disrupted in order to be fair to the rest of the people and i to restore stability to the social structure. The actions of the commission als

The Opening Case

A brief case opens each chapter and introduces the chapter concepts. Every Opening Case is re-examined throughout the chapter in The Opening Case Revisited.

Both our government and our legal system are designed to respo to the will of the people. Our government is also a system of che and balances. This is why the President could not ignore the vot the Senate but instead had to go forward and appoint the 9-11 Commission. As you read this chapter, revisit these issues in an attempt to see how the system works.

Chapter Outcomes

Succinct, crisply written objectives follow The Opening Case at the beginning of each chapter. The objectives describe what the students can expect to learn as a result of completing the chapter.

Chapter Outcomes

1. Enumerate the objectives of the law.
2. Clarify the operation of the law as a complex adaptive system.
3. Outline the content of the U.S. Constitution.
4. Explain the role of statutory law in the legal system.

New to the eleventh edition!

Business Law in the News uses articles from *BusinessWeek* and other news sources and ties today's headlines with business law concepts. Each article is enhanced with Questions for Discussion.

Business Law in the News

Disconnected: Lawyers and the Public Learn to Live Without Cellphones in the Courthouse

Most federal courthouses prohibit two items: weapons and cellphones.

Electronic devices are like a plague that has descended upon courts, and, like the most virulent germs, they survive by morphing into ever more sophisticated forms.

Pagers became cellphones and then picture phones. Laptops were trumped by PDAs (personal digital assistants, such as a BlackBerry). Both often have recording capabilities. And now stun guns come disguised as cellphones—but it is safe to assume that these fall into the weapons category and are banned.

When it comes to nonweapon electronic devices, lawyers and their clients had better check the local rules.

work to do, but they understand the ram breaking the rules." Taking a picture o sound is an ethical violation, Dodge said.

A now-retired traffic court judge County is reputed to have jailed three r phone offenders for contempt—one over

Besides protecting witnesses and pris marshals have added cellphone vigilan mission of protecting federal courts.

Billy Walker, judicial court security off Middle District of Florida, a deputy U.S said rules are consistent in four of the dis tions in Fort Myers, Orlando, Ocala and J No cellphones.

In Tampa, though, there's an experime that allows lawyers to check cellphones i

---

About the Law

In federal court, if even one defendant is a citizen of the same state as one of the plaintiffs, diversity cannot be established. In such a case, the law says that "diversity is not complete."

rated in Delaware and headquartered building in the Somerset, Ohio, school b took two years and cost the school ol officials discovered that three of the tually contained more asbestos than chool system $770,000 to have those ther company. The Somerset School l district court in Cleveland for dam- diversity, subject matter jurisdiction nsacted business in Ohio meant that an liction over that out-of-state corpora-

About the Law boxes provide additional clarification of chapter concepts.

Did You Know? boxes are interesting factoids directly linked to the chapter concept being discussed.

Did You Know?

Roman law was first codified into The Law of the Twelve Tables in 450 B.C. The Twelve Tables declared that all free citizens had certain fundamental rights.

Background Information The separation of

	Identifies the presiden Gives the president po
Article III	Establishes the Supre federal courts Provides for trial by ju Defines treason agains
Article IV	Defines interstate rela Sets up the full faith a public acts and proc Provides for extraditio
Article V	Outlines the method o
Article VI	Establishes the Const supreme law of the
Article VII	Provides for the origin

A Question of Ethics boxes challenge the student's understanding of previously discussed chapter examples by asking questions specifically relating to ethical dilemmas.

must always be present. If the actions of the tortfeasor are not the actual cause of the accident, they cannot be the proximate cause.

A Question of Ethics

In Example 5-10, when the Transglobal mechanics failed to prepare the landing gear properly, they could not foresee that the fire truck would have a blowout, smash into a light pole that would hit Carbonari's car, and damage both the car and the DVD player in the trunk. Therefore, legally, their conduct was not the proximate cause of the damage to the car and the DVD player. However, would Transglobal owe an ethical duty to reimburse Carbonari for the damages that were inflicted on his car and his DVD player? Explain.

Actual Harm The injured party in a lawsuit for negligence must show that actual harm was suffered. In most cases, the harm suffered is a physical injury and is, therefore, visible. Harm suffered due to fright or humiliation is difficult to demonstrate. Courts often deny damages in actions for negligence unless they can see an actual physical injury. Actual harm can also come in the form of property damage.

Examples are numbered throughout each chapter and use short vignettes to explain how concepts can be applied in real-life situations.

Example 4-4

The question of competency to stand trial was a key factor in a case in which Harold Gunther was prosecuted for the murder of one person and the attempted murder of two others. Listening at the door of an apartment, Gunther believed he heard three co-workers plotting against him. Convinced that he was about to be attacked, Gunther entered the apartment and assaulted his three co-workers, killing one and severely injuring the other two. Gunther consistently maintained that he was the intended target of a plot to destroy him. No evidence was ever presented that such a plot existed. In contrast, expert testimony indicated that Gunther was paranoid and delusional. Consequently, his defense attorney moved for a competency hearing. Despite the expert testimony, the judge in the case found Gunther competent to stand trial. The competency ruling was based on the fact that, despite Gunther's mental problems, he was capable of understanding the charges against him and was able to assist in his defense. Under state law, these were the only qualifications needed for a competency finding by the court. Gunther met these qualifications and was found competent to ~~trial.~~

and movies, is that motive is an element of criminal liability. Such is not the case. Establishing motive may help the prosecution persuade the jury that the accused is guilty, but proving an evil motive is not necessary for a criminal conviction.

Quick Quiz 4-2 True or False?

1. The two elements needed to create criminal liability are a criminal act and the requisite state of mind.

2. Individuals act with negligence when they act with the intention to cause the result that does in fact occur.

3. Motive is an element of criminal liability.

QuickQuiz boxes follow each numbered section and give students the chance to test themselves with three true/false questions. Answers are provided at the end of each chapter.

4-3 Specific Crimes

Statutory definitions and classifications of crimes vary from jurisdiction to jurisdiction.

service of process, 55
special jurisdiction, 47
specific performance, 61

summary judgment, 57
surrebuttal, 60

writ of certiorari, 50
writ of execution, 61

Questions for Review and Discussion

1. What is the difference between original jurisdiction and appellate jurisdiction? Between general jurisdiction and special jurisdiction?
2. Explain the basic structure of the federal court system. Over what two types of cases do the federal trial courts have jurisdiction?
3. Under what circumstances might the U.S. Supreme Court grant a writ of certiorari?
4. What is the extent of cyberspace jurisdiction?
5. What is the structure of a typical state court system?
6. What are the steps in the litigation p ning with the commencement of the through the execution of judgment?
7. What is the difference between a de set of interrogatories?
8. What is the nature of cyberspace dis
9. What is involved in an appeal?
10. What are the steps in a criminal pro ning with the arrest up through the s the defendant?

Questions for Review and Discussion provide a means for students and the instructor to re-examine and discuss the key points of law. All objectives listed at the beginning of each chapter are also reviewed.

Summary

4-1 A crime is an offense against the public at large. As such, a crime threatens the peace, safety, and well-being of the entire community. For this reason, crimes are punishable by the official governing body of a nation or state. A felony is a crime punishable by death or imprisonment in a federal or a state prison for a term exceeding one year. Some feloni~~es~~ by fine. A misdemeanor is a les~~ser~~ generally punishable by a prison~~ment~~ than one year.

robbery, and arson are the most common c property committed in the United States. N nature, business crimes are those carried ness or individual in the course of doing b tain a business-related advantage.

4-2 The two elements necess~~ary~~ liability are (a) an act and (b) mind. Generally speaking, a cri~~me~~ ted unless the criminal act na~~med~~ performed with the requisite stat~~e~~ criminal codes include four po~~ssible~~

Summary Numbered to match the outline at the beginning of the chapter and the main heads within each chapter, the Summary provides an encapsulated review of the chapter's content.

Key Terms

American Law Institute (ALI) test, 83
arson, 76
assault, 75
battered spouse syndrome, 86
battery, 75
bribery, 76
burglary, 76
crime, 69
defense of others, 85

embezzlement, 76
entrapment, 83
extortion, 76
felony, 71
forgery, 77
homicide, 74
irresistible impulse test, 83
kidnapping, 75
knowledge, 72

Key Terms Each key term is printed in boldface and defined when introduced in the text. A list of key terms and the page number of first usage appears at the end of each chapter. A glossary of the key terms is provided at the back of the text.

Cases for Analysis

When the trial of Martha Stewart began, her attorney and the attorney for codefendant, Peter Bacanovic, asked that *voir dire* be conducted in private. The court granted the request, so only the judge, the defendants, their attorneys, and the prosecutors were present. Reporters were supplied with transcripts of the *voir dire* proceedings, which were available on the day following the examination of the jurors. However, the identities of the jurors along with any individual items concerning those jurors were erased from the transcripts. In response, seventeen news companies asked the appellate court to reverse the order. The news agencies argued that the ruling made little sense since the court had excluded the press from a case that had a great deal of pu at its core. They also argued that closi was an additional step down a slipper they envisioned as eventually resulting plete closure of American courts to th other side argued that there was a com to close the *voir dire* process to make the prospective jurors would be open about questions concerning high-profi Martha Stewart. Should the appeals co the closing of *voir dire* in this case? E answer. *In re Application of ABC Inc.* (2d U.S. Cir. Ct. of App.). See also Yo "The Closed Voir Dire for Martha Ste *National Law Journal,* January 26, 20

Cases for Analysis have been updated extensively for the eleventh edition and were chosen for their relevance, case-of-understanding and interesting fact patterns. Many are abridgements of actual court decisions; others are hypothetical situations written to emphasize legal issues and concepts presented in the text.

urisdiction and special jurisdiction?
Explain the basic structure of the federal court sys-
em. Over what two types of cases do the federal
rial trial courts have jurisdiction?
Under what circumstances might the U.S.
Supreme Court grant a writ of certiorari?
4. What is the extent of cyberspace jurisdiction?
5. What is the structure of a typical state court system?

through the execution of judgmen
7. What is the difference between a
set of interrogatories?
8. What is the nature of cyberspace
9. What is involved in an appeal?
10. What are the steps in a criminal p
ning with the arrest up through th
the defendant?

Investigating the Internet

activities encourage students to seek additional information on the Internet.

Investigating the Internet

The Administrative Office of the United States Courts maintains a website
cludes the latest press releases from the federal courts. Access one of th
press releases and write a report on the issues contained therein. You mig
write a report on an article appearing in the *The Third Branch*, the monthl
produced by the federal courts and appearing on this website.

Part 1 Case Study

Planned Parenthood of Pennsylvania v. Casey
United States Supreme Court 112 S.Ct. 2791

The **Case Study** at the end of each of the nine parts begins with a summary of the facts of the case, followed by an excerpt from the court's opinion, and concludes with a series of questions.

Summary

The Pennsylvania state legislature passed a statute that limited a woman's right to have an abortion. Specifically, the statute included three provisions that made it more difficult for a woman to obtain an abortion than it had been prior to the enactment of the statute. The first provision required a woman to give her "informed consent" to the procedure. Informed consent was to be obtained by providing the woman with detailed information concerning abortion and then re-quiring her to undergo a twenty-four-hour waiting period before the abortion could be performed. A second provision demanded the informed consent of at least one parent of a juvenile seeking an abortion. The third provision compelled a married woman to notify her spouse of her plan to seek an abortion. The statute also allowed these provisions to be circumvented should a "medical emergency"

Two appendices provide critical material for the students: **The Constitution of the United States (Appendix A)** and Articles 1, 2, 2a, and 3 of the **Uniform Commercial Code (Appendix B).** Marginal references throughout the text refer students to the page of the appendix where the original source of the law being discussed can be found.

Appendix A

The Constitution o United States

Preamble

We the People of the United Stat
more perfect Union, establish Ju
Tranquility, provide for the commo
general Welfare, and secure the
ourselves and our Posterity, do or
Constitution for the United States

Article I

Section 1. All legislative Powers
vested in a Congress of the Unit
consist of a Senate and House of R
Section 2. **[1]** The House of
be composed of Members chosen
the People of the several States, an
State shall have the Qualifications requisite for Electors of
the most numerous Branch of the State Legislature.
[2] No Person shall be a Representative who shall not have
attained to the Age of twenty-five Years, and been seven
Years a Citizen of the United States, and who shall not.

Appendix B

Uniform Commercial Code (Articles 1, 2, 2a, and 3)

Article 1: General Provisions

Part 1: Short Title, Construction, Application
and Subject Matter of the Act

§1-101. Short Title. This act shall be known and may be
cited as Uniform Commercial Code.

**§1-102. Purposes; Rules of Construction; Variation
by Agreement.**
(1) This Act shall be liberally construed and applied to
promote its underlying purposes and policies.
(2) Underlying purposes and policies of this Act are
(a) to simplify, clarify and modernize the law
governing commercial transactions;
(b) to permit the continued expansion of commercial
practices through custom, usage and agreement
of the parties;
(c) to make uniform the law among the various

mistake, l
cause shal

§1-104. C
Act being
subject ma
repealed b
reasonabl

§1-105. T
(1) Excep
transa
and al
agree
other
duties
transa
state.
(2) Wher
specif
and a
tent p
laws r
Righ

equally divided.
[5] The Senate shall
President pro tempo
dent, or when he sha
the United States.

Supplements

Student Study Guide (ISBN: 0-07-296058-2)

Each chapter in the Study Guide begins with an outline to be completed by the student. Corresponding with the outline at the beginning of each text chapter, this learning activity reinforces the subject matter being studied. When completed, it also serves as a study aid to the student. The outline is followed by true/false questions covering important legal concepts. Next, a section entitled "Language of the Law" gives students practice in matching key legal terms with their definitions. Finally, ten hypothetical cases give students an opportunity to apply the law to cases. Answers to the objective questions and hypothetical cases are found in the back of the Study Guide.

Instructor's Edition (ISBN: 0-07-296059-0)

This instructional tool features teaching tips, answers to end-of-chapter questions, analyses of chapter cases, and solutions to case studies. In addition, annotations on text pages provide background information, related cases, state variations of specific laws, vocabulary terms, methods of getting students involved, interesting quotes, and suggested further readings.

For the eleventh edition, five segments from the "You Be the Judge DVD" are included with the Instructor's edition.
This exclusive DVD features interactive case videos that showcase courtroom arguments of business law cases. This interactive DVD gives students the opportunity to watch profile interviews of the plaintiff and defendant, read background information, hear each case, review the evidence, make their decision, and then access an actual, unscripted judge's decision and reasoning.

For your students, you may order the full eighteen-segment DVD packaged with the student text at a discount.
For more information on how to package this, please contact your sales representative.

Instructor's Manual (ISBN: 0-07-296060-4)
Printed Instructor's Test Bank (ISBN: 0-07-296061-2)
Instructor's Resource CD-ROM (0-07-296065-5)

Instructors are now able to choose between printed supplements or CD-ROMs. The Instructor material includes Lesson Plans, Lecture Notes and Outlines, Sample Syllabi, Test Bank (CD-ROM test bank written in ExamViewPro), and Conducting a Mock Trial. PowerPoint slides are also available on the Instructor's Resource CD-ROM.

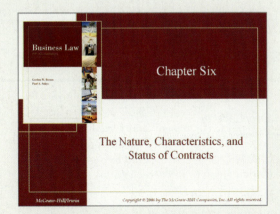

Online Learning Center (OLC)

www.mhhe.com/brown11e

More and more students are studying online. That's why we offer an Online Learning Center that follows *Business Law with UCC Applications* chapter-by-chapter. It doesn't require any building or maintenance on your part—it's ready to go the moment you or your students type in the URL.

A secured Instructor Resource Center stores your essential course materials to save you prep time before class. The Instructor's Manual, Lesson Plans, Lecture Notes and Outlines, PowerPoint slides, and sample syllabi are only a couple of clicks away. You can even access the "Conducting a Mock Trial" feature with ease!

Acknowledgments

We are grateful to the following individuals for their review feedback. We appreciate their ideas and suggestions.

Brother Norman Bradshaw
Alvin Community College

Ruthann Bergman
Pine Manor College

Woody Colbert
University of Advancing Computer Technology

Kimber Cramer
Davenport University

Ben Dunn
York Technical College

Alfred E. Fabian
Ivy Tech State College

Robert Huyck
The Utica School of Commerce

Varina Haney
Aiken Technical College

Linda Wilke Heil
Central Community College

Amy Hickman
Collins College

Richard Hudanick
Sanford Brown Business College

Jeffrey Kleeger
Florida Metro University–Orlando

Jennifer Labosky
Davidson County Community College

Jerry Lafferty
National Business College

Charity Lanier
Florida Metro University–Lakeland

Monica Lapkoff
Randolf Community College

M. Alan Lawson
Mount San Antonio College

Catherine McKee
Mount San Antonio College

Jane McNiven
Ivy Tech State College

Stephen Pan
Las Vegas College

Kathy Panther
Tri-County Community College

Susan Petit
Allentown Business School

Kathleen Saxton
Bryan & Stratton Bookstore

Margaret Stafford
Valley College

Vashti O. Varnado
Kendall College

Jack Verani
New Hampshire Community Technical College

We also extend special thanks to Jane A. Brown for her assistance in writing The Study Guide for the edition and to Sally Nelson, CPA of Nelson and Nelson, CPAs in Mt. Vernon, Ohio, for her assistance with the liability of accountants section in Chapter 40, Professional Liability.

Special thanks is also extended to the Business Law classes for Fall Quarter 2003 and Winter Quarter 2004 at North Central State College for pilot testing the Mock Hearing Process found in the ancillary materials for *Business Law with UCC Applications, 11e.*

About the Authors

Gordon W. Brown,

Professor Emeritus, North Shore Community College, Danvers, Massachusetts, is the author of *Legal Terminology* and *Administration of Wills, Trusts, and Estates,* and is co-author of *Understanding Business and Personal Law.* Mr. Brown received his law degree from Suffolk University. He is a member of the Massachusetts and federal Bars.

Paul A. Sukys
is a professor of law and legal studies at North Central State College in Mansfield, Ohio. He is co-author of *Understanding Business and Personal Law* and *Civil Litigation,* a textbook for paralegals. He is also the author of *Lifting the Scientific Veil: Science Appreciation for the Nonscientist,* which explores the relationships among science and other disciplines, focusing on the interaction of science and the law. He is currently pursuing his doctorate at The Union Institute and University of Cincinnati. Mr. Sukys received his law degree from Cleveland State University. He is a member of the Ohio Bar.

Dedication

This book is dedicated with much love and many thanks to our lovely wives,
Jane A. Brown and Susan E. Sukys.

Ethics, Law, and the Judicial System

Part One

Chapter 1   Ethics

The Opening Case
Enron and Social Responsibility

As often happens in such situations, the episode that came to be known as The Enron Case, captured the public's attention only after the Securities and Exchange Commission (SEC), an arm of the federal government, had announced that it was about to investigate a series of allegedly illegal transactions that had been carried out by officers at Enron, an energy management corporation that dealt primarily in natural gas. As a result of this investigation, Enron officials were compelled to make two shocking announcements. First, they reported that the corporation had evidently lost over 1 billion dollars in a relatively short period of time. Second, they announced that the corporate books had apparently been manipulated for at least four consecutive years, resulting in a picture that inflated Enron's net worth by almost 600 million dollars. After these two revelations, the value of Enron stock began to collapse from a high point of over 90 dollars per share to a record low of 26 cents per share. At that point, the house of cards that had been Enron toppled. Mass layoffs ensued; and a buyout engineered by Dynegy, Inc., collapsed. Adding insult to injury, the accounting firm of Arthur Andersen, which had acted as auditors for Enron, was indicted for allegedly shredding records that might have shown the accountants' complicity in the financial disintegration of Enron. As you read this chapter on ethics and social responsibility, ask yourself whether the Enron case is a strange aberration or an example of a corporation that simply got caught doing what thousands of other businesses do as a matter of course on a daily basis.

Chapter Outcomes

1. Define law and morality.
2. Distinguish between values and ethics.
3. Explain ethical relativism.
4. Describe the social contract theory.
5. Outline the steps in applying utilitarianism.
6. Apply the principles of rational ethics.
7. Identify the ethical character traits reflected in role model ethics.
8. Outline the arguments supporting social responsibility.
9. Explore the need for law in our society.
10. Clarify how the law and ethics are usually in harmony with one another.

1-1 Defining the Law, Morality, and Ethics

Ideally, everyone ought to know what the law is and why the law is an important aspect of our lives. Similarly, in a perfect world, everyone would know what the term "ethics" means and how it is different from the idea of morality. Of course, a brief look at any daily newspaper or a quick glance at the evening news will reveal that people hold widely diverse views on the difference between right and wrong. If this were not the case, if everyone thought exactly the same about right and wrong, there would have been no Enron scandal, no dispute over the Pledge of Allegiance, no allegations of wrongdoing against anyone, and no war with Iraq. Yet, in each of these cases, and others like them, many people's various opinions clash not only on how to handle each situation, but also on the issue of whether the actions themselves were right or wrong in the first place.

It is, therefore, no surprise that most legal textbooks and many treatises on ethics begin by defining these disciplines. This is in marked contrast to most other studies. Few physics textbooks pause to tell the reader what physics is. Fewer history books devote space to explaining the term history, and almost no math texts begin by defining math. However, that is as it should be. These disciplines and others like them, are fixed in our minds as implacable fields of study. In history, for example, the fact that John Kennedy was assassinated on November 22, 1963, is not open to debate. Nor is our understanding that such an event is historical fact. The same is true of the second law of thermodynamics in physics and the multiplication tables in mathematics. None of these facts can be open to debate, except in the most esoteric way. (See: Murphy, Jeffrie G., and Jules L. Coleman. *The Philosophy of Law.* Boulder, CO: Westview Press, 1990, p. 6; See also: Calhoun, John C. "A Disquisition on Government." In *Philosophy in America,* Eds. Paul Russell Anderson and Max Harold Fisch. New York: Appleton-Century-Crofts, Inc., 1939, pp. 356–357.)

The Law and Morality

Such is not the case with the law and morality. People *will* argue about whether the law is a form of civil management or a way to dictate individual behavior, whether it ought to be created by a national government or a regional state system, and whether it ought to change regularly or stay the same indefinitely. They will even argue about whether the rules made by the government demand absolute, unquestioned obedience or simply ask for occasional recognition as optional guiding principles. People will also argue about moral issues. They will argue about whether schools should censor textbooks, whether abortion should be permitted, and whether waging a preemptive war is morally correct. This is why we pause at the beginning of *Business Law with UCC Applications* to define the law and morality, and to distinguish between ethics and morals, concepts that many of us usually do not think about on a daily basis.

The **law** consists of rules of conduct established by the government of a society to maintain harmony, stability, and justice. It does this by defining the legal rights and duties of the people. The law also provides a way to protect the people by enforcing these rights and duties through the courts, the executive branch, and the legislature. The law is, therefore, a means of civil management. Certainly, the law usually cannot stop a person from doing wrong. However, the law can punish an individual who chooses to do that wrong, whatever it might be. The law, then, draws the line between conduct that is permissible and that which is not allowed, so people, at the very least, know that they can be punished if they choose to disobey the law.

In contrast, **morals** are values that govern a society's attitude toward right and wrong and toward good and evil. As a result, we ought to see morality as more fundamental than law. Therefore, morality ought to serve as a guide for those bodies within our society, such

An eminent lawyer cannot be a dishonest man. Tell me a man is dishonest, and I will answer he is no lawyer. He cannot be, because he is careless and reckless of justice; the law is not in his heart, is not the standard and rule of his conduct.

—Daniel Webster
 (1782–1852), American
 statesman

State Variations Most states have Good Samaritan laws that grant immunity from civil liability to people who provide emergency care to injured persons. There is no legal duty for a person to stop and give aid, but is there a moral duty?

Teaching Tips The use of fetal tissue for medical treatment is at the center of a fiery debate. Discuss the topic in class. Then ask the students to analyze it from a viewpoint of subjective ethics.

as the courts, the executive branch, the legislature, and the administrative agencies, which make, interpret, and enforce the law. Most of the time, these law-making, law-interpreting, and law-enforcing bodies will follow the belief that morality and legality ought to match up with one another. Indeed, there are even those philosophers of law who argue that morality is a necessary element of the law. They would say that you cannot have a philosophically valid law that is not grounded in morality.

Natural Law Theory

According to one system of legal thought, morality and the law are united in a common bond based on their intrinsic nature. This system of thought, which is generally known as **natural law theory,** sees an unbreakable link joining morality to the law in a fundamental way. This link exists because a law must, in its most basic form, be moral. Otherwise, it is not lawful. A law with an immoral purpose is not a law at all. Instead it is an anomaly that does not fit into our concept of either law or the legal process. It is of course, one thing to say that laws must be firmly grounded in morality and quite another to argue that legality and morality are always the same thing. There are, in fact, some laws that have no moral content whatsoever. Thus, a statute that requires a driver to have an operator's license, has no intrinsic moral substance. On the other hand, such a law is not immoral on its face either. The natural law theorist would say that a law must, at the very least, be morally neutral to have any integrity as a law. In a larger sense, it can also be argued that a law which decrees that people must be licensed to drive, while not intrinsically moral, contributes to the orderly and stable functioning of society, and is, therefore, moral because of its purpose and effect.

See Murphy, Jeffrie G., and Jules L. Coleman. *The Philosophy of Law.* Boulder, CO: Westview Press, 1990, pp. 11–12.

Value and Ethics

So far we have defined law as a set of rules created by the government to establish a means of civil management that directs people to do what is right and avoid what is wrong. The purpose served by the law includes the creation of order, stability, and justice. The assumption is that if these purposes are met, right will be served and wrong defeated. Moreover, we have also defined morals as those fundamental values that tell us the difference between right and wrong in the first place. What we have not explained, however, is where those values come from. This, then, is the job of ethics. Ethics is the attempt to develop a means of determining what these values ought to be and for formulating and applying rules that enforce those values.

Enron's CFO Andrew Fastow and his wife both faced prison time that would keep them from raising their children.

Ethical Decision Making

Ethical decisions are made in a variety of ways. Some people will say that they do not think about ethics, but instead act on instinct when faced with a moral dilemma. Others will say

that they try to act rationally and eventually do what they "believe" is right. Still others will say that they follow the rules that they learned in school, in their place of worship, or in their family setting. Some professions, businesses, and organizations attempt to solve ethical problems by developing long and complex guidelines, usually called rules of conduct or canons of professional responsibility. Such rules are often divided along certain levels of behavior. Some behaviors are encouraged; others are discouraged. Often disciplinary sanctions for rule violations are included as a part of these guidelines.

While such rules are admirable, they are often so complex that they are difficult to understand and even more difficult to follow. For example, under Ethical Consideration 7-4 of the Code of Professional Responsibility for attorneys, a lawyer is required to "urge

The Opening Case Revisited, Part I
A Lawyer's Ethical Responsibility

For a practical example of how these complicated guidelines sometimes contradict themselves, at least on the surface, let's return to the scenario in The Opening Case. One of the officers involved in the Enron Case was the chief financial officer (CFO) of the corporation. The CFO's wife was also involved in the case and was eventually indicted. The CFO and his wife wanted to avoid simultaneous prison terms because they had two young school age children at home. Accordingly, attorneys entered plea bargaining negotiations on their behalf. At one point, a plea bargaining deal had been negotiated that would permit the CFO's wife to receive a reduced sentence. The judge in the case, however, rejected the deal. At that point, the attorneys representing the CFO's wife were at the crossroads between Ethical Consideration 7-4, which encourages attorneys to urge any permissible construction of the law favorable to their client, and Disciplinary Rule 7-101(A) (1), which says that attorneys cannot fail to seek the lawful objectives of the client. The question facing the attorneys was whether they should continue to pursue plea bargaining negotiations even though the judge had expressed his displeasure with the previous version of the deal. Certainly, if they went forward with the negotiations, they risked further rejection by the judge. Such a rejection would certainly not meet the goals of the client. However, if they did not negotiate, they could have been accused of not pursuing a construction of the law that was most favorable to their client. Fortunately, for their client, the attorneys in this case saw no conflict and went forward with the plea bargaining negotiations. As a result, the CFO's wife was permitted to enter a guilty plea to a misdemeanor. Consequently, her attorneys had succeeded in guiding her through the complicated negotiation process. Not all attorneys can navigate their way through the Code of Professional Responsibility with successful results like this, however. Consequently, it is often simpler and more effective to have only a few guidelines that, when applied consistently, yield ethical results. To uncover these guidelines, we will examine five ethical theories: ethical relativism, social contract ethics, utilitarianism, rational ethics, and role model ethics. (See Johns, Carrie. "Lea Fastow Reaches New Plea Deal With Enron Prosecutors." *The Washington Post,* April 30, 2004, p. E-3; "Former Enron Assistant Treasurer Lea Fastow Sentenced to 12 months in Jail." Department of Justice News Release, May 6, 2004.)

any permissible construction of the law favorable to his client, without regard to his professional opinion as to the likelihood that the construction will ultimately prevail." However, the lawyer is also forbidden by Disciplinary Rule 7-101(A)(1) to "(f)ail to seek the lawful objectives of his client through reasonably available means." What happens then, when a lawyer follows EC 7-4 and offers a risky interpretation of the law that fails and results in a client's conviction? Has the lawyer followed EC 7-4, which urges the attorney to take risks, or has that lawyer violated DC 7-101, which mandates that attorneys must seek whatever goals the client has decided are important? Such contradictions, real or imagined, can cause confusion and will inevitably lead to unpredictable, uncertain, unreliable, and, sometimes, unjust results. (See *Code of Professional Responsibility: The Canons, The Ethical Considerations, The Disciplinary Rules.* Columbus: Ohio Bar Liability Insurance Co., 2003, pp. 65, 74.)

1-2 Ethical Theories

Throughout the history of philosophy many scholars have offered techniques for determining those values that ought to guide all ethical decisions. While these theories differ in their particulars, they all have one thing in common. Each theory is based on the assumption that people want to live ethical lives. If this were not the case, there would be no need to fashion these theories in the first place. Nevertheless, despite this common assumption, the theories differ greatly in their individual approaches to the problem of determining the nature of the values which underline ethical decision making.

Ethical Relativism

See Glater, Jonathan D. "In Recent Cases, It's the Cover-Up, Not the Crime." *The New York Times,* May 4, 2004, p. C-1.

Ethical relativism says that there are no objective or absolute standards of right and wrong. Rather, the standards used to distinguish between right and wrong change from circumstance to circumstance and from person to person. Thus, ethical rules are relative; that is, the rules vary depending upon the actor, the circumstances, and countless other factors that may affect a person's ethical judgments. Because relativism emphasizes the highly individualized nature of ethical decision making, it is also called subjective ethics.

Ethical relativism is a very common position among Americans because the United States is a country of immigrants from a wide variety of cultures, many of which have different ethical values. Because many Americans want to respect these different cultures and their value systems, they often conclude that each culture is right within its own world, even when the values of that culture clash with another. Moreover, the United States was founded on a tradition that allows and even encourages a free exchange of ideas, feelings, and opinions on all subjects, including ethics.

Martha Stewart, once famous for turning homemaking into an artform, was found guilty of obstruction of justice.

Shortcomings of Ethical Relativism When Martha Stewart explained to federal regulators why she sold her shares in ImClone, she may have seen nothing wrong in her explanation. In fact, she appears to have truly believed that she was justified in selling the shares when she did. Apparently, her attorneys agreed with her because they felt quite secure in defending her position in this matter. Apparently, the prosecutors and ultimately the jury disagreed. However, if Stewart, her attorneys, the prosecutors, and the jurors all believed in ethical relativism, they would all have to agree that both points of view would be equally correct from an ethical, if not a legal standpoint.

In reality, many of the people involved in the Martha Stewart case disagreed with one another. If they hadn't, there would have been no need for the prosecutors to pursue their action against Stewart. We also know that all those involved in the case were convinced of the ethical correctness of their positions. Yet, if they were ethical relativists, they would all have to admit that the others were equally correct in the stance that they took. Herein lies the chief stumbling block associated with ethical relativism. If ethical values change from person to person and from circumstance to circumstance, then no one can ever do, say, or think anything wrong. Moreover, no one can ever disagree with anyone just because the other person holds a different view on the morality of the action. In fact, if we pursue ethical relativism to its logical end, all ethical standards evaporate and any concept of right and wrong along with them.

Thus, after the verdict in the Martha Stewart case, Stewart and her attorney would have to say, "Well, it looks like the prosecutors and the jurors are ethically correct, even though we disagree with them." Of course, if the jurors really were dedicated ethical relativists, they would never have rendered a guilty verdict in the first place. They would have concluded, as loyal ethical relativists, that Martha Stewart had done nothing wrong because circumstances would have justified anything she told to the federal regulators. In fact, they would not even be able to judge her testimony because the concept of truth itself would have disappeared. This would also mean that the federal prosecutors could no longer pursue any case that involves lies, perjury, or dishonesty. Such concepts become meaningless in a world in which truth is relative. When stated in such straightforward terms the illogic of ethical relativism becomes painfully obvious.

Situational Ethics Still, certain aspects of relativism are appealing, including the notion that the ethical decisions of other individuals ought not to be judged without taking into consideration the special situation in which those individuals find themselves. This is why some people favor a variation of relativism which takes different situations into consideration, but does not necessarily use those different situations to completely exonerate the actor. This theory, which is known as **situational ethics,** argues that each of us can judge a person's ethical decisions only by initially placing ourselves in the other person's situation. This technique allows us to be aware of the various factors that led to the other person's situation. Such an approach encourages people to look at others with tolerance and patience, an outlook that all of us would like to see practiced by those who might be inclined to judge our ethical decisions. On the other hand, it would be more satisfying if we agreed on a single ethical standard for making such moral judgments. Consequently, we must look elsewhere for a more consistent set of ethical values.

Social Contract Theory

Social contract theory holds that right and wrong are measured by the obligations imposed on each individual by an implied agreement among all individuals within a particular social system. At the most fundamental level, social contract theory says that, for people to live together harmoniously, they must give up certain freedoms in order to receive certain protections in return. Thus, all individuals give up the freedom to do as they please and in return receive a guarantee that other individuals will curb their behavior, thus protecting everyone else in that society from random and indiscriminate actions. The existence of the implied social contract permits us to live together in peace and harmony. Naturally, for the social contract to work, most people must adhere to its implied precepts and those who do not must be punished. If this were not the case, then the social contract would disintegrate and the society would return to a "state of nature" in which each person must fend for himself or herself. As is true of ethical relativism, there are problems within social contract theory. One chief problem is that social contract theory is descriptive rather than prescriptive. A **descriptive theory** simply describes the values at work within a social system, rather than explaining how the values originated in the first place. In contrast, a **prescriptive theory** explains how to come up with the values that permit a society to run smoothly.

Of course, not everyone believes that social contract theory is prescriptive only. Some ethical theorists argue that social contract ethics is a prescriptive theory because it places a

The Opening Case Revisited, Part II
Enron and Social Contract Theory

If we apply a social contract analysis to the Enron example, we can see that the social rule which says that people should be truthful to one another was involved in the case. Such a rule limits our freedom to say whatever we want to one another, but it ensures that we can believe other people when they tell us something is true. Rules like this make the simplest personal exchanges possible. They also allow us to engage in commerce, politics, and diplomacy.

value on the obligation itself. Thus, the benefits that a person receives by knowing other people will not lie to him or to her gives rise to the obligation not to lie to anyone else. Social contract ethics, therefore, concentrates on each individual's obligation to everyone else and on the belief that, as long as these obligations are met, social stability will be preserved.

Utilitarianism

Instead of focusing on circumstances and situations, as ethical relativism does, **utilitarianism** focuses on the consequences of an action. Thus, the morality of an action is determined by its ultimate effects. The more good that results, the more ethical the action. Conversely, the more bad that results, the less ethical the action. Unlike ethical relativism, which is constantly shifting, utilitarianism seeks only one stable goal, the greatest good for the greatest number. Determining the greatest good for the greatest number, however, is not as simple as it sounds. For one thing we must resist the temptation to transform the greatest good for the greatest number principle into the "greatest good for me" principle. One way to avoid mistakes that can result from an improper application of utilitarianism is to follow these steps:

1. The action to be evaluated should be stated in nonemotional, fairly general terms. For example, "stealing another person's property" is emotional language; "confiscating property for one's own use" is somewhat less emotional.

2. Every person or class of people that will be affected by the action must be identified.

3. Good and bad consequences in the relation to those people affected must be considered.

4. All alternatives to the action stated in step 1 must be considered.

5. Once step 4 has been carried out, a conclusion must be reached. Whichever alternative creates the greatest good for the greatest number of people affected by the action is the one that ought to be taken.

Example 1-1

For a practical example of utilitarianism, consider the following case. Mannheim Electronics had developed a new sensor that, when installed in an automobile, would reduce the possibility of a collision with other vehicles. Mannheim attempted to convince the president of Mirkov Motors to have sensors installed in all of its vehicles. Mannheim argued that, although the cost of each vehicle would rise somewhat, and although the dividends paid to Mirkov's shareholders might decrease at least temporarily, many injuries could be prevented and many lives could be saved by the use of the sensors. The president of Mirkov argued that his duty was to the shareholders not the consumer. The president went on to say that he would prefer to spend corporate funds on other projects that would increase profits rather than on one that would reduce them. Is the position adopted by the Mirkov president ethical? A utilitarian approach to answering this question would follow these steps:

1. *Action stated in nonemotional, general language.* The action examined in the case can be stated in the following nonemotional, general language: "Delay the installation of a new safety device in an expensive, but popular consumer item, in order to save money and to secure dividends for the corporation's shareholders."

2. *Participants identified.* In this case, the participants include the president of Mirkov Motors; Mirkov employees, shareholders, suppliers, and customers; their families and friends; Mannheim employees, shareholders, suppliers, and customers; their families and friends; the potential victims; their families and friends; the actual victims; their families and friends; and society at large.

3. *Good and bad consequences for the participants.* If the sensors are not installed in Mirkov vehicles, production costs would remain at a steady, affordable level. As a result, Mirkov Motors would continue to make a profit, the president would keep his job, the shareholders would receive short-term dividends, and assembly line workers would remain employed. In contrast, the failure to install the sensors would have negative results. For instance, if enough sensor orders are not received, Mannheim shareholders might lose dividends and Mannheim employees might be laid off. In addition, accident victims in crashes involving Mirkov vehicles could be severely injured and might, as a result, bring suit against Mirkov. Such lawsuits could result in hefty damage awards that might wipe out long-term dividends for shareholders. Such suits might also result in massive recalls that could cost Mirkov a lot of money that could, in turn, result in a drastic reduction in profits. In a really severe case, the solvency of Mirkov might even be threatened.

4. *Alternatives examined.* One alternative would have been to take no action at all. The net effect of that decision, however, is the same as actively refusing to add the sensors. Another alternative would be for Mirkov to add the sensors to all vehicles. Another option would be to install sensors in some vehicles but not in others. A final choice might be to delay the final decision and, in the interim, weigh the cost of settling all lawsuits against the cost of installing the sensors. The objective of such a study would be to determine whether it is more cost-effective to install the sensors or settle a variety of lawsuits as the need arises.

5. *Conclusion.* What should be obvious from this extended example is that the difficult task of handling Mirkov's ethical dilemma can be dealt with in a direct and logical way by applying utilitarianism. Mirkov's refusal to install sensors could result in disastrous consequences over the long run. This is especially true if a huge lawsuit is filed that results in heavy damages or that leads to a recall of all Mirkov cars without the sensors. However, even if the cost of installing the sensors was much higher than the cost of avoiding the issue or paying off lawsuits on a case-by-case basis, the ethical thing to do is to install the sensors. The point of utilitarianism is *not* to focus narrowly on the good of one participant but, instead, to look at the greatest good for the greatest number of people affected by the action. In this case, the good produced for thousands of people who might be saved by the installation of the safety glass far outweighs the good counted in profits and dividends for Mirkov.

Despite the systematic approach of the utilitarian theory, many people are uncomfortable with it. One questionable aspect of utilitarianism is that, in business at least, it can be confused with utility thinking. **Utility thinking,** which is also referred to as **cost-benefit thinking,** looks only at corporate benefits and problems rather than the benefits and problems that will result for others outside the boardroom. Thus, in the Mannheim case, a study to determine whether it is more cost-effective to install the sensor or settle a variety of lawsuits as the need arises, might very well conclude that settling lawsuits on a case-by-case basis is more cost-effective for the corporation. Clearly, while such a result violates the basic tenets of utilitarianism, it would be a comfortable decision for those who run the corporation. Because of the questionable nature of utilitarianism, it would be wise to look at one more ethical theory. That is why we now turn our attention to rational ethics.

Rational Ethics

In contrast to relativism, social contract theory, and utilitarianism, **rational ethics** rejects the notion that ethical rules can change in any way. Rational ethics replaces the shifting standards of relativism, the prescriptive approach of social contract theory, and the results-oriented standards of utilitarianism with a system that is objective, logical, and relatively consistent. According to rational ethics, actions are either right or wrong regardless of the circumstances and regardless of the consequences. Rational ethics establishes objective rules of behavior that transcend personal preferences, cultural differences, and end results. For this reason rational ethics is often referred to as objective ethics. Rational ethics begins with the premise that only human beings are morally responsible for their actions. Animals, plants, and inanimate objects may cause injury or harm, but they are never held morally responsible because they are incapable of making rational decisions. The only thing that separates moral beings from those that are amoral is the rationality of the moral beings.

The Golden Rule and Rational Ethics As rational beings, people think for themselves and, in doing so, recognize their own self-worth as individuals. Along with self-worth comes a belief in certain inherent rights. These rights include the right to life, the right to be free from injury, the right to be treated fairly, the right to independent self determination, and so on. Rational beings recognize that they do not want to be killed or cheated. They do not want their freedom taken away without just cause and due process. Because they believe in their own inherent rights, they also recognize that all people share these same rights. Thus, each individual has a duty to refrain from violating the rights of all other human beings.

The Logical Premise of Rational Ethics As rational beings, people also realize that it is logical to establish rules that support the continued existence of society. A rule that destroys a society which tries to follow it would be an illogical rule. Consider the following rule: "False promises are morally correct as long as they are made to gain some advantage." A person who adheres to rational ethics would instantly recognize that such a rule is both illogical and immoral. If everyone in a society were to adopt such a rule, no one could make a promise, and no one would accept a promise, even if it were made. A society without promises would be a world without commerce, credit, diplomacy, or lasting personal relationships. Such a society would be illogical, and, therefore immoral.

Example 1-2

Let's return momentarily to the Mannheim case. Recall that Mannheim attempted to convince the president of Mirkov Motors to have a new sensor installed in all Mirkov vehicles. The Mannheim Corporation argued that, although the price of each vehicle might climb a bit, and although the dividends paid to shareholders would fall over the short term, many lives could be saved by the installation of the sensors. Under rational ethics is the plan to avoid installing sensors ethical? The Golden Rule of rational ethics states "Act so that you treat others as you believe you would want to be treated. Be sure to respect others as ends in themselves, not as a means to an end." In this situation that question becomes: "Would the managers of Mirkov want to be treated as they plan to treat those people who will ride in unsafe Mirkov vehicles?" Most people would quickly answer "no" to this question. Therefore, the refusal to install sensors in all Mirkov vehicles violates the Golden Rule and is unethical. The second question is: "Would a society which follows this rule survive?" If some people who have the power to make other people safe are rewarded for avoiding that responsibility, soon everyone with that same responsibility would also avoid it. Eventually, the concept of taking responsibility for one's actions would mean nothing, and the social structure would collapse. As a result, the plan to manufacture unsafe vehicles would be illogical and, therefore, unethical.

Role Model Ethics

A final theory for making moral judgments is known as the **role model theory.** This theory encourages people to pattern their behavior after admirable individuals whose activities provide examples of the proper way to act. One advantage of the role model theory is that it provides concrete examples of how to behave rather than an abstract system for determining principles of behavior. A downside to the role model theory is that it is still necessary to derive consistent characteristics from these role models. Sometimes this need to examine individual lives and to extract character traits from those lives can be difficult, contradictory, and controversial. Nevertheless, in most cases, the following ethical character traits can be distilled from these role models: honesty, fairness, compassion, and integrity. Table 1-1 provides an overview of these character traits.

Honesty The character trait of **honesty** means that a person is always open and truthful in his or her dealings with other people. Being honest is not always the easiest action to take in every situation. Yet, most of us, if given the choice, would prefer to deal with an honest person rather than a dishonest one. To characterize someone as an honest person is the highest of compliments. After all, it's no accident that Abraham Lincoln was nicknamed "Honest Abe." Also encompassed by honesty is the requirement that people be faithful to their word. Thus, an honest person is not only one who tells the truth but also one who can be trusted to do what he or she has promised to do. Possessing an honest character and being truthful, however, are not always the same thing. A person can be truthful without being honest.

"Augustine shares with the ancient philosophers the conception of ethics as an inquiry into the supreme good: that which we seek for its own sake, never for the sake of some further end, and which makes us happy. He also shares the conviction that all human beings by nature want to be happy, agreeing that happiness is a condition of objective well-being, not merely the pleasure a person might gain from satisfying whatever desires she happens to have, however deluded or self-destructive."

—Bonnie Kent, The Moral Life, In *The Cambridge Companion to Medieval Philosophy.*

"Spinoza and Hobbes agree in making the selfish desire for self-preservation the foundation of justice and duty. Without a strongly self-interested motive, they reasoned, human beings would have little incentive to obey the rules of social morality, much less restrain their desires to do whatever is in their power."

—Steven B. Smith, *Spinoza's Book of Life: Freedom and Redemption in the Ethics.*

Table 1-1 Ethical Characteristics	
Trait	**Definition**
Honesty	Honesty allows a person to be open and truthful with other people.
Fairness	Fairness allows a person to treat other people with justice and equality.
Compassion	Compassion allows a person to care for others.
Integrity	Integrity allows a person to do what is right regardless of personal consequences.

Example 1-3

Velma Hite has a copy of an important deed locked in her safe deposit box at the First National Bank of Gotham City. When Fred Henry asks her if she has the deed she tells him that she does not. Strictly speaking, she is being truthful because the deed is not in her immediate possession. Yet, since the deed is in her safe deposit box and, therefore, under her control and since she could produce it for Henry if she wished, she is not being honest with him.

Fair play is a jewel.

—Abraham Lincoln (1809–1865), American president

Fairness   The second ethical character trait is **fairness.** A fair person is one who treats people with justice and equality. A person who is fair minded can also be trusted to deal evenhandedly not only with friends and family, but also with his or her enemies. Since everyone wants to be treated fairly it stands to reason that they would admire a person who has the ability to exercise fairness. That is one reason why Martin Luther King, Jr., is admired by millions of people. His campaign against segregation was, in its most basic form, a demand for the fair treatment of everyone, not just minorities.

Example 1-4

Being fair generally requires determining how everyone can be treated in the same way. Edgar Collins was appointed to a committee which was supposed to determine who would be eligible to receive the Annual Faculty of the Year Award at South Central State College. Several of the committee members wanted to exclude those instructors who had not yet been awarded tenure. These committee members argued that nontenured faculty members should be excluded because their own departments had not yet determined whether they were fit to remain on the faculty at SC State. Collins argued that it would not be fair to exclude nontenured faculty because the requirements for tenure were different from those used to determine the winner of the faculty member of the year award. By making this argument, Collins is attempting to treat all faculty members equally and fairly.

Compassion   The third ethical character trait is compassion. **Compassion** means that people should always act with the intent of doing good. Another way of saying this is to note that people should always attempt to be kind to one another. Moreover, the trait of compassion means that people should respect other individuals and their right to make their own decisions regarding what is best for them. Individuals who have compassion would also try to preserve individual freedom and liberty. The ability to be understanding of other people's shortcomings and to be forgiving when they make mistakes would also be characteristics of the compassionate individual. Albert Schweitzer and Mother Teresa are often held up as models of compassion. This is because they both dedicated their lives to helping those in need.

Example 1-5

Acting with compassion often requires seeing things from another person's point of view. Harriet Farmer, the director of the Research and Development Department at Lewis, Inc., has had a lot of trouble with Yale Zimmerman, one of her lab assistants, who has had an impeccable work record for years. Zimmerman is consistently late for work, often leaves early, and frequently takes long, unwarranted breaks. Farmer clearly has grounds for firing Zimmerman. Instead, she takes the time to discuss the situation with him. As a result, she discovers that Zimmerman's sister is very ill and that Zimmerman is the only one who can care for her. To help Zimmerman, Farmer arranges some flex-time scheduling to allow Zimmerman the time that she needs to care for her sister. By exercising compassion, Farmer has helped another person, and has saved a valuable employee for the company.

Integrity The final ethical character trait is integrity. A person with **integrity** has the courage to do what is right regardless of personal consequences. People with integrity may be compelled to stand up for their convictions against the majority of the people. They may find themselves at great personal risk and may often suffer great personal loss. A person with integrity is often said to be a person with a high sense of his or her duty to do what is right and to avoid doing what is wrong. At the very least this would mean the duty not to violate the rights of all other people regardless of the circumstances or the consequences. Gandhi had been a relatively well-to-do attorney, when, because of his personal integrity and his deep sense of duty, he took up the cause of freedom and fought for the people of India. His unwavering dedication to the principle of nonviolent protest demonstrates his integrity.

Further Reading For more information about Mohandas Gandhi, **see** *Gandhi: Prisoner of Hope* by Judith M. Brown (Yale 1989) and *The Life of Mahatma Gandhi* by Louis Fischer (Easton Press 1988).

Example 1-6

In order to act with integrity a person must often place himself or herself in an unpopular position. Marena Burroughs was a student at Ashville University, a predominately conservative institution located in north central Indiana. When Burroughs applied for permission to hold an open forum to discuss opposition to the American occupation of Iraq she was turned down. Later, Burroughs discovered that she had been turned down for a work study position in the political science department at the university, had been expelled from her sorority, and had been eliminated from consideration for a presidential scholarship. Despite these difficulties, which she believed were directly related to her political stand, Burroughs continued to oppose the American occupation and even held her own open forum off campus. Burroughs' refusal to change her position in reaction to pressure from her school showed integrity.

Quick Quiz 1-2 True or False?

1. Utilitarianism focuses on the consequences of an action.
2. Rational ethics is a form of ethical relativism.
3. A fair person is one who treats people with justice and equality.

1-3 Social Responsibility in the Business Sector

So far our study of ethics has focused on individuals. This is natural since ultimately all ethical decisions, even those that drive governmental regulations and corporate policies, are made by individuals. On the other hand, the decisions made by individuals affect the policies and procedures carried out by institutions that have the power to affect many parts of our social structure. Aside from the government, which has an enormous amount of power, and which we will examine later, corporations carry a great deal of influence over the economy, the community, and the people. There are those who say that a corporation has no social responsibility beyond making a profit for its shareholders. This is, in fact, the traditional view of corporate responsibility. It is a view that has remained so ingrained in our system that, until recently, it was the only view built into statutory and common law. Recently, however, voices have been raised arguing that corporations have a high degree of social responsibility to those people affected by their decisions.

The Traditional Corporate Culture

Although all businesses affect the economy and the community, the greatest force in the American industrial state is the corporation, in general, and, in particular, the multinational corporation. The reality of corporate power is revealed by the fact that philosophers on both ends of the political spectrum can point to the corporation as a guiding force in modern civilization. For instance, in his treatise, *Individualism Old and New,* the pragmatic American philosopher, John Dewey, notes, "The United States has steadily moved from an earlier pioneer individualism to a condition of corporate dominance." Similarly, the theoretical philosopher, Herbert Marcuse, once remarked that no one, not even the former enemies of capitalism, can escape the influence of corporate power. In fact, Marcuse goes so far as to say that in the modern global marketplace "the socialist and communist systems are linked with capitalism." (See Dewey, John. *Individualism: Old and New*. New York: Capricorn Books, 1962; and Marcuse, Herbert. *Five Lectures: Psychoanalysis, Politics, and Utopia*. Trans. Jeremy J. Shapiro and Shierry M. Weber. Boston: Beacon Press, 1970.)

One reason that corporations have such power is that they are legal persons, created under the authority of federal and state statutes. This status as a "legal person" gives the corporation certain rights and abilities that other business entities do not always have. For instance, as legal persons they are accorded certain constitutional rights, such as the right not to be deprived of property without due process of law. They can also own property in their own name and can have lawsuits filed to protect them or to vindicate their rights. There are, of course, many types of corporations. Our focus will be on those corporations that are privately run to make a profit for their owners, who are referred to as shareholders. The traditional view says that privately owned corporations are created solely to make a profit for their shareholders. Consequently, the foremost job of any manager is to maximize those profits. In fact, under the traditional rule of shareholder dominance, the managers of a corporation could be held liable in a court of law for making decisions that did not guarantee that the shareholders would receive a maximum return on their investment.

Example 1-7

When Lynn Cummings discovered that the managers of a corporation in which she owned stock had made a decision that had caused shareholders to lose money in a merger plan, she sued, seeking a reversal of the merger or a suitable payment from the managers that would make up for her losses. Basically, Cummings second-guessed the way that the managers had made their decision, arguing that they had not done a proper job of researching the merger and had not placed the shareholders' profits first. The managers argued that they had made their decision based on the long-term benefits of the merger to everyone involved, including the local community and the economy of the nation and state. The court sided with Cummings, noting that the job of the managers was to look out for the shareholders' profits, not the long-term benefits to the community or the economy.

As we've already seen earlier in this chapter, the type of thinking promoted by the court in Example 1-7 is referred to as utility thinking or cost-benefit thinking. Using utility thinking, a corporate manager simply looks at the action he or she is about to take and asks whether the benefit to the shareholders will outweigh the cost to the corporation. If the shareholders' benefits offset corporate costs, then the action is taken. If not, the action is abandoned. Proponents of this position justify cost-benefit thinking in three ways. First, the profits to the shareholders must always come first. Second, it would be unfair to divert funds which belong to the shareholders to activities that do not directly benefit the shareholders. Third, a corporation's managers are accountable to the shareholders and to no one else. The problem with this approach is that it often results in actions that are clearly unethical.

Example 1-8

The managers of Stutzman-Hillier Pharmaceuticals, Inc., have received some disturbing reports that the corporation's latest weight loss drug, biomiocin, has had some unpredicted side effects which have caused problems for several people. The managers of Stutzman-Hillier order the accounting department to determine how much it would cost to recall all the biomiocin now on the market, to suspend manufacturing, and to conduct more tests on the drug's safety. The accountants report that it would be more cost-effective to simply leave the drug on the market and pay off anyone who is injured and brings a lawsuit against S-H Pharmaceuticals. Keeping the drug on the shelves will allow the corporation to continue to pay dividends to the shareholders. In contrast, if the drug were taken off of the market, the payment of dividends would be suspended pending the outcome of the new testing program. Consequently, the corporate managers decide to suppress the report on the side effects and to leave biomiocin on the shelves. This decision not only violates virtually every ethical standard that we've studied thus far, but also evades the corporation's social responsibility to consumers, to the government, to the shareholders, and to the public at large.

Reasons for Social Responsibility

The fact that corporate officers and directors have made such decisions should not be surprising. Nor should it be surprising that, until recently, the law supported such decisions. The idea that a corporation is a legal person did not spring full grown into the law when the first corporations were formed. In fact, it took jurists quite some time to see that corporations were neither partnerships nor miniature democratic states, but were, instead, vehicles for making a profit. Once jurists recognized the unique position that corporations hold within the hierarchy of business associations, however, they easily granted certain privileges to corporate entities. Despite this, as the jurists entered the modern age, they began to see that there are a number of reasons that corporations, like Stutzman-Hillier in Example 1-8, should accept social responsibility for their actions. Some of these reasons are built upon the legal advantages granted to corporations. Others are based on the idea that many corporations are powerful forces in their communities. Still, others focus on the self-interest of the corporation. Whatever the case, these arguments are being voiced more loudly and with more conviction with each passing fiscal year.

See Posner, Richard A. *Overcoming Law*. Cambridge: Harvard University Press, p. 285.

Legal Advantages Granted to the Corporation The first argument supporting corporate social responsibility is based on the fact that corporations are granted certain rights as a result of the incorporation process. For example, the corporate form offers limited liability to those who share in its ownership. This means that the personal assets of the corporate owners cannot be taken if the corporation defaults on a contract or commits a tort or a crime. In addition, under provisions of most incorporation statutes, a corporation is considered an artificially created person. This means that, under provisions of the U.S. Constitution and under those of most state constitutions, a corporation, like a natural person, cannot be deprived of life, liberty, or property without due process of law. This also means that a corporation can own property in its own name and can bring a lawsuit to vindicate its rights. Because corporations have all these rights, they owe an obligation to the public and to the community at large to act responsibly. In practical terms, this means that the decisions of corporate managers must not be narrowly focused on the profits of the shareholders.

Example 1-9

As part of a downsizing campaign, the Andrean-Harrison Corporation was about to close down operations in Tulsa. The company owned an office building and a small laboratory on the outskirts of Tulsa that are adjacent to thirty acres of undeveloped land. The corporation had a chance to sell the land at an outrageous price that would have made a substantial profit for the shareholders of the company. Rather than take advantage of this offer, Andrean-Harrison decided to donate the land to the city. The fact that the corporation was a legal person meant that it owned the land and could donate it to the city. Corporate officials acted responsibly in this case, taking advantage of the corporation's right to own land in its own name.

The Impact of Corporate Decision Making A second reason for demanding social responsibility from corporations is that corporate decision making clearly has an impact on more people than just the shareholders and the managers. Those who support corporate social responsibility often argue that many corporate decisions, such as the decision to open or to close a factory, will affect everyone in the local community. Those affected by such decisions include suppliers, consumers, employees, support businesses, and community members. Consequently, the argument goes, all of these groups should be taken into consideration when corporate managers make decisions. Some individuals who support this form of extreme corporate social responsibility would like to see representatives from the employees' union, from consumer protection groups, from environmental protection groups, and from the local chamber of commerce, on every corporation's board of directors. Others, however, argue that because corporate decisions impact upon more individuals and groups than just the shareholders and managers, those decisions should be made by an impartial group of corporate outsiders. Often the corporate outsiders named are governmental officials.

Getting Students Involved Discuss the following situation with students: A poor man's wife is dying of an unusual illness. Medication is available that will prevent her death and allow her to live a normal life, but the man cannot afford to buy it. He appeals to doctors, pharmacists, church groups, and government officials for money, but they all refuse him. As his wife's health continues to decline, the man, in desperation, breaks into a pharmacy and steals the medication. Is his conduct ethically correct? Should he be prosecuted?

Example 1-10

When the directors of Igar International Corporation were working on plans to diversify their operation, they considered opening a chemical plant in Santa Ana. Before making the decision, they sent a team of experts to Santa Ana to investigate the possibility of establishing an operation just within the city limits. Although the city officials promised Igar a tax abatement plan and agreed to donate several acres of land to the corporation, citizens' groups were against the plant because of environmental and health concerns. The corporation could have simply found a more receptive or, per-haps, a less vocal city in which to locate. However, instead of simply discarding their consideration of Santa Ana, they worked with the citizens' groups to meet their concerns. Ultimately the two sides could not agree on modifications to the plant and Igar went elsewhere. Nevertheless, the willingness of the company to dis-cuss the proposed changes in their operation reflects an understanding of the cor-poration's social responsibility based on the fact that corporate decisions have a far-ranging impact.

Enlightened Corporate Self-Interest Finally, there are those who argue rather convincingly, that accepting social responsibility is actually in the long-term best interests of the corporation. This argument, which is generally referred to as enlightened self-interest, is based on the notion that socially responsible corporations benefit by creating goodwill for themselves, thus motivating consumers to purchase their products, investors to buy their stock, and lawmakers to grant them further legal advantages. In addition, the corporation benefits because the community at large gains from such decisions. If the community at large is healthy, the argument goes, then the corporation which relies on that community will be healthy also.

Example 1-11

The president of Pilder and Wesselkamper International, Inc., decided to suspend negotiations with union representatives when he learned that they were about to demand a salary increase that he believed was untenable given the corporation's financial health, or lack thereof. The union threatened to file a complaint with the National Labor Relations Board, charging that the president and his staff were not cooperating with the collective bargaining process. The union also indicated that it was considering publishing an advertisement in *The New York Times* denouncing the president's decision and eventually would authorize a strike. The president continued to resist further negotiations and simply shut down operations. Eventually, the com-pany filed for bankruptcy and dissolved its operation. Neither of the parties involved in this case opted to pursue a course of enlightened self-interest, which resulted in the worst possible conclusion for all those involved.

Efforts to Promote Social Responsibility

As noted previously, the traditional view of a corporation says that its primary role is to make a profit for its shareholders. This means that corporate managers are obligated to make decisions that maximize those profits. Moreover, under the traditional role of corporate managers, those managers could be sued for making a decision that hurt the cor-poration's profits and thereby reduced or eliminated dividends. However, recent amend-ments to many corporate statutes have been designed to encourage corporate managers to make broader-based decisions. Thus, some statutes now permit managers to consider fac-tors beyond profit in making corporate decisions. These factors include the economic well-being of the nation, the state, and the local community; the interests of employees, consumers, and suppliers; and the betterment of the environment, the economy, and the overall social structure. These statutes generally hold managers immune from shareholder lawsuits, which claim that the managers did not put the shareholders' profits first.

Teaching Tips Explain to students that communica-tion between an attorney and a client is strictly confi-dential. There is one excep-tion: When a client confides in his or her lawyer that he or she is about to commit a crime, the attorney has a legal duty to disclose this information to the police. Lead the class in a discus-sion of how serious a crime would have to be before the attorney has an *ethical* duty to act. Would the attorney client privilege benefit pro-portionately if this exception were not in place?

Related Cases Attorneys are required to keep their clients' funds that are held in trust in accounts sepa-rate from their normal busi-ness accounts. An Indiana attorney was disbarred for commingling his clients' funds and his own per-sonal funds. The attorney had spent $18,000 of his clients' funds for his per-sonal use. *In re Frosh,* 643 N.E.2d 902 (IN).

Related Cases Paying the appropriate amount of taxes each year is difficult even for the most ethical person. However, in an ex-treme case, a Connecticut man was convicted of will-fully failing to pay income taxes when, for two years in a row, he submitted nearly blank personal in-come tax returns despite having received personal income. *U.S. v. Schiff,* 612 F.2d 73.

Example 1-12

The directors of Chindi-Mowry Enterprises, Inc., were under fire because of a takeover bid against Chindi-Mowry engineered by an alien corporation known as Rixensart Industries. To stave off the assault, the directors invited a friendly bid from Sandoff, Inc., a firm that promised not to dismantle Chindi-Mowry after the deal was entered. The final amount of the offer from Sandoff was less than that offered by Rixensart, and so those shareholders who sold their stock received less on the sale to Sandoff than they would have received had the directors endorsed the Rixensart plan. However, in making their decision, the directors were persuaded that the deal offered by Sandoff would save jobs, help the community, boost the national and state economy, and eventually result in a long-term gain for the corporation and for those shareholders who remained with the company.

Quick Quiz 1-3 True or False?

1. Cost-benefit thinking will always result in ethical decisions.

2. Corporations are not allowed to own property.

3. Some statutes allow corporate managers to consider factors beyond shareholder profits in making business decisions.

Business Law in the News
Innovation Is Job One

There was a time when 3M Co. epitomized U.S. innovation. For years, this great Midwestern company consistently generated up to a third of its annual profits from new products. Some time in the 1990s, the company that invented sandpaper, floppy disks, Scotch tape, and Post-it Notes lost its magic and got stuck. James McNerney, an alumnus of General Electric Co. who became chairman and CEO in 2001, is trying to light 3M's fire once again. Nothing is more important to 3M than his success.

McNerney's challenge is to show that he has the DNA for innovation. He is cutting costs, visiting customers, and introducing Six Sigma to boost management rigor and measure performance. He is focusing 3M's $1.1 billion annual research budget and 1,000 scientists and engineers on hot new growth markets in health care and high-tech displays for consumer electronics. But innovation is about embracing uncertainty and taking risks, and McNerney has yet

to show that he can do that. The GE way to success is through measurement—stating precise goals and surpassing them. 3M's success had been in taking commercial advantage of unexpected scientific discoveries.

America's challenge is to keep its innovation economy running. It is disturbing to see that the latest disruptive technology—camera cell phones—originated in Europe and Asia. Camera phones are remaking the digital camera, printer, film, and telephone industries. This is the heart of innovation: a fusion of new technologies that changes all kinds of behavior and businesses. The U.S., hobbled by incompatible cell-phone standards, is lagging.

It is worrisome as well to see the best and brightest foreign students turning away from U.S. universities because they can't get visas. One of the country's sources of innovation is this stream of young people, who come to study and stay to start companies, especially in high tech. Now many, particularly from Asia, are going to China.

Finally, it is disturbing to see that the issue of innovation is being virtually ignored in the Presidential campaign. Certainly it's important to talk about taxes, budget deficits, and Social Security. But the question underlying all of these is how best to get America to innovate, because that's the path to growth, jobs, income, and wealth.

McNerney's struggle to restart the 3M innovation machine is part of a larger fight to keep America at the leading edge of innovation. Both must be won.

Questions for Analysis

1. The editorial entitled "Innovation Is Job One" implies that corporations have a responsibility to take risks in research and development. Should CEOs risk short-term profits in favor of long-term gains, based on risky research projects? Explain.

2. The editorial also indicates that a corporation's social responsibility involves promoting what is best for the country. Should corporations voluntarily trade the best interests of shareholders for the best interests of the nation? Explain.

3. Should corporations be compelled by legislation to focus on national rather than corporate goals? Explain.

4. Should politicians build election campaign promises on a pledge to change corporate responsibility? Explain.

5. Should America's immigration regulations be relaxed to encourage an influx of international students or should those regulations protect American students first? Explain.

Source: BusinessWeek, April 12, 2004, p. 120.

1-4 The Relationship Between Law and Ethics

Thus far, we have seen that ethics and morals can be distinguished from one another. We have also looked at the ethical character traits honesty, fairness, compassion, and integrity. We have also defined values, examined the causes of unethical conduct, and determined how to develop an ethical lifestyle. Some people determine an ethical lifestyle as simply doing what is legal. Such a course of action may often result in ethical conduct. However, that is not always the case. Even when most people know that a particular type of conduct is illegal, that does not prevent some people from engaging in that conduct. For example, everyone knows that killing is illegal. Yet, that knowledge does not stop the national murder rate from climbing higher and higher each year. Similarly, everyone knows that child abuse, spousal abuse, and elder abuse are immoral, but that consensus has not eliminated the problem of abuse from our society.

The Need for Law in Our Society

The law is needed because, although people know better, they do not always follow these ethical principles. As noted earlier, the law consists of rules of conduct established by the government of a society to maintain harmony, stability, and justice in that society. It does this by defining the legal rights and duties of the people. It also provides a way to protect the people by enforcing these rights and duties through the courts and the legislature. Ethical principles can tell us what is right, but they cannot stop us from doing that which is wrong. The law also cannot stop us from doing wrong. However, the law can punish us if we choose to do wrong. The law draws the line between permissible and impermissible conduct, so that people, at the very least, are punished if they hurt or cheat one another.

Further Reading For an interesting discussion of various theories of morality and their applications in the law, see *Morality, Harm, and the Law,* by Gerald Dworkin (Boulder: Westview Press, 1994).

Getting Students Involved Politicians often speak about the country's loss of family values and ethics. Suggest that students write a report expressing their opinion on whether or not the government should attempt to change society's values and ethics by passing laws. Ask them to back up their opinions by including examples of how the government's efforts have or have not worked.

Ethical and Legal Harmony

In a perfect society, ethics and the law would always coincide. Our society is not perfect, however, and it is not likely to become perfect in the foreseeable future. Therefore, our society needs the law and the legal system to give it structure, harmony, predictability, and justice. However, ethical considerations should always form the foundation of law and the legal system. If the law is not founded upon ethics, it will rarely succeed in reaching its objectives. Ethics can lead the way in difficult situations or in areas of the social structure into which the law has yet to venture.

Quick Quiz 1-4 True or False?

1. The law cannot stop us from doing wrong, but it can punish us if we choose to do wrong.

2. In a perfect society, ethics and law would always coincide.

3. The law and the legal system need not be founded on ethical considerations.

Summary

1-1 The law consists of rules of conduct established by the government of a society to maintain harmony, stability, and justice. Morals involve the values that govern a society's attitude toward right and wrong. Ethics, in contrast, attempts to develop a means for determining what those values ought to be and for formulating and applying rules in line with those values.

1-2 Ethical relativism holds that there are no fixed or stable standards of right and wrong. Social contract theory holds that right and wrong are measured by the obligations imposed on each individual by an implied social agreement. Utilitarianism determines right and wrong by looking at the consequences of a person's actions. According to rational ethics, actions are either right or wrong regardless of the circumstances and regardless of the consequences. Role model theory encourages people to pattern their behavior after individuals whose activities provide a good example of how to act.

1-3 Corporations owe society a level of responsibility because the government has granted certain legal advantages to corporations. Another reason for expecting socially responsible decisions from corporate executives is that corporations have a great deal of power in the economic structure and with power comes responsibility. Finally, corporations should act responsibly because it is in their own best interest to do so.

1-4 In a perfect society, ethics and the law would always coincide. Our society is not perfect and is not likely to become so in the foreseeable future. Therefore, our society needs the law and the legal system to give it structure, harmony, predictability, and justice.

Key Terms

compassion, 12
cost-benefit thinking, 10
descriptive theory, 7
ethical relativism, 6
fairness, 12
honesty, 11

integrity, 13
law, 3
morals, 3
natural law theory, 4
prescriptive theory, 7
rational ethics, 10

role model theory, 11
situational ethics, 7
social contract theory, 7
utilitarianism, 8
utility thinking, 10

Questions for Review and Discussion

1. What is the difference between law and morality?
2. What is the difference between values and ethics?
3. What is ethical relativism?
4. What is social contract theory?
5. What are the steps in applying utilitarianism?
6. What are the principles of rational ethics?
7. What are the ethical character traits generally reflected in role model ethics?
8. What are the arguments supporting social responsibility?
9. Why is law needed in our society?
10. How is harmony established between the law and ethics?

Investigating the Internet

Two ethical codes that provide that an interesting contrast to the Public Relations Society Code mentioned earlier in this chapter are the American Marketing Association Code of Ethics and the Institute of Electrical and Electronic Engineers Code of Ethics. Access each of these codes on the Internet and write a paper comparing and/or contrasting selected provisions. As an alternative assignment, choose the code you find to be the most workable of the three and explain your choice.

Cases for Analysis

1. Officials of the United States Air Force negotiated a deal with Boeing under which the military would purchase 100 jets from the corporation. The plan was to modify the Boeing 767s so that they could operate as in-flight tankers. The inspector general of the Pentagon halted the deal when he discovered that the Air Force might have paid too much for the new tankers. The inspector general also complained that the Air Force should not, as a part of any contract, eliminate the military's power to audit the production process once the contract begins. Finally, the inspector general was concerned about the allegation that the Air Force officials had revealed how much Boeing's competitors had bid on the deal, allowing Boeing to underbid those competitors and, thus, clinch the deal. It was also revealed that, after she left her job with the Air Force, a certain official had allegedly obtained a job with Boeing. Did Boeing breach its social responsibility in its contract with the Air Force? Explain. Did the Air Force also breach its social responsibility? Explain. See Oppel, Richard. "Pentagon Says Changes Are Needed in Boeing Jet Deal." *The New York Times,* April 10, 2004, p. A-9.

2. After the war with Afghanistan, American military forces imprisoned a large number of foreign nationals in a prison at Guantánamo Bay in Cuba. These foreign nationals were held without due process of law, a right guaranteed by the U.S. Constitution. Labeling these foreign nationals as "enemy combatants," the government argued that, since they were not citizens, the constitutional right to due process did not apply to them. Attorneys representing the prisoners argued that the right to due process of law applies to all people, not just citizens. Applying rational ethics to this case, why is the argument made by the government unethical? Explain. Is there any ethical theory described in this chapter that might be used to defend the government's position? Explain. See Cole, David. "America's Prisoners, American Rights." *The New York Times,* April 20, 2004, p. A-23.

3. In the wake of the bombing of a passenger train in Madrid, Spain, the British government stepped up its antiterrorist activities and, as a result, in just over one month's time, arrested eighteen people who were suspected of terrorist activities. Under British antiterrorism statutes, the government is

permitted to imprison suspected terrorists even though no charges have been filed and no trial held. Applying social contract theory to this case, is the action taken by the British government ethical? Explain. Is there any ethical theory described in this chapter that might be used to defend the British government's position? Explain. See Cowell, Alan. "British Police Arrest 10 on Suspicion of Terror." *The New York Times,* April 20, 2004, p. A-3.

4. Yellowstone International Inc. has developed a line of lawn mowers that have a tendency to explode into flames. Since the mowers were first marketed 10 years ago, hundreds of people have been injured by mowers that have exploded into flames, often while they are not even in use. Yellowstone has stopped lawsuits by offering huge settlements to those people injured by the mowers. One such settlement, for example, topped $3 million. In these settlements, Yellowstone inserted a secrecy clause preventing the other party from revealing to the public any part of the incident. Should Yellowstone continue to market mowers knowing of their tendency to explode? Should the corporation settle these claims out of court? Should secrecy clauses be included in the settlement agreement? Are the injured parties acting ethically when they promise to keep quiet knowing what can happen to literally hundreds of other unsuspecting consumers? Explain all of your responses.

5. Philip Holden and Kurt Mueller were replacing the roof on Tom Harrelson's farmhouse when Mueller lost his balance and fell to the ground. When Holden could not revive Mueller, he placed his partner in their van and drove him to the Culver City Hospital. When they arrived at the hospital, while Mueller was being examined by the emergency room physician, Holden was questioned by the admissions clerk. During the admission process, Holden learned that Culver City Hospital has a policy of not treating patients who do not have health insurance. Neither Holden nor Mueller have such insurance. When the admissions clerk asked about insurance, Holden, who believed that his friend's life was hanging in the balance, told her that Mueller had insurance. When asked about Mueller's insurance card, Holden told the clerk that the card was back at Harrelson's farm. On the strength of Holden's answers Mueller was admitted. He underwent extensive surgery and a long period of recovery at the hospital. Eventually, his hospital bills total $65,897.52. These expenses are not covered by insurance. Neither Holden nor Mueller can afford to pay the bill. Instead of suing Holden and Mueller, the hospital turned the case over to the district attorney who charged both Holden and Mueller with fraud. Is the hospital's policy of turning away people without health insurance ethical? Did Holden face a genuine conflict of duties? What two duties did he have to balance? How might Holden have solved this ethical dilemma? Was Holden's lie about the health insurance ethical? Is the hospital's decision to turn the case over to the district attorney ethical? Is the district attorney's decision to prosecute ethical? Defend your answers.

6. The accounting firm of Thompson, Myers, and Polis was hired by Greystone Industries to prepare the company's annual audit. During the course of the audit, Larry Kenton discovered several irregularities in the bookkeeping process conducted by Gary Wentworth, Greystone's treasurer. The irregularities did not involve any illegalities and were relatively minor. Moreover, they did not amount to very much in terms of a monetary loss for the company. Nevertheless, if allowed to continue, the questionable practices could cost the firm thousands of dollars. When Kenton informs Fred Thompson, the senior partner in the accounting firm, Thompson tells Kenton not to bring the matter up. Thompson argues that Wentworth has a volatile temper and is likely to cancel the accounting firm's contract with Greystone if his bookkeeping techniques are questioned. When Kenton objects to this course of action, Thompson tells him that the decision is final. Is it ethical for Thompson to order Kenton not to reveal the bookkeeping discrepancies? What should Kenton do now that he has been ordered not to bring the matter to Wentworth's attention? Defend your answers.

7. William Yurchak, vice president of production for Dragonfly Enterprises, was passed over for what he believed was a much deserved promotion to the presidency. Instead of promoting Yurchak, the board of directors of Dragonfly, a firm that specializes in the development and production of recreational aircraft, decided to hire an outsider. Clyde Kellor, the chairman of the board of Vostok Incorporated, one of Dragonfly's chief competitors, offers Yurchak the presidency of Vostok. Although Yurchak still has three years to run on his contract with Dragonfly, he is tempted to take

Kellor's offer because he feels that he has been badly treated by Dragonfly, and because he could use the 50 percent raise that Kellor has offered him. Kellor has added one stipulation. He wants Yurchak to bring with him the plans for Dragonfly Six, the corporation's latest revolutionary aircraft. Was it ethical for the board of Dragonfly to hire an outsider as president? Is Kellor's offer to Yurchak ethical? Would the offer be ethical if Kellor had not added the request for the Dragonfly Six plans? What is the ethical course of action for Yurchak? Explain all of your answers.

8. Barbara McMahon is a reporter for *The Lake County Press*. McMahon is approached by Julie Bryant, a research scientist for the International Chemical Corporation. Bryant, who asks for and receives a promise of confidentiality from McMahon, informs the reporter that International Chemical has been disposing of its chemical waste product by illegally dumping it in the Lake County River. On the strength of Bryant's word alone, *The Lake County Press* runs a series of articles on the illegal dumping. The district attorney of Lake County elects to prosecute the president and board members of International. At the trial, McMahon is called as a witness and asked to reveal her confidential news source. The state in which Lake County is located does not recognize any journalist-news source privilege. The judge tells McMahon that if she does not reveal her source, she will be placed in jail until she does so. Was it ethical for Bryant to go to McMahon with her confidential story in the first place? Was it ethical for McMahon to print the news stories on the basis of Bryant's word alone? Would it be ethical for the judge to place McMahon in jail? What is the ethical course of action for McMahon? What is the ethical course of action for Bryant? Defend all of your responses.

Quick Quiz Answers

1-1	1. F	1-2	1. T	1-3	1. F	1-4	1. T
	2. F		2. F		2. F		2. T
	3. T		3. T		3. T		3. F

Chapter 2

Sources of the Law

The Opening Case
"The 9-11 Commission"

Shortly after the horrific attacks by Al Qaeda on the World Trade Center and the Pentagon on September 11, 2001, a call went out, requesting the appointment of an independent body to investigate events leading to that fateful day. The independent group would determine not only whether the tragedy could have been prevented, but also how to deter similar attacks in the future. President George W. Bush responded by stating that no investigative body would be formed by the government. He added that no public hearings would be conducted and that none of his staff members at the White House would ever testify before such a commission. In response, a group of individuals comprised mostly of family members of the victims of 9-11, bypassed the President completely and went to Congress to pressure legislators into forcing the executive branch to respond. At first Congress resisted. However, after the 9-11 families went to the press with their case, the Senate agreed to support the demand for an independent commission. The vote to approve this request was an overwhelming 90–8. In light of this pressure from the Senate, the President relented and appointed the 9-11 Commission to investigate government responsibility for foreseeing and preventing the 9-11 attacks and to determine how such attacks could be forestalled in the future. The events leading to the appointment of the commission underscore the complex interplay that occurs among the various levels of our government. In this case, the executive branch responded to pressure from the legislative branch which, in turn, had responded to legitimate demands from the people. As we shall see, this is as it should be. Both our government and our legal system are designed to respond to the will of the people. Our government is also a system of checks and balances. This is why the President could not ignore the vote by the Senate but instead had to go forward and appoint the 9-11 Commission. As you read this chapter, revisit these issues in an attempt to see how the system works.

Chapter Outcomes

1. Enumerate the objectives of the law.
2. Clarify the operation of the law as a complex adaptive system.
3. Outline the content of the U.S. Constitution.
4. Explain the role of statutory law in the legal system.

5. Defend the need to set up a system of uniform state laws.
6. Identify the latest cyberlaw statutes that have been added to the legal system.
7. State the role of common law in the legal system.
8. Describe how the principle of *stare decisis* provides stability to our legal system.
9. Differentiate between statutory interpretation and judicial review.
10. Account for the legislature's need to establish administrative regulations.

2-1 The Purpose and Operation of the Law

As explained in Chapter 1, the **law** consists of rules of conduct established by the government to maintain harmony, stability, and justice within a society. Ideally, the primary objectives of the law are to promote harmony, stability and justice. In everyday life the balance is not easy to maintain. Often justice must be sacrificed for harmony and stability. Sometimes the opposite is true.

The law is often a balancing act. One person's rights are enforced while another's are not. One group is allowed to act, which restrains the freedom of another group. One company's contract rights are upheld at the expense of another's. Balancing like this occurs frequently. Generally, the objectives of harmony, stability, and justice are kept in mind as such decisions are made. Because the law is made by people, it is not perfect. Legislators and judges bring their own personal prejudices and biases into the process. Nevertheless, most of them try to apply the law as objectively as possible. The law is made even more complex because it is not a fixed tradition but is, instead, a complex adaptive system that is constantly changing.

Cross-Cultural Notes
Legal systems in many Latin American countries have been shaped by the colonial history of the region. Since gaining independence, Brazil, Mexico, Venezuela, and Argentina, for example, have each retained a strong centralized government that is molded after colonial rule. Claiming to be democratic, these governments, like their colonial predecessors, often disregard or change the law when it becomes inconvenient.

Complex Adaptive Systems

The law acts as a constantly changing complex adaptive system. A **complex adaptive system** is a network of interacting conditions which reinforce one another while, at the same time, adjusting to changes from agents both outside and inside the system. The entire

The Opening Case Revisited
"The 9-11 Commission"

When the 9-11 Commission issued its findings in the summer of 2004, many government officials found that they could no longer conduct business as usual. Their professional and personal lives were disrupted by the commission's recommendations for reform in the executive branch, especially as those proposals affected the intelligence-gathering agencies of the government. The recommendations had the potential to cause disorder within those agencies, thus leading to a period of instability within the government. Nevertheless, any other ruling would have been unfair to the people of the United States who depend on these agencies for their safety and security and for the overall stability of the entire nation. This situation reveals the balancing act that the law and the government must engage in on a daily basis. In this case, the orderly lives of certain government officials had to be disrupted in order to be fair to the rest of the people and in order to restore stability to the social structure. The actions of the commission also demonstrate how the law works as a means for improving social control.

The 9-11 Commission was necessary in order to improve social control, even though the event caused great disruption for many government agencies.

purpose of a complex adaptive system is the survival and improvement of the system itself. Natural examples of complex adaptive systems include beehives, anthills, the neural network of the human brain, the operation of a cell, and any sufficiently advanced ecosystem. Social examples include the educational system, the technological community, the stock market, and the economy itself.

All complex adaptive systems, whether they are natural or social, share six basic attributes. First, every complex adaptive system operates as the result of the interaction of a variety of actors within the system itself. In an anthill, the actors are the various ranks of ants, each rank having its own independent, yet interactive function. In an economic network, the actors include producers and consumers, as well as intermediaries such as bankers, transporters, sellers, lawyers, and so on.

Second, in a complex adaptive system there is no central controlling actor. Instead, control of the system is dispersed among various actors, any one of which can be replaced by another, equally effective actor. Even those actors designated as a "chief" or central actor, have only nominal control over the entire complicated system. Thus, despite his or her apparent power, even the chairperson of the Federal Reserve System does not exercise complete control over the entire economic system.

Third, complex adaptive systems are just that; they are complex. This means that multiple levels of organization exist within the network. To be a true adaptive system, however, each lower level must contribute to the existence of the upper levels, and vice versa. Thus, in an economic system, those who sell a product at the upper levels cannot perform their job without the contribution of the laborer on the line at the lower levels of the system.

Fourth, the more experienced a complex adaptive system becomes, the more change it undergoes. This is the "adaptive" element within the complex system. As the system learns from the past, it changes to avoid making the same mistakes a second and third time. This is what happens, for instance, when the economic system learns how to avoid the disastrous type of stock market crash that wiped out so many people's life savings in 1929.

Fifth, as a part of this process, a complex adaptive system can infer the direction of future events and can often adjust to those changing events. Often this anticipation is more intuitive than conscious, thus making adaptation an encoded part of the system.

See Waldrop, M. Mitchell. *Complexity: The Emerging Science at the Edge of Chaos.* New York: Simon and Schuster, 1992, pp. 145–147.

Sixth, within each complex adaptive system certain levels of influence, called **embedded niches,** exist, which permit individuals inhabiting those niches to exercise a certain degree of limited power. Each niche is populated by experts upon whom others, outside that level, depend. Embedded niches permit the actors within those niches to exercise a great deal of power. Nevertheless, the power wielded within a niche is limited because each embedded actor still depends on other niches for knowledge and guidance beyond their areas of expertise. Thus, a complex adaptive system involves interdependent levels of influence.

The Law as a Complex Adaptive System

The law, or more properly, the entire legal framework, is a complex adaptive system exhibiting each of these six attributes. First, the law functions because of the interaction of a variety of agents within the legal system. Those agents include lawmakers, attorneys,

judges, administrators, paralegals, executives, and so on. Each agent has his or her independent job to do within the system, yet each agent depends on all of the other agents to
hold the entire system together as a functioning entity.

Second, as in all complex adaptive systems, in the law there is no central controlling
agent. Rather, control is distributed among a number of different agents. Even those
agents that may appear to be central controlling agents are not. Thus, the United States
Supreme Court, which may seem to have absolute authority, does not. The Supreme
Court has no police power of its own. Therefore, it cannot force other agents in the system to follow its dictates. Yet, most of the time, those dictates are followed, because the
existence of the entire complex adaptive system depends on granting the court a certain
degree of autonomy.

Third, as is true of all complex adaptive systems, the law is an intricate network of
interactive organizational levels, each of which depends on the others for the smooth operation of the entire network. Thus, within the law, Congress, for instance, depends on the
President and the President's Cabinet to carry out the law, while the organizational levels
depend on the courts to interpret the law, and to make certain that it affects individuals
according to a proper assessment of congressional and presidential intent.

Fourth, the more proficient the law becomes, the more easily it adapts to changing
social, political, and economic influences. As noted above, this is the "adaptive" attribute of
the law. Actors within the legal network learn from experience, and, as a result, modify the
law so that it will address contemporary issues. This is what happened, for instance, when
states passed laws to deal with surrogate parenting contracts, or when Congress created the
Securities and Exchange Commission to deal with abuses in the sale of stock.

Fifth, the law often infers the direction of future events and adjusts accordingly. This
is what happens when, anticipating problems with litigation, the law cooperates with the
institution of alternative dispute resolution techniques.

Finally, the legal system includes embedded niches, each of which is populated by
experts upon whom others, outside those niches, depend and who, in turn, depend on others
for knowledge and guidance outside their own embedded niche. Within the law, attorneys
depend on judges, who depend on law clerks, who depend on law professors, who depend
on legal assistants, and so on. Or, on the legislative side of the aisle, the President or governor depends on legislators, who depend on legislative aides, who depend on lobbyists,
who depend on clients, who depend on lawyers, who depend on paralegals, who depend on
law professors, who depend on graduate assistants, and so on.

The point of demonstrating that the law is a complex adaptive system is to show that,
like any complex adaptive system, the law has a life of its own. This explains why certain things happen in the law and others do not, despite human attempts to promote or to
stop them. A key result of examining complex adaptive systems is the conclusion that,
out of the self-interaction of the levels within the system, order emerges. Thus, what appears to be aimless and random activity at the local level, becomes organized and orderly
when the system is viewed as a whole. Disorder in the courtroom, on the floor of
Congress, or in the Oval Office, as well as among these embedded niches, is ultimately canceled out because an orderly process emerges from these lower-level interactions.
Throughout the text, we will often remind ourselves that the law is a complex adaptive
system. This will help us understand why certain objectives are met by the law while others are not.

Complex Adaptation and Cyberlaw

The realization that chaotic activity at the local level often resolves itself as order emerges
at the higher levels, allows us to be optimistic about the law. However, this view is not
meant to blind us to the injustices that still exist within the legal system itself. Thus, the law
continues to disappoint numerous people in many areas, including the inadequate way it

Talking Points Read the
following quotations on the
nature of the law. As you
read the quotations and
reflect on the ideas that
they represent, ask your-
self which of the positions
best reflects the development of the law as a com-
plex adaptive system.

*"The truth is, that the law is
always approaching, and
never reaching, consistency.
It is forever adopting new
principles from life at one
end, and it always retains
old ones from history at the
other; which have not yet
been absorbed or sloughed
off. It will become entirely
consistent only when it
ceases to grow."*

—Oliver Wendell Holmes,
Jr. "Early Forms of Lia-
bility." In *The Common
Law.*

*"The multi-layered charac-
ter of American law (legislation superimposed on com-
mon law, federal law superimposed on state law, and
federal constitutional law
superimposed on state and
federal statutory and common law), the undisciplined
character of our legislatures,
the intricacy and complexity
of our society, and the moral
heterogeneity of our population combine to thrust on
the courts a responsibility
for creative lawmaking that
cannot be discharged either
by applying existing rules to
the letter or by reasoning by
analogy."*

—Richard Posner.
Overcoming Law.

deals with discrimination, influence peddling, insider trading, runaway litigation, spousal abuse, bureaucratic red tape, religious intolerance, the drug trade, environmental protection, identity theft, consumer fraud, and racketeering to name a few. Nevertheless, the fact that many of the advances in the law happen despite the fact that people try to prevent them gives us reason to hope.

Digital Information Contracts   A case in point is the development of cyberlaw in the United States. The integration of computers into the economy has caused many problems at every level of the legal system. However, one of the most difficult questions to face lawmakers recently has been how to deal with **digital information contracts** (aka, **software contracts** and **cybercontracts**). The sale of the computer itself is not a problem since buying hardware is just like buying a television. A problem arises, however, with the sale of software which is, after all, the sale of information in a digital format. Thus, it is not the CD or the floppy disk that is for sale. Rather, it is the digital information on the CD or the floppy disk that is being sold. Until a few years ago, nothing in the law dealt with this form of property. How the legal world adjusted to this new phenomenon illustrates how the law operates as a complex adaptive system.

As with any complex adaptive system, there is no central controlling agent in the legal system that could shape digital information contract law. In fact, because of the nature of a complex adaptive system, several embedded niches within the legal system dealt with this problem simultaneously, causing confusion and inconsistency. The niche we will focus on here is the National Conference of Commissioners on Uniform State Laws, an independent organization, established to design model laws. Initially, the commissioners attempted to revise an existing model law, Article 2 of the Uniform Commercial Code (UCC) (see page 869). The commissioners should have been able to simply look at the old law, at the nature of software contracts and, through logical deduction, modify the old law to fit this new type of contract. Unfortunately, this did not happen.

Any attempt by the commissioners to revise existing law was hampered by the rapid pace at which computers and software changed, by the unique nature of digital information contracts, and by the fact that merchants had already created new techniques for the sale of digital information. Consequently, drafting a model law required that the framers detect the fundamental nature of digital information contracts, predict developments in digital information, and anticipate trends in the marketing of digital information. In short, they had to act like meteorologists developing a weather forecast that would be valid for several years.

Complicating matters for the commissioners was the fact that, before they took up their task, other embedded agents in the complex adaptive system of the law had been at work developing legal norms to deal with digital information contracts. These embedded elements included decisions made by the courts, laws passed by state legislatures, and the UCC itself. What emerged from the interaction of these agents was a series of unpredictable and, therefore, highly unsatisfactory rules for dealing with digital information contracts. Yet these rules could not be ignored in the revision of Article 2 of the UCC.

The Uniform Computer Information Transactions Act   What the commissioners discovered was that it was impossible to revise Article 2 of the UCC to meet the evolving state of digital information contracts. As a result, what emerged from the interaction of the embedded agents in the system was the first modern cyberlaw, the **Uniform Computer Information Transactions Act (UCITA). Cyberlaw** is a single law or a series of laws that deals exclusively with some aspect of computers and their attendant elements, such as their hardware and software. This particular cyberlaw arose from the interaction of the embedded agents within the complex adaptive legal system. As an emergent quality, it included many of the aspects that had characterized the other embedded agents. This new cyberlaw was, for example, flexible, in that it allowed merchants to create their own contracts. The UCITA, therefore, became a law that parties could refer to if something was ambiguous, had been ignored, or had been forgotten in the development of their individual digital information contracts. In addition, the commissioners took the unique nature of digital information into consideration and, as a result, characterized most cybercontracts as license agreements, rather than sale of goods contracts.

Complex Adaptation at Work The process involved in the development of cyberlaw shows how the attributes of a complex adaptive system are reflected in the legal system. First, like all complex adaptive systems, the legal system functions because of the interaction of a variety of agents within that system. In this case, the courts, legislatures, merchants, and the commissioners themselves were all involved in the process of making a new cyberlaw. Second, much of this interaction was caused by the fact that, as within all complex systems, in the legal system, there is no central controlling agent charged with dealing with digital contracts. This forced the embedded agents to work together in the creation of cyberlaw.

Third, as is true of all complex adaptive systems, the legal system is an intricate network of interactive organizational levels, each of which depends on the others for the consistent operation of the entire network. Thus, in this case, the commissioners had to deal with court decisions, with laws passed by the legislature, with provisions of the old UCC, and so on, in the writing of the new cyberlaw. Fourth, the legal system also showed that, like any complex system, it has learned to adapt to changing economic, social, and technological conditions. This is why the UCITA became a default code that parties can use when their own contracts fail to address something. Fifth, the legal system also demonstrated that it can infer the direction of future events. This is why the commissioners chose to characterize cybercontracts as license agreements. A **license agreement** permits the parties to pick and choose those rights that will move from the seller to the buyer of digital information, thus allowing them to adjust to future changes in the nature of that information. Finally, the embedded niches worked together to create a single cyberlaw, which emerged from the interaction of those niches. In this case the process continues to this day. As with all model laws, the UCITA becomes legally effective only when it is adopted by a state legislature. Thus far, only a few state legislatures have enacted it into law.

In order to take a more detailed look at how these embedded niches work together, we will now look at them individually. The four main sources of the law, and thus, the four main embedded niches are: (1) federal and state constitutions, (2) federal and state statutes, (3) court decisions, and (4) administrative regulations.

"Yet, to philosophy of law, exactly as to political philosophy, this law, as it is being handed down by constitutions, legislatures, courts and administrative agents, is only a matter of critique or justification. Whenever we ponder about justice in the transpositive sense of what ought to be law, we necessarily turn to the question of whether there are external, or absolute, or at least objective standards of justice."

—Arnold Brecht. "The Impossible in Political and Legal Philosophy." In *The Political Philosophy of Arnold Brecht.*

See Standby Committee. "Prefatory Note." *Uniform Computer Information Transaction Act.* National Conference of Commissioners on Uniform State Laws. http://www.law. upenn.edu/ bll/ulc/ucita/2002final.htm.

Quick Quiz 2-1 True or False

1. The law consists of rules of conduct established by the government to maintain harmony, stability, and justice within a society.

2. Cyberlaw is a single law or a series of laws that deals exclusively with some aspect of computers.

3. A license agreement permits the parties to pick and choose those rights that will move from the seller to the buyer of digital information, thus allowing them to adjust to future changes in the nature of that information.

2-2 Constitutional Law

The law has been defined as rules of conduct created by the government to maintain harmony, stability, and justice within a society. This definition is adequate but it is also somewhat limited. It does not explain where the government comes from or who gives it the power to make those rules.

In some societies, the government is represented by a hereditary monarchy. In others, the establishment of a government depends upon which political faction can muster the necessary power for taking control of that nation's resources. In the United States, the government was established by a constitution.

A **constitution** is the basic law of a nation or state. The United States Constitution provides the organization of the national government. Each state also has a constitution that establishes the state's governmental structure. The body of law that makes up a constitution and its interpretation is known as **constitutional law.**

The Articles of Confederation

The Constitution of the United States, as it exists today, is not the nation's first constitution. The first constitution was known as the **Articles of Confederation.** The Articles of Confederation were created to hold together a fragile coalition of states, each of which was determined to maintain its own independent existence. While the Articles of Confederation fulfilled a much needed function during the first years in the life of the United States, they contained certain weaknesses.

One of the primary weaknesses was the fact that the Confederation Congress, as the national legislature was known under the Articles, could not impose taxes or tariffs. While a common treasury was supposed to be supplied by the states in proportion to the value of land within each state, the states retained the power to levy and collect taxes. In essence, this meant that the Confederation Congress had to rely on the goodwill of the states in order to obtain money. Such revenues were rarely forthcoming. Some states paid nothing at all; others turned over a portion of what they owed, but rarely by the date the payments were due. Part of this problem was caused by the fact that the states were not about to trade one dictatorial central government for another and, therefore, simply ignored the national government.

Moreover, the desire to prevent the type of tyranny that the colonies had experienced under the rule of King George and the British Parliament, had led the Framers of the Articles to include other limitations on the national government. For instance, the Articles made no provision for any sort of chief executive to run the national government. Instead, the administrative power of the confederation was to reside in a Committee of the States appointed by Congress to operate when Congress was not in session. Moreover, all delegates to the Congress were appointed by the state legislatures and served at their pleasure. Several times, the national government found itself powerless to act, because some of the legislatures did not even bother to send delegates to Congress. In addition, while the Confederation Congress had the authority to regulate the value of any money created under its own authority or under the authority of a state, the states retained the power to issue their own currency.

Eventually these weaknesses made the establishment of any effective national government impossible. Consequently, in the summer of 1787, twelve of the thirteen states organized under the Articles sent delegates to a Constitutional Convention held in Philadelphia. The purpose of the convention was to revise the nation's first constitution, the Articles of Confederation. However, the Articles were so weak that the delegates decided instead to come up with a brand new constitution.

The Opening Case Revisited
"The 9-11 Commission"

When the 9-11 Commission began its hearings, a lot of people in the government were called to testify. Some of the individuals who were asked to appear before commission members, did so readily. Others, however, resisted. This was initially true, for example, of Condoleezza Rice, the President's National Security Adviser. After answering questions in private before the Commission, she refused to be placed under oath or to testify before the media. With the President's approval, Rice argued that forcing her to testify would violate the separation of powers between the executive and the legislative branches of the federal government. In contrast, some legal scholars argued that there could be no separation of powers issue because the 9-11 Commission was an independent investigative body rather than an arm of Congress. Still other scholars argued that, even if the Commission were an extension of Congress, compelling the President's National Security Adviser to testify would actually be a part of the checks and balances system built into the Constitution. Rice did eventually testify before the Commission. However, the President's legal team argued that the decision to allow her to testify should not be considered a precedent for later similar situations.

The Principles of the United States Constitution

The Constitution of the United States is based upon two fundamental principles that were supported by many of the delegates to the convention in Philadelphia. Those two principles promote, first, a separation of national powers among three distinct branches of government and, second, a system of checks and balances that allows each branch to oversee the operation of the other two branches. The principle of the separation of powers sets up the now familiar three branches of the national government: the executive branch, the legislative branch, and the judicial branch. The principle of checks and balances allows each branch to share in the power of the other two branches.

The Structure of the United States Constitution

The U.S. Constitution is divided into two parts: the articles and the amendments. The articles establish the organization of the national government. The amendments change provisions in the original articles and add ideas that the Framers did not include in those articles.

The Articles   The first three of the seven articles distribute the power of the government among the legislative, executive, and judicial branches. Article I establishes Congress as the legislative (statute-making) branch of the government. Article II gives executive power to the president, and Article III gives judicial power to the Supreme Court and other courts established by Congress. Article IV explains the relationships among the states, while Article V outlines the methods for amending the Constitution. Article VI establishes the U.S. Constitution, federal laws, and treaties as the supreme law of the land. Finally, Article VII outlines how the original thirteen states would go about ratifying the new Constitution. Table 2-1 outlines the content of each article in the Constitution.

The Amendments   The amendments to the Constitution establish the rights that belong to the people, change some of the provisions in the original articles, and add ideas that the Framers did not include in those articles. Thus, the amendments are attempts to

---

Background Information Only seven times in its entire history has the United States Senate exercised its authority under the Constitution and actually removed public officials from office. Those seven officials are: John Pickering, a district court judge (1804); West Humphreys, district court judge (1862); Robert Archbald, commerce court judge (1912–13); Halsted Ritter, district court judge (1936); Harry Claiborne, district court judge (1986); Alcee Hastings, district court judge (1989); and Walter Nixon, Jr., district court judge (1989).

"How can those who are invested with the powers of government be prevented from employing them, as the means of aggrandizing themselves, instead of using them to protect and preserve society . . . This, too, can be accomplished only in one way, and that is, by such an organism of the government—and, if necessary for the purpose, of the community also,—as will, by dividing and distributing the powers of government, give to each division or interest, through its appropriate organ, either a concurrent voice in making and executing the laws, or a veto on their execution."

—John C. Calhoun.
  "A Disquisition on
  Government." In *Philosophy in America: From The Puritans to James.*

U.S. Const. Articles
I–VII (see pages
856–860)

Our Constitution is an experiment, as all life is an experiment.

—Oliver Wendell Holmes
  (1841–1935), Supreme
  Court Justice

Further Reading A very practical work on the U.S. Constitution is *The Constitution of the United States with the Declaration of Independence and the Articles of Confederation* by R. B. Bernstein (New York: Barnes and Noble, 2002). Another book that discusses such concepts as the separation of powers in its original form is *The Second Treatise of Government* by John Locke (Mineola, NY: Dover 2002).

Did You Know?

Roman law was first codified into The Law of the Twelve Tables in 450 B.C. The Twelve Tables declared that all free citizens had certain fundamental rights.

Background Information The separation of governmental powers into the legislative, executive, and judicial branches marks a key difference between the American and British legal systems. In Britain, the Prime Minister is a part of the Parliament. Should the Prime Minister lose the official support of the House of Commons, he or she must leave office. This is not true of the President. (See Honore, Tony. *About Law: An Introduction*. Oxford: Clarendon Press, 1995, p. 31.)

U.S. Const. Amendments 1–27 (see pages 860–863)

Table 2-1 Articles of the U.S. Constitution

Articles	Content
Article I	Establishes the legislative branch of the federal government (the Congress) Defines the duties and powers of each house Outlines how Congress must conduct its business Lists legislative powers granted to Congress Lists powers denied to Congress Lists powers denied to the states
Article II	Gives executive power and responsibilities to the president Outlines the president's term of office, qualifications, and manner of election Identifies the president as commander in chief Gives the president power to make treaties
Article III	Establishes the Supreme Court and authorizes the establishment of other federal courts Provides for trial by jury for crimes Defines treason against the United States
Article IV	Defines interstate relations Sets up the full faith and credit clause obligating each state to recognize the public acts and proceedings of other states Provides for extradition of those accused of crimes in other states
Article V	Outlines the method of amending the Constitution
Article VI	Establishes the Constitution, federal laws, and federal treaties as the supreme law of the land
Article VII	Provides for the original ratification of the Constitution

fine-tune the Constitution and to update its provisions to meet the demands of a changing socioeconomic structure. The first ten amendments of the Constitution compose the Bill of Rights. They were added soon after the ratification of the Constitution by the original thirteen states. Other amendments that secure the rights of the people include the Thirteenth, which prohibits slavery; the Fourteenth, which guarantees equal protection of the law and due process; the Fifteenth, which guarantees voting rights; the Nineteenth, which extends voting rights to women; the Twenty-fourth, which prohibits poll taxes; and the Twenty-sixth, which extends the right to vote to eighteen-year-old citizens. Table 2-2 provides a more detailed look at the amendments.

The U.S. Constitution establishes the branches of government: executive, legislative, and judicial.

The Question of Democracy

The structure of the Constitution as described here does not set up a democracy. Instead it establishes a republic. The difference between a democracy and a republic is that, in a democracy, the people have direct control over the government whereas in a

Table 2-2 Amendments to the U.S. Constitution

The Bill of Rights		Pre-Civil War Amendments	Civil War Amendments	Early Twentieth-Century Amendments	Depression-Era Amendments	Modern Amendments
Amendment 1 Freedom of religion, speech, press, assembly	*Amendment 6* Procedures allowed in criminal cases	*Amendment 11* Lawsuits against the states	*Amendment 13* Slavery is abolished	*Amendment 16* The income tax is established	*Amendment 20* Terms of president, vice president, senators and representatives altered	*Amendment 22* President's terms limited to two
Amendment 2 The right to bear arms and set up a militia	*Amendment 7* Jury trials in common law cases guaranteed	*Amendment 12** President and vice president elected together	*Amendment 14* Equal protection of the law, due process, citizenship	*Amendment 17* Senators elected by direct election	*Amendment 21* Prohibition repealed	*Amendment 23* Washington, DC gets electors
Amendment 3 The quartering of soldiers in homes is prohibited	*Amendment 8* Bill of Rights guaranteed, cruel and unusual punishment prohibited		*Amendment 15†* Voting rights guaranteed	*Amendment 18‡* Prohibition established		*Amendment 24* Poll taxes outlawed
Amendment 4 Search and seizure by probable cause	*Amendment 9* People retain other rights			*Amendment 19* Women given right to vote		*Amendment 25* Disability of the president; vacancies in the vice presidency
Amendment 5 Grand juries, double jeopardy, self-incrimination, due process, and eminent domain	*Amendment 10* Powers reserved to states					*Amendment 26* Vote extended to 18-year-olds
						Amendment 27 Congress prevented from voting itself instant pay raises

*Altered somewhat by the Twentieth Amendment. †Voting age changed by Twenty-sixth Amendment. ‡Repealed by Twenty-first Amendment.

republic the people elect delegates to represent them. When the Framers wrote the Articles of Confederation in 1777 and when they designed the Constitution in 1787, they thought in terms of a republic rather than a democracy. Certainly, to the Framers the concept of republicanism meant that there would be no royalty in the American system. However, it also implied that the people would have some voice in the running of the government, even if it were an indirect voice. In fact, for the most part the voice of the people was an indirect voice, since the only delegates that the people elected directly were those in the House of Representatives.

Today, when most people speak of democracy, it is likely that they mean a form of republicanism in which there is competition among political parties to elect representatives on a regular basis, and in which the government's power to interfere in the rights of the people is limited. Despite the fact that democracy is a part of the rhetoric of politicians, not everyone agrees automatically that democracy is a good thing. Even American politicians are not as dedicated to democracy as it sometimes appears on the surface. For example, the first Constitution ratified for Iraq after Gulf War II limited the power of the Iraqi Congress to pass their own laws, something that is essential to democracy. In addition, some nations seem to prefer to have a less than democratic ruling process.

Even in the United States itself, many people express a disillusionment with democracy, evidenced by a perennially low voter turnout. Still, most people seem to prefer the

Business Law in the News
What Democracy? The Case for Abolishing the United States Senate

Americans believe in the idea of democracy. We fight wars in its name and daily pledge allegiance to its principles. Curiously, the fervor with which we profess our faith in democracy is matched only by the contempt with which we regard our politics and politicians. How interesting that we should so dislike the process that we claim to revere. Perhaps, however, our unhappiness with politics points to something significant; perhaps Americans dislike the daily reality of their political system precisely because it falls short of being a proper democracy. Indeed, in the last presidential election, we saw a man take office who did not win the popular vote. Money above all else shapes our political debate and determines its outcome, and in the realm of public policy, even when an overwhelming democratic majority expresses its preference (as for national health insurance), deadlocks, vetoes, filibusters, and "special interests" stand in the way. No wonder so few people vote in national elections; we have become a nation of spectators, not citizens.

The United States of America is not, strictly speaking, a democracy; indeed, the U.S. Constitution was deliberately designed to prevent the unfettered expression of the people's will. Yet the

Founders were not, as some imagine, of one mind concerning the proper shape of the new American union, and their disputes are instructive. The political dysfunction that some imagine to be a product of recent cultural decadence has been with us from the beginning. In fact, the document that was meant to prevent democracy in America has bequeathed the American people a politics of minority rule in which our leaders must necessarily pursue their unpopular aims by means of increasingly desperate stratagems of deceit and persuasion.

Yet hope remains, for if Americans have little real experience of democracy, they remain a nation convinced that the best form of government is by and for the people. Growing numbers of Americans suspect that all is not right with the American Way. Citizens, faced with the prospect of sacrificing the well-being of their children and grandchildren on the altar of supply-side economics, the prospect of giving up new schools and hospitals so that the colony in Iraq might have zip codes and modern garbage trucks, have begun to ask hard questions. Politics, properly understood as the deliberate exercise of citizenship by a free people, appears to be enjoying a renaissance, but the hard point must be made nonetheless that tinkering with campaign-finance reform is unlikely to be sufficient to the task. True reform becomes possible only if Americans are willing to return to the root of our political experiment and try again. And if democracy is our aim, the first object of our constitutional revision must be the United States Senate.

In America today, U.S. senators from the twenty-six smallest states, representing a mere 18 percent of the nation's population, hold a majority in the United States Senate, and, therefore, under the Constitution, regardless of what the President, the House of Representatives, or even an overwhelming majority of the American people wants, nothing becomes law if those senators object. The result has been what one would expect: The less populous states have extracted benefits from the rest of the nation quite out of proportion to their populations. As Frances E. Lee and Bruce I. Oppenheimer have demonstrated in their *Sizing Up the Senate,* the citizens of less populous states receive more federal funds per capita than the citizens of the more populous states. And what happens if the larger states, with a majority of the people, object? Not much. Today, the nine largest states, containing a majority of the American people, are represented by only 18 of the 100 senators in the United States Senate.

Questions for Analysis

1. In the article entitled "What Democracy?" how does the author explain that Americans simultaneously revere and dislike democracy?

2. According to the author, what is the primary factor that shapes the political debate in this country? Explain.

3. According to the author, "strictly speaking" is the United States a democracy? Why or why not?

4. Is the current wave of political dissatisfaction in this country a new phenomenon? Explain.

5. What is the "politics of minority rule" that the author refers to in the article?

democratic process, even if they are disillusioned by how democracy works in the "real" world. This loyalty to democratic ideals probably remains intact because, over the long haul, all other forms of government are even less satisfying than democracy. Part of this may be due to the fact that, in a democracy, there is always the opportunity to change leaders at election time, even if the opportunity is not often realized. It is also probably due to the fact that, in a democracy, the people's rights are recognized as an integral part of the governmental formula, even if the exercise of those rights is often imperfectly realized. (See Bernstein, R. B. *The Constitution of the United States with the Declaration of Independence and the Articles of Confederation*. New York: Barnes and Noble, 2002, p. 9; Giddens, Anthony. *Runaway World: How Globalization Is Reshaping Our Lives*. New York: Routledge, 2000, p. 100; Weisman, Steven R. "White House Says Iraq Sovereignty Could Be Limited. *The New York Times,* April 23, 2004, p. A1; Rosenfeld, Richard N. "What Democracy: The Case for Abolishing the United States Senate." *Harpers,* May 2004, pp. 35ff.)

State Constitutions

Each state in the union adopts its own constitution. A state constitution establishes the state's government. It also sets down principles to guide the state government in making state laws and conducting state business. Most state constitutions are patterned after the U.S. Constitution. However, state constitutions tend to be longer and more detailed than the U.S. Constitution, since they must deal with local as well as statewide matters.

The Principle of Supremacy

A basic principle of constitutional law is that the U.S. Constitution is the supreme law of the land. This principle of constitutional supremacy means that all other laws must be in

Further Reading Two excellent studies of the political situation that was present in Washington before the attacks on 9-11 are *Against All Enemies: Inside America's War on Terror* by Richard A. Clarke (New York: Simon and Schuster, 2004); and *The Price of Loyalty: George W. Bush, the White House, and The Education of Paul O'Neill* by Ron Susskind (New York: Simon and Schuster, 2004). A third book, *Worse Than Watergate* by John Dean (New York: Little Brown, 2004) looks at some other problems associated with the operation of the executive branch.

U.S. Const. Article VI (see page 860)

U.S. Const. Article II Sec. 4 (see page 858)

line with constitutional principles. If a law somehow conflicts with the Constitution, that law is said to be unconstitutional. If it does not conflict, it will be upheld by the court as constitutional.

Quick Quiz 2-2 True or False?

1. The present U.S. Constitution is the only constitution that the United States has ever had.

2. The principle of separation of powers was never adopted by the Framers of the U.S. Constitution.

3. The U.S. Constitution has been amended only ten times.

2-3 Statutory Law

Laws passed by a legislature are known as **statutes.** At the federal level, statutes are the laws made by Congress and signed by the president. At the state level, statutes are enacted by state legislatures, such as the Ohio General Assembly or the Oregon Legislative Assembly. Many statutes prohibit certain activities. Most criminal statutes are prohibitive statutes. For instance, Ohio criminal law prohibits hazing, which is defined as coercing someone into doing an act of initiation that has a substantial risk of causing mental or physical harm. Other statutes demand the performance of some action. For instance, Ohio statutory law requires all motor vehicle drivers and passengers to wear safety belts. Some statutes, such as those that create governmental holidays or that name state flowers, simply declare something.

Codes and Titles

Terms The word *code* comes from the Latin *codex*, referring to the trunk of a tree. In ancient times, laws were carved into wooden tablets made from tree trunks.

Statutes must be arranged, cataloged, and indexed for easy reference. This is done by compiling state and federal codes. A **code** is a compilation of all the statutes of a particular state or of the federal government. All federal statutes, for instance, are gathered in the United States Code (USC), while all Ohio statutory law is collected in the Ohio Revised Code (ORC). In general, codes are subdivided into **titles,** which are groupings of statutes that deal with a particular area of the law. Title 17 of the Ohio Revised Code, for example, covers corporations and partnerships. Often titles are subdivided into chapters, and chapters subdivided into sections. Thus, ORC 1701.03, *Purposes of a Corporation,* can be read from right to left as the third section of the first chapter of Title 17 of the ORC.

Uniform Laws

Getting Students Involved Have students write a short paper about the advantages and disadvantages of separating federal and state statutes. Encourage students to explore topics such as the uniformity of federal law and the responsiveness of state legislation.

Because many different statues are passed each year by the fifty state legislatures, there are important differences in state statutory law. This lack of similarity can cause problems when legal matters cross state boundaries. One solution to the problem of inconsistent statutory law is for all the state legislatures to adopt the same statutes. The National Conference of Commissioners on Uniform State Laws (NCCUSL) was founded to write these uniform laws. After a proposed uniform act is written by the commissioners, it is recommended to the state legislatures for adoption. Some states may adopt it, others may not. The most significant development in uniform state legislation has been the Uniform Commercial Code. The National Conference of Commissioners on Uniform State Laws maintains a website which includes the final drafts of all uniform acts that have been approved and recommended for adoption by the state legislatures.

The Uniform Commercial Code

The **Uniform Commercial Code (UCC)** is a unified set of statutes designed to govern almost all commercial transactions. The basic principles of commercial law were not changed by the UCC provisions. By defining and clarifying often misunderstood business and legal terms, the UCC helps parties involved in commercial transactions prepare their contracts. The District of Columbia, the Virgin Islands, Puerto Rico, and all the states, except Louisiana, have adopted the UCC. Louisiana, which still uses the Napoleonic Code, has adopted only four of the nine articles. For all practical purposes, therefore, the rules governing commercial transactions are the same throughout all of the states because of the UCC.

UCC (see pages 864–926)

Cyberlaw Statutes

As we have already seen, the advent of the Information Age has sparked the need for specific cyberlaw statutes that address the problems associated with e-commerce. **E-commerce** is the term that is applied to all electronic transactions. The National Conference of Commissioners on Uniform State Laws has responded to this challenge by creating several new uniform laws. Earlier in the chapter, we explored the significance of the Uniform Computer Information Transactions Act (UCITA), which is designed to deal directly with cyberlaw contracts that involve the sale or licensing of digital information. Another uniform cyberlaw approved by the commissioners for enactment by state legislatures is the Uniform Electronic Transactions Act (UETA). This uniform cyberlaw points out those principles which should be used in every state to make certain that e-commerce contracts (e-contracts) are enforceable.

Quick Quiz 2-3 True or False?

1. Laws passed by a legislature are known as amendments.

2. There is no difference between a code and a title.

3. E-commerce is the term that is applied to all electronic transactions.

2-4 Court Decisions

When most people think of the law, they think of the Constitution or of statutes passed by Congress and the state legislatures. While these two sources are important, they are not the only two sources of law in this country. The courts also make law in the following ways:

- common law
- interpretation of statutes
- judicial review

Common Law

The term *common law* comes from the attempts of early English kings to establish a body of law that all the courts in the kingdom would hold in common. At that time, judges in the towns and villages had instructions to settle all disputes in as consistent a manner as possible. The judges maintained this consistency by relying on previous legal decisions whenever they faced a similar set of circumstances. In this way, they established a body of common law. As the process continued, judges began to record their decisions and shared them with other judges. This body of recorded decisions became known as **common law.**

Background Information One of the medieval common law's most important contributions to modern times is the concept of the supremacy of law. Under common law, no ruler or government agency had the authority to overturn the decisions of the past, thus limiting their powers. Today, economics and social justice are protected by courts that look to precedent rather than solely to statutes.

Precedents, past decisions, form the basis of common law.

The process of relying on these previous decisions is called *stare decisis* (let the decision stand). The past decisions themselves are referred to as precedents.

The legal system of the United States, except Louisiana, is rooted in the common law of England. These roots derive from the early American colonists who came from England and were governed by the English monarchy. Over time, the English common law has become eroded in the United States by the passing of state statutes and court decisions that better meet the needs of today's society. Nevertheless, parts of the common law as it was practiced in England still exist in the laws of the United States today. Courts still apply the common law when there are no modern court decisions or statutes dealing with an issue in dispute.

Today's judges make decisions in the same way as their counterparts from the Middle Ages. They rely on precedent according to the principle of *stare decisis*. A **precedent** is a model case that a court can follow when facing a similar situation. There are two types of precedent: binding and persuasive. **Binding precedent** is precedent that a court must follow. **Persuasive precedent** is precedent that a court is free to follow or to ignore. Generally, whether a precedent is binding or persuasive is determined by the court's location. For instance, decisions made by the Florida Supreme Court would be binding in all Florida state courts but persuasive in all other states' courts.

The U.S. Supreme Court in 1993 emphasized the crucial role that precedent plays in the American legal system. In emphasizing the importance of precedent, the court outlined a series of questions that judges should ask as they contemplate whether or not to overturn a rule of law established in an earlier case. These questions include the following:

- Is the established rule still practical?
- Have so many people relied upon the rule that overturning it would cause difficulty and injustice?
- Is the rule still legally viable, or has it become merely a relic of an outdated and deserted legal doctrine?
- Is the rule still up to date, or has it become obsolete because of changes in society?

Only if judges can answer these questions satisfactorily should they consider overturning an established precedent.

Statutory Interpretation

A second way that court decisions make law is in the interpretation of statutes. When legislators enact a new statute, they cannot predict how people will react to the new law. Nor can they foresee all of its future ramifications and implications. Thus, when two or more parties have a dispute that challenges the statute, they may differ as to what the legislature had in mind when it wrote the statute. Also, legislators may have purposely made the language of a statute general. The job of reacting to unforeseen circumstances and making generalities fit specific circumstances falls to the courts. As a result, a judge may be called upon to determine how a certain statute should be interpreted.

Courts are not, however, free to interpret a statute at random. A court cannot interpret a statute unless it is faced with a case involving that statute. In interpreting a statute, a court looks to a variety of sources, including the legislative history of the statute and the old statute that the new statute replaced, if any. Naturally, the court also must review any binding precedent that interprets that statute. This is because the court must still rely upon previous cases when engaged in statutory interpretation, just as it does when deciding questions of common law.

Judicial Review

A third way that courts make law is through judicial review. **Judicial review** is the process of determining the constitutionality of various legislative statutes, administrative regulations, or executive actions. In exercising the power of judicial review, a court will look at the statute, regulation, or action and will compare it with the Constitution. If the two are compatible, no problem exists. However, if they are contradictory, one of the two must be declared void. Since the Constitution is the supreme law of the land, the Constitution always rules, and the statute, regulation, or action is ruled unconstitutional.

Naturally, in exercising the power of judicial review, the court also must review any binding precedent involved in the constitutional issue. This is because the court still must rely upon previous cases in judicial review, just as it does in common law and statutory interpretation. The lower courts in this country have the capacity to review issues of constitutionality and to interpret the meaning of provisions within the U.S. Constitution. However, the ultimate authority and, therefore, the final word on such issues rests with the United States Supreme Court.

Cross-Cultural Notes

Sweden was the first country to establish the office of *ombudsman,* a nonpartisan agency appointed by the *Rikstag* (parliament) that protects people from illegal or incompetent abuses of power by government officials and agencies. The office of ombudsman initiates its own investigation and responds to citizens' complaints. It ordinarily resolves problems through a combination of persuasion and publicity; however, it sometimes uses its authority to press charges.

Quick Quiz 2-4 True or False?

1. The process of relying on previous decisions is called *stare decisis.*

2. Common law originated in France.

3. Judicial review is another name for statutory interpretation.

Business Law in the News

House Sets Up Quick Elections If Its Members Die in Attack

Fearing that a terrorist attack on the Capitol could decimate the legislative branch, the House overwhelmingly approved a measure on Thursday that would provide for quick special elections if 100 or more of its members were killed.

The bill, which would allow for elections 45 days after a catastrophe, went to the Senate after it passed by a vote of 306 to 97. But its Republican sponsors refused to take up the politically thorny question of whether the Constitution should be amended to allow for temporary appointments to the House until special elections could be arranged.

"James Madison used the strongest of terms when stating the House must be composed only of those elected by the people," said Representative F. James Sensenbrenner Jr., the Judiciary Committee chairman and chief sponsor of the bill.

Mr. Sensenbrenner, a Wisconsin Republican, said amending the Constitution would "accomplish what no terrorist could, namely striking a fatal blow to what has otherwise always been 'the People's House.'"

Last June, an independent commission studying the so-called continuity of government issue recommended the constitutional amendments. Advocates

(Continued)

Business Law in the News (Continued)

say that without temporary appointments, scores of House seats could be left vacant in the aftermath of a terrorist attack, at precisely the time the nation needed its legislators most.

The fate of the bill in the Senate is unclear. Senator John Cornyn, Republican of Texas and a member of the Senate Judiciary Committee, said Thursday that he believed the Senate should defer to the House on the issue.

"If House members decide to rely solely on special elections to cure continuity problems in their chamber, I will not stand in their way." Mr. Cornyn said.

But he also said that legal experts in the field of continuity agreed that a constitutional amendment might be necessary.

Mr. Sensenbrenner said his committee would vote on the amendment issue in the near future. But Democrats, including Representative Nancy Pelosi of California, the House Democratic leader, said that by not allowing a vote on Thursday, Republicans were engaging in partisanship.

"I have been involved in politics my whole life," Mrs. Pelosi said, "and I cannot see where there is one grain of partisanship in continuity of government."

Thursday's vote came two and a half years after the Sept. 11, 2001, terrorist attacks, which were very much on lawmakers' minds during the debate. Many believe that one of the four hijacked flights, United Airlines Flight 93, which crashed in rural Pennsylvania, was headed for the Capitol.

With the terrorist attacks preceding the recent national elections in Spain and recent warnings by Condoleezza Rice, President Bush's national security adviser, that a similar attack could occur in the United States before the November elections, lawmakers said they felt compelled to act.

The measure would allow for special elections in "extraordinary circumstances," which the bill defines as occurring when the speaker of the House announces that there are more than 100 vacancies. Within 10 days of the announcement, the political parties of states with vacancies would be permitted to nominate candidates to run in a special election within 45 days.

Questions for Analysis

1. The article entitled "House Sets Up Quick Elections" reports on a measure taken by the House of Representatives to hold emergency elections within 45 days to fill vacancies in the House, should a national disaster occur. Is that measure an amendment, a statute, or a common law principle? Explain.

2. Why is the issue of a Constitutional amendment raised in this article? Explain.

3. Do you agree that a Constitutional Amendment would be required in this situation? Why or why not?

4. If a statute were passed providing for the appointment of interim representatives, and the statute was challenged in court, who would render the final decision on whether such a statute is constitutional? Explain.

5. What is the designation given to the process of reviewing the constitutionality of such a statute?

Source: Sheryl Gay. "House Sets Up Quick Elections If Its Members Die in Attack," *The New York Times,* April 23, 2004, p. A-14. Copyright © 2004. The New York Times Co. Reprinted with permission.

2-5 Administrative Regulations

Neither legislators nor judges can administer to all aspects of today's society. Moreover, legislators are generalists; they are rarely experts in all areas over which they have power. Since legislators are generalists, and since today's problems are so complex, statutory law, created by legislators, is very limited in what it can do. To broaden the power of statutory law, legislators delegate their power to others. They do this when they create administrative agencies.

Administrative Agencies

Federal administrative agencies administer statutes enacted by Congress in specific areas, such as communication, aviation, labor relations, working conditions, and so on. Similarly, agencies have been designated by the states to supervise intrastate activities. These agencies create rules, regulate and supervise, and render decisions that have the force of law. Their decrees and decisions are known as **administrative law.**

Administrative Procedures Act

Problems sometimes occur because administrative agencies have the power to make the rules, enforce the rules, and interpret the rules. To help prevent any conflict of interest that could arise from these overlapping responsibilities, Congress passed the federal Administrative Procedures Act. Similarly, most states have adopted a uniform law known as the Model State Administrative Procedures Act. Under these two acts, an administrative agency planning new regulations must notify the affected parties and hold hearings to allow those parties to express their views. These acts also allow the courts to review agency decisions and rulings.

State Variations States that have legalized gambling, such as Illinois, Iowa, Mississippi, Nevada, New Jersey, New Mexico, and South Dakota, regulate the industry with gaming commissions. These commissions are administrative agencies and, as such, are not constrained by the Constitution in regard to search and seizure questions.

Quick Quiz 2-5 True or False?

1. Together, legislators and judges can administer all aspects of today's society.

2. Most legislators are specialists.

3. The decrees and decisions made by administrative agencies are known as administrative law.

Summary

2-1 The law consists of rules of conduct established by the government to maintain harmony, stability, and justice within a society. Ideally, the primary objectives of the law are to promote harmony, stability, and justice. In everyday life the balance is not easy to maintain. The law, or more properly, the entire legal framework, is a complex adaptive system exhibiting each of the six attributes of such systems. First, the law functions as a complex adaptive system because of the interaction of a variety of agents within the legal system; second, as in all complex adaptive systems, in the law there is no central controlling agent; third, the law is an intricate network of interactive organizational levels, each of which depends on the others for the smooth operation of the entire network; fourth, the more proficient the law becomes, the more easily it adapts to changing social, political, and economic influences; fifth, the law often infers the direction of future events and adapts to those events; and sixth, the legal system includes embedded niches each of which is populated by experts upon whom others, outside those niches, depend and who, in turn, depend on others for knowledge and guidance outside of their own embedded niche.

2-2 A constitution is the basic law of a nation or state. The United States Constitution provides the organization of the national government. Each state also has a constitution that determines the state's governmental structure. The body of law that forms a constitution and its interpretation is known as constitutional law.

2-3 The laws passed by a legislature are known as statutes. At the federal level, these are the laws made by Congress and signed by the President. At the state level, statutes are enacted by state legislatures. Statutes must be arranged, cataloged, and indexed for easy reference. This is done by compiling state and federal codes. A code is a compilation of all the statutes of a particular state or of the federal government. Generally, codes are subdivided into titles, which are groupings of statutes that deal with a particular area of the law. Because many different statutes are passed each year by the fifty state legislatures, there are important differences in state statutory law throughout the nation. One solution to the problem of inconsistent statutory law is for the legislatures of all the states to adopt the same statutes. The National Conference of Commissioners on Uniform State Laws (NCCUSL) was founded to write these uniform laws. The Uniform Commercial Code (UCC) is a unified set of statutes designed to govern almost all commercial transactions. The Uniform Computer Information Transactions Act and the Uniform Electronic Transactions Act are two cyberlaw statutes recently approved by the commissioners for adoption by state legislatures.

2-4 Courts make law through common law, the interpretation of statutes, and judicial review.

2-5 Federal administrative agencies administer statutes enacted by Congress in specific areas, such as commerce, communication, aviation, labor relations, and working conditions. Similar agencies have been designated by the states to supervise intrastate activities. These agencies create rules, regulate and supervise, and render decisions. To help prevent any conflict of interest that could arise from these overlapping responsibilities, Congress passed the federal Administrative Procedures Act. Similarly, most states have adopted a uniform law known as the Model State Administrative Procedures Act. Under these two acts, an administrative agency planning new regulations must notify the affected parties and hold hearings at which those parties can express their opinions.

Key Terms

administrative law, 41
Articles of Confederation, 30
binding precedent, 38
code, 36
common law, 37
complex adaptive system, 25
constitution, 30
constitutional law, 30
cybercontracts, 28

cyberlaw, 28
digital information contracts, 28
e-commerce, 37
embedded niches, 26
judicial review, 39
law, 25
license agreement, 29
persuasive precedent, 38
precedent, 38

software contracts, 28
statutes, 36
titles, 36
Uniform Commercial Code (UCC), 37
Uniform Computer Information Transactions Act (UCITA), 28

Questions for Review and Discussion

1. What are the objectives of the law?
2. How is the law a complex adaptive system?
3. What are the functions of the articles and the amendments of the U.S. Constitution?
4. What is the role of statutory law in the legal system?
5. Why does this country need to set up a system of uniform state laws?
6. What are two of the most recent cyberlaw statutes added to the legal system?
7. What is the role of common law in the legal system?
8. How does the principle of *stare decisis* provide stability to our legal system?
9. What is the difference between statutory interpretation and judicial review?
10. Why does the legislature need to establish administrative regulations?

Investigating the Internet

Access the U.S. Historical Documents Archive on the Internet and write a research paper about one of the major U.S. historical documents listed there. As an alternative assignment, trace the evolution of American political thought as represented in these major documents.

Cases for Analysis

1. Two instructors in the Maine-Endwell Central School District requested a day of paid leave to observe a religious holy day. Under the terms of their contract, they were entitled to three days of leave for religious reasons. Despite this, the school board charged the instructors' time off against their personal days. The Maine-Endwell Teachers' Association brought suit on behalf of the instructors. At trial, the judge ruled in favor of the school board. The judge explained that the contract ran afoul of the First Amendment since that amendment specifically prevents the establishment of a government-approved religion. The First Amendment reads, in part, "Congress shall make no law respecting an establishment of religion, or prohibiting the free exercise thereof." The amendment, therefore, applies to the federal government. If this is true, how can the school board make its case since it is an arm of the state government? Explain. *Maine-Endwell Teachers Association. v. Board of Education,* No. 93831 (NY App. Div., 3d Dept.). (*See* Caher, John. "Panel Upholds Religious Leave." *National Law Journal,* January 26, 2004, p. 4.)

2. Members of the Ku Klux Klan asked for permission to hold a rally in New York outside the county courthouse. The government granted permission, but refused to permit the demonstrators to wear masks. The Klan members brought suit in the United States District Court arguing that the antimask statute violated the free speech provision of the First Amendment of the United States Constitution. The District Court judge agreed and struck down the mask prohibition as unconstitutional. The city appealed the decision. The appeals court overturned the district court's ruling, stating that sometimes one of the purposes of the law must be sacrificed to preserve another purpose.

Explain the balancing act that the court is engaged in here. *Church of the American Knights of the Ku Klux Klan v. Kerik* No. 02-9418. (2d U.S. Cir. Ct. of App.). (See Hamblett, Mark. "2d Circuit Upholds State Mask Ban." *National Law Journal,* January 26, 2004, p. 14.)

3. Chadha, an immigrant who had resided in the United States for more than seven years, was called before an immigration judge for a deportation hearing. The judge elected not to deport Chadha. When the action was brought to the House of Representatives by the Attorney General, the House elected to exercise its legislative veto and ordered Chadha deported. Chadha brought a lawsuit to escape deportation. He argued that the legislative veto was unconstitutional because it violated the separation of powers contemplated by the Framers in the writing of the Constitution. Specifically, Chadha argued the legislative veto allowed a single House of Congress to undo a provision of a law that had been voted upon by both Houses of Congress and which had been signed by the President. According to Chadha, in exercising the legislative veto, the House of Representatives was unilaterally amending a statute without the participation of either the Senate or the President, as required by the Constitution. Is Chadha correct in his argument? Does the fact that the Senate did not have to participate in the legislative veto violate the separation of powers principle? Does the fact that the President did not have to participate in the legislative veto violate the separation of powers principle? Explain each of your answers. *Immigration and Naturalization Service v. Chadha,* 462 U.S. 919 (U.S. Sup. Ct.).

4. Joe Hogan wished to enter the Mississippi University for Women, a school of nursing which

had, up to that point in time at least, restricted its enrollment to female students. Hogan, who was academically acceptable for admission to the university, was denied entry solely on the basis of his gender. While university officials offered to allow Hogan to audit courses, they would not permit him to earn credit for any of those courses. Hogan brought a lawsuit in federal district court. The district court supported the university, but the appeals court overturned that decision. The university elected to take the case to the United States Supreme Court. Read through the amendments to the Constitution and see if you can determine any rights that would be violated by the Mississippi University for Women's refusal to admit Hogan to its school of nursing. *Mississippi University for Women v. Hogan,* 458 U.S. 718 (U.S. Sup. Ct.).

5. Barbara Rome entered Flower Memorial Hospital in order to undergo a series of X rays. When she was ready for the X rays, she was assisted by a student radiological intern. The intern placed Rome on the X-ray table and strapped her onto the table correctly. However, the intern did not properly fasten the footboard which was located at the foot of the table. As a result of this error, Rome fell and was hurt when the table was raised. As a consequence, Rome brought a lawsuit against Flower Memorial Hospital alleging that the ordinary negligence of the intern had caused her injury. In contrast, the hospital argued that the lawsuit involved a medical claim as defined under the state's medical malpractice statute. Whether a case involves ordinary negli-

gence or a medical claim would determine whether the state's two-year statute of limitations for negligence or the state's one-year statute of limitations for medical claims would apply. This case clearly involves a difference of opinion on the interpretation of a statute. What sources might the court consider when interpreting the statute in question? *Rome v. Flower Memorial Hospital,* 635 N.E.2d 1239 (OH).

6. The Heart of Atlanta Hotel brought an action against the United States seeking a judgment that would declare Title II of the Civil Rights Act of 1964 unconstitutional. Congress's power to enact the Civil Rights Act is based upon Article I, Section 8, Clause 3, which gives Congress the power to regulate commerce among the states. The Heart of Atlanta Hotel argued that the statute was an unconstitutional extension of Congressional power. The motel also contended that the unconstitutional nature of the act especially applied to establishments like itself, which are incorporated and do business in only one state. On the other hand, since at any given time, three-fourths of the hotel's registered guests came from other states, the hotel clearly had an impact on interstate commerce. Do the lower federal courts have the authority to determine the constitutionality of Title II of the Civil Rights Act? What court has the ultimate authority to determine the constitutionality of the Civil Rights Act? Speculate on the outcome of this case. Do you think that the court should uphold the act? Explain. *Heart of Atlanta Hotel v. United States,* 370 U.S. 241 (U.S. Sup. Ct.).

Quick Quiz Answers

2-1	2-2	2-3	2-4	2-5
1. T	1. F	1. F	1. T	1. F
2. T	2. F	2. F	2. F	2. F
3. T	3. F	3. T	3. F	3. T

Chapter 3

The Judicial Process

The Opening Case
"Duck Hunting for Federal Jurisdiction"

When Vice President Richard Cheney convened a policy group to explore issues related to federal energy standards, he had no idea that he was about to ignite a firestorm, not over the policies themselves, but over the process used to develop those policies. Critics of the procedure charged that Cheney's energy advisory group was packed with friendly political contributors and biased energy industry representatives, many of whom were eager to push for federal funds to support their own agendas. Two vocal critics, the Sierra Club, a liberal organization, and Judicial Watch, a conservative group, joined forces in a rare show of cooperation, to file a lawsuit in federal court. The plaintiffs in the case filed under the Federal Advisory Committee Act, a congressional statute that mandates the public release of records from any commission that includes nonfederal employees in its membership. The vice president's attorneys argued that those advisers that concerned the plaintiffs were not official members of the group. Therefore, they concluded that the law did not apply them. The plaintiffs countered that the nonofficial status of the members made no difference under the law. The trial court agreed with the plaintiffs as did the court of appeals. The vice president's attorneys pressed for a hearing in the United States Supreme Court. Is this the type of case that should go to the Supreme Court? Why or why not? Under what grounds did the case get into federal court in the first place? Explain. An additional controversy arose when Justice Antonin Scalia did not recuse himself from the case, despite the fact that, while the lawsuit was pending, he had joined the vice president on a duck-hunting trip. Should Justice Scalia have refused to sit on the panel when it heard the case? Explain.

Chapter Outcomes

1. Distinguish between original jurisdiction and appellate jurisdiction and between general jurisdiction and special jurisdiction.
2. Outline the structure of the federal court system, and judge under what circumstances the federal court has jurisdiction to hear a case.
3. Recognize those cases which may be heard by the U.S. Supreme Court.
4. Determine the extent of cyberspace jurisdiction.
5. Identify the typical structure found in most state court systems.
6. Describe the civil litigation process.

7. Define discovery and explain the most commonly used discovery techniques.
8. Explain the nature of cyberspace discovery.
9. Detail the nature of an appeal.
10. Describe the steps in a criminal prosecution.

3-1   The Court System

The laws of our government are interpreted and enforced by a system of courts authorized by either the federal or a state constitution and established by legislative authority. **Courts** are judicial tribunals that meet in a regular place and apply the laws in an attempt to settle disputes fairly. Each of these official bodies is a forum for the party who presents a complaint, the party who answers the complaint, and the jury and/or judge who settles the dispute. As noted in the last chapter, the courts are an integral part of a complex adaptive system that is the law. As is true of all complex adaptive systems, the law is an intricate network of interactive organizational levels, each of which depends on the others for the smooth operation of the entire network. The courts make up one of these key organizational levels. Thus, within in the law, the executive branch (the President or the governor, and his or her executive assistants), the legislature (Congress or the various state assemblies), and the bureaucracy (those agencies that are charged with doing the "grunt work" of the law) depend on the courts to interpret the law, and to ensure that the law is carried out according to legislative and executive intent.

Also, as in all complex adaptive systems, the more experienced the law becomes, the more readily it adjusts to a shifting social and economic climate. This "adaptive" attribute of the law is seen in the court's willingness to interpret statutory law, to uphold the Constitution, and to address tough contemporary issues by hearing controversial cases. It can also be seen when the United States Supreme Court decides to tackle landmark cases like *Planned Parenthood v. Casey,* which is highlighted at the end of Part I in this text. As we shall see in *Planned Parenthood v. Casey,* the courts can generally be seen as the most stable of the embedded niches within the complex legal system, because the courts can be depended upon to consistently follow their own past decisions.

> *Integrity is the key to understanding legal practice. . . . Law's empire is defined by attitude, not territory or power process.*
>
> —Ronald D. Dworkin, professor of law, New York University

The Federal Court System

The federal court system is authorized by Article III of the U.S. Constitution, which states, "The Judicial Power of the United States, shall be vested in one supreme court, and in such inferior courts as Congress may from time to time ordain and establish." The present federal court system includes the Supreme Court, the courts of appeals, and the federal district courts.

U.S. Const. Article III (see page 859)

Court Jurisdiction

The authority of a court to hear and decide cases is called the court's **jurisdiction.** It is set by law and is limited as to territory and type of case. A court of **original jurisdiction** has the authority to hear a case when it is first brought to court. Courts having the power to review a case for errors of law are courts of **appellate jurisdiction.** Courts having the power to hear any type of case are said to exercise **general jurisdiction.** Those with the power to hear only certain types of cases have **special jurisdiction.** Examples of courts with special jurisdiction are probate courts and courts of claims. Courts also exercise subject matter jurisdiction and personal jurisdiction. **Subject matter jurisdiction** is the court's power to hear a particular type of case. **Personal jurisdiction** is the court's authority over the parties to a lawsuit.

Federal District Courts   Each state and territory in the United States has at least one federal district court. These courts are also known as *U.S. district courts.* The district courts are the courts of general jurisdiction in the federal system. Most federal cases begin

Teaching Tips   Discuss the pros and cons of electing and appointing judges.

The Opening Case Revisited
"Duck Hunting for Federal Jurisdiction"

When the Sierra Club and Judicial Watch decided to bring a lawsuit against Vice President Richard Cheney in federal courts, they had to first establish that the court had subject matter jurisdiction over the case. In this situation, the plaintiffs argued that the United States District Court in Washington, D.C., had subject matter jurisdiction over the case, based on the existence of a federal question. There are, in fact, two ways to approach the court's jurisdiction in this case. If, in fact, a federal statute is involved, then subject matter jurisdiction is established on that basis alone. The members of the vice president's legal team based their primary argument on this point, claiming that the statute itself did not permit the disclosure of the names of the nonfederal employees. However, it might also be argued that a constitutional issue exists because the vice president claimed that his right to executive privilege outweighed the legislative desire for the disclosure of his records. The vice president's legal team based their alternative argument on the separation of powers principle which underwrites the partition of the executive branch from the legislative branch. The legal team urged the Supreme Court to recognize a "zone of autonomy" that evolves from the Constitution's separation of powers principle and that permits the President to seek input from outside sources when he develops his legislative agenda. Some legal scholars argued that the vice president's claim in this case to complete executive privilege and to this "zone of autonomy" amounts to arguing that the vice president, and therefore by implication, the President, stand above the law. These scholars saw the Federal Advisory Committee Act as an expression of the checks and balances principle that sanctions the "watchdog" power that each branch holds over the other two. (See Greenhouse, Linda. "Administration Says a 'Zone of Autonomy' Justifies Its Secrecy on Energy Task Force." *The New York Times,* April 24, 2004, p. A14; Greenhouse, Linda. "Justices Hear Argument in Energy Task Force Case." *The New York Times,* April 28, 2004, p. A12; Krugman, Paul. "A Vision of Power." *The New York Times,* April 27, 2004, p. A25.)

Background Information Diversity jurisdiction allowing suits between citizens of different states was once regarded as highly necessary, for fear that the courts of a state would heavily favor its own citizens. Today's mobility and the national scope of business affairs seem to make this an anachronism. With federal courts busy implementing broad social policy and a reluctance to expand the federal courts, there is some support for eliminating this type of diversity jurisdiction, thereby forcing such cases back into state courts.

in the federal district court. Not all cases belong there, however. The federal courts have subject matter jurisdiction over two types of cases: those involving federal law and those involving diversity.

Federal district courts have subject matter jurisdiction over cases that concern a federal question. A **federal question** could involve the U.S. Constitution, a federal statute or statutes, or a treaty. A state law issue can be included in a suit involving a federal question if the state claim is part of the same situation that created the federal question. If the federal claim is thrown out by the federal court, the state law issue usually cannot stand by itself. The people bringing the lawsuit would have to take their case to a state court.

Subject matter jurisdiction in federal court also arises in cases of diversity, even when no federal law is involved. **Diversity cases** include lawsuits that are (1) between citizens of different states, (2) between citizens of a state or different states and citizens of a foreign nation, and (3) between citizens of a state and a foreign government as the plaintiff. For legal purposes, corporations are considered citizens of the state in which they are incorporated and the state where they have their principal place of business. Diversity cases must involve an amount over $75,000. Establishing subject matter jurisdiction may not be enough to get a case into federal court if the federal court does not have personal jurisdiction over a party.

Example 3-1

Friedman Construction Inc., which is incorporated in Delaware and headquartered in Pittsburgh, contracted to refit every school building in the Somerset, Ohio, school system with asbestos-free ceiling tiles. The job took two years and cost the school system approximately $2.5 million. Later, school officials discovered that three of the buildings had been refitted with tiles that actually contained more asbestos than the tiles that had been removed. It cost the school system $770,000 to have those three buildings refitted a second time by another company. The Somerset School System decided to sue Friedman in the federal district court in Cleveland for damages in the amount of $770,000. Because of diversity, subject matter jurisdiction exists. The fact that Friedman Construction transacted business in Ohio meant that an Ohio state court could exercise personal jurisdiction over that out-of-state corporation. The federal court must use the state long-arm statute, because there is no federal long-arm statute.

About the Law

In federal court, if even one defendant is a citizen of the same state as one of the plaintiffs, diversity cannot be established. In such a case, the law says that "diversity is not complete."

To answer the question posed in Example 3-1, the court must look at the Ohio state long-arm statute. A long-arm statute lists circumstances under which a court can exercise personal jurisdiction over an out-of-state defendant. Typically, these circumstances include the following:

- owning real property in the state
- soliciting business in the state
- having an office or a store in the state
- committing a tort within the state
- transacting business in the state

Some of the circumstances listed in the long-arm statute are relatively clear. Committing a tort in a state, for instance, leaves little room for misunderstanding. Other circumstances, however, such as "transacting business in the state" are not as precise. This is why personal jurisdiction under a state long-arm statute also requires meeting the required minimum contacts with the state. The concept of **minimum contacts** identifies the fewest number of contacts needed to allow the court to exercise jurisdiction over the out-of-state defendant. For example, let's say that a state allows the court to establish personal jurisdiction over any person who transacts business in the state. Now, suppose a person buys a newspaper at an airport during a layover in the state. Does the purchase of that single newspaper constitute "transacting business" in the state? The question turns on whether the purchase establishes a minimum contact with the state. In this case, the answer is probably no. In general, the courts exclude contacts that are passive or that do not rise to a level that would permit the person transacting the business to reasonably foresee that he or she would come under the court's jurisdiction as a result of that transaction. It is difficult to conclude that the casual purchase of a newspaper at an airport kiosk would lead a person to foresee that he or she has voluntarily submitted to the jurisdictional power of a state. Something more would have to be involved. For instance, if the person in question specifically targeted the airport layover time to conduct negotiations with a client, and if a contract resulted from those negotiations, then the minimum contacts requirement would have been met and jurisdiction established.

Teaching Tips   Ask students to pay attention to media coverage of various trial proceedings. Take a few minutes each class period to share cases being heard.

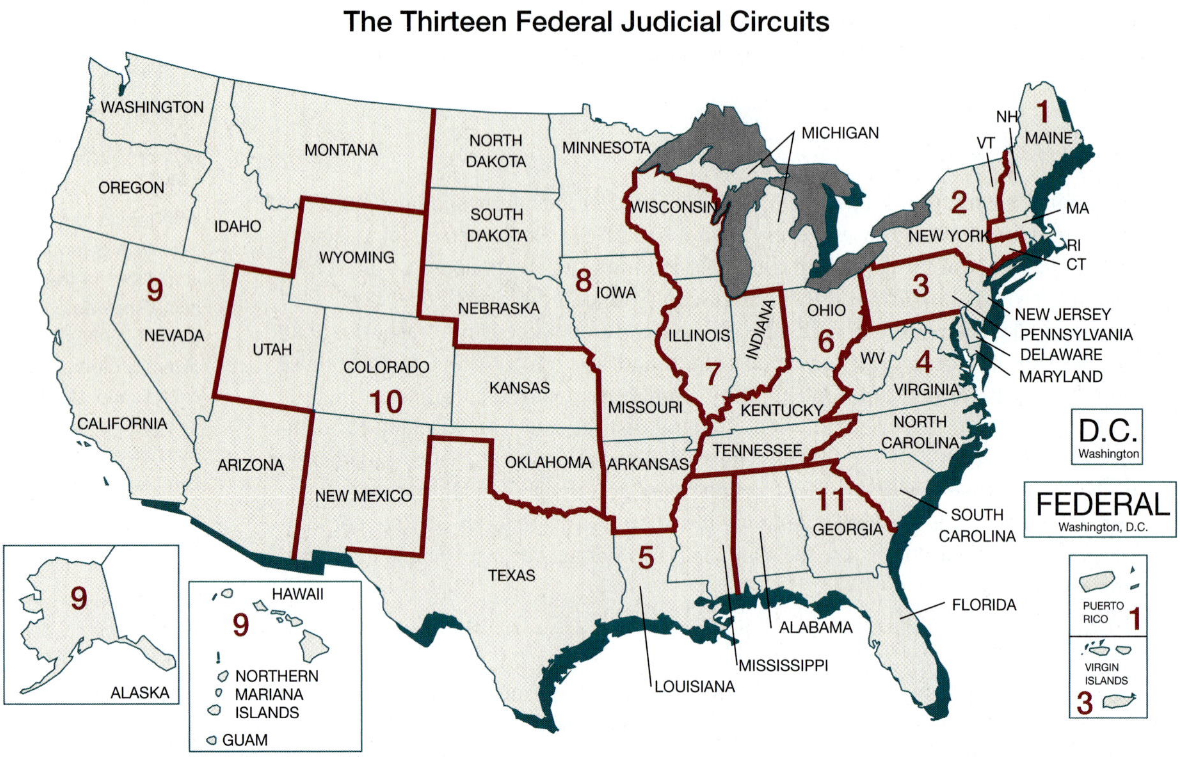

The Thirteen Federal Judicial Circuits

Figure 3-1 The U.S. federal court system is divided into thirteen circuits, including the Washington, D.C., and federal circuits. Each circuit has several district courts.

U.S. Courts of Appeals At present, there are thirteen U.S. courts of appeals within the federal court system (see Figure 3-1). Eleven of these appellate courts cover geographical groupings of states. For example, the Sixth Circuit Court of Appeals includes Michigan, Ohio, Kentucky, and Tennessee. The Fifth Circuit includes Texas, Louisiana, and Mississippi. There is also a special appellate court for the District of Columbia called the U.S. Court of Appeals for the District of Columbia.

In addition to these twelve appellate courts, organized on a geographical basis, there is a thirteenth appellate court that has special jurisdiction over certain types of cases. This court is known as the U.S. Court of Appeals for the Federal Circuit. This court hears cases appealed from the Court of International Trade, the U.S. Claims Court, and the U.S. Patent and Trademark Office, among others. This court can also hear certain types of appeals from the district courts.

U.S. Const. Article III
(see page 859)

The United States Supreme Court Established by the Constitution, the U.S. Supreme Court is the court of final jurisdiction in all cases appealed from the lower federal courts and in cases coming from state supreme courts. It has original jurisdiction in cases affecting ambassadors or other public ministers and consuls, and in cases in which a state is a party. The Supreme Court is composed of a chief justice and eight associate justices. They are appointed by the President with the consent of the Senate and hold office during good behavior.

In many situations, a case will reach the U.S. Supreme Court only if the court agrees to issue a writ of certiorari. A **writ of certiorari** is an order from the Supreme Court to a lower court to deliver its records to the U.S. Supreme Court for review. The Court will issue

Terms *Certiorari* is Latin for "to be informed of."

Business Law in the News
And Justice For All?

Windridge Pig Farm is based in New South Wales, Australia. The headquarters of F. Hoffmann-La Roche Ltd. is in Basel, Switzerland. So when Windridge and 11 other foreign companies filed a class action against Hoffmann-La Roche and more than three dozen overseas manufacturers of livestock vitamins for price-fixing in 2000, where was the case filed? In Washington, D.C.

As globalism becomes a fact of life, U.S. courts fast are becoming the forum of choice for victims abroad. Product-liability suits, civil antitrust claims, and human rights cases filed by overseas plaintiffs and based on alleged misdeeds that occurred outside of the U.S. all appear to be on the rise. Mexicans and Venezuelans, for example, have filed hundreds of lawsuits in the U.S. against Bridgestone/Firestone involving tires made, sold, and used in those countries. Although precise numbers are hard to come by, there are fears that the wave of foreign litigation could overburden American courts and expose companies to wider liability. "If anybody can sue in the U.S., it's a step in the direction of the U.S. becoming a world court," says former Federal Trade Commission Chairman Robert Pitofsky, a member of Hoffmann-La Roche's legal team.

But consumer activists, human-rights groups, and some businesspeople praise the development. Compared with their foreign counterparts, U.S. courts are transparent, efficient, and effective. They are the only available venues for certain types of consumer protection and corporate malfeasance claims. "The real question is how do we make multinational companies accountable for their actions," says former World Bank chief economist Joseph E. Stiglitz, who has filed an animus brief against Hoffmann-La Roche.

Cartel Profits

Now the U.S. Supreme Court is weighing in on the debate. On Apr. 27, the high court will hear arguments about whether the vitamin price-fixing lawsuit, *F. Hoffmann-La Roche Ltd. v. Empagran,* should proceed before an American judge. It is one of a trio of cases this term focusing on the issue of how far domestic courts should wade into international disputes. The U.S. Chamber of Commerce, which has filed briefs in all three, is asking the court to sharply curtail access to the American legal system.

In the livestock vitamin price-fixing case, Windridge and its supporters argue that the U.S. legal system is the only one in the world with sufficiently robust antitrust laws to deter global price-fixing.

Questions for Analysis

1. How can subject matter jurisdiction be established in a U.S. District Court in Washington, D.C., if both the plaintiff, Windridge, and the defendant, Hoffmann-La Roche, are based in foreign countries? Explain.

2. What are the advantages of permitting foreign plaintiffs to file claims within the federal court system? Explain.

3. What is the downside of permitting, or even encouraging, foreign plaintiffs to file claims within the federal court system? Explain.

4. Why would it be appropriate for the United States Supreme Court to hear the case of *F. Hoffmann-La Roche, Ltd. v. Empagran?* Explain.

5. What are the requirements of the type of class action lawsuit filed in *F. Hoffmann-La Roche, Ltd. v. Empagran?* Explain.

Author's Note: The U.S. Supreme Court ultimately decided that the federal court did not have jurisdiction in this case because the claim was based solely on the foreign effect of the alleged antitrust violation rather than on any effect within the United States.
Source: BusinessWeek, May 3, 2004, p. 76.

Background Information *Wisconsin v. Yoder* reinforced a standard for judging state statutes that impact upon the free exercise of religion. That standard requires states to show a "compelling interest" in any law that impacts upon religion. A "compelling interest" might be the preservation of human life or the protection of national security. A failure by the state to show such a compelling interest would render the statute unconstitutional. However, in 1990, the Supreme Court, in *Employment Division, Department of Human Resources of Oregon v. Smith,* altered the standard, stating that states would no longer be required to show a compelling interest in order to defend a statute that places an indirect burden upon religion. Many people objected to this change, so in 1993 Congress passed the Religious Freedom Restoration Act, which reinstated the compelling state interest standard.

Getting Students Involved Have students write research papers on one of the members of the current U.S. Supreme Court. Students should research the justice's career and the specifics of his or her appointment, including the President who selected the appointee, other potential choices at the time, and major issues or controversies surrounding the appointment.

Background Information When the Supreme Court was established, it was unclear whether it would have the power to declare laws unconstitutional. It wasn't until Chief Justice John Marshall asserted his authority that the court assumed this role. During Marshall's tenure (1801–1835), the Court overturned more than a dozen state statutes.

a writ of certiorari if several lower courts have dealt with an issue, but cannot agree on how it should be handled. If the case involves an issue that affects a large segment of society, the Court is likely to grant a writ. Finally, the Court may also hear a case if it involves a constitutional issue.

Applicable Law When a federal court hears a case involving only federal law or the U.S. Constitution, it must follow that federal law, the Constitution, and/or any line of federal precedent that can be used to interpret the situation. Circumstances are different in diversity cases or in federal law cases that also concern issues of state law. For instance, if a federal judge in Minnesota hears a diversity case between a Minnesota citizen and an Iowa citizen, would that judge use federal law, Minnesota law, or Iowa law? As a general rule, a federal court hearing a diversity case will apply the law of the state in which it is physically located.

Example 3-2

While walking on a railroad track in Pennsylvania, Tompkins was injured when he was struck by an open door protruding from one of the passing freight trains. The federal court had diversity jurisdiction because Tompkins was a citizen of Pennsylvania and the railroad company was formed in New York. Under Pennsylvania common law, Tompkins would have been considered a trespasser and would, therefore, lose the case. Tompkins, therefore, urged the court to ignore Pennsylvania law and apply what he called "general law." General law, according to Tompkins's attorneys, included principles of law that are of a universal nature and are thus not tied to any one state. The trial court and the appellate court agreed with Tompkins. The U.S. Supreme Court did not. The Court held that attempts to enforce this unwritten "general law" were confusing and inconsistent. The Court concluded that federal courts in diversity cases must use state substantive law.

State Court Systems

The courts of each state are organized according to the provisions of the state constitution. Despite differences from state to state, such as the names for similar types of courts, there are basic similarities. For example, each state has an arrangement of inferior, or lower-level courts that serve as limited jurisdiction trial courts. Higher-level trial courts with broader jurisdiction are also provided. In addition, each state has appellate courts to which questions of law (not questions of fact) may be appealed. Figure 3-2 provides a general outline of the federal and the state court systems.

State Trial Courts The state trial courts, also known as general jurisdiction courts, have the power to hear any type of case. They are often called superior courts, circuit courts, or courts of common pleas. Some states, notably New York, refer to them as supreme courts. These courts are usually organized around the counties of the state, so that each county has its own trial court of general jurisdiction. Most states also have other trial courts that are lower than the general jurisdiction courts. These limited jurisdiction courts usually hear only certain types of cases. For instance, a municipal court may be empowered to hear only those cases that involve municipal ordinances, criminal cases involving crimes within the city limits, and other cases that involve monetary claims of less than $10,000. Many localities have small-claims courts that hear civil cases involving small dollar amounts, ranging from $500 to $5,000, depending on state law.

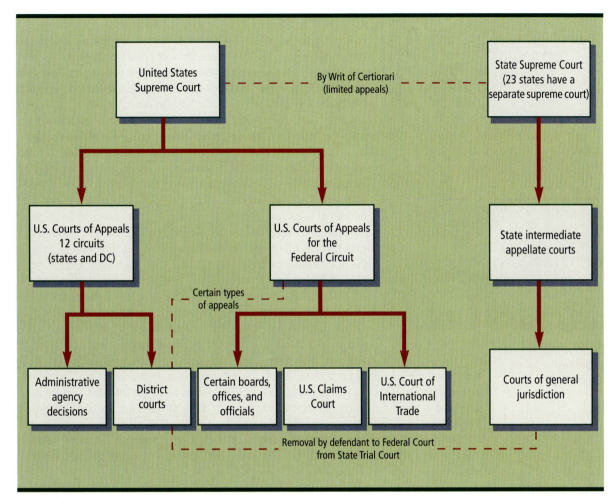

Figure 3-2 Federal and state court systems.

State Intermediate Appellate Courts State court systems provide for a variety of appellate court structures. Still, the purpose of the appellate courts remains the same, that is to hear appeals on questions of law from the lower courts. Usually, appeals are heard by a three-judge panel. The panel examines the records of the lower court, reads the written arguments submitted by the attorneys, studies the law on its own, and listens to the oral arguments of the attorneys. If the panel agrees with the lower court, it will affirm the decision of that court. However, if the panel disagrees with the lower court's decision, it can set aside or modify the decision of that court.

State Supreme Courts Twenty-seven states rely on their supreme court as their only appellate court. These states have no intermediate appellate courts. The other twenty-three states have both intermediate appellate courts and state supreme courts. Most supreme courts consist of a panel of from three to nine judges. As is true at the intermediate appellate level, the panel of judges examines the records of the lower court, reads the written arguments submitted by the attorneys, studies the law on its own, and listens to the oral arguments of the attorneys. The decisions of state supreme courts are final unless a federal issue or a constitutional right is involved.

Further Reading An excellent insight into the workings of the Supreme Court can be found in *The Center Holds: The Power Struggle Inside the Rehnquist Court,* by James F. Simon (New York: Simon and Schuster, 1995).

State Variations The highest court in California is called the Supreme Court, while New York refers to its top trial court as the Supreme Court.

State Variations The Alaska Supreme Court consists of three justices. By contrast, the Colorado Supreme Court consists of not less than seven justices, and can be increased to no more than nine members.

Cybertransactions must be handled on a case-by-case basis.

Cyberspace Jurisdiction

It is virtually impossible today to conduct business without being involved with computers. Even the most fundamental question of all, that is, Does the court have jurisdiction over an out-of-state defendant? has been complicated by Internet business transactions. Using the Internet, sellers can solicit business, negotiate terms of a contract, enter the contract, receive payment, and deliver the goods without ever physically entering a state. Does this type of activity reach the level of a minimum contract required to establish cyberspace jurisdiction? **Cyberspace jurisdiction** is the authority of a court to hear a case based on Internet-related transactions. While this area of law is still in its infancy, we can, nevertheless, extract at least one normative principle. This principle holds that, because of its basic nature, cyberspace jurisdiction is a moving target. To help attorneys and businesspeople hit this moving target, the courts have established a sliding scale on which several types of jurisdiction can be measured.

On one side of this scale are those cybertransactions that obviously involve minimum contacts. These would include cybertransactions carried out from beginning to end on the Internet. Those cybertransactions that involve solicitation, negotiation, payment, and delivery in cyberspace would, therefore, establish jurisdiction. On the other side of the scale are those cases that can establish that the defendant simply placed an inactive advertisement on the Web. Such inactive advertisements will usually not establish jurisdiction. The final type of case falls in that vast expanse on the scale between the two extremes. These cases concern cybertransactions that involve more than simple inactive advertising on the Internet. The courts have not established any single normative approach to such transactions and so the matter is still open to debate. This means that each situation must be handled on a case-by-case basis.

Quick Quiz 3-1 True or False?

1. Courts are judicial tribunals that meet in a regular place and apply the laws in an attempt to settle disputes fairly.

2. The authority of a court to hear and decide cases is called the court's jurisdiction.

3. The concept of minimum contacts identifies the fewest number of contacts needed to allow the court to exercise jurisdiction over the out-of-state defendant.

3-2 Civil Procedure

Although civil procedure differs from state to state, the following examination of common elements can simplify the task of analyzing the cases presented in this text. Keep in mind that this process involves civil lawsuits, rather than a criminal prosecution. In a civil lawsuit, one individual, organization, or corporation brings an action against another individual, organization, or corporation. The objective of a civil suit is usually to obtain money to compensate the victim. **Litigation** is another name for the process of bringing a case to court to enforce a right.

Commencement of the Action

The principal parties to a lawsuit are the plaintiff and the defendant. The **plaintiff** is the person who begins the lawsuit by filing a complaint in the appropriate trial court of general jurisdiction. The **defendant** is the person against whom the lawsuit has been brought and from whom a recovery is sought.

Filing the Complaint

Filing the Complaint   The **complaint** sets forth the names of the parties to the lawsuit, identifying them as plaintiffs or defendants. Generally, the complaint includes the addresses of all parties. The complaint also sets forth the following:

- the facts in the case from the plaintiff's perspective
- the alleged legal violations by the defendant
- the injuries that the plaintiff suffered
- the plaintiff's request for relief

If the plaintiff wants a jury trial, this information must also be specified on the complaint. In federal court, the complaint must also include a statement of jurisdiction. This will tell the court whether the case has been brought in federal court because of a federal question or because of diversity among the plaintiffs and the defendants.

Filing the Complaint   The complaint sets forth the names of the parties to the lawsuit, identifying them as plaintiffs or defendants. Generally, the complaint also includes the addresses of all parties. The complaint also sets forth the facts in the case from the plaintiff's perspective, the alleged legal violations of the defendant, the injuries that the plaintiff suffered, and the plaintiff's request for relief. If the plaintiff wants a jury trial this must also be specified on the complaint. In federal court, the complaint must also include a statement of jurisdiction. This will tell the court whether the case has been brought in federal court because of a federal question or because of diversity among the plaintiffs and the defendants.

There are times when the filing of a complaint would be pointless because the amount of recovery that any single plaintiff might receive in the case would be so low that the effort and expense of carrying out the suit would not be worth the potential award. In some instances, however, the potential number of plaintiffs injured by a transgression is so high that the cost of entering the action would be justified if all of those plaintiffs joined together. In such cases, it is possible for one representative party to file a lawsuit on behalf of all the members of a group of plaintiffs who share a single, similar injury. Such a case is called a **class action** law suit. The courts will permit a class action lawsuit provided (1) that it is not feasible for the members of the group to bring the suit on their own; (2) that the members of the group share common questions of law that can be tried together; and (3) that the class action approach is far better than forcing the plaintiffs to file separate actions.

Service of Process

The complaint is presented to the appropriate court officer, usually the clerk of courts. The clerk will then see that the defendant is served with a copy of the complaint and a summons. The *summons* names the court of jurisdiction, describes the nature of the action, and demands that the defendant answer the complaint within a specified period of time, usually between twenty and thirty days, depending on the state rules of civil procedure. Giving the summons and the complaint to the defendant is called **service of process.**

The Pre-Answer Stage

As noted, once the defendant has been served, he or she has twenty to thirty days to file an answer. Usually, however, the defendant will ask for and receive an extension of that time

Terms Trial by jury originated with the Saxons. An accused person would be set free if a number of people would come forward and swear that the accused was innocent. These people were called *juratores,* meaning "sworn witnesses" in Latin.

Getting Students Involved Invite professionals such as lawyers, judges, or paralegals to share their legal knowledge and experience with the class. Encourage students to prepare questions in advance, particularly ones regarding litigation procedures.

period. The time between service and the answer is termed the *pre-answer stage.* During this stage, the defendant will take some time to examine the nature of the claim that has been filed by the plaintiff. The defendant may, as a result of this initial examination, decide to file one or more pre-answer motions. A *motion* is a request for the court to rule on a particular issue. One possible motion is a motion for dismissal of the case for failure to state a claim for which relief can be granted. Some states call this a **demurrer.** Other motions to dismiss may be based on the grounds that the court lacks subject matter jurisdiction, that the court lacks personal jurisdiction, or that the court cannot hear the case because the statute of limitations has passed.

Example 3-3

Lauren Jensen agreed to purchase a desk for $295 from the Stephens Sisters Furniture Store. During a management change at Stephens, Jensen's order was lost, and the furniture was never delivered. Jensen never contacted Stephens, but instead purchased a similar desk for $495 at another store. Five years later, Jensen decided to bring suit against Stephens for breach of contract. She wants to recover the extra $200 that she paid to the second store. Stephens' attorney realizes that the state statute of limitations for such contracts is four years. As a result, she files a motion to dismiss for failure to state a claim for which relief can be granted. Some states call this motion a demurrer. If Stephens' attorney is correct, the suit will be dismissed.

The Answer

Cross-Cultural Notes
Saudi Arabia operates under Islamic law, or *sharia.* Under the Saudi system, persons suspected of a crime are arrested and held in detention while the Ministry of Justice investigates and decides whether to recommend prosecution. Trials are conducted with only the family of the accused present. Although no jury and no lawyers are allowed, Saudi Arabian judges are known for their incorruptibility and strict adherence to the standards of fairness stated in the Koran, the holy book of the Islamic religion.

The **answer** is the defendant's official response to the complaint. In the answer, the defendant admits or denies the allegations in the complaint. The defendant's answer can also include affirmative defenses. An **affirmative defense** is a set of circumstances that indicate that the defendant should not be held liable, even if the plaintiff proves all of the facts in the complaint. One affirmative defense is *assumption of the risk.*

Example 3-4

Carol Jennings took a cruise of the Mediterranean on the Underwood Cruise Line, a firm incorporated and doing business in the United States. While the cruise ship *Principia* was docked at a Greek island, Jennings joined a tour group. She was cautioned numerous times to remain with the tour group and not to wander off by herself because of the danger of being attacked and robbed. Nevertheless, Jennings ignored the warnings and left the tour group. While on her own, she wandered into a particularly dangerous part of the city where she was beaten and robbed. She later brought a lawsuit against the Underwood Cruise Line. In its answer to Jennings' complaint, the cruise line may wish to use the defense of assumption of the risk. Such a defense would argue that Jennings was aware of danger when she chose to abandon the tour group and wander off by herself. As a result, the cruise line might argue, she assumed the risk of being attacked and robbed.

The defendant's answer may also contain counterclaims and cross-claims. A *counterclaim* is a claim that a defendant has against a plaintiff. A *cross-claim* is a claim filed by a defendant against another defendant in the same case. At this time a defendant may also wish to file a *third-party complaint,* which is a complaint filed by the defendant against a third party not yet named in the lawsuit.

The Pretrial Stage

After the answer has been filed, the parties must await trial. During this waiting period, cleverly dubbed the pretrial stage, several activities can be carried out including the pretrial conference, discovery, and the filing of pretrial motions.

Pretrial Conference Some courts require cases to go to a pretrial conference after the complaint and the answer have been filed. A pretrial conference usually has two purposes. One is to discuss the possibility of settling the case without the need for a trial. Another is to decide on the details involved in bringing the case to trial. Such a conference is generally called a *case management conference.* Issues that might be discussed at a case management conference include the way that the parties will conduct discovery or the need to place a limit on the number of expert witnesses that will be called at trial.

State Variations Under Kansas law, the court may conduct a case management conference with counsel and any unrepresented parties to a lawsuit within forty-five days of the defendant's answer.

Pretrial Motions Several motions may be filed during the pretrial stage. One motion available at this time is a motion for **summary judgment.** Such a motion asks the court for an immediate judgment for the party filing the motion. This motion is filed when there is no genuine issue as to any material fact, and the party filing the motion is entitled by law to a favorable judgment. The motion cannot be filed without supporting legal arguments written out in a brief and accompanied by applicable supporting evidence.

Discovery **Discovery** is the process by which the parties to a civil action search for information that is relevant to the case. The objective is to simplify the issues and to avoid unnecessary arguments and surprises in the subsequent trial. Discovery techniques and tools include the following:

Related Cases Margaret Harmotta was on her way to a bingo game at the Immaculate Conception Church when she slipped in the snow-covered parking lot and injured herself. She sued the church and won, but the church appealed, claiming that some of the jurors should have been disqualified because they had a financial interest in the diocese. In the appealed suit, *Harmotta v. Bender* (601 A.2d 837), the court found in favor of Harmotta, concluding that jurors had only a remote interest in the diocese, since none was an actual member of the church.

> **Depositions** are oral statements made out of court under oath by witnesses or parties to the action in response to questions from the opposing attorneys. The answers are recorded by a court stenographer and can be used for later reference.
>
> **Interrogatories** are written questions that must be answered in writing under oath by the opposite party. Interrogatories cannot be given to witnesses. Only plaintiffs and defendants can be required to answer interrogatories.
>
> **Requests for real evidence** ask a party to produce documents, records, accounts, correspondence, photographs, or other tangible evidence. The request may also seek permission to inspect land.
>
> **Requests for physical or mental examination** ask a party to undergo a physical or a mental examination. Such requests can be made only if the physical or the mental condition of the party is in controversy; it must be a central concern to the lawsuit.
>
> **Requests for admissions** are made to secure a statement from a party that a particular fact is true or that a document or set of documents is genuine. An admission eliminates the need to demonstrate truthfulness of the fact or the genuineness of the documents at trial.

The discovery process cannot be taken lightly by the litigants. The rules of court provide severe penalties for those who fail to cooperate with discovery. Should a litigant withhold his or her cooperation, the other litigant can ask the court to compel the uncooperative party to respond to the discovery request. If the uncooperative party has a reason for not complying, then he or she may try to persuade the court of the validity of the refusal. If, for instance, the discovery request seeks information protected by the attorney-client privilege, the judge may refuse to compel the litigant to comply with the request.

If, however, the litigant cannot persuade the judge that the refusal is legally justified, the judge may impose severe penalties on the litigant. For example, the judge may elect to dismiss the lawsuit completely. The judge may also decide to render a default judgment against the uncooperative party. Reasonable expenses caused by the refusal to comply with discovery may also be assessed against the uncooperative party. These expenses may include attorney's fees. In many states, the rules allow the expenses to be assessed against either the attorney or the litigant.

Cyberspace Discovery Advances in technology have profoundly affected the process of discovery in civil litigation. These advances have affected both the way discovery is conducted and the amount and types of information available as part of the discovery process. For example, until recently most attorneys were unwilling to videotape depositions. Today the practice has become commonplace. **Cyberspace discovery** or **cyberdiscovery,** as it is sometimes called, is the search for evidence using computers. Cyberdiscovery has also become an accepted procedure in litigation today. The pervasive presence of the Internet has aided attorneys in the gathering of information. Some law firms today make it a conventional practice to conduct depositions using the Internet. The Internet has also become a tool for webconferencing about discovery procedures and problems. Some enterprising attorneys and paralegals have also found that the Internet can be used to send and to respond to interrogatories. The widespread use of mobile phones, the increased use of personal digital assistants (PDAs), the almost universal presence of fax machines in court houses and law offices, and the pervasive use of e-mail have all helped make discovery less costly and more effective than it has ever been before.

The widespread use of computers in business, government, and education has altered the way information is stored and, therefore, the way it can be retrieved during discovery. As a result, law firms must be ready to change the way they conduct discovery to ensure that important cyberevidence does not remain hidden because it is produced and stored in cyberspace. **Cyberevidence** involves any and all types of computer-generated data. This inevitably includes such diverse records as e-mail files, calendering programs, databases, and all other types of cyberrecords. Lawyers must also be prepared to warn clients about preserving such cyberrecords so as not to inadvertently destroy cyberrecords that should have been preserved. Many law firms have decided to employ their own cyberexperts to help them navigate the complex world of cyberspace, cyberrecords and cyberevidence.

The Civil Trial

Upon completion of discovery, the pretrial conference, and any hearings held on pretrial motions, the case is ready for trial. A trial by jury is an adversarial proceeding in which the judge's role is secondary to that of the jury's. Competition between attorneys permits the jury to sort out the truth and arrive at a just solution to the dispute.

Jury Selection Once it is decided that the case will involve a jury, the process of *voir dire* (to speak the truth) begins. In this process, the lawyers for both parties question prospective jurors to determine whether they will be allowed to sit on the jury. Prospective jurors may be rejected if they are unable to render an impartial judgment. One reason for rejecting a prospective juror is if he or she had a personal relationship with the litigant or with a witness.

Prospective jurors may also be rejected if they have a financial interest in the outcome of the trial. However, the financial interest must be a direct, substantial interest. Remote

Business Law in the News

Disconnected: Lawyers and the Public Learn to Live Without Cellphones in the Courthouse

Most federal courthouses prohibit two items: weapons and cellphones.

Electronic devices are like a plague that has descended upon courts, and, like the most virulent germs, they survive by morphing into ever more sophisticated forms.

Pagers became cellphones and then picture phones. Laptops were trumped by PDAs (personal digital assistants, such as a BlackBerry). Both often have recording capabilities. And now stun guns come disguised as cellphones—but it is safe to assume that these fall into the weapons category and are banned.

When it comes to nonweapon electronic devices, lawyers and their clients had better check the local rules.

One rule of thumb involving cellphones, though, seems to be consistent: If you bring it into court, one day it will ring—and it will cost you. Lawrence F. Clark, a Dauphin County, Pa., judge, recently ordered a bailiff to drop a ringing cellphone out of a five-story window onto a roof below. Fortunately, the bailiff had taken it away from its owner first.

But while lawyers and members of the public are getting the message about electronic gadgetry in the courthouse, an old prohibition looms over new technology—picture phones, recorders in laptops and PDAs.

The Illinois Supreme Court has long banned cameras and recording devices in courtrooms. In December, it clarified its definitions: "[T]he use of the terms 'photographs,' 'broadcasting,' and 'televising' include the audio or video transmissions or recordings made by telephones, personal data assistants, laptop computers, and other wired or wireless data transmission and recording devices."

The Cellphone Police

Deputy sheriffs are trained to spot the devices with those capabilities among members of the public, said Gary Dodge, court administrator for Illinois' 18th Judicial Circuit in DuPage County.

"If one is spotted, they're required to return them to their vehicles," Dodge said. "We're reluctant to take them away from attorneys, because they've got work to do, but they understand the ramifications of breaking the rules." Taking a picture or recording sound is an ethical violation, Dodge said.

A now-retired traffic court judge in DuPage County is reputed to have jailed three ringing cellphone offenders for contempt—one overnight.

Besides protecting witnesses and prisoners, U.S. marshals have added cellphone vigilance to their mission of protecting federal courts.

Billy Walker, judicial court security officer for the Middle District of Florida, a deputy U.S. marshal, said rules are consistent in four of the district's locations in Fort Myers, Orlando, Ocala and Jacksonville: No cellphones.

In Tampa, though, there's an experimental project that allows lawyers to check cellphones in lockers in the lobby of the federal building. Laptops are allowed by individual court order. PDAs are allowed if they do not have recording or photo-taking capabilities.

"It is a difficult task that requires each device to be screened," said Walker. "The ever-changing and evolving technology and the multifunctions of devices makes the delineation between acceptable and unacceptable devices difficult." Translation: He appreciates the fact that lawyers and the general public don't get hot-tempered when the lines to enter their federal buildings back up.

Questions for Analysis

1. While electronic devices have become commonplace in the legal arena, there are limits to their effectiveness. Should judges be permitted to confiscate mobile phones that ring during a court procedure? Explain.

2. Should judges be permitted to jail mobile phone users? Explain.

3. Why is there a controversy over picture phones in Illinois courtrooms? Explain.

4. How has the controversy over mobile phones and PDAs affected the daily operation of the federal courts? Explain.

5. Explain the Tampa experiment in relation to electronic devices. Is this an effective way to deal with the problem? Why or why not?

Prospective jurors may be selected or rejected based on their ability to render an impartial judgment.

financial interests in a trial will not disqualify a juror. Thus, the fact that the outcome of a trial may result in higher insurance rates would not disqualify a juror who has an insurance policy. Another reason might be if the prospective juror has had a past experience that would prevent him or her from being impartial in the present case. Thus, a juror who has had a bad experience with a psychologist, for instance, might be unable to impartially judge the actions of a psychologist who has been sued for malpractice.

In most lawsuits *voir dire* is conducted in the open. This means that the process is generally accessible to the press and the mass media. However, in cases that have attracted a lot of public attention the judge may order that the media's access to the *voir dire* process be limited. Often this means that news reporters will be limited to reading abridged copies of the transcript of the *voir dire* process after the process has been completed. The names of the jurors may also be censored along with personal data about those jurors. This limit on the access to *voir dire* usually occurs in notorious criminal trials, but it could also happen in high-profile civil lawsuits.

State Variations In Hawaii, as in many states, either party in a jury trial may challenge any prospective juror "for cause" and the court will then determine whether the juror can render an impartial decision.

Opening Statements

At the beginning of the trial, both attorneys have the opportunity to make an opening statement. In the *opening statement,* an attorney presents the facts in the case and explains what he or she intends to show during the trial. Attorneys are not permitted to argue their case in the opening statement. There is widespread disagreement, however, as to what constitutes "arguing the case" during the opening statement. Consequently, the degree of argument permitted during the opening statement often depends upon what the judge will allow.

Terms There is a courtroom tradition that all present stand up as a judge enters the courtroom. The bailiff usually calls out, *"Oyez! Oyez!* or "Hear ye! Hear ye!"

The Plaintiff's Case in Chief

The plaintiff's **case in chief** is the plaintiff's opportunity to present evidence that will prove his or her version of the case to the jury. The plaintiff's attorney calls witnesses and immediately subjects those witnesses to **direct examination.** Direct examination is designed to present the facts that will support the plaintiff's version of the facts. Opposing attorneys then have the chance to challenge the truthfulness of each piece of evidence presented. In this process of **cross-examination,** the witnesses answer questions of the defense attorney.

The Defendant's Case in Chief

After the plaintiff has ended the presentation of his or her case in chief, the defendant has the opportunity to present his or her case in chief. The defendant's attorney calls witnesses for direct examination and the plaintiff's attorney has an opportunity to cross-examine the defendant's witnesses.

The Rebuttal and the Surrebuttal

Once the plaintiff and the defendant have presented their cases in chief, each attorney may present evidence to discredit the evidence presented by the opposition and to reestablish the credibility of his or her own evidence. This step is called the **rebuttal.** The term **surrebuttal** is used in some states when referring to the defendant's rebuttal.

Closing Statements

After the rebuttals are completed, each attorney makes a closing statement. In this statement, the attorneys emphasize aspects of the testimony and other evidence they believe will best persuade the judge or jury.

Jury Instructions Since juries comprise many people who are not familiar with particular aspects of the law, someone must explain the law to the jury. This is one of the duties of the judge. Although the attorneys may suggest to the judge what instructions ought to be used, the judge makes the decision. The judge's instructions explain the rules of law that the jurors are to apply to the facts in reaching their decision.

Verdict and Judgment After receiving the judge's instructions, the members of the jury retire to a private room, where they apply the rules stated by the judge to the evidence presented by the witnesses. The jury eventually reaches a verdict. A **verdict** is a finding of fact. The verdict may be limited to the question of liability or it can be extended to include the issue of damages. **Liability** means that the defendant is held legally responsible for his or her actions. The term **damages** refers to the money recovered by the plaintiff for the injury or loss caused by the defendant. The verdict is entered by the judge in the court records, and the case is said to be decided. By the terms of the judgment, the defeated party either is required to pay the amount specified or to do a specific thing, such as perform the terms of the contract. Court costs are usually paid by the losing party.

In some cases, money will not be adequate to satisfy the plaintiff. In such cases, the plaintiff may seek an equitable remedy. An **equitable remedy** requires a party to do something or to refrain from doing something beyond the payment of money. One equitable remedy is **specific performance.** This would require a party to a contract to go through with the terms of the contract. Usually, specific performance is permitted only in cases involving real estate or unique, one-of-a-kind goods such as art objects or rare antiques. Another equitable remedy is an injunction. An **injunction** stops a party from doing something. For instance, an employer may seek an injunction against a former employee to prevent that employee from using a trade secret on his or her new job if that trade secret is the property of the original employer.

Further Reading For an interesting fictional account of the jury process see *The Runaway Jury* by John Grisham (Island Books, 1997).

The Appeal

An **appeal** is the referral of a case to a higher court for review. For an appeal to be successful, it must be shown that some legal error occurred. For example, a party could argue that some of the evidence that was admitted should have been excluded or that evidence that was not allowed should have been allowed. A party could also argue that the judge's instructions were erroneous or were stated in an inappropriate manner. Generally, an appeal is filed by the party which lost the case in the trial court. However, it is also possible that the party which prevailed at trial may wish to file an appeal. This is referred to as a **cross-appeal.** For instance, if the trial court upheld most of the claims made by the plaintiff, but denied one or two key claims, the plaintiff may wish to file a cross-appeal. It may also be advisable to file a cross-appeal if the trial court did not award the appropriate amount in damages, if it refused to grant attorney's fees, or if it allowed money damages but refused to permit equitable relief.

Getting Students Involved Have students go to the local courthouse and find out when a civil trial is set to be heard. Have them sit through at least a half-day's worth of the trial and then have them write a report on what they have observed.

See Bayer, Aaron S. "Appellate Law: The Cross-Appeal." *The National Law Journal,* Feb 9, 2004, p. 13.

Execution of the Judgment

In civil cases, if the judgment is not paid, the court will order the loser's property to be sold by the sheriff to satisfy the judgment. This order by the court is known as a **writ of execution.** Any excess from the sale must be returned to the loser. Execution of the judgment also may be issued against any income due to the loser, such as wages, salaries, or dividends. This is known as execution against income, or garnishment, and the proceedings are known as garnishee proceedings. Checking accounts are also subject to garnishment.

Quick Quiz 3-2 True or False?

1. In state court a complaint must include a statement of jurisdiction.

2. The defendants' answer must not include either counterclaims or cross-claims.

3. *Voir dire* must always be open to the press.

3-3 Criminal Procedure

The objectives of a criminal prosecution are to protect society and to punish the wrongdoer by a fine or imprisonment. The steps in a criminal prosecution include the following:

- the arrest and initial appearance
- the preliminary hearing
- the formal charges
- the arraignment
- the trial

The Arrest and Initial Appearance

Background Information *Miranda v. Arizona* established a criminal defendant's right to be informed of his or her rights. The U.S. Supreme Court has held that the protection of the public may outweigh the defendant's rights to be informed. Consequently, statements may be admissible at trial even if the defendant was not informed of his rights as long as those statements were taken to protect the public. Under Title II of the Omnibus Crime Control Act, a freely given confession is admissible in federal court, as long as the trial judge is convinced that the confession was genuinely voluntary.

A crime is an offense against the people. Once a law enforcement agency learns that a crime has been committed, the agency begins a criminal prosecution. The first step in a criminal prosecution is to gather evidence of the crime and to identify all possible suspects. When the law enforcement agency is convinced that it has ample evidence of both the crime and the identity of the suspect, an arrest warrant is issued and the suspect is arrested. At the time of arrest, the defendant must be informed of his or her rights. One of the principal rights of the accused is the right to be represented by counsel. This right is guaranteed by the Sixth Amendment to the Constitution. Another important right is the right to remain silent, which is protected under the Fifth Amendment which states that a criminal defendant cannot be compelled to be a witness against himself or herself. The U.S. Supreme Court has ruled that the Fourteenth Amendment to the Constitution requires that both the right to remain silent and the right to representation by counsel must also be protected by state governments. The defendant is then brought before a judge or a magistrate for an initial appearance, where once again the defendant is reminded of his or her rights. At this time, a preliminary hearing is also scheduled.

The Preliminary Hearing

A **preliminary hearing** is a court procedure during which the judge decides whether probable cause exists to continue holding the defendant for the crime. The government is represented by an attorney called the **prosecutor.** In some states, this government official is called the district attorney. During the preliminary hearing, the prosecution and the defendant are permitted to make arguments and to call witnesses. The case will move on to the next step if there is probable cause to hold the defendant. If not, the defendant is set free.

Further Reading Two excellent books provide more information about the grand jury system. *The Grand Jury: An Institution on Trial* by Marvin E. Frankel and Gary P. Naftalis, (Hill and Wang, 1978); and *The People's Panel* by R. D. Younger (Providence: American History Research Center, Brown University, 1963).

The Formal Charges

In the United States, formal charges against the defendant may be brought either by indictment or by information. Some states do not have a grand jury system and therefore can bring formal charges only by an information. In those states that use both, the indictment is usually used to bring formal charges for serious crimes.

An Indictment The federal courts and many state courts bring formal charges against the defendant by issuing an indictment. An **indictment** is a set of formal charges against a defendant issued by a grand jury. A *grand jury* consists of citizens who serve as jurors for a specified period of time to review a variety of criminal cases. The objective of a grand jury review is to determine whether probable cause exists to believe that a crime has been committed and that this particular defendant may have committed the crime. Grand jury proceedings are held in secret and are directed by the prosecutor or district attorney. If the grand jury finds probable cause exists, an indictment is issued.

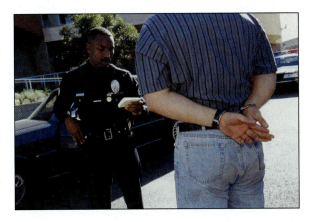

Defendants must be informed of their rights at the time of arrest. Two important rights are the right to representation by counsel and the right to remain silent.

An Information An **information** is a set of formal charges against a defendant drawn up and issued by the prosecutor or district attorney. No grand jury is involved in this process. Nevertheless, an information does the same thing that an indictment does. If the prosecutor has found that probable cause exists to believe that a crime has been committed and that this particular defendant committed the crime, an information is issued.

The Arraignment

The **arraignment** is a formal court proceeding, during which the defendant, after hearing the indictment or information read, pleads either guilty or not guilty. Should the defendant enter a guilty plea, a sentence may be imposed immediately. If the defendant enters a plea of not guilty, the case moves on to the trial.

The Criminal Trial

If the defendant has requested a jury trial, a jury is selected. After the jury has been seated, each side makes its opening statement. Opening statements are followed by the production of evidence by both the prosecution and the defendant. One very significant difference between a criminal trial and a civil trial is the burden of proof. In a civil trial the plaintiff must prove his or her case by a preponderance of evidence. In contrast, in a criminal case the prosecution must prove the defendant's guilt beyond a reasonable doubt. As is the case with civil procedure, the criminal trial is completed by the attorneys' closing statements and the judge's instructions to the jury. The jury members are then allowed to retire to deliberate and decide upon a verdict. In most states, a defendant can be found guilty only by the unanimous agreement of all of the jurors. A defendant who is found not guilty is released. One who has been found guilty is sentenced by the judge.

Getting Students Involved Discuss media coverage of local or national trials. Encourage students to describe cases they've followed in the news. Ask them if they think that media coverage of jury trials should be allowed during the proceedings or postponed until after the verdict is reached.

Background Information A defendant has the right to a jury trial, but may waive, or give up, this right and have the judge decide the facts.

Quick Quiz 3-3 True or False?

1. The objectives of a criminal prosecution are to protect society and to punish the wrongdoer by a fine or imprisonment.

2. The steps in a criminal prosecution include the arrest and initial appearance, the preliminary hearing, the formal charges, the arraignment, and the trial.

3. A crime is an offense against a single individual.

Summary

3-1   Courts are judicial tribunals that meet in a regular place and apply the laws in an attempt to settle disputes fairly. The federal court system is divided into three levels: the district courts, the courts of appeals, and the U.S. Supreme Court. State systems vary in structure but will often consist of several levels including lower-level limited jurisdiction trial courts, higher-level trial courts, intermediate appellate courts, and state supreme courts.

3-2   Litigation begins when the plaintiff files a complaint with the appropriate trial court. The defendant must then be given a copy of the complaint and a summons. During the pre-answer stage, the defendant may attempt to dismiss the lawsuit by filing certain pre-answer motions. In the answer stage, the defendant will file an answer, which may contain affirmative defenses, counterclaims, and/or cross-claims. The defendant, at this time, may also file third-party complaints. During the pretrial stage, conferences may be held, motions may be made, and discovery conducted. The trial includes the opening statement, each side's case in chief, the opportunity for rebuttal and s400surebuttal, the closing arguments, and the jury instructions. The jury then renders a verdict. Either party may

appeal the case if that party believes that a legal error was made during the trial that influenced the verdict unfavorably. If a judgment is not paid, the court may issue a writ of execution.

3-3   The steps in a criminal prosecution include the arrest and initial appearance, the preliminary hearing, the formal charges, the arraignment, and the trial. At the time of the arrest, the defendant must be informed of his or her rights. Immediately following the arrest, the defendant is brought before a judge or a magistrate for an initial appearance, at which time the defendant is again reminded of his or her rights. A preliminary hearing is also scheduled. A preliminary hearing is a court procedure during which the judge will decide whether probable cause exists to continue to hold the defendant pending formal charges. Formal charges against the defendant may be brought either by indictment or by information. The arraignment is a formal court proceeding, during which the defendant pleads guilty or not guilty. The trial includes the opening statement, each side's case, the closing arguments, and the jury instructions. The jury then renders a verdict.

Key Terms

affirmative defense, 56	cyberspace jurisdiction, 54	interrogatories, 57
answer, 56	damages, 61	jurisdiction, 47
appeal, 61	defendant, 55	liability, 61
appellate jurisdiction, 47	demurrer, 56	litigation, 54
arraignment, 63	deposition, 57	minimum contacts, 49
case in chief, 60	direct examination, 60	original jurisdiction, 47
class action, 55	discovery, 57	personal jurisdiction, 47
complaint, 55	diversity cases, 48	plaintiff, 55
courts, 47	equitable remedy, 61	preliminary hearing, 62
cross-appeal, 61	federal question, 48	prosecutor, 62
cross-examination, 60	general jurisdiction, 47	rebuttal, 60
cyberdiscovery, 58	indictment, 63	request for admissions, 57
cyberevidence, 58	information, 63	request for a physical or mental examination, 57
cyberspace discovery, 58	injunction, 61	

Questions for Review and Discussion

1. What is the difference between original jurisdiction and appellate jurisdiction? Between general jurisdiction and special jurisdiction?
2. Explain the basic structure of the federal court system. Over what two types of cases do the federal trial courts have jurisdiction?
3. Under what circumstances might the U.S. Supreme Court grant a writ of certiorari?
4. What is the extent of cyberspace jurisdiction?
5. What is the structure of a typical state court system?
6. What are the steps in the litigation process beginning with the commencement of the action, up through the execution of judgment?
7. What is the difference between a deposition and a set of interrogatories?
8. What is the nature of cyberspace discovery?
9. What is involved in an appeal?
10. What are the steps in a criminal prosecution beginning with the arrest up through the sentencing of the defendant?

Investigating the Internet

The Administrative Office of the United States Courts maintains a website which includes the latest press releases from the federal courts. Access one of the most recent press releases and write a report on the issues contained therein. You might instead write a report on an article appearing in the *The Third Branch,* the monthly newsletter produced by the federal courts and appearing on this website.

Cases for Analysis

1. When the trial of Martha Stewart began, her attorney and the attorney for codefendant, Peter Bacanovic, asked that *voir dire* be conducted in private. The court granted the request, so only the judge, the defendants, their attorneys, and the prosecutors were present. Reporters were supplied with transcripts of the *voir dire* proceedings, which were available on the day following the examination of the jurors. However, the identities of the jurors along with any individual items concerning those jurors were erased from the transcripts. In response, seventeen news companies asked the appellate court to reverse the order. The news agencies argued that the ruling made little sense since the court had excluded the press from a case that had a great deal of public concern at its core. They also argued that closing *voir dire* was an additional step down a slippery slope which they envisioned as eventually resulting in a complete closure of American courts to the press. The other side argued that there was a compelling need to close the *voir dire* process to make certain that the prospective jurors would be open and honest about questions concerning high-profile figures like Martha Stewart. Should the appeals court uphold the closing of *voir dire* in this case? Explain your answer. *In re Application of ABC Inc.,* No. 04-0220 (2d U.S. Cir. Ct. of App.). See also Young, Gary. "The Closed Voir Dire for Martha Stewart." *The National Law Journal,* January 26, 2004, pp. 1, 25.

2. After a conviction had been rendered in a Virginia court, one of the jurors remarked to a deputy sheriff as he was accompanying her to her car, that she would not park in a parking garage because she had once been robbed there. This was news to the deputy who knew that the jurors had been asked during *voir dire* whether they had ever been victimized in a crime. When the prosecutors were told about this remark, they reported it to the defendant's attorney, who filed a motion for a mistrial. When questioned again, the juror defended her answer by arguing that she had not grasped the meaning of the question at the time it was asked. In fact, she went on to say, if she had understood the question, she would have answered in the affirmative, because she had not wanted to serve on the jury in the first place. The defense argued that her past experience made her biased in the present case and that this robbed the defendant of his right to a fair trial. Should the judge grant a mistrial in this case? Explain. *Blevins v. Virginia,* No. 031022 (VA Sup. Ct.). See also Horrigan, David. "Conviction Stands Despite Juror's Lapse." *The National Law Journal,* January 26, 2004, p. 18.

3. The state of Alabama was required under provisions of its own constitution to reapportion its electoral districts every ten years. The state, however, had failed to reapportion districts for more than half a century. Since then the population of Alabama had grown to such an extent that severe inequalities existed among the electoral districts. The inequalities were so great in some cases that the votes of citizens in some parts of the state carried as much as ten times the weight of the votes of citizens in other parts of the state. This suit was brought in federal court on the grounds that the inequalities in voting power violated certain guarantees found in the U.S. Constitution. The defendants argued that the federal court should not interfere in what is essentially a state matter and that by doing so it would upset the delicate balance between the states and the federal government. Nevertheless, the federal district court struck down the apportionment scheme as unconstitutional. Does this case belong in the U.S. Supreme Court? Explain the reasons for your response. Should the Supreme Court uphold or overturn the federal district court's decision? Explain. *Reynolds v. Sims,* 377 U.S. 533 (U.S. Sup. Ct.).

4. Speculate on which of the following cases the U.S. Supreme Court might decide to review: a case involving a dispute over whether computer software can be copyrighted; a case involving an appeal of a zoning board's decision to limit the number of adult book stores on any single city block; a case involving the constitutionality of an abortion statute; a case involving an antitrust suit based on a violation of a federal antitrust statute between the National Football League and the United States Football League; a libel case against a small town newspaper involving allegations of the mayor's dishonesty; a case involving the placement of a religious scene on city property; a case brought by a steel company to enjoin employees from going on strike; a case involving the distribution of antiwar flyers at a private shopping mall; a case involving the search of a high school student's locker without her permission. In each case, give reasons for your answer.

5. Eight limited partners filed a lawsuit in the Lucas County Court of Common Pleas, alleging that the general partners in ten different limited partnerships had engaged in an extensive pattern of self-dealing that had involved converting partnership property for their own personal use. Also named in the lawsuit was the accounting firm of Donald J. Goldstein, C.P.A., a resident of Florida, and Goldstein, Lewis, and Company, a professional corporation located in Florida. The plaintiffs claimed that the accountant and the accounting firm had known of the general partners' misconduct and were therefore liable to the plaintiff for that malpractice. The accountant and the accounting firm decided to end the suit as quickly as possible. Consequently, they filed a motion for dismissal. The motion stated that the courts of Ohio lacked personal jurisdiction over them because they were from Florida. They further stated that they did not solicit business in Ohio, maintained no place of business in Ohio, had no license to act as accountants in Ohio, owned no property in Ohio, provided all services from Florida, and filed no documents with the state of Ohio. Consequently, they concluded that they fell outside the power of Ohio's long-arm statute. Conversely, the plaintiffs argued that the defendants transacted business in the state of Ohio on a continuing and ongoing basis by regularly submitting financial statements to the limited partners in Ohio, and by being actively involved in the decisions of the general partnership. Did the activities of the accountant and the accounting firm place them under the jurisdiction of the Ohio court according to the state "long-arm" statute? Explain. *Goldstein v. Christiansen,* 638 N.E.2d 541 (OH).

6. The criminal defendant in this case, a man named Gideon, broke into a pool room in Florida with the objective of committing a minor crime. Since Gideon was without any means of financial support, he could not afford an attorney. He asked for but was denied representation by a court appointed attorney. Consequently, he represented himself at trial. Ultimately, he was found guilty and sentenced to five years in prison. Gideon later challenged his conviction on the grounds that he had been deprived of his constitutional right to representation by an attorney. In opposition, Florida argued that, although all fundamental rights guaranteed by the federal government through the Bill of Rights should also be guaranteed by state governments, the right to legal representation was not such a fundamental right. In fact, the right to a court appointed attorney arose only when the criminal defendant has been accused of a very serious crime. The U.S. Supreme Court agreed to hear the case. How should the Supreme Court rule in this case? Is the right to an attorney a fundamental right that should also be guaranteed to criminal defendants by the states regardless of the seriousness of the crime? Explain. Examine the Constitution and find the Amendment which guarantees the right to representation by an attorney. Examine the Constitution and find the Amendment which extends that right to defendants in state criminal actions. *Gideon v. Wainwright,* 372 U.S. 355 (U.S. Sup. Ct.).

7. Ernesto Miranda was arrested in his own home for a serious crime and held in an interrogation room. He was not informed of his right to remain silent nor was he informed that he could be represented by an attorney. Eventually, after a two-hour interrogation conducted by two police officers, Miranda signed a statement which indicated that he had voluntarily confessed to the crime of which he was accused. On the basis of the confession, Miranda was found guilty. He appealed to the Arizona Supreme Court which affirmed the guilty verdict. Miranda asked the U.S. Supreme Court to hear his appeal. Is this the type of case that belongs in the U.S. Supreme Court? Explain the reasons for your response. Should the Supreme Court uphold or overturn the state court's conviction of Miranda? Explain the Constitution and find the Amendment which guarantees the right to remain silent when arrested for a criminal action. Examine the Constitution and find the Amendment which extends that right to defendants in state criminal actions. *Miranda v. Arizona,* 384 U.S. 436 (U.S. Sup. Ct.).

Quick Quiz Answers

3-1 1. T	3-2 1. F	3-3 1. T
2. T	2. F	2. T
3. T	3. F	3. F

Chapter 4

Criminal Law

The Opening Case

"Crime in the Streets or Crime in the Suites?"

The CEO of Adelphia Communications Corporation was prosecuted in federal court for a long list of abuses that involved such things as securities fraud, bank fraud, and conspiracy. The list of alleged offenses included some very complicated transactions that resulted in the concealment of a debt that topped the $2 billion dollar mark. The indictment reported that, in order to cover up the debt, false press releases had been issued, phony entries had been made in the books and records of the company, and misrepresentations had been made to Moody's Investors Service. The indictment also charged that the CEO had misled investors about the company's earnings, again by issuing false press releases, and other similar techniques. The CEO was also indicted for defrauding investors and creditors by covering up the alleged improper business relationships that existed between the company and the CEO, among others. A good portion of the public's attention was focused on these "improper business relationships" because they allegedly involved the type of extravagant spending that has been the focus of much attention lately. Several examples offered at trial included such things as the purchase of more than a dozen company cars, the acquisition of 3,600 acres of land for $26 million in company funds to protect the view of the forest in front of the CEO's home, and the use of company funds ($6,000) to fly two Christmas trees to New York for one of his children. The case against the CEO went to trial and he was ultimately found guilty of bank fraud, securities fraud, and conspiracy. As extraordinary as this case may seem at first, the Adelphia Case is actually only one of many similar cases involving high profile corporate defendants that have come to light in recent years. The case itself serves to focus our attention on the fact that, whenever we write or speak about criminal law in this country today, we must not be so narrowly focused that we think only of crime in the streets. Instead, any criminal law discussion must also include a look at "Crime in the Suites."

Chapter Outcomes

1. Explain the purpose of criminal law.
2. Enumerate the various categories and classes of crimes.
3. Describe the nature of an act within the meaning of criminal liability.
4. Identify the four mental states that can be found in the criminal code.
5. Distinguish motive from the required elements of criminal liability.
6. Enumerate and explain the various crimes against people.
7. Distinguish between embezzlement and larceny by false pretenses.
8. Define and explain the nature of cybercrime.
9. Explain the three standards for the insanity defense found in criminal law.
10. Outline the requirements of entrapment as a defense to criminal liability.

Opening Case Sources:
See *United States v. John Rigas,* et al., 2003 U.S. Dist. Lexis 13891, [Memorandum and Order by District Judge Leonard Sand]; Associated Press. "Update 6: Adelphia Founder Guilty of Conspiracy," *Forbes,* July 8, 2004; Erin Mcclam. "Guilty Verdict for Rigas." *Rocky Mountain News,* July 9, 2004.

4-1 Definition and Classes of Crimes

Perhaps one of the most discussed and least understood areas of the law is criminal law. Most people think they know a lot about criminal law, since they read about it frequently in the newspaper and view programs about it on television. In fact, there is a lot of misinformation spread in the media about criminal law and procedure. This section of the chapter will attempt to rectify some of these misconceptions by defining a crime and by explaining the various classes of crimes.

Definition of a Crime

A **crime** is an offense against the public at large. As such, a crime threatens the peace, safety, and well-being of the entire community. For this reason, crimes are punishable by the official governing body of a nation or state. Also, for this reason, the state or the federal government, representing the public at large, is the prosecution, that is, the one who brings the criminal action. The person accused of the crime is called the defendant. No act can be considered criminal unless it is prohibited by the law of the place where it is committed, and the law provides for the punishment of the offenders. These laws are created by the federal government and the governments of the fifty states.

As stated previously, the primary objective of criminal law is to protect the public at large, to preserve harmony and stability within society, and to discourage future disruptive conduct. In contrast, tort law is concerned with private wrongs that have caused injury to an individual's physical health and well-being, property, business, or reputation. Because tort law is concerned with private wrongs rather than public ones, its focal point is quite different from that of criminal law. Tort law focuses on compensating the victim, while criminal law seeks to punish the wrongdoer. When a tort is committed, the victim has a cause of action against the person who has committed the tort. This would allow the victim to recover money as compensation for any injuries that he or she has suffered. In contrast, when a crime is committed the government may prosecute the accused. It is possible, however, for a single act to be both a tort and a crime.

Terms The term *outlaw* dates back to Anglo-Saxon times when it was used to refer to criminals who were stripped of their privileges of citizenship and deprived of all protection by the law. An outlaw's property was given to the king and no matter what injury the outlaw might suffer, he or she had no legal redress. Mobs often made a sport of catching and killing outlaws, so an outlaw usually fled from civilization, often into desolate forests to join other outlaws. Some bands of outlaws became professional robbers to survive. Because of the violence and crime credited to outlaws, the term has come to stand for any criminal not yet detained by authorities.

Cross-Cultural Notes One of the earliest Chinese dynastic codes of law and one that greatly influenced future legislation was that of the T'ang dynasty of the seventh century A.D. It was composed of two sections: a body of statutes called *lu,* which amounted to a criminal code, and a collection of ordinances called *ling,* which was an administrative code.

Example 4-1

Marlowe Phillips invested $25,000 in a financial plan devised by his neighbor, Ted Franklin. Under the terms of the agreement between Phillips and Franklin, the former was to invest his money in prime real estate on Sanibel Island off the coast of Florida. After turning the money over to Franklin, Phillips discovered that the land is worthless.

(Continued)

> ## Example 4-1 (*Continued*)
>
> Phillips confronted Franklin several times and demanded a return of his money with no result. He then took his grievance to Chandler Raymond, the county prosecutor. After an extensive investigation, Raymond told Phillips that he did not have enough evidence to prosecute Franklin. Phillips confronted Franklin one last time. When Franklin still refused to pay, Phillips drove his SUV at top speed in Franklin's direction. Franklin jumped out of the way and saved himself at the last moment. Phillips's SUV continued on and hit Anne Turtledove, seriously injuring her. As a result, Phillips was prosecuted for criminal battery. However, battery is not only a crime, it is also a tort. Consequently, several months after Phillips was prosecuted for criminal battery, he was also sued by Turtledove in civil court for the tort of battery.

Criminal Law in the American System

Laws too gentle are seldom obeyed; too severe, seldom executed.

—Benjamin Franklin (1706–1790), American statesman and philosopher

As we saw in the last chapter, the American legal system actually consists of two systems, the federal system and the state system. Both systems are involved in the making and enforcing of criminal law statutes. However, since there are fifty states and the District of Columbia it is actually more accurate to say that the American system is made up of fifty-two systems. Nevertheless, it is helpful to limit any discussion of the law to an examination of the federal and state systems. We simply must remember that each state has its own code and its own procedures which, although similar in most respects to all other states, may have its own peculiarities.

State Variations In 1999, Texas led the nation in the number of executions, followed by Virginia, Missouri, and Arizona.

State Variations Between 1977 and 1999 eight states with death penalty laws have carried out no executions: Connecticut, Kansas, New Hampshire, New Jersey, New Mexico, New York, South Dakota, and Tennessee.

Background Information An ancient Anglo-Saxon pledging system for preventing crime still existed in seventeenth century England and was probably the origin of the modern system of posting bond in the United States. A person guilty or suspected of a crime was required to make a pledge of good behavior to the court. The pledge usually required a person to appear at a later court where it would be determined if the conditions for good behavior had been met. If not, the criminal would be fined.

Federal Criminal Law Another peculiarity about the American system is that the federal government has no express power in the Constitution allowing it to enact criminal law statutes or to establish a national police force. Yet, the federal government does enact criminal law statutes and has set up a national police force, in the guise of the Federal Bureau of Investigation (FBI). The federal government also has a cabinet level criminal law enforcement official called the attorney general who has the power to conduct federal criminal investigations. The existence of the federal criminal law system and the various national law enforcement agencies is made possible by the adaptive processes at work within the legal system itself.

Criminal Law as a Complex Adaptive System The resourceful way in which Congress has assumed a set of powers never granted to it by the Framers of the Constitution demonstrates how the law acts as a complex adaptive system. The process works something like this. The Framers of the Constitution intended that Congress have only those powers enumerated in Article I, Section 8 of the Constitution. Since the term "police power" is not mentioned anywhere in the Constitution, it is clear that the Framers did not intend to give that power to the federal government, but instead expected it to be reserved to the states. Consequently, Congress can create criminal law statutes only in those areas over which it has jurisdiction. For instance, Congress has the power to coin money, so it can set up laws against counterfeiting. Yet, as we've seen, Congress has created criminal law statutes in other areas beyond counterfeiting. Since there has been no constitutional amendment explicitly handing Congress police power, how did Congress get the power to create a set of criminal law statutes and a national police force?

The answer is that the law, as a complex adaptive system, did want any complex adaptive system does when faced with an obstacle—it adapted. The adaptation occurred when Congress extended its power through a generous interpretation of the Commerce Clause.

The Commerce Clause, found in Article I, Section 8, Clause 3 of the U.S. Constitution, permits Congress to pass laws that regulate commerce "among the several States." Congress simply used this clause to regulate interstate criminal activities, which, after all, typically have an impact on "commerce." Although the ultimate results were a long time coming, eventually the courts, through a series of cases, culminating in the classic case of *Wickard v. Filburn* (63 S.Ct. 82) gave their "stamp of approval" to the legislature's interpretation of the Commerce Clause. In a sense then, Congress and the Courts cooperated to give Congress police power, a power it does not really have. That power includes the authority to create federal criminal law statutes and to establish a national police force.

Classes of Crimes

Under common law, crimes were dealt with in the order of their seriousness: treason, felonies, and misdemeanors. Most states now divide offenses into felonies and misdemeanors. A **felony** is a crime punishable by death or imprisonment in a federal or a state prison for a term exceeding one year. Some felonies are also punishable by fine. Some states define a felony as a crime subject to "punishment by hard labor," as an "infamous crime," or as a "crime subject to infamous punishment." Manslaughter, armed robbery, and arson are examples of felonies.

Some states also have separate categories for their most serious crimes. For instance, a state might classify premeditated murder and murder as *special felonies* or *capital felonies,* if these two are the only two offenses that might result in a death sentence or in life imprisonment. States may also have a separate category for violent offenses. Sometimes these violent offenses are termed *aggravated felonies.* Assault with a deadly weapon might be an example of an aggravated felony.

A **misdemeanor** is a less serious crime that is generally punishable by a prison sentence of not more than one year. Included in this category are offenses such as disorderly conduct. Some states also have a separate category for their least serious offenses. The label for these least serious offenses varies, but two of the most common are *petty offenses,* and *minor misdemeanors.* Traffic violations and building code violations are usually within this classification.

Terms The word *capital* derives from the Latin *caput,* meaning *head.* Capital crimes in British law were usually crimes for which the criminal had his or her head chopped off. The first recorded use of the word *capital* appeared in a 1493 document: "To have capytal sentence & be beheaded." The term *capital punishment* was used about a century later in a declaration that commoners sentenced to death would be hanged, and nobles sentenced to death would have their heads chopped off.

Trials for felonies, such as Scott Peterson's trial for the murder of Laci Peterson and their unborn son, often draw media attention.

Quick Quiz 4-1 True or False?

1. A misdemeanor is a crime punishable by death or imprisonment in a federal or a state prison for a term exceeding one year.

2. The primary objective of criminal law is to protect victims.

3. It is impossible for a single act to be both a tort and a crime.

4-2 Elements of a Crime

The two elements necessary to create criminal liability are a criminal act and the requisite state of mind. Although it is difficult to generalize about both of these concepts, certain characteristics are common to each, regardless of jurisdiction. Nevertheless, keep in mind that criminal law is largely statutory in nature. Consequently, specific statutory definitions may vary from state to state.

A Criminal Act

Under American law, a crime cannot be committed unless some overt act has occurred. An individual cannot be accused of a crime for merely thinking of a criminal act. The act is such an important element to criminal liability that convictions may be avoided or overturned if defendants can show that the statute under which they were prosecuted is ambiguous in its description of the act. Often, such ambiguity will occur when the legislature passes a statute that creates a new offense, when the statute outlaws an activity that may be protected by the U.S. Constitution, or when the statute seeks to outlaw statutes or behavior that causes no imminent negative effect but which may eventually lead to great public harm. For instance, the courts have frequently held statutes that outlaw a status, such as drug addiction or vagrancy, to be void for vagueness. The courts have also struck down statutes that are overbroad. The language of a criminal statute is overbroad if the courts cannot determine what specific activity the legislature intended to outlaw.

Omissions and Refusals to Act   At times, the failure to act, an omission, or the outright refusal to act may be considered criminal. Generally, however, an omission must be coupled with a legally imposed duty. A railroad crossing gate operator, who knows that a train and an automobile are on a collision course at the crossing, yet fails to lower the crossing gate, would be held criminally liable for this omission. This is true even though, strictly speaking, the gate operator did not act, but, instead, failed to act.

Involuntary Movement or Behavior   Many states specifically exclude involuntary movement and behavior from their general definition of a criminal act. Convulsions, reflexes, movements during sleep or unconsciousness, or behavior during a seizure are all considered involuntary movement or behavior falling outside the limits of criminal liability. However, the mere fact that someone is unconscious during a seizure may not absolve that individual of criminal liability if that person knew that he or she might suffer the seizure, yet took no precautions to avoid harming people or property. A person who decides to drive an automobile knowing that she or he is subject to sudden, unpredictable epileptic seizures may be criminally liable if a seizure causes that person to lose control of the vehicle, and kill or injure someone.

The Requisite State of Mind

Generally speaking, a crime cannot be committed unless the criminal act named in the statute is performed with the requisite state of mind. Many state criminal codes include the following four states of mind:

- purpose
- knowledge
- recklessness
- negligence

Purpose   Individuals act with **purpose** when they act with the intention to cause the result that does in fact occur. For example, if a young man were to point a loaded gun at his ex-girlfriend with the intention of shooting her, and if he actually were to shoot her, he would have acted with purpose. Some states choose to call this mental state *intent.* Intent or purpose should not be confused with *premeditation,* which is often an added condition in the case of aggravated or first-degree murder. If the young man had also planned the shooting of his ex-girlfriend, stalked her, finally decided exactly when and where to shoot her, and then actually carried out this plan, he would have been acting with premeditation.

The Opening Case Revisited
"Crime in the Streets or Crime in the Suites?"

Recall in The Opening Case at the beginning of this chapter, that the CEO of Adelphia Communications Corporation was prosecuted in federal court for a long list of abuses that involved such things as securities fraud, bank fraud, and conspiracy. The list of alleged offenses included some very complicated transactions that resulted in the concealment of a debt that topped the $2 billion dollar mark. One of the key charges involved bank fraud. According to the United States Code:

"Whoever knowingly executes, or attempts to execute, a scheme or artifice—
(1) to defraud a financial institution; or
(2) to obtain any moneys, funds, credits, assets, securities, or other property owned by, or under the custody or control of, a financial institution, by means of false or fraudulent pretenses, representations, or promises shall be [guilty of a crime]."
18 U.S.C. Sec. 1344 (2000).

This statute clearly illustrates how the element of the required mental state fits into criminal liability. Many criminal law statutes will, like this one, specifically identify the mental state required to create criminal culpability. In this case the required mental state is *knowledge*.

Knowledge When people act with an awareness that a particular result will probably occur, they act with **knowledge.** For instance, if the young man discussed previously took a loaded gun to a crowded shopping mall and began to fire at random, not aiming at anyone in particular, he would be acting with the knowledge that he would probably hit a lot of people and either wound or kill those people. This awareness would be true even if he were to recite quite vigorously and loudly, "I really don't want to shoot anyone. I hope I don't hit anybody!" In other words, he would know that shooting a gun in a crowded mall might easily kill someone.

Recklessness **Recklessness** involves a perverse disregard of a known risk of negative consequences. People act recklessly when they are indifferent to a serious risk they know to exist. Two drivers who challenge one another to an illegal drag race on a public highway are acting recklessly. In other words, they have disregarded the possible serious consequences of their decision to engage in an illegal drag race.

Negligence People act with **negligence** when they fail to see the possible negative consequences of their actions. A young woman who cleans a hunting rifle without checking to see if it is loaded is acting with negligence. This is because she has not bothered to look for any possible negative consequences that could result from her actions. Criminal negligence should not be confused with negligence in tort law. Negligence in tort law is concerned with the compensation of accident victims (see Chapter 5). In contrast, negligence in criminal law is concerned with punishing the wrongdoer and protecting the public at large.

The Matter of Motive

Motive in criminal law is the wrongdoer's reason for committing the crime. One common misconception about criminal law, which is perpetuated by countless television programs

Cross-Cultural Notes
Saudi Arabia, which has one of the lowest crime rates in the world, follows Islamic law. Penalties for crimes are severe but largely misunderstood in the West. For example, although murderers are punished by public decapitation and thieves suffer amputation, criminal investigations are thorough and penalties are given for false accusations. The king must approve all death sentences, and, in accordance with the Koran, a criminal may be cleared if the victim's family offers forgiveness.

About the Law
The definition of many legal terms varies depending upon the area of the law in which they are used. For example, in tort law, negligence is defined in relation to four elements: duty, breach of duty, proximate cause, and actual harm.

and movies, is that motive is an element of criminal liability. Such is not the case. Establishing motive may help the prosecution persuade the jury that the accused is guilty, but proving an evil motive is not necessary for a criminal conviction.

Quick Quiz 4-2 True or False?

1. The two elements needed to create criminal liability are a criminal act and the requisite state of mind.

2. Individuals act with negligence when they act with the intention to cause the result that does in fact occur.

3. Motive is an element of criminal liability.

4-3 Specific Crimes

Statutory definitions and classifications of crimes vary from jurisdiction to jurisdiction. Nevertheless, several generalities can be drawn to simplify an examination of specific crimes. Crimes can be classified as crimes against people, crimes against property, and crimes involving business.

Crimes Against People

Crimes against people, most often referred to as *felonies,* include homicide, assault, battery, kidnapping, and hate speech.

Homicide Any killing of one human by another may be labeled as a **homicide.** Criminal homicide is either murder or manslaughter. When the unlawful killing is done with premeditation and deliberate intent, it is labeled as *aggravated murder, premeditated murder,* or *first-degree murder.* The definition of first-degree murder, or aggravated murder, differs from state to state. However, in general, first-degree murder involves one of the following circumstances: (1) killing someone with premeditation (thinking about it and planning it in advance); (2) killing someone in a cruel way, such as with torture; (3) killing someone while committing a major crime such as rape, robbery, or kidnapping.

If none of these conditions apply, the crime is known as *second-degree murder.* In most states, the distinction between first- and second-degree murder is important because first-degree murder usually carries the death penalty while second-degree murder does not. In contrast to murder, manslaughter is an unlawful killing without the intent to kill. A killing that results when a person acts in a state of extreme fright, terror, anger, or blind rage that destroys the ability to reason is known as *voluntary manslaughter.* When the unlawful killing results from negligence, the homicide is called *involuntary manslaughter.*

Example 4-2

Using a computer chat room David Walker, who was seventeen at the time, enticed nine-year-old Kenneth Richter to meet him at a secluded spot. Walker then kidnapped Kenneth and transported him to another state. Walker's intent had been to demand a ransom from Kenneth's family. Walker, however, was stopped by police and attempted

> to flee. In the ensuing car chase, Walker lost control of his vehicle and crashed into a guard rail killing Kenneth. Walker was later convicted of manslaughter. However, the judge, who had a long record of being lenient on minors, gave Walker a suspended sentence. Kenneth's father was in the courtroom when this was announced. In a state of extreme rage, Kenneth's father attacked and killed Walker. Even though Kenneth's father's actions were clearly intentional, they were performed in a state of extreme rage as a result of a reasonable provocation.

Assault and Battery **Battery** is the unlawful touching of another person. An accidental bumping of another person in a crowded hallway or in the school cafeteria line would not be battery, since the crime requires criminal intent or at least reckless behavior. Similarly, the touching that occurs between football players during a game would not be a battery despite its violent nature because all parties have consented to the contact, assuming that the contact is within the rules of the game. Battery usually involves the forceful use of a person's hand, knife, gun, or other weapon. However, a battery could also be committed by giving poison or drugs to an unsuspecting victim, spitting in someone's face, siccing a dog on someone, or even kissing someone who does not want to be kissed.

An **assault** is an attempt to commit a battery. The pointing or shooting of a gun at someone is the assault; the bullet striking the person is the battery. Some states no longer follow the common law distinction between assault and battery. Ohio, for example, has eliminated the term "battery" from its criminal code and substituted "assault" by itself.

Simple assault and battery are generally misdemeanors. *Aggravated battery* and *aggravated assault,* however, are felonies in most states. To qualify as an aggravated offense, the assault or battery would have to be committed with a deadly weapon, with the intent to murder, with the intent to commit rape, or with the intent to commit robbery. Some states call aggravated assault *felonious assault.*

Kidnapping The unlawful abduction of an individual against that person's will is known as **kidnapping.** It constitutes false imprisonment with the additional element of the removal of the victim to another place. Most state laws distinguish between simple kidnapping and the more serious offenses involving child stealing or demands for ransom.

Hate Speech In recent years, many legislative bodies have attempted to criminalize the use of certain symbols, writings, and speech intended to provoke outrage or fear on the basis of race, religion, color, or gender. These statutes and ordinances are frequently referred to as laws against *hate speech.* Such statutes are constitutional only if they are not content specific. Therefore, while it may be acceptable to draft a statute that outlaws any speech designed to rouse fear or outrage regardless of the content of that speech, it would be impermissible to outlaw speech aimed at inciting outrage or fear based solely on race, religion, color, gender, or any similar category.

State Variations Iowa, along with other states, requires a No Contact order be issued whenever there is an arrest for a domestic assault. Violation of the No Contact order carries a mandatory minimum seven days in jail.

Background Information A British statute of 1916 stated that only a person who broke into a dwelling between 9:00 p.m. and 6:00 a.m. with the intention of committing a felony could be considered a burglar.

Elizabeth Smart was kidnapped in June 2002 and was fortunate to have been found in March 2003.

Crimes Against Property

Burglary, arson, robbery, larceny, and extortion are the most common crimes against property committed in the United States today.

Burglary **Burglary** consists of a break-in of a dwelling or other building for the purpose of carrying out a felony. The slightest forced entry qualifies as a break-in. Inserting a stick through a window while remaining outside constitutes an entry. Entry through an open door or a window does not alone establish the act of burglary, but once the person is inside, the opening of an interior door would constitute a break-in.

Arson **Arson** is the willful and malicious act of causing the burning of another's property. Under rules established in the common law tradition, arson included only the burning of a person's home. Modern criminal statutes, however, have expanded the crime of arson to include the burning of other structures as well. In some states, arson also includes the burning of a house by its owner. The willful burning is often motivated by the intent to defraud an insurer of the property.

Robbery The act of taking personal property, including money, from the possession of another against that person's will, in that person's presence, and under threat to do great bodily harm or damage is **robbery.** When force is not used, robbery is committed when the victim is subjected to extreme fear.

Larceny A person who takes and carries away the personal property of another without the right to do so is guilty of **larceny.** Generally, the victim need not be actually present for larceny to occur. The value of the property taken—$50 in many states, as high as $300 in others—determines whether the theft is *grand larceny,* a felony, or *petty larceny,* a misdemeanor. Shoplifting is a form of larceny.

Extortion **Extortion** is taking another's property with consent when such consent is coerced by threat to injure the victim's person, property, or reputation. Extortion is sometimes called *blackmail.*

Crimes Involving Business

Nonviolent in nature, business crimes are those carried out by a business or individual in the course of doing business to obtain a business-related advantage. Covering a wide range of illegal practices, business crimes are directed against individuals, other businesses, the government, or the public.

Larceny by False Pretenses The taking of someone's money or property by intentionally deceiving that person is known as **larceny by false pretenses.** The false statements that are made must be calculated to mislead and must induce the victim to rely on them.

Embezzlement Individuals who wrongfully take property entrusted to their care have committed the crime of **embezzlement.** In contrast to larceny, in which the offender takes the property without permission, the embezzler gains possession of the property or the money by legitimate means in the ordinary course of business. The embezzler then either keeps the property or puts it to personal use. It is no defense for the embezzler to argue that it was his or her intention to return the property after using it or when the rightful owner requested its return.

Bribery The crime of **bribery** involves a corrupt agreement induced by an offer of reward. Central to the offense is the offering, giving, receiving, or soliciting of something of value to influence official action or the discharge of a public duty. Whether the recipient accepts or rejects the bribe does not absolve the person who made the bribe. If the intended recipient accepts the bribe, then the recipient would be guilty of *bribery acceptance.*

Business Law in the News
Former Baltimore Police Leader Pleads Guilty

A former Baltimore police commissioner pleaded guilty on Monday to using thousands of dollars in police money to pay for liquor, lavish meals and nights at fancy hotels.

The former commissioner, Edward T. Norris, 43, also pleaded guilty to filing a false federal income tax return in a plea agreement reached at Federal District Court in Baltimore. He had been scheduled for arraignment before Judge Richard Bennett on three tax charges added to his indictment but instead entered the pleas.

Thomas M. DiBiagio, a United States attorney, said that Mr. Norris had admitted spending as much as $30,000 from three off-the-books police accounts. The accounts were set up in the Depression era to benefit officers.

"Public officials who lie, cheat and steal undermine our fundamental right to fair and honest government," Mr. DiBiagio said. "We deserve better."

Mr. Norris declined to comment as he left the courtroom. His lawyer, David Irwin, said Mr. Norris "accepted full responsibility for the mistakes outlined in the charges to which he pled guilty."

Mr. Norris and his former chief of staff, John Stendrini, were accused of misusing the money between May 2000 and August 2002. Mr. Stendrini has pleaded not guilty. Although there were no written guidelines for the money in the account, it "was required to be used for the benefit of the Baltimore Police Department," the indictment, from December, said.

Mr. Norris pleaded guilty on Monday to conspiracy to misuse city police funds and one count of filing a false tax form. The other charges—misapplication of funds, making a false statement on a mortgage application and two more counts of filing a false statement on a tax return—will be dropped.

Mr. Norris, who is to be sentenced in June, faces 6 to 12 months in prison on the conspiracy count and 6 months in prison on the tax charge. He also may have to pay a fine of up to $250,000 and restitution of up to $30,000.

Questions for Analysis

1. The criminal case outlined in this news article was held in the Federal District Court in Baltimore. On what legal grounds was federal jurisdiction established in that court? Explain.

2. The terms extortion and larceny are often misused in criminal law. Why does this case not involve charges of extortion or larceny?

3. From the facts in the case, is it clear whether this crime is a felony or a misdemeanor? Explain.

4. Does the defendant's motive for appropriating the funds matter in this case? Explain.

5. Suppose that the police commissioner explained that he intended to return the funds that were appropriated. Would this be an adequate defense in this case? Explain.

Source: "Former Baltimore Police Leader Pleads Guilty," *The Associated Press,* March 8, 2004, p. A-12. Reprinted with the permission of The Associated Press.

Forgery Forgery is the false making or changing of a writing with the intent to defraud. The signing of another person's name to a check or other document without authority is forgery. Signing one's own name or pretending to be someone else of the same name is also forgery. Similarly, the creation of a fictitious identity, and the signing of the name of that fictitious person with fraudulent purpose is considered forgery.

In order for there to be a crime in these circumstances, there must be an intent to defraud, and the item forged must have some legal effect. Thus, it would not be fraud to write someone else's signature on a will that was never witnessed, because an unwitnessed will has no legal effect. Uttering a forged instrument is also a crime. *Uttering* means to offer a forged instrument to another person, knowing that it is forged and intending to defraud.

Background Information There have been a number of controversial cases in the United States involving the insanity defense. One of the first examples to spur national debate was in the trial of John W. Hinckley, Jr., who had tried to assassinate President Ronald Reagan in 1981.

Racketeer Influenced and Corrupt Organizations Act To prevent a criminal invasion of legitimate businesses, Congress enacted the Racketeer Influenced and Corrupt Organizations Act (RICO). Under provisions of this statute, conducting a legitimate business with the funds acquired from a "pattern of racketeering activities" can give rise to criminal liability. Many of the offenses that fall within the scope of "racketeering activity"—such as arson and robbery—are serious crimes. Others, however, are less sinister. For example, both mail fraud and wire fraud fall within the definition of racketeering activities. The provisions of RICO can give rise not only to criminal charges, but also to civil liability. Thus, it is not uncommon for individuals to seek damages in lawsuits filed against corporations that have violated RICO.

Quick Quiz 4-3 True or False?

1. In most states, the distinction between first- and second-degree murder is important because first-degree murder usually carries the death penalty while second-degree murder does not.

2. It is acceptable to draft a statute that outlaws speech aimed at inciting outrage or fear based solely on race, religion, color, gender, or any similar category.

3. Shoplifting is a form of larceny.

4-4 Cybercrimes

As is true of most other crimes, statutory definitions and classifications of cybercrimes vary from jurisdiction to jurisdiction. Moreover, in the case of cybercrimes the definitions are even more varied because there is no agreement on what constitutes a cybercrime (see Table 4-1). One approach to this task is to state that *cybercrimes* involve any criminal act that includes a computer. This approach, which is often referred to as *computer trespass* or *cybertrespass,* can solve many of the problems associated with cybercrime, if only by an indirect treatment of such crimes. Another way to classify cybercrimes is to distinguish between crimes committed with a computer and crimes committed against computers.

Cybertrespass

A different type of problem arises when crimes that are already on the books are committed with a computer. As noted above, one way to deal with this situation is to create a single, general offense called cybertrespass. *Cybertrespass* is defined as gaining access to a computer with the intent to commit a crime. In effect, in one single stroke, this technique incorporates the rest of a criminal code into this one crime making it an offense to use a computer to commit any other crime in the code. In a state that takes this approach, all criminal statutes, but especially those on fraud, embezzlement, blackmail, and theft become part of this one crime known as computer trespass.

Crimes Committed with a Computer

Another approach to dealing with cybercrime is to distinguish between using a computer to commit a crime and committing an offense against a computer or the owner of a computer. Cybercrimes that focus on the use of a computer include cyberextortion, cyberstalking, and cyberspoofing.

Table 4-1 State Cybercrimes

The General Approach

Cybertrespass—Gaining access to a computer with the intent to commit a criminal act.

Crimes Committed with a Computer

Cyberextortion—Gaining access to the computer records of a business or other institution and, in the process, uncovering the illegal, unethical, or negligent conduct of that organization and using that information to commit extortion.

Cyberstalking—Targeting an innocent victim for exploitation using that person's computer connections.

Cyberspoofing—Falsely adopting the identity of another computer user or creating a false identity on a computer website in order to commit fraud.

Crimes that Target Computers

Cyberterrorism—Using a computer to disrupt or destroy one of the critical elements of the nation's electronic infrastructure.

Cybervandalism—Attacking a computer system so that a website is completely destroyed or paralyzed.

Cybergerm Warfare—Using viruses to attack a computer system.

Identity Theft—Using a computer to steal credit card information, financial data, access codes, passwords, and debit card information to clean out a person's bank accounts, to run up credit card debt, to divert cash transfers, and to disrupt the financial and personal life of the victim.

Cyberextortion *Cyberextortion* or *cyberblackmail,* as it is often called, can occur when an experienced hacker gains access to the computer records of a corporation or other institution and discovers some sort of illegal, negligent, or unethical conduct which might embarrass or otherwise damage the reputation or the financial health of the target organization. The hacker can then contact the company, also often using the computer, to threaten exposure unless he or she is handsomely compensated.

Cyberstalking *Cyberstalking,* which is related to cyberblackmail, and which often either precedes or follows it, involves targeting individuals for exploitation using their computer connections. Cyberstalkers usually target vulnerable individuals who may be searching for a genuine confidant. Minors are most often targeted by cyberstalkers. After gaining the trust of the minor or other innocent victim, the cyberstalker arranges a meeting so that he or she can take direct advantage of the innocent party.

Cyberspoofing To commit *cyberspoofing,* a *cybercriminal* must falsely adopt the identity of another computer user or create a false identity on a computer website in order to commit fraud. A simple form of cyberspoofing involves adopting the identity of an e-mailer in order to defraud the recipients of the original e-mail. Another type of cyberspoofing involves creating phony websites or diverting users from legitimate websites in order to obtain credit card numbers, debit card numbers, passwords, or other confidential information to commit a wide variety of fraudulent activities. A third cyberspoofing method involves sending out phony e-mails that solicit buyers and, in the process, obtain credit card information, account numbers, passwords and so on. This last technique is known as *phising.*

Protect your information! Using stolen credit cards or other personal information, identity thieves can steal not only from you, but also from stores and banks.

Crimes That Target Computers

Cybercrimes that target computers attempt to disable the computer itself, to disable the system that it operates, or to confiscate and use information stored on the computer, sometimes after erasing the original genuine data. Crimes that target computers include cyberterrorism, identity theft, cybervandalism, and cybergerm warfare.

Cyberterrorism   *Cyberterrorism* involves using a computer to disrupt or destroy one of the critical elements of the nation's electronic infrastructure, such as power systems, the air traffic control system, water and sanitation systems, ground transportation systems, the nation's stock exchanges, the banking system, and the national defense system. Cyberterrorists could send a virus into a critical computer system that causes the entire electronic infrastructure to collapse.

Identity Theft   Another cybercrime that targets computers and computer information is known as identity theft. In *identity theft* a perpetrator, using one of the techniques noted above, steals credit card information, financial data, access codes, passwords, or debit card information. The perpetrator then passes himself or herself off as the victim. Using this technique, the identity thief can clean out bank accounts, run up credit card transactions, divert cash transfers, and generally disrupt the financial and personal life of the victim.

Cybervandalism   Sometimes expert cybervandals can attack a computer system so that a website is completely destroyed, or so that it is paralyzed to the extent that legitimate business can no longer be conducted on that site. This type of attack is known as *cybervandalism.* Often cybervandalism is used to cripple a business as a form of revenge for real or imagined wrongs, to exercise power over the business, or to hurt the owner of a business.

Cybergerm Warfare   When criminals use viruses to attack a computer system they are engaged in *cybergerm warfare.* Clearly viruses can be used to attack computer systems for many of the cybercrimes listed above. Thus, a cyberextortionist can threaten to unleash a virus into a company's computer system unless he or she is paid a certain amount of money. In effect, the cyberextortionist is using the virus to extract ransom money from the business. Similarly, a cyberterrorist or a cybervandal can use a virus to disrupt a computer system for political or psychological reasons.

Federal Cybercrimes

Many states have enacted legislation to combat these cybercrimes and other computer-related offenses. The federal government has also attempted to deal with the issue by passing a number of anticybercrime statutes including the Access Device Fraud Act; the Computer Fraud and Abuse Act; the No Electronic Theft Act; the CAN SPAM Act; the Racketeer Influenced and Corrupt Organizations Act (RICO); The Communications Assistance for Law Enforcement Act; The Identity Theft and Assumption Deterrence Act; The Multistate Anti-Terrorism Information Exchange; and The Wire and Electronic Communication Interception Act.

The Access Device Fraud Act   The objective of this federal statute is to make it unlawful to obtain money, property, or services through fraudulent use of a computer. Such use would include adding, deleting, or altering a computer program or data.

Computer Fraud and Abuse Act As noted previously in this chapter, the Computer Fraud and Abuse Act prohibits many of the things outlined above such as accessing protected computers for the purpose of committing fraud, theft, or trespass. Under provisions of the act, it is also forbidden to access one computer in order to invade and destroy another computer. The act makes it unlawful for any person to use a computer to gain access to secret information that could compromise national security with the intent to hurt the United States or help a foreign power.

The No Electronic Theft Act Although the federal authorities do not often invoke the No Electronic Theft Act (the NET Act), it is available as a way to deal with some forms of piracy on the Web. Penalties under the act include imprisonment and heavy fines that can go as high as $250,000.

The CAN SPAM Act Spam is the nickname for all of those pop-up advertisements that appear on computer screens while users are tapped into the Internet. The CAN SPAM Act is designed to deal with this problem as well as the problem of unsolicited commercial e-mail.

The Racketeer Influenced and Corrupt Organizations Act (RICO) When RICO was first passed as part of Title IX of the Organized Crime Control Act of 1970, Congress had no idea that it would ultimately be used to attack consumer fraud, consumer extortion, and corporate corruption. However, the fact that wire fraud falls within the definition of racketeering activities means that offenses committed by corporations on the Internet can be included within its realm of influence.

The Communications Assistance for Law Enforcement Act This act was set up to make electronic surveillance easier for law enforcement groups. Under certain provisions of the Communications Assistance for Law Enforcement Act, Internet providers must assist enforcement agencies in wiretap operations.

The Identity Theft and Assumption Deterrence Act This statute represents Congress's attempt to deal with the growing problem of identity theft in the United States today. As noted above, in identity theft a wrongdoer steals credit card information, financial data, access codes, passwords, and debit card information and then passes that information off as his or her own. However, the perpetrator need not actually work a computer to commit identity theft. Instead, he or she could use stolen or forged credit or debit cards to pass himself or herself off as the actual card holder.

The Multistate Anti-Terrorism Information Exchange This act, which is frequently referred to as the MATRIX Act, involves the cooperation of state and federal authorities in the compilation of files on subjects based on state drivers' licenses, tax files, marriage certificates, divorce decrees, and traffic offenses. States are permitted to get involved in the process on a voluntary basis.

Wire and Electronic Communication Interception Act This federal act is designed to protect the privacy of most wire and electronic communication attempts. Thus, under provisions of the act, a perpetrator cannot obstruct or interfere with wire or other electronic communication attempts, including communication attempts on the Internet.

See Ellis, Robert L. "New Digital Technologies and the Law." The Ohio State Bar Association Annual Conference, May 13, 2004, Cleveland, Ohio, pp. 3, 6, 10.

Quick Quiz 4-4 True or False?

1. Statutory definitions and classifications of cybercrimes have become uniform within all jurisdictions in the United States.

2. Cybertrespass is defined as gaining access to a computer with the intent to commit a crime.

3. After an identity theft incident, it often takes the victim months or years to reestablish his or her own credit, employment, and personal history.

4-5 Defenses to Criminal Liability

Since the essence of criminal liability lies within the two essential elements of an act and requisite mental state, a logical defense would be aimed at eliminating one or both of those elements. Most defenses attempt to do just that. The most common defenses are insanity, entrapment, justifiable force, and mistake. (See Table 4-2.)

The Insanity Defense

Although the insanity defense has been around for a long time, many people do not understand the nature of the defense. One of the key points of confusion is the difference between *competency to stand trial* and the *insanity defense itself*.

Further Reading For a better understanding of legal terminology, refer students to *Legal Terminology*, 4th edition by Gordon W. Brown (Upper Saddle River, NJ: Prentice Hall, 2004).

Competency to Stand Trial Criminal defendants are generally presumed to be mentally competent to stand trial. However, the issue of competency to stand trial can be raised if the court, the defense attorney, or the prosecutor suspects that the defendant is not competent. If the issue of competency is raised, the defendant will undergo psychiatric examinations to determine the level of competency. Generally, defendants are considered competent to stand trial if they understand the nature and the purpose of the charges against them, and if they are capable of aiding their attorneys in their defense. When defendants are found to be incompetent, they are usually given treatment to improve their competency level so that they can understand what is going on and can assist in their case.

Table 4-2 Criminal Liability and Defenses

Criminal Liability	Criminal Defenses

The act:
   Criminal behavior specifically
     outlined by statute
	Defenses to the act:
	   Act as defined is "status" only
	   Act as defined is ambiguous
	   Act as defined is overbroad

The mental state:
   Mental state specifically
     outlined by statute
     Purpose
     Knowledge
     Recklessness
     Negligence
	Defenses to the mental state:
	   Insanity
	   Entrapment
	   Justifiable force
	   Mistake

> ## Example 4-4
>
> The question of competency to stand trial was a key factor in a case in which Harold Gunther was prosecuted for the murder of one person and the attempted murder of two others. Listening at the door of an apartment, Gunther believed he heard three co-workers plotting against him. Convinced that he was about to be attacked, Gunther entered the apartment and assaulted his three co-workers, killing one and severely injuring the other two. Gunther consistently maintained that he was the intended target of a plot to destroy him. No evidence was ever presented that such a plot existed. In contrast, expert testimony indicated that Gunther was paranoid and delusional. Consequently, his defense attorney moved for a competency hearing. Despite the expert testimony, the judge in the case found Gunther competent to stand trial. The competency ruling was based on the fact that, despite Gunther's mental problems, he was capable of understanding the charges against him and was able to assist in his defense. Under state law, these were the only qualifications needed for a competency finding by the court. Gunther met these qualifications and was found competent to stand trial.

Not Guilty by Reason of Insanity (NGRI) Recall that a crime is defined in terms of the act and the required mental state. American law recognizes that individuals cannot be held responsible for their actions if they do not know what they are doing. In addition, it serves no practical purpose to imprison someone who needs the care of mental health professionals. For these reasons, insanity is recognized as a valid defense to criminal conduct.

The oldest test of insanity is the **M'Naughten Rule.** Under this rule, a defendant can be found NGRI, if at the time the criminal act was committed, he or she was suffering from a mental disease that was so serious that the defendant did not know the nature of the act, or did not know that act was wrong. Another test of insanity is the **irresistible impulse test.** This test holds that criminal defendants can be found NGRI, if at the time of the offense, they were stricken with a mental disease which prevented them from knowing right from wrong or compelled them to commit the crime.

A more recent insanity test has been developed by the **American Law Institute (ALI).** Under the ALI test, a person is not responsible if "as a result of mental disease or defect he lacks substantial capacity either to appreciate the criminality of his conduct or to conform his conduct to the requirements of law." The ALI test is plainly a relaxation of the usual insanity standard as expressed in M'Naughten and the irresistible impulse test because both of the older tests require "total" rather than "substantial" impairment. M'Naughten requires an inability to appreciate the wrongfulness of an action while the irresistible impulse test requires a thorough loss of self-control.

It is important to understand that people found not guilty by reason of insanity do not automatically go free. Instead, they are committed to institutions and must undergo periodic psychiatric examinations. Once they are found to be sane they may be released. Many people object to the fact that these individuals can look forward to release without serving any time in prison.

State Variations More and more states have adopted the American Law Institute version of the insanity test. At least seventeen states have adopted the ALI test, with five more states adopting a similar version of this test. At least nineteen states are currently using the M'Naughten Rule, or a modified version of it. There are a few other versions of this rule also, and a few states have dropped the insanity defense altogether.

Entrapment

If a law enforcement officer induces a law-abiding citizen to commit a crime, **entrapment** may be used as a defense. The person using the defense must show that the crime would not have been committed had it not been for the inducement of the officer. The defense of

Business Law in the News
High-Court Ruling Unleashes Chaos Over Sentencing

When the Supreme Court last month struck down tough sentencing guidelines used in Washington State, Justice Sandra Day O'Connor dissented. She feared the ruling would wreak havoc on the nation's federal courts.

She was right. Although the 5-4 ruling technically affects only one state's court system, the Justice Department is forcing prosecutors of federal crimes to draft indictments and sculpt plea bargains in compliance with it. That has thrown into confusion the sentencing of nearly 250 federal defendants every day. And tens of thousands of old cases are up in the air again as defense attorneys try to get long sentences thrown out.

Now Congress may step in with a bill that might fix the problem temporarily while legislators, prosecutors and the courts search for a permanent solution. "The criminal justice system has begun to run amok," Orrin Hatch, chairman of the Senate Judiciary Committee, said yesterday.

The June 24 Supreme Court ruling said that any factor increasing a criminal sentence must be admitted by the defendant in a plea deal or proved to a jury. The ruling came in the case of a Washington state man, Ralph H. Blakely Jr., who pleaded guilty to kidnapping his estranged wife. That crime in Washington state carries a maximum sentence of four years and five months. But the judge tacked on another three years and a month, based on the finding that Mr. Blakely acted with "deliberate cruelty." The Supreme Court said the tougher sentence violated the defendant's Sixth Amendment right to a jury trial.

The Blakely ruling has exposed concerns about the fairness of 20-year-old guidelines for sentencing federal defendants and reignited the question of how much authority Congress should have to mandate federal prison sentences.

Prosecutors can boost a defendant's recommended sentence under the guidelines by introducing examples of "relevant conduct" that, while not proved in court, appear to increase the gravity of the offense. Judges can ignore the recommended sentence, but few want to face the likelihood of being overturned on appeal. Long before Blakely, many federal judges were rebelling at what they saw as congressional encroachment on their turf. And defendants complained that they were handed mega-sentences without ever having a chance to challenge the facts that underpin them.

The Supreme Court's ruling has given new life to these protests. Lower-court decisions in the last few weeks have differed over whether the high court's ruling applies to federal cases.

Crime and Punishment

Milestones in federal sentencing rules:

- **1984:** Congress creates U.S. Sentencing Commission to standardize sentences.

- **1987:** First sentencing guidelines created by commission.

- **1995:** Commission members try to change cocaine sentences, but Congress says no.

- **2003:** With Feeney Amendment, Congress cracks down on judges who give lighter sentences.

- **June 2004:** Supreme Court rules in state case, Blakely v. Washington, that judges can't use information in sentencing not heard by jury or admitted to by defendant.

- **July:** Judges begin ruling that Blakely applies to federal courts, undermining federal sentencing guidelines.

Source: WSJ research

Questions for Analysis

1. What Constitutional Amendment is at the heart of the Supreme Court's ruling on sentencing in the Blakely Case? Explain.

2. In the Blakely Case, the Supreme Court ruled on the constitutionality of a case that was heard in the courts of the state of Washington. Why should this ruling trouble federal prosecutors? Explain.

3. Explain the Constitutional significance of the following quotation: "The June 24 Supreme Court ruling said that any factor increasing a criminal sentence must be admitted by the defendant in a plea deal or proven to a jury."

4. How is the separation of powers doctrine involved in this case? Explain.

5. Why do judges refrain from ignoring the recommended sentences in federal criminal cases? Explain.

Source: Laurie P. Cohen and Gary Fields. "Legal Quagmire: High-Court Ruling Unleashes Chaos over Sentencing," *The Wall Street Journal,* July 15, 2004, p. A1. Reprinted with permission.

entrapment is not available to a defendant who would have committed the crime even without the involvement of the officer.

Example 4-5

Lester Merrideth, a resident of Colorado Springs, placed a cryptic advertisement in the personal ads of a national newspaper that caters to mercenaries. The advertisement was actually a disguised offer seeking the services of a hit man. Terry Usalis, an officer in the Colorado Springs Police Department, recognized the advertisement for what it was and, along with his superiors, formulated a plan under which Usalis would pretend to be a hit man and would contact Merrideth. Usalis contacted Merrideth and set up a meeting at an obscure diner in Colorado Springs. At that meeting, Merrideth asked Usalis to murder his business partner. Usalis promptly arrested Merrideth. Merrideth will not be able to use the defense of entrapment because he would have attempted to hire a hit man regardless of the intervention of the police officer.

Background Information An investigation conducted by the FBI in 1978–1980 spurred public debate on the question of entrapment. The result of the investigation was the conviction of seven members of Congress and five other public officials for conspiracy, bribery, and other charges. FBI agents impersonating an Arab sheikh and other high-ranking officers had offered bribes in return for special favors. Their encounters were recorded on videotape. In 1982, a Senate panel criticized the FBI's handling of the investigation but found that no civil rights had been violated.

Justifiable Force

In general, the law will not condone the use of force to solve problems. Still, special circumstances may arise that justify the use of force. Three of these situations lead to the following defenses: self-defense, defense of others, and the battered-spouse syndrome.

Self-Defense When individuals have good reason to believe that they are in danger of death or serious injury, they can use force to protect themselves. This is known as **self-defense.** In some states, the person claiming self-defense must retreat, if possible, before resorting to force. However, a person does not have a duty to retreat before using force if the attack occurs in his or her own home. When self-defense is used in a criminal case, the defendant must show that he or she was not the one who started the altercation in the first place. Moreover, in all cases, the person claiming self-defense must not have used more force than necessary to stop the unprovoked attack.

Defense of Others If a person uses force to rescue another person who is the victim of an apparent attack, most states will allow the rescuer to escape criminal liability. This is known as **defense of others.** As in the case of self-defense, the rescuer must have good reason to believe that the victim was in danger of severe bodily injury or even death.

Getting Students Involved Help students understand the concept of self-defense by holding a mock trial. Think of a scenario or ask a group of students to create one whereby self-defense could be argued in a court of law. Write the scenario on a sheet of paper and hand out copies to the entire class. Ask for volunteers to play the various roles, including witnesses, judge, bailiff, prosecutor, defense attorney, defendant, and jury. When the trial is finished, ask students to write a report summarizing the events of the trial.

The Battered Spouse Syndrome The law also protects a married individual from being abused by his or her spouse. In most cases of spouse abuse, the wife is victimized by the violent outbursts of her husband. Many communities have established shelters where abused and battered wives can seek safety and receive counseling and legal services for themselves and their children. Wives who wish to protect themselves from the continual abuse caused by their husbands may seek legal help from the courts.

One such remedy is the *protective order.* Protective orders bar the abusing spouse from maintaining any contact with the victim. Such orders are enforced by the local police. Unfortunately, protective orders are not always effective. In some very severe cases, the victimized spouse has taken the law into her own hands and killed her tormentor. The set of circumstances that leads a woman to believe that the only way that she can escape death or severe bodily injury is to use force against her tormentor is called **battered spouse syndrome.** These circumstances are also known as *battered woman* or *battered wife syndrome.* Because the spouse has good reason to believe that she was in danger of death or severe bodily injury, battered spouse syndrome is considered a form of self-defense in some courts.

Mistake

Mistake is a defense to charges of criminal liability as long as the mistake destroys one of the elements necessary to that crime. If the mistake does not destroy an element, then it is not a valid defense. To be a successful defense, the mistake must be based on a reasonable belief. It would be no defense for a defendant to say that he shot his wife because he believed she was an invader from Mars. Note also that it is not a defense for an accused to say that he did not know that this particular conduct was prohibited by law. Nor is it a defense to a gambling charge for the defendant to argue that she did not know that the gambling law applied to her. Finally, the mistake must destroy the criminal nature of the act in the mind of the accused. It would be no defense for example, if a defendant argued that he injured an individual by mistake when he was actually trying to injure someone else.

Example 4-6

In Example 4-1 Marlowe Phillips drove his SUV at top speed in an attempt to injure Ted Franklin, who jumped out of the way and saved himself. Nevertheless, Phillips' SUV seriously injured Anne Turtledove. As a result, Phillips was prosecuted for criminal battery. Phillips would not be able to use the defense of mistake here by claiming that he intended to hit Franklin rather than Turtledove. Such a mistake would not destroy a key element here, that is, the intent to injure a person with the speeding vehicle.

Quick Quiz 4-5 True or False?

1. Most defendants who are found NGRI are released immediately.
2. A person does not have to retreat in his or her own home before resorting to force to repel an attack.
3. Mistake is never a defense to a charge of criminal liability.

Summary

4-1 A crime is an offense against the public at large. As such, a crime threatens the peace, safety, and well-being of the entire community. For this reason, crimes are punishable by the official governing body of a nation or state. A felony is a crime punishable by death or imprisonment in a federal or a state prison for a term exceeding one year. Some felonies are also punishable by fine. A misdemeanor is a less serious crime that is generally punishable by a prison sentence for not more than one year.

4-2 The two elements necessary to create criminal liability are (a) an act and (b) the requisite state of mind. Generally speaking, a crime cannot be committed unless the criminal act named in the statute is performed with the requisite state of mind. Many state criminal codes include four possible states of mind: (1) purpose, (2) knowledge, (3) recklessness, and (4) negligence. Establishing motive may help investigators pinpoint the guilty party, but proving an evil motive is not necessary for a criminal conviction. Conversely, establishing the existence of a good motive will rarely absolve a defendant of criminal liability.

4-3 Crimes against the people include homicide, assault, battery, kidnapping, and hate speech. Burglary, robbery, and arson are the most common crimes against property committed in the United States. Nonviolent in nature, business crimes are those carried out by a business or individual in the course of doing business to obtain a business-related advantage.

4-4 One approach to this task of defining cybercrime is to state that cybercrimes involve any criminal transgression that includes or impacts upon a computer. This approach is often referred to as computer trespass as cybertrespass. Another way to classify cybercrimes is to distinguish between crimes committed with a computer and crimes committed against computers. Crimes committed with a computer include cyberextortion, cyberstalking, and cyberspoofing. Crimes committed against computers include cyberterrorism, identity theft, cybervandalism, and cybergerm warfare. Another way to fight cybercrime is through the creation of federal anticybercrime statutes.

4-5 Since the essence of criminal liability lies within the two essential elements of act and requisite mental state, a logical defense would be aimed at eliminating one or both of those elements. Most defenses attempt to do just that. The most common defenses are insanity, entrapment, justifiable force, and mistake.

Key Terms

American Law Institute (ALI) test, 83
arson, 76
assault, 75
battered spouse syndrome, 86
battery, 75
bribery, 76
burglary, 76
crime, 69
defense of others, 85

embezzlement, 76
entrapment, 83
extortion, 76
felony, 71
forgery, 77
homicide, 74
irresistible impulse test, 83
kidnapping, 75
knowledge, 72

larceny, 76
larceny by false pretenses, 76
misdemeanor, 71
M'Naughten Rule, 83
negligence, 73
purpose, 72
recklessness, 73
robbery, 76
self-defense, 85

Questions for Review and Discussion

1. What is the purpose of criminal law?
2. What are the various categories and classes of crimes?
3. What is the nature of an act within the meaning of criminal liability?
4. What are the four mental states that can be found in the criminal code?
5. What is motive and how does it differ from the elements of criminal liability?
6. What are the various crimes against people?
7. What are embezzlement and larceny by false pretenses?
8. What are the various ways that the law has of dealing with cybercrime?
9. What are the three standards for the insanity defense found in criminal law?
10. What are the requirements of entrapment as defenses to criminal liability?

Investigating the Internet

The National Institute of Justice, which is the research arm of the United States Justice Department, maintains a website that deals with national criminal justice issues. The Racketeer Influenced and Corrupt Organizations Act (RICO) can be found on the Internet by accessing the Legal Information Institute (LII) of Cornell Law School. A source of state laws is StateLaw which is furnished by the Washburn School of Law.

Cases for Analysis

1. Three teenaged football players used a phony pistol in a robbery attempt at 2 a.m. on an early Friday morning. To their surprise, their planned target produced his own weapon. The intended victim fired at and shot one of the three robbers. The other two boys fled the scene leaving their injured teammate behind. The third football player and would-be robber died from the gunshot wound. The other two teenagers were later arrested and charged with murder. How can the other two boys be charged with murder when neither of them fired a weapon? Explain. The man who shot and killed the third robber was also charged with murder. What defense does the intended victim have in his case? Will he succeed in that defense? Explain. See Nichols, Jim. "Teens Admit Role in Player's Death, Lawyer Says." *The Cleveland Plain Dealer,* April 29, 2004, pp. A-1, A-14.

2. Angie Chen arranged with Mayflower to have her household goods moved from Atlanta to Chicago. At the time the contract was made, she was told that her bill would be no more than $1,749.89. When the truck arrived at her apartment in Chicago, additional fees were charged because of the alleged need for a shuttle truck. The final bill was for $2,549.89. When Chen tried to pay by credit card, the representatives of Mayflower refused to accept payment and threatened to impound and auction off her furniture and household goods to satisfy the amount that she allegedly owed the moving company. Chen later found out that this type of "bait and switch" scheme had occurred many times to other Mayflower customers. Consequently, she sued Mayflower under the RICO statute. How is it possible for a private plaintiff to bring a civil lawsuit under a criminal statute like RICO? Explain. *Chen v. Mayflower Transit, Inc.,* 99-C-6261 (N. D. Ill.); see also Harris, Andrew. "National Mover Faces RICO Suit." *The National Law Journal,* April 19, 2004, p. 4.

3. While at a party, Scott drank some punch which he did not know was laced with PCP. Subsequent to this event, he exhibited bizarre behavior and began to hallucinate. Believing that his life and the life of the President were in danger, he attempted to commandeer several motor vehicles. He was charged, tried, and convicted of two counts of attempted theft. Will Scott's conviction be overturned? Explain. *People v. Scott,* 194 Cal. Rptr. 633 (CA).

4. Katie Roberts was wasting away from the effects of an incurable disease. She asked her husband Frank to help her commit suicide. In response to her request, Roberts mixed poison and water and placed the mixture on a chair within her reach. She took the poison and died several hours later. Roberts admitted placing the poison within her reach, but denied having the required mental state for first-degree murder because he was responding to his wife's request and was motivated by love and mercy. Will Roberts prevail? Explain. *People v. Roberts,* 178 N.W.690 (MI).

5. Several teenagers taped the broken legs of a chair together in order to create a cross which they then ignited and placed on the lawn of an African-American family in the neighborhood. One of the teenagers, a minor, was charged with a misdemeanor under the St. Paul Bias Motivated Crime Ordinance. The St. Paul ordinance criminalized the placing on private property of any "symbol, object, appellation, characterization or graffiti . . . which one knows or has reasonable grounds to know arouses anger, alarm, or resentment in others on the basis of race, color, creed, religion or gender." The defendant argued that the ordinance was an unconstitutional violation of the First Amendment. The city contended that the statute was constitutional because it was necessary for the preservation of a compelling state interest, namely, the right of group members who have been discriminated against in the past "to live in peace where they wish." Is the St. Paul ordinance constitutional? Explain. *R.A.V. v. St. Paul,* 505 U.S. 1992 (U.S. Sup. Ct.).

6. Tomas Reese entered a fast-food restaurant before the restaurant had opened for business through an unlocked rear entrance. The door had been left unlocked by an accomplice who was an employee of the restaurant. After entering the restaurant, Reese pushed one employee against a soda machine and, while holding a gun to the neck of the manager, forced her to open the safe. Reese then locked the employees in a cooler and fled the scene with over $5,000. Has Reese committed burglary, robbery, or larceny? Explain. *State v. Reese,* 113 Ohio App. 3d. 642 (OH).

7. Cuttiford and Banks lived in the same duplex. Banks lived upstairs and Cuttiford lived downstairs. The two apartments shared a common internal stairway at the back of the duplex. A confrontation began between Banks and Cuttiford in the rear stairway of the duplex. Banks became rather violent and threatened Cuttiford and Cuttiford's wife. Cuttiford went to his apartment on the bottom floor and retrieved two guns from his bedroom. When he returned to the back door near the stairway, Banks told him, "You don't have the guts to use that, because you're going to have to use it because I'm going to kill you!" Banks then came at Cuttiford lunging from the common stairway into the kitchen of the Cuttiford apartment. Cuttiford then shot and killed Banks. At trial Cuttiford argued that he shot Banks in self-defense. The trial court refused to instruct the jury that Cuttiford did not have to retreat in his own home before acting to repel an attacker. The court apparently believed the prosecution which had argued that, since Banks and Cuttiford occupied the same duplex, Cuttiford had the duty to retreat before repelling Banks' attack. Was the trial court judge correct in his instruction to the jury regarding self-defense? Explain. *State v. Cuttiford,* 639 N.E.2d 472 (OH).

8. Cowen had on many occasions operated as a paid drug informant for the FBI and the Ventura Police Department. The Ventura police asked Cowen to keep in touch with them should he become involved in any deals. Subsequently, Cowen asked Busby to introduce him to any drug dealers he knew. Busby introduced Cowen to Mandell, who sold Cowen several samples of cocaine in anticipation of a $41,500 deal. Cowen then contacted the Ventura police. A police officer posed as Cowen's buyer and both Busby and Mandell were arrested and eventually turned over to the federal authorities. Busby was convicted of possession of cocaine with the intent to distribute it. He appealed this conviction, claiming that he had been entrapped by Cowen. Will Busby's entrapment defense succeed on appeal? Explain. *United States v. Busby,* 780 F.2d 804 (9th Cir.).

Quick Quiz Answers

4-1	4-2	4-3	4-4	4-5
1. F	1. T	1. T	1. F	1. F
2. F	2. F	2. F	2. T	2. T
3. F	3. F	3. T	3. T	3. F

Chapter 5   Tort Law

The Opening Case
"Hasta la Vista Publicity"

Shortly after the action movie hero, Arnold Schwarzenegger, became governor of California, a bobble-headed figure of him showed up for sale on Internet auctions and through an Ohio toy manufacturer known as Bosley Bobbers. The smiling, bobble-headed figure depicted the actor-turned-politician dressed in a suit and tie, wearing a bandoleer, and carrying a gun. The figure was priced at $19.99. However, $5 of the cost was sent to a cancer-fighting charity. After the bobble-headed duplicate of governor Schwarzenegger showed up in a Sacramento souvenir shop, Bosley Bobbers was contacted by Schwarzenegger's lawyers, and threatened with a lawsuit if Bosley and friends did not refrain from further marketing attempts. The company continued to manufacture and market the doll, and, as a result, a lawsuit was filed by Schwarzenegger. Attorneys for the former actor argued that, since Schwarzenegger still owns the rights to his own image, the sale of the bobble-headed figure violates the governor's rights. Bosley and company argued that the actor/governor is a public official who is subject to the type of political satire that the doll is designed to display. Can a public official control the rights to his or her image or is that right surrendered upon running for public office? Does this case involve the right to privacy or the right to publicity? If you were the judge in this case, would you find for Schwarzenegger or Bosley Bobbers? Questions like these will be addressed in this chapter on tort law.

Chapter Outcomes

1. Differentiate between the objectives of tort law and those of criminal law.
2. Discuss the element of duty.
3. Identify the principal intentional torts and outline the elements of each.
4. Determine the four elements of negligence.
5. Contrast contributory negligence, comparative negligence, and assumption of the risk.
6. Judge in a particular case whether the doctrine of strict liability applies.
7. Discuss the emerging concept of cybertort law.

8. Outline the various remedies available in tort law.
9. Discuss the concept of damage caps.
10. Identify the principal innovations suggested for contemporary tort reform.

5-1 Tort Law Defined

A **tort** is a private wrong that injures another person's physical well-being, emotional health, business, property, or reputation. The English word tort comes from the Latin word *tortus,* which can be translated as "twisted." A person who commits a tort and has, thus, engaged in this "twisted" behavior, is called a **tortfeasor.** The other party is alternately referred to as the injured party, the innocent party, the victim, or the plaintiff if a lawsuit has been filed. In the case of a lawsuit, the tortfeasor would be called a defendant.

Tort Law Versus Criminal Law

The primary purpose of tort law is to compensate the injured party's loss. Another objective is to protect potential victims by deterring future tortious behavior. In contrast, criminal law involves a public wrong, that is, a wrong that affects the entire society. Since criminal law is concerned with protecting the public, its focus differs from that of tort law. When a crime is committed, government authorities begin legal actions designed to remove the offender from society. It is possible, however, for a single act to be both a tort and a crime.

Respondeat Superior

Businesspeople must be especially aware of tort law because of the doctrine of *respondeat superior* ("let the master respond"). The doctrine of *respondeat superior* may impose legal liability on employers and make them pay for the torts committed by their employees within the scope of the employer's business. The theory behind this doctrine is that the injuries to persons and property are the hazards of doing business, the cost of which the business should bear. The loss should not be born by the innocent victim of the tort or by society as a whole (see Chapter 32).

> ### Example 5-1
>
> Lori Roberts worked as a cab driver for the Barrows Cab Service in New York City. One afternoon, she picked up Ted Franklin at LaGuardia Airport. While driving up Fifth Avenue, Roberts was cut off by another driver at an intersection. Enraged, Randall lost her concentration and ran a red light colliding with a car driven by Jerry Lancaster. Lancaster can sue both Roberts and Barrows Cab under the doctrine of *respondeat superior.*

The Element of Duty

One approach to the law is to think of legal liability in terms of elements. This approach emphasizes that no liability can be imposed against an individual unless all the elements are present. In tort law, the first element is duty. A **duty** is an obligation placed on individuals because of the law. The second element is a violation of that duty. A duty can be violated intentionally, through negligence, or under the theory of strict liability.

Opening Case Sources: See Hudak, Stephen. "Doll Shakes Up Schwarzenegger." *The Cleveland Plain Dealer,* April 2, 2004, p. 1; Broder, John. "Schwarzenegger Files Suit Against Bobblehead Maker." *The New York Times,* May 18, 2004, p. A-14.

Getting Students Involved Ask students if they have ever been victims of a tort. If so, did the torts involve damage to their physical well-being, their property, or their reputation? Ask students if the torts could also be categorized as crimes.

Background Information Much of British tort law developed over disputes about land ownership and between neighbors. Because land was typically divided into scattered parcels, disputes often arose between neighbors about boundaries and interference. A typical tort was a violent raid by one land owner on a neighbor's livestock or produce. Common law had remedies for those who wanted to enjoy their land properly. However, the Industrial Revolution brought new sources of danger to the individual. As cities became more crowded, tort laws were devised to address specific urban problems, such as assault. Offenses due to negligence such as carelessness with fire, spawned a new group of torts described as "negligence."

> *About the Law*
>
> The doctrine of *respondeat superior* is also known as vicarious liability.

Quick Quiz 5-1 True or False?

1. A person who commits a tort is engaged in "twisted" behavior.

2. The purpose of tort law is to protect the public at large.

3. Employers are never liable for the torts of their employees because such a move would violate the constitutional prohibition against double jeopardy.

5-2 Intentional Torts

Intentional violations of duty include a vast variety of intentional torts, all of which have their own individual elements. Table 5-1 summarizes the primary intentional torts.

Assault and Battery

Under U.S. tort law, assault and battery, though often closely associated with one another, are separate torts. An **assault** occurs when the victim is placed in fear or apprehension of immediate bodily harm by a tortfeasor who has the present apparent ability to inflict that harm. No actual physical contact is needed for an assault. The essence of the tort is in the fear or apprehension that is created in the victim.

Table 5-1 Intentional Torts

Tort	Definition
Assault	An assault occurs when the victim is placed on fear or apprehension of immediate bodily harm by tortfeasor who has the present apparent ability to inflict that harm.
Battery	A battery involves an offensive or harmful, unprivileged touching.
False imprisonment	When one party prevents another party from moving about freely, the first party has committed the intentional tort of false imprisonment.
Defamation	Any false statement communicated to others that harms a person's good name or reputation may constitute the tort of defamation.
Invasion of privacy	Invasion of privacy occurs when one person unreasonably denies another person the right to be left alone.
Misuse of legal procedure	Misuse of legal procedure occurs when one person brings a legal action with malice and without probable cause.
Intentional infliction of emotional distress	Intentional or reckless infliction of emotional distress occurs when an individual causes another to undergo emotional or mental suffering, even without the accompanying physical injury.
Disparagement	Disparagement involves any false statement communicated to others that somehow questions the quality of an item of property or that raises uncertainty as to who actually has legal ownership rights to the property in question.
Fraud	Fraud involves false statements or actions, or a combination thereof, that misrepresent facts so that an innocent party relies on those misrepresentations and suffers an injury or loss as a result.

Example 5-2

Terry Kline and Patrick Fisher were playing a friendly game of darts at the Wood Street Tavern one evening when they invited Fred Feeney and David Ballentine to join them. Unknown to either Kline or Feeney, Ballentine was intoxicated. After losing several games, Ballentine became enraged and tried to hit Kline by throwing several darts at him. In his intoxicated state, Ballentine's aim was poor, and he did not hit Kline. Nevertheless, Ballentine has committed an assault.

A **battery** involves an offensive or harmful, unprivileged touching. Naturally, if in Example 5-2, above, Ballentine had actually managed to hit Kline, he would have committed a battery. However, as the definition points out, a touching need not be harmful to be a battery. It is also interesting to note that a battery does not always require the touching of the actual person of the victim, if the tortfeasor touches something closely associated with that victim. So, if a prankster pulls a chair out from under someone before that person sits down, and the person falls to the floor, the joker has committed a battery. Or if he knocks a cafeteria tray out of a diner's hands, again he or she has committed a battery, despite the fact that the actual person or the victim has not been contacted.

Example 5-3

Lucy Pickett works as a nurse at Garner County Hospital. Because she knows that her patient, Jim Luger, is afraid of needles, she sneaked up behind him and injected him with an antibiotic that had been ordered by his primary physician. Despite her desire to help Luger, and her wish to save him from feeling unnecessary fear, Pickett has committed a battery.

False Imprisonment

When one party prevents another party from moving about freely, the first party has committed the intentional tort of **false imprisonment.** This tort is called *false arrest* in some states. The victim of false imprisonment need not be locked in a prison or a jail cell. All that is required is that the person's freedom of movement be restricted in some fashion. For example, a physician who refuses to return a patient's clothing until a partial payment is received for a long overdue bill has committed false imprisonment.

Store owners must be very careful about detaining suspected shoplifters, because such a detention could result in a false imprisonment lawsuit if not handled properly. Still, because of the growing problem of shoplifting in society today, most states have laws that allow storekeepers to detain a suspected shoplifter if they have reasonable grounds to suspect that a shoplifting incident has occurred. In addition, they must detain the suspect in a reasonable manner and for no longer than a reasonable length of time.

Defamation and Disparagement

Intentional torts such as battery, assault, and false imprisonment involve direct physical and psychological injury to an individual. This is not the only type of harm, however, that can be imposed upon individuals in tort law. Sometimes the injury that occurs results from words and hurts a reputation, which leads to monetary loss. Two of these word-oriented torts are defamation and disparagement.

Background Information Cases of assault were among the most common in colonial American courts, amounting to about 6 percent of tried offenses. A charge of assault could contain grounds for a civil suit for damages as well as for criminal prosecution. Although writings of the time reflect differing views on what defined assault, most describe what were then considered acceptable types of physical coercion: A parent could physically punish a child, a master could beat a servant, and a teacher could physically discipline a student. In general, colonial judges followed the British principle that considered an assault to be more than a tort if it caused bloodshed or broke the peace.

Getting Students Involved Have students research state laws that apply to shoplifting. Suggest that they also talk to store owners about how they handle shoplifters—what are responsible grounds for suspecting a person of shoplifting and what constitutes a reasonable method of handling a suspected shoplifter?

Defamation   Any false statement communicated to others that harms a person's good name or reputation may constitute the tort of **defamation.** To be defamatory, the statement must hold the victim up to ridicule, contempt, or hatred. Defamation in a temporary form such as speech is **slander;** in a permanent form, such as writing, movies, videocassette, or DVD, it is **libel.**

People can usually bring a libel suit whenever the permanent statement is damaging to their reputation, is false, and is communicated to a third party. However, under common law, individuals can bring slander lawsuits even if they have suffered no actual loss, if the false statements fall into one of the following categories:

1. An accusation that the victim of the slanderous statements has committed a very serious crime, such as murder or rape.

2. An accusation that the victim has a communicable disease, such as venereal disease.

3. An accusation that the victim has engaged in improprieties in a business, trade, or profession.

4. An accusation that an unmarried female victim has been unchaste.

Individuals may speak the truth without being sued successfully for defamation as long as it is done without spite or ill will. In addition, statements made by senators and representatives on the floor of Congress and statements made in a court of law are privileged. Privileged statements are not the proper subject of a defamation lawsuit. The idea behind creating these privileges is to promote the open debate of legislative and judicial matters.

The U.S. Supreme Court has given journalists the extra protection of the actual malice test when they write about public officials. Under the **actual malice test,** a public official must prove not only that the statement made or printed was false, but also that it was made with actual malice. **Actual malice** means that the statement was made or printed either with the knowledge that it was false, or with a reckless disregard for its truth or falsity. Later decisions expand the actual malice test to cover public figures. Public figures are people like television actors, sports figures, and rock stars, who seek out public fame and who are readily recognizable by the public at large.

What about the temporary public figure? Temporary public figures are people who are thrust involuntarily into the public view by some event beyond their control. Disaster victims, hostages, and rescuers are examples of temporary public figures. Generally, such people are held to the higher standard of actual malice as long as their notoriety lasts.

Disparagement   The tort of **disparagement** involves any false statement communicated to others that somehow questions the quality of an item of property or that raises uncertainty as to who actually has legal ownership rights to the property in question. Generally, in order to recover for a disparagement, the plaintiff must show an actual monetary loss. Such losses may include the loss of sales, money spent to correct the public's image of a product, or expenses spent on litigation due to the disparagement. The difference between defamation and disparagement is that in defamation the false charge is made about the victim's reputation while with disparagement the falsehood is made about a person's property or product. The falsehood usually casts doubt on the value of the product or on the property rights of the owner.

Example 5-4

Warren Barrington owned and operated Toys and Tots—From Two to Twelve, a toy store that specialized in educational toys for children between two and twelve years of age. Barrington and his wife, who operated the store as a partnership, did their best to market only original toys made out of natural materials. Electronic toys, computers, and toys made of plastic were strictly forbidden in the store. During the annual, National Toy and Model Association of America convention, Raymond Matthews, who owned a competitive shop, started several rumors, most of which suggested that many of the toys that were being shown by the Barringtons at the convention were not made of natural materials as advertised. He also suggested that those toys which were made of natural materials involved ideas stolen from him and that the Barringtons did not have the right to market them as they were doing at the convention. Matthews has clearly committed disparagement here. He has planted false reports about both the value of the Barrington's products and about the Barrington's property rights to the toys.

Fraudulent Misrepresentation

Another word-oriented tort is fraudulent misrepresentation. **Fraudulent misrepresentation,** or **fraud** as it is known in some states, occurs when false statements or actions, or a combination thereof, are made by one party in a way that causes another party to rely on those misrepresentations and then suffer an injury or loss as a result. Frequently, fraud involves a business relationship, and works to destroy the mutual assent that ought to exist between the parties who are involved in a contract. For that reason, it is discussed at length in Chapter 8. However, fraud is also a tort and need not involve a contract.

Example 5-5

Donna Gregory worked as the purchasing agent for South Central University in Union City, Indiana. While the university was in the process of building its new science center, she was charged with the responsibility of ordering all of the new equipment for the labs in the center. After coordinating all of the budget requests from all department heads, she entered into negotiations with Georgetown Scientific Instruments, Inc. Frank Jameson, a sales representative from Georgetown, told Gregory that the electron microscopes that she needed for the microbiology laboratory would be compatible with the computer system that she had also ordered from Georgetown. In addition, Jameson told Gregory that the microscopes were new, although he knew that they had been used for demonstration purposes at several universities in the Midwest. Jameson also told Gregory that the microscopes were portable and could easily be moved from one lab to another. Finally, he assured her that the microscopes were state-of-the-art models that would not be replaced for several years. In reality, a new model was already on the production line and would be out within six months. Since none of Jameson's representations proved to be true, and since Gregory relied on his promises when she entered the contract for the university, Jameson has committed fraud. This type of fraud involves a contract. The false representations made by Jamestown clearly destroy the mutual assent that should have existed between the two parties. As a result, the university has a clear cause of action against the scientific equipment company.

Invasion of Privacy

The courts in the United States have consistently held that people have a right to privacy. Consequently, a violation of that right would involve the tort of **invasion of privacy.** The right to privacy can be violated in several ways:

1. revelation of confidential records
2. intrusion
3. creating a false light
4. exploitation

Revelation of Confidential Records Individuals who, because of their jobs, work with confidential records containing private information must ensure that those records remain private. A failure to protect such confidential matters could result in an invasion of privacy lawsuit. Although it is not a violation of privacy for individuals to discuss confidential matters in a professional setting for professional reasons, it could be an invasion of privacy to discuss those same records in the professional setting for non-professional reasons. The motive of the person who releases the information does not matter.

Intrusion An individual's privacy can also be violated if there is an unwarranted intrusion into the person's expectation of privacy. The expectation of privacy changes depending on the situation. A person in a crowded mall has a very low expectation of privacy while a person who is in his or her own home has a very high expectation of privacy.

Creating a False Light Creating a false light is closely akin to defamation because it involves the publication of information about a person that paints him or her in a way that the majority of the population would see as disturbing. A fashion model who poses for photographs for a bathing suit catalog and finds her image printed in a sexually explicit magazine would have a cause of action for creating a false light.

Exploitation The courts have held that an individual holds the rights to his or her own likeness to make money. An invasion of privacy can occur when one party uses an individual's

The Opening Case Revisited

"Hasta la Vista Publicity"

Recall that in The Opening Case at the beginning of this chapter, a bobble-headed figure of Arnold Schwarzenegger showed up for sale on Internet auctions and through an Ohio toy manufacturer called Bosley Bobbers, directly after the former actor became governor of California. Shortly after the doll showed up in a Sacramento souvenir shop, Schwarzenegger's attorneys contacted Bosley Bobbers and threatened a lawsuit. The attorneys demanded that Bosley discontinue sales and turn over all copies of the doll still in their possession. Attorneys for the former actor argued that, since Schwarzenegger owned the rights to his own image, the sale of the bobble-headed figure violated the governor's right to publicity.

Author's Note: This case was later settled out of court. One of the terms of the settlement permitted Bosley to create a new bobble-headed figure of the governor, without the gun.

photo, likeness, or name without permission for advertising, marketing, or publicity. Some courts treat the misappropriation of a person's likeness as a separate tort, calling it an invasion of the right to publicity.

Intentional Infliction of Emotional Distress

In recent years the courts have recognized a tort called the **intentional or reckless infliction of emotional distress.** Before these more enlightened court decisions were handed down, victims who were injured emotionally by the wrongful acts of others could not recover damages without proving some sort of bodily injury. Today, in many states, someone who intentionally or recklessly causes another individual to undergo emotional or mental suffering will be responsible even without the accompanying physical injury. The actions complained of must be extreme and outrageous and must cause severe emotional suffering.

Example 5-6

Marc Christian, who gained notoriety as the live-in boyfriend of Rock Hudson, sued the estate of the late actor for the intentional infliction of emotional distress. Christian argued that he had been induced to continue having "high-risk" sexual relations with the late screen star because Hudson had failed to inform him that he had contracted AIDS. As a result of Hudson's misrepresentations, Christian contended that he suffered extreme emotional distress when he learned that Hudson was ill. This was true, Christian argued, despite the fact that he was not HIV positive himself. Although Hudson did not attempt deliberately to transfer the virus to Christian and did not plan to cause Christian emotional distress, the inherent harmfulness of Hudson's actions could easily amount to extreme and outrageous conduct.

Misuse of Legal Procedure

The intentional tort known as the **misuse of legal procedure** occurs when one person brings a legal action with malice and without probable cause. When the misuse of the legal procedure involves the filing of a false civil lawsuit, it is called **wrongful civil proceedings.** In contrast, when the misuse involves bringing false criminal charges, it is labeled **malicious prosecution.** Some states use only the term malicious prosecution to refer to both forms of the tort. All of the following conditions must be present for a lawsuit based on misuse of legal procedure to succeed.

1. The defendant (the person against whom the misuse of legal procedure suit has been filed) must have brought civil or criminal charges against the plaintiff at an earlier time.
2. The earlier case must have been resolved favorably for the plaintiff.
3. The plaintiff must prove that the earlier case was brought by the defendant with malice and without probable cause.

When these conditions are present, an individual may be able to recover damages from the defendant for making the innocent party the target of a legal action without a good cause.

A related cause of action, which can easily be confused with malicious prosecution, is abuse of process. **Abuse of process** occurs when a legal procedure is used for a purpose other than that for which it is intended. It differs from malicious prosecution in that there is no requirement that the earlier case be brought without probable cause or that the earlier

Business Law in the News
Lawyers Can Be Sued over Bad Cases

If a California attorney has good reason to suspect that a lawsuit has no merit after it has been filed, he would be wise to get out while the gettin's good.

In a case of first impression last week, the California Supreme Court ruled unanimously that lawyers could be sued for malicious prosecution if they continue to pursue a case after learning it isn't supported by probable cause.

"Continuing an action one discovers to be baseless harms the defendant and burdens the court system just as much as initiating an action known to be baseless from the outset," Justice Janice Rogers Brown wrote. "As the court of appeal in this case observed, 'It makes little sense to hold attorneys accountable for their knowledge when they file a lawsuit, but not for their knowledge the next day.'"

The ruling reinstates a malicious prosecution suit filed by Woodland Hills, Calif., lawyer Jerome Zamos against former client Patricia Brookes and her subsequent attorney, James Stroud. Zamos accused the two of persisting in pursuing a fraud action against him in spite of strong evidence that he had done nothing wrong.

Brookes had accused Zamos of misrepresenting her in a foreclosure suit in which she received a settlement of nearly $167,000.

Zamos offered documents from court hearings indicating that he had not misled Brookes in any manner: Los Angeles County Superior Court Judge Stephen Petersen even told Brookes she "couldn't have had a better lawyer" than Zamos.

The California 2d District Court of Appeal backed Zamos last year, even though the same court had held in two separate cases in 2002 that malicious prosecution was limited to the initiation of a suit, not the continuation.

In last week's opinion, the Supreme Court disapproved of both those cases—*Swat-Fame Inc. v. Goldstein,* 101 Cal. App. 4th 613, and *Vanzant v. DaimlerChrysler Corp.,* 96 Cal. App. 4th 1283.

"Confining the tort of malicious prosecution to the initiation of a suit without probable cause would be, we conclude, without support in authority or in principle," Brown wrote.

Brown noted that for 25 years the law—as stated in the Restatement (Second) of Torts—has held that anyone who continues a civil proceeding after learning there is no probable cause "becomes liable as if he had then initiated the proceeding." In addition, Brown pointed out, 13 states have agreed, including Colorado in 1932, and Pennsylvania in 1900.

Questions for Analysis

1. Identify the plaintiff(s) and the defendant(s) in the malicious prosecution case outlined in the story reprinted above.

2. Identify the nature of the lawsuit that preceded the malicious prosecution case. What was the final outcome of that original case?

3. What are the two negative consequences of unfounded lawsuits that the California Supreme Court sought to avoid by supporting the malicious prosecution claim in this case. Explain.

4. How did the California Supreme Court widen the scope of malicious prosecution in this case? Explain.

5. What evidence did the plaintiff in the malicious prosecution case offer to support the claim that the case was brought without a just cause? Explain.

case be resolved favorably for the plaintiff. The tort can involve either a criminal or civil case. Typically, abuse of process happens when a perfectly legal process is used as a pressure tactic to convince someone to do something he or she would not be inclined to do under ordinary circumstances.

Example 5-7

Janice Franklin and Karen Yalta were involved in the middle of a very difficult dissolution of their partnership. As a result of this problematic dissolution, as well as many other factors, the two young women did not like each other. Accordingly, Franklin filed a lawsuit against Yalta for defamation. The lawsuit was resolved in Yalta's favor. Yalta then sued Franklin for wrongful civil proceedings. Yalta won the case because she was able to prove that the original defamation suit against her was fabricated by Franklin who was motivated by hatred and ill will. This is an example of the misuse of legal proceedings. If Franklin had filed a defamation suit to force Yalta to agree to Franklin's terms in the dissolution, she would be involved in abuse of process. This would be true even if Franklin had legitimate reasons for filing the defamation suit.

Quick Quiz 5-2 True or False?

1. Assault and battery never exist simultaneously.

2. To be defamatory a statement need not be communicated to a third party.

3. The intentional infliction of emotional distress has yet to be recognized as a tort in any state jurisdiction.

5-3 Negligence

People and property are sometimes injured even when no one intends that the injury occur. Such an occurrence is usually labeled an accident. Although no one acted with intent, someone was injured. The victim has experienced pain and suffering, lost wages, and incurred medical or repair bills. Justice demands that the injured party be compensated. The part of tort law that is concerned with the compensation of accident victims is called **negligence.**

Elements of Negligence

The issue before the court in a negligence action is: Under what circumstances can the actions of an alleged tortfeasor be labeled negligent so that the tortfeasor will be held liable? Four elements must be present to establish negligence: legal duty, breach of duty, proximate cause, and actual harm. Table 5-2 gives an overview of these four elements.

Legal Duty A determination that a legal duty exists between the parties must be made in order to establish liability through negligence. This is solely a question of whether the tortfeasor should have reasonably foreseen a risk of harm to the injured party. Often today the concept of duty is not at issue in a lawsuit. However, there are some instances, often when a novel case comes before a court, that the legal duty of the defendant may be placed at issue.

Related Cases While helping a neighbor on his farm, Charles Tiede raised an auger that hit a high voltage electric power line, killing himself and two other workers. Tiede's wife brought a suit against the owner of the farm and the electric company. In *Tiede v. Loup Power District* (411 N.W.2d 312), the court ruled that, because Tiede had been warned about the dangers of the electrical wire and had even warned others about it, Tiede's contributory negligence precluded his wife from collecting any damages for his death.

Table 5-2 The Elements of Negligence

Element	Definition
Legal duty	A determination that a legal duty exists between the parties must be made in order to establish liability through negligence. This is solely a question of whether the tortfeasor should have reasonably foreseen a risk of harm to the injured party.
Breach of duty	The judge or the jury must determine whether the person accused of negligence has breached the duty owed to the victim. To determine if the alleged tortfeasor has met the appropriate standard of care, the court uses the reasonable person test.
Proximate cause	In order for the tortfeasor to be held liable, the unreasonable conduct must be the proximate cause of the victim's injuries. Proximate cause is the legal connection between the unreasonable conduct and the resulting harm.
Actual harm	The injured party in a lawsuit for negligence must show that actual harm was suffered.

Example 5-8

Rene Harrington was suffering from a psychological problem that led her to believe that she was being persecuted by many unknown enemies. She was especially fixated on several family members that she feared might do her harm. After several years of trying to live on her own, as the result of a doctor's advice, she moved back into her parents' home. Her parents cared for her for several months and, as a result, monitored her behavior regularly. Consequently, they were aware of her fears about the family, which she expressed on a regular basis. Despite this, they allowed her to move about their home freely, to stay at home unsupervised, and to frequently leave the house on her own. They also took her to visit friends and family members. On one such visit, at a birthday party, Rene poisoned the punch, which caused several people, including Ken Bartley, a family friend, to become severely ill. Bartley brought a lawsuit against Rene and her parents. One of the main questions before the court in the lawsuit was whether the parents, a third party in the case, had the duty to inform the people at the gathering about their daughter's illness and to warn them of the danger that they might be in because of her fears. The question of whether a parent has a duty in relation to his or her minor children had been answered by the court. The question of a parent's duty in relation to an adult child, however, had not been answered by the court before this case.

Related Cases A New Mexico police officer was found negligent when the officer stopped and then released a man who had been driving while intoxicated. The driver later caused an accident. The injured people were successful in suing the officer for a breach of his duty. *Blea v. City of Espanola,* 870 P.2d 755 (NM).

Related Cases When a drunken man tripped on a broken sidewalk in California and then sued for damages, the judge in the case stated that "a drunken man has as good a right to a perfect sidewalk as a sober man, and he needs one a good deal more."

Breach of Duty The judge or the jury must determine whether the person accused of negligence has breached the duty owed to the victim. A *breach of duty* occurs if the alleged tortfeasor has not met the appropriate standard of care. That is, he or she has failed to be careful enough under the circumstances. To determine if the alleged tortfeasor has met the appropriate standard of care, the court uses the *reasonable person test.* This test compares the actions of the tortfeasor with those of a reasonable person in a similar situation. If a reasonable person would not have done what the tortfeasor actually did, then the tortfeasor is liable. The reasonable person standard is an objective test. Circumstances may change but the standard of care applied by a reasonable person does not. How a reasonable person would behave in one set of circumstances may not be the same in another set of circumstances.

Example 5-9

Luigi Tarentino hired a limousine from Highland Limo Service so that he and his wife, Maybeth, could attend their high school reunion in style. When the limousine arrived, Tarentino told the driver to take them to the Regency Hotel. Once they were on the freeway, it became clear that the driver did not know how to reach the hotel. Every time the driver took a wrong turn, Tarentino attempted to correct him. The driver continued to ignore Tarentino's instructions. Eventually, the driver, who later said he was aggravated by Tarentino's frequent interruptions, stopped the limousine and told Tarentino and his wife to walk to their reunion. He then drove off and left his passengers several miles from the hotel in the middle of an ice storm. While walking to the hotel, Tarentino slipped on a patch of ice and fell and broke his arm. Later the Tarentinos learned that the driver had a long history of similar conduct, and that the limousine company had not done a proper search into the driver's work history before hiring him. The question to the jury was, "Would a reasonable person hire an employee who will be responsible for the safety of paying passengers without checking the work history of that potential employee?" The jury said no, and Highland was held liable for the injuries that befell Tarentino from this breach of duty to protect paying passengers from harm.

If the defendant in a particular case is a professional, such as a physician or an engineer, the circumstances—not the test—change. To determine whether the defendant acted reasonably, the jury would have to know how the reasonable professional would act under similar circumstances. Determining this may require the use of expert witnesses to testify as to the reasonable professional's conduct under the circumstances.

Proximate Cause It is not enough to simply show that the tortfeasor's actions were unreasonable. In order for the tortfeasor to be held liable, the unreasonable conduct must be the proximate cause of the victim's injuries. **Proximate cause** is the connection between the unreasonable conduct and the resulting harm. Proximate cause is sometimes referred to as *legal cause.* In determining proximate cause, the court asks whether the harm that resulted from the conduct was foreseeable at the time of the original action.

Related Cases A horse owner was found liable for damages caused by a runaway horse on a highway. The Mississippi Supreme Court ruled that the owner was negligent for not keeping the horse safely enclosed. *Carpenter v. Nobile,* 620 So.2d 961 (MS).

Example 5-10

Two Transglobal Airline mechanics failed to properly repair the landing gear of a TGA 747. As a result, the plane's landing gear collapsed on takeoff and the plane caught fire. Several passengers were injured. While racing to the scene of the crash, an airport fire truck blew a tire and hit a light pole. The pole fell onto Carbonari's car, smashing the trunk and damaging the new DVD player stored there. The injured passengers and Carbonari sued TGA and the mechanics. When the mechanics failed to properly prepare the landing gear, it would have been easy for them to foresee that their unreasonable conduct might cause the plane to crash on takeoff and injure some passengers. However, it would have been impossible for them to foresee that the fire truck would have a blowout and smash into a light pole that would hit Carbonari's car and damage both the car and the DVD player in the trunk. Therefore, the mechanics' conduct was the proximate cause of the injuries to the passengers but not to the damage to the car or the DVD player.

Note in Example 5-10 that the mechanics' actions were the actual cause of the damage to the car and the DVD player. In other words, had they repaired the landing gear properly, the fire truck would not have been on the runway; it would not have had the collision with the light pole; and the light pole would not have fallen on Carbonari's car. Actual cause must always be present. If the actions of the tortfeasor are not the actual cause of the accident, they cannot be the proximate cause.

A Question of Ethics

In Example 5-10, when the Transglobal mechanics failed to prepare the landing gear properly, they could not foresee that the fire truck would have a blowout, smash into a light pole that would hit Carbonari's car, and damage both the car and the DVD player in the trunk. Therefore, legally, their conduct was not the proximate cause of the damage to the car and the DVD player. However, would Transglobal owe an ethical duty to reimburse Carbonari for the damages that were inflicted on his car and his DVD player? Explain.

Related Cases A motorcyclist sued a truck stop restaurant after he hit a pothole in the parking lot and received head injuries. The appellate court found the motorcyclist 50 percent at fault for not wearing a helmet and for not avoiding the pothole. As a result, his damages award was cut in half. *Landry v. Roe,* 597 So.2d 14 (LA).

Actual Harm The injured party in a lawsuit for negligence must show that actual harm was suffered. In most cases, the harm suffered is a physical injury and is, therefore, visible. Harm suffered due to fright or humiliation is difficult to demonstrate. Courts often deny damages in actions for negligence unless they can see an actual physical injury. Actual harm can also come in the form of property damage.

Defenses to Negligence

Several defenses can be used by the defendant in a negligence case. These defenses include contributory negligence, comparative negligence, and assumption of the risk.

Contributory Negligence The defense of **contributory negligence** involves the failure of the injured party to be careful enough to ensure personal safety. Contributory negligence completely prevents the injured party from recovering damages. In other words, if the injured party's negligence contributed to personal injury, the tortfeasor wins. *Last clear chance* is the injured party's defense to a charge of contributory negligence. Under this doctrine, a tortfeasor may be held liable if the injured party can show that the tortfeasor had the last clear chance to avoid injury.

Did You Know?

Assumption of the risk can be raised as a defense in a case in which the plaintiff has been injured in a voluntary sports activity such as touch football. For a player in a touch football game to be found liable for injuries to another player, the first player would have to have caused the injuries intentionally or with a degree of recklessness beyond the usual action within such a sport.

Comparative Negligence To soften the harsh effects of contributory negligence, many states have adopted **comparative negligence** statutes that require courts to assign damages according to the degree of fault of each party. Rather than deny all recovery, the court weighs the relative degree of wrongdoing in awarding damages. If the tortfeasor was 80 percent negligent, the injured party may be allowed to recover 80 percent of the losses suffered. Some states have adopted the "50 percent rule." Under this rule, an injured party who was found to be more than 50 percent negligent cannot recover any damages from the tortfeasor.

Assumption of the Risk Another defense to negligence is *assumption of the risk,* which involves the voluntary exposure of the victim to a known risk. If the injured party was aware of the danger involved in a situation, and by his or her actions indicated a willingness to be exposed to the danger, then he or she has assumed that risk. An awareness of the extent of the danger is the court's primary consideration in awarding or denying damages.

5-4 Strict Liability

Under certain circumstances, the courts may judge a person liable for harm even though that person was not negligent and did not commit an intentional tort. This doctrine is known as **strict liability,** or absolute liability. In recent years, strict liability has also been applied to product liability cases.

Grounds for Strict Liability

Under strict liability, the court will hold a tortfeasor liable for injuries to a victim even though the tortfeasor did not intend the harm and was not, in any way, negligent. Strict liability is generally applied when the harm results from an ultrahazardous, or very dangerous activity. Such activities include using explosives and keeping wild animals. A number of dangerous activities, such as flying an airplane, operating X-ray equipment, and laying public gas lines, are not subject to liability without fault. These activities are recognized as essential to the economic health and welfare of the public.

Product Liability

Product liability is a legal theory that imposes liability on the manufacturer and seller of a product produced and sold in a defective condition. A product in **defective condition** is unreasonably dangerous to the user, to the consumer, or to property. Anyone who produces or sells a product in defective condition is subject to liability for the physical or the emotional injury to the ultimate consumer and for any physical harm to the user's property. The courts have regularly held that liability for a defective product extends to the producer of the product, the wholesaler, and the retailer. The seller or producer must be engaged in the business of selling such products. In addition, the product manufactured or sold must be expected to reach the ultimate consumer without substantial change in conditions under which it was originally manufactured or sold.

Product liability is not without its limits. In most states, product liability is not also available as a cause of action if the only property damaged is the defective property itself. In such a situation, the product owner must seek a remedy in sales law for breach of warranty. (Note: People who are injured by faulty products might also be able to bring a product liability lawsuit in negligence. This issue is discussed at length in Chapter 18.)

State Variations Among the states that have adopted the "50 percent rule" are Arkansas, Colorado, Connecticut, Hawaii, Idaho, Indiana, Kansas, Massachusetts, Minnesota, Montana, Nevada, New Jersey, Ohio, Oklahoma, Oregon, Pennsylvania, Texas, Vermont, West Virginia, Wisconsin, and Wyoming.

State Variations In Nebraska, any person engaged in the disposal of low-level radioactive waste is subject to strict liability in tort for property damage, bodily injury, or death resulting from such disposal.

In 2001, Bridgestone and Firestone recalled thousands of defective tires used on Ford Explorers.

Teaching Tips Students may confuse the concept of product liability with warranties. Explain that a person's rights under the product liability law are based on obligations of the seller or manufacturer rather than on warranty coverage included as part of an agreement. A seller or manufacturer can rarely, if ever, use contract terms to modify obligations imposed by product liability laws or to limit amounts a person can recover as damages. Thus, a person can use product liability laws to hold a seller or manufacturer liable for product defects, even if they are not covered in a warranty.

> ### Quick Quiz 5-4 True or False?
>
> 1. Keeping wild animals is an ultrahazardous activity.
> 2. Strict liability is also known as absolute liability.
> 3. Product liability is completely unrelated to strict liability and the two torts should never be confused with one another.

5-5 Cybertorts

The advent, growth, and development of computers has had a profound impact on the legal community. Computers have changed the way we do business and the way we communicate. They have given us access to a great deal of information on a global basis. They have made many aspects of our lives easier. Unfortunately, they have also provided unscrupulous individuals with many new ways to engage in criminal and tort activity. In the last chapter, we examined a new series of legal transgressions called cybercrimes. In this chapter, we change focus slightly to explore another group of legal problems referred to as cybertorts. We will look, first, at the nature of cybertort law and then at the problems associated with defining, describing, and preventing cybertorts.

The Nature of Cybertort Law

Cybertorts are peculiar in that they always involve information. A **cybertort** involves the invasion, distortion, theft, falsification, misuse, destruction, or financial exploitation of information stored in or related to an electronic device including but not limited to desktop PC's, laptops, mobile phones, mainframes, phonecams, personal digital assistants (PDAs), and home computers that stand alone or are part of a network. Cybertorts rarely, if ever, involve any harm to a party's physical well-being. Instead, the victim's reputation has been hurt because a false statement has been posted on the Internet; the victim's emotional state has been disturbed because his or her privacy has been invaded; or the victim has suffered monetary harm because his or her identity has been tampered with. We will focus on the first two injuries, that is, those that are caused by defamation and those that are caused by invasion of privacy.

Cyberdefamation

Cyberdefamation is the communication of false and destructive information about an individual through the use of an electronic device. Most legal moves thus far in the cyberdefamation arena have been designed to limit, rather than extend, liability for defamatory comments disseminated on the Internet. For example, when the courts were first involved in cyberdefamation, they easily extended liability for defamation from the party who posted a defamatory message on the Internet to the *Internet service provider (ISP)* such as America Online, who provided the vehicle for the posting. Thus, for instance, it was not difficult in one case for a court in New York to decide that the Prodigy Service Company was responsible when an investment banking firm sued for defamation after false statements were posted on a cyberbulletin board that was under Prodigy's control.

After the Prodigy case, however, the Communications Decency Act was enacted by Congress to protect ISPs from future defamation suits for false statements that are posted by other individuals on the net. Despite the passage of the law, many cases have been filed attempting to hold ISPs liable for defamatory postings. Few have succeeded. In one such case, AOL was found *not* liable for defamation despite the fact that the provider had been informed of the defamatory content of a posting and had substantially delayed its removal. Moreover, the protection granted to ISPs has gone far beyond protection for defamatory postings. The courts have also found that ISPs are not liable when hackers place a virus into the system, when piracy is involved on the Net, or when invasion of privacy takes place via a provider's link.

In another interesting development, the definition of an ISP has been expanded to include any company that has maintained an e-mail service for its associates. Although this latest interpretation does not involve the Communications Decency Act and although it was made by the Federal Trade Commissions rather than the courts, the tendency to protect ISPs is clear here. This does not mean that a victim of cyberdefamation has no recourse in the courts. Rather, it means that he or she must pursue the person who did the actual posting on the Web via the ISP. It is certain that such individuals are liable. Moreover, their identities are not protected by federal law.

Cyberinvasion of Privacy

A *cyberinvasion of privacy* is the unwelcome intrusion into private matters initiated or maintained by an electronic device. Since the state of computer technology is in a constant state of flux, it is not surprising that the law is uncertain about just what constitutes a cyberinvasion of privacy. Therefore, rather than speculate on the details of the law in this arena, we will instead spend some time exploring recent developments in computer technology that have the potential of causing a cyberinvasion of privacy. These technological developments include but are not limited to RFIDs, phonecams, E-911 locator devices, and cyberspyware.

Radio frequency identity devices (RFIDs) are tiny electronic chips that can be implanted in virtually any physical object from clothing to canned goods. Since the chips themselves carry no power source, they can be small enough to be sewn into fabric, fused into plastic, or implanted in most any other material. The chips contain an electronic code that can be activated by any RFID reading device which transmits a signal that is picked up by the RFID chip which answers the contact signal with its own coded return signal. Since the return signal is unique, the reader can identify the object in which the chip has been placed. The minuscule nature of these chips means that they can be implanted in clothing, cash, eyeglasses, shoes, and jewelry, making it possible to locate anyone, at any time, no matter where they are situated. The implications for invasion of privacy matters should be obvious. For example, if the Treasury Department opts to include RFIDs in paper money, it will no longer be possible for anyone to engineer a completely anonymous cash transaction. Thus, an inventor who wants the ingredients in a formula or the parts in a device to remain a trade secret would not be able to do so simply by purchasing those ingredients or those parts in cash. Cash transactions would also no longer protect people in the witness protection program or those carrying out legitimate covert operations for the government.

Although the widespread use of RFIDs has yet to be realized, at least as of the writing of this book, the same is not true of phonecams. A *phonecam* is a mobile phone which can transmit video and record digital photographs. These devices are available and affordable today. In fact their use has become so common that some lawmakers have already become concerned enough to consider legislation banning their use in certain situations and at certain locations. Again, the potential for the cyberinvasion of privacy should be obvious in this. Phonecams are small enough for a photographer to carry into areas that are generally considered private and into which carrying a large camera would not be permitted. Private areas such as a person's home or hotel room or semiprivate areas such as locker rooms and dressing rooms can now be invaded by people with phonecams that are no larger and no

Business Law in the News
Dealing with the Darker Side

What will be the social consequences of a world full of embedded RFID tags and readers? Will our privacy be further eroded as RFID technology makes it possible for our movements to be tracked and allows our personal information to be available in unprecedented detail? These and many other questions must be answered before RFID systems become commonplace.

One of the major worries for privacy advocates is that RFID tags identifying individual items purchased with credit or debit cards would link buyers to the specific items in the card's or the store's databases.

Another concern is that RFID equipment will produce automatic audit trails of commercial transactions: in a totally tagged world, it will be easier to detect when we lie about how we spent our time or what we did and where. This capability could have great consequences for the workplace, and the legal system might look to using logs kept by tag readers as courtroom evidence. We may need laws to specify who can access data logs and for what purpose. In Europe, the Data Protection Act already limits access to computer records of this kind, and the U.S. will probably enact similar legislation.

We will also have to grapple with the inevitable displacement of workers by RFID systems. Opposition to tagging could well come from the industrial labor force, which stands to lose significant numbers of jobs as industry adopts RFID tools able to perform tasks that now depend on human effort.

The backlash against perceived invasions of consumer privacy by RFID applications began in March 2003, when Philips Semiconductor announced that it was shipping 15 million RFID tags to the clothing manufacturer and retailer Benetton to be incorporated into labels during production.

Despite Philips's reassurances that tagged clothing could not be tracked outside Benetton stores, some industry experts said that criminals could increase the Benetton tags' tracking distance by creating more sensitive RFID readers. Privacy advocates worried that the tags could be scanned by RFID readers other than those in Benetton stores, which would allow people wearing the clothes to be monitored without their knowledge by, say, criminals or the government.

Similar concerns—that corporations might keep consumers' products under surveillance in purchasers' homes and on the streets—surfaced about a test of an in-store RFID inventory system that was planned by Wal-Mart and Gillette. To answer consumer concern, Gillette announced that it was embedding its RFID tags in packaging, not products, so purchasers would discard the tags with the packaging. But Declan McCullagh, a commentator who writes for computing publications and who favors RFID for its practical value, has written: "Future burglars could canvass alleys with RFID detectors, looking for RFID tags on discarded packaging that indicates expensive electronic gear is nearby. . . . [T]he ability to remain anonymous is eroded."

One way to avoid such possibilities is to put a kill switch into each RFID tag on a consumer item, which would allow the tag to be turned off after purchase.

McCullagh has suggested four requirements for the use of RFID tags on consumer products: Consumers should be notified when RFID tags are present in what they are buying (this could be done with a printed notice on a checkout receipt). All tags should be readily visible and easily removable. The tags should be disabled by default at the checkout counter. And, when possible, RFID tags should be placed only on the product's packaging, not embedded in the product.

Questions for Analysis

1. What concerns and worries have arisen in relation to the potential widespread use of RFID technology? Explain.

2. What is one possible use for RFID technology in the legal arena? Explain.

3. For what does the European Data Protection Act provide limits? Explain.

4. How have some of the concerns regarding RFID technology been addressed? Explain.

5. What requirements have been suggested for the use of RFID tags? Explain.

HOW RFID WORKS

RFID systems operate in both low frequency (less than 100 megahertz) and high frequency (greater than 100 megahertz) modes. Unlike their low-frequency counterparts, high-frequency tags can have their data read at distances of greater than one meter, even while closely spaced together. New data can also be transmitted to the tags, a process not shown here.

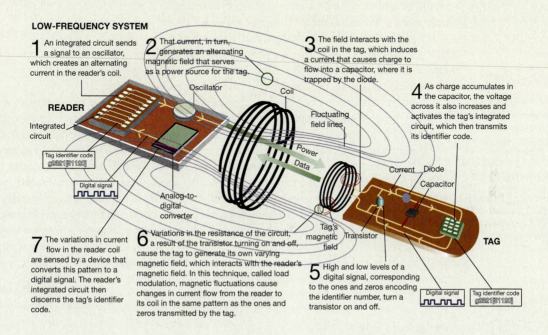

LOW-FREQUENCY SYSTEM

1 An integrated circuit sends a signal to an oscillator, which creates an alternating current in the reader's coil.

2 That current, in turn, generates an alternating magnetic field that serves as a power source for the tag.

3 The field interacts with the coil in the tag, which induces a current that causes charge to flow into a capacitor, where it is trapped by the diode.

4 As charge accumulates in the capacitor, the voltage across it also increases and activates the tag's integrated circuit, which then transmits its identifier code.

5 High and low levels of a digital signal, corresponding to the ones and zeros encoding the identifier number, turn a transistor on and off.

6 Variations in the resistance of the circuit, a result of the transistor turning on and off, cause the tag to generate its own varying magnetic field, which interacts with the reader's magnetic field. In this technique, called load modulation, magnetic fluctuations cause changes in current flow from the reader to its coil in the same pattern as the ones and zeros transmitted by the tag.

7 The variations in current flow in the reader coil are sensed by a device that converts this pattern to a digital signal. The reader's integrated circuit then discerns the tag's identifier code.

READER
Integrated circuit
Oscillator
Coil
Fluctuating field lines
Power
Data
Analog-to-digital converter
Tag's magnetic field
Current   Diode
Capacitor
Transistor
TAG
Tag identifier code
g3321[51120]
Digital signal
Tag identifier code
g3321[51120]
Digital signal

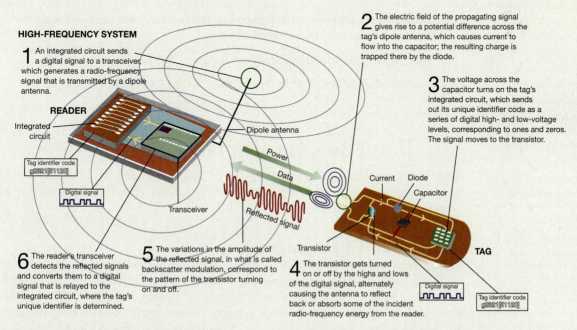

HIGH-FREQUENCY SYSTEM

1 An integrated circuit sends a digital signal to a transceiver, which generates a radio-frequency signal that is transmitted by a dipole antenna.

2 The electric field of the propagating signal gives rise to a potential difference across the tag's dipole antenna, which causes current to flow into the capacitor; the resulting charge is trapped there by the diode.

3 The voltage across the capacitor turns on the tag's integrated circuit, which sends out its unique identifier code as a series of digital high- and low-voltage levels, corresponding to ones and zeros. The signal moves to the transistor.

4 The transistor gets turned on or off by the highs and lows of the digital signal, alternately causing the antenna to reflect back or absorb some of the incident radio-frequency energy from the reader.

5 The variations in the amplitude of the reflected signal, in what is called backscatter modulation, correspond to the pattern of the transistor turning on and off.

6 The reader's transceiver detects the reflected signals and converts them to a digital signal that is relayed to the integrated circuit, where the tag's unique identifier is determined.

READER
Integrated circuit
Dipole antenna
Power
Data
Reflected signal
Transceiver
Current   Diode
Capacitor
Transistor
TAG
Tag identifier code
g3321[51120]
Digital signal
Tag identifier code
g3321[51120]
Digital signal

Source: Roy Want. "RFID: A Key to Automating Everything," *Scientific American,* January 2004. Copyright © 2004 Bryan Christie. Reprinted with permission.

more conspicuous than ordinary mobile phones. This increases the likelihood that unauthorized photos will be taken and sent to another person who is located far from the site at which the photo is taken. Since an individual's privacy is violated when there is an unwarranted intrusion into that person's expectation of privacy, the phonecam is an obvious threat to this right.

The *E-911 location identifier system* is an electronic chip located in a mobile phone that sends out a signal that is designed to ensure that EMS personnel can locate people who are unable or unwilling to reveal their exact locations when making an emergency call. It would be a limited, albeit an unwelcome, cyberinvasion if the E-911 locator was activated only when a 911 call is made. However, on newer model mobile phones, the E-911 locator is activated all the time. This means that, even when the owner of the phone has not dialed 911, the locator is on whenever the phone is on. As a result, the location of the mobile phone can be calibrated so long as the phone is switched on, allowing the holder of the mobile to be located at any time, thus diminishing his or her level of privacy.

Another threat to privacy is a new type of software that is referred to as cyberspyware. *Cyberspyware* or *cybersnoopware* as it is often called is a software program which, once it is installed in a computer, can keep a record of the keyboarding patterns established by the computer's user(s). Generally, the cyberspyware is not loaded into the computer as an end in itself. Rather, it is piggybacked onto software that has another, usually legitimate purpose that is unrelated to the snooping initiated by the spyware. Once the cyberspyware works its way into the host computer, however, the installer of the software can identify the user's passwords, credit card numbers, bank account numbers, debit card numbers, and so on. The software can also trail the Internet sites onto which the computer's user has logged, thus tracking his or her activity research activity, buying habits, hobbies, leisure time activities, sports and entertainment interests, and the like. Clearly, the antiprivacy implications of this type of software should be obvious.

For information on ISP's, RFIDs, phonecams, E-911 locator devices, and cyberspyware see Ellis, Robert. "New Digital Technologies and the Law." Presentation at the Ohio State Bar Association Conference, May 13–14, 2004, Cleveland, Ohio, p. 8. See also Want, Roy. "RFID: A Key to Automating Everything." *Scientific American,* January 2004, pp. 56–65.

Quick Quiz 5-5 True or False?

1. Cybertorts always involve information that has been invaded, distorted, stolen, falsified, or destroyed by an electronic device.

2. Most legal moves in cyberdefamation have been designed to extend liability.

3. The Communications Decency Act was enacted by Congress to protect ISPs.

5-6 Remedies for Torts

When a wrongdoer has injured another person by committing a tort, the victim can usually be compensated with money damages. However, at times the equitable remedy of an injunction is more appropriate.

The Right to Damages

Terms "Hedonic loss" is a controversial legal term that is being used in some cases to compute awards for personal injury and wrongful death. A federal court concluded for the first time that life's foregone pleasures—being with one's family, playing with friends on a summer day, watching the waves roll on a beach—constituted a whole new category for which damages could be awarded. The term was coined by a Chicago economist, Stan V. Smith. Smith presented complex economic models to estimate the monetary value of hedonic loss and to calculate the value of human life. For instance, Smith estimated the value of the life of a typical thirty-year-old to be between $500,000 and $3.5 million.

The compensation paid to the victims of a tort is known as **damages.** Damages can come in several forms. **Economic compensatory damages** are those that are directly quantifiable. These include damages awarded for lost wages, medical expenses, and expenses incurred in the repair or replacement of property. **Noneconomic compensatory damages** are those that result from injuries that are intangible and, therefore, not directly quantifiable. For example, damages resulting from pain and suffering, mental anguish, and loss of companionship are considered noneconomic. If the tortfeasor's acts are notoriously willful and malicious, a court may also impose punitive damages. These are damages above and beyond those needed to compensate the injured party. **Punitive damages** are designed to punish the tortfeasor so that similar malicious actions are avoided by others. For this reason, they are also referred to as *exemplary damages*. Some courts say that another purpose for punitive damages is to comfort the victim.

The Right to an Injunction

If a tort involves a continuing problem, such as the dumping of chemical waste into a river, the injured party may ask the court for an injunction. An **injunction** is a court order preventing someone from performing a particular act. If a tort involves some permanent fixture that harms the interests of the injured party, the court may order the wrongdoer to take positive steps to alleviate the problem. Thus, the court might order a company to clean up a landfill that has become a nuisance to neighborhood homes. If the company failed to complete the cleanup, it would be in contempt of court. Contempt of court is a deliberate violation of the order of a judge that can result in a fine or in jail time for the wrongdoer.

> ### Quick Quiz 5-6 True or False?
> 1. Economic and noneconomic compensatory damages are essentially the same thing.
> 2. Punitive damages are designed to compensate the victim of a tort.
> 3. An injunction is never granted by the court in any kind of tort case.

5-7 Tort Reform

Many of the common law rules regarding torts, have become obsolete in the modern world. For instance, under common law, if someone died from another's wrongful act, then the right to bring a suit died also. This rule originated because the king would execute the wrongdoer and would then take his or her property. As a result, there was no property left for the relatives of the wrongdoer's victim to recover in a tort suit. Modern statutes have, for the most part, eliminated this rule. Modern statutes have also taken steps to put a halt to some unfair practices that have, in recent years, found their way into American courts. One such practice is the excessive damage award.

Survival Statutes and Wrongful Death

Many state legislatures have revised common law by passing survival statutes. Survival statutes allow a lawsuit to be brought even if both the plaintiff and the defendant are deceased. Many states also have survival statutes that preserve the right to bring a lawsuit for personal injuries. This is true no matter what caused the death or deaths. Most states also allow such suits if the tort involves damage to personal or real property. However, there are some limitations placed on survival statutes. For instance, suits cannot be brought for libel or slander after the death of a defamed person because such a suit is for injury to a live person's reputation. Survival suits are brought or defended by the lawful representative of the estate of the deceased.

Unlike survival statutes, wrongful death statutes preserve the right to bring a lawsuit only if the death is caused by the negligence or the intentional conduct of the person who caused the death. Generally only family members who have lost the support of the deceased

Related Cases In *Pacific Mutual Life Insurance Co. v. Haslip* (IL S.Ct. 1032), the U.S. Supreme Court decided, seven to one, that punitive damages awarded by juries could not be limited.

State Variations In 1997, fourteen states adopted some type of civil justice reform, with Alaska and Iowa passing the most comprehensive packages.

State Variations In Connecticut, as in a few other states, monetary damages awarded for wrongful death are based on losses suffered by the deceased, not by the family members of the deceased. The jury is instructed to award damages first in terms of the deceased's loss of earning capacity; second, for his or her loss of employment of life; and third, for his or her pain and suffering experienced prior to death. Each loss is evaluated individually, and the award is paid to the estate of the deceased regardless of dependency.

State Variations In 1999, Alabama passed legislation that would put a cap on punitive damages awarded by juries.

State Variations In 1999, the Ohio Supreme Court struck down the state's three-year-old tort reform law which limited the amount of general and punitive damages that could be assessed in many civil cases. The Court stated the law ". . . usurps judicial power in violation of the Ohio constitutional doctrine of separation of powers."

In what was called "The Trial of the Century," O. J. Simpson was aquitted of murder charges in October 1995. In 1997, however, he was found liable in tort for the deaths of his ex-wife Nicole and her friend, Ron Goldman.

State Variations Top courts in Illinois, New Hampshire, Kentucky, Indiana, and Oregon have relied on provisions of state constitutions, such as guarantees of fair access to the courts, to strike down all or part of the new laws that were passed under the banner of tort reform.

Teaching Tips Lead the class in a discussion of modern tort reform. Use as an example the proposals mentioned on this page. Ask students for their own proposals and write them on the board or on an overhead. Then guide students in a discussion of these proposals, listing the pros and cons of each.

For more information on damage caps see Young, Gary. "'State Farm' Fires Up Debate—Once Again." *The National Law Journal,* May 3, 2004, p. 4.

have the right to bring a wrongful death suit. The definition of family members generally includes husbands, wives, children, and parents. Under wrongful death statutes, creditors, business partners, and the like have no right to bring a lawsuit.

Damage Caps

Another type of tort reform is for a state legislature to enact a specifically worded statute which places an upper limit on the amount of money that juries are permitted by law to award in a lawsuit. Often these **damage caps,** as they are called, apply only to noneconomic compensatory damages and punitive damages. Statutory damage caps relating to both noneconomic and punitive damages have been successfully inaugurated in a number of states. In other states, however, these caps have been struck down as an unconstitutional deprivation of equal protection.

It is also possible to combat excessive punitive damage awards in the courts. Some state courts have placed limits on punitive damages. The United States Supreme Court ruled in the case of *State Farm Mutual Automobile Insurance v. Campbell* that the due process clause of the U.S. Constitution protects defendants from unwarranted damage awards. The Court reiterated a set of guidelines that it had established in an earlier case. These guidelines include the following: (1) the heinous nature of the defendant's behavior in the case; (2) the level of inconsistency between just how badly the plaintiff was really (or possibly) hurt by the conduct of the defendant and the amount decided upon by the jury as a reward; and (3) the degree of variation between the amount set by law as a civil punishment involving similar transgressions, and the amount granted in the case at bar. Despite these guidelines, the court does not establish a dollar amount or a mathematical formula for determining damages. Some damage awards, however, are clearly too much. The court mentions an award of 500 times the compensatory damages as an example of an excessive award. In contrast, it points to a statutory award of triple damages as an appropriate amount.

Contemporary State Tort Reform

Other suggestions for reform at the state level involve statutory adjustments in tort law that include:

1. Appeal bond reform
2. Expert evidence reform
3. Forum shopping reform
4. Jury reform
5. Product liability reform

Appeal Bond Reform Many states require a defendant who has lost a case at trial to post an appeal bond before he or she is permitted to bring an appeal challenging a damage award. An *appeal bond* is the payment of a set sum of money into a protected account to secure the payment of that money to the plaintiff should the defendant's appeal be defeated. The fear is that, while the appeal is pending, the defendant might transfer funds to other parties, hide the funds in off-shore bank accounts, or simply spend the money outright, thus preventing the successful plaintiff from collecting the appropriate level of damages. To prevent this abuse, state law requires the payment of a bond that is equal to or slightly higher than the amount of the actual judgment.

Supporters of tort reform argue that the bond requirement has become overly burdensome on defendants because today some damage awards reach above the billion dollar mark. Consequently, they propose placing a cap on such bonds. The cap would simultaneously preserve the plaintiff's right to collect, while avoiding the burden that is placed on a defendant who must come up with an outrageously high bond just to preserve the right to appeal. Such a bond limit might reach $1 million for corporations and $100,000 for individuals or small business concerns.

Class Action Reform As we saw in Chapter 3, a class action lawsuit is brought on behalf of a large number of plaintiffs all of whom have suffered similar, related injuries at the hands of the defendant. Class action lawsuits are justified when the cost of bringing a lawsuit by a single individual far outweighs the small monetary award due that individual, should the suit succeed. Supporters of tort reform have argued that the requirements for bringing such lawsuits are so weak that they encourage attorneys to file such lawsuits in the hope of forcing corporate defenders to enter very lucrative settlement agreements. One reform measure would place a heavy fine on attorneys who file groundless class action lawsuits. Another would require the court of appeals to review the decision of any trial court to allow a class action lawsuit. A final reform measure would place a limit on the amount of money that could be collected by attorneys who represent clients in successful class action lawsuits.

Expert Witness Reform There is concern that some state courts have become too lenient in the scope and nature of expert testimony. When scientific evidence is distorted, exaggerated, misapplied, or misrepresented it is referred to as *junk science.* To control the use of junk science in the courtroom, reformers suggest tightening the requirements used by the court to determine the credentials and the qualifications of expert witnesses. Most reformers who promote changes in the guidelines point to the rules that are used in the federal court as good examples of the types of stringent procedures that ought to be used in the state courts to screen expert witnesses even before they enter the courtroom, let alone take the witness stand.

Forum Shopping Reform The technique of *forum shopping* is a process that some plaintiffs use to locate a jurisdiction that has a friendly track record for the type of lawsuit they are about to file. The objective is to ensure support for the legal position that the plaintiff intends to espouse in his or her argument before the court. There are, of course, limits to this tactic because there must be some jurisdictional nexus to the court before the plaintiff can even consider choosing that location for the suit. Nevertheless, the rules of state courts are liberal enough to allow them to become popular places for certain types of lawsuits.

There would seem to be little to complain about if a plaintiff is simply looking for a friendly location in which to file a case. However, if the practice gets out of hand, the courts in those locations may find that they have scheduled more cases than they can handle effectively. Supporters of reform have suggested that those courts which find themselves overburdened by cases that are not directly related to their home territory should tighten the class action filing requirements to discourage outside litigants from using their courts as friendly forums.

Jury Reform Like voting, jury duty should be seen as a civic responsibility. Unfortunately, for many people jury duty is viewed as a burden rather than a privilege. Much of this is due to the way the system is run, rather than to the concept of jury duty itself. At the heart of this difficulty is the fact that the process itself is unfair. On the one hand, the system makes escape easy for some people while, on the other, it makes the actual time served on the jury difficult and uncomfortable for those who fail to "escape." For example, often potential jurors can avoid jury duty by offering a specious excuse, or by simply failing to show up at the courthouse on the day they are ordered to. In contrast, those citizens who do show up often find themselves stuck on a jury, with little compensation, for an indefinite period of time.

Supporters of reform suggest that the rewards for serving on a jury should be increased, while the penalties for failing to serve when called should be intensified. These reformers also encourage courts to raise the amount of compensation that goes to jurors and to streamline procedures to shorten the actual time spent during a trial. Reformers would also revamp the court's oversight process and establish monitoring and follow-up procedures to track those jurors who are called to serve but who fail to show up at their designated times. Another suggested reform would change the pool of potential jurors to include both those adults who register to vote to those who hold a valid driver's license. This final change would vastly increase the number of people who are available for jury duty.

Product Liability Reform Some states have elected to revise the underlying theory of strict liability as it applies to product liability. These jurisdictions advocate transforming product liability into a cause of action based on negligence rather than strict liability. Should product liability become a negligence-based tort, the litigation process would require the plaintiff to show the existence of the elements of negligence including duty, breach of duty, proximate cause, and actual harm, elements that need not be shown in an absolute liability case. The objective is to make it more difficult for plaintiffs to succeed in product liability cases, thus discouraging them from filing these cases in the first place.

Opponents of such a change in the law point out that the original intent of product liability was to protect innocent consumers who are victimized by manufacturers who create unreasonably dangerous products. Moreover, the theory was grounded in strict liability rather than negligence because manufacturers hold complete control over the type of evidence that a plaintiff needs to prove a case based on negligence. Moreover, the objective of product liability is to make certain that manufacturers go above and beyond the call of duty to ensure that any product that they put on the market is as safe as possible for consumers to purchase and use. Changing the standard, the argument goes, would rob consumers of this fundamental level of protection.

For information on appeal bond reform, expert evidence reform, forum shopping reform, jury reform, and product liability reform see "Tort Reform: An Overview of State Legislative Efforts to Improve the Legal System." National Association of Mutual Insurance Companies, April 3, 2004. http://www.namic.org/reports/tortReform/overview.asp.

For more information on the federal tort reform bill see Coyle, Marcia. "Prospects Bright for Passage of Tort Bill." *National Law Journal,* January 16, 2004, p. 1.

Contemporary Federal Tort Reform

The concern over the recent increase in the number of tort lawsuits in the state courts has led to a demand for changes in the system that would make it easier for certain types of cases to enter the federal court system. Many of these proposals involve class action lawsuits that include plaintiffs from multiple states. These suggested reforms would give a federal court additional grounds to accept the removal of a case from the state court where it was originally filed. For example, it might be possible under these reform suggestions for a federal court to accept the removal of a case from the state court in which it was originally filed if the question at the heart of the case involved a national issue. In addition, the federal court might also accept removal if the defendant could demonstrate that the class action case was filed in a state jurisdiction as a direct result of forum shopping. One of the beliefs behind this attempt to empower the federal courts in class action tort suits is the idea that the federal courts are better equipped to deal with the problems associated with frivolous tort lawsuits. Whether or not this is actually true remains to be seen.

Tort Reform and the Complex Adaptive System

The interaction of the state legislatures, the state courts, and the federal courts in the tort law crisis, demonstrates how the law works as a complex adaptive system. In this case, the interaction begins with the state legislatures which, in response to concerns about our litigious society, enacted tort reform legislation to deal with the problem. The state legislators were, in part, responding to the strong lobbying efforts of the insurance industry and the American Medical Association, both of which demanded changes in the system. On the other hand, organizations like the American Association of Trial Lawyers, also exerted pressure on legislators not to overreact to the claims of the AMA and the insurance industry. Lobbying efforts such as these, however, are also a part of this complex adaptive process.

Focusing on damage caps as one aspect of tort reform will show the adaptive process at work. Damage caps limit the extensive damage awards that many juries have bestowed on plaintiffs in medical malpractice lawsuits. Damage caps were routinely placed in tort reform statutes by state legislatures. Frequently, such caps were challenged in the courts by plaintiffs who questioned their constitutionality. Consequently, the caps were often struck down by the court because they deprived certain plaintiffs of the equal protection of the law.

Eventually a third reactive agent in the complex system, the United States Supreme Court, entered the interplay of levels and readjusted the law's focus on damage awards. The Court began to see merit in an argument that defendants had cleverly borrowed from plaintiffs. If statutory damage caps deprive certain plaintiffs of equal protection because those caps limit the amount that those plaintiffs can recover when compared to other plaintiffs, then permitting consistently large awards against certain defendants can deprive those defendants of equal protection when compared to other similarly situated defendants. Thus, we see how three agents in the system, state legislatures, state courts, and the U.S. Supreme Court played off one another to address the problem of tort reform, thus permitting a change within the complex adaptive system of the law without being overwhelmed by it.

Quick Quiz 5-7 True or False?

1. Wrongful death and survival statutes are two legal terms that refer to the same legal concept.

2. Damage caps usually apply to noneconomic damages.

3. Tort reform is the province of the states only.

Summary

5-1 A tort is a private wrong that injures another person's physical well-being, emotional health, property, or reputation. A person who commits a tort is called a tortfeasor. The other party is alternatively referred to as the injured party, the innocent party, or the victim. The primary purpose of tort law is to compensate the innocent party by making up for any loss suffered by that victim. The doctrine of *respondeat superior* may impose legal liability on employers and make them pay for the torts committed by their employees within the scope of the employer's business.

5-2 The principal intentional torts include assault, battery, false imprisonment, defamation, disparagement, fraudulent misrepresentation, invasion of privacy, deprivation of publicity, intentional infliction of emotional distress, and malicious prosecution.

5-3 Negligence is the failure to exercise the degree of care that a reasonable person would have exercised in the same circumstances. Negligence includes four elements: duty of care, breach of duty through a failure to exercise the appropriate standard of care, proximate cause, and actual harm. Three defenses to negligence are contributory negligence, comparative negligence, and assumption of risk.

5-4 Under the doctrine of strict liability, when people engage in ultrahazardous activities, they will be liable for any harm that occurs because of that activity, regardless of intent, and regardless of care.

5-5 Cybertorts involve computer information that has been invaded, distorted, stolen, falsified, misused, destroyed, or exploited financially by an electronic device. Therefore, cybertorts rarely involve any harm to a party's physical well-being. Instead, the victim's reputation has been hurt because a false statement has been posted on the Internet, the victim's emotional state has

been disturbed because his or her privacy has been invaded, or the victim has suffered monetary harm because his or her identity has been tampered with.

5-6 Tort remedies include money damages and injunctions.

5-7 Survival statutes allow a lawsuit to be brought even if both the plaintiff and the defendant are deceased. Wrongful death statutes preserve the rights of third parties affected by the death of the deceased to bring a lawsuit. Suggestions for contemporary state tort reform include appeal bond reform, expert evidence reform, forum shopping reform, jury reform, and product liability reform. Suggestions for tort reform at the federal level focus on class action lawsuits.

Key Terms

abuse of process, 97
actual malice, 94
actual malice test, 94
assault, 92
battery, 93
comparative negligence, 102
contributory negligence, 102
cybertort, 104
damage cap, 110
damages, 108
defamation, 94
defective condition, 103
disparagement, 94

duty, 91
economic compensatory damages, 108
false imprisonment, 93
fraud, 95
fraudulent misrepresentation, 95
injunction, 109
intentional or reckless infliction of emotional distress, 97
invasion of privacy, 96
libel, 94
malicious prosecution, 97
misuse of legal procedure, 97

negligence, 99
noneconomic compensatory damages, 108
proximate cause, 101
punitive damages, 109
respondeat superior, 91
slander, 94
strict liability, 103
tort, 91
tortfeasor, 91
wrongful civil proceedings, 97

Questions for Review and Discussion

1. What is the difference between a tort and a crime?
2. What is the meant by the legal term duty?
3. What are the principal intentional torts?
4. What are the elements of negligence?
5. What are the differences among contributory negligence, comparative negligence, and assumption of the risk?
6. When does strict liability apply?
7. What is a cybertort?
8. What remedies are available in tort law?
9. What is a damage cap?
10. What innovations have been suggested for contemporary state tort reform?

Investigating the Internet

An variety of tort law principles can be located on the Internet by accessing the Legal Information Institute (LIT) of Cornell Law School. The Internet Law Library of the United States House of Representatives maintains a wide assortment of cases, statutes, and articles concerning tort law issues. A source of state laws is StateLaw which is furnished by the Washburn School of Law.

Cases for Analysis

1. At the height of the civil rights movement, *The New York Times* ran a full page advertisement entitled "Heed Their Rising Voices." The advertisement detailed police efforts in Montgomery, Alabama, to suppress the nonviolent civil rights demonstrations being carried on there by thousands of college students. The Police Commissioner of Montgomery, L.B. Sullivan, filed a lawsuit against *The New York Times,* alleging that he had been libeled by information carried in the advertisement. This was true, he argued, despite the fact that he was never mentioned by name. Should the court use the actual malice test in this case to determine whether the newspaper libeled the commissioner? Explain. *New York Times Co. v. Sullivan,* 376 U.S. 254 (U.S. Sup. Ct.).

2. The publishing firm of Secker and Warburg was set to publish the British edition of a book entitled, *House of Bush, House of Saud: The Secret Relationship Between the World's Two Most Powerful Dynasties,* when it suddenly pulled out of the arrangement. When questioned about their withdrawal from the deal, officials at Secker and Warburg admitted that they were apprehensive about publishing the book because the Saudi royal family had a record of bringing libel suits against publishers in the United Kingdom. The rationale for this type of forum shopping on the part of the royal family appears to be the fact that the United Kingdom has a tough libel law process. Under British libel law, the presumption is that the publication is false. The defendant then has the burden of proof to show that the allegedly libelous information was true. Does libel law in the United Kingdom differ from libel law in the United States? Explain. Lyall, Sarah. "Are Saudis Using British Libel Law to Deter Critics?" *The New York Times,* May 22, 2004, p. A15.

3. Five Commerce City police officers were summoned to break up a disturbance at a local party of teenagers. At the party, Ralph Crowe, who had consumed eight cups of beer and three cups of alcoholic punch, became rowdy and had to be detained by the officers. The police released Ralph after receiving the assurances of his brother Eddie that he would drive Ralph home. After leaving the party, Eddie allowed Ralph to take the wheel. Instead of going home, Ralph drove to the site of another party where he lost control of the car and ran down six people. The police officers were sued for negligence in releasing of Ralph. Did the five officers owe a duty to the six victims of Ralph's drunk-driving accident? Explain. *Leake v. Cain,* 720 P.2d 152 (CO).

4. Seventy-four years old at the time, Ramona Booker entered a drugstore by pushing her way through one door and then through a second. Both doors were extremely heavy so Booker was compelled to use both hands, causing her cane to drag on the ground. As she entered the second door, the tip of her cane caught on the exposed coil of a security device causing her to fall and injure herself. Booker brought a lawsuit against Revco DS, Inc., to recover for her injuries. Did the drugstore owe a duty to Booker and other customers to maintain a safe environment? Explain. Is Booker's lawsuit based upon allegations that the store owners committed an intentional tort or that they were negligent? Explain. What test would be used to judge whether the drugstore owners should be held liable for Booker's injuries? Explain. *Booker v. Revco DS, Inc.* 681 N.E.2d 499 (OH).

5. Queenway Tankers, Inc., Kingsway Tankers, Inc., East River Steamship Corporation, and Richmond Tankers, Inc. all chartered supertankers designed by Transamerican Delaval, Inc. Under terms of the

charters, each shipping company was financially responsible for many repairs to the tankers. From the start, there were problems with the tankers' turbines, which needed extensive and costly repairs. The plaintiffs brought a product liability suit against Delaval. The suit alleged that the manufacturing defects caused the damage. Should the shipping companies have prevailed in product liability against the manufacturer? Explain. *East River Steamship Corporation v. Transamerican Delaval, Inc.,* 106 S. Ct. 2305 (U.S. Sup. Ct.).

6. Myers was injured when she slipped and fell on an ice patch on the front walkway of the Canton Centre Mall. The mall is owned and operated by Forest City Enterprises. Forest City had employees who were responsible for clearing the ice off of the mall walkways every morning. On this particular morning, they had cleared the ice from the walkway a short time before Myers took her tumble. Nevertheless, an ice patch had formed, and Myers did fall, sustaining injuries. Cooper, one of the employees charged with the ice-removal task, theorized that water may have been splashed up onto the sidewalk by passing cars where it froze sometime after their initial cleaning of the day. According to Cooper, "the vehicles could have splashed this back up on there . . . we're constantly moving around the building at all times, so anything can be going on in this half of the building while you're over here doing this half coming around." Was Forest City negligent in failing to keep the sidewalk clear of ice at all times that winter? What test would be used to judge Forest City's conduct? Explain. *Myers v. Forest City Enterprises, Inc.* 635 N.E.2d 1268 (OH).

7. Michelle Wightman was driving toward a railroad crossing at which the gates were down and the lights flashing. Wightman noted a stopped train a short distance from the gate. Believing the stopped train to be the cause of the closed gate, she drove around the gate and was struck and killed by a train that suddenly appeared from behind the stopped train. The stopped train had blocked her view of the oncoming train. Both trains were owned and operated by Consolidated Rail Corporation (CRC). Wightman's mother brought a wrongful death lawsuit and a survivorship action against CRC. CRC claimed that Wightman's action of driving around the gates in violation of both state and city law regarding the operation of a motor vehicle at a railroad crossing constituted negligence on her part. CRC further argued that if Wightman had not crossed the tracks she would not have been struck by the train. Therefore, her actions were the sole cause of the accident and the railroad corporation should not be held liable for her death. The attorney for the plaintiff argued that the placement of the first train, blocking the view of the other track, contributed to the accident and that CRC should be held liable for Wightman's death. Should Wightman's own negligence be a complete bar to the plaintiff's recovery of damages in this case? Explain. *Wightman v. Consolidated Railroad Corporation,* 640 N.E.2d 1160 (OH).

Quick Quiz Answers

5-1	5-2	5-3	5-4	5-5	5-6
1. T	1. F	1. F	1. T	1. T	1. F
2. F	2. F	2. T	2. T	2. F	2. F
3. F	3. F	3. F	3. F	3. T	3. F

5-7
1. F
2. T
3. F

Part 1 Case Study

Planned Parenthood of Pennsylvania v. Casey
United States Supreme Court 112 S.Ct. 2791

Summary

The Pennsylvania state legislature passed a statute that limited a woman's right to have an abortion. Specifically, the statute included three provisions that made it more difficult for a woman to obtain an abortion than it had been prior to the enactment of the statute. The first provision required a woman to give her "informed consent" to the procedure. Informed consent was to be obtained by providing the woman with detailed information concerning abortion and then requiring her to undergo a twenty-four-hour waiting period before the abortion could be performed. A second provision demanded the informed consent of at least one parent of a juvenile seeking an abortion. The third provision compelled a married woman to notify her spouse of her plan to seek an abortion. The statute also allowed these provisions to be circumvented should a "medical emergency" require such a waiver.

Immediately before the act was to go into effect, several clinics that specialized in abortion procedures and one physician representing an entire class of physicians, filed a lawsuit in federal court, naming the Governor of Pennsylvania as a defendant in the suit and asking the court to stop the implementation of the statute. The plaintiffs also asked the Federal District Court to find the three statutory provisions unconstitutional. The District Court obliged. Accordingly, it issued an injunction forbidding the enforcement of the law. The Third Circuit Court of Appeals reversed the findings of the District Court. While the appellate court did find the spousal notification provision unconstitutional, it nevertheless upheld the other two provisions as constitutional.

The case then went to the United States Supreme Court. The Supreme Court agreed to hear the case because it represented an opportunity for the court to clarify some of the doubts, uncertainties, and controversy surrounding *Roe v. Wade*, 410 U.S. 113, the landmark case in which the Supreme Court upheld a woman's right to end her pregnancy during the beginning phases of that pregnancy. The Court also felt that it needed to address what the justices had begun to perceive as an attempt by the executive branch to compel the court to reevaluate the law as stated in *Roe v. Wade*. According to the majority opinion, the Justice Department had in five separate cases asked the Court to overturn *Roe v. Wade*.

The case of *Planned Parenthood of Pennsylvania v. Casey* is interesting for several reasons. First, it represents an unusual alliance among three justices, Sandra Day O'Connor, Anthony M. Kennedy, and David H. Souter. All three of these justices had been appointed by conservative presidents for their conservative legal philosophies. Nevertheless, all of them lent their support to *Roe v. Wade,* a development that was decidedly unexpected in most legal circles. Second, O'Connor, Kennedy, and Souter cooperated in the actual writing of the Court's opinion. Such a collaboration among justices in the writing of an opinion is rare. The customary procedure is for the Chief Justice, or the senior justice within the majority if the Chief Justice is a member of the minority, to appoint one justice to write the opinion of the majority. In this case, however, all three justices issued the opinion as joint authors. Finally, *Planned Parenthood of Pennsylvania v. Casey* stands, not only as a landmark redrafting of the legal principles found in *Roe v. Wade,* but also as a vivid example of the extraordinarily important role that precedent plays within the American legal system.

The Court's Opinion:

Justices Sandra Day O'Connor, Anthony M. Kennedy, and David H. Souter

After considering the fundamental constitutional questions resolved by *Roe,* principles of institutional integrity, and the rule of *stare decisis,* we are led to conclude this: the essential holding of *Roe v. Wade* should be retained and once again reaffirmed.

It must be stated at the outset and with clarity that *Roe*'s essential holding, the holding we reaffirm, has three parts. First is a recognition of the right of the woman to choose to have an abortion before viability and to obtain it without undue influence from the State. Before viability, the State's interests are not strong enough to support a prohibition of abortion or the imposition of a substantial obstacle to the woman's effective right to elect the procedure. Second is a confirmation of the State's power to restrict abortion after fetal viability, if the law contains exceptions for pregnancies which endanger a woman's life or health. And third is the principle that the State has legitimate interests from the outset of the pregnancy in protecting the health of the woman and the life of the fetus that may become a child. These principles do not contradict one another; and we adhere to each. . . .

Men and women of good conscience can disagree, and we suppose some shall always disagree, about the profound moral and spiritual implications of terminating a pregnancy, even in its earliest stage. Some of us as individuals find abortion offensive to our most basic principles of morality, but that cannot control our decision. Our obligation is to define the liberty of all, not mandate our own moral code. The underlying constitutional issue is whether the State can resolve these philosophical questions in such a definitive way that a woman lacks all choice in the matter, except perhaps in those rare circumstances in which the pregnancy is itself a danger to her own life or health, or as the result of rape or incest. . . .

[W]hen this Court reexamines a prior holding, its judgment is customarily informed by a series of prudential and pragmatic considerations designed to test the consistency of overruling a prior decision with the ideal of the rule of law, and to gauge the respective costs of reaffirming and overruling a prior case. Thus,

for example, we may ask whether the rule has proved to be intolerable simply in defying practical workability; whether the rule is subject to a kind of reliance that would lend a special hardship to the consequences of overruling and add inequity to the cost of repudiation; whether related principles of law have so far developed as to have left the old rule no more than a remnant of abandoned doctrine; or whether facts have so changed or come to be seen so differently, as to have robbed the old rule of significant application or justification.

Although *Roe* has engendered opposition, it has in no sense proven "unworkable," representing as it does a simple limitation beyond which a state law is enforceable. . . . But to do this (i.e., to ignore the issue of reliance) would be simply to refuse to face the fact that for two decades of economic and social developments, people have organized intimate relationships and made choices that define their views of themselves and their places in society, in reliance on the availability of abortion in the event that contraception would fail. . . . No evolution of legal principle has left *Roe*'s doctrinal footings weaker than they were in 1973. No development of constitutional law since the case was decided has implicitly or explicitly left *Roe* behind as a mere survivor of obsolete constitutional thinking. . . . We have seen how time has overtaken some of *Roe*'s factual assumptions: advances in maternal health care allow for abortions safe to the mother in later pregnancy than was true in 1973, and advances in neonatal care have advanced viability to a point somewhat earlier. But these facts go only to the scheme of time limits on the realization of competing interests, and the divergences from factual premises of 1973 have no bearing on the validity of *Roe*'s central holding, that viability marks the earliest point at which the State's interest in fetal life is constitutionally adequate to justify a legislative ban on nontherapeutic abortions. . . . Within the bounds of normal *stare decisis* analysis, then, and subject to considerations on which it customarily turns, the stronger argument is for affirming *Roe*'s central holding, with whatever degree of personal reluctance any of us may have, not for overruling it. . . .

Some guiding principles should emerge. What is at stake is the woman's right to make the ultimate decision, not a right to be insulated from all others in doing so. Regulations which do no more than create a structural mechanism by which the State, or the parent or guardian of a minor, may express profound respect for the life of the unborn are permitted, if they are not a substantial obstacle to the woman's exercise of the right to choose. Unless it has that effect on her right of choice, a state measure designed to persuade her to choose childbirth over abortion will be upheld if reasonably related to that goal.

Regulations designed to foster the health of a woman seeking an abortion are valid if they do not constitute an undue burden. . . . An undue burden exists, and therefore a provision of law is invalid, if its purpose or effect is to place a substantial obstacle in the path of a woman seeking an abortion before the fetus attains viability. . . . To promote the State's profound interest in potential life, throughout pregnancy the State may take measures to ensure that the woman's choice is informed, and measures designed to advance this interest will not be invalidated as long as their purpose is to persuade the woman to choose childbirth over abortion. (Following this standard, the Court decided that the informed consent provision and the parental notification provision did not pose an undue burden on the woman's right to choose to have an abortion. However, the spousal notification provision was overturned as creating an undue burden.)

Questions for Analysis

1. At one point in the opinion, O'Connor, Kennedy, and Souter write, "Some of us as individuals find abortion offensive to our most basic principles of morality, but that cannot control our decision. Our obligation is to define the liberty of all, not mandate our own moral code." Do you agree or disagree with the justices on this issue? Explain. Should judges allow their own moral code to control their legal decisions? Explain why or why not.

2. What ethical character traits are the justices exemplifying by taking this stand? What ethical character traits are they violating? Explain.

3. Are the justices submitting to the pressure of subjective ethics by taking this stand or are they seeking some sort of objective standard? Explain.

4. Why did Planned Parenthood of Pennsylvania bring this lawsuit to Federal District Court? What are the grounds for subject-matter jurisdiction in this case? Why is the governor of Pennsylvania named as a defendant in the lawsuit? Explain.

5. In what way is the decision in this case an example of a strongly independent federal judiciary? Explain.

6. What factors might have motivated the justices of the United States Supreme Court to decide to hear this case? Explain.

7. What are the four considerations that a court should look at when determining whether or not to overturn a line of precedent? Did any of these considerations apply in *Planned Parenthood of Pennsylvania v. Casey?* Explain.

8. Did the United States Supreme Court uphold or overturn *Roe v. Wade* in *Planned Parenthood of Pennsylvania v. Casey?* Explain.

9. According to the reasoning in this case, what two conflicting rights does the court attempt to reconcile in *Planned Parenthood of Pennsylvania v. Casey?* Explain.

10. When *Planned Parenthood of Pennsylvania v. Casey* was decided, both the pro-choice and the pro-life political factions said that the case hurt their positions on abortion rights. Speculate on why this was so.

Contract Law

Part Two

Chapter 6

The Nature, Characteristics, and Status of Contracts

The Opening Case

"To Compete or Not to Compete"

Yuri Kaleri, a research microbiologist, worked for Shanower Ecological Research Industries, Inc. After working for SERI for three years, he was asked to sign a noncompetition agreement, under which he promised not to work for another research facility in the United States for two years, should he ever decide to leave his job at SERI, in exchange for a one time bonus of $20,000. Although he thought it odd at the time, Kaleri noted that the agreement did not include any provision that would allow SERI to assign his noncompetition agreement to anyone else, even a company that might buy SERI. He assumed that omission was due to management's desire not to promise any of its employees anything should they wish to enter negotiations for the sale of SERI. When another company, Transeuro Research, Ltd., bought SERI, the new management team tried to get Kaleri to sign a new noncompetition agreement, which he refused to do. Kaleri left Transeuro and took a job at the Oppenheimer Research Corporation. Transeuro attempted to enforce the original noncompetition agreement that Kaleri had made with SERI. Transeuro argued that the noncompetition clause was part of Kaleri's overall employment agreement and that, since the overall employment contract had transferred to Transeuro, the noncompetition agreement had transferred along with it. Kaleri argued that the noncompetition agreement was a separate deal and could not be transferred. He pointed to the fact that the noncompetition agreement had been negotiated several years after his original employment contract, that it was written as a separate document, and that SERI had paid him extra consideration in the form of $20,000 to go along with the new deal. Since that noncompetition agreement had no assignment clause, the noncompetition agreement itself did not transfer to Transeuro with the sale of SERI. Transeuro brought suit against Kaleri and asked the court for an order that would uphold the noncompetition agreement. Was the noncompetition agreement a contract? Should the court uphold that agreement? Did Transeuro make a mistake when it failed to offer Kaleri compensation for the newly added noncompetition agreement? Will the court take away Kaleri's livelihood by preventing him from working for Oppenheimer? Questions like these are at the heart of contract law.

Chapter Outcomes

1. Distinguish between the will theory and the formalist theory of contract law.
2. Identify the six elements of a contract.
3. Explain the place of the UCC in contract law.
4. Distinguish contracts from other agreements made between different parties.
5. Explain the concept of privity and contract law.
6. Explain the nature of valid, void, voidable, and unenforceable contracts.
7. Contrast unilateral and bilateral contractual arrangements.
8. Outline the difference between express and implied contracts.
9. Discuss the difference between quasi-contracts and implied-in-fact contracts.
10. Explain how executory contracts differ from executed contracts.

For a situation that is very similar to The Opening Case, see: "Can't Assign Noncompete Without Workers' OK." *The National Law Journal,* April 26, 2004, p. 16, *Traffic Control Serv. Inc. v. United Rentals Northwest, Inc.* No. 40798, Nevada Supreme Court.

6-1　The Nature of Contracts

A **contract** is an agreement between two or more competent parties, based on mutual promises, to do or to refrain from doing some particular thing which is neither illegal nor impossible. The agreement results in an obligation or a duty that can be enforced in a court of law.

Example 6-1

Kristan Gregori was negotiating the sale of her restaurant, the Gregori Deli, to Tony Francisco. During the negotiation stage, Francisco asked Gregori to agree not to open a competing restaurant for five years anywhere in Jamestown. Gregori agreed. The sale of the restaurant was contingent upon Francisco selling his apartment building to Wellsian Real Estate Developers of Jamestown. That evening Gregori told her cousin, Betina, that she would take her out to dinner if the deal with Francisco was finalized. There are several agreements within this scenario. The first is the sale of the restaurant. This contract will only go into effect if the second contract between Wellsian and Francisco is finalized. The third agreement between Gregori and her cousin Betina is only a social agreement and cannot be enforced as law. The noncompetition agreement that Gregori has made with Francisco is a part of the overall agreement to sell the restaurant.

All parties to a contract must meet their responsibilities as specified in the contract.

The contracting party who makes a promise is known as the **promisor;** the one to whom the promise is made is the **promisee.** The party who is obligated to deliver on a promise or to undertake some act of performance is called the **obligor.** The contracting party to whom this party owes an obligation is called the **obligee.**

The Basic Objectives of Contract Law

In Example 6-1, the contract between Gregori and Francisco is valid because it was entered freely. Neither party was coerced into entering the agreement. Also, presumably, each side knew the terms of the contract and agreed to those terms without reservation. If for some reason in

Did You Know?

Prior to the advent of industrial capitalism in Britain, contract law was based on a fairness principle which required an exchange of property of equal value. With the rise of industrial capitalism, the fairness principle was replaced with the requirement that the parties to a contract freely agree to the terms of the contract regardless of the value of the property exchanged.

See Caudill, David S., and Steven Jay Gold. *Radical Philosophy of Law: Contemporary Challenges to Mainstream Legal Theory and Practice.* New Jersey: Humanities Press, 1995, pp. 144–145.

Cross-Cultural Notes As an eighteenth-century Hindu scholar, Jagannatha wrote about contract law in Hindu society. However, during the years when the British occupied India, Jagannatha's writings, as well as other Indian laws pertaining to business transactions, were ignored.

the future, Gregori believes that she did not receive enough for her restaurant, she will be unable to file a complaint against Francisco. Unless Francisco somehow defrauded or coerced her, the fact that Gregori did a poor job of negotiating and received too little for the deli will not matter to the court. This is because the underlying objective of contract law is to determine whether the parties entered the agreement freely. If the court determines that the parties willingly entered the agreement, then the contract is valid. If the court then determines that one of the parties violated this valid contract, that party will have to compensate the other party for any loss that results from that breach.

Usually, the courts will not make someone go through with a contract if they back out of the agreement. However, as noted above, the courts will compel a party who has failed to live up to his or her agreement to compensate the innocent party for any loss that results from that breach. As a general rule, the court's goal in the remedy phase of a contract dispute is to place the injured party in as good a position as he or she would have been in had the contract been carried out. There are built-in limitations to this theory, however. For instance, the innocent party is not permitted to take advantage of the breach by deliberately raising the level of damages that the other party will have to pay as a consequence of the breach. This is known as the principle of mitigation. We will examine the remedies available in contract law as well as the principle of mitigation in more detail in Chapter 14. For now, it is best to remember that the general principle of contract law is to put the parties in as good a position as they would have been in had the contract been fulfilled.

The Will Theory and the Formalist Theory

It is always important to remember that contracts are based on the willful acts of the parties involved in the agreement. Both parties freely enter the agreement understanding the obligations that they have assumed and the benefits due to them and they must therefore live up to those agreements. This is referred to as the **will theory** of contract law. At times, to outsiders, the terms of a contract may seem disproportionate or unfair. However, as long as the parties freely enter a legal agreement with equal bargaining power and with full contractual capacity, a valid contract will result. Principles of equity and justice enter the question only if a party's free will has been thwarted by fraud, misrepresentation, mistake, duress, undue influence, by something uncontrollable, or by some event or circumstance that could not be reasonably foreseen.

However, since it is impossible for the courts to actually invade the consciousness of the parties, the courts must use the outward actions and the words of the parties as their standard of judgment. Over the years, this need to look at outward actions and words has led to a formalist theory of contract law. Under the **formalist theory** of contract law, the courts look to see if certain elements exist. Those elements are offer, acceptance, mutual assent, capacity, consideration, and legality. If each element is present, then a contract exists, regardless of what the parties may argue after the fact.

Offer An offer is a proposal made by one party to another indicating a willingness to enter a contract. The person who makes an offer is called the offeror; the person to whom the offer is made is the offeree. (See Chapter 7.)

Acceptance In most cases, only a specifically identified offeree or his or her authorized agent has the right to accept an offer. Acceptance means that the offeree freely agrees to be bound by the terms of the offer. (See Chapter 7.)

Mutual Assent If a valid offer has been made by the offeror, and a valid acceptance has been made by the offeree, then mutual assent exists between them. If mutual assent has been destroyed, the relationship that results is said to be a defective agreement. (See Chapter 8.)

Table 6-1 The Six Elements of a Contract	
Element	**Explanation**
Offer	A proposal is made by one party (the offeror) to another party (the offeree) indicating a willingness to enter a contract.
Acceptance	The offeree agrees to be bound by the terms found in the offer.
Mutual assent	Offer and acceptance go together to create mutual assent or "a meeting of the minds." Assent can be destroyed by fraud, misrepresentation, mistake, duress, or undue influence.
Capacity	The law presumes that anyone entering a contract has the legal capacity to do so. However, minors are generally excused from contractual responsibility, as are mentally incompetent and drugged or intoxicated individuals.
Consideration	Consideration is the thing of value promised to the other party in a contract in exchange for something else of value promised by the other party. This mutual exchange binds the parties together.
Legality	Parties are not allowed to enforce contracts that involve doing something that is illegal. Some illegal contracts involve agreements to commit a crime or perform a tort. Others involve activities made illegal by statutory law.

Capacity   The fourth element necessary to a make a contract complete is capacity. Capacity is the legal ability to make a contract. (See Chapter 9.)

Consideration   The fifth element to any complete contract is the freely exercised mutual exchange of benefits and sacrifices. This willful exchange is called consideration. Consideration is the thing of value promised to the other party in exchange for something else of value promised by the other party. (See Chapter 10.)

Legality   The final element of a binding contract is legality. Parties cannot be allowed to enforce a contract that involves doing something that is illegal. (See Chapter 11.)

Contracts and the UCC

As discussed in Chapter 2, the Uniform Commercial Code (UCC) is a unified set of statutes designed to govern almost all commercial transactions. Article 2 of the UCC sets down the rules that govern sale-of-goods contracts. All other types of contracts, including employment contracts and real property contracts, are governed by common law rules and certain special statutory provisions. Fortunately, in many cases, common law rules and UCC provisions are the same. Those differences that do exist are pointed out in the discussion of general contract law in Part II. In Part III, Article 2 of the UCC and sale-of-goods contracts are discussed. Property law contracts are analyzed in Part IV and Part VII examines employment contracts.

Contracts and Other Agreements

All contracts are agreements, but not all agreements are contracts. An agreement may or may not be legally enforceable. To be enforceable, an agreement must conform to the law of contracts. The courts have never been agreeable to the enforcement of social agreements: dates, dinner engagements, or the like. Many states have extended this concept to include agreements to marry and agreements to live together without the benefit of a marriage contract.

Further Reading   For a thorough discussion of contract law and its historical background in the common law, read *The Common Law of Obligations,* by John Cooke and David Oughton (London: Butterworth, 1993).

Background Information   Many contracts are informally sealed with a handshake, a gesture commonly used to signify agreement. The handshake is a Western custom that is thought to have originated when hands were extended to show they held no weapons. The parties to the agreements then shook hands as a symbolic gesture of mutual trust.

State Variations   California, South Dakota, and many other states have defined the elements of a contract to be: (1) parties capable of contracting; (2) their consent; (3) a lawful object; and (4) a sufficient cause or consideration.

UCC (see pages 864–926)

Contracts and Privity

The general rule of contract law is that the parties to a contract must stand in privity to one another. **Privity** simply means that both parties must have a legally recognized interest in the subject of the contract if they are to be bound by it. Outside parties who do not have such an interest in the subject matter of the contract may not be bound by it. Their right to bring a lawsuit in the event of breach of contract would also be called into question.

Example 6-2

The Columbus Redbirds, a professional swim team, had a contract with the city to hold seven swim meets at the city's new nautorium in the downtown area. When the Redbirds corporation breached its contract and moved the team to Indianapolis, the city of Columbus sued. In another development following the inauguration of the original lawsuit, a group of three downtown hotels and fifteen restaurants joined together to bring a second lawsuit against the Redbirds for breach of contract. The city will have standing to bring its lawsuit because the city and the swim team were in privity. However, the hotels and the restaurants will not have standing to sue because they were not in privity under the terms of the original contract.

Despite this privity rule, it is possible for two or more parties to provide benefits to a third party. However, the law still makes a distinction between third parties who are intended beneficiaries and third parties who are incidental beneficiaries. In Example 6-2 above, the hotels and the restaurants are incidental, rather than intended beneficiaries. In contrast, a life insurance contract generally involves intended beneficiaries. Thus, when an insurance company makes a payment on a life insurance contract, that payment is to an intended beneficiary. Moreover, an exception to the general rule of privity exists in cases involving warranties and product liability. (See Chapter 16.)

Quick Quiz 6-1 True or False?

1. A contract results in a duty that can be enforced in a court of law.

2. The court's objective in the remedy phase of a contract dispute is to place the injured party in as good a position as he or she would have been in had the contract been carried out.

3. The law makes no distinction between intended and incidental beneficiaries.

6-2 Contractual Characteristics

Contractual characteristics fall into five different categories. These categories include: valid, void, voidable, and unenforceable; unilateral and bilateral; express and implied; informal and formal; and executory and executed. Any given contract would be classifiable in all five ways. Thus, for example, a single contract could be said to be valid, bilateral, express, formal, and executed, or any other acceptable combination of characteristics.

Valid, Void, Voidable, and Unenforceable Contracts

A **valid contract** is one that is legally binding and fully enforceable by the court. In contrast, a **void contract** is one that has no legal effect whatsoever. For example, a contract to perform an illegal act would be void. A **voidable contract** is one that may be avoided or canceled by one of the parties. A contract made by minors or one that is induced by fraud or misrepresentation are examples of voidable contracts. An **unenforceable contract** is one that, because of some rule of law, cannot be upheld by a court of law. An unenforceable contract may have all the elements of a complete contract and still be unenforceable.

Unilateral and Bilateral Contracts

A **unilateral contract** is an agreement in which one party makes a promise to do something in return for an act of some sort. The classic example of a unilateral contract is a reward contract. A person who promises to pay five dollars to the finder of a lost compact disc does not expect a promise in return. Rather, the person expects the return of the lost CD. When the CD is returned, the contract arises and the promisor owes the finder five dollars.

A Question of Ethics

Suppose you posted a reward notice that read, "Reward: $50 for the return of my lost college class ring." Suppose further that someone who did not know of the reward offer found your ring and returned it. Legally you would not have to pay the reward money to the person who found your ring because he or she did not know about your offer. However, would it be ethical not to pay the reward to the finder? Explain.

In contrast, a **bilateral contract** is one in which both parties make promises. Bilateral contracts come into existence at the moment the two promises are made. A **breach of contract** occurs when one of the two parties fails to keep the promise. When there is a breach of contract, the injured party has the right to ask a court of law to somehow remedy the situation. (Breach of contract and remedies are discussed in detail in Chapter 14.)

Express and Implied Contracts

A contract can be either express or implied. An **express contract** requires some sort of written or spoken expression indicating a desire to enter the contractual relationship. An **implied contract** is created by the actions or gestures of the parties involved in the transaction.

Express Contracts   When contracting parties accept mutual obligations either through oral discussion or written communication, they have created an express contract. Oral negotiations will, in many cases, be reduced to writing, but this is not always necessary.

A written contract does not have to be a long, formal preprinted agreement. While such lengthy, preprinted forms are common in some businesses, other less formal written documents are frequently used to show that a contract exists. For example, a written contract may take the form of a letter, sales slip and receipt, notation, or memorandum. A written contract may be typed, printed, keystroked, scrawled, or written in beautiful penmanship. In some situations, state laws require certain types of contracts to be in writing. (See Chapter 12.)

When a contract is placed in writing, it is essential that the content be as clear and unambiguous as possible. When faced with a dispute over an ambiguous clause, the court may be compelled to look at factual evidence to determine the actual intent of the parties. This

Related Cases   A manager of a nightclub called the Alligator Disco sued his employer to obtain a bonus that had been orally promised to him. The promise was not an enforceable contract, the court ruled, because the promise to pay an employee to do something that he or she was already obligated to do is considered a mere gratuity, not a contract. *DeVito v. Pokoik,* 540 N.Y.S.2d 858 (NY).

State Variations   In Nebraska, a surrogate parent contract (a contract by which a woman is to be compensated for bearing a child of a man who is not her husband) is void and unenforceable.

Background Information   In seventeenth century England, because people made many unsealed and, therefore, informal and unenforceable contracts, the power of local courts in contract disputes declined. Unsealed contracts were accepted as valid, provided there was consideration. Eventually, the Royal Court began to standardize obligations in contracts for special recurring relationships, such as those between landlord and tenant and between supplier and buyer.

About the Law

The law which declares which contracts must be in writing is called the Statute of Frauds. In its original form when it was passed by Parliament in 1677, it was known as the Act for the Prevention of Fraud and Perjuries.

may mean that a case that could have been dismissed early, will have to go to trial so that the court can make a factual determination of intent by looking at evidence beyond the terms in the writing.

When the law does not require a written agreement, an *oral contract* resulting from the spoken words of the parties will be enough. Parties to such an agreement, however, should anticipate the difficulty of proving the contractual relationship should disputes arise later. Nevertheless, expressing every agreement in writing, in anticipation of future need of proof, is impractical in the fast-paced modern world of business.

Implied Contracts One who knowingly accepts benefits from another person may be obligated for their payment even though no express agreement has been made. An agreement of this type can be either implied in fact or implied in law. A contract implied by the direct or indirect acts of the parties is known as an **implied-in-fact contract.** Pumping gas into a car at a self-service gas station is an example of an implied-in-fact contract. Since the parties to a contract enter that contract by an exercise of free will, the court follows an objective rule in interpreting the acts and gestures of a party. Under this concept, the meaning of one's actions is determined by the impression those actions would make upon any reasonable person who might have witnessed them, not by a party's self-serving claim of what was meant or intended by the actions.

> ### Example 6-3
>
> Herbert Ward watched workers employed by the Rice Lawn and Garden Greenhouse as they chemically treated his front lawn. In fact, Ward had no contract with Rice and had not ordered any chemical treatments of his property. The treatment should have been performed on another house at 750 Maple Street instead of at Ward's, which had an address of 570 Maple. Ward never stopped the work crew, even though he knew that a mistake had been made. Rice would be within its rights to believe that the work was being done with Ward's consent. In assessing damages for the cost of the improvement, the court would apply the objective concept rule. A reasonable person who might have watched Rice treat the front lawn would conclude that Ward had freely consented to the work.

An **implied-in-law contract** is imposed by a court when someone is unjustly enriched. It is used when a contract cannot be enforced or when there is no actual written, oral, or implied-in-fact agreement. Applying reasons of justice and fairness, a court may obligate one who has unfairly benefited at the innocent expense of another. An implied-in-law contract is also called a **quasi-contract.**

> ### Example 6-4
>
> Karl Rapp was found unconscious in his hotel room by Jan Stevens, the third-floor maid. She immediately called 911 and then notified Ken Kramer, the hotel manager. Kramer arranged to have Rapp placed in a hospital for emergency treatment. When Rapp regained consciousness, he refused to pay for the treatment, claiming that he was not aware of what was going on and had not agreed to what had been done to him. The case illustrates a quasi-contractual situation wherein it would be unfair to allow the injured person to benefit at the expense of the hospital. In any suit that might arise over this expense, a court would require Rapp to pay the fair value of the services rendered.

Cross-Cultural Notes
In China, judges may act as mediators in contractual disputes, often applying powers that exceed those of American judges. Officially, judges cannot confiscate foreign passports, but the practice still occurs in China. Recently several foreign businesspeople had their passports confiscated by judges when trade disputes with Chinese enterprises arose. The foreigners, nearly all of Chinese descent, were not allowed to leave until their companies settled the disputes by paying the claims.

Getting Students Involved Divide the class into small groups and have each group create one situation in which there is an implied-in-fact contract and one in which there is an implied-in-law contract, or quasi-contract. Have each group share their examples and identify each type of contract.

Cross-Cultural Notes
Traditionally, the Japanese seek harmony in all things. Japanese businesses, therefore, generally avoid litigation. Referring a dispute to a third party, such as a court, is considered an embarrassment. Evidence of this is the fact that there are only about 12,000 lawyers practicing in Japan. Three times more civil court cases are pending in California alone than in all of Japan. Experts in dealing with Japanese businesses suggest including in contracts a clause stating that, if a dispute arises, the parties will discuss the problem and settle it harmoniously.

The quasi-contract concept cannot apply, however, as a means of obtaining payment for an act that a party simply feels should be done. The concept also cannot be applied when one party bestows a benefit on another unnecessarily or through misconduct or negligence. A quasi-contract is not a contract in the true sense of the word because it is created by the court. It does not result from the mutual assent of the parties as do express or implied-in-fact contracts.

Business Law in the News

Comic's Creator Must Share Copyright

Applying a distinctive characters-based doctrine, the 7th U.S. Circuit Court of Appeals has ruled that the creator of the popular *Spawn* comic book series must share the copyright with a writer who collaborated in developing the series' storyline. *Gaiman v. McFarlane,* nos. 03-1331, 03-1461.

In 1992, Todd McFarlane began the *Spawn* comic book series. The titular Spawn—used in the plural and short for "Hellspawn"—were an army of the damned under the command of a devil, hoping to attack Heaven some day.

After early issues of *Spawn* were criticized for bad writing, McFarlane invited top comic book writers, including Neil Gaiman, to write for the series.

While McFarlane and Gaiman made no specific written agreement, according to the court, McFarlane orally promised to treat Gaiman "better than the big guys did," referring to industry leaders Marvel Comics and DC Comics.

Gaiman created new characters, including Medieval Spawn and Count Nicholas Cogliostro. Gaiman wrote the characters' dialogue and McFarlane illustrated the tales. Gaiman's edition of *Spawn* was a tremendous success, selling more than 1 million copies.

After Gaiman learned that McFarlane was considering selling the enterprise, Gaiman sued, seeking a declaratory judgment that he and McFarlane were joint owners of the copyrights on the characters by reason of their respective contributions to joint, indivisible work.

A Wisconsin federal court jury found for Gaiman, and the trial court entered a judgment declaring him to be the co-owner of the characters in question, ordering McFarlane to designate Gaiman the co-owner on undistributed copies in which the characters appear and awarding modest monetary relief.

McFarlane appealed, arguing that the characters were not copyrightable because they were stock characters under the scenes a faire doctrine.

The 7th Circuit rejected McFarlane's argument and affirmed the judgment, holding that the doctrine—which prohibits infringement actions for the use of "stock characters"—did not apply because both Medieval Spawn and the count were distinctive.

Noting those characters' unique traits, U.S. Circuit Judge Richard Posner proceeded to cite the stock characters from whom they were distinct, including "a drunken old bum," "a drunken suburban housewife, a fire-breathing dragon, a talking cat, a Prussian officer who wears a monocle and clicks his heels, a masked magician," and, of course, the stereotypical "gesticulating Frenchman."

Dated February 20, the decision was posted on March 12. Posner noted that one can see the characters at http://spawn.home.sapo.pt/characters.html.

Questions for Analysis

1. Who are the parties in this lawsuit? What was the subject matter of the arrangement between the two artists?

2. If you were required to defend the original writer/artist, what legal argument would you make in contract law? Explain.

3. If you were required to make a case for the second writer, what legal argument would you make in contract law? Explain.

4. What remedy did the second writer seek?

5. Who won the case and how did the court explain the result?

Informal and Formal Contracts

The law sometimes requires that contracts follow formalities prescribed by statute or by common law. These are called formal contracts. All others are classified as informal.

Informal Contracts

Any oral or written contract that is not under seal or is not a contract of record is considered an **informal contract.** An informal contract is also known as a *simple contract.* An informal contract generally has no requirements as to language, form, or construction. It comprises obligations entered into by parties whose promises are expressed in the simplest and, usually, most ordinary nonlegal language.

UCC 2-203 (see page 871)

Formal Contracts

Under common law principles, a **formal contract** differs from other types in that it has to be (1) written, (2) signed, witnessed, and placed under the seal of the parties, and (3) delivered. A *seal* is a mark or an impression placed on a written contract indicating that the instrument was executed and accepted in a formal manner. The UCC removed the requirement for the seal in sale-of-goods contracts. Some states, however, still require the use of the seal in agreements related to the sale and transfer of real property.

Today a person's seal may be any mark or sign placed after the signature intended to be the signer's seal. In states still requiring the seal or formal contract, it is sufficient to write the word *seal* after the signature.

Background Information The use of a seal or a signet ring has been associated with legal transactions for centuries. Roman lawyers displayed their rings at legal proceedings. Also, the use of a seal for the purchase of property was mentioned in the Old Testament: "And I bought the field of Hanameel, and weighed him the money, even seventeen shekels of silver. And I subscribed the evidence, and sealed it, and took witnesses, and weighed him the money in the balances" (Jeremiah 32:9–10).

Example 6-5

Audrey Kimmel signed an agreement with Corey Baumberger to buy seven acres of farmland owned by Baumberger just outside Bellville. Later that day, Baumberger found another interested buyer who was willing to pay seven times as much for the land as Kimmel had offered. Kimmel had signed the sales agreement without including any representation of the seal. In any state that required such formality in all real property contracts, Kimmel would now be helpless in attempting to enforce the original contract that he had made with Baumberger.

Getting Students Involved Have students analyze which contractual elements are present in a contract of record and which are not.

Contracts of Record

A special type of formal contract is known as a **contract of record.** Often, such a contract is confirmed by the court with an accompanying judgment issued in favor of one of the parties. The judgment is recorded, giving the successful litigant the right to demand satisfaction of the judgment. A contract of record is not a contract in the true sense of the word because it is court created. Although it does not have all of the elements of a valid contract, it is enforced for public policy reasons.

Example 6-6

Mortimer Byrne installed a new roof on Alexander Harper's house in Lakeside for the agreed-upon price of $7,500. Harper paid Byrne $4,000 so that he could secure materials. After the job was completed, Byrne then sent Harper a bill for $3,500. Harper sent Byrne a check for $2,500, on which was written "in full payment of all money owed." These words were in very fine print and not seen by Byrne. Byrne sued Harper in the small claims division of the Ottawa County Court of Common Pleas for the amount still owed. The court ruled in favor of Byrne and entered a judgment against Harper for the money owed. Entry of the judgment created a contract of record, which was enforceable against Harper.

The Opening Case Revisited
"To Compete or Not to Compete"

In The Opening Case, the court saw the original noncompetition as an executed agreement. Since the original agreement was executed, and could not be assigned, and since Kaleri had not entered a new noncompetition agreement with Transeuro, there was no way that Transeuro could stop Kaleri from working for Oppenheimer.

Executory and Executed Contracts

A contract that has not yet been fully performed by the parties is called an **executory contract.** Such a contract may be completely executory, in which case nothing has been done, or it may be partly executory, in which case the contract is partially complete. When a contract's terms have been completely and satisfactorily carried out by both parties it is an **executed contract.** Such contracts are no longer active agreements and are valuable only if a dispute about the agreement occurs.

Background Information Early Roman law, like Anglo-Saxon law and other early legal systems, recognized only executed contracts that involved face-to-face dealings and an exchange of property at the moment the deal was made. With the expansion of the Roman Empire and increased foreign trade, rules to address unfulfilled promises developed, allowing a new flexibility in commerce.

Quick Quiz 6-2 True or False?

1. A void contract is one that can be avoided by one or more of the parties.

2. A formal contract is also known as a simple contract.

3. A contract that has not yet been fully performed by the parties is called an executory contract.

Summary

6-1   A contract is an agreement between two or more competent parties based on mutual promises to do or to refrain from doing some particular thing which is neither illegal nor impossible. The six elements of a contract include offer, acceptance, mutual assent, capacity, consideration, and legality. Article II of the UCC covers sale-of-goods contracts; common law and special statutory provisions cover employment and real property contracts. To be enforceable, an agreement must conform to the law of contracts. The courts have never been agreeable to the enforcement of social contracts. Finally, the general rule of contract law is that the parties to a contract must stand in privity to one another.

6-2   Contractual characteristics fall into five different categories. These categories are: valid, void, voidable, or unenforceable; unilateral or bilateral; express or implied; informal or formal; and executory or executed.

Key Terms

bilateral contract, 127

breach of contract, 127

contract, 123

contract of record, 130

executed contract, 131

executory contract, 131

express contract, 127

formal contract, 130

formalist theory, 124

Questions for Review and Discussion

1. How did the present theory of contracts evolve?
2. What are the six elements of a contract?
3. What is the place of the UCC in contract law?
4. What is the difference between contracts and other agreements?
5. What is the nature of privity and contract law?
6. What are the differences among valid, void, voidable, and unenforceable contracts?
7. What is the difference between a unilateral and bilateral contract?
8. What is the difference between an express and an implied contract?
9. What is the difference between quasi-contracts and implied-in-fact contracts?
10. What is the difference between an executory contract and an executed contract?

Investigating the Internet

Access the website sponsored by QuickForm Contracts and follow the instructions for the drafting of a hypothetical contract. Use one of the examples in this chapter as the basis of your hypothetical contract. (Note: There is a small fee for the use of the forms at this site.)

Cases for Analysis

1. Several businesspeople secured a contract with the state of Massachusetts that permitted them to construct a bridge spanning the Charles River. The businesspeople intended to charge a toll for passage over the bridge to recover the expense of building the bridge and to make a sizable profit off its operation. Later another group of businesspeople made a similar contract. They too were permitted to build a bridge and to charge a toll. There was, however, a six-year limit on the tolls that would be charged on the second bridge, transforming it into a free bridge after the end of the six-year period. The first group of businesspeople realized that the existence of a free bridge would make their bridge worthless. Accordingly, they sued to prevent the second bridge from being constructed. They argued that the original contract that they had negotiated with the state implied that no other bridge would be built. The second group argued that, since there was no explicit agreement in the first contract preventing a second bridge from being built, the court, under the Contracts Clause of the Constitution, could not impair the rights that they had freely negotiated under the new contract to build a second bridge. The case ended up in the United States Supreme Court. How did the Supreme Court decide the case? Explain. *Proprietors of the Charles River Bridge v. Proprietors of the Warren Bridge,* 11 Pet. 420 (USSCt. 1837). See Friedman, Lawrence. "Economy and Law in the Nineteenth Century." *Law in America.* New York: The Modern Library, 2002, pp. 49–54.

2. The Borg-Warner Protective Services Corporation and Burns International Security Services contracted to provide security for the Cleveland

Institute of Art (CIA). Robert Adelman was struck by an object thrown by a CIA student from the roof of one of the Institute's buildings. Adelman sued both the CIA and the security corporations. The security corporations moved for summary judgment, arguing that they had contracted with CIA to protect the faculty and the students and that they, therefore, had no duty to protect pedestrians outside the buildings. Adelman argued that the contract specifically obligated the security corporations to control the activities of CIA students within the Institute's buildings. The disputed clause read that the security corporations agreed "to control the movement and activities of students within the buildings at all hours." The trial court granted the summary judgment motion and Adelman appealed. Should the appellate court reverse the decision of the lower court? Explain. If the case goes to trial, how will the court determine the meaning of the ambiguous clause? Explain. *Adelman v. Timman,* 690 N.E.2d 1332 (OH).

3. One of Stewart's clients gave him a check for $185.48. The check had been drawn up by the client's corporate employer and properly indorsed by the client. Nevertheless, the bank refused to cash the check for Stewart even though there was enough money in the account to cover the $185.48. Could Stewart sue the bank for not cashing the check as he requested? Explain. *J.E.B. Stewart v. Citizens and Southern National Bank,* 225 S.E.2d 761 (GA).

4. Vokes was told that she would become a professional dancer if she took a very expensive dancing course offered by Arthur Murray, Inc. She was also continually told that she had great talent. The contract called for payments amounting to a total of $31,000. As it turned out, she never became a professional dancer and, in fact, had little or no talent. She sued Arthur Murray, claiming that the Arthur Murray people misrepresented the facts in order to entice her to enter the contract. The court agreed and found in her favor. Would Vokes have the right to void the contract? Explain. *Vokes v. Arthur Murray, Inc.,* 212 So.2d 906 (FL).

5. Anderson, a farmer, orally agreed to buy a used tractor from the Copeland Equipment Company for $475. Copeland delivered the tractor to Anderson, who used it for eleven days. During this period, Anderson could not borrow enough funds to cover the purchase price. Anderson, therefore, returned the tractor to Copeland. Both parties agreed that their sales contract was canceled when the tractor was returned. However, Copeland later claimed that under the doctrine of quasi-contract, Anderson was required to pay for the eleven-days' use of the tractor. Do you agree with Copeland? Explain your answer. *Anderson v. Copeland,* 378 P.2d 1006 (OK).

6. B. L. Nelson & Associates, Inc., entered into a contract with the city of Argyle to design and construct a sanitary sewer collection and treatment facility for the city. The city attempted to get out of the contract by citing certain provisions of the state constitution. These provisions made it illegal for the city to enter a contract for services if it did not have the money to pay for these services. Since the city did not have the funds to pay Nelson, it argued that the contract was illegal and therefore void. Was the city correct? Explain. *B. L. Nelson & Associates, Inc. v. City of Argyle,* 535 S.W.2d 906 (TX).

7. Peters entered into a contract to purchase Dowling's business. The following terms were agreed to: (a) Peters would take over all of Dowling's executory contracts; (b) Peters would purchase Dowling's tools at an agreed-to-price; (c) Peters would accept full responsibility for all warranties made by Dowling on previous contracts; and (d) Dowling would remain as a consultant to the new firm for a period of five years. Analyze each part of this contract and classify each term according to whether it is executed or executory. *Wagstaff v. Peters,* 453 P.2d 120 (KS).

Quick Quiz Answers

6-1 1. T
2. T
3. F

6-2 1. F
2. F
3. T

Chapter 7 | Offer and Acceptance

The Opening Case
"The Hedge-Your-Bet Fund"

Fleming Summerfield retired with a modest retirement portfolio that he and his wife had accumulated over their forty-seven-year career as the owners and operators of Summerfield's Summerplace, a resort in Florida. Summerfield and his wife and her mother were enjoying retirement in Hawaii when they received an e-mail from Daniel Eldred, a financial advisor from Seattle. Summerfield was intrigued and went to a presentation Eldred made in San Francisco. Eldred made an eloquent presentation that involved an opportunity to invest in a hedge fund. A hedge fund is a short-term, high-risk investment that by law, cannot involve investors with a net worth of less than $1 million or a yearly income of less than $200,000. Based on these legal limitations, Summerfield did not qualify. Eldred did not tell Summerfield about the limitations and cheerfully took his money. Moreover, he promised Summerfield that he would receive millions of dollars in return for his investment and that there was absolutely no risk of loss involved in the investment opportunity. Summerfield and his wife agreed to go along with the deal and invested in the fund. Summerfield transferred $300,000 to the Hedge-Your-Bet Fund. At first, Summerfield made a slight gain of $45,000 and so he added more money into the fund. Then the market collapsed and the firms that were a part of Hedge-Your-Bet either lost a great deal of money or went under completely. Altogether, Summerfield lost $422,000. Eldred went bankrupt. Summerfield and several other investors joined in a lawsuit against Eldred claiming fraud, breach of contract, breach of fiduciary duty, and deceptive practices. In the relationship between Summerfield and Eldred, who was the offeror and who was the offeree? Since Eldred misled Summerfield, were the terms of the contract clear and definite? Was Eldred's e-mail an offer or an invitation to make an offer? These and other questions like them are explored in this chapter.

Chapter Outcomes

1. Explain how formalism guides the court in determining the elements of offer and acceptance.
2. Identify the three requirements of a valid offer.
3. Differentiate between a public offer and an invitation to trade.
4. Explain acceptance of an offer in the case of a unilateral contract and a bilateral contract.

5. Identify the role of the Uniform Commercial Code (UCC) in the law.
6. Define the mirror image rule.
7. Explain the UCC's concept of acceptance in contract law.
8. Relate the various means by which an offer can be revoked.
9. Explain what is meant by a firm offer.
10. Identify those statutes that affect the formation of cybercontracts.

For a situation similar to the facts in The Opening Case see: Arner, Faith, and Amy Borrus. "A Hedge Fund Too Good to Be True." *BusinessWeek,* May 10, 2004, pp. 102–104.

7-1 Requirements of an Offer

The first element of a valid contract is the existence of an offer. As explained in the previous chapter, an **offer** is a proposal freely made by one party to another indicating a willingness to enter a contract. The person who freely makes an offer is called the **offeror.** The person to whom the offer is made is called the **offeree.** As soon as the courts attempted to use the will theory of contract law, they could see how challenging it was to establish whether the offeror and offeree actually agreed to the terms of a contract. Because the actual intent of each party was out of reach, the courts had to examine behavior to determine that intent. This problem led the courts to establish a formalist approach. According to the formalism, if certain requirements are met, the court concludes that the parties intended to make and accept an offer. In the case of an offer, the courts established the following requirements. There must exist: (1) serious intent; (2) clear and reasonably definite terms; (3) and communication to the offeree. It is to a discussion of these requirements that we now turn.

Serious Intent

An offer is invalid if it is made as an obvious joke, during an emotional outburst of rage or anger, or under circumstances that might convey a lack of serious intent. The offeror's words or actions must give the offeree assurance that a binding agreement is intended. Serious intent is determined by the offeror's words and actions and by what the offeree had the right to believe was intended by those words and actions (see Table 7-1). It might be best to apply the following test to determine whether the offeror had serious intent. Ask whether the supposed offeror would, at the precise moment that the words are spoken or the actions taken, be prepared to be bound by those words or those actions. If the answer is "yes," a contract exists. If the alleged offeror says something like, "I'm looking for investors and I think you and your spouse fit the profile that I have in mind," no offer exists.

Related Cases A 1952 Virginia case arose from a conversation between two friends. Mr. Lucy offered his friend Mr. Zehmer $50,000 in cash for Zehmer's farm. Zehmer thought Lucy was joking, so he wrote up a note for the sale, saying he would accept the offer. Lucy raised the money the next day, and when Zehmer refused to sell, Lucy brought suit. Zehmer claimed he "was high as a Georgia pine" on liquor and that the agreement was "just a bunch of two dog-goned drunks bluffing to see who could talk the biggest and say the most." The court concluded that Zehmer's offer and actions would cause a reasonable person to assume he was serious and ruled that the contract was valid. *Lucy v. Zehmer,* 84 S.E.2d 516.

Table 7-1 Requirements of an Offer

Requirement	Explanation
Serious intent	The offeror's words must give the offeree assurance that a binding agreement is intended.
Clarity and reasonably definite terms	The terms of an offer must be sufficiently clear to remove any doubt about the contractual intentions of the offeror. Most courts require reasonable rather than absolute definiteness.
Communication to the offeree	The proposed offer must be communicated to the offeree by whatever means are convenient and desirable. The communication of the offer can be express or implied. Public offers are made through the media but are intended for one party whose identity or address is unknown. Invitations to trade are not offers.

Cross-Cultural Notes Chinese law on the formation of contracts requires that the price in a contract of sale be in accordance with prices decreed by the state price-control agency. For commodities that are allowed to fluctuate in price within a certain range, the buyer and the seller may negotiate and set a price within the range permitted. If a seller raises a price without authorization by the state, the seller must pay double the buyer's loss or assume other liability imposed by law.

The Opening Case Revisited
"The Hedge-Your-Bet Fund"

In The Opening Case, Eldred told Summerfield about the opportunity to invest in a hedge fund. Remember that hedge funds were governed by a legal requirement that eliminated investors with a net worth less than $1 million or a yearly income of less than $200,000. Because such rules existed, Eldred would have had to check to see if, in fact, Summerfield and his wife were qualified. In effect, then, his sales presentation was not an offer but an invitation to Summerfield and his wife to enter into a negotiation stage concerning the hedge fund. The fact that Eldred did not check on Summerfield's net worth, did not know about the legal requirements, or simply ignored them, would not matter. He could not have expected Summerfield to accept based on his own words of preliminary invitation. Certain key elements, including not only Summerfield's qualifications, but also how much he would invest, are missing. With such key elements missing, the words spoken by Eldred cannot be considered an offer.

The words appear to be inviting the other party to enter into a negotiation stage, rather than presenting that party with a valid, enforceable offer.

Clear and Reasonably Definite Terms

The communicated terms of an offer must be sufficiently clear to remove any doubt about the contractual intentions of the offeror. No valid offer will exist when terms are indefinite, inadequate, vague, or confusing. Again, as in the case of serious intent, it might be best to apply a test to determine whether the terms in the alleged offer are clear and definite enough. Ask whether the terms are so clear that, if there were a breach, the court would know how to assess a remedy. If the answer is "yes," the terms are probably definite enough. If the answer is "no," then some crucial term in the alleged offer must be too un-clear to create a contract.

Example 7-1

The Lindbergh-Sikorsky Aircraft Corporation e-mailed an offer to Kenneth Hiebel, the owner of the Triple R-Bar Ranch in Idaho. The e-mail stated, "Please consider this our offer to purchase 20,000 acres of your 61,200-acre ranch land near Harrington, Idaho. Our offering price is between $60,000 and $65,000 per acre. Please respond soon." If we apply the question above, we can easily see that this e-mail is not a legally effective offer. The terms are much too indefinite. The e-mail does not specify which of Triple R-Bar's acres Lindbergh-Sikorsky wants to purchase. Nor does it specify a set price per acre. If there were a breach of contract, the court would not know how to set damages. Would it use the $60,000 figure or the $65,000 figure or something in-between? If Lindbergh-Sikorsky asked for specific performance of the contract, the court would not know which acres to transfer to the aircraft company. All in all, the terms lack an appropriate level of clarity and definiteness to constitute an offer.

Degree of Definiteness In general, an offer should include points similar to those covered in a newspaper story—who, what, when, where, how much—if it is to be clear, definite, and certain. This means that the offer should identify (1) the parties involved in the contract, (2) the goods or services that will be the subject matter of the contract, (3) the price the offeror is willing to pay or receive, and (4) the time required for the performance of the contract. Most courts require reasonable rather than absolute definiteness. Offers will be upheld as long as the language is reasonably definite enough to enable the court to establish what the parties intended the terms to be so that, should there be a breach, a remedy can be set.

Example 7-2

Dr. Anita Hughes was developing a cold fusion reactor that would solve the energy problems of this country for decades to come. The Toledo Electric Illuminating Company sent a proposal to Hughes by fax, offering her a fair share of the profits if she would develop the fusion reactor for their exclusive use. On the next day, the National Atomic Research and Development Laboratories (NARDL) in Oakland also faxed Hughes a proposal offering not only to pay her $10,000,000 to develop the fusion reactor for them, but also to reimburse her for all expenses related to the development of the reactor and to give her 20 percent of the profits during the first ten years of the sale of the fusion reactors to domestic, foreign, and alien power companies. Of the two proposals, the Toledo proposition is much too indefinite to be considered a real offer. The NARDL proposal, however, is definite enough, even though a final dollar amount has not been settled upon. This is because the court has a way to figure out what the parties intended and what the final amount should be. If there were a breach of contract, the court would know how to set a remedy for the innocent party.

Offers and the UCC The UCC permits offers to omit certain information. It states that "even though one or more terms are left open, a contract for sale does not fail for indefiniteness if the parties have intended to make a contract and there is a reasonably certain basis for giving an appropriate remedy." Under this section of the UCC, cost-plus contracts, output contracts, requirement contracts, and current market price contracts are enforceable even though they are not complete in certain matters. A **cost-plus contract** does include a final price. The contract price is determined by the cost of labor and materials plus an agreed-to percentage or dollar markup. A **requirements contract** is an agreement in which one party agrees to buy all of the goods it needs from the second party. The term of a requirements contract must be carefully worded. If the agreement allows the buyer to purchase only those goods that the buyer desires or wishes, then the agreement is unenforceable. This is because the agreement is illusory in that the buyer is not really obligated to do anything. An **output contract** is an agreement in which one party consents to sell to a second party all of the goods that party makes in a given period of time. Finally, a **current market price contract** is one in which prices are determined by reference to the market price of the goods as of a specified date.

UCC 2-204 (3) (see page 871)

Teaching Tips Inform students about the Consumer Price Index (CPI), which is a measure of average price changes of consumer goods and services over time. Ask students how the CPI might be useful if they were formulating a current market price contract.

Communication to the Offeree

In order to be valid, an offer must be freely communicated to the offeree. The offeror's intentions may be communicated by whatever means are convenient and desirable. For example, the offer may be communicated orally, by mail, by fax machine, by e-mail, or by any other capable means. It may also be implied. The proposing party's acts and conduct are, in many cases, successful in communicating an intention to make an offer to another party witnessing them. When acts and conduct are sufficient to convey an offeror's intentions, an implied offer results.

Public Offers At times, an offer must be communicated to a party whose name, identity, or address is unknown. In such cases, the public offer is made. A **public offer** is one that is made through the public media but is intended for only one person whose identity or address is unknown to the offeror. A classic example of a public offer is an advertisement in a lost-and-found column in a newspaper. Although this is a public offer, it is legally no different from other types of offers.

Invitations to Trade By contrast, invitations to trade are not offers. An **invitation to trade** is an announcement published to reach many persons for the purpose of creating interest and attracting responses. Newspaper and magazine advertisements, radio and television commercials, store window displays, price tags on merchandise, for sale signs on houses and businesses, for rent signs, and prices in catalogs come within this definition. In the case of an invitation to trade, no binding agreement develops until a responding party makes an offer which the advertiser accepts. Nevertheless, in certain relatively rare circumstances, advertisements may be held to be offers. However, such advertisements would have to contain very particular promises, use phrases like "first-come, first-served," or limit the number of items to be sold. Since the number of people who can buy the product is very limited, the advertisement becomes an offer.

Bait and Switch Confidence Games Most of the time, an advertisement is not specific enough to constitute an offer. This is because it will generally lack certain key items. For one thing, the seller really does not promise to sell one, single individual item to a named or easily identifiable buyer in an advertisement. The seller may decide not to deal with a particular customer because that customer's credit rating is in bad shape, or because the seller has run out of the item that was advertised. Moreover, advertisements rarely contain all of the terms that will eventually become a part of the finished contract. On the other hand, sellers cannot engage in deliberately deceptive practices that entice buyers into their place of business if the seller actually has no intention of selling the item advertised at the price stated in the advertisement. This practice, which is referred to as the **bait and switch confidence game,** has been outlawed by the Federal Trade Commission. In addition, many, perhaps most, states have similar laws prohibiting bait and switch confidence games.

Quick Quiz 7-1 True or False?

1. The person who freely makes an offer is called an offeree.

2. An offer is valid only if it has (a) serious intent, (b) clear and reasonably definite terms, and (c) communication to the offeree.

3. No valid offer will exist when terms are indefinite, inadequate, vague, or confusing.

7-2 Acceptance of an Offer

The second major element in a binding contract is acceptance of the offer. As previously stated, **acceptance** means that the offeree agrees to be bound by the terms set up by the offeror. Only the offeree, the one to whom the offer is made, has the right to accept the offer. If another party attempts to accept, that attempt would actually be a new and independent offer.

Example 7-3

Friedman owned and operated Friedman Rare Books and Antiquities, a sole proprietorship which sold rare books, original manuscripts, and antiques to libraries, museums, galleries, and private collectors. Friedman met with Castillo and Bauer, the owners and operators of the Mather Rare Books Shoppe, and offered to sell them an original, first edition of Ezra Pound's *Cantos*. Hoffman, the owner of Seattle Rare Books and Antiquities, also learned that the edition was for sale. He called Friedman and, after inspecting the edition, bought it for $225,000. Friedman had mistakenly thought that Hoffman worked for the Mather shop. When he found that Hoffman worked for the nearly bankrupt Seattle book store, he refused to deliver the edition of *Cantos*. Hoffman and the Seattle book store sued. The court held that no contract resulted. Only Castillo and Bauer, the parties to whom Friedman had made the offer to sell, could accept it.

Unilateral contracts do not usually require oral or written communication of an acceptance. When the offeror makes a promise in a unilateral contract, the offeror expects an action, not another promise in return. Performance of the action requested within the time allowed by the offeror and with the offeror's knowledge creates the contract.

Example 7-4

Patrick Barnes and George Layton were employed by the Sailors' Maritime Service. When they expressed dissatisfaction with their jobs, their employer offered them a new contract whereby they would receive a 10 percent bonus on company profits if they remained with the firm. At times they discussed the terms of the new agreement with an official of Sailors' Maritime. Eventually, they decided that the offer was a good one and they continued on the job as usual. Sailors' Maritime later refused to pay the 10 percent bonus, claiming that its offer had never been accepted. The court ruled this to be a unilateral agreement and that their performance in remaining with Sailors' Maritime constituted acceptance.

In bilateral contracts, unlike unilateral ones, the offeree must communicate acceptance to the offeror. Bilateral contracts consist of a promise by one party in return for a promise by the other. Until the offeree communicates a willingness to be bound by a promise, there is no valid acceptance.

Example 7-5

Suppose in the previous example, Sailors' Maritime had said to Barnes and Layton, "We will consider your written acceptance to this new proposal as binding us to the payment of the 10 percent bonus." There would have been the intention of creating a bilateral contract, supported by mutual promises by both Sailors' Maritime, on the one hand, and Barnes and Layton, on the other.

Did You Know? Even though an auctioneer will say that the goods in an auction are being "offered for sale," the bidders at the auction are the parties who make the offer to buy those goods.

Talking Points In a landmark text entitled, *The Stages of Economic Growth: A Non-Communist Manifesto*, the economist, W. W. Rostow, contends that societies go through five stages of economic growth: the traditional economy; the pre-take-off economy; the take-off economy; the mature economy; and the high-mass consumption economy. He further contends that only the United States, western Europe, and Japan have entered stage five. How has contract law contributed to this economic growth in the United States, western Europe, and Japan?

The history of what the law has been is necessary to the knowledge of what the law is.

—Oliver Wendell Holmes (1841–1935), Associate Justice, U.S. Supreme Court

Getting Students Involved Challenge students to list mediums of communication through which an offer could be made and accepted. Encourage them to think of examples other than those mentioned in the text, such as telephone, fax, and letter. Ask students to discuss which medium might pose problems for contractual arrangements. Suggest that they informally survey several area businesses to find out the frequency with which they use each medium of communication to create their contracts.

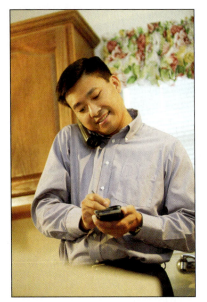

Technology such as
e-mail may help speed
the acceptance process.

Communication of Acceptance

Communication of acceptance of an offer may be either express or implied. In an express acceptance, the offeree chooses any method of acceptance, unless the offer states that an acceptance must be made in a particular manner. A stipulation such as "reply by fax" or "reply by e-mail" included in the offer must be carried out to have acceptance.

Face-to-Face and Telephone Communication No special problem as to the timing of acceptance usually arises if the parties are dealing face-to-face. The acceptance becomes complete and effective as soon as the offeror hears the words of acceptance spoken by the offeree. In a similar vein, if the parties are negotiating over the telephone, the acceptance becomes effective when the offeree speaks the words of acceptance into the telephone receiver (see Table 7-2). When the parties negotiate by mail, telegram, or fax, problems may arise, and the law provides certain rules as to when acceptance occurs.

Long-Distance Communication Under traditional common law principles, if a long-distance acceptance is made by an authorized method of communication, then the acceptance is effective when it is sent. An authorized means of communication is one that has been endorsed by the offeror. The endorsement can be made either expressly or by implication. An acceptance is expressly endorsed by the offeror if he or she specifies the means of acceptance to be used by the offeror. Under traditional common law rules an authorization of an acceptance is implied when the offeree accepts by the same means or by a means that is faster than that used to make the offer. Thus, an offer made through the mail is accepted when the acceptance is mailed or when it is sent by a faster means such as a private courier (FedEx or UPS), a fax, a phone call, an e-mail, or an in-person visit.

The Uniform Commercial Code It is important to remember that contract law is affected by changes made by the Uniform Commercial Code. The UCC was written by a group of legal experts known as the National Conference of Commissioners on Uniform State Laws. The NCCUSL is made up of legal experts, including attorneys, judges, and law professors. These experts also review legal developments in all fifty states. These specialists then condense the law as it appears in the states into a series of precise model

Table 7-2 Communication of Acceptance

Method Used	Legal Effect
Face-to-face communication	Acceptance is complete and effective when offeror hears the words of acceptance.
Telephone communication	Acceptance is complete and effective when offeror hears the words of acceptance.
Authorized means of communication	Acceptance is complete and effective when given to that same medium (e.g., mailed offer is accepted when acceptance is dropped in the mail).
Acceptance improperly dispatched	Acceptance is complete and effective when it actually reaches offeror.

codes. The model codes are in a form that can be directly enacted into law by the various state legislatures. The model code that most concerns us in contract law is the Uniform Commercial Code and the section of that code which is most crucial is Article 2, which covers the sales of goods.

The UCC asserts that a contract comes into existence if any reasonable means is used to communicate the acceptance. The UCC is quite explicit in noting that, to establish a contract for the sale of goods, unless otherwise indicated by the offeror or by the circumstances, the offeree may accept the offer in any manner and by any medium that is reasonable. A contract for the sale of goods then comes into existence when the acceptance is sent, as long as the method used to send it is reasonable. The actual text of this rule is found in UCC 2-206 (1) (a).

Unequivocal Acceptance

To be effective, an acceptance must be *unequivocal,* which means that the acceptance must not change any of the terms stated in the offer. Under common law this is known as the mirror image rule.

The Mirror Image Rule
Under the **mirror image rule,** the terms as stated in the acceptance must exactly "mirror" the terms in the offer. If the acceptance changes or qualifies the terms in the offer, it is not an acceptance. A qualified acceptance is actually a counteroffer. A **counteroffer** is a response to an offer in which the terms of the original offer are changed. No agreement is reached unless the counteroffer is accepted by the original offeror.

Example 7-6

Sally Kurtzman, chairperson of the board of Oakcrest Properties, LLC, offered to purchase an apartment building on Parkview Avenue from Enduring Dreams Developers, Inc., for $42 million. The managers of Enduring Dreams said that the deal sounded good to them and they were ready to finalize the details immediately, but they needed at least $47 million for the property. Under the mirror image rule, despite all of the positive rhetoric offered by the management of Enduring Dreams, they really have not made an acceptance. What they have done under the mirror image rule is made a counteroffer. Kurtzman and Oakcrest properties are now free to accept or reject Enduring Dream's counteroffer or to make a new offer.

Counteroffers Under the UCC
The UCC has changed the mirror image rule for sale-of-goods contracts. Under the UCC, as long as there is a definite expression of acceptance, a contract will come into existence even though an acceptance has different or additional terms. If the parties are not both merchants, the different or additional terms are treated as proposals for additions to the contract. If both parties are merchants, however, the different or additional terms become part of the contract unless (1) they make an important difference to the contract, (2) the offeror objects, or (3) the offer limits acceptance to its terms. This exception is discussed further in Chapter 15.

Implied Acceptance

Acceptance may result from the conduct of the offeree. Actions and gestures may indicate the offeree's willingness to enter into a binding agreement.

Unordered merchandise delivered by mail can be treated as a gift by the recipient.

Mailing of Unordered Merchandise Delivery of unordered merchandise through the mails is now considered nothing more than an offer to sell. In the past, unethical sellers attempted to treat the failure of the recipient to either return the goods or send money as an implied acceptance of the offer to sell goods. Complaints were made that this practice allowed unethical firms to use the mails to defraud consumers and to saddle recipients with unwanted merchandise. This led to corrective regulations that are now incorporated into the Postal Reorganization Act of 1970. By this act, the recipient of unordered merchandise delivered through the mails may treat such goods as a gift. The receiver has no obligation to pay for or return the goods or to communicate with the sender in any way.

Unordered Goods Not Delivered by Mail When unordered goods are delivered by agencies other than the post office, the common law rule is usually followed. In general, the receiver is not obligated to contact the sender or pay for the goods. There is an implied obligation to retain the goods and give them reasonable care over a reasonable period of time. After that time, the receiver may consider that the sender no longer claims the goods and may use or dispose of them as desired. Some states, however, have laws similar to the postal law that allows recipients of unordered goods to consider them a gift no matter how they were delivered.

A Question of Ethics

Suppose, after conducting a survey which revealed that most people did not know about their rights under the Postal Reorganization Act, a company began a mailing campaign that sent unordered merchandise to certain targeted groups. Would such a move be ethical? Explain.

Silence as Acceptance

As a general rule, silence is not an acceptance. If, however, both parties agree that silence on the part of the offeree will signal acceptance, then such an acceptance is valid.

Example 7-7

Sarah Jameson read an advertisement in *The Independent* inviting her to become a member of the New Era DVD Club. Jameson chose several DVDs that were listed in the advertisement. She paid only $1 for those DVDs and became a member of the DVD club. In doing so, she also agreed to purchase four more DVDs in a year's time. Under terms clearly specified in the advertisement, Jameson knew she would receive a brochure twelve times a year listing selections. The brochure would also identify the main selections which would be sent to her automatically unless she sent a reply form to stop the shipment. In effect, Jameson had agreed that, whenever she did not return the reply card, that silence would amount to acceptance of the main selections.

Business Law in the News
How Do You Sell a Golf Legend? Very Carefully

Maybe it's just coincidence, but the actor who portrays Jesus in Mel Gibson's *The Passion of the Christ* now has top billing in a movie about another famous figure whose followers can be pretty fanatical themselves. Their religion is golf, and the movie starring Jim Caviezel is *Bobby Jones: Stroke of Genius,* opening on Apr. 30.

To golfing purists, Jones is the epitome of the game as it was meant to be played—with mental acuity, physical grace, and immeasurable class. So when he dropped in his last tournament putt 74 years ago, Jones probably never dreamed that someday his signature would be on a bottle of shower gel and his image would be the engine of a thriving little empire. And the business of Bob Jones figures to get even better after the feel-good movie hits theaters.

The film depicts a sensitive Jones as he swings to victory in golf's major tournaments—the coveted grand slam—in the magical year of 1930. A career amateur, Jones captured 13 titles in the 21 major championships he played, a record even Tiger Woods must envy.

In 1986, his descendants formed Jonesheirs Inc. to cash in on commercial products. Decisions are now made by seven surviving grandchildren (Jones's three children are now deceased) who meet about once a year and kick around proposals via e-mail. "Not only does there have to be a tie-in to Bobby Jones, it has to be a product of great quality," says Bob Jones IV, a clinical psychologist in Atlanta.

It's true that some offers do get a thumbs-down. Recently, Jonesheirs said no to PGA Tour golfer and vintner David Frost, who wanted to put the Jones name on a wine label. Also nixed: a shotgun, comic strip, and computer game.

For clothes hounds with golf bags full of money, though, slipping on the Bobby Jones image is easy. In his prime, Jones seldom played in anything less formal than a dress shirt and necktie. In death, he has become considerably more laid-back. This year,

sportswear maker Hickey Freeman, a licensee since 1988, will sell over $30 million worth of pricey Jones duds for men and women. Kids' clothes are on the way. In Beverly Hills and Atlanta, you can even pop into a Bobby Jones store—Las Vegas and Honolulu outlets open next year—and pick up $325 silk golf jackets, $158 cotton golf shirts, or $85 swimming trunks.

If that hasn't maxed out your credit cards, the new Bobby Jones Golf Co. is introducing titanium drivers ($600–$650) and fairway woods ($400–$450) in May. It's not the first equipment deal: A line of Jones clubs in 1985 helped launch Callaway Golf Co. That deal ended in 2001.

Bob Jones toiletries and a $549.99 Bobby Jones Trophy Edition Motorola cell phone (now discontinued) may smack of hucksterism—"you don't think of cell technology being associated with Bob Jones," notes Bob IV. But the family approved because the deals were presented as ways to lift clothing sales. The phone came with $150 certificates for apparel.

Stroke of Genius is certain to spread the legend. And who knows? It may sell a few more Bobby Jones bathing suits.

Questions for Analysis

1. Who (or what) now controls the right to use the Bobby Jones name? Explain.

2. In a contract granting the right to sell Bobby Jones's merchandise, who is the offeror and who is the offeree? Explain.

3. Why would it be important to control the roles of offeror and offeree in such contracts? Explain.

4. Speculate on how the contract between Callaway Golf Co. and the Jones company might have ended.

5. If a customer were to purchase some Bobby Jones merchandise online, what law or laws would ensure that the electronic transaction was just as valid as a paper transaction?

Source: Mark Byman. "How Do You Sell a Golf Legend? Very Carefully," *BusinessWeek,* May 10, 2004, p. 48.

Teaching Tips Discuss actions or gestures that might lead an offeror to believe an offeree has accepted an offer. Remind the students that courts often use the standard of how a reasonable person might interpret someone's actions.

Terms The word *revoke* comes from the Latin *revocare*, meaning "to call again," which is formed from the Latin root *voclvox*, meaning voice. *Voclvox* is akin to the Old High German *giwahanen*, meaning "to mention."

Another exception to the general rule occurs when the offeree has allowed silence to act as an acceptance. The offeror cannot force the offeree into a contract by saying silence will mean acceptance. The offeree, however, can force the offeror into a contract if the offeror set up the silence condition.

Example 7-8

Jason Riley wanted to sell his 1962 Volkswagen. He wrote a letter to Rita Tenpenny offering to sell the Volkswagen to Tenpenny for $25,000. Riley ended the letter by stating, "If I don't hear from you by December 3 of this year, I will take your silence to mean you accept my offer." Tenpenny received the letter and did not reply. Although Riley could not bind Tenpenny to this contract, Tenpenny could hold Riley to his offer because Riley set up the silence condition himself.

Rejection of an Offer

A **rejection** comes about when an offeree expresses or implies refusal to accept an offer. Rejection terminates an offer and all negotiations associated with it. Further negotiations could commence with a new offer by either party or a renewal of the original offer by the offeror. Rejection is usually achieved when communicated by the offeree.

Quick Quiz 7-2 True or False?

1. An authorized means of communication is one that has been endorsed by the offeror.

2. Bilateral contracts consist of a promise by one party in return for a promise by the other.

3. Restatements present explanations of the law, whereas the model codes can be enacted into law by state legislatures.

7-3 Revocation of an Offer

Getting Students Involved Have students suggest how a contract could be worded to avoid a situation in which a revocation of an offer crosses in the mail with an acceptance of an offer.

A **revocation** is the calling back of the offer by the offeror. With the exception of an option contract and a firm offer (discussed in following text), an offer may be revoked anytime before it has been accepted. The offeror has this right, despite what might appear to be a strong moral obligation to continue the offer. An offer may be revoked by the following methods and circumstances:

- communication
- automatic revocation
- passage of time
- death or insanity of the offeror
- destruction of the subject matter
- the subsequent illegality of the contract

Revocation by Communication

An offer may be revoked by the offeror by communicating that intention to the offeree before the offer has been accepted. Revocation is ineffective if the acceptance has already been communicated, such as by mailing the acceptance in response to a mailed offer. Direct communication of revocation is not required if the offeree knows about the offer's withdrawal by other means.

Example 7-9

Michael Sukarno offered to sell a painting entitled *The Pond at Ville d'Array* by the French artist Camille Corot to Arthur Kroeber for $987,000. It was mutually agreed that the offer would remain open for five days. Three days later Kroeber read that Sukarno had sold the painting to the Rothman International Galleries for $1,200,000. Having learned of the sale, Kroeber would be aware that the offer had been withdrawn and at that point he could not accept. Suppose in this same case that the offer had been made in a letter received by Kroeber and, before any news of the sale to the Rothman International Galleries reached Kroeber, a letter of acceptance was mailed to Sukarno. Although the acceptance may not reach Sukarno for another day, acceptance was complete upon the mailing of the letter, and revocation would not apply.

Automatic Revocation

When the terms of an offer include a definite time limit for acceptance, the offer is automatically revoked at the expiration of the time stated.

Example 7-10

Uma Craig had just finished her new novel, *The Counterfeit Impostor,* when she offered to sell full publishing rights to Orascom Publishing for $25 million. Craig gave Orascom until May 20 to accept the offer. When Orascom did not accept Craig's offer by midnight on May 20, the offer was automatically revoked. Craig was not required to honor Orascom's acceptance on May 21. Instead, she was free to make a new offer to Orascom or to any other publisher.

Revocation by Passing of Time

When no time limit has been set, an offer will revoke automatically after the passing of a reasonable length of time. The time element is determined through a review of all facts and surrounding circumstances. Perishable characteristics of goods, price fluctuations, supply-and-demand factors, and other surrounding circumstances contribute to establish the reasonable time factor. For example, communicating an offer by fax or e-mail rather than by letter would ordinarily imply the need for haste in making acceptance.

Revocation by Death or Insanity

Death or insanity of an offeror automatically revokes an offer that has not yet been accepted. Both death and insanity preclude the possibility of a meeting of the minds. Revocation in both situations is immediate. Communication to the offeree is not required.

Terms In the Middle Ages, the *notrii,* or notaries, were those who understood early contract law well enough to draft agreements. The notary represented both parties of a contract and enabled them to put their accord into writing. A trained writer of contracts was also known as *magister,* Latin for master or *official,* and *scribus,* Latin for *scribe.* The legal profession began to develop fully in the late Middle Ages, with the emergence of a professional class of *loirs* (lawyers), *advocats* (advocates), or *procureurs* (procurers) who represented clients in legal matters.

Cross-Cultural Notes In the former Soviet legal system, most formal contracts were conducted between socialist organizations or between citizens and socialist organizations. Very few formal contracts were made between citizens. A ten-day limit was often set for agreeing or disagreeing with a contract proposed by a buyer or seller. If neither party refused the contract, it was considered accepted. Any precontract problems had to be filed within ten days with *Arbitrazh,* an administrative agency in charge of settling precontract disputes between socialist organizations.

Revocation by Destruction

Destruction of subject matter related to an offer automatically revokes that offer. Destruction of the subject matter removes any possibility of performing an anticipated agreement.

Revocation by Subsequent Illegality

Restrictive legislation that would make performing an anticipated agreement illegal automatically revokes an existing offer. Any agreement resulting from an attempted acceptance of such offers would be unenforceable.

Quick Quiz 7-3 True or False?

1. A revocation is the calling back of the offer by the offeror.

2. When the terms of an offer specify a time limit, the offer is automatically revoked by the expiration of that time limit.

3. Destruction of the subject matter related to the offer never revokes that offer.

Terms Some people mistakenly assume that an option contract necessarily involves a down payment. The term *down payment* dates from 1926 when buying on credit was at its peak. It is defined as a part of the full price that is paid at the time of purchase or delivery, with the balance promised later. An option contract, which requires consideration, is a binding promise to hold an offer open. The offeree has the choice to create a new contract by exercising the option during a specified time period.

About the Law

Although the Ch'ing Dynasty, which ruled China from 1644 to 1911, codified the law of criminal offenses, it left civil law, for the most part, in the hands of the family and clan.

7-4 Option Contracts and Firm Offers

An **option contract** is an agreement that binds an offeror to a promise to hold open an offer for a predetermined or reasonable length of time. In return for this agreement to hold the offer open, the offeror receives money or something else of value from the offeree. Parties to an option contract often agree that the consideration may be credited toward any indebtedness incurred by the offeree in the event that the offer is accepted. Should the offeree fail to take up the option, however, the offeror is under no legal obligation to return the consideration.

An option contract removes the possibility of revocation through death or insanity of the offeror. The offeree who holds an option contract may demand acceptance by giving written notice of acceptance to the executor or administrator of the deceased offeror's estate or to the offeror's legally appointed guardian.

Example 7-11

Takashi Osaka offered to sell Andras Galai a collection of rare Japanese prints for $755,000. Galai requested time to consider the offer, and Osaka agreed to hold the collection for Galai for one week in return for Galai's payment of $755. Osaka died several days later. When Galai tendered the $755,000, the executor refused to deliver the collection, claiming that death had revoked the offer. The court ruled otherwise, with judgment given to the offeree based upon the option agreement between Galai and the deceased.

UCC 2-205
(see page 871)

A special rule has been developed under the UCC. This rule holds that no consideration is necessary when a merchant agrees in writing to hold an offer open. This is called a **firm offer.** A firm offer may be made for a specified period of time. If no time limit is specified, then the offer may remain open for a reasonable amount of time. However, the upper limit for a firm offer is three months.

> ## Quick Quiz 7-4 True or False?
>
> 1. An option contract is an agreement that binds an offeror to a promise to hold an offer open.
>
> 2. Firm offers are outlawed by the Uniform Commercial Code.
>
> 3. Option contracts do not remove the possibility of a revocation through the insanity of the offeror.

7-5 Offer and Acceptance in Cybercontract Law

As is true of most areas of the law, contract law, in general, and the law of offer and acceptance, in particular, have been affected by the use of computers in the commercial setting. In many situations, the courts have taken orthodox laws that govern contracts and applied them to **cybercontracts,** that is, to contracts that are made by using computers either by e-mail or via the Internet, or contracts that involve computer-related products such as databases and software. This is true of the law as represented in the Uniform Commercial Code and the Restatement (Second) of Contracts. In addition, the courts must also be aware of several new approaches to cybercontract law as represented by federal law and by the model codes written by the National Conference of Commissioners on Uniform State Laws. The new rules are found in the federal Electronic Signatures in Global and National Commerce Act (E-Sign Act), the Uniform Electronic Transactions Act, and the Uniform Computer Information Transactions Act.

The E-Sign Act

The E-Sign Act was passed by Congress several years ago and represents an effort by the national legislature to make certain that commercial cyberdocuments are given the same credence as their paper counterparts. Simply stated, the act provides that cybercontracts that are entered on the Internet or via e-mail will be valid, provided that the parties to the cybercontract have agreed that electronic signatures will be used. As long as the cybercontract can be duplicated and stored, it will have the same validity as a paper contract. The act expressly applies to Article 2 (Sale of Goods Contracts) and Article 2A (Leases) of the UCC.

The Uniform Electronic Transactions Act

The Uniform Electronic Transactions Act (UETA) was written by the National Conference of Commissioners on Uniform State Laws to ensure that cybercontracts are given the same legal effect as their paper equivalents. The model act does not create any new rules applying to offer, acceptance, assent, consideration, capacity, and legality, but instead makes certain that the laws that govern these elements apply to cybercontracts just as they apply to paper contracts. There are three basic elements under the UETA. First, the participants must concur on the use of an electronic medium to create their contractual relationship. This is usually not a problem since the parties to a cybercontract are generally aware of the nature of their relationship when they sit down at the computer. Second, once the first requirement is met, the act says that the electronic record generated by the computerized transaction will have the same weight that a paper document would have in a traditional transaction. Finally, once the first requirement is met, the act acknowledges that an electronic signature is just as effective as a written signature on a paper document.

The Uniform Computer Information Transactions Act

The Uniform Computer Information Transactions Act (UCITA) arose when the NCCUSL and the ALI attempted to revise Article 2 (Sale of Goods Contracts) and Article 2A (Leases) of the UCC. Revising these articles to meet the demands of cybercommerce and cyber-contractual relationships proved very difficult. In fact the attempt was so difficult that the ALI dropped out of the process altogether, leaving the NCCUSL on its own. The NCCUSL then elected to write an entirely new act which came to be known as The Uniform Computer Information Transactions Act. One of the problems encountered by the NCCUSL in the writing of the new act was that many of the contracts that are entered into in cyberspace are more akin to licensing agreements than sales of goods contracts. The UCITA, therefore, covers such diverse areas as database contracts, software licensing agreements, customized software formulation, and the rights to multimedia commodities. Many of the legal questions associated with Internet-made cybercontracts are answered by the new act.

Offer and Acceptance in Cyberspace

In addition to the terms that are included in most other offers, a cyberofferor should insert the following terms in his or her offer: (1) payment criteria, (2) remedies that can be used by the offeree, (3) refund policies, (4) return procedures, (5) dispute settlement instructions, (6) the applicability of cybersignatures, (7) liability disclaimers if needed, and (8) provisions relating to the offeree's manner of acceptance. In general, the offeree's manner of acceptance in a cybercontract is manifested by having the party click on a box on the computer screen that states that he or she agrees to be bound by the terms of the contract. Sometimes this process of acceptance is referred to as a **"click-on" acceptance** or a **"click-on" agreement.** Otherwise, it is important to recall that, as explained above, when the agreement deals with goods, the provisions of Article 2 of the UCC will apply.

Quick Quiz 7-5 True or False?

1. The Uniform Electronic Transactions Act (UETA) was passed by Congress as a federal law.

2. The Electronic Signatures in Global and National Commerce Act was written by the National Conference of Commissioners on Uniform State Laws.

3. The process of accepting an online offer is often referred to as a "click-on" agreement.

Summary

7-1 As soon as the courts attempted to use the will theory to interpret contracts, they could see how challenging it was to establish whether the parties actually agreed to the terms of a contract. Because the actual intent of each party was out of reach, the courts established a formalist approach to the interpretation of contracts. According to

formalism, if certain requirements are met, the court concludes that the parties intended to make and accept an offer. Agreement is reached when an offer made by one party is accepted by another party. An offer is valid if it has serious intent, clear and reasonably definite terms, and communication to the offeree.

7-2   The second major part of mutual assent is the acceptance of the offer. Only the offeree has the right to accept the offer. Communication of the acceptance may be either express or implied. Under common law principles, to be effective an acceptance must not change any of the terms of the offer. This is known as the mirror image rule. The UCC has altered the mirror image rule. Acceptance may result from the conduct or actions of the offeree. However, as a general rule, silence cannot be made acceptance by the offeror.

7-3   At any time prior to acceptance, the offeror can withdraw the offer. Offers may be revoked by communication, by an automatic revocation, by the passage of time, by the death or insanity of the offeror, by the destruction of the subject matter, or by the subsequent illegality of the contract.

7-4   Some types of offers cannot be revoked by the offeror. These involve irrevocable or firm offers and option contracts.

7-5   The principal rules concerning the interpretation and the enforcement of cybercontracts are found in the federal E-Sign Act, the Uniform Electronic Transactions Act (UETA), and the Uniform Computer Information Transactions Act (UCITA).

Key Terms

acceptance, 138

bait and switch confidence game, 138

"click-on" acceptance or agreement, 148

cost-plus contract, 137

counteroffer, 141

current market price contract, 137

cybercontract, 147

firm offer, 146

invitation to trade, 138

mirror image rule, 141

offer, 135

offeree, 135

offeror, 135

option contract, 146

output contract, 137

public offer, 138

rejection, 144

requirements contract, 137

revocation, 144

Questions for Review and Discussion

1. How does formalism guide the court in determining the elements of offer and acceptance?
2. What are the three requirements of a valid offer?
3. What is the difference between a public offer and an invitation to trade?
4. What is the difference between the acceptance of an offer in a unilateral contract and the acceptance of an offer in a bilateral contract?
5. What is the role of the Uniform Commercial Code (UCC) in the law?
6. What is the mirror image rule?
7. What is the UCC's position on acceptance in contract law?
8. What are the various means by which an offer can be revoked?
9. What is a firm offer?
10. What statutes affect the formation of cybercontracts?

Investigating the Internet

Access the website sponsored by QuickForm Contracts and write a report on how to use the QuickForm website. (Note: There is a small fee for the use of the forms at this site.)

Cases for Analysis

1. An advertisement appeared in the *Chicago Sun-Times* for the sale of a Volvo station wagon at Lee Calan Imports, Inc., for $1,095. The advertisement had been misprinted by the *Sun-Times*. The actual price of the automobile was $1,795. O'Keefe showed up at Lee Calan and said he would buy the Volvo for $1,095. Lee Calan refused to sell the car for $1,095. O'Keefe sued, claiming that the advertisement was an offer that he accepted, creating a binding agreement. Was O'Keefe correct? Explain. *O'Keefe v. Lee Calan Imports,* 262 N.E.2d 758 (IL).

2. The Great Minneapolis Surplus Store published the following advertisement in a Minneapolis newspaper: "Saturday 9 A.M. 2 Brand New Pastel Mink 3-Skin Scarfs selling for $89.50—Out they go Saturday. Each . . . $1.00. 1 Black Lapin Stole. Beautiful, Worth $139.50 . . . $1.00. First Come First Served." Leftkowitz, the first customer admitted to the store on Saturday, tried to buy the Lapin stole. The store refused to sell, stating that the offer was for women only. Leftkowitz sued. Was the offer definite enough to allow Leftkowitz to tender a valid acceptance? Explain. *Leftkowitz v. Great Minneapolis Surplus Store,* 86 N.W.2d 689 (MN).

3. Morrison wanted to sell a certain parcel of land to Thoelke. He decided to make an offer by sending Thoelke a letter. When Thoelke received the letter, he decided to accept. He wrote a letter to Morrison saying that he would buy the land at the price quoted in the letter. Thoelke then mailed the letter. Before he received the letter from Thoelke, Morrison changed his mind and withdrew the offer to Thoelke. When Thoelke found out Morrison would not sell the land to him, he sued. Was Thoelke's letter a valid acceptance, binding Morrison to the sale? Explain. *Morrison v. Thoelke,* 155 So.2d 889 (FL).

4. Wholesale Coal Company ordered twenty-five carloads of coal from Guyan Coal and Coke Company. Guyan could not come up with twenty-five carloads. However, it did have seven carloads available. Before shipping the coal, Guyan wrote back to Wholesale stating, "You can be sure that if it is possible to ship the entire twenty-five carloads, we will do so. But under the circumstances, this is the best we can promise you." When Guyan heard nothing from Wholesale, it shipped the seven carloads. When Wholesale did not pay for the seven carloads, Guyan brought suit to compel payment. Wholesale countersued, claiming Guyan had not yet delivered the remaining eighteen carloads. Was Wholesale correct? Explain. *Guyan Coal and Coke Company v. Wholesale Coal Company,* 201 N.W. 194 (MI).

5. Tockstein wrote an offer to purchase a house owned by Rothenbeucher. Tockstein signed the offer and personally delivered it to Rothenbeucher. The offer included a condition that acceptance must be made within twenty-four hours. At the end of that twenty-four-hour period, the offer would be automatically revoked if Rothenbeucher had not accepted. Rothenbeucher signed the agreement within the twenty-four-hour period. However, he did not deliver the acceptance to Tockstein personally, as Tockstein had done with the offer. Instead, Rothenbeucher delivered the acceptance to his own real estate agent, who delivered it to Tockstein after the automatic revocation time. Tockstein claimed that the offer was automatically revoked when Rothenbeucher did not deliver it within the specified time period. Was Tockstein correct? Explain. *Rothenbeucher v. Tockstein,* 411 N.E.2d 92 (IL).

6. Gina Greenhouse was a representative of the Dollar-or-Less chain of discount strores. In that capacity, she wrote to Louis Bolick and promised him that he would be granted a franchise agreement with Dollar-or-Less as long as he would follow instructions and advice in preparing to open the store. Greenhouse wrote in the letter that Bolick did not have to reply if he agreed to these terms. Bolick received the letter and, according to Greenhouse's instructions, did not bother to reply. Instead, he began to make arrangements to open his store, part of which meant that he turned down a similar arrangement with Less-Than-A-Dollar, a chain of similar discount stores. Unfortunately, Greenhouse and Dollar-or-Less did not live up to the agreement. As a result, Bolick ended up without any contract, having turned down the arrangement offered by Less-Than-A-Dollar. Bolick sued Greenhouse and Dollar-or-Less. Greenhouse and Dollar-or-Less denied the existence of a contract, claiming that Bolick's silence in not answering Greenhouse's letter could not be construed as acceptance. Are they correct?

Quick Quiz Answers				
7-1 1. F	7-2 1. T	7-3 1. T	7-4 1. T	7-5 1. F
2. T	2. T	2. T	2. F	2. F
3. T	3. T	3. F	3. F	3. T

Chapter 8

Mutual Assent and Defective Agreement

The Opening Case

"Mutual Assent or Mutual Mistake?"

In June, at the beginning of the fiscal year for the Aero Technologies, CEO Jason Hewitt, declared that the firm would have to cut expenses in a number of critical areas. One of these areas was the cost of computer equipment. In response to this mandate, Victor Stennis, the Director of the IT Department, assigned Jake O'Connor the task of pricing a series of new scanners that the department had decided to purchase. O'Connor called several suppliers and indicated what his company needed. On the fifth call, O'Connor talked to Trisha Kimmel of Blumstein Diagnostics who told O'Connor that scanner "seventy-nine-nine" seemed to be the one that would fit the company's needs. Neither O'Connor nor Kimmel discussed the price of scanner "seventy-nine-nine," because it was clearly listed in the catalog as $150. O'Connor agreed to order 40 scanners from Blumstein. When O'Connor reported the contract to Stennis, the IT director was impressed by the deal that O'Connor had negotiated with Blumstein and countersigned the order. Both Stennis and O'Connor were quite surprised when, after the delivery of the scanners, they received a bill for $22,000 (40 scanners @ $500 per scanner) because they had expected a bill of $6,000 (40 scanners @ $150 per scanner). Investigation proved that, when Kimmel said she would send them forty units of scanner "seventy-nine-nine" she had meant #799, while O'Connor believed she was referring to scanner #79-9. Did any of Kimmel's statements amount to misrepresentation or fraud? Is there a difference between fraud and misrepresentation? Was this merely a case of mutual mistake or should O'Connor and Stennis have known better? Was O'Connor placed under too much pressure because of the budget crunch? The answers to these and other questions are found in this chapter.

Chapter Outcomes

1. Explain the nature of mutual assent.
2. Identify the ways that mutual assent can be destroyed.
3. List the elements that must be proved to establish fraud.
4. Identify those situations that can give rise to claims of passive fraud.
5. Distinguish between fraud and misrepresentation, and contrast the remedies available for each.
6. Discuss the difference between unilateral and bilateral mistakes.
7. Judge which types of mistakes provide appropriate grounds for getting out of the contract.
8. Explain the nature of physical and emotional distress.

9. Explain the elements of economic duress.
10. Explain how the existence of a confidential relationship is a key factor in establishing undue influence.

8-1 Mutual Assent

As we have seen, the courts are interested in whether contracts have been negotiated and entered freely. In Chapter 7 we focused on the fact that an offer is a proposal that is freely made by the offeror to the offeree. The proposal indicates the offeror's willingness to freely enter into a contract with the offeree. If the offer is seriously intended, clear and definite, and communicated to the offeree, then the offeree may accept or reject it. The second element of a contract is the acceptance. If the offeree does in fact accept the offer freely, then there is mutual assent between the parties. Mutual assent is the third element of a valid contract.

The Nature of Mutual Assent

Mutual assent means that the parties have had a "meeting of the minds." In other words, both parties know what the terms are and both have willingly agreed to be bound by those terms. Mutual assent may be reached quickly, as in buying a phonecam at the local electronics outlet store, or it may result from weeks of negotiations related to a multimillion-dollar purchase of real estate. Whatever the case, mutual assent evolves through the communication of an offer and an acceptance between the contracting parties.

The Destruction of Mutual Assent

After mutual assent has been reached, the law protects the contracting parties in their contractual relationship. If one party or the other discovers that he or she has been cheated or discovers that a mutual mistake placed the party at a great disadvantage, that party is no longer bound to the terms of the agreement. Each party to a contract is protected from the chicanery of the other or from certain mistakes that may have crept into their agreement and destroyed mutual assent. If mutual assent has been destroyed, the contract is said to be a **defective agreement** (see Tables 8-1 to 8-3). A *defective agreement* can arise as a result of fraud, misrepresentation, mutual mistake, duress, or undue influence. The remainder of this chapter covers each of these potentially destructive forces.

Terms *Chicanery* is a word that means "trickery." In terms of law, it usually involves artful or clever practice aiming to deceive.

Table 8-1 Agreements Made Defective by Falsehood

Falsehood	Definition	Remedy
Active fraud	Active fraud occurs when one party to a contract makes a false statement intended to deceive the other party and thus lead that party into a deceptively based agreement.	Rescission and money damages
Passive fraud (concealment or nondisclosure)	Passive fraud occurs when one party does not say something about certain facts that he or she is obligated to reveal. Obligations arise in situations involving hidden problems and fiduciary relationships.	Rescission and money damages
Misrepresentation	Misrepresentation occurs when a false statement is innocently made with no intent to deceive.	Rescission only

Table 8-2 Agreements Made Defective by Mutual Mistake

Mistake	Legal Effect
Mistake as to description	Rescission will be granted.
Mistake as to existence	Proof that subject matter was destroyed *before* the agreement was made gives grounds for rescission.
Mistake as to value	Rescission will not be granted since value is a matter of opinion, not fact.

Table 8-3 Agreements Made Defective by Force or Pressure

Type of Force or Pressure	Explanation	Legal Effect
Physical duress	Violence or threat of violence to person, family, household, or property	Contract voidable; rescission allowed
Emotional duress	Acts or threats that create emotional distress in the one on whom they are inflicted	Contract voidable; rescission allowed
Economic duress or business compulsion	Threats of a business nature that force another party without real consent to enter a commercial agreement	Contract voidable; rescission allowed
Undue influence	Dominant party in a confidential relationship uses excessive pressure to convince the weaker party to enter a contract to benefit the dominant one	Contract voidable; rescission allowed

Quick Quiz 8-1 True or False?

1. Mutual assent means that the parties have had a "meeting of the minds."

2. After mutual assent has been reached, the law protects the contracting parties in their contractual relationship.

3. If mutual assent has been destroyed, the contract is said to be a defective agreement.

8-2 Fraud and Misrepresentation

Fraud is a wrongful statement, action, or concealment pertinent to the subject matter of a contract knowingly made to damage the other party. Fraud, if proved, destroys any contract and makes the wrongdoer **liable** (i.e., legally responsible) to the injured party for all losses that result.

The Elements of Fraud

To destroy mutual assent on a claim of fraud, the complaining or innocent party must prove the existence of five elements. First, the complaining party will have to show that the other party made a false representation about some **material fact** (i.e., an important fact, a fact of substance) involved in the contract. A material fact is one that is very crucial to the terms of the contract. Second, it must be shown that the other party made the representation knowing of its falsity. Third, it must be shown that the false representations were made with the intent that they be relied upon by the innocent party. Fourth, the complaining party must demonstrate that there was a reasonable reliance on the false representations. Finally, it must be shown that the innocent party actually suffered some loss by relying on the false representation after entering the contract. A case involving either active or passive fraud must be based on these five elements.

Cross-Cultural Notes Britain's Serious Fraud Office (SFO) handles large, complex cases of fraud. It has the authority to compel witnesses to answer questions and produce papers. Critics are concerned that the SFO abuses its power by forcing incriminating statements from accountants and bankers who have confidential, or fiduciary, relationships with their clients.

Example 8-1

As director of acquisitions at the Royal International Museum, Sir Walter Osborne purchased two original paintings from Ms. Audrey Rumbaugh, a private collector. The first painting was *Early Morning After a Storm at Sea* by Homer Winslow; the second was *Brittany Coast* by Charles-Francois Daubigny. Rumbaugh, owner and primary sales representative for Rumbaugh International Galleries, told Osborne that she had purchased the paintings from another private collector seven years before, that the paintings were genuine, and that they were in their original frames. As it turned out, most of what Rumbaugh had told Osborne was false. The only thing that turned out to be true was that the two paintings were in their original frames. The paintings themselves were clever forgeries that Rumbaugh had purchased on the black market three weeks earlier. Both of the actual paintings were owned by the Cleveland Museum of Art. Osborne and the Royal Museum could sue Rumbaugh for a return of all the money paid to Rumbaugh and for any other damages that resulted from the falsely made statements. This is true because the false statements made by Rumbaugh had been material to the contract. Moreover, Rumbaugh had intended that the false statement lead Osborne and the Royal Museum into the contract and the false statements did, in fact, lead Osborne and the museum into the contract.

In the Royal International Museum example noted above, all five elements of fraud are present. First, Rumbaugh made false representations about several material facts. In the Royal Museum example, the genuineness of the paintings was clearly material to the contract. Second, Rumbaugh made the representations knowing they were false. Third, the statements made by Rumbaugh were designed to lead the museum representative into relying on them. Fourth, the Royal Museum representative reasonably relied on the statements in the purchase of the paintings. Finally, the museum actually suffered a financial loss because it paid a top price for two forgeries.

Further Reading For a look at business fraud in England, see *Serious Fraud Office*, by Brian Widlake (London: Little, Brown & Co.).

Active Fraud

Active fraud occurs when one party to a contract makes a false statement intended to deceive the other party and thus leads that party into a deceptively based agreement. The false statements made by Rumbaugh to the Royal Museum representative would fall into this category. Thus, Rumbaugh committed active fraud against the museum. False statements

About the Law

While the common law courts of England were quite willing to acknowledge fraud in tort law, they were not as willing to see its application in contract law.

about material facts may also include illustrations and models that specifically relate to the description, condition, and characteristics of the subject matter of the contract. These "statements" need not be confined to oral or written representations. Actions designed to deceive, such as turning back a car's odometer or painting over rust spots, are considered statements about the condition of the subject matter of the contract.

Example 8-2

Gabriel Hayden owned a motor boat that was docked at the Butler Reservoir. Hayden, however, was about to move to the city and so he was anxious to get rid of a boat for which he would have no use in the city. Kelly Rhodes, who was new in town, wanted to purchase a motor boat quickly so that she would have several weeks of summer weather left to enjoy the boat. Sensing that he could make a real killing on the deal, Hayden told Rhodes about the boat. Rhodes was impressed by Hayden's sales pitch but she wanted to see the boat first and take it for a test run on the reservoir. Hayden agreed. However, before Rhodes arrived the next day for the test run, Hayden patched up several obvious holes in the bottom of the boat with putty and poster board. Hayden knew the repairs would not make the boat seaworthy for longer than fifteen minutes, but he figured that would be enough time to fool Rhodes into thinking that the boat was in good condition. Deceived by the apparently good condition of the boat, Rhodes purchased it. The next time she took it out on the reservoir, the boat quickly sank. Even though Hayden never actually told any verbal lies to Rhodes, he would still have committed fraud.

Getting Students Involved Have students make lists of examples of sales puffery that they see daily in media advertising. Then have them explain why it is merely sales puffery and not a fraudulent statement.

Related Cases Dow Corning Corporation, the manufacturer of silicone breast implants, was the victim of thousands of lawsuits when a jury determined that the company was guilty of fraud and malice because of nondisclosure of hazards. The company had maintained that no scientific data was withheld from the Food and Drug Administration (FDA), who approved the use of the implants. However, further studies by the FDA were able to prove that Dow Corning knew of the implant's health risks, but withheld the information. One woman was awarded $7.34 million. Dow Corning filed for bankruptcy in 1995 due to the overwhelming number of lawsuits resulting from the case.

To be fraudulent, statements must involve facts. Opinions and **sales puffery** consist of the persuasive words and exaggerated claims made by salespeople to induce a customer to buy their product. As long as the comments are reserved to opinion and do not misstate facts, they cannot be considered fraud in a lawsuit even if they turn out to be grossly wrong.

Example 8-3

Fran Holiday, a sales clerk representing the Kellog Formal Wear Shoppe was trying to sell a tuxedo to Ken Oldacker. During the sales discussion, Holiday told Oldacker that (1) the tux came with two pairs of pants, (2) the tux was made of 100 percent wool, (3) the tux had a very rich texture (4) the tux looked very good on Oldacker, and (5) the tux would make him look like a cross between Ted Turner and Donald Trump.

The first two statements are statements of material fact and could be the basis of a lawsuit for fraud if they are proven to be false. The others are either opinions expressed by the seller or the persuasive puffing that might induce Oldacker to buy the tux and could not be used as the basis of a lawsuit for fraud.

Passive Fraud

As noted above, active fraud occurs when one party actually makes a false statement intended to deceive the other party in a contract. In contrast, **passive fraud,** which is generally called **concealment,** or **nondisclosure,** occurs when one party does not say something about certain facts that he or she is under an obligation to reveal. If this passive conduct is intended to deceive and does, in fact, deceive the other party, fraud results. In general, a party is not required to reveal every known fact related to the subject matter of a contract. Certain facts may be confidential and personal. For instance, someone offering a DVD for sale need not disclose why it is being sold or how much profit will be realized. Hiding a fact becomes concealment, however, under certain circumstances. These circumstances include hidden problems and fiduciary relationships.

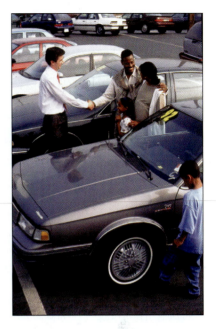

Hidden Problems As previously stated, in general a party is not under any duty to reveal everything about the subject matter of a contract. However, if the problem or defect is hidden and the other party cannot reasonably be expected to discover the defect, provided the problem involves some material fact, the offeror may be obliged to reveal it.

As long as comments are limited to a salesperson's opinion and do not misstate facts, the only act the salesperson would be guilty of is sales puffery.

Example 8-4

Franklin Bernstein had decided to purchase an apartment building in lower Manhattan near the World Financial Center, that he intended to convert into condominiums. Before finalizing the deal, he visited the building several times with a real estate agent representing the seller, Keyfitz Management, Inc. Each time Bernstein examined a different aspect of the building, concentrating first on the plumbing, then on the electrical system, then on the heating and air conditioning system, and so on. He also hired Guftanson Contractors, Ltd., to make thorough inspection of the entire building. What Bernstein did not know and, in fact, could not reasonably be expected to discover was that the foundation had been damaged when the World Trade Center had collapsed in 2001. Max Crowley, the actual owner, knew of the damage. However, he did not reveal the problem to Bernstein. Crowley had committed passive fraud or concealment because he did not reveal a serious hidden problem that Bernstein could not reasonably be expected to discover on his own.

Getting Students Involved Direct groups of students to create lists of relevant questions about types of goods that are likely to have hidden problems, such as used items. The list of questions should be designed to help students avoid being the victims of fraud in future transactions.

Some states have held that sellers are legally bound to reveal only problems so hidden that even an expert would not be able to uncover them. In these states, problems such as insect or rodent infestation would not be hidden problems because an expert could easily uncover them.

Fiduciary Relationships A **fiduciary relationship** is a relationship based upon trust. Such relationships exist, for example, between attorneys and clients, guardians and wards, trustees and beneficiaries, and boards of directors and corporations. If one party is in a fiduciary relationship with another party, then an obligation arises to reveal what otherwise might be withheld when the two parties enter an agreement.

A Question of Ethics

Suppose that you are showing your car to Tim Jorgenson, a potential buyer. You know that if Jorgenson takes your car out for a ride, he will notice that the front end rattles at speeds in excess of thirty-five miles per hour and that the brakes grind badly. Jorgenson, however, does not take the car on a test drive and, therefore, fails to detect any defects. Would you have an ethical duty to tell Jorgenson about the car's problems? Explain.

Terms *Fiduciary* is from the Latin *fiduciarius,* meaning *confidence* and *trust,* and the French *fidere,* "to trust." *Fidere* is also the origin of the pet's name *Fido,* which reflects the quality of loyalty associated with dogs.

State Variations The well-settled rule in Minnesota is that one cannot snap up an offer or bid knowing that it was made in error.

Example 8-5

Otto Groza was vice president of business and finance for the San Rafael Motor Corporation when he learned that Toth Properties Ltd. wanted to buy 12,000 acres of ranch land owned by San Rafael. Groza was the only one at San Rafael who knew that a new extension of the interstate was going to be located on the acreage owned by the company. Moreover, Groza knew that Toth wanted the land for an outlet mall and an adjoining hotel, and was willing to pay $19,000 per acre. Groza made a deal with Toth agreeing to sell the land at that price. He then went to the CEO and the board of San Rafael and offered to buy the farmland without revealing anything about the Toth deal. As a result, he purchased the acreage for $1,000 per acre and made an $18,000 profit on each acre he resold to Toth. Groza will be liable to San Rafael because he concealed a material fact that he was obligated to reveal because of his fiduciary relationship to the company.

Misrepresentation

Getting Students Involved Have students consider and discuss how misrepresentations could be unfair or possibly tragic even when the false statement was made with no intention to deceive.

Misrepresentation is a false statement made innocently with no intent to deceive. Innocent misrepresentation makes an existing agreement voidable and the complaining party may demand rescission. **Rescission** means that both parties are returned to their original positions, before the contract was entered into. Unlike cases based on fraud which allow rescission and damages, cases based on innocent misrepresentation allow only rescission and not money damages.

Example 8-6

Anthony Sanderson was browsing through eBay when he located what was labeled as a 1932 edition of *Brave New World* by Aldous Huxley, produced by Chatto and Windus, the London publisher which had printed the first edition of that landmark novel. The book was advertised as coming along with a companion book by Julian Huxley, entitled *If I Were Dictator,* published in 1934 by the London publishing house of Methuen. The seller was Juliette Straus, who set the minimum bid for the two volumes as GBP 8,700. Sanderson, who quickly bid on the two books, eventually won the auction with a successful bid of GBP 9,800. Later, after receiving the two books, Sanderson discovered that the copy of *If I Were Dictator* was actually a 1948 reprint of the original work. Without any indication of wrongdoing, Straus would be liable for nothing more than an innocent misrepresentation. In cases of this kind, the parties often renegotiate the purchase price if the agreement is affirmed.

If a party to an agreement makes an innocent misrepresentation and then later discovers that it is false, that party must reveal the truth. If the party does not reveal the truth, the innocent misrepresentation becomes fraud.

Quick Quiz 8-2 True or False?

1. Nondisclosure occurs when one party does not say something about certain facts that he or she is under an obligation to reveal.

2. A fiduciary relationship is a relationship based upon trust.

3. If a party to an agreement makes an innocent misrepresentation and then later discovers that it is false, there is no obligation for that party to reveal the truth, unless directed to do so by a court.

8-3 Mistake

When there has been no real meeting of the minds because of a mistake, mutual assent was never achieved and the agreement may be rescinded. As in misrepresentation, mistake permits rescission.

Terms *Mistake,* when used in the law of contracts, refers to a belief that is not in accord with the facts.

Unilateral and Bilateral Mistakes

A mistake made by only one of the contracting parties is a **unilateral mistake** and does not offer sufficient grounds for rescission or renegotiation. When both parties are mistaken, it is a **bilateral mistake.** A bilateral mistake, which is also called a **mutual mistake,** may permit a rescission by either the offeror or the offeree.

The Nature of Mistakes

Mutual mistakes are of several kinds. Some are universally accepted as grounds for rescission. Others are not grounds for rescission. Still others can give rise to lawsuits, but not in all courts or in all states.

Mistakes as to Description When both parties are mistaken in the identification and description of subject matter, there is a real mutual mistake and rescission will be granted.

Related Cases One of the most famous cases in contract law involves the sale of a cow in 1887. The parties agreed to the sale of the cow, both thinking that the animal was unable to produce any offspring. The price was for a fraction of that of a fertile cow. When it was discovered that the cow was, in fact, with calf, the seller refused to deliver as agreed. The court rescinded the contract, noting that the mutual mistake affected the substance of the whole consideration. *Sherwood v. Walker,* 33 N.W. 918.

The Opening Case Revisited
"Mutual Assent or Mutual Mistake?"

In The Opening Case, both O'Connor and Kimmel thought they were talking about the same item when, in fact, they were each referring to different scanners. The court ruled that there was enough ambiguity in the term "seventy-nine-nine" to see both interpretations (#79-9 and #799) as reasonable. As a result there was no "meeting of the minds" and mutual assent had been destroyed by mutual mistake!

State Variations In Georgia, if the consideration to a contract was given as a result of a mutual mistake of fact or law, the contract cannot be enforced.

Teaching Tips Students may not understand that value is relative. Discuss how disagreements over the monetary value of an item could be influenced by opinions on its artistic or sentimental value, for example, in contracts involving art or heirlooms. In such cases, a legally authorized and independent party, such as an assessor or appraiser, could set a price for the contested items based on their fair market value.

Mistakes as to Existence Proof that the subject matter had been destroyed before agreement was made gives grounds for rescission. Thus, if one accepted an offer to purchase a boat that both parties mistakenly believed to be berthed at a specified marina, the agreement would be voidable if it were proved that moments before acceptance the boat had been destroyed. Had the boat been destroyed after final acceptance, there would have been no mutual mistake and an enforceable contract would have resulted.

Mistakes as to Value When two parties agree on the value of the subject matter and later find they were both mistaken, this is a mutual mistake of opinion, not of fact. Mutual mistakes of opinion are not grounds for rescinding a contract.

Mistakes Through Failure to Read Document Failure to read a document or the negligent reading of a document does not excuse performance on the ground of a mistaken understanding of the document's contents. Exceptions may be made when conditions are printed on parking lot stubs, cleaner's tickets, hat check identifications, and the like. The law usually holds that these vouchers are given for identification purposes only. The courts generally are not favorable toward enforcing the fine-print conditions on the face or reverse side of such tickets.

Mistakes of Law Misunderstandings of existing laws do not give grounds for rescission. As often quoted, "Ignorance of the law is no excuse." Rescission may be allowed, however, when there have been mistakes related to the law of another state. In this way the courts interpret mistakes of law of a different state as mistakes of fact, not of law. Some states have now adopted statutes that completely remove the so-called ignorance-of-law concept. In those states, any mutual mistake of law is sufficient to bring about a rescission.

Quick Quiz 8-3 True or False?

1. When both parties are mistaken in the identification and description of subject matter, there is no mutual assent.

2. Even if the subject matter has been destroyed before an agreement has been made, the courts will not permit rescission.

3. Mutual mistakes of opinion are grounds for rescinding a contract.

8-4 Duress and Undue Influence

Background Information *Extortion* is an illegal means of forcing a person into a contract. It is a lay term for *duress*. The term *extortion* comes from the Latin *extorquere,* meaning "to wrench out."

Both duress and undue influence rob a person of the ability to make an independent, well-reasoned decision to freely enter a contractual relationship. Both of these conditions, therefore, strike at the heart of contract law. In general, **duress** may be viewed as an action by one party which forces another party to do what need not otherwise be done. Duress forces a person into a contract through the use of physical, emotional, or economic threats. In contrast, undue influence merely involves the use of excessive pressure. Moreover, undue influence also requires the existence of a special relationship generally of a confidential or fiduciary nature.

Physical and Emotional Duress

Physical duress involves either violence or the threat of violence against an individual or against that person's family, household, or property. If only threats are used, they must be so intense and serious that a person of ordinary prudence would be forced into the contract without any real consent. Threats of physical duress are relatively rare today. Perhaps more common are threats that create emotional duress. **Emotional duress** arises from acts or threats that would create emotional distress in the one on whom they are inflicted. It is generally necessary that the action threatened be either illegal or illicit. Wrongful exposure to public ridicule, threatened false attacks on one's reputation, or unjust efforts to prevent employment might constitute emotional duress. It might also be duress to threaten a person with criminal charges or with a civil lawsuit, if there are no grounds for using such intimidating tactics. On the other hand, it is not duress to promise to exercise a legal right, such as bringing a justified lawsuit, should someone not comply to a reasonable request.

The elderly are sometimes victims of duress by unscrupulous caregivers.

Example 8-7

Lynn and Tony Grayson contracted with Max Douglas, who agreed to have aluminum siding placed on the Grayson house. As a part of the agreement, the Graysons stated that the house had to be completed by Memorial Day weekend because they planned to have their daughter's high school graduation party at the house at that time. One week before the planned party, Douglas had still not started the project. When Lynn Grayson discussed this with him, Douglas said that he was still not certain that he could start that week, and was relatively certain that, even if he did start the project soon, he could no longer guarantee that the work would be done at the agreed time. Lynn stated that if he did not start that afternoon, she would find a contractor who would get the work done on time and would sue Douglas for whatever extra money it would cost her and her husband to get the house sided before the graduation party. This threat may cause Douglas distress, but because this is Lynn's legal right, there is no wrongful duress involved.

Economic Duress

Economic duress, also known as **business compulsion,** consists of threats of a business nature that force another party without real consent to enter a commercial agreement. In order to establish economic duress, the complaining party must demonstrate the existence of three elements. (1) The complaining party must first show that the other party was responsible for placing the complainant in a precarious economic situation and that the other party acted wrongfully in doing so. (2) The complainant must also show that there was no alternative other than to submit to the contractual demands of the wrongful party. (3) Finally, the innocent party must also show that he or she acted reasonably in entering the contract. If the plaintiff can prove the existence of these three elements, the court will rule the contract voidable on grounds of economic duress.

Business Law in the News
And Now, Your Fiscally Questionable All-Stars!

Baseball's owners love to complain about exorbitant salaries. But it's not as if they're making the best use of the money they've got. You'd think owners would shy away from being overly generous—but you'd be wrong. As baseball's best prepare to make their owners' investments look good, here are some of the guys whose seasons make their owners look plain bad. If only we could all get paid so much for doing so little.

	Kevin Brown PITCHER L.A. Dodgers	Charles Johnson CATCHER Fla. Marlins	Lee Stevens FIRST BASE Mont. Expos	Damion Easley SECOND BASE Detroit Tigers	Matt Williams THIRD BASE Ariz. D'backs	Neifi Perez SHORTSTOP K.C. Royals	Greg Vaughn LEFT FIELD T.B. Devil Rays	Carl Everett CENTER FIELD Texas Rangers	Derek Bell RIGHT FIELD Pitt. Pirates
Salary*	$15.7 mil.	$5.0	$4.0	$6.25	$9.5	$4.1	$8.75	$8.66	$4.75†
2001 team $ issue**	$68,887,000 operating loss, MLB worst	$60,547,000 revenue, third lowest	MLB-worst revenue of $34,171,000	Lost $10,694,000 and 96 games	$44,358,000 operating loss, second worst	$63,696,000 revenue, fourth lowest	Lost $17,880,000 and 100 games	$31,249,000 operating loss, fourth worst	Lost $5,879,000 and 100 games
Stats through 6/21	2-3, 4.06 ERA	.221 avg., 3 HR, 15 RBI	.191, 9, 30	.134, 1, 4	On disabled list	.226, 2, 22	.165, 8, 29	.200, 5, 18	Cut before season

*Figures obtained by the Associated Press from management and player sources.
†From media reports.
**Figures from Major League Baseball.

Questions for Analysis

1. If a major league baseball team is suffering financial setbacks due to the high salaries of its players, could it claim economic duress and void those expensive contracts? Explain.

2. Suppose that a major league baseball team is convinced by a player's agent to sign that player to a multimillion-dollar contract. Could that team claim undue influence in an attempt to void the contract? Explain.

3. If a major league baseball team signs a player for a multimillion-dollar contract, and that player turns out to be less than worth the money, could the team claim mistake of value in an attempt to void the contract? Explain.

4. Would the courts be likely to let a team void a contract for a multimillion-dollar baseball player if the player misrepresented his health? Explain.

5. Would the courts be likely to let a team void a contract based on mistake as to the description of the subject matter, if the player performed poorly? Explain.

Example 8-8

The owners and operators of the National Air Races negotiated a seven-year lease with the city of Macon for the use of the Macon City Airport. Each summer, during the Fourth of July weekend celebration, the National Air Races were held at the Macon City Airport. One week before the first race of the fourth year under the contract, Macon City officials informed the owners and operators of the National Air Races that they would no longer be able to use the Macon City Airport for the Fourth of July races unless they paid a substantial rent increase. The owners and operators of the Air Races, who had already sold at least 5,000 tickets per race, who had accepted entry fees from ninety-five pilots, and who had contracts with twenty concessionaires, could not find any other suitable airport within 120 miles of Macon. As a result, they agreed to the terms. Later the owners of the Air Races sued Macon to have the rent increase rescinded. The court ruled that the rent increase was voidable on grounds of economic duress.

Getting Students Involved The history of labor unions in the United States includes some rocky confrontations over employment contracts. Suggest that students work together in pairs to create scenarios in which a striking union member could claim economic duress in signing a labor contract.

Undue Influence

Undue influence occurs when the dominant party in a special relationship uses excessive pressure to convince the weaker party to enter a contract that greatly benefits the dominant party. To prove undue influence, it must be shown that a special relationship existed between the parties. A special relationship can generally be characterized as one of a confidential nature or one that has fiduciary elements. Examples of **confidential relationships** include the relationships of parent to child, guardian to ward, husband to wife, attorney to client, physician to patient, pastor to parishioner, and so forth. In most cases involving undue influence, one party in the special relationship has enough strength and leadership to dominate the other party, who is obviously weaker and dependent.

Did You Know?

It is possible for a party to ratify a contract made under duress if, after the duress has ended, the party makes a new promise to abide by the terms of the original agreement. In such a situation, the party ratifying the contract need not supply any new consideration.

Example 8-9

When Roger Armbruster was ten years old he was orphaned and inherited an enormous estate from his parents. Consequently, the court placed him under the then guardianship of his aunt, Georgette McCann. Over the years, Armbruster came to depend on his aunt for a variety of things, including her educational and financial advice. After he reached maturity, Armbruster still maintained a close relationship with his aunt. The two of them lived together and McCann handled all of Armbruster's financial affairs. At this time, McCann began to pressure Armbruster into signing over all his property to her in exchange for McCann's promise never to leave. McCann isolated Armbruster from relatives and friends and told him that everyone had abandoned him and that only she, McCann, cared about him. Convinced he had been completely abandoned by his family and friends, Armbruster signed over all his property. When Armbruster's half-sister found out what had happened, she took up her brother's cause and eventually convinced a court that in his weakened condition, Armbruster had submitted to McCann's excessive pressure in signing over all his property.

Teaching Tips Ask students to compare fiduciary relationships with the types of confidential relationships required in cases of undue influence.

Undue influence should not be confused with persuasion or some subtle form of inducement. Although one might be induced to enter into agreements through the urging of someone such as an employer, a professor, or an athletic coach, there is no undue influence if there is absence of the required confidential relationship. Persuasion and subtle induce-ment, while at times unethical, are not considered undue influence in the eyes of the law and do not, in and of themselves, provide a basis for rescinding agreements.

Quick Quiz 8-4 True or False?

1. Duress is an action by one party which forces another party to do what need not otherwise be done.

2. Economic duress is also known as business compulsion.

3. Undue influence should not be confused with persuasion or some subtle form of inducement.

Summary

8-1 Offer and acceptance go together to create mu-tual assent. Mutual assent means that both parties know what the terms are and have agreed to be bound by those terms. If mutual assent has been destroyed, the contract is said to be a defective agreement. A defective agreement can arise as a result of fraud, misrepresenta-tion, mutual mistake, duress, or undue influence.

8-2 Fraud involves a deliberate deception about some material fact that leads a party into an agreement that is damaging to that party. Active fraud occurs when one party makes a false statement intended to deceive the other party and thus leads that party into a deceptively based contract. The deception can involve an oral state-ment or an action that misleads the other party about a crucial fact. Passive fraud, or concealment or nondisclo-sure, occurs when one party does not say something that he or she is obligated to say. Misrepresentation is a false statement innocently made with no intent to deceive.

8-3 Unilateral mistakes, that is, mistakes made by one party, do not allow for rescission or renegotiation. When both parties are mistaken, it is a bilateral or a mutual mistake. A mutual mistake may allow for rescission by either party.

8-4 Duress and undue influence rob a person of the ability to make an independent, well-reasoned decision to freely enter into a contract. Physical duress involves vio-lence or threats of violence. Emotional duress arises from acts or threats that would create emotional distress in the individual who is the object of the threats or acts. Economic duress consists of threats of a business nature that force another party without real consent to enter into a contract. Undue influence involves a confidential rela-tionship. In most cases, undue influence involves the dominant party in the confidential relationship applying excessive pressure to the weaker party resulting in a con-tract that is of benefit to the dominant individual.

Key Terms

active fraud, 155

bilateral mistake, 159

business compulsion, 161

concealment, 157

confidential relationship, 163

defective agreement, 153

duress, 160

economic duress, 161

emotional duress, 161

fiduciary relationship, 157

fraud, 154

liable, 154

material fact, 155

misrepresentation, 158

mutual assent, 153

mutual mistake, 159

nondisclosure, 157

passive fraud, 156

physical duress, 161

rescission, 158

sales puffery, 156

undue influence, 163

unilateral mistake, 159

Questions for Review and Discussion

1. What is mutual assent?
2. How can mutual assent be destroyed?
3. What five elements must be proved to establish that a contract is defective because of fraud?
4. What situations can give rise to claims of passive fraud?
5. What is the essential difference between fraud and misrepresentation? How do the remedies for each differ?
6. What is the difference between unilateral and bilateral (mutual) mistake?
7. What types of mistakes provide appropriate grounds for getting out of a contract?
8. What is the nature of physical and emotional duress?
9. What are the elements of economic duress?
10. Why is the existence of a confidential relationship a key factor in establishing undue influence?

Investigating the Internet

Access the website sponsored by The National Fraud Information Center and write a report on how to disclose telemarketing fraud.

Cases for Analysis

1. Walker and Cousineau were both in the gravel business. Walker placed an advertisement for a tract of land, claiming that he had an engineer's report that indicated the land held at least 80,000 cubic yards of gravel. In fact, Walker knew the land contained much less gravel. Cousineau purchased the land and began to excavate it. After 6,000 cubic yards of gravel had been removed, the supply ran out. Cousineau sued Walker, asking the court to rescind the contract. Did Cousineau win the case? Explain. *Cousineau v. Walker,* 613 P.2d 608 (AL).

2. Young sold a residential lot to Sorrell without revealing that the lot had been filled. The landfill was not obvious, and Sorrell could not have been reasonably expected to detect it. When Sorrell discovered the landfill, he sued Young and asked the court to rescind the agreement. Young claimed he was under no obligation to reveal the fill to Sorrell. Was Young correct? Explain. *Sorrell v. Young,* 491 P.2d 1312 (WA).

3. Boskett offered to sell a 1916 dime to Beachcomber Coins, Inc. Beachcomber examined the coin carefully and agreed to pay Boskett $500 for it. Later, Beachcomber asked a representative from the American Numismatic Society to examine the coin. The coin turned out to be counterfeit. No evidence existed to indicate fraud on Boskett's part. Beachcomber sued Boskett for rescission and a return of the $500. Beachcomber claimed this bilateral mistake of fact created grounds for a rescission. Was Beachcomber correct? Explain. *Beachcomber Coins, Inc. v. Boskett,* 400 A.2d 78 (NJ).

4. Prisoners rioted at the Iowa State Penitentiary and held prison staff members as hostages. The warden agreed in writing that no reprisals would be levied against the rioting inmates. In exchange, the prisoners released the hostages. After the hostages were released, several of the prisoners were punished for the riot. One prisoner, Wagner,

was placed in solitary for thirty days. He also received 180 days of administrative segregation and the loss of 1,283 days of goodtime earned. On what legal grounds could the warden refuse to keep his promise to the inmates? Explain. *Wagner v. State,* 364 N.W.2d 246 (IA).

5. Loral Corporation had a contract with the U.S. government to manufacture radar sets. Loral subcontracted with Austin Instrument for the production of precision parts to be used in the radar sets. In the middle of production, Austin told Loral that it would deliver no more parts unless Loral agreed to pay Austin a good deal more than originally agreed upon. Loral could not obtain the same parts in time from any other company. As a result, Loral agreed to the price increase. After delivering the radar sets, Loral sued Austin and asked the court to rescind the price increase. Did the court grant Loral's request? Explain. *Austin Instrument, Inc. v. Loral Corporation,* 272 N.E.2d 533 (NY).

6. Vargas, an artist, had been under contract with *Esquire* magazine for several years. When the time came for a new contract, Vargas met with the president of the company and signed the new contract without reading it. Later, Vargas found out that the contract did not say what he thought it said. He sued *Esquire,* arguing that he signed the agreement only because he had relied upon the president of the company to look after his business affairs. Was this a case of undue influence? Explain. *Vargas v. Esquire, Inc.,* 166 F.2d 651 (7th Cir.).

Quick Quiz Answers

8-1	8-2	8-3	8-4
1. T	1. T	1. T	1. T
2. T	2. T	2. F	2. T
3. T	3. F	3. F	3. T

Chapter 9   Contractual Capacity

The Opening Case
"There Is Great Joy in Foothill"

Every spring, major league baseball teams conduct a draft during which they compete for the most talented young men playing baseball on the diamonds of the nation's high schools and colleges. Many of the young men who are drafted are not yet adults. In fact, some of them have not even graduated from high school at the time of the draft. Recently, for instance, the New York Yankees' first pick in the draft was Phil Hughes a right-handed pitcher from Foothill High School in Santa Ana, California. In the same draft, the Yankees also picked a catcher named John Poterson who played for Chandler High School in Arizona. Both of these young men were only seventeen years old at the time of the draft. As minors, they would have the legal capacity to void any contract that they might have negotiated with the Yankees. With that in mind, would it be wise for the Yankees, or any major league team, for that matter, to enter a contract with a ballplayer who has not yet reached eighteen years of age? Is there any way for the Yankees to protect themselves if they wanted to sign a minor like Hughes or Poterson? Would it be better to simply wait until they reach the age of majority? Is the age of majority the same in all fifty states? On what precise date does a person reach the age of majority? What would happen if Poterson and Hughes signed with the Yankees before reaching the age of majority and then, after becoming eighteen, changed their minds, and decided to sign with the Cleveland Indians? These questions and others like them are addressed in this chapter on capacity in contract law.

Chapter Outcomes

1. Describe the legal presumption regarding capacity.
2. Explain why the law allows minors to void contracts.
3. Differentiate between the age of minority and the age of majority.
4. Explain how the Constitution affects the age of majority.
5. Distinguish between emancipation and abandonment.
6. Assess the liability of a minor who lies about his or her age.
7. Describe the legal liability of minors in contracts involving necessaries.
8. Identify exceptions to the general rule about minors and contracts.
9. Explain the effects of mental impairment on contractual capacity.
10. Discuss the contractual capacity of drugged or intoxicated persons.

9-1 Minors' Rights and Obligations

The fourth element essential to a legally effective contract is the legal ability to enter into a contractual relationship. This legal ability is known as **capacity.** Because the will theory of contract law focuses on the free will of the parties, initially the law placed an enormous amount of emphasis on each party's contractual ability. Then when the law shifted from the will theory to the formalist theory, the law established a general presumption that anyone entering a contractual relationship has the legal capacity to do so. This means that someone enforcing an agreement does not have to prove that the other party had contractual capacity when the contract was negotiated and finalized.

However, this is a **rebuttable presumption;** that is, a defending party has the right to attack the presumption in order to rescind a contract. Under the current state of the law, for example, contracts entered by minors are voidable by the minor. The law allows minors the privilege to **disaffirm** (negate) a contract in order to protect them from adults who might take advantage of young people who do not fully understand their obligations. In effect, the privilege allows minors to get out of contracts they have entered before reaching adulthood. The law, therefore, protects minors by acknowledging that their immaturity and innocence may hinder their ability to choose freely in a wise and productive way. In effect, this move represents a step away from the purely formalist approach because it recognizes situations in which it would be unfair to hold a minor to an agreement that he or she did not understand as a direct result of his or her inexperience.

Minors are able to rescind most contracts.

For more details on the situations covered in The Opening Case see: Kepner, Tyler. "Catcher Is Only 17, but Yanks See Potential." *The New York Times,* June 7, 2004, p. C-23.

Teaching Tips Students may think that a minor cannot enter into a legal contract. The proof that a minor can is that the other party is legally bound by the contract. Emphasize that a minor can enter a legal contract and then void the contract.

Example 9-1

Terry Jacquet and Benjamin Olsen entered a contract which obligated Jacquet to sell her DVD player to Olsen. At the time, Jacquet was only seventeen years old. Before the DVD player was delivered or any money exchanged, Jacquet changed her mind. Olsen brought suit in small claims court against Jacquet. It would not be necessary for Jacquet to prove she had contractual capacity because the law presumes that such capacity exists. However, because the presumption is rebuttable, Jacquet could introduce evidence to show that, because she was a minor, she could rescind the contract.

About the Law

A rebuttable presumption is also known as a "disputable presumption."

When a minor indicates by a statement or act an intent not to live up to a contract, that minor is entitled to a return of everything given to the other party. This is true even when the property transferred to the minor under the contract has been damaged or destroyed. A few states will deduct something from the amount due back to the minor if the goods are damaged. Most states, however, deduct nothing.

State Variations In Oklahoma, if a minor between the ages of sixteen and eighteen contracts with respect to purchasing an automobile, such a minor must first restore consideration prior to disaffirming the contract.

Example 9-2

Alex DeNardo was sixteen years old when she purchased a set of fourteen volumes of *The Adventures of Nancy Drew* from BuytheBook, Inc. The set cost $849. After having the volumes in her possession for three days, she decided to return the books to BuytheBook. On the way to the store, DeNardo dropped several volumes into a puddle of water causing extensive damage to those volumes. Clyde Thistle, the store manager said it would take $400 to repair the damaged volumes and, even then, they would no longer be in mint condition, which they had been when DeNardo purchased them. Most states would allow DeNardo a full refund of $849 despite the damaged condition of the volumes. A few states would deduct $400.

Definition of Minority

U.S. Const. Amendment 26 (see page 863)

Terms *Minor* is Latin for *lessor* and comes from *minimus,* meaning *small* or *little. Majority* is from the Early French *majorite,* a derivative of the Old Latin *major,* meaning *greater.* The common term for someone who is no longer a minor is *adult,* which comes from the Latin *alere,* "to nourish" or "to begin to grow." The English words *old, elder,* and *adolescence* also come from the same Latin root.

State Variations In Alabama, Nebraska, and Wyoming, the age of majority is nineteen. In Mississippi, the age of majority is twenty-one. However, persons eighteen and older have the capacity to enter binding contractual relationships affecting personal property.

Getting Students Involved Why do minors need to be protected from contractual obligations any more than adults? Have two student groups prepare and present opposing arguments on this question. Then ask students what their real opinions are on this issue. Have them defend their viewpoints.

Minority, under common law, was a term that described persons who had not yet reached the age of twenty-one. Upon reaching that age, a person was said to have reached **majority.** Ratification and adoption of Amendment 26 to the U.S. Constitution in 1971 lowered the voting age in federal elections from 21 to 18. To avoid the confusion that would result from having two voting ages, the states started to enact new laws that enabled eighteen-year-olds to vote in state and local elections. Then states began to lower the age of majority to eighteen years for certain types of contracts. Now the age of majority in forty-nine states is eighteen. Only Nebraska has established nineteen as the age of majority. Still, there are other age requirements that differ from state to state in relation to other matters such as the legal ability to purchase alcoholic beverages, to enter a marriage, to buy tobacco products, and to operate motor vehicles. Recently, for instance, in response to outside influences from a variety of social organizations and governmental institutions, many states have raised the legal age for purchasing and consuming alcohol to twenty-one years.

Legal Age In some states, a person becomes an adult at the beginning of the day before his or her eighteenth (or in Nebraska his or her nineteenth) birthday. This strange quirk in the law occurs because the day on which a person is born is counted as the first day of life. Therefore, since the law does not consider fractions of days, on a person's eighteenth (or nineteenth) birthday, the person is really eighteen (or nineteen) years and one day old.

Example 9-3

Simon Kodera was born on September 9. State law required people to be twenty-one before they could purchase and consume alcoholic beverages. Since Kodera becomes twenty-one at any time on September 8, he would be legally allowed to celebrate at the local tavern on that date. Few bartenders and tavern owners know this rule, though, and so from a practical, not a legal, point of view, Kodera would probably have to wait until September 9 for his first (legal) drink.

Emancipation and Abandonment In some jurisdictions, minors who became **emancipated,** that is, no longer under the control of their parents, are responsible for their contracts. This means that they cannot void the contract despite their apparent minority. Emancipated minors include those who are married, those in the armed forces, and those who leave home and, in the process, give up all right to parental support. In certain states, minors are even allowed to ask the court for a legally sanctioned emancipation. In any of these cases, an emancipated minor is said to have **abandoned** the usual protective shield given them. Although minors in these categories are no longer protected from liability on their contracts, merchants are still reluctant to deal with them on a credit basis, fearing that they may still attempt to disaffirm, or repudiate, their contracted debts. Again, for practical, not legal, reasons, merchants require that minors get the signature of a responsible adult who will agree to guarantee payment of money owed.

Moreover, the hesitancy felt by some merchants in relation to emancipated minors is justified because a few states still hold to the opposite rule, that is, that emancipated minors do not give up the legal advantages associated with minority simply because they leave home or become married. To support this position, the courts in these jurisdictions note that the rule that allows minors to rescind contracts is based on the idea that minors are less experienced and less knowledgeable than adults about the consequences of their actions. It is, therefore, difficult to see why getting married or leaving home somehow bestows more common sense on a minor who does so. In fact, one court remarked that, getting married and leaving home may actually indicate that a minor has less good sense than another minor who does neither. Since this rule differs from state to state it would be a good idea to check on the rule of law in your jurisdiction.

A Question of Ethics

As noted in Example 9-2, most states would allow DeNardo a full refund when she returns the books, even though they have been damaged. Consequently, there would be nothing illegal about DeNardo accepting the entire amount. However, ethically, should DeNardo accept the full $849, or should she acknowledge her culpability and volunteer to deduct the $400 needed to repair the books? Explain.

Misrepresentation of Age

Minors sometimes lie about their age when making a contract. Despite the misrepresentation of age, most states will allow the minor to disaffirm or get out of the contract. From one perspective this makes sense, because the theory that supports a minor's right to rescind a contract is based upon the fact that the minor is immature and inexperienced. The fact that a minor lies about his or her age actually confirms the fact that the minor is both irresponsible and unworldly, otherwise he or she would not have attempted to get away with such a lie in the first place. Nevertheless, some jurisdictions do not permit the minor to get away with the lie. Some states require the minor to place the adult in the same situation that he or she was in before the contract. Others allow the adult to use tort law rather than contract law to sue the minor for fraud. Some states have also enacted statutes that allow recovery against a minor who is engaged in business and who misrepresents his or her age in a commercial contract. A number of states, for example, have statutes that deny disaffirmance if the minor has signed a written statement falsely asserting adult status. Without such a statute, the minor would be allowed to get out of the primary contract despite her or his signature on that primary contract or the contract asserting adult status.

State Variations In California, minors cannot disaffirm contracts for artistic or creative services or professional sports contracts if they have been judicially approved. Moreover, in Arkansas, when a minor borrows money for higher education, the contract is valid and binding as if the minor were full age.

9-2 Contractual Capacity of Minors

Executory contracts, those which have not been fully performed by both parties, may be repudiated by a minor at any time. A promise to deliver goods or render services at some future time need not be carried out by the minor who so decides. This privilege is not available to an adult who contracts with a minor.

If goods delivered to a repudiating minor are still in the minor's possession, it is the minor's duty to return them to the other party.

Example 9-4

Walt Andrews, who was seventeen years old, purchased a new computer from the Alpha-Omega Computer Company. Andrews paid $250 down and agreed to pay the balance in twelve monthly installments. Four weeks later, after he had taken the computer home, Andrews decided he didn't want it any longer. When Alpha-Omega Computer Company refused to take back the computer, Andrews sued the company in small claims court for the return of his down payment and the cancellation of the balance he still owed. In most states, Alpha-Omega Computer Company would be required to make the refund and cancel the debt. Andrews would have to return the computer set.

The Opening Case Revisited
"There Is Great Joy in Foothill"

Recall in the opening case that both of the young ballplayers chosen by the Yankees were less than eighteen years of age at the time of the draft. As minors, they would have the legal ability to rescind any contract that they might have entered with the Yankees. With that in mind, it would be wise for the Yankees, or any major league team who chooses a minor in the draft, to wait until the minor is eighteen to enter a contract with that ballplayer. Or, to avoid the problem altogether, a team might refuse to deal with minors at any time in any portion of the draft and simply focus on ballplayers who have reached the age of majority.

Contracts for Necessaries

Necessaries are those goods and services that are essential to a minor's health and welfare. Thus, necessaries can include clothing, food, shelter, medical and dental services, tools and equipment needed for the minor to carry out his or her business, and even, in some cases, educational expenses. If a minor makes a contract for necessaries he or she will be liable for the fair value of those necessaries. Despite the general tenor of this principle, if the necessaries have already been provided to the minor by parents or others, the rule does not apply. In addition, not everything that a party claims as a necessary will actually be a necessary. In order to determine whether goods and services qualify as genuine necessaries, the court will inquire into the minor's family status, financial strength, and social standing or station in life. Necessaries, then, are not the same to all persons.

Example 9-5

Angel Milavec had lived in Hawaii her entire life. Because she had started school one year before everyone else, she was only seventeen when she graduated from high school and entered college. The college she attended was in Chicago. Since she had never owned a winter coat, she purchased one in November from the Hawthorne Brothers Department Store, while she was still seventeen. This coat would be a necessary, and any attempt to repudiate the purchase would probably fail.

Technically, a minor's contract covering necessaries is not enforceable against the minor in the truest sense of the term. Instead, the minor is required to pay the fair value of the necessaries that have been provided by the adult. The fair value is determined by the court. This approach to the law is an extension of the concept of quasi-contract. Remember that when applying the concept of quasi-contract, the court will require the parties to act as if there were a contract, even though a true contract does not exist. The point of requiring the minor to pay the fair value of the item is to play it straight with adults who carry the risk of dealing with minors in relation to necessaries. Allowing the minor to get away with completely rescinding such contracts would amount to unfair enrichment of the minor. The concept of quasi-contract is aimed at preventing this type of unjust enrichment.

There is an interesting corollary related to the concept of necessaries that many people, including minors and the adults who deal with them, overlook. This is the standard which states that the rules related to necessaries apply only to executed contracts. An executed contract is one whose terms have been completely and satisfactorily carried out by both parties. In contrast, an executory contract is one that has not yet been fully performed by the parties. Wholly executory contracts calling for a future delivery or rendering of services may be repudiated by the minor. Thus, in the foregoing example, had Milavec's coat been ordered, but not delivered or paid for, she could have repudiated her agreement with no damages or monetary loss being assessed against her.

Technically, parents are liable for a contract executed by a minor, even a contract for necessaries, only when they cosign the agreements. When a parent, or anyone else for that matter, cosigns for a loan or for a contract involving installment payments, the cosigner becomes a guarantor. A guarantor promises to pay the other party's debts if that party does not settle those debts personally. This promise is known as a guaranty of payment. In contrast, if parents do not cosign a contract, they are not liable for that contract, even though the contract was made by their minor child. As might be expected, there is an exception to this general rule. If a parent had neglected or deserted the minor, the parent may be held liable to a third person for the fair value of the necessaries supplied by the third party to the minor.

Other Contracts Not Voidable

State Variations   In Arkansas, a bank may enforce a contract against a minor when the money was lent for the purpose of defraying the expense of the minor's higher education.

By statute and court decision, certain other types of contracts have been excepted from the general rule that the contracts of minors are voidable at the minor's option. For public policy reasons, minors may not at their option disaffirm a valid marriage or repudiate an enlistment contract in the armed forces based on a claim of incapacity to contract. Neither may a minor repudiate a contract for goods and services required by law; for example, minors may not repudiate payments for inoculations and vaccinations required for attendance at a university or college or required in securing a visa for travel in certain foreign lands. They may also be prevented from terminating contracts with banks and other financial institutions for educational loans. Some states also bar minors from repudiating agency contracts and insurance contracts. Others prevent minors from voiding contracts for psychological care, pregnancy care, the transfer of stocks and bonds, and contracts involving child support. This is a state-by-state issue, so it is wise to check your own state statutes to determine which of these contracts are not voidable by minors in your jurisdiction.

Shield or Sword Doctrine   If tempted to see the rescission rights of minors as unfair, we must keep in mind the original intent of the court in granting this power. As noted previously, the right to rescind contracts was given to minors as a protective device or "shield" against those unscrupulous adults who might try to take unfair advantage of the immaturity and inexperience of minors. This is precisely the type of situation that the law envisioned when it granted minors the "shield" which allows them to rescind contracts.

The problem with this protective device is that it can be exploited by minors who use it to rescind legitimate contracts. In effect, an unprincipled minor can take this safeguard, which is meant as a protective shield, and transform it into a sword that violates the rights of the other party. Fortunately, the courts are not oblivious to this type of abuse. Since the doctrine was never meant to allow minors to take advantage of innocent people, the courts have no difficulty denying rescission rights to minors when they use it as a weapon against another contracting party.

About the Law

Under the Napoleonic Code, people under thirty years of age could not marry without their father's permission. In addition, a father could have his child incarcerated for as long as six months on his word alone.

Example 9-6

Rene Higgins, who was seventeen, purchased a round-trip airline ticket from Transglobal Airlines for a trip from Portland, Oregon, to Daytona Beach, Florida, for spring break. When spring break was over, Higgins returned to Portland and, on arrival, demanded the return of all the money that she had paid for the round-trip ticket. Her demands were based on her rescission rights as a minor. Clearly, Higgins was using her right to rescind to take advantage of Transglobal Airlines. She was not using her rights as a minor as a protective shield, as the law intended. It is doubtful that Higgins will be permitted to recover money for her ticket.

Voidable Contracts and Innocent Third Parties Another curb on a minor's right to rescind contracts is provided by provisions in the UCC. These provisions protect the rights of an innocent third party who purchases goods from an individual who originally purchased those same goods from a minor. While individuals who buy goods from minors have voidable ownership rights, under the UCC, those same individuals can transfer valid ownership rights to an innocent third-party purchaser of those goods. Thus, rescission by a minor will not require the innocent purchaser to return the goods.

Example 9-7

Daniel Steiner, age sixteen, decided to sell his guitar to Vintage Instruments, Inc. Vintage then sold the guitar to Robert Cline, an innocent third-party buyer. Before Steiner became an adult, he decided to get back his guitar from Cline by disaffirming his contract with Vintage. Steiner would not be able to recover the guitar from Cline by disaffirming his contract with Vintage.

The UCC rule refers to the sale of personal property. In cases where a minor has sold real estate to one who subsequently sells it to an innocent third party, the minor, on reaching adulthood, may disaffirm the sale and recover the real property.

Ratification of Minors' Contracts

People may ratify their contracts made during minority only after reaching their majority—age eighteen, nineteen, or twenty-one or at any other age set by statute—or within a reasonable time thereafter. **Ratification,** or **affirmance,** is the willingness to abide by contractual obligations. It may be implied by using the item purchased, making an installment payment, paying off the balance of money owed on a previously voidable contract, by continuing to accept goods and services being provided under a contract, or just by doing nothing about the contract after reaching majority. Affirmation may also result from the person's oral or written declaration to abide by the contract. These acts as well as others ratify an existing agreement and elevate it to the status of one that is enforceable against an adult.

Disaffirmance of Minors' Contracts

An individual may disaffirm an agreement made during minority before or within a reasonable time after reaching adulthood. The exact period of time will vary depending on the nature of the contract and on applicable state and local laws. Failure to disaffirm within a reasonable period of time would imply that the contract had been ratified. The method of disaffirmance is fundamentally the same as the method of ratification. Disaffirmance may be implied by the acts of the individual after achieving majority, such as by a failure to make an installment payment. Similarly, an oral or written declaration of disaffirmance would achieve the same end. In general, there are no particular protocols attached to the act of disaffirmance by a minor. On the other hand, it is generally a good idea to make the disaffirmance in writing so that there is a record of the transaction should questions arise at a later time. This is especially true if the contract is disaffirmed after the minor has reached the age of majority (see Figure 9-1).

State Variations California, Georgia, and Mississippi have no age limits for entering into a marriage contract *with* parental consent. Mississippi is the only state that does not require age eighteen as the minimum before parties can marry *without* parental consent (males can marry at age seventeen, and females can marry at age fifteen). However, Mississippi does require parental notice if the parties are under age twenty-one. In Florida, Virginia, and the District of Columbia, parental consent is not required for parties age sixteen or older if they have been married before. In Alabama, previously married parties age fourteen or older can remarry without parental consent.

Cross-Cultural Notes British Parliament passed the Infant Relief Act in 1874, which protected persons under age twenty-one from their lack of experience and the persuasions of merchants and moneylenders. The act made contracts "absolutely void" for repayment of money loans and for goods other than necessaries. Even if the money was loaned to buy necessaries, the loan was void. However, if the money was actually spent on necessaries, the minor could be asked to pay the lender the same purchase price for the necessaries that the supplier received.

Related Cases Sixteen-year-old William Wallace purchased a car from Whitley's Discount Auto Sales. Wallace stated on the credit application that he was eighteen. Within eight months, Wallace had two car accidents. He decided to return the car and get his money back. The court held in *Gillis v. Whitley's Discount Auto Sales* (319 S.E.2d 661) that Wallace was entitled to the money he had paid, because in North Carolina misrepresentation of age does not bar a minor from disaffirming his contract.

17810 Windward Rd.
Terre Haute, IN 47811
September 9, 20 - -

Spectrum Electronics
433 East 310th Street
Willowick, IN 47812

Please take notice that I, Andrew Heinzmann, of 17810 Windward Road, Terre Haute, Indiana, hereby disaffirm the contract made on August 19, for the purchase of a Kurasaki compact disc player, model S-5293, from Spectrum Electronics, 433 East 310th Street in Willowick, Indiana.

On August 19, the date the contract was entered, I was seventeen years of age, a minor under the laws of Indiana.

I also demand a return of the $50.00 down payment that I gave you under the contract. I will return the compact disc player to your store at 1:00 p.m. on September 15.

Thank you for your understanding in this matter.

Sincerely,

Andrew Heinzmann

Andrew Heinzmann

Figure 9-1 This is a sample letter indicating a minor's disaffirmance.

Quick Quiz 9-2 True or False?

1. Executory contracts, those which have not been fully performed by both parties, may be repudiated by a minor at any time.
2. Ratification is the willingness to abide by contractual obligations.
3. Necessaries are the same for all persons.

Business Law in the News
Now It's a Girl Thing

Hollywood is smitten with teen girls—and not just as perky daughters or cute girlfriends on the big screen. From near-obscurity a decade ago, they have become the audience of choice for many filmmakers.

Witness the explosion of girl-power movies, from sappy romantic fantasies to snappy comedies. Among the top 10 box office draws over the May 8 weekend: *Mean Girls,* starring 17-year-old Lindsay Lohan as a home-schooled innocent who becomes queen bee of a high school clique; *New York Minute,* with teen stars Mary-Kate and Ashley Olsen as bickering twins on a madcap Manhattan adventure; and *13 Going on 30,* with Jennifer Garner as a girl thrust into the body and life of her older, successful self.

The sight of 10- to 18-year-old females queueing up at the ticket window is certainly good news for studios, which have watched other parts of their audience fragment or drift away to the Web. The success of 2001's *The Princess Diaries* and 2003's *Freaky Friday,* which grossed more than $100 million apiece in the U.S., took many by surprise. But it shouldn't have—this is a generation raised on seeing girl stars in music and TV, such as Mandy Moore and Hillary Duff, migrate to the big screen. It's a group that enters puberty younger than previous generations, gets independence early because of dual-career households, and is gaining in equality with boys in sports. The result: confident consumers who want to see images of themselves and their aspirations in movies, says Barb Martino, who runs G Whiz, a youth marketing agency. "They're enjoying teenhood," says Martino, "The girl teen and tween marketplace is probably more powerful than boys."

That said, it's also a group that can be tough to please. *New York Minute* has so far wooed mostly girls under 11, grossing a disappointing $6.2 million in its opening weekend. The Olsens' cutesy image may not play well with an older crowd. And *The Princess Diaries'* success has yet to be replicated in modern-day fairy tales, from *Ella Enchanted* to *The Prince & Me.* Maybe the formula just gets tired. Jarrod Moses, CEO of Alliance, an entertainment development company, figures that teen girls are "smart and cynical viewers [who] want aspirational, empowering, and funny stories." *Mean Girls* and *13 Going on 30* fit the bill. Ensemble casts, edgy scripts, and heartthrobs like Ashton Kutcher don't hurt, either.

Boyz 2 Men

Teen boys certainly have their particular tastes as well, but they tend to blend in with older male audiences. Action movies and video games attract a male fan base that ranges far beyond the teen years. Gross-out humor or featherbrained scripts—what Julie Friedlander of Zenith Media refers to as the "*Dumb and Dumber* franchise"—also have appeal for men beyond the teen years.

Cynics predict that Hollywood's fixation on teen girls could fade faster than a high school crush. Still, at a time when other groups seem tough to catch, aiming for a large, well-defined target audience has appeal. "Girls are at the forefront of everyone's mind these days," says Rachel Geller, chief strategic officer of youth marketer Geppetto Group. Even the odd frosty reception won't deter moviemakers from wooing this fickle audience.

Questions for Analysis

1. At the time that this article was printed, how old was the actress Lindsay Lohan, the star of *Mean Girls?*

2. Would Ms. Lohan's age prevent her from entering a contract? Explain.

3. The target market for movies such as *Mean Girls, New York Minute,* and *13 Going on 30* is ten- to eighteen-year-old girls. What problems might result for movie producers who target a market of individuals, most of whom have not reached the age of majority? Explain.

4. Would the courts be likely to protect a minor who sits through an entire film and then, based on the principle of minority, demands a refund? Explain.

5. Considering the principle of minority and its possible negative effects, why might the teen boy film market be safer for movie producers than the teen girl film market? Explain.

Source: Diane Brady. "Now It's a Girl Thing." *BusinessWeek,* May 24, 2004, p. 97.

9-3 Persons with Mental Impairments and Persons Drugged or Intoxicated

Persons deprived of the mental ability to comprehend contractual obligations have the right to disaffirm their contracts. Their rights are, in many respects, the same as the rights of minors. Agreements of mentally impaired persons are either valid, voidable, or void, depending on the seriousness of their disability and on whether they have been declared insane.

Persons Mentally Impaired

Under the orthodox rule of competency in contract law, a contract made by a person who is mentally infirm, has brain damage, is suffering from a physical illness such as Alzheimer's disease, or who suffers from a psychological disorder, may be voidable, if the person's impairment is severe enough to rob that person of the ability to understand the nature, purpose, and effect of that contract. However, mental retardation, a psychological disorder, a physical illness that affects the operation of the brain, or brain damage by themselves do not necessarily reduce a person's ability to enter into contracts. The question will be whether the mental problem existed at the time the contract was made and was so serious that the person did not understand the nature of the contract. If that is the case, the mentally impaired person may disaffirm any contract made under the influence of that mental impairment.

The incompetent person must return all consideration received. Another way to say this is to note that the mentally impaired individual person must restore the other party to the same position that he or she was in before the contract was entered. This is true especially when the other party had no knowledge of the person's mental impairment. If, on the other hand, the other party knew about the person's mental impairment and took advantage of that knowledge, there is no requirement to return the other party to the identical place that he or she was in before the original agreement was established.

A second rule is also recognized by the Restatement of Contracts and by some states. That rule says that a person's contractual obligations may be voidable if that person suffers from a mental impairment that prevents him or her from acting in a reasonable manner. This rule goes beyond the orthodox rule which requires that a person with an impairment be unable to comprehend the nature of the agreement. Under this version of the rule, a person may understand the nature of the contract but may, because of his or her impairment, be unable to stop himself or herself from entering the contract. In such a situation, as long as the contract has yet to be executed or, if executed, can be shown to be very unjust, the impaired person may void the contract. If the contract is executed or fair, the impaired party may still void the contract but must also return the other party to the place he or she was in before the contract was entered. If returning the other party to his or her precontract condition cannot be done, the court will decide on a fair alternative.

Persons Legally Insane

A person declared to be insane by competent legal authority is denied the right to enter contracts. Such persons will be under the care of a guardian who acts on behalf of the impaired person who has, in effect, become a ward of the court. Any contractual relationship with others results is nothing more than a void agreement. In most states, persons who knowingly take advantage of one declared insane are subject to criminal indictment and prosecution.

Persons Drugged or Intoxicated

A contract agreed to by someone under the influence of alcohol or drugs may be voidable. Incompetence related to either alcohol or drugs must be of such a degree that a contracting party would have lost the ability to comprehend or to be aware of obligations being accepted under the contract. A person who enters into a contract while in this condition may either affirm or disaffirm the agreement at a later time. Disaffirmance in such cases requires the return to the other party of all consideration that had been received. However, such a return may be refused when evidence indicates that the other party took advantage of the person's drunken or otherwise weakened condition.

Example 9-8

Fred Santos attended a private dinner party at the home of David Lampton, an antique collector who lived in suburban Poplar Heights. Unknown to Santos, the punch at the dinner party had been laced with alcohol. After drinking several glasses, Santos became highly intoxicated. While intoxicated, he entered into a contract in which he sold his antique silver set to Lampton. When Santos recovered, he sought to disaffirm the contract. Because his involuntary state of intoxication had robbed Santos of his ability to comprehend the contract he was making with Lampton, he would be allowed to get out of the agreement.

Quick Quiz 9-3 True or False?

1. In order for a contract to be voidable by a person with a mental impairment, the mental problem must exist at the time the contract was made.

2. A person declared to be insane by competent legal authority cannot be denied the right to enter contracts.

3. A contract made by a person who is intoxicated is completely void.

Summary

9-1   The fourth element essential to a legally effective contract is the legal ability to enter into a contractual relationship. This legal ability is known as capacity. Under the law there is a rebuttable presumption that anyone entering a contract has the legal capacity to do so. Since the presumption is a rebuttable, a party can attack it. Minors are allowed this privilege. Minority means that an individual has not yet attained the age of majority.

9-2   An exception to the rule about minors and contracts involves necessaries. Necessaries are those goods and services that are essential to a minor's health and welfare. Thus, necessaries can include clothing, food, shelter, medical and dental services, tools and equipment needed for the minor to carry out his or her business, and even, in some cases, educational expenses. By statute and court decision, certain other types of contracts have been excepted from the general rule that the contracts of minors are voidable at the minor's option. Different states have different rules in regard to these exceptions.

9-3   Contracts of persons who are mentally infirm or mentally ill, but not legally declared insane, may be valid or voidable, depending on the seriousness of the mental problem. Persons declared to be insane by competent legal authority are denied the right to enter into contracts, and contracts entered into may be declared void. Incompetence related to alcohol or drugs must be of such a degree that the contracting party has lost the ability to comprehend or to be aware of the obligations being accepted under the contract.

Key Terms

abandoned, 171	emancipated, 170	ratification, 175
affirmance, 175	majority, 170	rebuttable presumption, 169
capacity, 169	minority, 170	
disaffirm, 169	necessaries, 173	

Questions for Review and Discussion

1. What general presumption does the law make about a person's capacity to contract?
2. Why does the law allow minors to void contracts?
3. When does a person attain the age of majority?
4. How did Amendment 26 to the U.S. Constitution affect the age at which minors achieve majority?
5. What is the difference between emancipation and abandonment?
6. How do the states deal with minors who lie about their age when entering into contracts?
7. What is the legal liability of minors in relation to contracts for necessaries?
8. What are the other types of contracts that the law may except from the general rule that minors may void their contracts?
9. What is the legal effect of contracts made by persons who are mentally impaired?
10. What is the legal effect of contracts made by persons who are intoxicated or drugged?

Investigating the Internet

Access the Consumer Action and Information Center of Hawaii and write a report on the feature entitled "This Month's Issue."

Cases for Analysis

1. After she was married, Sherri Mitchell, a young woman of seventeen, was in an automobile accident in which she was hurt enough to require medical treatment. She was later approached by an insurance agent who offered her $2,500 as a settlement. All she had to do was sign a release that would absolve the insurance company of any complaint that she might have against it in regard to the accident. She agreed to accept the $2,500 and signed a release to that effect. However, she then changed her mind, and decided to void the agreement. She argued that since she was seventeen at the time that she signed the release, she was a minor and could, therefore, void the

contract. Is Mrs. Mitchell correct? Explain. *Mitchell v. State Farm Mutual Automobile Insurance Co.,* 963 S.W.2d (Ky. Ct. App.).

2. Jack Galloway was a construction worker. He was injured while working for Sunderland Construction. Subsequent to the accident, Galloway signed an agreement with his employer that granted Galloway compensation in exchange for his promise not to sue. Galloway is now trying to have the agreement voided. Evidence introduced proved that Galloway had an IQ of sixty-five and that he dropped out of school at age thirteen. When he dropped out of school, he was in the eighth grade but was doing less than sixth-grade-level work. Will Galloway's condition necessarily invalidate the contract? Explain.

3. Ken Olsen, who was seventeen, and had a part-time job, was in the market for a new computer system. He found a new Macintosh system for $2,900 at Macrotex, Inc. Beth Skidmore, an authorized sales representative for Macrotex, negotiated the deal with Olsen, knowing that he was only seventeen. Olsen paid $900 down and agreed to pay the balance over the next five years. Five days after he had purchased the computer system, Sarah Laurel, the owner of Macrotex, learned that Skidmore had sold the system to a minor. She told Skidmore to get the computer back and to cancel the deal. Skidmore called Olsen and told him that she needed to have the computer back. She told Olsen that since he was a minor she and Macrotex had the right to void the contract. Was Skidmore legally correct in this statement? What capacity, if any, does a minor have when entering a contract?

4. Anne Graham and Ted McCaslin entered into a contract which obligated Graham to sell her CD player to McCaslin. At the time, Graham was only seventeen. Graham turns the CD player over to McCaslin and receives $450 from him in return as agreed. Two weeks later Graham learns that McCaslin resold the CD player to Vaughn Winston for $550. Graham elects to rescind her contract with McCaslin and demands that Winston return the CD player to her. Will Winston be obligated to honor Graham's rescission demand? Explain.

5. Sperry Ford sold a car to Bowling when Bowling was only sixteen years old. Once Bowling had paid the full purchase price in cash, Sperry turned over the car and the certificate of title. After driving the car for only a week, Bowling discovered that the main bearing was burned out. When Bowling found out that repair costs would almost equal the price he'd paid for the car, he left the car on Sperry's lot and asked for his money back. Sperry Ford refused to give Bowling his money. Was Sperry justified in this refusal? Explain. *Bowling vs. Sperry,* 184 N.E.2d 901 (IN).

6. Quality Motors, Inc., refused to sell a car to Hays because he was only sixteen years old. However, Quality told Hays that they would sell the car to an adult and then show Hays how to transfer the title to his name. Hays agreed with the scheme and came back with a friend who was twenty-three. Quality sold the car to Hays's friend. Quality then gave Hays the name of a notary public who would transfer the title to Hays. After the transfer was accomplished, Hays's father found out about the deal and tried to get Quality Motors to take the car back. Quality replied that the car had been sold to an adult, so Hays could not disaffirm the contract. Is Quality correct? Explain. *Quality Motors v. Hays,* 225 S.W.2d 326 (AR).

7. The Bundy family entered a contract with Dalton to add vinyl siding to their house. Dalton assumed that the house belonged to the parents but later found out that it belonged to their daughter who was a minor. Dalton argued that the siding was a necessary and that the daughter should, therefore, be liable to him for its reasonable value. Was the vinyl siding a necessary? Explain. *Dalton v. Bundy,* 666 S.W.2d 443 (MO).

8. Lonchyna enlisted in the U.S. Air Force while he was still a minor. Three times he applied for and received educational delays that put off the beginning of his tour of duty. The last time, he claimed he could void the contract, since he'd entered into it when he was a minor. Was Lonchyna correct? Explain. *Lonchyna v. Brown, Secretary of Defense,* 491 F. Supp. 1352 (N.D. IL).

9. Darwin Kruse was a construction worker. He was injured while working for the Coos Head Timber Company. Subsequent to the accident, Kruse signed an agreement with his employer that granted Kruse compensation in exchange for his promise not to sue. Kruse is now trying to have the agreement voided. Evidence introduced proved that Kruse had an IQ of 83 and that he dropped out of school at age eighteen. When he dropped out of school, he was in the eighth grade but was doing less than sixth-grade-level work. Will Kruse's "slowness" necessarily invalidate the contract? Explain. *Kruse v. Coos Head Timber Co.,* 432 P.2d 1009 (OR).

10. Krasner shared office space with Berk for many years. Periodically, they renegotiated a contract that stipulated how rental payments would be divided between them. Before the most recent agreement was renegotiated, Krasner discovered that Berk was suffering from a serious case of senility that made him incapable of fully understanding the agreement. Nevertheless, Krasner negotiated with Berk, and they entered into the new contract. Sixty days later, Berk was forced to give up his business because of his mental problems. Berk then attempted to get out of the rental agreement based on his mental capacity. Would Berk succeed? *Krasner v. Berk,* 319 N.E.2d 897 (MA).

Quick Quiz Answers

9-1	9-2	9-3
1. T	1. T	1. T
2. F	2. T	2. F
3. F	3. F	3. F

Chapter 10 Consideration

The Opening Case
"Home Is Where the Perks Are"

When most people hear about the executive "perks" that are bestowed upon CEOs and other major officers of big-name corporations, they generally think that such spending is wasteful and extravagant. Recent research, however, seems to indicate that such impressions may be mistaken. The research, which was conducted by the International Monetary Fund (IMF) and the Wharton School, indicates that executive perks often make the high-ranking corporate officers more efficient, more productive, and more effective. Moreover, and perhaps more to the point, this high productivity on the part of major executives often translates into a higher success rate for the entire corporation. For instance, the IMF-Wharton study showed that providing a company jet for the CEO of a company which is headquartered in a rural area far from a major airport can make that CEO more productive by saving him or her an enormous amount of time traveling to and from distant airports. Similarly, providing a chauffeur service for a CEO in a big city area can help make that CEO more productive by transforming commute time into work time. If the IMF-Wharton study proves to be true, would it be advisable for companies to automatically include such "perks" in their executive compensation packages? Would this type of extra consideration be appropriate in every situation or should such packages be negotiated on a case-by-case basis? What would happen if an executive were promised an executive perk and then did not receive it? Would there be any legal basis for demanding that the promised "perk" be granted? Could a CEO make valid consideration of a promise to continue doing his or her present job in exchange for an additional set of executive perks? Questions like these involve the element of consideration, which is the subject of this chapter.

Chapter Outcomes

1. Explain the term consideration.
2. Describe the different types of detriment.
3. Identify the characteristics necessary for valid consideration.
4. Define the term unconscionable.
5. Explain whether a promise not to sue can be consideration.
6. Explain how a charitable pledge can be consideration.

7. Outline the procedure that a debtor and creditor may use to settle a claim by means of accord and satisfaction.
8. Identify those agreements which may be enforceable by a court of law even though they lack consideration.
9. Explain the doctrine of promissory estoppel.
10. Relate those agreements which, on the surface, appear to have consideration, but which the courts refuse to enforce.

Citation for Opening Case: Mehring, James. "An Unfair Rap for Perks? Two Researchers Insist They're Not All Bad." *Business-Week,* June 7, 2004, p. 32.

10-1 Requirements of Consideration

In the last three chapters, we have discussed four of the six elements of a contract: offer, acceptance, mutual assent, and capacity. A fifth element essential to any valid contract is the mutual promise to exchange benefits and sacrifices between the parties. This promise to exchange things of value is called **consideration.** It is the thing of value promised to the other party in exchange for something else of value promised by that other party. It is this promise to exchange valued items or services that binds the parties together. If an agreement has no consideration, it is not a binding contract. For example, a promise to give someone a birthday present is not a contract. Instead, it is a promise to make a gift because the giver receives nothing in exchange for the birthday present.

The Nature of Consideration

Consideration consists of a mutual exchange of gains and losses between contracting parties. In the exchange, what is a gain by the offeree is, at the same time, a loss to the offeror. Likewise, the gain bargained for by the offeror will finally result in a loss or a sacrifice by the offeree. The legal term used to designate the gain that each party experiences is that party's legal benefit. Similarly, the legal term used to describe the sacrifice that each party must experience is that party's legal **detriment.** A legal detriment can be any of the following: (1) doing something (or promising to do something) that one has a legal right not to do; (2) giving up something (or promising to give up something) that one has a legal right to keep; and (3) refraining from doing something (or promising not to do something) that one has a legal right to do. This last type of detriment is known as **forbearance.**

> ## Example 10-1
>
> Raymond Couch, a salesperson for the Taylor Hardware Distribution Company, was chosen to be a contestant on a new reality show called *The Ultimate Scare Game.* Couch has planned to spend his four-week vacation on the show. Couch is, perhaps, the most effective salesperson on the sales force at Taylor. Consequently, Audrey Taylor, the CEO of Taylor Hardware, offered to pay Couch a bonus of $25,000 for not appearing on the reality show, because to do so would put him at great risk. Couch agreed and gave up his place on the television program. Taylor would be legally bound to give Couch the $25,000. Since Couch had the legal right to go on the program, his sacrifice in giving up that opportunity is valid consideration. This is known as forbearance.

Note in the previous example that the act of giving up the *Scare Game* appearance may be highly beneficial to Couch's health and physical well-being because he will not be subjected to the tricks, antics, and pranks that are the mainstay of the show. However, the fact

Terms Another legal term for *consideration* is *quid pro quo,* which is Latin for "something in return for something."

Background Information Medieval English lawyers invented the verbs *agreare* and *barganizare* to describe the action of a contract, which previously had been described by the words *covenant* and *contract.* As the actions of contracts became more complex, however, these words lost their ability to describe contracts adequately and were replaced by the more common word *assumptio,* which means *undertaking.* The action of *assumpsit* was defined as "mutual agreement between the parties for a thing to be performed by the defendant in consideration of some benefit which must depart from or of some labor or prejudice which must be sustained by the plaintiff." It wasn't until the 1600s that the word *contract* regained widespread usage, taking on a broader, more useful definition.

Teaching Tips Point out to students that a binding contract involves each party in suffering a detriment and each in receiving a benefit. If you offer to sell your watch to a student for $25, you are promising to give up your legal right to keep your watch (your detriment) in exchange for the student's legal right to keep the $25 (the student's detriment). Your benefit is the promise of the money; the student's benefit is the promise of the watch.

that it is medically and physically beneficial does not change the fact that the sacrifice is a legal detriment since Couch has every right to appear on the show. The fact that each party has received a benefit and suffered a detriment means that the consideration has legal value.

The Characteristics of Consideration

Consideration has three characteristics: (1) The agreement must involve a bargained-for exchange; (2) the contract must involve adequate consideration; (3) the benefits and detriments promised must themselves be legal.

Bargained-for Exchange The law will not enforce an agreement that has not been bargained for. An agreement involves a **bargained-for exchange** when (1) a promise is made in exchange for another promise, (2) a promise is made in exchange for an act, or (3) a promise is made for forbearance of an act. The concept of bargaining means that each party will be hurt in some way if the other party fails to keep a promise. Conversely, each party gains something when the promises are kept and the exchange is made.

Example 10-2

Joanne Curtis agreed to loan Leo Fletcher her laptop so that Fletcher could give a PowerPoint presentation to a seminar of fifteen students. There was no understanding that Fletcher would pay for the use of the laptop. Curtis then refused to allow Flectcher to use the miniature computer. Although Curtis might have an ethical duty to lend Fletcher the laptop, their agreement was not an enforceable one in that it contained no bargained-for promise.

Adequacy of Consideration The fact that a contract has legal value is not the same as saying that it has adequate consideration. However, there are no specific requirements, other than being legal, concerning what one party may promise the other party in return for a pledge to deliver goods and services. The promise itself is adequate consideration when it represents something of value. Thus, the promise to assist another to repair an automobile would be something of value promised. The value placed on goods and services need not be street or market value. It is important only that the parties freely agreed on the value and the price. In general, the courts do not look into the adequacy of consideration; that is, they do not look to see whether the value of the consideration was fair to both parties. As we've seen this is because, in the wake of the Industrial Revolution, the courts no longer look to see if the things exchanged in a contract are of equal value. Courts let people make their own agreements, placing their own values on the goods or services exchanged. The court then enforces those agreements.

There are, however, exceptions to this general rule. In one exception, the courts will give a party relief when the consideration is so outrageous that it shocks the conscience of the court. A court may refuse to enforce a contract or any clause of a contract if it considers the contract or clause to be **unconscionable;** that is, where the consideration is so ridiculously inadequate that it shocks the court's conscience. This usually happens when there is a great inequality in bargaining power between the two

parties. In very specific matters, usually related to taxes, some states have adopted statutes dealing with adequacy. In general, though, courts remain reluctant to disturb the promises made by parties to an enforceable contract.

Legality of Consideration Consideration requires that the benefits and sacrifices promised between the parties be legal. Absence of legality renders the consideration invalid. Thus, a party cannot agree to do something that he or she does not have the legal right to do. Similarly, a party cannot promise not to do something which he or she has no legal right to do. Also, a party cannot make valid consideration out of a promise to stop doing something that was illegal to do in the first place.

Quick Quiz 10-1 True or False?

1. The fact that each party has received a benefit and suffered a detriment means that the consideration has legal value.

2. The legal term used to designate the gain that each party experiences is referred to as the party's legal benefit.

3. Consideration does not require that the benefits and sacrifices promised between the parties be legal.

10-2 Types of Consideration

Generally, consideration takes the form of money, property, or services. In certain special kinds of agreements and promises, however, the benefits and sacrifices are in some manner unique, and not immediately obvious to the casual observer. Significant among these agreements are promises not to sue and charitable pledges.

Money as Consideration

Money is the usual consideration offered by parties seeking another's promise or performance. The parties are free to negotiate privately the amount of money to be paid except when price structures have been established through administrative rulings or legislation. Historically, fuel, oil, natural gas, and other goods have been the subject of price controls. Rent controls in certain urban areas also limit the amount that landlords can charge. Generally, such controls prevent landlords from raising the rent above a maximum amount that has been established by law. Likewise, employers engaged in interstate commerce may not bargain with qualified employees for a wage rate less than that guaranteed by the federal Fair Labor Standards Act. This amount is referred to as the minimum wage.

Property and Services as Consideration

Before money was accepted as a medium of exchange, consideration consisted of property and services. In modern times, especially during recessionary or inflationary cycles, parties have sometimes found it more beneficial to enter into barter agreements than to base their promises on cash payments. The courts have held that barter agreements do contain valid consideration. For example, the exchange of services in return for the use of another's car or a promise to trade a watch for a typewriter represent benefits and sacrifices that constitute valid consideration to support a legally binding contract.

Pledges to charities for specific projects are enforceable contracts when the project begins.

Background Information In early America, contract law was less enforced and more flexible than land law or civil procedure. Consideration was regarded as an element that was not to be measured by the court. For purposes of the law of contract, the price determined by the parties was proof of the market value. In actual practice, however, judges were often sympathetic to the underdog in contract cases in which the uneducated or naive were manipulated by those who were more shrewd. As a result, rules of consideration were often bent.

Promises Not to Sue

A promise not to sue, when there is the right, or at least the apparent right, to sue, is enforceable when it is supported by consideration. Promising not to sue is a forbearance. A promise not to sue, in exchange for an amount of money is a customary way to settle or prevent a pending lawsuit. Settlements of this type are preferred to expensive and time-consuming litigation. Such settlements are also better than submitting a claim to alternate dispute resolution procedures, such as arbitration or mediation.

Example 10-3

Patrick Sullivan was injured in midtown Manhattan during a confrontation between the NYPD and a trio of bank robbers who were attempting to escape after robbing a midtown branch of Chemical Bank. Sullivan discussed his legal rights with an attorney who suggested that he might receive compensation from the NYPD if he brought suit against the city. When faced with the suit, the NYPD elected to offer Sullivan $250,000 if he would agree not to bring suit against the city. Sullivan agreed to these terms. The "thing of value" that Sullivan transferred to the city was his right to bring a lawsuit. A court would uphold this agreement on the basis of the promise between the parties.

Acceptance of an agreement not to sue, supported by consideration, terminates one's right to continue any lawsuit, presently or in the future, on grounds described in the agreement. A promise not to sue is commonly called a **release.** Agreements of this kind are usually negotiated and agreed upon before a suit is even filed. However, occasionally they are negotiated between attorneys after a lawsuit has been filed and sometimes even after a trial has begun. In such an event, the settlement is arranged in cooperation with the court and presiding judge. Interestingly enough, some states will uphold a promise not to sue, which is exchanged for consideration even if circumstances later indicate that the party granting the release really did not have the right to sue in the first place, as long as at the time of the agreement the exchange is made in good faith and fraud is not involved.

Charitable Pledges

Under traditional rules, charitable pledges are not enforceable as contractual obligations because they are not supported by consideration. The dependence of charitable institutions and nonprofit organizations upon the solicitation of contributions has encouraged the courts to enforce charitable pledges as though they were contractual obligations. Basically, there are three ways that the court's can seek to uphold charitable pledges. The first way involves actual consideration. This occurs when charitable contributions are made on the condition that the promisor be remembered for the gift by having his or her name inscribed in some way on a memorial associated with the project. Some courts see this promise to install a memorial to the pledgor as consideration.

A more contemporary approach is to use either promissory estoppel or public policy to support the claim. Promissory estoppel (see page 193) involves the detrimental reliance on a promise made by another party. If in reliance on a pledge or a series of pledges, a charity goes forward with a project, such as building an addition to the church hall or adding a wing to the synagogue, the courts will see the commencement of the project as evidence that the charity relied on the promises, and will stop the promisors from denying the effects of the promise. At times pledges are used for the general operation and maintenance of a charitable or nonprofit organization, rather than for a specific project.

When there is no promise to carry out a specific project, the courts have held that each pledge made is supported by the pledges of all others who have made similar pledges. This concept of consideration is used in support of all promises of money for undefined causes. The ultimate argument in this situation is that it would violate public policy to allow one pledgor to get away with denying his or her pledge when the other promisors relied on each other in making their individual pledges.

Quick Quiz 10-2 True or False?

1. Rent controls that limit the amount that landlords can charge tenants are unconstitutional.

2. If a party promises not to sue another party, and it is later discovered that the first party never really had the right to sue, the original promise not to sue is invalid in every state, and the consideration must be returned.

3. Even though charities depend on the solicitation of contributions, the courts have refused to enforce charitable pledges.

10-3 Problems with Consideration

Problems sometimes arise when the consideration involved in a contract is money and the parties disagree as to the amount of money that the debtor owes the creditor. How such problems are resolved depends upon whether the transaction involves a genuine dispute as to the amount owed. One way such disputes can be settled is by an agreement known as accord and satisfaction.

Disputed Amounts

A **disputed amount** is one on which the parties never reached mutual agreement. It may be difficult, at first, to see how the amount due under a contract can end up as the focal point of a dispute, until we recall that the law permits a certain degree of incompleteness in the final terms of an agreement, provided there is a way to settle on the eventual amount owed. For instance, when a contractor is hired to do work on a home or when an accountant is retained to figure out a client's taxes, the final amount owed is never laid out in absolute terms. Instead, the custom is to settle on an amount per hour, to estimate the number of hours that will be spent on the job, and then to settle on the final amount once the job is finished.

If a creditor accepts as full payment an amount that is less than the amount due, then the dispute has been settled by an **accord and satisfaction. Accord** is the implied or expressed acceptance of less than what has been billed the debtor. **Satisfaction** is the agreed-to settlement as contained in the accord. Only if the dispute is honest, made in good faith, and not superficial or trivial will the courts entertain arguments based on accord and satisfaction.

Getting Students Involved Ask students to compare the bargaining practices involved in accord and satisfaction to plea-bargaining in criminal cases.

State Variations In Alabama and California, an *accord* is an agreement to accept, in extinction of an obligation, something different from, or less than, that to which the person agreeing to accept is entitled.

State Variations California defines a *satisfaction* as acceptance, by the creditor, of the consideration of an accord which extinguishes the original obligation.

Example 10-4

Arthur C. Lewis hired C. S. Clarke to figure out his income tax for last year. During the initial consultation with Lewis, Clarke told him that his rate was $250 per hour. Clarke also estimated that the job appeared to be one that might take ten to twenty hours of intensive work. (The fact that Lewis turned all of his records over to Clarke in a shoe box, may have had something to do with this relatively high estimate, even though Clarke used a software package to do all his clients' returns.) When Clarke completed the work, he sent a bill to Lewis for twenty hours of work at $250 per hour for a total of $5,000. The number of hours included a five-hour seminar that Lewis took at the local college. When questioned about this, Clarke said that he had attended the seminar to learn how to deal with a problem that had cropped up in Lewis's return in relation to Lewis's limited liability company. Lewis did not believe that he should be charged with the time that Clarke spent at the seminar. Consequently, he deducted $1,250 from the bill and sent Clarke a check for $3,750. Lewis wrote the following notation on the check: "In full payment for all services involved in making out my tax return for last year." Clarke cashed the check and later sued Lewis's company in small claims court for the $1,250 balance. Clarke would not succeed in this lawsuit because he had already accepted a lesser amount, which had been offered by Lewis in good faith, in full payment of the amount in dispute.

Undisputed Amounts

Getting Students Involved Students may be aware that threats of costly lawsuits have changed the way many people do business in today's society. Involve students in a debate about the extent to which lawsuits protect businesses and the general public. Challenge them to predict how a forbearance, such as a promise not to sue, could affect various types of contracts.

An **undisputed amount** is one on which the parties have mutually agreed. Although a party may have second thoughts about the amount promised for goods or services rendered, the amount that was agreed to by the parties when they made their contract remains an undisputed amount. A part payment in lieu of full payment when accepted by a creditor will not cancel an undisputed debt.

Example 10-5

Bernice Stewart had new gutters and downspouts placed on her home, agreeing to pay the Hofstadter Home Improvement Company $2,625 for the parts and the labor charge for installation. A week later, before paying the $2,625, Stewart saw the same gutters and downspouts at the Port Clinton Home and Garden Show. She talked to the representative at the show who told her he would have been able to sell her the gutters and downspouts and have them installed for only $2,125. Stewart sent a check to Hofstadter for $2,125 with the notation "In full payment for the gutters and downspouts applied to my home." Hofstadter deposited the check and demanded payment of the balance of $500. Stewart would still be obligated to pay that balance.

In this situation, there was no good faith dispute over what Stewart owed to Hofstadter for the gutters, the downspouts, and their installation. The buyer was simply trying to get the work done at the lower price that was quoted to her by the other installation company. The sum of $2,625 was an undisputed amount, and the balance of $500 is still owed to Hofstadter.

Quick Quiz 10-3 True or False?

1. A disputed amount is one on which the parties never reached mutual agreement.

2. If a creditor accepts as full payment an amount that is less than the amount due, then the dispute has been settled by promissory estoppel.

3. An undisputed amount is one on which the parties have mutually agreed.

10-4 Agreements Without Consideration

As a general rule, an agreement without consideration will not be an enforceable contract. This is true because consideration is so important as the binding element within a contractual relationship. Nevertheless, some states eliminate the requirement of consideration in specific types of agreements. In contrast, there are certain promises which the courts always refuse to enforce because they lack even the rudimentary qualities of valid consideration, even though on the surface they may appear to offer that much-needed element.

Enforceable Agreements

As noted above, some states have chosen to eliminate the element of consideration in a few specifically named contracts. Unfortunately, as is frequently the case in such matters, there is no uniformity among jurisdictions as to the types of agreements subject to such laws. Still, some typical agreements falling into this category include promises under seal, promises after discharge in bankruptcy, debts barred by the statute of limitations, promises enforced by promissory estoppel, and options governed by the UCC (see Table 10-1).

Teaching Tips Remind students that the law cannot enforce moral obligations. Personal ethics may motivate a debtor to reaffirm debts and renew obligations to creditors. However, the law does not require it and has taken the position that it is more unethical for creditors to pressure a debtor whose debts have legally been discharged through bankruptcy than it is for the debtor to be unable to pay back debts.

Table 10-1 Agreements Without Consideration

Agreement	Legal Status
Promises under seal	Enforceable in some states for contracts not involving goods; unenforceable under the UCC for contracts involving goods
Promises after discharge in bankruptcy	Enforceable in most states
Promise to pay debts barred by statute of limitations	Enforceable
Promises enforced by promissory estoppel	Enforceable only if offeror knew that offeree would rely on the promise and offeree places himself or herself in a different and difficult position as a result of that promise
Option	Enforceable under the UCC if made by a merchant, in writing, stating the time period over which the offer will remain open
Illusory promises	Unenforceable
Promise of a gift	Unenforceable
Past considerations	Unenforceable
Preexisting duties	Unenforceable as a consideration in a new contract

Business Law in the News
Borrowing 101

It's panic time for a lot of families whose students head to college next month. Maybe your job suddenly feels insecure or the money you saved for tuition lies buried in the stock market.

For a crying towel, call the experts at the college aid office. This time of year, they're handing out lists of fast-money sources as if they were hankies.

You don't necessarily need a loan. At most schools you can gain some breathing room by paying your bill in monthly installments rather than writing a single, fat check when each semester starts. No interest is charged. If you owe $10,000, you might arrange for 10 monthly payments of $1,000 each. Your paycheck gets squeezed (for college parents, what's new about that?), but it often beats borrowing. Tuition-payment plans are usually managed by outside firms, such as Academic Management Services in Swansea, Mass., and Tuition Management Systems in Newport, R.I.

If borrowing seems inevitable, there couldn't be a better time. Interest rates on college loans have fallen to historic lows. Some parents make a combo choice, says Maureen McCarthy Mello, senior vice president for Academic Management Services. You pay part of the bill through a monthly plan and borrow the rest in a low-cost supplemental loan.

So which loan? By now, students should have their basic, government-backed Stafford Loan in hand. Undergraduates can borrow $2,625 to $5,500 a year, depending on how far along they are in school. The interest rate on Staffords just dropped to an amazing 4.06 percent for those repaying now (rates change each July 1). Payments are deferred as long as you're in school.

Homeowners love home-equity loans. Currently, you'd pay about 5 percent on a variable loan or 7 percent for a fixed rate—all tax-deductible.

If that's not an option, consider the government-backed PLUS loan for parents. You can borrow up to the full cost of school minus any financial aid such as grants and government loans. There's a credit check, but you don't have to put up collateral or meet any income requirements. The government's current variable rate for a PLUS: just 4.86 percent, and a 3 percent upfront fee that's deducted from the loan proceeds. The loan-guarantee agencies may tack on 1 percent more.

Some schools offer PLUS loans directly; others refer you to independent lenders. Either way, you should get a provisional OK within 24 to 48 hours. Repayments begin 60 days after you borrow the money. Private lenders may vary the terms of the PLUS.

Questions for Analysis

1. When a student enters a contract with the college of his or her choice, what form of consideration does the college promise to pay to the student? Explain.

2. What form of consideration does the student promise to pay to the college? Explain.

3. Why would a college grant students a plan that allows them to pay on the installment plan with no interest? What possible benefit does the college receive from such a plan? Explain.

4. When the federal government gives homeowners a tax break on their home equity loans, can a bank which grants such a loan label that tax break as a form of consideration? Explain.

5. If a tuition payment plan is managed by an outside management firm, is the student's contract with the college or the outside firm? Explain.

UCC 2-203 (see page 871)

Promises Under Seal A **seal** is a mark or an impression placed on a written contract indicating that the instrument was executed and accepted in a formal manner. Today a seal is usually indicated by the addition of the word seal or the letters L.S. (*locus sigilli,* meaning "place of the seal") following a party's signature. Years ago contracts under seal required no consideration. Some states still honor a promise under seal, but most have abolished this concept especially in relation to sale of goods contracts. In fact, the UCC has eliminated the use of the seal in all sale of goods contracts. On the other hand, a few states still require the use of the seal in real property and certain other types of transactions. Since there is no uniformity in this regard, it is advisable to research and consult the requirements in your jurisdiction.

Promises After Discharge in Bankruptcy

Persons discharged from indebtedness through bankruptcy may reaffirm their obligations, prompted perhaps by moral compulsion. In the past, reaffirmation has been the subject of abuse by creditors who used pressure against those whose debts have been excused. In response to this, Congress passed a bankruptcy reform act that makes it more difficult for creditors to extract such promises. The bankruptcy court must now hold a hearing when a reaffirmation is intended, informing the debtor that reaffirmation is optional, not required, and of the legal consequences of reactivating a debt. It is also up to the court to approve such reaffirmations. In addition, reaffirmation promises can also be rescinded as long as the cancellation comes within 30 days of the date on which the promise became enforceable. State laws, in most cases, provide that no new consideration need be provided in support of reaffirmation. Most states require that a reaffirmation be supported by contractual intent. Some states require the new promise to be in writing. However, when there is no such provision, an oral promise or reaffirmation is usually sufficient.

Debts Barred by Statutes of Limitations

State laws known as **statutes of limitations** limit the time within which a party is allowed to bring suit. The time allowed for the collection of a debt varies from state to state, usually from three to ten years. Some states allow more time for collection when the document of indebtedness is under seal, as in the case of a promissory note containing the seal of the maker. Debtors may revive and reaffirm debts barred by the statutes of limitations without the necessity of new consideration. Affirmation will result from the part payment of the debt. When a debt is revived, the creditor again is permitted the full term, provided by the statute of limitations, to make collection. Some states require a written reaffirmation when a debt made unenforceable by the statute of limitations is reactivated. Consequently, it would be best to check the rule in your jurisdiction.

Promises Enforced by Promissory Estoppel

The doctrine of **estoppel** denies rights to complaining parties that are shown to be the cause of their own injury. **Promissory estoppel,** then, is the legal doctrine that restricts an offeror from revoking an offer, under certain conditions, even though consideration has not been promised to bind an agreement. To be effective, promissory estoppel requires that the offeror know, or be presumed to know, that the offeree might otherwise make a definite and decided change of position in contemplation

Example 10-6

Dale Radcliff was arrested for a crime she did not commit. Kevin Rueters, her supervisor at Yellowstone Enterprises, told her that he had to suspend her. However, he also told her that if she were later found not guilty and released, she would have her old job with the same seniority and pay grade that she had when she left. Two months later, the charges were dropped and Radcliff tried to get her job back. Rueters refused to let her return to work. It took Radcliff four months to secure suitable employment. In a suit brought by Radcliff against Yellowstone to recover the pay she lost during those four months, the court ruled in her favor. Yellowstone and Rueters were stopped from denying the promise they'd made to Radcliff despite the absence of consideration from her because she had relied on that promise and had not looked for other work while suspended.

Background Information Although the seal was highly regarded in early contract law as proof of consideration, few people in the United States owned a seal, and literacy was high enough to undercut the need for the device. Thus, state statutes were passed that limited the meaning of the seal. In 1836, New York passed a statute that stated a seal was only "presumptive evidence of a sufficient consideration" and its effect could be "rebutted in the same manner and to the same extent as if [the] instrument were not sealed." Even today, however, the seal takes the place of consideration in Massachusetts.

Terms When people say they are going to go after someone in court, meaning they are going to sue someone, they are correctly translating the word sue from its early Latin root word *sequi,* which means "to follow," or "to come or go after."

State Variations The statute of limitations for breach of a sales contract in North Carolina is four years. For liabilities arising from general contracts, the limit is three years. The statute of limitations for forfeiture of a mortgage is ten years.

Terms Estoppel is a legal way to stop someone from making a claim or denial when previous actions or words to the contrary have been made. The term *estoppel* comes from the French word *estopail,* which literally means "a stopper."

Related Cases Danby guaranteed that the Osteopathic Association would receive credit for bank loans totaling $55,000. The Association, a charity, was using the funds to build a hospital. After the hospital had used $31,000 of the credit available, Danby became dissatisfied with the construction of the hospital and attempted to withdraw his guarantee for the rest of the promised funds. In *Danby v. Osteopathic Hospital Association of Delaware* (104 A.2d 903), the court ruled that, based on the doctrine of promissory estoppel, the guarantee could not be withdrawn. The hospital relied on the promise—it might never have agreed to a loan contract knowing funding might be withdrawn at any point in the project.

UCC 2-205 (see page 871)

Getting Students Involved Direct pairs of students to create three proposals for contracts—two that are enforceable and one that is unenforceable because it contains an illusory promise. Remind them that an illusory promise of consideration is usually phrased in ambiguous terms or may seem to mean something that it does not. Each pair of students can challenge another pair to identify which of the three proposed contracts is the one with the illusory promise.

of promises contained in the offer. Courts, in reaching this doctrine, have accepted the principles of justice and fairness in protecting the offeree from otherwise unrecoverable losses.

Although Yellowstone had received no consideration supporting the promise to hold open Radcliff's job for her while she was suspended, Radcliff had accepted the promise and had placed herself in a very different and difficult position through her reliance upon the promise. Had Yellowstone not made such a promise, Radcliff would no doubt have looked for another job after Yellowstone had suspended her.

Option An **option** is the giving of consideration to support an offeror's promise to hold open an offer for a stated or a reasonable length of time. The UCC has made an exception to the rule requiring consideration when the offer is made by a merchant. In such cases, an offer in writing by a merchant, stating the time period over which the offer will remain open, is enforceable without consideration. The offer, which is called a **firm offer,** or an **irrevocable offer,** must be signed by the offeror, and the time allowed for acceptance may not exceed three months. When the time allowed is more than three months, firm offers by merchants must be supported by consideration to be enforceable.

Unenforceable Agreements

The promises just described are exceptions to the general rule that consideration must support a valid contract. The exceptions are allowed by state statute or because the courts, in the interest of fairness or justice, find it inappropriate to require consideration. There are certain promises, however, which the courts will not enforce because they lack even the rudimentary qualities of valid consideration. Included in this category are promises based on preexisting duties, promises based on past consideration, illusory promises, and promises of future gifts and legacies.

Preexisting Duties A promise to do something that one is already obligated to do by law or by some other promise or agreement cannot be made consideration in a new contract. Such obligations are called **preexisting duties.**

The same rule of consideration applies to police officers, firefighters, and other public servants and officials who may pledge what appears to be some special service in exchange

The Opening Case Revisited
"Home Is Where the Perks Are"

Recall that, in The Opening Case at the beginning of this chapter, we learned that a study done by the International Monetary Fund (IMF) and the Wharton School indicated that executive perks often make corporate executives more proficient, more prolific, and more productive. In addition, the study also revealed that this high level of proficiency on the part of major corporate officers often results in a higher achievement rate for the whole company. Should the IMF-Wharton project be verified by subsequent studies, it might become more common for high-ranking corporate officers to negotiate more extensive perk packages. However, under the doctrine of preexisting duties, it would *not* be appropriate for a corporate executive, who is already on the job, to negotiate a new set of perks if he or she did not promise to assume some additional or different duties in exchange for those new perks. This is because, under the doctrine of preexisting duties, a party cannot make a set of preexisting duties consideration in a new contract.

for a monetary reward, when all they have actually promised is to execute the duties they are already obligated to perform. Suppose, for instance, that the local fire chief, in exchange for a monetary reward, promises an apartment owner that he or she will provide protection should a fire break out in the owner's building. Neither the fire chief nor the apartment owner could enforce such an agreement in court. The promise is based on the chief's empty guarantee to do what is already his or her job.

Past Consideration   A promise to give another something of value in return for goods or services rendered and delivered in the past, without expectation or reward, is **past consideration.** Only when goods or services are provided as the result of bargained-for present or future promises is an agreement enforceable.

Example 10-7

Gale Hansen wanted to have her hair dyed before her college graduation party, but could not afford to pay the $120 fee that was expected by the local hair dresser. Without any mention of payment, her friend Marianne Everett helped Hansen dye her hair. After seeing what a good job Everett did on her hair, Hansen told Everett that she'd give him $35 for helping her color her hair. Hansen's promise to Everett is not enforceable because Everett has already completed the work. Her consideration is, therefore, in the past.

Illusory Promises   An **illusory promise** is one that seems to be genuine but which on close examination, actually fails to obligate the promissor to do anything. A party who makes an illusory promise is the only one with any right to determine whether the other party will be benefited in any way. Illusory promises fail to provide the mutuality of promises required in establishing consideration.

Example 10-8

Pemberton Grocery agreed to buy such fruits and vegetables as it "might desire" for one summer season from Enchanted Farms, Inc. In return for this promise, Enchanted negotiated terms whereby it would give Pemberton a special schedule of discounts for the fruits and vegetables. The promise to buy as much as it "might desire" had actually obligated Pemberton to do nothing. Its promise was illusory because Pemberton might desire absolutely no fruits and vegetables and still keep its promise. The benefits that Pemberton was to derive from the schedule of discounts were not supported by a real or enforceable promise on Pemberton's part. A suit brought by either party to enforce this agreement would fail for want of consideration.

Future Gifts and Legacies   The promise of a gift to be given at some future time or in a will is not enforceable if no consideration is given for the promise. Included here are promises to provide gratuitous services or to lend one's property without expectation of any benefits in return.

Related Cases   A Porsche owner was experiencing problems with the automobile's clutch system, so he took the car in to be repaired. The new maintenance included a six-month warranty. When the Porsche owner soon after experienced the same problems, he took the car back to the shop, where he was promised the repair would be covered by the warranty. However, the repair shop later refused to pay for the repairs, asserting that the repair was due to driver abuse. The court ruled that the promise to repair was not supported by any new consideration and therefore did not constitute an enforceable contract. *Schupak v. Porsche Audi Manhattan,* 541 N.Y.S.2d 412 (NY).

A Question of Ethics

In Example 10-7, legally Hansen does not have to pay Everett a single penny, despite her promise to do so. However, is she ethically bound to keep her pledge and deliver to Everett the $35 that she promised to give her? Explain.

Quick Quiz 10-4 True or False?

1. An option is the giving of consideration to support an offeror's promise to hold an offer open for a stated length of time.

2. Although illusory promises provide the mutuality of promises required in establishing consideration, the courts will not enforce them due to the doctrine of unconscionability.

3. The promise of a gift to be given at some future time or in a will is completely enforceable even if no consideration is given for the promise.

Summary

10-1 The fifth element necessary to any valid contract is consideration. Consideration is the mutual exchange or promise to exchange benefits and sacrifices between contracting parties. Consideration has three requirements: (1) promises made during bargaining are dependent on the consideration to be received; (2) the consideration must involve something of value; (3) the benefits and detriments promised must be legal.

10-2 Generally, consideration takes the form of money, property, or services. There are certain special kinds of agreements and promises where the benefits and sacrifices are unique. Among these are promises not to sue and charitable pledges.

10-3 Problems sometimes arise when the consideration involved in a contract is money and the parties do not agree on the amount of money owed. If there is a genuine dispute, a creditor can accept an amount as full payment even though it is less than the amount claimed. Once the creditor has accepted the lesser amount, the dispute is settled by an act of accord and satisfaction. If the dispute is not genuine, accord and satisfaction do not apply.

10-4 As a general rule, contracts are not enforceable without consideration. However, some states eliminate the need for consideration in some agreements. These agreements include promises bearing a seal, promises after discharge in bankruptcy, debts barred by the statute of limitations, promises enforced by promissory estoppel, and options governed by the UCC. There are other agreements that seem to involve consideration but which the courts will not enforce. These agreements involve preexisting duties, past consideration, illusory promises, and gifts.

Key Terms

accord, 189

accord and satisfaction, 189

bargained-for exchange, 186

consideration, 185

detriment, 185

disputed amount, 189

estoppel, 193

firm offer, 194

forbearance, 185

Questions for Review and Discussion

1. What is consideration?
2. What are the different types of detriment?
3. What characteristics are necessary for consideration to be valid?
4. What is meant by the term unconscionable?
5. Can a promise not to sue be consideration?
6. How can a charitable pledge be consideration?
7. What is the procedure that a debtor and creditor may use to settle a claim by means of accord and satisfaction?
8. What agreements may be enforceable by a court of law even though they lack consideration?
9. What is the doctrine of promissory estoppel?
10. What agreements appear to have consideration but will not be enforced by the courts?

Investigating the Internet

Sources of information about contract law can be accessed from Contract Law from the WWW Virtual Law Library. As a research assignment, access this website and report those sources of information that might concern consideration.

Cases for Analysis

1. Aviation Electronics entered a contract with Sky Train Institute of Montana in which Aviation agreed to supply the institute with 17,000 component parts for the development of the institute's remote control bomber. The bomber had to be operational by December 3, otherwise the institute would lose a research grant from the Department of Defense. After delivering 5,000 of the parts, Aviation told Sky Train that it wanted an additional 4 million dollars beyond the original price agreed upon to deliver the remaining parts. Sky Train attempted to obtain the parts from other firms, none of which could fill the order in the time limit required by the DOD contract specifications. In order to make the deadline stipulated in the government contract, Sky Train reluctantly agreed to the new price demanded by Aviation. What "thing of value," if any, has Aviation transferred to the institute that it did not already owe the institute under the original contract? Explain.

2. Savaretti offered to pay his niece, Wilma, $2,000 if she would agree to give up eating meat and pastries and drinking caffeinated beverages for six months. Wilma agreed and gave up these activities for six months. At the end of those six months, Savaretti refused to give Wilma the $2,000 arguing that, since giving up caffeine, meat, and pastries were beneficial to her health, she suffered no detriment and was owed nothing. Wilma takes Savaretti to small claims court and demands payment of the $2,000. She argues that, since she had the legal right to consume the caffeine, meat, and pastries,

she suffered a legal detriment and was entitled to her money. How should the referee rule in this case? Explain.

3. Daniel Davidson told Velma Evans that he would hire her to work on an architectural job. He gave her a date to show up for work and told her to leave her present job. Relying on Davidson's statements, Evans left her job. Davidson never did let Evans begin work, and as a result, she was out of work for six months. Evans sued Davidson for the wages she lost during those six months. Davidson argued that since they'd never decided on the final terms of employment, no contract ever existed between the two of them. Evans argued that the principle of promissory estoppel should apply here. Is Evans correct? Explain.

4. Mers was arrested and charged with a felony. Dispatch Printing, his employer, told him that he had to be suspended. However, Mers was also told that he could return to work if the case against him was resolved in his favor. Relying on this promise, Mers did not seek other employment. The case ended in a hung jury and Mers reported back to work. Dispatch Printing, however, refused to let him work or to pay him any back pay. In a suit against Dispatch Printing, what legal argument might Mers use to compel Dispatch Printing to pay him for any losses due to his reliance on the promise to let him return to work when the case was ended in his favor? Explain. *Mers v. Dispatch Printing,* 483 N.E.2d 150 (OH).

5. The Mighty Fine Food Emporium agreed to buy such fruits and vegetables as it "might desire" for one summer season from Kennelsworth Farms and Vineyards. In return for this promise, Kennelsworth negotiated terms whereby it would give Mighty Fine a special schedule of discounts for the fruits and vegetables. Did the promise to buy as much as it "might desire" obligate Kennelsworth in any way? Are the benefits that Kennelsworth was to derive from the schedule of discounts supported by an enforceable promise on Kennelsworth's part? Would a suit brought by either party to enforce this agreement succeed? Explain each answer.

6. Graham O'Hanlon, without any mention of payment, helped his friend, Patricia Tippon, move from Westerville to Pepper Pike. The entire move took 48 hours to complete. At the end of the day, after she was in her new house, Tippon told O'Hanlon that she'd give him $200 for helping her move. Is Tippon's promise to O'Hanlon enforceable? Why or why not?

7. Vanoni Biological Supplies, Inc., contracted with the Hayden Institute to supply the Institute with 24,000 biological specimens for a series of experiments that the Institute has agreed to perform for the Maritime University of Columbia. The Institute must have the specimens by September 9 to meet the University's schedule. After delivering 12,000 of the specimens parts, Vanoni told the Institute that it wanted an additional $1,600 to deliver the remaining 12,000 specimens. Can Vanoni make the delivery of the remaining 12,000 specimens consideration in a new agreement with the Institute? Explain.

8. Seier agreed to pay $10,000 to Peek in exchange for all the stock in a corporation. The agreement was placed in writing. Nevertheless, when the time came for payment, Seier refused to live up to his end of the deal. His argument was that the stock was not worth the $10,000 that he had agreed to pay for it. Did the court listen to Seier's argument and attempt to determine the value of the consideration? Explain. *Seier v. Peek,* 456 So.2d 1079 (AL).

9. N. B. West Contracting Co., Inc., agreed to repave Koedding's parking lot. When the repaving work was done, Koedding was unsatisfied with the quality of the work. Consequently, he informed West of his intention to bring suit. West told Koedding that the lot would be resealed and that the job would be guaranteed for two years if Koedding agreed not to pursue the lawsuit, which had already commenced. Koedding agreed. After the repaving was completed a second time, Koedding was still not satisfied. Would the agreement not to sue operate to stop Koedding's lawsuit? Explain. *Koedding v. N. B. West Contracting Co., Inc.,* 596 S.W.2d 744 (MO).

10. Evans used his credit card to run up a $98.75 bill with the Rosen Department Store. When Rosen tried to collect, Evans wrote a check for $79.00. He wrote on the check that he meant it to be "full payment of all accounts to date." Rosen cashed the check. When Rosen sued Evans for $19.75 balance, Evans argued that under accord and satisfaction, the fact that Rosen cashed the $79.00 check meant that they had accepted that amount as full payment. Was Evans correct? Explain.

11. Jill Anderson agreed to purchase William and Teresa Dawson's flower shop for $75,000. Anderson paid the Dawsons $20,000 when the contract was signed. She also agreed to pay the balance of $55,000 at an interest rate of 8.5 percent

per year for five years. This meant that she would be making monthly installments of $1,128.41 to the Dawsons. During the negotiation stages of the contract, Anderson was told that all of the equipment in the store was in perfect condition. Moreover, the Dawsons told Anderson that she could expect a profit of $75,000 per year. Anderson discovered that the equipment needed extensive repair and that the financial condition of the business had been misrepresented so that she made considerably less than the $75,000 that the Dawsons had cited. Accordingly, Anderson sent a check to the Dawsons for $6,560.21. On the reverse side of the check she wrote, "Payment in full for University Flower Shop." This final check would mean that after making installment payments for more than a year and a half she had paid a total of $50,000 for the flower shop. In a letter that accompanied the check, Anderson indicated that, because she had been misled by the Dawsons on the condition of the equipment and the financial state of the business, the store had actually been worth only $50,000 at the time she purchased it. The Dawsons disagreed but negotiated the check and then brought suit against Anderson for breach of contract. Anderson argued that, when the Dawsons negotiated her check, the debt was discharged under accord and satisfaction. Is Anderson correct

here? Explain. *Dawson v. Anderson,* 698 N.E.2d 1014 (OH).

12. Tim W. Koerner and Associates, Inc., was a distributor for electrosurgical products for Aspen Labs, Inc. Zimmer U.S.A., Inc., purchased Aspen and replaced Aspen's distribution system with its own. Aspen remained in business as a subsidiary. Koerner sued Aspen and Zimmer, joined as defendants, trying to force them to honor a contract that Aspen and Zimmer had made compensating former Aspen dealers for their past efforts. Zimmer refused to honor the agreement. For whom did the court find and why? *Tim W. Koerner & Assocs., Inc. v. Aspen Labs, Inc.,* 492 F. Supp. 294 (S.W. TX).

13. Trisko purchased a loveseat from the Vignola Furniture Company. The loveseat arrived at Trisko's home in a damaged condition. Vignola agreed to repair the loveseat if Trisko agreed not to sue. Trisko agreed, but then later brought suit. Vignola argued that Trisko could not bring suit because he had promised not to sue them in exchange for the repair of the loveseat. Trisko argued that Vignola had a preexisting duty to deliver an undamaged loveseat. This preexisting duty could not, therefore, be consideration in a new agreement. Was Trisko correct? Explain. *Trisko v. Vignola Furniture Company,* 299 N.E.2d 421 (IL).

Quick Quiz Answers

10-1	10-2	10-3	10-4
1. T	1. F	1. T	1. T
2. T	2. F	2. F	2. F
3. T	3. F	3. T	3. F

Chapter 11 | Legality

The Opening Case
"Legal or Illegal? That Is the Question"

Everyone knows who Harry Potter is and how popular his books and movies have become over the last few years. What many people do not know, however, is that at least one version of the film *Harry Potter and the Sorcerer's Stone* exists, which does not present Harry and his friends in the same way that either his creator or the makers of his films intended. That version of the film, which is entitled *Wizard People, Dear Reader,* was developed by an Austin, Texas, comic book artist who simply added his own sound track to the original film. The new version of *The Sorcerer's Stone* is satiric, presenting Harry and his friends as less than sterling folks whose language and whose interpretation of the events in the film would not be endorsed by the "real" (reel?) Harry. Still, the new artistic version is a labor of love, not an attack on the character, and it has been featured at the New York Underground Film Festival. Moreover, the film has also been shown in a warehouse theater in Brooklyn to filmgoers for $7 each. Most people would see this satiric version of the film as falling within the fair use exception to the rules of copyright protection. Some people could argue, however, that this version of the film plus new sound track might be an infringement of the copyright held by Warner Brothers. If that is the case, then anyone who sold a ticket to the screening of *Wizard People, Dear Reader* might have been involved in an illegal contract. What would be the legal consequences, if any, of selling a ticket to this allegedly illegal screening? Chapter 11 on legality in contract law attempts to answer this and other questions.

Chapter Outcomes

1. State the effect of illegality on a contract.
2. Identify those contracts made illegal by statutory law.
3. Explain the rationale behind usury laws.
4. Identify those wagering agreements that may not be illegal under state law.
5. Explain the rules regarding licenses and illegality.
6. Describe when an agreement might be considered unconscionable.
7. Identify those statutes that make Sunday agreement illegal.
8. Explain the legal principle of public policy.
9. Enumerate the contracts made illegal by public policy.
10. Explain the consequences of illegal agreements.

11-1 Agreements to Engage in Unlawful Activity

The sixth requirement of a complete contract is legality. A contract may include a valid offer, an effective acceptance, mutual assent, competent parties, and valid consideration and still be invalid because the agreement involves doing something illegal. An illegal agreement is void. It has no legal effect. In general, the law will not aid either party to an illegal agreement. Ordinarily, the court will leave the parties to an illegal agreement where they placed themselves. If an illegal agreement is still executory, the court will not order it to be performed or award damages for breach of contract. If the illegal agreement has been executed, the court will not award damages or assist in having it annulled. The most obvious type of illegal contract is the one in which parties agree to perform some sort of unlawful activity. This activity could be a crime or a tort, depending upon the circumstances. However, when we use the term "unlawful activity" in this context, we are referring to activities that are clearly wrong in and of themselves. These unlawful activities include crimes and torts that most people would recognize as wrong, even if there were no statute, regulation, or court decision to tell them it was wrong.

Agreements to Engage in Tortious Activity

The law will not uphold any contract that obligates one of the parties to commit a tort. For example, a newspaper reporter who agrees to defame several politicians in return for a position as their opponent's press secretary would find no remedy in the law should her benefactor fail to follow through after the libelous story is printed. The agreement to commit a tort would be void in the eyes of the law. This approach only makes good sense. The law cannot lend its approval to a contract that breaks the law, no matter how complete it is in relation to the other five elements.

Agreements to Engage in Criminal Activity

In like manner, the law cannot honor any agreement if the purpose of the agreement is to commit a crime. If, for example, a storekeeper would pay a known criminal to vandalize the shop of a competitor, that storekeeper would not be able to sue the criminal for breach of contract should the criminal take the money and run. As strange as it may seem, the nature of criminality is not always as clear as might be imagined. Because criminal law involves serious offenses that can result in the loss of a person's freedom or, more seriously, the loss of a person's life, all criminal statutes must be drawn as precisely and as clearly as possible. A statute that is obscure or that outlines conduct that is ambiguous may be struck down by the court as void for vagueness. This would mean that a contract that involves the conduct that is allegedly outlawed by a vague statute might not be void.

For a detailed account of the story outlined in the Opening Case see: Werde, Bill. "Hijacking Harry Potter, Quidditch Broom and All." *The New York Times,* June 7, 2004, p. B5.

Teaching Tips Describe several examples of contracts and ask students to identify them as either legal or illegal. When discussing illegal contracts, have students consider whether any part of the contract is enforceable. Ask students their opinions about the consequences of enforcing illegal contracts.

State Variations It is unlawful in the state of Georgia to offer to buy or sell a human body or any part of a human body, except under limited circumstances.

Terms *Usury* is an archaic term for *interest* that is often used today to refer to exorbitant interest rates.

Business Law in the News

Beware Online Job—It's for a "Fence"

You're looking for work and post your resume on one of the online job boards.

You're contacted by a company looking for an "order verification specialist."

Trust me, this is one job you don't want. It's a little like being a mystery shopper, but you don't leave home.

Expensive items—HDTVs, computers, electronics—are shipped to you and you verify that each order is correct and properly packed and grade each against a checklist. Then you reship the merchandise to the company's eastern European office.

After a few packages, the shipments abruptly stop.

Then federal agents show up at your door and want to know why you've been receiving stolen goods. You find out that the "company" was using fraudulent credit cards to buy the merchandise.

It happened to a guy in North Olmsted, among others, and U.S. postal inspectors are warning Internet job seekers to watch out.

Although the job title may be "order verification specialist," "reshipper" or "product locator," a more accurate description is "fence."

Inspectors say the rings running the scams are based abroad, mainly in eastern Europe. Because they know electronics companies are wary about shipping goods overseas, they need to have an American address as an initial stopping point. If they can convince you that your job is to receive merchandise and then mail it overseas, they will have moved on to someone new by the time you or their corporate victims catch on.

When you're an honest person who's hungry for a paycheck, it might be difficult to believe a job offer could be a scam.

But here are some tips to protect yourself if you're going to post a resume:

- Be wary of any company that's based overseas, especially if it doesn't appear to have any physical location in the United States.

- You might check the Better Business Bureau www.bbb.org, which keeps track of complaints about companies. But no news isn't necessarily good news: If there's not a report, it may just mean the company hasn't operated long under the name it's given you.

- Be suspicious of jobs that require you to accept and ship out merchandise, especially expensive items. Ask yourself why orders aren't checked at the warehouse or why goods couldn't be directly sent to the company that ordered them.

- Be wary of checks issued from overseas. Because of U.S. banking rules, if you cash a foreign check, your bank will put the money in your account before it clears the foreign banks.

  Spend that money too quick and you may find you've spent cash that was never really there—and now you're facing bounced-check fees.

- Never agree to open a bank account on behalf of your new employer or to funnel company money through an account with your name on it.

Questions for Analysis

1. For many of us it seems far-fetched to imagine that we might be involved in a contract to commit a crime or a tort. This story shows how it is possible to unwittingly get caught up in such an arrangement. What are the illegal actions described in this news article?

2. What is the legal status of the contact that obligated the "order verification specialist" to check incoming packages? Explain.

3. Does this contract qualify as an *in pari delicto* contract? Explain.

4. How is the court likely to treat an attempt to enforce this contract? Explain.

5. What suggestions does the writer offer to avoid being caught up in these illegal schemes?

Example 11-1

Clark Richardson, a former adviser to the President, wrote a book entitled *The Cost of Honor: Against All Attack Plans of the Enemy*. Richardson entered a publishing agreement with Oakcrest Publications, Inc. When, following the terms of a secrecy agreement signed by all government employees, Richardson submitted the manuscript to the government for its approval, he was arrested and prosecuted under a recently passed federal criminal statute that made it a crime to publish any material that "placed the present administration in a bad light." Accordingly, Oakcrest declared the publishing contract illegal and, therefore, void and demanded that Richardson return the advance that the publishing company had paid him. Richardson refused. At trial, the judge declared that the statute was void for vagueness. Consequently, the publication of the book was legal; the contract itself was also legal and, was, therefore, binding on the publisher.

Agreements Made Illegal Under Statutory Law

Most people of good faith would know, even in the absence of any statute, regulation, ordinance, rule, or court decision, that the behavior outlined in the examples noted above would be wrong. It is difficult to imagine, for instance, that the shopkeeper would be surprised to discover that it is wrong to hire someone to destroy his competitor's property. Similarly, it is not easy to believe that the reporter who agreed to lie in print thought that her behavior was in any way admirable. In contrast, some activities that do not seem wrong on the surface may have been made wrong by specific statutory enactments. Therefore, the fact that some of these activities are illegal may catch us by surprise. For example, the shopkeeper, who knows vandalism is illegal, may be confused to learn that he cannot hold a garage sale without a license. Or the reporter who knows that libel is wrong may be amazed to learn that her Wednesday-evening poker game is not legal. For this reason, we will examine those activities that are wrong because a statute says they are wrong. These activities include usurious agreements, wagering agreements, unlicensed agreements, unconscionable agreements, and Sunday (Sabbath) agreements.

Usurious Agreements   The illegal practice of charging more than the amount of interest allowed by law is called **usury.** To protect borrowers from excessive interest charges, each state has passed laws which specify the rate of interest that may be charged in lending money. These interest rates vary from state to state. Agreements to charge more than is allowed by law are illegal. Special statutes, however, allow small loan companies, pawn shops, and other lending agencies accepting high-risk applicants for credit to charge a higher rate of interest.

Example 11-2

Derek Clapham had an outstanding balance of $70,000 on eight credit cards. Five of the companies were threatening legal action against Clapham. In a mild state of panic, if there really is such a thing, Clapham decided to consolidate his loans by

(Continued)

Teaching Tips A credit card statement lists the maximum amount of interest each state allows. Project this section of a statement on an overhead projector to illustrate the variety of interest rates that states charge.

Background Information Usury laws in the United States in the early part of the nineteenth century reflected economics at the time. Before the government put large amounts of public land up for sale, usury laws were used to keep interest rates from becoming too high and to encourage growth at a time when cash was scarce. After statehood was established, usury laws were abolished because the availability of government land created a demand for cash.

I think that your attention might well be directed to the burglar, rather than those who caught the burglar.

—John F. Kennedy to Earl Russell, October 26, 1962

Example 11-2 (*Continued*)

going to the Forest City Loan Company. Forest City agreed to loan Clapham the money but charged him 29 percent interest over a forty-eight month period. Although, the usual maximum interest rate in the state was 21 percent, a state statute specifically authorized this higher maximum rate for high-risk applicants such as Clapham.

So-called payday loans that come with a charge of over 800 percent per annum have become legal in some states. Payday loans are small loans that are given on a weekly basis for an extremely large fee.

Example 11-3

Jill Salkeld needed money to pay an outstanding bill. A storefront loan company in her neighborhood agreed to lend her $150 for one week at a charge of $29. Salkeld received the $150, paid the $29 fee and wrote a check to the loan company which the loan company agreed not to cash for one week. A week later, when Salkeld could not cover the check she had written, the loan company agreed not to cash the check again for another $29 fee. This scene repeated itself over and over for ten weeks, after which Salkeld had paid $290 and still owed the original $150 she had borrowed in the first place.

Many states provide for a different maximum interest rate when the loan goes to a business or when it involves a mortgage (see Chapter 30). Most states also have special usury statutes to monitor the interest charges by retailers and others when the contract involves an installment loan. Such statutes are often referred to as retail installment sales acts. Some transactions involve charges that appear to be interest, but are actually legitimate expenses that can be collected without violating usury laws. The fee for a title search, an

Payday loans are sometimes used as short-term credit for people who need money immediately, but which charge extremely high interest rates.

> **Payday Loan Regulations by State**
>
> States with regulations that exempt payday lenders:
> California, Colorado, Florida, Iowa, Kansas, Kentucky, Louisiana, Minnesota, Mississippi,
> Missouri, Nebraska, Nevada, North Carolina, Ohio, Oklahoma, South Carolina, Tennessee,
> Washington, and Wyoming.
>
> States with regulations that prohibit payday loans by setting maximum interest rates:
> Alabama, Alaska, Arizona, Arkansas, Connecticut, Georgia, Hawaii, Maine, Maryland,
> Massachusetts, Michigan, New Hampshire, Pennsylvania, Rhode Island, Texas, Vermont,
> Virginia, West Virginia, and Puerto Rico, U.S. Virgin Islands.
>
> States with regulations that permit payday loans and set no limits on small loan interest rates:
> Delaware, Idaho, Illinois, Montana, New Jersey, New Mexico, New York, North Dakota,
> Oregon, South Dakota, Utah, and Wisconsin.
>
> One state, Indiana, sets a maximum interest rate (36%), but allows payday loans by setting a
> minimum finance charge ($33).

Figure 11-1 State loan regulations.

appraisal of land, or a credit report would fall into this category. Such fees must be genuine; any attempt to disguise usury as a special fee will not be tolerated by the courts. (See Figure 11-1 for state statutes.)

> ## Example 11-4
>
> Matt Bourne decided to replace the siding on his house. To do so he went to the Emmet Financial Bank and applied for a loan. Fay Defalco, the loan manager of Emmet, told Bourne that they would need $2,500 up front to process the loan. This processing, she told Bourne, would involve a credit check, an appraisal of the value of the house, and a title search. In fact, these things were not done, and the $2,500 fee was simply a way to charge extra interest above the maximum rate. Such a scheme is illegal.

The legal consequences associated with charging too much interest depends upon the laws of the jurisdiction. Some states make the entire contract completely void. Other states allow the lender to collect only the principal with no interest at all. Others permit the lender to recover the principal and the interest up to what is actually allowed by law. Since these legal consequences vary from jurisdiction to jurisdiction, it would be wise to check the law in your state.

Wagering Agreements

Any agreement or promise concerning a wager or some other form of gambling is invalid and may not be enforced. States make exceptions when bets are placed in accordance with laws that permit horse racing, state lotteries, church-related or charitable games of bingo, and gambling casinos regulated by state authority. However, even in states where gambling is legal, it is frequently still illegal to borrow money to gamble.

Unlicensed Agreements

Certain businesses and professions must be licensed before they are allowed to operate legally. One reason for requiring a license is to provide a source of revenue, part of which is used to supervise the business or profession being licensed. A city ordinance requiring all residents to obtain a license before holding a yard

Related Cases Burke wrote a note promising to pay $200,000 to Byer. In exchange for this note, Byer agreed not to sue Burke for prior gambling losses. When Burke reneged on his promise, Byer sued to enforce the note. The court ruled for Burke and dismissed the case, stating "any note or contract with any part of the consideration thereof involving money won or lost at gambling is absolutely void (citing South Dakota statute 53-9-2)." *Byer v. Burke,* 338 N.W.2d 293 (SD).

State Variations Gambling debts are unenforceable even in Nevada, where state law permits gambling.

State Variations Not only are contracts made by certain unlicensed parties considered void in Missouri but some unlicensed agents may also be subject to criminal prosecution.

Getting Students Involved Have students work in pairs to investigate local licensing requirements for various businesses and professions. One member of the pair can interview business owners to learn about the licensing process and their personal views on licensing. The other member of the pair can find out about the requirements from local government officials.

or garage sale would fall into this category. Another purpose that the government has in licensing individuals is to provide supervision and regulation of businesses and professions that might inflict harm on the public if allowed to operate without such controls. Physicians; nurses; dentists; attorneys; engineers; architects; elementary, middle, and high school teachers; and others in public service must be supervised for the protection of the public. Courts distinguish between licenses purely for revenue and licenses for protection of the public. If a license is required simply to raise revenue, the lack of a license will not necessarily make a contract void. In contrast, if a licensing requirement is designed to protect the public, it is likely that unlicensed people will not be able to enforce their contracts.

Example 11-5

Sandra Abernathy was hired by the Catalina Steel Corporation in Detroit to work on certain industrial engineering projects. Abernathy, however, had never obtained a license to become a registered engineer. A Michigan statute prohibited people from performing engineering services without having the appropriate license. When Catalina refused to pay Abernathy for a job they felt was poorly done, she sued them for breach of contract. The court found in favor of the steel company. The court felt that public welfare allowed the state to regulate and license engineers in order to provide for public safety.

Teaching Tips Make a list on the board of local traders and professions that are licensed by the state. Discuss whether each license is for revenue or regulatory purposes. Also discuss the reasons behind licensing these professions but not others.

Teaching Tips Pose contractual scenarios to the class and direct students to think of examples of unconscionable agreements.

Unconscionable Agreements A court will not enforce a contract or any part of a contract that it regards as unconscionable. An agreement is considered unconscionable if its terms are so grossly unfair that they shock the court's conscience. When the court so desires, it will limit how the unconscionable clause in an agreement is carried out, provided it can do so without causing any unfair consequences.

Example 11-6

A telemarketer for the Wynette Kitchen Supply Company convinced Gina Jenkins, an 80-year-old widow who lived alone and who did not hear very well, to purchase a set of pots and pans for $9,000. The actual value of the set was about $500. When Jenkins's niece found out that the telemarketer had pressured her aunt into this grossly unfair agreement, she told her not to pay the outrageous amount. When she failed to pay her bill and demanded that Wynette take the pots and pans back, the company sued her. Because of the difference in bargaining power and the incredibly unfair price, it is likely that the court would refuse to enforce the contract.

About the Law

Under the Napoleonic Code, it was illegal for a woman to enter a contract for the acquisition of property without her husband's written consent.

Of course, the party seeking to uphold the contract is allowed to present evidence that would show that the agreement is not as unfair as it may, at first, appear. The court would look at the commercial setting as well as the purpose and the effect of the agreement to determine its overall fairness.

Sunday Agreements State statutes and local ordinances regulate the making and performing of contracts on Sunday. These laws are usually called **blue laws** because one of the first laws banning Sunday or Sabbath contracts was written on blue paper. Interestingly enough, the local legislative bodies had to act affirmatively to create statutes against

Sunday contracts because, under common law, these contracts were perfectly legal. Today, the enforcement of restrictive blue laws varies in different geographical areas. Certain states have eliminated uniform statewide laws regulating Sunday activities, but permit their counties and incorporated cities, towns, and villages to adopt their own ordinances under a concept known as **local option.** Thus, adjoining counties may have opposing laws, with one opting, by popular referendum, to permit Sunday sales and the other opting to make such sales illegal. Other states have rolled back these laws almost entirely, permitting most contracts while prohibiting or limiting only a few select Sunday contracts, such as those involving the sale of alcohol.

Where laws do restrict Sunday business, two rules are usually observed. First, agreements made on Sunday or any other day requiring performance on Sunday may be ruled invalid. Exceptions to this rule are those agreements necessary to the health, welfare, and safety of the community and its residents. Second, agreements made on Sunday for work to be done or goods to be delivered on a business day are valid and enforceable. However, some states still require that there be an affirmation of such agreements on a day other than Sunday if such agreements are to be enforceable. The enforcement of blue laws varies widely from state to state, county to county, and village to village. Some localities have restrictive laws but prefer not to enforce them, permitting all types of commercial activity without interference. Religious influences have been of major importance where enforcement is strict. Highly populated urban areas have almost entirely succumbed to the pressures of commercialism and have removed the Sunday blue laws from the books.

Quick Quiz 11-1 True or False?

1. Special statutes sometimes permit small loan companies to charge a higher rate of interest for high-risk applicants.

2. A court will usually enforce an unconscionable contract if the immediate threshold test is met, at least in relation to part of the agreement.

3. Wagering agreements are permitted in states with blue laws.

11-2 Agreements Contrary to Public Policy

The government has the power to regulate the health, safety, welfare, and morals of the public. This power emerges within the states simply because of their status as legitimate governing bodies. It has also become a part of the federal government's power under various interpretations of the U.S. Constitution. Any action that tends to harm the health, safety, welfare, or morals of the people is said to violate public policy. **Public policy** is that general legal principle that says no one should be allowed to do anything that tends to injure the public at large. Agreements most commonly invalidated as contrary to public policy are those to obstruct justice, interfere with public service, defraud creditors, escape liability, and restrain trade. Some of these agreements are prohibited by statute, such as those that suppress competition and those that interfere with public service. Consequently, they could have been listed and explained in the last section. Instead, these contracts are listed here with the other public policy–related contracts, because they share one thing in common, although such contracts are made between private individuals, they would hurt the entire social structure if the law enforced them in any way.

Background Information Some unusual laws have been enacted in an apparent attempt to keep Sunday as a holy day of rest and worship for Christians. Such laws can be found in the history of Evansville, Indiana, where hamburgers were not to be sold on Sundays, and in Louisiana, where it was unlawful to whistle on Sundays.

Did You Know?

Corbin on Contracts, one of the most respected treatises on contract law, begins its discussion of public policy by stating, "The loudest and most confident assertions as to what makes for the general welfare and happiness of mankind are made by the demagogue and the ignoramus."

Terms Thomas Wilde, Lord Chancellor of Great Britain, articulated public policy when he called it "that principle of the law which holds that no subject can lawfully do that which has a tendency to be injurious to the public, or against the public good."

Further Reading For an interesting discussion of some of the additional problems associated with the treatment of prisoners in the Afghanistan and Iraqi wars, see *Secret Trials and Executions: Military Tribunals and the Threat to Democracy* by Barbara Olshansky, published by The Open Media Pamphlet Series in New York, 2002.

In modern societies the notion of the common good or public good tends to be expanded to include a large number of things that have to do with the individual good of the members.

—Raymond Geuss,
  Princeton University,
  author of *Public Goods,
  Private Goods*

For a more detailed account of the story outlined in A Question of Ethics see: "The Roots of Abu Ghraig." *The New York Times,* June 9, 2004, p. A24; Lewis, Neil A., and Eric Schmitt. "Lawyers Decided Bans on Torture Didn't Bind Bush." *The New York Times,* June 8, 2004, p. 1.

A Question of Ethics

In March of 2003, as Gulf War II was underway, a task force of attorneys working for the administration in Washington developed a set of legal arguments demonstrating that the President of the United States and his appointees should not be bound by prohibitions against torture as outlined in international law and federal statutory law. The legal memorandum produced at that time was only one of a series of legal memos written by administrative legal teams. Each memo was aimed at proving that American officials did not have to abide by the Geneva Conventions and other international agreements outlawing torture. What all of these memos seem to have overlooked is the basic premise that the overall public good is preserved only when the good of individuals is also preserved. In denying basic human rights to Iraqi detainees, the attorneys had forgotten (or ignored) a fundamental reason that the United States had agreed to be bound by such laws in the first place; that is, to protect all soldiers, but especially our own, from such abuse.

Agreements to Obstruct Justice

Agreements to obstruct justice include agreements to protect someone from arrest, to suppress evidence, to encourage lawsuits, to give false testimony, and to bribe a juror. The category also includes a promise not to prosecute someone or not to serve as a witness in a trial. Any agreement promising to perform any of these activities would be void.

Example 11-7

Sarah Jurgens was shopping at the Otterbacher Grocery Outlet when she slipped and fell, breaking her arm. Sam Warner, who witnessed the entire incident, was paid $700 by the owners of Otterbacher to forget everything he'd seen. Warner later changed his mind and testified truthfully about the facts concerning the incident. The agreement made with the owners of the Otterbacher Grocery Outlet is void because it is considered against public policy. Any effort to hold him to it will be unsuccessful.

Agreements Interfering with Public Service

Agreements interfering with public service are illegal and void. Contracts in this group include agreements to bribe or interfere with public officials, to obtain political preference in appointments to office, to pay an officer for signing a pardon, or to illegally influence a legislature for personal gain.

Getting Students Involved After reviewing the agreements to obstruct justice, have students prepare a research paper on the accusations against President Clinton regarding obstructions of justice in his impeachment trial.

Example 11-8

Philip Olive entered into an agreement with Jim Martin, the state highway engineer, in which Martin agreed to use his influence to have the new state highway run adjacent to Olive's resort hotel. Olive paid Martin $9,000 for his promise to attempt to grant this request. This agreement is void and may not be enforced. The failure of the engineer to exert his influence would give Olive no rights in seeking the return of the $9,000 paid.

Agreements to Defraud Creditors

Agreements to defraud creditors, that is, agreements that tend to remove or weaken the rights of creditors are void as contrary to public policy. Thus a debtor's agreement to sell and transfer personal and real property to a friend or relative for far less than actual value would be void if done for the purpose of hiding the debtor's assets from creditors with a legal claim to them.

Example 11-9

Eugene Concord had failed to diversify his investment portfolio and, as a result, had begun to lose a great deal of his wealth as the dot-com stocks he had invested in began to fail during the second great stock market crash. Eventually, he was forced to declare bankruptcy. However, before doing so he sold his car and his van to his sister for $1,000 each. His objective was to protect these assets from the bankruptcy process so that they would not be sold to pay off debts owed to creditors. When the bankruptcy proceedings were over, he intended to buy back the van and the car for the same $2,000. Since the entire transaction was designed to defraud Concord's creditors, it would be void.

Agreements to Escape Liability

A basic policy of the law is that all parties should be liable for their own wrongdoing. Consequently, the law looks with disfavor on any agreement which allows a party to escape this responsibility. One device frequently used in the attempt to escape legal responsibility is the **exculpatory agreement.** Such an agreement is usually found as a clause in a longer, more complex contract or on the back of tickets and parking stubs. The exculpatory clause will state that one of the parties, generally the one who wrote the contract, will not be liable for any economic loss of physical injury even if that party caused the loss or injury.

Example 11-10

Sam Lawson, a truck driver who was represented by the Franklin Trucking Company, was sent to a transport job that would involve transporting several live animals, including an alligator, a tiger, and a bear. When Lawson arrived for the job, he was told he had to sign an additional contract with Hans Bimson, the owner of the animals. One of the clauses in the additional contract included an exculpatory clause that stated that Lawson and Franklin Trucking would hold Bimson blameless, should Lawson be injured by any of the wild animals. During the trip, Bimson and Todd Richards, the animals' trainer, were distracted by a problem with their travel schedule. While the two of them were focused on the difficulty with the schedule, the bear, which had been left unattended by both Bimson and Richards (Richards had worked with Bimson on numerous occasions and was frequently charged with supervising the animals) escaped and severely injured Lawson. Both Lawson and Franklin Trucking sued Bimson and Richards. Bimson pointed to the exculpatory clause and said he was not liable. The court disagreed saying that, while the exculpatory clause might excuse him from events that were not his fault or were beyond his control, it could not protect him from his own negligence, which, in this case, the court decided had contributed directly to Lawson's injuries.

Perhaps the sentiments contained in the following pages, are not yet sufficiently fashionable to procure them general favor; a long habit of not thinking a thing wrong, gives it a superficial appearance of being right, and raises at first a formidable outcry in defence of custom. But the tumult soon subsides. Time makes more converts than reason.

—Thomas Paine,
Common Sense

Cross-Cultural Notes
In Kenya, it is common practice to pay a bribe to a public official. For example, traffic tickets can be avoided by offering a police officer a small bribe. In addition, government officials often expect payments for granting government contracts or issuing licenses. While this form of corruption is illegal, wages for these officials are commonly so low that they view the acceptance of bribes as necessary.

This exculpatory clause is an example of the type that the courts have found to be a violation of public policy. Such exculpatory clauses are not favored by the law because they permit behavior to fall below acceptable standards, which was what happened in the Lawson case. A clause simply disclaiming liability in general terms is often insufficient to release a party from his or her own negligence. Still, some courts will enforce exculpatory clauses if they do not offend public policy and there is no inequality of bargaining power between the parties. On the other hand, whenever an exculpatory provision is ambiguous, confusing, vague, incomplete, or can be interpreted in different ways, the court will construe the clause against the party it was designed to protect.

Agreements in Restraint of Trade

The law tries to be a constant protector of the rights of persons to make a living and to do business freely in a competitive market. If persons enter into contracts that take away these rights, the law will restore the rights to them by declaring such contracts void. A **restraint of trade** is a limitation on the full exercise of doing business with others. Agreements which have the effect of removing competition or denying to the public services they would otherwise have or which result in higher prices and resulting hardship are **agreements in restraint of trade** and can be declared void.

Agreements to Suppress Competition

Any agreement made with the intent of suppressing competition, fixing prices, and the like is void as an illegal restraint of trade. Such agreements are unenforceable because they deprive the public of the advantages guaranteed in an economy based on freedom to contract, laws of supply and demand, and fair and honest business dealing. Agreements of this type may be legal and enforceable, however, if they do not violate the so-called **rule of reason standard** that is usually applied by the courts. The rule of reason is that such agreements are enforceable when they do not unreasonably restrict businesses from competing with one another.

To determine reasonableness, the courts will consider such facts as the history of the restraint, the harm that results (if any), the reason for the practice, and the purpose attained. On the other hand, there are standards set by antimonopoly statutes such as the Sherman Antitrust Act, which name certain practices, such as price fixing, which are inherently anticompetitive by their very nature. Such practices are termed **per se violations** and are prohibited whether or not anyone is actually harmed. (See the discussion of restraint of trade in Chapter 39. In addition to the Sherman Antitrust Act, Chapter 39 also covers the Clayton Act, the Robinson-Patman Act, and the Federal Trade Commission Act.)

Contracts Related to Copyright Infringement

A **copyright** is designed to protect the rights that attach to an artistic, literary, or musical work. A copyright holder is given the exclusive right to reproduce, publish, and sell a work that is set in a tangible medium of expression. Copyright owners also have the right to produce derivative works that come from the original copyrighted material. It would be illegal to enter a contract that would involve a promise to violate the rights of a copyright holder by agreeing to duplicate and sell copies of the original work. The Supreme Court has also declared it illegal for one party to provide a way for a second party to violate the copyright rights of a third party even if the provider of the means does not itself violate the original copyright. This offense has been termed **contributory copyright infringement.**

On the other hand, the law also recognizes that there are exceptions to the rule that protects the holder of a copyright. The key exception is known as **fair use.** Copying items for such purposes as criticism, comment, news reporting, teaching, scholarship, and research is permissible. Libraries and archives may reproduce single copies of certain

Musicians, such as Metallica's Lars Ulrich, sued Napster for copyright infringement in 2000 and brought the subject into the spotlight. Subsequently, people who download music illegally have faced legal action.

copyrighted materials for noncommercial purposes without obtaining permission from the copyright owners. Transforming a copyrighted work for purposes of parody and satire is also permissible.

Sale of Business When a business is sold, it is common practice for the agreement to contain covenants that restrict the seller from entering the same type of business. Such **restrictive covenants** in a contract for the sale of a business will be upheld by the court if they are reasonable in time and geographical area. What is reasonable is determined by a careful examination of the business being sold. For example, an agreement by the seller of a barbershop not to open a similar shop in the same community for the next three years would undoubtedly be reasonable. In contrast, a wider geographical area or longer period of time might not be allowed by the court.

Example 11-11

Vinnie Gerdel owned a neighborhood pizza and sub restaurant called the Leaning Tower of Pizza, which he sold to Fran Holden. A condition to the sale was a clause in the contract which prohibited Gerdel from opening another pizza and sub restaurant anywhere in Indianapolis for a period of five years. Gerdel sought to have this condition invalidated as contrary to public policy. The court ruled that the provision covered such an extensive geographical area and such a long period of time that it was unreasonable. The court revised the agreement allowing Holden to restrain Gerdel from opening a pizza and sub restaurant within five miles of the Leaning Tower for two years.

Restrictive Employment Covenants A restrictive employment covenant is an employment contract that limits a worker's employment options after leaving her or his present job. The objective of such a clause is to protect the present employer from an employee who might take trade secrets, customer lists, or other confidential material to a competitor. In a typical restrictive employment covenant (see Figure 11-2), an employee

Related Cases Dr. Herron signed an employment contract with Dr. Stringer that included a covenant not to compete within a 15-mile radius of the three veterinary offices if he left his employment. When he left, he filed suit to rescind the contract. The court agreed, stating that the covenant was unreasonable because the 15-mile radius was overbroad. The overwhelming majority of the former employer's clients lived much closer than 15 miles from at least one practice location and the radius reached into adjoining counties and another state. *Stringer v. Herron,* 424 S.E. 2d 547.

State Variations In Wisconsin, a contract provision that prohibits an employee or agent from competing with his or her employer or principal during the term of the employment or agency within a specified territory and during a specified time is legal and enforceable only if the restrictions imposed are reasonably necessary for the protection of the employer or principal.

The Opening Case Revisited

"Legal or Illegal? That Is the Question"

Recall that in The Opening Case at the beginning of the chapter, some people saw *Wizard People, Dear Reader* as a possible infringement of the copyright held by Warner Brothers. If that were the case, then anyone who sold a ticket to the screening of *Wizard People, Dear Reader* might have been involved in an illegal contract. However, this interpretation of the law would probably not hold up in court. It is likely that the court would rule that *Wizard People, Dear Reader* is a legitimate parody of *Harry Potter and the Sorcerer's Stone* and, therefore, protected by law.

Figure 11-2 The restrictive employment covenant in Example 11-12 would be upheld by the court. Note that the agreement is reasonable as to the type of work Angelitis is allowed to do (loan officer), the length of time involved (six months), and the geographical area covered by the prohibition (a five-mile radius from Hawthorne's location).

RESTRICTIVE EMPLOYMENT COVENANT

In consideration of my being employed by Hawthorne Savings and Loan, I, Vytataus Angelitis, the undersigned, hereby agree that when I leave the employment of Hawthorne, regardless of the reason I leave, I will not compete with Hawthorne, or its assigns or successors.

The phrase "NOT COMPETE" stated above means that I will not directly or indirectly work as a loan officer for a savings and loan association or any other financial institution that is in competition with Hawthorne.

This restrictive employment covenant will extend for a radius of five miles from the present location of Hawthorne at 6802 East 185th Street, Cleveland, Ohio. This covenant will be in effect for six months, beginning on the date of the termination of employment.

Signed this second of March, 20 – –.

Vytataus Angelitis

Employee

promises not to work for a competitor in the same field for a specified time period and within a specified geographical area after leaving the current job. Agreements like this are not favored by the law because they could deprive people of their livelihood and they could severely limit competition. Consequently, restrictive employment covenants must be reasonable in the type of work they prohibit, the length of time involved in the prohibition, and the geographical area covered by the prohibition. Naturally, reasonableness as to work, time, and geography will vary from case to case, depending upon the nature of the job involved in the prohibition.

Nondisclosure Agreements Some employers attempt to avoid the problems associated with restrictive employment covenants by using nondisclosure agreements. A **nondisclosure agreement** requires employees to promise that, should they leave their present place of employment, they will not reveal any confidential trade secrets that they might learn while on their current job. Because the limitation is placed on the use of confidential information rather than actual employment of the worker, such agreements do not deprive people of their employment and, therefore, do not constitute an extensive limit on competition.

While helpful, nondisclosure agreements are often not needed to protect trade secrets. The court will generally issue an injunction to prevent the revelation or the utilization of trade secrets if the employer can convince the court: (1) that the information revealed by the former employee was actually a trade secret; (2) that the secret information was crucial to the running of the employer's business; (3) that the employer had the right to use the trade secret; and (4) that the former employee came into possession of the trade secret while in a position of trust and confidence and in such a way that it would be unfair for the former employee to disclose that trade secret in a way that would hurt his or her former employer. Of course, it is also necessary to show that the employee actually revealed the confidential information to a competitor.

Example 11-12

Hawthorne Savings and Loan Association attempted to prevent Vytautus Angelitis from working as a loan officer for any other savings and loan association in competition with Hawthorne and located within five miles of the present location of Hawthorne. This prohibition was to last for six months after Angelitis left Hawthorne. Five weeks after leaving Hawthorne, Angelitis took a job at the Lithuanian Savings and Loan Company as a loan officer. The Lithuanian Savings and Loan is located about three miles from Hawthorne. Hawthorne tried to stop Angelitis, claiming his knowledge of their customer lists would hurt their business. Hawthorne pointed to the restrictive employment covenant prohibiting Angelitis from taking such a job. The court held that the restrictions in the covenant were reasonable as to time, location, and type of job. (See Figure 11-2.)

A Question of Ethics

Suppose in Example 11-12, the members of the board of directors of Hawthorne Savings and Loan Association knew the job Angelitis had taken with the Lithuanian Savings and Loan Company would not in any way realistically hurt their business.

(Continued)

> ### A Question of Ethics (*Continued*)
>
> Suppose further that the Hawthorne board members knew Angelitis had been out of work for five weeks and that he and his family had many past due bills that they could not pay unless Angelitis remained at Lithuanian. Legally, the Hawthorne board members can prevent Angelitis from working for Lithuanian. However, would it be ethical for them to do so? Explain.

Civil RICO Litigation Another approach that employers can take to protect themselves against the theft of trade secrets by former employees is to file a civil action under the Racketeer Influenced and Corrupt Organizations (RICO) Act. Of course, this technique is unlike the use of restrictive employment covenants and nondisclosure agreements because it is a reactive approach that happens after the trade secret has been revealed. Nevertheless, the fact that such technique has been approved of by the courts has strengthened the effectiveness of the other two techniques. Former employees who contemplate breaching a restrictive employment covenant or a nondisclosure agreement might think twice about doing so, if they know that their former employer might also bring a RICO action against them. This is because under RICO, employers can, in addition to their other remedies, receive triple damages, attorney fees, and reasonable court costs, should they prevail.

Quick Quiz 11-2 True or False?

1. Public policy says only the government should be allowed to do things that injure the public at large.

2. Per se violations of antitrust law are prohibited only if someone is actually harmed.

3. A nondisclosure agreement requires employees to promise that they will reveal trade secrets only when compensated properly.

11-3 Consequences of Illegality

Teaching Tips Before beginning the section on consequences of illegality, give students examples of the types of contracts discussed. Ask them whether they feel criminal acts have been committed in the agreements listed. Have students decide if the parties to those agreements should be prosecuted on criminal charges or if the contracts should simply be dissolved.

Illegality of contract, as in promises to commit criminal acts, not only serves to void existing agreements but may lead to indictment and prosecution when sufficient evidence warrants such an action. Persons who agree to commit criminal acts for a promised consideration are involved in what criminal law defines as a **conspiracy.** Agreements that do not violate criminal laws may still be invalid. Thus, many agreements considered contrary to public policy have been declared invalid as against the public good, but not illegal in terms of criminal liability. Both types of agreements fail to have the characteristics that permit legal enforcement.

In Pari Delicto Contracts

When both parties to an illegal agreement are equally wrong in the knowledge of the operation and effect of their contract, they are said to be ***in pari delicto*** (in equal fault). In such cases the court will give no aid to either party in an action against the other, and will award no damages to either. When the parties are not *in pari delicto,* relief will often be allowed if sought by the more innocent of the two. Although this rule is not applicable where one may be less guilty of premeditation (plotting or planning an illegal act) and intent to achieve a gain through known illegal acts, it may be applied when one party is not aware that a law is being broken and where there is no intent to do a wrong.

Example 11-13

Gary Kowalski was an out-of-work snowmobile salesman who needed a job quickly. Following the advice of his neighbor, Larry Perdue, he tried to find employment on the Internet. Kowalski logged onto the Net and found an advertisement placed by International Shipping for a job entitled "product repackager." He applied for and was granted the position. As part of his training, Kowalski had to send International $500 for a starter kit that contained his repackaging instructions and supplies. When he received the supplies, they did not appear to be worth $5, let alone $500. Unfortunately, Kowalski was now committed to the job because of the cash outlay and so he did as he was told. Kowalski's job was to receive packages in the mail from American companies, unpack those packages, inspect them, and then repackage them for shipment to foreign addresses. After receiving and resending twelve packages, the shipments stopped. The very next day, Kowalski was surprised by a visit from federal agents who accused him of fencing goods purchased with stolen credit card numbers. Kowalski was not aware of this fact, and in an action against International, the court would rule that Kowalski might recover his $500 as the parties were not *in pari delicto*.

Illegality in Entire Agreement

Sometimes an agreement will be partly legal and partly illegal. If the legal part of the agreement can be separated from the illegal part, the agreement is said to be divisible. The court will enforce the legal part, but not the illegal part. Likewise, if the main purpose of the agreement can be reached without enforcing the illegal part, the courts are likely to uphold the agreement.

The public good is in nothing more essentially interested than the protection of every individual's private rights.

—Sir William Blackstone (1723–1780), British jurist

Example 11-14

Fraser and Brambles Inc., a soap and cosmetics firm, entered a contract with Kavanaugh and Associates Advertising, Inc., a Dallas-based advertising agency. Under terms of the agreement, Kavanaugh was supposed to fashion a national ad campaign for the marketing of twelve new cosmetic products produced by Fraser and Brambles. One of the products was a new sunscreen that was denied approval by the federal Food and Drug Administration (FDA). The part of the contract that involved the sunscreen now involved an illegal product. The part of the contract for that product, however, would be divisible from the overall contract, Kavanaugh would still be able to sue for the compensation promised, separating the illegal product from the main purpose of the agreement to advertise the new product line for Fraser and Brambles.

In contrast, if the legal part cannot be separated from the legal part, it is termed indivisible and the entire agreement is void. Even though specific sections of the agreement may be legally enforceable, if standing alone, illegality of any part of the entire agreement renders it invalid.

Example 11-15

Suppose, in the last example, all the new products that Fraser and Brambles intended to place on the national market were denied approval by the FDA. In such a situation, it is quite likely that the court would then declare the agreement to be illegal in its entirety. This determination would mean that the court would have to deny the Kavanaugh Advertising Agency any rights whatsoever under the contract. This is true even if some of the clauses in the contract standing by themselves, such as time limits, or the amount of consideration to be paid to the ad agency, the timing of the advertising campaign, or the types of media to be used would be legal if the subject matter of the ad campaign itself had turned out to be legal.

Quick Quiz 11-3 True or False?

1. Persons who agree to commit criminal acts for a promised consideration are involved in what most state criminal codes define as a piracy.

2. When neither party to an illegal agreement knows that the substance of the contract is illegal, each party is said to be *in pari delicto*.

3. If the legal part of the agreement can be separated from the illegal part, the agreement is said to be divisible.

Summary

11-1   An agreement might have offer, acceptance, mutual assent, competent parties, and consideration and still be invalid if the objective of the agreement is to do something that is illegal. One type of contract that fails in illegality is the one in which the parties agree to do some otherwise illegal act. This illegal act could be a crime or a tort. Some agreements are made illegal by statute even though the activities themselves are neither crimes nor torts. These agreements include usurious agreements, wagering agreements, unlicensed agreements, unconscionable agreements, and Sunday (Sabbath) agreements.

11-2   Public policy is a general legal principle that says no one should be allowed to do anything that tends to hurt the public at large. Agreements found void for a violation of public policy include agreements to obstruct justice, agreements interfering with public service, agreements to defraud creditors, exculpatory agreements, and agreements in restraint of trade.

11-3   Contracts that involve illegal agreements are invalid. Moreover, promises to commit illegal acts may also lead to indictment and prosecution. If an entire agreement is illegal, no binding contract results. If only part of an agreement is illegal, the court may rescind only those parts found to be illegal. When both parties are equally at fault in creating an illegal agreement, the court will award no damages to either. When the parties are not in equal fault, relief will often be granted if sought by the innocent party.

Key Terms

agreements in restraint of trade, 210

blue laws, 206

conspiracy, 214

contributory copyright
infringement, 210

copyright, 210

exculpatory agreement, 209

fair use, 210

in pari delicto, 214

local option, 207

nondisclosure agreement, 213

per se violations, 210

public policy, 207

restraint of trade, 210

restrictive covenants, 211

rule of reason standard, 210

usury, 203

Questions for Review and Discussion

1. What is the effect of illegality on a contract?
2. What contracts have been made illegal by statutory law?
3. What is the rationale behind usury laws?
4. What wagering agreements are not illegal under state law?
5. What are the rules regarding licenses and illegality?
6. When is an agreement considered unconscionable?
7. What statutes make Sunday agreement illegal?
8. What is the legal principle of public policy?
9. What are the contracts made illegal by public policy?
10. What are the consequences of an illegal agreement?

Investigating the Internet

Sources of information about contract law can be accessed from under the Contract Law topic on the Legal Database website. As a research assignment, access this website and report those sources of information that might concern covenants not to compete.

Cases for Analysis

1. Shannon Audley, a professional model, signed an agreement before starting work on a photo shoot at Bill Melton's studio. The agreement stated: "I, Shannon Audley, realize that working with wild and potentially dangerous animals (i.e., lion, white tiger, hawk) can create a hazardous situation resulting in loss of life or limb. I take all responsibility upon myself for any event as described above that may take place. I hold Bill Melton and T.I.G.E.R.S. or any of their agents free of any or all liability. I am signing this of my own free will." During the photo shoot, Audley was bitten on the head by the adult male lion with which she had been posing. Audley brought suit against Melton. Would the exculpatory clause be upheld by the courts? Explain. *Audley v. Melton,* 640 A.2d 777 (NH).

2. Judy Myers and the Terminix International Company entered a contract in which Terminix agreed to inspect Myers' home and eliminate any termite problem found there. The service cost Myers an initial payment of $1,300, plus annual renewal fees of $85. Terminix failed to eradicate the termite infestation causing over $41,000 in damage to

the Myers' home. The contract contained a clause which required the parties to submit any disputes to arbitration under the American Arbitration Association (AAA). What the contract did not disclose was that Myers would be required to pay a filing fee to submit a claim to AAA. In this case, the filing fee amounted to $7,000. In a lawsuit filed for breach of contract, Myers asserted that the undisclosed filing fee requirement was unconscionable. Is Myers correct? Explain. *Myers v. Terminix,* 697 N.E.2d 277 (OH).

3. When Donald Kennedy worked for Bridgestone/Firestone (B/F), he entered a nondisclosure agreement by which he promised that, should he leave B/F's employ, he would not reveal any confidential trade secrets that he might learn while at B/F. When Kennedy left Bridgestone/Firestone, he went to work for the Hankook Tire Manufacturing Co., one of B/F's competitors. B/F elected to bring suit against both Hankook and Kennedy for breach of the nondisclosure agreement. Would this type of clause be upheld by the courts? Explain. *Bridgestone/Firestone, Inc. v. Hankook Tire Manufacturing Co., Inc.* 687 N.E.2d 502 (OH).

4. Asdourian obtained a contractor's license under the name "Artko Remodeling and Construction," which was the name under which he planned to incorporate his business. He signed the license application as the responsible managing party. Later, having not yet incorporated the business, Asdourian signed a contract under his own name to convert a garage into a restaurant for Mr. and Mrs. Araj. After completing the work and not being paid fully, Asdourian sued Mr. and Mrs. Araj for the money owed. They argued that they did not have to pay him because he did not have a contractor's license in his name. Do you agree? Why? *Asdourian v. Araj,* 696 P.2d 95 (CA).

5. A group of men known as the "last man's club" bought a hunting lodge in upstate New York for their headquarters. The men agreed that the land would belong to the last surviving member. The last surviving member was Crawford, who claimed exclusive title to the land. Crawford's claim was challenged by Quinn, the daughter of a deceased member of the club. Quinn argued that the agreement made by the club members was actually a wagering agreement and, therefore, was illegal. Was Quinn's claim correct? Explain. *Quinn v. Stuart Lakes Club, Inc.,* 439 N.Y.S.2d 30 (NY).

6. West was hired by the data processing department of the Alberto-Culver Company as a senior programmer. Since West had obtained the job through an employment agency, Alberto-Culver was supposed to pay the agency a fee. However, Alberto-Culver found out that the employment agency was not licensed, as was required by Illinois law. Because the employment agency was not licensed, Alberto-Culver claimed it did not have a duty to pay the agency fee. Was Alberto-Culver correct? Explain. *T.E.C v. Alberto-Culver Company,* 476 N.E.2d 1212 (IL).

7. Williams, as a regular customer of Walker-Thomas Furniture, would buy household goods on time payments. A clause in each installment contract indicated that an unpaid balance would affect all items ever purchased. In effect, this meant that if Williams ever missed a payment, the store could repossess all the items that Williams had ever bought from Walker, regardless of how long ago they were purchased. Williams missed one monthly payment, and Walker attempted to repossess everything that Williams had purchased over the last five years. Williams claimed that the default clause was unconscionable. Was he correct? Explain. *Williams v. Walker-Thomas Furniture Company,* 350 F2d 445 (DC Cir.).

8. Peeples was seriously injured when he fell from a scaffold set up by Donar Systems, his employer. At the time of the fall, the work was being done for the city of Detroit. The city claimed that it was not liable because Donar's employment contract contained a clause that absolved the city of any liability for negligence regardless of who was at fault. Peeples claimed that this was an illegal exculpatory clause and asked the court not to uphold it. Did the court comply with Peeples' request? Explain. *Peeples v. City of Detroit,* 297 N.W.2d 839 (MI).

9. The Topps Chewing Gum company and the Major League Baseball Players Association entered into exclusive five-year contracts for the services of the league's baseball players. Photographs of major league baseball players were to appear exclusively on baseball cards distributed by Topps with the sale of its chewing gum. The Fleer Corporation, a rival of Topps, brought suit for $16 million, alleging that the exclusive contracts would freeze out competition in this area and thus constituted "an illegal restraint on trade." Topps argued that Fleer could compete by seeking the agreements

with players still in the minor leagues. Thus, Topps concluded, their competitive efforts were not unreasonable. Was Topps correct? Explain. *Fleer Corporation v. Topps Chewing Gum, Inc.,* 501 F. Supp. 485 (E.D. PA).

10. Trecher worked for Columbia Ribbon and Carbon Manufacturing Co., Inc., as a salesperson for several years. His employment agreement included a restrictive employment covenant that said he could not obtain a similar job anywhere in the United States for two years after he left Columbia. Trecher left Columbia and was hired as a salesperson by A-1-A Corporation, one of Columbia's competitors. Columbia filed a lawsuit to stop Trecher from working for A-1-A based on the restrictive employment covenant. Did the court stop Trecher from working for A-1-A? Explain. *Columbia Ribbon and Carbon Manufacturing v. A-1-A Corporation,* 369 N.E.2d 4 (NY).

Quick Quiz Answers

11-1	11-2	11-3
1. T	1. F	1. F
2. F	2. F	2. F
3. F	3. F	3. T

Chapter 12

Written Contracts

The Opening Case
"Whose Debt Is It Anyway?"

When Franklin Rostow attempted to purchase a new DVD player from the Highgate Radio and Television Department Store, he found out that he did not have an appropriate credit line. He went to see his brother, Scott, who was in a position to cosign for his purchase. Scott Rostow went to Highgate and told the manager that he would pay for the DVD player if Franklin defaulted on any of his installment payments. Under those circumstances, the manager agreed to sell the DVD player to Franklin. What Scott did not realize, although he should have because it was clearly written in the preprinted contract, was that the contract contained an acceleration clause. Under the terms of the acceleration clause, if Franklin missed a single payment, the responsibility to pay the entire amount immediately shifted to Scott. Later that same day, Scott took his daughter, Barbara, to the Yardley Friedman Clothing Outlet. When they arrived at the store, he told the owner, Teri Boterus, that his daughter could use his credit account to purchase her back-to-school wardrobe, as long as she spent no more than $499. Teri agreed to this arrangement and Barbara went off on her spending spree. Although these two situations appear to be very similar, they are actually quite different. One of them requires a written agreement for enforceability; the other does not. Which of the two must be in written form? Questions such as this are addressed in Chapter 12, Written Contracts.

Chapter Outcomes

1. Point out the abuses that the Statute of Frauds was designed to eliminate.
2. Identify agreements that must be written under the Statute of Frauds.
3. List the information that must be in a written contract.
4. Explain the parol evidence rule.
5. Describe the exceptions under the parol evidence rule.
6. Explain the best evidence rule.
7. Explain the equal dignities rule.
8. Illustrate various methods of writing a signature.
9. Discuss the use of witnesses, acknowledgments, the seal, and recording.
10. Identify the most current cybercommerce laws.

12-1 The Statute of Frauds

Often when people hear the word *contract,* they immediately think of a piece of paper. Instead, they should think of an agreement, which may or may not be in writing. This is because many contracts do not have to be in writing to be enforceable. Most oral contracts are valid and upheld by the court. Although it may be desirable to put a contract in writing so that its terms are clear, only certain kinds of contracts are required to be in writing. This chapter discusses the **Statute of Frauds,** which is the law that requires certain contracts to be in writing to be enforceable.

Early British law permitted the enforcement of all oral contracts when they could be proven through testimony of witnesses. Witnesses were required to prove or disprove the existence of an oral agreement; the parties themselves were barred from testifying on their own behalf. Perjury was not uncommon at the time; consequently, numerous alleged contracts that a defendant was unable to disclaim were enforced. To correct this matter, the British Parliament in 1677 passed the Act for the Prevention of Frauds and Perjuries, later shortened to the Statute of Frauds. Some provisions of the Statute of Frauds were adopted into practice in the U.S. Courts after the colonies separated from England. Each state now has it own Statute of Frauds.

Contracts That Must Be in Writing

According to the Statute of Frauds, applicable in most states, six types of contracts must be in writing to be enforceable.

1. Contracts that cannot be completed within one year
2. Contracts transferring real property rights
3. Contracts for the sale of goods of $500 or more
4. Certain contracts entered by executors and administrators
5. Contracts by one party to pay a debt of another party
6. Contracts in consideration of marriage

The third contract on the list, contracts for the sale of goods of $500 or more, is actually included in the Uniform Commercial Code, rather than the Statute of Frauds. This is covered in more depth in Chapter 15.

Contracts That Cannot Be Completed Within One Year If the terms of a contract make it impossible to complete the agreement within one year, the contract must be in writing.

State Variations Under New York law, professional boxer Mike Tyson was held liable for $4.4 million in damages for breach of an oral contract with his trainer, in which he agreed that his trainer would represent Tyson "for as long as the boxer fights professionally."

State Variations In California, all contracts may be oral, except those contracts which are required by statute to be in writing.

Though the marriage agreement itself does not have to be written, some contracts associated with marriage do.

Example 12-1

Karen Quartermain entered an agreement with Kent Anderson in which they agreed that Anderson would become Quartermain's gardener for eight months beginning one month after Quartermain moved into her new home. Quartermain could not move into her new home, however, until Larry and Lena Jeffries, the present owners, moved out. The Jeffries promised to move out within one to three months. One month after the agreement, Quartermain told Anderson that she would not need his services. Anderson, who had relied on the contract and had not sought other employment and
(Continued)

Historical Note   That witnesses took bribes to perjure themselves in the King's Court should not be a surprise in light of the fact that Charles II, who was king when the Statute for the Prevention of Frauds and Perjuries was passed, frequently took bribes from the French monarch in exchange for directing British foreign affairs in favor of French interests. Charles's successor, James II, also had a habit of suspending the law for his own purposes, and when James II left the throne, Parliament created a completely fabricated tale about a voluntary abdication that never really took place. (See Woodward, E. L. *History of England from Roman Times to the End of World War I.* New York: Harper and Row, 1962, pp. 116–120.)

Terms   The word *statute* can be traced back to the thirteenth century Latin words *statuere,* which means "to set up," and *status,* meaning "the position of a person or thing in the eyes of the law."

Example 12-1 (*Continued*)

who now had a difficult time obtaining comparable employment, threatened to sue. Quartermain told Anderson to go ahead and sue. Privately, Quartermain told her husband, Manfred, not to worry because, since Larry and Lena Jeffries had three months to move out, the contract could not have been performed within one year. Since the contract could not have been performed within one year it should have been in writing. Since the contract was not in writing, Quartermain concluded, it was not enforceable. Kent told his wife, Mavis, that because Larry and Lena Jeffries *could* move out in less than one month, the contract *could be* performed within a year, and it did not have to be in writing to be enforceable.

In Example 12-1, Anderson is correct and Quartermain is wrong. Since the Jeffries family *could* have moved out within one month, or less for that matter, the contract *could have been* performed within one year. If Larry and Lena Jeffries actually did move out within the first month, Anderson would begin work one month later. The term of employment from that point would have run eight months. Therefore, the entire contract could have been performed within ten months. Recall that the operative words in the statute state that contracts "not to be performed" within one year must be in writing. If it is possible to perform a contract within one year, then it falls outside the statute and no writing is required. That was the case here.

Contracts Transferring Real Property Rights   Under the Statute of Frauds, conveyances of real property must be in writing to be enforceable. This provision covers the sale of land; however, it also covers trusts that are created by one party, the trustor, permitting a second party, the trustee, to possess and control the land for the advantage of a third party, the beneficiary. Whether the provision includes leases is problematic, since some jurisdictions permit short leases, generally those that will last less than a year, to be oral. Most states, however, are relatively clear that leases that are designed to last longer than one year must be in writing to be enforceable. Moreover, it is not enough that the lease actually be in writing; the writing must also be presented to the court for it to be enforceable.

Example 12-2

Walt Nicklesworth entered a lease agreement with Marblehead Properties, under which Nicklesworth used the property located at 5293 Lake Shore Boulevard as a used book store. The terms of the lease included a right of first refusal under which Nicklesworth could purchase the property if Marblehead ever decided to sell. Two years into the five-year lease, Marblehead sold the property to Daniel O'Donnell. Nicklesworth brought suit for breach of contract. At trial, no one could produce a written copy of the lease for the judge. The judge dismissed the case because the Statute of Frauds required a writing and none could be produced at court.

It is also important to understand that when a party owns land, he or she owns a bundle of rights that can be distributed among various other parties. Thus, it is possible, for example, for the owner of a parcel of land to divide the rights to that land among several different parties. One party might hold a lease to a house on the land allowing her to live there, a second could have an easement that permits him to cross the land, a third might own the right to mine the land, and so on. The Statute of Frauds requires a writing for each of these different transactions. The object of this requirement is to make certain that there is a way to follow the trail of each of these rights to determine who owns them, should a dispute arise concerning them.

Example 12-3

In 1919, Pasha Patel owned several acres of land in the Upper Peninsula of the state of Michigan. Half a pond was located on Patel's land. The other half of the pond was located on land owned by Brooke Brookhaven. For a small bit of consideration, Patel transferred the right to cut ice on her side of the pond each winter to Fred Xavier. The contract was oral and was supposed to last for the next five winters. Each day from early October to late March, Xavier would cut the ice and remove it. He would then carefully carve the ice into large cubes that fit perfectly into the ice boxes located in the rental cabins dotting the upper peninsula. (This is 1919 remember.) He then sold the ice to the cabin renters. One summer Brookhaven drained her part of the pond. In October this meant that ice was sparse and what was available was sunk into the mud at the bottom of the lake and was thus unusable for carving and sale. Xavier brought suit against Brookhaven arguing that her action in draining the lake, made his interest in the property worthless. The court asked for a copy of the written contract transferring the right to cut the ice to Xavier. When Xavier could not produce one, the judge dismissed the case.

An exception to the rule that contracts for the sale of land must be in writing is called **part performance** or **equitable estoppel.** The exception applies when a person relies on an owner's oral promise to sell real property and then makes improvements on the property or changes his or her position in an important way. The plaintiff in such a case must prove three elements to succeed in a lawsuit. First, the plaintiff must show that he or she made the improvement relying on the original promise and without suspecting that the other party intended to renege on the agreement. Second, the plaintiff must show that any other remedy, such as restitution for the amount spent, is not enough to satisfy his or her effort or outlay of funds. Finally, the plaintiff must show that the part performance itself is evidence of the existence of the contract.

Example 12-4

Jake Iafigliola agreed in an oral contract to sell Dwight Zuer a run-down parcel of storefront property for $50,000. The storefront was located across the street from the site of a new Wal-Mart that was about to be established in the neighborhood. Relying on Iafigliola's agreement, Zuer spent $20,000 improving the premises so that he could move his video and DVD rental business into the storefront. Iafigliola then backed out of the deal. Zuer sued, asking the court to order Iafigliola to go through with the contract. Iafigliola argued this was a real property contract and it had to be in writing to be enforceable. Zuer asked the court to apply the part performance doctrine. Zuer made the following case. First, Zuer argued that he had made the

(Continued)

Background Information Throughout history, requiring orderly form for certain agreements has proved necessary. Possibly the oldest set of laws written on contracts is in the Babylonian Code of Hammurabi. According to the code, a person who obtained property without a written contract had committed a crime. Similarly, under Roman Law, a contract that did not adhere to the legal form could not be enforced.

Teaching Tips Give students some examples of contracts that will take more than one year to perform, such as an apartment lease, a construction contract, or a contract for employment. Make up dates for the contracts, for the start of performance on the contracts, and for the completion of the performance. Ask students which of the three dates one year is measured from according to the Statute of Frauds.

Related Cases Boothby, a top executive for a shoe company, was lured away by a competitor's agent to work for the rival firm. The agent assured Boothby orally that his position at the firm would be permanent. After three years, Boothby was fired. He filed suit against the firm, claiming breach of contract. The company defended by claiming that the statute of frauds prohibited the enforcement of the oral agreement. The court ruled in Boothby's favor, stating that the statute of frauds "does not apply to contracts which may be performed within, although they may extend beyond, one year." *Boothby v. Texon, Inc,.* 608 N.E. 2d 1028 (MA).

Example 12-4 (*Continued*)

improvements relying on the original promise. Second, he pointed out that any other remedy, such as restitution for the amount spent, would not be enough, because he clearly wanted the storefront in the lot across from the new Wal-Mart. Third, Zuer argued that the fact that he spent $20,000 to improve the storefront could not be explained in any other way other than his reliance on the contract. The court agreed and allowed the lawsuit even without the writing.

The courts do not require a writing for a contract in which the owner of land agrees to improve the land for the use of another party who has already received a partial interest in the land. In such a situation, the courts believe that, once the real interest in the land has been transferred, the contract to improve the land does not create a new interest. Instead, the new contract is solely a promise to provide labor and to make changes in the land. It, therefore, falls outside the statute and no writing is required.

Example 12-5

Rene Collins owned a piece of land in rural Pennsylvania, just outside Streetsboro. Frederick Dewey received an easement across Collins's land. The easement, which was supposed to last for five years, was executed in a written document. After the first year, Dewey asked Collins to lay gravel on the small road that constituted the easement. Collins said that she would not lay the gravel herself, but would permit Dewey to do so and would reimburse him for the expense. Dewey laid the gravel and presented Collins with the bill. Collins refused to reimburse Dewey as agreed. In contract Collins argued that, since there was no writing, the contract, which involved land, was unenforceable. The referee disagreed, concluding that the agreement to lay gravel did not create a new interest. Instead, it simply involved a commitment to pay for improvements to land in which Dewey already owned an interest.

Contracts for the Sale of Goods of $500 or More Under the UCC, contracts for the sale of goods (moveable items) for $500 or more must be in writing to be enforceable. However, there are four exceptions to this rule. Oral contracts for the sale of goods of $500 or more will be enforced in situations involving the following:

1. oral contracts between merchants when a written confirmation has been received by one party and not objected to by the other party
2. specially manufactured goods that cannot be resold easily
3. admissions in court
4. executed agreements

These exceptions are discussed in more detail in Chapter 15. Under international law (the United Nations Convention on Contracts for the International Sale of Goods), contracts for the sale of goods need not be in writing.

Certain Contracts Entered by Executors and Administrators An *executor* is a person who is named in a will to oversee the distribution of the estate of a deceased according to the provisions outlined in the will. An *administrator* is a person named by the court to do the work of an executor if none is named in the will or if the executor cannot or will not perform those duties. As a general principle of law, neither an executor nor an administrator is personally liable for the debts of the decedent's estate. Executors and administrators must pay the debts of the estate, to be sure, but out of the assets of the estate, not out of their own pockets. Thus, any promise to pay the debts of the estate using the executor's or the administrator's own funds is unenforceable without a writing.

Example 12-6

Max Quinn was named to be the executor of his sister's estate. One of his sister's creditors, Nancy Trautman, demanded immediate payment of a debt of $6,600 owed by the deceased. To protect his sister's good name, he promised Trautman that he would pay her the amount owed out of his own funds if the estate could not cover that amount. Trautman refused to agree unless Quinn placed the agreement in writing. Quinn agreed. After things calmed down, Trautman tried to collect the debt. Quinn refused to pay. Trautman would be able to enforce the promise because she has written evidence of Quinn's agreement to pay the debt.

Contracts by One Party to Pay a Debt Incurred by Another Party

A promise made by one party to pay another person's debts, if that person fails to pay the debt, falls within the statute and must be in writing to be enforceable. Several terms are used to describe these types of transactions. They are alternately referred to as a **guaranty of payment,** a **guaranty contract,** and a **collateral contract.** The promisor is usually called a **guarantor.** Often in a commercial setting the guarantor is referred to as a **cosigner.** The person to whom the promise is made is the **obligee** and the person who owes the original debt is referred to as the **obligor.** It is crucial to distinguish between guaranty contracts and original contracts.

The Opening Case Revisited
"Whose Debt Is It Anyway?"

In The Opening Case at the beginning of this chapter, Scott Rostow involved himself in two contracts. The first was with the Highgate Radio and Television Department Store. In this contract he agreed to pay for a DVD player, purchased by his brother, Franklin, if Franklin defaulted on any of his installment payments. Under those circumstances, the manager had agreed to sell the DVD player to Franklin. Later that same day, Scott took his daughter, Barbara, to the Yardley Friedman Clothing Outlet. When they arrived at the store, he told the owner, Teri Boterus, that his daughter could use his credit account to purchase her back-to-school wardrobe, as long as she spent no more than $499. Teri agreed to this arrangement and Barbara went off on her spending spree. Although these two situations appear to be very similar, they are actually quite different. The first agreement, the one with Highgate, is a guaranty contract, and, therefore, falls win of the Statute of Frauds, and requires a writing. In the second contract, Scott is the primary debtor; thus, a writing is not needed.

Terms *Executor, executive,* and *executioner* all come from the Latin word *sequi,* meaning "to follow."

Teaching Tips When students wonder about how a purely English law like the Statute of Frauds, became so ingrained within the American legal system, it might be helpful to refer to Lawrence Friedman's observations in his book *Law in America*: "(T)he colonies were poor in legal sources; few law books were published in the colonies, and lawyers and judges relied very much on English materials (not that these were themselves at all common in the colonies). William Blackstone's *Commentaries on the Laws of England,* published in the middle of the eighteenth century, became a wild best-seller in legal circles on the American side of the Atlantic. Here, in limpid and elegant English, and in the short space of four volumes, was a skeleton key to the mysteries of English Law: a guide to its basic substance." (See Friedman, Lawrence M. *Law in America: A Short History.* New York: The Modern Library, 2002, p. 31.)

Terms Both *valid* and *valiant* come from the Latin word *valere,* which means "to be strong and worthy."

Related Cases A prenuptial agreement should have complete disclosure of each party's assets. One prenuptial agreement was declared invalid because the groom's assets were not fully disclosed. The bride only knew that her husband-to-be was wealthy, and the evidence suggested that she underestimated the extent of his wealth. *Sogg v. Nevada State Bank,* 832 P.2d 781 (NV).

An exception to this rule is known as the primary objective test. Under the **primary objective test** (which is also referred to as the **leading objective test** and the **main purpose test**) if the promise to pay another party's debt is actually made to obtain a gain for the guar-antor, then there is no need for a writing to enforce the promise. Suppose, for instance, that Hans McKnight, the owner of Scottish Inn, depends upon the Hometown Bakery for the inn's sub buns for its lunch trade. Suppose further, that McKnight knows that the Hometown Bakery has had some financial trouble and may have to shut down its operation if it cannot pay Jakub's Supply for its regular flour shipment. If McKnight promises Jakub's that, if they continue to supply Hometown with flour, he will pay the bill, that promise falls under the primary objective test and need not be in writing to be enforceable.

Contracts in Consideration of Marriage   Agreements made in consideration of marriage must be in writing to be enforceable. This part of the statute does not refer to the marriage contract itself, or to engagement promises to marry, which are almost always oral. Rather, it refers to promises made by parties before marriage, in which they accept additional obligations not usually covered in the marriage vows. A **prenuptial agreement** (which is also referred to as a **premarriage agreement** and an **antenuptial agreement**) involves two people who are planning marriage, and who agree to change the property rights that they possess by law in a marriage (see Figure 12-1). Such promises are enforce-able only if they are in writing and are agreed upon prior to the marriage.

Example 12-7

Griff Forester and Gina Chambers entered a prenuptial agreement in which Forester promised that he would have no claim on Chambers's property or business should they divorce. Chambers agreed to give Forester $90,000 each year for the remainder of his life in the event of their divorce. She also promised to transfer $200,000 into Forester's account the moment that he agreed to the contract. This contract falls within the statute and, therefore, would have to be in writing to be enforceable.

Although this point is not directly related to the Statute of Frauds, it is good to know that a court is more likely to uphold a prenuptial agreement that includes a provision for consideration. The agreement in Example 12-7 contains the element of consideration and is, therefore, likely to be upheld in court, provided it was in writing in the first place.

Other Contracts   Each state has enacted special statutes outlining other agreements that must be in writing. Other contracts that are usually required by special statutes to be in writing include the release of a party from debt (general release) and the resumption of obligations after bankruptcy. In addition, some states require real estate listing contracts and insurance binders to be in writing. Other contracts that require a writing under the UCC are contracts for the sale of securities (stocks and bonds) and agreements creating security interests (see Chapter 30).

The Contents of a Writing

Just what is meant when the statute states that "the agreement must be in writing"? The statute requires only that the agreement be in writing—nothing more. The writing should be intelligible. It may be embodied in letters, memos, telegrams, invoices, and purchase orders sent between the parties. It may be written on any surface suitable for the purpose of recording the intention of the parties, as long as all the required elements are present.

Prenuptial Agreement

Agreement made this 10th day of June, 20 - -, between Joseph Taft of 1273 Holly Lane, Amesburgh, PA, and Susan Jacobs, of 299 Oak Lane, Amesburgh, PA.

Whereas a marriage is shortly to be solemnized between the parties hereto:

Whereas Susan Jacobs now owns a large amount of property and expects to acquire from time to time additional property under a trust established by her uncle, Henry Jacobs;

Whereas Joseph Taft has agreed that all of the property now or in the future owned by Susan Jacobs, or her estate, shall be free of all rights that he might acquire by reason of his marriage to her.

It is agreed as follows:

1. Susan Jacobs shall have full right and authority, in all respects the same as she would have if unmarried, to use, enjoy, manage, convey, mortgage, and dispose of all of her present and future property and estate, of every kind and character, including the right and power to dispose of same by last will and testament.

2. Joseph Taft releases to Susan Jacobs, her heirs, legal representatives, and assigns, every right, claim and estate that he might have in respect to said property by reason of his marriage to Susan Jacobs.

IN WITNESS WHEREOF the parties have hereunto set their hands and seals the day and year first above written.

Joseph Taft
_____

Susan Jacobs
_____

Figure 12-1 Contracts made in consideration of marriage must be in writing to be enforceable.

State Variations In California, Oregon, and Washington, the enforceibility of a prenuptial agreement depends upon whether both parties were represented by independent counsel at the drafting and signing of the agreement.

State Variations Many states' laws require certain contracts to be in writing. For example, in Colorado, outfitters and guides must provide their clients with written contracts. In California, it is illegal to build a swimming pool with third-party financial assistance without first having a written contract from the third party. In Massachusetts, contracts for customer goods or services over $25 made away from the place of business of the seller (such as through door-to-door selling) must be in writing to be enforceable.

Elements of a Writing To be absolutely complete, a written agreement, or **memorandum,** as it is often called, should contain the following elements:

- terms of the agreement
- identification of the subject matter
- statement of the consideration promised
- names and identities of the persons to be obligated
- signature of the party sought to be bound to the agreement

Example 12-8

For several weeks, Mary Shapiro and Harry Whitehall discussed making an agreement under which Shapiro would lease from Whitehall several hundred acres of pasture land outside Mt. Vernon for grazing her horses. Shapiro said that she needed the agreement to last for five years, but Whitehall wanted to grant only a year-by-year lease that would be renewable at the end of each year. Eventually, they compromised on a three-year lease that would be renewable at the end of the second year. Since they had been squabbling about the terms for so long, once the agreement was reached, Shapiro wanted to reduce it to writing. The moment that they agreed to the compromise, however, the two of them were standing in the parking lot at the local Wal-Mart. Shapiro pulled an envelope out of her back pocket and noted the conditions and terms of the agreement. She then handed the envelope to Whitehall who signed it and returned it to Shapiro who, because it was starting to rain, quickly stuck it in her back pocket without adding her signature. The two of them then parted company. The deal went through without a hitch until the end of the second year, when Whitehall refused to allow Shapiro to use his land any more despite the terms of the original agreement. Shapiro had to find a replacement pasture that cost her twice as much. She sued Whitehall for the difference. In court, Whitehall claimed that the writing that Shapiro had produced was invalid because it was written on an old envelope and because Shapiro had not signed it. The court held that the envelope-contract satisfied the requirements of the Statute of Frauds. The fact that the contract was handwritten on an envelope made absolutely no difference as long as all of the terms were present. Moreover, the fact that Shapiro's signature was missing made no difference because Whitehall was the party sought to be bound.

It has been held that the words on a check given in payment for a purchase can often satisfy the requirements of a memorandum. A check identifies the parties and is signed by one party on the front and by the other party on the back. All that is necessary is to write some additional words on the memo line of the check to set forth the terms of the contract and to identify the subject matter and the agreed price.

Example 12-9

Frank Jameson and Gary Muldovan entered an agreement whereby Muldovan agreed to grant Jameson an easement across his land for five years. Jameson gave Muldovan a check for $4,000. Jameson wrote on the check that it was payment for the five-year easement granted by Muldovan for his land located at 433 East 310th Street in

Willowick, Ohio. In a subsequent dispute, Muldovan did not deny the existence of the contract. However, he argued in a summary judgment motion that the contract was not enforceable because it involved real property rights and, therefore, had to be in writing. The court said that the check itself was evidence of a contract by one obligated to grant the easement rights because it described the terms of the agreement, the subject matter, and the price to be paid.

Quick Quiz 12-1 True or False?

1. A contract is said to be outside the statute if it requires a writing to show that the two objectives of the Statute of Frauds have been met.

2. An administrator is a person who is named in a will to oversee the distribution of the estate of a deceased according to the provisions outlined in the will.

3. Agreements made in consideration of marriage must be in writing to be enforceable.

12-2 Legal Rules for Written Contracts

Operating as a complex adaptive system, the legal system has developed certain basic criteria that make the construction and interpretation of written contracts as flawless as possible. These criteria act very much the way basic axioms or rules work in mathematics. Therefore, we could characterize these rules as unquestioned assumptions about the text of a writing that must be followed when an attorney, a magistrate, or a judge interprets a writing that claims to contain the terms of a contract. These four rules are: (1) the standard construction rule, (2) the parol evidence rule, (3) the best evidence rule, and (4) the equal dignities rule. The first two rules, the standard construction rule and the parol evidence rule, cover the interpretation of contracts, whereas the last two, the best evidence rule and the equal dignities rule, govern their enforcement.

The Standard Construction Rule

Appropriately, the first of the interpretation rules is the most critical and the most fundamental of the four. The **standard construction rule** guides the entire interpretation process by directing the interpreter of a contract to first determine the principal objective of the parties in the making of the contract. The *principal objective* is the primary or the main goal that the parties hoped to accomplish by entering the agreement in the first place. Once this principal objective is stated, then everything else must be interpreted in order to promote that principal objective. In line with this rule, the law also says that common words used in the contract are given their expected, everyday definition and technical terms or professional slang will be given their technical or professional definitions. The standard construction rule also says that any standard operating procedures that are used in the parties' professions or trades should also be followed whenever there is any doubt about what procedure should be used in the contract.

Since the standard construction rule is the most fundamental guideline involved in the interpretation of written contracts, it also guides the interpreter on matters of ambiguity and misinterpretation. The rule says that whenever an ambiguous term, clause, or line is found

Terms Although the word *evidence* is most closely related to the Latin *videre*, meaning "to see," it also is associated with the Greek *eidenai*, which means "to know."

Background Information An early case that invoked the parol evidence rule took place in 1806 when the buyer of a ship sued the seller for making a false claim that the ship would be copper-fastened. The bill of sale included no such provision. The court ruled that when a written contract is in force, "everything in parol becomes thereby extinguished."

in a prewritten or preprinted contract, that ambiguity is interpreted against the party who wrote the contract. This approach should encourage those people who draft contracts to do so in clear and unambiguous terms, because if they draft a clause that is ambiguous it will be interpreted against them. Thus, there is no profit in making things difficult to understand in any written contract.

The Parol Evidence Rule

Under the **parol evidence rule,** evidence of oral statements made before signing a written agreement is usually not admissible in court to change or to contradict the terms of a written agreement. Following oral discussion and negotiation, parties may reduce their agreements to some written form. When this is done, only the terms, conditions, and promises included in the writing will be allowed as evidence in court. This provision is enforced because the court presumes that the parties will have put everything they agreed to in the writing.

Example 12-10

Emily Twaine purchased a $1,250 desktop computer from Krell, Inc. Before all of the documents of sale were signed, the salesperson promised that she would get round-the-clock tech support from Krell technicians whenever she had a problem with her computer or any of the software associated with the computer. Krell subsequently refused to take care of any problems that Twaine had with the computer. The court ruled that the salesperson's oral warranty statements were not admissible in court because they were not contained with the other conditions in the written sales agreement.

Getting Students Involved In your discussion of exceptions to the parol evidence rule, encourage students to think about activities that they are involved in on a regular basis that require written contracts. Ask them to share their ideas of universal practices in those areas that might not be included in a written contract.

Exceptions to the Parol Evidence Rule The parol evidence rule will not apply when unfair and unjust decisions might result from its application. In cases in which a written agreement is incomplete, oral evidence may be used to supply the missing terms. Similarly, when a written contract is obscure or indistinct in certain of its terms, oral evidence may be used to clarify those terms. Also, if a written agreement contains a typographical or clerical error of some sort, the court will allow oral evidence as to the true intent of the parties.

Example 12-11

Edgar Bulwark was hired as an independent contractor to produce a series of magazine and journal articles that would appear under the name of a famous, and very busy, newspaper columnist. The written agreement had an error that indicated that Bulwark would receive $500 per article. The actual amount of consideration was supposed to be $5,000. The court would likely allow oral evidence to correct this obvious error.

In general, the courts allow a party to a written agreement to introduce oral testimony to show that the contract is void or voidable due to a lack of mutual assent or contractual capacity. The courts are willing to allow such testimony because it does not affect the terms of the agreement. Rather, it seeks to discredit the entire transaction. Thus, it is permissible to introduce oral evidence as to fraud, duress, misrepresentation, mistake, and undue influence. Similarly, it is appropriate to offer oral testimony as to a party's minority or mental incompetence.

Example 12-12

James Staniland contracted with Richard Morris, to purchase an original painting by Henrietta Stein, an artist who was a part of the Dadaist movement in Paris during the 1920s. After signing the written contract, Staniland took the painting and had it placed in the lobby of his business office. After one week, a customer spotted the painting and told Staniland that it was a forgery and that he had been defrauded by Morris. When Staniland took the witness stand during the trial, he was permitted to introduce evidence of the oral statements made by Morris that led him to the fraudulent conclusion that the painting was a genuine work by Stein. The court allowed the testimony because it did not affect the terms of the agreement. Rather, it sought to discredit the entire transaction.

If a written agreement is dependent upon some event before it becomes enforceable, then oral evidence may be offered concerning that condition precedent. A **condition precedent** is an act or promise that must take place or be fulfilled before the other party is obligated to perform his or her part of the agreement. The courts allow this type of oral evidence because, like the oral evidence involving assent and capacity, it does not have an impact upon the terms of the agreement, but it does on the enforceability of the entire contract.

Example 12-13

Asa Pierce agreed with Jay Lauretig to lease Lauretig's warehouse. The terms of the lease were laid out in a lengthy, detailed written agreement. However, as a condition precedent, a credit history and background check by Lauretig on Pierce would have to come back flawless; otherwise the deal would be canceled. When the Search and Discover Detective Agency reported that Pierce had both a bad credit rating and two criminal convictions on drug charges, Lauretig refused to go through with the contract. At court, the judge permitted oral testimony about the credit check and the criminal background search because they were precedent conditions that had to be met before the contract went into effect.

Oral evidence may be used to prove that the parties orally agreed to rescind or modify the terms of a written contract after entering into it. Subsequent negotiations to change or rescind the agreement are permitted, and evidence to that effect does not undermine the spirit of the parol evidence rule. However, if the change in the contract involves an agreement that would have to be in writing under the Statute of Frauds, then a writing would be required. Similarly, if the original written contract requires later modifications to be in writing, then that written requirement will rule.

Teaching Tips Ask students to think about the consequences of not having in writing any of the contracts described under the Statute of Frauds. Ask them to consider what would happen to the parties involved in each situation. Make sure the class understands that a failure to comply is not a crime and there is no punishment. Point out that the contract is simply not enforceable.

Example 12-14

George Laurie Construction entered into a contract with Terry and Sherrie Popson the terms of which indicated that Laurie Construction was to place aluminum siding, downspouts, and gutters on the Popson vacation house on Kelley's Island. The agreement was written out in a long, preprinted contract with blanks for the pertinent

(Continued)

> ## Example 12-14 (Continued)
>
> individual information. All of the appropriate blanks were filled in, the contract was signed by all the parties, and the job began on schedule. Once Laurie was on the job for three days, Sherrie Popson decided that she wanted a window placed on the house. She discussed the cost of the additional work with George Laurie who agreed to make the change indicated. The additional terms were not put in writing. After the job was completed, the Popsons paid the original amount but did not pay the added cost of the new window. The small claims court allowed testimony as to the terms involving the window because those terms represented negotiations subsequent to the original agreement to change the original terms.

UCC 1-205, 2-202, 2-208 (see pages 868, 871, and 872)

As a final exception to the parol evidence rule, the UCC allows oral testimony about how the parties have done business together over a long time period. The UCC makes allowance for this type of testimony because, from a practical point of view, parties often get so used to dealing with each other in a particular way that they neglect to include certain terms in their written agreements. Similarly, some practices are so universal in a particular trade, business, or industry that the parties feel no need to include such universal practices in their written contracts. Accordingly, the UCC allows oral testimony to supplement a written agreement as to these practices.

Teaching Tips Invite students to discuss their own related experiences in which oral understanding superceded written agreement. For example, students may cite job descriptions as agreements that commonly evolve in this way. Ask students if they think oral evidence should be more restrictive or whether it should not impact at all on the enforceability of a contract.

> ## Example 12-15
>
> St. Clair Printing, Inc., and the Commonwealth Chemical Company have been doing business for twenty years. St. Clair prints all labels, business cards, letterheads, invoices, and purchase orders for Commonwealth. During their long time working together, St. Clair has always delivered orders to Commonwealth. When a new foreman took over the bindery and delivery operation for St. Clair, he decided that there would be no deliveries to any customers outside a five-mile radius of the print shop. As a result, Commonwealth did not receive an important order of labels and lost several big orders. When Commonwealth sued St. Clair for breach of contract, St. Clair pointed out that there was nothing mentioned in the written contract about delivery responsibilities falling to St. Clair. However, because of their twenty-year history of consistently dealing with one another, the court, allowed oral testimony about past practices to supplement the written contract.

The Best Evidence Rule

Under the **best evidence rule** the courts generally accept into evidence only the original of a writing, not a copy. Under this rule, a written instrument is regarded as the primary or best possible evidence. Thus, the best evidence rule concurs with and supports the parol evidence rule.

The Equal Dignities Rule

The **equal dignities rule,** which is followed in some states, provides that when a party appoints an agent to negotiate an agreement that must be in writing, the appointment of the agent must also be in writing. In contrast, the appointment of an agent to negotiate an agreement that the law does not require to be in writing may be accomplished through an oral agreement.

Example 12-16

A state statute required that all agreements for the sale of real property be in writing. Lisa Genoa, whose apartment building was for sale, was leaving the country for three months. To expedite the sale of the building, Genoa orally appointed Anthony Young to sign a contract if a buyer were found for the apartment building. Because of the equal dignities rule, any contract that Young should sign with a potential buyer would be unenforceable. Genoa's appointment of Young as her agent should have been in writing.

Quick Quiz 12-2 True or False?

1. Whenever an ambiguous term is found in a preprinted contract, that ambiguity is interpreted in favor of the party who wrote the contract.

2. The principal objective is the main goal that the parties hope to accomplish by entering an agreement.

3. Parol evidence is another term for written evidence.

12-3 Formalities of Construction

Certain formalities are usually followed in the formation of other than the simplest kinds of written agreements. While the Statute of Frauds may necessitate nothing more than the briefest written disclosure of promises, conditions, and terms, plus the signature(s) of the obligated party or parties, usually contracts in general commercial and consumer use are carefully written, researched for legal compliance, and signed. Furthermore, leases and contracts for the sale of real property may have additional requirements of content and formality that extend beyond these formalities.

Signature Requirements

Written agreements should be, but need not be, signed by both parties. If signed by only one party, any obligation on the agreement would be limited to that party alone. Parties should use their usual signatures, that is, the signatures used in other matters in the regular course of business. However, any mark that the signer intends to be a signature will be the legal signature of that person. Although it is unusual, a party may adopt any name desired in creating a contractual obligation as long as the party intends to be bound by that signature. Thus, a well-known actress may sign a hotel register using a name other than her real name as a means of protecting her privacy. A signature may be a full name or initials, and it may be printed, typewritten, or stamped, as with a rubber stamp. However made, a signature must be made with the intent to be bound thereby.

Facsimile Signatures With the increased use of facsimile (fax) machines, methods have been adopted to bypass the best evidence rule by giving authentication to signatures sent by way of facsimile machines. A facsimile signature will be acceptable on a contract

Background Information In medieval England, the use of written contracts for dealing with goods and money frequently caused disputes in the courts. A defendant's seal on a contract was often enough to enforce the contract according to the terms within. If the defendant protested, however, that the seal was not his, the matter would be resolved in combat.

if the contract states that facsimile signatures are valid. More commonly, however, people will fax copies of signed documents to other parties and follow it up by sending the original signed documents by overnight mail or express delivery. Some states have enacted statutes allowing certain facsimile signatures.

Example 12-17

Massachusetts has enacted the following statute relative to residence insurance agents: "A facsimile of a signature of any such resident agent imprinted on any property or casualty insurance policy issued by mail, computer modem or facsimile machine, so-called, shall have the same validity as a written signature. (Mass. Gen. Laws Chapter 92, s. 43)

In addition, some states have adopted the **Uniform Facsimile Signatures of Public Officials Act.** This law allows the use of facsimile signatures of public officials when certain requirements are followed.

In cases in which a party cannot sign the written agreement due to illness, physical disability, or some other physical reason, another person may sign for that person. The signature should be followed by a statement indicating that the contracting party was physically unable to sign the document and that a signature was placed on the document by another person in the contracting party's presence and at the request of the contracting party. The person who has signed for the contracting party then signs the document (see Figure 12-2). Persons who lack the ability to read or write are often obliged to sign contracts. In such situations, the law accepts the person's mark, usually an X, properly witnessed, as a valid signature (see Figure 12-3).

Witnesses and Acknowledgments

Witnesses are required in the signing of a will and sometimes a deed, but in most other documents their signatures are at the option of the contracting parties. To ensure that no misunderstanding will arise as to the acceptance and signing of a written agreement, the use of witnesses is advised. Certain official documents, such as a certificate of title to a motor vehicle and a deed to real property, require the owner's signature and an **acknowledgment**

Getting Students Involved Assign students the task of finding out how to become a notary public and what services can be performed in that capacity. They should investigate legal requirements, cost, necessary training, and time limitations for the position.

Figure 12-2 The signature for an incapacitated person bears a witness's name.

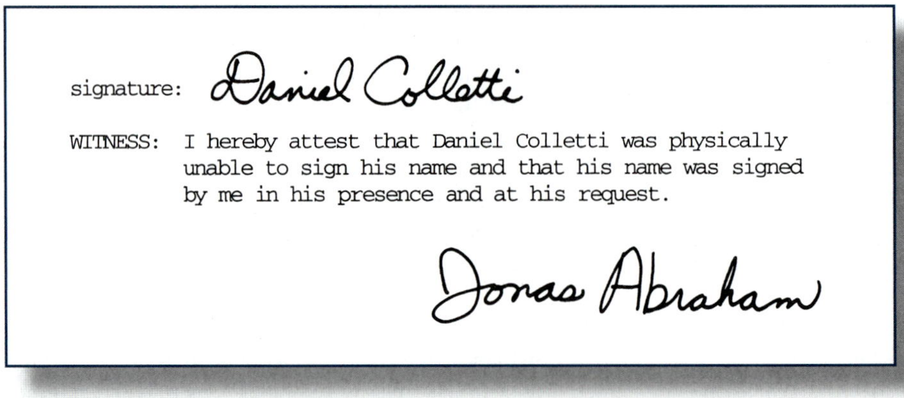

signature: *Daniel Colletti*

WITNESS: I hereby attest that Daniel Colletti was physically
          unable to sign his name and that his name was signed
          by me in his presence and at his request.

          Jonas Abraham

Her

Samantha X Cunningham

Mark

WITNESS: I hereby attest that Samantha Cunningham made her
mark as her signature and that, at her request, I
added her name to her mark.

Lindsay Quartermain

Figure 12-3 The signature (*X*) of a person who does not know how to write has been witnessed.

by a notary public that the signature was the person's free act and deed. The notary witnesses the signing of the document and then acknowledges this act by signing the document and adding the official seal to it. A notary is not authorized to read the document being signed and may be prevented from doing so.

Seal

Some states still make use of a seal when a formal contract is signed. Contracts for the sale and transfer of real estate sometimes come within this category. Historically, the seal was a carefully designed coat of arms, or other suitable design, mounted in a ring and used to impress markings in melted sealing wax placed on a document. As noted in Chapter 10, modern practice has dispensed with this custom, and today's seal is usually nothing more than the word *seal* or the initials *L.S.* for *locus sigilli* (place of the seal) printed or written next to the signature. In some states, a seal furnishes consideration in a contract that otherwise has none.

Recording

As a protection to lenders and to persons selling goods through installment contracts and the like, the law provides that certain documents be recorded in a public office for inspection by anyone wishing to know about them. For example, when money is loaned on a motor vehicle, the lender may record that transaction in the appropriate public office to protect his or her interest in the vehicle. The recording requirement is discussed in detail in Chapter 30.

Quick Quiz 12-3 True or False?

1. Written agreements must always be signed by both parties to the contract.

2. Facsimile signatures are not acceptable in any state.

3. The seal has become an outmoded means of proving the existence of a contract and, as a result, is no longer used in any state.

12-4 Cybercommerce and the Requirement of a Writing

Cybercommerce, or e-commerce as it is often called, involves transacting business by one of a wide variety of electronic communication techniques. One of the most common cybercommerce techniques involves buying and selling directly on the Internet, by accessing a company's website. Some companies, such as Amazon.com, have made a name for themselves by perfecting this cybercommerce technique. Other enterprises, such as eBay, have made a business of providing a marketplace for pulling buyers and sellers together in a cyberauction setting (see Chapter 15). Others, such as PayPal, provide financing support for other transactions. Still others, such as Orbitz and Priceline.com, have found a niche in the marketplace by providing access to bargain services on airlines and at hotels. There are, of course, problems associated with buying and selling on the Internet. One of these problems involves the difficulty of authenticating the identity of the person on the other side of an Internet connection. Another involves the question of how to deal with the fact that electronic transactions do not produce paper documents the same way that traditional transactions do. In both cases, the law has done what any complex adaptive system does; it has reacted and provided some solutions to these difficulties.

Verification Problems

Many cyberconsumers are attracted to the Internet because they can shop for a wide variety of products that might not be available from stores and businesses in their own hometowns. Buyers also have the additional advantage of being able to do all of this shopping from the comfort and security of their home or office. In addition, sellers also have many advantages when they do business on the Internet. Among those advantages is the fact that, through its website, a business can reach an enormous number of potential customers in a relatively short period of time. However, these advantages can also give rise to problems because firms that transact business on the Internet often deal with customers who are strangers to those firms. This is also a problem on auction sites such as eBay because the buyers and the sellers do not know one another. Questions can then arise as to the identity of a stranger and his or her authority to enter a contract.

These problems can be solved in a number of ways. For example, the parties can avoid the problem altogether by adding a term that delays the creation of the contract until the identities of the parties can be verified by some means other than by computers. Or a business might elect to use its website only as an advertisement site. These solutions are unsatisfactory to most businesspeople, however, because they eliminate the advantages of doing business on the Internet. Another technique is for the parties to an Internet transaction to individually customize the verification process for each contract. However, in the interests of efficiency and cost, it would be preferable to have a process that applies to all contracts.

A possible solution to this problem is the use of digital signatures. A **digital signature** is an encoded message that appears at the end of a contract that is created online. The receiver of the encoded message can use that encryption to authenticate both the identity of the sender and the content of the message. The digital signature is provided by a party known as a **certification authority.** It is the job of the certification authority to provide businesses with digital signatures and to make certain that those signatures are kept current. Those businesses and legal practitioners who promote the use of digital signatures hope that the courts and/or the legislatures will institute a principle which states that the use of a digital signature creates a rebuttable presumption that the signature is authentic and terms of the transaction have not been altered in transmission.

Business Law in the News
Just Click On the Dotted Line

Three years ago, just as the Internet bubble burst, Congress passed a law that was supposed to usher in a new era of e-commerce, one in which a wide variety of transactions would be sealed by a digital signature. For a host of technical, legal, and cultural reasons, almost nothing happened. But now, notaries public, the keepers of one of the nations' hoariest legal traditions, are getting ready to move into the digital era, opening the door to much broader use of e-signatures on contracts and other documents.

The digital signature most likely to dominate will strongly resemble the pen-and-ink kind. On May 28, the National Notary Assn., a professional organization of more than 200,000 notaries, will endorse a new system called the Electronic Notary Journal of Official Acts (ENJOA).

This will let notaries use computer files instead of paper logbooks to record their witnessing of official signings. The $550 ENJOA hardware-software package will save a digital record of the signature along with the notary's records and supporting information on signers, including digital photos and thumbprint scans. The heart of the system is Interlink Electronics' ePad, a device that resembles those used to sign credit card transactions at retailers such as Home Depot, but which provides greater protections against forgery. Legal documents themselves remain overwhelmingly paper and will be signed the old-fashioned way. But the ability of software such as Adobe Acrobat to add digital signatures to facsimiles of paper documents means that full electronic signing is not far off.

This is not the way most advocates of digital signatures expected things to work out. Three years ago, the dominant notion involved a mathematical procedure known as public key cryptography. Cryptographic signatures were designed so that they would not only positively identify the signer but would guarantee that the document had not been altered in any way since being signed.

It was a technically elegant solution, but its unfamiliarity was a huge drawback. Nothing about the signature itself, which appeared on an electronic document as either an icon or as a long string of random characters, resembled a "real" signature. Furthermore, for the process to work, the recipient of a digitally signed document had to verify the signature by checking the signer's "public key"—another long string of characters—against a database of keys maintained by a trusted third party. Companies such as VeriSign and Entrust provide public key services, but the mechanisms to assign keys to individuals have not developed.

Although we may be years away from a time when a digital key becomes a common part of anyone's identity, cryptographic signatures do play a vital role in e-commerce. For example, when Web browsers load secure pages, they check a signed digital "certificate" to make sure that the page on which you enter your credit-card number really does belong to Amazon.com. Businesses that do extensive online commerce use public-key signatures to validate purchase orders, invoices, and other electronic contract documents exchanged with their partners.

For signing actual documents, however, it's much more likely that a system based on digitized handwritten signatures will prevail. Devices such as the Interlink ePad do a lot more than just capture an image of a signature. They measure both the pressure and velocity of the stylus tip as you sign, which makes forging a signature difficult. Both images of the signature and the collected data can become part of the electronic version of any document signing.

Still, it will probably take some time before that stack of papers you face at a real estate closing will be replaced by a digitally signed electronic document. The rituals of signing documents have their roots in antiquity and won't change quickly. "The speed at which it happens will depend not on the technology, which is already here, but on its acceptance," says Milton G. Valera, president of the National Notary Assn. At last, however, we do seem to be moving forward.

(Continued)

Cybercommerce Legislation

Cybercommerce legislation has taken many forms over the last decade. However, the three most influential acts have been the E-Sign Act, the Uniform Electronic Transactions Act (UETA), and the Uniform Computer Information Transactions Act (UCITA).

The E-Sign Act The E-Sign Act is a federal act designed to deal with problems associated with cybercommerce, especially problems related to the recognition of electronic contracts and electronic signatures. Basically the act states that, if the parties to a contract have voluntarily agreed to transact business electronically, then the electronic contract that results will be just as legally acceptable as a paper contract. The act also notes that the parties must be able to store and reproduce the electronic record of the contract. Otherwise, the e-record will not be legally sufficient under the act. The final word here is that under provisions of the E-Sign Act, cybercontracts and cybersignatures are just as legitimate as their paper counterparts. There are a few documents that are not covered by the statute. These include court records, eviction notices, health insurance cancellations, wills, foreclosure notices, prenuptial contracts, and divorce papers. However, sale and lease of goods contracts as covered by the Uniform Commercial Code are also included in the E-Sign Act.

[UETA 2(8).]

The Uniform Electronic Transactions Act (UETA) The Uniform Electronic Transactions Act establishes the same type of legal parity between electronic records and paper records as does the E-Sign Act. It does not establish any new guidelines governing contracts just because they are entered electronically. The approach, therefore, is not to establish the differences between electronic contracts and paper agreements. Instead, the act focuses on the similarities, and, as a result, states that, once the parties to a contract have voluntarily agreed to enter a transaction using an electronic medium, the agreement that results in electronic form, including the electronic signatures, will be just as valid as a paper agreement. The UETA applies only to transactions, that involve some sort of commercial, business, or governmental matter. The act also states that if an act, such as the Statute of Frauds requires a writing and a signature, then an electronic record and an electronic signature will fulfill that requirement. The UETA defines an electronic signature as, "an electronic sound, symbol, or process attached to or logically associated with a record and executed or adopted by a person with the intent to sign the record."

The Uniform Computer Information Transactions Act (UCITA)

The Uniform Computer Information Transactions Act (UCITA) focuses on certain types of contracts, that is, those involved in the sale or lease of computer software, computer databases, interactive products, multimedia products, and any other type of computer information. The UCITA is in line with the basic provisions of the E-Sign Act and the UETA, in that it also declares that any transaction that is entered into using an electronic medium, is just as valid as a paper agreement. Very few states have adopted the UCITA and so its importance at the present time remains in doubt. Nevertheless, it would be wise to check on the applicability of the statute in your jurisdiction.

Quick Quiz 12-4 True or False?

1. The E-Sign Act is a model act designed to deal with problems associated with cybercommerce.

2. The Uniform Electronic Transactions Act was passed by Congress to deal with the legality of electronic transactions.

3. The UCITA is not in line with any of the provisions of the E-Sign Act or the UETA.

Summary

12-1 The Statutes of Frauds outlines six types of contracts that must be in writing to be enforceable. These six include contracts that cannot be completed within one year; contracts transferring real property rights; contracts for the sale of goods of $500 or more; certain contracts entered by executors and administrators; contracts by one party to pay a debt incurred by another party; and contracts in consideration of marriage.

12-2 The legal system has developed certain basic criteria that make the construction and interpretation of written contracts consistent. These four criteria are (1) the standard construction rule, (2) the parol evidence rule, (3) the best evidence rule, and (4) the equal dignities rule.

12-3 Certain formalities are followed in the formation of contracts. Written agreement need not be signed by both parties. However, any agreement signed by only one party would obligate only that party. Facsimile signatures are allowed on a contract if the contract states that such signatures are valid. Some states have statutes allowing facsimile signatures. Persons who are illiterate usually sign written contracts with an X. Such

signatures should be witnessed. Witnesses are not required when parties enter written agreements. However, to avoid misunderstanding the use of witnesses is still advisable. Some states still make use of the seal when a party enters a contract. Most, however, have disposed of the custom. The law provides that some documents must be recorded in a public office for inspection by the public.

12-4 Cybercommerce involves transacting business by one of a wide variety of electronic communication techniques. One of the most common cybercommerce techniques involves buying and selling directly on the Internet, by accessing a company's website. There are problems associated with buying and selling on the Internet. One of these problems involves the difficulty of verifying the identity of the person on the other side of an Internet connection. Another involves the question of how to deal with the fact that electronic transactions do not produce paper documents. In both cases, the law has provided some solutions to these difficulties. Three laws that address these problems include: the E-Sign Act, the Uniform Electronic Transactions Act (UETA), and the Uniform Computer Information Transactions Act (UCITA).

Key Terms

acknowledgment, 234

antenuptial agreement, 226

best evidence rule, 232

certification authority, 236

collateral contract, 225

condition precedent, 231

cosigner, 225

digital signature, 236

equal dignities rule, 232

equitable estoppel, 223

guarantor, 225

guaranty contract, 225

guaranty of payment, 225

leading objective test, 226

main purpose test, 226

memorandum, 228

obligee, 225

obligor, 225

parol evidence rule, 230

part performance, 223

premarriage agreement, 226

prenuptial agreement, 226

primary objective test, 226

standard construction rule, 229

Statute of Frauds, 221

Uniform Facsimile Signatures of
Public Officials Act, 234

Questions for Review and Discussion

1. What abuses did the Statute of Frauds attempt to eliminate?
2. What agreements must be written under the Statute of Frauds?
3. What information must be in a written contract?
4. What is the parol evidence axiom?
5. What are the exceptions under the parol evidence axiom?
6. What is the best evidence axiom?
7. What is the equal dignities axiom?
8. What are the various methods of writing a signature?
9. How are witnesses, acknowledgments, the seal, and recordings used today?
10. What are the most current cybercommerce laws?

Investigating the Internet

Access the Equality in Marriage website and report on the tips offered there for the writing of a prenuptial agreement.

Cases for Analysis

1. Harold Perdue entered an individually negotiated employment contract with Nicholas Paynter. Under terms of the contract, Perdue was to work for Paynter as a private investigator in Paynter's newly established firm known as Eye-Spy Investigations. The employment contract was on a trial basis and was to last for nine months. That nine-month period was set to begin one month after Paynter had set up shop. However, Paynter could not begin his operation until the contractors finished remodeling his office. Johnson Contractors, Ltd., had promised to have the office completed within one to three months. One month after the contract had been finalized, Paynter notified Perdue that he had hired someone else and that his services were no longer needed. Perdue, who had relied on the contract, had turned down several other lucrative offers that had since been filled by other operatives. Moreover, Perdue was now having trouble getting a similar job. Perdue threatened to bring suit against Paynter. Paynter told Perdue to go ahead and sue. Privately, Paynter believes that he

is immune to a lawsuit because, since Johnson Construction had three months to finish remodeling the office, the contract could not have been performed within one year. Perdue argued that, because Johnson could have finished in less than one month, the contract could be performed within a year, and it did not have to be in writing to be enforceable. Who is correct here? Explain.

2. Meng, a vice-president at Boston University, resigned his position to protest what he regarded as the unethical and unprofessional behavior of the University's president, John Silber, in terminating a recently renewed contract with Linkage Corporation. Silber orally promised Meng, as a severance package when he resigned, fourteen months of salary and benefits, and free tuition for two of his children if either should attend the university. Was the oral promise enforceable? Explain. *Meng v. Trustees of Boston University,* 96-9776 Appeals Court (MA).

3. As part of an employment agreement, Bazzy orally promised to give Hall an option to buy 1,000 shares of company stock at $20 per share. Hall brought suit against the company when it refused to sell the stock to him. What legal argument may Bazzy's company use to refuse to sell the stock to Hall as agreed? *Hall v. Horizon House Microwave, Inc.,* 506 N.E.2d 178 (MA).

4. Anna Wilson was assistant manager of a Montgomery Ward store. When Montgomery Ward announced that it would be closing the store, the manager quit, leaving Wilson in charge. A district manager orally promised Wilson that if she stayed on and assisted in the closing of the store, she would receive a sum of money calculated according to a certain formula. Wilson stayed on and managed the closing of the store (which took two months) in addition to her regular duties. Montgomery Ward refused to pay her the money, claiming that the oral promise was unenforceable. Was the store correct? Why or why not? *Wilson v. Montgomery Ward,* 610 F. Supp. 1035 (DC IN).

5. Curtis Hendrix orally agreed to compensate Beverly Spertell for services rendered in connection with their living together out of wedlock.

Later, when suit was brought to collect the money, Hendrix argued that the oral contract was unenforceable under the Statute of Frauds. Do you agree with Hendrix? Explain. *Spertell v. Hendrix,* 461 N.Y.S.2d 823 (NY).

6. Lawson hired Konves to conduct extensive audits of her eighty-seven boutiques, located throughout the United States. As part of the agreement, Lawson required Konves to spend one week at each boutique. Konves demanded a written agreement before she would agree to Lawson's terms. Why was Konves correct in making this demand?

7. Butler leased a certain piece of property from Wheeler with an option to purchase it at a later date. The agreement was handwritten and consisted of two separate documents, each listing part of the transaction. Butler later attempted to purchase the property but Wheeler refused to sell, claiming that the agreement was unenforceable because it was contained in two documents. Was Wheeler correct? Explain. *Butler v. Lovoll,* 620 P.2d 1251 (NV).

8. Ray's Motor Sales sold a mobile home to Hathaway. Before the written contract was signed, the salesperson told Hathaway that Ray's would take care of any problems that Hathaway might have with the mobile home. This promise was not included in the written document. When Hathaway had problems with the mobile home, he asked Ray's to take care of them. Ray's refused to be of any assistance. Could Hathaway enforce Ray's promise? Explain. *Hathaway v. Ray's Motor Sales,* 247 A.2d 512 (VT).

9. Madden sued the president and board of directors of Georgetown College on a number of different issues involving breach of contract and negligence. One question before the court was whether the contract was under seal. The question was crucial because it affected the statute of limitations. In this case, the word *seal* was printed on the page. However, it was not next to the signatures but an inch above and to the left, over the word *attest.* Was this a sealed contract? Explain. *President of Georgetown College v. Madden,* 505 F. Supp. 557, (D. MD).

Quick Quiz Answers

12-1	1. F	12-2	1. F	12-3	1. F	12-4	1. F
	2. F		2. T		2. F		2. F
	3. T		3. F		3. F		3. F

The Opening Case

"Your Assignment, Should You Choose to Accept"

When Sara and Patrick Sullivan decided to buy a summer cottage on the lake they went directly to Oak Island Reality in Lakefield. Sherri Collins, a real estate agent with Oak Island, showed the Sullivans several properties. However, once the couple saw a ranch house located at 206 Saffron, they knew that they had found their summer home. Collins arranged for the Sullivans to meet with Rene Fulton, a loan officer at the Boulder City Bank, a local financial institution, that was so small it had only two branches: the main branch in downtown Boulder City, and a branch in nearby Port Hillary. Because the Sullivans had an excellent credit history and were in good shape financially, the mortgage went through without any problems. The Sullivans received a payment book that they were to use to make their $1,487 payment each month. Patrick got into the regular habit of stopping by the Boulder City office each month to pay the mortgage in cash. Then, seemingly out of the blue, the Sullivans received a notice informing them that their mortgage had been assigned to the Fourth Sixth National Bank, a Toledo-based financial institution. Under the assignment, the Sullivans would have to mail their mortgage payment to Fourth Sixth National in Toledo. Patrick, who in the past had experienced very poor service from Fourth Sixth, and from banks in Toledo in general, refused to acknowledge the assignment and continued to pay the Boulder City Bank. Hank Nugent, a new teller with Boulder, continued to accept the cash payments from Patrick. When Fourth Sixth National threatened to foreclose on the Sullivans' mortgage for nonpayment, the Sullivans argued that they had continued to pay Boulder City. The Boulder City Bank, however, had no record of the payments and denied that they had received anything from the Sullivans. The bank also could not locate Hank Nugent, who no longer worked for the Boulder City Bank, and who had left Boulder City for parts unknown. Who is responsible for the Sullivans' loss? Did the Sullivans have the right to ignore the Fourth Sixth assignment and continue to pay Boulder City or should they have recognized the assignment, despite their misgivings? Questions such as these are addressed in this chapter.

Chapter Outcomes

1. Explain the legal rights given to intended beneficiaries.
2. Identify the legal rights given to incidental beneficiaries.
3. Explain the assignment of rights.
4. Explain the delegation of duties.
5. Identify the three parties in an assignment.
6. Indicate who is responsible for giving notice of an assignment.
7. Explain the obligations of the parties to an assignment.
8. Identify contracts that cannot be assigned.
9. Explain the nature of a novation.
10. Distinguish between a novation and an assignment.

13-1 Contracts and Third Parties

A **third party** is a person who may, in some way, be affected by a contract but who is not one of the contracting parties. A third party, also known as an **outside party,** is at times given benefits from a contract made between two or more other parties. A third party receiving benefits from a contract made by others is known as a **beneficiary.** Although not obligated by the agreement made between those in privity, third parties may have the legal right to enforce the benefits given them by such agreements.

Intended Beneficiaries

A beneficiary in whose favor a contract is made is an **intended beneficiary.** With exceptions in some states, an intended beneficiary can enforce the contract made by those in privity of contract. Those who are most frequently recognized to be intended beneficiaries and who have the right to demand and enforce the benefits promised are creditor beneficiaries, donee beneficiaries, and insurance beneficiaries.

Creditor Beneficiaries A **creditor beneficiary** is an outside third party to whom one or both contracting parties owe a continuing debt of obligation arising from a contract. Frequently, the obligation results from the failure of the contracting party or parties to pay for goods delivered or services rendered by the third party at some time in the past.

Example 13-1

Annette Marquard owed Floyd Hodges a balance of $1,236 for the vinyl siding that Hodges put on her house. On another contract, Marquard agreed to resolve some problems that Vince Castele was having with his computer on the condition that Castele would give Marquard's $250 fee to Hodges toward payment of the $1,236 debt. The second contract made Hodges a creditor beneficiary with the right to demand payment from Castele if the $250 is not paid.

Donee Beneficiaries A third party who provides no consideration for the benefits received and who owes the contracting parties no legal duty is known as a **donee beneficiary.** However, the contracting parties owe the donee beneficiary the act promised; if it is not forthcoming, the donee beneficiary may bring suit. The consideration that supports this type of agreement is the consideration exchanged by the parties in privity of contract.

State Variations In North Dakota, a contract made expressly for the benefit of a third person may be enforced by the third person at any time before the parties to the contract rescind it.

Background Information Under common law, abstract rights such as collections or lawsuits were not routinely transferred to other parties, and a transferee could not sue for the right to do so. With the development of contract law during the 1800s, the value of transferring abstract rights became evident in the marketplace, and the practice more common.

Teaching Tips Ask students to think of contracts that involve third parties. Have them confirm that each contract they suggest involves an actual third party rather than all contracting parties.

Teaching Tips One of the justifications for the rights of third persons in contracts is the idea that the law in general, and the law of contracts in particular, should endorse distributive justice. Distributive justice promotes the belief that the law has a responsibility to make certain that, when a case is decided, even a contract case, one of the factors that must be taken into consideration is the effect that it will have on how wealth and resources are distributed in the community. In fact, some legal authorities go so far as to argue that distributive justice "must be taken into account if the law of contracts is to have even minimum moral acceptability." (See Murphy, Jeffrie G., and Jules L. Coleman, *Philosophy of Law: An Introduction to Jurisprudence,* Boulder, CO: Westview Press, 1990, p. 165.)

Teaching Tips Ask students if any of them have ever been either an intended or an incidental beneficiary to a contract. Also ask if any of them have ever entered into a contract that was designed to benefit a third party or that unintentionally benefited a third party. Remind them that insurance contracts and collective bargaining agreements involve third-party beneficiaries.

Example 13-2

Carl Carpenter agreed to landscape Wade Shepherd's property for $600. Carpenter, however, wanted Shepherd to pay the $600 fee to Carpenter's daughter. The daughter would be the donee beneficiary. If Shepherd failed to pay her the $600, Carpenter's daughter would have the right to bring suit to collect the money.

Insurance Beneficiaries An individual named as the beneficiary of an insurance policy is usually considered a donee beneficiary. The beneficiary does not have to furnish the insured with consideration to enforce payment of the policy. In some cases, an insurance beneficiary may also be a creditor beneficiary. This situation occurs in consumer or mortgage loans when the creditor requires the debtor to furnish a life-term insurance policy naming the creditor as the beneficiary. The policy will pay the debt if the debtor dies before the loan has been repaid (see Chapter 29).

Incidental Beneficiaries

An **incidental beneficiary** is an outside party for whose benefit a contract was not made but who would substantially benefit if the agreement were performed according to its terms and conditions. An incidental beneficiary, in contrast to an intended beneficiary, has no legal grounds for enforcing the contract made by those in privity of contract.

Example 13-3

Mark Faber owned a hotel and restaurant in downtown Indianapolis. The Brotherhood of Aerospace Workers (BAW) had a contract with the city for the use of the municipal auditorium for the union's annual convention. One week before the convention, the union announced that it was canceling the meeting. The move was a clear violation of BAW's contract with the city. Faber brought suit against the BAW for damages due to lost business caused by the breach. The court dismissed the case on a motion for summary judgment. The court ruled that Faber was an incidental beneficiary and, therefore, had no grounds upon which to bring the suit against the union.

Quick Quiz 13-1 True or False?

1. Third party rights were set down in an organized fashion for the first time in the Uniform Commercial Code.

2. The principle of privity stopped many judges from establishing third party rights.

3. Incidental and intended beneficiaries have the same rights.

13-2 The Law of Assignment

When people enter contracts, they receive certain rights and they incur particular duties. It is completely accepted today that, with some exceptions noted later and unless the contract itself provides otherwise, these rights and duties can be transferred to others. An **assignment** is a transfer of a contract right and a **delegation** is a transfer of a contract duty.

Terms *Assignment* has its origins in the Latin word *signare,* meaning "to mark or sign." *Delegate* is also from a Latin word, *legare,* which means "to send as emissary." To differentiate between the two words, think of a delegation as the sending of an emissary and an assignment as a signing over of rights to a third party.

Example 13-4

Fred Fisher wanted to purchase Steve Ruppert's dry cleaning business. Ruppert, however, refused to sell to Fisher because of a long-standing dispute between the two businesspeople. Instead, Ruppert entered a written agreement to sell the business to Hazel Harding. Nothing in the contract said the contract could not be assigned to another party. Before the deal was carried out, Harding assigned her rights under the contract to Fisher. Ruppert was now contractually bound to sell the business to Fisher even though he did not want to. If Ruppert refused to sell the business to Fisher, he would be in breach of contract and would suffer the legal consequences, undoubtedly intensifying the bad blood that already existed between Fisher and him.

Assignment and Delegation Distinguished

In general, rights are *assigned* and duties are *delegated.* In most cases, both are governed by the same rules. If A is owed money by B, A may assign to C the right to collect the money. On the other hand, if A has agreed to pay B to harvest 200 acres of wheat for a price, B may delegate the duty of harvesting to C. Restrictions against the delegation of duties are presented later in this chapter.

Getting Students Involved On the board, illustrate the rights and duties of parties involved in a contract. Draw a line between two points, A and B, representing the two parties in a contract, to show privity of a contract. Draw another line from A to X to show that either party in the contract can transfer his or her rights or duties to a third party. When duties are transferred, such an assignment is called a *delegation.* Next, point out that if A transfers all rights and duties to X, A will still be responsible to B. If B would agree, A could be released from the contract and privity would exist between X and B, creating a novation.

Example 13-5

Lee Wesley agreed to lay asphalt on the sidewalk in front of Walter Lerro's house for $4,000. Plans and specifications were provided by Lerro. Wesley would have the right to delegate the duties involved in laying the asphalt to another contractor. Similarly, the new party might assign to another the right to collect the $4,000 from Lerro after the job was ended.

Parties to Assignment

Three parties are associated with any assignment. Two of the parties are the ones who entered the original agreement. The party who assigns rights or delegates duties is the **assignor.** The outside third party to whom the assignment is made is the **assignee.** The remaining party to the original agreement is the **obligor.**

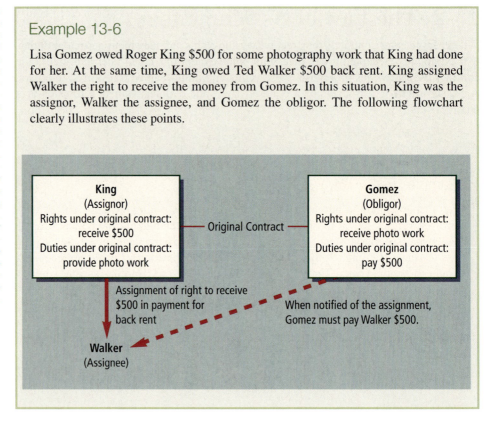

Example 13-6

Lisa Gomez owed Roger King $500 for some photography work that King had done for her. At the same time, King owed Ted Walker $500 back rent. King assigned Walker the right to receive the money from Gomez. In this situation, King was the assignor, Walker the assignee, and Gomez the obligor. The following flowchart clearly illustrates these points.

Consideration in Assignment

Consideration is not required in the assignment of a contract. When there is no supporting consideration, however, the assignor may repudiate the assignment at any time prior to its execution. In the previous example, the consideration supporting King's assignment is found in the rental agreement between King and Walker.

In addition, when no consideration is given for an assignment, creditors of the assignor may have the assignment rescinded on the ground that it is a fraudulent conveyance. A **fraudulent conveyance** is a transfer of property with the intent to defraud creditors. If the $500 assignment to Walker in Example 13-6 had been a gift instead of for payment of back rent, King's creditors could have had the assignment rescinded, because they could rightfully anticipate the money coming from Gomez.

Assignment Methods

To be valid, an assignment must follow certain accepted procedures designed to protect all of the parties. Form of assignment, notice of assignment, and the rights of parties in successive or subsequent assignments must conform to practices established by case law and state statutes.

Form of Assignment
Assignment may be accomplished through written, oral, or implied agreements between the assignor and the assignee. Parties to an assignment must

observe the requirement provided by the equal dignities rule discussed in Chapter 12. Under that rule, the law requires that if the agreement by the original parties must be in writing, the assignment, too, must be in writing.

Example 13-7

Alexis Amenott agreed in writing to sell his collection of antique glassware to Francis Joliet for $1,600. The written contract was executed properly following the requirements of the Statute of Frauds. Joliet then made an oral assignment of the contract to Daniel Parenti. Sometime later Joliet had second thoughts and decided to renege on the assignment. When Parenti tried to enforce the assignment, he discovered, much to his dismay, that because the assignment had not been in writing, the court could refuse to enforce it.

Some state and federal laws require certain types of assignments to be in writing (Figure 13-1).

Figure 13-1   This is the type of assignment that Joliet should have made to Parenti in Example 13-7. Why was the contract between Joliet and Amenott required to be in writing?

<u>Assignment</u>

For value received, I, Francis Joliet, of 4444 Flowers Road, Lewiston, Maine, hereby assign, transfer, and set over to Daniel Parenti, of 2441 Kenwood Circle, Bainesville, Maine, all my rights and interests in and to a contract with Alexis Amenott, dated March 2 of this year, a copy of which is attached hereto, subject to all terms and conditions thereof. In witness whereof, I have executed this assignment at 97 Erieview Plaza, Mercedes, Maine, on May 4, 20 - -.

F. Joliet
Francis Joliet, Assignor

<u>Acceptance of Assignment</u>

Daniel Parenti hereby accepts the foregoing assignment, subject to all terms and conditions therefore.

Daniel Parenti
May 4, 20 - -   Daniel Parenti, Assignee

Notice of Assignment An assignment is valid at the time it is made. As a measure of protection against subsequent assignments, the assignee should give notice of the assignment to the obligor. Although this is an obligation of the assignee, either party may give notice. Once notice is received, the obligor should deal with the assignee. If notice is not given, it would be normal practice for the obligor to render performance to the other original contracting party, the assignor. If due notice has been given and the obligor makes payment to the assignor, the obligor is not excused from making payment to the assignee.

Figure 13-2 This was the format used by Bryant, Inc., in the case described in Example 13-8, to notify Newfield of the assignment from Pendleton.

Bryant, Inc.
6225 St. Clair Avenue
Cleveland, OH 44103

June 15, 20 - -

Mr. Carl Newfield
750 Maple Street, Apt. 4-C
Lakewood, Ohio 44117

Dear Mr. Newfield:

You are hereby notified that Pendleton Architects Limited of Euclid, Ohio, has assigned to Bryant, Inc., all rights to its claim against you in the amount of $750.

You are further notified to direct all payments to Bryant, Inc., at the above address to ensure credit for payment.

Sincerely yours,

Norbert Bryant

Norbert Bryant
Vice-President

A Question of Ethics

Joliet's oral agreement in Example 13-7 to assign the contract to Parenti was unenforceable because of the equal dignities rule. Is the equal dignities rule just and fair? How do you feel about the legality of someone breaking an oral promise? Why does the law have such a provision? Is it ethical? What has happened to the old fashioned saying that a person's word is his or her bond?

Example 13-8

Carl Newfield owed Pendleton Architects Limited $750 as a final payment for architectural work. Pendleton, in turn owed Bryant, Inc., a substantial sum. As partial payment of that amount, he assigned Newfield's debt to Bryant. As the assignee in this case, Bryant sent a letter to Newfield indicating that the debt that he owed to Pendleton should now be paid to Bryant, Inc. Figure 13-2 presents a copy of the letter that Bryant sent to Newfield informing him of the assignment. Newfield would now be legally required to adhere to the assignment.

Subsequent Assignments Should the assignor make a subsequent assignment of the same right, the courts must decide which of the two assignees has a superior right and claim against the obligor. A majority of the states hold that the first assignee has a superior right even if a later assignee was the first to give notice of the assignment to the obligor. A minority of courts hold that whichever assignee was first to give notice of assignment has a superior right and claim to any assigned benefits.

Getting Students Involved Have students investigate local laws to find out which assignee prevails in claims against the obligor—the one to give first notice or the first to receive assignment. Discuss the possible difficulties and benefits of having assignees share assignments equally.

Quick Quiz 13-2 True or False?

1. A delegation is the transfer of a contractual right.

2. The equal dignities axiom has no application in the law of assignment.

3. It is the responsibility of the assignor to give notice of the assignment to the obligor.

13-3 Assignment Rights, Duties, and Restrictions

Rights can be assigned and duties can be delegated. While this rule seems simple enough, disputes still arise concerning both assignment and delegation. What is generally in dispute is whether a particular right or duty can be transferred, and if, so what legal effects arise from that transfer.

About the Law

An assignment, rather than a negotiation occurs when a check is transferred to a third party without a required indorsement.

Rights and Duties of the Assignee

The rights and duties of the assignee are the same as those previously held by the assignor under the original contract. It is fair to say that the assignee "steps into the shoes" of the assignor. Claims the assignor may have had against the obligor now belong to the assignee.

The Opening Case Revisited

"Your Assignment, Should You Choose to Accept"

When the Sullivans received a notice informing them that their mortgage had been assigned to the Fourth Sixth National Bank, they were obligated to make their mortgage payment to the new bank. The Sullivans had no choice in this matter. They had been notified by Fourth Sixth Bank of the assignment and they were, therefore, legally obligated to honor that assignment. In essence, Fourth Sixth Bank had "stepped into the shoes" of Boulder City Bank in relation to the Sullivan mortgage, and the Sullivans could ignore that assignment only at their own risk.

Also, defenses the obligor may have had against the assignor's claims may now be used against the assignee.

The assignee's duty in an assignment is to give notice of the assignment to the obligor. The obligor is allowed a reasonable time to seek assurance that an assignment has been truly made. Making the assignment in writing reduces the possibility of one's fraudulent representation as an assignee.

Example 13-9

Quitter appeared at the payroll department of the Meadville Delivery Company and told the paymaster that one of Meadville's drivers, Stalker, had made an assignment of part of his paycheck to her. Under terms of the assignment, Quitter was to receive $150 of the money that Meadville owed to Stalker. Meadville, the obligor, would not have to pay Quitter the $150 until the paymaster had a reasonable amount of time to verify the assignment.

Liabilities and Warranties of the Assignor

The assignor is obligated to any express and implied warranties that serve to protect either the assignee or the obligor. A **warranty** is a promise, statement, or other representation that a thing has certain qualities.

Warranties to the Assignee The assignor is bound by an implied warranty that the obligor will respect the assignment and will make performance as required by the original agreement between the assignor and the obligor.

Example 13-10

Suppose, in the Quitter-Stalker assignment, that the Meadville Trucking Company had been either unwilling or unable to pay Quitter the $150. Stalker would be bound by an implied warranty to Quitter that the $150 would be paid. If the assignment were a gift to Quitter, there would be no enforceable warranty in the absence of consideration between the assignor and the assignee.

Warranties to the Obligor If the assignor delegates to an assignee duties owed the obligor, there is an implied warranty that the duties delegated will be carried out in a complete and satisfactory manner.

Example 13-11

Heinecken delegated the duties under a contract for the remodeling of Donohue's kitchen to Edberg. Edberg's work was unsatisfactory. In fact after careful investigation, Donohue discovered that the work done by Edberg was far below what was considered satisfactory in the home remodeling profession. Donohue sued Heinecken for the amount of money Donohue subsequently spent to have the kitchen done properly. The court awarded that money to Donohue, stating that Heinecken had breached the implied warranty that duties delegated will be carried out in a complete and satisfactory manner.

Restrictions on Assignments

While most contracts may be assigned, those for personal and professional services may not. The right of assignment may also be restricted by agreement of the original parties to the contract and, in certain cases, by law.

Restrictions on Personal and Professional Service Contracts A party may not delegate duties that are of a personal or professional nature. *Personal,* in this context, means "other than routine." Musicians or artists, for example, could not delegate their services to someone else. They are chosen for their ability or artistic talent. Professional services are those rendered by physicians, lawyers, certified public accountants, ministers, and others. People in these occupations are selected because of their special abilities, and their services could not be delegated to someone else. In contrast, routine services may usually be delegated. These are services performed by electricians, mechanics, woodworkers, plumbers, waitstaff, bankers, publishers, and others whose skills and abilities are judged according to the usual customs and standards of the marketplace.

Restrictions Imposed by Original Contract Parties to a contract may include a condition that will not allow its assignment. Some courts have held that a restriction against assignment of a debt owed by the obligor robs the assignor of a property right guaranteed by law and would be contrary to public policy. Other courts have permitted this restrictive condition. If, in Example 13-11, Donohue had included a condition against assignment, the assignment to Edberg would have been void.

Restrictions Imposed by Law Assignment, in special situations, may be restricted by law or declared void because it is contrary to public policy. Thus, members of the armed services may not assign any part of their pay except to a spouse or family member. Police officers, persons elected or appointed to public office, and others are likewise restricted from making assignment of their pay or of duties that they have been especially chosen to perform.

Novation and Assignment

Sometimes a party to a contract will assign all rights and delegate all duties to a third party (the assignee). Once this happens, the assignee will work directly with the obligor, performing the duties and receiving the benefits.

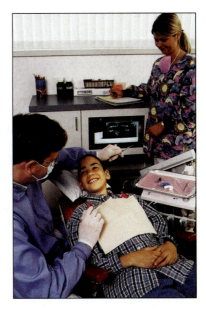

Contracts for professional services cannot be assigned.

Business Law in the News
What's Next, Free Popcorn?

The Hottest New Stop on Hollywood's marketing rounds is a tiny cable channel called G-4. Sure, it currently reaches barely one-fifth of households. But studios in search of a big opening weekend for action or science-fiction flicks love the 12-to-34-year-old gamers who tune in to the 24-hour channel; they're twice as likely to see a movie on its opening weekend as the overall population. That fact has helped G-4 sign up 70 movie advertisers this year—twice the total in 2003, says Charles Hirschhorn, CEO of G-4 Media LLC.

For studio execs, attracting first-weekenders has become crucial. If a movie doesn't open big right away, it is quickly muscled out by the next blockbuster. For years, Hollywood has relied heavily on network-TV advertising to bring in the crowds. But that is no longer enough. The under-25s who make up nearly a third of the moviegoing public these days are abandoning the networks for cable, the Web, and video games. The change has left the studios scrambling to find new ways to reach their most avid audience. "People don't sit at home and watch *Friends* any longer," says Jeffrey Godsick, Twentieth Century Fox's executive vice-president for marketing. "Our biggest job now is to go and find them."

The stakes are always high this time of year, as Hollywood prepares to roll out its biggest-budget flicks for the summer. But this popcorn season looks especially fraught. For starters, the money at stake has soared. The average cost of making and marketing a film now tops $100 million. What's more, studios are cramming the schedule with 44 movies, according to Exhibitor Relations Co., up from 40 last year.

The risks are higher, too. Following a handful of big-time flops in the summer of '03, including *Lara Croft Tomb Raider: The Cradle of Life,* the studios are releasing fewer sequels this year. Instead, they're rolling out dozens of original films with lesser-known actors, including Walt Disney Co.'s *The Village,* which features Joaquin Phoenix. Such films often require heftier marketing budgets than sequels, which feature known characters and themes.

10-Minute Clips

Against this wildly competitive backdrop, the studios are trying a range of new marketing tactics. When they do turn to TV, they're going well beyond the traditional 30-second trailer. Most studios are offering extensive free footage in hopes of duplicating the success Universal reaped by airing the first 10 minutes of *Dawn of the Dead* on the USA Network in March. And Hollywood is ramping up its use of special programs. As part of Disney's efforts to promote *The Village,* director M. Night Shyamalan is hosting a screening of his previous film *Unbreakable* on ABC and showing clips of the new flick during commercial breaks.

Gadgetry is helping studios reach people, too. Sony Pictures Entertainment, which gave away 500,000 DVDs containing 10 minutes of its hit film *Hellboy* to Best Buy shoppers in March, may do the same for summer releases. Research had shown that Best Buy's TV and computer shoppers were likely opening-day moviegoers. To lure teen girls, Fox plans to send out cell-phone ring tones and text messages with theater times for its Will Smith thriller *I, Robot,* and for *Dodge Bail,* a Ben Stiller comedy.

The studios, following audiences to the Web, have also boosted online ads. Last year, Yahoo! Inc. put up ads for 131 movies, up from 74 in 2002, according to Jim Moloshok, the portal's senior vice-president for media and entertainment, Yahoo! recently launched a major blitz for *Shrek 2,* including linking the green ogre to ticketing site Fandango.

Will any of this help Hollywood avoid a repeat of last summer's doldrums? That depends on whether it offers up better flicks. Ticket sales are up around 9% this year, but Mel Gibson's *The Passion of the Christ* accounts for much of that increase. Mel got those numbers by enlisting churches eager to bus folks to the movie. There's a lesson here: When it comes to filling seats, sometimes you have to go where the audience is.

Questions for Analysis

1. Why is it crucial for movie advertisements to attract as many first weekenders as possible for a first-run feature film? Explain.

2. What has happened that has caused movie studios to change their advertising tactics? Explain.

3. Could one marketing firm delegate its duty to run an advertising campaign for a new feature film to another agency? Explain. Could G-4 delegate its duty to present a trailer for a new film to another cable network? Explain.

4. Suppose a movie studio discovers that the best way to market its upcoming big-budget film is to advertise with G-4. If it does not enter a contract with another television network as a result, could the network, as a third party beneficiary, bring a lawsuit? Explain.

5. What if a movie studio pulls a movie that was supposed to run for one month out of that theater after only a week's run? Does the pizza restaurant next door to the theater have a cause of action as a third party beneficiary? Explain.

Source: Ronald Grover. "What's Next, Free Popcorn?" *BusinessWeek,* May 3, 2004, p. 56.

Nevertheless, the assignor will remain in privity of contract with the obligor and will be liable to the obligor if the assignee does not perform or performs improperly.

Teaching Tips Write several short descriptions of contracts and have students determine if they are assignable or not. This exercise could be used as a quiz.

Example 13-12

Allgood Canning Company entered into a contract to sell 1,000 cases of baked beans to Superfine Market for a specific price. Shortly thereafter, Allgood delegated its duty to ship the beans and assigned its rights to receive the money to Fastway Canning Company. The beans Fastway shipped turned out to be bad. If Superfine were to bring suit for damages, it would have to be brought against Allgood because that was the company with which it had contracted. There was no privity between Superfine and Fastway.

Teaching Tips After reviewing the difference between assignment and delegation, describe various contracts and have students differentiate between rights assigned and duties delegated. Include examples of novation and contracts that would not be assignable because of types of restrictions that students have learned about in previous sections.

In contrast, if all three parties agree, the assignor can be released from liability at the time of the assignment, and privity of contract can exist between the assignee and the obligor. Such an arrangement is called a **novation,** which is a substitution, by mutual agreement, of a new party for one of the original parties to a contract. If, in the above case, Superfine and Fastway had agreed to release Allgood from responsibility under the original contract, a novation would have occurred. Privity of contract then would have been between Superfine and Fastway. Superfine's only recourse upon receiving the bad beans would have been to bring suit against Fastway since, by mutual consent, Allgood was discharged.

State Variations The Louisiana legislature has defined a novation to be the extinguishment of an existing obligation by the substitution of a new one.

Quick Quiz 13-3 True or False?

1. The phrase "assignment of a contract" means the same thing as the phrase "assignment of rights."

2. Personal and professional duties are just as transferable as all other duties.

3. Novations have been outlawed under the Restatement of Contracts.

Summary

13-1 Third parties are at times given benefits through a contract made between two other parties. Some contracts are made specifically to benefit a third party. Such a third party is known as a third party beneficiary. Three types of intended beneficiaries include creditor beneficiaries, donee beneficiaries, and insurance beneficiaries. Some third parties benefit from a contract even though the contract was not made for their benefit. These parties are known as incidental beneficiaries.

13-2 The transfer of contract rights to a third party outside of the original agreement is an assignment. In general, rights are assigned and duties are delegated. However, the rules apply to both transfers in the same way. The party who assigns rights or who delegates

duties is the assignor. The outside third party to whom the assignment is made is the assignee. The remaining party to the original agreement is the obligor. The assignee must give notice of assignment to the obligor.

13-3 The rights and duties of the assignee are the same as those held by the assignor under the original agreement. Contracts for personal or professional services cannot be assigned. Assignments also can be limited by agreement. A novation occurs when two contracting parties agree to replace one of the parties with a new party. The new party (the assignee) agrees to enter the contract with the remaining original party (the obligor), causing a privity of contract between them.

Key Terms

assignee, 245

assignment, 245

assignor, 245

beneficiary, 243

creditor beneficiary, 243

delegation, 245

donee beneficiary, 243

fraudulent conveyance, 246

incidental beneficiary, 244

intended beneficiary, 243

novation, 253

obligor, 245

outside party, 243

third party, 243

warranty, 250

Questions for Review and Discussion

1. What are the legal rights given to intended beneficiaries?
2. What are the legal rights given to incidental beneficiaries?
3. What is an assignment of rights?
4. What is a delegation of duties?
5. Who are the three parties in an assignment?
6. Who is responsible for giving notice of an assignment?
7. What are the obligations of the parties to an assignment?
8. What contracts cannot be assigned?
9. What is the nature of a novation?
10. How does a novation differ from an assignment?

Investigating the Internet

Access the website for the National Conference of Commissioners on Uniform State Laws, and conduct a search for the Uniform Fraudulent Conveyors Act. Report on any planned revisions to this Act.

Cases for Analysis

1. Lyla Prendergast hired Rene Jolas to paint portraits of the Prendergast family. The commission was to consist of one portrait that involved the entire family to include Mr. and Mrs. Prendergast; their three children, Brittany, Bryce, and Stephen; Stephen's wife, Gwenyth; and Bryce's husband, Peter. Jolas was also to do an individual portrait of each family member. Jolas did the family portrait himself and the individual portraits of Mr. and Mrs. Prendergast. However, because he had other commitments, Jolas delegated the duty to do the other portraits to Jack Fleming. This delegation was unknown to Mrs. Prendergast. When the portraits were unveiled, Mrs. Prendergast was satisfied with the portraits of herself and her husband and of the family, but she did not believe that the other portraits were up to the talent of Jolas. Nevertheless, she took the portraits and paid Jolas. Several months later, while at dinner, the Prendergast family was discussing the portraits and Mrs. Prendergast finally figured out that the other portraits had been done by Fleming. When she protested to Jolas, he argued that since there was no clause in their contract forbidding the delegation, it was his right to make such a transfer. Mrs. Prendergast argued that he had no such right. Who is correct here? Explain.

2. The Louisville Thoroughbreds, a professional soccer team, entered a seven-year agreement with the city to hold twenty-six soccer matches each year at the city's outdoor stadium in the downtown area. The Thoroughbreds lived up to their end of the agreement for the first four years. However, by the end of the fourth year, the owner of the Thoroughbreds threatened to move the team to Tampa Bay because the city had not made the agreed-to repairs and improvements to the stadium. The city argued that the improvements had to be made only if the overall attendance for five years running passed the 1 million mark. The Thoroughbreds argued that the team had reached the million mark each year and that the five-year rule was, therefore, inoperative. When the city continued to avoid making the repairs and improvements, the Thoroughbreds corporation moved the team to Tampa Bay, as promised. The city sued the team. In a parallel development following the filing of the original lawsuit, a group of seven downtown hotels and twelve restaurants joined together to bring a second lawsuit against the Thoroughbreds for breach of contract. The Thoroughbreds filed a summary judgment motion to dismiss the second lawsuit, arguing that the hotels and the restaurants did not have standing to sue because they were not in privity under the terms of the original contract and were, therefore, only incidental beneficiaries under the contract with the city. The hotels and restaurants argued that they were in fact intended beneficiaries, because the whole idea of having a professional soccer team in the downtown area was to stimulate business in that part of town. Who will prevail in the summary judgment motion? Explain.

3. Leslie and Roland lived together without being married and had one child. In addition, Leslie had two children from an earlier marriage. After a four-year relationship, Roland brought court proceedings to evict Leslie and to obtain custody of their child. Leslie hired a lawyer who brought a breach of contract action on her behalf against Roland. Shortly thereafter, Leslie and Roland settled both lawsuits by themselves without the attorney's participation. They agreed that Leslie and the three children would return to live with Roland and that he would support them. Roland also agreed to pay Leslie's legal fees. Can the attorney recover his legal fees from Roland under the agreement between Leslie and Roland? Why or why not? *Margolies v. Hopkins,* 514 N.E.2d 1079 (MA).

4. Under a divorce decree, Blackston was ordered to pay $600 a month in child support to his former wife. The decree provided that the payments were to be paid to the clerk of the court's office. The clerk of the court assigned the right to receive the payments to the Department of Human Resources. Who was obligated to notify Blackston of the assignment? *Blackston v. State Ex Rel. Blackston,* 585 So.2d 58 (AL).

5. Gary Jones retained the law firm of Irace and Lowry after being injured in a motorcycle accident. Later, Jones required surgery after dislocating his shoulder in an unrelated incident. Having no money to pay the surgeon, Jones signed a letter requesting that the money from the accident settlement be assigned to Dr. Herzog for treatment of a

shoulder injury that occurred at a different time. The law firm was notified of the assignment. When the settlement was received by the law firm, Jones instructed the firm to pay the money to him rather than to the surgeon. It did, and the surgeon was never paid. Could Dr. Herzog recover the money owed him from the law firm? Why or why not? *Herzog v. Irace,* 594 A.2d 1106 (ME).

6. The Chicago Tribune Syndicate and Press Service, Inc., had a contract to furnish the old Washington Post Company with four comic strips. These strips included *The Gumps, Gasoline Alley, Winnie Winkle,* and *Dick Tracy.* The *Washington Post* went bankrupt, and the bankruptcy trustee assigned the right to receive these comic strips to the reorganized company owned by Meyer. The Tribune Syndicate claimed that the contract could not be assigned. Accordingly, they canceled it and sold the rights of those strips to the *Washington Times.* Was the contract to furnish the comics assignable? Explain. *Meyers v. Washington Times Co.,* 76 F.2d 988 (DC Cir.).

7. Powder Power Tool Corporation negotiated a collective bargaining agreement with the International Association of Machinists. The agreement went into effect on August 24. Employees, however, were to receive a wage increase retroactive to April 1. Several workers who had been employed on April 1 at the old wage scale were not working on August 24. These workers assigned their rights to the retroactive wage increase to Springer. The corporation refused to pay Springer, claiming that the former employees were not parties to the contract, and, as incidental beneficiaries, could not bring suit to enforce the contract. Was the corporation correct? Explain. *Springer v. Powder Power Tool Corporation,* 348 P.2d 1112 (OR).

8. Copeland contracted with McDonald's Systems, Inc., for a franchise. Copeland was granted the fast-food outlet franchise for Omaha. McDonald's also gave Copeland first refusal rights for any plans to open other franchise outlets in Omaha. Copeland exercised the right several times, opening several additional outlets. He then sold the franchise to Schupack and assigned to Schupack the right to open new McDonald's outlets in Omaha. When Schupack tried to exercise the first refusal right, McDonald's objected, claiming its relationship with Copeland developed through a special confidence in Copeland's ability to manage and promote its new franchise outlets. Was McDonald's correct? Explain, *Schupack v. McDonald's Systems, Inc.,* 264 N.W.2d 827 (NE).

9. Timbercrest built a house for the Murphys. After occupying the house for a while, the Murphys complained of several problems. Timbercrest fixed the problems, and the Murphys had no further complaints. The Litwins bought the house from the Murphys three years later. When the house was sold, neither the Litwins nor the Murphys were aware of any problems. After living in the house for two years, the Litwins became aware of several problems. The Litwins then contacted the Murphys and had the Murphys assign them their rights under the original construction agreement with Timbercrest. The Litwins then sued Timbercrest, claiming Timbercrest had breached its contract with the Murphys by not providing them with a house free of defects. Were the Litwins correct? *Litwins v. Timbercrest Estates, Inc.,* 347 N.E.2d 378 (IL).

10. Nolan wrote the song "Tumbling Tumbleweeds" and, in an agreement with Sam Fox Publishing Company, transferred all rights to the song to the company. In return, Nolan was to receive royalties according to terms laid out in the agreement. Sam Fox later assigned all rights and interests in "Tumbling Tumbleweeds" to Williamson Music, Inc. Was it necessary for Sam Fox to obtain Nolan's consent before making the assignment to Williamson? Explain. *Nolan v. Williamson Music, Inc.,* 300 F. Supp. 1311 (S.D. NY).

Quick Quiz Answers

13-1	1. F	13-2	1. F	13-3	1. F
	2. T		2. F		2. F
	3. F		3. F		3. F

Chapter 14   Discharge and Remedies

The Opening Case
"A High-Speed Tram for Nottingham?"

For many of us in the United States, Nottingham is the imaginary home of the legendary Robin Hood. However, for the Carillon Corporation, a British-based construction firm, Nottingham turned out to be the source of serious, if unexpected problems. Carillon Corporation is responsible for running 25 percent of the railway service in Great Britain, and so it was a safe bet to succeed when it was awarded a new contract to construct an inner-city express tram facility in Nottingham. Carillon landed the £80 million project shortly after it split from the Tarmac Group, its parent corporation. The Nottingham tram project was proceeding on schedule in midsummer when, unexpectedly, experts had difficulty during the testing stages of the new system. The problem seemed to be focused on the attempt to integrate the new high-speed tram system with the existing Nottingham rail network. The "glitch" in the integration of the Nottingham systems delayed the inauguration of the high-speed tram for several months and cost Carillon £10 million. Carillon had no choice but to absorb the loss and forge ahead. What would have happened to this contract had it occurred in the United States? What if the rail system could never be integrated with the existing Nottingham system? Could Carillon have claimed impossibility of performance and pulled out of the contract? Does the frustration of purpose doctrine apply in such a case? Would commercial impracticability apply in this situation? How does the fact that the operation of the high-speed tram system will be late affect the performance of the contract? These are some of the questions addressed in this chapter on discharge and remedies.

Chapter Outcomes

1. Explain the concept of reasonable time in the performance of a contract.
2. Relate what constitutes satisfactory performance of a contract.
3. Outline the difference between complete and substantial performance.
4. Distinguish among conditions precedent, concurrent, and subsequent.
5. Define tender of performance.
6. List the ways that a contract can be discharged by nonperformance.

7. Clarify the concept of anticipatory repudiation.
8. Enumerate the types of damages available in the event of a breach of contract.
9. Describe mitigation of damages.
10. Contrast specific performance with injunctive relief.

For a detailed account of the story outlined in The Opening Case see: Stevenson, Rachel. "Carillon to Take £10m Hit After Tram Costs Spiral." *The Independent,* July 11, 2003, p. 21.

14-1 Discharge by Performance

Most contracts are discharged by **performance,** which means that the parties do what they agreed to do under the terms of the contract. When performance occurs, the obligations of the parties end. Sometimes, however, the parties do not perform in a timely or satisfactory manner. At other times, they perform partially but not completely. At still other times, they do not perform at all.

Time for Performance

When the time for performance is not stated in the contract, the contract must be performed within a reasonable time. A **reasonable time** is the time that may fairly, properly, and conveniently be required to do the task that is to be done, with regard to attending circumstances. Whether a task is performed within a reasonable time or not is a question of fact to be decided by the jury in a jury trial or by the judge in a nonjury trial.

Example 14-1

Rostow Aviation, Ltd., entered a contract with Futuregraphics, Inc., for the design and implementation of a new website for Rostow. The website was supposed to be up and operational for Rostow within sixty days of the making of the contract. Futuregraphics was one week late in the completion of the website. Rostow attempted to rescind the agreement claiming that time was of special importance. The court ruled, however, that it had not been clearly established that time was essential for the completion of the website. Since time was not essential to satisfactory performance of the agreement, Rostow was held to the contract.

A Question of Ethics

The court held Rostow to the contract in Example 14-1 even though Futuregraphics was one week late in fulfilling its part of the agreement. Since time really wasn't essential to the agreement, and since Rostow presumably knew that, was it ethical for Rostow to raise the issue of Futuregraphics' lateness in the first place? If time had been important to the completion of the website, didn't Rostow have a responsibility to raise the issue of time before the contract was finalized? If Futuregraphics knew it was running behind schedule, did it not have a duty to notify Rostow and offer some sort of compensation for the breach? Explain your answers.

When the time for performance is stated in the contract but there is nothing to indicate that time is of particular importance, the court will usually allow additional time to perform.

When the time for performance is stated in the contract and there is something special about the contract that indicates that time is essential, the time for performance will be strictly enforced.

Example 14-2

Spectrum Images, Inc., entered a contract with the entire Carter City school system for the design, production, and distribution of the yearbooks for each of the system's three high schools. A very strict schedule was developed for each high school yearbook staff specifying when the manuscript, art, and photos had to be delivered to Spectrum, when the material had to be read and returned, and when the page proofs had to be read, corrected, and returned to Spectrum. The yearbooks were to be delivered to each high school ninety days after Spectrum had received all page proofs so that they would be ready for distribution on graduation day for each of the high schools. In such a situation, it is clear that time is an important factor in this agreement.

Similarly, when the phrase "time is of the essence" is included among the terms of a written contract, the time period will be enforced. The phrase makes it clear that the time element is of the utmost importance to the parties.

Some contracts use a "best efforts" clause so as not to commit parties to a date but instead to commit them to do their best to perform by a certain date. A *force majeure* clause provides for the intervention of unforeseen circumstances. Such a clause usually limits those circumstances to extreme or unusual events, such as acts of God, strikes, and government regulations.

Satisfaction of Performance

Satisfactory performance exists when either personal taste or objective standards have determined that the contracting parties have performed their contractual duties according to the agreement. Satisfactory performance is either an express or implied condition of every contract. Sales agreements for consumer goods often express this condition by including the words "money back if not entirely satisfied." In other contracts, satisfaction may be

The Opening Case Revisited
"A High-Speed Tram for Nottingham?"

In The Opening Case at the beginning of the chapter, we learned that Carillon Corporation landed an £80 million project to add a high-speed tram to the Nottingham railway system. The Nottingham tram project proceeded on schedule until midsummer when, unexpectedly, experts had difficulty integrating the new high-speed tram system with the existing Nottingham rail network. The snag in the integration of the Nottingham systems delayed the inauguration of the high-speed tram for several months. The system, which was supposed to be operational in November, did not get up and running until the new year. A *force majeure* clause might have protected Carillon from losses resulting from this unexpected delay. Whether Carillon would benefit from such a clause would depend on whether the unforeseen incompatibility of the two railway networks was on the list of unexpected difficulties that would excuse nonperformance by a specified date.

carefully defined according to the expectations of the parties. When there is no express agreement, the law implies that work will be done in a skillful manner and that the materials or goods will be free of defects. Ordinarily, the parties may be discharged from a contract only if there has been satisfactory performance.

Sometimes, one person will agree to do something to another person's satisfaction. Services rendered in a beauty salon or barbershop, photographs taken at a studio, and portraits painted by an artist are in this classification. Regardless of the skill and application of the person doing the work dissatisfied customers may, on the basis of their personal judgment and satisfaction, refuse to make payment.

Example 14-3

Christine Droulliard commissioned Jean Luc Velliquette to sculpt a marble statuette for the front lawn of her summer residence. Velliquette, who was quite confident in his skills and talent as an artist, told Droulliard that, unless she was satisfied with his work, she would not have to pay for the statuette. Droulliard's personal taste and judgment would be the determining factor as to satisfaction in this situation. If Droulliard should not like the statuette, she would not have to pay Velliquette for his services. Moreover, Velliquette would not be discharged from the obligations or freed from his liability until he performed satisfactorily according to Droulliard's personal taste and preferences.

Satisfactory performance of contracts not involving personal taste is determined by objective standards. Contracts for the sale of mechanical devices and services offered by tradespeople are of this type.

Example 14-4

Hutchinson Construction, Ltd., contracted with Baymount Beach Entertainment, Inc., to construct a new high-speed roller coaster for the summer opening of Baymount's amusement park in Idlewild, New Jersey. Because of a serious defect in the construction plans, the scaffolding for the roller coaster would not support the weight of the cars. As a result, it was impossible for Baymount to commission the ride and the roller coaster could never be used safely. When Hutchinson sued for nonpayment, Baymount countersued, demanding that Hutchinson remove the structure so that the entertainment company could hire a new construction firm to build a new roller coaster for the next season. The court used an objective standard here and the decision went to Baymount.

Complete and Substantial Performance

Complete performance occurs when all the parties fully accomplish every term, condition, and promise to which they agreed. **Substantial performance** occurs when a party, in good faith, executes all promised terms and conditions with the exception of minor details that do not affect the real intent of their agreement. Complete performance terminates an agreement, freeing the parties of any further obligation to one another. Ordinarily, substantial performance also serves to discharge the agreement but with a difference.

A party who complains that performance has been substantial, but not complete, has the right to demand reimbursement from the offending party to correct those details that were not performed.

Example 14-5

McLaughlin Construction, Inc., was the primary contractor for the construction of a new engineering center for South Central State College. The construction of the center was supposed to be completed within one year, and the doors were to open in time for the fall term. The building was, in fact, completed by fall, but the architect for McLaughlin had committed an error in his plans. Apparently, he had failed to take into consideration the stress that would be placed on the floor-to-ceiling windows in the building's lobby. As a result, several floor-to-ceiling cracks developed in the floor-to-ceiling windows. An inspection by the state engineers demonstrated that there was no danger to anyone in or near the building. Nevertheless, the cracked windows were quite unsightly, and they leaked heavily when it rained. Consequently, the college demanded that the construction company make repairs at its own expense. The company refused and the college threatened to rescind the entire contract. Instead, cooler heads prevailed and the college went out and hired another construction firm to make adjustments to the stress so that the floor-to-ceiling windows would be the show piece they were supposed to be. When the college asked for and was refused reimbursement for the additional expense, it sued McLaughlin. The court held that there had been substantial performance of the original contract. However, because the cracked windows were shown to be caused by an error on the part of the McLaughlin architect, the court awarded reimbursement costs to the college.

Contractual Conditions

Some contracts have conditions or terms that determine the rights and duties of the parties prior to performance, during performance, and following performance. Conditions may be classified as conditions precedent, conditions concurrent, or conditions subsequent.

Condition Precedent
A **condition precedent** is a condition that requires performance of certain acts or promises before the other party is obligated to pay money or to give other consideration agreed to. In a *unilateral contract,* the performance of a condition precedent serves as the offeree's acceptance of the offer. In a *bilateral contract,* it is a promise that if not performed leads either to rescission or to termination of the entire agreement.

> ## Example 14-6
>
> Pressler, a third-year law student, signed an agreement to accept a position with a law firm. The members of the firm agreed to hire Pressler on the condition that she receive her law degree and pass the bar examination in their state. Earning the law degree and passing the bar examination are conditions precedent to the performance of the obligation of the law firm in giving Pressler the position.

Condition Concurrent A condition that requires both parties to perform at the same time is a **condition concurrent.** A promise to deliver goods supported by the buyer's promise to pay on delivery is a very common condition concurrent. Real estate sales agreements, by custom, usually state that the owner-seller will deliver a good and complete deed to the real property on the buyer's presentation of either cash or a certified check for the amount of the purchase price. Failure of either to do as promised concurrently would be a breach of the express contract condition.

Condition Subsequent A **condition subsequent** is one in which the parties agree that the contract will be terminated on a prescribed event occurring or not occurring. An agreement between a builder and a client stating that contract performance would terminate if a required building permit were not obtained from the issuing public authority within sixty days after the contract is signed is a condition subsequent. Some warranties included in contracts are also illustrative of these conditions.

> ## Example 14-7
>
> Luben Metcalf agreed to remodel a garage for Trisha Graham for $15,000. Both parties signed a written agreement. One clause in the agreement stated that Metcalf guaranteed that the improvements would be free from defects for twelve months after the work was completed. Graham agreed to pay for the improvements upon completion. Metcalf's guarantee constituted a condition subsequent, that is, a condition that applies after both parties have performed their primary obligations under the contract.

A condition subsequent is commonly contained in a fire insurance policy, for example. The insured typically agrees in the policy that the report of a fire loss must be made within thirty days of the loss or the insurer will be free of obligation to reimburse for loss.

Tender of Performance

Tender of performance means to offer to do what one has agreed to do under the terms of the contract. If someone has agreed to sell a parcel of land for $40,000, for example, tender of performance would be offering to give a signed deed to the buyer at the agreed time. Similarly, **tender of payment** would be presenting the $40,000 to the seller at the agreed time.

It is important to make tender even if one knows that the other party is not going to perform the contract. This provision is necessary in some states to test the other party's

State Variations In Montana and Oklahoma, when a breach of duty has caused no appreciable detriment to the affected party, he or she may still recover nominal damages.

Related Cases A contract dispute arose between a seed corn grower and a seed corn buyer. Due to an infestation of shattercane, the grower was unable to fulfill the terms of the contract, so the buyer sued. The court ruled that a clause in the contract that allowed for the grower to release certain acres of fields if certain events occurred, such as infestation, was a condition subsequent. Once infestation occurred, the grower was no longer obligated to supply the full amount of seed corn. *Schmidt v. J. C. Robinson Seed Co.,* 370 N.W.2d 103.

Terms One form of the legal term *tender* describes an action. It refers to presenting something, usually money or service, for acceptance. As a noun, tender is the offer itself and not the payment or service that will satisfy the obligation in question. Have students look on a dollar bill for the statement "This note is legal tender for all debts, public and private."

State Variations It is the law in nearly every state that a purchaser of real estate is entitled to specific performance of a contract to purchase property, because every piece of property is considered unique.

willingness and ability to perform. If neither party has made tender, a court would hold that a breach of contract has not been established. Thus, neither party would be in a position to bring suit against the other.

People who must perform acts (such as selling goods or performing services) are excused from performing if they make proper tender and it is rejected. On the other hand, people who must pay money are not excused from paying if their tender of payment is rejected. They are merely excused from paying further interest on their obligation.

Quick Quiz 14-1 True or False?

1. Very few contracts are discharged by performance.

2. A condition precedent is a condition that requires performance of certain actions before the other party to the contract is obligated.

3. Tender of performance means to offer to do what one has agreed to do under the terms of the contract.

14-2 Discharge by Nonperformance

Nonperformance may be defined as failing to fulfill or accomplish a promise, contract, or obligation according to its terms. Sometimes the failure to perform makes a party vulnerable to legal action. However, not every instance of nonperformance results in a legal action. Sometimes, nonperformance results from mutual agreement between the parties. At other times, nonperformance is excused because of conditions that make performance impossible or by operation of law. Nevertheless, under certain circumstances nonperformance will result in a breach of contract. Discharge by nonperformance often comes about in the following ways:

- discharge by agreement
- discharge by impossibility

- discharge by operation of law
- discharge by breach of contract

Discharge by Agreement

Parties to a contract may stipulate the time and conditions for termination and discharge as part of their agreement. They also may subsequently agree not to do what they had originally promised. The latter is the case when there is a mutual rescission of the contract, a waiver of performance by one or more of the parties, a novation, or an accord and satisfaction to liquidate an outstanding debt or obligation.

Termination by Terms of the Contract During contract negotiation, parties may agree to certain terms that provide for automatic termination of the contract. For example, a professional athlete may contract with management that their agreement will be terminated if for any reason the player becomes either physically or mentally incapable of rendering full performance.

Mutual Rescission Contracting parties may, either before or after performance commences, rescind their contract as a result of further negotiation and by their mutual assent.

Mutual rescission, in the majority of cases, requires both parties to return to the other any consideration already received or to pay for any services or materials already rendered.

Termination by Waiver When a party with the right to complain of the other party's unsatisfactory performance or nonperformance fails to complain, **termination by waiver** occurs. It is a voluntary relinquishing (waiver) of one's rights to demand performance. A waiver differs from a discharge by mutual rescission in that a waiver entails no obligation by the parties to return any consideration that may have been exchanged up to the moment of rescission. Discharge by waiver, when made, is complete in itself.

Novation By novation, the parties to a contract mutually agree to replace one of the parties with a new party. The former, original party is released from liability under the contract. Novation is discussed in detail in Chapter 13.

Accord and Satisfaction An accord and satisfaction is a resulting new agreement arising from a bona fide dispute between the parties as to the terms of their original agreement. The mutual agreement to the new terms is the accord; performance of the accord is the satisfaction—thus, accord and satisfaction. The accord, although agreed to, is not a binding agreement until the satisfaction has been made. The original agreement is not discharged, therefore, until the performance or satisfaction has been provided as promised. Accord and satisfaction is discussed in Chapter 10.

General Release A **general release** is a document expressing the intent of a creditor to release a debtor from obligations on an existing and valid debt. A general release terminates a debt and excuses the debtor of any future payment without the usual requirement that consideration be given in return.

Discharge by Impossibility

Occasionally, it becomes impossible to perform a contract. For example, when the subject matter of a contract, without the knowledge of the parties, had been destroyed before the contract was entered into, the contract would be discharged.

Example 14-8

While working in Seattle, Nancy McFadden agreed to purchase a condominium in Tampa belonging to Walter and Wilma Sterkel for $580,000. The contract was drawn up and signed and McFadden gave the Sterkels a certified check. Neither party knew that a hurricane had destroyed the condo the night before at its Florida location. Although no one realized it at the time the parties entered the contract, performance was impossible. Both parties were discharged of any promise of performance and the Sterkels, of course, had to return the check.

Conditions that arise subsequent to the making of a contract may either void the agreement or make it voidable by one of the parties. Discharge through impossibility of performance may, in some situations, be allowed only if the specific and anticipated impossibility has been made a condition to the agreement.

When the exact subject matter of an executory contract has been selected by the parties and later is destroyed, the performance obligation is discharged. In contrast, when the contract is not specific in the description or the location of the subject matter, a promisor is not

The Court has fulfilled two principal functions since the New Deal era: (1) legitimating the transformation of property that has occurred in the modern capitalist economy; and (2) managing social conflict by enduring formal, but limited, representation for select groups, primarily before the administrative agencies of the modern state.

—Carl Swidorski, "Constituting the Modern State: The Supreme Court, Labor Law, and the Contradictions of Legitimation," in *Radical Philosophy of Law: Contemporary Challenges to Mainstream Legal Theory and Practice*

Teaching Tips Discuss the different ways in which contractual agreements are discharged and examples of performance and nonperformance. Use the examples in the text to start students thinking and talking about their own experiences with contracts.

Terms *Rescission* means *cancellation* or *cutting off*. The Latin origin of *rescind* contributed to the development of the word *shed*, which means, among other things, "to cast off."

Related Cases Erber was in an automobile accident and suffered injuries that were covered by his auto insurance policy. Erber stated that he had been too ill following the accident to make the claim, and more than nine months passed before he was aware of the benefits to which he was entitled. After he became aware of his entitlement to coverage, he waited another 14 months before filing the claim. The North Carolina insurance company refused to pay the claim. Erber contested their refusal. The court found Erber's 14-month delay unacceptable, relieving the insurer of its obligation to perform.

discharged if the subject matter intended for delivery is destroyed. In this case, the promisor is obligated to locate and deliver subject matter of the same kind and quantity that could be secured elsewhere. Any financial losses due to the misfortune must be borne by the promisor.

When the performance of a contract promise requires execution of acts declared illegal because of existing common law, statute, or public policy, the contract is void from its inception. When the performance of a contract is made illegal through the passing of laws subsequent to the formation of the contract, the contract is likewise declared void and the parties are discharged.

Death, insanity, or disability of a party obligated to perform an act that requires a special talent or skill terminates and discharges an agreement. This includes promises to perform by musicians, artists, writers, skilled craftspeople, and certain professionals. When promised services are to be performed for the personal benefit of a promisee, the death of the promisee will also terminate the agreement. When contract promises relate to services that may be performed by others and do not demand the personal services of the contracting party, performance is not excused through death, insanity, or disability. The guardian of the party involved or the estate of the deceased may be held liable for performance.

Frustration-of-Purpose Doctrine   The **frustration-of-purpose doctrine** releases a party from a contractual obligation when performing the obligations would be thoroughly impractical and senseless. The doctrine is applied only in those cases in which a party recognizes and understands possible risks and accepts them in contemplation of performance.

Example 14-9

George Gaverick rented a fiftieth-floor apartment for the night of December 31. The apartment had a balcony overlooking Times Square in midtown Manhattan. The rental period was for only twenty-four hours and the landlord knew that the purpose of the contract was to allow Gaverick an unrestricted view of Times Square for the city's New Year's Eve celebration. Unfortunately, a terrorist alert canceled the entire Times Square celebration that year. Since the apartment was of no use to Gaverick the purpose of the agreement was frustrated and Gaverick would not have to pay the rent.

Commercial Impracticability   Although not identical to the frustration of purpose doctrine a related concept is known as **commercial impracticability.** Under this doctrine, the courts may excuse the nonperformance of one party to a contract because an unforeseen and very severe hardship has arisen that would place an enormous amount of hardship on that party. Commercial impracticability is not the same as impossibility because the party still can perform the contract. It is just that the performance itself would cause a great deal of adversity. Also with commercial impracticability, the purpose of the contract is not undermined by the unforeseen event and so the frustration of purpose doctrine does not apply. Nevertheless, under this relatively modern doctrine, some parties may escape performance if the unforeseen event was truly unforeseen and was not in any way the fault of the party seeking an escape from performance.

Discharge by Operation of Law

The performance of a promised act may be discharged by operation of law. Some law that causes the parties to be discharged from their obligations, such as bankruptcy or the statute of limitations, comes into play.

The Opening Case Revisited Once Again
"A High-Speed Tram for Nottingham?"

In The Opening Case at the beginning of the chapter, we learned that the Nottingham tram project conducted by Carillon Corporation hit an obstacle in midsummer when engineers unexpectedly discovered that the new high-speed tram system could not be properly integrated with the existing Nottingham railway network. The complication delayed the inauguration of the high-speed tram for several months and cost Carillon £10 million. Unfortunately for Carillon, this situation does not excuse its performance under any of the prevailing theories. First, the snag does not qualify as an impossibility because the contract could still be performed. Moreover, because the purpose of the contract, establishing a high-speed tram in Nottingham, could still be carried out, albeit with some difficulty, there was no frustration of purpose. Finally, even if the difficulty was unforeseen, it is not of such a magnitude to make the project commercially impractical. In fact, ultimately the main hardship for Carillon was the £10 million loss which seems devastating, but which apparently was not, since the company still made a profit that year.

Bankruptcy Through the provisions of the Bankruptcy Reform Act (see Chapter 31), a discharge in bankruptcy from a court will be allowed as a defense against the collection of most, but not all, debts of the bankrupt. Therefore, most contractual obligations to pay money come to an end when a party files for bankruptcy.

Statute of Limitations State statutes providing time limits within which suits may be brought are known as statutes of limitations. Each state sets its own time limits. In general, actions for collection of open accounts (charge accounts) must be brought within three to five years, written agreements usually within ten years, and judgments from ten to twenty years. Those states requiring the seal on certain contracts have still other limitations and requirements that are much broader than those applied to simple contracts. The time limit for bringing suit for breach of a sales contract is four years under the Uniform Commercial Code. The statute of limitations does not technically void the debt, but it gives the debtor a defense against any demand for collection.

Discharge by Breach of Contract

When there is a breach of contract, the injured party has the right to a remedy in court. There are several ways in which a breach may occur.

Deliberate Breach of Contract A breach of contract results when one of the parties fails to do what was agreed to under the terms of the contract. When time is of the essence, there is a breach if performance is not completed within the time limits agreed to by the parties. A breach also results if the performance has been negligent or unskillful. The services rendered must adhere to the standards of skill as determined by the custom of the marketplace. Wrongful performance or nonperformance discharges the other party from further obligation and permits that party to bring suit to rescind the contract or to recover money to compensate that party for any loss sustained. Such compensation is known as *damages*.

> ### Example 14-10
>
> Newel Yurchak, an internationally renown violinist, contracted to perform at Carnegie Hall on January 19. Carnegie Hall and the Carnegie Foundation had brochures and posters printed and had notice of the performance posted on its website. Carnegie also had advertisements aired on NPR and public television. On the day before the performance, Yurchak informed Carnegie that he was not going to perform. Through Yurchak's nonperformance, the contract between him and Carnegie was discharged. Moreover, Carnegie could seek damages from Yurchak on grounds of breach of contract.

Repudiation and Anticipatory Breach An **anticipatory breach** occurs when a party to a contract either expresses or clearly implies an intention not to perform the contract even before being required to act. The repudiation must indicate a deliberate refusal to perform according to the terms of the contract. Breaches of this kind are also called *constructive breaches*. The injured party may either commence suit at the time of the anticipatory breach or await the date agreed to for performance, thus giving the breaching party time to reconsider and begin performance.

Abandonment of Contractual Obligations Stopping performance once it has begun is called **abandonment of contractual obligations.** Leaving or deserting a party's obligations discharges the other party from any promises made and permits a suit for damages. A temporary, or short-lived, interruption of performance is not deemed to be abandonment. To constitute abandonment, the promisor must have inexcusably interrupted performance with the obvious intention of not returning to complete the obligations promised.

> ### Quick Quiz 14-2 True or False?
>
> 1. A general release is a document expressing the intent of a creditor to release a debtor from obligations on an existing and valid debt.
>
> 2. With commercial impracticability, the purpose of a contract is undermined by an unforeseen event.
>
> 3. Stopping a performance once it has begun is called abandonment of contractual obligations.

14-3 Remedies

A breach of contract releases the injured party from any obligations under the contract and gives that party the right to ask a court of law for a remedy. The usual remedy for breach of contract is the payment of damages in the form of money. At times, however, the payment of money damages is not enough to satisfy the injured party. In such situations, the injured party will ask the court for rescission, specific performance, or an injunction.

Damages

Damages describe money awarded to parties who have been victimized or have suffered injury to their legal rights by others. Damages are of different kinds, and the nature of a claim usually determines what type of damages will apply. In some states, by statute or judicial rule, juries are charged with two decisions: They must decide which party is to be given favorable judgment and how much is to be awarded in damages. Appeals to a higher court are allowed when the amount of damages awarded appears to be unreasonably low or excessively high.

Actual or Compensatory Damages

Actual damages are the sum of money equal to the real financial loss suffered by the injured party. Since they are intended to compensate the injured party, actual damages are also called **compensatory damages.** Thus, damages awarded for nondelivery of promised goods or services would be an amount equal to the difference between the price stated in the contract and what the promisee would have to pay elsewhere. Should the same goods or services be conveniently available elsewhere at the same or at a lower price, no actual loss could be claimed.

Example 14-11

Zach Sedgard entered a contract with Will Conte in which Sedgard promised to construct a fence around Conte's property for $4,890, including materials and labor. Sedgard refused to honor his promise, arguing that the prices for his materials had gone up so high that it was impossible for him to construct the fence without losing a great deal of money. Conte hired Fred Winchester to complete the job for him. Winchester charged Conte $5,890. Should Conte sue Sedgard for breach of contract—the actual damages would be $1,000, the difference between the $4,890 that Sedgard agreed to and the $5,890 that Conte was charged by Winchester, another equally competent and reputable builder?

Incidental and Consequential Damages

Incidental damages and consequential damages are awarded for losses indirectly, but closely, attributable to a breach. **Incidental damages** cover any expenses paid out by the innocent party to prevent further loss. **Consequential damages** result indirectly from the breach because of special circumstances that exist with a particular contract. To recover consequential damages, the injured party must show that such losses were foreseeable when the contract was made.

Example 14-12

Raymond Tremayne contracted to purchase a fishing boat from the Chappell Marine Center. Chappell knew that Tremayne intended to use the boat to take his catch to the market. Chappell also knew that Tremayne's livelihood depended on catching a certain number of fish during the summer months and getting those fish to market. Nevertheless, on the day that Tremayne was to pick up the boat, Chappell told him that the boat would not be available as agreed. As a result, Tremayne had to rent a boat to do his fishing. In addition, it took him some time to rent a boat, outfit it properly, and get it in the water. Consequently, his profit margin fell drastically that season. In a suit against Chappell, Tremayne could ask the court to compel the boat dealer to reimburse him for all rental charges on the replacement boat. Such out-of-pocket expenses are labeled incidental damages. He could also ask to be reimbursed for the lost profits. Such foreseeable losses are called consequential damages.

Background Information When a plaintiff wins in a dispute, the plaintiff is left with the job of collecting any damages awarded. A plaintiff may use a deposition or interrogatory to search for assets or to force the defendant to sell real estate or other property to satisfy the remedy demanded. Each of these measures involves more legal action.

Background Information Contracts may include a disclaimer limiting liability for consequential damages. Such disclaimers typically include phrases such as "Seller's liability shall be limited to the repair or replacement of defective parts." However, contracts eliminating all rights to consequential damages will usually not hold up in court.

Getting Students Involved For class discussion or a short writing assignment, ask students to imagine the consequences of requiring those who breach contracts to pay punitive damages in addition to compensatory damages. Students should consider how this requirement would affect the number of contracts that would be written and what the economic repercussions would be. Remind them that any added costs in taking a risk not only can deter the production of new products or activities but also can force businesses into bankruptcy.

Punitive or Exemplary Damages

Damages in excess of actual losses suffered by the plaintiff awarded as a measure of punishment for the defendant's wrongful acts are **punitive damages,** also called *exemplary damages*. They are in the nature of court-ordered punishment rather than compensation for a known loss. Punitive damages are awarded when a defendant is guilty of abusive and dishonest practices in consumer transactions that are unconscionable and contrary to the public good.

Nominal Damages

Token damages awarded to parties who have experienced an injury to their legal rights but no actual loss are **nominal damages.** The common law usually awarded six cents to the successful plaintiff when no actual losses were shown. In today's practice, the award is usually one dollar.

Example 14-13

The United States Football League (USFL) sued the National Football League (NFL), alleging that the NFL had engaged in unfair competitive practices that violated federal statutory law. The USFL also claimed that the NFL had intentionally interfered with certain USFL contractual relationships and even with some potential contracts. The jury decided that the NFL had been involved in some unfair competitive practices but that this had not hurt the USFL. As a result, the USFL was awarded one dollar in nominal damages. This figure was raised to three dollars, since the statute that was violated allowed for three times the damages awarded.

Present and Future Damages

Damages may be awarded for present injuries and for others that might reasonably be anticipated in the future. Thus, a party charged with fraud in the sale of a building infested with termites may be held liable for all damages revealed at the time of the suit and for damages that would reasonably be forthcoming as the result of the undisclosed and concealed infestation of the property.

Speculative Damages

Courts do not allow **speculative damages.** These damages are computed on losses that have not actually been suffered and that cannot be proved; they are damages based entirely on an expectation of losses that might be suffered from a breach. They differ from future damages in that speculative damages are not founded on fact but only on hope or expectation. Their basis is nothing more than a calculated guess as to the gains one might have received had there not been a breach.

Damages Under *Quantum Meruit*

The doctrine of *quantum meruit* (as much as one had earned) is important in assessing damages in cases founded on contracts implied-in-law, or quasi-contracts. Thus, where there has been no express or implied mutual agreement, a court will at times impose an obligation against a party who has been unjustly rewarded at the innocent expense of another. Damages awarded are in an amount considered reasonable in return for the benefits the one party derived through the quasi-contract relationship.

Liquidated Damages

Parties may stipulate (agree) as a condition of their contract the amount of damages that might be assessed if there is a breach. Damages agreed to in the initial contract are called **liquidated damages.** Liquidated damages must be realistic and in proportion to the losses that might be reasonably anticipated should there be a breach. When liquidated damages are found to be excessive or unreasonable, a court will disregard them and leave the matter of setting damages to the discretion of a jury.

Mitigation of Damages

The injured party has an obligation to do what is reasonably possible to mitigate the damages, that is, to keep damages to a minimum. A party who has been wronged by another's breach must exercise reasonable precautions to prevent the damages from becoming unfairly and unreasonably burdensome to the other party.

Equitable Remedies

When money in the form of damages is not enough to provide a fair and just award to the injured party, the court may grant one of the equitable remedies. Rather than simply order the breaching party to pay damages, a court issuing an equitable remedy compels the breaching party to perform an act or to refrain from performing an act. The two most common equitable remedies are specific performance and injunctive relief.

Specific Performance

A decree of **specific performance** is a court order calling for the breaching party to do what he or she promised to do under the original contract. The courts order specific performance only when the subject matter of a contract is unique or rare. The classic example of unique subject matter calling for specific performance is a contract for the sale and transfer of title to land, since each piece of land is unique. However, unique or rare subject matter could also include such items as antiques, family heirlooms, original works of art, and special animals, for example, a particular race horse. Obviously, an award of monetary damages would not provide the injured party satisfaction in any of these situations.

Contracts for personal services are rarely enforced through specific performance. Demanding that an unwilling party perform promised personal services would be contrary to Amendment 13 of the U.S. Constitution, which prohibits human servitude. A remedy in cases of this kind, however, may be found through injunctive relief.

Injunctive Relief

An **injunction** is an order issued by a court directing that a party do or refrain from doing something. An injunction may be either temporary or permanent. A temporary injunction is issued as a means of delaying further activity in any contested matter until the court determines whether a permanent injunction should be entered or the injunction should be removed entirely. One who disobeys an injunction does so under penalty of contempt of court.

Cross-Cultural Notes In Japan, the understanding of an agreement is more important than any written contract. Very few disagreements are settled through litigation. The Japanese approach to a contract is that it will be executed in good faith rather than through precise interpretation of a written agreement. Any unforeseen circumstances that arise to make an agreement impossible to perform are solved through further negotiation.

Teaching Tips Before discussing equitable remedies, pose contractual disputes for the students and ask them to decide on appropriate remedies. Keep a list on the board of students' ideas for equitable remedies. In cases in which some equitable remedy is appropriate and students only suggest awards of damages, ask them to consider whether any further action might be necessary to resolve the dispute in question.

Further Reading For a book that explains in plain language what a contract is, and the different situations where one is needed, see *Everyday Contracts: Protecting Your Rights* by Theresa Meehan (New York: Holt, 1989).

Quick Quiz 14-3 True or False?

1. Actual damages are also called compensatory damages.

2. Punitive damages cover any expenses paid out by the innocent party to prevent further loss.

3. The courts order specific performance only when the subject matter of a contract is unique or rare.

Summary

14-1 Most contracts are discharged by performance, which means that the parties do what they agreed to do. When the time for performance is not stated in a contract, it must be performed within a reasonable time. When the time is stated, the court will allow additional time to perform unless something indicates that time is of the essence—then, time for performance will be strictly enforced. Unless the parties agree otherwise, satisfactory performance will be determined by objective standards. Substantial performance will discharge the agreement with the right to reimbursement for correcting details that were not completed. Conditions may determine the rights and duties of the parties prior to performance, during performance, and following performance. It is important to make tender of performance to test the other party's willingness and ability to perform. If neither party makes tender, a breach of contract is not established.

14-2 Nonperformance can also discharge contractual obligations. Not every instance of nonperformance results in a breach of contract. Parties can agree to discharge a contractual obligation by terms in the contract, mutual rescission, waiver, novation, accord and satisfaction, and general release. Contractual obligations can also be discharged when it becomes impossible to perform a contract. The frustration-of-purpose doctrine releases a party from a contractual obligation when performing the obligation would be impractical and senseless. These obligations can also be discharged by operation of law under principles of bankruptcy, and the statute of limitations. When contractual obligations terminate by agreement or by operation of law, no liability falls to either party. However, when breach of contract comes from a deliberate breach, a repudiation of contractual obligation, or an abandonment of performance, liability will result.

14-3 A breach of contract relieves the injured party from any obligation under the contract. Breach of contract also gives the injured party the right to ask a court of law for a remedy, usually in the form of damages. Injured parties are required to mitigate their damages. When money will not be sufficient relief, the injured party may ask for specific performance or for injunctive relief.

Key Terms

abandonment of contractual obligations, 268

actual damages, 269

anticipatory breach, 268

commercial impracticability, 266

compensatory damages, 269

complete performance, 261

condition concurrent, 263

condition precedent, 262

condition subsequent, 263

consequential damages, 269

frustration-of-purpose doctrine, 266

general release, 265

incidental damages, 269

injunction, 271

liquidated damages, 271

mutual rescission, 265

nominal damages, 270

performance, 259

punitive damages, 270

reasonable time, 259

satisfactory performance, 260

specific performance, 271

speculative damages, 270

substantial performance, 261

tender of payment, 263

tender of performance, 263

termination by waiver, 265

Questions for Review and Discussion

1. What does the term reasonable time mean in the performance of a contract?
2. What constitutes satisfactory performance of a contract?
3. What is the difference between complete and substantial performance?
4. What are the differences among conditions precedent, concurrent, and subsequent?
5. What is tender of performance?
6. What are the ways that a contract can be discharged by nonperformance?
7. What is the concept of anticipatory repudiation?
8. What are the types of damages available in the event of a breach of contract?
9. What is mitigation of damages?
10. What is the difference between specific performance and injunctive relief?

Investigating the Internet

Access the Find Law website and conduct a search for recent articles or cases on contract law and damages. Report on the developments described in that case or article.

Cases for Analysis

1. When Kent contracted to have his new house constructed, he specifically noted that the plumbing must be made by Reading manufacturers. After the house had been completed, Kent did an inspection tour during which he discovered that, although much of the plumbing had come from Reading, there were some parts that did not. After making his discovery, Kent demanded that the non-Reading plumbing fixtures be ripped out and replaced with the supplies he had specified in the contract. In addition, Kent refused to pay the contractor until the proper plumbing supplies were added to the house. The contractor brought suit against Kent, arguing that, although there were minor deviations from certain specified parts of the contract concerning the plumbing fixtures, he had, nevertheless, substantially performed his end of the deal. Kent stuck to his strict construction of the contract and labeled the contractor's performance as unsatisfactory. He, thus, claimed to be released from the agreement, unless the contractor lived up to every term in the original agreement. Who should prevail in this case? Explain. *Jacob and Young v. Kent,* 129 N.E. 889.

2. The Morin Building Products Company was commissioned by Baystone Construction to install aluminum siding on the walls of Baystone's factory. Once the project was finished, Baystone inspected the job and expressed dissatisfaction primarily because the siding lacked an appropriately uniform finish. Morin argued that, based on an objective judgment of the work, the siding that the company had installed fit quite well with the utilitarian function of the business. Baystone argued that a standard of satisfactory performance should be used to judge the results of the siding job and because Baystone was not satisfied, the court should rule that Morin had not properly performed. Who will prevail in this case? Explain. *Morin Building Products Company v. Baystone Construction,* 717 F2d 413.

3. Sai Grafio agreed to paint Gerald Weaver's and Katherine Brewer's house for $5,650. Weaver and Brewer paid for the paint job in installments but stopped payment on the final $1,845 check, claiming that Grafio had breached the contract by doing a poor job. The lower court judge found that the only defect in the paint job was a footprint left

on the roof that would cost $50 to repair. How much money, if any, and under what legal theory, did the court allow Grafio to recover the money owed for the paint job? *Weaver v. Grafio,* 595 A.2d 983 (DC).

4. Kvassay contracted in writing to sell 24,000 cases of baklava at $19 per case to Great American Foods, Inc., over a one-year period. Great American breached the contract after Kvassay had delivered 3,000 cases. The contract contained the following clause: "If Buyer refuses to accept or repudiates delivery of the goods sold to him, under this Agreement, Seller shall be entitled to damages, at the rate of $5.00 per case, for each remaining to be delivered under this contract." Kvassay used the $5.00 figure after calculating that he would earn a net profit of $3.55 per case if the contract were fully performed. When the contract was breached by Great American, Kvassay sued for $105,000 ($5 × 21,000 cases not delivered). What is the legal name for the clause in the contract? What argument might Great American use to have the clause declared void? *Kvassay v. Murray,* 808 P.2d 896 (KS).

5. Arthur Murray, Inc., and Parker entered a series of contracts under which Arthur Murray agreed to teach Parker how to dance. Under the terms of each agreement, refunds were impossible and the lessons could not be canceled. After the contracts were entered, Parker suffered a permanent disability that made it physically impossible for him to dance. When Arthur Murray refused to refund any part of Parker's money, he sued to rescind the contracts on grounds of impossibility. Arthur Murray claimed that the nonrefund clause must be upheld by the court. Was Arthur Murray correct? Explain. *Parker v. Arthur Murray, Inc.,* 295 N.E.2d 487 (IL).

6. Shaw leased a service station from Mobil Oil. Shaw's monthly rent was based on his purchase of gasoline from Mobil. He was to pay 1.4 cents per gallon or a $470 minimum monthly rent. Each month Shaw would have to purchase 33,572 gallons to meet this minimum. In July, Shaw ordered 34,000 gallons. This would have allowed him to meet more than the minimum rent. Mobil, however, could deliver only 25,678 gallons. Nevertheless, Mobil attempted to collect the $470 minimum monthly rent. Shaw brought suit against Mobil, claiming that his payment of the $470 minimum and Mobil's delivery of at least 33,572 gallons were conditions concurrent. Shaw argued that since Mobil had not met its part of the bargain, he

was not obligated to meet his because Mobil's failure was a breach of contract. Was Shaw correct? Explain. *Shaw v. Mobil Oil Corporation,* 535 P.2d 756 (OR).

7. Bob Pagan Ford, Inc., hired Smith to work as a car salesperson in Galveston County. As part of his contract, Smith agreed not to work as an auto salesperson in Galveston County for three years after leaving his employment with Bob Pagan Ford. Smith worked for Bob Pagan for only a few months. He then left and took a sales job with another dealership in Galveston County. Was injunctive relief an appropriate remedy in this case? Explain. *Bob Pagan Ford, Inc., v. Smith,* 638 S.W.2d 176 (TX).

8. Kucha sold a house to Pilder for $75,293. The agreement was in writing as required by the Statute of Frauds. As part of the contract, Kucha agreed to pay for the remodeling of the sunporch. However, when Kucha found out that it would cost $12,728 to do the remodeling, he refused to sell the property. Pilder sued to compel Kucha to go through with the deal. Kucha argued that under the circumstances the court could not force him to sell under any equitable remedy. Was Kucha correct? Why or why not?

9. The Congress-Kenilworth Corporation hired Erickson Construction to build its new concrete water slide, Thunder Mountain Rapids. The project was completed and was opened to the public. When Congress-Kenilworth discovered extensive cracking of the concrete flumes within the water slide, the corporation refused to pay the amount due under the contract. The operation of the structure as a water slide was not affected by the cracking. Erickson sued to recover the amount due under the contract. Erickson claimed that under the doctrine of substantial performance, Congress-Kenilworth should pay for the amount due under the contract, less an amount needed to offset the defects. Was Erickson correct? Explain. *W. E. Erickson Construction, Inc., v. Congress-Kenilworth Corporation,* 477 N.E.2d 513 (IL).

10. The Commonwealth of Massachusetts entered into a contract with John J. Paonessa Company, Inc., for resurfacing and improvements on Route 128. Part of the contract called for replacing the grass median strip with bituminous concrete surfacing and precast, concrete barriers. The contracts had provisions that allowed the Commonwealth to make modifications for items found to be unnecessary. Paonessa subcontracted with Chase Precast

Corporation to supply 25,800 linear feet of double-face median barrier. However, the Commonwealth deleted the median barriers from the contract after a group of angry residents complained about using concrete barriers instead of the grass median strip. Chase, at the time, had produced about half of the required barriers and stopped producing any more. The company was paid for all of the barriers it had produced but sued Paonessa for the amount of profits it had lost from the cancellation of the contract. Under what legal theory may Paonessa be excused from completing the contract with Chase? Explain. *Chase Precast v. John J. Paonessa Co.,* 554 N.E.2d 868 (MA).

Quick Quiz Answers

14-1	14-2	14-3
1. F	1. T	1. T
2. T	2. F	2. F
3. T	3. T	3. T

Part 2 Case Study

Wilcox v. Trautz
Supreme Judicial Court of Massachusetts
693 N.E.2d 141 (MA)

Summary

Carol Wilcox and John Trautz, lived together as an unmarried couple for twenty-five years, beginning when they were both in their twenties. During that period, Wilcox contributed $25 a week toward general household expenses. She performed household duties including all the food and clothes shopping which she paid for solely from her earnings. When Wilcox became involved in another relationship, Trautz sought legal advice regarding the parties' rights with respect to the assets acquired during their relationship. They signed an agreement providing, among other things, that "each party's earnings and property is his or hers alone, and the other party shall have no interest in the property of the other." The assets, all in Trautz's name, included a house, valued at $180,000; an amphibious airplane, valued at $55,000; various bank accounts totaling $1,300; individual retirements accounts; and a one-half share of real estate in Maine, valued at $15,000. Wilcox had no assets other than a small bank account, the other one-half share of the Maine real estate, household furniture, clothing, and jewelry. The lower court judge held that the agreement was invalid and that, to prevent unjust enrichment, Wilcox was entitled to damages of approximately $30,000. Trautz appealed.

The Court's Opinion

Justice Greaney

We have not previously passed on the validity of written agreements between two unmarried cohabitants that attempt to define the rights of the parties as to services rendered and property acquired during their relationship. Our early decisions precluded the enforcement of an agreement between unmarried parties if the agreement was made in consideration that the parties should cohabit. More recently, we have held valid oral promises between unmarried cohabitants so long as "illicit sexual relations were [not] an inherent aspect of the agreement or a 'serious and not merely an incidental part of the performance of the agreement.'" *Margolies v. Hopkins,* 514 N.E.2d 1079 (1987).

Social mores regarding cohabitation between unmarried parties have changed dramatically in recent years and living arrangements that were once criticized are now relatively common and accepted. "As an alternative to marriage, more couples are choosing to cohabit. These relationships may be of extended duration, sometimes lasting as long as many marriages. In many respects, these cohabitation relationships may be quite similar to conventional marriages; they may involve commingling of funds, joint purchases of property, and even the birth of children." With the prevalence of nonmarital relationships today, a considerable number of persons live together without benefit of the rules of law that govern property, financial, and other matters in a marital relationship. Thus, we do well to recognize the benefits to be gained by encouraging unmarried cohabitants to enter into written agreements respecting these matters, as the consequences for each partner may be considerable on termination of the relationship or, in particular, in the event of the death of one of the partners. "In recent years, increased attention has focused on the advisability of unmarried couples entering into cohabitation contracts in which they . . . detail the financial consequences of dissolution." This may be especially important in a jurisdiction like Massachusetts where we do not recognize common law marriage, do not extend to unmarried couples the rights possessed by married couples who divorce, and reject equitable remedies that might have the effect of dividing property between unmarried parties.

Courts in other jurisdictions have concluded, as we did in *Margolies v. Hopkins, supra,* that an express agreement between adult unmarried persons living together is unenforceable only to the extent that it explicitly and inseparably is founded on sexual relations. . . . Furthermore, such agreements are not invalid merely because the parties may have contemplated the creation or continuation of a nonmarital relationship when they entered into the agreement. As the New York Court of Appeals stated in *Morone v. Morone,* 413 N.E.2d 1154, "[t]he theory of these cases is that while cohabitation without marriage does not give rise to the property and financial rights which normally attend the marital relation, neither does cohabitation disable the parties from making an agreement within the normal rules of contract law." Although none of these cases specifically concerns a written agreement between unmarried cohabitants attempting to resolve issues such as the parties' rights as to property, earnings, and services rendered, the principles they announce also apply to such an agreement. Implicit in these principles is tacit acknowledgement that unmarried cohabitants may agree to hold real property jointly or in common, agree to create joint bank and other accounts, do the same for investments, and, of course, make testamentary dispositions. These financial and property arrangements stem from a relationship that involves sexual cohabitation, but, in creating them, the parties are principally motivated by an intention to hold, or dispose of, property in a mutually acceptable way in order to manage day-to-day matters and to avoid litigation when the relationship ends. Such financial planning is enforceable according to the usual rules of contract. It makes no

sense to uphold these arrangements between unmarried cohabitants, but to withhold enforcement of written agreements between the same parties when they attempt to settle the financial and other consequences if they should separate.

To the extent we have not previously done so, we adopt the view that unmarried cohabitants may lawfully contract concerning property, financial, and other matters relevant to their relationship. Such a contract is subject to the rules of contract law and is valid even if expressly made in contemplation of a common living arrangement, except to the extent that sexual services constitute the only, or dominant, consideration for the agreement, or that enforcement should be denied on some other public policy ground. We shall no longer follow cases in this Commonwealth to the contrary.

Nothing we say here today is intended to derogate from the clear distinction we have made in our cases between the legal rights of married and unmarried cohabitants. . . . Nor should anything we have said be taken as a suggestion or intimation that we are retreating from our prior expressions regarding the importance of the institution of marriage and the strong public interest in ensuring that its integrity is not threatened. We have never recognized common law marriage in this Commonwealth, nor have we "permitted the incidents of the marital relationship to attach to an arrangement of cohabitation without marriage." We do not do so now. . . .

We conclude that the plaintiff and the defendant were free to contract with respect to property, financial, and other matters relevant to their relationship, and that the specific agreement at issue is valid and enforceable. It is undisputed that the parties, both adults, had the capacity to contract and understood each other's financial worth prior to the execution of the agreement. Moreover, the plaintiff was advised to seek counsel regarding the agreement and chose not to do so. There was no claim of fraud, overreaching, or unconscionability. The plaintiff is employed and makes no assertion that as a result of the agreement, she will be unable to support herself. The judge found that the plaintiff was not forced or coerced to sign the agreement.

Finally, we note that the plaintiff voluntarily entered into a relationship with the defendant, and continued to live with him for many years despite her knowledge that he was unlikely to marry her. The agreement she signed essentially tracked the living arrangement she had shared with the defendant for twenty-five years, in which they maintained separate legal and financial identities, and did not merge their financial affairs. There is no evidence that during the course of their relationship, the plaintiff was the "weaker" of the two cohabitants, or that she had been dissatisfied with the way they managed their affairs.

The judgment is vacated, and a new judgment is to be entered declaring the agreement to be valid and enforceable and disposing of the damages claim in the defendant's favor.

So ordered.

Questions for Analysis

1. On what occasion would the court's early decision preclude the enforcement of any agreement between unmarried parties.

2. What was required in more recent decisions for oral promises between unmarried cohabitants to be valid?

3. Why does the court believe it should recognize the benefits to be gained by encouraging unmarried cohabitants to enter into written agreements?

4. What is the theory of the cases holding that express agreements between adult unmarried persons living together are enforceable?

5. What view does the court adopt regarding contracts of unmarried cohabitants?

Sales and Consumer Protection

Part Three

Chapter 15 | Sale and Lease of Goods

The Opening Case
"An Eventful Day"

Jorge Ramos's day began with an interview for a job as manager for a new Wal-Mart store that would be opening soon in his community. That afternoon, just as he was about to leave to go to an antique auction, Ramos received word that he had been given the job as store manager. Elated, he attended the auction and bid an exceptionally high amount for an antique table. The auctioneer refused to sell the table at that price, however, believing that it was worth even more money. Ramos felt that since nothing had been said about the auctioneer's right to refuse the highest bid, it should have been sold to him for the amount he bid. Things improved that evening, however, when a private party agreed to buy Ramos's second-hand car that he had advertised for sale in the newspaper. Did the Uniform Commercial Code govern Ramos's employment agreement? Did the auctioneer have the legal right to refuse to sell the antique table to Ramos? Did the Uniform Commercial Code govern Ramos's agreement to sell the car to the private party?

Chapter Outcomes

1. Determine when to apply the law of sales under the UCC.
2. Describe the special rules for sales contracts.
3. Explain the four exceptions to the rule requiring contracts for the sale of goods costing $500 or more to be in writing.
4. Judge, in a given situation, whether a writing satisfies the requirements of the UCC.
5. Contrast an auction with reserve with an auction without reserve.
6. Determine, in the case of a bulk transfer, whether the four requirements of the UCC have been met.

15-1 The Sale and Lease of Goods

In the previous nine chapters, you studied general contract law, which governs contracts for such things as real estate, employment, and personal services. In Chapters 15 through 18, you will study a different type of law—the law of sales—that governs the sale and lease of goods. It is a very old law that grew from the customs and practices of businesspeople, merchants, and mariners in early English times. It has gone through many changes over the years and is now part of the Uniform Commercial Code (UCC), which has been adopted, either in whole or in part, by every state in the United States.

Goods are defined as all things (other than money, stocks, and bonds) that are movable. They include the unborn young of animals, growing crops, timber, and minerals if they are to be sold separately from the real property. Office furniture, mobile homes, human blood, milk, numismatics, wedding pictures, electricity, waste paper, kerosene, Christmas trees, ships, airplanes, horses, soybeans, polyethylene film, a printing press, and a book of recipes have all been held to be goods by the courts.

Goods that are not yet in existence or not yet under the control of people are called **future goods.** They include fish in the sea, minerals in the ground, goods not yet manufactured, and commodities futures.

UCC 2-105(1)
(see pages 869–870)

Background Information Louisiana has adopted parts of the UCC but not Article 2. The state's laws regarding sale of goods are patterned after the French legal system as opposed to the British system, part of Louisiana's legacy as a former French territory.

UCC 2-105(2)
(see page 870)

Example 15-1

Byron, Ltd., contracted to sell its cotton crop to Deep Southfield, Inc., before the crop had been planted. This agreement to sell a commodity at a certain time in the future for a certain price was legally enforceable. Under the UCC, it is called a contract to sell future goods.

Whenever anyone buys food in a supermarket, gasoline at a gas station, clothing at a shopping mall, a meal at a restaurant, or even a daily newspaper, a sale of goods occurs. In fact, several sales contracts usually occur for a particular item before the item reaches the consumer and, sometimes, even after it reaches the consumer.

Example 15-2

The Matthew Allen Corporation manufactures lawn mowers. The company enters into sales contracts with its suppliers every time it purchases parts and materials to make the mowers. In addition, the company enters into sales contracts with wholesalers when it sells the mowers. Similarly, wholesalers enter into sales contracts when they sell the mowers to retailers. In the same manner, retailers enter into sales contracts when they sell the mowers to consumers. Going even further, consumers enter into sales contracts when they sell their second-hand lawn mowers to other private parties. All of these contracts are governed by the UCC.

Teaching Tips One point that may confuse students is the domain of the UCC. When teaching this chapter, be sure that students differentiate between the sale of goods and that of services. Remind them, in brief, that goods are *moveable* property and are governed by the UCC. Services fall under the common law of contracts.

The Opening Case Revisited
"An Eventful Day"

Ramos's employment agreement was not governed by the UCC because it was not a contract for the sale of goods. Rather, it was a contract for services, which is governed by the common law of contracts. His agreement to sell the car to the private party was governed by the UCC because it was a contract for the sale of goods.

UCC Article 2
(see page 869)

UCC 2A-101-531
(see page 888)

Related Cases In *Danilow Pastry, Inc., v. Yoss Brothers Baking Corp.,* NY L.J., Yoss Brothers charged that Danilow was in violation of the UCC when, prior to going out of business, Danilow sold off delivery routes without notifying creditors. The court ruled in Danilow's favor because delivery routes are not goods and therefore are not covered by UCC regulations.

Teaching Tip Ask the students to name some goods they see around the classroom. Stress that a contract for any of these items would be governed by the UCC. Be alert for items that would be classified as fixtures rather than goods and explain the difference to the class.

Article 2 of the UCC applies whenever people buy or sell goods. This law applies to sales of goods between private parties and to sales of goods by businesspeople or merchants. To determine whether the UCC applies, ask if this is a contract for the sale of goods. If the answer is yes, apply the law under the UCC. If the answer is no, apply the common law of contracts discussed in Chapters 6–14 (see Table 15-1).

Leases of Goods

The leasing of goods is governed by Article 2A of the Uniform Commercial Code. This includes leasing such things as automobiles, trucks, machinery, computers, furniture, electronic equipment, and all types of tools. Many of the rules that are found in the UCC relating to the sale of goods (discussed in the following chapters) also apply to the leasing of goods under Article 2A of the UCC.

Contracts for Both Goods and Services

When a contract includes both goods and services, the dominant element of the contract determines whether it is a contract for goods or a contract for services. If the sale of goods is dominant, as when someone purchases a furnace and has it installed, the law under the UCC applies. In contrast, if the performance of services is dominant, as when someone has a furnace repaired and a few new parts are installed, the common law of contracts applies instead.

Table 15-1 Different Laws Apply to Different Transactions

Transaction	Applicable Law
Contract for the sale of real estate	General contract law (sometimes referred to as common law) and real property law
Contract for employment	General contract law and employment law
Sale of goods between two private parties	UCC (Article 2)
Sale of goods by a merchant to a consumer	UCC (Article 2) and state consumer protection laws
Sale of goods between two merchants	UCC (Article 2)
Contract for a mixture of goods and services—consisting mostly of goods	UCC (Article 2)
Contract for a mixture of goods and services—consisting mostly of services	General contract law
The leasing of goods	UCC (Article 2A)
International sales of goods	United Nations convention on Contracts for the International Sale of Goods (CISG)
Sale of stock on the stock market	UCC (Article 8)
The writing of a check, promissory note, or draft	UCC (Article 3)

Individuals, as well as businesses, lease automobiles today.

Getting Students Involved Let students discover the intricacies of leasing firsthand by contacting a local automobile dealer and comparing the legalities and costs of leasing with buying. Students should find out who holds title to the car, who's liable for both unavoidable damages and those caused by the lessee, and who holds the warranty on the car. They should factor in taxes, additional dealer costs, and maintenance estimates. This activity will be more interesting if you assign specific autos in a wide price range so that there will be a variety of results to share in class.

State Variations By statute, California has declared that the procurement, processing, distribution, or use of whole blood for the purpose of transfusion is a service by each participant and is not a sale of such blood for any purpose.

Quick Quiz 15-1 True or False?

1. Forty-nine states have adopted, either in whole or in part, the Uniform Commercial Code.

2. Money, stocks, and bonds are movable items that are not goods.

3. The dominant element of a contract determines whether it is a sales contract or a services contract.

UCC 2-106(1)
(see page 870)

Teaching Tip Since many students will own their own cars, point out that a car is a good and that a contract for the purchase or sale of a car would be governed by the UCC, whether the seller is a merchant or a private party.

15-2 Contract for Sale

A **sale** is a contract in which ownership of goods is transferred by the seller to the buyer for a price. Thus, every time you buy goods and receive ownership of them, a sale occurs. A **contract for sale** includes both a present sale of goods and a contract to sell goods at a future time.

A gift is not considered a sale because, although title passes, it is not given for a price. Similarly, a bailment (as when an item is left at a store to be sold on consignment) does not meet the definition of a sale because title does not pass between the parties. Bailments are discussed in Chapter 21.

Teaching Tip Review the special rules for sales contracts. Discuss who benefits from each special rule.

Teaching Tips Ask students to bring to class copies of sales contracts they have signed. Reproduce the small print on some of the contracts and distribute these to the students. Discuss clauses that should be crossed out by the buyer before signing the contract.

Quick Quiz 15-2 True or False?

1. Every time anyone buys goods and receives title to them, a sale occurs.

2. A contract for sale includes both a present sale of goods and a contract to sell goods at a future time.

3. A gift is considered to be a sale.

15-3 Special Rules for Sales Contracts

The fundamental rules of contract law, discussed in the previous nine chapters, are used as a base in the UCC, but the UCC is often more flexible. Some special rules for sales contracts follow.

Good Faith

UCC 1-203
(see page 868)

Under the UCC, every contract or duty imposes an obligation of good faith. In other words, the parties to a sales contract must act and deal fairly with each other.

Course of Dealings and Usage of Trade

UCC 1-205
(see page 868)

When the parties have dealt with each other before, their prior dealings give special meaning to sales contracts. Similarly, and **usage of trade,** that is, any method of dealing that is commonly used in the particular field, is given special meaning. Unless the parties express otherwise, a course of dealings or usage of trade may be used to supplement or qualify the terms of a sales contract.

Formation of a Sales Contract

UCC 2-204(1)(2)
(see page 871)

A contract may be made in any manner that shows that the parties reached an agreement. It may be oral (with some exceptions) or in writing, or it may be established by the conduct of the parties. An enforceable sales contract may come about even though the exact moment of its making cannot be determined and even though some terms are not completely agreed upon.

Example 15-3

Cargill, Inc., entered into a written contract with Fickbohm for the purchase of a certain amount of corn at $1.26 a bushel. The parties had orally agreed that the corn would be delivered sometime between June 1 and July 31, but the delivery date was omitted from the writing. Fickbohm failed to deliver the corn and argued that the contract was unenforceable because the delivery date had been omitted from the writing. The court disagreed, saying that the contract was enforceable even though all the terms were not set forth in the writing.

Offer and Acceptance

UCC 2-206(1)(a)
(see page 871)

Background Information In England, post office rules prevent the sender of a letter from retaking possession of it once it has been mailed. The practice of forming contracts from the date when they are mailed (a law common to both England and the United States) seems to have evolved from this peculiarity of the English postal system.

To establish a contract for the sale of goods, unless otherwise indicated by the offeror or the circumstances, the offeree may accept the offer in any manner and by any medium that is reasonable. A contract for the sale of goods comes into existence when the acceptance is sent, as long as the method used to send it is reasonable.

Example 15-4

Goodwin sent a letter by the U.S. Postal Service to Callaghan, offering to buy ten file cabinets for $700 if Callaghan would ship them promptly. Callaghan accepted the offer by e-mail. The contract came into existence when the e-mail was sent.

Unless the buyer indicates otherwise, an order or other offer to buy goods for prompt shipment may be accepted by either a prompt shipment or a prompt promise to ship. In Example 15-4, Callaghan could have accepted the offer by promptly shipping the file cabinets instead of by promising to ship them. Under this rule, the goods that are shipped may be either conforming or nonconforming goods. **Conforming goods** are those that are in accordance with the obligations under the contract. **Nonconforming goods** are those that are not the same as those called for under the contract or that are in some way defective.

UCC 2-206(1)(b)
(see page 871)

UCC 2-106(2)
(see page 870)

Firm Offer

The UCC holds merchants to a higher standard than nonmerchants. A **merchant** is a person who deals in goods of the kind sold in the ordinary course of business or who otherwise claims to have knowledge or skills peculiar to those goods. Although most rules under the UCC apply to both merchants and nonmerchants alike, some rules apply only to merchants. One such rule involves a firm offer.

UCC 2-104(1)
(see page 869)

No consideration is necessary when a merchant promises in writing to hold an offer open for the sale or lease of goods. Known as a **firm offer,** the writing must be signed by the merchant, and the time period for holding the offer open may not exceed three months. This differs from the general rule of contract law (discussed in Chapter 7), which requires consideration in an option contract.

UCC 2-205
(see page 871)

Related Cases Refer students to Example 7-11 on page 146 in which Galai gave $755 for an option to buy a rare print collection. Point out that if Osaka had been a merchant and the promise to hold the offer open had been in writing, no consideration would have been necessary.

Example 15-5

Sunrise Supply Co. offered to sell Jones a pool filter for $150. This price was especially good for that product. Although he wanted the filter, Jones thought that he might be transferred to another location. He needed four weeks to decide whether to buy the filter. Sunrise agreed in writing to hold the offer open to Jones for four weeks. Although Jones provided no consideration for holding the offer open, it was a firm offer and could not be revoked by Sunrise. Sunrise's firm offer also came within the UCC's three-month limit.

UCC 2-305(1)
(see pages 872–873)

Related Cases A scrap metal salvaging company entered into an output contract with a metal manufacturer. The contract stipulated that the manufacturer would ship all of its scrap metal to the salvager. When the manufacturer stopped shipping the scrap metal, the salvager sued. The manufacturer claimed that the contract should be ruled invalid because it did not name the amount to be shipped. The court ruled against the manufacturer, stating the agreement to purchase all of the manufacturer's scrap metal was not too indefinite to be enforced. This was a valid output contract. *Cohen v. Wood Bros. Steel Stamping,* 519 N.E.2d 1068.

Open-Price Terms

Another change that the UCC has made is that a contract for the sale of goods may be established even though the price is not settled. Such **open-price terms** may occur when the parties intend to be bound by a contract but fail to mention the price or decide to set the price later. Under the non-UCC law, no contract would come about because the terms are not definite. The UCC allows such a contract to come into existence. If the parties cannot agree on the price at the later date, the UCC requires that the price will be reasonable at the time the goods are delivered.

Example 15-6

Ayers contracted to buy chicken feed from Sparton Grain & Mill Co. As part of the contract, Sparton agreed to buy and market all of Ayers's eggs. The price that Ayers was to pay for the feed was not mentioned. The court held that the UCC requires the price to be a reasonable one when no price is quoted.

Output and Requirements Terms

UCC 2-306
(see page 873)

Sometimes, a seller will agree to sell "all the goods we manufacture" or "all the crops we produce" to a particular buyer. This agreement is known as an **output contract.** At other times, a buyer will agree to buy "all the oil we need to heat our building" (or some similar requirement) from a particular seller. This agreement is called a **requirements contract.** Such contracts often were not allowed under common law because the quantity of the goods to be bought or sold was not definite. The UCC allows output and requirements contracts for the sale of goods, as long as the parties deal in good faith and according to reasonable expectations.

Example 15-7

Spencer Oil Co. agreed to sell to Lopaz Manufacturing Co. all the heating oil Lopaz would need during the next year. Spencer knew that Lopaz used about 5,000 gallons of oil each year. During the summer, Lopaz enlarged its building to an extent that it would require 25,000 gallons of heating oil during the next year. Spencer would not be bound to supply that amount of oil to Lopaz because it was far beyond the amount it expected to supply.

Additional Terms in Acceptance

UCC 2-207
(see page 871)

Related Cases A software purchaser sued a software manufacturer after discovering problems with the product. On the software box was a sales agreement and a warranty disclaimer. The manufacturer argued that the combination of these two items shielded it. The court disagreed, holding that the warranty disclaimer was an additional term to the contract because it materially altered the contract. 939 F.2d 91.

Under the general rules of contract law, an acceptance of an offer must be an absolute, unqualified, unconditional assent to the offer. If the acceptance differs in the slightest from the offer, it is considered a rejection. The UCC changes this rule somewhat. A contract for the sale of goods occurs even though the acceptance states terms that are additional to or different from those offered or agreed upon (unless acceptance is made conditional on assent to the additional terms). The additional terms are treated as proposals for additions to the contract if the parties are not both merchants. If both parties are merchants, the additional terms become part of the contract unless they materially alter it, the other party objects within a reasonable time, or the offer limits acceptance to its terms.

This rule is intended to deal with two typical situations. The first is when an agreement has been reached either orally or by informal correspondence between the parties and is followed by one or both of the parties sending formal acknowledgments or memos that contain additional terms not discussed earlier.

Example 15-8

Cobb and Sons, Inc., reached an oral agreement with Valley Theatres, Inc., for the sale of an air-conditioning system. Later, Cobb put the agreement in writing, signed it, and sent it to Valley for its signature. Valley signed the writing but added additional terms relative to the date of completion of the contract. Since both parties were merchants, the additional terms would become part of the contract unless Cobb objected to them within a reasonable time. Had one of them not been a merchant, the contract would have to come into existence without the additional terms, and the added terms would have been treated as proposals for additions to the contract.

The second situation in which this rule applies is one in which a fax or letter intended to be the closing or confirmation of an agreement adds further minor suggestions or proposals, such as "ship by Thursday" or "rush."

> ## Example 15-9
>
> Cal-Cut Pipe and Supply, Inc., offered in writing to sell used pipe to Southern Idaho Pipe and Steel Co., specifying a delivery date. Southern Idaho accepted by sending a check but changed the delivery date. Cal-Cut mailed a confirmation containing the original delivery date with the postscript, "We will work it out." The court held that there was a binding contract between them despite the conflicting delivery terms.

Modification

Under the general rules of contract law, if the parties have already entered into a binding contract, a later agreement to change that contract needs consideration to be binding. The UCC has done away with this rule in contracts for the sale of goods. An agreement modifying a contract for the sale of goods needs no consideration to be binding. Any such modification may be oral unless the original agreement is in writing and provides that it may not be modified except by a signed writing. Any such clause in a form supplied by a merchant to a nonmerchant, however, must be separately signed (such as in the margin) by the nonmerchant to be effective.

UCC 2-209(1)
(see page 872)

UCC 2-209(2)
(see page 872)

> ### Quick Quiz 15-3 True or False?
>
> 1. Under the UCC, a contract comes into existence when the acceptance is sent if the method used is reasonable.
>
> 2. No consideration is necessary to establish a firm offer when a consumer promises in writing to hold an offer open for the sale or lease of goods.
>
> 3. Under the UCC, a contract for the sale of goods may be established even though the price is not settled.

15-4 Form of Sales Contracts

Many sales contracts are oral rather than written. They are often made by telephone; or at a store counter; or face-to-face between private parties or businesspeople, or both. As long as the price is under $500, an oral contract for the sale of goods is enforceable. Millions of such contracts are made daily by people in our society.

If the price is $500 or more, a sales contract must be in writing to be enforceable. This rule, however, has four exceptions.

UCC 2-201(1)
(see page 870)

State Variations Louisiana law is an exception to the rule that sales contracts over $500 need to be in writing. In general, Louisiana does not require such written contracts except in the case of certain transactions, such as securities.

> ## Example 15-10
>
> Deena Sampson agreed to buy a car from Ted Words for $2,500. The agreement was oral and called for payment of the full amount in cash upon delivery of the car the next day. Unless one of the exceptions in the discussion to follow applies, the oral contract cannot be enforced by either party because it was not evidenced by a writing of any kind.

UCC 2A-201
(see page 891)

A lease of goods, under the UCC, must be in writing if the total payments to be made under the lease are $1,000 or more.

Exceptions to the General Rule

There are four exceptions to the requirement that contracts for the sale of goods for $500 or more and the lease of goods for $1,000 or more must be in writing to be enforceable. These exceptions involve the following:

1. oral contracts between merchants in which a confirmation has been received by one party and not objected to by the other party
2. specially manufactured goods
3. admissions in court
4. executed contracts

UCC 2-201(2)
(see page 870)

Oral Contracts Between Merchants An exception to the general rule occurs when there is an oral contract between two merchants. If either merchant receives a written confirmation of the oral contract from the other merchant within a reasonable time and does not object to it in writing within ten days, the oral contract is enforceable.

Example 15-11

David Brown, the owner of Molly's Pub, telephoned Northeast Supply Co. and placed an order for $760 worth of merchandise. Later that day, he mailed a written confirmation of the order. Northeast Supply Co. received the confirmation and made no objection to it, making the oral contract enforceable.

UCC 2-201(3)
(see page 870)

Related Cases *Flowers Banking Co.* entered an oral contract with R-P Packaging for specialized cellophane wrapping material imprinted with the Flowers Banking name and unique artwork. When Flowers refused the goods, R-P sued. The court ruled that because these were specially manufactured goods, the oral contract was enforceable. *Flowers Banking Co. of Lynchburg, Inc., v. R-P Packaging, Inc.,* 329 S.E.2d 462.

Specially Manufactured Goods Another exception occurs when goods are to be specially manufactured for the buyer and are not suitable for sale to others in the ordinary course of the seller's business. If the seller has made either a substantial beginning in manufacturing the goods or has made commitments to buy them, the oral agreement will be enforceable.

Example 15-12

Lifetime Windows, Inc., entered into an oral agreement to manufacture fifteen over-sized windows for Harold Cohen for the price of $3,000. The windows were such an odd shape that no one else would have a need for them. When the windows were manufactured, Cohen refused to take them on the ground that the oral contract was unenforceable. The court held against Cohen, however, and enforced the oral agreement. The windows were specially manufactured and were not suitable for sale to others.

UCC 2-201(3)(c)
(see page 870)

Admissions in Court If the party against whom enforcement is sought admits in court that an oral contract for the sale of goods was made, the contract will be enforceable. The contract is not enforceable under this exception, however, beyond the quantity of goods admitted.

Executed Contracts When the parties carry out their agreement in a satisfactory manner, the law will not render the transaction unenforceable for want of an agreement in writing. Executed contracts (those that have been carried out) need not be in writing; the writing requirements apply only to contracts that are executory, that is, not yet performed. This provision means that contracts for goods that have been received and accepted need not be in writing.

If there has been a part payment or a part delivery, the court will enforce only that portion of the agreement that has been performed.

UCC 2-201(3)(c)
(see page 870)

Example 15-13

Gilmore orally agreed to sell Nash three electric guitars and a powerful amplification system for $1,900. Delivery was to be made in ten days, at which time Nash agreed to have the money ready for payment. If Gilmore had delivered one of the three guitars to Nash, the court would enforce payment for that one instrument.

Requirements of Writing

The writing that is required to satisfy the UCC must indicate that a contract for sale has been made between the parties and must mention the quantity of goods being sold. It must also be signed by the party against whom enforcement is sought (the defendant). A writing is acceptable even though it omits or incorrectly states a term agreed upon. However, a contract will not be enforceable beyond the quantity of goods shown in such writing. For that reason, it is necessary to put the quantity of goods to be bought and sold in the written agreement. Although a paper similar to the one shown in Figure 15-1 may be used, an informal note, memorandum, or sales slip will satisfy the writing requirements.

Interestingly, the trend in other countries is to eliminate the requirement that a sales contract be in writing. Great Britain, for example, after having such a requirement for 277 years, did away with it in 1954. The international sales law also has no writing requirements for a sales contract; instead, a sales contract may be proved by any means. The international sales law, called the United Nations **Convention on Contracts for the International Sale of Goods (CISG),** applies to sales between parties whose places of business are in different countries that have adopted the law. The United States adopted the international sales law in 1988.

UCC 2-201(1)
(see page 870)

State Variations Under the Illinois Motor Vehicle Leasing Act, a lease of a motor vehicle must be in writing and printed in at least 8 point type.

Further Reading A book that takes a thorough look at the CISG and explains international trade and trade terms is *Contracts of Sale in International Trade Law,* by Lakshman Marasinghe (Singapore: Butterworths, 1992).

Quick Quiz 15-4 True or False?

1. A lease of goods must be in writing if the total payments to be made under the lease are $500 or more.

2. Contracts for goods that have been received and accepted for $500 or more need not be in writing.

3. A required writing under the UCC must indicate the quantity of goods being sold.

CONTRACT FOR SALE OF GOODS

AGREEMENT made by and between Ozzie Caldwell (Seller), and Geordi Hasenzahl (Buyer).

It has been agreed between the two parties that:

1. Seller agrees to sell, and Buyer agrees to buy the following described property: one regulation-size pool table now located at the residence of Ozzie Caldwell, RD #1, Box 118, Ashberry, Kentucky.

2. Buyer agrees to pay Seller the total price of $850.00;

   payable as follows:

   $600.00 deposit herewith

   $250.00 balance by cash or certified check at time of transfer

3. Seller warrants he has full legal title to said property, authority to sell said property, and that said property shall be sold free and clear of all claims by other parties.

4. Said property is sold in "as is" condition. SELLER HEREBY EXCLUDES THE WARRANTY OF MERCHANTABILITY AND FITNESS FOR A PARTICULAR PURPOSE.

5. Parties agree to transfer title on February 7, 20 - -, at RD #1, Box 118, Ashberry, Kentucky, the address of the Seller.

6. This agreement shall be binding on the parties, their successors, assigns, and personal representatives.

7. This writing is intended to represent the entire agreement between the parties.

Signed under seal this nineteenth day of January, 20 - -.

Geordi Hasenzahl
_____
Buyer

Ozzie Caldwell
_____
Seller

Figure 15-1 With four exceptions, contracts for the sale of goods of $500 or more must be in writing to be enforceable. A formal writing such as this is not necessary to satisfy the writing requirements of the UCC, however.

15-5 Auction Sales

In an auction sale, the auctioneer presents goods for sale and invites the audience to make offers, which are known as bids. This process is similar to an invitation to trade. Bidders in the crowd respond with their offers. The highest bid (offer) is accepted by the auctioneer, usually by the drop of the gavel together with the auctioneer's calling out the word *sold.* If, while the gavel is falling, a higher bid comes from those in the crowd, the auctioneer has two options: to declare the goods sold or to reopen the bidding.

An auction sale is "with reserve" unless the goods are expressly put up without reserve. In an **auction with reserve,** the auctioneer may withdraw the goods at any time before announcing completion of the sale if the highest bid is not high enough. In an **auction without reserve,** after the auctioneer calls for bids on an article or lot, that article or lot cannot be withdrawn unless no bid is made within a reasonable time. In either case, a bidder may retract a bid until the auctioneer's announcement of completion of the sale. A bidder's retraction does not revive any previous bid.

The practice of planting persons in the crowd for the purpose of raising bids by innocent purchasers is not allowed. Except in a forced sale, such as by a sheriff, if a seller (or the seller's agent) makes a bid at an auction without notifying other bidders, a buyer has two options. Under the UCC, a buyer may either avoid the sale or take the goods at the price of the last good-faith bid prior to the completion of the sale. In a forced sale, as when a sheriff auctions property on foreclosure or to satisfy a lien creditor, the owner is allowed to bid on the property being sold.

Auctions on the Internet provide the opportunity to buy and sell goods worldwide as well as locally. An Internet auction can be either person-to-person or business-to-person. In person-to-person auctions, sellers offer items directly to consumers. The highest bidder must deal directly with the seller to arrange for payment and delivery. In contrast, operators of business-to-person auctions have control of the items being offered and take charge of payment and delivery of goods bought and sold.

The Opening Case Revisited
"An Eventful Day"

The auctioneer had the right to refuse to sell the antique table to Ramos for the amount of Ramos's bid. Because the terms of the auction were not announced, it was an auction with reserve allowing the auctioneer to withdraw the goods if the highest bid is not high enough.

Terms The word *auction* comes from the Latin phrase *auctio sub hasta* or "under the spear." After a battle, Roman soldiers would group behind a spear thrust into the ground and bid for the spoils of war.

UCC 2-328(2) (see page 877)

UCC 2-328(3) (see page 877)

Background Information Auctions have been a part of human culture for as long as there has been recorded history. Modern auctions closely resemble those of Roman times. In fact, some practices, such as holding up fingers for a bid, come from the Roman model. The story of Apponius, who acquired the emperor Caligula's goods by nodding off during an auction, started the myth that a simple nod or other inadvertent gesture might commit the auction goer to a purchase.

Be sure you know the "language of the auction" before participating in one.

Further Reading For more information on the ins and outs of auctions, look for *An Insider's Guide to Auctions,* by Sylvia Auebach (Reading, MA: Addison-Wesley Publishers, Inc., 1981), and *Auction Action! A Survival Companion for Any Auction Goer,* by Ralph Roberts (Blue Ridge Summit, PA: Tab Books, 1986).

UCC 2-328(4) (see page 877)

Business Law in the News
Tony Auctions for Everybody

Picture an auction of fine art, and you might imagine a crowd of dapper aristocrats in a lush wood-paneled room. As the auctioneer presents a painting by some brand-name Impressionist, buyers scratch their noses or tug their ear lobes to signal a secret bid. When the bidding stops, a hush envelops the room as the auctioneer calls out "Going, going, gone" and lowers his hammer.

At all these auctions, price points are far lower than those at more exclusive sales. Items sold in 2003 at Bonhams' twice-monthly lower-end events, for example, went for an average of just $522. "We are trying to educate the public and demystify the whole process," says Laura King Pfaff, chairman of Bonhams & Butterfields.

Good Deals

Of course, plenty of goods beat expectations. A pair of 20th century rock crystal and green quartz lamps that Christie's thought would bring in between $8,000 and $12,000 actually went for more than $33,000 last October. At the same sale, a Danish serving cabinet from the 1950s sold for $2,629, way above the $500 estimate. A South Seas pearl, diamond, and platinum necklace auctioned off by Bonhams in December exceeded the $5,000 estimate by a cool $2,638.

Even then, experts say these can be good deals. Why? Because buying that same item at a retail store costs a lot more. The necklace from Bonhams, for instance, would have retailed for about $25,000. That's why auction regulars say it's important to ask specialists at the auction to identify dealers in the crowd, and then watch how they are bidding. They will pay a price only up to the point at which their markups are still large enough. So if you're willing to outbid the dealers by 10%, you can get a good value. "I always hope and pray that my competition is a dealer," says Louis Webre of Doyle New York, who sometimes bids on behalf of absent clients.

None of this means that Christie's and others are looking to compete with eBay. Indeed, live auctions offer a very different experience. "People can view everything before a sale. They can touch it, turn it around, and ask specialists on the floor questions," says Heather Johnson, director of Christie's monthly house sales, which offer moderately priced items. "Then on the day of the auction, you might get a bargain or you could bid against someone who will pay anything to get the item. You never know."

Pointers for Novices

The you-are-there pitch resonates with many consumers who still feel uncomfortable making purchases online or buying goods sight unseen. "There may be better prices on eBay, but you can't see anything in person, so it's much easier to make a mistake," says Ed Berberian, a collector of Native American artifacts in Los Angeles who regularly shops at live auctions and on eBay.

In addition to specialists on hand to assist buyers during previews and sales, most auction houses put their catalogs, as well as tutorials that walk buyers through the auction process, on their Web sites. They explain everything from previewing items, known as lots, to bidding. Apart from the basics, attendees can pick up little-known pointers at these events, such as how to discern how much certain items may fetch. Since several like items are often sold, finding a lot similar to the one you want to buy that sells early in the auction will indicate how much your item is likely to go for later.

Some other important things to know: Most items come to auction on consignment, either through estates or because of divorce, and are sold as is. That means the inventory at each sale changes, and the items offered can be a wide-ranging mix. It's important to examine items closely for size and flaws during previews, which are usually held a few days before the auction.

Appraisers assign each lot a value range. When the sale begins, the auctioneer will start bidding below the low estimate. All lots will be sold—even under their estimated prices—unless sellers place minimum reserve prices on them. Many buyers are surprised to find that the so-called hammer price, which is the final bid, is not the final cost. All auction houses tack on a buyer's premium, which can be anywhere from 5% to 20% of the winning bid. In addition, buyers need to factor in taxes and shipping.

You need not be at the auction to take part. Most auctioneers allow bidding by phone, fax, or online.

Questions for Analysis

1. Why is it important to identify dealers in the crowd at an auction?

2. How does the experience at a live auction differ from the experience at an eBay auction?

3. Why is it easier to make a mistake when buying on eBay than at a live auction?

4. What are some advantages to shopping at a live auction?

5. Why may the so-called hammer price not be the final cost at a live auction?

Source: Linda Himelstein. "Tony Auctions for Everybody," *BusinessWeek,* February 9, 2004, p. 89.

Internet auction fraud is alarming. Sometimes sellers don't deliver the goods or they deliver something less valuable than they advertised. At other times, sellers don't disclose everything about a product or they fail to deliver it when they say they will. The Federal Trade Commission (FTC) provides helpful information about Internet auctions in its free brochures and its website.

Did You Know?

The federal government auctions cars, trucks, real estate, airplanes, boats, jewelry, office equipment, heavy equipment and many other items. For information about government auctions, log onto the Internet and, using the search engine *Excite,* type in the words "government auction." You may find something you need at a bargain price.

Quick Quiz 15-5 True or False?

1. In an auction sale, the auctioneer makes offers to sell goods to members of the audience.

2. In an auction sale "without reserve," the auctioneer may withdraw the goods at any time before announcing completion of the sale.

3. The practice of planting persons in the crowd for the purpose of raising bids by innocent purchasers is allowed.

Summary

15-1 The Uniform Commercial Code (UCC), which contains the law of sales, has been adopted, either in whole or in part, by every state in the United States. Article 2 of the UCC applies whenever people buy or sell goods. It applies to transactions between private parties as well as to transactions by business people or merchants. Article 2A applies to leases of goods. When a contract includes both goods and services, the dominant element of the contract governs whether it is a contract for goods or a contract for services.

15-2 A contract for sale includes both a present sale of goods and a contract to sell goods at a future time.

15-3 The following special rules that are different from general contract law apply to sales contracts.

- Every contract or duty imposes an obligation of good faith.

- Prior dealings and usage of trade may be used to supplement or qualify the terms of a sales contract.

- A sales contract may be made in any manner that shows that the parties reached an agreement.
- Unless otherwise specified, an offeree may accept an offer in any way that is reasonable, including a prompt shipment of the goods.
- A written promise by a merchant to hold an offer open needs no consideration to be binding.
- A sales contract may be made even though the price is not settled. If the parties cannot agree on a price, it will be a reasonable price at the time of delivery.
- Output and requirements contracts are allowed in sales contracts as long as the parties deal in good faith and according to reasonable expectations.
- A sales contract may result even when an offeree adds different or additional terms from those offered or agreed upon. The different terms do not become part of the contract unless the parties are both merchants and no objection is made to them within a reasonable time.
- No consideration is necessary to modify a contract for the sale of goods.

15-4 With four exceptions, a contract for the sale of goods for $500 or more and the lease of goods for $1,000 or more must be in writing. The exceptions are: oral contracts between merchants in which a confirmation has been received by one party and not objected to by the other party, specially manufactured goods, admissions in court, and executed contracts. A required writing must indicate that a contract for sale has been made between the parties and must mention the quantity of goods sold. The writing must be signed by the party against whom enforcement is sought. The United Nations Convention on Contracts for the International Sale of Goods (CISG) applies to sales between United States business and foreign businesses. The law is similar in many ways to the UCC.

15-5 In an auction sale, offers are made by the people in the audience. The acceptance takes place when the auctioneer bangs the gavel. In an auction with reserve, the auctioneer need not accept the highest bid. In an auction without reserve, the auctioneer must accept the highest bid.

Key Terms

auction with reserve, 291
auction without reserve, 291
conforming goods, 285
contract for sale, 283
Convention on Contracts for the International Sale of Goods (CISG), 289

firm offer, 285
future goods, 281
goods, 281
merchant, 285
nonconforming goods, 285
open-price terms, 285

output contract, 286
requirements contract, 286
sale, 283
usage of trade, 284

Questions for Review and Discussion

1. The law of sales applies to what types of contracts?
2. Name three items that are considered goods. Name one item that is a future good.
3. When a contract includes both goods and services, what determines whether it is a contract for goods or a contract for services?
4. What does a contract for sale include?
5. Describe three special rules that apply to sales contracts.
6. Compare an option contract with a firm offer. How do they differ?
7. When must a sales contract be in writing? When must a lease of goods be in writing?
8. What four exceptions apply to Question 7?
9. What are the requirements of a writing, when one is required, under the UCC?
10. Compare an auction with reserve with an auction without reserve. At what point is the reserve status established?

Investigating the Internet

Log onto the Uniform Commercial Code Locator at **http://www.law.cornell.edu/ uniform/ucc.html.** This links to state statutes that correspond to Articles of the UCC. Find the statutory location of UCC Articles 2 and 2A in your state. Check, also, to see if there are any proposed revisions of the articles.

Cases for Analysis

1. Alberto Parreira, a lobsterman, contracted in writing to sell Sam Adams one thousand pounds of fresh lobsters at a particular price during the following season. A few months later, when lobsters became plentiful and the price went down, Adams tried to get out of the contract. He argued that the contract was not enforceable because the lobsters had not yet been caught when the contract was made. Do you agree with Adams? Why or why not?

2. Harnois entered into an oral contract with Neverson to lease a compact computer and a printer for three months for $600. In an attempt to rescind the contract, Harnois claimed that the contract was unenforceable because it was not in writing. Do you agree with Harnois? Why or why not?

3. Missouri Farmers Association (MFA) entered into a contract to spray all but a 14-foot strip of Mr. McBee's 51-acre soybean field. The field was to be sprayed for cockleburr, and MFA was to select the chemical and method to be used for spraying. The evening before the beans were sprayed, they were a good color and height. The evening after they were sprayed, they were brown, crumbly, and dry. Except for the 14-foot un-sprayed strip, the beans died within two or three days after the spraying was done. Did the UCC cover this transaction? Why or why not? *Missouri Farmers Assoc. v. McBee,* 787 S.W.2d 756 (MO).

4. Curry entered into a contract to sell four wheel bearings to Litman for $300. Before the contract was carried out, Curry told Litman that the cost of bearings had increased and that he would have to change the price to $400. Litman agreed to pay $400 for the bearings. Later, Litman refused to pay the additional $100, claiming that Curry gave no consideration for Litman's promise to pay the extra money. Was Litman correct? Why or why not?

5. Coleman bid $2,050 for a D-7 tractor at a public auction. Nothing was stated that the auction was with reserve. The auctioneer yelled "Sold," accept-

ing Coleman's bid. Later, the owner of the tractor refused to sell it for $2,050, saying that the auction was with reserve and that he could refuse to accept the bid. Did the owner have to sell the tractor to Coleman for $2,050? Why or why not? *Coleman v. Duncan,* 540 S.W.2d 935 (MO).

6. Ferguson agreed to sell to R. L. Kimsey Cotton Co., Inc., all the cotton produced by Ferguson on a specified parcel of land at an agreed price. The agreement was in writing and contained other terms. Later, Ferguson argued that the agreement was invalid because the quantity and subject matter were vague and indefinite. Was Ferguson correct? Why or why not? *R. L. Kimsey Cotton Co., Inc., v. Ferguson,* 214 S.E.2d 360 (GA).

7. Carolina Transformer Co., Inc., brought suit against Anderson for several thousand dollars owed them for the purchase of transformers. Anderson testified in court that he had orally negotiated the contract and had reached a final agreement with Carolina for the purchase of the transformers. Anderson argued, however, that he was not responsible because under the UCC, a contract for the sale of goods of $500 or more is not enforceable unless it is in writing. Do you agree with Anderson? *Carolina Transformer Co. v. Anderson,* 341 So.2d 1327 (MS).

8. O'Brien placed a telephone order for twenty shipments of lettuce from Soroka Farms. Soroka Farms shipped the lettuce to a cooler, where it was held under cold storage. It was later shipped on O'Brien's orders directly to O'Brien's customers. O'Brien refused to pay for the lettuce, arguing that the contract was not enforceable because it was over $500 and was not in writing. Do you believe that the oral contract was enforceable in this case? Why? See also *O'Day v. George Arakelian Farms, Inc.,* 540 P.2d 197 (AZ).

9. Representatives of a fish marketing association (AIFMA) and a fish company (NEFCO) met at

Bristol Bay, Alaska, to negotiate a marketing agreement for the forthcoming fishing season. At this meeting, NEFCO's agent, Gage, signed an agreement that contained the price that was to be paid for the fish and other details about the transaction. It omitted the quantity of fish was to be purchased. Later, when suit was brought on the agreement, NEFCO argued that it was unenforceable because the written agreement failed to mention the quantity. Do you agree with NEFCO? Explain. *Alaska Indus Fish Mktg. Assoc. v. New England Fish Co.,* 548 P.2d 348 (WA).

Quick Quiz Answers

15-1	15-2	15-3	15-4	15-5
1. F	1. T	1. T	1. F	1. F
2. T	2. T	2. F	2. T	2. F
3. T	3. F	3. T	3. T	3. F

Chapter 16

Title and Risk of Loss in Sales of Goods

The Opening Case

"The Wandering Cockapoo"

Before leaving on a six-week, cross-country camping trip, Charlie Jones dropped off his beloved cockapoo, named Indiana, at a kennel to be cared for while he was away. The kennel was part of a reputable pet supply store in the community that also sold kittens, dogs, hamsters, and other small animals as part of its routine business. When Jones returned from his trip, he went to the kennel to pick up Indiana and was told that a salesperson had mistakenly sold the dog to a woman named Claudia Crocker who was unaware that the dog belonged to Jones. During the six weeks that Jones was away, Crocker became very attached to the cockapoo, and refused to give it up. Who has title to the dog? Does Jones have a cause of action against Crocker for its return?

Chapter Outcomes

1. Contrast voidable title with void title.
2. Discuss the rights of the parties when goods that are entrusted to merchants are sold to others in the ordinary course of business.
3. Determine, in a given case, when title to goods passes from the seller to the buyer.
4. Decide, in different situations, whether the buyer or the seller of goods must bear the risk of loss.
5. Compare a sale on approval with a sale or return.
6. Describe when buyers and sellers of goods have insurable interests in those goods.

16-1 Void and Voidable Title

Title is the right of ownership to goods. People who own goods have title to them. Sellers sometimes give a bill of sale to a buyer as evidence that the sale took place. A **bill of sale** is a written statement evidencing the transfer of personal property from one person to another. It does not prove, however, that the seller had perfect title to the goods. The goods may have been stolen, obtained by fraud, purchased from a minor or incompetent person, or entrusted with the seller by the true owner and sold by mistake. The question that arises in such cases is whether an innocent purchaser for value receives good title to the goods. The answer to this question depends on whether the seller's title to the goods was void or voidable and whether the goods had been entrusted to a merchant.

Void Title

With the exception of voidable title, buyers of goods acquire whatever title their sellers had to the property. If a seller has **void title** (no title at all), a buyer of the goods obtains no title to them.

Example 16-1

A thief entered Rodriguez's apartment and stole her brand-new 42-inch plasma TV set, which had just been purchased that day and had not yet been removed from its carton. The thief sold the set to Guthrie, an innocent purchaser, who believed that the thief was the real owner of the set. Rodriguez would have the legal right to the return of the television set from Guthrie if its whereabouts were located. Guthrie's only right of recourse would be against the thief for the money paid for the set. Anyone who buys stolen goods receives no title to them.

The continued sale of the stolen property through several innocent buyers would not in any way defeat the real owner's right to the property. The rights of possession and title of successive buyers of stolen property can never be any better than the rights of the thief, who had no title to them.

Innocent purchasers may bring suit against the person from whom stolen goods were purchased for breach of warranty of title. This remedy is explained in Chapter 18.

Voidable Title

Anyone who obtains property as a result of another's fraud, misrepresentation, mutual mistake, undue influence, or duress holds only voidable title to the goods. **Voidable title** means title that may be voided if the injured party elects to do so. This kind of title is also received when goods are bought from a minor or a person who is mentally impaired. Some people refer to voidable title as title that is valid until voided.

Anyone with voidable title to goods is able to transfer good title to others. According to the UCC, "A person with voidable title has power to transfer a good title to a good faith purchaser for value."

Example 16-2

Dayton bought an expensive surround speaker system from Merchandise Mart on a thirty-day charge account. In making the purchase, Dayton made several fraudulent statements to the store's credit department. Although the set was bought by fraudulent means, a resale by Dayton to an innocent purchaser for value would cut off the right of Merchandise Mart to demand the return of its former property. Although the store cannot recover the goods, it may bring an action against Dayton for any loss suffered due to the fraud.

Entrusting Goods to a Merchant

People often entrust goods that belong to them to merchants. For example, they leave their watches with jewelers and their television sets with stores to be repaired. When this occurs, if the merchant sells the goods in the ordinary course of business to a third party who has

Teaching Tips Clarify for students the difference between *void* and *voidable* title. A void title is no title. If Marco buys a car from Corinne, who has void title, Marco has no title to the car, even though he paid for it, because Corinne had no title to give. A voidable title is a title that can be voided. If Tran buys a mountain bike from Jaleel, who has a voidable title to the bike, Tran acquires good title to the bike because, at the moment of sale, Jaleel's title to the bike was voidable but not void.

Did You Know?

A multimillion-dollar masterpiece painted by Monet entitled "Nympheas, 1904" that had been plundered by the Nazis during World War II was identified by the granddaughter of its owner when it was displayed at the Boston Museum of Fine Arts in 1998. The museum had borrowed the painting from a French museum. Upon learning that it was stolen, the French government returned the painting to the heirs of its rightful owner.

UCC 2-403(1) (see page 878)

UCC 2-403(2) (see page 878)

Teaching Tips In discussing who retains title of stolen goods, it is worth pointing out the low statistics of recovered merchandise. The best way to deal with theft is to prevent it whenever possible and to insure goods for their full worth. Remind students that it is a bigger challenge to recover stolen goods than to claim title to them.

State Variations Maine, like many states, has adopted UCC 2-403, which provides that a person who entrusts goods to a merchant who deals in goods of that kind gives the merchant power to transfer all rights of the entrustor to a buyer in the ordinary course of business.

State Variations If a lessee in Minnesota entrusts leased goods to the lessor who is a merchant dealing in goods of that kind, a subsequent lessee of those goods under a lease entered into after the entrustment and in the ordinary course of business takes those goods free of the existing lease contract.

The Opening Case Revisited
"The Wandering Cockapoo"

Crocker received good title to the cockapoo when she bought it in the ordinary course of the pet supply store's business. Jones's cause of action would be against the pet supply store that owned the kennel for money damages that he suffered from the loss.

no knowledge of the real owner's rights, the third party receives good title to them. The original owner who entrusted them to the merchant loses title to the goods altogether, but may bring an action against the merchant for money damages caused by the loss.

The reason for this rule of law is to give confidence to people who buy in the marketplace. People can be assured that they will receive good title to property (except stolen property) that they buy from a merchant who deals in goods of that kind in the ordinary course of business.

A Question of Ethics

How would you defend the rule of law exemplified in The Opening Case from an ethical point of view?

Quick Quiz 16-1 True or False?

1. *Void title* means title that may be voided if the injured party elects to do so.

2. *Voidable title* means no title at all.

3. The reason for the law giving good title to people who buy entrusted goods from merchants is to give confidence to people who buy in the marketplace.

16-2 The Passage of Title and Risk of Loss

It is not unusual for goods to be stolen, damaged, or destroyed while they are awaiting shipment, are being shipped, or are awaiting pickup after a sales contract has been entered into. When something happens to the goods, it becomes necessary to determine who must suffer the loss: the seller or the buyer. The rules for determining risk of loss are contained in the UCC. Except when goods are to be picked up by the buyer and in a few other cases, whoever has title to the goods bears the risk of loss.

UCC 2-509
(see page 880)

UCC 2-501(1)
(see page 878)

Goods must be identified to the contract before title can be transferred to the buyer. **Identified goods** are specific goods that have been selected as the subject matter of the contract. Once goods are identified, title passes to the buyer when the seller does whatever is required under the contract to deliver the goods. Contracts calling for the seller to deliver the goods are either *shipment contracts* or *destination contracts*.

Shipment Contracts

A **shipment contract** is one in which the seller turns the goods over to a carrier for delivery to the buyer. The seller has no responsibility for seeing that the goods reach their destination. In a shipment contract, both title and risk of loss pass to the buyer when the goods are given to the carrier.

UCC 2-401(2)
(see page 877)

Getting Students Involved Have students work in teams to create lists of common situations in which property is transferred into the temporary possession of another. Have students discuss each situation on their lists in light of title. Could title ever be transferred (such as in the death in a hospital of a person with no will and no relatives)? In each situation would title be void or voidable?

Example 16-3

Underwood was employed by Kentucky Cardinal Dairies to pick up milk from various farmers and deliver it, in the farmers' cans, to the dairy. When no one was looking, he poured some of the milk from the farmers' cans into his own cans and sold it to another dairy. He was charged with unlawfully taking milk "which was the property of Kentucky Cardinal Dairies." In his defense, he argued that the milk was still the property of the farmers because it had not yet reached the dairy. The court disagreed, holding that title to the milk passed to the dairy the moment it was picked up by Underwood because that was the time and place of shipment.

UCC 2-319
(see page 875)

Shipment contracts are often designated by the term *f.o.b. the place of shipment* (such as f.o.b. Chicago). The abbreviation **f.o.b.** means "free on board." When goods are sent **f.o.b.** followed by **the place of shipment,** they will be delivered free to the place of shipment. The buyer must pay all shipping charges from there to the place of destination. The terms indicate that title to the goods and the risk of loss pass at the point of origin. Delivery to the carrier by the seller and acceptance by the carrier complete the transfer of both title and risk of loss. Thus, the buyer accepts full responsibility during the transit of the goods. (See Table 16-1.)

Who assumes the risk of loss for custom-made furniture awaiting delivery to the customer?

Table 16-1 Abbreviations

Abbreviation	Meaning
f.o.b. New York	Free on board to New York (This would be a *shipment contract* if shipped from New York.)
f.o.b. Los Angeles	Free on board to Los Angeles (This would be a *destination contract* if shipped from New York.)
c.o.d.	Collect on delivery
c.i.f.	Cost of goods shipped, insurance, and freight
c.f.	Cost of goods shipped and freight
f.a.s.	Free alongside vessel or at a dock

Teaching Tips Emphasize the rule that allows a merchant to give good title to someone who buys goods that have been entrusted to the merchant. Give the example of leaving a watch with a jeweler for repairs and later discovering that the jeweler has sold it by mistake.

Teaching Tips Help students remember the meanings of *c.f., c.i.f., c.o.d., f.a.s. vessel, f.o.b. the place of destination,* and *f.o.b. the place of shipment.* Have students work in pairs to come up with ways to communicate the meaning of one term to the other students. The pairs might, for example, draw cartoons illustrating the meaning of a term, act out the meaning of a term, or come up with a play on words for a term's abbreviation to help classmates remember what the term means.

UCC 2-401(2)
(see page 877)

UCC 2-319
(see page 875)

Example 16-4

Joshua Nichols of Hartland, Maine, shipped a pair of live chimpanzees to Osgood, a zoologist in Ellensburg, Washington. Terms of the shipment were f.o.b. Hartland, Maine. During the shipment, the carrier was involved in an accident, and the chimpanzees escaped. Osgood would suffer the loss because title and risk of loss passed to her in Hartland, Maine. Undoubtedly, Osgood would place a claim against the carrier in its obligation as insurer of goods accepted for shipment.

Destination Contracts

If the contract requires the seller to deliver goods to a destination, it is called a **destination contract.** Both title and risk of loss pass to the buyer when the seller tenders the goods at the place of destination. **Tender** means to offer to turn the goods over to the buyer.

Destination contracts are often designated by the terms **f.o.b.** followed by **the place of destination** (such as f.o.b. Tampa); goods shipped under such terms belong to the seller until they have been delivered to the destination shown on the contract. Similarly, the risk of loss remains with the seller until the goods are tendered at destination. Tender at destination requires that the goods arrive at the place named in the contract, the buyer is given notice of their arrival, and a reasonable time is allowed for the buyer to pick up the goods from the carrier.

Example 16-5

Suppose, in Example 16-4, the shipment to Osgood had been made under terms of f.o.b. Ellensburg, Washington. Title and risk would not have passed at the shipping point. Nichols would have had to suffer the loss, and Osgood would have had no obligation for payment.

When terms of shipment do not specify shipping point or destination, it is assumed to be a shipment contract. Adding the term **c.o.d.** (collect on delivery) instructs the carrier to retain possession until the carrier has collected the cost of the goods.

UCC 2-320
(see page 875)

The term **c.i.f.** (cost, insurance, and freight) instructs the carrier to collect all charges and fees in one lump sum. This sum includes the cost of goods shipped, insurance, and freight charges to the point of destination. The term **c.f.** means that insurance is not included in the sum.

UCC 2-319(2)
(see page 875)

The term **f.a.s. vessel** (free alongside vessel) at a named port requires sellers to deliver the goods, at their own risk, alongside the vessel or at a dock designated by the buyer.

No Delivery Required

UCC 2-401(3)(b)
(see page 877)

UCC 2-509(3)
(see page 890)

When the contract calls for the buyer to pick up the goods, title passes to the buyer when the contract is made. Risk of loss, on the other hand, passes at different times depending on whether the seller is a merchant. If the seller is a merchant, the risk of loss passes when the buyer receives the goods. If the seller is not a merchant, the risk of loss passes to the buyer when the seller tenders the goods to the buyer (see Table 16-2).

Table 16-2 Passage of Title and Risk of Loss

Terms of Contract	Title Passes	Risk of Loss Passes
Shipment contract	When goods are delivered to carrier	When goods are delivered to carrier
Destination contract	When goods are tendered at destination	When goods are tendered at destination
No delivery required	When contract is made	*Merchant seller:* When buyer receives goods; *Nonmerchant seller:* When seller tenders goods to buyer
Document of title	When document of title is given to buyer	When document of title is given to buyer
Agreement of the parties	At time and place agreed upon	At time and place agreed upon

Example 16-6

Rivera agreed to sell her Aurora fiberglass kayak to Gray for $2,500. Gray paid for the kayak and said that he would pick it up from Rivera's yard the next evening. Gray was called out of town, however, and did not pick up the kayak, which had been made ready for him. The kayak was stolen a week later from Rivera's yard. Gray must suffer the loss because the kayak had been tendered to him. Had Rivera been a merchant, she would have had to assume the loss because Gray had not yet received possession of the kayak.

Fungible Goods

The UCC defines **fungible goods** as "goods of which any unit is, by nature or usage of trade, the equivalent of any like unit." Wheat, flour, sugar, and liquids of various kinds are examples of fungible goods. They have no important characteristics that identify them as coming from a particular supplier and they are usually sold by weight or measure. Title to fungible goods may pass without the necessity of separating goods sold from the bulk. Under the UCC, "an undivided share of an identified bulk of fungible goods is sufficiently identified to be sold although the quantity of the bulk is not determined."

Example 16-7

Logan Trucking Co. owned a large fuel storage tank that was partially filled with diesel fuel. The exact quantity of fuel in the tank was not known. The company was going out of business. Interstate Trucking Co. contracted to buy half of the fuel in the tank, and Union Trucking Co. contracted to buy the other half. Both buyers agreed to send their own trucks to pick up the fuel. Title passed to the buyers when the contract was made even though the exact quantity of each sale was unknown and neither buyer had taken a share of the fuel from the entire lot.

Documents of Title

Sometimes, when people buy goods, they receive a document of title to the goods rather than the goods themselves. They then give the document of title to the warehouse or

Teaching Tips Use Table 16-2 as a guide for conducting a class discussion on the difference between passage of title and risk of loss. Stress that the terms are the same except when no delivery is required; the difference then depends on whether the seller is a merchant. Ask the class for examples of the latter situation.

UCC 2-105(4) (see page 870)

Terms The root word *fungi* refers to function, which relates to the broader definition of *fungible* as *interchangeable*. One unit of something fungible can function the same as any other unit.

Terms A *bill of sale* is not actually a bill. It is simply a receipt indicating that title has transferred from seller to buyer. A bill of sale prevents the seller from denying that the sale took place.

carrier that is holding the goods and receive possession of them. A **document of title** is a paper giving the person who possesses it the right to receive the goods named in the document. Bills of lading and warehouse receipts, as explained in Chapter 21, are examples of documents of title. An automobile title certificate has not been given the legal status of a document of title, as the term is used in the UCC.

UCC 2-401(3)(a)
(see page 869)

When a document of title is used in a sales transaction, both title and risk of loss pass to the buyer when the document is delivered to the buyer.

Example 16-8

Manchez stored a large quantity of wheat in a grain elevator and, in return, was given a warehouse receipt. Later, Manchez sold the wheat to Rodney. Upon receipt of the money for the wheat, Manchez signed and delivered the warehouse receipt to Rodney. Rodney received title to the wheat when the document was delivered to her.

Agreement of the Parties

UCC 2-401(1)
(see page 869)

The parties may, if they wish, enter into an agreement setting forth the time that title and risk of loss pass from the seller to the buyer. With one exception, title and risk of loss will pass at the time and place agreed upon. If the agreement allows the seller to retain title after the goods are shipped, title will pass to the buyer at the time of shipment regardless of the agreement, and the seller will have a security interest in the goods rather than title. A security interest gives the seller a right to have the property sold in the event that the buyer fails to pay money owed to the seller (see Chapter 31).

Example 16-9

Raymond agreed to sell Glover her John Deere tractor for $12,000. The agreement called for Glover to pay $3,000 down and the balance in monthly installments for two years. Under the terms of the agreement, title to the tractor would not pass to Glover until the $12,000 was paid in full. Since Raymond delivered the tractor to Glover on the day that the agreement was signed, title passed to Glover at that time regardless of the terms in the contract. The effect of those terms was to give Raymond a security interest in the tractor for the balance of the money owed to her.

Revesting of Title in Seller

UCC 2-401(4)
(see page 869)

Buyers, after entering into sales contracts, sometimes refuse to accept the goods that are delivered or are otherwise made available to them. In all such cases, title to the goods returns to the seller. This is true whether or not the buyer's rejection of the goods was justified. Similarly, title to goods returns to the seller when the buyer accepts the goods and then for a justifiable reason decides to revoke the acceptance. A justifiable reason for revoking an acceptance would be the discovery of a defect in the goods after having inspected them.

UCC 2-510
(see page 880)

When the seller sends goods to the buyer that do not meet the contract requirements and are, therefore, unacceptable, the risk of loss remains with the seller. For situations in which the buyer accepts the goods but later discovers some defect and rightfully revokes the acceptance, the passage of risk of loss depends upon whether the buyer is insured. If the buyer has insurance, that insurance will cover the loss. If there is no insurance, the risk of loss remains with the seller from the beginning.

UCC 2-510(3)
(see page 880)

When the buyer breaches the contract with regard to goods that have been identified to the contract, the seller may, to the extent of having no insurance coverage, treat the risk of loss as resting with the buyer.

International Sales

The rules governing international sales are given in the United Nations Convention on Contracts for the International Sale of Goods (CISG). The international law does not address questions dealing with the passage of title because the laws of each country vary considerably. However, the rules governing the passage of risk of loss are addressed in the international law and are quite similar to those found in the UCC.

Quick Quiz 16-2 True or False?

1. With a few exceptions, whoever has title to goods also bears the risk of loss.

2. When a contract calls for a non-merchant buyer to pick up the goods so that no delivery is required, the risk of loss passes to the buyer when the contract is made.

3. Fungible goods must be separated from the bulk before title to them can pass to a buyer.

16-3 Sales with Right of Return

Because of competition and a desire to give satisfaction, goods are sometimes sold with the understanding that they may be returned even though they conform to the contract. Determination of ownership and risk of loss while such goods are in the buyer's possession is sometimes necessary. Sales with the right of return are of two kinds: sale on approval and sale or return.

Sale on Approval

A sale that allows goods to be returned even though they conform to the contract is called a **sale on approval** when the goods are primarily for the buyer's use. When goods are sold on approval, they remain the property of the seller until the buyer's approval has been expressed. The approval may be indicated by the oral or written consent of the buyer or by the buyer's act of retaining the goods for more than a reasonable time. Using the goods in a reasonable and expected manner on a trial basis does not imply an acceptance. Grossly careless use and a failure to inform the seller of the buyer's intent to return, however, could constitute an acceptance.

Goods held by the buyer on approval are not subject to the claims of the buyer's creditors until the buyer decides to accept them. In addition, the risk of loss remains with the seller until the buyer has accepted the goods.

Sale or Return

A sale that allows goods to be returned even though they conform to the contract is called a **sale or return** when the goods are delivered primarily for resale. When such a sale occurs, the buyer takes title to the goods with the right to revest (reinstate) title in the seller after a specified period or reasonable time. In such cases, the buyer must accept all of the

---

Background Information The CISG has several notable exceptions in the contracts that it covers. It does not apply to goods bought for personal, household, or family use or to contracts that mainly supply services. Nor does it cover liability of the seller for death or injury caused by the goods sold. The risk of loss passes to the buyer when the goods are handed over to the first carrier for transmission to the buyer unless the seller agrees to hand them over at a particular place. If the seller agrees to hand the goods over to a carrier at a particular place, the risk of loss passes to the buyer at that time. Sometimes, goods are sold when they are in transit. When this kind of sale occurs (with some exceptions) the risk of loss passes to the buyer when the contract is made. In all other situations, the risk of loss, in general, passes when the buyer takes over the goods.

UCC 2-326
(see page 877)

State Variations Alaska, Arkansas, Colorado, Michigan, and New Mexico have each exempted works of fine art from the sale on approval section of the UCC. In these states, fine art becomes the property of the buyer on receipt.

UCC 2-327
(see page 877)

UCC 2-326
(see page 877)

Related Cases In *Mahler v. Allied Marine,* (513 So.2d 677), Mahler had a one-week period within which to accept or reject a yacht under a sale-on-approval agreement. Allied Marine regarded Mahler's overdue silence as acceptance. The court found in favor of Allied, stating that the buyer must respond within the specified time which had been specifically negotiated by the parties.

obligations of ownership while retaining possession of the goods. Goods held on sale or return are subject to the claims of the buyer's creditors.

While in the buyer's possession, the goods must be cared for and used in a reasonable manner, anticipating their possible return in the same condition as when received, after making allowance for ordinary wear and tear. Also, the goods must be returned at the buyer's risk and expense.

Example 16-10

Butcher owned a gift shop in which she sold other people's goods on consignment. Hanson delivered a dozen handmade braided rugs to Butcher with the understanding that she would be paid for any that were sold. Any rugs that did not sell after three months would be returned to Hanson. This agreement was a sale or return because the rugs were delivered primarily for resale. Butcher would be required to pay Hanson for any rugs that were damaged, lost, or stolen while in Butcher's possession.

Quick Quiz 16-3 True or False?

1. Goods that are sold *on approval* are subject to the claims of the buyer's creditors until the buyer decides to accept them.

2. Goods that are sold *on approval* remain the property of the seller until the buyer's approval has been expressed.

3. Goods that are sold on *sale or return* are not subject to the claims of the buyer's creditors.

16-4 Insurable Interest

UCC 2-501(1) (see page 878)

Teaching Tips Ask students if they ever returned merchandise that they ordered from a catalog. Have any students who had this experience explain what the seller required him or her to do to return the merchandise. Next ask students what would have happened if the merchandise had been lost in the mail on its way back to the seller.

People must have an insurable interest in property to be able to place insurance on it. An **insurable interest** is the financial interest that an insured party has in the insured property. Buyers may place insurance on goods the moment a contract is made and the goods are identified to the contract. At this point, buyers receive an insurable interest in the goods they buy. They obtain an insurable interest even though they later reject or return the goods to the seller. Notwithstanding the buyer's right to insure the goods, sellers retain an insurable interest in goods as long as they still have title to them. Insurable interests are discussed in more detail in Chapter 29.

Example 16-11

While shopping on vacation in an antique store in Connecticut, Maniff, who lived in Nevada, came upon a Native American totem pole that she liked. She decided to buy the totem pole on the condition that the antique dealer would ship it f.o.b. Winnemucca, Nevada. The dealer agreed. Maniff received an insurable interest in the totem pole when it was identified to the contract. At the same time, the dealer retained an insurable interest in it until it was tendered at its destination in Winnemucca. Both Maniff and the antique dealer could insure the totem pole.

Summary

16-1 Anyone with void title to goods, such as a thief, can never give good title to another person. Anyone with voidable title, such as someone who buys goods from a minor, may transfer good title to a good faith purchaser for value. When goods are entrusted to a merchant who sells them without authority to someone in the ordinary course of business, the purchaser obtains good title.

16-2 With few exceptions, such as when goods are to be picked up by the buyer, whoever has title to the goods bears the risk of loss. Goods must be identified to the contract before title can be transferred to the buyer. Once goods are identified, title passes to the buyer when the seller does whatever is required under the contract to deliver the goods. In a shipment contract, both title and risk of loss pass to the buyer when the goods are given to the carrier. In a destination contract, both title and risk of loss pass to the buyer when the seller tenders the goods at the place of destination. When the contract calls for the buyer to pick up the goods, title passes to the buyer when the contract is made. If the seller is a merchant, the risk of loss passes when the buyer receives the goods. If the seller is not a merchant, the risk

of loss passes to the buyer when the seller tenders the goods to the buyer. Title to fungible goods may pass without the necessity of separating goods sold from the bulk. When a document of title is used, both title and risk of loss pass to the buyer when the document is delivered to the buyer. In general, the parties may establish by agreement the time and place for the passage of both title and risk of loss. Title returns to the seller when the buyer refuses to accept the goods. Similarly, the risk of loss remains with the seller when the goods that are shipped do not meet the contract requirements.

16-3 Goods sold on approval remain the property of the seller until the buyer's approval is expressed. In addition, the seller retains the risk of loss. In contrast, in a sale or return, the buyer takes title to the goods but is given the right to return the goods to the seller at a later time. The buyer must care for the goods in a reasonable manner and suffer the risk of loss.

16-4 Buyers have an insurable interest in goods the moment a contract is made and the goods are identified to the contract. In addition, sellers retain an insurable interest in goods as long as they still have title to them.

Key Terms

bill of sale, 298
c.f., 302
c.i.f., 302
c.o.d., 302
destination contract, 302
document of title, 304
f.a.s. vessel, 302

f.o.b., 301
f.o.b. the place of destination, 302
f.o.b. the place of shipment, 301
fungible goods, 303
identified goods, 300
insurable interest, 306
sale on approval, 305

sale or return, 305
shipment contract, 301
tender, 302
title, 298
voidable title, 299
void title, 299

Questions for Review and Discussion

1. What is the difference between void title and voidable title? Explain.
2. What are the rights of an innocent purchaser of stolen goods?
3. What are some examples of people who have voidable title to goods?
4. What are the rights of the owner of goods who entrusts the goods to a merchant who sells them in the ordinary course of business?
5. When do title and risk of loss pass to the buyer in a shipment contract?

6. When do title and risk of loss pass to the buyer in a destination contract?

7. When do title and risk of loss pass to the buyer when the contract calls for the buyer to pick up the goods?

8. When do title and risk of loss pass to the buyer when a document of title is used?

9. What is the difference between a sale on approval and a sale or return?

10. When may buyers place insurance on goods they purchase?

Investigating the Internet

Information about the UN Convention on Contracts for the International Sale of Goods (CISG) can be found at **http://www.ita.doc.gov/legal/cisg.html.** Although the CISG follows the UCC rather closely, there are some differences.

Cases for Analysis

1. Wheel Sports Center entered into a sales contract agreeing to deliver a motorcycle to Ramos for the price of $893. Ramos paid the full price for the motorcycle and immediately had it insured and registered in his name. However, before it was delivered to Ramos, the motorcycle was stolen from Wheel Sports Center. Who must suffer the loss, Wheel Sports Center or Ramos? Why? *Ramos v. Wheel Sports Center,* 409 N.Y.S.2d 505 (NY).

2. Estes purchased a late-model Chevrolet Caprice sports coupe from Howard, an automobile dealer in Mississippi. Later, it was discovered that the vehicle had been stolen from a Chevrolet dealership in Florida and, after a circuitous route, eventually had come to rest in Mississippi. The bill of sale to the vehicle had been forged. Estes contended that he has good title to the vehicle because he bought the auto from a dealer. Was Estes correct? *Allstate Ins. Co. v. Estes,* 345 So.2d 265 (MS).

3. Brown, who operated Jack's Skelly Service Station, was sued by his former wife for child support payments. During the trial, the question arose as to who owned the gasoline in the service station tanks, Brown or Brown's supplier, Martin. Brown had entered into a "special Keep-Full motor fuel sales agreement" under which Martin agreed to deliver to Brown's place of business Skelly motor fuel. The agreement stated that title to the fuel "shall be and remain with Martin until removed from the tanks through and by means of computing pumps." Who owned the gas in the tanks, Brown or Martin? Why? *Stewart v. Brown,* 546 S.W.2d 204 (MO).

4. Fanning, who was seventeen years old, sold her bicycle to Gerard, an adult, for $75. The next day, Gerard advertised the bicycle for sale in the classified section of a local newspaper and sold it for $150. The person who bought the bicycle was unaware that it had belonged to Fanning. When Fanning discovered what Gerard had done, she attempted to get the bicycle back from the person who bought it, claiming that Gerard had voidable title to the bicycle. Does Fanning have the legal right to the return of the bicycle? Why or why not?

5. Harold Marcus entered into a contract with Corrigan's Yacht Yard & Marine Sales, Inc., to trade in his 34-foot Silverton power boat toward a later-model Mainship boat. He delivered his Silverton boat to the yacht yard at the time of the contract in November. The new boat was not to be delivered until the following April. The yacht yard sold the Silverton boat to William Heiselman soon after receiving it. When the yacht yard was unable to deliver the Mainship boat to Marcus in April, Marcus took back his Silverton boat. Who had title to the boat, Marcus or Heiselman? Explain. *Heiselman v. Marcus,* 488 N.Y.S.2d 571 (NY).

6. Gallo entered into a contract in October to deliver 3,500 heifers to Weisbart's ranch between May 1 and October 1 of the next year. Gallo experienced difficulty in raising the heifers due to rising costs and a severe winter, and his bank foreclosed on the cattle before they could be delivered to Weisbart. Weisbart claimed that sale of the cattle occurred in

October when the contract was made and that title passed to him at that time. Do you agree with Weisbart? Why or why not? *Weisbart & Co. v. First Nat'l. Bank,* 568 F.2d 391 (5th Cir.).

7. Mann bought a Lincoln Continental Mark IV automobile from Kilbourn American Leasing, Inc., for $6,500 cash. He received by mistake from Kilbourn a title certificate for a similar but different vehicle. Kilbourn later borrowed money from a bank and gave the correct title certificate for Mann's car to the bank as security for the loan. The bank claims that Mann does not have title to the car because he did not receive the title certificate. Was the bank correct? Why or why not? *National Exch. Bank v. Mann,* 260 N.W.2d 716 (WI).

8. Eberhard Manufacturing Company sold goods to Brown Industrial Sales Company without agreeing on who would bear the risk of loss. The contract contained no f.o.b. terms. Eberhard placed the goods on board a common carrier with instructions to deliver them to Brown. The goods were lost in transit. Who suffered the loss, Eberhard or Brown? Why? *Eberhard Mfg.Co. v. Brown,* 232 N.W.2d 378 (MI).

9. Henry Heide, Incorporated, received a warehouse receipt for 3,200 100-pound bags of sugar that it bought from Olavarria. The corporation withdrew 800 bags of the sugar from the warehouse (where thousands of pounds were stored), but when it returned for the balance, it discovered that the warehouse was padlocked and empty. Some 200,000 pounds of sugar had mysteriously disappeared from it. Henry Heide, Incorporated, carried insurance for such a loss, but its insurance company refused to pay, claiming that the corporation had no insurable interest in the sugar. Do you agree with the insurance company? Why or why not? *Henry Heide, Inc., v. Atlantic Mut. Ins. Co.,* 363 N.Y.S.2d 515 (NY).

Quick Quiz Answers

16-1	16-2	16-3
1. F	1. T	1. F
2. F	2. F	2. T
3. T	3. F	3. F

<table>
<tr>
<td>

Chapter 17

</td>
<td>

Performance and Breach of the Sales Contract

</td>
</tr>
</table>

The Opening Case
"Bitter Sunshine"

Garden-fresh Produce Co., located in Fairlawn, New Jersey, ordered 50 bushels of oranges from Sunripe Citrus of Immokalee, Florida. The fruit was shipped c.o.d. When it arrived, the shipper would not allow it to be inspected until it was paid for. Garden-fresh paid for the shipment, opened the boxes, and discovered that they contained grapefruit, not oranges. When notified of the mistake, Sunripe told Garden-fresh to sell the grapefruit, and that it would send a replacement shipment as soon as possible. Garden-fresh, however, threw away the grapefruit. Did Garden-fresh have the right to inspect the shipment before paying for it? Could it rightfully throw away the grapefruit?

Chapter Outcomes

1. Discuss, in general, the obligations of the parties to a sales contract.
2. Determine whether the requirements for tender of delivery and tender of payment have been met in given cases.
3. Explain the buyer's right to inspect goods.
4. Describe the buyer's rights and duties when improper goods are delivered.
5. Judge, in given cases, whether the seller has the right to correct an improper tender of delivery.
6. Compare the remedies that are available to the seller with those available to the buyer when sales contracts are breached.

17-1 Obligations of the Parties

The obligations of the parties to a sales contract are simple and straightforward. The seller is obligated to turn the goods over to the buyer, and the buyer is obligated to accept and pay for them, both acting in accordance with the terms of the contract. In addition, all parties must act in **good faith,** which means that they must act honestly.

The court need not enforce a contract or part of a contract that it finds to be unconscionable. An **unconscionable contract** is one that is so one-sided that it is oppressive and gives unfair advantage to one of the parties. Unequal bargaining power, the absence of a meaningful choice by one party, and unreasonably one-sided terms, when put together, are indications of unconscionability.

When disputes arise between parties who have dealt together in the past, the court often looks to their past dealings to give meaning to the

Business Law in the News
Coke's Decade of Arrogance

For a company whose flagship product has long stood as a global icon of American optimism and success, Coca-Cola Co. has spent much of the past decade beset by inner doubt and turmoil. After a glorious 16-year run under legendary Chairman Roberto C. Goizueta—Coke's shares soared 3,500% by the time of his unexpected 1997 death—the former high-flier has come crashing back to earth. Regulatory investigations, a divisive employee discrimination suit, and economic woes in key Asian and Latin markets have left profits weak. Against this backdrop, Coke CEO Douglas N. Daft's surprise Feb.19 announcement that he will retire after just five years isn't so surprising. Daft's efforts to rebottle the old magic at Coke fell short of expectations.

In *The Real Thing: Truth and Power at the Coca-Cola Company,* reporter Constance L. Hays of *The New York Times* makes a compelling case that Coke's struggles in recent years aren't so much the result of downturns in those key global markets—something the company might prefer that you believe—as the repercussions from the hubris that built up in Coke over the 1990s. Hays is an intrepid sleuth, able to craft a colorful narrative by gaining the confidence of the normally tight-lipped Coke executives and bottlers. However, her focus on events of the mid- and late-1990s is a liability. The book gives short shrift to the trials and tribulations Coke suffered after Daft took the helm in late 1999. As a result, any reader looking for insights into Daft's resignation will be disappointed.

Hays begins with a tedious retrospective of Coke's early history, starting with Asa Candler's purchase of the Coca-Cola recipe in 1888 from another Atlanta pharmacist. That's followed by an equally plodding account of the evolution of Coke's bottling network. But slowly, Hays reaches the crux of her argument: That a ruinous arrogance crept in over the decades, causing the company to cease dealing in good faith with a number of key constituents, including its bottlers and regulators.

The author chronicles the lengthy campaign to buy out and retire the independent bottlers that were the company's best assets but that Coke execs viewed instead as irritants. She also shows how Coke failed to pay proper homage to European regulators, who got their revenge by vetoing some key acquisitions that could have helped sustain the company's growth rate. As growth began to slow, Coke increasingly tried to make its numbers through debilitating price hikes on the concentrate it sells to bottlers, who handle the actual mixing, packaging, and distributing of the product. After their spectacular rise under Goizueta, Coke's shares fell into a painful spiral under successors M. Douglas Ivester and Daft, even now trading at 40% below the all-time high set back in 1998. The company began blaming each disappointing quarter on a confluence of unfortunate circumstances—everything from unfavorable currency translations and economic weakness in South America to rainy European summers that dampened demand for its products. Hays's narrative comes to a crescendo in late 1999: Ivester was forced to resign after a series of fateful events, including an overblown contamination scare in Belgium—for which Coke only grudgingly apologized—and a revolt by some key bottlers.

Questions for Analysis

1. What is the crux of Hays's argument as to the cause of Coke's falling profits?

2. As growth began to slow, what did Coke do to try to make its numbers?

3. In what way does this article relate to the contents of this chapter?

Source: Dean Foust. "Coke's Decade of Arrogance," *BusinessWeek,* March 15, 2004, p. 22.

State Variations In North Carolina, if a sales contract, or any portion of the contract, is determined to be unconscionable, the court may: (1) refuse to enforce the contract, or (2) enforce the contract without the unconscionable clause, or (3) limit the application of any unconscionable clause to avoid an unconscionable result.

UCC 1-205
(see page 868)

Related Cases Wine World had an oral contract with Brand to sell wine to Brand for distribution. This type of contract in the wine industry was customarily sealed with a handshake. In 1989, Wine World terminated the contract. Brand asserted that custom and usage in the wine industry dictated that a distributorship could only be terminated for poor performance or failure to pay invoices. The court noted that the custom and usage of the industry was relevant to prove an implied term of an oral contract. However, in this case, the custom had ceased by 1989, so the termination was upheld. *Varni Bros. Corp. v. Wine World, Inc.,* 41 Cal.Rptr.2d 740 (1995).

Teaching Tips The CISG has similar provisions for international sales. Under that law, the parties are bound by practices they have established between themselves. In addition, unless they agree otherwise, the parties must follow the methods of dealing in international trade that are widely known and regularly observed by parties in the same type of trade. CISG Article 9.

disputed transaction. When interpreting the meaning of contracts, the court may also consider any usage of trade, that is, any particular methods of doing business, that are commonly used in that field. Although terms that are expressly stated in a contract will usually control the contract's meaning, the parties' past dealings and usage of trade are often considered to supplement or qualify the express terms.

Example 17-1

Associated Hardware Supply Company negotiated with Big Wheel Distributing Company for the purchase of merchandise. The parties could not agree on pricing the goods. Associated Hardware wanted to pay cost plus 10 percent, while Big Wheel insisted on the dealers' catalog price less 11 percent. Although the parties exchanged letters, there was never any formal agreement on pricing. Over a two-year period, Associated Hardware ordered goods from Big Wheel amounting to more than $850,000, paying for them on a catalog-less-11-percent basis. Later, when an additional $40,000 was owed for merchandise purchased, Associated Hardware refused to pay, claiming that no agreement had been reached as to the pricing of the goods. Finding in favor of Big Wheel, the court attached great weight to the way the parties had dealt in the past. It held that the parties' course of dealing for the two-year period governed the sale of the remaining merchandise.

Quick Quiz 17-1 True or False?

1. According to the law of sales contracts, all parties must act in good faith, which means they must act honestly.

2. Fraud and duress are indications of unconscionability.

3. The parties' past dealings are never considered to supplement the terms of an express contract.

17-2 Tender of Performance

When the seller offers to turn the goods over to the buyer and when the buyer offers to pay for them, **tender of performance** occurs. It is the offering by the parties to do what they have agreed to do under the terms of the contract. Tender is necessary in order to test the party's ability and willingness to perform his or her part of the bargain. The seller must make tender of delivery, and the buyer must make tender of payment. If a party fails to make tender and the other breaches the contract, the one not making tender cannot bring suit.

Tender of Delivery by Seller

To be in a position to bring suit on a sales contract, the seller of goods must make **tender of delivery,** that is, offer to turn the goods over to the buyer. Failure to make this offer is an excuse for buyers not to perform their part of the bargain.

UCC 2-507
(see page 880)

Manner of Seller's Tender To make proper tender, the seller must put and hold conforming goods at the buyer's disposition during a reasonable hour of the day.

Example 17-2

Gipsum Canning Co. agreed to sell 1,000 cases of canned beets to Green Grocers for $8.40 a case. Before shipping the goods, however, Gipsum was offered $9.60 a case from another company. Gipsum delivered the 1,000 cases of beets to Green Grocers's loading platform at three o'clock in the morning. Finding no one there, Gipsum took the goods and sold them to the other company at the higher price. When sued, Gipsum claimed that Green Grocers had breached the contract by not accepting the goods when they were tendered at the loading platform. The court disagreed, saying that Gipsum did not put and hold the goods at the buyer's disposition during a reasonable hour of the day.

In addition, the seller must notify the buyer that the goods are being tendered. It is the responsibility of the buyer, on the other hand, to furnish facilities that are suitable for receiving the goods.

UCC 2-503(1)(b)
(see page 879)

Shipment Contract In a shipment contract, the seller must put the goods in the possession of a carrier and contract with that carrier for their transportation. Any necessary documents must be sent to the buyer, who must be promptly notified of the shipment.

UCC 2-504
(see page 879)

Goods in Possession of Warehouse Sometimes, goods are in the possession of a warehouse and are to be turned over to the buyer without being moved. When this situation occurs, tender requires that the seller either tender a document of title covering the goods or obtain an acknowledgment by the warehouse of the buyer's right to their possession.

UCC 2-503(4)
(see page 879)

Teaching Tips For international sales, the seller must deliver the goods, hand over any documents relating to them, and transfer the property in the goods, as required by the contract. If the seller is not bound to deliver the goods to a particular place, the seller must hand the goods over to the first carrier for transmission to the buyer. If there is no carrier involved, the seller must place the goods at the buyer's disposal. CISG Articles 30–34.

Example 17-3

Spiegel purchased 5,000 cases of canned onions from Ingalls at a price that was much lower than the wholesale market price of the same product. The cases of onions had been stored by Ingalls at the East Side Storage Warehouse. Spiegel wished to continue storing the onions at the same warehouse, as she had no immediate use for them. Ingalls notified East Side Storage Warehouse that the onions had been sold to Spiegel. Tender occurred when the warehouse acknowledged to Spiegel that it was now holding the cases of onions for her instead of for Ingalls.

Tender of Payment by Buyer

Although the seller is obligated to deliver the goods to the buyer, this obligation stands on the condition that the buyer make tender of payment unless otherwise agreed. **Tender of payment** means offering to turn the money over to the seller. Such tender may be made by any means or in any manner that is commonly used in the ordinary course of business. The seller has the right to demand payment in legal tender but must give the buyer a reasonable time to obtain it. **Legal tender** is money that may be offered legally in satisfaction of a debt and that must be accepted by a creditor when offered.

UCC 2-511(1)
(see page 880)

Teaching Tips Discuss with the class the meaning of *legal tender*. Point out that, under the UCC, tender of payment may be made by a check; however, the seller may demand legal tender and give the buyer a reasonable time to obtain it.

Example 17-4

Thompson Computer Sales agreed to sell a computer to Rubin for $6,000 c.o.d. When the equipment was delivered, Rubin offered to pay Thompson with a check. This was a sufficient tender of payment because checks are commonly used in the ordinary course of business. Thompson did not have to accept Rubin's check if it did not wish to do so. If the company refused to take the check, however, it would have to give Rubin a reasonable amount of time to obtain legal tender.

Payment by check is conditional under the UCC. If the check clears, the debt is discharged. If the check is dishonored, the debt is revived.

When a contract requires payment before inspection, as when goods are shipped c.o.d., the buyer must pay for them first, even if they turn out to be defective when they are inspected. Of course, if the defect is obvious, the buyer would not have to accept or to pay for the goods. Payment by the buyer before inspecting the goods does not constitute an acceptance of them. Upon discovering a defect and notifying the seller, the buyer may use any of the remedies that are mentioned later in this chapter against the seller for breach of contract.

Seller must make tender of delivery, and buyer must make tender of payment.

UCC 2-511(3)
(see page 880)

UCC 2-512
(see page 881)

Quick Quiz 17-2 True or False?

1. *Tender of performance* is the offering by the parties to do what they have agreed to do under the terms of the contract.

2. A party who fails to make tender cannot bring suit if the other party breaches the contract.

3. *Tender of payment* is money that may be offered legally in satisfaction of a debt and that must be accepted by a creditor when offered.

17-3 Buyer's Rights and Duties upon Delivery of Improper Goods

UCC 2-513
(see page 881)

UCC 2-106(2)
(see page 870)

Except when goods are shipped c.o.d. or when the contract provides for payment against a document of title, the buyer has the right to inspect the goods before accepting them or paying for them. The inspection may take place after the goods arrive at their destination. Expenses of inspection must be borne by the buyer but may be recovered from the seller if the goods do not conform to the contract and are rejected by the buyer. Goods conform to a contract when they are in accordance with the obligations under the contract.

When defective goods or goods not of the kind specified in the contract are delivered, the buyer may elect to reject them all, accept them all, or accept any commercial unit or units and reject the rest. A **commercial unit** is a single whole for the purpose of sale, the

The Opening Case Revisited
"Bitter Sunshine"

Garden-fresh had no right to inspect the shipment before paying for it because it was sent c.o.d. It could do so only after paying for the goods.

division of which impairs its character or value on the market. For example, a commercial unit may be a single article (as a machine) or a set of articles (as a suite of furniture or an assortment of sizes). It may be a quantity (as a bale, gross, or carload) or any other unit treated in the marketplace as a single whole item.

Rejection

A rejection occurs when a buyer refuses to accept delivery of goods tendered. A rejection must be done within a reasonable time after delivery or tender to the buyer. After a rejection, the buyer may not claim ownership of the goods. In addition, the buyer must notify the seller of the particular defect in the goods so as to give the seller an opportunity to correct the defect. If the goods are in the buyer's possession, the buyer must hold them with reasonable care long enough for the seller to remove them. A buyer who is not a merchant has no other obligation regarding goods that are rightfully rejected.

Buyer's Duties in General If the seller gives no instructions within a reasonable time after being notified of the rejection, the buyer may store the goods for the seller, reship them to the seller, or resell them for the seller. In all cases, the buyer is entitled to be reimbursed for expenses.

Merchant Buyer's Duties A special duty comes into existence when a buyer who is a merchant rejects goods. Merchant buyers have a duty after the rejection of goods in their possession or control to follow any reasonable instructions received from the seller with respect to the goods. If there are no such instructions, they must make reasonable efforts to sell the goods for the seller if they are perishable or threaten to decline speedily in value.

Merchants who sell rejected goods are entitled to be reimbursed either by the seller or from the proceeds of the sale for reasonable expenses of caring for and selling the goods. They are also entitled to such commission as is usual in the trade or, if none, to a reasonable sum not exceeding 10 percent of the proceeds of the sale.

The Opening Case Revisited
"Bitter Sunshine"

Garden-fresh should not have thrown the grapefruit away. The company had a special duty to follow Sunripe's instructions to sell the grapefruit, and it would have been entitled to receive its usual commission.

Teaching Tips In the case of international sales, the buyer must examine the goods within as short a period as is practicable in the circumstances. This inspection may be done after the goods arrive at their destination when the goods are shipped by carrier. CISG Article 38.

UCC 2-601
(see page 881)

Teaching Tips Before beginning this section, propose scenarios in which the students are buying certain goods. Ask students if they know their rights in each situation.

UCC 2-602
(see page 881)

UCC 2-604
(see page 882)

Related Cases The owner of a bowling alley began having some trouble with the second-hand pinspotters he had recently bought. He notified the seller in a letter, outlining the several problems. The seller, when sued, claimed that the buyer did not reject the pinspotters and therefore could not sue for damages. The court ruled that the buyer's letter of dissatisfaction was particular enough to put the seller on notice of defects. *Bonebrake v. Cox,* 499 F.2d 951.

UCC 2-603(1)
(see page 881)

UCC 2-603(2)
(see page 882)

Acceptance

UCC 2-606
(see page 882)

Teaching Tips Inform students that if a buyer of computer software and hardware not only failed to reject those goods, but also retained and used them for a period of time, the court would declare these actions as acceptance under UCC 2-606(1)(c).

Once goods have been accepted, they cannot be rejected. Acceptance of goods takes place when the buyer, after a reasonable opportunity to inspect them, does any of the following:

- signifies to the seller that the goods are conforming, that is, that they are in accordance with the obligations under the contract
- signifies to the seller a willingness to take them even though they are not conforming
- fails to reject them
- performs any act that is inconsistent with the seller's ownership

> ## Example 17-5
>
> Kandy Corp. bought concrete-forming equipment from Economy Forms Corp. Kandy used the equipment for six months before notifying Economy that it was inadequate. The court held that the use of the forms in construction was an act inconsistent with the seller's ownership and constituted an acceptance of the goods by Kandy.

UCC 2-607(3)
(see page 882)

When the buyer accepts goods and later discovers something wrong with them, the buyer must notify the seller within a reasonable time after the discovery. The failure to give proper notice will prevent the buyer from having recourse against the seller.

Revocation of Acceptance

UCC 2-608
(see page 882)

Teaching Tips Under international law, the buyer must notify the seller within a reasonable time after discovering a lack of conformity of the goods. If such notice is not given, the buyer loses the right to claim that the goods did not conform to the contract. Even then, any such notice must be given to the seller no later than two years after the goods were actually handed over to the buyer. CISG Article 39.

If a buyer has accepted goods on the assumption that their nonconformity would be corrected by the seller and the seller does not do so, the buyer may revoke the acceptance. This revocation must be made within a reasonable time after the buyer discovers the nonconformity. A revocation of an acceptance is not effective until the buyer notifies the seller of it. Buyers who revoke an acceptance have the same rights and duties with regard to the goods involved as if they had rejected them.

> ## Quick Quiz 17-3 True or False?
>
> 1. Buyers have no right to inspect goods before paying for them when they are shipped c.o.d.
>
> 2. After a rejection of goods, the buyer must notify the seller of the particular defect in the goods so as to give the seller an opportunity to correct the defect.
>
> 3. Merchant buyers have a duty after the rejection of goods in their possession to follow any reasonable instructions received from the seller with respect to the goods.

17-4   Seller's Right to Cure Improper Tender

UCC 2-508
(see page 880)

Sellers may sometimes **cure** an improper tender or delivery of goods; that is, they may correct the defect that caused the goods to be rejected by the buyer. When the time for performance has not yet expired, the seller has the right to cure the defect and make a proper tender within the contract time. If the time for performance has expired, the seller is allowed to have an additional amount of time to substitute a conforming tender if the seller had reasonable grounds to believe that the goods that were delivered were acceptable. In all cases, sellers must notify buyers that they are going to cure the improper tender or delivery.

Example 17-6

Caravan Motel ordered ten dozen bath towels from samples shown by Fleming Towel Company's representative. The representative made a mistake in writing up the order. As a result, the towels that were delivered were inferior to those shown to Caravan at the time the order was given. Caravan rejected them. Because the Fleming Towel Company had reasonable grounds to believe that Caravan Motel would accept the towels that were delivered, it was allowed additional time to substitute correct towels for the ones that were delivered. When it learned of the rejection, Fleming Towel Company was required to notify the motel that it intended to cure the nonconforming delivery.

The seller does not have the right to cure improper tender when a buyer accepts nonconforming goods, even though the buyer may later sue the seller for breach of contract. The seller has the right only when the buyer either rejects the goods tendered or revokes an acceptance of the goods.

Quick Quiz 17-4 True or False?

1. When time for performance has not yet expired, the seller may cure a defect and make proper tender within the contract time.

2. If the time for performance has expired, the seller is never allowed time to cure a defect.

3. The seller has the right to cure improper tender even when the buyer accepts nonconforming goods.

17-5 Breach of Contract

Breach of contract occurs when one of the parties fails to do what was agreed upon in the contract. When this happens, the other party to the contract has specific remedies available under the UCC. All parties must attempt to mitigate the damages; that is, to keep them as low as possible.

Anticipatory Breach

Sometimes, one of the parties will notify the other party before the time for performance that he or she is not going to conform. This is known as *anticipatory breach* (see Chapter 14). It is a breach committed before there is a present duty to perform the contract. Under older contractual law, the injured party in such a case had to wait until the actual time for performance before bringing suit or taking some other action. It was necessary to wait for the actual time for performance in order to know for sure that the other party was, indeed, not going to perform. Under the UCC, when either party repudiates the contract before the time for performance, the injured party may take action immediately

Related Cases Hal-Tuc, Inc., contracted to have Central District Alarm install new surveillance equipment at their place of business. When the equipment malfunctioned, Hal-Tuc discovered that Central Alarm had installed used equipment instead. Central Alarm attempted to cure with new equipment, citing UCC 2-508(2). However, the court allowed Hal-Tuc to rescind the contract because Central Alarm did not live up to its end of the original contract. *Central Dist. Alarm, Inc. v. Hal-Tuc, Inc.,* 886 S.W.2d 210.

Teaching Tips Under international law, the seller may cure any defect in the goods if the goods were delivered before the date of delivery. Up to that date, the seller may deliver any missing part, make up any deficiency in the quantity of goods delivered, or replace any defective goods without being in breach of contract. However, the seller may exercise this right only if it does not cause the buyer unreasonable inconvenience or expense. CISG Article 37.

Terms *Breach* refers to a failure to perform in a manner expected. In the context of contracts, it is simply a failure to do what the contract states.

UCC 2-610
(see page 883)

Terms An *anticipatory breach,* also called a *constructive breach,* is a clear and absolute refusal to perform what is stipulated by a contract before the time for performance.

if waiting would be unjust or cause a material inconvenience. Any of the remedies for breach of contract are available to the aggrieved party in addition to the right to suspend his or her own performance.

Example 17-7

Baily ordered ten steel I-beams to be made to order from Midwest Steel Co., for use in a building that Baily was going to begin building in six months. Midwest Steel agreed to deliver the I-beams on or before that date. Two months before the delivery date, Midwest Steel notified Baily that it would not be able to fill the order. Baily could treat the contract as having been breached and use any of the buyer's remedies that are available to him under the UCC.

Seller's Remedies When Buyer Breaches

When a buyer breaches a sales contract, the seller may select from a number of remedies. Table 17-1 is a list of remedies sellers may employ when the buyer breaches.

UCC 2-703(a)
(see page 884)

Background Information Under international law, the buyer may declare the contract voided if there is a fundamental breach, but the seller is given an opportunity to remedy the defect. The rules governing damages for breach are similar to those found in the UCC.

Withhold Delivery of Goods   If the goods have not been delivered, the seller has a right to keep them upon learning of the buyer's breach.

Stop Delivery of the Goods   If, after shipping the goods, the seller discovers that the buyer is **insolvent** (unable to pay debts), the seller may have the delivery stopped. This right is known as **stoppage in transit** and is permitted after goods have been shipped but before they have reached their destination.

The seller must give information to the **carrier** (the transportation company) to satisfy the latter that the buyer is insolvent. In addition, the seller must accept responsibility for any damage suffered by the carrier for not completing the shipment. If the insolvency information is incorrect, both the seller and the carrier could be sued for damages.

The seller may also stop delivery of a carload, truckload, or planeload or of larger shipments of express or freight when the buyer repudiates or fails to make a payment that is due before delivery or otherwise breaches the contract. If the seller has issued a

UCC 2-705
(see page 885)

Terms Those who are *insolvent* are those unable to pay their debts. In opposition is the term *liquid*, referring to something that is capable of producing or converting into cash.

Teaching Tips Use Table 17-1 as a guide for conducting a class discussion on the seller's remedies when the buyer breaches a sales contract.

Table 17-1 Seller's Remedies When the Buyer Breaches

1. Withhold delivery of any goods not yet delivered.
2. If the buyer is insolvent, stop delivery of any goods that are still in the possession of a carrier.
3. Resell any goods that have been rightfully withheld, and then sue the buyer for the difference between the agreed price and the resale price.
4. If the goods cannot be resold, sue the buyer for the difference between the agreed price and the market price.
5. Sue the buyer for the price of any goods that were accepted by the buyer.
6. Cancel the contract.

document of title, the seller can stop delivery only by surrendering the document to the carrier. If the buyer has received the document, delivery of the goods cannot be stopped in transit.

Resell the Goods The seller may resell the goods or the undelivered balance of them. In the case of unfinished manufactured goods, a seller may either complete the manufacture and resell the finished goods or cease manufacture and resell the unfinished goods for scrap or salvage value. In such cases, the seller must use reasonable commercial judgment to avoid losses. After the sale, the injured party may sue the other for the difference between what the property brought on resale and the price the buyer had agreed to pay in the contract.

UCC 2-706(1)
(see page 885)

UCC 2-704(2)
(see page 884)

Resale may be a public or private sale. If it is a private sale, the seller must give the buyer reasonable notice of intention to resell the goods. If it is a public sale, it must be made at a place that is normally used for public sales, if such a place is available. In addition, if the goods are perishable or threaten to decline in value speedily, the seller must give the buyer reasonable notice of the time and place of resale.

UCC 2-706(4)(b)
(see page 885)

A purchaser who buys in good faith at a resale takes the goods free of any rights of the original buyer. Furthermore, the seller is not accountable to the buyer for any profit made on the resale. The seller who chooses to do so may buy the goods at the resale.

UCC 2-706(4)(d)
(see page 885)

Recover Damages The seller may retain the merchandise and sue the buyer for either the difference between the contract price and the market price at the time the buyer breached the agreement or the profit (including overhead) that the seller would have made had the contract been performed. In either case, the seller is also entitled to *incidental damages*. These damages are reasonable expenses that indirectly result from the breach, such as expenses incurred in stopping delivery of goods, transporting goods, and caring for goods after the buyer's breach.

UCC 2-708
(see page 885)

UCC 2-710
(see page 886)

Sue for Price The seller may sue for the price of any goods that the buyer has accepted. Similarly, upon the buyer's breach, the seller may bring suit for the price of goods that cannot be resold at a reasonable price. In addition, the seller may sue the buyer for the price of any lost or damaged goods after the risk of their loss has passed to the buyer. The seller who sues the buyer for the price must hold for the buyer any goods that are under the seller's control. The goods may be sold, however, at any time resale is possible before the collection of a judgment in the case. The net proceeds of any resale must be credited to the buyer. Any goods that are not resold become the property of the buyer if the buyer pays for them as a result of a court judgment.

UCC 2-709
(see page 886)

> ### Did You Know?
>
> Retail e-commerce sales in the first quarter of 2004 were $15.5 billion, up 28 percent from the first quarter of 2003.

Cancel the Contract The seller can cancel the contract. This cancellation occurs when the seller puts an end to the contract because the other party breached. When cancellation takes place in this manner, the seller may use any of the remedies mentioned for breach of contract.

Buyer's Remedies When Seller Breaches

UCC 2-106
(see page 870)

When the seller breaches the contract by failing to deliver goods or by delivering improper goods, the buyer may cancel the contract and recover any money paid out. The buyer may also choose any of the remedies outlined in Table 17-2.

Cover the Sale The buyer may **cover** the sale, that is, buy similar goods from someone else. The buyer may then sue the seller for the difference between the agreed price and the cost of the purchase. Cover must be made without unreasonable delay.

UCC 2-711
(see page 886)

UCC 2-712
(see page 886)

Teaching Tips Use Table 17-2 as a guide for conducting a class discussion on the buyer's remedies when the seller breaches a sales contract.

Cross-Cultural Notes Deposits are commonly used in China to assure contract performance. If the depositor does not meet the terms of the contract, the other party has the right to retain the deposit. If the party accepting the deposit defaults, it is required to pay back twice the original deposit amount.

State Variations In Iowa, like other UCC states, the burden is upon the buyer to establish any breach with respect to the goods accepted.

Table 17-2 Buyer's Remedies When the Seller Breaches

1. Cancel the contract.

2. Sue the seller for the return of any money that has been paid.

3. Cover the sale—that is, buy similar goods from someone else and sue the seller for the difference between the agreed price and the cost of the purchase.

4. Sue the seller for the difference between the agreed price and the market price at the time the buyer learned of the breach.

5. If nonconforming goods have been accepted, notify the seller that they do not conform to the contract. Then, if no adjustment is made, sue the seller either for breach of contract or for breach of warranty.

6. When goods are unique or rare, sue for specific performance.

Example 17-8

Flamme Bros. contracted to deliver a specific quantity of corn to Farmers' Union Co-op Co., a cooperative grain elevator. When Flamme Bros. failed to deliver the corn, Farmers' Union bought corn from its members over a two-week period. The court held that this was cover of the contract without unreasonable delay. Farmers' Union recovered the difference between the agreed price of the corn from Flamme Bros. and the price it paid to the farmers for the corn it bought.

UCC 2-713
(see page 886)

UCC 2-715
(see page 887)

UCC 2-718(1)
(see page 887)

Sue for Breach When a seller breaches a contract by not delivering the goods, the buyer may sue for damages if any were suffered. The measure of damages is the difference between the price that the parties agreed upon and the price of the same goods in the marketplace on the date the buyer learned the breach. In addition, the buyer may sue for incidental and consequential damages.

Damages for breach of contract may be liquidated, that is, agreed upon by the parties when they first enter into the contract. Liquidated damages will be allowed by the court if they are reasonable. These damages are discussed in more detail in Chapter 14.

UCC 2-714(2)
(see page 886)

Keep Goods and Seek Adjustment When improper goods are delivered, the buyer may keep them and ask the seller for an adjustment. If no adjustment is made, the buyer may sue the seller for either breach of contract or breach of warranty, whichever applies. The amount of the suit would be the difference between the value of the goods contracted for and the value of the goods received. Warranties are discussed in Chapter 18.

Background Information In order to be found reasonable by a court, liquidated damages must be realistic and in proportion to the losses anticipated in the event of a breach. If the court finds them unreasonable, they will be disregarded, and a jury will have to set damages.

Example 17-9

Bare Essentials, Inc., ordered twenty dozen swimsuits from a swimsuit manufacturer. The suits that were delivered were different from the samples shown by the manufacturer's representative. Since the store needed the swimsuits for the spring trade, it decided to keep them. If no adjustment is made by the manufacturer, Bare Essentials, Inc., can sue the manufacturer for damages (including loss of profits) that were suffered because of the breach of the express warranty that the goods would be the same as the sample.

Sue for Specific Performance When the goods are unique or rare, the buyer may ask the court to order the seller to do what he or she agreed to do under the contract terms. This request is known as an action for specific performance of the contract. A decree of specific performance, if granted by the court, would require the seller to deliver to the buyer the goods described in the sales agreement. This type of action is permitted only when an award of money will not give the buyer sufficient relief. Contracts for *objets d'art,* rare gems, antiques, and goods described as one-of-a-kind come within the scope of this type of action. Under the UCC, the decree of specific performance may include the payment of the price, damages, or other relief as the court may deem just. Specific performance is discussed in more detail in Chapter 14.

UCC 2-716(1)
(see page 887)

Buyers have a right of replevin for goods that have been identified to the contract if, after a reasonable effort, they are unable to buy the goods elsewhere. A **writ of replevin** is a court action that allows a person entitled to goods to recover them from someone who has them wrongfully.

UCC 2-716(3)
(see page 887)

State Variations In some states (e.g., Massachusetts), the writ of replevin is no longer used.

Statute of Limitations

Nearly all lawsuits have a time limit within which suit must be brought. If the time limit is exceeded, the action is forever barred. In general, an action for breach of a sales contract must be brought within four years after the date of the breach. The parties may, if they wish to do so, provide for a shorter time period, not less than one year, in their sales agreement. They may not, however, agree to a period longer than four years.

UCC 2-725
(see page 888)

A Question of Ethics

What ethical question arises from the debtor's point of view when the time for bringing suit against the debtor runs out under the statute of limitations?

Quick Quiz 17-5 True or False?

1. When a buyer breaches a sales contract, the seller may, among other things, resell any goods that have been rightfully withheld, and then sue the buyer for the difference between the agreed price and the resale price.

2. When a seller breaches a sales contract, the buyer may always sue the seller for specific performance of the contract.

3. In general, a lawsuit for breach of a sales contract must be brought within six years after the date of the breach.

Summary

17-1 Sellers and buyers must follow the terms of their contract and act in good faith.

17-2 Tender of performance is necessary in order to test the other party's ability and willingness to perform. Tender of delivery requires the seller to make conforming goods available to the buyer at a reasonable hour of the day. Tender of payment may be made by any means that is commonly used in the ordinary course of business. The seller may demand legal tender if he or she gives the buyer a reasonable time to obtain it.

17-3 Except when goods are shipped c.o.d. or when the contract provides for payment against a document of title, the buyer has the right to inspect goods before accepting or paying for them. When improper goods are delivered, the buyer may elect to reject all of them, accept all of them, or accept any commercial unit or units and reject the rest. Rejection of goods must be done within a reasonable time, and the buyer must notify the seller of the reason for the rejection. Even after

accepting goods, buyers may revoke an acceptance if the goods were accepted on the assumption that their nonconformity would be corrected or if their nonconformity could not be easily detected.

17-4 Sellers may cure defects or nonconformities that caused the goods to be rejected by the buyer.

17-5 When a buyer breaches a sales contract, the seller may withhold delivery of any goods not yet delivered, under certain circumstances stop goods that are in transit, resell the goods or the undelivered balance of them, retain the goods and bring suit for damages, bring suit for the price of any goods that the buyer has accepted, or cancel the contract. When a seller breaches a sales contract, the buyer may cancel the contract and recover any money paid out, buy similar goods from someone else and sue the seller for the difference in price, sue the seller for damages for nondelivery, keep the goods and deduct the cost of damages from any price still due, or sue for specific performance if the goods are rare or unique.

Key Terms

carrier, 318

commercial unit, 314

cover, 319

cure, 316

good faith, 310

insolvent, 318

legal tender, 313

stoppage in transit, 318

tender of delivery, 312

tender of payment, 313

tender of performance, 312

unconscionable contract, 310

writ of replevin, 321

Questions for Review and Discussion

1. What are the obligations of parties to a sales contract? Describe them in general terms.
2. Why is tender of performance necessary?
3. What is required of the seller in making tender of delivery? What form of payment may be used by the buyer in making tender of payment? When may the seller demand legal tender?
4. What is the right of the buyer to inspect goods that are received under a sales contract? Explain.
5. What three choices does a buyer have when defective or nonconforming goods are delivered?
6. Describe the manner in which buyers must reject goods if they decide to do so. After a rejection, what may buyers do with goods in

their possession? What special duty applies to a merchant buyer?

7. When can a seller correct an improper tender of delivery?

8. How does older contractual law compare with the UCC as it applies to anticipatory breach?

9. What remedies are available to a seller when a buyer breaches a sales contract? Explain.

10. What remedies are available to a buyer when a seller breaches a sales contract? Explain.

Investigating the Internet

Log onto the 'Lectric Law Library's Law Practice Forms by going to **http://www.lectlaw. com/forms.htm.** Click "Our Main Forms Room." Then, scroll down to "Business & General Forms," and look for forms that are of interest to you.

Cases for Analysis

1. Kathleen Liarkos purchased a used Jaguar XJS automobile from Pine Grove Auto Sales. After experiencing various mechanical problems, she discovered that the vehicle's odometer had been turned back. Liarkos notified the seller that she revoked her acceptance of the vehicle. When is this remedy available to a buyer? *Liarkos v. Mello,* 639 N.E.2d 716 (MA).

2. P&F Construction Corporation ordered 338 door units for an apartment condominium project from Friend Lumber Corporation. The doors were delivered to the job site three weeks after they were ordered. Each door unit came wrapped in clear plastic. Three and one-half months after receiving the door units, P&F Construction notified Friend Lumber that the doors were one quarter inch off size. P&F refused to pay Friend Lumber the balance due. What rule of law may Friend Lumber use to recover the money owed? *P&F Const. v. Friend Lumber Corp.,* 575 N.E.2d 61 (MA).

3. William Young had cut evergreen boughs and sold them exclusively to Frank's Nursery & Crafts, Inc., for ten years. Upon receiving a $238,000 order for 360 tons of boughs from Frank's, Young obtained cutting rights from many farmers, repaired his machinery, and made seventy-five new hand tyers to tie the evergreen bundles. Several months later, Frank's reduced its order to less than $60,000 for about 70 tons of boughs. Young delivered the 70 tons of boughs and sued Frank's for breach of contract. How were Young's damages computed? *Young v. Frank's Nursery & Crafts, Inc.,* 569 N.E.2d 1034 (OH).

4. Herman Googe agreed to buy an automobile from Irene Schleimer. Later, Googe changed his mind and refused to buy the car. Schleimer, without making tender of delivery, brought suit against Googe for breach of contract. Did Schleimer recover damages? Explain. *Schleimer v. Googe,* 377 N.Y.S.2d 591 (NY).

5. Mr. and Mrs. Aldridge bought a motor home from Sportsman Travel Trailer Sales, located in Texas. Two years later, after traveling more than 14,000 miles on trips to Louisiana, Colorado, and California, they attempted to reject the motor home, claiming that it was defective. Could they return the vehicle and recover damages? Explain. *Explorer Motor Home Corp. v. Aldridge,* 541 S.W.2d 851 (TX).

6. Dehahn agreed to sell and Innes agreed to buy for the price of $35,000 a 35-acre gravel pit, a back hoe, a bulldozer, a loader, two dump trucks, and a low-bed trailer. Since Dehahn had recently lost his bid for reelection as road commissioner in the town, he was required to remove the equipment from town property. He moved the equipment to a field owned by Innes across from the driveway to Innes's home and left the keys in the vehicles. Later, Innes canceled the contract and refused to make any payments. When sued, Innes argued that Dehahn failed to make tender of delivery of the equipment. Do you agree with

Innes? State why or why not. *Dehahn v. Innes,* 356 A.2d 711 (ME).

7. Formetal Engineering Co. placed an order with Presto Manufacturing Co., Inc., for 250,000 polyurethane pads to be used in making air-conditioning units. The pads were to be made according to samples and specifications supplied by Formetal. When the pads arrived, Formetal discovered that they did not conform to the sample and specifications in that there were incomplete cuts, color variances, and faulty adherence to the pads' paper backing. Formetal notified Presto of the defects and said that it was rejecting the goods and returning them to Presto. The goods, however, were never returned. Was the rejection proper? Explain. *Presto Mfg. Co. v. Formetal Eng'g. Co.,* 360 N.E.2d 510 (IL).

8. City National Bank of Crete agreed to sell and deliver to Goosic Construction Company a set of concrete forms for the sum of $200, which Goosic paid. The forms had been repossessed at an earlier time by the bank and were stored at another location. When Goosic arrived at the storage location to pick up the forms, a Mr. Roberts claimed a storage lien and refused to allow Goosic to take possession of the goods. Goosic never received the forms, which had a fair market value of $1,500. Did the City National Bank make proper tender of delivery? If Goosic Construction Company won the case, how much would it recover? Give reasons for your answers. *Goosic Const. Co. v. City Natl. Bank,* 241 N.W.2d 521 (NE).

9. Sagebrush Sales Co. sold building materials to Pace, a retail lumber dealer. As the goods were unloaded at Pace's lumberyard, Pace noticed that two of the truckloads contained materials that he had not ordered. He nevertheless permitted the unordered goods to be unloaded without objection and wrote on his copy of the invoice "not ordered." Pace then telephoned Sagebrush's office and asked why they were sending him extra lumber. The employee replied that he did not know, but that he would have the salesperson call Pace. No further complaint was made by Pace to Sagebrush. The goods were placed into Pace's inventory and offered for sale to the public. Pace made a partial payment for the goods but refused to pay the full amount, claiming that he had not accepted the unordered goods. Do you agree with Pace? Why or why not? *Pace v. Sagebrush Sales Co.,* 560 P.2d 789 (AZ).

10. Carolyn McQueen bought a new Fiat Spider from American Imports, Inc. The deal included a $500 trade-in allowance on McQueen's Oldsmobile, and McQueen borrowed the money to buy the car from a credit union. She paid for the Fiat by check and promised to deliver an Oldsmobile for trade-in the next week. Two days later, the Fiat overheated. McQueen had also discovered that neither the speedometer nor the odometer functioned properly. American Imports, Inc., towed the car to its garage, replaced a broken fan belt, and tightened a nut on the speedometer that also controlled the odometer. After the repairs were made, McQueen refused to take the car, saying that she wanted a new one. She stopped payment on the check. When sued for the purchase price, McQueen claimed that she had revoked her acceptance of the Fiat and could, therefore, cancel the contract. Was McQueen within her rights? Why or why not? *American Imports, Inc., v. G.E. Emp. West. Region Fed. Credit Union,* 245 S.E.2d 798 (NC).

Quick Quiz Answers

17-1	17-2	17-3	17-4	17-5
1. T	1. T	1. T	1. T	1. T
2. F	2. T	2. T	2. F	2. F
3. F	3. F	3. T	3. F	3. F

Chapter 18

Warranties and Product Liability

18-1 Warranty Protection

Express Warranties • Implied Warranties • Warranty of Title • Duty to Notify Seller of Defective Product

18-2 Exclusion of Warranties

Consumer Protection • Human Blood and Tissue

18-3 Privity Not Required

18-4 Product Liability

Negligence • Strict Liability

The Opening Case
"The Jewel"

While browsing through a used-car lot, Vega was approached by a fast-talking salesperson who said, "I've got a beauty that just came in. Take a look at that baby," pointing to a shiny, red Mustang. "It's a jewel, and I can let it go at a good price. You won't find a better car for the money anywhere."

"What'll it get for mileage?" Vega asked.

"I guarantee you'll get 35 miles per gallon driving in the city with that beauty."

Vega bought the Mustang, and discovered, after a few weeks, that the car's mileage averaged 19 miles per gallon in city driving instead of the 35 miles the salesperson had guaranteed.

Four months later, Vega returned to the used-car lot and reminded the salesperson of the guarantee. The salesperson responded, "Oh, we don't make guarantees. Take a look at your sales slip."

Vega saw that the salesperson had written the words *as is* on the sales slip.

Are the words, "It's a jewel," and "You won't find a better car for the money anywhere," considered warranties? Is the salesperson's oral guarantee of 35 miles per gallon a warranty? If so, can Vega recover on it?

Chapter Outcomes

1. Describe the three ways in which an express warranty may be created.
2. State the requirements of the Magnuson-Moss Warranty Act.
3. Compare the meaning of a "limited" warranty with that of a "full" warranty.
4. Recognize the ways in which warranties may be excluded.
5. Differentiate between the implied warranty of fitness for a particular purpose and the implied warranty of merchantability.
6. Explain the warranty of title.
7. Describe the duty to notify sellers of a defective product.
8. Determine the persons to whom warranties are made under the laws of your state.
9. State why it is often difficult for a consumer to win a product liability case on the theory of negligence.
10. Explain what an injured party must prove to recover from the manufacturer of a dangerous and defective product.

18-1 Warranty Protection

Have you ever bought something that did not work when you took it home? Have you ever purchased an item that turned out to be damaged or broken when you opened the box? Have you ever paid for something that you wanted for a particular purpose, only to find that it would not do the job? Has a salesperson ever made a statement or a promise about a product that did not come true? Have you ever found an impurity or a foreign substance in food that you bought in a store or ate in a restaurant? The UCC gives you protection in all of these types of situations under its law of warranties. A warranty is another name for a guarantee.

Express Warranties

An **express warranty** is an oral or written statement, promise, or other representation about the quality of a product. Express warranties arise in three different ways: by a statement of fact or promise, by a description of the goods, and by a sample or model.

In states that have adopted Article 2A of the UCC, express warranties arise when goods are leased in exactly the same way that they arise when goods are sold.

UCC 2-313
(see page 874)

UCC 2A-210
(see page 893)

UCC 2-313(1)(2)
(see page 874)

Statement of Fact or Promise Whenever a seller of goods makes a statement of fact about the goods to a buyer as part of the transaction, an express warranty is created. The seller's statement is treated legally as a guarantee that the goods will be as they were stated to be. This is true whether the seller is a merchant or not. If the goods are not as they were stated to be, the seller has breached an express warranty.

> ### Example 18-1
>
> Wambach went into a furniture store and told the clerk that he wanted a mahogany table. The clerk showed Wambach a table and said that it was made of solid mahogany. Soon after buying it, Wambach learned that the table was made of pressed wood covered by a mahogany veneer. The statement by the clerk was an express warranty that the table was made of solid mahogany. Wambach would be able to sue the store for breach of express warranty if the store refused to remedy the situation.

Teaching Tips Before introducing any of the material from the chapter, ask students to share their own experiences with warranties and company negligence. Assign half of the class members the role of devil's advocate in the discussion. For example, if a student shares a story about false promises from a salesperson, the devil's advocates should defend the salesperson's position.

Terms The word *warrant* has its origins in *very* or *true*.

An express warranty also occurs when a seller makes a promise about the goods to a buyer. The promise must relate to the goods and be part of the transaction.

Manufacturers often include express warranties with the products they sell. They are usually found inside the package containing the product and are sometimes referred to as guarantees.

Teaching Tips From a seller's point of view, the best express warranties are those that take away more rights than they give. When a statement explains what a product *can* do, it implies all that it *cannot* do. Use examples of real warranties from products you've bought or from advertisements so that students can examine and define what warranties truly promise.

> ### *The Opening Case Revisited*
> #### "The Jewel"
>
> The salesperson's statement that Vega will get 35 miles per gallon driving in the city is an express warranty. The fact that it is oral makes no difference other than that it may be difficult for Vega to prove.

Business Law in the News

Not Your Father's . . . Whatever

When it comes to young car-buyers, the '70s and '80s haunt Detroit like a ghost. During the oil shock, the Big Three were late making the move toward small, fuel-efficient cars, and handed a new generation of penny-pinchers to Toyota and Honda. Later, U.S. auto brands compounded their error, offering horrible styling and quality to newly affluent baby boomers. Many fled to Mercedes-Benz and BMW. The resulting love affair fueled import growth for almost 30 years. The Big Three bled market share and eventually had to kill struggling brands like Oldsmobile and Plymouth.

That epic shift in loyalties explains why U.S. and foreign auto makers devote so much attention to Generation Y, today's 16- to 24-year-olds. The group already buys 850,000 cars a year, about 6% of U.S. vehicle sales. According to Toyota, about 63 million kids will be driving by 2010. "This generation is bigger than the boomers," says James Press, COO of Toyota Motor Sales USA Inc. "We need to build the same relationship with them that we have with their parents."

Imports still have an edge with kids. Because Toyota, Honda, Nissan, and Hyundai refresh their small-car lineups more frequently than Detroit, many of their models boast younger average buyers. But no brand—import or domestic—has truly locked up the loyalty of the youth market, despite millions spent on wild designs and brash marketing. The most aggressive looks, from cars like the Pontiac Aztek, Chrysler PT Cruiser, and Toyota Echo compact, all struck out with kids. Honda Motor Co.'s boxy Element hit the market with a splash last year, but it has lured more fortysomethings than hipsters. "A big mistake car companies make is they assume that because kids have three piercings that they want to drive something obnoxious," says Wesley R. Brown, an analyst at Iceology, a trend research firm.

Long Warranties

In truth, carmakers are discovering yet again that the primary selling points for kids are the same as 30 years ago: price and value. The average sticker price for a new car sold to buyers under age 24 (most of them buy used cars) is $15,000, says CNW Marketing Research Inc. Says Eric Noble, president of The Car Lab, which has studied the market for auto makers: "A youth car is just a cheap car."

Little surprise that two South Korean cars—Hyundai Motor Co.'s $10,000 Accent and $13,000 Elantra—have the youngest average buyers of any on the market, at age 24. It helps a lot that Hyundai has seriously improved the styling of its cars in recent years. But the company's biggest advantage comes from playing up its long warranties. Hyundai guarantees its cars for five years and 60,000 miles—at least a year longer than a standard warranty. Engines and transmissions carry a 10-year, 100,000-mile warranty. Says Hyundai Motor America marketing director Paul Sellers: "That removes one element of risk." It also keeps ownership costs low for years.

Questions for Analysis

1. According to this article, what errors did U.S. auto brands make in the '70s and '80s when it comes to young car buyers?

2. Why do U.S. and foreign auto makers devote so much attention to generation Y?

3. What are the selling points that car makers are discovering for kids?

4. What is Hyundai's biggest attraction to young buyers?

Source: David Welch. "Not Your Father's . . . Whatever," *BusinessWeek,* March 15, 2004, pp. 82–83.

Formal words such as *warranty* or *guarantee* do not have to be used to create an express warranty. A seller may not intend to make a warranty, but if the language used by the seller is a statement of fact or a promise about the goods and is part of the transaction, an express warranty is created. Advertisements often contain statements and promises about goods that are express warranties.

The Opening Case Revisited
"The Jewel"

The salesperson's statement to Vega that "It's a Jewel" and "You won't find a better car for the money anywhere" are examples of puffery and would not be considered an express warranty.

Example 18-2

Tuffco Auto Polish was advertised as a safe, noncorrosive polish, manufactured to the highest standards required of finishes. Myron bought a can of the polish, and it ruined the finish of her new car. Myron could have sought damages against the seller, claiming that the advertised statements were warranties made to any prospective purchaser.

Warranties are based on statements of fact. Opinions of salespersons and exaggerated and persuasive statements are not included. Courts have long recognized the temptation of salespersons to indulge in sales puffery or to extol their wares beyond the point of fact. Buyers must use good judgment in separating a seller's statements of fact from statements that are opinion or puffery. Such statements as "this is the best television set on the market" or "this VCR is a good buy" are examples of sales talk or puffery. They are not express warranties.

Description of the Goods   Any description of the goods that is made part of the basis of the bargain creates an express warranty that the goods will be as described.

UCC 2-313(1)(b)
(see page 874)

Example 18-3

Kiley ordered a gas grill from a catalog. The catalog description said that the grill contained a swing-away warming rack. The grill that was delivered, however, had a fixed warming rack. Kiley could have had a cause of action against the seller for breach of express warranty if the seller refused to remedy the situation.

Sample or Model   It is a common practice of salespeople to show samples of their products to prospective buyers. When a sample or model becomes part of the basis of the bargain, an express warranty is created. The seller warrants that the goods that will be delivered are the same as the sample or model.

UCC 2-313(1)(c)
(see page 874)

Advertising Express Warranties   The Federal Trade Commission has established specific rules for advertising express warranties on goods that are sold in interstate commerce:

- An advertisement stating that a product is warranted must tell you how to get a copy of the warranty before you buy the product.

- Advertisers who use expressions such as "Satisfaction Guaranteed," "Money-Back Guarantee," and "Free Trial Offer" must refund the full purchase price of their product at the purchaser's request. Any conditions, such as the return of the product, must be stated in the ad.

Related Cases In a bar, a father and his daughter became curious about an advertised alcoholic concoction called a Watermelon. They queried the bartender who responded, "They're great." The pair then ordered and drank what they believed to be two Watermelon shots. In fact, they drank dishwashing liquid and chemical lye. They sued, and the court ruled that the bartender's statement was an express warranty. *Cott v. Peppermint Twist Management Co., Inc.,* 856 P.2d 906.

Getting Students Involved Have students write an advertisement or a sales pitch for any item they choose. Instruct them to include a mix of warranty details and sales puffery in their descriptions. Ask students to exchange their ads and look for examples of fact and hype.

Teaching Tips Point out to students that some warranties include a disclaimer exempting the seller from responsibility for anything that is not included in the warranty. This exemption helps guard against claims made on the basis of what a seller might have said or promised but did not write down. However, any statement of fact or promise, whether oral or written, creates an express warranty under the UCC.

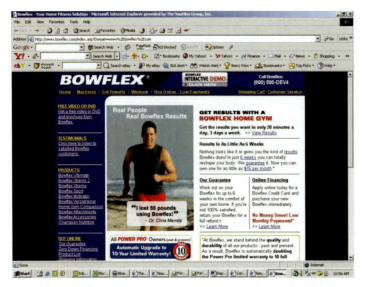

Have you ever taken advantage of a money-back guarantee?

• Advertisers who warrant products for a lifetime must fully explain the terms of their promises, such as "Good for as long as you own the car."

Magnuson-Moss Warranty Act

The federal Magnuson-Moss Warranty Act is designed to prevent deceptive warranty practices and to provide consumers with more information about warranties that are made on products they buy. The act applies only when written warranties are made voluntarily on **consumer products.** These products are defined as tangible personal property normally used for personal, family, or household purposes. Because it is a federal law, the act affects only warranties on products that are sold in interstate commerce.

Under the act, when a written warranty is given to a consumer on goods costing more than $10, the warranty must disclose whether it is a full or a limited warranty. When goods cost more than $15, the written warranty must be made available before the consumer decides to buy the product. The writing must express the terms and conditions of the warranty in simple and readily understood language.

A **full warranty** is one in which a defective product will be repaired without charge within a reasonable time after a complaint has been made about it. If it cannot be repaired within a reasonable time, the consumer may have either a replacement of the product or a refund of the purchase price. The consumer will not have to do anything unreasonable to get warranty service, such as ship a heavy product to the factory. A full warranty applies to anyone who owns the product during the warranty period, not only the original buyer. A full warranty must also state its duration, for example, a "full one-year warranty."

Example 18-4

Kienitz bought an electric range manufactured by a well-known firm. Attached to the box containing the range were several papers, one of which read as follows: "Full one-year warranty. If your range fails because of a manufacturing defect within one year from the date of original purchase, we will repair the product without charge to you. Parts and service labor are included. Service will be provided in your home in the forty-eight contiguous states, the state of Hawaii, or in the District of Columbia." This paper was a full warranty.

A **limited warranty** is any written warranty that does not meet all of the requirements for a full warranty. The consumer is not given the absolute, free-of-charge repair or replacement of a defective product, as is given in the full warranty. Something less than a complete remedy is given to the consumer.

Examples of limited warranties are those that cover only parts, not labor, allow only a *pro rata* (divided proportionately) refund or credit in the case of a defect rather than a full refund, require the buyer to return a heavy product to the store for service, or cover only the first purchaser.

Implied Warranties

Under the UCC, an **implied warranty** is a warranty that is imposed by law rather than by statements, descriptions, or samples given by the seller. It arises independently and outside the contract. The law annexes it, by implication, into the contract that the parties have made. Implied warranties are designed to promote high standards in business and to discourage harsh dealings. There are three types of implied warranties: the implied warranty of merchantability, the implied warranty of fitness for a particular purpose, and the implied warranty that is derived from a course of dealing or usage of trade.

Merchantability One of the most beneficial warranties, from the point of view of a buyer, is the implied **warranty of merchantability.** This warranty provides that, unless excluded in one of the ways discussed, whenever a merchant sells goods, the merchant warrants that the goods are merchantable. This warranty is given when the seller is a merchant with respect to goods of that kind. It is given by manufacturers, wholesalers, and retailers whenever they sell goods to give assurance that products sold by them are fit for the purpose for which the goods are to be used. The warranty of merchantability is not given by someone who is not a merchant.

A warranty of merchantability is a valuable protection for consumers.

UCC 2-314(1)
(see page 874)

> ## Example 18-5
>
> Perez bought a second-hand car for $3,500 from Osgood, a private party. Perez drove the car home, parked it in her driveway, and turned off the engine. The next morning, the car would not start. The automobile mechanic who was called to try to start the car informed Perez that it would cost $1,200 to repair the car so that it would start properly. Perez cannot recover from Osgood for breach of warranty of merchantability because Osgood was not a merchant.

To be merchantable, goods must at least pass without objection in the trade under the contract description; if fungible goods, be of fair average quality; be fit for the ordinary purposes for which such goods are used; be of the same kind, quality, and quantity; be adequately contained, packaged, and labeled as the agreement may require; and be in conformance with any promises or statements of fact made on the container or label.

UCC 2-314(2)
(see page 874)

> ## Example 18-6
>
> If Osgood had been a merchant in Example 18-5, Perez could have recovered from Osgood for breach of warranty of merchantability. An automobile that will not start is not fit for the ordinary purposes for which automobiles are used and is, therefore, not merchantable.

A claim for breach of warranty of merchantability can be made only when a defect exists at the time the goods are purchased.

Example 18-7

Haven Hills Farm purchased a truck tire from Sears, Roebuck. On a trip from Mississippi to Alabama, the tire blew out, causing the truck to turn on its side, destroying 11,862 dozen eggs. At the time of the blowout, the tire was four and one-half months old and had been driven 30,000 miles. Haven Hills claimed that Sears was liable for breach of the implied warranty of merchantability. It argued that Sears sold the tire in a defective condition. In finding in favor of Sears, Roebuck, the court held that there was no evidence of a defect in the tire at the time it left the control of the manufacturer or seller.

Day-old chickens with bird cancer; contaminated blood received in a blood transfusion; applesauce that was inedible because of poor taste and smell; contaminated cheese; and food containing impurities are a few examples of goods that the courts have held to be nonmerchantable.

Fitness for a Particular Purpose   Sometimes buyers will have the seller select goods for them rather than select them themselves. They rely on the seller's knowledge and experience to choose the product after telling the seller of the particular use they have for the goods. This arrangement creates the implied **warranty of fitness for a particular purpose.** When the buyer relies on the seller's skill and judgment to select the goods, the seller impliedly warrants that the goods will be fit for the purpose for which they are to be used.

UCC 2-315
(see page 874)

Example 18-8

McGuire purchased a television set in a store that had a sign on the wall declaring, "No refunds! All sales final!" McGuire told the clerk that she needed a cable to connect the new set to her VCR. The clerk went to the shelf, selected a cable, and told McGuire that the cable would do the job. That evening, McGuire discovered that the cable would not fit the VCR. Even though the sign said that all sales were final, McGuire would be able to return the cable. McGuire relied on the store clerk's judgment in selecting the cable, which created an implied warranty that the cable would connect to the VCR.

UCC 2-314(3)
(see page 874)

Usage of Trade   Other implied warranties may arise from ways in which the parties have dealt in the past or by usage of trade. For example, when a person sells a pedigreed dog, there is an implied warranty that the seller will provide pedigree papers to evidence conformity of the animal to the contract. The reason this implied warranty arises is that providing such papers has become a well-established custom or practice of the trade.

Teaching Tips Under international law, the seller must deliver goods that are of the quantity, quality, and description required by the contract. The goods must be contained or packaged in the manner that is required by the contract. Unless the parties agree otherwise, the goods must also be fit for the purposes for which goods for the same description would ordinarily be used. CISG Article 35.

The Opening Case Revisited
"The Jewel"

The four-month delay by Vega to inform the car dealer of the breach of warranty would probably be found by a court to exceed the reasonable time period within which the dealer must be notified.

Warranty of Title

Whenever goods are sold, either by a merchant or a private party, the seller warrants that the title being conveyed is good and that the transfer is rightful. This warranty is known as the **warranty of title.** It includes an implied promise that the goods will be delivered free from any liens (claims of others) about which the buyer has no knowledge. When anyone buys goods that turn out to be stolen, the rightful owner will be entitled to the return of the goods. The innocent purchaser may sue the seller for breach of warranty of title.

UCC 2-312(1)
(see page 874)

Related Cases An automobile dealership unknowingly purchased a stolen car and then sold the car. Since the rightful owner did not agree to this transfer, the court ruled that the subsequent sale of a stolen car by a dealer constituted a breach of warranty of good title. *Robinson v. Durham,* 537 So.2d 966.

Example 18-9

Lopez bought a racing bicycle from Perkins at a yard sale for $125. Shortly thereafter, Lopez learned that the bicycle had been stolen from Garcia. Garcia, the true owner, would be entitled to the return of the bicycle. Lopez's rights would be against Perkins for breach of warranty of title.

When the buyer is aware that the person selling the goods does not personally claim title to them, the warranty of title is not made by the seller. Such is the case, for example, in sheriff's sales and sales by personal representatives of estates.

Teaching Tips Under international law, the seller must deliver goods that are free from any right or claim of a third party. This rule does not apply, however, when the buyer enters into a contract knowing that others have rights or claims to the goods. CISG Articles 41–44.

Duty to Notify Seller of Defective Product

To recover money damages for breach of warranty, buyers of defective goods must notify the seller of the defect within a reasonable time either after the discovery or after the defect should have been discovered. Failure to do so will prevent them from recovering damages for breach of warranty.

UCC 2-607(3)(a)
(see page 882)

Quick Quiz 18-1 True or False?

1. No warranty of title is given when goods are sold by a private party.
2. An implied warranty occurs when a seller makes a promise about the goods to a buyer.
3. Whenever a merchant sells goods, unless it is excluded, the merchant warrants that the goods are merchantable.

18-2 Exclusion of Warranties

To exclude the implied warranty of merchantability in states that allow it, the word *merchantability* must be used in the disclaimer. If the exclusion is in writing, it must be in large, bold type so that it is conspicuous. To exclude the implied warranty of fitness for a particular purpose, the exclusion must be in writing and also be conspicuous.

UCC 2-316(2)
(see page 874)

Example 18-10

Valdez bought a used car from Kinkaid Motors, Inc., for $2,095. Printed on the sales slip, which Valdez signed, were the following words in large, bold capital letters: "THE SELLER HEREBY EXCLUDES THE WARRANTY OF MERCHANTABILITY

(Continued)

UCC 2-316(3)(a)
(see page 874)

> ## Example 18-10 (*Continued*)
>
> AND FITNESS FOR A PARTICULAR PURPOSE." Two days later, when the car broke down, Valdez had no recourse against the car dealer for breach of either implied warranty.

A common practice in the sale of used cars, lawnmowers, electrical appliances, and similar merchandise is for the seller to stipulate that the goods are being sold as is. The use of expressions such as *as is, with all faults,* and others is another way to exclude implied warranties. However, those words do not exclude express warranties or the warranty of title.

> ## A Question of Ethics
>
> In Example 18-10, Valdez signed away his rights to warranty protection. Is the practice of excluding warranties on the sale of goods ethical?

UCC 2-316(3)(b)
(see page 874)

Implied warranties may also be excluded under the UCC by having buyers examine the goods. When buyers have examined the goods, the sample, or the model as fully as they desire (or have refused to examine them when given the opportunity), there is no implied warranty as to defects that an examination would have revealed.

Under the Magnuson-Moss Warranty Act, any clause purporting to exclude or limit consequential damages for breach of warranty must appear conspicuously on the face of the warranty. **Consequential damages** are losses that do not flow directly and immediately from an act but only from some of the consequences or results of the act.

> ## Example 18-11
>
> Souci bought a freezer made by a reputable manufacturer. The freezer carried a full one-year warranty. The following sentence appeared in boldface type on the face of the warranty: "In no event shall this company be liable for consequential damages." Shortly after buying the freezer, Souci filled it with $1,500 worth of meat. Several days later, the freezer stopped working owing to a defect in its manufacture. Under the warranty, the company would have to repair or replace the freezer, but it would not be responsible for the loss of the meat. This loss would be considered consequential damage, which the company had effectively disclaimed.

>
>
> ### *The Opening Case Revisited*
> "The Jewel"
>
> The words *as is* written on the sales slip would not operate to exclude the express warranty made by the dealer because such language excludes only implied warranties.

Consumer Protection

The Magnuson-Moss Warranty Act places limits on the exclusion of implied warranties to consumers. Under the act, if either a full or limited express warranty is made to a consumer, the implied warranties of merchantability and fitness for a particular purpose may not be excluded during the warranty period. This law also applies if the seller gives the buyer a service contract.

In addition, many states have protected consumers even further by saying that implied warranties cannot be excluded when goods are sold to consumers. If the sale of the car to Valdez in Example 18-10 had taken place in Connecticut or Massachusetts, Valdez would have had legal recourse against Kinkaid Motors. Those states and eleven others do not allow sellers to exclude implied warranties when goods are sold to consumers.

Human Blood and Tissue

In some states, including Florida and Massachusetts, a statute provides that the procurement, processing, storage, and distribution of human blood are considered a service rather than a sale, and warranties do not apply. The Massachusetts statute reads as follows:

> The implied warranties of merchantability and fitness shall not be applicable to a contract for the sale of human blood, blood plasma, or other human tissue or organs from a blood bank or reservoir of such other tissues or organs. Such blood, blood plasma, or tissue or organs shall not for the purposes of this Article be considered commodities subject to sale or barter, but shall be considered as medical services. [MASS. GEN. L. ch. 106 §2-316(5)]

Quick Quiz 18-2 True or False?

1. The word *merchantability* must be used to disclaim the warranty of merchantability and it must be written in large, bold type.

2. If a buyer examined the goods, no implied warranty of merchantability is made as to defects that an examination would have revealed.

3. Implied warranties may not be excluded when a seller gives either a full or limited express warranty to a consumer.

18-3 Privity Not Required

Under earlier law, warranties extended only to the actual buyer of the product, that is, the one with whom the seller had dealt or was in privity of contract. People who were injured by defective products had no remedy against the seller for breach of warranty unless they themselves had purchased the goods. Thus, if children were injured by foreign objects in food that had been bought by their parents, the children could not recover for injuries because they had not purchased the goods. The UCC has abolished the requirement of privity. Instead, it provides three alternatives from which a state may choose. In all of the alternatives, warranties extend to people who would normally be expected to use the goods as well as to those who actually buy them.

> *Alternative A* A seller's warranty, whether express or implied, extends to any natural person who is in the family or household of his buyer or who is a guest in his home if it is reasonable to expect that such person may use, consume, or be affected by the goods and who is injured in person by breach of the warranty. A seller may not exclude or limit the operation of this section.

Related Cases In *Tarulli v. Birds in Paradise, N. Y. L. J.* (July 20, 1979), the buyer of a Moluccan cockatoo claimed that the seller had breached warranty by refusing to replace the bird, which had died of anemia less than four weeks after purchase. The sales agreement provided a two-day period in which the buyer could have the bird examined by a veterinarian and exchanged should any serious health problem be found. Tarulli failed to have the cockatoo examined, despite being urged to do so by the seller. Had the bird's health been checked, the anemia would most likely have been detected. The court determined that because the buyer had refused to examine the goods, no warranty existed.

State Variations In Delaware, the implied warranties of merchantability and fitness are not applicable to the sale of human tissue or organs from a reservoir of such tissue or organs.

Teaching Tips Under international law (CISG), buyers must notify sellers within a reasonable time after discovering any lack of conformity of the goods. CISG Article 39.

Teaching Tips Ask students if anyone they know has ever been injured by using a defective product. Discuss the circumstances in the class.

Terms *Privity* refers to a relationship between people with a legal interest in the same property, contract, or other transaction.

UCC 2-318
(see page 875)

Table 18-1 UCC Alternatives to Privity

State	Alternative	State	Alternative	State	Alternative
Alabama	B	Kentucky	A	North Dakota	C
Alaska	A	Louisiana	NA	Ohio	A
Arizona	A	Maine	OV	Oklahoma	A
Arkansas	A	Maryland	A	Oregon	A
California	NA	Massachusetts	OV	Pennsylvania	A
Colorado	B	Michigan	A	Rhode Island	OV
Connecticut	A	Minnesota	C	South Carolina	A
Delaware	B	Mississippi	A	South Dakota	B
District of Columbia	A	Missouri	A	Tennessee	A
Florida	A	Montana	A	Texas	OV
Georgia	A	Nebraska	A	Utah	C
Hawaii	C	Nevada	A	Vermont	B
Idaho	A	New Hampshire	OV	Virginia	OV
Illinois	A	New Jersey	A	Washington	A
Indiana	A	New Mexico	A	West Virginia	A
Iowa	C	New York	OV	Wisconsin	A
Kansas	B	North Carolina	A	Wyoming	B

NA—None Adopted.　OV—Own Version.

Related Cases In *Languilli v. Bumble Bee Seafood, Inc.,* (604 N.Y.S.2d 1020), Languilli broke a tooth on a one-half inch tuna bone that had come from a can of tuna fish. Defendants asserted lack of privity and moved to dismiss the case. The court, however, denied the motion because Languilli was claiming actual physical injury, and his claim of breach of implied warranty did not have to prove privity.

State Variations In Texas, the law does not specify whether anyone other than the buyer is entitled to take advantage of warranties. Texas statutes allow the courts to decide on this matter.

Alternative B　A seller's warranty, whether express or implied, extends to any natural person who may reasonably be expected to use, consume, or be affected by the goods and who is injured in person by breach of the warranty. A seller may not exclude or limit the operation of this section.

Alternative C　A seller's warranty, whether express or implied, extends to any person who may reasonably be expected to use, consume, or be affected by the goods and who is injured by breach of the warranty. A seller may not exclude or limit the operation of this section with respect to injury to the person of an individual to whom the warranty extends.

Most states have adopted one of the alternatives provided in the UCC. A few states, however, have written their own version of the law. Table 18-1 indicates the alternative that has been adopted by each state.

Quick Quiz 18-3 True or False?

1. Today, warranties extend only to the actual buyer of a product.

2. The UCC has retained the requirement of privity of contract.

3. Under the UCC, warranties extend to people who would normally be expected to use the goods as well as to those who actually buy them.

18-4 Product Liability

One of the most important areas of law for consumers today is known as **product liability.** Under this law, which is a tort rather than a breach of contract, a buyer or user of a product who is injured because of the product's unsafe or defective condition may recover damages from the manufacturer, the seller, or the supplier of the goods. Injuries to persons or damage to property caused by defects in design and manufacture give consumers a right to seek recovery under the law of product liability.

Product liability suits are usually based on either of two legal theories, negligence or strict liability—both of which are tort actions.

Negligence

One legal theory that is available to people who are injured by faulty products is negligence. This tort, which is explained more fully in Chapter 5, may be defined as the failure to exercise that degree of care that a reasonably prudent person would have exercised under the same circumstances and conditions. In order to recover for negligence in a product liability case, it is necessary to prove all of the following: that there was a negligent act on the part of the manufacturer or supplier of the goods; that injuries were suffered by someone who used the goods; and that the injuries were caused by the negligent act.

Example 18-12

Lee Boyd Malvo and John Allen Muhammad were convicted of murder in the Washington, D. C./Virginia-area sniper shootings in which ten people were killed. It was alleged that 17-year-old Malvo strolled into Bull's Eye Shooter Supply and walked out with a 3-foot-long, .223-caliber Bushmaster rifle, a civilian version of the military M-16. Suit was brought by the victims' families for the negligent distribution of weapons against the gun dealer as well as against the gun's manufacturer, Bushmaster Firearms. In a settlement, Bull's Eye Shooter Supply agreed to pay $2 million to eight plaintiffs, and Bushmaster Firearms agreed to pay $550,000.

It is not easy for an injured consumer to win a case on the theory of negligence because injured parties usually have no evidence of a negligent act by the manufacturer. They were not present when the goods were made and normally have very little information about the manufacturing process. Injured parties are often more successful in bringing suit for breach of warranty of merchantability rather than negligence.

Strict Liability

Under the doctrine of strict liability, it is not necessary to prove a negligent act on the part of the manufacturer or seller when someone is injured by a defective product. **Strict liability** is a legal theory,

Manufacturers must make products as safe as possible or risk product liability suits.

Teaching Tips This law, however, does not apply to international sales. Article 5 in the CISG states that it does not apply to the liability of the seller for death or personal injury caused by the goods to any person.

State Variations In 1999, a California jury awarded $107 million in compensatory damages to six people who had been burned in a crash when their car exploded in flames in a rear-end collision. The jury also awarded $4.9 billion in punitive damages.

Getting Students Involved Divide the class into small groups and assign each a corporation or industry to investigate for examples of negligence. Have the students delegate responsibilities within their groups and make a short presentation of their findings to the class. Reports may include specific cases such as the Exxon *Valdez* oil spill or the Ford Pinto's faulty gas tank, or more general trends, such as the rise in tamperproof packaging. Encourage the class to find examples of corporate responsibility as well as negligence.

Getting Students Involved Hold a brief discussion in class on the idea of abolishing strict liability laws, encouraging students to explain their opinions. Bring into the discussion such factors as insurance costs, lawyer's fees, alternative assistance for the needy, and consequences to business.

Getting Students Involved CISG Article 5 limits the seller's liability for death or personal injury caused by the goods in any form. The purpose of the exclusion is to leave issues of personal liability to applicable national law. What problems would this cause an American suing a foreign corporation? How would a judgment be collected?

State Variations The North Carolina legislature has abolished strict liability in tort in product liability actions in that state.

adopted by two-thirds of the states, which imposes liability on manufacturers or suppliers for selling goods that are unreasonably dangerous, without regard to fault or negligence. The principle consideration under the doctrine of strict liability is the safety of the product, not the conduct of the manufacturer or supplier of the goods. Under this rule of law, manufacturers have the duty to design reasonably safe products. They must also give proper instructions for the product's use and provide warnings of possible danger.

It is difficult to recover damages under the strict liability doctrine. People who are injured or who suffer property damage from a defective product may recover from the manufacturer or seller only if they can prove all of the following:

1. The manufacturer or seller sold the product in a defective condition.
2. The manufacturer or seller was engaged in the business of selling the product.
3. The product was unreasonably dangerous to the user or consumer.
4. The defective condition was the proximate cause of the injury or damage.
5. The defective condition existed at the time it left the hands of the manufacturer or seller.
6. The consumer sustained physical harm or property damage by use or consumption of the product.

The defective condition may arise through faulty product design, faulty manufacturing, inadequate warning of danger, or improper instructions for the product's use.

Example 18-13

Stewart stood on the lifting platform of a forklift and caused it to raise him to a rack 16 feet above the floor level so that he could inventory some ball bearings. Suddenly, the lift apparatus failed. The platform fell to the floor, and Stewart was seriously injured. The cause of the failure was attributed to negligent repair work performed a few days earlier by Scott-Kitz Miller Co., a company responsible for maintenance of the equipment. Scott employees had removed some bolts holding the lift guide and reinserted them backward. In this position, the bolts protruded in such a way that when an attempt was made to lower the raised platform, the lift assembly would hang at the top of the mast, then fall to the floor. The court held that the forklift was defectively designed. It would have required very little effort or expense to design the bolts so that they could not accidentally be inserted backward.

The manufacturer's and seller's liability extends to all persons who may be injured by the product. Injured bystanders, guests, or others who have no relationship to the product, the seller, or the manufacturer may seek damages caused by defects in the offending product.

Example 18-14

Ryder Truck Rental rented a truck to Jackson. While Jackson was waiting for a light to change, the truck moved forward owing to a faulty brake system. Martin, in another car, was injured when the truck hit her car. The Delaware Supreme Court ruled, on appeal, that Ryder could be held liable even without proof of its negligence. It was only necessary for the injured party to prove that the truck had an unreasonably dangerous product design that caused personal injury or property damage to the plaintiffs.

Business Law in the News
How to Put the Right Cap on Punitive Damages

In an important but split decision, *State Farm v. Campbell,* the U.S. Supreme Court in April held that "the Due Process Clause [of the 14th Amendment] prohibits the imposition of grossly excessive or arbitrary punishments on defendants in tort cases. This was the second High Court ruling in the past few years that rightly objected to steep punitive damage awards.

Punitive damages are often added to compensatory damages awarded to victims of drunk drivers, medical malpractice, defective goods, and others who suffer because of careless or irresponsible behavior. There is no controversy about the fact that incompetent doctors, intoxicated or reckless drivers, and companies that produce dangerous and shoddy products should have to pay for the harm they cause.

But compensatory damages alone may not be enough to deter harmful actions. It is not always possible for victims to detect careless medical practices, dangerous goods, and other behavior. Moreover, some victims may be unwilling to file lawsuits because of the sizable expense in time and money, the discomfort of having to testify in court, and the uncertainty that they will win even legitimate cases. So punitive damages are often valuable; they help encourage such lawsuits and deter dangerous behavior.

Given that punitive damages are desirable, how big should they be? In his dissent in the State Farm case, Justice Antonin Scalia argued that the determination of punitive damages should continue to be left to individual judges and juries because the Supreme Court cannot devise a "principled application" that determines what these damages should be in different circumstances.

Unfortunately, under the present system, the principle that juries sometimes use is the depth of defendants' pockets. The Utah jury in the State Farm case awarded the Campbells $2.6 million in compensatory damages and $145 million in punitive damages. On appeal, the Utah Supreme Court reduced compensatory damages to $1 million but allowed the punitive ones. Punitive damages, therefore, amounted to 145 times compensatory—a ratio that is far too high.

State Farm may have misled the Campbells, but its behavior was not especially reprehensible. It assured the Campbells they had no liability and no need to hire counsel to defend Curtis Campbell against charges he caused a serious auto accident. When the jury returned a large judgment against him, State Farm at first refused to pay but eventually relented and paid.

Excessive punitive damage awards are not harmless transfers of wealth: They damage the functioning of the U.S. economy and judicial system. Companies pass these costs on to consumers via higher prices. In addition, large punitive damages encourage expensive class-action law firms, driven by the prospect of big contingency fees, to pursue unwarranted suits.

The challenge is to find rules to set punitive damages that are neither too weak nor clearly excessive. The Supreme Court indicated in the State Farm case that the ratio of punitive to compensatory damages should generally be in the single digits. Antitrust laws have established this ratio at 3 to 1 in private suits against companies engaged in monopolistic business practices. Although trebling damages is a rigid rule, it can be administered consistently and is a reasonable standard to apply in tort cases as well.

Strict limits on the ratio of punitive to compensatory damages would elevate the importance of accurate measurement of compensatory harm. For example, loss of life in automobile accidents caused by drunk drivers, or wrong statements by producers of drugs that cause severe harm or death to inappropriate users, damage victims and their heirs in ways that go far beyond the loss of future earnings. Although economists have developed techniques to gauge the monetary value to individuals of the loss of future activities due to wrongful deaths, juries have been reluctant to rely on them.

One might agree either with the majority of justices in the State Farm case that the 14th Amendment implies restrictions on punitive damages, or with Justice Ruth Bader Ginsburg, who argued in her dissent that federal courts should defer to state legislators in the setting of punitive damages. But unless more is

(Continued)

Business Law in the News *(Continued)*

done at the judiciary or legislative levels to limit these damages, the American tort system will continue to be costly and arbitrary.

Questions for Analysis

1. What was the holding of the U.S. Supreme Court in *State Farm v. Campbell?*

2. For what reasons may compensatory damages not be enough to deter harmful actions?

3. What did Justice Scalia argue in his dissent in the State Farm case?

4. What was the ratio of compensatory damages to punitive damages in the case?

5. In what ways do excessive punitive damage awards damage the functioning of the U.S. economy and judicial system from the viewpoint of this article?

6. What examples are given to illustrate how strict limits on the ratio of punitive damages to compensatory damages would elevate the importance of accurate measurement of compensatory harm?

Source: Gary S. Becker. "How to Put the Right Cap on Punitive Damages," *BusinessWeek,* September 15, 2003.

Background Information In common law, it is assumed that a buyer who inspects the goods will be aware of any defects. Before the practice of issuing warranties became standard, the Latin term *caveat emptor,* meaning "let the buyer beware," applied to sales transactions. Government regulations, warranties, and liability suits have since created a situation of *caveat venditor,* or "let the seller beware."

Duty to Warn Sometimes a duty is placed upon manufacturers to warn consumers that harm may result from a product. Unavoidably unsafe products may require a warning to inform the consumer of possible harm. If the warning is adequate, consumers may be required to use the product at their own risk. A warning must specify the risk presented by the product and give a reason for the warning. When the danger that is presented by a product is obvious, however, no duty to warn exists because a warning will not reduce the likelihood of injury.

Punitive Damages In addition to recovering damages to compensate them for their losses, injured parties in strict liability cases sometimes recover punitive damages. These are a monetary penalty imposed as a punishment for a wrongdoing.

Quick Quiz 18-4 True or False?

1. Strict liability laws impose liability on manufacturers or suppliers for selling goods that are unreasonably dangerous.

2. Only people who are in privity of contract may seek damages for injuries caused by defects in products.

3. Manufacturers sometimes have a duty to warn consumers of possible harm that may result from the use of a product.

Summary

18-1 Express warranties arise by a statement of fact or promise, by a description of the goods, and by a sample or model. Federal law requires that written warranties on consumer products be labeled as either full or limited warranties.

When merchants sell goods, they warrant that the goods are merchantable. In addition, when a buyer relies on the seller's skill and judgment in selecting the goods, the seller warrants that the goods will be fit for the purpose for which they are to be used. Other warranties may arise from ways in which parties have dealt in the past.

When goods are sold, either by a merchant or a private party, the seller warrants that the title is good and that there are no liens on the goods.

To be able to sue for breach of warranty, a buyer of defective goods must notify the seller of the defect within a reasonable time after discovering the defect.

18-2   Except when express warranties are made, sellers may exclude the warranties of merchantability and fitness for a particular purpose. Such an exclusion must be in writing and conspicuous. The words *as is* and *with all faults* serve to disclaim implied warranties but not the warranty of title. However, many states protect consumers by saying that implied warranties cannot be excluded when goods are sold to consumers. In addition, the distribution of human blood and tissue is considered a service rather than a sale in some states, making warranties under the UCC inapplicable.

18-3   Warranties extend to people who would normally be expected to use the goods as well as to those who actually buy them.

18-4   Buyers who are injured from unsafe or defective products may sometimes recover damages from the manufacturer, seller, or supplier of the goods under product liability laws. Lawsuits are brought under either of two theories, negligence or strict liability.

Key Terms

consequential damages, 334

consumer products, 330

express warranty, 327

full warranty, 330

implied warranty, 331

limited warranty, 330

product liability, 337

strict liability, 337

warranty of fitness for a particular purpose, 332

warranty of merchantability, 331

warranty of title, 333

Questions for Review and Discussion

1. In what three ways may express warranties be created?
2. Under the Magnuson-Moss Warranty Act, what must be done when a written warranty is given to a consumer?
3. What is the difference between a full warranty and a limited warranty?
4. When does the implied warranty of fitness for a particular purpose arise? When and by whom is the warranty of merchantability given?
5. What is the warranty of title that is made by a seller of goods? Explain.
6. What special rules must be followed to exclude the warranties of merchantability and fitness for a particular purpose? In what other ways may warranties be excluded?
7. What notice must buyers of defective goods give to recover damages for breach of warranty?
8. What provision does the UCC make relative to privity of contract under the law of warranties?
9. Why is it often difficult for a consumer to win a product liability case on the theory of negligence?
10. What must an injured party prove to recover from a manufacturer for strict liability?

Investigating the Internet

The Internet has a site explaining the lemon laws of most states at "Lemon Law America."

342

Part Three   Sales and Consumer Protection

Cases for Analysis

1. Caswell bought a gas grill to give to his friend, Kile, as a birthday present. The grill exploded the first time it was used due to a factory defect, and Kile was injured. The manufacturer of the grill argued that it was not responsible for Kile's injuries because Kile had not purchased the grill. There was no privity of contract between Kile and the manufacturer. How would you decide?

2. Shaffer ordered a glass of rosé wine at the Victoria Station Restaurant. As he took his first sip of wine, the glass broke in his hand, causing permanent injuries. Shaffer brought suit against the restaurant for breach of warranty of merchantability. The restaurant's position was that, since it did not sell the wine glass to Shaffer (only its contents), it was not a merchant with respect to the glass, and therefore made no warranty. Do you agree with the restaurant? Why or why not? *Shaffer v. Victoria Station, Inc.,* 588 P.2d 233 (WA).

3. McCoy bought an antique pistol from the Old Fort Trading Post for $1,000. Later, the gun was taken from McCoy by the police when they learned that it was stolen property. The police turned the gun over to the rightful owner. McCoy notified the Old Fort Trading Post of what had happened and asked for the return of his money, but the owner of the business refused to give him a refund. What remedy, if any, did McCoy have against the owner of the trading post? Explain. *Trial v. McCoy,* 553 S.W.2d 199 (TX).

4. Werner purchased a sloop from Montana for $13,250. During the negotiations before the sale, Montana had told Werner that the sloop would "make up" when placed in the water and would become watertight. Werner placed the sloop in the water and allowed sufficient time for the planking to swell to form a watertight hull, but it still leaked and could not be sailed. He then discovered extensive dry rot in the hull and learned that the cost of repairs would be substantial. Montana refused to take the sloop back and refund Werner's purchase price. Did Werner have a cause of action against Montana? If so, on what grounds? Explain. *Werner v. Montana,* 378 A.2d 1130 (NH).

5. Romedy bought a car from Willett Lincoln-Mercury, Inc. He did not inspect it until four or five days after it was delivered to him. Three weeks later, he notified the dealer that the car

did not contain the equipment that the dealer had said it would contain. He did, however, continue to make payments on the car. Later, he brought suit against the dealer for breach of warranty. Did he recover damages? Explain. *Romedy v. Willett Lincoln-Mercury, Inc.,* 220 S.E.2d 74 (GA).

6. Mr. And Mrs. Benfer bought a mobile home from Thomas, a mobile home retailer. Prior to the purchase, Thomas had told them that the type of mobile home he carried had a one-quarter-inch sheathing on the siding that made it better than cheaper units. Thomas showed them a model of the mobile home that he carried and pointed out to them the grade of plywood sheathing that was on the model. When the mobile home was delivered to them, they were given several written warranties signed by the manufacturer, Town & Country Mobile Homes, Inc., including one that specifically warranted that the mobile home was sheathed with one-quarter-inch plywood beneath the prefinished aluminum exterior wall surface. Later, the Benfers discovered that their mobile home did not contain this sheathing. Did they have a cause of action against the retailer, Thomas? Why or why not? *Town & Country Mobile Homes, Inc., v. Benfer,* 527 S.W.2d 523 (TX).

7. Hensley bought a used Plymouth automobile from Colonial Dodge, Inc. The following language was written in small print on the back of the purchase agreement: "No warranties, expressed or implied, are made by the dealer with respect to used motor vehicles or motor vehicle chassis furnished hereunder except as may be expressed in writing by the dealer." After driving only three or four blocks, Hensley noticed that the windshield wipers and the brake lights were not working properly. He returned the car to the dealer to correct the problems. When he next received the car, it started to lose compression and slowed down to 20 or 25 miles per hour before he got halfway home. The engine sounded as if it were "missing quite badly." After arriving home, which was about six miles from the dealer's place of business, Hensley was unable to get the car started again. An investigation revealed that the car needed a new engine, which the dealer

refused to provide. Did Hensley recover damages from the dealer for breach of warranty? Why or why not? *Hensley v. Colonial Dodge, Inc.,* 245 N.W.2d 142 (MI).

8. Paul and Cynthia Vance invited Carl and Jeanne Leichtamer to go for a ride in the Vances's four wheel drive jeep at an "off the road" recreation facility called the Hall of Fame Four-Wheel Club. The club had been organized by a jeep dealer who showed films to club members of jeeps traveling in hilly country. This activity was coupled with a national advertising program of American Motor Sales Corporation encouraging people to buy jeeps that could drive up and down steep hills. As the jeep went up a 33-degree sloped, double-terraced hill, it pitched over from front to back and landed upside-down. The Vances were killed, and the Leichtamers were severely injured. The jeep was equipped with a factory-installed roll bar attached to the sheet metal that housed the rear wheels. When the vehicle landed upside down, the flat sheet metal gave way, causing the roll bar to move forward and downward 14 inches. The Leichtamers argued that the weakness of the sheet metal housing upon which the roll bar had been attached was the cause of their injuries. The manufacturer claimed that the roll bar was provided solely for side-roll protection, not pitchover, as occurred in this case. Did the Leichtamers recover against the manufacturer on a theory of strict liability? Why or why not? *Leichtamer v. American Motors Corp.,* 424 N.E.2d 568 (OH).

9. Michael P. Babine was injured when he was thrown from an "El Toro" mechanical bull that he rode at a nightclub. The club had placed mattresses around the bull to cushion the fall of riders, but the mattresses were not adequately pushed together. Babine was thrown off during his ride, and hit his head on the floor where there was a gap between the mattresses. Before riding the bull, Babine had signed a form releasing the nightclub from liability for injuries sustained from the activity. The mechanical bull had been manufactured for the purpose of being a training device for rodeo cowboys, and it was purchased second-hand by the nightclub. Babine sought to recover damages from the manufacturer under the theory of product liability. Did he succeed? Why or why not? *Babine v. Gilley's Bronco Shop, Inc.,* 488 So.2d 176 (FL).

Quick Quiz Answers

18-1	18-2	18-3	18-4
1. F	1. T	1. F	1. T
2. F	2. T	2. F	2. F
3. T	3. T	3. T	3. T

Consumer Protection

The Opening Case
"Double Trouble"

While browsing through a large used-car lot, Randy Falco saw a sharp-looking, four-year-old Toyota Tundra double-cab pickup that he liked. A large sign on the vehicle gave the price, but nothing indicated the kind of warranty, if any, that went with it. When Falco took the truck out for a test drive, the salesperson said that it was fully warranted but gave no details. Falco decided that he would think it over and left. Later that day, he discovered that his wallet was missing. He returned to the used-car lot and, much to his relief, found the wallet on the ground next to the vehicle he had driven. Later that evening, he discovered that his VISA card was missing from the wallet. He notified VISA of the loss by telephone. In spite of his prompt notice, a thief was able to charge purchases totaling $1,600. What law did the used-car lot violate? Will Falco be legally responsible for paying the full $1,600 back to the credit card company?

Chapter Outcomes

1. Discuss the Federal Trade Commission (FTC) Act and explain how the act is enforced.
2. Describe four federal laws designed to prevent unfair or deceptive acts.
3. Identify several FTC rules designed to protect the consumer.
4. State the purpose of the Consumer Product Safety Act.
5. Explain how consumers can benefit from the Consumer Leasing Act.
6. Identify and state the purpose of six consumer credit laws.

19-1 Federal and State Consumer Protection Laws

Consumer protection laws apply to transactions between someone conducting a business and a consumer. A **consumer** is someone who buys or leases real estate, goods, or services for personal, family, or household purposes. Thus, people who buy or rent things for personal use from a business are protected by consumer protection laws. On the other hand, if they buy the same things from another consumer or for business use, they are not, with some exceptions, protected by the consumer protection law.

State consumer protection offices provide information and help to enforce state consumer protection laws. They sometimes assist consumers

A Question of Ethics

Today, there are many federal and state consumer protection laws. Why do you think these laws are necessary?

Teaching Tips Ask students to list different types of money transactions they have performed in the last week. Discuss whether any of these transactions would be covered by consumer protection laws or the UCC.

Terms Students will easily differentiate between *interstate* and *intrastate* commerce if they know that *inter* is a prefix meaning "between" and *intra* means "within."

Background Information FTC regulations cannot be enforced by an individual. However, since the FTC defines unfair practices in its trade regulation rules, consumers are legally protected from such practices in any agreements they enter.

Getting Students Involved Ask each student to bring to class the details of one FTC investigation. Suggest that they check the Internet. Ask the students how many of the investigations they found involved consent orders and how many involved complaints. What were the outcomes of the investigations? Is there any correlation between whether the investigations involved complaints or consent orders and their outcomes?

with individual problems. Consumer protection offices are located in state and county offices, and, in some cities, the mayor's office.

Federal consumer protection law stems from the Federal Trade Commission Act which states that "unfair or deceptive acts or practices in or affecting commerce are hereby declared unlawful." The act defines **commerce** as "commerce among the several states or with foreign nations . . . or the District of Columbia." Thus, the act applies to businesses that sell real estate, goods, or services in interstate commerce or that somehow affect interstate commerce. **Interstate commerce** is business activity that touches more than one state. Purely local business activity, which has no out-of-state connections, called **intrastate commerce,** is not governed by the FTC Act.

Example 19-1

Ortega owned a farm on which he grew a variety of vegetables. He sold the vegetables to a local store and also to consumers who stopped at his roadside stand. Since his business was purely local, it would not be governed by the FTC Act. Instead, his business would be regulated by the consumer protection laws, as well as other laws, of his own state.

The Federal Trade Commission (FTC) investigates violations of the FTC Act. If the FTC believes a violation of the law occurred, it may attempt to obtain voluntary compliance by entering into a consent order with the violating company. A **consent order** is an order under which the company agrees to stop the disputed practice without necessarily admitting that it violated the law. If an agreement cannot be reached, the FTC may issue a complaint. This action begins a formal hearing before an administrative law judge. If a violation of law is found, a cease and desist order or other appropriate relief may be issued.

Example 19-2

Jay Norris, Inc., made false claims about a number of products listed in its mail-order catalogs and advertisements. It described a "flame gun" that would dissolve the heaviest snowdrifts and whip through the thickest ice; the product did neither. A roach powder was described as completely safe to use and as never losing its killing power, even after years; the powder was neither safe to use nor very deadly to roaches. Cars were listed as carefully maintained and thoroughly serviced; they were former New York taxicabs, many in poor condition. The FTC issued a cease and desist order prohibiting Jay Norris, Inc., from representing the safety or performance characteristics of any product unless such claims were fully and completely substantiated by competent and objective material available in written form.

Consumers may bring individual or class-action lawsuits against businesses for violating FTC rules. A **class-action lawsuit** is one that is brought by one or more plaintiffs on behalf of a class of persons. Usually, suit must be brought within one year after the violation. Alternate dispute resolutions are also available for resolving this type of problem (see Chapter 42).

Quick Quiz 19-1 True or False?

1. Consumer protection laws apply to transactions between someone conducting a business and a consumer.

2. A consumer is someone who buys or leases real estate, goods, or services for personal, family, or household purposes.

3. Intrastate commerce is business activity that touches more than one state.

19-2 Unfair or Deceptive Acts or Practices

Related Cases In *Our Fair Lady Health Resort v. Miller* (564 SW.2d 410), a suit was brought against Our Fair Lady for deceptive practices. Miller was told, upon enrolling as a new member of the resort, that her signed contract would not be binding if she canceled within three days. When Miller attempted to cancel the contract before the trial period was up, Our Fair Lady refused, stating that the contract had already been "sent in." The court ruled in favor of Miller on the grounds that the ratification of the contract had not been established.

Getting Students Involved Have students write to their state's consumer protection office for copies of consumer protection literature. What are the most common complaints filed in their state? What are the results of these complaints?

Terms A *dun* is a type of immature fly. The act of *dunning* means to pester someone without relief, just as some flies do.

The FTC Act prohibits unfair or deceptive acts or practices. The FTC and the courts have determined that certain activities are unfair or deceptive. They include fraudulent misrepresentations, sending unordered merchandise, bait-and-switch schemes, and odometer tampering.

Fraudulent Misrepresentations

It is unfair or deceptive for a seller to make a *fraudulent misrepresentation,* that is, a statement that has the effect of deceiving the buyer. A misrepresentation usually occurs when the seller misstates facts important to the consumer.

Making false statements about the construction, durability, reliability, safety, strength, condition, or life expectancy of a product is a deceptive practice. It is also deceptive to fail to disclose to a buyer any fact that would cause the buyer not to enter into the contract.

You may see ads like the following in newspapers and magazines: "Would you like to earn hundreds of dollars a week at home in your leisure time? Many people are supplementing their income in a very easy way. Let us tell you how. . . ."

An offer like this may sound very attractive, particularly if you are unable to leave your home to work. But, be cautious about work-at-home ads, especially ones that promise you large profits in a short period of time. While some work-at-home plans are legitimate, many are not. Home employment schemes are some of the oldest kinds of classified advertising fraud.

Unordered Merchandise

Except for free samples clearly and conspicuously marked as such and merchandise mailed by charitable organizations soliciting contributions, it is a violation of the postal law and the FTC Act to send merchandise through the mail to people who did not order it. Similarly, it is illegal to send a bill for such unordered merchandise or to send **dunning letters,** that is, letters requesting payments.

People who receive unordered merchandise through the mail may treat it as a gift. They may keep the merchandise or dispose of it in any manner they see fit without any obligation whatsoever to the sender. In addition, senders of unordered merchandise must attach a statement to the package informing recipients of their right to keep and use the goods.

Bait-and-Switch Schemes

A **bait-and-switch scheme** is an alluring but insincere offer to sell a product or service that the advertiser in truth does not intend or want to sell. Its purpose is to switch customers from buying the advertised merchandise in order to sell something else, usually at a higher price or on a basis more advantageous to the advertiser.

The FTC law prohibiting bait-and-switch activity states, "No advertisement containing an offer to sell a product shall be made when the offer is not a *bona fide* effort to sell the advertised product."

Any of the following activities could indicate a bait-and-switch scheme:

- the refusal to show, demonstrate, or sell the product offered in accordance with the terms of the offer
- the "put down" of the product by acts or words of the seller
- the failure to have available at all outlets listed in the advertisement a sufficient quantity of the advertised product to meet reasonably anticipated demands
- the refusal to take orders for the advertised product to be delivered within a reasonable period of time
- the showing of a product that is defective, unusable, or impractical for the purpose represented in the advertisement

Related Cases A commercial for a carpet store advertised 150 square feet of nylon carpet for $77 plus a "free gift" of an upright vacuum cleaner. Upon visiting the home for measurement, the salesperson would disparage the advertised product and push for the more expensive line of products. There was also no "free gift." The court ruled that this was a classic bait-and-switch scheme and buyers could sue as a consumer fraud class action against the carpet supplier.

Odometer Tampering

The federal Odometer Law prohibits people from disconnecting, resetting, or altering the odometer of a motor vehicle to register any mileage other than the true mileage driven. Anyone who sells a car or even gives it away, unless it is over 25 years old, must provide the new owner with a written statement disclosing the odometer reading at the time of the transfer. If the seller has reason to believe that the mileage reading on the odometer is incorrect, the disclosure statement must indicate that the actual mileage traveled is unknown.

An odometer must be set at zero if it is repaired and cannot be adjusted to show the true mileage. In addition, the car owner must attach to the left door frame a written notice showing the true mileage before the repair or replacement and the date that the odometer was set at zero. It is illegal for anyone to alter or remove any such notice attached to the door frame of a car.

Quick Quiz 19-2 True or False?

1. A misrepresentation usually occurs when the seller misstates facts important to the consumer.

2. People who receive unordered merchandise through the mail must either return the merchandise or pay for it.

3. An odometer must be set at zero if it is repaired and cannot be adjusted to show the true mileage and a written notice of the date of repair and the true mileage must be attached to the left door frame of the car.

19-3 The FTC Trade Regulation Rules

To correct wrongdoings in the marketplace, the FTC has established trade regulation rules that must be followed by companies that transact business in interstate commerce. Some of these rules are discussed here.

Used Car Rule

State Variations In New York, at the time of purchase or lease of a used motor vehicle from a dealer, the dealer shall provide to the consumer a notice, printed in not less than 8 point boldface type, entitled "USED CAR LEMON LAW BILL OF RIGHTS."

Further Reading For an excellent overview of consumer protection and the purchase of an automobile, read *Lemonaid! A Layperson's Guide to the Automotive Lemon Laws* by Andrew A. Faglio (New York: Oceanna Publications, Inc., 1991).

Buying a used car? Be sure to read the Buyer's Guide on the window before you purchase.

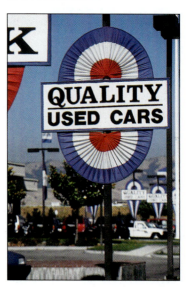

Many consumer complaints involve the purchase of a used car. To remedy this situation, the FTC established the **Used Car Rule.** The rule requires used-car dealers who sell more than five used vehicles in a twelve-month period to place a window sticker, called a **Buyer's Guide,** in the window of each used car they offer for sale. The Buyer's Guide provides the following information:

- A statement that the car is sold *as is* if it is sold with no warranties. (Some states do not allow used cars to be sold *as is* by car dealers.)

- A statement that the car is sold with implied warranties only if that is the case (see Chapter 18).

- A statement telling whether the warranty is "full" or "limited" (see Chapter 18) and citing the length of the warranty period if the car is sold with an express warranty. In addition, the guide must list the specific systems that are covered by the warranty and must state the percentage of the repair costs the buyer will be required to pay.

- A statement that tells consumers not to rely on spoken promises.

- A suggestion that consumers ask whether they may have the vehicle inspected by their own mechanic either on or off the premises.

- A list of the fourteen major systems of an automobile and some of the principal defects that may occur in these systems.

Dealers are required to put a Buyer's Guide on all used vehicles they offer for sale, including automobiles, light-duty vans, and light-duty trucks. The guide becomes part of the sales contract and overrides any contrary provision that may be in the contract.

Cooling-Off Rule

The FTC has established the **Cooling-Off Rule** to give consumers an opportunity to change their minds after signing contracts with people who come to their houses. Under this rule, sales of consumer goods or services over $25 made away from the seller's regular place of business, such as at a customer's home, may be canceled within three business days after the sale occurs. This rule requires the seller to give the buyer two copies of a cancellation form, one of which the buyer may send to the seller any time before midnight of the third business day after the contract was signed, canceling the contract. The law also applies to consumer product parties given in private homes and to sales made in rented hotel rooms or restaurants.

The Opening Case Revisited
"Double Trouble"

The used-car lot violated the FTC's used-car rule by not placing a buyer's guide on the window of the truck, providing information about the warranties that went with the vehicle.

Example 19-3

Nesbit saw an advertisement in a local newspaper advertising Oriental rugs for sale at a local motel. She went to the motel, purchased an Oriental rug, and was given a sales slip saying that all sales were final. The company violated the FTC rule. It did not provide her with a cancellation form that she could use to cancel the contract within three days. Although the FTC cannot resolve individual complaints, it does want to know about them. Nesbit should have notified her state consumer protection office and should have sent a copy of her complaint to the Enforcement Division, Federal Trade Commission, Washington, DC 20580.

Under the laws of some states, such as New York, the three-day right to cancel does not begin until the seller gives the buyer a written notice of the right to cancel. Until such notice is given, the buyer may use any means to notify the seller of the cancellation of the contract.

The Cooling-Off Rule does not apply to sales made at the seller's regular place of business, sales made totally by mail or phone, and sales under $25. In addition, it does not apply to sales for real estate, insurance, securities, sales for emergency home repairs, or sales involving arts and crafts sold at fairs or other locations.

Negative Option Rule

When consumers subscribe to a magazine, CD club, or other plan that sends products on an ongoing basis, the Negative Option Rule applies. Under such plans, sellers regularly send announcements describing the current selection. If the subscriber does nothing, the seller will ship the selection automatically. If the subscriber does not want the selection, he or she must tell the seller not to send it, and there is a deadline for notification. Under the Negative Option Rule, sellers must tell subscribers:

- How many selections they must buy, if any.
- How and when they can cancel the membership.
- How to notify the seller when they do not want the selection.
- When to return the "negative option" form to cancel shipment of a selection.
- When they can get credit for the return of a selection.
- How postage and handling costs are charged.
- How often they will receive announcements and forms.

Antispam Law

The **Can Spam Act** is an attempt by the federal government to reduce the use of unsolicited e-mail, commonly known as **spam,** on the Internet. Under the law, unsolicited commercial e-mail messages must be truthful and must not use misleading subject lines or incorrect return addresses. E-mail containing pornography must be specifically labeled in the subject line. In addition, spammers cannot harvest e-mail addresses from chat rooms and other sites without permission. The law authorizes the FTC to establish a "do-not-e-mail registry," and provides for fines of $250 for each e-mail violation.

Antislamming Law

Slamming is the illegal practice of changing a consumer's telephone service without permission. New consumer protection rules created by the Federal Communications Commission (FCC) provide a remedy if you've been slammed.

Business Law in the News

Now Spam Is Being Outsourced

Everyone knows that China and South Korea have become export powerhouses for everything from baseball gloves to semiconductors. But watch out, world: The Asian powers are fast becoming major exporters of an item you don't want to import—Internet spam. In early September, Chinese officials were scheduled to hold an antispam summit in Beijing with top executives from some of America's biggest Net companies, including America Online Inc., eBay, Yahoo!, and Microsoft. With reason: More than 25% of the junk e-mail sent around the globe now originates from servers in China and South Korea. "It won't be long before China produces the same amount of spam as the U.S.," frets York Ma, chairman of the Hong Kong Internet Service Providers Assn.

This is one export Asia—especially China—has to curtail fast. If not, it could endanger the security of the global Net. Junk e-mail dangerously clogs the cyberways, of course. Net executives worry, too, that spammers using China as a base will team up with hackers and virus writers, which would be "very destructive," says Li Boda, e-mail manager at Chinese portal Sohu.com.

What's frustrating to many companies is that governments have been slow to react even as Asian spam has been growing explosively. A survey by Sophos PLC, a British Internet security firm, found that between February and August of this year, the flow of junk e-mail coming out of China and Hong Kong almost doubled, from 6.24% of the global output to 11.63%, while the amount from South Korea went from 5.8% to more than 15%.

Some spam conveyors are renting servers in China, but others are remotely hijacking Asian PCs without their owners' knowledge to use as vehicles for transmitting billions of e-mails. Spam artists are moving operations to Asia to avoid a crackdown in the U.S. Internet service providers such as AOL and EarthLink Inc. have filed suits against spammers. The so-called Can Spam Act, which took effect in January, has erected new legal hurdles. "As crackdowns are happening in the U.S., spammers are going offshore," says Gregg Mastoras, senior security analyst at Sophos. "Mostly it involves being in an environment where nobody is going to come shut you down."

Why Asia? South Korea has the world's most advanced broadband infrastructure, allowing spammers to take advantage of its high-speed connections. And China, while it boasts fewer broadband hookups, is largely unregulated. "China is a safe harbor for spammers," says Andy Lake, director of sales and operations for Greater China and Southeast Asia for MessageLabs, the British e-mail security company. "There's not a lot of control over the infrastructure." Asia's rise as a spamming center is drawing the attention of industry big guns. "What we really need to do is agree across all nations what are the areas that are wrong no matter where you are," says Ryan Hamlin, general manager for antispam technology and strategy at Microsoft Corp.

By Bruce Einhorn, with Chen Wu in Hong Kong, Brian Grow in Atlanta, and Moon Ihlwan in Seoul

Questions for Analysis

1. For what reason did Chinese officials hold an antispam summit with some of America's top executives from Net companies?

2. Why is it important that Asia act fast to curtail the use of spam?

3. For what reasons are spam artists moving operations to Asia?

Source: Bruce Einhorn. "Now Spam is Being Outsourced," *BusinessWeek,* September 13, 2004, p. 54.

If you have been slammed and HAVE NOT paid the bill of the carrier who slammed, you do NOT have to pay anyone for service for up to 30 days after being slammed. This means you do not have to pay either your authorized telephone company (the company you actually chose to provide service) or the slamming company. You must pay any charges for service beyond thirty days to your authorized company, but at that company's rates, not the slammer's rates.

If you have been slammed and HAVE paid your phone bill and then discover that you have been slammed, the slamming company must pay your authorized company 150 percent of the charges it received from you. Out of this amount, your authorized company will then reimburse you 50 percent of the charges you paid to the slammer. For example, if you were charged $100 by the slamming company, that company will have to give your authorized company $150, and you will receive $50 as a reimbursement.

With these rules, the FCC has taken the profit out of slamming and protected consumers from illegal charges.

Mail, Telephone, Internet, or Fax Rule

The FTC has established a rule to protect consumers who order goods by mail, telephone, Internet, or fax machine. Under the rule, sellers must ship orders within the time promised in their advertisements. If no time period is promised, sellers must either ship the order within thirty days after they receive it or send the consumer an option notice. The option notice tells the consumer of a shipping delay and gives the consumer the option of agreeing to the delay or of canceling the order and receiving a prompt refund. Instructions on how to cancel the order must be included in the notice. In addition, the seller must provide a free means for the consumer to reply.

Telemarketing Sales Rule

The FTC's Telemarketing Sales Rule is designed to protect consumers from abusive and unscrupulous telemarketers. The rule has established the *Do Not Call Registry* (see Figure 19-1) that makes it easier for consumers to reduce the number of unwanted sales calls they get. The rule also requires telemarketing firms to identify themselves on

Terms The word *unscrupulous* describes someone without principles or something that would result from a lack of principles.

Figure 19-1 Once your number is registered, how long will it remain in the National Do Not Call Registry?

NATIONAL
DO NOT CALL
REGISTRY

Place your telephone number on the National Do Not Call Registry by calling toll-free 1-888-382-1222 (TTY: 1-866-290-4236) or going online to donotcall.gov. Registration is free.

Placing your telephone number on the Do Not Call Registry will stop all telemarketing calls except those from political organizations, charities, and people making surveys. You can expect fewer calls within three months of the date you sign up for the registry. Your number will stay in the registry for five years, until it is disconnected, or until you delete it from the registry. You may renew your registration after five years.

Telemarketers are required to search the registry every three months and avoid calling any phone numbers that are on the registry.

If you receive telemarketing calls after you have registered your telephone number and it has been in the registry for three months, you can file a complaint at donotcall.gov or by calling toll-free 1-888-382-1222 (TTY: 1-866-290-4236). You will need to provide the date of the call and the name or phone number of the company that called you. Telemarketers who disregard this law can be fined up to $11,000 for each call they make.

Have you added your phone number to the Do Not Call Registry?

Caller ID technology. The name displayed by a telemarketer on a Caller ID must either be the business trying to make a sale or the company making the call. The display must also include a phone number that consumers can call and ask that the company no longer call them.

Under the Telemarketing Sales Rule:

- It is illegal for a telemarketer to call a consumer if the consumer has asked not to be called.

- Calling times are restricted to the hours between 8 A.M. and 9 P.M.

- Telemarketers must tell the consumer that it is a sales call, the name of the seller, and what they are selling before they make their pitch. If it is a prize promotion, they must tell the consumer that no purchase or payment is necessary to enter or win.

- It is illegal for telemarketers to misrepresent any information, including facts about their goods or services, earnings potential, profitability, risk or liquidity of an investment, or the nature of a prize in a prize-promotion scheme.

- Before consumers pay, telemarketers must tell them the total cost of the products or services offered and any restrictions on getting or using them or that a sale is final or nonrefundable.

- It is illegal for telemarketers to withdraw money from a consumer's checking account without the consumer's express, verifiable authorization.

- Telemarketers cannot lie to get consumers to pay, no matter what method of payment is used.

- Until the services are delivered, consumers do not have to pay for (1) *credit repair* (promises to change or erase accurate negative information from a consumer's credit report; (2) *recovery room* (promises to recover previously lost money to telemarketing scams); or (3) *advance-fee loans* (promises to guarantee a loan for a fee paid in advance).

Consumers who have the slightest doubt about a telephone offer should ask for written information about the product, service, investment opportunity, or charity that is the subject of the call. They should resist high-pressure sales tactics and talk to a family member or friend before responding to the call. Consumers should never give out their bank account or credit card number to anyone who calls them. Similarly, they should never send money by courier, overnight delivery, or wire to anyone who insists on immediate payment.

900-Telephone-Number Rules

The 900 telephone number is used sometimes in telemarketing because the consumer, rather than the seller, pays the phone charge. Some consumers have been charged excessively for 900-number services or have not received the services advertised. Some 900-number scams disclose a cost per minute but do not reveal that you must listen for many minutes to hear all of the information. Other 900 services use announcers who speak so quickly that you need to call back to understand the message.

Some scams promote 900-prefix numbers for job or housing information. Once you place—and pay for—the call, you are told that the job or house is already taken. Some television promotions encourage children to call 900 numbers for "free" gifts or stories. Teenagers may call 900-number talklines to chat with other teens—usually at a cost-per-minute charge. They sometimes make these calls without telling their parents or not understanding that the phone calls cost money. Parents have received phone bills of thousands of dollars.

FTC regulations require that people who dial 900-prefix numbers be warned of the cost of the calls and be given a chance to hang up before being charged. In addition, telephone companies must block service to 900-prefix numbers if requested by the customer. Telephone customers must be sent pay-per-call disclosure statements annually, and any prefix other than 900 is prohibited for use as a pay-per-call service. Telephone companies cannot disconnect phone service to customers who refuse to pay for 900-number calls, and rules have been established for resolving billing disputes.

Popular telephone psychic Miss Cleo is a mere paid spokeswoman for Miss Cleo's Mind and Spirit Psychic Network. Millions have called the 900 number expecting Miss Cleo herself but talked to her "associates" instead.

Quick Quiz 19-3 True or False?

1. Dealers are not required to put a buyer's guide on all used vehicles they offer for sale.

2. Sales of consumer goods or services over $25 made away from the seller's regular place of business may be canceled within three business days after the sale occurs.

3. The seller, rather than the consumer, pays the phone charge when a 900 telephone number is used.

19-4 Consumer Product Safety Act

To protect consumers from dangerous products, Congress passed the Consumer Product Safety Act. The act established the Consumer Product Safety Commission (CPSC) to protect consumers from unreasonable risk or injury from hazardous products. The act covers products or component parts, American-made or imported, that are manufactured or distributed for sale to a consumer for personal use, consumption, or enjoyment.

Cross-Cultural Notes
The Saudi Arabian government enforces health and sanitation regulations on all imported foods. Any products containing narcotics, alcohol (including pharmaceutical drugs containing alcohol traces), and pork are strictly forbidden.

Example 19-4

Hundreds of people were being killed and thousands were being injured while riding on three-wheel, all-terrain vehicles (ATVs). The vehicles, which have large, soft tires, were designed for off-road use. Because of so many deaths and injuries, the commission banned the sale of new three-wheel ATVs in the United States in 1987. In addition, the commission required manufacturers of ATVs to spend over $8 million advertising to the public the safety problems with the three-wheel vehicles.

The commission can order the recall of products found to be inherently unsafe and dangerous. It has the authority to impose civil fines for violations of its standards and cease and desist orders. Private citizens, acting in their own behalf, may bring suit to establish or enforce a safety rule if the commission fails to act. Information may be obtained from the commission, and unsafe products may be reported by telephoning its hotline: 1-800-638-CPSC.

19-5 Consumer Leasing Act

The Consumer Leasing Act is a federal law requiring leasing companies to inform consumers of all of the terms of a lease of personal property. Consumers can use the information to compare one lease with another or to compare the cost of leasing with the cost of buying the same property.

The law applies only to personal property leased by an individual for a period of more than four months for personal, family, or household use. It does not cover daily or weekly rentals, leases for apartments or houses, or leases to anyone for business purposes.

Example 19-5

Guzman decided that her business could be managed much more efficiently if it had a computer. The cost of buying a computer, however, was more than Guzman could afford. She considered leasing one. The Consumer Leasing Act would not apply to Guzman's lease, because the computer was for business rather than personal use. She would be able to make a better decision, however, if she asked the leasing company for the same information the company would be required to provide to a consumer.

The law requires that consumers be given a written statement informing them of the full cost of the lease including the cost of any necessary licenses, taxes, or other fees. Consumers must be informed of any insurance requirements and of any penalties for late payment. They must also be told who is responsible for maintaining and servicing the property. In addition, they must be told whether or not they can buy the property, and, if so, when and at what price. The law also places a limit on the amount of a **balloon payment** (a very large final payment) to no more than three times the average monthly payments.

Advertisements of leases are also regulated by law. If an advertisement mentions the amount or number of payments, specifies a particular down payment, or states that no down payment is required, it must also disclose the total of regular payments, the consumer's responsibility at the end of the lease, and whether the consumer may purchase the property.

Quick Quiz 19-4 & 19-5 True or False?

1. The requirements of the Consumer Leasing Act apply to overnight rentals of videos from a video store.

2. The Consumer Leasing Act applies to the leasing of a copy machine to a business.

3. Consumers must be told, when they lease property, whether nor not they can buy it and, if so, when and at what price.

19-6 Consumer Credit Laws

People buy more on credit today than ever before. They borrow money from banks, credit unions, finance companies, and automobile manufacturers. They have charge accounts with stores, restaurants, and major oil companies. They often have more than one nationally recognized credit card. Due to this extensive use of credit, Congress has found it necessary to pass federal laws to protect the consumer.

Truth in Lending

Because lending institutions and businesses charge different rates of interest to consumers, if often pays to shop around before borrowing money or buying on credit. To help consumers know the truth about the cost of borrowing money, Congress passed the Truth-in-Lending Act. Under this act, lenders must disclose two important things to borrowers: the **finance charge** (the actual cost of the loan in dollars and cents) and the **annual percentage rate (APR)** (the true rate of interest of the loan). With this information, consumers can compare the cost of a loan from different lenders before deciding where to borrow. Surprisingly, the APR sometimes turns out to be greater than would appear at first glance.

Example 19-6

Hana borrowed $100 for one year and agreed to pay a finance charge of $10. If she kept the $100 for the year, and at the end of the year paid back the full amount together with the $10 finance charge, the APR would be 10 percent. If, on the other hand, she paid the $110 in twelve monthly installments of $9.17 each, the APR would be 18 percent. The latter rate is higher because during the course of the year she would have the use, on the average, of only about half of the $100.

The APR is computed with the use of a complicated mathematical formula. Tables provided by the Federal Reserve Banks are helpful in determining the exact APR on any loan.

The Truth-in-Lending Act regulates the advertising of credit terms. If an advertisement mentions one feature of credit, such as the amount of a down payment, it must also mention all other important terms, such as the terms of repaying the loan. Whenever an advertisement mentions a finance rate, it must be stated as an APR, and that term must be used.

Equal Credit Opportunity

The Equal Credit Opportunity Act was passed by Congress to ensure that all consumers are given an equal chance to receive credit. The law makes it illegal for banks and businesses to discriminate against credit applicants because of their sex, race, marital status, national origin, religion, or age or because they get public assistance income. The law must be followed by anyone who regularly extends credit, including banks, credit unions, finance companies, credit card issuers, and retail stores. Some of the rights to consumers under the act are as follows:

1. People who apply for credit may not be asked to reveal their sex, race, national origin, or religion; whether they are divorced or widowed; their marital status, unless they are applying for a joint account or a secured loan (marital status may, however, be asked in the states of Arizona, California, Idaho, Louisiana, Nevada, New Mexico, Texas, Washington, and Wisconsin—all of which are community property states [see Chapter 20]); information about their spouse, except in community property

states, unless the spouse is also applying for credit or will use the account; their plans for having or raising children; and whether they receive alimony, child support, or separate maintenance payments if they will not be relying on that income.

2. When deciding to extend credit, creditors must not consider the applicant's sex, marital status, race, national origin, or religion; consider the applicant's age, unless the applicant is a minor or is considered favorably for being over 62; refuse to consider public assistance income in the same manner as other income; and refuse to consider income from part-time employment, pensions, or retirement programs.

3. Applicants may apply for credit under the name given to them at birth, their married name, or a combination of both. They may receive credit without a cosigner if they meet the creditor's standards. In addition, applicants have a right to know within thirty days whether their application for credit has been accepted or rejected. If rejected, they have a right to know the reasons for the rejection within sixty days.

4. People may bring suit in a federal district court either individually or with others against creditors who violate this law. If they win, they may be awarded their actual losses plus attorney's fees, court costs, and punitive damages (damages designed to punish the wrongdoer).

Unauthorized Use of Credit Cards

Sometimes credit cards are lost, stolen, or used by people who have no authority to use them. Under the Truth-in-Lending Act, credit cardholders are not responsible for any unauthorized charges made after the card issuer has been notified of the loss, theft, or possible unauthorized use of the card. Such notice may be given to the card issuer by telephone, letter, or any other means. Even then, credit cardholders are responsible only for the first $50 of any unauthorized charges. Debit cards do not have this built in protection (see Chapter 28).

The credit cardholder can avoid the $50 liability if the credit card issuer has not included on the card a method to identify the user of the card, such as a signature, a photograph, or other means of identification. Card issuers must notify cardholders in advance of the potential $50 liability.

Credit card issuers are not allowed to send out unsolicited credit cards unless they are a renewal or substitute for a card already in use.

Fair Credit Reporting

The Fair Credit Reporting Act was passed by Congress to ensure that consumers are treated fairly by credit bureaus and consumer-reporting agencies. A consumer has the right to know all information (other than medical information) that is in its files about that consumer. A consumer also has the right to know, in most cases, the source of the information that is on file. In addition, a consumer has the right to be told the name of anyone who received a credit report in the past year (two years if the credit report relates to a job application).

The Opening Case Revisited
"Double Trouble"

If the charges occurred before VISA received notice of the theft, Falco will be liable for $50 of the unauthorized charges. If the charges occurred after VISA had received notice, Falco would have no liability.

Consumers who wish to know what information a credit bureau has on file about them can order a credit report on the Internet or from the following sources:

- Equifax, P.O. Box 740256, Atlanta, GA 30374 (800) 685-1111
- Trans Union, P.O. Box 1000, Chester, PA 19022 (800) 916-8800
- Experian, P.O. Box 949, Allen TX 75013 (888) 322-5583

There may be a fee of up to $9.00 for the report. If errors are found, credit bureaus must investigate and then correct or delete information that is inaccurate, incomplete, or obsolete. If the credit bureau retains information that the consumer believes to be incorrect, the consumer's version of the facts must be inserted in the file. Also, creditors are required to tell consumers the specific reasons for the denial of credit.

Fair Credit Billing

Errors are sometimes made in bills sent out by retail stores, credit card companies, and other businesses that extend credit. To make it easier for billing errors to be corrected, Congress has passed the Fair Credit Billing Act (FCBA). The law establishes a procedure for the prompt handling of billing disputes.

Under the act, when consumers believe an error has been made in a bill, they must notify the creditor within sixty days after the bill was mailed. The notice must identify the consumer and give the account number, the suspected amount of error, and an explanation of why the consumer believes there is an error. The creditor must acknowledge the consumer's notice within thirty days. Then, within ninety days, the creditor must conduct an investigation and either correct the mistake or explain why the bill is believed to be correct.

Another provision of the act gives consumers protection when they buy unsatisfactory goods or services with credit cards. If you have a dispute with a credit card purchase, do not pay the bill for the disputed item. Instead, notify the credit card issuer by telephone immediately. The credit card issuer will put the disputed amount on hold and send you a form to fill out explaining the dispute. The credit card issuer will attempt to resolve the dispute and inform you of the results. Then, if the problem is not corrected and suit is brought by the credit card issuer, the consumer may use as a defense the fact that unsatisfactory goods or services were received. For this law to apply, the initial transaction must have taken place in the consumer's state or within 100 miles of the consumer's mailing address. Creditors may not give cardholders a poor credit rating for exercising their rights under this act.

Background Informa-tion Many financial experts agree that consumers who find an error on their credit card statement should report the error in writing. A clearly written, businesslike letter explaining the problem creates a paper trail, which will help if the problem becomes complicated. Also the documentation will exist as a record of the number of times errors occur.

Fair Debt Collection Practices

Under the Fair Debt Collection Practices Act specific rules must be followed by companies that are in the business of collecting debts for others. Some of these rules are as follows:

1. When trying to locate someone, a debt collector may not communicate by postcard or tell others that the consumer owes money.

2. When the debt collector knows that the consumer is represented by an attorney, the debt collector may communicate only with the attorney.

3. A debt collector may not communicate with the consumer at any unusual or inconvenient time or place. Unless there are circumstances to the contrary, the convenient time for communicating with a consumer is between the hours of 8 A.M. and 9 P.M.

4. A debt collector may not communicate with the consumer at the consumer's place of employment if the debt collector knows that the employer prohibits such communication.

5. A debt collector may not communicate, in connection with the collection of a debt, with any person other than the consumer, the consumer's attorney, the creditor's attorney, or a consumer-reporting agency.

Getting Students Involved Invite the collection officer of a local bank and a representative of a local collection agency to your class. Have each describe their methods of collecting debts. Prepare students in advance to question the officers about what strategies they can legally use to collect on debt without the Fair Debt Collection Practices Act.

6. If a consumer notifies a debt collector in writing that the consumer refuses to pay the debt or wishes the debt collector to cease further communication, the debt collector must cease communication, except to notify the consumer of a specific action.

7. Debt collectors may not harass consumers or use abusive techniques to collect debts. The use or threatened use of violence or other criminal means to harm the person, property, or reputation of the consumers is not allowed. In addition, debt collectors may not use obscene or profane language or publish a list of those who allegedly refuse to pay debts. It is also illegal for a debt collector to cause a telephone to ring or to engage in repeated telephone conversations with the intent to annoy the consumer.

Debt collectors who violate this law may be sued for actual damages, punitive damages, and attorneys' fees.

Quick Quiz 19-6 True or False?

1. Lenders must disclose the finance charge and the annual percentage rate of loans to borrowers to help borrowers compare the cost of a loan from different lenders.

2. It is illegal for banks and businesses to discriminate against credit applicants because of their sex, race, marital status, national origin, religion, age, or because they get public assistance income.

3. Credit cardholders are responsible for all unauthorized charges made before the card issuer has been notified of the loss, theft, or unauthorized use of the card.

Summary

19-1 Consumer protection laws apply in transactions between a business and a consumer. State consumer protection offices help to enforce state consumer protection laws and sometimes assist consumers with individual problems. The FTC Act makes unfair or deceptive acts or practices in or affecting commerce unlawful. The federal law applies to businesses that deal with interstate commerce or that affect interstate commerce.

19-2 Unfair or deceptive acts or practices are prohibited by the FTC Act. Consumers need to be alert for telemarketing fraud and work-at-home schemes. Only free samples and items sent by charities may be mailed to people who did not request them. People who receive unordered merchandise through the mail may treat the merchandise as a gift. Bait-and-switch schemes are prohibited. True odometer readings on cars must be disclosed to buyers.

19-3 The FTC has established rules to help correct wrongdoings in the marketplace. The Used Car Rule

requires dealers to inform buyers of the warranties that go with the car by placing a Buyer's Guide in the window of each used car offered for sale. The Cooling-Off Rule gives consumers three days to change their minds when they enter into contracts away from the place of business of the seller. The Negative Option Rule protects consumers when they subscribe to magazines, CD clubs, or other plans that send products on an ongoing basis. The Can Spam Act is designed to reduce the use of unsolicited e-mail on the Internet. The FTC's anti-slamming law provides a remedy for consumers whose telephone service is changed without their permission. The Mail, Telephone, Internet, or Fax Rule requires sellers to ship orders within the time promised in their advertisements. If no time period is promised, they must ship orders within thirty days. If they cannot do so, they must give consumers the option to cancel the order and receive a refund. The Telemarketing Sales Rule helps protect consumers from abusive and deceptive telemarketers. Consumers can place their telephone numbers on the national Do Not Call Registry to stop most telemarketing calls. The FTC requires people who dial 900-prefix numbers to be warned of the cost of the call. The FTC also allows customers to block such services if requested.

19-4   The Consumer Product Safety Commission establishes safety standards for consumer products. The commission has the power to recall unsafe products and to impose fines on violators.

19-5   The Consumer Leasing Act requires companies that lease personal property to consumers for longer than four-month periods to disclose the full cost of the lease as well as other details of the transaction.

19-6   Many laws protect consumers who apply for or obtain credit. Lenders must make certain disclosures before lending money. It is illegal for creditors to discriminate against credit applicants because of their sex, race, marital status, national origin, religion, or age or because they get public assistance income. Credit cardholders are not responsible for any unauthorized charges made after the card issuer has been notified of the loss, theft, or possible unauthorized use of the card. Even then, cardholders are responsible only for the first $50 of any unauthorized charges. Consumers have the right to know all information about themselves (other than medical information) that is on file with a credit bureau. They also have a right to know the name of anyone who received a credit report in the past six months. A procedure has been established for the prompt handling of billing disputes dealing with charge accounts. Debt collectors are prohibited from harassing or abusing debtors when they attempt to collect debts.

Key Terms

annual percentage rate (APR), 355

bait-and-switch scheme, 347

balloon payment, 354

Buyer's Guide, 348

Can Spam Act, 349

class-action lawsuit, 346

commerce, 345

consent order, 345

consumer, 344

Cooling-Off Rule, 348

dunning letters, 346

finance charge, 355

interstate commerce, 345

intrastate commerce, 345

slamming, 349

spam, 349

Used Car Rule, 348

Questions for Review and Discussion

1. To what transactions do consumer protection laws apply?
2. What acts are declared unlawful by the Federal Trade Commission Act?
3. Name and describe four unfair or deceptive acts.
4. Describe the Used Car Rule, the Cooling-Off Rule, and the Mail, Telephone, Internet, or Fax Rule.
5. Highlight the main features of the Telemarketing Sales Rule, the 900-Telephone-Number Rules, the Negative Option Rule, the antispam law, and the antislam law.
6. Explain the purpose of the Consumer Product Safety Act and describe the powers of the Consumer Product Safety Commission.
7. What benefits do consumers receive from the Consumer Leasing Act?
8. What two important things must lenders disclose to borrowers under the Truth in Lending Act and what does the Equal Credit Opportunity Act prohibit?
9. How are credit cardholders protected under the Truth in Lending Act? What protection are credit cardholders given under the Fair Credit Billing Act?
10. List three rules that must be followed by debt collecting companies under the Fair Debt Collecting Practices Act.

Investigating the Internet

Full text versions of hundreds of the best federal consumer publications available can be found by visiting the Consumer Information Center website at: **www.pueblo.gsa.gov.** Pick a subject of interest to you by clicking one of the categories listed or click "search" to find your particular subject. Be sure to check out "Special Stuff" to see great information that isn't currently in their catalog. You may view the full text versions of the publications free or you can purchase printed copies at their online ordering site.

Cases for Analysis

1. Emerson told a store clerk that she needed some furniture right away to furnish her empty condo. The clerk showed Emerson a leather couch and chair, and said that they were in stock and could be delivered the following Friday. Emerson bought the items, paying for them with her credit card. The furniture was not delivered Friday as promised, and Emerson was told by the store that it could not be delivered for a month. What would you suggest that Emerson do to remedy the situation?

2. Barrett owned some apartment buildings that he operated for business purposes. He did not live in any of the apartments. The Adirondack Bottled Gas Corp. supplied the apartment buildings with a propane-tank storage system. A dispute arose, and in a suit against Adirondack, Barrett claimed that the consumer protection law applied to the transaction. Do you agree with Barrett? Why or why not? *Barrett v. Adirondack Bottled Gas Corp.,* 487 A.2d 1074 (VT).

3. Harriet Glantz lost her job. She was unable to find work for several months and fell behind in the payment of her debts. A debt collector telephoned her at 11:45 p.m., used profanity, and threatened to "take care of her" if she didn't pay the amount owed. Were Glantz's rights violated? Explain.

4. Ingram went to a used car lot in a large city and bought a used car. On his way home from the lot, the car that he had purchased broke down. The engine stopped running altogether. The used car lot refused to fix the car because the salesperson had written "as is" on the sales slip. Ingram had not been informed that the car was sold to him as is. Was a consumer protection law violated? Explain.

5. Prior to his marriage, Edward Garber had been in financial difficulty and had a poor credit rating.

His wife, Natalie, applied for a credit card in her family name, fearing that she would be turned down if she used her married name of Garber. She was told that she must use her married name on a credit application. Could Natalie have used her family name when she applied for credit? Explain.

6. Horack bought a used Mustang from a used car lot. The odometer showed that the car had been driven only 30,000 miles. Later, while cleaning her car, Horack found a service receipt showing that the actual mileage on the car a year earlier was 45,000 miles. Was a law violated? Explain.

7. Carboni's Master Card bill contained several charges that she had not made. Upon investigation, she discovered that her credit card was missing from her wallet. She immediately notified the bank of the lost credit card. The unauthorized charges on the bill that she received amounted to $375. Did Carboni have to pay the full amount of the bill? Explain.

8. Delores Bierlein paid a $200 deposit toward the rental of the Silver Room at Alex's Continental Inn for her wedding reception. Later, Delores canceled the reception because her fiancé was transferred from Ohio to New York. The inn refused to refund Delores's deposit. The consumer protection law of that state requires suppliers to furnish receipts when they receive deposits. Delores was not given a receipt for her $200 deposit. When she sued for the return of the $200 deposit, the question arose as to whether this transaction fell within the consumer protection law. Do you think it does? Explain. *Bierlein v. Alex's Continental Inn, Inc.,* 475 N.E.2d 1273 (OH).

9. In response to a radio advertisement, Mr. and Mrs. Lancet telephoned Hollywood Decorators, Inc., and arranged for Mr. Wolff, a company representative,

to visit their home. During Wolff's visit, the Lancets signed a contract for interior decoration and paid a $1,000 deposit. Two days later, the Lancets canceled the contract by telephone and asked for the return of their deposit. Twelve days after that, the Lancet's attorney wrote a letter to the company renewing the cancellation. Were they bound by the contract they signed? Why or why not? *Hollywood Decorators, Inc., v. Lancet,* 461 N.Y.S.2d 955 (NY).

10. After receiving an unsuccessful surgical procedure designed to facilitate weight loss, Gatten brought

suit against the physician for violation of the state consumer protection law. That law read in part, "unfair methods of competition and deceptive practices in the conduct of any trade or commerce are unlawful." Gatten based her case on statements made to her about her course of treatment and the probable results of that treatment. Does the unsuccessful treatment by a physician fall within the consumer protection law? Explain. *Gatten v. Merzi,* 579 A.2d 974 (PA).

Quick Quiz Answers

19-1	19-2	19-3	19-4 & 19-5	19-6
1. T	1. T	1. F	1. F	1. T
2. T	2. F	2. T	2. F	2. T
3. F	3. T	3. F	3. T	3. F

Part 3 Case Study

Circuit City Stores, Inc. v. Commissioner of Revenue
Supreme Judicial Court of Massachusetts
439 Mass. 629 (MA)

Summary

Circuit City allowed customers to purchase items in Massachusetts and pick them up at a New Hampshire store, allowing them to avoid the 5 percent Massachusetts sales tax. Circuit City credited the sales to its Massachusetts stores and gave employees in those stores commissions for them. The Massachusetts Commissioner of Revenue assessed Circuit City $172,460 for these sales during a three-year period. Circuit City paid the tax in full and filed an application for an abatement, which was denied.

The Commissioner of Revenue asserts that title passed at the cash register in Massachusetts when Circuit City received payment and the receipt was handed to the customer. Circuit City takes the position that title did not pass until the purchased merchandise was physically placed in the customer's hands in New Hampshire. This is an appeal to the state's highest court.

The Court's Opinion

Justice Greaney

Our tax statutes provide no explicit definition of the term "title," and so we look for guidance to the Uniform Commercial Code (UCC), incorporated into the General Laws as Chapter 106. See *Associated Testing Lab., Inc. v. Commissioner of Revenue,* 429 Mass. 628; *Sherman v. Commissioner of Revenue,* 24 Mass. App. Ct. 64. See also 830 Code Mass. Regs. § 64H.6.7 (passage of title for sales tax purposes defined as in UCC). Section 2-401 of the UCC instructs on the concept of title. With respect to situations, as here, where "matters concerning title become material," § 2-401 (2) provides that, "[u]nless otherwise explicitly agreed title passes to the buyer at the time and place at which the seller completes his performance with reference to the physical delivery of the goods."

We discern no explicit agreement between the parties concerning passage of title. Circuit City claims that testimony at the hearing with respect to its handling of alternative location sales (i.e., that Circuit City does not book the sale, credit the sale, or consider the sale to have occurred until the product is physically released to the customer) indicates an understanding between the parties that the transaction that takes place in Massachusetts constitutes, not a concluded sale, but only an order for merchandise. We disagree. The events transpiring at the cash register in Massachusetts reflect a significant degree of understanding between Circuit City and its customers that a sale, and not a mere deposit on an order, has occurred. The customer sales receipt, although not a document of title, contains a description of the item or items purchased, as well as the time and date of the sale. The record suggests that, in an ordinary case, any period of warranty relevant to the purchase begins as of this date. The purchase price reflected on the receipt represents full consideration paid for the merchandise. From the vantage point of the customer, the sales receipt represents proof of his or her right to the purchased merchandise. The fact the sale is credited to the Massachusetts store, and the commission accorded the sales associate in Massachusetts, in our view, is indicative of an intent on Circuit City's part that more than an order for merchandise takes place in Massachusetts.

The physical retention of the merchandise by Circuit City is not dispositive of "the time and place at which the seller completes his performance with reference to the physical delivery of the goods" under the UCC. G. L. c. 106, § 2-401 (2). Section § 2-503 (1) describes acceptable methods of a seller's tender of delivery and states the following: "Tender of delivery requires that the seller put and hold conforming goods at the buyer's disposition and give the buyer any notification reasonably necessary to enable him to take delivery. The manner, time and place for tender are determined by the agreement and this Article, and in particular . . . tender must be at a reasonable hour, and if it is of goods they must be kept available for the period reasonably necessary to enable the buyer to take possession. . . ."

Under common law as well, title may pass although the goods are still in the actual possession of the vendor. See *Bristol Mfg. Co. v. Arkwright Mills,* 213 Mass. 172. As under the UCC, the inquiry centers, not on physical transfer of the goods, but on whether goods are placed within the actual or constructive possession of another. See *Mitchell v. LeClair,* 165 Mass. 308 ("Under a contract of sale, when the goods have been . . . appropriated and set apart, the vendor has done that which by the terms of the agreement makes the whole consideration payable; and so long as he remains ready to do whatever else is to be done to give the vendee the benefit of his purchase, he is entitled to receive the agreed price without deduction on account of his retention of his lien upon the property").

Here, Circuit City performed its obligations with respect to delivery when the sale was entered as an alternative location sale into Circuit City's DPS system and the purchased merchandise was "reserved" for the customer at the designated location. It was the customer from that point on who assumed responsibility for acquiring physical receipt of the purchased merchandise. The time of such receipt was placed by Circuit City within the customer's control and packaged as a sales option offered as part of Circuit City's over-all philosophy to "wow the customer." See R.A. Anderson, *Uniform Commercial Code § 2.401.90* (3d ed. rev. 2002) (seller always obligated to deliver goods, but performance of this duty may range from merely making goods available to buyer, shipping

goods to buyer, delivering goods at specified destination, making delivery of documents of title, or transferring title without delivery of goods or documents).

It is clear that, under the UCC, no title can pass under a contract for sale "prior to their identification to the contract." G. L. c. 106, § 2-401 (1). This was also true in common law. See *G.E. Lothrup Theatres Co. v. Edison Elec. Illuminating Co.,* 290 Mass. 189, 193 (1935) ("title cannot pass until goods are set apart and appropriated to the contract"). We reject, however, Circuit City's argument that "identification to the contract" cannot be made in alternative location sales prior to the time that the merchandise is physically removed from inventory and the serial number is scanned in the New Hampshire store. The reserve notation marked on the customer sales receipt for the purchased merchandise sufficiently reflects its status of being set aside, or identified, to that particular transaction. The Circuit City district manager described the reserving system as moving merchandise to a "phantom" location to await customer pick up, and, indeed, the situation presented to the customer is just as though the merchandise actually is set aside and waiting for the customer at the pick-up counter. The purchased merchandise in the alternative location sales at issue is, by its nature, fungible. Because customers do not choose items in a store such as Circuit City by a particular serial number, but only by make and model, identification by serial number is unnecessary to the sale. See *Chokel v. First Nat'l Supermarkets, Inc.,* 421 Mass. 631; *Cushing v. Breed,* 14 Allen 376, 380. . . .

We conclude that the alternative location sales in issue were taxable in Massachusetts under G. L. c. 64H, §2.

Questions for Analysis

1. What does Section 2-401 of the UCC instruct on the concept of title?

2. What does Circuit City claim that the testimony indicates?

3. What does the court say the sales receipt represents?

4. Under a contract of sale, according to *Mitchell v. LeClair,* when has the vendor done that which makes the whole consideration payable?

5. When did the court say that Circuit City performed its obligations?

6. When did the court say the merchandise was identified to the contract?

7. What was the holding of the Court?

Property

Part Four

The Opening Case

"A Happy Birthday?"

Angelique had a wonderful twenty-first birthday celebration. Her boyfriend gave her a digital camera, and her sister gave her a $50 gift certificate to a popular restaurant. Angelique's grandfather telephoned her from Florida to say his present to her was his convertible sports car. She could pick it up at his winter home in Florida any time. The next day, she received news that her grandfather had passed away in Florida before she had had time to pick up the car. She let a year go by before going to the restaurant to use the gift certificate and was told that the certificate had expired. She and her boyfriend ate there anyway, but after leaving the restaurant, Angelique realized that she had left her digital camera at their table. She learned from the restaurant manager that another party had found the camera and was supposed to have returned it to her. Later, the police found the camera at a pawn shop and identified it as hers. Is Angelique entitled to her grandfather's car? Could the restaurant keep the money that had been paid for the gift certificate? What duty did the restaurant owe to Angelique concerning her camera? Can she recover the camera from the pawn shop?

Chapter Outcomes

1. Give examples of tangible and intangible personal property.
2. Describe the methods of owning property with others.
3. Differentiate among lost property, misplaced property, and abandoned property.
4. Identify the requirements of a completed gift.
5. Explain the law that applies to stolen property.
6. Discuss the law of patents, copyrights, and trademarks.

20-1 Personal Property

Broadly defined, **personal property** is everything that can be owned other than real estate. It is divided into two kinds, tangible and intangible.

Tangible personal property is property that has substance and that can be touched, such as a book, a pair of jeans, or a television set. Also called goods, or **chattels,** tangible personal property is movable and includes animals and crops.

Intangible personal property, on the other hand, is property that is not perceptible to the senses and cannot be touched. Accounts receivables and stock certificates are examples of intangible personal property. Another name for this type of property is **chose in action,** which means evidence of the right to property but not the property itself. In addition to the items mentioned, chose in action includes money due on a note or contract, damages due for breach of contract or tort, and rights under insurance policies.

Ownership of Personal Property

When personal property is owned solely by one person, it is said to be owned in **severalty.** When it is owned by more than one person, it is said to be held in **cotenancy.** The types of cotenancies discussed here are tenancy in common, joint tenancy, and community property. Other forms of cotenancies are examined under real property in Chapter 22.

When two or more people own personal property as **tenants in common,** each cotenant's share of the property passes to his or her heirs upon death. In contrast, when two or more people own personal property as **joint tenants,** (sometimes referred to as **joint tenants with the right of survivorship**), each cotenant's share of the property passes to the surviving joint tenants upon death. Nine states recognize **community property,** which is property (except a gift or inheritance) that is acquired by the personal efforts of either spouse during marriage and which, by law, belongs to both spouses equally. The states that recognize community property are the following: Arizona, California, Idaho, Louisiana, Nevada, New Mexico, Texas, Washington, and Wisconsin. Spouses can leave their half of the community property by will to whomever they choose. If they die without a will, their share passes to their surviving spouse.

Lost, Misplaced, and Abandoned Property

The finder of lost property has a legal responsibility, usually fixed by statute, to make an effort to learn the identity of the owner and return the property to that person. Advertising the property in a general circulation newspaper is usually evidence of the finder's honest effort to locate the owner. Statutes in many states provide that if the finder of lost property has made an effort to locate the owner and has not been successful within a period specified by law, the property then belongs to the finder.

If lost property is found on the counter of a store, on a table in a restaurant or hotel, on a chair in a washroom, or in some similar public or semipublic place, it is considered not to be *lost* but to have been *misplaced.* It is reasonable to suppose that the owner will remember leaving it there and return for it. For this reason, the finder may not keep possession of the article but must leave it with the proprietor or manager to hold for the owner. If the property is found on the floor or in the corridor or any other place that would indicate it was not placed there intentionally, the finder may retain possession of the article while looking for the true owner. In this case, it is not likely that the owner would recall where it was lost.

Example 20-1

While walking along a beach one morning, Carlow noticed a plastic bag near the edge of the water. She opened the bag and discovered that it contained a large sum of money. In the bag with the money was a bank deposit slip made out in the name of a nearby seafood restaurant. Carlow had a legal duty to return the money to the restaurant.

The Opening Case Revisited
"A Happy Birthday?"

Misplaced Property Angelique's camera was misplaced rather than lost and should have been retained by the restaurant for Angelique to pick up.

State Variations
$800,000 dumped on a Florida highway by a Brink's armored truck was not considered to be lost or abandoned property under that state's law. The bad news for those people who ran off with $650,000 of the money is that they could be considered guilty of theft.

Suppose the bank deposit slip had not been in the bag and Carlow was unsuccessful in an attempt to find the rightful owner. After making a sincere effort to locate the real owner, and after a period of time set by state statute, Carlow would become the owner of the money.

When property is found and turned over to officials of a state, without any claim registered by the finder, the property becomes the property of the state after a period of time set by statute. The same rule applies to bank deposits and other claims that have been abandoned by persons in whose names such claims were registered. In these latter instances, a period of up to twenty years may be required to establish the right of the state to take title. In some states, gift certificate money that is unclaimed after a certain number of years is supposed to be transferred to the state under the abandoned property law. When property reverts to the state, it is said to **escheat.** Some states have statutes that remove gift certificates from their abandoned property law, treating them in different ways.

Abandoned property is property that has been discarded by the owner without the intent to reclaim ownership of it. Courts require clear and convincing evidence of both the desertion of the property by the owner as well as the owner's intent not to return to it before determining that property was, indeed, abandoned. With some exceptions, anyone who finds abandoned property has the right to keep it and obtains good title to it, even as against the original owner.

Old shipwrecks are often the subject of abandoned property cases. If an abandoned shipwreck is found outside the boundaries of a state, either the law of finds or the law of salvage applies. The *law of finds* gives ownership to the finder if all of the following apply: (a) the property is abandoned, (b) the finder intends to acquire the property, and (c) the finder has possession of the property. The *law of salvage* gives a **salvor** (one who salvages) the right to compensation for assisting a foundering vessel. **Salvage** is the reward given to persons who voluntarily assist a sinking ship to recover its cargo from peril or loss. By contrast, if an abandoned shipwreck is found in the submerged land of any state of the United States, the Abandoned Shipwreck Act of 1987 applies rather than the *law of finds* or the *law of salvage.* This Act gives states the right of ownership to shipwrecks found beneath their waters.

The Opening Case Revisited
"A Happy Birthday?"

Abandoned Property In states that treat unclaimed gift certificates as abandoned property, Angelique would be entitled to the value of the gift certificate if she claimed it before it became the property of the state.

> ### Example 20-2
>
> In 2004, the federal court awarded full ownership of a Civil War–era shipwreck to Odyssey Marine Exploration. The salvage company agreed to pay $1.6 million to an insurance company that had paid claims when the ship sank. The *SS Republic* was a side-wheel steamer that went down in 1865 while en route from New York to New Orleans after fighting a hurricane for two days. The salvage company discovered the shipwreck 1,700 feet below the surface of the Atlantic Ocean approximately 100 miles off the Georgia coast. Among other relics, the ship contained $400,000 (face value) of gold and silver coins, which may now be worth up to $180 million.

Gifts of Personal Property

People often make gifts of personal property. There are three requirements for a gift to be completed: the **donor** (the one giving the gift) must intend to make a gift, the gift must be delivered to the **donee** (the one receiving it), and the donee must accept the gift. Once all three requirements are met, the gift cannot be taken back by the donor. It is known as an absolute gift, or **gift *inter vivos*** (between the living).

The gift of an engagement ring is a conditional gift, given in contemplation of marriage. Most courts hold that the donor of an engagement ring is entitled to its return if the engagement is broken by mutual agreement or by the donee. A few courts allow the return of the ring even when the donor breaks the engagement. These courts theorize that it is better to break the engagement without penalty than to have an unhappy marriage.

Uniform Transfers to Minors Act Problems can easily arise when gifts are given to minors. Sometimes, parents or guardians use such gifts for themselves rather than for the minor. At other times, donors make gifts to minors and then change their minds and take the gifts back. Gifts to minors are often used as tax shelters. Formerly, wealthy parents in high tax brackets often made gifts to their minor children as a way to shift unearned income to lower-bracket taxpayers. The IRS has changed this practice with the so-called kiddie tax. Under current income tax rules, the first $750 of unearned income (dividends and interest) of a child under the age of fourteen is not taxed. On the other hand, unearned income between $750 and $1,500 is taxed at the child's income tax rate and, above that, at the parent's income tax rate.

The Uniform Transfer to Minors Act (UTMA), which has been adopted by most states, also prevents some of these problems. The act establishes a procedure for gifts to be made to minors. Under the procedure, minors are assured that gifts to them will either be used for their benefit or made available to them when they become adults. The income from gifts that are given to minors is taxable according to the kiddie tax rules mentioned above. The UTMA allows money, securities, real property, and tangible and intangible personal

State Variations In California, New York, and Wisconsin a donor who breaks an engagement is still allowed to recover the engagement ring. The theory being that the ring was given solely in contemplation of marriage, and once the marriage is called off the gift must be returned.

Getting Students Involved Have students work in groups to think of imaginary but possible situations in which the rights of a donor, a minor donee, or the parents or guardians of a minor donee could be violated if it weren't for the Uniform Transfers to Minors Act. Have the groups share their findings.

State Variations In the territory of Puerto Rico, every gift made by a person having no children or descendents is revoked if the donor, after the gift, has or adopts children, even if after the donor's death.

The Opening Case Revisited
"A Happy Birthday?"

No Car for Angelique Angelique would not be entitled to her grandfather's car because it had not been delivered to her before he passed away.

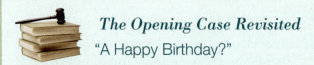

The Opening Case Revisited
"A Happy Birthday?"

Angelique Is the Owner Angelique can recover her camera from the pawn shop because it was stolen from her, and she is the true owner.

property to be transferred to a custodian for the minor's benefit. The age of twenty-one rather than eighteen is used as the age when the custodianship terminates, because the IRS uses that age to terminate certain trusts.

Gift *in Causa Mortis* A gift given during one's lifetime, in contemplation of death from a known cause, is a **gift *in causa mortis.*** A gift *in causa mortis* is conditional, and it is ineffective if the donor does not die as expected or if death is caused by circumstances other than those feared.

Getting Students Involved Break the class into small groups. Have them discuss what problems a court would face in a case in which there was an alleged gift *in causa mortis.* Would there be problems of proof if there was no written proof? How could this problem be rectified?

Example 20-3

Rossano was seriously ill following an abdominal operation. Realizing that death might be near, Rossano signed over a savings account to Hall, giving Hall the savings book with necessary notations of assignment. Rossano did die three weeks later, not because of the surgery but because of an automobile accident. Rossano's executor may declare the gift *in causa mortis* void and demand the return of Rossano's savings for the benefit of the estate.

Stolen Personal Property

Related Cases Goods obtained through fraud or misrepresentation are different from those stolen. In the case found in Example 16-2, p. 299, Dayton would be able to transfer good title for the speaker system he bought fraudulently. If he had stolen the speaker system outright, the title would always be void.

Although a presumption of title to goods usually follows possession of them, it is possible for a person to have possession of goods without having title, just as it is possible for a person to have title without having possession. Thus, a thief acquires no title to goods that are stolen and, therefore, cannot convey a good title. The true owner never relinquished title to the goods, and even an innocent purchaser, who acquired the goods in good faith and for value, would be obliged to return the goods to the owner. Title to stolen goods never left the true owner, and possession can always be regained by that owner if the goods can be found, no matter in whose possession they may be at the time.

Quick Quiz 20-1 True or False?

1. If lost property is found on a table in a restaurant, it is considered to be misplaced rather than lost.

2. Under the kiddie tax, a child's unearned income over $1,500 is taxable at the parent's income tax rate if the child has not reached age fourteen.

3. An innocent purchaser who buys stolen goods from a thief acquires good title to the stolen goods.

20-2 Intellectual Property

An original work fixed in a tangible medium of expression is **intellectual property.** It includes patents, copyrights, and trademarks. To encourage innovation and creativity, the government has enacted patent, copyright, and trademark laws. These laws give special rights to the owners of intellectual property.

Patents

A **patent** is a grant from the government that gives an inventor the exclusive right to make, use, and sell an invention for a period set by Congress, generally twenty years from the date the patent application was filed. When the period expires, the subject matter of the patent becomes **public domain;** that is, owned by the public and not protected by copyright. A patent may not be obtained if the subject matter of the patent would be obvious to a person having ordinary skill in the field. To be patentable, a device must be useful and must consist of some new idea or principle not known before. It must be a discovery as distinguished from mere mechanical skill or knowledge. There are three types of patents:

- utility patents
- design patents
- plant patents

A **utility patent** is a patent granted to someone who invents or discovers any new and useful process, machine, article of manufacture, or composition of matter, or any new and useful improvement thereof.

Example 20-4

A microbiologist invented a bacterium capable of breaking down crude oil. The U.S. Patent and Trademark Office denied a patent on the bacterium, claiming that it was alive and therefore not patentable. On appeal, the U.S. Supreme Court held that the live, human-made bacterium is patentable. The court said that such a microorganism is a "manufacture" or "composition of matter" within the meaning of the patent law.

A **design patent** is a patent granted to someone who invents a new, original, and ornamental design for an article of manufacture. In contrast to a utility patent, which protects the way an article is used and works, a design patent protects the way an article looks. Both design and utility patents may be obtained on the same invention if it has ornamental as well as functional characteristics. Design patents are granted for fourteen years instead of the twenty-year period that is given for other types of patents.

A **plant patent** is a patent granted to someone who invents or discovers and asexually reproduces any distinct and new variety of plant. Asexually grown plants are those that are reproduced by means other than from seeds, such as by the rooting of cuttings, by layering, budding, grafting, inarching, and so forth.

To obtain a patent, an inventor must file an application with the U.S. Patent and Trademark Office. The application is examined by the office, and a search is made for a similar device that has already been patented. Inventors may avoid disappointments by conducting preliminary searches themselves before filing patent applications. A search room is located in the Patent and Trademark Office in Arlington, Virginia, where the public may search and examine all U.S. patents granted since 1836. In addition, patent depository libraries are

Did You Know?

You can order printed copies of patents issued since 1974 for $2.49 each on the Internet by going to: **http://edisonpatents.com/.**

located in almost every state in the United States (at large public or university libraries) and are available for public use. For search purposes, patents are arranged according to a classification system of over 400 classes and more than 120,000 subclasses.

To be legally protected, a patented item must be marked with the word *patent* followed by the patent number. If this is not done, anyone making the same item without knowledge of the patent cannot be sued for damages. Some inventors put the words *patent pending* or *patent applied for* on their products. These words have no legal effect, however, other than informing others that an application for a patent has been filed. Patent protection does not begin until the patent is actually granted.

Any unauthorized making, using, or selling of a patented invention during the term of the patent is known as a **patent infringement.** A federal court can issue an injunction ordering an infringing party to discontinue the infringement. In addition, the court can order the infringing party to pay money damages to the owner of the patent.

Further Reading For answers to frequently asked questions on ideas, inventions, and patents by a registered patent agent log onto **http://patent-faq.com/.**

Cross-Cultural Notes Japan has developed a computerized system for filing and searching for patents. Previously, a patent search could take as long as thirty-six months. For more information log onto the Japanese Patent Office Homepage at **http://www.jpo-miti.go.jp/homee.htm.**

Example 20-5

In 1991, a federal court ordered Eastman Kodak Company to pay Polaroid Corporation $925 million damages for infringing on seven of Polaroid's patents on instant cameras and film. Previously, in 1985, the court ruled that there was an infringement and ordered Kodak to discontinue manufacturing and selling its instant camera products.

Some new products, such as drugs, must go through a governmental review period before they can be marketed. Because the products cannot be sold while they are being reviewed, the review period is not counted as part of the twenty-year term of the patent.

Universities, small companies, and nonprofit organizations are allowed to retain ownership of patents gained as a result of federal grants and contracts. The law does not provide this benefit to large corporations, however.

Transfers of Patent Rights Like other personal property, a patent may be sold, given away, or passed on to others through inheritance. The transfer of a patent is accomplished by the use of an assignment (see Chapter 13), which must be in writing. An assignment may transfer the entire interest in the patent to another or it may assign a part interest, such as a one-half interest or a one-sixteenth interest, to another. To be effective, as to subsequent purchasers of a patent, an assignment must be recorded at the Patent and Trademark Office within three months from its date.

In addition to being owned by individuals (including corporations), patents may be owned jointly by two or more people. Any joint owner of a patent interest, no matter how small a share, may make and use the invention without regard to the other owners unless they have agreed otherwise. Similarly, unless they have agreed otherwise, any joint owner may sell his or her interest in the patent without regard to the other owners.

Cross-Cultural Notes Brazil does not recognize patents on drugs.

International Law Most foreign countries have their own patent laws, which differ from U.S. laws. Anyone wishing to obtain a patent in a foreign country must file an application with that country's patent office. A treaty, called the Paris Convention for the Protection of Industrial Property, is adhered to by ninety-three countries including the United States. Under the treaty, each country guarantees to citizens of the other countries the same rights in patent and trademark matters that it gives to its own citizens. In addition, the treaty gives priority rights to people who apply for patents. This priority right means that when a patent application is first filed in a member country the applicant may, within one year (six months in the case of a trademark), apply for protection in all other member countries. The latter applications are regarded as having been filed on the same date as the first application was filed.

Another treaty, called the Patent Cooperation Treaty, which is adhered to by forty-one countries including the United States, provides for centralized filing procedures and a standardized application form.

Copyrights

A **copyright** is a right granted to an author, composer, photographer, or artist to exclusively publish and sell an artistic or literary work for the life of the author plus 70 years. In addition to books, magazines, and newspapers, works that may be copyrighted include such things as computer software, graphic arts, architectural designs, motion pictures, and sound recordings.

Example 20-6

A music-swapping service, Napster, Inc., allowed Internet users to search each other's hard drives for music files and download the songs in a compressed digital file format. Napster was forced to discontinue its online file-swapping business, however. The federal court held that the company infringed on at least two of the copyright holder's exclusive rights: the rights of reproduction and distribution.

Originality is a requirement for something to be copyrighted. Mere facts, standing alone, cannot be copyrighted because they are not original. If, however, facts are selected, coordinated, and arranged in an original manner, the presentation of them may be copyrighted.

The law allows some copying to be done without permission under the **fair use doctrine.** This doctrine provides that copyrighted material may be reproduced without permission if the use of the material is reasonable and not harmful to the rights of the copyright owner. The duplication of copyrighted materials for profit by a copyshop would not be a fair use because it would adversely affect the potential market for the copyrighted work. Copying items for such purposes as criticism, comment, news reporting, teaching, scholarship, and research is permissible. Libraries and archives may reproduce single copies of certain copyrighted materials for noncommercial purposes without obtaining permission of the copyright owner.

Example 20-7

Universal City Studios, Inc., and Walt Disney Productions, Inc., brought suit against Sony Corporation of America, manufacturers of Betamax. Universal and Disney claimed that Sony infringed on their copyrights by manufacturing and selling Betamax videotape recorders, allowing people to tape record their copyrighted films at home. The U.S. Supreme Court held in favor of Sony. The court said that noncommercial recording of material broadcast over the public airwaves that is intended for home use only is a fair use of copyrighted works and does not constitute copyright infringement.

The Computer Software Copyright Act includes computer programs among "writings" to which exclusive rights can be granted. The act defines a computer program as "a set of statements or instructions to be used directly or indirectly in a computer in order to bring about a certain result." Under the act, it is not an infringement for the owner of a copy of a computer program to make another copy provided that its duplication is essential in the use of a particular machine.

Teaching Tips Write to Information and Publications Section, Copyright Office, Library of Congress, Washington, DC 20559, or telephone (202) 278-8700 to obtain information and forms for obtaining a copyright. Write to the Commissioner of Patents and Trademarks, 2021 Jefferson Davis Highway, Arlington, VA 22202, for information on patents and trademarks. Distribute the materials and use them as a guide for discussion. Invite a patent attorney to visit the class to answer any questions.

Background Information Certain uses of copyrighted material are legal and regarded as "fair use." There are no definitive rules for fair use, but generally a court's decision is based on the purpose of use, nature of work copied, amount of work used, and effect on the market value of the copyrighted work. If works are copied for commercial gain, copyright laws are more likely to be enforced than those used for education. Making single copies from library materials is regarded as fair use.

Related Cases In
Fantasy, Inc., v. Fogerty (644
F. Supp. 1345), Fantasy
owned exclusive rights to
John Fogerty's 1970 song
"Run Through the Jungle."
In 1984, Fogerty wrote and
copyrighted, "The Old Man
Down the Road." Fantasy
claimed that "Old Man"
was simply "Jungle" with
different words. A California court found that if the
two songs were substan-
tially similar, then Fantasy
should prevail. A jury determined, after listening to
Fogerty's demonstration,
that the two songs were
different.

In the case of *Lotus Development Corp. v. Paperback Software International,* the federal court held that the copyright on the Lotus 1-2-3 spreadsheet program was infringed by the spreadsheet program VP-Planner. The court held that the organization, sequence, and structure of Lotus 1-2-3's menu commands were protected by its copyright. However, in a 1995 case, *Lotus Development Corp. v. Borland International Inc.,* the court held that Lotus's drop-down menu lists on computer screens could not be copyrighted. The court said that the Lotus menu command hierarchy is an uncopyrightable method of operation.

A Question of Ethics

Piracy is a form of copyright infringement. It includes the duplication, forgery, or direct distribution of software in a manner that violates the author's copyright. Can piracy be justified from an ethical standpoint?

Original material appearing on a website may be protected by copyright; however, a domain name may not be copyrighted. The Internet Corporation for Assigned Names and Numbers (ICANN), a nonprofit organization, administers the assignment of domain names through accredited registers. Procedures for registering the contents of a website can be found in Circular 66, *Copyright Registration for Online Works,* put out by the U.S. Copyright Office.

Copyright registration is accomplished by completing a simple form (see Table 20-1 and Figure 20-1) and sending it with a small fee and a copy of the work to the U.S. Copyright Office in Washington, DC. In the past, it was necessary to put the following notice on the work: © or the word *copyright* followed by the date and the name of the owner. This requirement became optional in 1989, however, when the United States adhered to the Berne Convention for the Protection of Literary and Artistic Works. Authors' and artists' works now have worldwide copyright protection as a result of the United States's adherence to three treaties: the Pan American Convention, the Universal Copyright Convention, and the Berne Convention.

The Digital Millennium Copyright Act was enacted by Congress in 1998, bringing copyright law into the digital age. The Act implements the provisions of two international treaties, which will give writers, artists, and other creators of copyrighted material global protection from piracy in the new millennium. Among other things, the Act:

- Makes it a crime to circumvent antipiracy measures built into commercial software.
- Outlaws the manufacture, sale, or distribution of code-cracking devices used to illegally copy software.

Table 20-1 Commonly Used Copyright Forms

Use This Form	To Obtain a Copyright For
TX	Published or unpublished nondramatic literary works
PA	Published or unpublished works of the performing arts
SR	Published or unpublished sound recordings
VA	Published or unpublished works of visual arts
SE	Serials (newspapers, magazines, newsletters, annuals, journals, etc.)
RE	Renewal of copyright

Copyright Office fees are subject to change. For current fees, check the Copyright Office website at *www.copyright.gov*, write the Copyright Office, or call (202) 707-3000.

C Short Form TX
For a Nondramatic Literary Work
UNITED STATES COPYRIGHT OFFICE

REGISTRATION NUMBER

TX _____ TXU _____
Effective Date of Registration

Application Received

Deposit Received
One _____ | Two

Fee Received

Examined By

Correspondence ❏

TYPE OR PRINT IN BLACK INK. DO NOT WRITE ABOVE THIS LINE.

Title of This Work: Alternative title or title of larger work in which this work was published:	**1**	
Name and Address of Author and Owner of the Copyright: Nationality or domicile: Phone, fax, and email:	**2**	Phone ( ) Fax ( ) Email
Year of Creation:	**3**	
***If work has been published,* Date and Nation of Publication:**	**4**	a. Date _____ _____ _____ *(Month, day, and year all required)* Month Day Year b. Nation
Type of Authorship in This Work: Check all that this author created.	**5**	❏ Text (includes fiction, nonfiction, poetry, computer programs, etc.) ❏ Illustrations ❏ Photographs ❏ Compilation of terms or data
Signature: Registration cannot be completed without a signature.	**6**	*I certify that the statements made by me in this application are correct to the best of my knowledge.** Check one: ❏ Author ❏ Authorized agent **X** _
OPTIONAL **Name and Address of Person to Contact for Rights and Permissions:** Phone, fax, and email:	**7**	❏ Check here if same as #2 above. Phone ( ) Fax ( ) Email

8 Certificate will be mailed in window envelope to this address:	Name ▼ Number/Street/Apt ▼ City/State/ZIP ▼	Complete this space only if you currently hold a Deposit Account in the Copyright Office.
		9 Deposit Account #_____ Name _____ DO NOT WRITE HERE Page 1 of ___ page

*17 U.S.C. § 506(e): Any person who knowingly makes a false representation of a material fact in the application for copyright registration provided for by section 409, or in any written statement filed in connection with the application, shall be fined not more than $2,500.

Rev: August 2003—30,000 Web Rev: August 2003 ♻ Printed on recycled paper

U.S. Government Printing Office: 2003-496-605/60

Figure 20-1 *Copyright Application.* Copyright forms with instructions and current fees can be found on the Internet.

- Exempts nonprofit libraries, archives, and educational institutions under certain circumstances.

- Limits Internet service providers from copyright infringement liability for simply transmitting information over the Internet.

- Limits liability of nonprofit institutions of higher education when they serve as online service providers for copyright infringement by faculty members or graduate students.

- Requires that licensing fees be paid to record companies for the use of musical recordings.

Trademarks

A **trademark** is any word, name, symbol, or device adopted and used by a manufacturer or merchant to identify the goods and distinguish them from those manufactured or sold by others. (See Figure 20-2.) It is different from a patent in that it does not apply to an invention or manufacturing process. Rather, it applies to the name or mark used to identify a product. The function of a trademark is to identify the source of a product, that is, the one who makes it. Coke, for example, is made only by the Coca-Cola company, and Wheaties are made only by General Mills. In a 1995 case involving green-gold SUN GLOW pads, the U.S. Supreme Court held that color alone can fit a definition of a trademark as a symbol to distinguish one brand from a competitor. Owners of trademarks have the exclusive right to use the particular word, name, or symbol that they have adopted as their trademark. Trademarks can be established in three different ways: under the common law, under a state statute, or under the Federal Trademark Act of 1946.

Common Law Trademarks Under the common law, trademarks may be established by usage rather than by registration with the state or federal government. To claim such a mark, the party must demonstrate that use of the mark has been of such quality and for such a duration that it has come to identify goods bearing it as originating from that party. The mark must have developed a secondary meaning—not merely identification of the product but rather identification of its producer.

Figure 20-2 The function of a trademark is to identify the source of a product. What is the source of this product?

The Underwood *devil* is thought to be the oldest registered food trademark still in use in the United States. William Underwood started a small condiment business in Boston in 1822, which mushroomed into a lucrative canned-food venture during the Civil War. Underwood's canned foods were among the staples that pioneers took with them on their way west. In 1867, Underwood's sons developed a process they called "deviling," in which they mixed ground ham with special seasonings to make a uniquely tasting food product. In 1870, the company obtained a patent on its world-famous trademark. The trademarks for Samson's (a man and a lion), Nabisco's Cream of Wheat, General Electric's GE Medalion, Carnation brand condensed milk, and Pabst Milwaukee Blue Ribbon Beer are all over one hundred years old.

Business Law in the News
Piracy Wars: Hollywood Turns Its Guns on Tech

For three years, Hollywood and Silicon Valley have maintained an uneasy truce. Beset by illegal copying, makers of movies, music, and software focused on file-swappers—not companies that made the technology pirates use. But all that changed in April, after a U.S. District Court in California threw out the studios' case against Grokster Ltd., saying the company could not be blamed if its software was used to make illegal copies. West Indies-based Grokster and other file-swapping networks thumbed their noses at movieland, trumpeting on their Web sites that a U.S. court had deemed them legit.

Those boasts broke the détente—and now Hollywood & Co. want revenge. On June 22, top Senate Judiciary Committee members Orrin Hatch (R-Utah) and Patrick Leahy (D-Vt.), took aim at Grokster and its ilk with legislation that would make it a crime to "induce" people to violate copyright—by implying, for example, that downloading pirated music is legal. Hatch and Leahy have the backing of Senate Majority Leader Bill Frist (R-Tenn.), Minority Leader Tom Daschle (D-S.D.), recording and movie industry heavies, and even Microsoft Corp.

That might be enough to squash the Groksters of the world, but the Inducing Infringement of Copyrights Act of 2004 is stirring up formidable opposition. In a July 6 letter to Hatch, 43 tech companies and trade groups, including Intel, eBay, Google, MCI, Sun Microsystems, and Verizon Communications said the bill could let content owners use lawsuits to kill off nascent technologies they find threatening. It might even undo the Supreme Court's 1984 Betamax decision, which declared that makers of VCRs couldn't be held liable if people used the machines to tape TV programs. "This gives Hollywood an extremely powerful litigation tool that will freeze investment in technology," says Philip S. Corwin, a lobbyist for Sharman Networks, distributor of KaZaA file-sharing software.

File-Swapping Marches On

CONTENT OWNERS SAY they have no beef with gadgets such as DVD burners or Apple Computer Inc.'s iPod. Sure, Hollywood has sparred over such devices before—witness the heat Apple took for its edgy "Rip. Mix. Burn." ad campaign a few years back. But this time, "the target is the bad actors that have hijacked technology," says Mitch Bainwol, a former Frist aide who now runs the Recording Industry Association of America, which helped draft the bill.

Hollywood wouldn't be calling in its chits if it weren't suffering setbacks. The RIAA has spent millions of dollars suing thousands of individuals over illegal file-swapping, but peer-to-peer downloads still measure in the millions. And political pushback is building. In the House, Representative Joe Barton (R-Tex.)—who is sympathetic to consumer complaints that content owners are overreaching—has replaced a starstruck Billy Tauzin (R-La.) as chairman of the Energy & Commerce Committee. And electronics makers are joining forces with P2P companies and consumer groups to try to turn back limits on copying. "The whole fight is escalating," says Gary Shapiro, CEO of the Consumer Electronics Assn. "This is a battle royal."

Hollywood vs. the Valley—a clash of titans indeed. But for the movie, music, and software industries, the real foe is technology—and all the campaign contributions in the world can't hold back that tide.

Questions for Analysis

1. Until recently, what group has been targeted in an attempt to stop illegal copying?

2. Why are such companies as Intel, eBay, and Google opposed to the passage of the Inducing Infringement of Copyright Act of 2004?

3. Why are some groups afraid to undo the Supreme Court's 1984 Betamax decision?

4. According to this article, what is the real foe of the movie, music, and software industries?

Source: Lorraine Woellert. "Piracy Wars: Hollywood Turns Its Guns on Tech," *BusinessWeek,* July 19, 2004, p. 45.

> ## Example 20-8
>
> Powers, who published a small newspaper, decided to name the paper the *Daily Planet*. D. C. Comics, Inc., publishers of the Superman comic book, brought suit to stop Powers from using that name. Evidence was introduced to show that the *Daily Planet* first appeared in the Superman story in 1940. Since then it has played a key role, not only in the Superman story, but also in the development of the Superman character. In addition, D. C. Comics, Inc., has used the Superman character in connection with many products born of the Superman story. These products have included school supplies, toys, costumes, games, and clothes. The court enjoined Powers from using the name *Daily Planet*. It held that D. C. Comics, Inc., had demonstrated an association of such duration and consistency with the *Daily Planet* that it had established a common law trademark in that name. The *Daily Planet* has, over the years, become inextricably woven into the fabric of the Superman story.

State Trademark Statutes Although the U.S. Constitution gives exclusive control to the federal government over patents and copyrights, it is silent about trademarks. Therefore, federal laws apply only to trademarks that are used in interstate commerce. Each of the fifty states has statutes that regulate the use of trademarks in intrastate commerce, that is, within the boundaries of the state. Although there has been an attempt to make the trademark laws of each state uniform, they differ substantially.

The Federal Trademark Act of 1946 The Federal Trademark Act of 1946, called the Lanham Act, provides for registration of trademarks with the U.S. Patent and Trademark Office. To be eligible for registration, the goods or services must be sold or used in more than one state or in this and a foreign country. A trademark cannot be registered if it consists of immoral, deceptive, or scandalous matter; matter that may disparage or falsely suggest a connection with persons, living or dead, institutions, beliefs, or national symbols, or which may bring them into contempt, or disrepute; the flag or coat of arms or other insignia of the United States or of any state or municipality, or of any foreign nation, or any simulation thereof; the name, signature, or portrait of any living individual, except with that person's written consent; the name, signature, or portrait of a deceased President of the United States during the life of a surviving spouse, if any, except by the written consent of the spouse; or a mark that so resembles a mark registered in the Patent and Trademark Office or a mark or trade name previously used in the United States by another and not abandoned, as to be likely to cause confusion when applied to the goods of the applicant, or to cause mistake, or to deceive.

An application to register a trademark may be filed six months before the mark is used in commerce. This reserves the mark so that no one else can use it during the reservation period. No registration will be issued, however, until the mark is actually used in commerce, which means "the bona fide use of a mark in the ordinary course of trade." One automatic extension of the six-month reservation period is allowed and other extensions are available upon a showing of good cause. The reservation period before the actual use of the mark in commerce may not exceed three years, however. In addition, to prevent trafficking in trademarks, the reservation of a trademark may not be sold or assigned to anyone other than a successor to the business of the applicant. A trademark registration remains in force for ten years and may be renewed for additional ten-year periods, unless it is canceled or surrendered by nonuse.

Anyone who registers a trademark may give notice that the mark is registered by displaying the following with the mark: "Registered in U.S. Patent and Trademark Office" or "Reg. U.S. Pat. & Tm. Off." or the letter R enclosed within a circle, thus: ®.

Companies can lose their trademark protection if the marks are used as a generic term by a large segment of the public for a long period of time.

Background Information Protecting copyrights, trademarks, and patents is a business in itself. For example, registered patent lawyers are available for conducting patent searches, and the American Society of Composers and Publishers, which protects musical copyrights, hires services to research how often copyrighted works are used.

Further Reading For an excellent overview of intellectual property law, read *Copyright and Trademark Law for the Non-Specialist,* by Chairman Richard Dannay (New York: Practicing Law Institute, 1995).

Cross-Cultural Notes The characters, visual features, and names of comic strips are protected by trademarks. Licensing programs have been established that allow certain companies to borrow the trademarks for advertising purposes. The worldwide popularity of comic strips make these trademarks—from Peanuts chopsticks in Japan to Garfield frozen lasagna in Brazil—a big international business.

> ## Example 20-9
>
> In the 1980s, the Murphy Door Bed Co. was refused a trademark registration for its Murphy bed. The court held that the name Murphy bed had been appropriated by the public to designate a type of bed that folds into a wall or closet.

Former trademarks that have been lost by becoming generic terms by a large segment of the public include cornflakes, cube steak, dry ice, escalator, high octane, kerosene, lanolin, linoleum, nylon, raisin bran, shredded wheat, trampoline, and yo yo.

Companies often use a word such as *brand* after the name of their product in their advertisements to remind people that the product name is a registered trademark. They also place advertisements in writers' magazines and other journals (such as the one shown in Figure 20-3) pointing out that fact.

Terms   *Public domain* is a term that refers to property rights belonging to the community at large. Property in the *public domain* (e.g., Big Brother, nylon) is unprotected by copyrights or patents and can be used by anyone.

Figure 20-3 Why does Xerox not want its name used indiscriminately? (Reprinted with permission of the Xerox Corporation.)

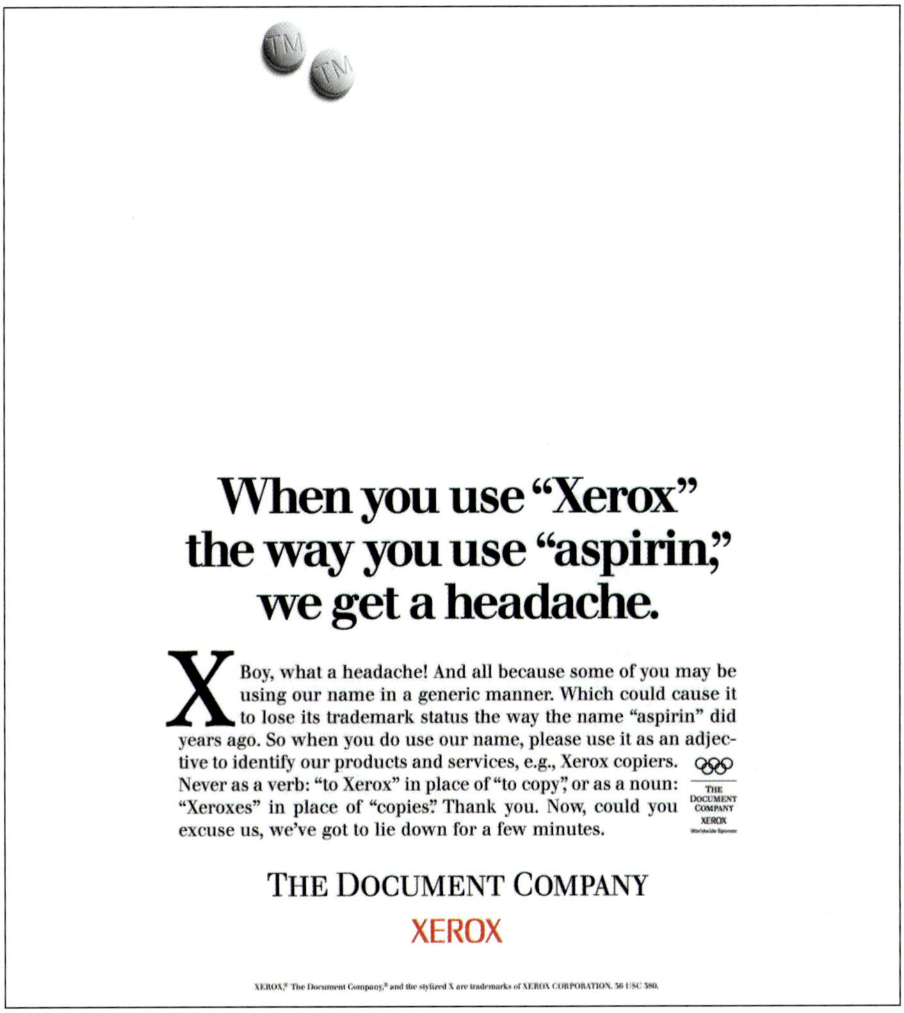

When you use "Xerox" the way you use "aspirin," we get a headache.

XBoy, what a headache! And all because some of you may be using our name in a generic manner. Which could cause it to lose its trademark status the way the name "aspirin" did years ago. So when you do use our name, please use it as an adjective to identify our products and services, e.g., Xerox copiers. Never as a verb: "to Xerox" in place of "to copy," or as a noun: "Xeroxes" in place of "copies." Thank you. Now, could you excuse us, we've got to lie down for a few minutes.

THE DOCUMENT COMPANY
XEROX

XEROX,® The Document Company,® and the stylized X are trademarks of XEROX CORPORATION. 56 USC 380.

Quick Quiz 20-2 True or False?

1. A patent gives an inventor the exclusive right to make, use, and sell an invention for a period set by Congress, generally twenty years from the date the patent was granted.

2. A copyright gives the exclusive legal right to reproduce, publish, and sell a work for the life of the author plus seventy years.

3. A federally registered trademark remains in force for ten years but may be renewed for additional ten-year periods.

Summary

20-1 Personal property is everything that can be owned except real estate. Anyone who finds lost property must make a reasonable effort to find the owner. Misplaced property must be turned over to the manager of the place where it is found. Abandoned property is property that has been intentionally discarded by the owner and may be kept by a finder. The Abandoned Shipwreck Act gives states the right to shipwrecks beneath their waters. For a gift to be completed, the donor must intend to make a gift, it must be delivered to the donee, and the donee must accept the gift. A thief acquires no title to goods that are stolen and, therefore, cannot convey a good title to others.

20-2 A patent gives the owner the exclusive right to make, use, or sell an invention for a term set by Congress, generally twenty years from the date the patent application was filed. Copyrights give their owners the exclusive right to publish their work for the life of the author plus seventy years. Trademarks, which protect product names and marks, may be established either by usage or by registration. Registered trademarks remain in force for ten years and may be renewed.

Key Terms

abandoned property, 368

chattels, 366

chose in action, 367

community property, 367

copyright, 373

cotenancy, 367

design patent, 371

donee, 369

donor, 369

escheat, 368

fair use doctrine, 373

gift *in causa mortis,* 370

gift *inter vivos,* 369

intellectual property, 371

joint tenants, 367

joint tenants with the right of survivorship, 367

patent, 371

patent infringement, 372

personal property, 366

plant patent, 371

public domain, 371

salvage, 368

salvor, 368

severalty, 367

tenants in common, 367

trademark, 376

utility patent, 371

Questions for Review and Discussion

1. What is community property, and how many states recognize it?
2. When may someone who finds lost property claim ownership of it?
3. How has the Abandoned Shipwreck Act of 1987 affected the law of finds and the law of salvage?
4. What are the requirements for a gift to be completed?
5. What assurances are minors and donors given by following the procedures of the Uniform Transfers to Minors Act?
6. What kind of title is given by a thief who sells stolen goods to an innocent person? Explain.
7. What do patents protect?
8. What do copyrights protect?
9. What is the protection given by the registration of a trademark?
10. How can companies lose their trademark protection? Name some products that have lost trademark protection in this way.

Investigating the Internet

Log onto the U.S. Copyright Office's website at **www.copyright.gov** to find information, including forms and current fees, about copyrighting original material that you would like to protect.

Cases for Analysis

1. Susan Lacroix's Yerf-Dog go-kart was stolen from her driveway one evening when she went inside to have dinner. The thief placed an advertisement in the newspaper, and sold it to Ronald Casey for half of what it was worth. Later, Lacroix recognized the kart in Casey's yard and identified it as hers through its serial number. In a suit brought by Lacroix for the return of the go-kart, Casey argued that he now had title to the kart because he paid for it without knowledge that it had been stolen. Is Casey's argument sound? Explain.

2. Rural Telephone Service Company published a telephone directory consisting of white and yellow pages. Rural obtained data for the directory from its telephone customers who provided their names and addresses when they applied for telephone service. Feist Publications, Inc. specialized in publishing more extensive telephone directories covering a much larger area than Rural's coverage. When Rural refused to license its white pages listings to Feist for a directory covering eleven different telephone service areas, Feist extracted the listings it needed from Rural's directory and published them without Rural's consent. Is Feist liable for copyright infringement? Why or why not? *Feist Publications, Inc. v. Rural Tel. Service Co.,* 499 U.S. 340 (U.S. Sup. Ct).

3. Michigan Document Services, Inc., a commercial copyshop, reproduced without permission substantial segments of copyrighted works of scholarship, bound the copies into "course-packs," and sold them to students for use in fulfilling reading assignments given by professors at the University of Michigan. The company argued that it could legally do this under the "fair use" doctrine of the copyright law. Do you agree? Explain. *Princeton University Press v. Michigan Document Services, Inc.,* 99 F.3d 1381 (6th Cir.).

4. Pollard found a valuable first edition that someone had dropped on the street. She took the book home,

placing it with others in a collection of first editions. The owner's name could not be found in the lost book, and Pollard made no effort to locate the owner. Did she thus have title to the book? Explain. See also *Doe v. Oceola,* 270 N.W.2d 254 (MI).

5. Vincent Hartwell admired a valuable book collection on his uncle's bookshelf. To Hartwell's surprise, his uncle said that he planned to give the books to Hartwell as a gift and that he could have them at that moment. Hartwell replied that he was living in a dormitory and had no place to keep the collection. His uncle said, "Consider the books yours. I'll keep them here, and when you're ready for them, come and get them." Hartwell thanked his uncle and left for school. His uncle died a week later. Hartwell's cousin, Kathleen Lane, inherited the uncle's entire estate. She claimed that the valuable book collection belonged to her. Who was the legal owner, Hartwell or Lane? Explain.

6. In the course of writing a research paper for one of her classes, Kirby copied a number of pages from several books at the library. She took the copies home to continue her research in a more relaxed atmosphere. A friend in her law class told Kirby that she had violated the copyright laws by copying the pages from the various books. Was the friend correct? Why or why not?

7. In his will, Gavegnano left all his tangible personal property to his daughter, Caroline. At the time of his death, he owned nineteen thoroughbred horses. In addition, a cashier's check made payable to him for $33,000 was found among his belongings. The lower court judge held that the horses and the check were tangible personal property and should be given to Caroline under the terms of the will. Caroline's brothers appealed the decision, claiming that neither the horses nor the check were tangible personal property. Were Caroline's brothers correct? Explain. *Pagiarulo v. National Shawmut Bank,* 233 N.E.2d 213 (MA).

Quick Quiz Answers

20-1 1. T   20-2 1. F
      2. T   2. T
      3. F   3. T

Chapter 21 | Bailments

The Opening Case
"A Rough Night's Sleep"

The Rosiers were guests at the Gainesville Holiday Inn. Before retiring for the night, they locked their outside door but did not secure the chain latch. At about 1:30 A.M., they awoke to find a ski-masked burglar in the room at the foot of their bed. Mr. Rosier jumped from the bed and tackled the intruder. A struggle ensued. Mr. Rosier was stabbed twice, and Mrs. Rosier was also injured. In a suit brought by the Rosiers against the Inn, a security expert testified that the type of lock used in the door was a low-grade, residential lock. The expert said that the industrywide standard was a mortise lock, which when locked from the inside would secure the door with a dead bolt and could not be opened by a maid's passkey or a duplicate room key. Was the Inn responsible to the Rosiers for their injuries?

Chapter Outcomes

1. Determine when a bailment occurs.
2. Name and describe the principal types of bailments.
3. Explain innkeepers' duties of care to their guests.
4. Describe the liability imposed upon common carriers for damages to goods transported by them.
5. Discuss the duties and obligations of carriers toward passengers and their baggage.
6. Identify the classes of warehouses and describe their rights and duties.
7. Explain a warehouser's lien.

21-1 Bailments of Personal Property

A **bailment** is the transfer of possession and control of personal property to another with the intent that the same property will be returned later. Renting a movie from a video shop, borrowing a friend's car, and leaving clothes at the cleaners are examples of bail-ments. The person who transfers the property is the **bailor.** The person to whom the property is trans-ferred is the **bailee.** In a bailment, neither the bailor nor the bailee intends that title to the property should pass. The bailee has an obligation to return the same property to the bailor, or to someone the bailor desig-nates, at a later time. A bailment does not occur when the person in possession of the property has no control over it. For example, it is not a bailment when someone parks a car in an unattended parking area. (See Figure 21-1.)

When you rent a DVD, you have the responsi-bility as the bailee to return that DVD to the place from which you rented it.

Example 21-1

Sewall parked his car in the same parking lot he used each day. He paid the atten-dant, locked the car, and took the keys with him. The attendant remained on duty only in the morning and left the lot unattended for the rest of the day. There were several entrances and exits to the lot. When Sewall returned for his car, he discovered that it had been stolen. The court held that this was not a bailment. The attendant had exercised no control over the vehicle whatsoever. Instead, it was simply a rental of a parking space. Sewall lost the case against the parking lot owner because he could not prove that the employees had committed a negligent act.

Terms Although the terms *bail, rent, lease, lend,* and *borrow* are often used in-terchangeably to refer to a form of bailment, each is regulated by its own spe-cific set of laws that ex-tends beyond or replaces regular bailment laws. For example, in many states, leasing is now regulated by Article 2A of the UCC guidelines for sales con-tracts rather than by bail-ment laws because many leasing agreements in-clude an option to buy (see Chapter 15).

In contrast, courts have held it to be a bailment when someone parks a car in a garage or lot that has an attendant present at all times to check cars going in and out.

Example 21-2

Eduardo drove his car to the entrance of the public parking garage at Logan Inter-national Airport in Boston. He entered the garage through a gate by taking a ticket from a machine, drove into the garage, parked and locked his car, and took the keys with him. The exit from the garage was attended at all times. When Eduardo returned four days later, he discovered that his car had been stolen. The court held that this was a bailment because the parking garage had possession and control of the vehicle. Eduardo recovered the value of the car from the parking garage be-cause the garage could not prove that it had used reasonable care to prevent the theft of the car.

When an individual loans goods to another with the intention that the goods may be used and later replaced with an equal amount of different goods, it is not a bailment. Instead, it is known as ***mutuum.***

THIS IS A SELF-PARKING FACULTY CLAIM CHECK. PLEASE BE CAREFUL in parking your car so that you do not damage your own car or those of your fellow parkers. PARK AT YOUR OWN RISK. THIS IS NOT A BAILMENT. EMPLOYEES NOT AUTHORIZED TO ACCEPT DELIVERY OF YOUR CAR.

This check is a Contract of Lease between Middletown Parking Authority, Lessor, and you as Tenant, for a parking space. By renting the space, you agree that there is no Bailor-Bailee relationship between you and the Lessor. Term of lease from hour to hour, rental as payable.

1. Lessor is not responsible for personal property; and Lessor assumes no liability for fire, theft, or casualty except from its own negligence.

2. Any suits or actions against Lessor for any claim arising out of this lease shall be filed within ninety (90) days of date of occupancy of the leased premises.

MIDDLETOWN PARKING AUTHORITY
FIRST & MAIN STREETS

**PLEASE PAY CASHIER
BEFORE GETTING IN YOUR CAR**

Figure 21-1 The small print on this parking-garage ticket states that it is not a bailment. Some states, including Massachusetts, have statutes making disclaimers on signs and tickets in parking lots and garages void as against public policy.

Getting Students Involved Have students keep lists of the temporary transactions of personal property in which they are involved over a course of a week. Next, have them determine which of their transactions are bailments and which are *mutuums*. For each bailment, students should identify the bailor and the bailee and determine if the bailment is involuntary, gratuitous, for the sole benefit of the bailor, for the sole benefit of the bailee, or for mutual benefit. For each mutual benefit bailment, students should identify if the bailment is a pledge, contract for the use of goods, contract for the custody of goods, or contract for work or service on goods.

Example 21-3

Susan Chin borrowed a cup of flour from her neighbor. She used the flour in a cake that she made that evening. She returned a cup of flour to her neighbor the next day after shopping at a grocery store. The loan of the flour was a *mutuum* rather than a bailment because the parties did not intend that the identical particles of flour that were borrowed would be returned.

Quick Quiz 21-1 True or False?

1. It is a bailment when someone parks a car in an unattended parking lot.

2. In a bailment, the bailor intends to pass title to the bailee.

3. A mutuum is the transfer of possession and control of personal property to another with the intent that the same property will be returned later.

21-2 Principal Types of Bailments

There are three principal types of bailments: bailments for the sole benefit of the bailor, bailments for the sole benefit of the bailee, and mutual-benefit bailments. In the first two types, called **gratuitous bailments,** property is transferred to another person without either party's giving or asking for payment of any kind. Such bailments lack consideration; therefore, they may be rescinded at any time by either party. Parties to such agreements usually consider them only as favors. In reality, however, definite legal responsibilities are placed upon both the bailor and the bailee.

Bailments for Sole Benefit of Bailor

When possession of personal property is transferred to another for purposes that will benefit only the bailor, **bailments for the sole benefit of the bailor** result.

Example 21-4

Conte agreed to deliver Higgins's watch to a jewelry shop, which she would pass on the way to work. Higgins gave her the watch, and she placed it in a briefcase with other valuables. Conte was promised no payment for this act. It was a favor. It was also a bailment for the sole benefit of the bailor.

In a bailment for the sole benefit of the bailor, the bailee owes a duty to use only *slight care,* since the bailee was receiving no benefit from the arrangement. The bailee was required only to refrain from **gross negligence.** This is very great negligence—much more serious than ordinary negligence.

Example 21-5

The Martins asked two girls, Bell and Christian, to live in their home during the Martins's vacation. The contents of the house were badly damaged by fire when one of the girls left a pan of grease unattended on a range burner. This was a gratuitous bailment for the sole benefit of the bailor. Bell and Christian were not liable for damage to the Martins's property because they were not grossly negligent.

The bailee has no implied right to use the bailor's property in a bailment for the sole benefit of the bailor. Use without permission is technically a tort of conversion on the part of the bailee; it would make the bailee liable for any damages that might result, even if the bailee had used great care and was not guilty of negligence. (Conversion is the civil wrong that arises when one unlawfully treats another's property as one's own.)

Example 21-6

Lindstrom agreed to care for Holbart's car while Holbart was absent from the city. Although permission to use the car had not been given. Lindstrom drove the car many times to save having to walk.

If Lindstrom had become involved in an accident as a result of the unauthorized use of Holbart's car, he would have been liable to Holbart for damages. In a case like this, it would not even be necessary for the bailor to prove lack of care by the bailee.

Background Information When Samuel Clemens (Mark Twain) asked to borrow a book from a neighbor, the neighbor agreed, but said, "I must ask you to read it here. I make it a rule never to let any book go out of my library." Several days later, when the neighbor asked to borrow Clemen's lawnmower, Clemens replied, "Why certainly. You're more than welcome to it. But I must ask you to use it here. You know that I make it a rule."

Further Reading *Simple Contracts for Personal Use,* by Stephen Elias (Berkeley, CA: Nolo Press, 1991), contains examples of different types of contracts, including contracts to store and lend personal property.

Getting Students Involved Ask students to think of examples of types of property that might commonly be involved in the tort of conversion in a bailment for the sole benefit of a bailor. Invite students to share experiences they may have had in which someone used their property without permission while temporarily storing it or caring for it.

In a bailment for the sole benefit of the bailor, the bailor has a duty to reimburse the bailee for any expenses the bailee might have in the care of the property.

Bailments for Sole Benefit of Bailee

Transactions in which the possession of personal property is transferred for purposes that will benefit only the bailee are gratuitous **bailments for the sole benefit of the bailee.**

Example 21-7

Martin asked Kahn if she might use the latter's car for a trip she planned to make to Kansas City. Kahn agreed to lend the car, asking nothing in return for this favor. The bailment was created for the sole benefit of the bailee, Martin.

In a bailment for the sole benefit of the bailee, the bailee is required to use *great care* because possession of the goods was solely for the bailee's benefit. The bailee is responsible for **slight negligence,** which is the failure to use that degree of care that persons of extraordinary prudence and foresight are accustomed to use.

Example 21-8

Perez borrowed her aunt's car and used it to drive 7,000 miles on a cross-country trip. At no time during the entire trip did she check the oil in the engine. This resulted in damage to the motor. Since Perez did not exercise great care, she will be responsible for any repairs resulting from her negligence.

In this type of bailment, the bailee has the right to use the property for the purposes for which the bailment was created. Use for other purposes or use over a longer period of time than provided for in the agreement will make the bailee responsible for any damages that may result to the property, regardless of the amount of care exercised.

Example 21-9

Robbins used Castro's chainsaw to cut up a small tree that fell during a storm. The cutting of the tree was all that Castro had agreed to allow Robbins to do with the saw. Robbins decided to cut up other timber awaiting the fireplace. Through no fault of Robbins's, the saw's engine caught fire. Even though Robbins was not responsible for the fire, he was obligated to reimburse Castro for the damage because he used the saw for a purpose other than that to which was agreed.

Any *ordinary* and *expected expense* incurred in the use of another's property must be borne by the bailee. For example, gas and oil for the operation of the chainsaw in Example 21-9 should be paid for by Robbins. On the other hand, repairs and adjustments not caused by ordinary use or damages not attributed to the bailee's negligence become the responsibility of the bailor. The bailee is not obligated to replace parts that break down because of the gradual use and depreciation of the other's property over an extended period. If the chainsaw had simply worn out through no fault of Robbins, he would not have been responsible.

Example 21-10

Swanson, with Oberly's permission, took Oberly's motorcycle on a trial ride. Every precaution was taken to avoid damage. Nevertheless, on the way home, the front tire blew, and Swanson found it necessary to buy a new tire. The old tire had been badly worn in many places. The blowout was not caused by Swanson's negligent use. Oberly, the bailor, would be responsible for any *unusual* and *unexpected* expenses resulting from the tire blowout, including the obligation of reimbursing Swanson for the tire.

Mutual-Benefit Bailments

When personal property is transferred to a bailee with the intent that both parties will benefit, a **mutual-benefit bailment** results. The ordinary bailments involving business transactions are usually mutual-benefit bailments in which the business person is paid for the services.

Renting an item such as a car or a videotape, leaving a car at a garage to be repaired or a suit to be cleaned at a cleaners, placing one's property in storage, and leaving a diamond ring at a pawn shop (a *pledge*) in exchange for a loan of money are examples of mutual-benefit bailments.

Example 21-11

Cohen borrowed $7,400 from the American Arlington Bank. As security for the loan, the parties signed a bailment agreement making the bank the bailee of Cohen's valuable painting of King George III of England, allegedly one of three portraits of the king by eighteenth-century painter George Ramsey. The painting was hung in the office of the bank's vice president. This agreement was a pledge because the bank had possession and complete control over the painting while the loan was outstanding. The UCC governs the subject of pledges, which is discussed in more detail in Chapter 30.

A **consignment contract** is a type of mutual benefit bailment in which the **consignor** entrusts goods to the **consignee** for the purpose of selling them. If the goods are sold, the consignee, known as a *factor,* will forward the proceeds, less a fee, to the consignor. If they are not sold, they will be returned.

In a mutual-benefit bailment, the bailee owes a duty to use *reasonable care.* **Reasonable care** means the degree of care that a reasonably prudent person would use under the same circumstances and conditions. The bailee is responsible for **ordinary negligence,** which is failing to use the care that a reasonable person would use under the same circumstances.

Example 21-12

Champine stored his boat, motor, and trailer in Field's building for the winter for $10. Champine expressed some doubts about the soundness of the building, particularly concerning the structure of the roof. Field assured him that the building was safe. The

(Continued)

When people take their possessions to a pawn shop, they receive money in the form of a loan from the pawnbroker. If the money is repaid with interest by a specified date, people can require their belongings. If not, the pawnbroker can sell the item.

Did You Know?

Pawnbroking, a type of mutual-benefit bailment, began at least 3,000 years ago in ancient China. The borrower deposits an item of personal property, such as a watch, ring, or musical instrument with the pawnbroker as collateral for a loan. When the loan is repaid with interest on or before the due date, the personal property is returned to the borrower. If the borrower defaults, the collateral becomes the property of the pawnbroker, who sells it at retail usually below the market price.

Example 21-12 (Continued)

roof collapsed after a winter snowstorm, damaging Champine's boat. In allowing Champine to recover from Field, the court said that the relationship imposed a duty on the bailee to use ordinary care, which he failed to do.

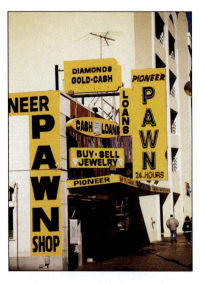

Many courts, today, apply the reasonable care standard to all types of bailments including bailments for the sole benefit of the bailor and bailments for the sole benefit of the bailee.

In a mutual-benefit bailment, the bailee must use the property only for the express purposes permitted by the bailor as provided for in the contract of bailment. The rental of a car, tools, or formal wear, for example, implies the right of reasonable use. Failing to use the property as agreed makes the bailee responsible for any damages that might result, regardless of the degree of care that was exercised.

Example 21-13

Smith rented a tuxedo from the Valet Shop. While wearing it, he crawled under a friend's car to make an adjustment to the brakes. Smith was liable to the Valet Shop for the resulting damage to the suit. The bailed property had not been used for the purposes permitted by the bailor. A reasonably prudent person would know that one does not crawl under a car while wearing a rented tuxedo.

Quick Quiz 21-2 True or False?

1. A bailment for the sole benefit of the bailee is a gratuitous bailment.

2. In a bailment for the sole benefit of the bailor, the bailee has an implied right to use the bailor's property.

3. In a mutual-benefit bailment, the bailee owes a duty to use reasonable care.

21-3 Burden of Proof

Sometimes items are damaged, lost, or stolen when they are in the possession of a bailee. In the past, the bailor had to prove that the bailee was negligent to recover against the bailee for damages. This was very difficult to do because the bailor was not in a position to know what caused the loss because the bailee had possession of the property at the time. Most courts today shift the burden of proof in bailment cases to the one who is in the best position to know what happened; that is, to the bailee. Today, when items in the possession of a bailee are damaged, lost, or stolen, the burden is on the bailee to prove that it was not negligent.

Terms The legal phrase *burden of proof* has two meanings. First, it describes the responsibility of the party who must present evidence to prove or disprove a relevant and material fact in a court case. Second, *burden of proof* refers to the amount of proof that is required for a favorable decision to be rendered in a case. Depending on the type of case, there are three levels of the amount of required proof. Most civil cases, such as negligence cases, require only enough evidence to favor one party. Some civil cases, however, demand a higher level of proof—"clear and convincing evidence." Criminal cases require that the proof results in a decision that is "beyond a reasonable doubt."

Example 21-14

Edwards took her Cadillac automobile to the Crestmont Cadillac garage to have a tire changed and the wheels aligned. When she returned later to pick up the car, she learned that it had been stolen from the garage. The court held Crestmont responsible. It had not used reasonable care in preventing the car from being stolen. The court said that a bailee is presumed to be negligent when it fails to redeliver the bailed property unless it can prove that it was not negligent.

Refer again to Examples 21-1 and 21-2. In the former example, which was not a bailment, the burden was on Sewall to prove that the parking lot owner was negligent. In contrast, Example 21-2 involved a bailment, placing the burden on the parking garage (the bailee), to prove that it was not negligent.

21-4 Special Bailments

Certain types of bailees, including innkeepers, common carriers, and warehousers have extraordinary obligations in addition to the duties imposed on all bailees.

Background Information Travel in the Middle Ages involved a great deal of risk, in part because of unscrupulous innkeepers who robbed travelers. In England, to make travel safer, government officials were assigned to inspect inns and arrest criminals. As a result, the English inn evolved into a safe haven for the traveler. The common law guiding innkeepers in England influenced the law in the United States.

Innkeepers

An **innkeeper** is the operator of a hotel, motel, or inn that holds itself out to the public as being ready to entertain travelers, strangers, and transient guests. A **transient** is a guest whose length of stay is variable. A lodger is discussed in Chapter 23.

To assist travelers in obtaining accommodations, the common law imposed the duty upon innkeepers to accept all people who requested a room if one was available. In addition, innkeepers were considered to be insurers of their guests' property. With exceptions, this is still the law today.

Related Cases *Heart of Atlanta Hotel v. U.S.* (379 U.S. 241) was the first challenge to the 1964 Civil Rights Act. The Atlanta Hotel refused to rent rooms to African Americans who contended that the unavailability of accommodations made interstate travel difficult for them. The motel defended itself on the grounds that it had a constitutional right to choose customers. The Supreme Court of the United States upheld the Civil Rights Act on the grounds that discrimination put a burden on interstate commerce and that Congress had a right to remove such obstructions as long as its means were constitutional.

Example 21-15

Section 7, Chapter 140 of the Massachusetts General Law reads, "An innholder who, upon request, refuses to receive and make suitable provision for a stranger or traveler shall be punished by a fine of not more than fifty dollars."

The Civil Rights Act of 1964 prohibits discrimination in the selection of guests for reasons of race, creed, color, sex, or ethnic background. People may be turned away when all rooms are occupied or reserved. In addition, innkeepers may refuse to accommodate people whose presence might endanger the health, welfare, or safety of other guests or the safety of the establishment itself.

Innkeeper's Duty of Care Innkeepers must use reasonable care in protecting their guests from harm. They are responsible for injuries to their guests caused by the inn's negligence or the negligence of employees.

The Opening Case Revisited
"A Rough Night's Sleep"

The lower court held that since the Rosiers failed to secure the chain latch to the outside door, the inn was not responsible. The court of appeals reversed the lower court's decision, holding that a jury should decide whether the motel used reasonable care in protecting its guests.

Innkeepers must respect their guests' rights of privacy. Guests are guaranteed exclusive and undisturbed privacy of rooms assigned by the hotel. Interruption of the guests' privacy through unpermitted entry by hotel employees or other guests creates a liability in tort for invasion of privacy.

Teaching Tips Invite a hotel or motel manager to talk to the class. Ask the manager to bring copies of the notice from the hotel that sets the terms for the safekeeping of valuable items. Ask students to discuss how this notice addresses the innkeeper's duty of care. Encourage a discussion on this topic and about the legal cases in which the manager has been involved.

Cross-Cultural Notes Many Japanese hotel rooms have only a sliding door with no lock. While some hotels have safes, in others the hotel managers take valuables home for safekeeping. These safety standards rarely cause problems because Japanese society puts great value on trust.

Example 21-16

Nash stopped at the Riverside Motel for the night. After taking a shower, she opened the bathroom door and discovered a couple bringing suitcases into her room. The motel clerk had assigned the room to another couple by mistake. Nash may seek damages against the motel for invasion of privacy.

Innkeepers have a greater duty of care toward their guests' property than is imposed in the usual mutual-benefit bailment. With exceptions (as follows), innkeepers are held by law to be insurers of their guests' property. The insured property includes all personal property brought into the hotel for the convenience and purpose of the guests' stay. In the event of loss, the hotelkeeper may be held liable, regardless of the amount of care exercised in the protection of the guests' property.

Safety and privacy are important concerns for hotel, motel, and inn guests.

> ## Example 21-17
>
> Upon checking into the Concord Hotel, Mr. and Mrs. Modell placed two diamond rings in the hotel's safe-deposit vault. Later, Mrs. Modell withdrew the rings from the vault to wear that evening. When she went to return them later than night, she was told by the desk clerk that the vault was closed until the next morning. That night, the Modells' room was broken into, and the rings were stolen. The hotel was held liable for the loss of the rings because it did not provide a place for their safekeeping.

Innkeepers are not liable as insurers in these four cases:

1. Losses caused by a guest's own negligence.
2. Losses to the guest's property due to acts of God or from acts of the public enemy.
3. Losses of property due to accidental fire in which no negligence may be attributed to the hotelkeeper. This exception also includes fires caused by other guests staying at the hotel at the same time. Such persons, even though on other floors, are called fellow guests.
4. Losses arising out of characteristics of the property that cause its own deterioration.

> ## Example 21-18
>
> At the Village Hotel, guests were advised to lock their doors whenever leaving their rooms and bellhops instructed guests in the use of the locks. Hamlin left the hotel without locking the room door, and property was stolen from his room. The hotel was not liable for this loss.

In most states, innkeepers are further protected by laws limiting the amount of claim any guest may make for a single loss. The limit is usually $500 or less, depending upon the state in which a hotel is located. These laws also give the innkeeper the right to provide a safe or vault for the better protection of the guests' valuables. A guest who does not use the safe provided for valuables will be personally responsible for losses and may not seek recovery from the innkeeper.

Innkeeper's Lien and Credit Card Blocking Innkeepers have a lien on their guests' property. A **lien** is a claim that one has against the property of another. If a guest cannot pay the bill, the innkeeper is permitted to take possession of the guest's property as security for payment at some later date. Payment of the bill releases the property and terminates the right of lien.

Credit card blocking is a common method used by hotels to secure payment for a room. Under this system, guests are asked for a credit card when they register. The hotel then contacts the card issuer electronically with the estimated cost of the bill. If the card issuer approves the transaction, the guest's available line of credit is reduced by the estimated amount. This procedure is known as a block (or authorization). The final actual charge for the room will replace the block within a day or two after the guest checks out. If the guest pays the final charge with cash, check, or a different

Teaching Tips Have students go to the library and research articles from newspapers across the country concerning fires or robberies that took place in hotels. Ask the students to analyze each article and determine if they think the innkeeper was liable to the guests.

State Variations New York, Ohio, and many other states limit a hotel's liability for theft of a guest's personal property if the hotel provides a safe or safe deposit box for their guests, provides adequate notice of these safes, and states clearly the ramification of not placing articles in them.

State Variations North Carolina applies a slightly different standard to the amount guests can claim. For any value over $100, guests must notify the innkeeper in writing with an itemized list. The innkeeper is then liable for the full amount reported.

Related Cases The hotel chain Days Inn had a sign clearly posted informing guests they could deposit their valuables in the office safe. When a guest's money and diamonds were stolen, he sued the hotel for liability. The court ruled that the sign was enough to protect the hotel from suit. *Bischoff v. Days Inn of America*, 568 F.Supp. 1065.

Background Information The origin of the word *hotel* in American culture dates back to the late eighteenth century when the owners of the famous Tontine Tavern changed its name to the City Hotel, to invoke the more fashionable French word *hotellerie*.

credit card, however, the block will remain on the original credit card for as long as fifteen days.

Carriers

The events of September 11, 2001, changed the lives of Americans in many ways, most notably in the field of transportation. Two months following 9/11, the President signed into law the Aviation and Transportation Security Act (ATSA), which among other things established a new Transportation Security Administration (TSA) within the Department of Transportation. The TSA protects the nation's transportation systems to ensure freedom of movement for people and commerce. Soon after, Congress established the Department of Homeland Security, which oversees the Coast Guard, Customs Service, Immigration and Naturalization Service, and the TSA. Collectively, these organizations are responsible for protecting our nation's transportation system and supervising the entry of people and goods into the United States. (See Figure 21-2.)

Carriers are businesses that undertake to transport persons, goods, or both. If a carrier holds itself out to the general public to provide transportation for compensation, it is called a **common carrier.** Like hotels, common carriers cannot turn away people who ask for their services with exceptions for security reasons.

Common carriers of goods are insurers of all goods accepted for shipment. They are liable as insurers regardless of whether or not they have been negligent. The Carmack Amendment to the Interstate Commerce Act states that a carrier is liable for damage to goods transported by it unless there is proof that the damage comes within one of the following exceptions:

- acts of God (e.g., floods, tornadoes, cyclones, earthquakes)
- acts of the public enemy (wartime enemies, terrorists, and the like)
- acts of public authorities
- acts of the shipper
- the inherent nature of the goods (such as perishable goods, evaporating and fermenting liquids, and diseased animals)

Figure 21-2 The Transportation Services Index measures the movement of freight and passengers.

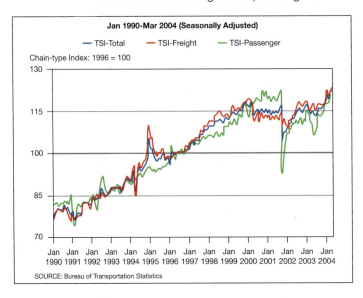

State Variations In Iowa, a person may file with the state department of transportation a complaint against a common carrier that has violated the law and the amount of damages caused by the violation. The carrier must contest the complaint or satisfy the claim.

Example 21-19

Whitehall Packing Co. engaged Amway Truck Lines to transport forty barrels of fresh meat from its plant in Wisconsin to Howard Johnson's in New York. The federal government required plastic liners in the barrels, and Howard Johnson's would not allow dry ice in them. The refrigerator unit in Amway's truck operated properly. The truck experienced delays and took longer than its normal running time for the trip. When it arrived in New York, the meat in the barrels had an off, or gassy, odor and was not considered acceptable by the U.S. government inspector. An expert meat inspector testified that the barreled meat was smothered because of the use of the plastic liners and the absence of dry ice. Some hanging meat in the same truck was found to be in perfect condition. Although there was no evidence that Amway was negligent, the court held it responsible, saying that it was an insurer of the meat.

In addition to being insurers, common carriers of goods must accept *without discrimination* all goods offered to them for shipment. Under the Interstate Commerce Act, discrimination either through the selection of customers or through the use of preferential rates is illegal. Exceptions to the rule against discrimination are as follows:

1. A common carrier is not required to accept goods of a type that it is not equipped to carry.
2. The carrier may refuse goods that are inherently dangerous and that would create hazards beyond the control of the carrier's usual safety facilities.
3. The common carrier may refuse goods that it does not represent itself as hauling.
4. The carrier may refuse goods that are improperly packed. Proper packaging is determined by the type of goods being shipped, the length of the haul, and the usual custom of the trade.
5. The carrier may refuse goods that are not delivered at the proper place and time.

Common carriers will not be excused from liability for losses due to strikes, mob violence, fire, and similar causes. Labor unions are required to give notice of impending strikes weeks in advance of the strike dates to allow carriers to reject shipments that might be damaged by delays caused by strikes. The carrier is required to ship goods by the proper route, protect them during shipment, and deliver them to the proper person.

Carriers may limit the amount of their liability to the value stated on the **bill of lading,** which is the written contract between a common carrier and a shipper.

Teaching Tips Discuss reasons why a common carrier's liability is that of an insurer of goods. Review the exceptions to this general rule.

Terms Make sure students do not confuse *bill of lading* and *airbill*. An airbill is simply a bill of lading for goods shipped by airplane.

UCC 7-309(2)

Teaching Tips Overnight mail carriers, such as Federal Express, list liability limitations on their packaging. Make copies of the limitations listed on a Federal Express envelope and distribute them to students. Ask students how much Federal Express would be liable for the loss of goods worth $300. How much would Federal Express be liable for the loss of goods worth $700 but not declared as such? What would be their liability for goods worth and declared to be worth $480 for which a greater charge has been paid?

Example 21-20

Mrs. Bratton hired Allied Van Lines, Inc., to transport her household goods from Ohio to Florida. When the goods were picked up, Mrs. Bratton signed a bill of lading that contained a provision limiting the carrier's liability to $1.25 per pound (which amounted to $4,500) or the actual value of the goods as written on the bill of lading. There was a place on the bill of lading for Mrs. Bratton to fill in the actual value of the goods ($10,630). She failed to do this. The shipment was destroyed in transit. Mrs. Bratton argued that since she did not read the document and was unaware of any provision affecting the carrier's liability, she was not bound by the words in the bill of lading. The court held that a bill of lading containing a limitation of the carrier's liability is binding even though the shipper had not read it.

UCC 7-307

A common carrier has the right to the payment of fees agreed upon for the shipment of the goods and a lien on all goods shipped for the amount of the shipping charges due. Should the shipper and the party receiving the goods fail to pay the charges, the carrier has the right to sell the goods at public sale.

Related Cases TRW contracted with Federal Express to ship goods. Federal Express in turn contracted with Great Western Airlines to deliver the goods. The Great Western plane crashed and TRW sued both Great Western and Federal Express. The court ruled that Great Western was a connecting carrier and was liable to TRW for actual damages. *Akwright-Boston Manufacturing Mutual Ins. Co. v. Great Western Airlines, Inc., 41 UCC Rep. Serv. 962.*

Example 21-21

Hanlon Book Company ordered paper from Maine Paper Company. The paper was shipped from Bangor, Maine, under terms that transferred title to the paper when delivered to the carrier. Hanlon Book Company refused to pay shipping costs when informed of the arrival of the shipment. Notice was finally given to both firms of the carrier's intention to sell the paper to recover shipping charges. At a public sale, the paper brought a high bid of $2,237. The carrier deducted shipping costs and turned over the balance to the Hanlon Book Company.

49 U.S. Code 44901(a)

49 U.S. Code 44902

Related Cases In *Cestell v. American Airways* (88 S.W.2d 976), the court decided that common carriers of passengers may refuse transport to passengers that have contagious diseases because the health of the other passengers would be endangered.

State Variations Whether a school bus operator is considered a common carrier varies among states. In Massachussets, for example, a court ruled that a bus operator was a common carrier and was strictly liable for damages in a case in which a bus driver raped a student. *Gallant by Gallant v. Gorton*, 581 F.Supp. 909.

49 U.S. Code 44902(b)

Common Carriers of Passengers A **passenger** is defined as a person who enters the premises of a carrier with the intention of buying a ticket for a trip. One continues to be a passenger as long as one continues the trip. This relationship is terminated after one has reached the destination printed on the ticket and has left the premises of the carrier.

Prior to 9/11, common carriers had an obligation to accept all passengers who sought passage over their lines. This has changed. By order of the U.S. Congress, the Federal Aviation Administration (FAA) has established regulations that require the screening of passengers and property before entering an aircraft, to search for dangerous weapons, explosives, and other destructive substances. Passengers who do not consent to the screening must be refused transportation.

The TSA's approach to security includes thorough screening of baggage and passengers by highly trained screeners, fortified cockpit doors in all airliners, thousands of federal air marshals aboard a record number of flights, and armed federal flight deck officers. A program was developed by the government to confirm the identity of passengers and keep terrorists off commercial aircraft but was rejected before it became operational (see Talking Points on the following page, "Airport Screening System Rejected"). Known as the Computer Assisted Passenger Prescreening System (CAPPS II), the program would have enabled airport security officials to access a list to identify and detain particular travelers. After receiving many complaints and lawsuits about the program's potential for breach of privacy, the government shelved the plan and is attempting to develop a different model to assure travelers' security.

Common carriers may not discriminate in the selection of passengers on the basis of race, color, national origin, religion, sex, or ancestry. Carriers may refuse passengers: (1) when all available space is occupied or reserved, (2) if they are disorderly, intoxicated, insane, or infected with a contagious disease, or (3) since 9/11, when the carrier decides a passenger "is or might be inimical to safety."

A passenger who has boarded a plane that has not taken off must leave the plane if told to do so by an authorized airline representative. **Racial profiling,** the act of targeting a person for criminal investigation primarily because of racial or ethnic characteristics, may not be a motivating factor in a carrier's decision to refuse transportation.

A carrier must exercise reasonable care in the protection of passengers. Injuries that are reasonably foreseeable or preventable and that result from the carrier's negligence give a passenger a right to sue for damages. However, if injuries are not reasonably foreseeable or preventable, the carrier is not responsible.

Talking Points

Airport Screening System Rejected

In July 2004, an airport screening system that was about to go into effect was suddenly scrapped as being too invasive of the public's right to privacy.

Under the planned Computer Assisted Passenger Prescreening System (CAPPS II), airlines would have asked passengers for a slightly expanded amount of reservation information, including full name, date of birth, home address, and home telephone number. The system would have verified the identity of passengers and conducted a risk assessment using commercially available data and intelligence information. It would then have assigned one of the following risk scores to each passenger:

- unknown risk
- no risk
- elevated risk
- high risk

Government employees would not have viewed the commercially available data, and intelligence information would have remained behind the government firewall. Once the proposed system had computed a traveler's risk score (in about five seconds), it would have sent an encoded message to be printed on the passenger's boarding pass indicating the appropriate level of screening and sent to screeners at security checkpoints. Appropriate law enforcement officers would have been notified when a traveler was identified as having known or suspected links to terrorism or had an outstanding federal or state warrant for a violent crime.

The Transportation Security Administration (TSA) plans to make changes in the proposed program to address the privacy issues. What is your opinion of the plan that was scrapped?

Did You Know? According to the Department of Homeland Security, 730 million people travel on commercial aircraft and more than 700 million pieces of baggage are screened for explosives each year. Additionally, 11.2 million trucks and 2.2 million rail cars cross into the United States from Canada and Mexico each year. Also, 7,500 foreign flag-ships make 51,000 calls in U.S. ports annually.

Example 21-22

Three men who were intoxicated boarded a commuter train around midnight. They were talking loudly and making a lot of noise. A conductor saw them and told them not to bother passengers. At the next stop, while the conductor let passengers on and off the train, the men went to another car. There, they assaulted, hit, and kicked a passenger. As soon as the conductor reboarded the train, he sought out the three men, discovered what they had done, and had them arrested. In a suit brought by the injured passenger against the carrier, the court held in favor of the carrier. The court said that the incident occurred so quickly and unexpectedly that the conductor, acting with the highest degree of care under the circumstances, could not have averted it.

Related Cases Political activist Ralph Nader sued Allegheny Airlines for fraudulent misrepresentation because it failed to inform him of its overbooking practices and failed to give him the boarding priority it had promised. Although he had been told that he had a "confirmed reservation," when Nader arrived at the check-in area, he was told that his flight had been overbooked. Nader was awarded $10 in compensatory damages and $25,000 in punitive damages. *Nader v. Allegheny Airlines, Inc.,* 462 U.S. 1978.

Bumped Airline Passengers When an airline flight is overbooked, the airline must first find volunteers willing to give up their seats for ones on the next available flight. If there are not enough volunteers, other passengers may be denied a seat in accordance with the airline's priority rules. Airlines are required to establish and publish priority rules for determining which passengers holding confirmed reservation space will be denied boarding on an oversold flight.

Background Information Airlines claim that many passengers make reservations they never keep, necessitating overbooking. The average domestic flight is overbooked by 10 to 20 percent. At holiday times, that percentage may double. According to the U.S. Department of Transportation, bumping disrupts the plans of about 765,000 passengers yearly.

A Question of Ethics

Why do you think airlines overbook some of their flights? Although the practice is legal, is it ethical?

Business Law in the News
Travelers, Prepare to Be Smelled

It greets travelers with discreet puffs of air, just enough to dislodge a trace of explosives from skin, hair, or clothing. And it can detect them right through shoes. It's the latest bomb-sniffing technology, and it may be coming to a train station or airport near you.

On May 3, the U.S. Transportation Security Administration announced a 30-day trial at Amtrak's New Carrollton (Md.) station, testing a system made by General Electric. It's also looking at the Sentinel II, the system built by British security company Smiths Group. The devices, which cost up to $150,000, are used in nuclear power plants in the U.S. and Canada. Britain's Heathrow and Manchester Airports are testing them.

Travelers walk through a gate similar to a metal detector where currents of air circulate, then get sucked back into the machine for analysis, which takes eight seconds. It's sensitive enough, says Bill Mawer, president of Smiths Detection North America, a unit of the British company, to foil a would-be shoe bomber whose sneakers are still on and laced.

The TSA already uses 3,500 desktop baggage detectors at the nation's airports. But they depend on security guards taking swipes off suspicious passengers' bags to test for explosives. The Sentinel does the job on everyone, no muss, no fuss.

Questions for Analysis

1. Would discreet puffs of air blown against your skin be disturbing as you proceed through a security check point?

2. What kind of security measures, if any, do you currently find most disturbing?

Source: Catherine Yang. "Travelers, Prepare to Be Smelled," *BusinessWeek,* May 24, 2004, p. 16.

Passengers who are denied boarding involuntarily, that is, bumped, may be entitled to compensation. If the airline can arrange alternate transportation that is scheduled to arrive at the passenger's destination within one hour of the original arrival time, there is no compensation. However, if the alternate flight gets to the destination between one and two hours late, the passenger is entitled to a cash payment equal to the price of one fare up to $200. This amount is doubled if the passenger is more than two hours late.

Passengers may refuse all compensation and bring private legal action. Federal regulations state: "The passenger may decline the payment and seek to recover damages in a court of law or in some other manner." In 1994, the U.S. Supreme Court confirmed that passengers who are bumped from a scheduled flight may sue the carrier for damages.

Passengers' Baggage Since 9-11, dangerous weapons, explosives, destructive items, and items that may be deemed to present a potential threat cannot be carried on board an aircraft. Many items that cannot be hand-carried may, however, be carried in the luggage compartment of planes. The law has no requirement for returning banned items that are left at airport security checkpoints. In addition, those who attempt to bring banned items through airport checkpoints are subject to civil penalties of up to $1,100 per violation as well as criminal penalties. Passengers must also declare any hazardous materials that they are carrying. Violators of federal hazardous materials regulations may be subject to a civil penalty of up to $27,000 for each violation and, in appropriate cases, criminal penalties.

In conjunction with the carrying of passengers, a carrier is obliged to accept a reasonable amount of baggage. Excess baggage may be shipped by a passenger or payment of additional fees. Baggage limits vary with different air-lines. Personal luggage carried aboard an airline and kept at one's seat does not generally come within the weight limits permitted each passenger.

When a baggage car or baggage compartment is available for checking luggage, the carrier is considered an insurer of the luggage checked by the passengers and left in these places. Property kept by passengers at their seats or in overhead compartments places upon the carrier the obligation of exercising ordinary care for its safety.

Federal rules place limits on the liability of airlines for lost luggage. For travel wholly within the United States, the maximum liability of an airline for lost luggage is $2,500 per passenger. Excess valuation may be declared on certain types of articles. However, some carriers assume no liability for fragile, valuable, or perishable articles.

Airport security in the United States is much more thorough because of ongoing security concerns.

Warehousers

When goods are stored in a warehouse, the relationship of bailor and bailee is created between the owner of the goods and the warehouser. The UCC defines a **warehouser** as a person engaged in the business of storing goods for hire. A **warehouse** is a building or structure in which any goods, but particularly wares or merchandise, are stored. A **warehouse receipt** is a receipt issued by a person engaged in the business of storing goods for hire.

UCC 7-102(h)

UCC 1-201(45)

Although both common carriers and warehousers are mutual-benefit bailees, they perform different functions. Common carriers are engaged in moving goods. Warehousers keep goods in storage. At times, however, one or the other will perform both functions.

Warehousers may be classified as public and private warehousers. A **public warehouser** is one who owns a warehouse where any member of the public who is willing to pay the regular charge may store goods. Grain elevators in the Midwest, used to store farmers' grain, are sometimes established as public warehouses. A warehouser whose warehouse is not for general public use is a **private warehouser.** Most warehousers fall into this latter category.

Sometimes, businesspeople will borrow money using goods that they have stored in a warehouse as security for the loan. The one who lends the money is given the warehouse receipt. If the debt is not paid, the holder of the receipt may obtain possession of the goods that are in storage. This practice is called **field warehousing.**

UCC 7-204(1)

A warehouser must use that amount of care that a reasonably careful person would use under similar circumstances. Failure to use such care is negligence and makes the warehouser liable for losses or damages to the goods.

> ## Example 21-23
>
> Bekins Warehouse stored Keefe's household goods in its warehouse beneath some sprinkler system pipes. It did not inspect the area before placing the goods there. One of the pipes was unconnected, and water from the pipes leaked onto Keefe's goods, damaging them. Bekins's failure to inspect the area of storage was a negligent act that made Bekins responsible for the loss.

Related Cases A warehouser is liable for items not accounted for even if no warehouse receipt is issued. The duty remains and burden shifts to the warehouser to explain the loss or disappearance of the goods. *Kearns v. McNeill Bros. Moving & Storage Co. Inc.,* 509 A.2d 1132.

The parties may limit the amount of liability of the warehouser by including terms to that effect in the storage agreement or warehouse receipt.

UCC 7-204(2)

Teaching Tips In class, compare the liability limitation terms in the storage agreements on warehouse receipts of different local private warehouses. Do any of them differ? If so, discuss how the differences can be explained—by the warehousers' locations, facilities, or fees, for example.

Example 21-24

The warehouse receipt given by Bekins to Keefe in Example 21-23 limited Bekins's liability to ten cents per pound per article. The limitation was enforceable even though it was not specifically called to Keefe's attention when the warehouse receipt was signed.

UCC 7-206

If goods are not removed from a warehouse at the end of a storage period, the warehouser may sell them. Before doing so, however, the warehouser must notify the owner that they are going to be sold and must give that person the right to redeem them. If no time for storage is fixed in the agreement, the warehouser must give at least thirty days' notice to the owner before selling the goods.

UCC 7-209

A warehouser has a lien on the goods that are in the warehouser's possession. A **warehouser's lien** is the right to retain possession of the goods until the satisfaction of the charges imposed on them. The lien is for the amount of money owed for storage charges, transportation charges, insurance, and expenses necessary for the preservation of the goods. The lien is a possessory one. It is lost when the warehouser voluntarily delivers the goods or unjustifiably refuses to deliver them. If the owner of the goods owes the warehouser money for the storage of other goods, the warehouser has a lien for the other debt only if it is so stated in the warehouse receipt.

UCC 7-210(1)

If the person who stored the goods is a merchant in the course of business, the warehousers's lien may be enforced by a public or private sale at any time or place and on any terms that are commercially reasonable. Notice must be given to all persons known to claim an interest in the goods. The notice must include a statement of the amount due, the nature of the proposed sale, and the time and place of any public sale (see Figure 21-3).

UCC 7-210(2)

If the person who stored the goods is not a merchant, more complicated rules must be followed to enforce the warehouser's lien. In addition to giving notice to all persons known to claim an interest in the goods, the nonmerchant must also advertise the pending sale in a local newspaper. Notices and advertisements must contain specific information set forth in the UCC.

UCC 7-210(3)

Related Cases When Miller was evicted from her apartment, she put her property in storage. At the end of the storage period, the storage company sent notice to Miller's last known address and then posted, seven days later, a notice of the sale of Miller's goods. The court ruled that the notice was insufficient, because it did not give Miller the proper ten-day notice. Miller received damages for the loss of property plus punitive damages. *Miller v. Henshaw,* 808 P.2d.715.

Figure 21-3 Before this warehouser's lien sale is held, notice must be given to all persons known to have an interest in the goods.

PUBLIC AUCTION
Warehouser's Lien Sale
To be held at
The Carriage House
NORTH BROADWAY, ELMWOOD, N.H.

Wednesday, July 1 at 6:30 p.m.

Preview at 5 p.m.
We have moved the sale for the convenience of the sale 12 containers with inventory of the following merchandise; living room sets, kitchen sets, bedroom sets, chests of drawers & more; Washer, dryers & refrigerators. Also, a large assort. of TV's, stereos, lamps, mirrors, shelves, glass, a lg. number of box lots, dishes, bric-a-brac & much, much more.
Terms: cash or check w/ preapproval

E.B. MAPLE, Auctioneers N.H. Lic. 112
34 Main St., Elmwood, N.H. 555-1200

Quick Quiz 21-4 True or False?

1. Innkeepers may turn away strangers and travelers if they desire, even when they have rooms available.

2. Common carriers are insurers of goods accepted for shipment only when they are negligent.

3. With a few exceptions, bumped airline passengers must be offered alternate transportation plus the money back for their tickets.

Summary

21-1 A bailment occurs whenever someone transfers possession and control of personal property to another with the intent that the same property will be returned later.

21-2 The principal types of bailments are: bailments for the sole benefit of the bailor, bailments for the sole benefit of the bailee, and mutual-benefit bailments. Under modern law, bailees owe a duty to use reasonable care with the goods in their possession. Former law, still followed in some states, required the bailee to use great care in a bailment for the sole benefit of the bailee, slight care in a bailment for the sole benefit of the bailor, and ordinary care in a mutual-benefit bailment.

21-3 When goods are lost or damaged while in the possession of a bailee, the burden is on the bailee to prove that no negligence was involved; if this proof cannot be made, the bailee will be held responsible for the loss.

21-4 Innkeepers are required to accept all guests unless there are no vacancies. They must respect their guests' right of privacy. With exceptions, innkeepers are

insurers of their guests' property. In most states, however, they are protected by laws limiting their liability to a specific dollar amount. Innkeepers have a lien on guests' property for the amount of any unpaid bills.

The Transportation Security Administration (TSA), under the Department of Homeland Security, is responsible for protecting our nation's transportation system. The TSA's approach to security includes thorough screening of baggage and passengers, fortified cockpit doors, and the use of air marshals.

Common carriers of goods are liable as insurers of the goods they ship regardless of whether or not they have been negligent. They are not responsible for damages caused by acts of God, acts of the public enemy, acts of public authorities, acts of the shipper, and the inherent nature of the goods. With some exceptions, bumped airline passengers are entitled to a payment of denied boarding compensation.

Public warehousers must accept goods for storage by any member of the public willing to pay for the service. Private warehouses are not for general public use. Warehousers must use reasonable care in storing goods. They have a lien on goods until storage charges are paid.

Key Terms

bailee, 385
bailment, 384
bailments for the sole benefit of the bailee, 388
bailments for the sole benefit of the bailor, 387
bailor, 385
bill of lading, 395
carriers, 394
common carrier, 394
consignee, 389

Questions for Review and Discussion

1. What are the principal types of bailments? Give an example of each.
2. How does the standard of care imposed on a bailee today differ from the degrees of care recognized in former years?
3. How has the burden of proof shifted, under today's law, when items in the possession of a bailee are damaged?
4. What obligation does an innkeeper have to accept guests?
5. What is a common carrier's liability for damage to goods it transports?
6. What does the Transportation Security Administration's approach to security include?
7. Describe the screening system known as CAPPS II.
8. What are the two classes of warehousers? Explain their differences.
9. What duty of care is owed by a warehouser to the owner of stored goods?
10. Explain the warehouser's lien. What amount of money does it involve? When is it lost?

Investigating the Internet

A great deal of information is available on the Internet about airline security, prohibited carry-on luggage, and racial profiling. To locate the information, go to a search engine such as **www.google.com** and key in any of those terms.

Cases for Analysis

1. Schaeffer boarded a 30-passenger, single-aisle turboprop airplane carrying two pieces of baggage. When asked by a flight attendant to surrender one carry-on for proper storage, he refused and became verbally abusive. The captain of the plane decided not to depart with the disruptive passenger on board because he was concerned about the safety of the flight. When asked to leave the plane, the passenger refused, and the Port Authority police were called to remove him. Must a passenger who has boarded a plane that has not taken off leave the plane when told to do so by an authorized representative? Explain. *Schaeffer v. Cavallero,* 54 F.Supp.2d 350 (S.D.N.Y.).

2. Joe Scott left his automobile with Purser Truck Sales, Inc., to be repaired. Purser Truck Sales turned the automobile over to Lonz Radford to make the repairs. The car was demolished

while in the possession of Radford. In a suit brought by Scott against Purser, the trial court held in favor of Purser due to the fact that Scott presented no evidence indicating that Purser was negligent. Was the trial court correct? Why or why not? *Scott v. Purser Truck Sales, Inc.,* 402 S.E.2d 354 (GA).

3. Grabert stored his Cessna 175A aircraft in Noel's hangar for $30 a month. The Cessna required a key to be started, and the key was left either in the plane's ignition or hung on a knob on the instrument panel. At night the hangar was locked. A key to the hangar door was left outside on the top of a meter box so that aircraft owners could get to their planes at any hour of the day or night. Cameron, a part-time employee of the airport, stole the plane one night when he was off duty. He did not have a pilot's license. The plane crashed, and Cameron was killed. Was the owner of the airport liable for the destruction of the plane? Explain. *Grabert v. James C. Noel Flying Service, Inc.,* 360 So.2d 1363 (LA).

4. Donovan, who was seventeen, was hired by Schlesner as a gas station attendant. This job included pumping gas, keeping the station clean, washing windows, and taking care of customers. Donovan was also required to keep the books to reflect the sale of such items as gas, milk, and candy. Schlesner deducted money from Donovan's pay each week for shortages that appeared from the books. In a suit that Donovan brought to recover the money so deducted, Schlesner claimed that Donovan was a bailee of the goods that were sold in the gas station. Do you agree with Schlesner? Why or why not? *Donovan v. Schlesner,* 240 N.W.2d 135 (WI).

5. F-M Potatoes, Inc., stored potatoes for Suda. The oral agreement provided for a storage rental price of 40 cents per hundredweight to February 1 and an additional 10 cents per hundredweight to April 1. F-M Potatoes, Inc., controlled the temperature and atmospheric conditions of the warehouse. Suda stored 13,000 hundredweight of potatoes in the warehouse. The potatoes spoiled because F-M Potatoes failed to maintain the proper temperature and atmospheric conditions. F-M Potatoes, Inc., argued that the arrangement was a lease rather than a bailment, and hence it was not liable for the spoilage. Do you agree? Explain. *F-M Potatoes, Inc., v. Suda,* 259 N.W.2d 487 (ND).

6. James Reed and Deborah Addis, husband and wife, were the only guests at the Red Inn in Provincetown, MA. An owner of the inn checked the building at 12:30 A.M., found the windows closed and the doors locked, and left. Shortly thereafter, the guests were awakened by a fire alarm. They ran down the stairs and found the premises dark and full of smoke. The dining room was afire. The guests tried to leave by the door they had entered earlier, but it was locked. Other efforts to escape from the first floor were unsuccessful. Ultimately, they returned to the second floor, forced open a window, and jumped out, causing both to be injured. An investigation showed that the fire had been set by an arsonist. Did the inn have a duty to protect the guests from a fire set by an arsonist? Why or why not? *Addis v. Steele,* 648 N.E.2d 773 (MA).

7. Poroznoff was living in a room at the YMCA on a week-to-week basis. It was his only residence. While there, he became drunk and disorderly and was arrested by the police. On his return to the YMCA, he found that his room was locked. He was told by the management not to reenter the building. Poroznoff argued that since the room at the YMCA was his only residence, he was not a transient guest. He claimed that he had rights of a tenant. Do you agree with Poroznoff? Why or why not? *Poroznoff v. Alberti,* 401 A.2d 1124 (NJ).

8. A state agency attempted to inspect Blair Academy's dormitories as hotels under the state's hotel and multiple-dwelling law. The law of that state defined a hotel as any building "which contains 10 or more units of dwelling space or has sleeping facilities for 25 or more persons and is kept, used, maintained, advertised as, or held out to be, a place where sleeping or dwelling accommodations are available to transient or permanent guests." Did Blair Academy's dormitories come within that state's definition of a hotel? Explain. *Blair Academy v. Sheehan,* 373 A.2d 418 (NJ).

9. A storage company stored Conrad's household furniture for $25 a month. Conrad made the first payment, left town, and paid nothing for five months. The storage company sold Conrad's furniture at an auction without notifying Conrad or advertising the sale in the newspaper. Conrad claims that his rights were violated by the storage company's sale of the goods. Do you agree with

Conrad? Why or why nor? See also *Poole v. Christian*, 411 N.E.2d 513 (OH).

10. Fairchild made plane reservations for a flight to Chicago. She arrived at the airport one hour before the scheduled departure time and was told that her flight had been overbooked and that there were no remaining seats on the plane. The airline asked for volunteers to give up their seats but not one volunteered. What are Fairchild's rights?

Quick Quiz Answers

21-1	21-2	21-4
1. F	1. T	1. F
2. F	2. F	2. F
3. F	3. T	3. T

Chapter 22 — Real Property

The Opening Case
"The Dream House"

Matt and Jan were excited. They were about to make the largest purchase of their lives—their first home. It was a pretty house, beautifully landscaped with newly planted trees. Inside, the floors were covered with wall-to-wall carpeting, and the windows had new curtains. One side of the property formed the bank of a stream. Another side was bordered by a fence covered with roses. Many questions came to mind as they entered into this important transaction. Did the curtains and wall-to-wall carpeting go with the house? Were the rose bushes and newly planted trees included in the purchase? What rights would they have to the stream and the water flowing through it, and at what point in the stream was the property line? What kind of deed would they receive? Who would own the property if one of them died?

Chapter Outcomes

1. Explain what constitutes real property.
2. Identify three ways of creating an easement.
3. Differentiate between freehold and leasehold estates.
4. Describe the different types of co-ownership of real property.
5. Identify three methods of acquiring title to real property.
6. Give an example of a nonconforming use of real property and discuss the granting of a variance.
7. Explain eminent domain.

22-1 The Nature of Real Property

Real property is defined as the ground and everything permanently attached to it. It includes building, fences, and trees on the surface; earth, rocks, and mineral under the surface; and the airspace above the surface.

Trees and Vegetation

Trees, flowers, shrubs, vineyards, and field crops that grow each year without replanting (perennials) are considered real property. These plants have been planted and cultivated with the intention that they remain as a part of the real estate. Once planted and growing, such improvements to the land are called *fructus naturales* (fruit of nature).

The Opening Case Revisited
"The Dream House"

The newly planted trees and the rose bushes on the property that Matt and Jan were about to purchase were included in the purchase. Since they both are perennials (*fructus naturales*), they are part of the real property.

In contrast, crops or garden plantings that produce flowers, vegetables, or other harvest only for the year in which they are planted (annuals) are called *fructus industriales* (fruit of industry). These are treated as personal property rather than real property.

Example 22-1

When the Freeman farm was sold early in the spring, the new owner was deeded "all the real property consisting of what is known as the Freeman farm." A 25-acre section of winter wheat had been planted the fall prior to the sale and would be ready for harvest the following July. Unless the parties agreed otherwise, the wheat crop would not be part of the sale of the farm because it is an annual plant and it would be treated as personal property. The wheat crop would still belong to whoever planted it.

A tree belongs to the person on whose land the trunk is located. People who own adjoining land have the right to cut off trespassing tree branches in their airspace and trespassing roots at the boundary line of their property. Whenever property owners dig down at the very edge of their own property, however, they must provide support to their neighbor's land so that it does not cave in.

Air Rights

In early England, landowners owned the airspace above their property to "as high as the heavens." This law changed with the increased use of the airplane. Modern court decisions have held that landowners own the airspace above their land to as high as they can effectively possess or reasonably control. This height usually extends as high as the highest tree or structure on their property. It is a trespass for anyone to run wires through someone else's airspace or to use another's airspace in any way without permission. Electric and telephone companies must obtain easements for the right to run wires through the airspace of property owners (see page 411).

Congress has enacted legislation that gives the public the right of freedom of transit through the navigable airspace of the United States. The **navigable airspace,** subject to FAA regulations, is the space above 1,000 feet over populated areas and above 500 feet over water and unpopulated areas. In airport cases involving planes landing and taking off, the courts try to strike a balance between the landowners' rights to the exclusive possession of their airspace free from noise and exhaust fumes and the public need for air travel.

Air rights are valuable and are often sold to interested buyers, particularly in land-depleted metropolitan areas. For example, in New York City, developers bought air rights over the access to the George Washington Bridge and constructed multistory buildings. Two privately owned buildings have been constructed in the airspace over the Massachusetts

Turnpike near Boston. Use of air rights becomes important when land is no longer avail-able for new buildings. The private use of airspace also becomes a tax source for otherwise untaxable land owned by a city or state government.

Subterranean Rights

Unless excluded in the deed, the owner of land has exclusive title to material below the surface of the land. The right extends to a point determined to be the exact center of the earth. These subterranean rights are often sold to corporations exploring for coal, oil, or other mineral deposits. Taking out oil or minerals from below the surface would constitute trespass if such rights were not obtained from their owners.

> ## Example 22-2
>
> McGee's house and lot were adjacent to land on which a small industrial plant had been built. McGee discovered that the plant owners had driven drainage pipes under-ground from the plant into her land. She may charge the plant owners with trespass. She can also sell this right to the plant or demand that the practice be stopped and the pipes be removed.

A landowner must not dig a cellar or other excavation so close to the boundary of a neighbor as to cause the neighbor's land to cave in or the neighbor's building to be dam-aged. A person excavating who fails to shore up the adjoining land is liable to the neighbor for damages.

Water Rights

People who own land along the bank of a river or stream are called **riparian owners.** They have certain rights and duties with respect to the water that flows over, under, and beside their land. Owners of land through which a stream flows own the soil beneath the water. If a nonnavigable stream is a boundary line between two parcels of land, the owner on each side owns to the center of the stream. If the stream is navigable, however, each owner owns only to the bank of the stream, and the bed is owned by the state. A navigable stream in some states is defined as one that ebbs and flows with the tide. In other states, it is defined as a stream that is capable of being navigated by commercial vessels.

Although property owners may own the land under a stream, they do not own the water itself. Their right to the use of the water depends on the doctrine followed in their state. Most states east of the Mississippi River follow the riparian rights doctrine. Under this doctrine, owners of land bordering a stream have equal rights to use the water passing by or through their property. Each riparian owner may make reasonable use of the water for domestic purposes such as drinking, cooking, and bathing. In addition, they may use the water for irrigation purposes if it does not interfere unreasonably with the use being made by other riparian owners downstream. Owners may not sell the water from the stream to outside third parties.

Some states west of the Mississippi, where water is less plentiful, follow the prior appropriation doctrine. This doctrine follows a seniority system. The first person to make beneficial use of the water has the right to take all he or she is able to use before anyone else has any rights to it. If there is water left over, the next person in seniority may use all the water that can be put to beneficial use.

Other states west of the Mississippi follow a combination of the riparian rights doctrine and the prior appropriation doctrine.

The Opening Case Revisited
"The Dream House"

The rights that Matt and Jan would have to the bed of the stream would depend on whether the stream is navigable as defined by that state's law. If it were navigable, they would own to the bank of the stream. On the other hand, if it were nonnavigable, they would own to the center of the stream. Matt and Jan's legal use of the water flowing through the stream depends on whether that state follows the *riparian rights* doctrine or the *prior appropriation* doctrine.

In New England states, a small pond (under ten acres) is owned by the person who owns the ground underneath. In contrast, a great pond (ten acres or more) is owned by the state, and private abutters own the land only to the lower water mark. Great ponds are usually accessible to the public for swimming, boating, and fishing.

Percolating water is water that passes through the ground beneath the surface of the earth without any definite channel. It consists of rainwater that slowly oozes and seeps through the soil or water that infiltrates the banks or bed of a stream. Subterranean water is water that lies wholly beneath the surface of the ground. It may be either percolating water or water that flows in underground channels or lies still in underground lakes. Common law gave property owners the absolute right to percolating water below their land. Under modern statutes, however, property owners may draw only the water that is reasonably required to satisfy their needs. Other property owners damaged by unreasonable use may seek an injunction against such use in a court of equity.

Rainwater on the surface of the earth may not be artificially channeled to an abutter's property without permission of the abutter. Unless a drainage easement is obtained to drain water onto another's land, surface water must be left to its natural watercourse.

Fixtures

When personal property is attached to real property, it is known as a **fixture** and becomes part of the real property. Built-in stoves and dishwashers, kitchen cabinets, and ceiling light fixtures are examples of fixtures. Disagreements sometimes occur over whether an item is a fixture.

Example 22-3

The Rodriguezes bought a house from the Smiths. After the closing, when they moved in, the Rodriguezes discovered that the Smiths had taken with them the wall-to-wall carpeting in the living room. The Rodriguezes had expected the carpeting to go with the sale of the house as part of the real property. The Smiths treated the carpeting as personal property and took it with them.

In deciding whether or not an item is a fixture, the courts ask the following questions: Has there been a temporary or permanent installation of the personal property? Can it be removed without damaging the real property?

Another question asked is has the personal property been adapted to the intended use of the real property?

Terms The origin of the word *property* is the Latin *proprius,* meaning *own.* Its use as a noun to delineate ownership of items dates to the fourteenth century.

Example 22-4

In Example 22-3, if the carpeting were tightly nailed to the floor, there is a good chance that it would be held by the court to be a fixture. The same would be true if the carpeting covered plywood flooring. In both cases, the carpeting would be considered part of the real property and belong to the new buyers.

If the living room were oddly shaped and the carpeting were cut to fit that shape, it would be further evidence that the carpeting was a fixture. It had been adapted to be used in that odd-shaped room.

Also, the court would ask what was the intent of the party at the time the personal property was attached to the real property?

There is nothing which so generally strikes the imagination and engages the affections of mankind, as the right of property, or that sole and despotic dominion which one man claims and exercises over the external things of the world in total exclusion of the right of any other individual in the universe.

—Sir William Blackstone (1723–1780), British jurist

Example 22-5

Franklin complained to her landlord that the kitchen in her apartment needed to be modernized. The landlord gave her permission to improve the kitchen as long as it could be done without cost to him. Franklin installed cabinets, a built-in stove, and an under-the-counter dishwasher. She also bought a new refrigerator. Even though Franklin paid for them, the cabinets, stove, and dishwasher would be fixtures and would belong to the landlord. The refrigerator, which was not built-in, would remain the personal property of the tenant.

Trade fixtures are those items of personal property brought upon the premises by the tenant that are necessary to carry on the trade or business to which the premises will be devoted. Contrary to the general rule, trade fixtures remain the personal property of the tenant

The Opening Case Revisited
"The Dream House"

The best way for Matt and Jan to handle the question of whether the curtains and wall-to-wall carpeting go with the house is to write specifically in the purchase and sale agreement, before they sign it, that the items are or are not included in the sale. If it is not written in the agreement and the matter goes to court, a judge or jury will seek answers to the following questions:

- Has there been a temporary or permanent installation of the curtains and carpeting? Temporary items would not be fixtures.

- Can they be removed without damage to the real property? If so, they may not be fixtures.

- Have they been adapted to the intended use of the property?

- What was the intent of the owner when the curtains and carpeting were placed in the house?

or occupier of the property and are removable at the expiration of the term of occupancy. Trade fixtures are not treated as part of the real property.

Quick Quiz 22-1 True or False?

1. Landowners do not own the airspace above their land.

2. Unless excluded in the deed, landowners own the land under their property to the center of the earth.

3. Fixtures are considered to be part of real property unless they are trade fixtures.

22-2 Easements

An **easement** (also called a **right of way**) is the right to use another's land for a particular purpose. Easements are used to give people the right to pass over another's land, to run wires through another's airspace, to drain water onto another's property, and to run pipes underneath someone else's ground. The one who enjoys the easement and to whom it attaches is called the **dominant tenement.** In contrast, the one on whom the easement is imposed is called the **servient tenement.**

Example 22-6

Hatfield owned a long, narrow strip of land that ran between a lake and a highway. She decided to sell the front half of the lot that bordered the highway to McCoy and keep the back half that bordered the lake for her own use. To give McCoy the ability to reach the lake, an easement was placed in the deed granting McCoy the right to "pass and repass" over Hatfield's property to reach the lake. In this easement, McCoy is the dominant tenement and Hatfield is the servient tenement. Also, to give Hatfield the ability to reach the highway, an easement was placed in the deed, reserving to Hatfield the right to "pass and repass" over McCoy's property to reach the highway. In this easement, Hatfield is the dominant tenement and McCoy is the servient tenement.

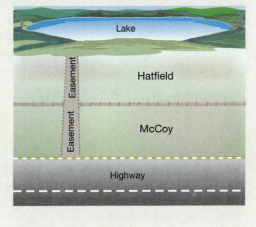

An easement may be created in three ways: by grant, by reservation, and by prescription. To create an easement by grant, the owner of the land signs a deed, giving the easement to the dominant tenement and keeps the remainder of the land. To create an easement by reservation, the owner of the land grants to another person the entire parcel of land except for the

Easements may be necessary to accommodate underground utilities and cable television.

easement that he or she keeps. An **easement by prescription** is an easement that is obtained by passing over another's property without permission openly and continuously for a period of time set by state statute (twenty years in many states). People claiming easements by prescription must show that they used (but did not possess) part of another's property openly, notoriously, and in a hostile manner for the prescribed period. This proof is similar to that used in adverse possession, which is discussed later in this chapter.

Once an easement is created, it runs with the land. This condition means that future owners will have the right to use the easement unless one of them gives it up by a deed or by not using it for a long period of time.

Terms A legal easement may exist even if it isn't in writing. For example, the law allows people access to their homes so, if the only access is by crossing through another landowner's property, the law will grant permission through an "easement by necessity." Thus, Eli has a legal right to cross Adrienne's property if it is the only way to reach his own property.

Example 22-7

By warranty deed in 1907, Jesse Horney conveyed the northern portion of his real estate to Wayne County Lumber Company. That deed included the following provision: "Said Jesse Horney hereby conveys to Wayne County Lumber Company the right of ingress and egress for teams and wagons in conducting their business through an open driveway along the South line to South Main Street." The property was conveyed to a different lumber company in 1930 and to a third lumber company in 1943. Later, in a dispute over the easement, the court held that the easement ran with the land and belonged to the third lumber company. In this case, Horney's property was the servient tenement. The lumber company's property was the dominant tenement.

A profit *à prendre* is a special type of easement with the added privilege of removing something of value from the servient property. For example, the right to enter another's property and remove sand, gravel, soil, or the like is called a profit *à prendre*. This right may be created by deed, will, or adverse use.

Example 22-8

The Bates Company and Sawyer executed an agreement that provided that Bates could enter upon Sawyer's land and remove sand, gravel, and stone. Bates agreed to pay Sawyer a set rate per cubic yard or short ton for all the sand it removed. The agreement stated, "Sawyer will not grant to anyone else the privilege of removing sand and stone from said parcel during the period hereof . . . but Sawyer reserves to herself, her successors and assigns, the right during said period . . . to go on and use said tract of land for any purpose they may desire, but without unreasonable interference with the rights of said Bates." The court held that Bates possessed a profit *à prendre* under the agreement.

22-3 Estates in Real Property

An estate is the interest or right that a person has in real property. A leasehold estate comes from a lease and is an interest in real estate. In a freehold estate, the holder owns the land for life or forever. Anyone having a freehold estate may transfer that interest to another by sale, gift, will, or by dying without a will. Freehold estates are either estates in fee simple or life estates.

Terms *Estate* comes from the Middle English *estat*, which is a form of the Latin *stare*, meaning "to stand." It is related to the Greek *histani*, meaning "to cause to stand" or "set." In its oldest known sense, *estate* implies a rank or standing. In early England, people were held in low or high estate. Later, *estate* came to refer to assets and liabilities, including land, left by a person at death.

Estates in Fee Simple

Anyone owning real property outright—that is, forever—is said to have an **estate in fee simple.** The estate descends, on the death of the owner, to the owner's heirs. The owner of an estate in fee simple has absolute ownership in the real estate, with the right to use or to dispose of it as desired, so long as the use of it does not interfere with other's rights.

Example 22-9

When the Landers bought the land on which to build their house, they received an estate in fee simple from the former owners. They thus received full rights to the property. They may sell it, give it away, or use it as they wish. The only restrictions are those contained in the deed or required of them by law.

Related Cases A wife gave her husband a life estate to some property. The husband leased the land to a pipeline company to mine the land. After he died, his children brought suit because the pipeline company was depleting the land's value. The court ruled against the children, starting that the mineral lease was not so unconscionable as to support forfeiture of the life estate. *Moore v. Vines,* 474 S.W.2d 437.

Life Estates

A person who owns real property for life or for the life of another owns an interest in real property called a **life estate.** Such an estate may be created by deed, by will, or by law. When the terms of a deed or will state that the property is to pass at the end of a life estate to someone other than the grantor or the grantor's heirs, the future interest is a **remainder estate.**

Example 22-10

Rosengard deeded her farm to Kinkaid for life. The deed stated that upon Kinkaid's death the property was to pass to Honig in fee simple. Kinkaid owns a life estate in the farm. Honig owns a remainder estate until Kinkaid's death, then an estate in fee simple.

The owner of a life estate may convey that interest to another. Thus, in Example 22-10, if Kinkaid conveys his interest to Jenkins, Jenkins will own a life estate for the duration of Kinkaid's life, after which the property will belong to Honig. When the terms of a deed or a will state that property is to return to the grantor or to the grantor's heirs at the expiration of a life estate, the future interest is a **reversion estate.**

Life estates are sometimes created by operation of law. Dower and curtesy are examples. Years ago, in England, **dower** was the right that a widow had to a life estate in one-third of the real property owned by the husband during the marriage. **Curtesy** was the right that a widower had, if children of the marriage were born alive, to a life estate in all real property owned by the wife during the marriage. The rights of dower and curtesy were in addition to rights given to spouses under the law of wills.

Example 22-11

Before her marriage, Clark received title to an old house through a will left by her grandfather. While her husband had no rights in this property at the time of their marriage, such rights arose at the birth of their first child. Her husband thereafter had the right of curtesy should Clark die while she was still married to him.

Many states have either done away with common law dower and curtesy altogether or have modified them to reflect modern-day needs.

Quick Quiz 22-3 True or False?

1. An estate in fee simple descends, on the death of the owner, to the owner's heirs.
2. The owner of a life estate may not convey that interest to another.
3. Dower and curtesy are examples of life estates created by operation of law.

22-4   Co-ownership of Real Property

Real property may be owned individually or by two or more persons known as **cotenants.** The cotenant relationships are:

- tenancy in common
- joint tenancy
- community property
- tenancy by the entirety
- tenancy in partnership

Tenancy in Common

When two or more persons own real property as **tenants in common,** each person owns an undivided share of the whole property. A cotenant's share of the property transfers to that cotenant's heirs upon death rather than to the surviving cotenants. Each cotenant is entitled to possession of the entire premises. This is known as unity of possession. Tenants in common have the right to sell or to deed away as a gift their share in the property without permission of the other cotenants. When this action occurs, any new owner becomes a tenant in common with the remaining cotenants. One cotenant's interest is not necessarily the same as another cotenant's interest.

> ## Example 22-12
>
> Ingalls and Carpenter owned a parcel of real property as tenants in common. When Ingalls died, his three children inherited his estate equally. The children became tenants in common (each owning a one-sixth interest) with Carpenter, who owned a one-half interest in the property.

Tenants in common may separate their interests in the property by petitioning the court for a partition of the property. If the court allows the petition, either it will divide the property into separate parcels so that each cotenant will own a particular part outright, or it will order the property sold and divide the proceeds of the sale among the cotenants. Creditors may reach the interest of a tenant in common by bringing a lawsuit against that particular cotenant and, if successful, by having that cotenant's interest sold to pay the debt.

By statute in most states, co-ownership of property by two or more persons is considered to be a tenancy in common unless the relationship is expressly indicated as a joint tenancy or a tenancy by the entirety.

Joint Tenancy

When two or more persons own real property as **joint tenants,** the estate created is a single estate with multiple ownership. Each tenant owns the entire estate, subject to the equal rights of the other joint tenants. Four unities must be present to create a joint tenancy: time, title, interest, and possession:

1. The unity of time means that all owners must take title at the same time.
2. The unity of title means that all owners must derive title from the same source.
3. The unity of interest means that all owners must have equal interests in the property.
4. The unity of possession means that all owners must have the equal right to possess the property.

Upon the death of one joint tenant, the entire ownership remains in the other joint tenants and does not pass to the heirs or devisees of the deceased cotenant. For this reason, joint tenants are often identified as joint tenants with the right of survivorship.

> ## Example 22-13
>
> If Ingalls and Carpenter, in Example 22-12, had owned the parcel of real property as joint tenants instead of as tenants in common, Carpenter would have owned the entire property outright when Ingalls died. Ingalls's three children would not have been entitled to any interest in the real property whatsoever.

A joint tenant may deed away his or her interest to a new owner without permission of the other joint tenants. The new owner, in such a case, becomes a tenant in common with the remaining joint tenants. As in the case of a tenant in common, a joint tenant may petition the court for a partition of the estate, which would end the joint tenancy. Creditors

Further Reading Students can read about the intricacies of property rights and learn how to research legal issues in Attorney Cora Jordan's book, *Neighbor Law: Fences, Trees, Boundaries, and Noise* (Berkeley, CA; Nolo Press, 1991).

Related Cases A husband and wife bought a piece of property that they owned by joint tenancy. They later divorced, and when the husband died, the estate sued to sell the husband's half. The court ruled that after the divorce both parties continued to own an undivided 50 percent interest in the property. Under Alabama law, the divorce decree did not destroy the joint tenancy with right to survivorship. *Porter v. Porter,* 472 So.2d 630.

may levy upon the interests of a joint tenant on execution and take over that particular joint tenant's interest as a tenant in common with the remaining joint tenants. To levy on execution means to collect a sum of money by putting into effect the judgment of a court.

Community Property

Community Property is property (except a gift or inheritance) that is acquired by the personal efforts of either spouse during marriage and which, by law, belongs to both spouses equally. The law originated in Spain, was embraced by Mexico, and is presently followed in Puerto Rico and nine U.S. states (see Figure 22-1). While state laws differ, they all operate on the theory that both spouses contribute equally to the marriage—that all property acquired during the marriage is the result of the combined efforts of both of them. Although one spouse earns all the money to acquire the property, all the property acquired is considered to be community property.

With differences among the community property jurisdictions, couples may enter into agreements that declare property that would otherwise be community property to be the separate property of either the husband or the wife. Similarly, they may do the opposite and declare their separate property to be community property. Even though Alaska is not a community property state, Title 34, Chapter 77 of the Alaska Statutes allows married couples to enter into a community property agreement.

In community property jurisdictions, each spouse can make a will leaving half the community property to whomever he or she chooses. If a spouse dies without a will, the deceased's half will pass according to intestate law discussed in Chapter 24. Upon divorce, community property is divided equally and becomes owned by the couple as tenants in common.

Tenancy by the Entirety

A **tenancy by the entirety** may be held only by a husband and wife and is based upon the common law doctrine known as unity of person. Under this very old doctrine, a

Figure 22-1 Community property jurisdictions.

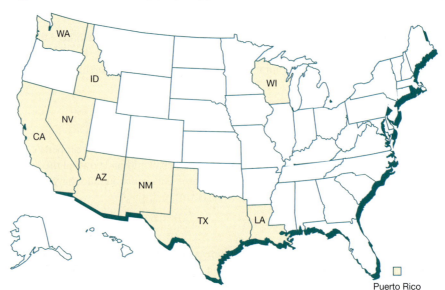

Puerto Rico

husband and wife were regarded, in law, as one. In theory, each spouse owned the entire estate, which neither could destroy by any separate act. The husband, however, had the entire control over the estate, including the exclusive right to possession and the right to all rents and profits. Upon the death of either spouse, the surviving spouse owned the entire estate outright. Although an individual creditor of the husband could levy and sell on execution the husband's interest in the tenancy, the property always remained subject to the wife's survivorship right, and if the husband died before the wife, the creditor lost that interest. The wife's right of survivorship was not attachable by her individual creditors.

Example 22-14

The DeVoes owned their home together as tenants by the entirety in a state that still followed the old common law rules. While driving a car titled in his name alone, Mr. DeVoe caused an accident resulting in serious injury to another person. The injured person obtained a judgment against Mr. DeVoe that far exceeded his insurance coverage. DeVoes' house was sold by the sheriff to satisfy the judgment, and they had to move out. Five years later, however, when Mr. DeVoe died, Mrs. DeVoe became the outright owner of the property because she survived Mr. DeVoe. Her right of survivorship in the property could not be taken from her. The person who bought the property at the sheriff's sale lost all ownership interest in it when Mr. DeVoe died.

State Variations Marital property in those states that recognize tenancies by the entirety is divided equally. Massachusetts has an amended version that treats husbands and wives equally.

Related Cases Two spouses gave a third person an option to buy property they held in tenancy by the entirety. However, one of the spouses died before the option was exercised. The court ruled that because the offer to sell was made by the tenants by the entirety together and not as individuals, the offer lapsed on the death of one. *Beall v. Beall,* 434 A.2d 1015.

Had the judgment in Example 22-14 been against Mrs. DeVoe instead of Mr. DeVoe, the property could not even have been attached by the injured person. Thus, from a practical point of view, ownership as tenants by the entirety protected both spouses from losing their real property when a judgment was obtained against either spouse individually.

Although the husband, acting alone, could not convey or encumber the *entire estate,* the husband could convey or encumber his interest in the property held as tenants by the entirety. Since the husband had the exclusive right to possession, he could sell the property or give a mortgage on it without the wife's consent. However, as in the DeVoe case above, anyone buying the property or receiving a mortgage on it would lose all ownership interest should the wife survive the husband.

In the event that husband and wife were divorced, the tenancy by the entirety no longer existed and they then become tenants in common, with separate and equal rights in the property.

Some states have done away by statute with tenancy by the entirety. Other states have enacted statutes giving equal rights to husbands and wives who own property as tenants by the entirety. Still other states require both spouses to consent to a valid mortgage on property owned as tenants by the entirety.

Tenancy in Partnership

Ownership of real property by partners is called a tenancy in partnership and is governed by the Uniform Partnership Act in those states that have adopted it. This type of co-ownership of real property is discussed in Chapter 36.

Table 22-1 summarizes the differences among the various cotenant relationships.

Table 22-1 Cotenant Relationships

	Tenants in Common	Joint Tenants	Tenants by Entirety	Tenants in Partnership	Community Property
1. Who can be cotenants	Any number of people	Any number of people	Only husband and wife	Only partners	Only husband and wife
2. At death, deceased's share goes	To deceased's heirs*	To surviving cotenants	To surviving spouse	To surviving partners	To deceased's heirs*
3. Title	Separate title for each cotenant	One title to the entire property	Husband has title (under the doctrine of unity)†	Title is in the partnership	Title is in the community
4. Division of ownership interests	Cotenants can have equal or unequal interests	All interests must be equal	Interests equal; husband has the right to control and manage†	Interest same as partnership interest	Both interests equal
5. Right to possession of entire premises	Equal with all cotenants	Equal with all cotenants	Husband only†	Equal with all partners for partnership business only	Equal with both spouses
6. Right to convey ownership interest	May convey to another without permission of cotenant	May convey to another but will end joint tenancy relationship	Husband may convey to anyone; wife's interest is protected†	May convey only with consent of copartners	May convey personal property without spouse's permission; must have written permission to convey real property
7. Right to partition the property	Yes	Yes	No	No	No
8. Owner's separate interest reachable by creditors	Yes	Yes	Husband's only†	No	No. Whole community only, depending on state law

*Either by will or the law of intestate succession if the deceased had no will.
†At common law. States have either abolished this type of tenancy or amended it to give equal rights to men and women.

The Opening Case Revisited

"The Dream House"

The answer to the question of who would own the property if either Matt or Jan died depends on how they took title as cotenants. If they took title as tenants in common, the deceased person's heirs would become the owners of the property, either through a will or the law of intestate succession. In contrast, if they took title as joint tenants or tenants by the entirety, the surviving spouse would automatically own the property outright. If it was community property, the deceased person's heirs would own half and the surviving spouse would own the other half.

Quick Quiz 22-4 True or False?

1. When three people own property as tenants in common and one of them dies, the deceased's share of the property passes to the surviving tenants in common.

2. When three people own property as joint tenants and one of them dies, the deceased's share of the property passes to his or her heirs.

3. Three people cannot own property as tenants by the entirety.

22-5 Methods of Acquiring Title to Real Property

Title to real property may be acquired by sale or gift, will or descent, or occupancy.

Title by Sale or Gift

Ownership and title to real property are most frequently transferred from one owner to another by sale or by gift. This action is done by transferring a written instrument called a deed. The person transferring title is the **grantor.** The person to whom the title is transferred is the **grantee.** A deed becomes effective when it is delivered to the grantee. A deed to real property may be bestowed as a gift from the owner or through a sale. In the case of a gift, consideration is not given by the grantee for the deed.

General Warranty Deed   A **general warranty deed,** sometimes called a full covenant and warranty deed, contains express warranties under which the grantor guarantees the property to be free of encumbrances created by the grantor or by others who had title previously. It is the most desirable form of deed from the point of view of the grantee because it warrants (gives assurances) that title is good.

Special Warranty Deed   A **special warranty deed** contains express warranties under which the grantor guarantees that no title defect arose during the time that the grantor owned the property, but not otherwise. No warranties are made as to defects that arose before the grantor owned the property.

Bargain-and-Sale Deed   A **bargain-and-sale deed** is one that transfers title to property but contains no warranties. The form of the deed is the same as that of a warranty deed except that the warranties are omitted. Since a bargain and sale necessarily involves the idea of a valuable consideration, this type of deed is not valid without consideration. It could not be used to convey a gift of real property.

Quitclaim Deed   A **quitclaim deed** (also called a deed without covenants) is one that transfers to the buyer only the interest that the seller may have in a property. This type of deed merely releases a party's rights to the property. It contains no warranties. It is used when one gives up some right in the property, such as an easement or dower and curtesy, or to cure a defect in the chain of title.

Title by Will or Descent

When people die owning real property solely in their own name or with others as tenants in common, title passes to their heirs at the moment of death. If they die with a will, title passes to the people named in the will. If they die without a will, title passes to the heirs, as tenants in common, according to the laws of intestacy discussed in Chapter 24. A deed is not used when title passes to heirs in this manner. Instead, the records of the probate court establish title to the property. A deed may be used, however, by the personal representative of an estate to transfer title to real property to another. This may be done in many states by authority granted in a will or by a license issued by the court.

Title by Adverse Possession

Title to real property may be obtained by taking actual possession of the property openly, notoriously, exclusively, under a claim of right, and continuously for a period of time set by

Related Cases   Ono purchased land from Coos County under a land sale contract. The contract required the county to deliver a "good and sufficient quitclaim deed." When Ono discovered a mortgage was recorded against the property, Ono sued the county to recover the amount of the mortgage lien. The court dismissed the suit, stating that the contract simply required that the deed be in a form adequate to convey whatever title the county held, without a guarantee of marketable title. *Ono v. Coos County,* 792 P.2d 476.

State Variations   In New Hampshire, no title to any real property or to any interest in real property may be acquired by or against a railroad by adverse possession.

State Variations   In California, Idaho, and Montana, persons in adverse possession of property for five years, who have paid the taxes on the land, may claim ownership. Twelve states require adverse possession for twenty years to claim ownership, while Ohio and Pennsylvania uphold a twenty-one-year term of residence.

The Opening Case Revisited

"The Dream House"

The kind of deed that Matt and Jan will receive often depends upon the kind that is commonly used in that state and the kind that the grantor is willing or able to give. The general warranty deed gives the most protection, followed in descending order by the special warranty deed, the bargain and sale deed, and the quitclaim deed.

state statute. This method of obtaining title to real property is called **adverse possession.** To establish such ownership rights, claimants must prove the following:

- that they have had continuous use of the property for twenty years (or a period set by state statute)
- that this use has been without interruption by the owner
- that it was without the owner's permission
- that it was with the owner's knowledge

Proof of these facts in court will give a person superior rights over the one in whose name a deed is recorded. A court of equity has the power to declare the one claiming under adverse possession to be the new owner.

Example 22-16

Wilhelm and Kupersmith were next-door neighbors. Not realizing where the true property line was, Wilhelm built a garage and driveway two feet onto Kupersmith's land. He used the garage and driveway continuously, with Kupersmith's knowledge, for the next twenty-two years. The error was discovered when Kupersmith sold her property to a new owner who had it surveyed. Wilhelm, through court action, was able to obtain title to the land on which the garage and driveway were located by adverse possession.

Quick Quiz 22-5 True or False?

1. A general warranty deed is the most desirable form of deed for a grantee to receive.

2. If a person dies without a will, title passes to the heirs as tenants in common without the use of a deed.

3. A quitclaim deed releases a party's rights to property and contains no warranties.

22-6 Zoning Laws

Zoning laws regulate the uses that may be made of properties within specified geographical areas or districts. Residential zoning prohibits properties from being used for commercial purposes within a given area. Multifamily zoning permits construction of apartment buildings. Limited-commercial zoning allows the construction of small stores but restricts the building of large shopping malls and commercial centers. Industrial zoning allows the building of factories, and agricultural zoning allows farming in a particular area. Zoning laws help to keep property values from declining and protect against the undesirable use of neighboring property.

A Question of Ethics

In Example 22-16, Wilhelm became the legal owner of land that he did not purchase. What do you think is the purpose of this law? Is it ethical?

State Variations   In Nebraska, a person may acquire title to the land of another by adverse possession through actual, continuous, open, and exclusive possession under claim of ownership for a period of ten years.

Teaching Tips Lead students in a discussion of situations in which adverse possession would affect title to the land.

Getting Students Involved   Divide students into teams and instruct them to obtain copies of surrounding local zoning ordinances, and zoning maps, if possible. Then have the teams put together a report that shows how zoning among the various municipalities differs.

State Variations In Illinois, towns may zone land that lies up to one-and-a-half miles beyond their boundaries.

Background Information The right of the state to take property by eminent domain was well established in the American colonies. Most land was taken to make public improvements, such as to build roads. However, because land was abundant and cheap, unimproved land was often taken without consideration. It was not until 1875, in *Kohl v. United States*, 91 U.S. 367, that the Supreme Court granted the federal government the right to take property directly in its own name. The Fifth Amendment clause reading "nor shall private property be taken for public use, without just compensation" was interpreted by the Court as a concession to take private property, granting the government the right to secure privately owned land for the building of government structures. Most constitutional theorists agree that the clause was actually meant as a restriction.

Business Law in the News
Who Says Wal-Mart Is Bad for Cities?

The Wal-Mart at the Baldwin Hills Crenshaw Plaza in South Central Los Angeles sits across the street from the kind of stores you'll find in any struggling big-city neighborhood. There's Lili's Wigs and King's Furniture and Mama's House, which promises the "Best Soul Food in Town." Last year, Wal-Mart Stores Inc. took over a space that had been vacant since Macy's left five years ago. Since then, it has lured black and Latino shoppers with low prices on everything from videos to toothpaste. And now that people can stay in the neighborhood for bargains, something else interesting is happening: They're stopping at other local stores, too.

"The traffic is definitely there. We're seeing more folks," says Harold Llecha, a cashier at Hot Looks, a nearby clothier. The same is happening at other nearby shops, say retailers. They acknowledge that these shoppers don't always buy from them. On some items, Wal-Mart prices can't be beat. And a handful of local shops have closed. But the larger picture is that many that were there before the big discounter arrived are still there. There are new jobs now where there were none. And a moribund mall is regaining vitality. In short, Wal-Mart came in—and nothing bad happened.

Opening a Wal-Mart in neighborhoods underserved by retailers should be a no-brainer. Yet opposition to Wal-Mart is fierce. In June, the Los Angeles City Council considers a law that will ban big-box retailers with grocery stores (read: Wal-Mart Supercenters) from poor neighborhoods. There, the issue is Wal-Mart's low wages and benefits. But opposition comes for other reasons, too. In April, Inglewood (Calif.) voters shot down Wal-Mart when it wanted to circumvent local zoning laws. In Chicago, the issues are wages and land use. In New Orleans, design was a flash point.

But for hard-pressed urban neighborhoods, having a Wal-Mart is probably a good idea. People like the bargains—and the jobs. And with fewer small-town sites left, Wal-Mart's march into cities will only pick up. Ten years ago, it had only 13 stores in cities with more than 1 million people. Today it has 38, with more on the way. Even Los Angeles Councilman Eric Garcetti, prime backer of the L.A. bill, says: "We're not saying to Wal-Mart that we don't want you under any condition. But we want to bring them to Los Angeles in a way that supplements the economic development policies we have." He fears that supercenters could put local supermarkets, often the key to neighborhood upgrades, out of business.

A new Wal-Mart can indeed gut a small burg's downtown. But urban big-box retailing is so new that economists are just beginning to get a handle on it. A 2003 study by Emek Basker at the University of Missouri found that five years after the opening of Wal-Marts in most markets, there is a small net gain in retail employment in counties where they're located, with a drop of only about 1% in the number of small local businesses. That is consistent with what seems to have happened in Baldwin Hills. Basker has also found significant price benefits: Retail prices for many goods fall 5% to 10%.

While Big Labor blasts the discounter for its nonunion workforce, where a Wal-Mart worker might earn half what a union counterpart makes, even critics suggest that a Wal-Mart job might pay no worse than one at a local mom-and-pop. "Many small businesses are comparable in wages to Wal-Mart," says Stacy Mitchell, a researcher at the Institute for Local Self-Reliance in Minneapolis.

In Austin, a poor area of Chicago, the employment Wal-Mart would provide looms large. "It's real simple: we need those jobs, and we need them bad," says Alderman Emma Mitts, in whose ward a new Wal-Mart (without a supermarket) may go. She knows unions dislike Wal-Mart. But for her, the bottom line is this: "I can't monitor them unless they're here." Finally, there is the tax benefit. Urban stores capture sales taxes that might end up in the suburbs. Even so, some critics say that offering incentives to land a Wal-Mart may yield only a small return for a city. San Diego gave Wal-Mart $9.5 million to open a store in an old mall. A study by the Center on Policy Initiatives found that the city reaps tax benefits of only $250,000 annually. It isn't a lot, but as co-author David Karjanen puts it: "The question becomes whether something is better than nothing."

It probably is. Nothing is wrong with more jobs, lower prices, and more tax revenues. Wal-Mart's critics should acknowledge that. But Wal-Mart could improve the handling of its urban engagements with more flexibility and a keener ear for local concerns. The company should not be saying, as it does, that it has no urban strategy.

That's a mistake. Wal-Mart needs a well-thought-out plan to ease its entry into cities. One idea: It could take the bold step of revising its wage scale. Costco Wholesale Corp., for instance, is mostly non-union. But it offers better pay, so it rarely provokes the ire a Wal-Mart does. The company would do well to consider more flexibility in its store design, too. What looks O.K. in a former cornfield can set a city dweller's teeth on edge. Most important, it needs to talk early and often with the communities it wants to be in—a lesson Wal-Mart seems only now to be learning. "I think there was a point in the company's history when we were less sensitive to local needs,

but we have gotten better," says Robert S. McAdam, Wal-Mart's vice-president for state and local government relations. Many observers would argue that it could do a whole lot more.

Questions for Analysis

1. In short, what happened when Wal-Mart took over vacant space in a struggling neighborhood in South Central Los Angeles?

2. What are some reasons for the fierce opposition Wal-Mart faces sometimes when it attempts to open a store in a poor neighborhood?

3. What were some findings in the study by Emek Basker of the University of Missouri in 2003?

4. What are some suggestions offered to Wal-Mart by the authors of this article?

Source: Robert McNatt, Ronald Grover, and Wendy Zellner. "Who Says Wal-Mart Is Bad for Cities," *BusinessWeek,* May 10, 2004, pp. 77–78.

Newly passed zoning laws do not apply to existing uses of the land. Such uses are called **nonconforming uses** if they are not allowed under the new zoning law. They may continue in existence but may not be enlarged or changed in kind.

By appeal to the local zoning board, variances may be given to individuals or businesses when justified and reasonable. A **variance** is an exemption or an exception that permits a use that differs from those allowed under the existing ordinance. Variances are granted in special circumstances to protect property owners who might otherwise suffer a hardship if zoning laws were applied and enforced arbitrarily.

Decisions of a local zoning commission may be appealed to county commissioners, a county court, and to the highest court in the state.

Further Reading *Property Rights and Eminent Domain,* by Ellen Frankel Paul (New Brunswick, NJ: Transaction Books, 1987), offers readers a thorough history of eminent domain and current theories and applications of this right in such areas as environmental politics.

In Chicago, residents of the suburbs surrounding O'Hare International Airport are actively protesting airport expansion that threatens homes, cemeteries, and other private property.

22-7 Eminent Domain

All ownership of private property is subject to the government's superior rights if property is needed for purposes of public use. **Eminent domain,** also called **condemnation,** is the right of federal, state, and local governments, or other public bodies, to take private lands, with compensation to their owners, for public use. The right is exercised for such purposes as new highway construction, public parks, state hospitals, and to reinvigorate depressed areas.

The right of eminent domain is not available to persons or businesses when taken for private profit. In such situations, property may be acquired only through mutual agreement and for consideration acceptable to the owner. Eminent domain is at times extended to public utilities when it can be shown that denial of a right-of-way for electric, telephone, gas, or

other lines may interrupt construction of installations providing needed services to an entire community.

When private property is taken by eminent domain proceedings, the owner must be paid the fair value of what has been taken. The owner is not required to accept an amount offered by those assessing the value of the property. But if an offer is refused, the owner must then seek greater compensation through action in the state or federal courts.

Example 22-17

Interstate 95 was designed to cut a swath through a residential section of Chester. Hundreds of homes, businesses, and churches lay in the path of the new highway. Kovach refused to accept the $89,500 offered by assessors for his property. An appeal was made through the county court, with Kovach claiming a fair value of $115,000; this amount would provide the family with a similar home in a comparable neighborhood of the same city. The court might accept the assessors' figure as final; might increase the amount offered; or, in some instances, might reduce the $89,500 if it were considered excessive when reviewed.

In 1987, the U.S. Supreme Court held that property owners must be compensated by the government when regulations that are unduly burdensome deprive them of the use of their land.

Example 22-18

The First English Evangelical Lutheran Church of Glendale sought compensation from the County of Los Angeles, claiming that a flood control ordinance deprived the church of the use of a 21-acre parcel of land in a canyon alongside a creek. The ordinance had been passed after a forest fire denuded the hills upstream from the property and a flood had killed several people and destroyed some buildings on the land. The church had previously used the land as a campground and recreational area for handicapped children. The Supreme Court held that the church was entitled to compensation if it could prove that the regulation preventing the use of the land was unduly burdensome. The court's decision was based on the Fifth Amendment to the U.S. Constitution, which states that private property may not "be taken for public use, without just compensation."

Quick Quiz 22-6 and 22-7 True or False?

1. Newly passed zoning laws do not apply to *nonconforming uses;* that is, existing uses of the land.

2. Exceptions to zoning laws are unfair and, therefore, not allowed.

3. Eminent domain is the right of federal, state, and local governments to take private lands, without compensation to their owners, for public use.

Summary

22-1 Real property is the ground and everything permanently attached to it. It includes the airspace above the surface to as high as the owner can use and the ground under the surface. Although property owners may own the land under a stream, they do not own the water itself. Their rights to use of the water vary, depending on the doctrine of law followed in their state. Property owners may use only that amount of subterranean water that is reasonably required to satisfy their needs. Rainwater may not be artificially channeled to an abutter's property without permission of the abutter. Fixtures are personal property that are so permanently attached to real property that they become part of the real property.

22-2 Easements give people the right to pass over another's land, to run wires through another's airspace, to drain water onto another's property, and to run pipes underneath another's ground. Easements run with the land.

22-3 An estate in fee simple is the greatest interest that one can have in real property. It descends to one's heirs upon death and can be disposed of in any manner during one's lifetime. In contrast, a life estate lasts only for someone's life. At the owner's death, the estate either reverts to the former owner or passes on to someone else.

22-4 People may own real property individually or with others. When two or more people own real property as tenants in common, the interest of a deceased owner's

share passes to the heirs upon death. In contrast, when two or more people own real property as joint tenants or tenants by the entirety, the interest of a deceased owner's share passes to any other cotenants upon death. Only a husband and wife can own property as tenants by the entirety, and the property is protected from creditors unless both the husband and wife are debtors.

22-5 A deed is used to transfer real property by sale or gift. The records of the probate court, instead of a deed, establish title to property when an owner dies. Title to real property may be gained by adverse possession. This action requires possession of another's property openly, notoriously, exclusively, under a claim of right, and continuously for a period of time set by state statute.

22-6 Zoning laws regulate the uses that may be made to properties within specified geographical areas. Newly passed zoning laws do not apply to nonconforming uses, which are uses that were in existence before the zoning law was passed. Nonconforming uses may not be enlarged or expanded. Variances may be issued by boards of appeals to people who suffer undue hardship from zoning laws.

22-7 Eminent domain is the right of federal, state, and local governments, or other public bodies, to take private lands for public use. Owners must be paid the fair value of the property taken.

Key Terms

adverse possession, 421

bargain-and-sale deed, 420

community property, 416

condemnation, 423

cotenants, 414

curtesy, 414

dominant tenement, 411

dower, 414

easement, 411

easement by prescription, 412

eminent domain, 423

estate in fee simple, 413

fixture, 409

general warranty deed, 419

grantee, 419

grantor, 419

joint tenants, 415

life estate, 413

navigable airspace, 407

nonconforming uses, 423

quitclaim deed, 420

real property, 406

remainder estate, 413

reversion estate, 414

right of way, 411

riparian owners, 408

servient tenement, 411

special warranty deed, 419

tenancy by the entirety, 416

tenants in common, 414

trade fixtures, 410

variance, 423

zoning laws, 421

Questions for Review and Discussion

1. What type of vegetation is considered real property? What type is considered personal property?
2. Under modern court decisions, to what extent do landowners own the airspace above their land?
3. What questions are asked in deciding whether an item is a fixture?
4. In what three ways may an easement be created?
5. How does a freehold estate differ from a leasehold estate?
6. What is the difference between common law dower, and common law curtesy?
7. In each of the following tenancies, who owns the property when a cotenant dies: a tenancy in common, a joint tenancy, and a tenancy by the entirety?
8. In what three ways may title to real property be acquired?
9. Describe a nonconforming use of real property. When might a variance be given?
10. What is eminent domain?

Investigating the Internet

Visit the American Bar Association's website at **http://www.abanet.org.** At that site look for "Business and Reference Resources" to find answers & legal questions.

Cases for Analysis

1. Aloi sold a section of her land to Bell, including in the deed an easement allowing Bell to cross Aloi's property to reach the newly acquired parcel. Three years later, Aloi sold his property to Cadd. Shortly thereafter, following an argument, Cadd put a chain across Bell's right of way, saying that he had not given permission for Bell to cross his land. How should the court rule on this matter and why?

2. Alfonso DiFilippo and his brother, Pasquale, owned a parcel of real property as tenants in common. Pasquale died in 1961 leaving a life estate in the property to his widow, Annie, with the remainder estate when Annie dies to Alfonso. Annie died in 1985. Alfonso died in 1969, leaving his interest in the property to his wife, Maria. What interest did Maria own in the property when she died in 1981? *DiFilippo v. DiFilippo,* 640 N.E.2d 1120 (MA).

3. When its lease expired, Kingston Frameworks made plans to move to another building. Preparations were made to remove shelving, mat and glass cutters, display boards, benches, and other fixtures that had been built into the store when the lease first started. All the shelves and fixtures were specially designed for the picture-framing business. The landlord told the owners of Kingston Frameworks to stop removing the items from the property. Could they remove the shelves and other fixtures that were paid for and installed by them during their tenancy? Why or why not? See also *George v. Town of Calais,* 373 A.2d 553 (VT).

4. Smith and Dudley are next-door neighbors. The branches of a large maple tree on Smith's property hang over Dudley's driveway, dripping sap onto Dudley's car. Smith refuses to trim the branches overhanging Dudley's driveway, saying that she does not want to spoil the beauty of the tree. What are Dudley's legal rights in this situation?

5. The Eisenmanns purchased a 90-acre tract of land on which they drilled a 179-foot-deep irrigation well. When the well was completed, they began pumping water at the rate of 650 gallons per minute. Two of the surrounding landowners, the Prathers (whose well was 121 feet 10 inches deep) and the Furleys, lost the use of their wells the next day. A third neighbor, the Zessins, lost the use of

their well three days later. The surrounding landowners sought money damages for the loss of the use of their wells from the Eisenmanns. Did they recover these damages? If so, how much? Explain. *Prather v. Eisenmann,* 261 N.W.2d 766 (NE).

6. Two years after Jean Russell was divorced from Billy Russell, Jean signed a quitclaim deed conveying her interest in their jointly owned real property to Billy. Later, she tried to have the deed set aside on the ground that Billy gave her no consideration. Was she successful? Why or why not? *Russell v. Russell,* 361 So.2d 1053 (AL).

7. Soon after Walter and Elsie Wienke were married, Walter conveyed property that he owned on Ridgewood Drive to himself and Elsie as tenants by the entirety. At the same time, Elsie conveyed property that she owned on Harlan Street to herself and Walter as tenants by the entirety. Twelve years later, Elsie conveyed the Harlan Street property by warranty deed to Colonial Discount Corporation. Walter objected to this sale and did not sign the deed. Colonial Discount Corporation sold the property to Danny and Glenda Lynch. Walter Wienke contended that a conveyance by one tenant by the entirety was inoperative. Do you agree with Walter? Why or why not? *Wienke v. Lynch,* 407 N.E.2d 280 (IN).

8. Richard and Olive Misner began to develop a campground on land that they owned on Olive Lake. The zoning law in existence at the time allowed campgrounds to be built in that area.

A year later, however, the county rezoned the area to "agricultural and lake resort" use, which did not permit campgrounds. At the time the new law went into effect, the Misners had built ten campsites with facilities and three primitive campsites on their property. When they continued to use and expand the campground after the new zoning law was passed, neighbors complained that they were violating the law. Could the Misners continue to use and expand the property as a campground? Explain. *Misner v. Presdorf,* 421 N.E.2d 684 (IN).

9. The Lowell Five Cents Savings Bank took a second mortgage from Stephen Coraccio on property owned by Stephen and his wife, Nancy, as tenants by the entirety. Stephen defaulted on the mortgage, and the bank began foreclosure proceedings against him. Nancy did not know of the mortgage and did not assent to it. She learned of the mortgage only after reading the foreclosure notice in the newspaper. Can a husband give a mortgage on property owned with his wife as tenants by the entirety without the wife's consent? Explain. *Coraccio v. Lowell Five Cents Sav. Bank,* 612 N.E.2d 650 (MA).

10. Walter and Emma Barrett jointly executed a warranty deed conveying three lots of land to Chandler and Jean Clements as joint tenants with the right of survivorship. Six years later, Jean Clements conveyed her one-half undivided interest in the property to Wheeler. Chandler claimed that Jean could not sell her interest to another person without his approval. Was he correct? *Clements v. Wheeler,* 314 So.2d 64 (AL).

Quick Quiz Answers

22-1	22-2	22-3	22-4	22-5	22-6 & 22-7
1. F	1. F	1. T	1. F	1. T	1. T
2. T	2. T	2. F	2. F	2. T	2. F
3. T	3. T	3. T	3. T	3. T	3. F

Chapter 23   Landlord and Tenant

The Opening Case
"The Apartment"

In their junior year of college, Ana Perez and Katherine O'Neil decided to rent an apartment rather than to continue to live in the dormitory. They knew two students who were leaving college with six months remaining on their lease and decided to take over their apartment. After the first month, things started going wrong. They came home from school late one afternoon to find their landlord in their apartment waiting for them. When they rejected the landlord's improper advances, he demanded the rental payment that was due, and declared that the rent would be double after that. Perez and O'Neil paid the rent that was due. When they returned home the next day, they found that the electricity had been shut off. This time, the landlord told them that they had been evicted. He said that he had leased the apartment to the prior occupants and had not given his permission for Perez and O'Neil to live there. Can two students take over another student's apartment without the landlord's permission? Can a landlord legally enter a tenant's apartment without permission, raise the rent without giving notice, and disconnect the apartment's electricity?

Chapter Outcomes

1. List the five elements necessary to create the landlord-tenant relationship.
2. Compare the landlord-tenant relationship with licenses and lodging.
3. Define the four types of leasehold interests.
4. Discuss the law regarding options to renew, options to purchase, assignments, and subletting.
5. Explain the duties of landlords and tenants.
6. Describe the methods used to evict tenants.

23-1 The Landlord-Tenant Relationship

The landlord-tenant relationship is a contractual arrangement whereby the owner of real property allows another to have temporary possession and control of the premises in exchange for consideration. The agreement that gives rise to the landlord-tenant relationship is called a **lease.** The property owner who gives the lease is the **lessor** or **landlord,** and the person to whom the lease is given is the **lessee** or **tenant.** There are five elements necessary for the creation of the landlord-tenant relationship:

1. consent of the landlord to the occupancy by the tenant
2. transfer of possession and control of the property to the tenant in an inferior position (in subordination) to the rights of the landlord
3. the right by the landlord to the return of the property, called the right of reversion
4. the creation of an ownership interest in the tenant known as a leasehold estate
5. either an express or implied contract between the parties that satisfies all the essentials of a valid contract (mutual assent, competent parties, consideration, lawful purpose)

Although rent is usually paid by the tenant to the landlord for the arrangement, it is not essential to the creation of the landlord-tenant relationship.

23-2 Leasing Versus Other Relationships

Other relationships that may be compared with the landlord-tenant relationship are licensing and lodging.

Leasing Compared with Licensing

A lease differs from a license in that a lease gives an interest in real property and transfers possession, whereas a **license** gives no property right or ownership interest in the property but merely allows the licensee to do certain acts that would otherwise be a trespass.

Example 23-1

The city of Topeka was given a gift of 80 acres of land for use as a public park by the heirs of Guilford G. Gage. The deed that was signed by the heirs contained a condition that the property would revert to them if the property were ever deeded or leased to a third party. After the park was established, the city granted the exclusive right to McCall to construct and operate, for a period of five years, a miniature train on the premises. Under the agreement, McCall was subject in virtually all respects to the control of the city, and either party could terminate the arrangement by giving thirty days' notice. The heirs of Gage claimed that the transaction was a lease and that the property should be returned to them. In holding that McCall had a license rather than a lease, the court said that all McCall had was "the exclusive right to operate as the City may dictate."

Since a license confers a personal privilege to act and not a present possessory estate, it does not run with the land and is usually not transferable. It may be made orally or in writing and may be given without consideration. In addition, a license need not delineate the specific space to be occupied.

In contrast, a lease gives the tenant exclusive possession of the premises as against all the world, including the owner. It describes the exact property leased and states the term of the tenancy and the rent to be paid. In addition, in some states, a lease must be in writing.

Permission to sell Christmas trees at a gas station, to hold dance parties in a hall, and to place a sign on the outside of a building have all been held to be licenses rather than leases.

Terms *Lease* comes from the Latin *laxare,* meaning "to loosen." The owner of leased property is, in effect, loosening hold on it.

Terms *Tenant* comes from the Latin word for *hold.* When a landlord lets another person hold the lease to a building or apartment, that person is known as a tenant.

Teaching Tips Write examples of different types of properties on the board and ask students to identify which could involve leasing arrangements. Your list might include *house, flat, condominium, co-op, time-share, duplex, apartment,* and *loft.*

Teaching Tips Explain to students that a lease is merely a contract. Review the requirements of a binding contract and apply these requirements to the formation of a lease.

Cross-Cultural Notes
Many employers in Kenya provide employees and families with housing, from small single-room dwellings called *cubes* to fully equipped houses. Certain government agencies, such as the department of education, may offer housing subsidies to people when their employers do not.

Leasing Compared with Lodging

A **lodger** is one who has the use of property without actual or exclusive possession of it. A lodger is a type of licensee, with a mere right to use the property. The landlord retains control of the premises and is responsible for its care and upkeep. Unlike a tenant, a lodger has no right to bring suit for trespass or to eject an intruder from the premises. One who lives in a spare room of a house, for example, whose owner retains direct control and supervision of the entire house, is a lodger.

Quick Quiz 23-1 & 23-2 True or False?

1. In a landlord-tenant relationship, the tenant has an ownership interest in the property.

2. A license gives no ownership interest in the property to the licensee.

3. A lodger is a type of licensee, with a mere right to use the property.

23-3 Types of Leasehold Interests

The interest conveyed by a lease is called a **leasehold estate,** or a **tenancy.** There are four kinds of leasehold estates:

1. tenancy at will
2. tenancy for years
3. periodic tenancy
4. tenancy at sufferance

Tenancy at Will

Teaching Tips Write the different types of leases on the board and discuss the uses of each. Include a discussion of how long each of the various leases may last. Finally, have the students think of likely scenarios in which each of the four leases would be used.

A **tenancy at will** is an ownership interest (estate) in real property for an indefinite period of time. No writing is required to create this tenancy, and it may be terminated at the will of either party by giving proper notice. The notice requirement to terminate a tenancy at will varies from state to state. It ranges from the time between rent periods to thirty days' written notice from the next day that rent is due.

The rule generally followed in this country is that a tenancy at will comes to an end when the property is sold by the landlord to a third party. The notice required by state law must be given to the tenant in any event.

Tenancy for Years

A house she hath, 'tis made of such good fashion,
The tenant ne'er shall pay for reparation,
Nor will the landlord ever raise her rent
Or turn her out of doors for nonpayment:
From chimney tax this cell is free
To such a house who would not tenant be?

—17th Century English tombstone

A **tenancy for years** is an ownership interest (estate) in real property for a definite or fixed period of time. It may be for one week, six months, one year, five years, ninety-nine years, or any period of time, as long as it is definite. Such a tenancy automatically terminates on the expiration of the stated term. A tenancy for 100 years or more creates an estate in fee simple, transferring absolute ownership to the tenant. For this reason, leases are sometimes written for ninety-nine-year periods.

In some states, a tenancy for years may be oral if the term is shorter than one year; otherwise, it must be in writing. Other states require all tenancies for years to be in writing. A tenant who remains in possession of the premises at the expiration of the term with permission of the landlord, but without a new lease, is a tenant at will in some states. In other states, such a tenant is known as a periodic tenant.

Periodic Tenancy

A **periodic tenancy,** which is also known as a **tenancy from year to year** (or month to month, or week to week), is a fixed-period tenancy that continues for successive periods until one of the parties terminates it by giving notice to the other party.

Unless the landlord or the tenant gives advance notice of an intention to terminate the lease, it will be automatically renewed at the end of each fixed period for the same term. Advance notice varies from state to state, but it generally is defined as a period of three months for periodic tenancies of one year or longer and "one period" for periodic terms of less than a year.

State Variations Common law rules hold that before terminating a lease, a landlord must give a six-month notice to a year-to-year tenant, a one-month notice to a month-to-month tenant, and a one-week notice to a week-to-week tenant. North Carolina statutes differ markedly from common law rules in that they require a landlord to give a one-week notice to a month-to-month tenant and a two-day notice to a week-to-week tenant. To compute the time period, days are counted beginning with the day after notice was served and ending with the last day of the rental period.

Example 23-2

Pasco's year-to-year lease expired on December 31. On November 15, she gave her landlord notice of her intention to terminate the lease. In her state, three months' notice is necessary to terminate a year-to-year tenancy. Pasco's landlord, therefore, could hold her to an additional year.

The death of a tenant who holds a periodic tenancy does not terminate the tenancy. Rather, the interest of the tenant passes to the personal representative of the deceased's estate.

Example 23-3

Wilson was in possession of rental property originally leased to his father on a month-to-month basis. After the father's death, the landlord notified Wilson to vacate the premises on the grounds that the tenancy had ceased automatically. When Wilson refused to leave, criminal trespass charges were filed against him. He was found not guilty. The court held that his father's interest in the premises passed to him and that he was entitled to proper notice to end the month-to-month tenancy.

A periodic tenancy may be created impliedly by a landlord accepting rent from a tenant for years whose lease has expired or who is wrongfully in possession. Some states treat the latter situation as a tenancy at will.

Tenancy at Sufferance

A **tenancy at sufferance** arises when tenants wrongfully remain in possession of the premises after their tenancy has expired. It often comes about at the expiration of the term of a tenancy for years or when a tenancy at will has been properly terminated and the tenant remains in possession. Such a tenant is a wrongdoer, having no estate or other interest in the property. A tenant at sufferance is not entitled to notice to vacate and is liable to pay rent for the period of occupancy. A periodic tenancy or a tenancy at will may come about, however, instead of a tenancy at sufferance if a landlord accepts rent from a tenant whose tenancy has expired.

Background Information A landlord has no responsibility to give a tenant at sufferance notice to vacate, and a tenant at sufferance has no responsibility to give a landlord notice of termination. However, many lease contracts stipulate that, upon termination of the lease, both parties will be held to the same terms to avoid situations of no responsibility.

> ## Example 23-4
>
> Sutherland, an attorney, rented a suite of rooms in the Metropolitan Building in Chicago that she used for law offices. When her two-year lease expired, she negotiated with the owner of the building for a new lease. The negotiations extended over a period of several months, and the parties could not reach agreement. The landlord accepted rent each month from Sutherland during the period of negotiations. Sutherland was not a tenant at sufferance during the negotiation period because the landlord accepted rent from her during that time. A month-to-month tenancy was created. The landlord was required to give Sutherland a month's notice to end the tenancy.

> ## Quick Quiz 23-3 True or False?
>
> 1. A tenancy at will is an ownership interest in real property for a definite period of time.
>
> 2. A lease for 100 years or more transfers absolute ownership of the property to the tenant.
>
> 3. A periodic tenancy automatically renews at the end of each period unless the landlord or tenant gives advance notice to terminate it.

23-4   The Lease Agreement

Background Information Landlord-tenant law began in England, where all land was once held by the king. Lords were given plots of land in exchange for services, usually military, performed for the king. After the twelfth century, tenants were allowed to hold land for specific periods under sealed contracts, but they didn't have much recourse if the king breached the contract and decided to reclaim the property. Not until the thirteenth century were tenant rights protected by writ.

State Variations Iowa allows landlords to require up to two months rent for security deposits. Minnesota law requires landlords to pay interest on security deposits.

The agreement between a lessor and a lessee, called a lease, creates the landlord-tenant relationship. It provides the tenant with exclusive possession and control of the real property of the landlord. Since the lease is a contract, the general rules of contract law apply to it.

> ## Example 23-5
>
> Piccarelli, a representative of Mister Donut, expressed interest in leasing Tull's property. He sent a letter to Tull describing the "rudiments of our deal" and concluding with an expression of hope "that in the very near future preliminaries will be completed." This was followed by a form of lease sent by Piccarelli to Tull for the latter's approval. Tull signed the lease, after changing it materially, and returned it to Mister Donut for a countersignature. Nothing further was done, and the transaction never materialized. Tull's building was vandalized and burned after his tenants were evicted in anticipation of leasing the property to Mister Donut. When Tull sued Mister Donut, the court held that no contract and thus no lease came about. The initial letter was no more than an agenda for further discussion. The first draft of the lease sent by Piccarelli to Tull was an offer, and the revised document was a counteroffer that was never accepted by Mister Donut.

The essential requirements of a lease are: (1) a definite agreement as to the extent and bounds of the leased property, (2) a definite and agreed term, and (3) a definite and agreed price of rental and manner of payment (see Figure 23-1).

Example 23-6

Schumacher leased a retail store to a tenant for a five-year term. The renewal clause stated that "the Tenant may renew this lease for an additional period of five years at annual rentals *to be agreed upon;* Tenant shall give Landlord thirty (30) days written notice, to be mailed certified mail, return receipt requested, of the intention to exercise such right." The tenant gave timely notice to renew the lease, but the parties could not agree on the rent for the new term. The court held that the agreement to renew the lease was unenforceable because the amount of rent was uncertain.

Figure 23-1   This is an example of a lease.

LEASE

This lease made the 20th day of August, 2005, between ROBERT VICKERS, herein called Landlord, and ETHEL LOPAZ, herein called Tenant, witnesseth:

The Landlord leases to the Tenant the following described premises: Four rooms and a bath on the first floor of the premises located at 17 Rosebud Terrace, Ashmont, New Hampshire, for the term of one year commencing at noon on the first day of September 2005 and ending at noon on the 31st day of August, 2006.

The Tenant agrees to pay to the Landlord the sum of $6,000 for the said term, in eleven (11) monthly payments as follows: The first and last months' rent of $1,000, plus a security deposit of $500, payable on September 1, 2005, and $500 on the first day of each month thereafter.

The Landlord agrees that the Tenant on paying the said rent and performing the covenants herein contained shall peaceably and quietly have, hold, and enjoy the premises for said term.

The Tenant agrees that at the expiration of the time mentioned in this lease she will give peaceable possession of the said premises to the Landlord in as good a condition as they now are, the usual wear, unavoidable accidents, and loss by fire excepted, and will not make or suffer any waste thereof, nor assign this lease, nor sublet, nor permit any person to occupy the same, nor make or suffer to be made any alteration therein, without the consent of the Landlord in writing having first been obtained, and that the Landlord may enter to view and make improvements, and to show the premises to prospective tenants or purchasers.

The covenants herein shall extend to and be binding upon heirs, executors, and administrators of the parties to this lease.

IN WITNESS WHEREOF, the parties have hereunto set their hands and seals the day and year first above written.

Robert Vickers
Robert Vickers

Ethel Lopaz
Ethel Lopaz

Rent Control

Some large communities have passed rent control laws to keep rents within an affordable range. These laws limit what landlords can charge for rental property and often contain procedures that must be followed before tenants may be evicted. In a number of areas, rent control laws have caused landlords to turn their apartments into condominiums, leading to shortages in rental apartments. Such laws differ from place to place. Some states, including Massachusetts, have done away with rent control laws altogether.

Security Deposits

Most leases for apartments call for a security deposit to protect the lessor against nonpayment or property damage.

In addition to the first month's rent, landlords often require either a security deposit or the last month's rent, or both, to be paid at the beginning of a tenancy. The deposit protects landlords against damages to their property as well as nonpayment of rent. Due to abuses of such deposits by landlords, state legislatures have passed laws regulating security deposits on residential property. Such laws spell out the rights of tenants and make it easier for tenants to prevail in court. Although these laws differ from state to state, the following characteristics are commonly found: most states limit security deposits to 1, 1½, 2, or 2½ months' rent, and most states require that security deposits be placed in interest-bearing accounts. The interest is either paid to tenants on an annual basis or accrued in their favor. Security deposits may not be commingled with other money belonging to the landlord. Also, the landlord is given a specific period, usually thirty days after the lease ends, to account for the security deposit and return the balance due to a tenant. Many states have now "put teeth" into the law providing for double or triple damages, court costs, and attorney's fees for tenants whose security deposits were wrongfully withheld.

State Variations In Colorado, a landlord's willful retention of a security deposit can render a landlord liable for treble the amount of that portion of the security deposit wrongfully withheld from the tenant, together with reasonable attorney's and court costs.

Related Cases Some college students who had rented an apartment, began having trouble paying the rent after one of the students moved out. The landlord finally evicted them and also sued them not only for unpaid past rents but also future rents, according to the terms of the lease. The students attempted to defend by voiding the lease, arguing that it was unconscionable because the terms so strongly favored the landlord. The court ruled in the landlord's favor, however, noting that the students had read and signed the lease and could have understood its terms. *Nyen v. Park Doral Apartments,* 535 N.E.2d 178.

> ## Example 23-7
>
> Santos rented a $450-per-month apartment from Hollis for a term of two years. When Santos's tenancy ended, Hollis refused to return any of the $450 security deposit to Santos, claiming that the damages to the apartment fully offset the amount of the deposit. Santos hired a lawyer, who brought suit against Hollis. The landlord was able to demonstrate only $70 in damages to Santos's apartment. The court found that Hollis had wrongfully withheld $380 of Santos's security deposit. The court awarded Santos a judgment for double damages of $760 plus attorney's fees of $200. With court costs, the landlord was forced to pay over $1,000.

Landlords of commercial property may also require security deposits, but the consumer protection statutes do not usually cover commercial leases.

Option to Renew or to Purchase

Many leases contain a provision allowing the lessee to have the option to renew the lease for one or more additional periods. An option to renew gives the lessee the right, at the end of the lease, to a new lease for an additional period. The new lease is on the same terms as

Business Law in the News
The Mouse Takes Manhattan

Before Hollywood, there was New York's 42nd Street, birthplace of American mass-market entertainment. Beginning in 1899, a burst of construction on a single mid-Manhattan block created the greatest concentration of playhouses America has ever seen or likely will see again. No place has ever evoked the glamour of big-city nightlife as vividly as did "naughty, bawdy, gaudy" 42nd Street, stomping ground of legendary impresarios Oscar Hammerstein I and Florenz Ziegfeld Jr.

Starting in the 1930s, 42nd Street's fame gradually soured into infamy as the glitzy musicals of its golden age were supplanted by burlesque revues and B movies. XXX fare descended on 42nd Street with a vengeance in the late 1960s when a vending-machine salesman named Martin J. Hodas adapted the peep show machine to pornographic use. A conspicuous property-value sinkhole amid the world's costliest stand of skyscrapers, 42nd Street affronted the custodians of New York's economy no less than its guardians of public morality.

Many schemes to restore 42nd Street to "respectability" were floated over the next few decades, but redevelopment did not gain traction till the mid-1990s, when government officials struck a catalytic deal with the Walt Disney Co. to restore the New Amsterdam Theatre.

The willingness of Disney CEO Michael D. Eisner, a native New Yorker, to take a flyer on the New Amsterdam was rooted in his own nostalgic memories of 42nd Street. . . .

The transaction was tightly wrapped in financial and legal complications, but its essence was this: The state would make a $26 million capital investment in the New Amsterdam in the form of a subsidized loan to Disney, which would invest $8 million in equity. Taking into account a federal tax credit, the company's net investment would amount to less than $3 million. Still, Eisner and crew did not get everything they wanted; most important, Disney was unable to purchase the New Amsterdam outright, settling instead for a 49-year lease. . . .

No longer is 42nd Street midtown's economic Dead Zone; it has been integrated into the city's economy, radiating financial benefits to businesses and property owners throughout the area. Still, there remains a patchwork quality to 42nd Street's revival. Many smaller retailers have struggled. And in transplanting a glitzy theme-park culture into the heart of the big city, 42nd Street's redevelopers have enhanced its tourist appeal at the cost of alienating many New Yorkers.

But for the Walt Disney Co., 42nd Street has proven an unqualified triumph. Eliminating every trace of the damage done to the New Amsterdam by its previous owners' neglect, Disney restored the theater to a condition approximating its original splendor. In late 1997, the company reopened the New Amsterdam with a live adaptation of its hit film *The Lion King.* An arresting fusion of middlebrow storytelling and avant-garde costuming and design, the drama won uniformly laudatory reviews. And, ranking high on the list of the longest-running hits in Broadway history, *The Lion King* continues to play to full houses on the new 42nd Street.

Questions for Analysis

1. Beginning in 1899, what area of New York City created the greatest concentration of playhouses America has ever seen?

2. How did the area change beginning in the 1930s?

3. What happened to the area in the late 1960s?

4. What motivated Disney's CEO to restore the New Amsterdam Theater and what type of ownership did Disney acquire?

5. What was the cost to many New Yorkers of enhancing the area's tourist appeal?

6. What proof is there of Disney's success in this venture?

The Opening Case Revisited
"The Apartment"

In The Opening Case, the lease could be assigned or sublet to Ana and Katherine unless there was a clause in the lease that stated otherwise. In any event, the acceptance of rent from the students amounted to an implied acceptance of their tenancy.

the old one with the possible exception of an increase in the rent. To exercise the option, the lessee must notify the lessor on or before the date set forth in the lease to do so.

A lessee may, if the lease so provides, be given an option to purchase the property. This option is an agreement by the lessor to sell the property to the lessee for a stated price. To exercise the option, the lessee must notify the lessor, within the time period stated in the lease, of the decision to purchase the property.

Example 23-8

Larson purchased a parcel of real property for $19,140 and leased it to the Panhandle Rehabilitation Center. The lease was for ten years and contained an option to buy for $19,000. After leasing the premises for five years and spending $5,000 to improve it, Panhandle notified Larson of its intention to exercise its option. By this time, the property was worth $38,000. Larson refused to sell the property to Panhandle for $19,000. The court ordered her to do so.

Assignment and Subletting

An assignment of a lease occurs when the interest in the leased premises is transferred by the lessee to another person for the balance of the term of the lease. The new party, called the assignee, steps into the shoes of the tenant, or assignor, and is liable for all of the original tenant's obligations and is entitled to all of the original tenant's rights under the lease. In contrast, it is called a **sublease,** or **underlease,** if the transfer is for a part of the term but not for the remainder of it.

A lease may be assigned or sublet unless the lease states otherwise. Many leases are written so that they require landlord approval for an assignment or a sublease. However, in some states the landlord cannot withhold such approval unreasonably. An assignment or sublease will be held valid if the landlord accepts rent over a period of time from either an assignee or a subtenant.

Quick Quiz 23-4 True or False?

1. Most states require that security deposits be placed in interest-bearing accounts with the interest belonging to the tenant.

2. A lessee may be given either an option to renew the lease or an option to purchase the property but not both.

3. A sublease occurs when the interest in the leased premises is transferred by the lessee to another person for the balance of the term of the lease.

23-5 Landlord's Duties

A good lease agreement will carefully spell out the respective rights and duties of the landlord and the tenant. However, state and local laws may restrict or expand upon what is set forth in the lease.

Duty to Refrain from Discrimination

A landlord may not discriminate in selecting tenants on the grounds of race, creed, color, or sex. In most states a landlord may restrict rentals to persons without children, but may not restrict a married couple's freedom to bear children during the leasehold.

> ### Example 23-9
>
> The Stimsons, a married couple, rented a luxury apartment from Chester Realty Associates. A condition inserted in the lease read, "The lessee agrees that if a child or children are born to the tenants during the period of the lease, the lease will be automatically terminated without the necessity of notice from the landlord." This condition is not enforceable against the Stimsons. Persons may not be denied the freedom of bearing children through contracts made with a landlord or others.

Duty to Maintain the Premises

When real property is rented for dwelling purposes, there is an implied warranty, called the **warranty of habitability,** that the premises are fit for human habitation. This provision means that the landlord warrants that there are not defects vital to the use of the premises for residential purposes. Examples of defects are unsafe electrical wiring, a malfunctioning heating or cooling system, broken windows, a leaking roof, and infestation of insects.

> ### Example 23-10
>
> Jefferson leased an apartment for one year from Berman. A series of breaks in underground heating pipes caused the tenant to receive intermittent heat for two months. Finally, in early October, the pipe burst completely, and the tenant was without heat and hot water for two weeks. The court held that even though the landlord was not at fault, the warranty of habitability had been breached. Jefferson was not required to pay rent during the period that the apartment had no heat.

Many municipalities have adopted ordinances to protect tenants from unsafe or unhealthy conditions created by a landlord's refusal to make necessary repairs. Building inspectors, health authorities, and other public officials are empowered to make inspections and demand improvements when they are contacted by dissatisfied tenants. In many cases, ordinances permit the tenant to cease payment of rent for the period during which the landlord fails to make the repairs or improvements needed.

The majority of states hold that a landlord has a duty to clear common entryways of natural accumulations of snow and ice. Some states, nevertheless, still follow the older rule that the landlord owes no duty to tenants to clean common entryways of ice and snow unless there is an agreement on the part of the landlord to do so.

Teaching Tips Ask student volunteers to contact government officials and tenant associations to find out about local laws governing rental property, landlord and tenant responsibilities, subletting, and damages to property. Have the volunteers report their findings to the class.

State Variations In Arizona, a person who knowingly refuses to rent a dwelling to a tenant because the tenant has children is guilty of a petty offense.

Related Cases A landlord tried to evict an unmarried female tenant on the grounds that she was using the premises to engage in sexual activity with a male friend. The court refused to evict, noting that the tenant was not acting illegally, since this was not a commercial activity and she was not, therefore, participating in prostitution. *Edward v. Roe*, 327 N.Y.S.2d 307.

Further Reading For an international view of landlord-tenant relations, see *The Regulation of Rental Contracts in the Housing Market* by Franz Hubert (Frankfurt: Peter Lang, 1991).

Duty to Deliver Peaceful Possession

The tenant is entitled to the exclusive peaceful possession and quiet enjoyment of the rental premises. **Quiet enjoyment** is the right of a tenant to the undisturbed possession of the property. The landlord may not interfere with the tenant's rights of possession as long as the tenant abides by the conditions of the lease and those imposed by law.

Example 23-11

Smith Grocery & Variety, Inc., leased one store in a two-store mall from Northern Terminals, Inc. The lease entitled Smith to the use of the parking areas (between fourteen and twenty spaces) abutting the leased premises. Five months after Smith opened for business, Northern Terminals added an additional store to the mall without increasing the mall's parking facilities. Smith's business declined due to the severe parking shortage caused by the opening of a Triple-S Blue Stamp Redemption Center in the new addition. The court held that Northern Terminals, Inc., breached the covenant of quiet enjoyment. There was a substantial interference with the lessee's use of the premises, which was caused by the lessor's taking away of the parking spaces.

The right to exclusive possession by the tenant makes the landlord a trespasser should there be any unauthorized entry by the landlord into the rented premises.

Example 23-12

Benson & Childs rented a skylight suite for their architecture offices. The lease gave the owner permission to enter only when a request had been made or in the event of extreme emergency. The landlord entered the offices late one evening for what he termed was his regular safety and fire inspection. Benson & Childs may treat the landlord's trespass as a breach of their right to sole possession, giving them the right to terminate the lease and charge the landlord in either a civil or a criminal complaint.

A tenant who is wrongfully evicted is not required to return and may consider the lease as ended. An **eviction** is an act of the landlord that deprives the tenant of the enjoyment of the premises. It is called an **actual eviction** when the tenant is physically deprived of the leasehold. When the tenant is deprived of something of a substantial nature that was called

The Opening Case Revisited
"The Apartment"

In The Opening Case, the landlord violated Ana's and Katherine's right to exclusive, undisturbed possession of the premises by going into the apartment without permission. The landlord also committed a constructive eviction by shutting off the electricity.

for under the lease, it is termed a **constructive eviction.** The tenant is justified in abandoning the premises without paying rent when a wrongful eviction occurs. The tenant must mitigate (lessen) any damages, however, if possible.

Example 23-13

Sound City, U.S.A., was interested in renting space in a shopping center. An inspection of the premises disclosed portions of the ceiling tile missing or hanging loose, water marks on the ceiling, and bare fluorescent light fixtures. As a result, Sound City included in its one-year lease an addendum (addition) whereby the landlord agreed to repair and paint the ceiling tile, cover the light bulb fixtures, panel the south wall, and erect a partition. Sound City moved into the shopping center, but after three months and many complaints the repairs were never completed. It then moved out. The landlord brought suit for the remaining nine months' rent. The court held against the landlord, saying that there had been a constructive eviction. The physical appearance of the store was an important factor in the successful operation of Sound City's business. The failure to repair the premises properly in accordance with the lease rendered the premises unsuitable for the purpose for which they were rented.

Quick Quiz 23-5 True or False?

1. When real property is rented for dwelling purposes, there is an implied warranty of habitability, which means that snow will be cleared from common entryways.

2. A tenant is entitled to quiet enjoyment of the property, which means that walls between adjoining apartments must be soundproof.

3. A landlord is never considered a trespasser on the leased property.

Background Information Under rent control programs, landlords lose some traditional rights, such as the right to determine the amount that rents will be raised. Laws differ among municipalities, but, under most programs, a landlord can only raise rents a predetermined percentage each year.

23-6 Tenant's Duties

The tenant has the duty to pay rent to the landlord. In addition, the landlord has the right to remove, through court procedures, a tenant for nonpayment of rent, disorderliness, or illegal or unpermitted use of the premises.

A tenant has the duty to observe the valid restrictions contained in the lease. Leases may impose duties of all kinds as long as they are legal and do not deny a tenant's constitutional rights. Failure to abide by the restrictions agreed to at the time of the signing of the lease gives the landlord the right to seek eviction of the tenant.

Terms Tenants who hold property under rent control are called *statutory tenants* because of the statutes imposing public policy on housing accommodations.

Teaching Tips Obtain at a law library or on the Internet a copy of the landlord-tenant statutes of your state. Distribute copies of the statutes to students and use them as guides for a discussion of landlord-tenant laws.

Example 23-14

Bogg's lease states that he cannot paint any exterior woodwork or walls without first getting written permission from the landlord. Painting these surfaces, even though doing so improves the property, gives the landlord the right to terminate Bogg's lease.

Unless agreed otherwise the tenant must turn over to the landlord all fixtures (except trade fixtures belonging to a business) that have been made a permanent part of the real property by the tenant during the leasehold.

Example 23-15

Dr. Hembly installed partitions in the rented house, dividing the living room for consultation offices. New lighting fixtures were installed, as well as a built-in air-conditioning system. Hembly would be barred from removing the additions at the expiration of her lease or upon her eviction, as they had become real property.

Tenants also have a duty to avoid damaging or destroying the property; that is, commit waste. **Waste** is defined as substantial damage to premises which significantly decreases the value of the property.

Quick Quiz 23-6 True or False?

1. A landlord has the right to remove by force a tenant for nonpayment of rent.
2. Tenants must comply with valid restrictions contained in the lease.
3. Tenants cannot commit waste, that is, damage the premises in such a way that its value is decreased significantly.

23-7 Tort Liability

When a person is injured on leased property, the one who is in control of that part of the premises where the injury occurs usually is responsible if the injury was caused by that person's negligence. The landlord, for example, is responsible for injury to others that may be caused by a defect in the common areas, such as hallways and stairways.

Example 23-16

Wilson sustained serious injuries when she fell on a defective step while descending the front stairway of her apartment building. The landlord was held liable for Wilson's injuries because she was negligent in failing to keep the steps in a reasonably safe condition.

Although landlords are not guarantors of the safety of persons in a building's common area, they are not free to ignore reasonably foreseeable risks of harm to tenants and others lawfully on the premises. Landlords must take reasonable steps to guard against foreseeable criminal acts of third parties.

Example 23-17

Whittaker was an editorial assistant for a publishing company that leased space in an office park building. One Sunday, she drove to the office park and let herself into the building with a key that she was entitled to have. While attempting to unlock a door to the publishing company's office, she was attacked from behind by an unknown person. The assailant threatened Whittaker, blindfolded her, and took her to an adjoining area where he raped her. In a suit brought by Whittaker against the owner of the building, the court held that the landlord had no duty to Whittaker to provide protection because the random act of violence was not foreseeable.

Tenants are responsible, in most cases, for reasonably foreseeable injuries to persons caused by defects in the portion of the premises over which they have control.

Example 23-18

While visiting a friend's second-floor apartment, Ward fell down a single step leading to the bathroom. In a suit brought against the landlord for her injuries, Ward lost the case. The court said that the tenant was the responsible occupier of the premises. Any duty owed to the tenant's guest relative to the step was owed by the tenant, not the landlord.

23-8 Eviction Proceedings

States today do not allow landlords to use force to evict tenants. Instead, they must make use of statutory remedies that are available to them. Some states do, however, recognize the right of landlords to enter wrongfully held premises and take over possession if it can be done peacefully.

A Question of Ethics

It is illegal in every state for a landlord to use force to evict a tenant. What ethical considerations are implied in this law?

Ejectment is the common law name given to the lawsuit brought by the landlord to have the tenant evicted from the premises. This older remedy is still available in many states; however, it is time-consuming, expensive, and subject to long delays.

Unlawful detainer is a legal proceeding that provides landlords with a quick method of evicting a tenant. The proceeding is referred to by different names in different states, including the following: summary process, summary ejectment, forcible entry and detainer, and dispossessory warrant proceedings. The remedy provides landlords with a quick method of regaining possession of their property and protects tenants from being ousted by force and violence. Strict notice requirements must be followed by the landlord, after which

Background Information In New York and Houston, 5 percent of landlords control over half the rental properties.

Cross-Cultural Notes After the Communist revolution in China, many changes were made to correct what were viewed as the injustices of imperialism. For example, "eternal lease rights" to land had previously barred the Chinese from raising rents for foreigners or terminating leases, so housing on such property had been let at prices that were unfair to landlords. Most private leases were subsequently eliminated.

The Opening Case Revisited
"The Apartment"

In The Opening Case, the landlord could not raise the rent until the expiration of the lease and could not evict Ana and Katherine without having grounds to do so and without following proper procedures under state law.

both parties are given their day in court. If a forcible eviction becomes necessary, it is done by the sheriff under the supervision of the court.

Example 23-19

Several months after Koonce fell behind in her rent payments, her landlord brought summary process proceedings against her. The court issued an execution (an order to carry out its judgment) giving the landlord possession, rent arrearages, and costs. Armed with the execution, a sheriff went to the premises and removed three fans, a stereo system, a record collection, a digital clock radio, a double-bed quilt, an iron, and a portable tape recorder. He also left a note saying that execution would be carried out if the rent were not paid up. The court held that this was an improper procedure. It was the duty of the sheriff, once the execution was placed in his hands, to remove all Koonce's possessions, sell such of them as were necessary to satisfy the execution, and make the rest of her possessions available to her. Piecemeal exercise of an execution was not permissible.

Quick Quiz 23-7 & 23-8 True or False?

1. Tenants are responsible, in most cases, for reasonable foreseeable injuries to persons caused by defects in the portion of the premises over which they have control.

2. Landlords may usually use force to evict tenants.

3. Strict notice requirements must be followed by a landlord to evict a tenant.

Summary

23-1 The landlord-tenant relationship is a contractual arrangement whereby the owner of real property allows another to have temporary possession and control of the premises in exchange for consideration.

23-2 A lease differs from a license in that a lease conveys an interest in real property and transfers possession, whereas a license conveys no property right or interest but merely allows the licensee to do certain acts that would otherwise be a trespass. A lodger, a type of licensee, has the use of property without the actual or exclusive possession of it.

23-3 A tenancy at will is an ownership interest (estate) in real property for an indefinite period of time. A tenancy for years is an estate for a definite period of time, no matter how long or how short. A periodic tenancy is a tenancy that continues for successive periods until one of the parties terminates it by giving notice to the other party. A tenancy at sufferance arises when tenants wrongfully remain in possession of the premises after their tenancy has expired.

23-4 The lease creates the landlord-tenant relationship. Since it is a contract, the general rules of contract law apply to it. State laws often regulate security deposits on residential property. A lease may be assigned or sublet unless the lease states otherwise.

23-5 A landlord may not discriminate in selecting tenants on the grounds of race, creed, color, or sex.

Premises that are rented for residential purposes must be fit for human habitation. Tenants are entitled to peaceful possession and quiet enjoyment.

23-6 Landlords have the right to evict tenants for nonpayment of rent, disorderliness, and unpermitted use of the premises. Tenants must observe the valid restrictions in a lease and not commit waste.

23-7 When someone is injured, the person in control of that part of the premises where the injury occurs is responsible if negligent.

23-8 Peaceable entry, ejectment, and unlawful detainer are the principal methods available to landlords to regain possession of their premises. Of these, unlawful detainer (called by different names in different states) is the most commonly used method. This remedy provides landlords with a quick method of regaining possession of their property and protects tenants from being ousted by force and violence.

Key Terms

actual eviction, 438

constructive eviction, 439

ejectment, 441

eviction, 438

landlord, 428

lease, 428

leasehold estate, 430

lessee, 429

lessor, 428

license, 429

lodger, 430

periodic tenancy, 431

quiet enjoyment, 438

sublease, 436

tenancy, 430

tenancy at sufferance, 431

tenancy at will, 430

tenancy for years, 430

tenancy from year to year, 431

tenant, 429

underlease, 436

unlawful detainer, 441

warranty of habitability, 437

waste, 440

Questions for Review and Discussion

1. What are the five elements that are necessary for the creation of the landlord-tenant relationship?
2. How does a lease compare with a license and with lodging?
3. In what ways do the following tenancies differ: tenancy for years, periodic tenancy, tenancy at will, and tenancy at sufferance? Explain.
4. What are the three essential requirements of a lease?
5. How does the assignment of a lease compare with the subletting of a lease?
6. When and by whom is the implied warranty of habitability made?
7. What duties do landlords have under a lease?

8. What duties do tenants have under a lease?

9. What are the obligations of the tenant and the landlord when someone is injured on leased property?

10. What are the three principal methods available to landlords to regain possession of premises when tenants fail to leave at the end of a tenancy? Describe each method.

Investigating the Internet

On the Net, key in the words "law about landlord tenant." This should bring you to the Legal Information Institute's landlord-tenant website, which includes, among other things, state-specific laws on that subject.

Cases for Analysis

1. Bech owned a building in which Cuevas resided as a tenant at will. Alleging that Cuevas had committed waste, Bech delivered a letter to Cuevas ordering her to vacate the premises in two days. The law of that state required a thirty-day notice to evict a tenant at will. Must Cuevas vacate the premises? Explain. *Bech v. Cuevas,* 534 N.E.2d 1163 (MA).

2. The following language was in a handwritten agreement signed by Harold and Saul and their respective wives: "Saul & Zelda get the option to rent the lower level of the Hope Chest store when their lease expires. If they do take it, they will pay the same rate of rent per square foot that Harold is paying for his store. Saul & Zelda will do all the fixing up at their expense. Entrance to upper level has to be maintained from Newbury Street—similar to how it is now. Saul and Zelda have to let Harold know six months ahead of time: (lease expires by May 31, 1987 so that Saul and Zelda have to let Harold know by Nov. 31, 1986). Saul and Zelda cannot use the name Simon or Simon's on anything with the Simon name as a name for their store. Too confusing." Does the language contain the essential elements of a lease? Explain. *Simon v. Simon,* 625 N.E.2d 564 (MA).

3. Goldstein rented an apartment from Dunbar as a tenant at will. She paid her rent on time and took good care of the premises; she was never disorderly. Dunbar decided to evict Goldstein and rent the apartment to a college friend who was moving to the area. He sent Goldstein a proper notice to quit. Goldstein claimed that she could not be asked to leave because she had done nothing wrong. Do you agree with Goldstein? Explain. See also *Ralo, Inc., v. Jack Graham, Inc.,* 362 So.2d 310 (FL).

4. Sarah H. Brown and Sandy F. Soverow agreed to rent separate apartments from Osborn, the owner of an apartment complex called Nob Hill Apartments, which was being constructed. Since their single apartments were not yet completed, Brown and Soverow agreed to rent one larger apartment in the complex and live in that until their separate apartments were finished. A fire occurred in the apartment shortly after Brown had put some leftover livers and gizzards for her dogs on the electric stove and had left the apartment. In the lawsuit that followed, the contention was made that Brown and Soverow were lodgers rather than tenants. Do you agree with the contention? Explain. *Osborn v. Brown,* 361 So.2d 82 (AL).

5. Alabama Outdoor Advertising Co., Inc., leased part of a lot from All State Linen Service Co. to erect a commercial advertising sign. The term of the lease was for "indefinite years, beginning 1st day of January, 1973, and ending year to year thereafter." When All State sold the lot, it was argued that Alabama's lease was a tenancy at will and, therefore, came to an end when the lot was sold. Do you agree with this argument? Why or why not? *Industrial Mach., Inc., v. Creative Displays, Inc.,* 344 So.2d 743 (AL).

6. Nash rented an apartment from Short for $500 a month. Nash always paid his rent on time. He fell

behind, however, when his company went out of business and he lost his job. At a point when the amount in arrears reached $1,000, Short pushed Nash out of the apartment and padlocked the door. Nash claimed that Short violated the law by using force to evict him. Short claimed that he had a right to do so. For whom would you decide? Why? See also *Sempek v. Minarik,* 264 N.W.2d 426 (NE).

7. Friedman's tenancy came to an end on June 30. His landlord did not return or account for any portion of Friedman's security deposit until the following September 1. A statute in that state requires landlords to either return or account for security deposits within thirty days after the termination of a tenancy. Failure to do so entitles the tenant to an award of damages equal to three times the amount of the security deposit plus 5 percent interest from the date when the payment became due, together with court costs and reasonable attorney's fees. Was Friedman entitled to recover from the landlord? *Friedman v. Costello,* 412 N.E.2d 1285 (MA).

8. Elmer and Bonnie Cummings, as lessors, entered into a lease with Leo and Glen Ward for the rental of a building from March 16, 1966, to July 31, 1974. The lease provided that there could be no assignment without the written consent of the lessors. In October 1966, the Wards assigned the lease to Robert and Alice Smith with no written consent from the Cummingses. The Cummingses accepted rent from the Smiths for five years without objection. Was the assignment valid? Why or why not? *Smith v. Hegg,* 214 N.W.2d 789 (SD).

9. Sorrells rented a single-family dwelling house from Pole Realty Company. When eviction proceedings were brought against her for nonpayment of rent, Sorrells claimed that there had been a breach of the implied warranty of habitability. Pole Realty Company argued that the warranty of habitability did not apply to the rental of single-family residences. Do you agree? Explain. *Pole Realty Co. v. Sorrells,* 417 N.E.2d 1297 (IL).

10. The Kings leased a residential dwelling from a partnership called JA-SIN. The lease agreement provided that the tenants were to "take good care of the house" and "make, at their own expense, the necessary repairs caused by their own neglect or misuse." A guest of the Kings, Sharon Ford, tripped on a loose tread on one step while descending an outside stairway and sustained personal injuries. Who was responsible, the landlord or the tenant? Give the reason for your answer. *Ford v. JA-SIN,* 420 A.2d 184 (DE).

Quick Quiz Answers

23-1 & 23-2	23-3	23-4	23-5	23-6
1. T	1. F	1. T	1. F	1. F
2. T	2. T	2. F	2. F	2. T
3. T	3. T	3. F	3. F	3. T

23-7 & 23-8
1. T
2. F
3. T

Chapter 24   Wills, Trusts, and Estates

The Opening Case
"The Solemn Promise"

Elliott Preston lived alone all of his adult life. His only heirs were several distant cousins who hardly knew him. He lived in a well-kept house in the suburbs. When Preston grew too old to care for himself, two special friends, Dana and Ida Long, took care of him. They cooked his meals, cleaned his house, and took care of his personal needs. Preston told the Longs on several occasions that he had a living will and that when he died, his house would belong to them. Preston died intestate. Will Dana and Ida Long inherit Preston's house?

Chapter Outcomes

1. Give details about the sources of probate law and its relevance to business entities.
2. Discuss the types and purposes of advance directives.
3. Determine whether a person who makes a will has the capacity to do so.
4. Explain the formal requirements for executing a will.
5. Compare the protection of children with the protection of spouses under the law of wills.
6. Identify the different methods of revoking or changing a will.
7. Decide, in different situations, who will inherit the property of someone who dies without a will.
8. Ascertain the lawful heirs when an inheritance depends upon the exact time of death.
9. Describe the steps to be taken by an executor or administrator in settling an estate.
10. Differentiate among the various types of trusts and determine when they might be used.

24-1 Sources and Relevance of Probate Law

The term **probate** refers to the process of handling the will and the estate of a deceased person. Each state has its own laws passed by its legislature, different from other states, governing the writing of wills and the settling of estates. For this reason, it is necessary to check one's own state law to ascertain the rules for writing a will and to determine how property passes when someone dies. In an attempt to standardize and modernize the different state laws on this subject, the Uniform Probate Code has been set up, but only sixteen states have made this part of their law at this time (Figure 24-1).

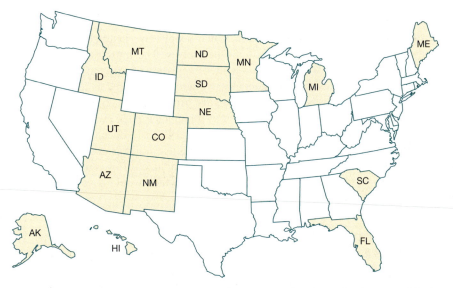

Figure 24-1 States that have made the Uniform Probate Code part of their state law.

Relevance of Probate to Business

Since probate matters deal with the handling of people's estates, and since all businesses are owned by people in one way or another, the subject of probate law is relevant to all forms of business entities. When sole proprietors die, for example, the assets of their businesses pass to their heirs according to their states' probate laws. When owners of a corporation, that is, stockholders, die, their solely owned shares of stock pass to their heirs in a similar fashion. The death of a partner in a partnership form of business automatically dissolves the partnership. In such event, the deceased partner's estate has the right either to be paid the value of the partner's share or to have the partnership ended.

Quick Quiz 24-1 True or False?

1. Each state has its own laws passed by its legislature, different from other states, governing the writing of wills.

2. The subject of probate law is relevant to all forms of business entities.

3. When sole proprietors die, the assets of their businesses pass to their heirs according to their states' probate laws.

24-2 Preliminary Matters and Probate Terminology

It is not uncommon for people to prepare for possible future misfortune by making advance arrangements for handling them while they are still mentally and physically able to so. A good time to do this is when a will is executed because all the necessary documents can be prepared, signed, and witnessed simultaneously.

Advance Directives

Advance directives are written statements in which people give instructions for future medical care if they become unable to do so themselves. The most common type of advance directive is the **living will,** which is a written expression of a person's wishes to be allowed to die a natural death and not be kept alive by heroic or artificial methods. Another vehicle that is used for this purpose is the **health care proxy**—a written statement authorizing an agent to make medical treatment decisions for another in the event of incapacity.

A **durable power of attorney** (discussed in Chapter 33) is a document authorizing another person to act on one's behalf with words stating that it either is to survive one's incapacity or is to become effective when one becomes debilitated. This is not the same as an ordinary *power of attorney,* discussed in Chapter 32, which would have questionable effect upon one's incapacity.

Probate Terminology

A **will,** also called a **last will and testament,** is a formal document that governs the transfer of property at death. A person who dies with a will is said to die **testate.** A person who dies without a will is said to die **intestate.** The giving away of one's property by will is known as testamentary disposition.

A person who makes a will is called a **testator** if a man or a **testatrix** if a woman. (The masculine forms of terms like *testator* are used for purposes of discussion. They refer to people of either sex.) Personal property that is left by will is called a **bequest** or legacy except in states that have adopted the Uniform Probate Code. Real property that is left by will is known as a **devise.** Those who receive property by will are referred to as beneficiaries. They are also known as **legatees** if they receive personal property and as **devisees** if they receive real property under a will. In states that have adopted the Uniform Probate Code, the term *devise* refers to both real and personal property, and the term *devisee* refers to a person who receives a gift of either real or personal property. The term **heir** is a broader term referring to one who inherits property either under a will or through one dying without a will.

Quick Quiz 24-2 True or False?

1. A living will is a written expression of a person's wishes to leave property to someone at death.

2. A man who makes a will is called a testatrix.

3. Except in states that have adopted the Uniform Probate Code, the term *bequest* refers to personal property that is left by will.

24-3 Dying with a Will

Any person who has reached the age of adulthood (eighteen years) and is of sound mind may make a will. The issue of soundness of mind is raised only when someone contests a will on that ground. In determining whether a testator was of sound mind when making a will, the court asks the following questions: When making the will, did the testator know, in a general way, the nature and extent of the property he or she owned? Did the testator know who would be the natural recipients of the estate? Was the testator free from delusions that might influence the disposition of the property? Did the testator know that he or she was making a will? If all of these questions are answered in the affirmative, the court will find that the testator was of sound mind when making a will.

Example 24-1

At the time of the execution of his will, Stein was suffering from loss of memory. His son observed his father's failing health and mental illness over a period of time. He once observed his father's failure to recognize his own wife. Stein's daughter once observed her father's failure to recognize her and another relative, both of whom he saw frequently. The court disallowed the will, saying, "The testator did not have mind and memory sound enough to know and understand the businesses upon which he was engaged at the time of execution."

Did You Know?

It can be risky to draft one's own will or even to use a pre-printed generic will found in a stationery store. The law of wills is very technical, and unique language is often used in the drafting of wills that may not be fully understood by lay people. In addition, the law of wills varies considerably from state to state, making a generic will unreliable in many cases.

Requirements for Executing a Will

The laws governing the making and signing of wills are not uniform throughout the United States because they are a product of state statute. Nevertheless, a will that is properly executed according to the laws of one state will be given full faith and credit in another state. The laws are highly technical and require strict adherence to detailed formalities. Many lawsuits have occurred over the years because people have attempted to make their own wills without consulting a lawyer. Often, in such cases, a technicality causes the will to be disallowed by the court, and the true wishes of the deceased are not carried out.

Formal Requirements   With the exception of a nuncupative will discussed later, a will must be in writing, signed by the testator, and attested in the testator's presence by the number of witnesses established by state law (Figure 24-2). Each of the particular statutory requirements of the state where the will is made must be met for a will to be valid.

Example 24-2

Dugan's will contained the following clause: "All United States Savings Bonds in safety deposit box #559 Farmers Bank 10th and Market Sts., Wilmington, Del., to be given to the people and places as marked." When Dugan died, a number of U.S. Savings Bonds were found in his safe-deposit box. There was also a handwritten list of the names of various individuals and organizations and, beside each name, serial numbers, dates, and face amounts corresponding to specific bonds. Further specific notations were written on small slips of paper and attached to each bond with a rubber band. The court held that there was no effective testamentary transfer of the bonds. Neither the list, the envelopes, nor the small slips of paper satisfied the statutory requirements for executing a will. They were not properly signed and witnessed. Dugan's wishes as stated in the will were never carried out.

Background Information   Although wills are referred to in the Bible, the right to dispose of property through a will did not come about until the Romans distributed property to heirs in formal ceremonies. The Anglo-Saxons also had rituals to divide property. The ecclesiastical courts of the Middle Ages became involved in the creation of wills when clergymen started recording the bequests of those to whom they were delivering last rites. These bequests usually concerned only the division of personal property. In England, the Statute of Wills (1540) and the Wills Act (1837) broadened individuals' rights to include disposal of both personal and real property.

A will may be typewritten or handwritten or it may consist of a filled-in form. It need not be under seal. The will offered for probate must be the original and not a copy. In a case in which a testator executed both an original and a carbon copy of a will and then later canceled only the carbon, the court held that it could be presumed that the testator also intended to cancel the original. Problems of this nature can be avoided by executing only the original will itself.

A will must be signed by the testator. The place of the signature on the will and the requirement as to who must be present at the signing vary from state to state. In some states, a will must be signed at the end of the instrument; in other states, the signature may be

LAST WILL AND TESTAMENT
OF
JUDITH M. DORE

I, JUDITH M. DORE, of Salem, County of Essex, Commonwealth of Massachusetts, make this my Last Will and Testament, hereby revoking all earlier wills and codicils.

ARTICLE I

I give, devise, and bequeath all my estate, real, personal, and mixed and wherever situated to my husband, PETER DORE, if he is living on the thirtieth day after my death.

ARTICLE II

If my husband, PETER DORE, is not living on the thirtieth day after my death, I give and devise all of my property of every kind and wherever located which I own at the time of my death or to which I am then in any way entitled in equal shares to my children, ALAINA DORE and DAVID DORE, but if either of them shall not be living, his or her share thereof shall pass to his or her issue then living by right of representation, and in default of such issue then his or her share shall pass to the survivor of them.

I, the undersigned testator, do hereby declare that I sign and execute this instrument as my last will, that I sign it willingly in the presence of each of said witnesses, and that I execute it as my free and voluntary act for the purposes herein expressed, this 15th day of January, 2005.

_____
Judith M. Dore

We, the undersigned witnesses, each do hereby declare in the presence of the aforesaid testator that the testator signed and executed this instrument as her last will in the presence of each of us, that she signed it willingly, that each of us hereby signs this will as witness in the presence of the testator, and that to the best of our knowledge the testator is eighteen (18) years of age or over, of sound mind, and under no constraint or undue influence.

_____   _____
(Witness)   (address)

_____   _____
(Witness)   (address)

COMMONWEALTH OF MASSACHUSETTS
COUNTY OF ESSEX

On this 15th day of January, 2005, before me, the undersigned notary public, personally appeared JUDITH M. DORE, proved to me through satisfactory evidence of identification, which was a current Massachusetts driver's license, to be the person whose name is signed on this instrument, and acknowledged to me that she signed it voluntarily for its stated purpose.

_____
Charles E. Jones, Notary Public

Figure 24-2 These are sample portions of a formal will drafted according to Massachusetts law. The laws of each state are not the same on the subject of wills.

placed anywhere on the paper. Similarly, some states require a will to be signed in the presence of witnesses, whereas others allow a will to be signed privately if the testator acknowledges to the witnesses when they sign that it is his or her signature. Testators who are not able to write may make a mark, such as an X, attested to by the required number of witnesses. If the testator's condition makes movement impossible, as in paralysis, another person may sign for the testator. This must be done at the request of the testator, in the testator's presence, and in the presence of the witnesses.

With the exception of some wills that are handwritten, wills must be witnessed by the number of witnesses prescribed by state law. Almost every state today requires that a will be witnessed by two witnesses. Witnesses must sign in the presence of the testator and, in some states, in each other's presence. Since the witnesses may be called upon to attest to the genuineness of the testator's signature and soundness of mind, it is advisable that witnesses be younger than the testator. In some states, no age requirements are given for witnesses. Instead, minors may witness a will as long as they are of sufficient understanding and are competent to testify in court as to the facts relating to the execution of the will. In other states, witnesses must have reached a certain age, such as fourteen, sixteen, or eighteen, to qualify as a witness.

In many states, persons and their spouses who witness a will may not receive gifts under the will unless there are still other witnesses. The failure to observe this provision may result in their being disinherited.

Example 24-3

Delbert executed a will leaving all of his property to his three step-daughters, Jane, Noreen, and Frances, who had been very close to him during his lifetime. Jane's husband was one of the subscribing witnesses to the will. When Delbert died, Jane received nothing from her step-father's estate. A statute in that state makes void any testamentary gift to a subscribing witness or spouse of such a witness.

Some states protect beneficiaries who witness a will by allowing them to inherit up to the amount that they would have inherited had the deceased died without a will. In Example 24-3, had Delbert died in such a state, Jane would have inherited up to the amount she would have inherited had Delbert died without a will.

A Question of Ethics

Contrary to her step-father's wishes, Jane, in Example 24-3, received nothing under her step-father's will when he died. Would Noreen and Frances have an ethical duty to share their inheritance with Jane?

Need for Accuracy Certain words often used in wills may have a legal interpretation that is different from their everyday meaning. Care must be taken to describe each bequest and devise in a manner that will satisfy the legal definition. For instance, a testator may use the word *heirs* when really meaning *children*. The differences in the meanings of the two words could result in much dispute and expensive litigation. It is also important to avoid ambiguous language.

Example 24-4

Sparacio made a will leaving his property to his daughter, Mary, and his friend, Eileen, "as in their mutual agreement they decide." The court held that the will was invalid. It was impossible to determine under the terms of the will how much to give Mary and how much to give Eileen.

State Variations Twenty-nine states permit holographic wills. Maryland and New York only permit them for soldiers and sailors.

Background Information The briefest will ever recorded was written by Karl Tausch of Langen, Hesse, Germany. It said, *Vse zene,* which is Czechoslovakian for "all to wife." Another will was scratched into a metal identification tag worn by a British soldier who had been lost at sea. A microscope had to be used to see the letters, which read, "All to mother."

Informal Wills   A *holographic will* is one that is not witnessed but is written entirely in the handwriting of the testator. About half the sates in the United States treat holographic wills as valid. The other half do not recognize them because of the lack of witnesses.

Example 24-5

Sedmak resided in Pennsylvania. The following handwritten document was found among his papers when he died:

> My Brother Mil   Oct 6, 72
> Please see that Zella Portenar receives $5,000 from my savings account it is in the Western Savings Bank.
>
>   George A. Sedmak
>   or Alexander Sedmak

The Pennsylvania court held the unwitnessed document to be a valid holographic will.

Oral wills made by persons in their last illness or by soldiers and sailors in actual combat are nuncupative wills. *Nuncupative wills* are valid only in some states and are restricted to the giving of personal property only. Testators must indicate their bequests and must state that those hearing the statements are to be considered witnesses to the oral will.

Protection of Spouses

Most state laws contain various devices that are designed to give protection to surviving family members when a spouse dies. Some states provide for a **family allowance,** sometimes called a **widow's allowance,** which is an amount of money taken from the decedent's estate and given to the family to meet its immediate needs while the estate is being probated. The amount of the allowance is either a fixed, statutory amount, or discretionary with the court and is not chargeable against other benefits given to the family members. Another family protection is the **homestead exemption,** which puts the family home beyond the reach of creditors up to a certain limit. Still another protective device that is provided by some states is known as **exempt property,** which is certain property of a decedent that passes to the surviving spouse or children and is beyond the reach of creditors. In some states, for example, $3,500 worth of personal property passes automatically to the surviving spouse or, if none, to surviving children equally. The rights of dower (for a widow) and curtesy (for a widower) are also available in some states, providing the surviving spouse with certain property rights in real property owned by the deceased spouse.

Wills protect the rights of family members and assure the smooth transfer of property.

In addition to the rights mentioned, surviving spouses are assured a share of a deceased spouse's estate. A surviving spouse who does not like the provisions of a deceased spouse's will may choose to take a portion of the estate set by state statute rather than accept the amount provided in the will. In some states, this sum is referred to as a spouse's **forced share.** In other states, it is called a spouse's **elective share.** The amount the surviving spouse will receive varies from state to state. In some states, it is the amount the spouse would have received had the deceased spouse died without a will. In other states, the amount is computed by the use of a different formula.

Protection of Children

Children who can prove that they were mistakenly (rather than intentionally) left out of a parent's will are protected by the laws of most states. Forgotten children will receive the same share that they would have received had their parent died without a will. This situation does not mean that a parent may not disinherit a child. Parents are not obligated to leave children anything, but, to avoid litigation, such an intention should be shown in the will. A testator who wishes to disinherit a child should name the child in the will and make the statement that the child was intentionally omitted. By doing so, the omitted child cannot claim to have been mistakenly omitted from the will.

Adopted children, under modern laws, are given the same legal rights as natural children. They inherit from their adopting parents. In contrast, stepchildren, unless they have been adopted by a stepfather or stepmother, do not inherit from a stepparent. Children who have been taken into the family for one reason or another, but never legally adopted, have no right of inheritance.

> ## Example 24-6
>
> Carlos and Malana Hernandez, who had two children of their own, took into their home three preschool children whose parents had been killed in an accident. The couple developed a special closeness toward one of the children, adopting him through legal proceedings. Only the adopted child would have rights equal to those of the Hernandez's natural children.

Revoking and Changing a Will

With variations from state to state, a will may be revoked (canceled) in any of the following ways: (1) burning, tearing, canceling, or obliterating the will with the intent to revoke it; (2) executing a new will; and (3) in eleven states, subsequent marriage of the testator. The eleven states are Connecticut, Georgia, Kansas, Kentucky, Massachusetts, Nevada, Oregon, Rhode Island, South Dakota, West Virginia, and Wisconsin. In most states, the divorce or annulment of a marriage revokes all gifts made under a will to the former spouse and revokes the appointment of the former spouse as executor of the will.

Sometimes testators wish to make slight changes in a will. They may do so by executing a new will or by executing a **codicil,** which is a formal document used to supplement or change an existing will. A codicil must be executed with the same formalities as a will. It must be signed by the testator and properly witnessed. In addition, it must refer to the existing will to which it applies.

> ## Example 24-7
>
> Rueda made a will giving her entire estate to her husband. Later, Rueda enjoyed unusual financial success and felt inclined to leave $100,000 toward a new church building under construction in her parish. Rueda's attorney prepared a codicil, which Rueda formally executed in the presence of two witnesses. The bequest to the church contained in the codicil became an integral part of the will itself.

A properly executed codicil has the effect of republishing a will. It is said that a codicil breathes new life into a will, which means that the codicil will reestablish a will that had

Related Cases A mother died with a will naming her sole surviving daughter as beneficiary. Her previously-deceased daughter had three children who sued to receive a share, claiming that they were mistakenly left out of the will. The surviving daughter attempted to show an earlier will that explicitly stated the granddaughters were to receive nothing. The court ruled in the granddaughters' favor, stating that the previous will had been revoked and there was no evidence in the final will that the granddaughters had been omitted intentionally. *Armstrong v. Butler,* 553 S.W.2d 453.

Background Information Under Roman law, a child was entitled to "legitime," which was his or her share of parents' property, and parents could not contest the child's right. Louisiana is the only state to still abide by legitime.

Getting Students Involved Bring numerous copies of a will to class. Divide the class into groups and distribute the copies among the groups. Have each group choose a method of revoking or changing the will relative to any of the three ways listed in the text. Then have the students discuss what problems are created by that type of revocation. What problems will a court encounter years in the future in trying to ascertain the will's intent?

Further Reading *Administration of Wills, Trusts, and Estates,* by Gordon W. Brown (West Legal Studies, Delmar Learning, 2003) is written in a style similar to this book and contains much information about wills, trusts, and estates.

been formerly revoked or improperly executed. If, for example, a will is witnessed by only one person in a state that requires two witnesses, the will is invalid. However, if a properly signed and witnessed codicil is added at a later date, the will becomes valid.

Contesting a Will

Only persons who would inherit under an earlier made will or under the law of intestacy (described later in this chapter) are allowed to contest a will. A will may be contested on any of three grounds: improper execution, unsound mind, and undue influence.

When the formal requirements for executing a will are not followed precisely, a will may be contested on the grounds that it was executed improperly. Since lay people are not usually aware of the formal requirements for executing a will, it can be risky for them to make their own.

Another ground to contest a will is to allege that the testator was of unsound mind. When such an allegation is made, the burden is on the person presenting the will to the court to prove that the testator was of sound mind. This may be done by testimony and affidavits of witnesses and by testimony of the deceased's physician.

A will may also be attacked and held to be invalid if a probate court finds that the testator made the will under circumstances of undue influence. When persons come under the influence of another to the degree that they are unable to express their real intentions in a will, the will may be declared invalid. The court must distinguish between undue influence and the kindness, attention, advice, guidance, and friendliness shown toward the testator by the one named in the will.

Getting Students Involved After explaining that only interested persons may contest a will, have students brainstorm reasons why this may be a good or bad requirement.

Teaching Tips Emphasize the risks involved in making a will without legal consultation from a qualified estate-planning attorney.

Example 24-8

Smolak executed a will prepared by a lawyer whom he had selected and with whom he had conferred several times before the date on which the will was signed. His niece, Sandra, was the major beneficiary under that will. A week later, he executed another will under which his nephew Michael and Michael's brother were named principal beneficiaries. This will was done at the same time that Smolak executed a deed conveying his farm to Michael and Michael's brother (which conveyance he later sought to rescind, claiming that it was procured by fraud). The second will was executed at the office of a lawyer employed by Michael. Michael had made arrangements for a conference between his lawyer and Smolak. Michael attended that conference and also attended the execution of the resulting will. Smolak never conferred privately with Michael's lawyer concerning the second will and therefore never had an opportunity to express his true intentions out of earshot of his nephew. The court held that the second will was procured through undue influence and was, therefore, void.

Quick Quiz 24-3 True or False?

1. Any person who has reached the age of twenty-one and is of sound mind may make a will.

2. The will offered for probate may be a copy if the original cannot be found.

3. A surviving spouse may choose to take a portion of the estate set by state statute rather than accept the amount provided in the deceased spouse's will.

24-4 Dying Without a Will

When people die without a will, their property passes to others according to the various state laws of **intestate succession.** These state laws, which are not the same, contain the rules governing the allocation of intestate property. Personal property is treated differently from real property. *Personal property* is dispersed according to the law of the state where the deceased permanently resided (his or her domicile) at the time of death and passes to the personal representative to be distributed to the heirs. In contrast, *real property* passes according to the law where the property is located and passes directly to the heirs upon the death of the owner. The personal representative receives title to real property only when it must be sold to pay debts of the estate.

The following steps are taken to ascertain who will inherit from someone who dies without a will:

- Determine the rights of the surviving spouse, if any.
- Determine the rights of the other heirs.

State Variations Iowa has state laws that are generous to spouses in cases of intestacy. If the deceased leaves no children or only children from marriage to the surviving spouse, the spouse receives the whole estate. If the deceased leaves children that are not the spouse's, then the spouse receives $50,000 plus half of the estate, over that amount, and the children receive the rest.

Rights of the Surviving Spouse

Under a typical state statute, if a person dies intestate, the rights of the surviving spouse are as follows: If the deceased is survived by **issue** (children, grandchildren, great grandchildren), the surviving spouse is entitled to one-half of the estate. If the deceased is survived by no issue but by blood relatives, the surviving spouse is entitled to $200,000 plus one-half of the remainder of the estate. If the deceased is survived by no issue and no blood relatives, the surviving spouse is entitled to the entire estate. Keep in mind that this particular formula will differ from state to state.

State Variations Many states, including Arkansas, Connecticut, Georgia, Nevada, and Virginia have statutes that provide that a beneficiary who has murdered the deceased shall not receive any benefits from the deceased's will.

Rights of Other Heirs

Under the same typical state statute, if a person dies intestate, the property will pass, subject to the rights of the surviving spouse, as follows: If the deceased is survived by issue, the property passes in equal shares to the deceased's children, with the issue of any deceased child taking that child's share. If the deceased is survived by no issue, the property passes in equal shares to the deceased's father and mother or the survivor of them. If the deceased is survived by no issue and no father or mother, the property passes to the deceased's brothers and sisters, with the issue of any deceased brother or sister taking that brother's or sister's share. If the deceased is survived by no issue and

Terms The word *heir* comes from the Middle English *eir* and the Old French *hoir*, both derived from the Latin *heres,* akin to the Greek *cheros,* meaning "bereaved."

The Opening Case Revisited
"The Solemn Promise"

Dana and Ida Long will not inherit the house that Preston promised them because he died intestate. A living will is not the same as a "last will and testament." Instead, the property will pass according to the law of intestate succession in the state where the house is located—undoubtedly to his distant cousins. The Longs will be entitled to receive, under a theory of unjust enrichment, the monetary value of the services they rendered to Preston when he was too old to care for himself.

Terms Medieval kings instituted the doctrine of primogeniture—the eldest son's right to inheritance—to ensure that their offspring held land and, therefore, power. Primogeniture was abolished in the United States shortly after the Revolutionary War.

no father, mother, brother, or sister, or issue of any deceased brother or sister, the property passes to the deceased's **next of kin** (those who are most nearly related by blood). If the deceased is survived by no blood relatives and no surviving spouse, the estate **escheats** to (becomes the property of) the state. In all states, the property of a person who dies without a will goes to the state only when there is no surviving spouse, issue, or kindred (see Figure 24-3).

Example 24-9

Henrietta Johnson died intestate. She was survived by her husband, Arnold, a daughter, Bertha, and two grandchildren, Candice and Daniel, who were the children of her deceased son. Under the state statute mentioned above, Arnold will inherit 50 percent of the estate, Bertha will inherit 25 percent, and Candice and Daniel will each inherit 12½ percent.

Figure 24-3 This is an example of the way intestate property is distributed under a typical state statute (Massachusetts).

If the Deceased Is Survived by:	A Surviving Spouse (if any) Receives:	Any Remainder Is Distributed:
Issue (lineal descendants such as children, grandchildren, great grandchildren)	One-half of the estate	Equally to the deceased's children. If any children are also deceased, their children divide their deceased parents' share equally.
No issue but by kindred (blood relatives)	$200,000 plus one-half of the remainder of the estate	Equally between the deceased's father and mother or to the survivor of them. *However, if both parents are deceased, then:* Equally among the deceased's brothers and sisters. If any brothers or sisters are also deceased, their children divide their deceased parents' share equally. *However, if there are no living brothers or sisters or nieces or nephews, then:* Equally among the deceased's *next of kin* (those who are most nearly related by blood, including aunts, uncles, and cousins).
No issue and no kindred	The entire estate *However, if there is no surviving spouse, issue, or kindred, then:* The entire estate *escheats* to (becomes the property of) the state.	

24-5 Simultaneous Death

When two people die in a common disaster so that it is impossible to determine who died first, the Uniform Simultaneous Death Act often comes into play. This law contains rules that are followed when the inheritance of property depends upon the time of death, and there is nothing to indicate that the parties died other than at the same time. The following rules are followed:

1. The separately-owned property of each person passes as if he or she had survived unless a will or trust provides otherwise. For example, if a husband and wife die together in a plane crash, the husband's individually-owned property passes to his heirs as though his wife were not living at the time of his death. Similarly, the wife's individually-owned property passes to her heirs as though her husband were not living at the time of her death.

2. Property owned jointly by both of the deceased is distributed equally. In the above example, half of the couple's jointly owned property will pass to the husband's heirs; the other half will pass to the wife's heirs.

3. When the beneficiary of an insurance policy dies at the same time as the deceased, the proceeds of the insurance policy are payable as if the insured had survived the beneficiary. Suppose, in the above example, the wife was the beneficiary on the husband's life insurance policy. The wife would be regarded as deceased at the time of the husband's death. The proceeds of the policy will go to the husband's estate unless an alternate beneficiary is named in the policy.

Further Reading *Wills: A Do-it-Yourself Guide* by Theresa Meehan Rudy and Jean Dinneo (Washington, DC: Holt, Inc., 1992) is a thorough handbook for drafting and updating a will.

State Variations In West Virginia and many other states, a competent adult 18 years of age or older may execute a living will governing the withholding or withdrawal of life-prolonging intervention from himself or herself. It is the responsibility of the declarant to provide for notification to his or her attending physician of the existence of the living will.

Example 24-10

John F. Kennedy, Jr., and his wife, Carolyn Bessette Kennedy were killed in 1999 when their plane crashed into the ocean off the coast of Martha's Vineyard. The Uniform Simultaneous Death Act did not apply because the gifts to the spouses in each will were prefaced by the phrase "if she (or he) is living on the thirtieth day after my death."

Quick Quiz 24-5 True or False?

Under the simultaneous death act,

1. If a husband owns a house in his own name and he and his wife die at the same time in an accident, one-half the value of the house will pass to his wife's heirs.

2. If a husband and wife own a house jointly, and he and his wife die at the same time in an accident, one-half of the value of the house will pass to his wife's heirs.

3. If a husband names his wife as the only beneficiary of a life insurance policy, and he and his wife die at the same time in an accident, the proceeds of the policy will go to the wife's estate.

24-6 Settling an Estate

Background Information Probate proceedings can be quite expensive, as much as 10 percent even in uncomplicated cases. The costs of probate pale next to the federal estate taxes on estates worth more than $1,500,000 in 2005, $2,000,000 in 2006 through 2008, and $3,500,000 in 2009. Federal estate taxes range from 47 to 50 percent. There is no estate tax for the year 2010; however, the tax is reinstated automatically on estates over $1,000,000 in 2011 unless Congress votes to change it. A surviving spouse does not have to pay estate taxes on inheritances received from a deceased spouse.

Further Reading For a more in-depth discussion of trusts see Chapters 8 and 9 of *Administration of Wills, Trusts, and Estates*, 3rd ed., by Gordon W. Brown (West Legal Studies, Delmar Learning, 2003).

When people die owning assets, their estates must be **probated,** that is, settled under the supervision of the court. The court that supervises the procedure is called a probate court in some states and a surrogate court, or orphan's court, in others.

The first step in probating an estate is to determine whether the deceased left a will. If a will exists, it usually names a personal representative called an **executor** (male) or **executrix** (female) who is the person named in the will to carry out its terms. If there is no will, or if the executor or executrix named in the will fails to perform, someone must petition the court to settle the estate. That person, if appointed, is called an **administrator** (male) or **administratrix** (female). In states that have adopted the Uniform Probate Code (see Figure 24-1), executors and administrators are called **personal representatives.**

Before an executor or administrator is appointed, notice of the petition for appointment is published in a newspaper and sent to all heirs, legatees, and devisees. Anyone with grounds to object may do so. Witnesses are sometimes asked to testify or to sign affidavits about their knowledge of the execution of the will. Testimony is not necessary when all heirs and next of kin assent to the allowance of the will and no one contests it.

To ensure faithful performance, the executor or administrator is required to post a bond. A **bond** is a promise by the executor or administrator (and the sureties, if any) to pay the amount of the bond to the probate court if the duties of the position are not faithfully performed. **Sureties** are persons or insurance companies that stand behind executors or administrators and become responsible for their wrongdoing. In some states, a bond is not required if the will indicates that the executor or administrator need not post bond. In other states, a bond is always necessary, but sureties are not required if the will so dictates.

When a satisfactory bond has been filed, the court issues a certificate of appointment called letters testamentary to an executor or letters of administration to an administrator. The executor or administrator, called a **fiduciary** (one in a position of trust), is then authorized to proceed. The fiduciary's job consists of gathering the assets, paying the debts and taxes, and distributing the remaining assets in accordance with the will or the law of intestate succession.

Business Law in the News
The Many Lives of the Death Tax

You might think the estate tax is going to its grave. But while the federal government is slated to phase out its "death tax" by 2010, 18 states plus the District of Columbia have opted to retain it within their borders. They join a handful of others with separate inheritance taxes—imposed on the heirs rather than the estates. As a result, the estates of wealthy residents of these states could still wind up paying thousands of dollars in taxes.

For some taxpayers, this amounts to "a huge tax increase," says Laurie Hall, head of private client practice at Boston law firm Palmer & Dodge LLP. Consider the situation in New York. In 2004, New Yorkers will be able to leave heirs $1.5 million without paying Uncle Sam a dime. But because New York's estate-tax exclusion is $1 million, someone with a $1.5 million taxable estate will owe the state $64,400, says Blanche Lark Christerson, a director at Deutsche Bank Private Wealth Management. In 2009, the federal exemption rises to $3.5 million. But a $3.5 million taxable estate will owe New York $229,200, Christensen says. "The states are taking away a significant amount of the benefit of the reduction in federal estate taxes," says Hall.

The states are imposing these taxes in part to replace revenues lost by the declining federal estate tax. Unbeknownst to most taxpayers, Uncle Sam effectively shares its estate-tax revenue with the states. Starting in 2002, though, the feds began reducing the states' allocation, which will fall to zero in 2005.

The new state levies take many forms. Some states, including New Jersey and New York, are freezing estate-tax exclusions. In 2004, for example, New Jersey's exclusion will remain at $675,000, even as the Federal government allows taxpayers to shelter $1.5 million. (One caveat: Smaller estates which pass to heirs aside from spouses, children, and parents could still be liable for a separate inheritance tax.)

Other states, such as Vermont, are conforming to the federal government's estate-tax exclusion—which is rising from $1 million in 2003 to $3.5 million in 2009 (table). But if your estate exceeds those limits, watch out. A growing number of states are now forcing taxpayers to pay a state levy of up to 16% on top of the federal government's tax of up to 49%—the maximum for 2003. For the next two years, a partial credit will reduce that burden to some extent.

Still other states have adopted different approaches. Massachusetts is allowing its estate-tax exclusion to rise but to thresholds below the federal limits. In 2003, Massachusetts taxpayers can shield $700,000 from state estate tax. That's scheduled to rise to $850,000 in 2004, $950,000 in 2005, and $1 million in 2006—where it is slated to stay, says Hall. Illinois, meanwhile, is following the federal limits. But it will freeze its exclusion at $2 million starting in 2009, says Carol Harrington, a partner at McDermott, Will & Emery in Chicago.

Some help is on the way. Starting in 2005, the Internal Revenue Service will let estates deduct state taxes from their federal returns. In 2005, this will effectively reduce the total tax bite such that those in the top state estate-tax bracket—which kicks in at $10.04 million—will pay only 8.5% instead of 16%, says Leonard Adler of JPMorgan Private Bank in Palm Beach, Fla.

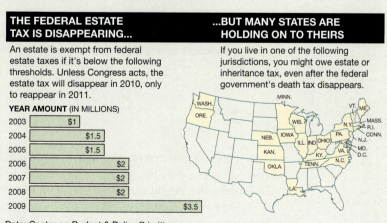

THE FEDERAL ESTATE TAX IS DISAPPEARING...

An estate is exempt from federal estate taxes if it's below the following thresholds. Unless Congress acts, the estate tax will disappear in 2010, only to reappear in 2011.

YEAR	AMOUNT (IN MILLIONS)
2003	$1
2004	$1.5
2005	$1.5
2006	$2
2007	$2
2008	$2
2009	$3.5

...BUT MANY STATES ARE HOLDING ON TO THEIRS

If you live in one of the following jurisdictions, you might owe estate or inheritance tax, even after the federal government's death tax disappears.

Data: Center on Budget & Policy Priorities

Illustration by Christoph Niemann; Charts by Roger Kenny; Robert Neubecker

(Continued)

Business Law in the News *(Continued)*

Defensive Strategies

Taxpayers can take some defensive steps. The most dramatic move: Relocate to a state with no estate tax, such as Florida or California. Another tactic is for spouses to change their wills to give their children or other heirs the maximum they can protect from state estate tax when the first spouse dies. In the case of a New York resident, for example, that would translate into a bequest of $1 million in 2004. Still, that means the New Yorker won't use $500,000 of the $1.5 million federal estate tax exclusion. If the surviving spouse dies before the federal tax expires in 2010 and has an estate that's above the federal exemption threshold, that $500,000 could be taxed by the IRS at rates of up to 49%.

Another approach is to put that $500,000 into a "contingent marital trust." That way, says Harrington, the executor can decide whether to pay or defer state estate taxes, depending on factors including the survivor's needs and the outlook for tax rates at the time. The best advice: Consult with a knowledgeable attorney or tax adviser.

Questions for Analysis

1. Why could the estates of some wealthy taxpayers wind up paying thousands of dollars in taxes?

2. What happened to the states' allocation of some of the federal estate taxes?

3. What are some of the forms that state estate taxes are now taking?

4. What help did the IRS give to taxpayers in 2005?

5. What are some defensive steps that taxpayers can take to lower the federal estate tax?

Source: Anne Tergesen. "The Many Lives of the Death Tax," *BusinessWeek,* December 22, 2003, p 96.

Teaching Tips Help students understand the similarities and differences between wills and trusts by explaining that both are legal means of transferring assets to other people. A will names an executor to distribute the assets, while a trust names a trustee to do the same thing after holding the assets according to the trust's terms. However, a will is carried out upon a person's death, whereas the execution of a trust can remain open long afterward. Moreover, a will is a public record (anyone can examine a person's debts and assets), and a trust (except a testamentary trust) is private. Wills are subject to probate taxes. Trusts may avoid probate taxes, and they are becoming more popular as a method of saving taxes.

Quick Quiz 24-6 True or False?

1. If a husband and wife die at the same time in an automobile accident, the separately-owned property of each spouse passes as if he or she had died first unless a will or trust provides otherwise.

2. Testimony of witnesses is not necessary when all heirs and next of kin assent to the allowance of the will and no one contests it.

3. In the context of settling an estate, a *bond* is a certificate of indebtedness obligating the issuer to pay the bondholder interest plus the principal on the maturity date.

24-7 Trusts

A **trust** is a legal device by which property is held by one person (the **trustee**) for the benefit of another (the beneficiary). The person who sets up the trust is called the *settlor.* The property that is held in trust is the *corpus,* or *trust fund.*

When a trust is established, title is split between the trustee, who holds legal title, and the beneficiary, who holds equitable, or beneficial, title. This separation allows the trustee to manage the trust property for the benefit of the beneficiary. Trusts are established to save taxes, to provide for the needs of young children, and to prevent money from being squandered, among other reasons.

Property is often placed in trust so that it will be preserved for future generations. In such cases, only the income is given out during the life of the trust, with the principal held in relatively safe investments. The rule against perpetuities prevents trusts (except charitable trusts) from lasting indefinitely. This rule in many states requires trust property to become owned by the beneficiary outright not later than twenty-one years after the death of some person alive at the creation of the trust.

Types of Trusts

The two principal types of trusts are testamentary trusts and living trusts. A **testamentary trust** is a trust that is created by a will. It comes into existence only upon the death of the testator. The terms of the trust together with the names of the trustee and beneficiaries are set out in the body of the will itself.

Example 24-11

Emile Hanson died, leaving four grown sons and daughters. His children had never demonstrated any real ambition and had depended heavily on prospects of receiving large legacies from the estate. Hanson feared that his heirs would quickly spend their inheritances and have nothing to support themselves in the years ahead. He therefore provided for this possibility in his will by placing all assets in trust. The assets would remain intact, safely invested, and a small income would be paid from the trust income to the children. Hanson's purpose was realized in that the estate would be preserved and the surviving children would not squander their inheritance.

In a trust, such as the one illustrated in Example 24-11, provision must be made for final distribution of the trust's assets when the purpose of the trust has been served. For example, Hanson could have the trust property go to a church, college, or some other worthy nonprofit organization on the death of the last surviving child. He also could have designated a grandchild or grandchildren as the ultimate beneficiaries.

A **living trust,** also called an *inter vivos* trust, comes into existence while the settlor is alive. It is established by either a conveyance in trust or a declaration of trust. In a **conveyance in trust,** the settlor conveys away the legal title to a trustee to hold for the benefit of either the settlor or another as beneficiary. In a **declaration of trust,** the settlor holds the legal title to the property as trustee for the benefit of some other person (the beneficiary) to whom the settlor now conveys the equitable title. A living trust may be either irrevocable or revocable. If it is *irrevocable,* the settlor loses complete control over the trust and cannot change it. The advantage of an irrevocable trust is that the income from the trust is not taxable to the settlor, and estate and inheritance taxes are avoided. The disadvantage of such a trust is that it can never be rescinded. The settlor can never get back that which has been put in an irrevocable trust regardless of the circumstances. A *revocable* living trust may be taken back or changed at any time during the settlor's lifetime. It has neither estate tax nor income tax advantages; however, it can serve the purpose of relieving the cares of management of money or property as well as other purposes.

A spendthrift is one who spends money profusely and improvidently. A *spendthrift trust* is designed to provide a fund for the maintenance of a beneficiary and, at the same time, to secure the fund against that person's improvidence or incapacity. In some states, all trusts are considered to be of this type. In others, a clause must be placed in the trust instrument to the effect that the beneficiary cannot assign either the income or the principal of the trust and neither the income nor the principal can be reached by the beneficiary's creditors. Spendthrift trusts are not permitted in some states.

Further Reading Two estate-planning attorneys offer a comprehensive look at living trusts, and how to create them in *Loving Trusts: The Right Way to Provide for Yourself and Guarantee the Future of Your Loved Ones* by Robert A. Esperti and Renno L. Peterson (New York: Viking, 1994).

Teaching Tips Invite a trust officer of a local bank and an estate-planning attorney to talk to your class about the advantages of creating a trust. Ask these experts to explain how the rules in your state vary from other states regarding trusts.

Put not your trust in money, but put your money in a trust.

—Oliver Wendell Holmes (1809–1894), physician, author, and father of U.S. Supreme Court justice of the same name

Background Information The modern spendthrift trust evolved because of unjust restrictions on the property rights of married women under British common law. Up until the nineteenth century in England, a woman's property was automatically transferred to her husband upon marriage. Sometime after 1700, however, fathers began to set up spendthrift trusts for their daughters' property. Today, spendthrift trusts are not allowed in England, although some trusts protective of beneficiaries are permitted.

A charitable, or public, trust is one established for charitable purposes, such as the advancement of education; relief to the aged, ill, or poor; and the promotion of religion. For the trust to be valid, the identity of the person to be benefited must be uncertain. The rule against perpetuities does not apply to a charitable trust.

A *sprinkling trust,* or *spray trust,* allows the trustee to decide how much will be given to each beneficiary rather than have the settlor make the decision. The advantage is that the trustee can compare the tax brackets of the beneficiaries long after the settlor is dead and cause a smaller tax liability to occur by giving more money to those beneficiaries in the lowest tax brackets. It also has built-in spendthrift provisions. The chief objection to this type of trust is that it gives the trustee too much control.

Obligations of the Trustee

Getting Students Involved Divide students into teams and assign each team one type of trust (testamentary, living, spendthrift, charitable, or sprinkling). Have these teams research their trust's history, local requirements and limitations, and current usage. Then have each team give a presentation as to the benefits of their trust.

The trustee is obligated by law to use a high standard of care and prudence in the investment of funds held by the trust. If real property is held in trust, it is the trustee's obligation to supervise and care for the property. When economic and other reasons indicate the need to shift trust assets to safer areas of investment, it becomes the duty of the trustee to make such changes. If investments selected by the trustee fail, the trustee is held liable unless a court rules that the action was taken with prudence and caution.

The trustee relationship is one of great and continuing responsibility. Appointment as a trustee should not be accepted by those without the knowledge and background that would afford prudent and good management. Banks, trust companies, and other kinds of fiduciary corporations offer professional services in the administration of trusts. They provide professional investment services and generally give maximum security and benefit for the fees charged.

Quick Quiz 24-7 True or False?

1. When a trust is established, title to the trust property is held completely by the trustee.

2. A *spendthrift* is one who is frugal and careful about spending money.

3. Trustees are obligated by law to use an average standard of care when investing funds for the trust.

Summary

24-1 Because each state's law is different on the subject of probate law, it is necessary to check one's own state law when dealing with probate matters. Furthermore, the subject of probate law is relevant to all forms of business entities.

24-2 Living wills and health care proxies are used to provide instructions for future medical care when one is no longer capable of doing so. A durable power of attorney authorizes another person to act on one's behalf even after one's incapacity. The

terms *will, last will and testament, testate, intestate, testator, testatrix, bequest, devise, legatees, devisees,* and *heir* are frequently used in the field of probate law.

24-3 Any person who has reached adulthood and is of sound mind may make a will. Wills must be in writing, signed by the testator, and attested in the testator's presence by two witnesses in most states. In some states, no formalities are necessary when a holographic will is made. Oral wills by soldiers and sailors in combat may be used to bequeath personal property. Probate laws of each state are not the same.

Surviving spouses are given protection through such provisions as a family allowance, a homestead exemption, exempt property, and the rights of dower and curtesy. They are also assured of a share of a deceased spouse's estate by taking an elective share instead of the amount provided by the will. Children who can prove that they were mistakenly (rather than intentionally) omitted from a parent's will may be able to receive an intestate share of their parent's estate. Adopted children, under modern laws, are given the same legal rights as natural children.

A will may be revoked by burning, tearing, canceling, or obliterating the will with the intent to revoke it; by executing a new will; and in some states, by the subsequent marriage of the testator. The divorce or annulment of a marriage revokes all gifts made under a will to the former spouse. A codicil must be executed with the same formalities as a will. It has the effect of republishing a will that was formerly revoked or improperly executed. A will may be contested on the grounds of improper execution, unsound mind, and undue influence.

24-4 When people die without a will, their property passes to others according to the law of intestate succession, which varies from state to state. Personal property is dispersed according to the law of the state where the deceased was domiciled and passes to the personal representative for distribution. Real property passes according to the law where the property is located and goes directly to the heirs.

In finding out who will inherit, determine the rights of the surviving spouse, if any, followed by the rights of the other heirs.

24-5 Special rules apply when people die simultaneously: Separately owned property passes as if its owner had survived the other person. Property owned jointly by both decedents is distributed equally. Insurance proceeds are payable as if the insured survived the beneficiary when they both die at the same time.

24-6 When people die owning assets, their estates must be probated. Heirs are notified, and an executor or administrator is appointed by the probate court. This fiduciary then gathers the assets, pays the debts and taxes, and distributes the remainder in accordance with the will or the law of intestate succession.

24-7 Trusts are used, among other reasons, to save taxes, to provide for the needs of young children, and to prevent money from being squandered easily. They may be created to take effect while a person is alive or after a person dies. When a trust is established, title is split between the trustee, who holds legal title, and the beneficiary, who holds equitable or beneficial title. The trustee manages the trust fund for the beneficiary.

Key Terms

administrator, 458	executrix, 458	living will, 448
administratrix, 458	exempt property, 452	next of kin, 456
advance directives, 448	family allowance, 452	personal representatives, 458
bequest, 448	fiduciary, 458	probate, 446
bond, 458	forced share, 452	probated, 458
codicil, 453	health care proxy, 448	sureties, 458
conveyance in trust, 461	heir, 448	testamentary trust, 461
declaration of trust, 461	homestead exemption, 452	testate, 448
devise, 448	intestate, 448	testator, 448
devisees, 448	intestate succession, 455	testatrix, 448
durable power of attorney, 448	issue, 455	trust, 460
elective share, 452	last will and testament, 448	trustee, 460
escheats, 456	legatees, 448	widow's allowance, 452
executor, 458	living trust, 461	will, 448

Questions for Review and Discussion

1. Why is it necessary to check one's own state laws before writing a will or determining how property passes when someone dies?
2. In what way is the subject of probate law relevant to a sole proprietorship? A corporation? A partnership?
3. What is the difference between a living will and a health care proxy, and how do they differ from a durable power of attorney?
4. Who may make a valid will?
5. What questions does the court ask in determining whether a testator was of sound mind when making a will?
6. In general, what are the formal requirements for executing a will?
7. What are some devices that are designed to give protection to family members when a spouse dies?
8. What must omitted children prove in order to inherit under a parent's will? What provisions should be made in a will by a testator who wishes to disinherit a child?
9. How are adopted children protected under modern inheritance laws?
10. In what ways may a will be revoked?
11. Following the statute shown in Figure 24-2, who will inherit from, and in what amount, the estate of a person who dies intestate survived by a spouse and two children ($60,000 estate); a spouse and a father and mother ($400,000 estate); a spouse and no blood relatives ($90,000 estate); three children ($90,000 estate); a brother and two children of a deceased sister ($90,000 estate); no blood relatives and no surviving spouse ($90,000 estate); and a spouse and a ninety-year-old aunt ($500,000 estate)?
12. What three special rules apply when people die simultaneously?
13. What are the steps that must be taken to settle an estate? Explain.
14. How and for what reason is title to property split when a trust is established? Explain.

Investigating the Internet

Visit the Legal Information Institute of Cornell University at **www.law.cornell.edu.**
At that site, click "Law About," then, under the alphabetical listing, click "Estates and Trusts."

Cases for Analysis

1. Miguel Ruiz, who had a wife and two small children, did not have a will. A friend told Miguel that he should have a will because if he died without one, everything he owned would go to the state. Was the friend correct? Explain.
2. Ling Lee, who had two children, made a will leaving one dollar to her husband, Seung, and the balance in equal shares to her two children. When Ling died, her husband, Seung, claimed that he was legally entitled to more than one dollar. Do you agree with Seung? Explain.
3. D. W. Elmer, a hospital patient, was seriously ill and unable to write his name. He executed his will, however, by making a belabored *X* on the paper in the presence of witnesses. Can a signature on a will made by an *X* be valid? Explain. *In re Estate of Elmer,* 210 N.W.2d 815 (ND).
4. James and Wanda Barns, husband and wife, were killed in a head-on automobile collision. It was impossible to determine who died first, and neither one had a will. The couple owned the following items as joint tenants: The house in which they resided and its furnishings, a savings account, and a checking account. James owned a car and some Lucent stock separately in his name. Wanda owned a car and a certificate of deposit separately

in her name. James was survived by two children of another marriage; Wanda was survived by one child of another marriage. Who will inherit their property?

5. Julia Dejmal executed her will while a patient in St. Joseph's Hospital. The will was witnessed by Lucille and Catherine Pechacek. Catherine was nineteen years old and was employed as an assistant X-ray technician at the hospital. The age of majority at the time in that state was twenty-one. It was contended that the will was not valid because one of the witnesses to it was a minor. Do you agree with the contention? Why or why not? *Matter of Estate of Dejmal,* 289 N.W.2d 813 (WI).

6. Lazer, a wealthy seventeen-year-old, learned that he was suffering from AIDS. He wrote a will leaving everything he owned to a friend he had met in school. Two years later, when Lazer died, his parents claimed that the will was not valid. Do you agree with Lazer's parents? Explain.

7. Santiago, a widower, made a will leaving one dollar to his son, Carlos, and the balance in equal shares to his other children, Benito and Angelita. The estate, after deducting debts, taxes, and expenses, amounted to $90,000. When Santiago died, Carlos claimed that he was legally entitled to $30,000 from his father's estate. Was Carlos correct? Why or why not?

8. Evidence was introduced in court to show that, at the time she executed her will, Blanch Robinson suffered from schizophrenia. She had delusions as to having had a love affair with Nelson Eddy and was suspicious, mistrustful, and perhaps deluded about her friends and acquaintances. Dixon, who had been left out of the will, contended that Robinson lacked the mental capacity to make a will. Do you agree with Dixon? Explain. *Dixon v. Fillmore Cemetery,* 608 S.W.2d 84 (MO).

9. Walsh, as settlor, executed a declaration of trust, naming himself as trustee and giving himself the income from the trust during his lifetime. After his death, the income was to be paid to his second wife for her life, and upon her death, to his two children, Edward and Margot. Upon their deaths, the income was to be paid to the children of Edward and Margot, after which it terminated. The trust expressly provided that the settlor had not made any provisions for his third child, Patricia, because "previous provisions had been made in her behalf." After executing the instrument, Walsh transferred to the trust the family residence, three farms, and a checking account. Patricia argued that the trust was testamentary, and therefore, invalid because it failed to comply with the statute of wills. Was this a testamentary or an *inter vivos* trust? Explain. *First Nat'l Bank v. Hampson,* 410 N.E.2d 1109 (IL).

10. Whitman Winsor's will read in part: "I give, devise, and bequeath all my property, real and personal, to my daughter Lucy T. Winsor. . . . I deem it only right and just that my said daughter Lucy T. Winsor shall have all my property . . . because she has lived with me and cared for me for many years, and it is my will that all shall be hers." Winsor had another daughter, Caroline, who was not provided for in the will. Is Caroline entitled to an intestate share of her father's estate? Why or why not? *Hauptman v. Conant,* 400 N.E.2d 272 (MA).

Quick Quiz Answers

24-1	24-2	24-3	24-4	24-5	24-6
1. T	1. F	1. F	1. T	1. F	1. F
2. T	2. F	2. F	2. T	2. T	2. T
3. T	3. T	3. T	3. F	3. F	3. F

24-7
1. F
2. F
3. F

Part 4 Case Study

Kapner v. Meadowlark Ranch
Court of Appeal of California
2d Civil B163525 (CA)

Summary

Meadowlark Ranch Association (MRA) sold a 5-acre portion of its 437-acre ranch to Sylvan Kapner, together with a 1/80th undivided interest in a 60-foot-wide roadway parcel through which a 20-foot-wide paved road meanders. Fifteen years later, Meadowlark had its roadways surveyed and discovered that portions of Kapner's driveway, gate, and perimeter fence encroached onto the paved portion of the roadway. When notified of the encroachments, Kapner refused to remove them or sign an encroachment agreement. The proposed agreement would allow the encroachments to remain, subject to their removal at Kapner's expense should the need arise.

Kapner filed an action against Meadowlark for quiet title. The lower court found in favor of Meadowlark and against Kapner. The judgment required Kapner to sign the encroachment agreement or to remove the encroachments.

The Court's Opinion

Gilbert, P.J.

Kapner contends the trial court erred in finding he has not acquired a prescriptive easement over the areas enclosed by his improvements.

A prescriptive easement requires use of land that is open and notorious, hostile to the true owner and continuous for five years. *Warsaw v. Chicago Metallic Ceilings, Inc.,* 35 Cal.3d 564 (1984). Unlike adverse possession, a prescriptive easement does not require the payment of taxes. *Gilardi v. Hallam,* 30 Cal.3d 317 (1981). It is not an ownership right, but a right to a specific use of another's property. *Mehdizadeh v. Mincer,* 46 Cal.App.4th 1296 (1996). But Kapner's use of the land was not in the nature of an easement. Instead, he enclosed and possessed the land in question.

To escape the tax requirement for adverse possession, some claimants who have exercised what amounts to possessory rights over parts of neighboring parcels, have claimed a prescriptive easement. Courts uniformly have rejected the claim. See *Mesnick v. Caton,* 183 Cal.App.3d 1248 (1986); *Silacci v. Abramson,* 45 Cal.App.4th 558 (1996); *Mehdizadeh v. Mincer, supra,* 46 Cal.App.4th at pp. 1304–1308.) These cases rest on the traditional distinction between easements and possessory interests. See, e.g., *Mehdizadeh,* at pp. 1305–1306.

Kapner relies on *Hirshfield v. Schwartz,* 91 Cal.App.4th 749 (2001). There the court declared an equitable easement over a fenced-in area by balancing the hardships. The case does not involve the claim of a prescriptive easement. In any event, to the extent *Hirshfield* can be read as allowing the creation of a prescriptive easement over an area the claimant possessed, we decline to follow it.

We are required to observe the traditional distinction between easements and possessory interests in order to foster certainty in land titles. Moreover, the requirement for paying taxes in order to obtain title by adverse possession is statutory. The law does not allow parties who have possessed land to ignore the statutory requirement for paying taxes by claiming a prescriptive easement.

Because Kapner enclosed and possessed the land in question, his claim to a prescriptive easement is without merit. . . .

Kapner contends the trial court cannot grant implied powers to the MRA. Kapner's contention is based on the theory that the trial court erred when it found the MRA has the power and authority to protect the ownership rights of its members in the roadway. But the recorded declaration of protective covenants and restrictions expressly places the duty on the MRA to maintain the roadway. The imposition of the duty necessarily carries with it the power to carry it out. One cannot maintain a roadway by allowing obstructions on it. Thus, the MRA had the power to act to remove obstructions placed on the roadway parcel by Kapner.

Kapner contends the MRA's claims are barred by the three-year statute of limitations for trespass. . . .

Here the MRA's cross-complaint alleges, and Kapner does not dispute, that Kapner and the other members of the MRA are tenants in common in the roadway parcel. "A trespass is an invasion of the interest in the exclusive possession of land, as by entry upon it. . . ." *Wilson v. Interlake Steel Co.* 32 Cal.3d 229 (1982). Kapner has not invaded the other parcel owners' right to exclusive possession of the roadway parcel. They have no right to exclusive possession as against Kapner. All tenants in common have the right to share equally in the possession of the entire property. A tenant in common cannot trespass on the commonly owned property. Thus, the statute of limitation for trespass does not apply here.

Where one cotenant unlawfully excludes other cotenants from a part or all of the cotenancy, the cause of action is properly characterized as an action for possession. See *Noble v. Manatt,* 42 Cal.App. 496 (1919). A cotenant who claims exclusive possession may bar a cause of action brought by other cotenants by proving he has adversely possessed the property. But here the trial court found Kapner did not prove adverse possession. Kapner does not challenge that finding on appeal.

Nor is the MRA's claim barred by the five-year statute of limitations for the enforcement of covenants restricting the use of real property or the four-year statute for actions on a written instrument. The MRA is not seeking to enforce a contract or restrictive covenant. Instead, the MRA is seeking to enforce the rights inherent in common property ownership. Even without a covenant, Kapner has no right to exclude the other cotenants from any portion of the roadway parcel.

Kapner contends waiver and laches bar any recovery under the MRA's cross-complaint. Waiver of the right to enforce a covenant may occur where substantially all of the landowners have acquiesced in a violation so as to indicate an abandonment. *Bryant v. Whitney,* 178 Cal. 640 (1918). Kapner claims that 35 of 54 landowners in Meadowlark Ranch have encroachments in the roadway parcel. But shortly after a survey disclosed the extent of the encroachments, the MRA sent letters requiring the offending landowners to either remove the encroachments or sign an encroachment agreement. That does not indicate waiver or abandonment. Kapner cites one case in which the MRA consented to an encroachment. But one or a few waivers will not suffice. There must be a sufficient number of waivers so that the purpose of the general plan is undermined. The trial court was not required to find a waiver. Moreover, as we have stated, the MRA's action is not based on a specific covenant or restriction but on the property rights of its members as tenants in common.

Laches may bar equitable relief where the party seeking relief has delayed enforcing a right and there is prejudice arising from the delay. In determining whether laches applies, the court should weigh the competing equities and grant or deny relief depending on the balance of those equities.

The trial court was not required to find delay. A former MRA board member testified that prior to the 2001 survey, nobody really knew where the boundary lines were. Nor was the trial court required to find prejudice. Even had the MRA acted the day after Kapner's improvements were completed, he would still have had to move them. Kapner asserts he spent money to maintain the improvements. But he does not point to any such evidence in the record, nor does he specify how much he spent. Finally, the trial court could take into account in balancing the equities that when Kapner was a member of the MRA's board he was instrumental in forcing other members to remove their encroachments. . . . The judgment is affirmed.

Questions for Analysis

1. What does a prescriptive easement require under California law?

2. What is the difference between an easement by prescription and adverse possession?

3. Why did the court hold that Kapner did not acquire a prescriptive easement?

4. How did the court respond to Kapner's contention that the MRA did not have the power and authority to protect its members' ownership rights in the roadway?

5. Why cannot a tenant in common be a trespasser on property owned in common with other cotenants?

6. For what reason did the court rule there was no waiver of MRA's rights to enforce a covenant?

7. Look up the meaning of *laches* in the Glossary. Why was the trial court not required to find delay?

Negotiable Instruments

Part Five

<table>
<tr><td>

Chapter 25

</td><td>

Purpose and Types of Negotiable Instruments

</td></tr>
</table>

The Opening Case
"The Student Loan"

Dennis Gullible loaned a friend he had met in class $125 to buy a textbook, knowing that she was expecting an income tax refund check very shortly. Thankful for the loan, the friend wrote on a piece of paper "IOU $125" and signed it. Gullible showed the IOU to another classmate who told him that it wasn't legal and wrote the following note to use instead: "Thirty days after date, I promise to pay to the order of Dennis Gullible $125 out of the proceeds of my income tax refund." A few days after signing the replacement note, Gullible's friend received a letter from the IRS saying that she had made an error on her income tax return and that she owed the IRS an additional sum of money. Was the IOU a negotiable instrument? Was the replacement note negotiable?

Chapter Outcomes

1. State the purpose of negotiable instruments.
2. Identify the two kinds of negotiable instruments that contain a promise to pay money.
3. Identify the two kinds of negotiable instruments that contain an order to pay money.
4. Differentiate among certified checks, bank drafts, cashier's checks, traveler's checks, and money orders.
5. Name the parties to each kind of negotiable instrument.
6. Judge whether specific instruments contain the requirements of a negotiable instrument.

25-1 Purpose of Negotiable Instruments

Throughout history, people have had a need to transact business without carrying around large sums of money. In the Middle Ages, for example, merchants carried gold and silver with them as they traveled from one fair to another buying goods. They were in constant danger of being robbed, and needed a safer and more convenient method of exchanging their gold and silver for the goods they bought. A system was developed by which merchants could deposit their precious metals with goldsmiths or silversmiths for safekeeping. When the merchants bought goods, instead of paying for them with gold or silver, they simply filled in a piece of paper, called a bill of exchange (now known as a draft). The bill of exchange ordered the goldsmith or silversmith to give a certain amount of the precious metal to the person who sold the goods. That person would then take the bill of exchange to the goldsmith or silversmith and receive payment. In a similar fashion throughout history, people have borrowed money from one another, necessitating an orderly system of procedures and laws governing credit transactions.

The law of negotiable instruments has developed to meet these needs. Checks, drafts, and notes are used conveniently and safely as a substitute for money and to obtain credit in today's society. With the rapid development of e-commerce and electronic banking, computer and electronic technology is now being used as a substitute for checks and other paper transactions as well as for actual check processing through the banking system. As a result, it is estimated that the number of checks written in the United States will decline greatly during the next decade.

The law of negotiable instruments is found in Article 3 of the UCC. This article was originally drafted in 1952. Since that time, many new developments have occurred in the commercial field. In order to adapt to modern technology and practices, Article 3 of the UCC was revised in 1990. All states except New York, and South Carolina have adopted the revised article.

Under the UCC, a **negotiable instrument** is a written document that is signed by the maker or drawer and that contains an unconditional promise or order to pay a fixed amount of money on demand or at a definite time to the bearer or to order. There are two basic kinds of negotiable instruments: notes (including certificates of deposit) and drafts (including checks).

> ### Quick Quiz 25-1 True or False?
>
> 1. In the Middle Ages, a bill of exchange was a paper that ordered a goldsmith or silversmith to give a certain amount of gold or silver to a person who sold goods.
>
> 2. A bill of exchange is now known as a note.
>
> 3. The vast majority of states have adopted the 1990 revised Article 3 of the UCC.

25-2   Promise Instruments

Two types of negotiable instruments contain a *promise* to pay money. They are *notes* and *certificates of deposit.*

Notes

A **note** (often called a promissory note) is a written promise by one party, called the *maker,* to pay money to the order of another party, called the *payee.* People who loan money or extend credit as evidence of debt use notes. When two or more parties sign a note, they are called *comakers.*

A **demand note,** as its name implies, is payable whenever the payee demands payment (Figure 25-1). A holder of a demand note may decide to collect the balance due at any time and for any reason. A time note, on the other hand, is payable at some future time, on a date named in the instrument. Unless a note is payable in installments, the principal (face value) of the note plus interest must be paid on the date that it is due. In an **installment note,** the principal together with interest on the unpaid balance is payable in installments (series of payments) at specified times.

Getting Students Involved To introduce Part 5, Negotiable Instruments, ask students to discuss how they manage and use money. Have them explain how and why they conduct particular transactions such as borrowing money and writing and cashing checks. Discuss various problems that arise when people exchange money, and ask students to predict how such problems are addressed by the law.

UCC Revised (1990) 3-104(e)-(j) (see page 909)

Background Information As traders at commercial fairs of the Middle Ages bought items from one another, the amounts due were recorded in the sellers' books and were countersigned by the purchasers. At the end of the fair, individuals settled debts. Balances were paid in cash at first, but eventually it became customary for a debtor to sign a document agreeing to pay the creditor at a certain date. These documents were the forerunners of the modern bills of exchange.

UCC Revised (1990) 3-104(e) (see page 909)

UCC Revised (1990) 3-108(a) (see page 910)

No. 381   Boston, Massachusetts, October 1, 20 —
On demand, the undersigned, for value received, promise(s) to pay to the order of
CAMBRIDGE TRUST COMPANY

Two thousand four hundred and 00/100 ————— Dollars,
at its offices in Boston, Massachusetts, together with interest thereon from the
date thereof until paid at the rate of 6 percent per annum.

Address 100 Bedford Street   Victor Powell
Waltham, Massachusetts

Figure 25-1 A demand note is payable whenever the payee demands payment.

Certificates of Deposit

UCC Revised (1990)
3-104(j) (see page 909)

A **certificate of deposit (CD)** is an instrument containing an acknowledgment that a bank has received a sum of money and a promise by the bank to repay the sum of money. A CD is a note of the bank. CD's are written for a specific time period, such as six months, one year, two years, or five years. Banks pay higher interest for longer-term CD's and more interest than regular savings accounts because the depositor cannot withdraw the money before the due date without penalty. Some banks allow a one-time early withdrawal from a CD without penalty.

Background Informa-tion The first demand notes were the first series of U.S. currency put into circulation. In 1861, at the start of the Civil War, an act of Congress authorized the U.S. Treasury to issue legal tender notes in de-nominations of $5, $10, and $20. They were called demand notes because they carried the statement "The U.S. promises to pay the bearer . . . on demand." These demand notes were also known as "green-backs" because they were green on one side.

Quick Quiz 25-2 True or False?

1. People who loan money or extend credit as evidence of debt use notes.

2. A time note is payable whenever the payee demands payment.

3. A CD is a note of the bank.

25-3 Order Instruments

Two other types of negotiable instruments contain an *order* to pay money. They are *drafts* and *checks*.

Drafts

UCC Revised (1990)
3-104(e) (see page 909)

In contrast to notes, which are *promises* to pay money, drafts are *orders* to pay money. They are more complicated than notes because they involve three parties rather than two. The most common type of draft in use today is the check, but this was not always the case. For example, in *A Farewell to Arms*, a novel that is set in Italy during World War I by Ernest Hemingway, one of the characters, an American major, discusses with his friend, Rinaldi, the possibility of going to Milan:

Terms The word *draft* comes from the Middle English *draught*, which is akin to the Old English *dra-gan*, meaning "to draw" or "to drag," and the Latin *tra-here*, "to pull" or "to draw."

> The tickets are very expensive. I will draw a sight draft on my grandfather, I said. A what? A sight draft he has to pay or I go to jail. Mr. Cunningham at the bank does it. I live by sight drafts. Can a grandfather jail a patriotic grandson who is dying that Italy may live? Live the American Garibaldi, said Rinaldi. Viva the sight drafts, I said.

A **draft** (also called a **bill of exchange**) is an instrument in which one party writes an instrument ordering a second party to pay money to a third party. The one who draws the draft (that is, the one who orders money to be paid) is called the *drawer*. The one who is ordered to pay the money is called the *drawee*. The one who is to receive the money is known as the *payee*.

Example 25-1

In Hemingway's story mentioned earlier the major would be the drawer of the draft and his grandfather would be the drawee. The story doesn't name the payee of the draft, but it could be the railroad ticket office or a bank in Italy—whoever is to receive the money. If this were a check, the person who signed the check would be the drawer, the bank would be the drawee, and the one to whom the check is written would be the payee.

A draft may be presented by the holder to the drawee for payment or for acceptance. When a draft is presented for payment, the drawee may decline to pay it unless it has been accepted. If the drawee refuses to pay an unaccepted draft, the draft is dishonored, and the drawee has no liability for refusing to pay it. In contrast, when a draft is presented for acceptance, the drawee is asked to become liable on the instrument. **Acceptance** is the drawee's signed agreement to pay a draft as presented. If the drawee refuses to accept the draft, it is dishonored and, again, the drawee has no liability. Drawees are liable on drafts only when they accept them; that is, agree to become liable on them.

To accept a draft, the drawee need only sign the draft across the face of the instrument. It is customary, however, when accepting a draft, for the drawee to write "accepted" across the face of the instrument, followed by the date and signature. An acceptance must be written on the draft itself; it may not be written on a separate piece of paper. By accepting a draft, the drawee agrees to pay the instrument at a later date when it becomes due.

Sight and Time Drafts A **sight draft** (Figure 25-2) is payable as soon as it is presented to the drawee for payment. A **time draft** (Figure 25-3) is not payable until the lapse of a particular time period stated on the draft. Drafts that are payable "thirty days after sight" and "sixty days after date" are examples of time drafts.

Figure 25-2 A sight draft is payable as soon as it is presented to the drawee for payment. How do you know that this draft has not been accepted by the drawee?

UCC Revised (1990) 3-409 (see page 920)

Terms The term *bill* is derived from the Latin *billa,* meaning "seal." During the Middle Ages, bill came to refer to any commercial document.

Background Information Over the years, checks have served surprising purposes. For example, in 1867, the United States paid for the territory of Alaska with a check for $17,200,000 made out to His Imperial Majesty the Tsar of all the Russias. Checks have also assumed unexpected forms. In 1970, British humorist A. P. Herbert received as a payment from the editor of *Punch* magazine a check written on the side of a cow. When Herbert cashed in his cow, the bank paid him in full.

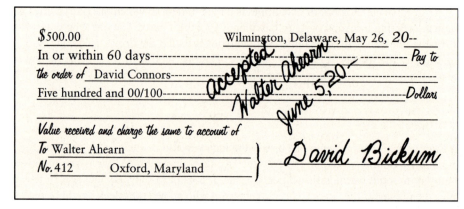

Figure 25-3 A time draft is not payable until the lapse of a particular time period stated on the draft. How do you know that this draft has been accepted by the drawee?

Domestic and International Bills of Exchange A **domestic bill of exchange** is a draft that is drawn and payable in the United States. A draft that is drawn in one country but is payable in another is called an **international bill of exchange,** or **foreign draft.**

Checks

UCC Revised (1990) 3-104(f) (see page 909)

A **check** is a draft drawn on a bank and payable on demand. It is the most common form of a draft. It is drawn on a bank by a drawer who has an account with the bank and is made to the order of a specified person or business named on the check or to the bearer. A check is a safe means of transferring money, and it serves as a receipt after it has been paid and canceled by the bank.

Teaching Tips Obtain from a local bank various types of blank, voided copies of checks for students to examine as checks are discussed in the text.

In the check shown in Figure 25-4, Evans is the drawer; she has an account in the Western National Bank. Alicia Adams Fashions, Inc., is the payee. Western National Bank, on which the check is drawn, is the drawee.

Ownership of a check may be transferred to another person by indorsement by the payee. In this manner, a check may circulate among several parties, taking the place of

Figure 25-4 All elements of a sample check are identified.

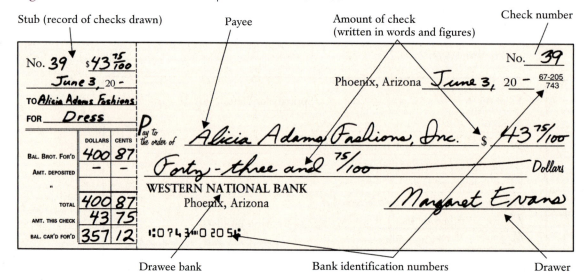

Business Law in the News
Checks Check Out

A funny thing happens when you write a check at some Wal-Marts: It gets handed right back to you. Hoping to speed payments, reduce costs, and cut fraud, the world's largest retailer now scans paper checks for pertinent information such as the bank and account number—and then gives them back to customers in the checkout line.

Remember the old saw, the check's in the mail? Drop it. Digital processing technologies such as those used by Wal-Mart Stores Inc. and the skyrocketing adoption of online bill payment are reshaping the $30 billion business of printing, transporting, and processing checks. Driving the transformation are banks, credit-card companies, and merchants eager to simplify an antiquated system that involves as many as 28 middlemen. They have plenty of motivation: Handling an online payment costs only 10¢, roughly one-third that of processing a paper check, according to Atlanta consultant Global Concepts. The result: The number of checks written annually should decline by about one quarter by 2007, to 30 billion, estimates researcher Celent Communications LLC. "This is a transformational moment," says Jonathan Wilk, senior vice-president at Bank of America Corp.

The age-old practice of printing checks and shuttling them around the country in armored cars is in upheaval. No. 1 check printer Deluxe Corp. is closing three of its 13 printing plants and fighting for its margins by pushing higher-priced check designs and fraud-prevention services. One of the Web's unlikeliest victims is AirNet Systems Inc., in Columbus, Ohio, which gets nearly 70% of its $140 million in revenues from flying checks between cities on Learjets. AirNet is shifting its focus to passenger charters and express shipments of donor organs. "We've seen this bogeyman coming," says Wynn D. Peterson, AirNet's vice-president for corporate development.

Fostering Loyalty

And he's coming fast. This year, 65 million U.S. consumers are paying some of their bills online, almost twice as many as last year, according to Gartner. And that's expected to jump to 73 million in four years. This growth is a boon for companies such as Wells Fargo, American Express, and Sprint, which work with online bill payment pioneers CheckFree Corp., edocs Inc., and others. Gartner figures that the average company with 1.9 million customers can cut $26 million in costs per year by persuading customers to receive and pay their bills over the Web.

Cost savings are just the start. Customers are more likely to stay with a bank if they pay bills online there. At Wells Fargo & Co., customers who pay bills online are 75% less likely to leave the bank than other customers. "No doubt, the benefits far outweigh the expenses," says Jim Smith, executive vice-president for consumer Internet products at Wells Fargo.

Even when payments are not made online, paper checks are going digital. Behind this modernization is the Check Clearing for the 21st Century Act, known as Check 21. This law, which goes into effect in October, is expected to kick off a mass adoption of check imaging by putting electronic images of checks on equal legal footing with paper originals for the first time. Even banks that aren't equipped to handle digital checks have to accept printouts of them, known as "substitute checks," as payment. During the past three years, startups Viewpointe Archive Services, Endpoint Exchange, and NetDeposit have rolled out software and services that convert checks into digital files so they can be stored and swapped electronically. Banks could reap big savings. The cost of upgrading to digital check handling will reach $1.9 billion next year, but the industry could save $2.1 billion annually from the shift, estimates Celent.

The changes will allow the banking behemoths to compete more fiercely with community banks. The corner florist and local Wal-Mart typically do business with a nearby bank because they want to get credit for their daily deposits as quickly as possible. With digital check processing, proximity no longer

(Continued)

money. A bank must honor a check when it is properly drawn against a credit balance of the drawer. Failure to do so would make the bank liable to the drawer for resulting damages.

Background Information As long ago as the fourteenth century, it was common practice for bankers to issue receipts confirming deposits. Although made out in the depositors' names, such receipts could be presented to third parties as instruments of payment, serving the function of what would eventually become checks.

Related Cases Duncan Savings & Loan Association issued a money order for $24,190 to McAffrey Funeral Home. When the instrument was presented by the First National Bank of Nocona for payment, Duncan Savings and Loan refused payment because McAffrey had put a stop payment on the money order. The court ruled that a drawer bank (Duncan Savings & Loan) on a personal money order is liable notwithstanding a stop payment order unless able to prove a valid defense. The S&L could not assert a defense, so it was required to pay on the order. *First National Bank of Nocona v. Duncan Savings & Loan Association,* 656 F.Supp. 358.

A Question of Ethics

Along with their bill, credit card companies often include blank checks for customers to make payable to anyone they wish, thus increasing the amount owed to the credit card issuer usually at an exceptionally high rate of interest. The practice is legal; is it ethical?

Form for Checks Banks provide regular and special printed check forms. These check forms display a series of numbers printed in magnetic ink, which make it possible to process checks speedily and accurately by computers. The first set of figures is the bank's Federal Reserve number. This number is followed by the bank's own number. The second set of numbers is the depositor's account number. The use of printed forms is not required however. Any writing, no matter how crude, may be used as a check if it is a draft drawn on a bank and payable on demand.

Example 25-2

While on a fishing trip in the Maine woods, Nichols lost his belongings when his canoe tipped over. A camper sold Nichols a jacket, some camping equipment, and enough food to make it to the nearest town. Since Nichols had lost his money, he wrote out a check on a piece of notebook paper ordering his bank to pay to the order of the camper $80. Although unusual, this writing amounted to a valid check that would have to be honored by Nichols's bank.

Figure 25-5   The State Street Bank became primarily liable when it certified this check.

Certified Checks

A **certified check** is a check that is guaranteed by the bank. At the request of either the depositor or the holder, the bank acknowledges and guarantees that sufficient funds will be withheld from the drawer's account to pay the amount stated on the check. A prudent person would request a certified check when involved in a business transaction with a stranger rather than accept a personal check.

UCC Revised (1990)
3-409(d) (see page 920)

A certified check, under the UCC, is "a check accepted by the bank on which it is drawn." The UCC places no obligation on a bank to certify a check if it does not want to do so, and the refusal to certify is not a dishonor of the check. When a check is certified, the drawer is discharged regardless of when it was done or who obtained the acceptance. Figure 25-5 illustrates a certified check.

UCC Revised (1990)
3-414(c) (see page 921)

Bank Drafts and Cashier's Checks

A **bank draft,** sometimes called a **teller's check,** or *treasurer's check,* is a check drawn by one bank on another bank in which it has funds on deposit in favor of a third person, the payee. Many banks deposit money in banks in other areas for the convenience of depositors who depend upon the transfer of funds when transacting business in distant places. When the buyer is unknown to the seller, such checks are more acceptable than personal checks.

UCC Revised (1990)
3-104(g)(h)
(see page 909)

A **cashier's check** is a check drawn by a bank upon itself. The bank, in effect, lends its credit to the purchaser of the check. It is the equivalent of a promissory note of the bank. Courts have held that payment cannot be stopped on a cashier's check because the bank, by issuing it, accepts the check in advance. People who will not accept personal checks will often accept cashier's checks. Such a check may be made payable either to the depositor, who purchases it from the bank, or to the person who is to cash it. If the check is made payable to the depositor, it must be indorsed to the person to whom it is transferred.

Many people pay monthly bills by check. Others prefer automatic payments to be made electronically by their banks.

Traveler's Checks

A **traveler's check** is similar to a cashier's check in that the issuing financial institution is both the drawer and the drawee. The purchaser signs the checks in the presence of the issuer when they are purchased. To cash a check, the purchaser writes the name of the payee in the space provided and countersigns it in the payee's presence. Only the purchaser can negotiate traveler's checks, and they are easily replaced by the issuing bank if they are stolen. Traveler's checks are issued in denominations of $10 and up, and the purchaser of the checks ordinarily pays a fixed fee to the issuer.

UCC Revised (1990)
3-104(i) (see page 909)

UCC Revised (1990)
3-104(f) (see page 909)

Money Orders A **money order** is a type of draft that may be purchased from banks, post offices, telegraph companies, and express companies as a substitute for a check. Instead of being drawn on an individual's account as is a check, however, a money order is drawn on the funds of the organization that issues it. That organization promises payment from its own funds. Purchasers of money orders fill in their name and address and the name of the payee on the instrument. They are given a receipt along with the money order. If the money order is lost and the purchaser has the receipt, it will be replaced if it has not already been cashed. U.S. Postal Service money orders can be purchased for an amount up to $1,000. U.S. International Postal Service Money Orders are often used to send money to foreign countries. Telegraphic money orders may be used to send money quickly. Under the UCC, a *bank* money order is a check, even though it is described on its face as a money order, and payment can be stopped on it like an ordinary check.

Quick Quiz 25-3 True or False?

1. A drawee is required to pay an unaccepted draft when it is presented for payment.

2. A cashier's check is a check drawn by a bank upon itself.

3. A stop-payment order can be placed on a money order.

25-4 Parties to Negotiable Instruments

The following are parties to negotiable instruments:

- the maker or comaker
- the drawer
- the issuer
- the drawee
- the payee
- the bearer

- the holder
- the holder in due course
- the indorser
- the indorsee
- the acceptor

UCC Revised (1990)
3-103 (see page 908)

A **maker** is a person who signs a note; that is, a person who promises to pay. **Comakers** are two or more people who sign the same note promising to pay. A **drawer** is a person who signs a draft; that is, the one who orders payment. An **issuer** is either a maker or a drawer of an instrument. A **drawee** is a person ordered in a draft to make payment. A **payee** is a person to whom a note or draft is payable.

UCC 1-201(5)
(see page 912)

UCC Revised (1990)
3-109(a) (see page 908)

UCC 1-201(20)
(see page 912)

A **bearer** is a person who is in possession of a negotiable instrument that is payable to bearer or to cash. A person who is in possession of an instrument that has been indorsed in blank (by the payee's signature alone) is also a bearer. A **holder** is a person who is in possession of a negotiable instrument that is issued or indorsed to that person's order or to bearer. A *holder in due course* is a holder of a negotiable instrument who is treated as favored and is given immunity from certain defenses. A detailed discussion of holders in due course can be found in Chapter 27.

An **indorser** is a person who indorses a negotiable instrument. This is done in most cases by signing one's name on the back of the paper. The different kinds of indorsements are discussed in Chapter 26.

UCC Revised (1990)
3-204 (see page 913)

An **indorsee** is a person to whom a draft, note, or other negotiable instrument is transferred by indorsement. An **acceptor** is a drawee of a draft who has promised to honor the draft as presented by signing it on its face. (See Figure 25-6.)

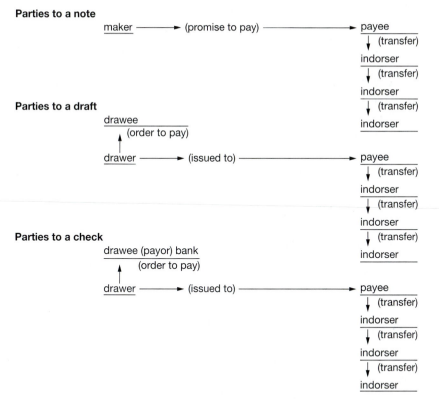

Figure 25-6 This diagram illustrates the relationship of the principal parties to negotiable instruments.

Quick Quiz 25-4 True or False?

1. A maker is a person who signs a draft.

2. A holder is a person who is in possession of a negotiable instrument that is issued or indorsed to that person's order or to bearer.

3. A bearer is a person who is in possession of a negotiable instrument that is payable to bearer or to cash.

25-5 Requirements of Negotiable Instruments

To be negotiable, instruments must:

- be in writing
- be signed by the maker or drawer
- contain an unconditional promise or order to pay
- be made out for a fixed amount of money
- be payable on demand or at a definite time
- except for checks, be payable to order or to bearer

UCC Revised (1990)
3-104(a) (see page 909)

As will be seen in Chapter 26, instruments that do not meet all of these requirements can be transferred to others by assignment. They cannot, however, be transferred by negotiation.

Written Instrument

UCC 1-201(46)
(see page 912)

Terms Forgery consists of making a false written instrument with the intent to defraud, altering a genuine instrument in any way, or *uttering* a forged instrument. In this sense, the word *utter* means "to offer" or "to pass for value in return."

UCC Revised (1990)
3-401(a)(b) (see page 918)

UCC Revised (1990)
3-402 (see page 918)

A negotiable instrument must be in writing (see Figure 25-7). This includes printing, typewriting, pen or pencil writing, or any other tangible form of writing. A negotiable instrument written in pencil is, however, an invitation to alteration by forgery. If forgery should happen, the person who drew the instrument would be responsible for any loss caused by the negligent drawing of the instrument.

Signature of Maker or Drawer

To be negotiable, an instrument must be signed by the maker or drawer. Any writing, mark, or symbol is accepted as a signature so long as it is the writer's intent to be a signature. It may be handwritten, typewritten, printed, or produced by a machine.

A signature may be made by an agent (one who represents and acts for another) or other representative. No particular form of appointment is necessary to establish such authority. Agents who sign their own names to an instrument are personally obligated if the instrument neither names the person represented nor shows that the agent signed in a representative capacity. The signature may appear in the body of the instrument as well as at the end.

Unconditional Promise or Order to Pay

UCC Revised (1990)
3-104(a) (see page 909)

To be negotiable, an instrument must contain no conditions that might in any way affect its payment. Statements requiring that certain things be done or that specific events take place prior to payment make the instrument a simple contract rather than negotiable paper.

Example 25-3

Chung signed the following note to the Chu-Tai Appliance Co.: "I promise to pay to the order of Chu-Tai Appliance Co. $550 sixty days after the delivery of my new refrigerator." This instrument is not negotiable because it is conditional upon the delivery of the refrigerator.

Figure 25-7 The requirements of negotiability are indicated on this ninety-day note.

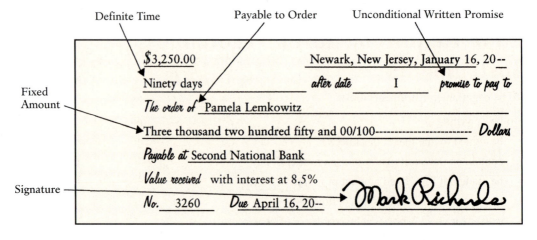

The Opening Case Revisited
"The Student Loan"

The IOU is not negotiable because it is neither a promise nor an order to pay. The note is not negotiable because it is conditional. Payment will be made only if the income tax refund is a sufficient amount and is actually received. The note could be made negotiable if it were changed to read, "to be charged to the proceeds of an income tax refund." This wording does not affect negotiability, since the friend's general credit is relied upon and the reference to the income tax refund is simply a record-keeping instruction following payment.

Related Cases Intending to make a loan, X gave Y a check for $2,000, but neglected to sign the check. The following day Y deposited the check to his account and delivered to X a note promising to pay back the $2,000. A year later Y defaulted and X sued the bank for cashing his check without his signature. The court ruled against X stating that the bank was relieved from liability, since X, by accepting interest payments from Y and later making written demand to Y for payment, received the benefit of the bank's payment of the check. *Spec-Cast, Inc. v. First National Bank and Trust Co. of Rockford,* 538 N.E.2d 543.

An instrument is conditional, and thus not negotiable, if it states that it is subject to any other agreement. The same is true if an instrument states that it is to be paid only out of a particular fund. This latter rule does not apply to instruments issued by government agencies. An instrument may state that it "arises out of" another agreement without being conditional. Similarly, a negotiable instrument may indicate a particular account that is to be charged.

In addition to being unconditional, a negotiable instrument must contain a promise to pay (as in a note) or an order to pay (as in a draft). A writing that says "Due Karen Osgood $600" or "IOU $600" is not negotiable because it is neither a promise nor an order to pay.

UCC Revised (1990) 3-106(b) (see page 910)

Fixed Amount of Money

A negotiable instrument must be payable in a fixed amount or sum certain of money. This stipulation means an amount of money that is clearly known. *Money* is defined as a medium of exchange adopted by a domestic or foreign government as part of its currency. Thus, a fixed amount of money need not be money of the United States.

UCC Revised (1990) 3-104(a) (see page 909)

UCC 1-201(24) (see page 912)

UCC Revised (1990) 3-107 (see page 910)

Example 25-4

In exchange for a commissioned painting, Emil Hauser, of Stuttgart, Germany, sent a note to Ann Maggio, of New York City, which read, "Ninety days after date, I promise to pay to the order of Ann Maggio 5,000 deutsches marks (signed) Emil Hauser." The note was negotiable. On the due date, it would probably be paid in American dollars according to the exchange rate of marks and dollars as of the date of payment.

Did You Know?

In a step towards having one currency for Europe, eleven members of the European Union introduced the euro in 1999. The euro replaced national currencies in 2002. The initial countries participating were Belgium, Germany, Spain, France, Ireland, Italy, Luxembourg, the Netherlands, Austria, Portugal, and Finland.

Payable on Demand or at a Definite Time

Negotiable instruments must be made payable on demand or at a definite time. This requirement makes it possible to determine when the debtor or promisor can be compelled to pay. Without this information, the present value of an instrument cannot be determined.

Demand Paper An instrument is payable *on demand* when it so states, or when it is payable "on sight" or "on presentation." The key characteristic of demand instruments is that the holder can require payment at any time by making the demand upon the person who is obligated to pay.

UCC Revised (1990)
3-108(a) (see page 910)

UCC Revised (1990)
3-108(b) (see page 910)

Definite-Time Paper Certainty as to the time of payment of an instrument is satisfied if it is payable on or before a stated date. Instruments payable at a fixed period after a stated date or at a fixed period after sight are also considered to be payable at a definite time. In each instance, a simple mathematical calculation makes the maturity date certain. The expressions "one year after date" and "thirty days after sight" are definite as to time. An undated instrument payable sixty days after date is negotiable as a demand paper.

A promise to pay only upon an act or event, the time of whose occurrence is uncertain, is not payable at a definite time. Thus, an instrument payable when a person marries, reaches a certain age, or graduates from college or one payable within a specific period of time after a named person's death is not negotiable.

Payable to Order or to Bearer

Negotiable instruments, except for checks, must be payable to order or to bearer. The words *to the order of* and *to bearer* are called the words of negotiability. Article 3 of the UCC was revised in 1990 to allow checks (but not other instruments) that are not payable to order or to bearer to be negotiable. Thus, a check, but no other instrument, payable "to Mary Harris" is negotiable in all states except New York and South Carolina, which have not adopted the revised Article 3.

UCC Revised (1990)
3-104(c) (see page 909)

UCC Revised (1990)
3-109(b) (see page 910)

UCC Revised (1990)
3-109(a) (see page 910)

Payable to Order An instrument is payable to order when it states that it is payable to the order of any person with reasonable certainty. The maker or drawer may state "Pay to the order of Mary Doe," "Pay to Mary Doe or order," or "Pay to Mary Doe or her assigns." An instrument may be payable to the order of the maker or drawer; the drawee; a payee who is not the maker, drawer, or drawee; two or more payees; an estate, trust, or fund; an office or officer by title; or a partnership or an unincorporated association.

Payable to Bearer An instrument is payable to bearer when it states that it is payable to bearer or the order of bearer, a specified person or bearer, cash or the order of cash, or any other indication that does not designate a specific payee. An instrument is payable to bearer when it does not state a payee. An instrument made payable to both, such as "Pay to the order of Anthony Andrews or bearer," is payable to order unless the bearer words are handwritten or typewritten.

(A negotiable instrument) is a key which in the hands of a rightful owner is intended to unlock the door of the warehouse, floating or fixed, in which the goods may chance to be.

—Charles S. C. Bowen (1835–1894), British Judge

Example 25-5

Joseph Andrews signed a promissory note that stated, "I promise to pay Ray Brown" a certain amount of money. The note was not negotiable because it was not payable to order or to bearer. The person to whom the note was transferred by Brown was not entitled to the special protection that would have been available had the note been negotiable.

Dates and Controlling Words

UCC Revised (1990)
3-113 (see page 911)

The omission of the date does not affect the negotiability of an instrument. When the date is omitted, the date on which the instrument is received is considered to be the date of issue. An instrument may be predated or post-dated without affecting its negotiability. Handwritten terms control typewritten and printed terms, and typewritten terms control printed terms. Words control figures, except where words are ambiguous (capable of being understood in more than one way). The numbering of, or the failure to number, an instrument does not affect its negotiability.

Quick Quiz 25-5 True or False?

1. Instruments that do not meet all of the requirements of negotiability are void.

2. A signed writing that reads "I promise to pay to John Gore $500" is negotiable.

3. A signed writing that reads "Pay to the order of Janet Giron $2,000 when she graduates from college" is negotiable.

Summary

25-1 The purpose of negotiable instruments is to allow people to transact business without carrying around large sums of money and to allow them to borrow money more easily. Computer and electronic technology is now being used as a substitute for checks and other paper transactions.

25-2 A note is a written promise by one party to pay money to another party. A certificate of deposit is the acknowledgment by a bank of the receipt of money and a promise to pay the money back on the due date, usually with interest.

25-3 A draft is an instrument by which the party creating it orders another party to pay money to a third party. A check is a draft drawn on a bank and payable on demand.

25-4 The parties to a draft are the drawer, drawee, and payee. The parties to a note are the maker and payee. A bearer is a person who is in possession of a negotiable instrument that is payable to bearer or to cash. A holder is a person who is in possession of an instrument that is issued or indorsed to that person's order or to bearer. A holder in due course is a holder of a negotiable instrument who is treated as favored and is given immunity from certain defenses. An indorser is a person who indorses a negotiable instrument. An indorsee is a person to whom an instrument is transferred by indorsement. An acceptor is a drawee of a draft who has promised to honor the draft by signing it on its face.

25-5 To be negotiable, an instrument must be in writing and have the signature of the maker or drawer, an unconditional promise or order to pay, for a fixed amount of money, payable on demand or at a definite time, and payable to order (except checks) or to bearer. Predating, postdating, or the omission of the date does not affect the negotiability of an instrument. Words control figures, except where words are ambiguous.

Key Terms

acceptance, 473

acceptor, 478

bank draft, 477

bearer, 478

bill of exchange, 473

cashier's check, 477

certificate of deposit (CD), 472

certified check, 477

check, 474

comakers, 478

demand note, 471

domestic bill of exchange, 474

draft, 473

drawee, 478

drawer, 478

foreign draft, 474

holder, 478

indorsee, 478

indorser, 478

installment note, 471

international bill of exchange, 474

issuer, 478

maker, 478

money order, 478

negotiable instrument, 471

note, 471

payee, 478

sight draft, 473

teller's check, 477

time draft, 473

trade acceptance, 473

traveler's check, 477

Questions for Review and Discussion

1. What is the purpose of negotiable instruments?
2. What are the two kinds of negotiable instruments that contain a promise to pay money?
3. What are the two kinds of negotiable instruments that contain an order to pay money?
4. Who are the parties to a note? Who are the parties to a draft?
5. How do the following notes differ from one another: demand note, time note, and installment note?
6. When is a drawee liable on a draft?
7. What form must be used to write a check?
8. How does a bank draft differ from a cashier's check?
9. What is the obligation of a bank to certify a check?
10. What is the difference between a bearer of a negotiable instrument and a holder?

Investigating the Internet

Go to "Uniform Commercial Code Locator" at **http://www.law.cornell.edu/ uniform/ucc.html.** Click Article 3 Commercial Paper. Then, click the name of your state to find your state law on that subject. Write a report on your findings.

Cases for Analysis

1. Haas deposited two checks totaling $42,000 into his account at the Meridian Bank and, at the same time, purchased a $35,000 money order. He then went to the Trump Plaza and Casino where he received cash for the money order for gambling purposes. The next day, the two checks were returned to the Meridian Bank unpaid with a notation "account closed." The bank put a stop-payment order on the money order and refused to pay it when it was presented by Trump Plaza for payment. Trump argued that payment could not be stopped on a money order. Do you agree with Trump? Why or why not? *Trump Plaza Associates v. Haas,* 692 A. 2d 86 (NJ).

2. Gail Sak wanted to give her niece, Kim Ryan, a gift of money for her twenty-first birthday, which was two weeks away. Since she was leaving for a trip to Europe the next day, Sak gave Ryan a check dated that day reading, "Pay to the order of Kim Ryan when she reaches the age of twenty-one (signed) Gail Sak." Was the check negotiable? Why or why not?

3. In exchange for legal services rendered to her by the law firm of Westmoreland, Hall, and Bryan, Barbara Hall wrote the following letter: "I agree to pay to your firm as attorney's fees for representing me in obtaining property settlement agreement and tax advice, the sum of $2,760, payable at the rate of $230 per month for twelve (12) months beginning January 1, 1970. Very truly yours, Barbara Hall Hodge." Was the letter a negotiable instrument? Give the reason for your answer. *Hall v. Westmoreland, Hall & Bryan,* 182 S.E.2d 539 (GA).

4. Barton signed a promissory note promising to pay to the order of Scott Hudgens Realty & Mortgage, Inc., the sum of $3,000. The note stated, "This amount is due and payable upon evidence of an acceptable permanent loan . . . and upon acceptance of the loan commitment." Was the note negotiable? Why or why not? *Barton v. Scott Hudgens Realty & Mortg.,* 222 S.E.2d 126 (GA).

5. Melanie E. Regan wrote the following words on a sheet of notebook paper in her own handwriting: "Twenty years from date, I, Melanie E. Regan promise to pay to the order of Ryan M. Brown $10,000 without interest." She did not sign the paper at the end. Is the instrument negotiable? Why or why not?

6. In 1969, Gentilotti wrote a check payable to the order of his five-year-old son for $20,000. The check was postdated to 1984. It was delivered to the child's mother, who kept it for the child. The check was indorsed by the father, as follows: "For Edward Joseph Smith Gentilotti / My Son / If I should pass away / The amount of $20,000.00 dollars / Shall be taken from / My Estate at death. / S. Gentilotti 11-25-69." Gentilotti died in 1973. Was the check negotiable? Explain. *Smith v. Gentilotti* 359 N.E.2d 953 (MA).

7. Joshua Nichols drew the following draft on his Uncle David Nichols and gave it to Natalie Brown in payment for a used car: "To David Nichols: On demand, pay to the order of Natalie Brown $7,000 (signed) Joshua Nichols." When Brown presented the draft to David Nichols for payment, the latter refused to pay it, arguing that the UCC did not require him to do so. Is Nichols correct? Why or why not?

8. James Ahmed gave William Cooper a draft that read, "To Esther Blum: Ninety days from date, pay to the order of William Cooper $5,000 (signed) James Ahmed." Cooper telephoned Blum to see if she would honor the draft. Blum said that she would and, to show her good faith, wrote Cooper a letter saying that she would honor the draft. Was the draft accepted by Blum? Explain.

9. Norek reported to his insurance company that his car had been stolen. The insurance company delivered to Norek a draft drawn on itself and payable through the First Pennsylvania Bank in the amount of $5,878.63. The draft was payable to Norek and to General Motors Acceptance Corporation (GMAC), which held a security interest on the car. Upon receiving the draft, GMAC released its lien on the vehicle and gave Norek the title certificate. Soon thereafter, it was discovered that the automobile had not been stolen and that Norek's claim was fraudulent. The insurance company stopped payment on the draft. GMAC claims that the draft was a check. Do you agree with GMAC? Why or why not? *Gen. Motors Accept. v. Gen. Acc. Fire & Life,* 415 N.Y.S.2d 536 (NY).

10. Duester bought a combine and grain platform on credit. He could not pay the amount owed when it became due. To avoid having the combine repossessed, Duester went to the bank for a cashier's check. An authorized teller made out a check payable to John Deere Company in the amount of $8,455.84 and signed it. Since the bank had recently established a policy requiring two signatures on a cashier's check, the teller excused herself to request a loan officer to come to the counter to sign the check. When the teller returned with the loan officer, Duester and the check were not there. Outside the bank, Duester gave the check to an agent of the John Deere Company who had come to repossess the equipment. When the check was presented for payment, however, the bank refused to pay it. Must the bank pay the cashier's check? Explain. *John Deere Co. v. Boelus State Bank,* 448 N.W.2d 163 (NE).

Quick Quiz Answers				
25-1 1. T	25-2 1. T	25-3 1. F	25-4 1. F	25-5 1. F
2. F	2. F	2. T	2. T	2. F
3. T	3. T	3. T	3. T	3. F

Transferring Negotiable Instruments

The Opening Case

"A Watertight Case"

Drinkwater, who was seventeen years old, bought a second-hand boat from Diaz for $650, paying for it by personal check. The transaction took place late on Friday afternoon, so Diaz kept the check over the weekend. Meanwhile, the boat had developed a leak and sunk while Drinkwater was trying it out. Fortunately, Drinkwater swam safely to shore. He telephoned his bank early Monday morning and stopped payment on the check. That afternoon, Diaz indorsed the instrument and cashed it at her bank, which was not the bank on which it was drawn. The check was returned to the bank that had cashed it marked "payment stopped." Can that bank recover its money from Drinkwater? From Diaz?

Chapter Outcomes

1. Differentiate between an assignment and a negotiation of an instrument.
2. Explain why the concept of negotiability is one of the most important features of negotiable instruments.
3. Name and describe four kinds of indorsements.
4. Identify the implied warranties that are made when people indorse negotiable instruments.
5. Explain the contract that is made when people indorse negotiable instruments.
6. Determine the indorsement required on instruments with more than one payee.
7. Describe the legal effect of a forged or unauthorized indorsement, and recognize three exceptions to the unauthorized indorsement rule.

26-1 Transferring Instruments

When an instrument is first delivered by the maker or drawer for the purpose of giving rights to any person, it is said to be *issued*. When the person to whom it is issued delivers it to a third party, it is *transferred*. Instruments can be transferred by assignment or by negotiation.

Assignment

An **assignment** is the transfer of a contract right from one person to another. Negotiable instruments are assigned either when a person whose indorsement is required on an instrument transfers it without indorsing it or when it is transferred to another person and does not meet the requirements of negotiability. In all such transfers, the transferee has only the rights of an assignee and is subject to all defenses existing against the assignor (see Chapter 13).

An assignment of negotiable instruments also occurs by operation of law when the holder of an instrument dies or becomes bankrupt. In such cases, title to the instrument vests in the personal representative of the estate or the trustee in bankruptcy.

Negotiation

A **negotiation** is the transfer of an instrument in such form that the transferee becomes a *holder* (a person who is in possession of an instrument issued or indorsed to that person, to that person's order, to bearer, or in blank). In contrast to an assignment, a negotiation gives greater rights to transferees.

If an instrument is payable to order, such as "pay to the order of," it is known as **order paper.** To be negotiated, order paper must be indorsed by the payee and delivered to the party to whom it is transferred. If an instrument is payable to bearer or cash, it is called **bearer paper** and may be negotiated by delivery alone, without an indorsement. When order paper is indorsed with a blank indorsement, it is turned into bearer paper and may be further negotiated by delivery alone.

UCC Revised (1990)
3-105 (see page 909)
and 3-203 (see
page 912)

Teaching Tips   Review with students the various restrictions on assignments as discussed in Chapter 13.

State Variations   A New York law states that it is illegal to arrest a dead man for debts.

UCC Revised (1990)
3-201 (see page 912)

A negotiable bill or note is a courier without luggage.

—John B. Gibson
(1780–1853), American
judge

Terms   The word *negotiable* comes from the Latin verb *negotiare,* meaning "to carry on business." It is also derived from *negotium,* which means *business* and is a combination of *neg,* meaning *not,* and *otium,* meaning *leisure.*

Example 26-1

Albright sold 100 cases of beans to Brodie for $12 a case. In exchange, Brodie gave Albright a promissory note, promising to pay the $1,200 in six months at 6 percent per annum interest. The note was not negotiable, however, because it read "I promise to pay to Albright" instead of "I promise to pay to the order of Albright." To obtain needed cash, Albright transferred the note to her bank. This transfer was an assignment rather than a negotiation because the note did not contain the proper words of negotiability discussed in Chapter 25. Brodie refused to pay the bank the amount due on maturity because the beans he had received from Albright were defective. They were not merchantable. Since the transfer of the note was an assignment rather than a negotiation, the bank was subject to the same defense as Albright and could not enforce payment of the note. Its only recourse was against Albright. Had the note been negotiable, the bank could have received greater rights than its transferor had. It could have forced Brodie to pay the note even though Brodie received bad beans.

Quick Quiz 26-1 True or False?

1. Instruments can be transferred only by negotiation.

2. A negotiation of an instrument gives greater rights to transferees than an assignment.

3. Osgood gave Rowe a check that read "Pay to the order of bearer $100." Rowe could negotiate the check without indorsing it.

26-2 The Concept of Negotiability

The concept of negotiability is one of the most important features of negotiable instruments. Largely because of this feature, negotiable instruments are highly trusted and are used daily by millions of people. When an instrument is transferred by negotiation, the person receiving the instrument is provided with more protection than was available to the person from whom it was received. The person receiving the instrument is able, in many instances, to recover money on the instrument even when the person from whom the instrument was received could not have done so.

Instruments that do not meet all of the requirements of negotiability cannot be negotiated. However, they can be transferred by assignment, which is governed by the ordinary principles of contract law. People who receive instruments by assignment are not given the special protection provided those who receive instruments by negotiation, because they cannot be *holders in due course,* explained in Chapter 27.

Terms *Indorse* is an alternate spelling of *endorse.* Both terms developed from an Old French word combining *en,* meaning *on,* and *dos* derived from the Latin *dor-sum,* which means *back.* Thus, *endorse* means "to put on the back." Today, under the UCC, an indorsement may be on either side of the instrument, although it is usually placed on the back.

UCC Revised (1990) 3-204(a) (see page 913)

26-3 Negotiation by Indorsement

An instrument is indorsed when the holder signs it, thereby indicating the intent to transfer ownership to another. Indorsements may be written in ink, typewritten, or stamped with a rubber stamp. They may be written on a separate paper (rider, or ***allonge***) as long as the separate paper is so firmly affixed to the instrument that it becomes part of it. Although the UCC does not require indorsements to be on any particular side of the paper, for convenience purposes they are usually placed on the back of the instrument. Anyone who gives value for

Business Law in the News

There Goes the Cheap Money

Eastman Chemical Co. may not be a household name, but as the credit flowed freely on Wall Street, the Kingsport (Tenn.) maker of specialty chemicals was able to borrow for a song. Last May, when the Eastman Kodak Co. spin-off acquired a rival's resins business, the company covered the $244 million purchase mostly by issuing commercial paper—30-day, renewable notes with a mere 2.5% interest rate. And although Eastman originally planned to replace the paper with longer-term debt, management became loath to give up that great rate. Instead, it just rolled the notes over every month.

But with the spate of big-name bankruptcies and accounting scandals sending tremors through the credit markets, Eastman's chief financial officer, Albert J. Wargo, moved recently to change that. He traded in $400 million of Eastman's short-term borrowing for longer-term notes costing 7%. While the move will cut a hefty $18 million out of Eastman's pretax profits this year, Wargo takes solace that rates remain historically low. "The short-term markets are not as stable as they used to be," he sighs. "I'm willing to suffer a little pain right now because at some point in the future, rates will be higher."

Wargo has plenty of company. Since the fall, Moody's Investors Service, Standard & Poor's, and other rating agencies have applied tougher scrutiny to corporate balance sheets—effectively pushing many borrowers out of the volatile short-term lending market. At the same time, the prospect of economic recovery has convinced most execs that a rise in interest rates is inevitable. The combination has sent chief financial officers throughout Corporate America scrambling to shore up balance sheets with more stable debt and lock in today's low rates while they can. The latest to go long: AOL Time Warner Inc., which on Apr. 3 sold $6 billion in bonds, largely to reduce its short-term obligations.

The massive shift has sent the value of outstanding commercial paper of nonfinancial companies in the U.S. falling sharply: From a peak of $315 billion in November, 2000, it has dropped to some $172 billion today. Analysts expect it could contract further in coming months. And another corporate blowup could cause the commercial paper market to dry up even more. "If the commercial paper market were to shut down, AOL and lots of other companies could have real problems," says Philip Olesen, a fixed-income analyst at UBS Warburg.

The trouble is, bolstering the balance sheet with more stable debt comes at a considerable expense. With the equity markets largely closed to issuers and with bankers tightening credit as well, many borrowers are issuing long-term bonds at rates that are double, or even triple, what they were paying on the short end. Louise Purtle, head of U.S. credit strategy at Credit-Sights, a New York research firm, estimates that General Electric Capital Corp.'s recent sale of $11 billion of longer-term bonds in order to begin scaling back its massive $100 billion exposure to the commercial paper market will raise its borrowing costs by as much as $100 million this year alone. Analysts estimate that similar shifts on the part of AOL and Verizon Communications could raise those companies' borrowing costs by $300 million and $100 million, respectively. That could trim about 3% off of AOL's earnings this year and trim Verizon's by 1%.

Add that up for every company making the switch, and the collective toll on corporate profits—and the U.S. economy—could be huge. David Wyss, chief economist at S&P, estimates that the shift out of commercial paper and into bonds could raise Corporate America's borrowing costs overall by as much as $30 billion this year.

While that's just a fraction of the $752 billion in pretax profits that Corporate America earned last year, it's still enough to shave as much as two-tenths of a percentage point off of gross domestic product this year. And that means plenty of money that might otherwise have gone into capital spending, new product development, or marketing will be diverted to debt payments. "It's just one more nick against the recovery," says Wyss.

Of course, the sudden rush into bonds illustrates just how many companies let their balance sheets get out of whack in the 1990s. Many companies quietly used commercial paper to slash borrowing costs and bolster sagging profits. Indeed, new commercial paper borrowing equaled roughly 18% of nonfinancial cor-

porate long-term borrowing in 2000, about twice the level of 1995.

There's a simple reason why. With short maturities—from 1 to 270 days—commercial paper was originally intended to help cover short-term funding needs such as payrolls. But when the annualized interest cost for commercial paper fell as low as 1.75% in the late 1990s, many companies began using it to finance longer-term projects such as constructing new factories.

But while it's cheap, commercial paper is an inherently risky form of borrowing. If questions of financial health arise, a company may find itself unable to roll over short-term notes. The reason: Securities & Exchange Commission regulations require that money-market funds—the main buyers of commercial paper—keep at least 95% of their assets in the highest-grade commercial paper. As a result, companies such as Tyco International Ltd. and Kmart Corp. were suddenly shut out of the commercial paper market when they were downgraded by the rating agencies. The ensuing liquidity squeeze was a big reason the latter was forced to file for Chapter 11 on Jan. 22. "Investors in commercial paper have zero tolerance for credit risk," says Jack Malvey, chief global fixed-income strategist at Lehman Brothers Inc.

Despite the higher costs, many managements say that there is a bright side to debt rejiggering. Thanks to 11 Federal Reserve rate cuts last year, investment-grade companies can still borrow at just above 6%—a fraction of the 11% rate those same borrowers would have paid coming out of the 1991 recession. To every debt cloud, a silver lining.

Questions for Analysis

1. Where did Eastman Chemical Co. get the $244 million to buy a rival's resin business?

2. Why do you think that Eastman's chief financial officer traded $400 million of Eastman's short-term borrowing for longer-term notes?

3. What did the sudden rush to bonds illustrate?

4. Why did new commercial borrowing increase so much between 1995 and 2000?

5. Why is commercial paper an inherently risky form of borrowing?

Source: Dean Foust and Margaret Popper, with Amy Barrett, Peter Elstrom, and bureau reports. "There Goes Cheap Money," *BusinessWeek,* April 15, 2002, p. 44.

Some merchants prefer to avoid potential problems with negotiable paper, and do not accept personal checks.

an instrument has the right to have the unqualified indorsement of the person who transferred it unless it is payable to bearer.

Regulation CC, issued by the Federal Reserve Board under the Competitive Banking Act, has established standards for check indorsements (Figure 26-1). Under the regulation, the back of a check is divided into specific sections designed to protect the indorsement of the depository bank (the bank of first deposit). The first one-and-one-half inches from the trailing edge of the check is reserved for the payee's indorsement.

Negotiation is effective to transfer an instrument even when it is transferred by a minor, a corporation exceeding its powers, or any other person without capacity; obtained by fraud, duress, or mistake of any kind; part of an illegal transaction; or made in breach of duty. Any

Figure 26-1 Regulation CC has issued check indorsement standards.

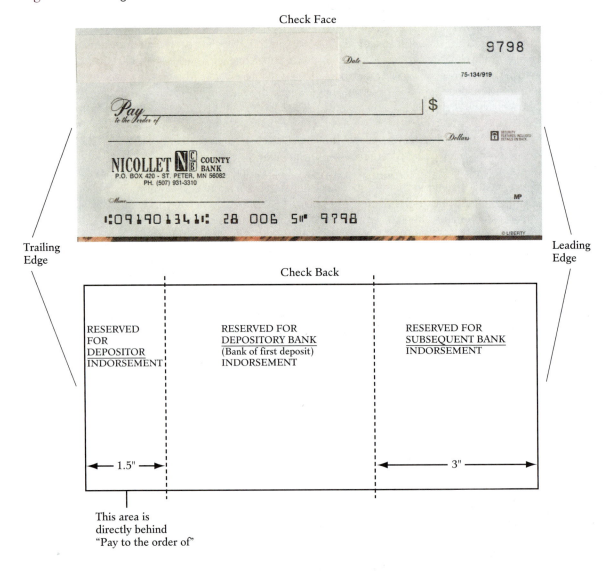

such negotiations, however, may be rescinded except as against a holder in due course (defined and explained in Chapter 27), who is given special protection.

There are four commonly used types of indorsements: blank indorsements, special indorsements, restrictive indorsements, and qualified indorsements.

UCC Revised (1990) 3-202(a) (see page 912)

Blank Indorsements

A **blank indorsement** consists of the signature alone written on the instrument. No particular indorsee (person to whom an instrument is indorsed) is named. When an instrument is indorsed in blank, it becomes payable to bearer and may be transferred by delivery alone. If the instrument is lost or stolen and gets into the hands of another holder, the new holder can recover its face value by delivery alone. For this reason, a blank indorsement should be used only in limited situations, such as at a bank teller's window. A blank indorsement turns order paper into bearer paper and may be transferred by delivery alone.

UCC Revised (1990) 3-205(b) (see page 913)

Teaching Tips Remind students that if an instrument is indorsed in blank and is subsequently lost, it can be cashed by anyone. If the instrument is a check, a bank will upon request, put a "stop payment" order on the check so that an unintended holder of the instrument cannot cash it.

> ## A Question of Ethics
> As part of its direct-mail advertising, a company included a $100 check payable to the recipient. Printed on the back of the check were these words: "By indorsing this check, the indorsee agrees to purchase . . ." Is this marketing practice ethical?

Getting Students Involved Prepare a blank form of a check and distribute a copy of it to each student. Working in small groups, students should practice writing special, blank, and restrictive indorsements. Have the members of each group inspect each other's checks.

Example 26-2

Carol Barcley received her first paycheck from the restaurant where she worked as a part-time hostess. She took the check to the bank where she indorsed it in blank at the teller's window. This was a proper time and place to use a blank indorsement, since there was no likelihood that the check would get lost or stolen.

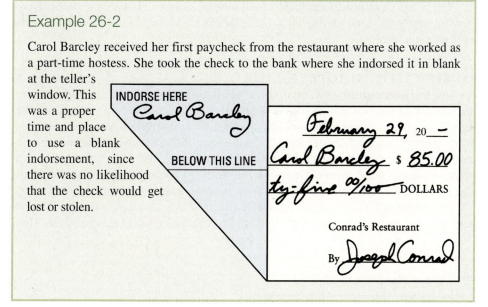

When an instrument is made payable to a person under a misspelled name or a name other than that person's own, the payee may indorse in the incorrect name, in the correct name, or in both. Signatures in both names may be required by a person paying or giving value for the instrument.

UCC Revised (1990) 3-204(d) (see page 913)

Special Indorsements

A **special indorsement** (also called an **indorsement in full**) is made by writing the words *pay to the order of* or *pay to* followed by the name of the person to whom it is to be transferred (the indorsee) and the signature of the indorser. When indorsed in this manner, the instrument remains an order instrument and must be indorsed by the indorsee before it can be further negotiated.

UCC Revised (1990) 3-205(a) (see page 913)

Example 26-3

Frank Cully withdrew $3,500 from his savings account to buy a car from Glendale Motors, Inc. When he made the withdrawal, Cully received a check from the bank payable to him for $3,500. He took the check to Glendale Motors, indorsed it with a special indorsement and received title to the car. A special indorsement (indorsement in full) creates order paper, which requires the signature of the indorsee. Since the check could not be legally transferred or negotiated further until Glendale indorsed it, all parties were protected.

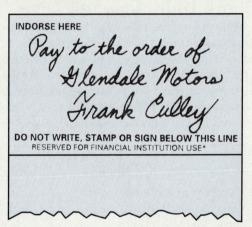

The holder of an instrument may convert a blank indorsement into a special indorsement by writing the same words (*pay to the order of a person* or *pay to a person*) above the indorser's signature.

Restrictive Indorsements

A **restrictive indorsement** limits the rights of the indorsee in some manner in order to protect the rights of the indorser. Indorsements for deposit or collection are restrictive indorsements designed to get an instrument into the banking system for the purpose of deposit or collection. When a check is indorsed "for deposit only," as in Figure 26-2, the amount of the instrument is credited to the indorser's account before it is negotiated further. Retail stores often stamp each check "for deposit only" when it is received. This wording provides protection in the event the check is stolen. Checks mailed to the bank for deposit should always be indorsed in this way.

An indorsement that purports to prohibit further transfer, such as "pay Olga Peterson only," may be further negotiated after the directions in the indorsement are carried out. Thus,

Figure 26-2 A restrictive indorsement limits the subsequent use of the instrument.

after Olga Peterson is paid, any holder of the instrument may continue to negotiate it. A restrictive indorsement does not prevent further transfer or negotiation of the instrument.

A **conditional indorsement,** a type of restrictive indorsement, purports to make the rights of the indorsee subject to the happening of a certain event or condition. A person paying the instrument or taking it for value, however, may disregard the condition.

UCC Revised (1990) 3-206(b) (see page 913)

Example 26-4

Gallo wished to transfer a dividend check that he received to his grandson, James Ingram, as a birthday gift (see indorsement at right). Since Gallo did not want Ingram to cash the check before his eighteenth birthday, a conditional indorsement was used. However, under the UCC, a bank or anyone else who gives Ingram money or value for the check will not be affected by the condition.

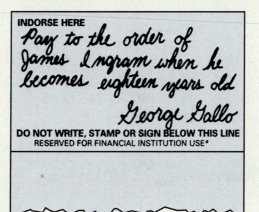

INDORSE HERE

Pay to the order of James Ingram when he becomes eighteen years old

George Gallo

DO NOT WRITE, STAMP OR SIGN BELOW THIS LINE
RESERVED FOR FINANCIAL INSTITUTION USE*

Qualified Indorsements

A **qualified indorsement** is one in which words have been added to the signature that limit the liability of the indorser. By adding the words *without recourse* to the indorsement, the indorser is not liable in the event the instrument is dishonored, that is, not paid by the maker or drawer. (See Example 26-5.)

UCC Revised (1990) 3-415(b) (see page 921)

Example 26-5

A $25,000 check was made payable to Attorney Samuel Brock in payment of a client's claim. Brock indorsed the check to the client, George Rose, "without recourse." By using this indorsement, Brock would not be responsible for payment if the check failed to clear because a qualified indorsement limits the contractual liability of the indorser.

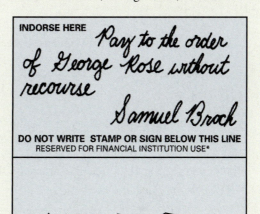

INDORSE HERE

Pay to the order of George Rose without recourse

Samuel Brock

DO NOT WRITE STAMP OR SIGN BELOW THIS LINE
RESERVED FOR FINANCIAL INSTITUTION USE*

Terms The phrase "foot the bill" comes from the practice of signing one's name at the bottom of a bill to indicate acceptance of payment. However, the current popular usage of the phrase indicates an acceptance to pay, making it similar to an indorsement.

Background Information Before alternative systems of identifying customers were introduced, clerks at Barclays Bank in London wrote short descriptions of customers next to their sample signatures. One description given is "short man; whiskers all round his face; one tooth out in front; looks like a coal heaver."

Quick Quiz 26-2 and 26-3 True or False?

1. A blank indorsement should be used only in limited situations, such as a bank teller's window.

2. A special indorsement creates bearer paper and can be negotiated without further indorsement.

3. Checks mailed to the bank for deposit should always be indorsed with a blank indorsement.

26-4 Obligations of Indorsers

Indorsements have a threefold significance. In addition to being necessary to negotiate order paper, they create obligations on the part of the indorser. These obligations come in the form of implied warranties and a contractual promise to pay subsequent holders of the instrument.

Warranties of Indorsers

UCC Revised (1990) 3-416 (see page 921)

Cross-Cultural Notes
It is a serious crime in Mexico to issue a check knowing that there are insufficient funds to cover it. If the check is for more than 3,000 pesos, the indorser may be sentenced to more than five years in prison and may have to pay at least 20 percent of the amount of the check to the innocent party for damages.

An indorser who receives consideration for an instrument makes five warranties to subsequent transferees of the instrument. These five warranties are as follows.

First, the indorser is entitled to enforce the instrument. This warranty gives assurances to subsequent holders that the person indorsing it did not steal it or come into possession of it in an unlawful manner.

Example 26-6

State National Bank accepted a check from Lawless for deposit to her account. The check contained a blank indorsement by Anthony Fiore in addition to Lawless's indorsement. The bank later discovered that Lawless had found the check in a supermarket. A stop payment order had been issued by the real owner, Anthony Fiore. Lawless, by her indorsement, had warranted that she was the true owner of the check. She would be held liable on this warranty for any loss suffered by the bank.

The second warranty is that all signatures are authentic and authorized.

Example 26-7

A check made payable to Jones was indorsed by his stepmother, who forged his signature and cashed the check at the Commonwealth Bank & Trust Co. The bank had a cause of action for the recovery of the money from Jones's stepmother on the ground of breach of warranty that all signatures are authentic and authorized.

The Opening Case Revisited:
"A Watertight Case"

The bank cannot recover the $650 from Drinkwater because he was a minor when he entered into the contract. He could have used the defense of minority against anyone who sued him on the contract. The bank, however, can recover the $650 from Diaz. By indorsing the check, she impliedly warranted that there were no defenses that she could have used to defend herself, including Drinkwater's defense of minority.

A third warranty is that the instrument has not been altered. The indorser warrants that there has been no alteration or other irregularity.

Example 26-8

Cushing wrote a check payable to the order of Daly for five dollars and delivered it to Daly. Daly altered the check to read $500, indorsed it, and cashed it at a bank. Cushing would have to pay only the original amount of the check (five dollars) unless it could be shown that she was negligent in writing it so that it could be easily altered. The bank's recourse would be against Daly for breach of this warranty.

A fourth warranty states that the instrument is not subject to a defense of any party which can be asserted against the indorser. A qualified indorser (one who uses the words *without recourse,* as shown in Example 26-5) does not make this warranty. Such an indorsement warrants only that the indorser has no knowledge of a defense that may be used, such as Drinkwater's defense of minority in the Opening Case of this chapter.

The last warranty provides that the indorser has no knowledge of the bankruptcy of the maker, acceptor, or drawer.

Contract of Indorsers

Unless an indorsement states otherwise (as by words such as *without recourse*), every indorser agrees to pay any subsequent holder the face amount of the instrument if it is **dishonored** (not paid by the maker or drawee). To enforce this obligation, it is necessary for the holder to do two things. The holder of an instrument must first present it for payment to the maker or drawee when it is due. If that person refuses to pay the instrument, it is said to be dishonored. The holder must then notify the indorser or indorsers of the dishonor. If the holder is a bank, notice must be given by midnight of the next banking day. Holders other than banks must give notice within thirty days after the dishonor. Failure by the holder to make presentment and to give timely notice of dishonor to an indorser has the effect of discharging that indorser from liability on the contract to pay subsequent holders of the instrument.

Related Cases An employee had a corporate officer sign checks made out for small amounts to a bank (and told the officer they were for company debts). She then altered the checks to substantially increase the amount and cashed the checks. The company sued the bank that cashed the checks, alleging violations of all the warranties of indorser. The court ruled that when a check has been materially altered and negotiated in an increased amount, the measure of damages is the difference between the raised amount and the amount for which the checks were originally written. The bank had to pay the difference. *Sun 'N Sand, Inc. v. United California Bank*, 582 P.2d 920.

Terms If a person is required by law to pay on a negotiable instrument, he or she may be said to have to "shell out." This colloquialism dates to colonial America when money was scarce, and people often paid debts in shelled corn.

Getting Students Involved Have students talk with a local bank official, police officer, and prosecuting attorney to see what happens when a check is dishonored. What criminal ramifications are possible? What steps will a police officer or prosecutor take before filing criminal charges? What civil ramifications are possible?

UCC Revised (1990) 3-415(a) (see page 921)

UCC Revised (1990) 3-503(c) (see page 924)

UCC 415(a)
(see page 921)

Getting Students Involved Students may be surprised to discover that a bank can supply the missing indorsement of a customer without notification so that operations can run more smoothly. Have small groups discuss the ethics of laws that permit otherwise illegal practices in the interest of efficiency. Encourage the groups to create some scenarios that illustrate the need for such laws and some that challenge those laws.

Example 26-9

When Ralph Brownlee received his paycheck, he indorsed it in blank and gave it to his mother, Sandra Jones, in payment for room and board. Sandra, in turn, indorsed the check and gave it to Robert Allen for work done on her house. Robert indorsed it and asked his sister, Diana Sklar, to drop it off at the Security Loan Company for him on her way to work. Security required Diana to indorse the check, even though it was applied to her brother's loan. The check bounced, and a substitute check was returned to Security Loan marked "insufficient funds." Security Loan had the right to demand payment from any of the indorsers shown on the back of the check if it gave them proper notice. The obligation of an indorser is owed to a person entitled to enforce the instrument or to a subsequent indorser who paid the instrument.

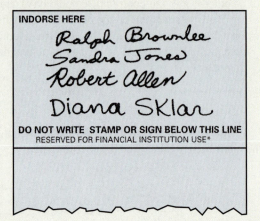

Quick Quiz 26-4 True or False?

1. Indorsers of negotiable instruments warrant that the maker or drawer is still alive.

2. Indorsers of negotiable instruments warrant that the maker or drawer is a reputable person.

3. Indorsers of negotiable instruments agree to pay any subsequent holder the face amount of the instrument if it is not paid by the maker or drawer.

26-5 Multiple Payees, Missing and Forged Indorsements

UCC Revised (1990)
3-110(d) (see page 910)

UCC 3-116

If an instrument is payable to either of two payees, as in "pay to the order of Eric Foss *or* Betty Foss," the indorsement of only one of the payees in necessary to negotiate it. On the other hand, if an instrument is payable to both of two payees, as in "pay to the order of Eric Foss *and* Betty Foss," the indorsement of both payees is necessary for a proper negotiation.

Example 26-10

Middle States Leasing Corporation drew a check payable to the order of two payees. Interpace Corporation and United Leasing Services, Inc., in the sum of $150,000. United Leasing Services, Inc., indorsed the check and received the entire proceeds from the drawee bank without the indorsement of Interpace Corporation on the instrument. Because the instrument was not indorsed by both payees, the bank was held responsible to Middle States Leasing Corporation for the entire amount of the check.

A bank that has taken an instrument from a customer to send through the bank collection process may supply any indorsement of the customer that is necessary to title. This rule is designed to speed up bank collections by eliminating the necessity to return to a depositor any items that were not indorsed. Such an indorsement may not be supplied by a bank, however, if the instrument contains the words *payee's indorsement required.*

UCC 4-205

Unauthorized or Forged Indorsements

An unauthorized signature or indorsement is one made without actual, implied, or apparent authority. With three exceptions and unless ratified (approved afterward), an unauthorized or forged signature does not serve as the signature of the person whose name is signed. It has no effect. In addition, when an instrument is paid on a forged indorsement, the tort of conversion takes place. For example, when a bank pays proceeds to a forger and the payee's wishes are not carried out, the bank is held liable for converting the payee's funds. **Conversion** is the wrongful exercise of dominion and control over another's personal property.

UCC Revised (1990) 3-403(a) (see page 918)

Related Cases A husband signed his wife's name to a promissory note without her knowledge or permission. The holder of the note sued both the husband and the wife to enforce the note. The court ruled that the wife was not liable for the note because an unauthorized signature is wholly inoperative as that of the person whose name is signed, unless that person later ratifies it. The wife neither signed nor ratified the note. *In re Grove,* 4 UCC Rep. Serv.2d 515.

Example 26-11

Seventeen checks payable to the Mott Grain Company, totaling $40,520.93, were deposited to the personal bank account of Baszler, the company's manager. Baszler disappeared with the money but was later found and convicted of embezzlement. Nine of the checks contained restrictive indorsements, requiring them to be deposited in the company's bank account. The remainder of the checks bore blank indorsements, such as "Mott Grain Co./Verson Baszler." Baszler's only authority was to deposit the checks in the Mott Grain Co.'s account. The bank was held liable to the grain company, in conversion, for the amount of all of the checks.

There are three exceptions to the general rule that an unauthorized indorsement has no effect. The exceptions are designed primarily to promote negotiability of negotiable instruments. They are as follows.

Imposters   An imposter is someone who impersonates another. When an instrument is issued to an imposter on the false belief that the imposter is the payee, the indorsement by any person in the name of the payee is treated as an effective indorsement. This rule places the loss, in such a case, on the one who is in the best position to prevent it—the maker or drawer of the instrument.

UCC Revised (1990) 3-404(a) (see page 919)

Example 26-12

Covington was induced in a fraudulent oil-land scheme to issue a cashier's check to an imposter under the false belief that the imposter was a person named Baird. The imposter's indorsement of the name Baird on the check was held by the court to be

(Continued)

Background Information The maker or drawer of an instrument does not have to meet the impostor to be held liable for any payments made. Fraud perpetrated through the mail is no exception to the rule.

> ### Example 26-12 (*Continued*)
>
> effective to negotiate the instrument. The bank that paid the check was not held liable in conversion, and the check was considered to be properly negotiated. The indorsement by the imposter was treated as an effective indorsement.

UCC Revised (1990) 3-404(b)(i) (see page 919)

No Interest Intended; Fictitious Payee   When the maker or drawer of an instrument intends the payee to have no interest in the instrument or the payee is a fictitious person, an indorsement by any person in the name of the payee is effective.

> ### Example 26-13
>
> Gordon loaned $5,000 to Wolf, intending Wolf to have the entire interest in the money. He made the check payable jointly, however, to Wolf and Wolf's wife, Norma. When the check was cashed, Norma's indorsement was forged. The court held that the forged indorsement was valid because Gordon did not intend Norma to have any interest in the instrument.

UCC Revised (1990) 3-405 (see page 919)

Padded Payrolls   When an agent or employee of the maker or drawer pads the payroll by supplying the employer with fictitious names, an indorsement by any person in the name of each fictitious payee is effective. This rule places the burden of preventing this type of fraud on the party who is in the best position to prevent it—either the drawer (if a draft) or the maker (if a note).

State Variations   Only 26 states have specific statutes that impose restrictions on payroll indorsements.

> ### Example 26-14
>
> Harrison, the payroll clerk for Industries, Inc., made out payroll checks for ten employees who did not exist and had her employer sign them. She negotiated the ten checks by indorsing them in the names of the fictitious payees. The indorsements by Harrison were effective. Industries, Inc., not the bank, had the burden of preventing this type of fraud, which it was in a position to avoid. Industries, Inc., would be liable for any losses suffered as a result of the padding of the payroll.

> ### Quick Quiz 26-5   True or False?
>
> 1. A check that is payable to "Thomas Scanlon and Jo Dee Scanlon" must be indorsed by both Thomas and Jo Dee to be negotiated.
>
> 2. A bank that has taken an instrument from a customer to send through the bank collection process may supply any indorsement of the customer.
>
> 3. Without exception, a forged signature does not serve as the signature of the person whose name is signed.

Summary

26-1 Negotiable instruments that do not meet all of the requirements of negotiability cannot be negotiated. They can only be transferred by assignment. People who receive instruments by assignment are not given the special protection provided those who receive instruments by negotiation. To be negotiated, order paper must be indorsed by the payee and delivered. In contrast, bearer paper may be negotiated by delivery alone.

26-2 When an instrument is transferred by negotiation, the person receiving the instrument may obtain more protection than was given to the person from whom it was received.

26-3 When an instrument is indorsed in blank, it becomes bearer paper. When an instrument is indorsed in full, it becomes order paper. A restrictive indorsement limits the subsequent use of an instrument. A qualified indorsement limits the liability of the indorser.

26-4 An indorser who receives consideration for an instrument warrants that he or she has good title to the instrument, all signatures are genuine or authorized, the instrument has not been materially altered, no defense of any party is good against the indorser, and he or she has no knowledge of any insolvency proceedings of the maker, acceptor, or drawer. Unqualified indorsers agree to pay subsequent holders the amount of an instrument if timely presentment is made, if the instrument is dishonored, and if they are given proper notice.

26-5 Instruments payable to one payee *or* another payee require the indorsement of only one of the payees. In contrast, instruments payable to one payee *and* another payee must be indorsed by both payees. A bank taking an instrument for deposit may supply a customer's missing indorsement.

With three exceptions and unless ratified, an unauthorized or forged signature does not serve as the signature of the person whose name is signed. A bank commits the tort of conversion when it pays money to a forger. Exceptions occur when an instrument is issued to an imposter, a payee is not intended to have an interest in an instrument, and a payroll is padded with fictitious names.

Key Terms

allonge, 488
assignment, 486
bearer paper, 487
blank indorsement, 491
conditional indorsement, 493

conversion, 497
dishonored, 495
indorsement in full, 491
negotiation, 487
order paper, 487

qualified indorsement, 493
restrictive indorsement, 492
special indorsement, 491

Questions for Review and Discussion

1. What is the difference between an assignment and a negotiation of an instrument?
2. Describe the concept of negotiability. What protection is available in many instances to a transferee of an instrument that has been negotiated?
3. What is the difference between a blank indorsement and a special indorsement?

4. Why should a blank indorsement be used only in limited situations, such as at a bank teller's window?
5. How does a restrictive indorsement differ from a qualified indorsement?
6. What warranties are made by an indorser who receives consideration for an instrument?

7. What contract does an indorser make with subsequent holders of a negotiable instrument?

8. What indorsements are necessary to negotiate an instrument that is payable to one person *and* another person and an instrument that is payable to one person *or* another person?

9. What are the legal consequences that arise when an instrument is paid on a forged indorsement?

10. What are the three exceptions to the general rule that any unauthorized indorsement is not effective?

Investigating the Internet

Go to **www.google.com** on the Net and key in the words "indorsements of negotiable instruments." Look for information about indorsements from the sites that are listed.

Cases for Analysis

1. David Shin, a silver collector, ran short of cash. He borrowed $1,500 from Vinnie Gaff, giving Gaff the following note: "Thirty days from date, I promise to pay to the order of Vinnie Gaff $1,500 worth of silver (signed) David Shin." Gaff indorsed the note and gave it to Kia Lai in exchange for services rendered by Lai. What legal term describes the transfer of the note from Gaff to Lai? Explain your answer.

2. Powell, intending to write a check to Thompson Electric, Inc., instead made it payable to the order of "Thompson Electric." Thompson Electric, Inc., indorsed the check with its name correctly spelled. Was the indorsement valid? Why or why not? *State v. Powell,* 551 P.2d 902 (KS).

3. Tufi forged the payee's name on the front of a U.S. Treasurer's check. When convicted of a forgery he appealed, contending that a signature on the front of a check cannot be an indorsement. May an indorsement be written on the front of an instrument? Explain. *United States v. Tufi,* 536 F.2d 855 (9th Cir.).

4. Morse wrote a check for $2,500 payable to Reynolds for services rendered. Reynolds fraudulently raised the check to $5,500, indorsed it "without recourse," and deposited it in her bank account. Later, when the alteration was discovered, Reynolds argued that she was not responsible because her indorsement was qualified. Do you agree with Reynolds? Why or why not? See also *Wolfram v. Halloway,* 361 N.E.2d 587 (IL).

5. Sanders borrowed $5,000 from Waskow, giving Waskow a promissory note that read, "One year from date, I promise to pay to the order of James Waskow $5,000, without interest (signed) Mary Sanders." Six months later, Waskow died. The unindorsed note was in the possession of Waskow's landlord, who claimed that Waskow had given him the note in payment of back rent. Was the landlord a holder of the note? Why or why not? See also *Smathers v. Smathers,* 239 S.E.2d 637 (NC).

6. When checks were received by Palmer & Ray Dental Supply, Mrs. Wilson, a company employee, indorsed them with a rubber stamp reading: "Palmer & Ray Dental Supply" (followed by the company's address). Mrs. Wilson deposited some of the checks in the company's account but cashed the rest, keeping the money for herself. The company contended that the indorsements were restrictive and, therefore, that the bank should not have cashed them. Were the indorsements restrictive? Explain. *Palmer & Ray Dental Supply, Inc., v. First Nat'l Bank,* 477 S.W.2d 954 (TX).

7. Commercial Credit Corporation issued a check payable to Rauch Motor Company. Rauch indorsed the check in blank and delivered it to a bank. The bank typed a very long special indorsement payable to Lamson on two legal-size sheets of paper and stapled them to the checks. May an indorsement be written on a separate paper and stapled to the checks? Explain. *Lamson v. Commercial Credit Corp.,* 531 P.2d 966 (CO).

8. The indorsement of the payee of a check drawn by Funding Systems Leasing Corporation was forged. Below the forged indorsement was added the signature of another person that was not forged. The check was deposited with the Sumiton Bank, which claimed to be a holder. Was the bank a holder? Why or why not? *Sumiton Bank v. Funding Sys. Leasing Corp.,* 512 F.2d 774 (5th Cir.).

9. The United States of America issued a check of the U.S. Treasury in the amount of $49,314.47 payable to two companies: Floors, Inc., and American Fidelity Fire Insurance Company. Floors, Inc., indorsed the check with a rubber stamp indorsement, "For Deposit Only, Floors, Inc.," deposited it in its account in the Peoples National Bank, and later withdrew the money. Was the check properly negotiated? Why or why not?

What tort, if any, did the Peoples National Bank commit? Explain. *Peoples Nat'l. Bank v. American Fidelity Fire Ins.,* 386 A.2d 1254 (MD).

10. Darrell Davis was in possession of a promissory note signed by his deceased father which read: "1 year after date for value received, the under-signed maker promises to pay to the order of _____ $12,000. [signed] Aubrey Davis." The name of the payee was left blank. Darrell alleges that his grandmother was the holder of the note and that she transferred it to him prior to her death so that he could collect it for her. Although the note was not indorsed, Darrell argues that bearer paper may be negotiated by delivery alone and need not be indorsed. Is the note bearer paper? Explain. *Davis v. Davis,* 838 S.W.2d 415 (KY).

Quick Quiz Answers

26-1	26-2 & 26-3	26-4	26-5
1. F	1. T	1. F	1. T
2. T	2. F	2. F	2. T
3. T	3. F	3. T	3. F

Chapter 27

Holders in Due Course, Defenses, and Liabilities

The Opening Case

"A Flat Screen Fiasco"

"Look honey!" Kevin said to his wife, Kelly, as he looked closely at the classified section of the local newspaper. "This is too good to be true! Somebody's selling their 50-inch Plasma HDTV for $1,000."

"Really? Let me see," reaching for the paper. "You're right! That's an awfully low price. It's even got a built-in HD tuner. I'll call the number."

Later that evening, Kevin and Kelly decided to buy the set and gave the seller a $1,000 check. "It'll take a few days for your check to clear. I'll call you when it does, and you can come and get the set. It's pretty heavy. You'll need a pickup truck and someone to help you carry it."

Four days later, after not hearing from the seller, Kevin and Kelly went to the seller's apartment and found it empty. Later, they learned that their check had been cashed at a check-cashing business, and $1,000 had been withdrawn from their bank account before they could stop payment on it. Can the couple recover the $1,000 from the check-cashing business?

Chapter Outcomes

1. State the requirements of being a holder in due course and describe the special protection given to such a holder.
2. Name six personal defenses.
3. Discuss the protection given to people who sign consumer credit contracts.
4. Name six real defenses and explain the significance of a real defense.
5. Differentiate between primary liability and secondary liability and list the parties who are primarily liable and secondarily liable.
6. Describe the conditions that must be met to hold a secondary party liable.

27-1 Holder in Due Course

A basic principle of contract law is that people cannot transfer greater rights than they have themselves. This rule, however, does not apply to the law of negotiable instruments. People who are *holders in due course* of negotiable instruments can receive even more rights than those who held the instruments before them. Largely for this reason, negotiable instruments are used frequently and passed liberally from one person to another.

Example 27-1

Alan Andrews sold his sports car to Elizabeth Barlow for $2,500. To make the sale, Andrews told Barlow that the radiator was brand new and that the brakes had been relined two weeks earlier; however, this was not true. Barlow gave Andrews a check for $2,500. While driving the car home, Barlow became aware of the fraud and stopped payment on the check. Andrews, however, had indorsed the check and given it to Catherine Cain, a holder in due course. Cain could collect the full $2,500 from Barlow. Even though Barlow was defrauded, she cannot use that defense against a holder in due course because such holders are protected against this kind of fraud. Her cause of action would have to be against Andrews, who committed the fraud.

A **holder in due course** is a *holder* who takes an instrument:

UCC Revised (1990) 3-302(a)(2) (see page 914)

- For value.
- In good faith.
- Without notice that anything was wrong with the underlying transaction.

Holder

To be a holder in due course, the person in possession of the instrument must first be a **holder.** To be a holder means that the instrument must have been issued or indorsed to that person or to that person's order or to bearer.

UCC Revised (1990) 1-201(20) (see page 912)

Example 27-2

John and Nancy Augustine contracted with Hanover Homes Corporation for the construction of a house. They obtained a commitment for a mortgage loan from a lending company, which issued checks periodically as the construction progressed. The checks were made payable to John, Nancy, and Hanover Homes Corporation. The last check that was issued by the lending company was deposited in Hanover's bank account without Nancy's indorsement on it. The bank that received the check for deposit was not a holder because, without Nancy's indorsement, the check was not issued or indorsed to it, to bearer, or in blank. Since the bank was not a holder, it could not be a holder in due course.

Teaching Tips Emphasize the importance of the holder-in-due-course concept in the law of negotiable instruments. Discuss with the class the various problems financial institutions would encounter if there were no holder-in-due-course rules.

Value

A person must give value for an instrument in order to qualify as a holder in due course. Thus, if an instrument is transferred to a person as a gift, that person would not qualify as a holder in due course. People give value for instruments when they give the consideration that was agreed upon or when they accept instruments in payment of debts.

UCC Revised (1990) 3-303 (see page 914)

Good Faith

To be a holder in due course, the holder must take the instrument in good faith. Good faith means *honesty in fact* and fair dealing. It requires that the taker of a commercial instrument act honestly. If the taker is negligent in not discovering that something was wrong with the paper, this does not establish lack of good faith.

UCC 1-201 (19) (see page 912)

UCC Revised (1990) 3-103(a)(4) (see page 908)

Background Informa-tion Courts of "equity," or fairness, which developed in medieval England, coexisted with common law courts in the United States until the late 1800s. It was in the courts of equity that such maxims as "He who seeks equity must do equity" and "He who seeks equity must have clean hands" were developed as precedents.

> ### Example 27-3
>
> Leo's Used Car Exchange purchased three cars at a car auction from Villa, paying for them with two checks totaling $15,150. Villa presented the checks to a bank and asked the teller to give him cash, since he was going to another auction and needed it. The teller did so without obtaining the bank manager's approval, which was against the bank's policy. Shortly thereafter, Leo's Used Car Exchange stopped payment on the checks because title to the three cars was not clear. The lower court held that the bank that cashed them was not a holder in due course because of the teller's negligence in not obtaining the manager's approval before cashing the checks. The appellate court reversed the lower court's decision, holding that good faith means honesty in fact. The court said, "Nothing in the definition suggests that, in addition to being honest, the holder must exercise due care to be in good faith." Since the bank was a holder in due course, it was able to recover the $15,150 from the drawer of the checks, Leo's Used Car Exchange.

Without Notice

UCC Revised (1990) 3-302(a)(2) (see page 914)

To be a holder in due course, a holder must not have notice of any claim or defense to an instrument or notice that an instrument is overdue or has been dishonored. A holder has notice of a claim or defense if the instrument bears visible evidence of forgery or alteration. The same is true if the instrument is so incomplete or irregular as to make its legal acceptance doubtful. Notice of a claim or defense is also considered given if the holder knows that the obligation of any party is voidable.

Teaching Tips Show the students how to diagram a negotiable instrument case whenever they read one in order to help them understand it. Write this diagram on the chalkboard:

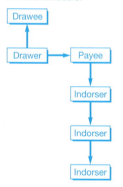

Tell the students to put names from the case in the diagram to identify the drawer, drawee, payee, and indorsers.

> ### Example 27-4
>
> Susan Luft, who was seventeen years old, borrowed $350 from Henry Minkus. She gave Minkus a promissory note, promising to pay the money back in ninety days. Minkus indorsed the note and sold it at a discount to Applebee, telling Applebee that it came from a minor. Applebee was not a holder in due course because she knew that Luft was a minor and could disaffirm the contract to pay back the money.

A holder has notice that a demand instrument is overdue when more than a reasonable length of time has elapsed since it was issued. A check is overdue ninety days after its date. For other instruments, such as a note or draft, what is a reasonable time depends upon the circumstances of each case.

UCC Revised (1990) 3-304 (see page 915)

> ### Example 27-5
>
> Genaro misplaced a check that he had received for cleaning out a neighbor's attic. He found the check four months later and cashed it at a nearby video shop. The video shop was not a holder in due course because it took the instrument when it was more than ninety days old.

Knowledge of some facts does not in itself give the holder notice of a defense or claim. For example, the fact that an instrument is postdated or antedated does not prevent someone from being a holder in due course; neither does completing an incomplete instrument constitute having such notice, unless the holder has notice of any improper completion.

Holder Through a Holder in Due Course

A holder who receives an instrument from a holder in due course acquires the rights of the holder in due course even though he or she does not qualify as a holder in due course. This stipulation is called a **shelter provision.** It is designed to permit holders in due course to transfer all of the rights they have in the paper to others.

UCC Revised (1990) 3-203(b) (see page 912)

Example 27-6

Irwin gave Hill a $150 check in payment for an antique chair. Hill indorsed the check and gave it to McGraw in payment for a debt. Since McGraw took the check for value, in good faith, and without notice, he was a holder in due course of the instrument. McGraw indorsed the instrument with a special indorsement and gave it to his niece as a graduation present. McGraw's niece was not a holder in due course because she did not give value for the instrument. However, she had the rights of a holder in due course because she received the check from a holder in due course.

The shelter provision does not apply to a holder who has committed fraud or an illegal act.

Quick Quiz 27-1 True or False?

1. A holder is a person who is in possession of a negotiable instrument that is issued or indorsed to that person's order or to bearer.

2. Able bought a book from Baker and gave Baker a $25 check. Baker indorsed the check and gave it to Charlie in payment of a debt. Charlie was not a holder in due course of the check.

3. Charlie indorsed the check he received from Baker (above) and gave it to David as a birthday gift. David had the rights of a holder in due course of the check.

Getting Students Involved Have students divide into teams and go to different financial institutions to research what fees are assessed against a check which has been dishonored. Then have the students research what recourse the financial institution has to recover the lost money.

State Variations In Iowa, after a ten-day notice is sent on a check with insufficient funds, criminal theft charges may be brought against the writer of the check if the check has not been covered.

UCC Revised (1990) 3-305(b) (see page 915)

27-2 Personal Defenses

The favorable treatment that holders in due course receive is that they take instruments free from all claims to it on the part of any person and free from all personal defenses of any party *with whom they have not dealt.* **Personal defenses** (also called **limited defenses**) are defenses that can be used against a holder, but not a holder in due course of a negotiable instrument. (The terms *personal defense* and *limited defense* came from the common law and are not used in the UCC.) The most common personal defenses are breach of contract, failure or lack of consideration, fraud in the inducement, lack of delivery, and payment (see Table 27-1).

Breach of Contract

Negotiable instruments are often issued in exchange for property, services, or some other obligation as part of an underlying contract. Sometimes, when this occurs, the party to

Table 27-1 Most Common Personal Defenses	
Defense	**Description**
Breach of contract	One of the parties to a contract has failed to do what he or she has previously agreed to do.
Failure of consideration	One of the parties to a contract has failed to furnish the agreed consideration.
Lack of consideration	No consideration existed in the underlying contract for which the instrument was issued.
Fraud in the inducement	The drawer or maker of an instrument is persuaded to enter into a contract because of a misrepresentation of some fact regarding the item purchased.
Lack of delivery of a negotiable instrument	A payee forcibly, unlawfully, or conditionally takes an instrument from a maker or drawer. The maker or drawer did not intend to deliver the instrument.
Payment of a negotiable instrument	The drawer or maker of an instrument has paid the amount of the instrument.

Getting Students Involved Discuss whether a holder in due course should have real defenses for failure of consideration and breach of contract. Remind students that a holder in due course may have obtained the negotiable instrument in question from another holder in due course and not from the maker.

whom the instrument was issued breaches the contract by failing to perform or by doing so in an unsatisfactory manner. If suit is brought on the instrument by a holder against the maker or drawer, the latter may use breach of contract as a defense. Because breach of contract is a personal defense, however, it may not be used if the holder of the instrument is a holder in due course unless the parties dealt with one another.

Lack or Failure of Consideration

Lack of consideration is a defense that may be used by a maker or drawer of an instrument when no consideration existed in the underlying contract for which the instrument was issued. The ordinary rules of contract law, discussed in Chapter 10, are followed to determine the presence or absence of consideration in such a case.

A Question of Ethics

As part of their direct-mail advertising, companies sometimes include what appears to be a check but when examined carefully, lacks one of the requirements of negotiability such as the words, "Good only when applied to the purchase of . . ." Is this marketing practice ethical?

Example 27-7

Lowell, without any mention of payment, helped his friend, Ransom, move from Cambridge to Gambier. At the end of the day, after he was in his new apartment, Ransom told Lowell that he'd give him some money for helping him move. The next day, Ransom gave Lowell a $200 check. Lowell cashed the check at a local bar and promptly left town. Ransom then stopped payment on the check. Ransom's promise to pay Lowell was not enforceable because Lowell had completed the work when the promise was made—it was past consideration. The local bar could recover the $200 from Ransom, however, because it was a holder in due course and not subject to the personal defense of lack of consideration.

The Opening Case Revisited

"A Flat Screen Fiasco"

Kevin and Kelly cannot recover the $1,000 from the check-cashing business because that business was a holder in due course of the instrument. It took the check for value (the $1,000), in good faith, and without notice that anything was wrong with the underlying transaction. The defense of failure of consideration (not receiving the plasma HDTV) cannot be used against a holder in due course.

Failure of consideration is different. It is a defense that the maker or drawer has available when the other party breaches the contract by not furnishing the agreed consideration.

Both lack of consideration and failure of consideration are personal defenses. They may not be used against a holder in due course.

Fraud in the Inducement

There are two kinds of fraud: fraud in the inducement and fraud as to the essential nature of the transaction. The first is a personal defense; the second is a real defense, discussed on page 508. The five elements of fraud are explained in depth in Chapter 8. When someone is induced by a fraudulent statement to enter into a contract, that person may have the contract rescinded. However, he or she may not use that defense against a holder in due course. A holder in due course can cut through the defense of fraud in the inducement and collect from the person who was defrauded. In Example 27-1 on page 503, Barlow had to pay Cain, a holder in due course of the check, even though she had been induced by fraud to write the check to Andrews.

Lack of Delivery

Every commercial instrument may be revoked by its maker or drawer until it has been delivered to the payee. *Delivery* is the voluntary transfer of possession of an instrument from one person to another. If the transfer of possession is not voluntary, the instrument has not been "issued." Thus, in the event a payee forcibly, unlawfully, or conditionally takes an instrument from a drawer, the drawer has the defense of lack of delivery. The payee therefore may be denied the right to collect on the instrument. If the payee negotiates the instrument to a holder in due course, however, this defense is cut off.

Terms *Induce* has its origins in the Latin term *inducere*, which means "to draw" or "to lead."

Fraud is the homage that force pays to reason.

—Charles Curtis (1860–1936), U.S. Vice-President, 1929–1933

Example 27-8

Morse wrote out a check payable to the order of Smith, intending to give it to Smith after Smith had completed a certain amount of work. Smith discovered the check on Morse's desk and took it without doing any work at all. Smith was not entitled to the check; however, if she negotiated the check to a bank, store, or private party for value, in good faith, and without notice (a holder in due course), Morse would have to honor the check even though Smith failed to do the required work.

Payment

Payment of an instrument by a maker or drawee usually ends the obligations of the parties. However, if a negotiable instrument is negotiated to a holder in due course after it has been paid, it will have to be paid again. This rule is because payment is a personal defense, which cannot be used against a holder in due course. Because of this rule, anyone who pays a demand instrument should have it marked "paid" and take possession of it. This requirement is not as important with a time instrument, unless it is paid before its due date, because no one can be a holder in due course of a past-due instrument.

Consumer Protection

The protection that is given to holders in due course was not always fair to consumers who bought on credit in the past.

Example 27-9

In 1975, Ruby Merlin bought a car from a used car dealer. She paid a small amount down and signed a consumer sales contract agreeing to pay the balance in twenty-four monthly installments. The used car dealer negotiated the contract (which was actually a promissory note) to a finance company and received payment immediately. The next day, the car's transmission stopped working, and the dealer refused to fix it. Merlin would still have to pay the finance company the full amount due on the note because the finance company was a holder in due course and was not subject to personal defenses.

In 1976, the FTC adopted the **holder in due course rule.** Under this rule, holders of consumer credit contracts who are holders in due course are subject to all claims and defenses that the buyer could use against the seller, including personal defenses. Thus, if the situation described in Example 27-9 were to occur today, Merlin's defense that the car's transmission did not work could be used against the finance company, even though it was a holder in due course. When sellers of consumer products have arrangements with financial institutions to finance their customer's purchases, the financial institutions are subject to the customer's personal defenses. They lose their protection as holders in due course.

Quick Quiz 27-2 True or False?

1. Personal defenses are defenses that can be used against a holder in due course but not a holder of a negotiable instrument.

2. The most common personal defenses are infancy and illegality.

3. If a negotiable instrument is negotiated to a holder in due course after it has been paid, it will have to be paid again.

27-3 Real Defenses

UCC Revised (1990) 3-305(a)(1) (see page 915)

Some defenses can be used against everyone, including holders in due course. These defenses are known as **real defenses** or **universal defenses.** The terms *real defense* and *universal defense* come from the common law and are not used in the UCC. No one is required to pay an instrument when they have a real defense. Real defenses include infancy and mental incompetence, illegality and duress, fraud as to the essential nature of the transaction, bankruptcy, unauthorized signature, and alteration (see Table 27-2).

Defense	Description
Infancy and mental incompetence	The maker or drawer of the instrument was a minor or mentally incompetent.
Illegality	The underlying contract for which the instrument was issued was illegal.
Duress	The instrument was drawn against the will of the maker or drawer because of threats of force or bodily harm.
Fraud as to the essential nature of the transaction	A false statement was made to the maker or drawer about the nature of the instrument being signed.
Bankruptcy	An order for relief was issued by the federal court that ended all the debtor's outstanding contractual obligations.
Unauthorized signature	Someone wrongfully signed another's name on an instrument without authority to do so.
Material alteration	The amount of the instrument or the payee's name was changed wrongfully after it was originally drawn by the maker or drawer.

Table 27-2 Most Common Real Defenses

Infancy and Mental Incompetence

A minor (person under the age of eighteen) or mental incompetent need not honor a negotiable instrument if it was given in payment for a contract that the minor or mental incompetent may disaffirm on the grounds of minority or incompetency. This rule is true even if the instrument comes into the hands of a holder in due course. Similarly, persons who have been found insane by a court are not liable on a negotiable instrument, since their contracts are void.

Illegality and Duress

An instrument that is associated with duress or an illegal act, such as twisting one's arm or drug trafficking would be void and uncollectible by anyone, even a holder in due course. This provision is true even though the holder in due course is unaware of the illegal acts or conditions.

> ### Example 27-10
>
> The Condado Aruba Caribbean Hotel loaned Tickel, who resided in Colorado, $20,000. The money was loaned for the purpose of gambling at the hotel's casino in Aruba, Netherlands Antilles, where gambling is legal. Tickel wrote two checks to repay the debt, each of which was returned for insufficient funds. When suit was brought on the checks, the Colorado court held that gambling debts are unenforceable in that state even against a holder in due course. Tickel was not liable on the checks that he had written to the hotel.

Fraud as to the Essential Nature of the Transaction

Fraud as to the essential nature of the transaction is more serious than fraud in the inducement. When this type of fraud occurs, the defrauded party has no knowledge or opportunity

Teaching Tips Have students recall the different elements of a contract, and remind them if one required element is missing, the contract is invalid. Then discuss how real defenses are similar in that, if one is present, it also will void a negotiable instrument.

Terms Legally, the term *duress* refers to any conduct that deprives a victim of free will. All transactions entered into under such conditions are legally voidable by the victim. *Duress* comes from the Latin word meaning *hard*.

to learn of the true character or terms of the matter. Because of its seriousness, it is a real defense and may be used against anyone, even a holder in due course.

Example 27-11

Duffy, who was almost blind, was asked by Ingram to sign a receipt. Duffy signed the paper without having had it read to him. The paper was actually a note promising to pay Ingram $2,500. Duffy would not be required to pay the note, even to a holder in due course, because this kind of fraud is more critical than fraud in the inducement, which was explained earlier.

Bankruptcy

Bankruptcy may be used as a defense to all negotiable instruments, even those in the hands of a holder in due course. Holders of such instruments will receive equal treatment with other similar creditors when the debtor's assets are collected and divided according to the bankruptcy law. This law is explained in more detail in Chapter 31.

Unauthorized Signatures

UCC Revised (1990) 3-403(a) (see page 918)

Related Cases In Example 31-1 on page 581, Strasser was forced into involuntary bankruptcy by three of his creditors. Since the court accepted the petition, any claims from holders in due course of instruments that Strasser had issued would have been discharged along with the debts owed to all his creditors.

Whenever someone signs another's name on an instrument without authority, it is a forgery. Unless ratified, it does not operate as the signature of the person whose name is signed. Instead, it operates as the signature of the person who signed it, that is, the wrongdoer.

Example 27-12

With no authority to do so, Parks signed Brown's name on a note, promising to pay Rivera $3,000 in ninety days. The note was negotiated by Rivera to a holder in due course. Brown would not have to pay the money to the holder in due course because the unauthorized signature is a real defense. Parks had committed a crime. The holder in due course could recover from Rivera who, in turn, could recover from the wrongdoer, Parks.

Alteration

UCC Revised (1990) 3-407 (see page 920)

Sometimes negotiable instruments are altered after they leave the hands of the maker or drawer. Usually, the alteration involves changing the payee's name or raising the amount of an instrument. The alteration of an instrument may be used as a real defense. Unless an instrument is written negligently so that it can be easily altered, makers and drawers are not required to pay altered amounts. They must pay only the amount for which the instrument was originally written.

Example 27-13

Martinez wrote out a check in a proper manner for $315 and gave it to Video Sales in payment for a DVD player. Video Sales raised the check to read $815. Martinez's bank honored the altered check. Martinez could seek reimbursement from his bank for $500, the difference between the original and the altered amount.

Any person who negligently contributes to a material alteration of an instrument or an unauthorized signature may not exercise the defense of alteration or lack of authority against a holder in due course, a drawee, or other payor who pays the instrument in good faith. For example, using a pencil to write a check or not being careful to keep the figures compact and clear gives a dishonest holder an opportunity to alter the amount. The careless writer would be without defense.

Writing a check with a pencil makes alteration of the check by a dishonest person much easier.

UCC Revised (1990) 3-406 (see page 919)

Quick Quiz 27-3 True or False?

1. No one with a real defense is required to pay an instrument.

2. Fraud in the inducement is more serious than fraud as to the essential nature of the transaction.

3. If a check is written with an erasable pen and later altered by a wrongdoer, the drawer of the check would not be responsible for any loss because alteration is a real defense.

27-4 Liability of the Parties

No person is liable on an instrument unless that person's signature or the signature of an authorized agent appears on the instrument. Parties to negotiable instruments have different liability depending on their function.

UCC Revised (1990) 3-401 (see page 918)

Terms *Liable* is related to the term *ligature,* which refers to something that is used to bind two things together.

UCC Revised (1990) 3-412, 3-413 (see page 920)

Makers, Acceptors, and Certain Drawers

The following are obligated to pay an instrument without reservations of any kind:

- The maker of a note.
- The issuer of a cashier's check or other draft in which the drawer and the drawee are the same person.
- The acceptor of a draft.

Other Drawers and Indorsers

Other drawers and indorsers have limitations on their obligation to pay an instrument. The drawer of a draft that has not been accepted is obligated to pay the draft to anyone who is entitled to enforce it; however, if a bank accepts a draft, the drawer is discharged. If a drawee other than a bank accepts a draft and it is later dishonored, the obligation of the drawer is the same as an indorser stated here.

Indorsers are obligated to pay an instrument only when the following conditions are met: (1) The instrument must be properly presented to the drawee or party obliged to

UCC Revised (1990) 3-414, 3-415 (a)(c) (see page 921)

Cross-Cultural Notes
In Mexico, a check must be presented for payment within fifteen days of issuance. After fifteen days, the drawer cannot be held liable. For checks that are made payable in different towns, the time limit is extended to thirty days.

UCC Revised (1990)
3-501 (see page 923)

UCC Revised (1990)
3-502 (see page 923)

About the Law

Formerly, it was necessary to send a protest to drawers and indorsers when a draft payable outside the United States was dishonored. A *protest* is a certificate of dishonor that states that a draft was presented for acceptance or payment and was dishonored, together with the reasons given for refusal to accept or pay, and made under the hand and seal of a United States consul or notary public. Today, under the Revised (1990) UCC, a protest is no longer required but may still be used.

UCC Revised (1990)
3-503 and 3-504
(see page 924)

pay the instrument, and payment must be demanded; (2) the instrument must be dishonored, that is, payment refused; and (3) notice of the dishonor must be given to the secondary party within the time and in the manner prescribed by the UCC. If all three of these conditions are not met, drawers of drafts and indorsers are discharged from their obligations.

Presentment **Presentment** means a demand made by a holder to pay or accept an instrument. Presentment may be made by any commercially reasonable means, including an oral, written, or electronic communication. If requested by the person to whom presentment is made, the person making presentment must exhibit the instrument and provide identification.

Dishonor *Dishonor* means to refuse to pay a negotiable instrument when it is due or to refuse to accept it when asked to do so. An instrument is dishonored when proper presentment is made and acceptance or payment is refused. Dishonor also occurs when presentment is excused and the instrument is past due and unpaid. The presenting party has recourse against indorsers or other secondary parties after notice of dishonor has been given.

Example 27-14

A note was presented to Baker for payment on the date specified. Baker refused to honor it, claiming the note was a forgery. The holder would have to proceed against the indorsers in order to obtain payment. The note was dishonored when Baker refused to pay it.

Notice of Dishonor Obligations of indorsers and drawers of instruments may not be enforced unless they are given notice of the dishonor or notice is excused. Notice of dishonor may be given by any reasonable means including an oral, written, or electronic communication, and is sufficient if it reasonably identifies the instrument and indicates that the instrument has been dishonored or has not been paid or accepted. The return of an instrument given to a bank for collection is sufficient notice of dishonor.

Nonbank holders must give notice of the dishonor to the drawer and indorsers within thirty days following the day of dishonor. Banks taking instruments for collection must give notice before midnight of the banking day following the day the bank was notified of the dishonor. Delay in giving notice of dishonor is excused when the holder has acted carefully and the delay is due to circumstances beyond the holder's control. Presentment and notice of dishonor are also excused when the party waived either presentment or notice of dishonor.

Quick Quiz 27-4 True or False?

1. Indorsers never have liability to pay.

2. Presentment can be made by oral, written, or electronic communication.

3. Notice of dishonor must be given by nonbank holders to indorsers within thirty days following the day of dishonor.

Summary

27-1   A holder in due course is a holder who takes the instrument for value, in good faith, without notice that it is overdue or has been dishonored, and without notice of any defenses against it or claim to it. Good faith means honesty in fact. A holder who receives an instrument from a holder in due course receives all the rights of the holder in due course.

27-2   Personal defenses can be used against a holder, but not a holder in due course. The most common personal defenses are breach of contract, lack or failure of consideration, fraud in the inducement, lack of delivery, and payment. Holders of consumer credit contracts who are holders in due course are subject to all claims

and defenses that the buyer could use against the seller, including personal defenses.

27-3   Real defenses can be used against anyone, including a holder in due course. Real defenses are infancy and mental incompetence, illegality and duress, fraud as to the essential nature of the transaction, bankruptcy, unauthorized signature, and alteration.

27-4   Makers of notes and acceptors of drafts have an absolute liability to pay. Indorsers have a liability to pay only if an instrument is presented properly for payment, the instrument is dishonored, and proper notice of dishonor is given to the secondary party.

Key Terms

failure of consideration, 507

holder, 503

holder in due course, 503

holder in due course rule, 508

lack of consideration, 506

limited defenses, 505

personal defenses, 505

presentment, 512

real defenses, 508

shelter provision, 505

universal defenses, 508

Questions for Review and Discussion

1. What are the requirements for being a holder in due course?
2. What is the purpose of the shelter provision and when will it not apply?
3. Why are personal defenses sometimes called limited defenses? Identify the most common personal defenses.
4. What protection is given to consumers who sign consumer credit contracts?
5. What is the significance of real defenses? Explain.
6. Name the parties to an instrument who are obligated to pay without reservation. When are indorsers obligated to pay instruments?
7. How may presentment be made?
8. When is an instrument dishonored?
9. In what way may notice of dishonor be given?
10. When must nonbank holders give notice of dishonor to the drawer and indorsers?

Investigating the Internet

Look for answers to your questions about holders in due course by keying in the words *holder in due course* at any of the following search engines: Google, Yahoo!, Alta Vista, Lycos, Netscape, MSN, AOL, Ask Jeeves, All the Web, Homepage Hotbot Web Search, LookSmart, and others that you find helpful.

Cases for Analysis

1. Without authority to do so, Allen signed Baker's name on a note, promising to pay Cohen $5,000 in 30 days. The note was negotiated to Davidson who was a holder in due course. Will Davidson be successful in recovering the $5,000 from Baker in court? Why or why not?

2. Refrigerated Transport Co., Inc., employed a collection agency to collect some of its overdue accounts. The collection agency indorsed, without authority, checks made payable to Refrigerated Transport and deposited them in the agency's own checking account. Was the bank that accepted the checks for deposit a holder in due course? Why or why not? *Nat'l Bank v. Refrigerated Transp.,* 248 S.E.2d 496 (GA).

3. Andersen entered into a franchise agreement with Great Lake Nursery, under which Andersen was to grow and sell nursery stock and Christmas trees. Great Lake was to provide trees, chemicals, and other items. Andersen signed an installment note that read in part "For value received, Robert Andersen promises to pay to Great Lake Nursery Corp. $6,412." Great Lake indorsed the note and transferred it to First Investment Company. Later, Andersen stopped making payments because Great Lake filed bankruptcy and failed to perform its part of the franchise agreement. May Andersen use failure of consideration as a defense when sued by First Investment Company on the note? Why or why not? *First Inv. Co. v. Andersen,* 621 P.2d 683 (UT).

4. In exchange for an asphalt paving job, Paulick gave Bucci a note promising to pay to the order of Bucci $7,593 in six months with 10 percent per annum interest. Payment was not made on the due date, and Bucci brought suit. Paulick used failure of consideration as a defense, claiming that the paving job was improperly done. The court held that Bucci was a holder in due course because he had taken the instrument for value, in good faith, and without notice of any claims or defenses of Paulick's. Could Paulick use the defense of failure of consideration against Bucci? Why or why not? *Bucci v. Paulick,* 149 A.2d 1255 (PA).

5. Carolyn Brazil wrote a check to a contractor who agreed to make certain improvements on her home. She wrote the check in reliance on the contractor's false representation that the materials for the job had been purchased. They, in fact, had not been purchased. Brazil had the bank on which the check was drawn stop payment on it. Another bank, which cashed the check and became a holder in due course of the instrument, attempted to recover the amount of the check from Brazil. Could it do so? Explain. *Citizens Nat'l Bank v. Brazil,* 233 S.E.2d 482 (GA).

6. As part of the purchase price for a 9,040-acre ranch, Kirby gave Bergfield a $20,000 check drawn on the Bank of Bellevue. Bergfield had her banker telephone the Bank of Bellevue to inquire about Kirby's account balance to be sure that the check was good. It was learned that there was not enough money in Kirby's account to cover the check. Bergfield continued to hold the check and did not present it to the Bank of Bellevue for payment. Later, Bergfield argued that the telephone call to the bank was a presentment and demand for payment of the check. Do you agree? Why or why not? *Kirby v. Bergfield,* 182 N.W.2d 205 (NE).

7. Haik transferred his stock in Petrocomp, an oil exploration company, to Rowley in exchange for five $10,000 promissory notes. The notes were signed by Rowley and indorsed by Rowley's son, Stephen. Rowley failed to pay the notes when they became due. No presentment for payment was made by Haik on the due date nor was a timely notice of dishonor given to Rowley's son, Stephen. Could Haik hold Stephen liable on the notes as an indorser? Explain. *Haik v. Rowley,* 377 So.2d 391 (LA).

8. David and Nettie Weiner signed seven promissory notes, totaling $89,000, in their capacity as president and secretary of NMD Realty Co. In addition, they indorsed each note on the reverse side with their individual signatures. Each note contained the following provision: "The Maker and indorser or indorsers each hereby waives presentment, demand, and notice of dishonor." The Weiners claimed that, because they are secondarily liable, the bank may not proceed against them individually until after presentment, notice of dishonor, and protest have occurred. Do you agree with the Weiners? Explain. *Bank of Delaware v. NMD Realty Co.,* 325 A.2d 108 (DE).

9. Rutherford purchased real property from Ethel Stokes for $35,000. He paid $5,000 down and signed a promissory note for the balance. The note was secured by a deed of trust (a type of security interest, discussed in detail in Chapter 30). When payments on the note were overdue, Stokes considered foreclosing on the property. Prior to doing so, however, she negotiated the note to Craig, who purchased it at a discount with notice that it was in default. Was Craig a holder in due course of the note? Why or why not? *Matter of Marriage of Rutherford,* 573 S.W.2d 299 (TX).

10. Bolton wrote a check for $20,000 to his daughter. Joyce, intending to make a gift. The check was drawn on the State Bank of Wapello and was mailed to Joyce in Maryland, where she was living. Joyce received the check, indorsed it, and mailed it to her bank in Baltimore with instructions to use it to establish a certificate of deposit in joint tenancy with her father. Was Joyce a holder in due course of the check? Explain. *Matter of Estate of Bolton,* 444 N.W.2d 482 (IA).

Quick Quiz Answers

27-1	27-2	27-3	27-4
1. T	1. F	1. T	1. F
2. F	2. F	2. F	2. T
3. T	3. T	3. F	3. T

<table>
<tr><td>

Chapter 28

</td><td>

Bank Deposits, Collections, and Depositor Relationships

</td></tr>
</table>

The Opening Case
"Off on a Taxing Vacation"

When Jason McCoy returned home from work on Friday afternoon at 5:35, he found that the $2,500 federal income tax refund check he had been waiting for had arrived in the mail. It was perfect timing. McCoy had the following week off and needed the money for a vacation he had planned for that week. He raced out the door, hopped into his car, and sped to the bank, getting there just before it closed (the bank's cut-off hour was 2:00 p.m.) and deposited the check into his account. He spent the weekend leisurely packing for the trip, and stopped by the bank to withdraw the needed funds as he left for vacation on Monday. To his dismay, he heard the teller say, "I'm sorry, Mr. McCoy, we can't give you the money until tomorrow." Was the bank within its rights to hold McCoy's money another day?

Chapter Outcomes

1. Name the different terms used to describe banks during the bank collection process.
2. Outline a check's life cycle.
3. Describe the principal feature of the Check 21 Act.
4. Discuss the protection given to consumers by the Electronic Fund Transfer Act.
5. Explain the duties of a bank relative to honoring orders, death of a customer, forged and altered checks, availability of funds, and the midnight deadline.
6. Explain the duties of a depositor relative to bad checks and examining accounts.
7. Compare an oral stop-payment order with a written stop-payment order.
8. Describe the insurance coverage that protects bank accounts.

28-1 Bank Deposits and Collections

The tremendous number of checks handled by banks and the countrywide nature of the bank collection process require uniformity in the law of bank collections. For this reason, Article 4 of the UCC contains rules and regulations for handling bank deposits and collections.

Bank Descriptions

During the bank collection process, banks are described by different terms, depending on their particular function in a transaction. Sometimes a bank takes a check for deposit. At other times, it pays a check as a drawee. At still other times, it takes a check for collection only. The different terms that are used to describe banks and their meanings are as follows: **Depositary bank** is the first bank to which an item is transferred for collection even though it is also the payor bank. **Payor bank** describes a bank by which an item is payable as drawn or accepted. It includes a drawee bank. **Intermediary bank** defines any bank to which an item is transferred in the course of collection except the depositary or payor bank. **Collecting bank** means any bank handling the item for collection except the payor bank. **Presenting bank** is any bank presenting an item except a payor bank. **Remitting bank** describes any payor or intermediary bank remitting for an item.

UCC 4-105

A Check's Life Cycle

The life cycle of a check begins when the drawer writes a check and delivers it to the payee. The payee may take the check directly to the payor bank (the bank on which it was drawn) for payment. If that bank pays the check in cash, its payment is final, and the check is returned to the drawer with the next bank statement. However, it is more likely that the check will be deposited in the payee's own account in another bank. That bank, known as the depositary bank, acts as its customer's agent to collect the money from the payor bank. Any settlement given by the depositary bank in this case is **provisional** (not final). It may be revoked if the check is later dishonored. The check is sent (sometimes through an intermediary bank) to a collecting bank, which presents the check to the payor bank for payment. If it is honored by the payor bank, the amount will be deducted from the drawer's account and a substitute check will be returned to the drawer with the next bank statement. If the check is dishonored for any reason, a substitute check will be returned to the payee via the same route that it was sent and all credits given for the item will be revoked (see Figure 28-1).

UCC 4-213

UCC 4-201

Teaching Tips Have students bring in a number of their own canceled checks. Select a few of them to diagram on the board the various institutions through which the checks have been. Then have the students discuss what steps in the cycle are common to all checks and what steps are not as common.

The Check 21 Act

Named for the twenty-first century, the **Check 21 Act** brings the check-clearing method into the modern age by the use of electronic check processing. This could not be done prior to this 2004 law because of the legal requirement that original checks be presented to the drawee bank for payment. Under this law, a new negotiable instrument called a substitute check is used. A **substitute check** (also called an image replacement document or IRD) is a paper reproduction of both sides of an original check that can be processed just like the original check. Under the new law, banks are not required to use substitute checks, but when they do so for consideration, they make the following warranties:

- The substitute check contains an accurate image of the front and back of the original check.
- It is the legal equivalent of the original check.
- No drawer, drawee, indorser, or depositary bank will be asked to pay a check that it already has paid.

Example 28-1

Suppose that the Rowley bank, in the example given in Figure 28-1 illustrating the life cycle of a check, has elected to use electronic check processing including substitute checks as a method of clearing checks. When it receives the original check deposited by
(Continued)

Example 28-1 (*Continued*)

Rubio, it can transfer the check information electronically to the Federal Reserve Bank of San Francisco. That bank can create a substitute check to present to the Oakland Bank where it is deducted from Rubio's account. Under the law, the Oakland Bank is required to accept the substitute check. As a result, instead of transporting the original check across the country by plane or truck, the Rowley, Massachusetts, bank can collect the substitute check at a much faster pace, using only local California transportation.

Figure 28-1 The life cycle of Rubio's check is traced through its collection and clearinghouse routes. Before the Check 21 Act became effective in October 2004, the check in this example would have had to be physically transported by plane or truck around its entire route.

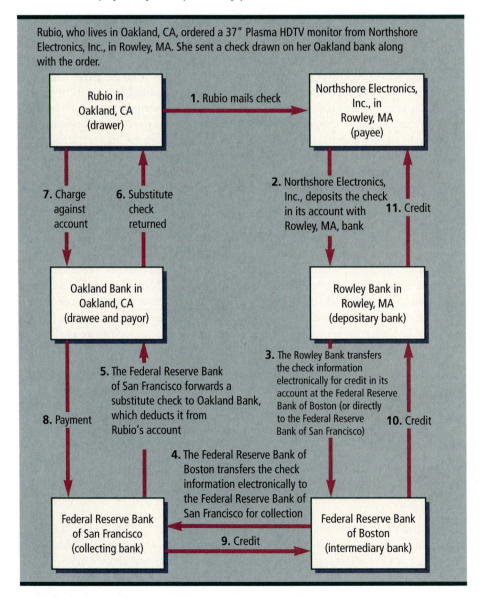

Original Check No Longer Returned Many banks in the past automatically returned canceled checks with their monthly bank statements to their customers even though the UCC does not require that original checks be returned unless a customer requests them. The Check 21 Act, which takes precedence over the UCC, changes this rule. Under the Check 21 Act, the customer has a right only to a paper substitute check that is a reproduction of the front and back of the original. Bank customers no longer have an absolute right to see their original canceled checks.

UCC 4-406 (a)(b)

Consumer Protection To protect consumers from losses related to substitute checks, the Check 21 Act includes a consumer's right to claim an *expedited credit*. This right exists if the consumer asserts in good faith the following four facts:

- The bank charged the consumer's account for a substitute check that was given to the consumer.
- Either the check was not properly charged to the consumer's account, or the consumer has a warranty claim with respect to the substitute check.
- The consumer suffered a resulting loss.
- The production of the original check or a better copy of the original check is necessary to determine the validity of any claim.

If the consumer makes a claim within forty-five days after receiving the bank statement or substitute check, the bank must investigate it and make any necessary recredit to the consumer's account. If the bank needs more than ten days to investigate and resolve the complaint, the bank must recredit the consumer's account for an amount up to $2,500 while it completes its investigation. The bank must recredit any remaining balance greater than $2,500 no later than forty-five days after the consumer submits the claim.

Quick Quiz 28-1 True or False?

1. A *collecting bank* is any bank to which an item is transferred in the course of collection except the depositary or payor bank.

2. If the payor bank pays a check in cash, its payment is final.

3. Under the Check 21 Act, bank customers no longer have an absolute right to see their original canceled check.

28-2 Electronic Banking

Electronic banking (also called **electronic fund transfers** or **EFTs**) use computers and electronic technology as a substitute for checks and other banking methods. People can go to automatic teller machines (ATMs) 24 hours a day to make bank deposits and withdrawals. They can pay bills by phone, have deposits made directly to their bank accounts, and pay for retail purchases directly from their bank accounts.

Some banks have arrangements for payment by **e-check** (sometimes called *electronic check conversion*), which is a system in which funds are electronically transferred from a customer's checking account, eliminating

Consumers are protected against lost or stolen ATM cards provided they notify their bank of the loss or theft.

the need to process a paper check. Under one system, the customer writes out an ordinary check and gives it to a merchant when making a purchase. After obtaining the customer's written authorization, the merchant passes the check through an instrument that reads the information on the check and converts the payment from a paper check to an electronic funds transfer. The merchant then voids the check and returns it to the customer with a receipt. Payment by e-check is cheaper to process and usually is accomplished sooner.

An **ATM card** is used together with a personal identification number (PIN) to gain access to an automatic teller machine either on or off the bank premises. In contrast, a **debit card** (also called a *check card* or *cash card*) is used to electronically subtract money from a bank account to pay for goods or services. Debit cards are used at stores rather than at ATM machines and usually require the use of the customer's signature rather than a PIN. Many banks now use a combination ATM-debit card that performs both functions.

There are two kinds of debit cards: online and off-line. *On*line debit cards make an immediate transfer of money from the customer's bank account to the merchant's bank account. *Off*-line debit cards record a debit against the customer's bank account, which is processed later.

A debit card offers less protection than a credit card. Unlike a credit card, a debit card payment cannot be stopped if a purchase is defective or if an order is not delivered. In addition, your liability for the unauthorized use of your ATM or debit card is limited to $50 only if you notify the issuer within two business days of the loss or theft of the card. Your liability increases to $500 if notice is delayed beyond that time, and it becomes unlimited when notice is not given within 60 days. The unauthorized use of an ATM card is a criminal offense punishable by a $10,000 fine and/or ten years in prison.

Example 28-2

A thief stole Hockmeyer's purse from a grocery store shopping cart. Three days later, Hockmeyer notified the bank that her ATM card was missing. By then, however, the thief had found the card along with Hockmeyer's secret identification number and had withdrawn $800 from her account. Because the bank was notified within three days of the theft, Hockmeyer lost $500. Had she notified the bank within two business days of the theft, she would have lost only $50.

Regulation E, issued by the Federal Reserve Board under the Electronic Fund Transfer Act, establishes the basic rights, liabilities, and responsibilities of consumers who use electronic fund transfer services and of financial institutions that offer these services. Transactions covered under the regulation include:

• Point-of-sale purchases.

• Automated teller machine transfers.

• Telephone-initiated transfers requiring an entry password (PIN).

• Transfers resulting from debit card transactions requiring an entry password (PIN).

• Internet banking.

Under the act, consumers are entitled to receive a written receipt whenever they use an automated teller machine. In addition, the transaction must appear on the periodic statement sent to the consumer. The consumer has sixty days to notify the bank of any error on the periodic statement or terminal receipt. After being notified, the bank has ten business days to investigate the error. If the bank needs more time, it may take up to forty-five days

Business Law in the News
The Virtually Cashless Society

Edward L. Farrell III is a card-carrying American. The 37-year-old Montclair (N.J.) resident and father of two maxes out merchant-reward programs using whatever plastic he can. A bank auditor, Farrell uses his ShopRite card to earn grocery discounts and rewards at Continental Airlines Inc. He reloads his Starbucks Corp. cash card with his Chase Manhattan Bank debit card—which deducts the expense from his bank account—to accumulate even more miles. His one conundrum: how to keep his coffee intake under control now that he can waltz into any Starbucks, "swipe and leave," he says. "I'm trying to limit it to once a day."

These days, just about any expense can be paid for with some type of card. Live in a $5,000-a-month luxury rental in Manhattan? Charge it automatically to your credit card each month. Stepping into a McDonald's for a Happy Meal? A swipe of your debit card covers the $1.99 charge.

Slackening growth and fierce competition, especially for customers who carry big balances, have banks and credit-card companies scrambling into untapped markets for plastic. Visa, MasterCard, and American Express want customers to make regular payments—such as for rent, gym memberships, utilities, and day-care center fees—with a card instead of a check. And they want consumers to pull out their debit cards instead of small bills at convenience stores, gas stations, and theaters.

All eyes are on the debit card. Even though there are twice as many credit cards as debit cards, debit cards will generate 16.5 billion transactions (excluding ATM withdrawals) in 2003, a 22% jump over last year and the first time debit will outpace credit transactions. Credit cards will grow 8%, the first year of single-digit growth in two decades. By 2007, debit-card purchases could top $1 trillion, forecasts *The Nilson Report,* a payments industry newsletter. And the amount spent on debit cards will increase 130%, vs. 49% for credit cards. Indeed, debit use is growing so fast at Visa, where it accounts for more than half the transactions, vs. 7% a decade ago, that it no longer calls itself a credit-card company but a "payments company."

Merchants' Choice

Why the fast growth in debit-card business? Consumers save time, feel more secure carrying fewer dollars, and track their spending better. Lost or stolen cards are quickly replaced by the bank. Merchants avoid credit risk and the costs of late payments, postage, employee theft, and check-clearing fees. More important, customers—who are costlier to acquire than to retain—are more loyal. In some markets, cable giant Cox Communications Inc. persuaded up to 20% of its 6.3 million subscribers to pay with plastic and found that renewals jumped. "There was no need for any other incentive programs," says Warren Jones, director of competitive strategy and customer retention at Cox.

Questions for Analysis

1. Why does Visa no longer call itself a credit-card company?

2. Why has the debit card business grown so fast?

3. Which type of card do you prefer to use, a debit or credit card? Explain.

Source: Mara Der Hovanesian. "The Virtually Cashless Society," *BusinessWeek,* November 17, 2003, p. 125.

to complete the investigation, but only if the money in dispute is returned to the consumer's account.

Since the Electronic Fund Transfer Act is a consumer protection law, it does not apply to transactions between banks and other businesses. A different law, Article 4A of the UCC, has been adopted by many states to govern EFTs that are made by banks and businesses. Under the UCC, a business that orders money to be sent electronically is called the *originator.* The business that is to receive the money is called the *beneficiary.*

UCC 4A-103-505

UCC 4A-104

UCC 4A-103

Example 28-3

Data Control, Inc., sold a computer system to Western Sales, Inc., for $2 million. When the system was installed, Western Sales ordered its bank to pay $2 million to Data Control. Since both companies had accounts in the First National Bank, the bank simply debited Western Sales' account and credited Data Control's account for $2 million. Western Sales was the originator; Data Control was the beneficiary. If Data Control had had a different bank, the First National Bank would have ordered that bank, called the beneficiary's bank, to credit Data Control's account for $2 million.

Businesses that deal with large sums of money need to be able to make quick transfers to avoid a loss of interest, among other reasons. EFTs help to meet this need.

Quick Quiz 28-2 True or False?

1. Consumers have thirty days to notify the bank of any error on the periodic statement received for the use of an ATM.

2. A consumer's liability for the unauthorized use of an ATM card is limited to $500 if notice of the loss or theft of a card is given the issuer within two business days.

3. The unauthorized use of an ATM card is a criminal offense punishable by a $500 fine and/or five years in prison.

28-3 The Bank-Depositor Relationship

The relationship between the drawee bank and its customer is that of both debtor and creditor and agent and principal. The relationship arises out of the express or implied contract that occurs when the customer opens a checking account with the bank. The bank becomes a debtor when money is deposited in the bank by the customer. At this time, the customer is owed money by the bank and is, therefore, a creditor. When an **overdraft** occurs, that is, when the bank pays out more than the customer has on deposit, the debtor-creditor role reverses, and the bank becomes the creditor.

UCC 4-201

UCC 4-212

The bank acts as the customer's agent when it collects or attempts to collect checks or other negotiable instruments made payable to the customer. If the items are deposited in the customer's account, any settlement made by the bank with the customer is provisional. A provisional settlement may be revoked by the bank if an item that the bank is attempting to collect is dishonored. The bank may charge back the amount of any credit given for the item to its customer's account or obtain a refund from its customer.

Example 28-4

Baker Company deposited in its checking account a check it had received in the mail from a customer. Baker Company's bank credited its account for the amount of the check and sent it through the clearinghouse for collection. The check was returned to the bank because of insufficient funds. Baker Company's bank charged back (debited) the amount it had credited to Baker Company's account.

The Bank's Duties

The bank owes a duty to its depositors to honor orders and to protect funds. However, these duties carry strict limitations.

Duty to Honor Orders The drawee bank is under a duty to honor all checks drawn by its customers when there are sufficient funds on deposit in the customer's account. If there are insufficient funds on deposit, the bank may charge the customer's account even if it creates an overdraft. If a bank fails to honor a check because of a mistake on its part, the bank is liable to the customer for any actual damages the customer suffers. The drawee bank has no liability to the holder of the check, however, unless it is certified.

UCC 4-401

UCC 4-402

Getting Students Involved Recently the federal government has allowed banks to get into different areas of business. Have students research whether banks in their states have taken advantage of these opportunities. Do local laws allow banks to operate across state lines?

Example 28-5

Rougier, who had $178 in her checking account, wrote out a check for $78.42 and mailed it to the telephone company in payment of a telephone bill. Due to a mistake on its part, Rougier's bank dishonored the check and returned it to the telephone company marked "insufficient funds." As soon as the error was discovered, the telephone company was notified and the check was redeposited and honored by the bank. Since Rougier suffered no loss, the bank was not liable for dishonoring the check. Had Rougier's telephone been disconnected because of the dishonored check, the bank would have been liable to her for the cost of restoring service. The bank was not liable to the telephone company.

A bank is under no obligation to a customer to pay a stale check unless it is certified. A **stale check** is a check that is presented for payment more than six months after its date. A bank, however, may honor a stale check without liability to its customer if it acts in good faith.

UCC 4-404

Example 28-6

The Chemical Bank paid a check that had been written by New York Flameproofing Co., ten years earlier on a check form no longer used by that company. The account on which the check was drawn had been closed for seven years, and the company's address written on the check had changed seven years earlier. In holding against the bank for paying the check, the court said that such payment was a reckless disregard of due care so much as to constitute bad faith. The bank was liable for the amount paid.

The drawee bank is not liable to a holder of a check for dishonoring the instrument unless it is certified. The holder's recourse is against the drawer or indorsers on their secondary liability.

Death or Incompetence of Customer The drawee bank is not liable for the payment of a check before it has notice of the death or incompetence of the drawer. In any event, a bank may pay or certify checks for ten days after the date of death of the drawer. This rule permits holders of checks that are drawn shortly before the drawer's death to cash them without the necessity of filing a claim with the court handling the deceased's estate.

UCC 4-405

Forged and Altered Checks

A **forgery** is the fraudulent making or alteration of a writing. A forgery is committed when a person fraudulently writes or alters a check or other form of negotiable instrument to the injury of another. The commission of forgery is a crime, subject to a fine and imprisonment. The offering of a forged instrument to another person when the offeror knows it to be forged is also a crime, known as **uttering.** If a bank, in good faith, pays the altered amount of a check to a holder, it may deduct from the drawer's account only the amount of the check as it was originally written.

Example 28-7

Lane wrote out a $400 check, in a nonnegligent fashion, to the order of Robinson in payment for repairs to Lane's house. Robinson raised the check to $4,000. If Lane's bank pays the full $4,000 to Robinson, it can deduct $400 from Lane's account, but no more. The bank must either get the money back from the wrongdoer, Robinson, or suffer the loss. The bank would be able to deduct the full $4,000 from Lane's account if the alteration was facilitated by Lane's carelessness in writing the check.

The depositor is also protected against a signature being forged. When a checking account is opened, the depositor must fill out a signature card, which is permanently filed at the bank. Thereafter, the bank is held to know the depositor's signature. The bank is liable to the depositor if it pays any check on which the depositor's signature has been forged.

Availability of Funds

In the past, banks were not uniform in the amount of time they required before they would make funds available to their depositors. Some banks held funds longer than others, and many banks did not disclose their holding policy to their customers.

Example 28-8

Remez received a check from her father, who lived in a distant city. She deposited it in her checking account and was told by the teller that she would not be able to draw a check on the funds for ten days. Remez's friend inquired at her own bank about its holding policy and was told that it would have made the funds available in five days.

To address the issue, Congress passed the Competitive Banking Act. Under the act, the Federal Reserve Board of Governors issued Regulation CC. The regulation has required banks to make funds available to depositors according to a prescribed schedule (Table 28-1). Funds from checks drawn on the U.S. Treasury, or any state or local government, and any bank draft, cashier's check, or postal money order must be made available on the next business day following the banking day of deposit; and funds from checks drawn on banks within the same Federal Reserve district must be made available within two business days following the banking day of deposit; and funds from checks drawn on banks outside the bank's Federal Reserve district must be made available within five business days following the banking day of deposit. A *business day* is defined under Regulation CC as Monday

Table 28-1 Availability of Funds You Deposit in Your Bank	
Type of Check	**Funds Must be Made Available for Withdrawal**
"On us" check [drawn on your bank]	1st business day* after the banking day† of deposit
Local check (except $100‡) [drawn on a bank in same check-processing region]	2nd business day* after the banking day† of deposit
Nonlocal (except $100‡) [drawn on a bank in a different check-processing region]	5th business day* after the banking day† of deposit
Electronic payment	1st business day* after the banking day† of deposit
Cashier's check	1st business day* after the banking day† of deposit
Certified check	1st business day* after the banking day† of deposit
Government check	1st business day* after the banking day† of deposit
U.S. Postal Service money order	1st business day* after the banking day† of deposit

*Monday through Friday except most federal holidays.
†Any business day (up to the bank's cutoff hour) when the bank is open for substantially all of its banking activities.
‡The first $100 (or the total amount of the deposit if less than $100) must be made available on the 1st business day after the banking day of deposit.

through Friday except most federal holidays. A *banking day* is any business day (up to the bank's cutoff hour) when the bank is open for substantially all of its banking activities.

Example 28-9

Edna Chase deposited a $500 local check that was payable to her in her bank at 3 p.m. on Monday. The bank's cutoff hour for the day's transactions was 2 p.m. Because the deposit was made after the bank's cutoff hour, it was considered received on Tuesday. The first $100 must be made available to Chase by Wednesday, and the remaining $400 must be made available by Thursday, the second business day after the banking day of deposit.

The Opening Case Revisited
"Off on a Taxing Vacation"

Was the Bank Within Its Rights? Yes. The deposit was made after the bank's cutoff hour on Friday, and Saturday and Sunday are not business days, so the deposit is considered to have been made on Monday—the next banking day. Because the funds are from a U.S. Treasury check, they must be made available by the first business day following the banking day of deposit, which is Tuesday.

Exceptions are made for new accounts, accounts that are repeatedly overdrawn, and deposits of a suspicious nature. In addition, some state laws require even shorter time periods for banks to make funds available.

Regulation CC also requires banks to disclose in advance their policy for making funds available to depositors. Such disclosures must be made when the account is initially opened and on conspicuously visible notices at teller stations in the bank.

Midnight Deadline Payor banks are required to either settle or return checks quickly. If they do not do so, they are responsible for paying them. If the payor bank is not the depositary bank, it must settle for an item by midnight of the banking day of receipt.

Example 28-10

LaPierre wrote a check to Kimberly Motors for $2,500 in payment for a secondhand car. The payor of the check (the bank on which it was drawn) was the National Bank & Trust Co. Kimberly Motors deposited the check into its account in the Southwest Mutual Bank (the depositary bank), which sent it on for collection. LaPierre's car broke down before she reached home that evening. She immediately stopped payment on the check. The National Bank & Trust Company must return the check to the Southwest Mutual Bank, with a notation that payment has been stopped, before midnight of the day that it received the check. If it keeps the check longer than that, it will be liable for payment.

If the payor bank is also the depositary bank, it must either pay or return the check or send notice of its dishonor on or before its midnight deadline. In this case, the bank's **midnight deadline** is midnight of the next banking day following the banking day on which it receives the relevant item.

Example 28-11

If the National Bank & Trust Company in Example 28-10 had also been the depositary bank, it would have had an extra day to handle the check. The bank would have had until midnight of the next banking day to return the check to Kimberly Motors with the notation that payment had been stopped.

The Depositor's Duties

Depositors, in general, owe a duty to the banks in which they have checking accounts to have sufficient funds on deposit to cover checks that they write. They must also examine their bank statements and canceled checks promptly and with reasonable care and notify the bank quickly of any discrepancies.

Bad Checks Most states have statutes making it larceny or attempted larceny for a person to issue a check drawn on a bank in which the person has insufficient funds. Such statutes usually have the following provisions that must be observed in the prosecution of anyone issuing a *bad check,* sometimes called an *NSF check*. The payee has the obligation of informing the drawer of the nonpayment of the check, together with notice of the provisions of the bad-check law and of the party's legal rights and obligations. After receiving notice of nonpayment, or dishonor, the drawer is given a specified number of days, usually five or ten, in which to make the check good, without fear of prosecution. Failure to make full payment of the check within the number of days allowed by statute serves as presumption of guilt that the drawer issued the check with full knowledge of the facts and with intent to defraud.

A Question of Ethics

Is there ever a situation when it would be ethical to write a check when you know there are insufficient funds in the bank to cover it?

Example 28-12

State National Bank received Yoder's check for $120 due on an installment note it held. After it was deposited, the check was returned to State National with the notification "insufficient funds." The bank's collection department sent a registered letter to Yoder in which responsibility under the bad-check statute was explained. Failure on the part of Yoder to make the check good within the period of time indicated would result in a criminal complaint being lodged against Yoder through the office of the state's prosecuting attorney.

Bad-check statutes are effectively used as a means of collection. Most bad-check writers make an effort to make full payment of the check when advised that they are subject to prosecution. (See Figure 28-2.)

Many banks offer overdraft protection service to their depositors, which covers small overdrafts that are usually caused by the mistake of the drawer in balancing the checkbook. This is important under the Check 21 Act because checks may have a shorter float time than in the past. With this service, the bank honors small overdrafts and charges the depositor's account. This service saves the drawer the inconvenience and embarrassment of having a check returned to a holder marked "insufficient funds."

Duty to Examine Accounts

The UCC imposes a duty on depositors to examine their bank statements and canceled checks promptly and with reasonable care when they are received from the bank. They must report promptly to the bank any forged or altered checks. If they do not do so, depositors cannot hold the bank responsible for losses due to the bank's payment of a forged or altered instrument.

The exact time within which a depositor must notify a bank is not established except in the case of the same wrongdoer forging or altering more than one check. In that case, the bank must be notified of the wrongdoing within thirty days after the depositor receives the bank statement.

Related Cases An employee of the Mid-American Clean Water Systems forged a number of checks from Mid-American's business account. Mid-American sued the bank for reimbursement of lost funds. The court ruled that it was Mid-American's own negligence that contributed to the repeated forgeries because Mid-American was slow to report the forgeries and also did not supervise the employee adequately. Thus, the bank was not held liable. *In re Mid-American Clean Water Systems, Inc.,* 22 UCC Rep. Serv. 272.

Teaching Tips To facilitate class discussion, obtain copies of your state's criminal code that applies to writing bad checks and distribute the copies to students. Invite a prosecuting attorney to discuss policies of his or her office with respect to bad checks and explain what fines, restitution, and jail penalties are possible for those charged with passing bad checks.

UCC 4-406

Background Information "Smart cards" hold a microcomputer chip and digital memory that can be accessed with a personal identification number. Each card can hold extensive records for a wide range of applicants, from bank accounts to car maintenance. A super smart card has a mini-keyboard that enables the cardholder to have access to the card's records directly.

Date: _____

Check Maker's name
Address

Dear Check Maker:

You are hereby notified that your

check number _____ ,

dated _____ ,

and drawn on _____ (bank) _____ ,

in the amount of $ _____ ,

made payable to _____ ,

has been returned unpaid.

You should be advised that the check deception law, I.C. § 35-43-5-5, provides that:

"A person who knowingly or intentionally issues or delivers a check for the payment of or to acquire money or other property, knowing that it will not be paid or honored by the credit institution upon presentment in the usual course of business, commits check deception, a Class A misdemeanor."

The maximum penalty for a class A misdemeanor is one year in prison and a fine of $5,000.00.

Please be advised that if you do not make arrangements to pay this check within the next ten (10) days, this case will be sent to the Marshall County Prosecuting Attorney's Office for the preparation of criminal check deception charges.

Sincerely,

(your name and address)

Marshall County Prosecutor's Office—revised 8/99

Figure 28-2   This is a sample letter used in the State of Indiana notifying the drawer of a bad check that criminal charges will be brought if the check is not paid.

Example 28-13

Applegard's checkbook was stolen from her desk without her knowledge. The thief filled out three of the stolen checks, forged Applegard's signature, and cashed them. Applegard must notify the bank of the forgery within thirty days after she receives the bank statement. If she does not do so and her bank suffers a loss, her bank will not be liable for paying the forged checks.

The absolute limit for notifying a bank of a forged or altered check is one year from the time the depositor receives the bank statement. The limit is three years, however, in the case of a forged indorsement on a check.

Antedated and Postdated Checks A check may be antedated or postdated. It is antedated when it is written and dated on one day and delivered at a later time. A check is postdated when the drawer delivers it before its stated date. However, a bank may charge a postdated check against a customer's account unless the customer has notified the bank of the postdated check within a reasonable time for the bank to act on it. Any such notice by a customer to a bank is effective for the same time periods allowed for stop-payment orders discussed below. If a check is undated, its date is the date that it was first given to someone.

UCC 4-401(c)

Stop-Payment Rights

Drawers may order a bank to stop payment on any item payable on their account. The stop-payment order must be received in time and in such a manner as to afford the bank a reasonable opportunity to act on it. An oral order is binding upon the bank for fourteen calendar days only, unless confirmed in writing within that period. A written order is binding for only six months, unless renewed in writing. The burden of establishing the fact and amount of loss resulting from the payment of an item contrary to a binding order to stop payment is on the customer.

UCC 4-403

UCC 4-403(3)

Bank's Right of Subrogation If a bank fails to stop payment on a check, it is responsible for any loss suffered by the drawer who ordered the payment stopped. The bank, however, may take the place of any holder, holder in due course, payee, or drawer who has rights against others on the underlying obligation. This right to be substituted for another is known as the bank's right of **subrogation.** It is designed to prevent loss to the bank and unjust enrichment to other parties.

UCC 4-407

Teaching Tips Ask students if it is possible to stop payment on a cashier's check used to buy from a catalog merchandise that arrived in defective condition. Remind them to think carefully about who is the drawer and who is the drawee of the check.

Example 28-14

Jervey was induced by fraud to enter into a contract with Glidden. As part of the transaction. Jervey wrote and delivered a check to Glidden for $1,500. When Jervey discovered the fraud, she immediately ordered her bank to stop payment on the check. The bank, by mistake, ignored the stop-payment order and paid the $1,500 to Glidden. The bank must return the $1,500 to Jervey but may sue Glidden for fraud under its right of subrogation.

Insured Accounts

The Federal Deposit Insurance Corporation (FDIC) insures deposits in banks as well as in savings and loan associations. The basic insurance coverage protects individual bank accounts for up to $100,000 and joint accounts for up to an additional $100,000. Revocable trust and payable on death bank accounts are protected for up to $100,000 for each beneficiary who is a close relative and named in the account records. (See Table 28-2).

Further Reading For more information on the FDIC and alternative ways of keeping money safe, read *Safe Money in Tough Times,* by Jonathan Pond (New York: Dell, 1991).

Background Informa-tion The FDIC will not separately insure multiple accounts in the same bank. For example, savings and checking accounts held in the same person's name that have a total balance of over $100,000 are only insured for the first $100,000, no matter how much is in each account.

Table 28-2 How a Husband, Wife, and One Child May Have Insured Accounts Totaling $1,000,000

Individual Accounts:	
Husband	$ 100,000
Wife	$ 100,000
Child	$ 100,000
Joint Accounts:	
Husband and Wife	$ 100,000
Husband and Child	$ 100,000
Wife and Child	$ 100,000
Revocable Trust Accounts:	
Husband as Trustee for Wife	$ 100,000
Husband as Trustee for Child	$ 100,000
Wife as Trustee for Child	$ 100,000
Wife as Trustee for Husband	$ 100,000
	$1,000,000

Quick Quiz 28-3 True or False?

1. The bank acts as the customer's principal when it collects checks or other negotiable instruments made payable to the customer.

2. The drawee bank has no liability to the holder of a check unless it is certified.

3. The commission of forgery is a crime, subject to a fine and imprisonment.

Summary

28-1 If a payee cashes a check at a payor (drawee) bank, the payment is final. If, instead, the payee deposits a check in his or her bank, which sends it to the payor bank for collection, any payment is provisional. The Check 21 Act establishes a *substitute check,* which may be returned to bank customers in place of the canceled original check. This makes check clearing much quicker by the use of electronic processing.

28-2 Consumers who use EFTs have sixty days to notify the bank of an error; thereafter, the bank must investigate. A consumer's liability for the unauthorized use of an ATM card is limited to $50 if notice of the loss or theft of a card is given the issuer within two business days. The consumer's liability increases to

$500 when notice is withheld beyond two business days and becomes unlimited when notice is not given within sixty days. Article 4A of the UCC governs EFTs made by banks and businesses.

28-3 The drawee bank must honor all checks (except stale checks) drawn by its customers when there are sufficient funds on deposit. Failure to do so makes the bank liable to the customer for any actual damages the customer suffers. The drawee bank has no liability to the holder of a check unless it is certified. Banks may pay checks for ten days after the death of a drawer. Banks are responsible for paying altered or forged checks. Banks must make funds available to depositors according to a specific schedule. In addition, banks must pay or return checks on or before their midnight deadline. Depositors must examine their bank statements and canceled checks promptly. It is a crime to write a check with insufficient funds in the bank. Oral stop-payment orders are binding upon the bank for fourteen days: written orders to stop payment are binding for six months. Bank accounts are insured by the FDIC up to $100,000 for individual accounts and up to an additional $100,000 for joint accounts.

Key Terms

ATM card, 520

Check 21 Act, 517

collecting bank, 517

debit card, 520

depositary bank, 517

e-check, 519

electronic fund transfers (EFTs), 519

forgery, 524

intermediary bank, 517

midnight deadline, 526

overdraft, 522

payor bank, 517

presenting bank, 517

provisional, 517

remitting bank, 517

stale check, 523

subrogation, 529

substitute check, 517

uttering, 524

Questions for Review and Discussion

1. What is the difference between a *depositary bank* and a *payor bank*?
2. What is the life cycle of a check that is deposited in the payee's bank?
3. What is the principal feature of the Check 21 Act?
4. In what way are consumers protected by the Electronic Fund Transfer Act?
5. How do EFTs help to meet the needs of businesses that deal with large sums of money?
6. What is the liability of a bank for dishonoring an uncertified check due to a mistake on its part to its customer? To a holder of the check? In the case of a stale check?
7. What is the bank's responsibility as to the payment of checks after the death of the drawer? The payment of forged and altered checks?
8. When must banks make funds available to depositors for checks drawn on the U.S. Treasury? A bank draft? A cashier's check? Checks drawn on banks within the same Federal Reserve district? Checks drawn on banks outside the bank's Federal Reserve district?
9. What crimes may occur when someone writes a check with insufficient funds? Why is it important for depositors to examine their bank statements promptly?
10. How does an oral stop-payment order compare with a written stop-payment order as it affects the bank's obligations?
11. How may a husband, wife, and one child have insured accounts totaling $600,000 in a bank?

Investigating the Internet

At the time the manuscript for this book was written, the Check Clearing for the 21st Century Act (the *Check 21 Act*) had been passed by Congress and signed by the President but was not to go into effect until October 28, 2004. Look on the Internet for up-to-date information about this law, especially how it is working from the point of view of both the banker and the bank's customers. Key in any of these words to do your research: Check 21 Act, Clearing for the 21st Century Act, substitute checks, image replacement documents (IRDs).

Cases for Analysis

1. Arthur Woods died holding an annuity payable on his death to his wife, Dorothy. In payment of the annuity, a checking account for $24, 900 was established in Dorothy Woods's name. The bank sent the checkbook and account statements to Woods's attorney, who had requested that the account be established for Woods. Six unauthorized checks bearing Dorothy Woods's forged signature were drawn on her checking account. Woods discovered the forgeries a year later when she received the checkbook and bank statements from her attorney. She notified the bank of the forgeries fifteen months after they had been written. Was the bank responsible for paying the forged checks? Why or why not? *Woods v. MONY Legacy Life Insurance Company,* 84 N.Y.2d 280 (NY).

2. Kelco bought a truck from Felton, paying for it with a cashier's check she had obtained from her bank. On her way home, the truck broke down. Kelco immediately telephoned her bank and told it to stop payment on the cashier's check. Later, Kelco discovered that her bank had not stopped payment on the cashier's check and instead had paid it. Did Kelco have a claim against the bank? Explain. See also *Taboada v. Bank of Babylon,* 408 N.Y.S.2d 734 (NY).

3. Granite Corp. sent a check to Overseas Equipment Co. When the check was reported lost, Granite wrote to its bank telling it to stop payment on the check. Granite then sent the money to Overseas Equipment Co. by wire. Thirteen months later, the check turned up and Granite's bank paid it. Did the bank violate its duty to stop payment on the check? Explain. *Granite Equip. Leasing Corp. v. Hempstead Bank,* 326 N.Y.S.2d 881 (NY).

4. While in the hospital during his final illness, Norris wrote out a check and gave it to his sister. She deposited it in her bank account. Norris died before the check cleared, and his bank refused to pay it. May a bank honor a check when it knows of the death of the drawer? Explain. *In re Estate of Norris,* 532 P.2d 981 (CO).

5. On June 18, Templeton deposited in his bank account a $5,000 check that was payable to his order. The check reached the drawee bank through normal banking channels on June 22. That bank had received a stop-payment order on the check on May 15 and, therefore, refused to honor it. It kept the check until June 28, when it returned it to Templeton with the notification that payment had been stopped. Did the drawee bank violate a duty it owed to Templeton? Explain. *Templeton v. First Nat'l Bank,* 362 N.E.2d 33 (IL).

6. In payment for services rendered, one of Stewart's clients gave him a check for $185.48 that had been drawn by the client's corporate employer and had been made payable to the order of the client. Although properly indorsed by the client, the drawee bank flatly refused to cash the check for Stewart. The bank acknowledged that the check was good, that is, that there were sufficient funds in the account. Could Stewart sue the bank for refusing to honor the check? Why or why not? *Stewart v. Citizens & Nat'l Bank,* 225 S.E.2d 761 (GA).

7. Fitting wrote an $800 check on her account with Continental Bank. A bank employee had mistakenly placed a hold on the account, causing the bank to dishonor the check when it was presented for payment. Fitting was unable to prove that she suffered damages because of the dishonor. Could she recover damages from the bank? Explain. *Continental Bank v. Fitting,* 559 P.2d 218 (AZ).

8. Roberta Lunt deposited a $625.00 nonlocal check payable to her with a teller at her bank at 10:30 a.m. on Monday. The next day, Tuesday, she went to the bank to withdraw $300 and was told by the teller that she could have only $100 from the check she had deposited the day before. When must the funds be made available to Roberta? Explain why.

Part 5 Case Study

Triffin v. Dillabough and American Express
Supreme Court of Pennsylvania
670 A.2d 684; 716 A.2d 605

Summary

Three American Express money orders were stolen from one of its agents, and 100 others were stolen while being shipped to a different agent. When stolen, all of the money orders contained the preprinted signature of the chairman of American Express, but they were blank as to amount, sender, and date.

Stacy Anne Dillabough presented two of the stolen money orders for payment at Chuckie Enterprises, Inc. (Chuckie's), a check-cashing operation in Philadelphia. The money orders were in the amounts of $550 and $650, respectively, and listed Dillabough as the payee and David W. (last name undecipherable) as the sender. Two months later, Robert Lynn presented another one of the stolen money orders for payment at Chuckie's in the amount of $200, which listed himself as payee and Michael C. Pepe as the sender.

After being cashed at Chuckie's, the money orders traveled the regular bank collection routes and were returned to Chuckie's bearing the stamp "REPORTED LOST OR STOLEN—DO NOT REDEPOSIT." American Express refused to pay Chuckie's the face amounts of the money orders. Chuckie's then sold them to Triffin, a commercial discounter. By written agreements, Chuckie's assigned all of its right, title, and interest in the money orders to Triffin.

In court, Triffin obtained judgments by default against Dillabough and Lynn. In a trial with American Express, the court found that the money orders were not negotiable instruments and entered a judgment in favor of American Express. On appeal, the Superior Court reversed the trial court and held that the money orders were negotiable instruments and that Triffin had the status of a holder in due course, entitling him to recover the face amount of the money orders from American Express.

The Court's Opinion

Madame Justice Newman

The Superior Court has described the purpose of negotiable instruments and the Commercial Code as follows:

> A negotiable instrument is an instrument capable of transfer by indorsement or delivery. Negotiability provides a means of passing on to the transferee the rights of the holder, including the right to sue in his or her own name, and the right to take free of equities as against the assignor/payee. [Citations omitted.] The purpose of the Commercial Code is to enhance the marketability of negotiable instruments and to allow bankers, brokers, and the general public to trade in confidence. [Citations omitted.] As a matter of sound economic policy, the Commercial Code encourages the free transfer and negotiability of commercial paper to stimulate financial interdependence.

Manor Bldg. Corp. v. Manor Complex Assocs., 645 A.2d 843. With these principles in mind, we turn to a discussion of the American Express money orders at issue here.

The threshold question is whether the money orders qualify as negotiable instruments under Division Three of the Commercial Code, 3101, *et seq.,* which governs negotiability.[1] Both parties agree that if the money orders are not negotiable instruments then Triffin's claims against American Express must fail. Initially, we note that the Commercial Code does not specifically define the term "money order," nor does it provide a descriptive list of financial documents that automatically qualify as negotiable instruments. Instead, 3104(a) sets forth the following four-part test to determine if a particular document qualifies as a negotiable instrument:

A. Requisites to negotiability. Any writing to be a negotiable instrument within this division must:

   (1) be signed by the maker or drawer;

   (2) contain an unconditional promise or order to pay a sum certain in money and no other promise, order, obligation or power given by the maker or drawer except as authorized by this division;

   (3) be payable on demand or at a definite time; and

   (4) be payable to order or to bearer.

The Superior Court described the face of the money orders in question as follows:

> Prior to being stolen[,] the American Express money orders read: "AMERICAN EXPRESS MONEY ORDER . . . CHASE SAVINGS BANK . . . DATE (blank). PAY THE SUM OF (blank), NOT GOOD OVER $1,000, TO THE ORDER OF (blank). Louis V. Gerstner, Chairman. SENDER'S NAME AND ADDRESS (blank). Issued by American Express Travel Related Services Company, Inc., Englewood, Colorado. Payable at United Bank of Grand Junction, Downtown, Grand Junction, Colorado."

The first requisite of negotiability, a signature by the drawer or maker, "includes any symbol executed or adopted by a party with present intention to authenticate a writing." § 1201. "Authentication may be printed,

stamped or written; it may be by initials or by thumbprint. . . . The question always is whether the symbol was executed or adopted by the party with present intention to authenticate the writing." Additionally, section 3307(a)(2) states that when the effectiveness of a signature is challenged, it is presumed to be genuine or authorized unless the signer has died or become incompetent. Here, the drawer, American Express, affixed the pre-printed signature of Louis Gerstner, its then Chairman, to the money orders in question before forwarding them to its agents. American Express does not argue that Gerstner's signature was affixed to the money orders for any reason other than to authenticate them. Accordingly, the money orders satisfy the first requisite for negotiability.

The second requisite, American Express argues, is lacking because the money orders do not contain an unconditional promise or order to pay. Specifically, American Express claims that a legend it placed on the back of the money orders qualifies an otherwise unconditional order on the front directing the drawee to "PAY THE SUM OF" a specified amount "TO THE ORDER OF" the payee. The legend provides as follows:

IMPORTANT
<u>DO NOT CASH FOR STRANGERS</u>

THIS MONEY ORDER WILL NOT BE PAID IF IT HAS BEEN ALTERED OR STOLEN OR IF AN INDORSEMENT IS MISSING OR FORGED. BE SURE YOU HAVE EFFECTIVE RECOURSE AGAINST YOUR CUSTOMER.

PAYEE'S INDORSEMENT

According to American Express, this legend renders the order to pay conditional on the money order not being altered, stolen, unindorsed or forged and destroys the negotiability of the instrument.

We disagree. In a factually similar case, the Louisiana Court of Appeal construed a legend on the back of an American Express money order similar to the one at issue here. *Hong Kong Importers, Inc. v. American Express Co.,* 301 So.2d 707. The legend there stated "CASH ONLY IF RECOURSE FROM INDORSER IS AVAILABLE. IF THIS MONEY ORDER HAS NOT BEEN VALIDLY ISSUED OR HAS BEEN FRAUDULENTLY NEGOTIATED, IT WILL BE RETURNED." The money order also had the following language printed on its face: "KNOW YOUR INDORSER CASH ONLY IF RECOURSE IS AVAILABLE." The Louisiana Court held that the legend on the back and the language on the front did not convert the money order into a conditional promise to pay, but merely operated as a warning to the party

---

[1] Although the Commercial Code has been revised since the transactions in this case occurred, its basic provisions survived the 1992 amendments. We expect that this Opinion will provide guidance for transactions conducted pursuant to the Commercial Code as amended in 1992.

cashing the money order to protect himself against fraud. Although *Hong Kong* was decided before Louisiana adopted the Uniform Commercial Code, we find its rationale to be persuasive and applicable to § 3104.

American Express attempts to distinguish *Hong Kong* by asserting that the legend in this case is more specific because it explicitly conditions payment on the money orders not being altered, stolen, unindorsed or forged. This argument misses the point. "Any writing which meets the requirements of subsection [(a)] and is not excluded under Section [3103] is a negotiable instrument, and all sections of this [Division] apply to it, *even though it may contain additional language beyond that contemplated by this section.*" § 3104, Comment 4 (emphasis added). An otherwise unconditional order to pay that meets the section 3104 requirements is not made conditional by including implied or constructive conditions in the instrument. § 3105(a)(1). Moreover, purported conditions on an otherwise negotiable instrument, that merely reflect other provisions of the law, do not vitiate negotiability. *State v. Phelps,* 608 P.2d 51 (Ariz. Ct. App. 1979). Here, the alleged conditions on the back of the money orders are nothing more than a restatement of American Express' statutory defenses against payment because of alteration, absence of signature, and forgery. Contrary to American Express' claims, expressing those statutory defenses in a legend with the conditional phrase "THIS MONEY ORDER WILL NOT BE PAID IF . . ." does not elevate the legend to a condition for the purposes of 3104(a) because it is merely a restatement of the defenses present in the Commercial Code. The legend is simply a warning that American Express has reserved its statutory defenses. Whether these defenses are effective against Triffin is a separate question to be answered after resolving the issue of negotiability. We hold, therefore, that the money orders contain an unconditional order to pay, and satisfy the second requisite of negotiability.

The third requisite, that the writing be payable on demand or at a definite time, and the fourth requisite, that the writing be payable to order or bearer, are clear from the face of the money orders and are not disputed by the parties. Thus, the American Express money orders qualify as negotiable instruments pursuant to § 3104.

American Express contends that even if the money orders are facially negotiable, they should not be viewed as negotiable instruments because they were never issued or otherwise "placed in the stream of commerce." Issue is defined as "[t]he first delivery of an instrument to a holder or a remitter." § 3102. Delivery is defined as the "voluntary transfer of possession." § 1201. American Express argues that because the money orders were incomplete when stolen and subsequently completed without authorization, the money orders were never delivered and it should have no liability for them.

Authorized completion and delivery, however, are not listed as requisites to negotiability in section 3104. Moreover, section 3115 specifically permits the enforcement of incomplete and undelivered instruments and provides as follows:

A. General rule. When a paper whose contents at the time of signing show that it is intended to become an instrument is signed while still incomplete in any necessary respect it cannot be enforced until completed, but when it is completed in accordance with authority given it is effective as completed.

B. Unauthorized completion. *If the completion is unauthorized the rules as to material alteration apply (section 3407), even though the paper was not delivered by the maker or drawer,* but the burden of establishing that any completion is unauthorized is on the party so asserting [emphasis added].

Section 3407 provides that the defense of unauthorized completion discharges a party from liability to any person *other than a holder in due course.* § 3407(a)(2); § 3407(b). "A subsequent holder in due course may in all cases enforce the [negotiable] instrument according to its original tenor, and when an incomplete instrument has been completed, he may enforce it as completed." 3407(c). Additionally, section 3305 provides that a holder in due course takes a negotiable instrument free from the defense of non-delivery. § 3305, Comment 3.

When read together, sections 3115, 3407 and 3305 demonstrate that unauthorized completion and non-delivery do not prevent enforcement of an otherwise negotiable instrument. Instead, the three sections permit a holder in due course to enforce the undelivered instrument as completed. . . .

The next question then, is whether Triffin has the rights of a holder in due course who can enforce the negotiable money orders.

Section 3302(a) describes a holder in due course as follows:

A. General rule. A holder in due course is a holder who takes the instrument:

(1) for value;

(2) in good faith; and

(3) without notice that it is overdue or has been dishonored or of any defense against or claim to it on the part of any person. § 3302(a).

Because the trial court held that the money orders were not negotiable instruments, it never answered the question of Triffin's status as a holder in due course. . . .

Triffin obtained the money orders from Chuckie's pursuant to a written agreement by which Chuckie's assigned all of its right, title and interest in the money orders to Triffin. Triffin could not become a holder in due course in his own name because he had notice of American Express' defenses when he took the money orders from Chuckie's. § 3302(a)(3). However, Triffin could acquire the *status* of a holder in due course from Chuckie's through the assignment if Chuckie's was a holder in due course because a transferee acquires whatever rights the transferor had, even if the transferee is aware of the defenses to enforcement. § 3201. Therefore, the focus of our inquiry is whether Chuckie's was a holder in due course.

The parties do not dispute that Chuckie's took the money orders for value. Paul Giunta, the owner of Chuckie's, testified that he paid Dillabough and Lynn the face value of the money orders, minus a two percent fee. Thus, section 3302(a)(1) is satisfied. The second element of section 3302(a), good faith, is defined as "[h]onesty in fact in the conduct or transaction concerned. § 1201. The evidence established that Giunta recognized Dillabough and Lynn from previous transactions and required them to present photographic identification. Additionally, although the trial court did not discuss each element of Chuckie's holder in due course status, it did opine in a discussion of its legal conclusions on the record that Chuckie's acted in good faith. Moreover, American Express does not argue that Chuckie's failed to act in good faith. Based on Giunta's actions, we cannot say that the trial court erred in concluding that Chuckie's acted in good faith. Therefore, section 3302(a)(2) is satisfied. Regarding section 3302(a)(3), there was no evidence presented that Chuckie's had any notice that the Dillabough and Lynn money orders were stolen when he cashed them. Accordingly, the record demonstrates as a matter of law that Chuckie's was a holder in due course. Because Triffin stands in Chuckie's shoes as its assignee, Triffin has attained the status of a holder in due course. §3201.

American Express further contends that even if Triffin qualifies as a holder in due course, the money orders are still not enforceable because the legend on their backs limits the "tenor" of the instruments. Pursuant to § 3413(a), American Express claims that it is only obligated to pay an instrument "according to its tenor." The 1979 Commercial Code does not define "tenor." The 1992 amendments to section 3413(a), however, substitute the word "terms" for the word "tenor." § 3413(a). Therefore, it appears that no substantive change was intended by the substitution of the word "terms" for the word "tenor" and we will treat these words synonymously. Thus, American Express is

essentially arguing that each money order should be enforced according to its terms, which state that the money order "WILL NOT BE PAID IF IT HAS BEEN ALTERED OR STOLEN OR IF AN INDORSEMENT IS MISSING OR FORGED."

As previously discussed, the legend on the back of the money orders is merely a warning that restates American Express' defenses against persons other than holders in due course in the event of alteration, theft, lack of indorsement or forgery. These defenses are ineffective against a holder in due course. § 3305; § 3407(c). Because Triffin has attained holder in due course status through the assignment of the money orders from Chuckie's, American Express cannot enforce the defenses against him. Accordingly, American Express is liable to Triffin for the face value of the money orders.

The Order of the Superior Court is affirmed.

Dissenting Opinion

Mr. Justice Castille

The majority concludes that appellee Robert J. Triffin ("appellee") is entitled to recover the value of the money orders at issue because the money orders were negotiable instruments and because appellee was a holder in due course of those negotiable instruments. However, since the money orders at issue contained express conditional language which precluded negotiability under the relevant statute, I must respectfully dissent from the majority's conclusion. . .

At issue here is the second of the four statutory prerequisites to negotiability, the requirement of an "unconditional" promise or order. Regarding this prerequisite, section 3105 provides:

A. Unconditional promise or order. A promise or order otherwise unconditional is not made conditional by the fact that the instrument:

(1) is subject to implied or constructive conditions;

. . . The comment to section 3105 states:

> 1. . . . Nothing in [paragraph (a) subsection (1)] is intended to imply that language may not be fairly construed to mean what it says, but implications, whether of law or fact, are not to be considered in determining negotiability.

Thus, the statute clearly distinguishes between language which creates an implied condition and language which creates an express condition. The latter renders a promise or order non-negotiable while the former does not. This conclusion derives further support from the revised § 3106(a), which provides that

> . . . a promise or order is unconditional unless it states (1) an express condition to payment. . . .

Here, the operative language in the money orders at issue clearly created an "express" condition and thereby rendered the money orders non-negotiable. The language at issue . . . explicitly conditions payments on the money orders' not being altered or stolen and the indorsements' not being missing or forged. The use of the word "if" renders the condition an express one, since "if" by definition means "on *condition* that; in case that; supposing that." Webster's New World Dict., 2d College ed. (emphasis added).

Furthermore, the official comment to revised section 3106 explains what the code intends by drawing the distinction between implied and express conditions:

> If the promise or order states an express condition to payment, the promise or order is not an instrument. For example, A states, "I promise to pay $100,000 to the order of John Doe *if* he conveys title to Blackacre to me." The promise is not an instrument because there is an express condition to payment. However, suppose a promise states, "In consideration of John Doe's promise to convey title of Blackacre I promise to pay $100,000 to the order of John Doe. That promise can be an instrument if [section 3104] is otherwise satisfied.

Accordingly, the use of the word "if" creates an express condition which otherwise might be lacking, and thereby precludes a money order from being a negotiable instrument under the statute. The language at issue in this case created the same type of express condition which is embodied in the Comment; consequently, the language precludes the money orders from being negotiable instruments.

The reasons proffered by the majority to justify its departure from this seemingly inescapable statutory logic are strained. First, the majority cites a case, decided by the Louisiana Court of Appeal in 1974, in which a condition incorporating the word "if" was construed not to bar negotiability. In that case, the Louisiana Court did not evaluate the significance of the word "if" or the significance of the condition which that word introduced. Moreover, in 1974, Louisiana had not yet adopted Article III of the Uniform Commercial Code ("UCC"). Hence, it appears that the Louisiana decision was decided against the backdrop of the Code of Napoleon. See *9 to 5 Fashions, Inc. v. Petr L. Spurney,* 538 So.2d 228, 233 (La. 1989)(discussing roots of Louisiana's civil code in the

Napoleonic code). Pennsylvania, on the other hand, has adopted Article III of the UCC, which speaks directly to the issue presented in this case, as explained supra. A decision by an intermediate Louisiana appellate court interpreting French legal principles should not override the explicit statutory guidance furnished by the Pennsylvania legislature on an issue of Pennsylvania law.

The majority also seizes on Comment 4 to § 3104, which states that "any writing which meets the requirements of subsection [(a)] and is not excluded under Section [3103] is a negotiable instrument, and all sections of this [Division] apply to it, *even though it may contain additional language beyond that contemplated by this section*" (emphasis added by majority). Since, as explained supra, the money orders contained language which precluded them from satisfying subsection (a), the quoted language from Comment 4 does not further the majority's argument.

Finally, the majority attempts to support its conclusion by referring to the principle that "purported conditions on an otherwise negotiable instrument, that merely reflect other provisions of the law, do not vitiate negotiability." The majority contends that the language at issue amounts merely to a restatement of appellant's statutory defenses against payment where there has been alteration (§ 3407), theft (§ 3306(4)), absence of signature (§ 3401) and forgery (§ 3404). The majority overlooks the fact that all of these statutory defenses are, by their own terms, ineffective against holders in due course. On the other hand, the language at issue here—which categorically states that the money order will not be paid if it was stolen—is operative even against holders who have taken in due course. As noted in the Comment to section 3105(a)(1), conditional language may be fairly construed to mean what it says. By its plain terms, the language at issue here sweeps beyond the scope of appellant's statutory defenses, and therefore does more than simply "reflect other provisions of the law."

In sum, the statute at issue in this case is devoid of ambiguity, and the application of that statute to these facts compels a conclusion contrary to that reached by the majority. Consequently, I respectfully dissent.

Mr. Justice Cappy joins this dissenting opinion.

Questions for Analysis

1. What did the court say is the four-part test to determine whether a particular document qualifies as a negotiable instrument? Were these basic requirements changed by the 1990 UCC revision?

2. What does the definition of a signature on a negotiable instrument include?

3. How did the court respond to American Express's argument that the following words created a condition: "this money order will not be paid if it has been altered or stolen or if an indorsement is missing or forged"?

4. Why does the fact that the money orders were completed without authorization and not delivered have no effect on negotiation of an instrument?

5. Why could Triffin not become a holder in due course?

6. Why could Triffin acquire the status of a holder in due course?

7. In his dissenting opinion, what argument did Mr. Justice Castille use to try to persuade the other justices on the court that the money orders were not negotiable?

8. Do you agree with the dissenting opinion? Why or why not?

Insurance, Secured Transactions, and Bankruptcy

Part Six

Chapter 29

The Nature of the Insurance Contract

The Opening Case
"Double Indemnity"

Marisa and Joseph St. Jean were married in 2001. Marisa took out a life insurance policy on Joseph's life, naming herself as beneficiary. She continued to pay the premiums even after they were divorced in 2003. The divorce judgment contained an order that the couple's late-model Infinity that was registered and insured in their names jointly "shall belong to Joseph outright." Joseph was killed in 2004 while driving the Infinity at a high rate of speed on an interstate highway without wearing a seat belt. The Infinity was totaled. The couple had not gotten around to removing Marisa's name from the insurance policy as a co-owner of the Infinity. Could Marisa collect on the life insurance policy? The automobile insurance policy?

Chapter Outcomes

1. Identify the contractual elements that are necessary to make an insurance agreement binding.
2. Describe the principal types of life insurance.
3. Identify exemptions from risk and optional provisions that may be part of a life insurance policy.
4. Describe the kinds of losses that are covered by fire insurance, marine insurance, and homeowner's and renter's insurance.
5. Differentiate among the principal kinds of automobile insurance and determine which insurance covers a particular loss.
6. Describe the benefits that are often included in health insurance policies.
7. List the steps to be followed in applying for, obtaining, and maintaining an insurance policy.
8. Judge whether an insurance policy can be canceled in given situations.

29-1 The Insurance Contract

Although life has always been full of risks and uncertainties, it has become even more so since 9/11. A process called risk management is used by many businesses to identify, analyze, control, and communicate risks of all kinds, from the making of an accounting error to having the company's security compromised. Hazards such as accidents, fire, and illness pose a constant threat to our well-being. The principal protection against losses from such hazards is insurance. The purpose of insurance is to spread the losses among a greater number of people. (See Table 29-1.) **Insurance** is

Table 29-1 Examples of Risk Management Strategies

Risks		Strategies for Reducing Financial Impact
Personal Events	**Financial Impact**	
Disability	• Loss of income • Increased expenses	• Savings and investments • Disability insurance
Death	• Loss of income	• Life insurance • Estate planning
Property loss	• Catastrophic storm damage to property • Repair or replacement • Cost of theft	• Property repair and upkeep • Auto insurance • Homeowner's insurance • Flood or earthquake insurance
Liability	• Claims and settlement costs • Lawsuits and legal expenses • Loss of personal assets and income	• Maintaining property • Homeowner's insurance • Auto insurance

Source: Brown, Gordon W., *Understanding Business and Personal Law,* 11th ed. Glencoe/McGraw-Hill p. 752.

a transfer of the risk of economic loss from the insured to the insurance company. Small contributions made by a large number of individuals can provide sufficient money to cover the losses suffered by a few as they occur each year. The function of insurance is to distribute each person's risk among all others who may or may not experience losses.

Parties to an Insurance Contract

The parties to an insurance contract are the insurer, or underwriter; the insured; and the beneficiary. The **insurer** accepts the risk of loss in return for a **premium** (the consideration paid for a policy) and agrees to **indemnify,** or compensate, the insured against the loss specified in the contract. The **insured** is the party (or parties) protected by the insurance contract. The contract of insurance is called the **policy.** The period of time during which the insurer assumes the risk of loss is known as the life of the policy. A third party, to whom payment of compensation is sometimes provided by the contract, is called the **beneficiary.**

Contractual Elements

Insurance policies, like other contracts, require an offer, an acceptance, mutual assent, capable parties, consideration, and a legally valid subject matter. The application filled in by an applicant is an offer to the insurer who may then accept or reject the offer. To have mutual assent, the parties must have reached agreement on the terms of the contract. A party to a contract must also be capable of understanding the terms of the agreement. Consideration arises from the premiums paid by the insured and the promise of the insurer to pay money to the beneficiary upon the happening of a certain event. Finally, the subject matter must not be tainted with illegality. For example, a fire insurance policy written on a building in which the owners permitted the illegal manufacture of fireworks would be void in the event of a fire.

Insurable Interests

A person or business applying for insurance must have an insurable interest in the subject matter of the policy to be insured. An **insurable interest** is the financial interest that a

Teaching Tips There are some people who do not believe they need insurance because they say they never get sick and never have to go to the doctor. They feel that they can save the money they do not spend on insurance to pay for emergencies. Ask students to debate the merits and the faults of this argument.

Terms The term *assurance* was used for all forms of *insurance* in the sixteenth century. *Assurance* is still used by many companies overseas in the same way that *insurance* is used in the United States.

Teaching Tips Discuss with students the types of risks that exist in your community for which insurance can be obtained. Ask students to classify these examples on the board according to the types of policies that will cover the risks.

policyholder has in the person or property that is insured. In the case of life insurance, all people have an insurable interest in their own lives as well as the lives of their spouses and dependents. Business partners have an insurable interest in each other because they could suffer a financial loss if a partner dies. Likewise, a corporation can have a financial interest in its key employees for the same reason. In the case of property insurance, anyone who would suffer a financial loss from damage to property would have an insurable interest in that property. For life insurance, the insurable interest must exist at the time the insurance is purchased. In contrast, for property insurance, the insurable interest must exist at the time of loss.

Subrogation

Insurance companies have the right to step into the shoes of the party they compensate and sue any party whom the compensated party could have sued. This substitution of one person in place of another relative to a lawful claim is known as **subrogation.**

Quick Quiz 29-1 True or False?

1. The purpose of insurance is to spread losses among people who can most afford it.

2. An application filled in by an insurance applicant is a binding contract on the insurer.

3. Anyone can obtain insurance on another person or property regardless of the relationship.

29-2 Types of Insurance

It is possible to obtain insurance against almost any risk if an individual or business is willing to pay the price. The premium charged will depend on the risk involved. Life insurance, property insurance, and health insurance are discussed here.

Life Insurance

Life insurance is an insurance contract that provides monetary compensation for losses suffered by another's death. Anyone has an insurable interest in the life of another if a financial loss will occur if the insured dies. For example, an insurable interest exists if the person who buys the insurance is dependent on the insured for education, support, business (partners), or debt collection. A life insurance policy will remain valid and enforceable even if the insurable interest terminates. It is necessary only that the insurable interest exists at the time the policy was issued.

The Opening Case Revisited
"Double Indemnity"

Marisa was able to collect on the life insurance policy. Because of the divorce, she no longer had an insurable interest in Joseph's life when he died; however, she did have an insurable interest at the time the policy was originally issued.

Premiums for life insurance are based on several factors, including the age and health of the insured, the coverage, and the type of policy. It is less expensive to buy life insurance at a young age because the death rate for young people is very low, and their health is usually at its peak.

If an individual takes out insurance on himself or herself, it is not necessary for the beneficiary to have an insurable interest in the insured's life. However, if a person takes out life insurance on someone else, that person must have an insurable interest in the insured's life.

The principal types of life insurance are straight life, limited-payment life, term, and endowment insurance.

Cross-Cultural Notes
Many African societies view children as a form of life insurance because children are expected to care for their parents in old age.

Straight Life Insurance

Straight life insurance, which is also known as **ordinary life insurance,** or **whole life insurance,** requires the payment of premiums throughout the life of the insured and pays the beneficiary the face value of the policy upon the insured's death. The amount of the premium is determined by the age of the insured at the time of purchase and normally stays the same throughout the life of the policy. The younger the insured, the lower the premium because the company expects to collect many years' worth of premiums.

Straight life insurance contains an investment feature known as the *cash surrender value.* The cash surrender value usually builds up slowly at first, but in later years it approaches the face amount of the policy. At some stated point (usually at the age of ninety-five or a hundred) it equals the face value of the policy. An insured can cancel a straight life policy at any time and receive its cash surrender value. Straight life insurance also contains a feature called a *loan value,* which is an amount of money that may be borrowed against the cash surrender value of the policy, usually at a relatively favorable rate of interest. During inflationary times, when bank interest rates are high, insurance policies are often excellent sources for loans at low interest rates.

Example 29-1

At age eighteen LaPlume purchased a straight life insurance policy with a face value of $20,000. The premiums were quite modest. At some later time, LaPlume could borrow on the policy or trade it in for its cash surrender value. Or, LaPlume could continue premium payments until death. If LaPlume died while a loan was outstanding, the insurance company would deduct the amount of the loan from the amount it paid to LaPlume's beneficiary.

A form of straight life insurance, called **universal life insurance,** allows the policy owner flexibility in choosing and changing terms of the policy. Within certain guidelines, the policy owner can modify the face value of the policy as well as the premiums in response to changing needs and circumstances in the policy owner's life. Under a typical universal life policy:

- Premiums may be increased or decreased within policy limits.
- The amount of insurance may be increased, subject to evidence of insurability, or decreased subject to set minimums.
- The owner may borrow up to the maximum loan value at a prearranged interest rate. Policy loans reduce the cash surrender value and death benefit.
- Withdrawals may be made from the cash surrender value.

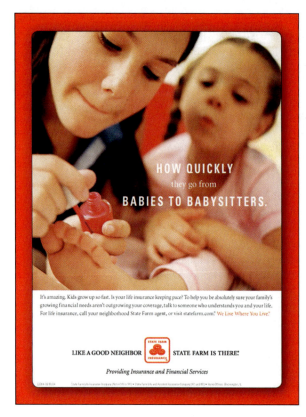

HOW QUICKLY
they go from
BABIES TO BABYSITTERS.

It's amazing. Kids grow up so fast. Is your life insurance keeping pace? To help you be absolutely sure your family's growing financial needs aren't outgrowing your coverage, talk to someone who understands you and your life. For life insurance, call your neighborhood State Farm agent, or visit statefarm.com.® We Live Where You Live.®

LIKE A GOOD NEIGHBOR   STATE FARM IS THERE.®

Providing Insurance and Financial Services

Many families include life insurance in their long term financial planning.

Limited-Payment Life Insurance **Limited-payment life insurance** provides that the payment of premiums will stop after a stated length of time—usually ten, twenty, or thirty years. The amount of the policy will be paid to the beneficiary upon the death of the insured, whether the death occurs during the payment period or after. Because of the limited number of payments made by the insured, the premiums are proportionately higher than those for straight life; however, the cash surrender value grows faster than that of straight life insurance.

Term Insurance **Term insurance** is issued for a particular period, usually five or ten years. The time period is known as the term. Term insurance is the least expensive kind of life insurance because term policies have no cash or loan value, as others do. Term insurance offers protection alone, in contrast to straight life, which combines protection with a savings plan. Premiums for term insurance, unlike those for straight life, commonly go up at the end of each term. It costs a twenty-five-year-old relatively little to buy term insurance. By the age of sixty, however, the insured must pay much higher premiums for this same coverage. But by that time, ordinarily, the insured's overall financial responsibility to others has lessened and thus less coverage may be needed.

Term insurance is often renewable at the end of each period simply by paying the increased premium, without need for a new medical examination. In addition, many term insurance policies are *convertible;* that is, they can be converted to straight life policies without taking a new medical examination—allowing protection throughout the insured's lifetime.

A modified form of term insurance is *decreasing term insurance.* The premium stays constant from year to year, but the amount of protection (death benefit) decreases over the years. This type of insurance is widely used to cover the outstanding balance of a home mortgage.

Endowment Insurance **Endowment insurance** is a type of protection that combines life insurance and investment so that if the insured outlives the time-period of the policy, the face value is paid to the insured. If the insured does not outlive the time-period of the policy, the face value is paid to the beneficiary. Because this type of policy builds up a cash value more rapidly than other policies, the premium is higher.

Example 29-2

Swenson, aged eighteen, purchased a $20,000 face value, twenty-year endowment policy. His beneficiary will get $20,000 if Swenson dies before age forty-one. If he survives, Swenson will get a check for $20,000 at age forty-one.

Annuity An **annuity** is a guaranteed retirement income that is purchased by paying either a lump-sum premium or making periodic payments to an insurer. The insured may choose either: (a) to receive an income for a certain fixed number of years, with a beneficiary receiving whatever is left of the annuity when the insured dies, or (b) to receive payments as long as the insured lives and, upon death, losing whatever is left of the annuity.

Exemptions from Risk Many life insurance policies contain clauses that exempt the insurance company from liability in certain situations. For example, policies often do not cover the insured when riding in an airplane, violating the law, or working in certain dangerous occupations.

A number of jurisdictions have held that beneficiaries cannot receive the benefits from a life insurance policy when the insured is legally executed. These courts base their reasoning on the theory that it would be against public policy for beneficiaries to receive insurance proceeds in such cases. They also note that death by legal execution is not one of the risks assumed by the insurance company. In contrast, other courts allow beneficiaries to receive life insurance benefits in cases of execution because denial of recovery is not a deterrent to crime.

In most cases, the courts allow a beneficiary to receive benefits under a life insurance policy when the insured is murdered, except when the murderer is also the beneficiary. A beneficiary who murders the insured forfeits all rights under the life insurance policy.

Most policies provide that beneficiaries can recover for a death caused by suicide if the suicide occurs more than two years after the policy was taken out. They may not recover, however, when the policy contains a provision preventing such recovery or when the life insurance was purchased by someone planning suicide or who was insane. One example of a named beneficiary who could recover would be a creditor of the insured.

Life insurance policies usually include an exemption from liability in times of war. The exemption states that the insurer will not be liable on the policy if the insured is killed while a member of the armed forces, generally outside the continental United States, and from service-connected causes.

Optional Provisions Life insurance policies have many optional provisions that may be purchased by the insured. Three popular options are double indemnity, waiver of premium, and guaranteed insurability.

For an additional premium, the insured may purchase a benefit known as **double indemnity,** or accidental death benefit. This option provides that if the insured dies from accidental causes the insurer will pay double the amount of the policy to the beneficiary. Death must occur within ninety days of the accident for this benefit to apply.

The *waiver of premium* option excuses the insured from paying premiums if he or she becomes disabled. Some insurance policies automatically include the waiver in their provisions; others offer it as an extra-cost option.

A *guaranteed insurability* option allows the insured to pay an extra premium initially in exchange for a guaranteed option to buy more insurance at certain specified times later on. The additional insurance can be purchased with no questions asked; thus, no new medical examination is required even if the insured develops a serious illness before exercising the option.

Property Insurance

Property insurance can be purchased to protect both real and personal property. To establish the existence of an insurable interest in property, the insured must demonstrate a monetary interest in the property. This monetary interest means that the insured will suffer a financial loss if the property is damaged or destroyed. Unlike life insurance, this insurable interest must exist when the loss occurs.

Property insurance can be less expensive by the use of a **deductible,** which is an amount of any loss that is to be paid by the insured. It can be a specified dollar amount, a percentage of the claim amount, or a specified amount of time that must elapse before benefits are paid. The bigger the deductible, the lower the premium charged for the same coverage.

The Opening Case Revisited
"Double Indemnity"

Marisa was not able to collect on the automobile insurance policy. Her insurable interest in the Infinity came to an end when the court ordered that the Infinity belonged to Joseph outright.

Coinsurance Clauses

Coinsurance is an insurance policy provision under which the insurer and the insured share costs, after the deductible is met, according to a specific formula. Most property and inland marine policies have a coinsurance clause, which limits the insurance company's liability for a loss if the property is not insured for its full replacement value. For example, if a homeowner's insurance policy has an 80 percent coinsurance clause, the building must be insured for 80 percent of its replacement value to receive full reimbursement for a loss (see Figure 29-1).

Fire Insurance

A fire insurance policy is a contract in which the fire insurance company promises to pay the insured if some real or personal property is damaged or destroyed by fire. A fire insurance policy is effective on delivery to the insured, even before the premium is paid. Even an oral agreement will make fire insurance effective.

The insurer's liability under a fire policy usually covers losses other than those directly attributed to fire. Under most policies, claims may also be made for losses from water used to fight the fire; scorching; smoke damage to goods; deliberate destruction of property as a means of controlling a spreading fire; lightning, even if there is no resultant fire; riot or explosion, if a fire does result; and losses through theft or exposure of goods removed from a burning building.

Marine Insurance

Marine insurance is one of the oldest types of insurance coverage, dating back to the Venetian traders who sailed the Mediterranean Sea. **Ocean marine insurance** covers ships at sea. **Inland marine insurance** covers goods that are moved by land carriers such as rail, truck, and airplane. Inland marine insurance also covers such

Figure 29-1 Here is a typical coinsurance clause found in an insurance policy. It limits the insurer's liability for a loss if the property is not insured for its full replacement value.

TYPICAL COINSURANCE CLAUSE

"The insurance company will pay that part of a loss that the insurance carried bears to 80 percent of the replacement cost of the building."

It would cost $100,000 to replace Felipe Garcia's house. If he insured it for $60,000, the insurance company would pay only three-fourths of any loss, computed as follows:

$$\frac{\text{Amount of insurance carried}}{\text{Percent of replacement cost}} = \frac{\$60,000}{80\% \text{ of } \$100,000} = \frac{\$60,000}{\$80,000} = \frac{3}{4}$$

A fire partially destroys the building, causing $40,000 worth of damage. Because of the coinsurance clause, Garcia would recover $30,000 (¾ of the loss) from the insurance company.

items as jewelry, fine arts, musical instruments, and wedding presents. Customers' goods in the possession of bailees, such as fur-storage houses and dry cleaners, are also covered by inland marine insurance.

A *floater policy* is one which insures property that cannot be covered by specific insurance because the property is constantly changing in either value or location. A personal property floater, for example, covers personal property in general, wherever located.

Homeowner's and Renter's Insurance

Many of the leading insurance companies offer a combination policy known as the **homeowner's policy.** This insurance gives protection for all types of losses and liabilities related to home ownership. Among the items covered are losses from fire, windstorm, burglary, vandalism, and injuries suffered by other persons while on the property. **Renter's insurance** protects tenants against loss of personal property, against liability for a visitor's personal injury, and against liability for negligent destruction of the rented premises.

Background Information Renters can purchase insurance to cover their personal property and their liability to others for personal injuries. The only items such policies don't cover are dwellings rented, which are covered by landlords' insurance policies.

Flood Insurance

Flooding can be caused by heavy rains, melting snow, inadequate drainage systems, failed protective devices such as levees and dams, as well as by tropical storms and hurricanes. Nevertheless, most commercial, homeowner's, and renter's insurance policies, do not cover flood damage. To obtain such coverage, special flood insurance must be obtained from an insurance agent.

Most flood insurance is backed by the National Flood Insurance Program (NFIP) established by Congress in response to the high cost of taxpayer-funded disaster relief for flood victims and the amount of damage caused by floods. Communities that agree to manage flood hazard areas by adopting minimum standards can participate in the NFIP. On the other hand, communities that do not participate in the program cannot receive flood insurance, federal grants and loans, federal disaster assistance, or federal mortgage insurance for the acquisition or construction of structures located in flood hazard areas of their community. Most lending institutions require borrowers to obtain flood insurance when they buy, build, or improve structures in Special Flood Hazard Areas (SFHAs). Lending institutions that are federally regulated or federally insured must determine if the structure is located in an SFHA and must provide written notice requiring flood insurance.

Automobile Insurance

Automobile insurance provides for indemnity against losses resulting from fire, theft, or collision with another vehicle and damages arising out of injury by motor vehicles to the person or property of another. The following are the most common types of automobile insurance:

- bodily injury to others
- no-fault insurance
- bodily injury caused by an uninsured auto
- bodily injury caused by an underinsured auto
- medical payments
- property damage to someone else's property
- collision insurance
- comprehensive coverage
- substitute transportation insurance
- towing and labor insurance

Bodily injury to others (**bodily injury liability insurance**) covers the risk of bodily injury or death to

Most private property can be insured to reduce the risk of loss.

pedestrians and to the occupants of other cars arising from the negligent operation of the insured's motor vehicle. Under liability insurance, the insurer is liable for damages up to the limit of the insurance purchased. The insurance company must also provide attorneys for the insured's defense in any civil court action.

No-fault insurance, currently required in twelve states[1] and the District of Columbia, places limitations on the insured's ability to sue other drivers, but allows drivers to collect damages and medical expenses from their own insurance carriers regardless of who is at fault in an accident. This coverage helps to cut down on fraudulent and excessively high claims. It also eliminates costly litigation needed to determine the negligence or lack of negligence of people involved in automobile accidents.

Bodily injury caused by an uninsured auto (**uninsured-motorist insurance**) provides protection against the risk of being injured by an uninsured motorist. The coverage applies when the person who caused the accident was at fault and had no bodily injury liability insurance to cover the loss. It protects the insured, the insured's spouse, relatives in the same household, and any other person occupying an insured automobile. It also protects people who are injured by hit-and-run drivers. No coverage is provided to persons injured in an automobile used without the permission of the insured or the insured's spouse. Uninsured-motorist insurance provides no reimbursement for damages to the insured's property.

Bodily injury caused by an underinsured auto (**underinsured-motorist insurance**) provides protection against the risk of being injured by an underinsured motorist. For an insured to collect this insurance, someone without enough bodily injury coverage must have caused the accident.

Medical payments insurance pays for medical (and sometimes funeral) expenses resulting from bodily injuries to anyone occupying the policyholder's car at the time of an accident. In some states, it pays for the medical bills of all family members who are struck by a car or who are riding in someone else's car when it is involved in an accident.

Property damage to someone else's property (**property damage liability insurance**) provides protection when other people bring claims or lawsuits against the insured for damaging property such as a car, a fence, or a tree. The person bringing the claim or suit must prove that the driver of the motor vehicle was at fault.

Collision insurance provides against any loss arising from damage to the insured's automobile caused by accidental collision with another object or with any part of the roadbed. Liability under collision insurance is limited to the insured's car.

Comprehensive coverage provides protection against loss when the insured's car is damaged or destroyed by fire, lightning, flood, hail, windstorm, riot, vandalism, or theft. The insurance company's liability is limited to the actual cash value of the vehicle at the time of the loss.

Substitute transportation insurance reimburses up to specified limits for car rental or transportation costs, including taxi, bus, and train fare, while your car is undergoing covered repairs.

Towing and labor insurance reimburses up to specified limits for towing and labor charges whenever your car breaks down, whether or not an accident is involved.

Health Insurance

With the increasingly high costs of prescriptions, other medical products, and services, affordable health insurance is a foremost need in today's society. Many people obtain health insurance through a group insurance plan where they work. Others have individual plans

---

[1]FL, HI, KS, KY, MA, MI, MN, NJ, NY, ND, PA, UT.

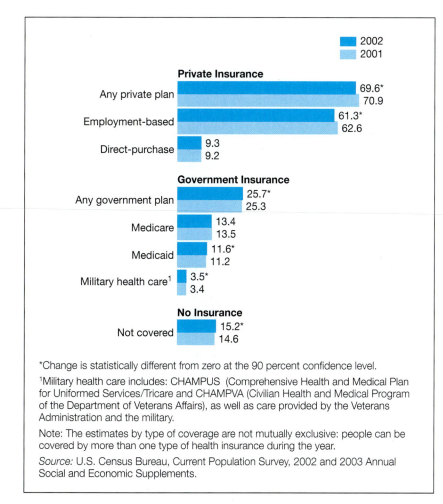

Figure 29-2 Type of health insurance and coverage status: 2001 and 2002 (in percent).

- Among the entire population eighteen to sixty-four years old, workers were more likely to have health insurance (82.0 percent) than nonworkers (74.3 percent). Among those in poverty, workers were less likely to be covered (52.6 percent) than nonworkers (61.9 percent).
- Compared with 2001, the proportion who had employment-based policies in their own name decreased from 56.3 percent to 55.2 percent in 2002.
- Young adults (eighteen to twenty-four years old) were less likely than other age groups to have health insurance coverage—70.4 percent in 2002, compared with 82.0 percent of those 25 to 64 and, reflecting widespread medicare coverage, 99.2 percent of those 66 and over.
- Spells without health insurance, measured on a monthly basis, tend to be short in duration—about three-quarters (74.7 percent) were over within one year.

that they purchase directly from an insurer. Still others have government health insurance plans through government employment, Medicare, and Medicaid (see Figure 29-2). Health insurance policies often include the following benefits:

- physician care
- prescription drugs
- inpatient and outpatient hospital care
- surgery
- dental and vision care
- long-term care for the elderly

Major medical coverage pays for expenses beyond those covered by a basic plan, including long-term hospitalization and catastrophic illness.

HMOs and PPOs Health Maintenance Organizations (HMOs) contract with doctors and other health care professionals to provide health care services for their members.

Members pay monthly premiums and must choose from a list of doctors provided by the HMO. HMOs encourage their members to have regular checkups, immunizations, and other forms of early treatment. In this way, it is hoped that people will be less likely to require more expensive kinds of treatment. Many different kinds of organizations sponsor HMOs, including doctors, community groups, insurance companies, labor unions, and corporations.

A Preferred Provider Organization (PPO) is a group of health care providers, such as doctors or hospitals, who provide care for groups of employees at reduced rates. PPOs are usually sponsored as part of an employer's group health plan. Employees choose among the health care providers on the PPO list when they need treatment. Choosing a non-PPO provider reduces the benefits paid to the insured under the plan.

Medicare and Medicaid   People 65 and over who are covered by Social Security are eligible for **Medicare,** a federally funded health insurance program. Medicare Part A helps pay for inpatient hospital care. Medicare Part B pays for 80 percent of doctors' and other medical services. Many people buy their own medigap insurance to cover the 20 percent not covered by Medicare.

Medicaid is a health care plan for low-income people. State governments administer Medicaid, which is funded by both state and federal funds.

Disability Insurance   Disability insurance pays benefits when one can't work because of a disability. Total, or long-term, disability pays if the insured can't perform normal job duties for a year or longer; partial, or short-term, disability pays for a few months of being disabled.

Long-Term Care Insurance   Long-term care insurance helps pay for home care, whether provided by family and friends or through professional home care organizations, when an insured becomes chronically ill. It also helps cover care received in adult day care, assisted-living facilities, and nursing homes. Benefits are usually payable when an insured is unable to perform certain daily living activities without assistance, such as eating, bathing, dressing, or using the bathroom.

Legal Protection   A variety of state and federal laws help make it easier for people with preexisting conditions to obtain and keep health insurance. A federal law known as HIPAA (Health Insurance Portability and Accountability Act) sets national standards for all health plans. Among its specific protections, HIPAA:

1. Limits the use of preexisting condition exclusions.
2. Prohibits group health plans from discriminating by denying coverage or charging extra for coverage based on a person's or family member's past or present poor health.
3. Guarantees certain small employers, and certain individuals who lose job-related coverage, the right to purchase health insurance.
4. Guarantees, in most cases, that employers or individuals who purchase health insurance can renew the coverage regardless of any health conditions of individuals covered under the insurance policy.

Another federal law known as COBRA (the Consolidated Omnibus Budget Reconciliation Act) allows employees to keep their group insurance for a specific period of time after being laid off. Under COBRA, employees who have been laid off pay their own premiums but can shift to another group plan upon starting a new job.

Business Law in the News
A License to Cherry-Pick

Diana Peek has lost almost everything except her life, and she blames her health insurer for much of that. When the 43-year-old former secretary in Mt. Vernon, Ill., was diagnosed with a brain tumor in October, 2002, she was fully insured for just $162 a month. But her insurer, RightCHOICE Managed Care Inc., which had just been taken over by industry giant WellPoint Health Networks Inc., had announced that it soon would stop providing individual health insurance in Illinois. Customers could shift to another WellPoint unit, UNICARE Life & Health Insurance Co., but that required a medical review unless they were applying for UNICARE's most basic plan.

Suddenly, Peek's brain tumor was a preexisting condition, and UNICARE's best plans wouldn't cover her. She was forced into the basic plan, which covered a much smaller share of her expensive treatments than RightCHOICE would have done. What's more, her premiums nearly tripled, to $472 a month.

Like Peek, some 12,000 customers lost their RightCHOICE coverage. Peek and two other former RightCHOICE customers filed a class action last year against WellPoint and UNICARE. But the law may not be on their side, and WellPoint has moved to dismiss the case. Ken Ferber, a spokesman for the Thousand Oaks, Calif., company, said in a written response to *BusinessWeek:* "WellPoint believes that its actions were in compliance with insurance and other laws, and therefore it will vigorously defend itself in this case."

Health insurers apparently have found a legal loophole big enough to drive a truck through. It allows them to buy another company and then dump the costliest individual policyholders and cherry-pick the healthiest, most profitable ones. According to the laws of 46 states, if a company pulls out of a state's health-insurance market for individuals, it can't return for at least five years. But the state laws don't forbid another company with the same parent from picking up the business. "It's technically legal, but a violation of the spirit of the law," says Kansas Insurance Commissioner Sandy Praeger, who chairs the health-insurance and managed-care committee at the National Association of Insurance Commissioners. The association is due to discuss the issue for the first time at a meeting in San Francisco on June 14, which could step up pressure on states to close the loophole.

Absent action, the problem seems certain to grow as the industry consolidates and companies seek to rationalize overlapping businesses. At the same time, the ranks of individual policyholders have grown as employers limit coverage by their group health plans. The number of people buying health insurance on their own rose to 16.8 million in 2002, from 16.1 million in 2000, according to Deborah J. Chollet, a health policy analyst at Mathematica Policy Research Inc., a Princeton (N.J.)-public policy group. A *BusinessWeek* tally shows that in the last three years, health insurers have culled, or attempted to cull, as many as 28,700 people from their rolls—or forced them to pay steep premium hikes to keep their coverage—after a merger or acquisition.

Few Safeguards

Regulators say there are few real safeguards for individuals when an insurer closes a plan after an acquisition. "We see movement across the health-insurance industry to privatize the good risk and socialize the bad risk," says Scott B. Lakin, director of the Missouri Dept. of Insurance. Indeed, in 32 states, people who don't qualify for private-health insurance end up in state-run high-risk insurance pools and are forced to pay much higher premiums. Just six states, including New York and Massachusetts, guarantee that state residents losing their individual health insurance at one company will be picked up by another offering similar premiums and benefits.

Even if more states finally focus on this issue, any action will come too late for Peek. Today, terminally ill and unable to work, she lives on a $919 monthly disability check and financial help from her 25-year-old daughter. Her car and mobile home were repossessed last year. In recent months, her neighbors have taken collections to help cover her

(Continued)

Business Law in the News (*Continued*)

spiraling treatment costs. In March, no longer able to afford her UNICARE coverage, she dropped if for Medicaid, the government-run health insurance for the poor.

In an era of rapidly rising health-care costs, weeding out costly customers may seem to be smart business. But a merger made sundae-sweet by such tactics can only mean a very bitter cherry for those forced to join the millions who, like Peek, are uninsured or underinsured.

Questions for Analysis

1. According to this article, what is the legal loophole that health insurers apparently have found?

2. As indicated by a *BusinessWeek* count, what have health insurers done in the last three years to increase profits?

3. What health-insurance industry movement has been noticed by the Missouri Department of Insurance?

Source: Brian Grow. "A License to Cherry-Pick," *BusinessWeek,* May 17, 2004, pp. 96–97.

Quick Quiz 29-2 True or False?

1. An insured can cancel a straight life policy at any time and receive its cash surrender value.

2. Term insurance is the most expensive kind of life insurance.

3. With property insurance, unlike life insurance, an insurable interest must exist when a loss occurs.

29-3 Form of the Insurance Contract

In most states, insurance contracts come in a standard form. These standard forms are carefully drafted by an insurance commissioner with help from the state's legal advisers. In this way, the consumer-buyer is protected from deception or fraud. As an additional protection to consumers, some states now require that insurance contracts must be written in clear, understandable language and printed in a readable typeface. Insurance policies, nevertheless, are **adhesion contracts**—that is, contracts drawn by one party that must be accepted as is on a take-it-or-leave-it basis.

Application

The first step in obtaining an insurance policy is to fill in an application. The application is an offer made by the applicant to the insurance company. As with any offer, the offeree, in this case the insurance company, may accept or reject the offer.

Binders

The waiting period between the offer and the acceptance opens the insured to potential risk. To avoid this risk, the insured can arrange to have the insurer issue a binder. A **binder,** or binding slip, will provide temporary insurance coverage until the policy is formally accepted. The binder will include all of the usual terms that would be included in the actual policy to be issued.

Premiums

An insurance contract differs from most other contracts in that it requires the payment of premiums. The amount of the premium is determined by the nature and character of the risk and by how likely the risk is to occur. The premium increases as the chance of loss increases. Thus, a premium on a fireproof building in a city with a fire department will be much lower than the premium on a barn located where firefighting equipment is not available.

Lapse

When the insured stops paying premiums, an insurance contract is said to lapse. This may not mean, however, that the contract will terminate automatically on the date that the last premium is paid. It may also not lapse automatically if the insured makes a delayed payment. Although state laws differ, most states allow for a grace period in which the insured may make payments to keep life and health insurance policies in force. Beyond this period, however, the insurance contract will lapse and the policy will terminate. Automobile and property insurance policies usually have no grace periods and will terminate when a premium is not paid when due.

Quick Quiz 29-3 True or False?

1. An insurance binder provides permanent insurance coverage.

2. Insurance premiums increase as the chance of loss increases.

3. An insurance contract will terminate automatically if a premium payment is not paid on time.

29-4 Cancellation of Insurance Policies

Under certain conditions, the insurer is given a legal right to forfeit, or cancel, an insurance policy. Proof of a forfeiture permits cancellation either before a loss or at the time the claim is made on a policy. Among grounds permitting forfeiture are a breach of warranty and a concealment or misrepresentation of a material fact by the insured (Table 29-2). Neither the

Table 29-2 Cancellation of Insurance Policies

Grounds for Cancellation	Explanation
Warranty violation	Insured fails to abide by restrictions especially written into the policy
Concealment	Insured deliberately withholds fact of material importance to insurer's decision to issue a policy
Misrepresentation	Insured gives false answers to questions in the insurance application that materially affect the insurer's risk

Related Cases After Dewar completed an application for automobile insurance, he submitted a check to cover the premium for the first two months, for which he was issued a binder. The agent for Statewide Insurance Corporation assured him his insurance became in effect "immediately." Dewar's check bounced, but before the insurance company could terminate the binder, Dewar was involved in an accident. The Arizona Supreme Court ruled that Dewar was covered for the damages because of the agent's representation that the policy was in effect immediately, and because the policy's termination does not take effect until after the insured has received notice. *Statewide Ins. Corp. v. Dewar,* 694 2d 1167.

Teaching Tips Explain to students that insurance companies calculate the amount of a premium based on the extent of the risk. This risk is determined by the principle of large numbers, which states that if a large number of people or businesses are exposed to the same risk, a predictable number of losses will occur. The insurance company calculates these figures and determines the appropriate amount of the premium. Because insurance companies are private businesses, they are motivated by profit. Premiums are set high enough to cover expected losses and still earn a profit for the insurance company.

Terms While the word *policy* in an insurance context might seem to be related to the general definition of *policy* as "a plan of action," the two words actually have different origins. The insurance *policy* evolved from Latin, Greek, and Italian words for *demonstration,* whereas the *policy* of planning comes from a Latin word for *administration.*

insured nor the insurer may deny statements or acts previously made or committed that might affect the validity of the policy.

Warranties

A *warranty* is an insured's promise to abide by restrictions, especially those written into a policy that are intended to be conditions precedent to the existence of coverage. By statute in many states, an insurance company has the burden of proof in establishing that a warranty has been breached (broken) by the insured. If this is proved, the insurer may cancel the contract or refuse payment of loss to the insured or to a beneficiary.

Example 29-3

Nicole Duffy, a well-known NASCAR driver, applied for life insurance after being involved in several racing accidents. Community Life was aware of these accidents, and Duffy agreed not to race while the policy remained in force. Duffy was killed while racing in an important race. Community Life could rescind any obligation to pay Duffy's beneficiaries.

Concealment

Fraudulent concealment is any intentional withholding of a fact that would be of material importance to the insurer's decision to issue a policy. The applicant need only give answers to questions asked. However, the insured may not conceal facts that would be material in acceptance of a risk.

Example 29-4

VanDorn, an insurance agent for Canadian Life, inspected Kalintor's building before issuing a fire insurance policy. Kalintor did not show VanDorn the basement, which was filled with flammable chemicals. After the policy was issued, Kalintor's building burned to the ground. Canadian Life later learned of the secret lab and was permitted to cancel Kalintor's policy.

Misrepresentation

If an insured party gives false answers, or *misrepresentations,* to questions in an insurance application that materially affect the risk undertaken by the insurer, the contract is voidable by the insurer. A representation is material if the facts represented influence the insurer's decision to issue the policy or the rate of premium to charge.

Example 29-5

The Clark family applied for fire insurance from the Alabama Farm Bureau Mutual Casualty Insurance Company. The Clarks answered no when asked whether they had ever been arrested. When their house was destroyed by fire and they attempted to

Background Information Lotus Development Corp., Levi Strauss, and MCA are among the companies that formally recognize the concerns of lesbian and gay employees, including providing insurance benefits for their partners. When lesbian and gay employees at Lotus approached the company's management with a request to extend benefits, the self-insured policies were easily adapted. However, the insurance company that provided supplemental coverage for Lotus balked at the idea of covering lesbian and gay couples. When the employees at Lotus submitted a report to the insurance company showing that the costs for treating AIDS were similar to those for treating heart disease, the insurer agreed to cover them.

Background Information In 1991, the New York City Police Department conducted a three-and-a-half month investigation of forty-nine abandoned vehicles. The investigation resulted in forty-nine arrests for insurance fraud. Such fraud schemes might involve individuals stripping their own cars of radios, seats, hoods, and other parts and then abandoning the cars only to "find" them later after reporting them stolen. Insurance companies then would reimburse the owners for the allegedly stolen parts.

collect under the policy, an investigation revealed that the Clarks had both been arrested on previous occasions. The court upheld the Farm Bureau's denial of benefits due to this deliberate material misrepresentation.

Although all jurisdictions agree on the effects of a deliberate deception, there is disagreement as to the effects of an innocent misrepresentation. A majority of the states hold that the intent of the insured is irrelevant. Even an innocent misrepresentation would make the policy voidable by the insurer. A minority of the states would not allow the insurer to deny coverage to an insured whose misrepresentation was unintentional.

Fraud includes the pretense of knowledge when knowledge there is none.

—Benjamin N. Cardozo (1870–1938), American jurist

Example 29-6

Folk took out an insurance policy with Countryside Casualty. When asked if he had any physical impairments, Folk, who suffered from epilepsy, said no. When Folk was killed in an automobile accident, his estate attempted to collect the insurance. Countryside, which had discovered Folk's epilepsy, refused to pay, claiming he had misrepresented his physical health. Evidence indicated that Folk genuinely did not consider his epilepsy, which was controlled by drugs, to be a physical impairment. In a majority of states, Folk's belief would make no difference. The policy would still be voidable by Countryside. In a minority of states, Folk's innocent misrepresentation would not allow Countryside to deny recovery under the policy.

Related Cases Durham took out homeowner's insurance on his house. He later built a workshop addition to his house and used it as a business. The homeowner's insurance had a clause that excluded such structures, but the agent, who had seen the workshop addition, never mentioned the clause to Durham. The structure was badly damaged by a fire, and Durham sued to have the insurance cover the loss. The court ruled that the agent's knowledge of the structure waived the insurance company's right to strictly construe the contract. *Durham v. Cox,* 310 S.E.2d 371.

Estoppel

An insurer may not deny acts, statements, or promises that are relevant and material to the validity of an insurance contract. This bar to denial is called an *estoppel.* When an insurer has given up the right to cancel a policy under certain circumstances by granting the insured a special dispensation, the insurer cannot deny that dispensation when the chance to cancel or deny liability arises.

Example 29-7

Maxwell, an insurance agent for Fidelity, called on MacLaine, who wanted fire insurance to cover her new cabin. The cabin was heated by a woodburning stove that, according to Fidelity's specifications, was located too close to a wooden wall. Maxwell told MacLaine not to worry about those specifications. He then falsified the measurements on the application. Two weeks later, MacLaine's cabin burned to the ground. Due to Maxwell's behavior, Fidelity would be estopped from denying its liability to MacLaine under the policy.

When the insurance company gives up one of its rights in order to help the insured, the company has made a *waiver.* A waiver, which is actually a form of estoppel, can be implied from the conduct of the insurance company. For example, when an insurance company cashes the check of a lapsed policy, it has, in effect, given up or waived its right to cancel that policy. Once a right has been waived, the insurer may not later deny its waiver.

Quick Quiz 29-4 True or False?

1. An insurance company may refuse to pay for a loss if it can prove that the insured breached a warranty to abide by certain restrictions.

2. If an insured gives false answers to questions in an insurance application, the insurance company can do nothing about it unless it discovers the fraud before any loss.

3. An insurer may not deny acts, statements, or promises that are relevant and material to the validity of an insurance contract.

Summary

29-1 Insurance is a transfer of the risk of economic loss from the insured to the insurer. Insurance policies require the elements of a contract: offer, acceptance, mutual assent, capable parties, consideration, and legality. The parties to an insurance contract include the insurer, the insured, and the beneficiary.

29-2 It is possible to obtain insurance for a variety of risks. Life insurance provides funds to a beneficiary on the death of the insured. A beneficiary must have an insurable interest when the policy is issued, but need not have that interest when the insured dies. The principal types of life insurance are straight life, limited-payment life, term, and endowment insurance. Principal types of property insurance include fire, marine, homeowner's, flood, and automobile insurance. In the case of property insurance, the insured must have an insurable interest when the loss occurs. Health insurance helps pay for such things as physician care, prescription drugs, inpatient and outpatient hospital care, surgery, dental

and vision care, and long-term care for the elderly. Federal laws include HIPAA that sets national standards for all health plans, and COBRA that allows employees to keep group insurance for a specific period after being laid off.

29-3 The first step in obtaining an insurance policy is to fill in an application. A binder provides temporary insurance coverage between the time the application is made and the time the policy becomes effective. Premiums are the consideration or payment an insured gives the insurer for its acceptance of risk. A lapse occurs when the insured stops paying premiums.

29-4 Under certain conditions, the insurer is given a legal right to cancel an insurance policy. Grounds permitting cancellation include breach of warranty, concealment of material facts, and misrepresentation on an application. Under the estoppel rule, an insurer is not allowed to deny certain statements, activities, or waivers.

Key Terms

adhesion contracts, 552

annuity, 544

beneficiary, 541

binder, 552

bodily injury liability insurance, 547

coinsurance, 546

collision insurance, 548

comprehensive coverage, 548

deductible, 545

double indemnity, 545

endowment insurance, 544

homeowner's policy, 547

indemnify, 541

inland marine insurance, 546

insurable interest, 541

insurance, 540

insured, 541

Questions for Review and Discussion

1. What contractual elements are found in an insurance policy?
2. Name and describe the principal types of life insurance.
3. What are four situations that might permit the insurer to deny paying life insurance claims?
4. Why are the waiver of premium option and the guaranteed insurability option popular optional provisions of life insurance policies?
5. In what ways do requirements of insurable interests differ in property insurance and life insurance?
6. What are the seven situations in which an insurer's liability under a fire insurance policy may extend beyond the damage caused directly by the fire? List the five examples of the losses that might be covered by a homeowner's policy.
7. Name seven kinds of automobile insurance. What are the risks covered by each of these policies?
8. What benefits are often included in health insurance policies? How does Medicare differ from Medicaid?
9. What is the first step in obtaining an insurance policy? Describe the device used to protect the insured between the time of this first step and the time the policy is actually obtained by the insured.
10. Why do insurance premiums differ from one insured to another? What happens when an insured fails to maintain a policy by missing a premium payment?
11. How might breach of warranty, concealment, and misrepresentation be used by an insurance company to cancel a policy?

Investigating the Internet

Go to **www.google.com** and key in "glossary of insurance terms." Select one of the glossaries that appear and check the meaning of any terms that you are curious about or interested in.

Cases for Analysis

1. Juan Ramos's wife, Maria, became concerned after a violent storm caused disastrous flooding in a community not too far down the river from where their house was located. She felt comforted when her husband told her that they were fully protected against flooding by their homeowner's insurance policy. The following spring, a flood caused serious damage to their home, and Juan's insurance

agent told him that his homeowner's policy did not cover flood damage. What recourse do the Ramoses have against the insurance company?

2. Al Zuni Trading, Inc., purchased a one million dollar life insurance policy on the life of one of its officers, Thomas McKee. Three months later, McKee resigned from the company. Two years later, McKee died. Did Al Zuni Trading, Inc., have an insurable interest in the life of McKee and thus be entitled to the million dollars? Explain. *In Re Al Zuni Trading, Inc.,* 947 F.2d 1403 (9th Cir.).

3. U.S. Aviation Underwriters issued an aircraft insurance policy to Cash Air, Inc., covering its employees. The policy stated that to be covered under the policy, the aircraft must be "flown only by a pilot or pilots described on the Coverage Summary page." Each policy coverage page stated that a pilot not named in the policy must be one who holds "an AA commercial pilot certificate with AA multi-engine and instrument ratings who has flown a minimum of 2,500 hours as pilot in command, at least 1,000 hours of which shall have been in multiengine aircraft and at least 25 hours of which shall have been in Piper PA 31-350 aircraft." Peter Covich, an employee of Cash Air, Inc., did not meet the pilot experience requirements when the Piper Seneca airplane he was piloting crashed, causing personal injuries and property damage. Must the insurance company pay for the loss? Explain. *U.S. Aviation Underwriters v. Cash Air,* 568 N.E.2d 1150 (MA).

4. Victory Container Corporation was owned by the three Radin brothers. Two of those brothers also owned the Warrensburg Paper and Board Corporation. Victory had no direct ownership of the Warrensburg plant, however. Nevertheless, Victory took out a fire insurance policy on the Warrensburg plant. When the Warrensburg property was damaged, Victory attempted to collect under the policy. Did Victory have an insurable interest in the Warrensburg property? Explain. *Victory Container Corporation v. Calvert Fire Insurance Company,* 486 N.Y.S.2d 211 (NY).

5. Avrit and Schuring entered an agreement to purchase a certain property. Each paid $1,000 as a down payment. They were later to pay an additional $25,000. The seller of the property was to maintain insurance until the deal was finalized. Avrit and Schuring also obtained an insurance policy on the property. Before the deal was finalized, fire damaged the property. Avrit and Schuring attempted to collect on their policy, but the insurance company claimed that Avrit and Schuring had no insurable interest at the time of the fire. Did Avrit and Schuring have an insurable interest between the time of the down payment and the time the deal was finalized? Explain. *Avrit v. Forest Industries Insurance Exchange,* 696 P.2d 583 (OR).

6. Martin Searle's life insurance policy contained a standard suicide clause. Under the clause, Allstate would not be liable to the beneficiary, Alice Searle, should Martin commit suicide within the first two years of the policy even if Martin were insane at the time of his death. Martin committed suicide ten months after the policy went into effect. Allstate refused to pay Alice any benefits under the policy. Alice sued the company, claiming that her husband had been mentally deranged at the time of the suicide and did not realize the consequences of his action. Allstate argued that the sanity clause removed the issue of mental incapacity from the case. Who would prevail in a majority of states? Explain. *Searle v. Allstate Life Insurance Company,* 212 Cal. Rptr. 466 (CA).

7. Bayer took his car to Whitaker's auto repair shop for repairs. Whitaker took the car for a test drive, with Bayer seated in the passenger seat. During the test drive, a car operated by another person drove on the wrong side of the road and collided with Bayer's vehicle, injuring Bayer. Neither Bayer's vehicle nor the vehicle owned by the wrongdoer was insured. Whitaker carried insurance on his own vehicles, including uninsured-motorist insurance. Could Bayer recover from Whitaker's insurance company under the uninsured-motorist provision of the policy? Why or why not? *Bayer v. Travelers Indemnity Co.,* 267 S.E.2d 91 (VA).

8. Riggins contacted the Hartford Insurance Company and asked for an all-risk policy for his truck. An underwriter for Hartford agreed to the policy and issued a binder on March 28. On April 2, before the full policy had been executed, Riggins left on a trip, hauling liquor. Sometime during the trip, the liquor was stolen. Hartford refused to pay, arguing that the final policy that would have been issued would not have covered the hauling of liquor. Riggins argued that the all-risk binder was in effect at the time of the theft, and that he was, therefore, covered even though the final policy would not have covered him. Was Riggins correct? Explain. *Hilt Truck Lanes, Inc., v. Riggins,* 756 F.2d 676 (8th Cir).

9. When Sidney Henry applied for insurance with State Farm, he was asked whether he had ever had

recurrent indigestion or a hernia. Henry answered no to each question. In fact, he had experienced recurring indigestion and it had been diagnosed as either an ulcer or a hernia. The policy was issued. Eight months later, Henry died of cancer of the esophagus. When Eula Henry applied for benefits, State Farm denied her request. Eula argued that the misrepresentations were not material because her husband died from cancer, not the illnesses he was questioned about. Was Mrs. Henry correct? Explain. *Henry v. State Farm,* 465 So.2d 276 (LA).

10. On January 13, Lax made out a check to State Farm Insurance to pay for her automobile insur-ance, which had lapsed sixty-two days earlier. Unfortunately, she forgot to mail the check. On January 22, Lax was killed when trying to pass a truck. The check was found in the wreckage and taken to a State Farm agent who mailed it to the main office. The main office, with knowledge of the accident, cashed the check. The beneficiaries argued that State Farm's conduct in cashing the check with knowledge of the accident constituted a waiver of its right to cancel the policy due to her failure to pay by the due date. Were the beneficiaries correct? Explain. *VanHulle v. State Farm,* 254 N.E.2d 457 (IL).

Quick Quiz Answers

29-1	1. F	29-2	1. T	29-3	1. F	29-4	1. T
	2. F		2. F		2. T		2. F
	3. F		3. T		3. F		3. T

Chapter 30

Mortgages and Other Security Devices

The Opening Case

"An Awesomely Secure Feeling"

Owen, a retail appliance dealer, borrowed money from a bank which took a security interest in all of Owen's present and after-acquired inventory and equipment. The bank perfected its security interest by filing. Later, still short of cash, Owen bought some inventory from a wholesaler who also took and perfected a security interest in the inventory that was purchased. Still later, Owen bought a computer on credit from a computer store which also took and perfected a security interest in the computer. Finally, Owen sold a stove and a microwave oven on credit to Cook, a customer, and took a purchase-money security interest in both items. Cook sold the microwave to a friend and paid nothing to Owen for either item. Whose security interest will prevail (a) between the bank and the wholesaler? (b) between the bank and the computer store? (c) between the bank and Cook? (d) between Owen and Cook's friend?

Chapter Outcomes

1. Differentiate between a secured and an unsecured loan and explain why a creditor needs a security interest when lending money or extending credit.
2. Identify six types of mortgages and decide which will best suit a particular fact situation.
3. Outline the legal effect of recording a mortgage and the priorities involved when more than one mortgage is held and recorded on the same property.
4. Describe and distinguish between the rights and duties of the mortgagor and the rights and duties of the mortgagee.
5. List the requirements of a security agreement and describe the events that must occur for a security agreement interest to attach.
6. Decide whether security interests are perfected in cases involving various kinds of collateral.
7. Determine who will have priority when several parties claim a security interest in the same property.
8. Discuss what rights a secured party has when a debtor defaults by failing to make payments when due.

30-1 Necessity of Security Devices

Security is the assurance that a creditor will be paid back for any money loaned or for credit extended to a debtor. Debts are said to be secured when creditors know that somehow they will be able to recover their money. Lenders of money and people who extend credit often require a security device to protect their financial interests. A security device is a way for creditors to get their money back in case the borrower or debtor does not pay. A **secured loan** is one in which creditors have something of value, usually called *collateral,* from which they can be paid if the debtor does not pay. In general, if creditors aren't paid the debt owed to them, they can legally gain possession of the collateral. The collateral is then sold, and the money is used to pay the debt. The right to use the collateral to recover a debt is called the creditor's **security interest.** If creditors lend money but do not require collateral, they have made an unsecured loan. An **unsecured loan** is one in which creditors have nothing of value that they can repossess and sell to recover the money owed to them by the debtor. Both real property and personal property can be used to secure a debt.

30-2 Real Property as Security

When real property is used as security for a loan, a device known as a mortgage is used to establish collateral for the loan. A **mortgage** is a transfer of an interest in property for the purpose of creating a security for a debt. The one who borrows the money (the **mortgagor**) conveys his or her interest in the property to the lender (the **mortgagee**) while at the same time retaining possession of the property. The borrower signs a promissory note (explained in Chapter 25) as evidence of the loan in addition to a mortgage instrument. The mortgage creates a legal claim to the property. This legal claim, also called a *lien,* gives the lender the right to have the property sold if the debt is not paid. Once the land is sold and the debt is paid, the mortgagor's obligation to the mortgagee is over. However, if the sale of the property does not satisfy the whole debt, the mortgagor will still owe the balance.

> ## Example 30-1
>
> Mayo bought a house for $144,000. Of this sum, she put up $50,000 in cash. Mayo then took out a $95,000 loan from the Unicorp Bank to cover the rest of her purchase. When Mayo could not meet the mortgage payments, Unicorp foreclosed and sold the house for $6,593 less than what was owed. Mayo would be personally liable for the $6,593, plus interest, until the debt was paid.

Mortgage Costs

There are many costs connected with obtaining a mortage. Initially, a potential borrower must pay a mortgage application fee, an appraisal fee, a credit report fee, and an inspection fee. If the loan is approved, the borrower often pays an origination fee, which is a charge for issuing the loan. Sometimes, the borrower pays interest in a lump sum up front, called points, to get a lower rate of interest. A point is a one-time charge equal to 1 percent of the principal amount borrowed. Thus, if three points are charged on an $80,000 mortgage, the borrower will be required to pay a one-time fee of 3 percent of $80,000, which amounts to $2,400. If all IRS requirements are met, points are tax deductible.

Other items charged to the borrower include charges for document preparation, attorney's fees, title insurance, surveyor fees, termite inspection, mortgage insurance, and homeowner's insurance.

Terms *Debt* is a modification of the French *dette,* derived from the Latin *debitum,* meaning "to owe." Oddly, *debt,* which first appeared in the fifteenth century, was later promoted by language reformers as the correct spelling of *dette.*

Background Information *Mort* means *dead* and *gage* means *pledge.* Originally, a mortgage was a "dead pledge," meaning that the mortgagor could not use the property during the term of the mortgage and would lose it altogether on default. Today, a mortgagor can use the property during the term of the mortgage.

Did You Know?

The chances of a borrower defaulting on mortgage payments can increase dramatically with life-changing events. They jump:

- 54 percent if the borrower has an unexpected drop in income.
- 26 percent if the borrower gets divorced from his or her spouse.
- 6 percent for each additional household member after the first two.

Teaching Tips Invite a real estate agent to class to discuss the local real estate market. Direct the discussion toward the closing of a real estate transaction, including the various mortgage costs.

Types of Mortgages

There are many different types of real property mortgages (Table 30-1). Some of the most common mortgages are the conventional, the variable-rate, the graduated-payment, the balloon-payment, the Federal Housing Administration (FHA) and Veterans Administration (VA), and deeds of trust.

Conventional Mortgage   A **conventional mortgage** involves no government backing by either insurance or guarantee. The loan is made by private lenders, and the risks of loss are borne exclusively by them. In the past, conventional mortgages had fixed interest rates that stayed the same during the life of the mortgage regardless of fluctuations in the economy. Changes in recent years, however, have resulted in the creation of variations to the fixed-interest-rate mortgage.

Variable-Rate Mortgage   A **variable-** or **flexible-rate mortgage** has a rate of interest that changes according to fluctuations in the index to which it is tied. The index rate may be the bank's prime rate or the Federal Reserve Board discount rate. As the index rate goes up and down, so does the rate of interest charged on the loan. This rate may be more or less than the index rate, but varies with it.

The obvious advantage of the variable-rate mortgage is the drop in the amount of the mortgage payment when the rate drops. However, mortgage payments can also rise when

Table 30-1   Some Methods of Financing a House

Type	Description
Fixed-Rate Mortgage	Fixed interest rate, usually long-term; equal monthly payments; including principal and interest, until debt is paid is full
Variable- or Flexible-Rate Mortgage	Interest rate changes based on a financial index, resulting in possible changes in monthly payments, loan term, and/or principal; some plans have rate or payment caps
Balloon-Payment Mortgage	Monthly payments based on fixed interest rate, usually short-term; payments may cover interest only with principal due in full at term's end
Graduated-Payment Mortgage	Lower monthly payments rise gradually then level off for duration of term; with flexible interest rate, additional payment changes possible, if index changes
Shared-Appreciation Mortgage	Below-market interest rate and lower monthly payments in exchange for a share of profits when property is sold or on a specified date; many variations
Assumable Mortgage	Buyer takes over seller's original, below-market rate mortgage
Seller Take-Back	Seller provides all or part of financing with a first or second mortgage
Wraparound Mortgage	Seller keeps original low-rate mortgage; buyer makes payments to seller who forwards a portion to the lender holding original mortgage; offers lower effective interest rate on total transaction

the rate rises. In general, a change in payments, either up or down, does not occur without some advance warning. Also, variable-rate mortgage agreements must include a maximum rate that cannot be exceeded. In addition, the frequency of these changes in the rate is usually restricted by the terms of the mortgage agreement.

Graduated-Payment Mortgage

A **graduated-payment mortgage** has a fixed interest rate during the life of the mortgage; however, the monthly payments made by the mortgagor increase over the term of the loan. In the first years of the mortgage, the payments are low. The payments gradually increase over time, usually reaching a plateau at which the payments remain fixed. This type of mortgage is advantageous for young people, whose income may be expected to increase as their mortgage payments increase.

Balloon-Payment Mortgage

A **balloon-payment mortgage** has relatively low fixed payments during the life of the mortgage followed by one large final (balloon) payment. The mortgage has a fixed interest rate, but it is written for a short time period, such as five years. At the end of the time period, the mortgagor usually must find new financing, either with the same or with a different lender, at the current interest rate.

Reverse Mortgage

A **reverse mortgage** is a type of loan that allows home owners, over the age of 62, to convert some of the equity in their home into cash while retaining ownership of their home. The loan is repaid when the borrower dies or the property is sold.

FHA and VA Mortgages

Some mortgages, although given by private lenders, are backed by federal agencies. The FHA and the VA are responsible to the lending institution in the event of a mortgagor's default and foreclosure on an FHA or VA mortgage. The U.S. government, through these agencies, reimburses the mortgagee for any loss and takes over the property. Such properties are then offered for sale to interested buyers to recover the government's loss. The Government National Mortgage Association (Ginnie Mae), through its *Mortgage-Backed Securities* program, guarantees the money provided by investors will be paid back.

Another way the federal government is involved with home mortgages is through two government agencies: the Federal Home Loan Mortgage Corp. (Freddie Mac), and the Federal National Mortgage Association (Fannie Mae). These agencies are federally chartered corporations with publicly traded stock that are set up to encourage investment in home mortgages. Many banks and mortgage companies make their profits on points and then sell their mortgages to Freddie Mac or Fannie Mae. The banks and mortgage companies that originate the loans are also paid to service them—that is, collect the monthly payments and foreclose when necessary.

Deed of Trust

In some states, a deed of trust is used instead of a mortgage. In a conventional mortgage, the mortgagor conveys all or part of his or her interest in the property directly to the mortgagee. Under a **deed of trust,** the mortgagor conveys his or her interest in the property to a disinterested third party, known as a trustee. The mortgagor remains on the property, but the trustee holds certain rights to that property as security for the mortgagor's creditors. If the debtor defaults, the trustee can sell the property for the benefit of those creditors. The provisions of many deeds of trust allow the trustee to sell the property without going to court. For this reason, some legal authorities do not consider a deed of trust a true mortgage, since true mortgages require a foreclosure action for the sale of the property (see page 568).

(see page 568).

Teaching Tips   Discuss the value of shopping carefully for the best interest rates when taking on a mortgage. One lending firm reported that in any given week across the United States, the spread between the highest and lowest thirty-year fixed-rate mortgage is about two percentage points. By borrowing at the low end of such a range, a person could save nearly $200 a month on a $150,000 loan, or about $77,000 over the life of the loan.

Terms   A conventional mortgage is often referred to as a *fixed-rate mortgage.* A flexible-rate mortgage is the same as an *adjustable-rate mortgage (ARM).*

Not all mortgages are the same. Each type is designed to meet the needs of specific groups of borrowers.

Federal Protection

The Real Estate Settlement Procedures Act (RESPA), a federal law, gives consumers protection when they apply for a loan. Under this law, the lender must give the consumer a copy of a booklet that explains the real estate settlement procedure. The lender must also give the consumer an estimate of the costs that will be incurred in obtaining the loan. Later, a uniform settlement statement must be filled out, which shows the exact cost of the settlement. Consumers have the right to see the completed form on the day before the closing if they wish. The lender must also give the consumer a truth-in-lending statement showing the true costs of the interest and finance charge on the mortgage loan.

Another federal law, the Private Mortgage Insurance (PMI) Act, requires homeowners to take out private mortgage insurance when they take out a mortgage with less than a 20 percent down payment. This insurance protects the lender from default losses in the event a loan becomes delinquent. The law provides two situations in which borrower-paid PMI may be canceled, automatically or by request:

- *Automatically.* In general, when the homeowner's equity position reaches 22 percent of the original value of the property, the lender must automatically cancel the PMI. The borrower must be current in making payments for automatic cancellation to apply. Different requirements exist for high-risk mortgage loans.

- *By request.* Homeowners can request cancellation of the PMI when their equity position reaches 20 percent of the original value of the property, if they meet certain criteria.

Recording the Mortgage

Like a deed, a mortgage must be in writing and delivered to the recorder's office in the county where the property is located. Recording a mortgage notifies any third party who may be interested in purchasing the property or in lending money to the owner that the mortgagee has an interest in the real property covered by the mortgage. If the mortgage is not recorded and a later mortgage is given on the same property, the new mortgage is superior to the first. The second mortgagee must not know about the first mortgage and must record the mortgage properly. A failure to record the first mortgage, however, would not remove the obligation of the mortgagor to the first mortgagee. The debt would simply be unsecured.

Example 30-2

Klein needed $20,000 to cover several bad investments. She obtained the money from the Newman Financial Bank by giving the bank a first mortgage on her house. The bank failed to have the mortgage properly recorded. Silver later bought the house from Klein. Since Silver found no mortgage against the property recorded in the county recorder's office, he took the house free of the mortgage. Klein, however, still owed the bank $20,000 plus interest.

Junior Mortgages

Sometimes an owner of real property may execute a junior mortgage on the property. A **junior mortgage,** also called a **second** (or subsequent) **mortgage,** is a mortgage subject to a prior mortgage. For example, if a homeowner wants to improve the mortgaged property and needs another loan to do so, he or she may use the property as security for another loan. If this transaction occurs, the mortgagor is said to have executed a second mortgage on the property. Some people have three or more mortgages on one parcel of property. If all the mortgages are recorded, the holders of second and subsequent mortgages may exercise their rights against the property only after prior mortgages have been paid off. Thus, if the first mortgagee causes the property to be sold and is paid off in full, the second and subsequent mortgages are paid out of the proceeds that remain. The first mortgagee acts as a trustee of the surplus funds for the benefit of the junior mortgagees.

Example 30-3

Zelentz wanted to add a new bedroom onto his house but did not have the ready cash. His house was already mortgaged to Mercedes Savings and Loan for $80,000. Nevertheless, he decided to take out a second mortgage with Cuyahoga Savings. Cuyahoga loaned Zelentz $10,000 because he pledged his home as security should he fail to repay the loan. When Zelentz defaulted on the mortgage to Mercedes and the loan from Cuyahoga, Mercedes caused the house to be sold for $90,000. Since Mercedes held the first mortgage, it was paid first. After Mercedes had its $80,000, Cuyahoga would collect its $10,000.

Holders of first mortgages sometimes enter into a **subordination agreement** in which they agree to allow their mortgage to be reduced in priority to a person holding a second mortgage. Their mortgage is **subordinated;** that is, placed in a lower order than the second mortgage. The agreement is recorded at the Registry of Deeds and has the effect of turning a second mortgage into a first mortgage and turning a first mortgage into a second mortgage.

A **home equity loan** is an example of a junior mortgage. It is either an outright loan or a line of credit made available to homeowners based on the value of the property over and above any existing mortgages. Such a loan takes advantage of the equity that has built up in one's home over a period of time. Home equity loans are often used to consolidate credit card balances or other debts that have higher interest rates. Unlike interest paid on a credit card balance, interest paid on a home equity loan is tax deductible.

Rights and Duties of the Mortgagor

By law and by agreement, the mortgagor has certain rights and certain duties in conjunction with the mortgage. First, the mortgagor has the right to possess the property. Also, the mortgagor has the right to any income produced by the property. For instance, the mortgagor would be entitled to any rent proceeds gained from leasing all or part of the property. The mortgagor could, however, assign this right to the mortgagee which is sometimes done as a condition to executing the original mortgage agreement.

In addition, the mortgagor has the right to use the property for a second or third mortgage. Finally, the mortgagor has the **equity of redemption,** that is, the right to pay off the mortgage in full, including interest, and to thus discharge the debt in total.

In addition to these rights, the mortgagor also has certain duties. Chief among these duties is to make payments on time. Mortgagors must also preserve and maintain the mortgaged property for the benefit of the mortgagee's interest and security. Similarly, the mortgagor is often required to insure the property for the benefit of the mortgagee to the amount of the mortgaged debt.

The mortgagor must pay all taxes and assessments that may be levied against the property. Frequently, the mortgagor will ease the burden of these obligations by paying a percentage of the insurance premium and taxes each month along with the mortgage payment. The mortgagee holds the money in an escrow account. An escrow account is a special account into which money is deposited before the payment of the insurance or taxes is due.

Cross-Cultural Notes In Japan, housing-loan companies were set up in the 1960s to provide mortgages for individual home-owners. In the late 1980s, as banks began to issue more home loans, the housing-loan companies began to lend heavily to property developers. Many of these developers assumed too much risk and were unable to repay the loans, so by 1992, many of the housing-loan companies were experiencing financial difficulties. Ultimately, the banks that were financing the housing-loan companies had to assume the bad debts.

Getting Students Involved When interest rates on loans drop, people often take out home equity loans, which are junior mortgages. Have students research local financial institutions to see how competitive the equity loan rates are. What is the great tax advantage of a home equity loan as opposed to an unsecured loan?

Further Reading Peter G. Miller's *The Common-Sense Mortgage, How to Cut the Cost of Home Ownership by $100,000 or More* (New York: Harper-Perennial, 1991) is an excellent reference on the choices available in customized home financing.

State Variations Connecticut, Minnesota, Massachusetts and Washington still follow the English Common Law rule that grants the mortgagee legal "title" to the property until the mortgage has been satisfied or foreclosed.

Business Law in the News
¡Hola, Amigo! You're Approved

When José Octavio Cano, 60, moved to Houston from Mexico with his wife and teenage son early last year, he boasted a valid work visa and a hefty salary. But without a credit history in the U.S., the programming executive for Spanish-language Liberman Broadcasting Corp. couldn't buy a home. Instead, he was paying more than $2,000 a month in rent—a huge waste, he felt.

Then, last July, General Motors Acceptance Corp.'s mortgage-lending unit launched Settle America, a home-loan program catering to new immigrants. It was Cano's lucky day. By considering his rent- and utility-payment history instead of the usual credit score, GMAC accepted a smaller downpayment than normal, just 3%, and lent him $320,000 to buy a four-bedroom house with a pool.

As lenders look to keep lucrative mortgage-origination income flowing, they are often bending age-old credit rules to appeal to America's fast-growing immigrant population. Just 48% of Hispanics own a home, vs. 68% for the overall population. Says Anna L. Paulson, senior economist at the Federal Reserve Bank of Chicago: "This is where the growth in the [housing] market is going to come from."

Banks are trying to exploit that potential by tailoring their requirements to meet the needs of immigrant groups, though anyone can apply for these loans. Wells Fargo & Co. allows the incomes of a spouse and an unlimited number of aunts, uncles, and cousins to count for up to 30% of the income that is needed to qualify for a loan. It will also accept as much as 30% of qualifying income to be in cash, though normally it wouldn't accept any. Such concessions recognize the realities of the lifestyles of new immigrants. They're more than twice as likely to have members of their extended family living with them than non-Hispanic whites, according to the Census Bureau. Besides, many Hispanics are paid in cash for jobs such as landscaping and housecleaning. Wells Fargo's mortgage lending to Hispanics has more than tripled since 1997, to $5.1 billion.

More than 200 mortgage lenders have jumped on the bandwagon, especially since 2000, when Fannie Mae and Freddie Mac started to buy loans with less stringent status and income requirements than before. For example, GMAC's program allows borrowers to put down as little as $1,000. Cash gifts from family members or communal funds also can be used as downpayments. At Bank of America Corp., first-time mortgages to Hispanics rose 30.1% last year, in part because it now allows up to four family members on an application. "The whole household functions as a middle-class unit," says former Housing & Urban Development Secretary Henry G. Cisneros, now chairman of American CityVista, a homebuilding joint venture with KB Home that largely targets Hispanics.

In fact, some lenders are even rushing to sign up Hispanics with a questionable legal status in the U.S. Undocumented immigrants, mostly from Mexico, apply for an Internal Revenue Service ID number. Using that in conjunction with a Mexican consular ID recognized by more than 70 financial institutions, they apply for a mortgage. Chicago's Second Federal Savings has made $15 million in such loans and expects to issue up to $10 million worth each month this year.

Lending to immigrants can be risky. Cash-based incomes are hard to verify. And immigrant mortgages are still so new that many can't be packaged for resale as mortgage-backed securities, which banks use to spread some of their lending risks. So banks are stepping up counseling for immigrant homeowners and training loan officers to scrutinize mortgage applications from recent arrivals more closely.

They may be worrying too much. On home loans insured by the Federal Housing Authority, Hispanics had a default rate of 1.15% in 2002, and Asians just 0.59%, vs 2.78% for whites, according to a study last year by the Congressional Budget Office. Says GMAC Executive Vice-President Rick A. Gillespie: "There are qualified people who are outside the [homeownership] walls, but they are quality customers." Now, José Cano and many other immigrant homeowners can say "*bienvenido a mi casa.*"

Questions for Analysis

1. Why was José Octavio Cano unable to buy a house when he first moved to Houston from Mexico even though he earned a large salary?

2. What change did GMAC make that allowed Cano to obtain a mortgage?

3. What have Wells Fargo, GMAC, and Bank of America done to allow some families to qualify for a loan?

4. How are some undocumented Hispanic immigrants able to obtain mortgage loans?

5. In what way is lending to immigrants risky?

6. In 2002, what was the default rate of FHA insured home loans to (a) Hispanics? (b) Asians? (c) Whites?

Source: Brian Grow. "¡Hola, Amigo! You're Approved," *BusinessWeek,* April 12, 2004, p. 84.

The money stays in the account until the time comes to pay the insurance or tax. The mortgagee then takes the money out of the account and makes the payments.

Rights and Duties of the Mortgagee

The mortgagee has the unrestricted right to sell, assign, or transfer the mortgage to a third party. Whatever rights the mortgagee had in the mortgage are then the rights of the assignee. The only way the mortgagor could stop the mortgagee from assigning the mortgage is to pay the mortgagee everything owed on the mortgage. Sometimes an assignment by the mortgagee to another mortgagee can cause unforeseen problems for the mortgagor.

Example 30-4

The Chamberlins financed the purchase of their house through the Midway Savings Bank, a local bank with only four branches, all in the city of Bromfield. The Chamberlins made their mortgage payments faithfully each month, in person, at the branch on their street. Without warning, they received notice that Midway had assigned their mortgage to the Unicorp Mortgage Corporation, a multimillion-dollar financial institution headquartered in New York. Although the Chamberlins had no desire to deal with Unicorp, they had no choice in the matter. The only way they could avoid dealing with Unicorp would be to make full payment of the mortgage debt.

Background Information In the fourteenth and fifteenth centuries, British common law mortgages gave the mortgagee the right to title and immediate possession of the property at any time. However, if the mortgagor paid the loan on the property in full on a specific day, known as the *law day,* the mortgagor had the right to enter and repossess the property. If the mortgagor did not make the final payment on the law day, all rights to the property were forfeited, even if the mortgagor tried to make the payment but could not locate the mortgagee to do so. By the seventeenth century, the courts had begun allowing the mortgagor to redeem the property within a reasonable time after law day, a practice that became known as the mortgagor's "equity of redemption."

Mortgagees have the right to receive each installment payment as it falls due. Frequently, mortgagees will include a term in the mortgage agreement allowing an **acceleration** of the debt if the mortgagor fails to meet an installment payment. This term means that a default on one installment payment will make the entire balance due immediately, giving the mortgagee the right to collect the full amount. In general, a clause allowing acceleration must be executed in good faith. In other words, before invoking the acceleration clause, the mortgagee must genuinely believe that the mortgagor will not be able to make good on the debt and that the mortgagee's security interest is therefore threatened. If the matter ends up in court, the mortgagor will have the burden of proving that the mortgagee did not act in good faith.

Background Informa-tion In the seventeenth century, British courts be-gan to make provisions for upholding the rights of both mortgagees and mortgagors. Mortgagors were granted the right to a reasonable time in which to redeem their property after defaulting. However, if a mortgagor did not pay the loan on a specific day and did not bring a suit to redeem the property, a mortgagee could present a bill to the courts that in-cluded the details of the mortgagor and default. The court would then order the mortgagor to pay the debt within a fixed period of time. Failure to comply with a court order meant that the mortgagor's right to redeem was barred for-ever, a practice known as *strict foreclosure*.

U.S. Const. Amend-ment 14 (page 861)

Related Cases Laber took out a mortgage on property that included a gas station and other build-ings. The mortgage had a clause that stated that the buildings could not be de-stroyed without the con-sent of the mortgagee, and it contained an acceleration clause in the event of de-fault. Laber, however, razed the buildings and the mort-gagee sued to foreclose and accelerate. The court ruled that even though the vacant lot was worth more than the amount due on the mortgage, once the mortgage's terms were breached, the mortgagee was entitled to foreclosure. *Laber v. Minassian*, 511 N.Y.S.2d 516.

State Variations South Dakota statute specifically requires that the Sheriff's mortgage foreclosure sale take place on the front steps of the courthouse.

A Question of Ethics

The Chamberlins' mortgage, in Example 30-4, was assigned by their local bank to a multimillion-dollar financial institution headquartered in New York. The assignment was done without the Chamberlins' consent, and they had no desire to deal with the distant bank. The assignment of the mortgage by the bank was legal; however, was it ethical? Explain your response.

If the mortgagor has defaulted or has failed to perform some other agreement in the mortgage, the mortgagee has the right to apply to a court to have the property sold. This right is called **foreclosure.** It takes priority even when the mortgagor files for bankruptcy. Since, in a majority of jurisdictions, a mortgage is a lien on the land, a foreclosure is an equitable action. The mortgagor does not have a right to a jury trial in a foreclosure action.

A mortgage is foreclosed when the mortgagee proves the amount of the unpaid debt (including interest and other charges) and the property is sold by and under the direction of a court. The proceeds from the sale are then applied to the payment of the debt. Any money remaining after the claims of the mortgagee have been satisfied goes to the mortgagor or to the second and subsequent mortgagees.

The mortgagee's financial interest in mortgaged property gives rise to certain consti-tutional rights. Under Amendment 14 to the U.S. Constitution, mortgagees cannot lose their interest in property without due process of law.

Example 30-5

Northmore Bank and Trust made a $456,000 loan to Perez. It secured that loan with a mortgage on a warehouse owned by Perez. The county commissioners wanted the Perez property for an expansion of the county airport. The county paid Perez a nominal amount for the warehouse and then had it demolished. Northmore received no notice of the demolition until after the building had been torn down. Northmore sued the county, claiming that its constitutional due process rights had been violated. The court agreed with Northmore's claim.

Mortgagees also have certain duties imposed by law. Both state and federal legisla-tion prohibits lenders from discriminating against borrowers because of race, creed, color, sex, or ethnic background. Such legislation imposes a duty to use nondiscriminatory cri-teria in approving and disapproving mortgage applications. For example, a lender may not refuse a mortgage to a prospective borrower simply because that borrower is a woman. Similarly, a lender could not refuse a mortgage to a borrower because that borrower is Hispanic. The mortgagee also has the duty to respect all rights properly claimed by the mortgagor.

Purchase by Mortgage Takeover

Mortgages often contain a clause providing that if the property is sold, the mortgage becomes due and payable. If the mortgage does not contain such a clause, the property may be sold with the mortgage remaining on it. In such takeovers, the transfer of title to a new buyer is subject to the buyer's payment of the seller's mortgage at the existing rate of interest.

In purchasing a property already mortgaged, the buyer will either **assume the mortgage** or take the property **subject to the mortgage.** When buyers decide to assume the mortgage, they agree to pay it. When they take the property subject to a mortgage, the seller agrees to continue paying the debt.

Quick Quiz 30-1 & 30-2 True or False?

1. A security device is a way for creditors to get their money back in case the borrower or debtor does not pay.

2. A home equity loan is an example of a junior mortgage

3. The mortgagor has the right to possess the mortgaged property and to any income produced by the property unless otherwise assigned.

30-3 Personal Property as Security

Article 9 of the UCC brings all personal property security devices, or security interests, together under one law. The property that is subject to the security interest is called **collateral.** A security interest is created by a written agreement, called a **security agreement,** which identifies the goods and is signed by the debtor. The lender or seller who holds the security interest is known as the **secured party.** A security interest is said to *attach* when the secured party has a legally enforceable right to take that property and sell it to satisfy the debt. It is said to be **perfected** when the secured party has done everything that the law requires to give the secured party greater rights to the goods than others have.

The following definitions apply to secured transactions:

- **Consumer goods** are goods that are used or bought for use primarily for personal, family, or household purposes. **UCC 9-102(23)**

- **equipment** are goods other than inventory, farm products, or consumer goods. **UCC 9-102(33)**

- **farm products** are crops or livestock or supplies used or produced in farming operations. **UCC 9-102(34)**

- **inventory** are goods other than farm products held for sale or lease, or raw materials used or consumed in a business. **UCC 9-102(48)**

- **fixtures** are goods that are so related to real estate that an interest arises in them under real estate law. **UCC 9-102(41)**

- **purchase money security interest** is a security interest taken by a lender or a seller of an item to secure its price. **UCC 9-103**

- **buyer in the ordinary course of business** is a person who in good faith and without knowledge that the sale is in violation of ownership rights or security interest of a third party buys goods in ordinary course from a person in the business of selling goods of that kind, not including a pawnbroker. **UCC 1-201(9) (see page 867)**

Security Agreement

A security agreement is an agreement that creates a security interest. It must be in writing, signed by the debtor, and contain a description of the collateral that is used for security. **UCC 9-105(l)**

Teaching Tips Inform students that one of the questions that should be asked when shopping for a mortgage is whether the lending institution intends to service the loan. "Servicing the loan" means that the institution lends the money and keeps the loan, takes payments, and then returns the note when paid in full. When mortgages are sold to the secondary market, problems may arise.

Getting Students Involved Ask students to create lists of everything they own that might be considered collateral by a lending institution. Then have students form small groups to discuss whether each of their items would or would not be regarded by banks as collateral, based on each item's assumed value according to general society.

Example 30-6

Moody Industries contracted to purchase certain robotics equipment from Universal. Moody's president signed a promissory note identifying Universal as a secured party. When Moody filed for bankruptcy, Universal claimed to have a security interest in the robotics equipment. Since the promissory note did not describe the collateral, Universal did not hold a valid security interest in the equipment.

If Universal had provided enough information about the collateral to allow the court to identify it without a detailed description, the result would have been different. Had Universal made reference to the equipment by including certain purchase order or invoice numbers, the court could have identified the equipment and would have upheld the validity of the security agreement.

Attachment of a Security Interest

UCC 9-203

To be effective, a security interest must be legally enforceable against the debtor. This is known as **attachment.** Attachment occurs when three conditions are met. First, the debtor has some ownership or possessive rights in the collateral. Second, the secured party (or creditor) transfers something of value, such as money, to the debtor. Third, the secured party takes possession of the collateral or signs a security agreement that describes the collateral.

Example 30-7

Conroy loaned Lightfoot $5,000 for six months at 8 percent interest. Lightfoot secured the debt by giving Conroy several uncut diamonds that Lightfoot owned. Conroy agreed to return the diamonds when Lightfoot paid the debt. The security interest was legally enforceable because all three conditions were met. First, Lightfoot had ownership rights in the diamonds. Second, Conroy gave Lightfoot something of value (the $5,000). Finally, Conroy took possession of the diamonds. The security interest would also have attached if Lightfoot had kept the diamonds but signed a security agreement describing them.

UCC 9-204

Creditors may obtain security interests in property acquired by the debtor after the original agreement is entered. The creditor does this by placing a provision in the security agreement that the security interest of the creditor also applies to goods the debtor acquires at a later time. It is known as a **floating lien.** This is important to creditors who take security interests in goods, such as food items, that are sold and replaced within short periods of time. The lien is lost when the goods are sold but is regained as soon as the debtor takes possession of the new property.

Perfection of a Security Interest

When a security interest attaches, it is effective only between debtor and creditor. Such creditors, however, will want to make certain that no one else can claim that collateral before they do if the debtors fail to pay them back. To preserve the right to first claim on the collateral, creditors must perfect their interest. A security interest can be perfected in one of three ways: by filing a financing statement in the appropriate government office, by attachment alone, or by possession of the collateral.

Perfection by Filing Security interests in most kinds of personal property are perfected by filing a financing statement in a public office. The office may be a central one (secretary of state's office) or a local one (county recorder or city clerk) where the debtor resides or has a place of business. The proper office for filing depends on the type of collateral and varies from state to state.

A financing statement must give the names of the debtor and the secured party. It must be signed by the debtor and give the address of the secured party from which information concerning the security interest may be obtained. It must also give a mailing address of the debtor and contain a statement indicating the types, or describing the items, of collateral. When the financing statement covers such things as fixtures, crops, timber, minerals, oil, and gas, the statement must also contain a description of the real estate concerned.

UCC 9-302

Example 30-8

Dig Big Excavator, Inc., was the low bidder on a job to clear a 50-acre wood lot on which a shopping center was to be built. The company borrowed $40,000 from the Second National Bank to purchase some equipment it needed for the job. To secure the loan, the bank required Dig Big's president to sign a security agreement that described the equipment that was purchased. The security agreement was perfected when the bank filed this UCC financing statement with the secretary of state's office and the city hall where the business was located.

UCC FINANCING STATEMENT
FOLLOW INSTRUCTIONS (front and back) CAREFULLY

A. NAME & PHONE OF CONTACT AT FILER [optional]
Cary Havitall, (603) 907-1234

B. SEND ACKNOWLEDGMENT TO: (Name and Address)
Second National Bank
42 Main Street
E. Hampstead, NH 03826

THE ABOVE SPACE IS FOR FILING OFFICE USE ONLY

1. DEBTOR'S EXACT FULL LEGAL NAME-insert only one debtor name (1a or 1b)-do not abbreviate or combine names

1a. ORGANIZATION'S NAME				
Dig Big Excavator, Inc.				
1b. INDIVIDUAL'S LAST NAME	FIRST NAME	MIDDLE NAME		SUFFIX

1c. MAILING ADDRESS	CITY	STATE	POSTAL CODE	COUNTRY
205 Hunt Pond Rd.	Sandown	NH	03873	USA

1d. SEE INSTRUCTIONS	ADD'L INFO RE ORGANIZATION DEBTOR	1e. TYPE OF ORGANIZATION	1f. JURISDICTION OF ORGANIZATION	1g. ORGANIZATIONAL ID #, if any [X] NONE

2. ADDITIONAL DEBTOR'S EXACT FULL LEGAL NAME-insert only one debtor name (2a or 2b)-do not abbreviate or combine names

2a. ORGANIZATION'S NAME				
2b. INDIVIDUAL'S LAST NAME	FIRST NAME	MIDDLE NAME		SUFFIX

2c. MAILING ADDRESS	CITY	STATE	POSTAL CODE	COUNTRY

2d. SEE INSTRUCTIONS	ADD'L INFO RE ORGANIZATION DEBTOR	2e. TYPE OF ORGANIZATION	2f. JURISDICTION OF ORGANIZATION	2g. ORGANIZATIONAL ID #, if any [ ] NONE

3. SECURED PARTY'S NAME (or NAME of TOTAL ASSIGNEE of ASSIGNOR S/P) - insert only one secured party name (3a or 3b)

3a. ORGANIZATION'S NAME				
Second National Bank				
3b. INDIVIDUAL'S LAST NAME	FIRST NAME	MIDDLE NAME		SUFFIX

3c. MAILING ADDRESS	CITY	STATE	POSTAL CODE	COUNTRY
42 Main Street	E. Hampstead	NH	03826	USA

4. This FINANCING STATEMENT covers the following collateral:

North Star Hydraulic 20-ton log splitter
30 HP Nortrac tractor #N644L3
18 HP 1.5 ton Mini Excavator #EX77304
30 HP Nortrac Bulldozer #721H35

5. ALTERNATIVE DESIGNATION [if applicable]:	LESSEE/LESSOR	CONSIGNEE/CONSIGNOR	BAILEE/BAILOR	SELLER/BUYER	AG. LIEN	NON-UCC FILING

6.	This FINANCING STATEMENT is to be filed [for record] (or recorded) in the REAL ESTATE RECORDS. Attach Addendum [if applicable]	7. Check to REQUEST SEARCH REPORT(S) on Debtor(s) [ADDITIONAL FEE] [optional]	All Debtors	Debtor 1	Debtor 2

8. OPTIONAL FILER REFERENCE DATA

FILING OFFICE COPY — UCC FINANCING STATEMENT (FORM UCC1) (REV. 05/22/02)

UCC 9-302(1)(d)

Perfection by Attachment Alone   A purchase money security interest in *consumer goods* is perfected the moment it attaches with the exception of motor vehicles and fixtures. Security interests on motor vehicles are perfected by making a note of the lien on the certificate of title issued by the state government. Security interests on fixtures are perfected by filing a financing statement at the registry of deeds where the land is located.

UCC 9-302(3)(b)

State Variations Security interests in certain collateral may not be perfected by the filing of a UCC financing statement. For example, a security interest in a motor vehicle may only be perfected by noting the lien on the certificate of title.

Example 30-9

Sabatini purchased a new 34″ widescreen HDTV for $1,999.99 from Steinbeck's TV Outlet. To pay for the TV, she borrowed the money from the Atlantic Finance Company, which took a security interest in the TV by entering into a security agreement with Sabatini. Since this was a purchase money security interest and the TV set was a consumer good, the security interest would become perfected the moment it attached; that is, when Sabatini signed the agreement, received the TV set, and Steinbeck received payment from the finance company.

UCC 9-313

Perfection by Possession   A security interest may be perfected when the secured party (the creditor) takes possession of the collateral. This is called a *pledge*. The borrower, or debtor, who gives up the property, is the pledgor. The secured party, or creditor, is the pledgee. A secured party who has possession of the collateral must take reasonable care of the property. The debtor must reimburse the secured party for any money spent to take care of the property.

Teaching Tips Auto mechanics can perfect a lien on a car they fixed by retaining possession of the car. This is technically called a mechanic's lien, and it applies to any type of item fixed. The party that fixed the item may keep it until the debt is paid in full. Often it is the only leverage available to the shop.

Example 30-10

After Sabatini paid off the debt to the Atlantic Finance Corporation, she decided to buy a compact disc player. This time she borrowed the money from her cousin, Colter, who agreed to lend Sabatini the money only if he could have her VCR as security until she repaid him. Colter's security interest in the VCR became perfected when he took possession of it.

Priorities and Claims

Sometimes, two or more parties claim a security interest in the same collateral. At other times, unsecured parties claim that they have better rights than secured parties. The UCC helps resolve these conflicts. The following are some of the provisions, stating who prevails over whom in particular situations:

UCC 9-312(3)

1. A perfected *purchase money security interest* in inventory has priority over a conflicting security interest in the same inventory.

UCC 9-312(4)

UCC 9-307(1)

UCC 9-301(1)(c)

2. A *purchase money security interest* in collateral other than inventory has priority over a conflicting security interest in the same collateral if it is perfected when the debtor receives the collateral or within ten days thereafter.

UCC 9-307(2)

3. Buyers of goods in the ordinary course of business (except farm products) prevail over security interests in the seller's inventory.

UCC 9-301

UCC 9-312(5)(a)

UCC 9-312(5)(b)

4. Buyers of farm products in the ordinary course of business, to the extent that they pay for and receive collateral without knowledge of the security interest, take precedence over nonperfected security interests.

UCC 9-601

5. Buyers of *consumer goods* take free of perfected security interests of which they have no knowledge.

The Opening Case Revisited

"An Awesomely Secure Feeling"

(a) Between the bank and the wholesaler, the wholesaler will prevail because a perfected purchase money security interest in inventory has priority over a conflicting security interest in the same inventory (rule 1 on previous page).

(b) Between the bank and the computer store, the computer store will prevail because the purchase money security interest was in collateral other than inventory (a computer) but was perfected when the collateral was received (rule 2 on previous page).

(c) Between the bank and Cook, Cook will prevail because buyers of goods in the ordinary course of business prevail over security interests in the seller's inventory (rule 3 on previous page).

(d) Between Owen and Cook's friend, Cook's friend will prevail because buyers of consumer goods take free of perfected security interests of which they have no knowledge (rule 5 on previous page).

Teaching Tips Students may mistakenly believe that as long as they make some type of payment on a loan, even if it is much smaller than their fixed installment, their creditor cannot force them to pay in court or turn over their accounts to a collection bureau. Remind students that a loan is a contract and that the terms of the contract regarding periodic payments cannot be altered without the consent of all involved parties.

6. In all other cases, a perfected security interest prevails over an unperfected security interest.

7. Conflicting security interests rank according to priority in time of filing or perfection.

8. When two or more parties have unperfected security interests in the same collateral, the first to attach prevails over the other parties.

Collateral may be repossessed by the lender if a borrower defaults on a loan.

Default of the Debtor

If a debtor defaults by failing to make payments when due, the secured party may satisfy the debt by taking possession of the collateral. Because of the difficulties of doing this, the perfection of a security interest by possession, as in a pledge, is better than other types of perfection. Collateral may be repossessed without going through the court if it can be done without causing a disturbance; otherwise, the creditor must use legal process.

After repossessing the goods, the secured party (the creditor) may sell them at a public auction or private sale. The terms of the sale must be reasonable, and the debtor must be given notice of the time and place of any public auction so that he or she may bid on them personally. If the goods are consumer goods and the debtor has paid 60 percent or more of the cash price of a purchase money security interest, the secured party cannot keep the goods. They must be sold.

Quick Quiz 30-3 True or False?

1. A security interest is perfected when the secured party has a legally enforceable right to take that property and sell it to satisfy the debt.

2. Security interests in most kinds of personal property are perfected by filing a financial statement in a public office.

3. Buyers of goods in the ordinary course of business (except farm products) prevail over security interests in the seller's inventory.

Summary

30-1 Individuals and institutions that lend money need some assurance that they will have their money returned to them. Security devices serve as this means of assurance.

30-2 Purchases of real property are generally secured by a mortgage. A mortgage is a transfer of an interest in property for the purpose of creating a security for a debt. Some common types of mortgages include the conventional mortgage, the variable-rate mortgage, the graduated-payment mortgage, the balloon-payment mortgage, FHA and VA mortgages, and deeds of trust.

30-3 When personal property is purchased on credit, the seller frequently retains a security interest in the property. Property that is subject to a security interest is called collateral. A security interest is created by a written agreement called a security agreement, which identifies the goods and is signed by the debtor. To be effective between debtor and creditor, a security interest must be made legally enforceable. This legality is known as attachment. To be effective against third parties who might also claim the secured property, the creditor must perfect the security interest. Perfection is accomplished by filing a financing statement, by attachment alone in certain cases, or by taking possession of the collateral.

Key Terms

acceleration, 567
assume the mortgage, 569
attachment, 570
balloon-payment mortgage, 563
buyer in the ordinary course of business, 569
collateral, 569
consumer goods, 569
conventional mortgage, 562
deed of trust, 563
equipment, 569
equity of redemption, 565
farm products, 569
fixtures, 569

flexible-rate mortgage, 562
floating lien, 570
foreclosure, 568
graduated-payment mortgage, 563
home equity loan, 565
inventory, 569
junior mortgage, 564
mortgage, 561
mortgagee, 561
mortgagor, 561
perfected, 569
purchase money security interest, 569
reverse mortgage, 563

second mortgage, 564
secured loan, 561
secured party, 569
security agreement, 569
security interest, 561
subject to the mortgage, 569
subordinated mortgage, 565
subordination agreement, 565
unsecured loan, 561
variable-rate mortgage, 562

Questions for Review and Discussion

1. Why do creditors frequently require security devices when lending money or extending credit?
2. In what principal way does a conventional mortgage differ from an FHA or a VA mortgage?
3. What are the differences among a variable-rate mortgage, a graduated-payment mortgage, and a balloon-payment mortgage?

4. Why is it important to record a mortgage in a public office in the county where the property is located?
5. What are four rights that belong to a mortgagor? What are four rights that belong to a mortgagee?
6. In the purchase of real property, what is the difference between assuming a mortgage and taking property subject to a mortgage?

7. What elements must be included in a security agreement?
8. Explain the reason for perfecting a security interest. What are the different ways this may be done?
9. What rules are found in the UCC for determining who prevails over whom when secured

and unsecured parties lay claim to the same collateral?
10. What rights and responsibilities does a secured party have if a debtor defaults by failing to make payments when due?

Investigating the Internet

On the Net, key in the phrase "The Mortgage Professor's Website." This will lead you to an enormous amount of helpful, practical, and up-to-date information about mortgages. Known as "The Mortgage Professor" by his nationally syndicated newspaper column readers, Wharton School of Business professor emeritus Jack Guttentag presents the latest mortgage information. Also included are online calculators to help you determine such things as what price you can afford to pay for real property.

Cases for Analysis

1. Sanchez bought a house for $100,000, paying $10,000 down and financing the balance through a local bank. As part of the closing costs, Sanchez was required to take out private mortgage insurance to protect the bank in case she defaulted on the mortgage. She had an excellent credit rating and always paid her mortgage payments when they were due. Two years after buying the property, she received an inheritance and used the money to pay an additional amount of $10,000 to the bank toward the principal of the loan. Hoping to cut down on her monthly payments, she asked the bank to cancel the mortgage insurance, but the bank refused. Does Sanchez have any rights in this situation? Explain.

2. Robert and Sherrell Bergeron gave a first mortgage on their property to First Colonial Bank and a second mortgage to Ford Motor Credit Company. When the Bergerons were unable to pay the mortgage, the bank foreclosed. The property was sold at a foreclosure sale for more money than the Bergerons owed to the bank. The Bergerons claim that they are entitled to the surplus funds from the sale. Do you agree? Explain. *First Colonial Bank for Savings v. Bergeron,* 646 N.E.2d 758 (MA).

3. When the Prestons took out a variable mortgage with the First Bank of Marietta, their interest rate was 9 percent. The agreement allowed First Bank

to raise or lower the interest rate at any time, provided that the Prestons received thirty days' advance notice. When the bank raised the interest rate to 11 percent, the Prestons refused to pay, arguing that the agreement was unenforceable, since it set no limit on what interest rate they might be forced to pay. Were the Prestons correct? Explain. *Preston v. First Bank of Marietta,* 473 N.E.2d 1210 (OH).

4. The Woolseys ran a mink farm that was mortgaged to the State Bank of Lehi. The agreement included provisions that allowed acceleration and foreclosure if the Woolseys failed to pay their obligations under the contract. The Woolseys defaulted on several payments, and the bank foreclosed. The couple demanded a jury trial on the foreclosure action. They also argued that the bank had not acted in good faith in its acceleration and foreclosure. Were the Woolseys entitled to a jury trial? Explain. Who had the burden of proof in demonstrating the bank's good faith in accelerating payments and demanding foreclosure? *State Bank of Lehi v. Woolsey,* 565 P.2d 413 (UT).

5. Bloom executed a real estate mortgage in favor of Lakeshore Commercial Finance Corporation on September 16. On October 4, Bloom executed another mortgage on the same described real estate in favor of Northridge Bank. Northridge, without notice of the mortgage to Lakeshore, recorded its

mortgage at 9:28 A.M. on October 25. On that same date, at 3:07 P.M., the prior mortgage executed in favor of Lakeshore was recorded. Bloom defaulted on the mortgages. The value of the real estate was insufficient to satisfy both mortgages fully. Which party had first rights to the property, Lakeshore or Northridge? Why? *Northridge Bank v. Lakeshore Com. Fin. Corp.,* 365 N.E.2d 382 (IL).

6. Cramer's mortgage contained a provision requiring her to pay monthly tax and insurance payments into an escrow account held by the bank in addition to principal and interest. Cramer paid the principal and interest regularly, but refused to pay the tax and insurance escrow payments. The bank brought foreclosure proceedings. Did it have the right to foreclose on Cramer's mortgage? Explain. *Cramer v. Metro. Sav. & Loan Ass'n.,* 258 N.W.2d 20 (MI).

7. Matthews Motors sold a Buick Riviera to Jenkins for $11,500. Matthews then borrowed money from Owensboro National Bank, using the Buick as collateral. When Matthews defaulted on the loan, the bank attempted to repossess the Buick from Jenkins. Jenkins refused to surrender the automobile, claiming that he and not Matthews owned it. The bank brought suit, asking the court to force Jenkins to turn over the Buick. Should the court grant the bank's request? Why or why not? *Owensboro National Bank v. Jenkins,* 328 S.E.2d 399 (GA).

8. Giant Wholesale agreed to supply Hendersonville Food Center with groceries if the owner, William Page, would guarantee all debts incurred by Hendersonville. Page agreed, and a security agreement was drawn up. The security agreement gave Giant a security interest in Hendersonville's groceries and equipment. Giant failed to properly file a financing statement. When Hendersonville ran into financial difficulty, Page turned over the checking account to Giant. When this maneuver did not work, Giant repossessed all of Hendersonville's inventory. Page later went bankrupt. Gray, the bankruptcy trustee, brought a suit against Giant, claiming that the inventory was part of Page's property and thus subject to the bankruptcy proceeding. Gray argued that since the financing statement had not been filed, Giant's security interest had not been perfected. Was Gray correct? Explain. *Gray v. Giant Wholesale,* 758 F.2d 1000 (4th Cir.).

9. U.S. Electronics, a Missouri corporation with a place of business in DeKalb County, Georgia, borrowed money from a Missouri bank. The corporation gave the bank a security interest in all of its machinery and equipment. The bank filed a financing statement in Fulton County rather than in DeKalb County as required by law. U.S. Electronics defaulted on the loan and fell behind on its rent. The corporation's landlord obtained a judgment against it for past-due rent, becoming a lien creditor. The landlord claimed priority over the bank to the proceeds of a sheriff's sale of the machinery and equipment, arguing that the bank's security interest was not perfected. Do you agree? Why or why not? *United States v. Waterford No. 2 Office Center,* 271 S.E. 2d 790 (GA).

10. Lallana bought a car on credit from a dealer who assigned the contract and the security agreement to Bank of America. When Lallana failed to make several payments, the bank repossessed the car. The bank notified Lallana that if she did not redeem the car or reinstate the contract within 15 days, it would sell the car. The bank then sold the car at a public auction for $5,000 and sued Lallana for $11,249, the balance due on her loan. The Kelly Blue Book's estimated retail value of the car at the time of the auction was $14,820. Did the bank give Lallana proper notice of the sale? Why or why not? *Bank of America v. Lallana,* 960 P.2d 1133 (CA).

Quick Quiz Answers

30-1 & 30-2	1. T	30-3	1. F
	2. T		2. T
	3. T		3. T

Chapter 31

Bankruptcy and Debt Adjustment

The Opening Case
"Unexpected Difficulties"

Brenda Ford left her job as an electronics engineer at Huvel Engineering to open her own electronics firm under the name Ford Corporation. Ford's firm manufactured and sold a line of new lightweight satellite dishes that could easily be mounted on almost any kind of structure. After a year of only marginally successful sales, Ford ran into some unexpected difficulties. First, Huvel Engineering brought suit against her for patent infringement. The litigation process was not only expensive, it was also enormously time consuming. Second, Ford's main supplier, Tech Electronics, had labor difficulties that stopped all shipments to Ford for six months. Unable to pay her personal debts or the debts of the business, Ford turned to federal bankruptcy law, seeking some sort of remedy. Could Ford be forced into bankruptcy by her creditors? Would Ford be forced to close down her business or could she make other arrangements under the law? Could any of her property be saved if she were forced into bankruptcy?

Chapter Outcomes

1. Identify the source of congressional power to create a bankruptcy law.
2. Describe ordinary bankruptcy and distinguish between the voluntary and involuntary methods of filing for bankruptcy.
3. Name the property exemptions that a debtor is allowed before beginning the sale of property.
4. Recognize those debts that have priority payment status under the Bankruptcy Code.
5. List debts that cannot be discharged by a bankruptcy debtor.
6. Outline the reorganization process as it pertains to individuals and businesses under Chapter 11 of the Bankruptcy Code.
7. Explain the debt adjustment process available to family farmers under Chapter 12 of the Bankruptcy Code.
8. Summarize the options available to individual debtors in Chapter 13 of the Bankruptcy Code.

31-1 Bankruptcy's History

Bankruptcy is the legal process by which the assets of a debtor are sold to pay off creditors so that the debtor can make a fresh start financially. This definition pinpoints the two most crucial objectives of bankruptcy law.

First, the law protects the creditors who have lent money or extended credit to the debtor by making certain that the debtor's money is divided fairly. Second, the law gives debtors an escape from their financial burdens and allows them to build new lives.

These objectives have not always been the case in the history of bankruptcy law. Early laws favored creditors. In addition to losing all of their property, debtors were often put in debtor's prison and sometimes, although not in the United States, put to death. The first federal bankruptcy law in the United States was enacted in 1800. Under that law, only creditors could begin a bankruptcy proceeding, and only merchants could qualify as debtors. That law lasted only three years before Congress repealed it. In 1840, debtor's prisons were abolished in the United States and, a year later, Congress passed a bankruptcy law that lasted only two years. Following the turmoil of the Civil War, Congress enacted a third bankruptcy law in 1867 that lasted eleven years. It wasn't until 1898 that permanent bankruptcy legislation came about in the United States with a law that gave businesses protection from creditors and lasted, with modifications during the Great Depression, for eighty years. The Bankruptcy Reform Act of 1978 again brought major changes, making it easier for businesses and individuals to obtain bankruptcy relief. It was in 1978 that the presently popular Chapters 11 and 13 (discussed later) were created, allowing businesses and individuals to reorganize and keep on going. In addition, debtors were allowed to keep more of their assets, giving them a better chance to make a fresh start with their activities. The 1994 Bankruptcy Reform Act continued honing the law and created the National Bankruptcy Commission to study the subject and make recommendations.

Over the years, bankruptcy law has progressed from punishing debtors, favoring creditors, and dealing solely with merchants to today's more liberal fresh-start approach to both businesses and consumers. As Table 31-1 illustrates, the number of nonbusiness bankruptcy filings today far exceeds the number of business filings.

Teaching Tips Assign a short research paper on the history of bankruptcy laws with an emphasis on how the laws have responded to the various economic problems of the country.

Constitutional Authority

The U.S. Constitution gives the federal government jurisdiction over bankruptcy proceedings by stating that "Congress shall have the Power . . . To establish . . . uniform laws on the subject of Bankruptcies throughout the United States." Congress exercised this power when it enacted the Bankruptcy Code which is found in Title 11 of the United States Code (USC).

U.S. Const., Article I, Sec. 8 (see page 857)

Table 31-1   Business and Nonbusiness Bankruptcy Filings (Years Ended March 31, 1999–2004)

Year	Total	Nonbusiness	Business
2004	1,654,847	1,618,062	36,785
2003	1,611,268	1,573,720	37,548
2002	1,504,806	1,464,961	39,845
2001	1,307,857	1,271,865	35,992
2000	1,301,205	1,263,096	38,109
1999	1,419,199	1,378,071	41,128

Source: Statistics are from the Administrative Office of the Courts, U.S. Department of Justice.

Restoring Credit After Bankruptcy

A personal bankruptcy filing remains on a debtor's credit report for ten years and has a detrimental effect on the ability to establish a line of credit. However, most debtors who file bankruptcy have already established a poor credit rating anyway, and filing bankruptcy gives them an opportunity to begin anew. A good number of their debts become discharged, which improves their debt-to-income ratio—a factor that potential creditors look at carefully. The more time that elapses after the bankruptcy filing, the easier it is to reestablish credit.

Many people in this situation switch from credit cards to debit cards, which is like paying cash because, instead of being a charge, money is withdrawn instantly from one's bank account (see Chapter 28). Some banks offer *secured credit cards* in which customers deposit money in the bank to guarantee that their credit card charges will be paid. Until their credit is reestablished, their credit limit is the same as the amount of their bank deposit. Credit card issuers sometimes allow debtors to continue using their credit cards if they agree in writing, after the bankruptcy filing, to pay off the old debt. Often, this also requires an agreement by the debtor to pay the credit card balance each month without carrying a balance.

People who are able to make a down payment and have steady income may be eligible for a mortgage loan as soon as two years following a discharge in bankruptcy.

31-2 Ordinary Bankruptcy—Chapter 7, Bankruptcy Code

When most people use the word *bankruptcy,* they are referring to the type of ordinary bankruptcy provided for in Chapter 7 of the Bankruptcy Code. Under ordinary bankruptcy, debtors are forced to sell most of their property and use the cash to pay their creditors a portion of the amount owed each one. This process is also called **liquidation.** See Table 31-2 for the types of bankruptcy procedures.

Commencing the Action

Ordinary bankruptcy may begin in one of two ways. Either the debtor files a petition or the debtor's creditors band together and file a petition to force the debtor to sell property and pay them off. The first type of filing is called a *voluntary filing.* The second type of filing is known as an *involuntary filing.*

Voluntary Proceedings If debtors are alert enough to realize that their financial position can never improve without some drastic action, they may decide to file a bankruptcy petition on their own. To do so, such debtors would go to the nearest federal district court. The government provides official forms for the filing of a bankruptcy petition. The form asks debtors to name all of their creditors and to indicate how much money they owe those creditors. The form also requires a listing of their property and a statement of income and expenses. Finally, the form asks debtors to list all of the property that they feel should be exempt from the sale when it comes time later in the bankruptcy proceeding to sell what they own.

Involuntary Proceedings Under Chapter 7 of the Bankruptcy Code, the creditors of a debtor can force that debtor into an involuntary bankruptcy proceeding if the debtor continuously fails to pay bills as they become due. The ability to pay is not the issue. If the debtor has enough money to pay bills but for some reason refuses to do so, an involuntary petition can be filed by creditors. Three creditors must file the petition if the debtor has twelve or more creditors. The combined debt owed the three must exceed $11,625. A single creditor who is owed a debt of more than $11,625 can also file if the debtor has fewer than twelve creditors.

Table 31-2 Types of Bankruptcy Procedures

Chapter	Who Can File?	When Used?	Special Features
Chapter 7: Ordinary Bankruptcy	Everyone is eligible except banks, railroads, and insurance companies; filing can be voluntary or involuntary	Used when debtor wants to discharge most debts and begin with a clean slate	Debtor's property is liquidated; some property is exempt; some debts cannot be discharged
Chapter 11: Reorganization	Individuals, partnerships, and corporations can file; railroads can file; only commodity brokers and stockbrokers cannot; filing can be voluntary or involuntary	Used when debtor, usually a business, wants to continue operating, but needs to reorganize and liquidate debts	Debtor-in-possession feature; debtor files plan within 120 days; plan must be fair, equitable, and feasible; creditors can also file plans; confirmation needed
Chapter 12: Family Farmer Debt Adjustment	Family farmers can file, including partnerships and corporations; debt ceiling of $1.5 million	Used when debtor is a family farmer who needs a debt adjustment plan to keep the farm running	Debtor-in-possession feature; debtor files plan within 90 days; plan lasts three years (with two-year possible extension); plan must be confirmed
Chapter 13: Individual Debt Adjustment	Individuals only; no corporations or partnerships; no involuntary filings allowed; debt ceiling of $450,000.	Used when an individual debtor with a steady income voluntarily decides to adopt a debt adjustment plan	Only the debtor can file a plan; payments must start 30 days after plan submitted; a few debts cannot be discharged; plan lasts three years (with two-year possible extension)

Example 31-1

Strasser had an excellent job with a high salary and a promise of continued advancement. However, he made several miscalculations in the stock market that severely damaged his financial picture. Consequently, although he owned a lot of property, he had little cash on hand. This situation caused him to fall behind on his payments to most of his fourteen creditors. Three of those creditors, the Bromfield Department Store, the Mariano Oil Company, and the Financial Bank, filed an involuntary bankruptcy petition against Strasser in federal court. Since Strasser owed the three of them more than $11,625, the petition was accepted.

Involuntary petitions cannot be filed against farmers, charities, or cities. Debtors can contest any petition filed involuntarily.

The Opening Case Revisited
"Unexpected Difficulties"

Into Bankruptcy Ford could be forced into bankruptcy by her creditors if she owed more than $11,625 and the proper number of creditors as mentioned filed the petition.

Order for Relief

An **order for relief** is the court's command that the liquidation begin. In a voluntary filing, the petition itself becomes the order for relief. In an involuntary case, the court does not issue the order immediately because the debtor is allowed a certain period of time to contest the filing. At this time, a **bankruptcy trustee** is also named by the court. The trustee is charged with the responsibility of liquidating the assets of the debtor for the benefit of all interested parties.

A Question of Ethics

A limited partnership that had been established solely to buy, develop, and sell a certain parcel of Florida real estate filed a voluntary petition for bankruptcy. The court appointed Marvin J. Bloom as trustee to the Debtor's bankruptcy estate. Bloom sought to employ his own real estate firm as a consultant to assist in the sale of the Debtor's property. What ethical question arises in this case?

Automatic Stay

The moment a petition for bankruptcy is filed, an **automatic stay** goes into effect. This is a self-operating postponement of collection proceedings against the debtor. Further efforts by creditors against the debtor to collect debts must stop immediately. Among other things, the stay prohibits creditors from beginning or continuing:

- lawsuits
- foreclosure sales
- collection proceedings
- repossession activities

Automatic stay applies to both voluntary and involuntary petitions. It does not apply to a lawsuit to establish paternity or to establish or modify an order for alimony, maintenance, or support. Creditors who ignore the stay can be held in contempt of court.

Example 31-2

Easterbrook found himself so deeply in debt that he could pay very little on his bills. One of his creditors, Linden Musical Supplies, told him that it was about to file a lawsuit against him. At that point, Easterbrook filed a voluntary bankruptcy petition in federal court. Since he filed voluntarily, the voluntary petition was considered the order for relief. At this time, the automatic stay provision of the Bankruptcy Code went into effect. If Linden Musical Supplies carried out its planned action, it could be held in contempt of court.

Federal Exemptions

Under the fresh-start approach of the federal Bankruptcy Code, debtors are permitted to exempt or exclude certain items of property from the bankruptcy process, which means that the property is kept by the debtor and cannot be sold to pay the debtor's outstanding bills. Exemptions can be doubled for married couples who file jointly. The following exemption amounts were in effect in 2004 and are subject to adjustment at three-year intervals after that to reflect the change in the Consumer Price Index, rounded to the nearest $25.

Homestead and Household Exemptions The Bankruptcy Code allows debtors to keep a maximum of $17,425 in equity in the debtor's place of residence and in property used as a burial ground. This is known as the **homestead exemption.**

State Variations The amount of a person's homestead exemption varies from state to state. Arizona allows a homestead exemption of $100,000, while Wyoming allows a homestead exemption of $10,000.

Example 31-3

Carlson purchased a home for $120,000 by placing $15,000 down and borrowing the balance from the East Savings and Loan Association. East held a first mortgage on the property. Carlson was later forced to file for bankruptcy. Under the homestead exemption, she would be allowed to exempt up to $17,425 in equity in her home. Since she only has a little over $15,000 in equity, this would be safe from her creditors.

Debtors can also keep a maximum of $925 for any individual item of furniture, household goods, clothes, appliances, books, crops, animals, or musical instruments. The total of all exemptions taken in this category cannot exceed $9,300. Debtors are also allowed to exempt $1,150 in jewelry beyond the $9,300 set aside for the other household items mentioned previously. In addition, they may keep any other property not exceeding the value of $925 plus up to $8,725 of any unused amount of the $17,425 homestead exemption.

Necessities Congress allows debtors to maintain a minimum standard of living by exempting certain necessary items of property. For example, debtors are allowed to exclude a maximum of $1,750 in professional tools, instruments, and books. In addition, they can exempt up to $2,775 in a motor vehicle. Finally, any medical supplies that have been prescribed for the health of the debtor can be excluded.

State Variations Florida has one of the most lenient debtor's laws in the United States. In 1847, state founders included a provision in the state constitution that made it illegal for a creditor to evict a homeowner from his or her land as long as the citizen kept current on the mortgage or owned the property. In Florida, debtors also may keep all wages, annuities, partnership profits, pension plans, and property owned jointly with a spouse.

Benefits and Support Payments Again, to allow debtors to maintain a minimum standard of living, Congress allows the exclusion of certain benefits and support payments. For instance, alimony and child support payments can be excluded. Benefits received under Social Security or a disability program are also exempt. Profits that are due under profit-sharing, pension, and annuity plans may be excluded. Furthermore, debtors are allowed to protect payments due to them under certain court orders. For example, if someone owes a debtor damages resulting from a personal injury tort case, those damages are exempt up to $17,425. Finally, any life insurance contracts carried for the benefit of a relative or approved beneficiary that have yet to mature are protected.

The Opening Case Revisited
"Unexpected Difficulties"

What's Exempt? If Ford were forced into bankruptcy, the property listed under Federal Exemptions, or the exemptions provided by her state law, could be saved and not taken by the bankruptcy trustee.

State Exemptions

The Bankruptcy Code allows states to use a list of exemptions created by the state legislature rather than the federal exemptions. Often the broad categories of exempt property will stay the same. However, the maximum dollar amount allowed under each category will vary from state to state. States that enact their own list of exemptions generally do so to protect their own citizens. The dollar amounts included in the state statutes usually will be a more accurate assessment of property values within each state. This is true because the state legislators are more flexible in such matters than members of Congress who must consider property values across the entire country.

Property Distribution

After the order for relief is granted, a trustee will be appointed to sell the debtor's property to obtain cash. The trustee then distributes the cash among the debtor's creditors according to set priorities. Recall that the debtor is required to list all creditors and the amounts owed to each on the petition form. The trustee uses this form in the distribution process.

The Bankruptcy Code provides a priority list that indicates which categories of debts are paid first (Table 31-3). Each category must be paid in full before moving on to the next category.

State Variations The states that allow their citizens to choose between the federal exemptions or their states' exemptions are Arkansas, Connecticut, District of Columbia, Hawaii, Massachusetts, Michigan, Minnesota, New Jersey, New Mexico, Pennsylvania, Rhode Island, South Carolina, Texas, Vermont, Washington, and Wisconsin. For updates, go to: **http://www.americanbankruptcy.com/bkexemptions/**.

State Variations The amount of a person's personal property exemption varies from state to state. The specific items and total value of a debtor's personal property that may be claimed as exempt is set out by state statutes.

Terms A secured creditor who repossesses collateral shortly before a debtor files for bankruptcy may not be able to keep it. Payments and repossessions that occur just before filing are called *preferences*. In general, a preference is more than $600 that is paid or transferred in property to a creditor. The trustee can sue the creditor for the amount of the preference and make it a part of the bankruptcy estate so that it can be distributed evenly among all creditors.

Table 31-3 Payment Priorities	
Debt	**Explanation**
Secured debts	Creditors with security interests take their collateral first.
Administrative debts	Bankruptcy trustee and others involved in bankruptcy process are paid next.
Certain unsecured debts	All unsecured debts after an involuntary petition has been filed, but before order for relief has been granted, are paid next.
Wages	Employees are paid next; maximum, $4,650 per employee.
Benefit plans	Contributions owed on employee benefit plans are paid next; maximum, $4,650 per employee.
Workers in the fishing and farming industries	Owner-operators of fish storage processing plants pay worker creditors next; owner-operators of grain storage plants pay farmer creditors next; both up to $4,650.
Deposits and advances	Deposits made for purchase or lease of property are paid next, as are advances made for personal, family, and household services; maximum, $2,100.
Alimony and support	Paternity, alimony, maintenance, and support payments are made next.
Taxes	Certain taxes are paid next.
Remaining unsecured creditors	All other unsecured creditors are paid from any balance remaining.
Debtor	If anything is left, it goes back to the debtor.

Secured Creditors Some of the creditors on the list will be creditors who have secured loans (see Chapter 30). Since secured creditors have the right to take the collateral to satisfy the debt, the collateral is not sold by the trustee. Although there are some narrow exceptions to this rule, most secured creditors are protected. In contrast, creditors who are owed unsecured debts are called unsecured creditors.

Example 31-4

Perez purchased a digital camera from Digicam Corp. Perez financed the deal by signing a security agreement with the company. Under the agreement, Digicam retained a security interest in the property allowing it to repossess the camera if Perez defaulted on the loan. Digicam was a secured creditor. The digital camera was the collateral.

Exceptions to Discharge

Once the trustee has run through all the aforementioned creditors, the debtor's debts are said to be discharged, which means that the debts are wiped away and the debtor is allowed to begin again. If the bankruptcy debtor does not have enough money to cover the debts, they are, nevertheless, considered discharged. However, there are some exceptions to this general rule. Some debts cannot be discharged. In other words, even though the debtor has gone through the entire bankruptcy proceeding, money may still be owed to certain creditors.

Debts Created by Misconduct Certain debts that have fallen into the debtor's lap because of misconduct cannot be charged in bankruptcy. For example, any debts that arose because of the debtor's fraudulent behavior cannot be discharged. Similarly, the debtor cannot escape legal liability for any debt that arose from willful and malicious misconduct. Finally, if the debtor knew about a debt that was not on the original list of debts, then that unlisted debt cannot be discharged.

Debts Enforced by the Government Certain debts that the debtor owes the government will remain on the books even after the bankruptcy proceeding has ended. These include certain back taxes, student loans that do not impose a hardship on the debtor, and many government fines and penalties. Similarly, several types of court-enforced debts cannot be discharged including alimony and child support and any legal liability that resulted from a court-ordered judgment for driving while intoxicated. Finally, any debts that were not discharged under a previous bankruptcy cannot be discharged under the new bankruptcy proceeding.

Debts Created by Excessive Spending Congress also refuses to allow bankruptcy debtors to discharge any excessive expenditures that occur around the time of the bankruptcy filing. This measure prevents people from running up big bills unnecessarily because they think they will not have to pay the full amount due on these bills when their assets are finally distributed. Thus, debts for luxury items that top $500 in value cannot be discharged if those items were purchased within ninety days before the order for relief was granted. Likewise, the debtor cannot discharge any cash advances that total more than $1,000 if those advances were obtained within twenty days of the relief order.

Example 31-5

Caswell finally realized that his financial problems were out of control. Consequently, he decided to file for bankruptcy on the following Monday. That Friday, he went to the Monroe National Bank and used his bank card to withdraw a cash advance of $1,500. He spent that money on a weekend in Atlantic City and then filed for bankruptcy on Monday. Caswell would not be allowed to discharge that $1,500, since it was a cash advance that was made within twenty days of the relief order.

Quick Quiz 31-1 & 31-2 True or False?

1. The U.S. Constitution gives state courts jurisdiction over bankruptcy proceedings.

2. Under Chapter 7 bankruptcy, debtors are forced to sell most of their property and use the cash to pay their creditors a portion of the amount owed each one.

3. The Bankruptcy Code allows states to use a list of exemptions created by the state legislature rather than the federal exemptions.

31-3 Reorganization—Chapter 11, Bankruptcy Code

Chapter 11 of the Bankruptcy Code provides a method for businesses to reorganize their financial affairs and still remain in business. If allowed to continue in operation, companies may be able to overcome their difficulties without having to sell most of their property. In **reorganization,** a qualified debtor creates a plan that alters the repayment schedule. A Chapter 11 filing is available to anyone who could file under Chapter 7. This includes individuals, partnerships, and corporations. In addition, unlike Chapter 7, Chapter 11 also allows railroads to file. The only individuals specifically excluded from filing under Chapter 11 are commodity brokers and stockbrokers.

Chapter 11 is advantageous for partnerships and corporations because it allows them to stay in business while the financial problems are cleared up. Like a Chapter 7 filing, a Chapter 11 filing may be voluntary or involuntary. Chapter 11 also shares the Chapter 7 automatic stay provision. However, reorganization under Chapter 11 also has some unique features of its own.

Filing for Chapter 11 bankruptcy, as United Airlines did in 2002, allows companies to make changes in their operations and hopefully strengthen their businesses while resolving their financial problems.

Special Features of Chapter 11

One of the most attractive features of Chapter 11 for business debtors is that the business continues to operate after the filing. Under Chapter 11, a debtor is frequently referred to as

Business Law in the News

On a Wing and a Prayer

For a brief moment, it looked as if Enron Corp. might make daring investors rich again. On July 11, the once-high-flying energy trader filed its bankruptcy reorganization plan. In the next four days, the stock shot up 70%, to 8.2¢, as volume spiked to 13.8 million shares a day, eight times its average. Go-go postings popped up on Internet message boards, urging everyone to hurry and buy shares.

Offering the opposite view, though, were other messages warning would-be purchasers to steer clear. They noted that, under Enron's plan, its equity would disappear, as company executives all along have said. In a posting on Lycos Inc.'s Raging Bull Web site, buzzbee20 cautioned: "I got out today. Lost a bundle but not all. My advice, my friend—get out and stay out." Sure enough, Enron stock began slipping a week later and now sells once again for 5¢ a share.

These days, investors are spoiled for choice when it comes to bankrupt companies. After a three-year explosion of corporate failures, more than 400 public companies are now in Chapter 11, figures PricewaterhouseCoopers LLC—an all-time record. Included are many big, familiar names such as insurer Conseco Inc. and airline UAL Corp. Indeed, eight of the 12 largest bankruptcy filings in U.S. history, measured by assets, are now being sorted out in court—as the companies continue to trade in the so-called pink-sheet and bulletin-board markets. What's more, the shares often go for pocket change, so even a penny-a-share price rise can bring a market-beating return.

Very occasionally, stocks in tottering outfits do maintain at least some value when the companies exit bankruptcy. But the harsh reality is that, in almost every reorganization, what money companies can scrape together goes to creditors first, often in the form of new equity, leaving old shareholders empty-handed. "If you purchase stock in a bankrupt company, it is highly likely that your investment not only will not rise in value, but that you'll be holding worthless shares," says Susan F. Wyderko, director of investor education and assistance at the Securities & Exchange Commission.

So why do people still buy? One reason is the temptation of a quick buck held out on Internet message boards and in spam. Some companies in Chapter 11 even push their own stock, such as U-Haul International Inc. parent Amerco. And because these stocks often are volatile, investors can score with well-timed buys.

Besides, many investors believe that the companies can turn themselves around, so they figure the stocks must be a good investment. Even when brokers or the companies warn that today's shares will be voided, many investors simply choose to ignore them.

The SEC is seeing a sharp rise in complaints from shareholders who got wiped out in bankruptcy reorganizations. That's due in part to Kmart Corp. After filing for Chapter 11 protection in January, 2002, the discount retailer announced on Apr. 22, 2003, that the bankruptcy court had approved its reorganization. The next day, 133 million shares were traded, up from a daily average of 21 million, and in a week the stock price doubled, to 12¢. On Raging Bull's Kmart message board, some posters urged investors to hold on to their shares. "This could be a great opportunity!!" cheered dadgummit. "I may just be a buyer here." But only two weeks later, the shares lost all their value as the Troy (Mich.) company emerged from Chapter 11 and ownership of the company was transferred to its creditors.

Now, as other big names prepare to leave Chapter 11 behind, SEC officials say many more investors undoubtedly will find that they, too, have been left holding the bag. Conseco plans to emerge in September, and Enron, UAL, and WorldCom (now known as MCI) are all planning to come out in the next few months. Each has warned that its stock will be worthless, yet shares in UAL, for one, still fetch 47¢.

In rare cases, shareholders do get something. For instance, when Peregrine Systems Inc., a San Diego software company, emerged from bankruptcy on Aug. 7, its equity holders received a third of its new shares.

Still, Dethy says most investors should avoid companies in bankruptcy court. "To make money,

(Continued)

Business Law in the News *(Continued)*

things have to get substantially better, and that doesn't usually happen," he says. "The vast majority of these do not work out." That's something to remember the next time some spam shows up pushing a Chapter 11 stock.

Questions for Analysis

1. What will most likely happen if you purchase stock in a bankrupt company according to the director of investor education and assistance at the Securities and Exchange Commission?

2. Why do people buy stock in bankrupt companies?

3. Why does Douglas L. Dethy, who made money buying and selling bankrupt companies, advise most investors to avoid buying stock in such companies?

Source: Michael Arndt and Mara Der Hovenesian. "On a Wing and a Prayer," *BusinessWeek,* September 1, 2003, pp. 82–83.

Cross-Cultural Notes In most European and Asian countries, if a company misses payments to creditors and renegotiation is infeasible, a trustee is appointed before liquidation.

Background Information During the first 100 years after the Constitution gave Congress the right to enact bankruptcy laws, few were passed. At the time, bankruptcy was seen as immoral. However, after a period of financial panic in 1893, a permanent bankruptcy law was passed in 1898 that allowed businesses and individuals to erase their debts by paying what they could and liquidating. The law was amended in 1938 to include a reorganization option.

Cross-Cultural Notes Great Britain employs a technique of bankruptcy management known as an administration order, which was written into British law in 1987. The law permits a troubled company's creditors to appoint a team of specially licensed bankruptcy accountants to fire existing management, take over operations of the company, and orchestrate a reorganization of assets. Thus, expensive and time-consuming litigation is eliminated.

a **debtor-in-possession** because the debtor continues to run the firm. However, if the problems of the business have been caused by poor judgment, mismanagement, or dishonesty, a trustee may have to step in to perform certain tasks. If appointed, the trustee would have to examine the debtor's financial position and provide the court, creditors, and tax authorities with financial information as necessary.

After the filing of the petition and the issuance of an order for relief, a **primary committee** is set up to work with the debtor on a reorganization plan. Membership on the committee generally consists of the debtor's unsecured creditors. Often the seven creditors to whom the debtor owes the most will make up the committee membership. It is also possible for the court to create other committees if membership on the primary committee fails to represent all those with legitimate claims against the debtor. These secondary committees also work with the debtor and, if appropriate, help set up the reorganization plan.

The Reorganization Plan

When a Chapter 11 petition is filed, the debtor has 120 days to devise a reorganization plan. The plan must outline how the debtor intends to reorganize the payment of debts. If the debtor lets the 120 days pass without taking any action or if the debtor creates a plan that is rejected, then a plan may be proposed by anyone involved in the reorganization effort. The 120-day period may be shortened or lengthened by the court.

Plan Qualifications   The Bankruptcy Code requires fairness, equity, and feasibility in the creation of a reorganization plan. The plan will group various claims against the debtor into classes and explain how each creditor in the class will be treated. The law requires equal treatment for all creditors grouped in a class. In addition, the law requires that the plan be feasible. This means that there must be a good chance that the plan will actually work. The law does not require an absolute guarantee of success. A plan may be difficult to implement because of labor or supply problems and still be feasible within the meaning of the law.

Plan Approval   The plan must be approved by the creditors before it can go into effect. However, the code does not require unanimous approval by the creditors. Instead, more than one-half of the creditors in each class must accept the plan before it is officially

The Opening Case Revisited
"Unexpected Difficulties"

Planned Reorganization Ford would not be forced to close down her business if she could develop a reorganization plan under Chapter 11 of the Bankruptcy Code that is confirmed by the court and placed into operation.

approved. There is one exception to the rule: If the plan has not changed the standard legal rights of the members of a class, then no approval is required from that class. Such a class of creditors in this case is termed an **unimpaired class** because the creditors' collection rights have not been impaired by the reorganization process.

Example 31-6

The Miller Chemical Company filed for reorganization under Chapter 11 of the Bankruptcy Code. One class of creditors included unsecured creditors who were owed $2,000 or less. A second class included unsecured creditors who were owed over $2,000. The plan called for a complete repayment of all Class 1 creditors according to the terms of their original contracts. This provision made Class 1 an unimpaired class. The Class 2 creditors would have a choice. They could receive either a 60 percent repayment on the date of confirmation or 100 percent repayment extended over four years. The extended repayment plan called for a 30 percent repayment on the date of confirmation and seven 10 percent payments at six-month intervals. More than one-half of the Class 2 creditors would have to approve the plan. In contrast, the Class 1 creditors had no approval rights, since Class 1 was unimpaired.

> **Did You Know?**
>
> According to a plan approved by the federal bankruptcy court, Enron's creditors, who are owed 66 billion dollars, will receive approximately 20 cents on the dollar.

Confirmation and Discharge The court will hold a hearing on the confirmation of the reorganization plan. A **confirmation** officially places a plan in operation. After confirmation, all property dealt with in the plan is free and clear of all claims of creditors and equity security holders. The debtor is discharged from any debts that arose before the date of confirmation.

Quick Quiz 31-3 True or False?

1. Chapter 11 of the Bankruptcy Code provides a method for businesses to reorganize their financial affairs and still remain in business.

2. The automatic stay provision found in Chapter 7 of the Bankruptcy Code is not used in Chapter 11 proceedings.

3. A trustee is appointed to run the firm when a business files a Chapter 11 bankruptcy petition.

31-4 Family Farmer Debt Adjustment— Chapter 12, Bankruptcy Code

Recognizing the grave financial difficulties facing family farmers, Congress enacted the Family Farmer Debt Adjustment Act in 1986. The act is designed to help farmers create a plan for debt repayment that will allow them to keep their farms running. Thus, Chapter 12 is an alternative to the ordinary bankruptcy procedure provided for by Chapter 7. Under the act, a **family farmer** is defined as one who receives more than one-half of the total income from the farm. In addition, 80 percent of the farmer's debt must result from farm expenses.

Chapter 12 has some important characteristics that allow individuals to file debt adjustment plans. First, Chapter 12 sets a $1.5 million debt ceiling. Second, Chapter 12 is open to partnerships and corporations as long as a farm family owns at least half of the farm business.

Chapter 12 Procedures

Like a filing under Chapters 7 and 11, a filing under Chapter 12 creates an automatic stay of debt collection as soon as the order for relief is issued. It is possible for creditors to ask the court to exempt them from the stay. However, a hearing on such a motion would have to be held, and the creditors would have to show why the court should grant exemptions.

As is the case in Chapter 7 and 11, the court may appoint a trustee to handle the farm's finances. The Chapter 12's trustee has duties similar to those of Chapter 7 and 11 trustees. In general, under Chapter 12, the farmer remains a debtor-in-possession. If the farmer is removed as debtor-in-possession, the trustee takes over.

The Adjustment Plan

Unlike the Chapter 11 debtor, who has a 120-day deadline to devise a reorganization plan, the Chapter 12 farm debtor is limited to ninety days. The clock starts running toward that ninety-day deadline when the order for relief is granted. Debtors, however, can file for an extension.

Contents of the Plan The Chapter 12 plan must include several provisions. First, the plan must include a provision that requires the debtor to turn over at least part of any future income to the trustee. Second, the plan must make certain that all priority claims are

The family farm, a vanishing breed in the United States.

paid in full. It is possible, of course, for a priority creditor to surrender this right voluntarily. Priority claims for Chapter 12 are identical to those named for Chapter 7. Third, if the claims of creditors are grouped into classes, then each creditor in a class must be treated identically. Fourth, the plan must not take longer than three years to complete unless the time is extended by the court. The maximum extension is for two years.

Plan Confirmation A hearing must be held to confirm the plan. This hearing must be set up no longer than forty-five days after the debtor has filed the plan. Unlike Chapter 11 creditors, Chapter 12 creditors have no prior input while the plan is being constructed. Secured creditors have approval power after the plan is written. Unsecured creditors do not have this right. However, unsecured creditors can object to the plan at the hearing. The court may still confirm the plan over the objections.

Example 31-7

Brey, who owned a dairy farm, filed for debt adjustment under Chapter 12. Two months after the relief order was issued by the court, Brey filed an adjustment plan. Under the plan, unsecured creditors owed over $300 would receive 100 percent of the amount owed to them over a three-year period. They would receive 20 percent immediately and 10 percent at regular intervals. Kozlo Supply Co. objected to the plan. However, since Brey was turning over 100 percent of her disposable income to the trustee for debt repayment, the court did not support Kozlo's objection.

The debtor can begin to make payments under the plan before its confirmation. Such payments would go to the trustee, who would hold them pending the plan's confirmation.

31-5 Adjustment of Debts—Chapter 13, Bankruptcy Code

Sometimes debtors overextend their credit. They have regular income, but they cannot pay all their bills. If given time, they may eventually be able to pay at least part of the amount they owe to each creditor. Chapter 13 of the Bankruptcy Code permits an individual debtor to develop a repayment plan and, upon completion of payments under the plan, to receive a discharge from most remaining debt.

Only individual debtors can take advantage of Chapter 13 provisions. Neither corporations nor partnerships can file under its provisions. However, sole proprietorships can file under Chapter 13, as long as they meet the statute's other requirements. These requirements hold that the debtor's liabilities cannot surpass $250,000 in unsecured debts or $750,000 in secured debts. Also, the debtor must have an already established steady income. Only voluntary filings are permitted under Chapter 13. The automatic stay provision clicks into place under Chapter 13 when the relief order is issued. A trustee oversees the Chapter 13 process. If Chapter 13 does not work out under certain circumstances, the individual can convert to a Chapter 7 bankruptcy, which changes the repayment plan to a liquidation.

The Chapter 13 Plan

It is the debtor's responsibility to file a debt readjustment plan under Chapter 13. Like Chapter 12, Chapter 13 requires the debtor to

Terms Chapter 13 bankruptcy is sometimes referred to as "wage earners' bankruptcy."

Further Reading *How to File for Bankruptcy,* by Stephen Elias, Albin Renauer, and Robin Leonard (Berkeley, CA: Nolo Press, 1991), is a complete guide to filing for bankruptcy.

By using credit cards responsibly, one can help avoid insurmountable debt.

transfer future income to the trustee in order to satisfy outstanding debts. Although the debtor need not turn over all future income, some portion of it must go to the trustee. Like a Chapter 12 plan, the Chapter 13 plan must make certain that priority debtors receive full payment.

Also, like Chapter 12, if the plan sets up groups of creditors, all group members must be treated equally. Finally, Chapter 13 debtors must also abide by the three-to-five-year rule requiring that the payment plan be completed within three-to-five years. If the debtor files for an extension, the most the court will grant is two years.

Plan Confirmation

Like Chapter 12 creditors, Chapter 13 creditors have no prior input while the plan is being created. Secured creditors have approval powers, but unsecured creditors do not. Unsecured creditors may, of course, object to the plan at the hearing. However, like Chapter 12, Chapter 13 will not allow the court to uphold an objection if the debtor plans to turn over 100 percent of all disposable income to the trustee for debt repayment.

Payments The debtor must start payments within thirty days of submitting the plan to the court. If the court has yet to hold its hearing, the debtor pays the trustee. The trustee holds the money until the court upholds or rejects the plan.

Discharge Once the amounts agreed to under the plan are paid, all remaining debts are discharged. The list of debts that cannot be discharged under Chapter 13 is much shorter than those included under Chapter 7. Only alimony, child support, and priority claims must be satisfied in full under Chapter 13. Every other debt may be discharged one way or another.

Quick Quiz 31-4 & 31-5 True or False?

1. Chapter 12 of the Bankruptcy Code provides a method for individual debtors to develop a repayment plan and, upon completion of payments under the plan, to be discharged from most remaining debt.

2. Sole proprietors can file bankruptcy under Chapter 13 of the Bankruptcy Code, but corporations and partnerships cannot.

3. Under Chapter 13 of the Bankruptcy Code, secured creditors have approval powers of a repayment plan but unsecured creditors do not.

Summary

31-1 Bankruptcy is the legal process that allows a debtor to get a fresh start by selling personal property to pay off creditors. The U.S. Constitution gives the federal government jurisdiction over bankruptcy proceedings. The Bankruptcy Code enacted by Congress is found in Title 11 of the USC.

31-2 Chapter 7 of the Bankruptcy Code covers ordinary bankruptcy which is also called liquidation. In ordinary bankruptcy, the trustee sells the debtor's property and uses the cash to pay creditors a portion of the amount owed to each one. Such a process can be either voluntary or involuntary.

31-3   Reorganization under Chapter 11 of the Bankruptcy Code allows debtors to overcome financial difficulties without selling *all* their property. Instead, a reorganization plan is drawn up that changes the debtor's payment schedule. The new schedule allows the debtor to maintain personal property while paying creditors.

31-4   Chapter 12 of the Bankruptcy Code applies to family farmers in financial difficulty. Under Chapter 12, a family farmer can maintain the farm while drawing up a debt adjustment plan to satisfy creditors.

31-5   Chapter 13 of the Bankruptcy Code applies only to individual debtors with established steady incomes. Such debtors can prepare a debt readjustment plan that will provide for repayment of all outstanding debts.

Key Terms

automatic stay, 582

bankruptcy, 578

bankruptcy trustee, 582

confirmation, 589

debtor-in-possession, 588

family farmer, 590

homestead exemption, 583

liquidation, 580

order for relief, 582

primary committee, 588

reorganization, 586

unimpaired class, 589

Questions for Review and Discussion

1. What is the source of power that enables Congress to create federal statutory law dealing with bankruptcy and other debt adjustment procedures?
2. How does a debtor voluntarily institute a bankruptcy proceeding? Under what conditions can the debtor's creditors institute an involuntary proceeding?
3. Outline the automatic stay process. How does it fulfill the objectives of the Bankruptcy Code?
4. What are the classes of property that can be exempted from sale when a debtor files for bankruptcy?
5. What are the priority of claims on a debtor's assets once the debtor's property has been sold and reduced to cash?
6. Which debts cannot be discharged under a bankruptcy proceeding?
7. What is the purpose of Chapter 11 provisions of the Bankruptcy Code?
8. Who may approve a Chapter 11 reorganization plan? Name any exceptions to this rule.
9. What are the criteria that must be met in order for a debtor to qualify for a Chapter 13 filing under the Bankruptcy Code?
10. In what ways does a Chapter 12 debt adjustment procedure differ from a Chapter 13 procedure?

Investigating the Internet

The United States Congress is in the process of amending the Bankruptcy Code. *Excite, Yahoo!,* and *Lycos* are among the search engines that can give you up-to-date information on changes in the bankruptcy law. Also, see *Bankruptcy in Brief* at **http://www.moranlaw.net/TOC.htm.**

Cases for Analysis

1. Soon after the birth of their second child, misfortune fell on the lives of Kurt and Leah Lyons. Kurt got laid off, the landlord raised their rent, they received notice that their car was about to be repossessed, and dunning letters arrived daily from credit card companies. Reluctantly, the couple filed for personal bankruptcy. Their disappointed parents told them that the bankruptcy would remain on their credit rating for the rest of their lives, that they would never again be able to establish a line of credit or obtain a mortgage to buy a house. Were Kurt and Leah's parents correct? Explain.

2. Lisa and William Leeper filed a Chapter 13 bankruptcy petition. One of the unsecured debts they listed on their bankruptcy petition was an amount owed to the Pennsylvania Higher Education Assistance Authority to attend college under a guaranteed student loan program. Will the loan to attend college be discharged by the bankruptcy court? Explain. *Leeper v. Pennsylvania Higher Education Assistance Agency,* 94-3372 & 94-3373, U.S. Court of Appeals (3rd Cir.).

3. When a Florida court dismissed Nellie Cortez's voluntary bankruptcy petition, it ordered her not to file another petition "under any chapter of the Bankruptcy Code for a period of twelve months." Two months later, an involuntary bankruptcy petition was filed in California by Cortez's stepfather, Thomas Bronkovic. The California court dismissed that case, finding that Cortez had colluded with her stepfather and that the case was, in fact, her own "voluntary" petition rather than her stepfather's "involuntary" petition. While the California case was pending, FDIC brought suit against Cortez to enforce certain promissory notes. Did FDIC violate the automatic stay provision of the Bankruptcy Code? Why or why not? *Federal Deposit Insurance Corporation v. Cortez,* 96-6047, U.S. Court of Appeals (2nd. Cir.).

4. Dyana Landrin was convicted of grand larceny after she admitted she took nearly $19,000 from the Community Mutual Savings Bank while she was employed as a teller. The county court ordered her to pay restitution to the bank—that is, return the money. Before paying restitution, Landrin filed a petition for relief under Chapter 7 of the Bankruptcy Code. Is the money owed to the bank discharged by the bankruptcy petition? Explain. *In re Landrin,* 93-B-20920 (Bankr. S.D. NY).

5. Three creditors filed an involuntary bankruptcy petition against the Manchester Lakes Association alleging that the association was not paying its bills when they came due. Manchester fought the petition, arguing that its general partner, Dominion Federal Savings and Loan, had enough money to pay these bills as they came due, even though it was not doing so. Should the court refuse to grant the order for relief if the debtor could prove it had the ability to pay its bills? Explain. *In re Manchester Lakes Association,* 47 B.R. 798 (Bankr. E.D. VA).

6. Finding itself in great financial difficulty, Fidelity Mortgage Investors filed a voluntary bankruptcy petition in a New York bankruptcy court. When the petition was filed, the automatic suspension went into effect. Ignoring the suspension, Camelia and Farnale, two of FMI's creditors, filed suit against FMI in a Mississippi federal court. As a result, FMI was forced to pay out enormous sums of money in its own defense on the Mississippi case. FMI then returned to the bankruptcy court in New York and asked that both Camelia and Farnale be held in contempt of court for ignoring the suspension. Should the New York bankruptcy court hold Camelia and Farnale in contempt? Explain. *Fidelity Mortgage Investors v. Camelia Builders, Inc.,* 550 F.2d 47 (2nd Cir.).

7. When the Rahls filed for bankruptcy, they attempted to exclude their entire silverware set from the bankruptcy sale by listing each piece at a value far under the $200 maximum allowed for each item of individual household goods at that time. Had they listed the silverware as one item it would have been worth more than $6,000. Thus, the entire set would not have been exempt. By listing each piece of silverware separately, the total value did not exceed $4,000 and the entire set could be saved. Should the court force the Rahls to list the silverware set as one item, thus limiting the exemption to $200? Explain. *In the Matter of Rahl,* 14 B.R. 153 (Bankr. E.D. WI).

8. Dubuque stole more than $4,000 from his employer, U-Haul. He later pled guilty to "theft by unauthorized taking or transfer." The court sentenced him to pay back the stolen money. When

Dubuque filed for bankruptcy, U-Haul claimed that this debt would qualify as an exception to discharge. Was U-Haul correct? Explain. *In re Dubuque,* 46 B.R. 156 (NH).

9. U.S. Truck Company, Inc., filed for a reorganization under Chapter 11 of the Bankruptcy Code. When the reorganization plan was presented for confirmation, one creditor objected to the plan. The creditor argued that the debtor was facing a possible strike and a new labor contract, both of which could place an additional strain on the debtor's finances. These potential labor problems, the creditor concluded, made the plan unfeasible. U.S. Truck admitted that the labor problems existed but noted that the company had recently rebounded from its financial problems to become very successful. Moreover, the labor union had just ratified two previous labor contracts by a 95 percent majority vote. U.S. Truck concluded that these factors made the plan workable and that was enough under the code, since the code did not require a guarantee of success. Was the conclusion correct? *In the Matter of U.S. Truck Co., Inc.,* 47 B.R. 932 (Bankr. E.D. MI).

Quick Quiz Answers

31-1 & 31-2	31-3	31-4 & 31-5
1. F	1. T	1. F
2. T	2. F	2. T
3. T	3. F	3. T

Part 6 Case Study

In re: Lisa A. Bloch, Debtor Plaintiff v. Windham Professionals, et al., Defendants
United States Bankruptcy Court for the District of Massachusetts
257 B.R. 374

Summary

Lisa A. Bloch filed for bankruptcy relief seeking a discharge of her student loan obligations. A forty-one-year-old woman with no dependents, Bloch attended a number of prestigious universities and colleges including Radcliffe, Cornell, Harvard, and Princeton. Her graduate education, a master's degree in public administration from Suffolk University in Boston, was financed through five promissory notes totaling $41,863, which have been assigned to the defendant, Educational Credit Management Corp. (ECMC).

While in Boston, she established a pattern of sporadic, full-time employment supplemented by part-time clerical assignments arranged by temporary employment agencies. The evidence at trial suggested that Bloch has an impressive educational résumé, and an abundance of marketable skills, including a considerable computer background and some management experience. After obtaining her master's degree, she moved to Seattle, Washington, without a job and incurred moving expenses of approximately $5,000. Her employment woes continued in Seattle where she failed to obtain permanent work. Her testimony revealed that she survived for the last year by living with friends and paying expenses by accepting a gratuitous $4,000 loan. Bloch admits she has no physical or mental disabilities that would hinder her from working full time, but for some unexplained reason, either a personality issue, or perhaps wanderlust, she has not been employed in any one full-time position for longer than a year since attaining her master's degree.

At the time of the trial, Bloch worked less than 30 hours per week at $20 per hour, earning approximately $2,350 per month gross pay. She testified that she was reluctant to seek additional evening or weekend employment because it would impede her search for a permanent full-time position. She presented evidence showing her current monthly living expenses to be approximately $2,200.

At trial, Bloch expressed optimism about an improvement in her job prospects, a desire to repay her outstanding loans, and acknowledged that she only brought this action as a result of her frustration in dealing with the various student loan agencies.

The Court's Opinion

Joel B. Rosenthal, United States Bankruptcy Judge

Section 523(a) (8) of the Bankruptcy Code states:

> A discharge under sections 727, 1141, 1228(a), 1228(b), or 1328(b) of this title does not discharge an individual debtor from any debt for an educational benefit, overpayment or loan made, insured or guaranteed by a governmental unit, or made under any program funded in whole or in part by a governmental unit

or nonprofit institution, or for an obligation to repay funds received as an educational benefit, scholarship or stipend unless excepting such debt from discharge under this paragraph will impose an undue hardship on the debtor and the debtor's dependents. . . .

(T)he issue . . . is whether the Debtor has met her burden of proving that excepting her student loan obligations from discharge will cause her "undue hardship."

This Court has adopted the "totality of the circumstances" test. . . . In *Dolan v. American Student Assistance, et al.,* 256 B.R. 230, this Court stated that a debtor seeking discharge of student loans under §523(a) (8) "must prove by a preponderance of the evidence, that (1) his past, present, and reasonably reliable future financial resources; (2) his and his dependents' reasonably necessary living expenses, and; (3) other relevant facts or circumstances particular to the debtor's case are such that excepting the student loans from discharge will prevent the debtor from maintaining a minimal standard of living, even with the advantage of a discharge of his other pre-petition debts." By making specific findings as to each of these matters, the Court must then determine if excepting a debtor's student loans from discharge will impose an "undue hardship" on that debtor and the debtor's dependents. Having stated the applicable analysis for "undue hardship" in this Court, I now turn to this Debtor's request for relief.

A. The Debtor's Past, Present and Reasonably Reliable Future Financial Resources

While it may be true the Debtor's past and present income are insufficient to pay her student loans and still maintain a minimal standard of living, the Debtor has nonetheless not proven to the Court's satisfaction that her prospects for increasing her future income are so bleak as to warrant a discharge of her student loans. . . . The Debtor currently makes $2,350 per month, and the Debtor's current living expenses suggest her past and present income have not been enough to service her student loans. The Court believes, though, that the Debtor could significantly enhance her future income by exploiting her educational credentials and the job skills she has acquired in past employment. Although highly educated, the Debtor's résumé and testimony indicate a presently unstable and uninspiring employment history, but the Court is convinced this will change, particularly in light of the favorable economic conditions present in Boston and Seattle, as well as the Debtor's portable credentials and job skills.

Furthermore, the Court believes the Debtor could do more to maximize her income by increasing the length of her work week. The Debtor admitted she works an average of only 29.5 hours per week. The Debtor has failed to show that this is reasonable given her economic circumstances and abilities. A 29.5 hour work week is a personal choice she has made and is not linked to any physical or mental disability, nor is it motivated by a need to care for any dependents. The Debtor stated her unwillingness to take part-time evening or weekend work because she says this would interfere with her job search. The Court finds this explanation unconvincing. It is not at all unreasonable to expect this Debtor to supplement her income by taking part-time weekend or evening work in order to meet her student loan obligations. . . . An increase in the Debtor's work hours, either at a part-time job or at her present temporary position, would raise her monthly income, possibly allowing her to make some effort at repayment of her student loans. The Debtor's strong educational background, coupled with her transferable skills and talents should assist her in her search for employment. Based on her education, and her articulate pro se presentation in this adversary proceeding, the Court is confident that the Debtor will bounce back by finding employment commensurate with her education. Therefore, the Court concludes the Debtor's past, present, and reasonably reliable future financial resources will allow her to pay her student loan obligations and still maintain a minimal standard of living.

B. The Debtor's Reasonably Necessary Living Expenses

In addition to the Court's conclusion that the Debtor's future income prospects will allow her to repay her student loans without undue hardship, the Court likewise finds the Debtor has not done all she can to minimize her reasonably necessary living expenses, and as such the Court denies her the relief requested. . . . The Court's review of the Debtor's living expenses leads to the conclusion that her living expenses are, for the most part, modest. The Debtor could however reduce her substantial rent expense in some manner with a resultant monthly savings of perhaps hundreds of dollars. For example, the Debtor could reduce her rent expense by taking a more affordable apartment, or perhaps by taking in a roommate in her present home. Either of these options would help ease her present financial burdens. Thus, the Court finds the Debtor has not done all she can to minimize her reasonably necessary living expenses such that she is entitled to a discharge of her student loans for "undue hardship" under §523(a) (8).

C. The Debtor's Other Relevant Facts or Circumstances

While the Court has already concluded the Debtor has not taken steps to maximize her current income and minimize her expenses, the Court also looks to see if there are facts or circumstances unique to the Debtor's case that warrant granting a discharge of her student loans, notwithstanding the Court's conclusions above. In this case, the Debtor has failed to present evidence of any facts or circumstances that would lead this Court to conclude that excepting her student loans from discharge would impose an undue hardship. On the contrary, the Debtor's facts and circumstances militate against granting a discharge. For example, the Debtor has no dependents that might place a burden upon her monthly income or expenses. . . . Also, the Debtor is fortunately not burdened with any handicap or disability that precludes her from any of the vocational fields the Debtor is qualified to enter. Additionally, the Debtor has continually professed a willingness to repay her outstanding student loans, and but for the purported inflexibility of the lenders' policies would enter into a payment arrangement to meet those obligations.

As the Court can find no compelling reason to grant this Debtor a discharge of her student loans, the Court must find for the defendant, ECMC, and leave the prevailing party with the suggestion that it work with this Debtor to reach a transitional agreement until the Debtor's employment situation changes.

Questions for Analysis

1. What must a debtor prove to be excepted from the rule that a student loan obligation cannot be discharged in bankruptcy?

2. What is the name of the test that the court has adopted to determine whether an exception exists?

3. What three points must a debtor prove to meet the test?

4. Summarize the court's opinion on each point.

5. What was the decision of the court?

Agency and Employment

Part Seven

<table>
<tr><td>

Chapter 32

</td><td>

The Principal and Agent Relationship

</td></tr>
</table>

The Opening Case
"Bidding Is Such Sweet Sorrow"

Once Jake Burdett discovered the advantages of hunting for vintage comic books on eBay, he made a habit of checking for back issues of The Green Arrow, his favorite superhero. One afternoon, while browsing through eBay, he discovered that the entire run of The Green Lantern-Green Arrow series by Dennis O'Neil and Neal Adams from the 1970s was up for auction. All thirteen issues were advertised for sale in mint condition. Burdett was anxious to bid but, because he was on a tight budget, he watched the bidding contest without entering it. His plan was to wait until the last second and then, in the final minute of the auction, enter the bidding by making an outrageously high bid that other bidders would be unable to reach in time during the last few seconds. During that last minute of the bidding, Burdett entered his first and final bid of $500. Burdett did not, however, realize that the cyberprocess he had entered would permit the bids to jump until the maximum bid was reached. Another bidder had entered a bid of $450. At the end of the bidding process, Burdett won the comics, but he ended up owing $450.50 for the collection, an amount he really could not afford. The cyberprocess that Burdett entered when he bid for the comics is a form of proxy bidding, which is carried on by a bot. A bot is driven by a software program which allowed Burdett's bidding to continue without human intervention until his maximum bid was reached. Without realizing it, Burdette had given a cybernetic entity the power to negotiate the purchase of the comics in his place. It appears then that Burdett created a cyberagent which had the authority to bind him to a contract. On the other hand, the User Agreement that eBay publishes states quite explicitly that entering a cyberbidding process does not create an agency relationship. Who is correct here? Is an agency relationship created when eBay users enter the automatic cyberbidding process? Or does eBay's simple statement that no agency relationship exists, make it so? Questions like this are explored in this chapter on the law of agency.

Chapter Outcomes

1. Describe the nature of the agency relationship.
2. Outline the doctrine of vicarious liability.
3. Distinguish among the different types of principals.
4. Differentiate among the different type of agents.
5. Explain the liability of agents.
6. Clarify the liability of principals.

7. Illustrate how agents relate to business associations.
8. Disclose how agency relationships are created.
9. Explain the purpose of the Uniform Compute Transactions Act.
10. Describe the goal of the Uniform Electronic Transactions Act.

32-1 The Law of Agency

In an essay entitled, "How Culture Changes," the anthropologist George Peter Murdock of Yale University, explains, "It is a fundamental characteristic of culture that, despite its essentially conservative nature, it does change over time and from place to place." The fact that the law is a part of this process of change has been a recurring theme throughout this book. The emergence of the law of agency within our culture is another prime example of this tendency toward change within the legal complex adaptive system. Many of the changes that we have seen throughout the book emerge because the law must adapt to deal with shifts in culture and social norms caused by technology, political conflict, economic problems, and interpersonal relationships. The emergence of the law of agency, in contrast, was precipitated by a different set of circumstances. The law of agency emerged because people are limited in the amount of work they can handle, in the knowledge they can retain, and in their physical ability to travel from one place to another.

See: Murdock, George Peter. "How Culture Changes." In *Man, Culture, and Society*. Edited by Harry L. Shapiro. New York: Oxford University Press, 1960, p. 247.

The Nature of Agency

Because the law of agency developed in response to human limitations, it was forced to borrow many of its principles from other, older and more well-developed areas of the law. Thus, in agency law, concepts that are found in tort law, contract law, trust law, and remedies can also be found in agency. On the other hand, the law of agency has been around long enough to have developed its own rules. Thus, the concept of vicarious liability, for example, while involving tort law, nevertheless, arose because of agency. The same is true of concepts such as inherent agency power, undisclosed principals, and the ratification of agency authority. Because the law of agency has its own principles, rules, doctrines, and concepts all of which emerged independently and belong only to agency, it is said to be *sui generis,* that is, a law unto itself.

Agency is a legal relationship in which one party, the **agent,** is authorized to act for and under the control of the second, the **principal,** in negotiating and making contracts with a third party. The **third party** is that individual with whom the agent deals for the principal. The principal must indicate in some manner that the agent is to act for and under the control of the principal. An agency relationship is always **consensual** because the agent must agree to act for the principal. The agency relationship is *fiduciary* because the agent and principal trust one another. The relationship may or may not arise because of a contract; however, it is always consensual. If an agency relationship does not result from a contract, it a **gratuitous agency** and the agent is a **gratuitous agent.** Once an agency relationship has been created, certain obligations, rights, and liabilities arise that relate to the principal, the agent, and the third party. Except for the obligation to compensate the agent in a contractual relationship, the obligations, rights, and liabilities remain the same regardless of whether the agent is contractual or gratuitous.

Teaching Tips Ask students to think of certain situations in which they have made contracts through third parties. Agency relationships are not always recognized as involving agency, so you might offer some examples. For instance, salespeople act as agents for their employers when they make contracts with customers.

Within the scope of the agency, principal and agent are one.

—Oliver Wendell Holmes (1841–1935), Supreme Court Justice

State Variations In Pennsylvania, an employer is responsible for the negligence of all employees acting within the scope of their employment.

Example 32-1

Several individuals were hired by Taylor Toys, Inc., to serve as sales representatives to introduce Taylor's new line of action figures based on major league baseball players just in time for the All Star Game. These representatives visited toy stores at
(Continued)

> ### Example 32-1 (*Continued*)
>
> malls, interviewed store managers, and, in many cases, obtained orders for the new action figures. This arrangement constituted an agency relationship in which Taylor Toys (the principal) is liable for the actions of its sales representatives (the agents) in their dealings with its many customers (the third parties).

Principal-Agent Relationship

In an agency relationship, the agent has the authority to represent the principal (see Figure 32-1). This means that the principal is liable for the agent's acts when the agent deals with third parties for the principal. In the principal-agent relationship, the agent performs duties for the principal that require the exercise of judgment and discretion and that result in a contract. Any person legally capable of entering into a contract may be a principal. Anyone appointed by the principal may be an agent. Even a minor or one who is mentally limited may be an agent, inasmuch as the acts of such persons are considered to be those of the principal.

Employer-Employee Relationship

The legal principles governing the relationship of principal and agent and of employer and employee are basically the same. The main distinction between the two relationships is the agent's authority to contract. While an agent always has some sort of power to enter contracts on behalf of a principal, an employee does not always have this power. An employee who merely performs mechanical acts for the employer under the employer's direction is not an agent. In contrast, a person who is an employee and who does have the power to enter contracts for the employer would have the status of an agent even without a formally executed contract of agency. Not all agents are employees of their respective principals, however. A real estate broker who is appointed by a homeowner to sell a house is an agent but not an employee.

Master-Servant Relationship

The terms *master* (employer) and *servant* (employee) are not outdated, but continue to be used in some legal circumstances. A **master** is a person who has the right to control the

Figure 32-1 The agent has the authority to represent the principal in an agency relationship.

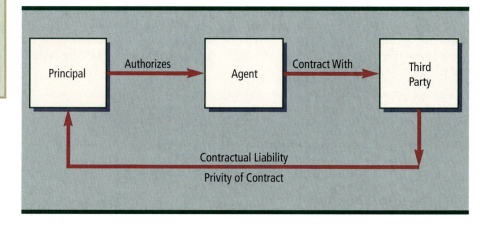

activities of another person. The person whose activities are controlled is called the **servant.** A servant who also has the right to conduct the business of the master is also an agent. In common usage, the terms *employer* and *employee* refer to the master-servant relationship. The terms *master* and *servant* are used instead of *employer* and *employee* in a legal setting when questions of tort liability arise.

For a detailed look at the works quoted in Talking Points see: Means, Richard L. *The Ethical Imperative: The Crisis in American Values.* New York: Doubleday, 1970, p. 175; Dewey, Thomas. *Individualism Old and New.* New York: Capricorn Books, 1962, p. 74.

Talking Points

In his book, *The Ethical Imperative,* the philosopher, Richard L. Means makes the following observation: "There are those who seem to believe that society does not exist in any real sense. Ayn Rand and her followers broadcast that it is only the individual who truly exists, and that the true nature of the individual is to maximize his or her own self-interest, economic profit, and personal satisfaction. This is called 'objectivism' by the true believer in 'Randian philosophy.' Such a view seems widespread in American culture."

In contrast, the American philosopher Thomas Dewey in his book, *Individualism: Old and New,* points out, "Our material culture, as anthropologists would call it, is verging on the collective and corporate."

In light of these two quotations, and the study of agency in this chapter, explore the following two questions: Does the law of agency promote collective behavior by allowing persons, including corporate, governmental, and institutional organizations to operate on a massive scale through its agents? Or does it promote individualism by allowing individuals to extend their own influence beyond their immediate physical restraints?

Proprietor-Independent Contractor Relationship

An **independent contractor** is a party who contracts to do a job and retains complete control over the methods employed to obtain final completion. The party for which an independent contractor works is often referred to as a **proprietor.** Independent contractors are not subject to the control of the proprietor. They maintain all required business licenses and permits and pay all job-related expenses; they are obligated only to get the job done. The proprietor has the right to specify the results of the job in question. Moreover, he or she has the right to inspect and approve, or disapprove, the results of the independent contractor's performance. Independent contractors are not employees; however, they may be agents. The distinction depends upon whether the independent contractor has the right to enter a contract on behalf of the proprietor. For instance, an individual might hire a financial expert to buy and sell stocks in his or her name. The financial expert would be an independent contractor as well as an agent. However, the expert would not be an employee.

Most famous personalities use an agent to represent them, especially in compensation matters.

Why the Distinctions Are Significant

The distinctions among these relationships frequently can be crucial in determining the nature and the extent of legal liability. It is important to note, however, that the names themselves are not controlling. Instead, it is the true nature of the relationship that is critical. Calling a servant an independent contractor does not transform the nature of the relationship if the master still controls the servant's conduct.

Contractual Liability   An agent is appointed by a principal to negotiate and enter into contracts on behalf of the principal. This means that the principal is bound to the terms of those contracts.

Unless an employee is also an agent, he or she has no power to negotiate and enter contracts for the employer. Moreover, an independent contractor has no power to bind the proprietor to a contract, unless expressly authorized to do so.

Tort Liability   The distinction between master-servant and proprietor-independent contractor relationships is especially critical in determining the nature and the extent of tort liability. Even though everyone is responsible for their own tortious conduct, there are times when the law will hold not only the tortfeasor, but also the person who engaged the tortfeasor, liable for the tort. This type of liability is called **vicarious liability.** Vicarious liability is based on the principle of *respondeat superior* (let the master, or the superior, respond). In most instances, a court will apply this principle when it is faced with a master-servant relationship because the master has the right to control the physical conduct of the servant (see Figure 32-2).

The concept of master-servant liability, in fact the entire concept of agency law itself, from a historical perspective arose from those Roman laws that dealt with masters and slaves. Under traditional Roman law, if a slave committed an offense against an innocent party, the slave owner was required to surrender the slave to the victim. Eventually, however, the law allowed the slave owner to pay the victim a sum of money so that the owner could retain the services of a valuable slave. Soon the custom became to sue the owner directly since, in most cases, the owner would prefer to keep the slave and pay the victim. Later, the Roman courts also began to hold innkeepers and ship owners directly liable

Figure 32-2 This chart shows the flow of principal/employer tort liability under the *respondeat superior* doctrine.

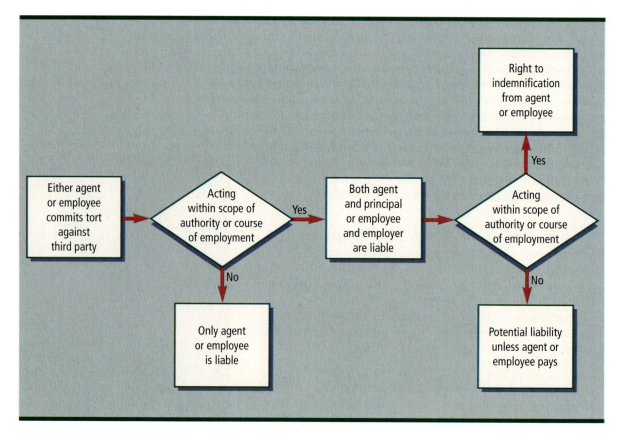

for torts committed by those who worked for them, on the basis of the idea that both ship owners and innkeepers held a high duty to those who traveled on their ships or who stayed at their inns. Often, a case was brought directly against the ship owner or the innkeeper, on the basis of the idea that they had a responsibility to make sure they had the best workers in their employ. As we shall see shortly, these two doctrines are still part of the law today in the form of nondelegable duties and the ideas of negligent hiring and negligent retention. (See page 608.) Moreover, since ship owners and innkeepers were just as likely to have free people working for them as slaves, the courts saw vicarious liability in terms of all workers, not just slaves. Nevertheless, the terms master and servant remain with us still today.

Example 32-2

Quentin Carraway was employed as a delivery driver for the St. Clair Printing Co. His supervisor, Ken Popson, was one of the owners of the company. Popson was responsible for setting the driving schedules. Every morning Popson would post a list of the companies that were to receive deliveries from St. Clair. The posted list would also include both the contents of the delivery and the order in which the packages were to be delivered. Popson also had all of the paperwork compiled so that all the drivers had to do was pick up the packing slips and invoices, load the packages, and get on the road for the day. Popson, however, never checked to see whether the drivers actually followed his suggested order and so some of the drivers, including Carraway, would decide on their own routes and would change the order of the deliveries to fit the route, rather than the other way around. When Carraway had an accident that injured several individuals and damaged several vehicles, the victims sued St. Clair on the basis of vicarious liability. Since Popson had the *right* to control the delivery drivers, the fact that Carraway had changed the suggested order of the deliveries would not absolve the company of liability.

In order to apply the doctrine of *respondeat superior* in a tort case, two questions must be answered. First, is the alleged tortfeasor a servant or an independent contractor? This first question often can be answered simply by looking at the degree of control that the hiring person has over the hired person. A master has the right to control the activities of a servant. A proprietor does not have the right to control independent contractors.

If the degree of control is unclear or in dispute, the court can apply other guidelines to determine whether the hired person is a servant or an independent contractor. For example, independent contractors usually have the power to choose their own workers and to discharge them on the job. They usually provide their own equipment and tools and are responsible for performing the entire job, including cleaning up. Workers paid by the hour are usually considered servants. Those who are paid by the job are usually independent contractors. Most of the time if working hours are set by the hiring person, the worker is a servant. A worker who determines his or her own hours is most often an independent contractor. Painters, physicians, and plumbers are examples of independent contractors when they are in business for themselves. They can lose this status and become employees, however, if they are hired as members of an employer's staff.

If the court determines that a master-servant relationship does exist, then it will turn to the next question, that is, the scope of employment. The **scope of employment** involves the range of activities for which the servant is engaged. In order for the doctrine of *respondeat superior* to apply, a tort must be committed while the worker was performing a task for

For a more detailed explanation of the development of agency law see: Holmes, Oliver Wendell, Jr. *The Common Law*. New York: Barnes and Noble Books, 2004, pp. 6–12.

State Variations In 1998, the U.S. Supreme Court ruled that employers in all states are vicariously liable for the sexually harassing acts of their supervisors, even if victims don't suffer adverse, tangible job-related consequences.

State Variations In Tennessee, an employer of a therapist may be liable if sexual misconduct occurred and the employer fails to take reasonable action when the employer knows or should have known of such misconduct, or the employer fails to make inquiries of a former employer of the therapist concerning past sexual misconduct of the therapist.

Getting Students Involved With help from students, create a list of occupations that are often performed by independent contractors. Then have the students choose one of the occupations listed and research the responsibilities involved, compiling a list of the costs of being an independent contractor in that occupation. Remind students to take into account personal expenses, such as insurance and taxes, as well as costs of the occupation, such as hiring subcontractors, renting space, and purchasing materials.

which he was hired, or at least one that he or she was authorized to perform by his or her employer. To determine whether a servant was operating within the scope of employment, ask the following questions:

1. Was the action committed by the employee authorized by the employer?
2. Where did the action take place?
3. Were the employer's interests promoted by the action?
4. Did the employer supply the instrumentality used in the action?
5. Was this action performed by other employees on a regular basis?
6. Was the action committed by the employee criminal?

Example 32-3

Anne Rutgers works as a cab driver for the Starshine Cab Company. While on a routine run transporting a passenger from New York's La Guardia Airport to the Marriott Marquis Hotel on Times Square, she collided with a car driven by Ian Harrington. Harrington wanted to sue both Rutgers and the Starshine Cab Company. He did so under the doctrine of vicarious liability because Rutgers was (a) an employee under the control of the cab company and (b) was operating within the scope of her employment.

If we apply the six factors listed above, the outcome of the case becomes obvious. First, Rutgers' activity of driving a cab was authorized by her employer. Second, the incident took place in midtown Manhattan, where Rutgers is authorized to drive. Third, the business of her employer was advanced by transporting a passenger from the airport to a hotel. Fourth, she was using a cab owned by the company. Fifth, she was driving a cab, which was something that she did on a regular basis. Finally, there was nothing criminal about her action. If several of the questions listed above led to opposite answers, a different decision might result. Consider, for instance, the following example.

Example 32-4

Suppose in the example cited above, after the accident in midtown, Rutgers got off work and, instead of returning the cab to the company garage as she was supposed to, she drove the cab to New Jersey to visit some friends and to have a drink or two in a neighborhood bar to calm her nerves. If in that situation she were to leave the bar and collide with a pedestrian, or anyone else for that matter, she would be operating outside the scope of her employment and the cab company would not be liable for her negligence.

In these two examples, the result is clear. Not all cases, however, offer this type of clarity. Consider, for instance, the following example.

Example 32-5

Raymond Meyers was employed as an accountant for the Enson-McKnight Aeronautics Company. He worked in the tax department of the manufacturer determining how to handle taxation problems for the company's branches in Europe and

South America. In July at the company's Independence Day picnic held on company grounds, Tony Enson, the president and CEO of the company, tried to convince Meyers to drive one of the company-owned golf carts in a golf cart race. Meyers did not want to get into the race and argued that he had no experience driving a golf cart. Nevertheless, the president insisted. Again Meyers refused. Finally, when it was clear that the president was about to get very angry with Meyers, he agreed to enter the race. Meyers lost control of the golf cart and drove into a group of passers-by injuring several of them. The victims sued both Meyers and Enson-McKnight on the basis of vicarious liability. The company argued that it should not be held liable since operating a golf cart was outside the scope of Meyers's employment as a tax accountant. The plaintiffs argued that, since Meyers was essentially ordered by the president to drive the company-rented golf cart at the company-sponsored picnic in a company-controlled race, the doctrine of vicarious liability applies.

No definitive answer exists in this case. Both sides have valid arguments. The defendants can argue quite convincingly that the employee, who was a tax accountant at the company, was not acting within the scope of his employment when he drove a golf cart into the group of passers-by. Moreover, the company can argue that driving a golf cart does not further the business of the aeronautics company. On the other hand, the plaintiffs can argue, with equal conviction, that since the accountant was ordered by the president of the company to drive a company-rented golf cart at a company-sponsored picnic, on company-owned property, he was essentially operating within the scope of his employment.

Most of the time vicarious liability is applied to negligence cases, because workers are not usually hired to commit intentional torts. There are, of course exceptions to this rule. If, for example, a servant commits a tort intending to further the master's business, as when a bouncer at a casino uses force to eject an unruly patron, then the master may be liable for battery. Or, if a security guard at a department store detains an innocent shopper by locking him or her in a room for several hours, the owner of the store might be liable for false imprisonment. Moreover, if the master could reasonably foresee that the servant might commit the intentional tort, as might be the case with a bouncer in a casino or a security guard in a department store, then the master may be liable for that tort.

The law also makes a distinction between intentional torts that cause actual physical harm and those that do not result in such harm. In the case of a physical tort the master will always be liable, assuming all of the other tests are met. However, in nonphysical torts the master is liable only if the servant possessed actual or apparent authority. Actual authority, as we shall see later at length, is real authority that exists because of some communication between the principal and the agent. Apparent authority exists when the principal has led a third party to the reasonable belief that a nonagent has certain agency powers.

When a master loans a servant to another master, the servant is referred to as a **borrowed servant.** In such a situation a question may arise as to which master should bear the loss caused by the servant's tort. The answer to this question depends on which one had control of the servant when the tort occurred. Other circumstances such as whose work is being performed and who supplies the tools and the place of work are relevant in answering this question. The skill of the worker, the length of time the worker has been aiding in the other's business, and the manner in which the worker is paid

The master is only liable when the servant is acting in the course of employment. If he was going out of his way, against his master's implied commands, when driving on his master's business, he will make his master liable; but if he was going on a frolic of his own, without being at all on his master's business, the master will not be liable.

—*Joel v. Morison,* 6 Car. & P. 501, 503, 172 Eng. Rep. 1338, 1339 (Ex. 1834)

Independent contractors are not employees of the homeowner.

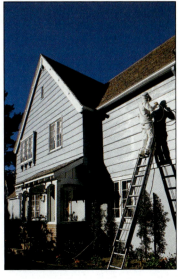

may also be relevant to show the ease with which control over a worker is shifted from one master to another.

Example 32-6

Fred Anderson was regularly employed by Georgetown Construction as a bulldozer driver. Georgetown subcontracted the building of several airfields throughout the south to Riverdell Construction. Riverdell was so impressed with Anderson's work that the company requested that he be permitted to join them on six more jobs. Georgetown agreed. Anderson showed up to work at sites completely controlled by Riverdell every day for eighteen months. Whenever special training was needed, he received it from Riverdell. He used Riverdell's equipment and tools and, when the Riverdell crew was on the road, he stayed with them at their hotel at Riverdell's expense. Riverdell figured out Anderson's wages and paid him, later getting a reimbursement for that amount from Georgetown. Anderson rarely contacted or was contacted by Georgetown for that entire eighteen-month period. During the nineteenth month, Anderson lost control of the bulldozer, which smashed into a truck driven by Victor Lazlo. Lazlo wants to sue both Anderson and Riverdell, but Riverdell claims that Anderson is not its employee. Under these circumstances, it is likely that the court would rule that Anderson is the borrowed employee of Riverdell. The key factor is that Riverdell had complete control over the activities of Anderson and had exercised that control extensively for eighteen months.

Related Cases Difficulties resulting from borrowed servants are not new. In 1826, a country gentleman, who had just arrived in town without means to get around, hired a carriage with horses and a driver from a stablekeeper. The driver negligently drove the gentleman's coach into another vehicle. The judges of the King's Bench divided two to two on the question of liability of the gentleman. *Laugher v. Pointer,* 5 B & C 547.

In some situations, the court may hold the proprietor liable for the torts of the independent contractor. For instance, in some jurisdictions, if a proprietor is negligent in checking an independent contractor's qualifications and, consequently, hires someone who is incompetent, the proprietor may be held liable should an innocent third party be injured by the negligence of the incompetent independent contractor. The court may hold the proprietor liable for the **negligent hiring** of the incompetent independent contractor. Similarly, a proprietor may be liable for the **negligent retention** of an incompetent independent contractor if, after hiring the independent contractor, the proprietor learns that the contractor is incompetent and does not dismiss the contractor. A proprietor may also be open to liability when the independent contractor has been hired to perform a nondelegable duty. A **nondelegable duty** is one that the proprietor cannot delegate, or pass off, to another party.

Example 32-7

Since it was suffering from a fiscal shortfall, Airflight Airlines, Inc., had elected to hire an independent maintenance firm to service its entire fleet of jet aircraft. The independent firm, Jackson Maintenance, Inc., made several serious errors that caused one of Airflight's planes to lose a wheel on a landing. The crash landing injured several passengers. Both Airflight and Jackson Maintenance were sued by the injured passengers. Even though Airflight could show that Jackson Maintenance was an independent contractor, the airline company could not escape liability for the accident because a common carrier, such as an airline company, cannot delegate its duty to protect its passengers.

Sovereign Immunity **Sovereign immunity** is a doctrine preventing a lawsuit against government authority without the government's consent. The doctrine is no longer as important a defense for government torts as it once was. It no longer protects government from liability, at least when the injury is caused by the government acting in its capacity as a commercial being rather than that of a supreme government. The doctrine has been abolished in some states by judicial decision and in others by legislation.

Federal Tort Claims Act The Federal Tort Claims Act of 1946 limits the federal government's sovereign immunity. Whenever a federal employee harms a third party or private property while driving a motor vehicle in the course of employment, the federal government is liable. However, the 1946 law explicitly preserves governmental immunity for a vaguely defined category of "discretionary" actions by officials.

> ## Example 32-8
>
> In 1982, a federal district court judge held that radioactive fallout from above-ground nuclear tests had caused at least nine people and perhaps dozens of others to die of cancer. The judge ruled that the federal government must pay damages under the Federal Tort Claims Act, explaining that while the high-level decision to conduct the tests had been discretionary, and thus was immune from liability, officials had conducted the tests in a negligent manner by failing to monitor radiation adequately or to warn residents of neighboring areas in Nevada, southern Utah, and northern Arizona who lived downwind from the test site about radiation hazards and how to reduce them. A federal appeals court, however, held that all aspects of the testing program were conducted in accordance with discretionary decisions of the Atomic Energy Commission and were thus immune from liability. The U.S. Supreme Court in 1988 refused to hear an appeal from the appellate decision.

Criminal Liability The principal or employer ordinarily is not liable for an agent's or employee's crimes, unless the principal or employer actually aids or participates in their commission. The commission of a crime usually requires a state of mind that is specified in the criminal statute. Thus, if the principal or employer had not authorized the crime, the courts would conclude that the requisite mental state has not been shown.

A principal or employer will be held criminally liable for acts done by an agent or employee to further an illegal business. In addition, most states have enacted statutes that hold a principal or employer liable for certain crimes committed by their agents or employees, even though they acted disobediently. Examples of such statutes are those that penalize the sale of impure foods or alcoholic beverages. Principals or employers may also be penalized for the acts of managerial or advisory persons who are acting in the scope of authority or

> ## A Question of Ethics
>
> In Example 32-8, a federal appeals court decided that the discretionary nature of the atomic tests conducted by the U.S. government made the federal government immune from liability. This ruling meant that legally the government did not have to compensate anyone injured as a result of those tests. However, was it ethical for the government to ignore the claims of the injured parties? Explain.

Terms Sovereign immunity developed from the theory that the King of England, as the supreme ruler, was immune from lawsuits. The word *sovereign* comes from Old French and from Latin *super,* meaning "to be above."

State Variation Most states have passed statutes that provide procedures for citizens to sue the state. Iowa passed the Tort Claims Act, which lists under what circumstances a citizen may sue the state. It also describes the procedure that should be used.

Getting Students Involved Have students discuss whether the U.S. government should be liable for all improper actions or only those that are allowed under the Federal Tort Claims Act. Does the historical background of sovereign immunity have any relevance today?

employment, unless they act in disobedience of instructions and not for the purpose of serving the principal or employer.

Despite the fact that principals can, in some cases, be held liable for the criminal activity of their subordinates, they will generally be fined but not imprisoned. This is because most states have enacted laws that will prevent imprisonment for vicarious crimes.

Quick Quiz 32-1 True or False?

1. Agency is an area of the law which arose because of the physical restraints imposed on people by the natural rules of the universe.

2. When a master loans a servant to another master, the servant is known as an independent contractor.

3. Most states have enacted laws that will prevent imprisonment for vicarious crimes.

32-2 Principles of Agency

Now that the different types of relationships involved in business have been discussed, the focus of the chapter can return to the principal-agent relationship. Several key guidelines help the courts to distinguish among different types of principals and among the different types of agents. Other principles help explain how agency law relates to minors and how it relates to business organizations.

Types of Principals

There are three types of principals. A **disclosed principal** is one whose identity is known by third parties dealing with that principal's agent. When an agent does not reveal the existence of an agency relationship but appears to act in his or her own behalf rather than for another, an **undisclosed principal** exists. A **partially disclosed principal** exists when the agent, in dealing with third parties, reveals the existence of an agency relationship but does not identify the principal.

Types of Agents

Teaching Tips Explain that an agent works for and on the behalf of a principal and is subject to the principal's control. Review the three types of principals and ask students to suggest examples of each type.

Agents are generally classified according to the scope of their responsibility. A **general agent** is a person who is given broad authority to act on behalf of the principal in conducting the bulk of the principal's business activity on a daily basis.

Example 32-9

Jay Crockett, manager of the Inverness New and Used Car Shop hired Thompson Decorators, Inc., to redecorate the showroom at Inverness. Crockett also employed two new used car salespeople to work the showroom on the weekends. As a general agent, Crockett has the authority to take these independent actions which protect and promote the interests of the dealership.

A **special agent** is a person who is authorized to conduct only a particular transaction, to conduct a series of related transactions, or to perform only a specified act for the principal. Examples are real estate brokers, lawyers, and accountants who are retained to do a specific job and whose authority is restricted to those acts necessary to accomplish it.

A **factor,** or common merchant, is a special agent who is employed to sell merchandise consigned for that purpose. The factor has possession of the goods and sells them for and in behalf of a principal. A factor who guarantees the credit of a third party to a principal and guarantees the solvency of the purchaser and performance of the contract is known as *del credere* **agent.** In the event of default, the *del credere* agent is liable to the principal.

Example 32-10

Edna Freeman hired Leonard Tenpenny to act as her agent in the sale of several antiques. The contract of agency included a promise by Tenpenny that Freeman would not suffer any loss because of any sales on credit that Tenpenny made with third parties. Shortly after, Tenpenny sold a rare first edition of one of Louis Bromfield's novels valued at $50,000 to Robert Fisher on credit. Fisher later declared bankruptcy. As a *del credere* agent, Tenpenny had guaranteed the credit of Fisher and is liable to Freeman for the value of the book.

Liability of Principals

The principal is liable on all contracts that a general or special agent may enter into with third parties, as long as the agent acts within the authority conferred by the principal. An undisclosed principal can be held liable for the acts of the agent once the identity of the principal is disclosed. Once the principal's identity is revealed, a third party may sue either the principal or the agent. Following this election, however, the third party cannot later decide to sue the other, unless the principal was undisclosed at the time the choice was made.

Liability of Agents

When an agent is not known to be an agent and is acting as a principal, the agent can be held liable as a principal. When a person is known to be an agent, but it is not known for whom the agent acts, the third party can also hold the agent liable. In addition, when an agent exceeds the authority conferred by the principal, the agent can be made personally liable.

Minors and Agency

A principal may not use the infancy of an agent as a reason for avoiding a contract made by that agent. The principal who is a minor may generally avoid or accept a contract made by an agent to the same extent that he or she could have had the principal dealt directly with the third party. However, state statutes are not universal in the way they treat the business contracts of minors. Some state courts have held that a minor who is sufficiently mature to run a business may not avoid business-related contracts made while running the business.

Example 32-11

Lew Shaver, a minor who owned a sports card shop, hired Quilla Henderson, an adult, as shop manager. Henderson contracted with a supply house to purchase six new display cases for the shop. Shaver refused to accept delivery or to pay for the cases. In the event the court interprets this transaction to be reasonably related to the carrying on of Shaver's business, it could hold that the purchase agreement was binding on Shaver.

Business Associations and Agency

Almost every executive of a business firm acts as the firm's agent in some capacity. For example, a purchasing agent is authorized to make agreements to buy equipment and supplies. A salesperson may be authorized to complete sales agreements. The treasurer can dispense the firm's money. The operation of partnerships and corporations illustrates the application of agency law.

Partnerships The Uniform Partnership Act and the partners' agreement govern partnership operations. Every partner in a partnership is an agent of that partnership for the purpose of its business. Thus, partners as agents are liable for the contracts that each makes in behalf of the business. The appointment of an agent by one partner is binding on all other partners.

Example 32-12

Yuri Korolyov and Sergei Leonov operated the Russian Space Collectibles Shop as partners. During Leonov's vacation, Korolyov ordered a large selection of cosmonaut hats. Although Leonov was not present and might disagree with the selection of merchandise, he will be liable for his share of the expense. Korolyov was acting as agent for the partnership, representing both himself and Leonov.

Corporations The corporation is an artificial person created by state statute, which authorizes it to provide and deliver products and/or services by means of agents acting in its behalf (see Chapter 37). All aspects of agency law pertaining to wrongful acts committed by agents against third parties or their property also apply to corporations. A corporation, being a legal entity only, cannot act for itself. All officers and employees are either agents or servants of the corporation, the principal.

Quick Quiz 32-2 True or False?

1. A partially disclosed principal exists when the agent, in dealing with third parties, reveals only the existence of the agency but not the identity of the principal.

2. A principal may not use the minority of an agent to avoid a contract made by that minor agent.

3. Corporations never need to deal through agents.

32-3 Creation of the Agency Relationship

An agency is created by some action or conduct on the part of the principal. A would-be agent cannot by conduct alone or by any statement establish an agency relationship. It is, therefore, wise for a third party, when dealing with an agent to determine the nature and extent of the agent's authority. An agency relationship is generally created by the following methods:

- appointment
- implication
- necessity
- operation of law
- estoppel
- ratification

Agency by Appointment

The usual agency relationship is created by an expressed agreement in which the agent is appointed to act for and on behalf of the principal. The agreement may be oral or written in the form of a power of attorney. A **power of attorney** is an instrument in writing by which one person, a principal, appoints another as agent and confers the authority to perform certain specified acts on behalf of the principal. It establishes the authority of the agent to third parties with whom the agent may deal.

Getting Students Involved Obtain from a stationery store standard forms for a power of attorney and have students examine them. Discuss the forms' terminology and have each student complete a form, giving power of attorney to an imaginary person. Be sure to void the forms at the end of class.

Example 32-13

Olga Stepford employed Samuel Benson as an agent to develop a recently purchased tract of land in Texas. Specifically, she wanted to drill for oil on the land. She executed a power of attorney authorizing Benson to contract for the purchase or sale of any property and to execute any necessary leases affecting the Stepford's interest in the Texas property. Benson also had the power to hire drillers to search for the oil. Benson hired The Tornado Drilling Company to commence drilling operations. Two weeks into the drilling, Eddie Krebs, the owner of Tornado, came to Benson and asked for a loan so that he could make some outstanding late payments on his drilling equipment. If he failed to make the payments, his equipment would be repossessed and the drilling would stop. Benson made the loan using Stepford's funds. Krebs later defaulted on the loan and left the country, vanishing without a trace. When Stepford attempted to hold Benson liable for the lost funds loaned to Krebs, the agent argued that the power of attorney granted him by Stepford empowered him to make the loan. In an interpretation of the terms of the power of attorney, the court reasoned that Benson's power to purchase, sell, lease, and hire drillers did not include the power to make a loan.

Equal-Dignities Rule In most states, the equal-dignities rule provides that when a principal authorizes an agent to enter into a written contract on behalf of the principal, the agent's authority to do so must also be in writing. The rule generally applies when the type of contract that the authorized person is to negotiate for another is required by the Statute of Frauds to be in writing.

Agency by Implication

An agency by implication may be created voluntarily by any conduct or actions of the principal and agent that reflect the intent to create an agency relationship, even though such intent is not expressed orally or in writing. Any conduct or words of the principal that give another cause to believe that the principal approves of that person acting as agent is sufficient to create an agency. Allowing a person to act as an agent knowingly and without objection is also viewed as permission to act as an agent.

Agency by Necessity

An agency by necessity is created lawfully when circumstances make such an agency necessary. If, for example, a real estate broker contracts for the repair of burst water pipes in the absence of the owner whose property the broker has been employed to sell, the court would hold that an agency of necessity had been created in order to prevent loss to the owner (principal).

Cross-Cultural Notes In the former Soviet Union, all artists and authors were required to use the services of VAAP, the government literary agency. VAAP held a monopoly on representation of literary talent. With the breakup of the Soviet Union, artists and authors gained the freedom to make their own independent contracts.

Agency by Law

The courts may create or find an agency when there is none if it appears from the facts that a necessity or desired social policy is involved. A child to whom a parent has failed to provide the necessities of life may be declared by the court an agent of the parent for the purpose of purchasing necessities the parent failed to provide. Under such an agency relationship, the parent would be bound by such contracts as long as they are reasonable.

Example 32-14

Andy Farmington, the father of six children, placed an advertisement in the classified section of the local newspaper stating that he would no longer be responsible for any bills unless contracted by him. He then abandoned his family. His wife, Emily Farmington, bought food and clothing for the children and herself. She also took the two youngest children to the doctor, and purchased the antibiotics ordered by the doctor for the children. Mrs. Farmington charged everything to her husband. Under these circumstances, Mrs. Farmington had become an agent by necessity, and her husband would be responsible for contracts made by her for all reasonable necessaries of life.

Agency by Estoppel

An agency by estoppel is created when one person is falsely represented to be an agent when no such agency relationship exists, or when an agent is falsely represented to possess authority outside the scope of his or her actual authority. Agency by estoppel is also known as apparent authority. The conduct of the agent alone cannot create apparent authority. The principal must willfully, negligently, or by silence give the false impression to a third party that another is the principal's agent. It is also possible for apparent authority to be created when the principal willfully, negligently, or by silence permits an actual agent to act outside the scope of his or her actual authority when dealing with a third party. Further, having dealt with the apparent agent in reliance on the false impression, the third party must be damaged by the fact that an actual agency relationship did not exist or by the fact that an actual agent did not possess the authority he or she appeared to have. In such a case, the principal is barred (estopped) from denying the apparent agency relationship. Apparent authority is covered in more detail in Chapter 33.

Agency by Ratification

Agents sometimes perform acts on behalf of the principal that exceed their authority. In such cases, the principal for whom the agent claimed to act may either ignore the transaction or ratify it. **Ratification** occurs when the principal approves the unauthorized act performed by an agent or by one who has no authority to act as an agent. Although an agent generally is personally liable to third parties for actions in excess of the agent's authority, this is not true when the third party knows that the agent has exceeded the proper level of authority.

In addition to an intent to ratify, certain other conditions must be fulfilled for ratification to be valid: The principal must have the capacity to ratify and must have knowledge of all the material facts. The act to be ratified must be legal and must have been done on behalf of the principal. Moreover, the ratification must apply to the entire act of the agent, and ratification must occur before the third party withdraws. The principal cannot accept the benefits of an unauthorized act and then refuse to accept the obligations that are part of it. The principal becomes bound as though the agent had authority to act.

Cyberagency and Authority

The Uniform Computer Information Transactions Act (UCITA) is valuable because it clearly establishes the nature of a cyberagent. According to UCITA, a *cyberagent* (also referred to as *electronic agents* and *e-agents*) can be characterized as a computer program that acts without human intervention to begin an activity, to answer cybermessages, to deliver or accept *cybermail,* or to enter cybercontracts, as a representative of an individual who does not intervene in the action taken by the cyberagent at the actual time of the cyberagent's activity. It is clear, then, that a *bot* (*robot, shopping bot, cyberbot* or *e-bot*) which searches cyberspace for the lowest price in a contract, sifts through the net for the best accommodations, hunts cyberspace for the most economical plan, or spontaneously responds to a bidding process during a cyberauction, is a cyberagent. The UCITA makes it clear that a principal, now termed a *cyberprincipal,* who places authority in the "hands" of a cyberagent will be liable for the cybercontracts entered by that cyberagent, even if the cyberprincipal remains ignorant of what the cyberagent has done because the cyberprincipal either ignores or forgets about the automated process.

Another model act, The Uniform Electronic Transactions Act (UETA), has legitimized the use of cyberagents by certifying that contracts made by cyberagents will have the same binding effect as contracts created by human agents. The net effect of these provisions is to guarantee that a company that has used a cyberagent to receive and process an order sent by a cyberagent will not be able to deny the effectiveness of that cybercontract. The provisions also state that once an individual has received an e-mail he or she is considered to have received notice of a cybercontract even if that person ignores or trashes the e-mail without opening or reading it. The UETA also says that cyberagents must be programmed to give the other party a confirmation that the cybercontract has been entered. Otherwise the cybercontract is voidable by that party.

Quick Quiz 32-3 True or False?

1. The equal dignities rule has been outlawed in most states.

2. An agency by estoppel is created when one person is falsely represented to be an agent when no such agency relationship exists.

3. Ratification occurs when the principal approves the unauthorized act performed by an agent.

Summary

32-1 Agency is the legal fiduciary relationship that exists when the principal authorizes the agent to create, modify, or end contractual relations involving the principal and third parties. The contracts that the agent negotiates are between the principal and third parties, and the principal is bound to perform them as if the principal had personally executed the agreement.

The courts are often called upon to distinguish among relationships between principal and agent, employer and employee, master and servant, and proprietor and independent contractor. The main difference between the principal-agent and employer-employee relationships is the agent's authority to contract. The terms master (employer) and servant (employee) are used when questions of tort liability arise. Even though all people are responsible for their own tortuous conduct, there are times when the law will hold not only the actual tortfeasor, but also the person who engaged the tortfeasor, liable for the tort. The name given to this type of liability is vicarious liability.

32-2 Any person legally capable of entering into a contract may be a principal. There are three kinds of principals—disclosed, undisclosed, or partially disclosed. Anyone may be appointed an agent. Agents are commonly classified as general agents, special agents, or factor and *del credere* agents. A principal is liable on all contracts that a general or special agent enters into as long as the agent acts with the authority of the principal. An agent acting as a principal can be held liable as a principal. Partnerships, corporations, and other businesses all act through agents.

32-3 An agency relationship generally may be created by appointment, implication, necessity, or operation of law. Under certain circumstances, the principal may be legally prevented (estopped) from asserting that the agent's act was unauthorized. Ratification by the principal of an unauthorized act by another person does not create agency, but it has the effect of agency. When the principal does not ratify another's unauthorized act, the person who acted without authority is personally liable on the contract.

Key Terms

agency, 601
agent, 601
borrowed servant, 607
consensual, 601
del credere agent, 611
disclosed principal, 610
factor, 611
general agent, 610
gratuitous agency, 601
gratuitous agent, 601

independent contractor, 603
master, 602
negligent hiring, 608
negligent retention, 608
nondelegable duty, 608
partially disclosed principal, 610
power of attorney, 613
principal, 601
proprietor, 603
ratification, 614

scope of employment, 605
servant, 603
sovereign immunity, 609
special agent, 610
sui generis, 601
third party, 601
undisclosed principal, 610
vicarious liability, 604

Questions for Review and Discussion

1. What is the nature of the agency relationship?
2. What is vicarious liability?
3. What are the different types of principals?
4. What are the different type of agents?
5. How does liability flow to agents?
6. How are principals liable?
7. How do agents relate to business associations?
8. How are agency relationships created?
9. What is the purpose of the Uniform Compute Transactions Act?
10. What is the purpose of the Uniform Electronic Transactions Act?

Investigating the Internet

Access Agency Law on the Brainy Encyclopedia website and find the entry on Hollywood agencies and management companies and write a report on one of those agencies or companies.

Cases for Analysis

1. A delivery truck driver who worked for the *Evening Star* in Washington, D.C., was on his route when he was commanded by a police officer to follow a traffic violator in order to apprehend him. The police officer then jumped onto the side of the truck and held on for the duration of the chase. During the high-speed pursuit, Balinovic was injured when the truck collided with his car. Balinovic wanted to sue both the driver and the *Evening Star* under the theory of vicarious liability. Would vicarious liability apply here? Was the driver a servant of the *Evening Star?* Was the driver operating within the scope of employment? Explain. *Balinovic v. Evening Star Newspaper Co.,* 113 F.2d 505 (D.C. Cir.).

2. Janet Young worked in an administrative capacity for the International Brotherhood of Locomotive Engineers. She was given a ten year contract by John Sytsma, the president of the union. The president regularly engaged in hiring union employees without consulting with either the executive committee or the advisory board of the union. In addition, the president entered into other contracts on behalf of the union. Although these powers were not specified in the constitution, the union knew that he dealt with the hiring of employees and that he routinely entered nonemployment contracts on behalf of the union. Sometime after Sytsma was defeated in a reelection bid, Larry McFather, the new president, discharged Young. McFather argued that Sytsma did not have the capacity to enter a ten year employment contract with Young because the authority to do so was not specified in the union's constitution. In addition, McFather pointed out that the contract had been entered during the union's convention, during which the power to govern the union falls to the delegates at the convention. In response, Young argued that the past practices of the union led her to the reasonable belief that the president had the power to grant her the employment contract. She also argued that even though the power to hire employees was not in the union constitution, the power to do so was implied by the powers of the president to preside over the union's administrative matters. Is Young correct on either of these points? Explain. *Young v. International Brotherhood of Locomotive Engineers,* 683 N.E.2d 420 (OH).

3. Mularchuk was employed as a part-time reserve police officer for the borough of Keansburg, New Jersey. He was never given any training, and he was not required to submit to any training with respect to the revolver he carried. A quarrel arose between McAndrew, who had car trouble, and a towtruck driver who McAndrew had called for assistance. Mularchuk proceeded to make arrests and, in the course of events, shot and seriously injured McAndrew. Was the borough of Keansburg liable to McAndrew under the doctrine of *respondeat superior?* Explain. *McAndrew v. Mularchuk,* 162 A.2d 820 (NJ).

4. Food Caterers, Inc., had a franchise agreement with Chicken Delight, Inc. Carfiro was employed by Food Caterers to deliver hot chicken bearing the trademark "Chicken Delight." While making a delivery, Carfiro was involved in an accident that killed McLaughlin. In a suit naming Chicken Delight, the franchiser, as defendant, the McLaughlin estate argued that Carfiro was an agent of Chicken Delight, since Carfiro was acting for the benefit of the company. There was no evidence, however, that Carfiro was hired, paid, instructed by, or even known by Chicken Delight. The decision was for whom and Why? *Estate of McLaughlin v. Chicken Delight, Inc.,* 321 A.2d 456 (CT).

5. While Elliot was an inmate at the state-run Chillicothe Correctional Institution, he was hit in the face by Turner, a corrections officer at the institution, and, therefore, a state employee. Elliot brought a lawsuit against the state under the doctrine of *respondeat superior.* The state argued that since Turner had acted recklessly in striking Elliot, his actions were outside the scope of his employment. Therefore, the state concluded, the court should dismiss Elliot's claim against it. Were Turner's actions outside the scope of his employment as a prison guard? Explain. *Elliot v. Ohio Department of Rehabilitation and Correction,* 637 N.E.2d 106 (OH).

6. Nielson had limited authority to purchase cattle for his principal, Hauser Packing Company. Christensen, who knew of Nielson's limited authority and who also knew that Nielson was exceeding that authority, nevertheless contracted with Nielson to sell cattle to the packing company. When the packing company refused to accept the

cattle, Christensen brought suit against Nielson for damages, showing that Hauser Packing Company refused to ratify the unauthorized act of its agent. The judgment was for whom and why? *Christensen v. Nielson,* 276 P. 645 (UT).

7. Hoddeson entered the showroom of the Koos Brothers Furniture Store, along with her aunt and four young children. She was met by a man dressed in a suit. He asked if he could help her and she consented. He showed her several pieces of bedroom furniture, including a mirror that she liked very much. She eventually decided on several pieces of furniture and gave the man cash in the amount of the purchases. He then told her that the items that she had requested were out of stock, but that they would be shipped very soon. The furniture items were never shipped to the Hoddesons who eventually found out that there was no record of either the transaction or the alleged sales clerk. The Hoddesons brought suit against Koos Brothers. What argument can the Hoddesons use that might persuade the court that Koos Brothers should be held liable for their loss? Explain your response. *Hoddeson v. Koos Brothers,* 135 A.2d 702 (NJ).

Quick Quiz Answers

32-1	32-2	32-3	32-4
1. T	1. T	1. F	1. T
2. F	2. T	2. T	2. F
3. T	3. F	3. T	3. T

Chapter 33   Agency Operation

The Opening Case
"Tarzan and the Agent"

In 1918 Edgar Rice Burroughs, the creator of Tarzan, entered a contract with Pliny P. Craft, the owner of Monopol Pictures, under which Monopol Pictures would produce a film entitled *The Return of Tarzan*. Almost immediately after the contract had been signed, problems arose. Craft complained that another film company's production of a film entitled *The Romance of Tarzan* had used so many scenes from *The Return of Tarzan* that his rights to that film had been severely damaged. A compromise was reached under which Craft was guaranteed the right of first refusal to all future Tarzan films, provided that Monopol Pictures produce at least one Tarzan film first. This did not, however, stop the trouble between Craft and Burroughs. Eventually, another compromise was reached under which Craft was given the rights to a second Tarzan film entitled *The Son of Tarzan* provided he produce the first film, *The Return of Tarzan,* by July 1, 1919. When Craft failed to meet the deadline, Burroughs sold the rights to *The Son of Tarzan* to another film company. Enraged, Craft sued Burroughs for $100,000. Burroughs retained a lawyer named Benjamin H. Stern to represent him. Stern entered negotiations with Craft on Burroughs's behalf, sending several letters to Craft and his attorney. In one of those letters, Stern suggested that Burroughs would be agreeable to reaching a settlement with Craft. This infuriated Burroughs who had no intention of settling the case, something that Burroughs believed Stern should have known. Consequently, when Burroughs received a bill from Stern for $1,000, he not only refused to pay what he considered to be an exorbitant amount, but also discharged Stern as his attorney. Did Stern, as Burroughs's agent, have the implied actual authority to settle the Craft case out of court? Did he have the apparent authority to do so on the basis of something Burroughs communicated to Craft? Did Stern disobey Burroughs's instructions when he offered a settlement? Did Burroughs violate his duty to compensate Stern by refusing to pay the $1,000? Was Burroughs justified in terminating the agency relationship? As you read Chapter 33, Agency Operation, consider whether Burroughs handled his agency relationship with Stern in the best possible, legal way.

Chapter Outcomes

1. Distinguish between express and implied agency authority.
2. Define apparent authority.
3. Explain the consequences of an unauthorized delegation of agency authority.
4. Indicate when an agent can legally appoint a subagent.
5. Enumerate the duties of an agent to the principal.
6. List the remedies available to a principal.
7. Clarify the duties that a principal has in relation to an agent.
8. Disclose the remedies of an agent.
9. Name the ways than an agency relationship can be terminated.
10. Identify who is entitled to a notice that an agency has ended.

For a detailed account of the events outlined in The Opening Case see: Porgres, Irwin. *Edgar Rice Burroughs: The Man Who Created Tarzan*. 2 Vols. New York: Ballantine Books, 1975. pp. 488–494.

33-1 Scope of an Agent's Authority

Agents may perform only acts that have been authorized by the principal. Agents who exceed their delegated authority become personally liable. Unauthorized actions do not bind the principal unless those actions can be reasonably assumed by a third party to be within the scope of the agent's authority. Authority granted to an agent may be express, implied, or apparent.

Express Authority

The agent's **express authority** is the authority that the principal voluntarily and specifically sets forth as oral or written instructions in the agency agreement. Sometimes referred to as *actual authority,* express authority may also be indicated by conduct, as when a sales representative informs the principal of travel plans and no objection to them is expressed.

Talking Points

Oliver Wendell Holmes, Jr., one of the most powerful and influential legal minds of the nineteenth century, and his twenty-first-century counterpart, Richard Posner, have some very interesting ideas on the nature of agency. After reading the following quotations, consider the underlying implications that these ideas have on human nature, in general, and the concept of freedom, in particular, especially as these ideas relate to agency and employment.

"That is the progress of ideas as shown by history; and that is what is meant by saying that the characteristic feature which justifies agency as a title of law is the absorption *pro hac vice* of the agent's individuality in that of his principal."—Oliver Wendell Holmes, Jr., *The Common Law.* New York. Barnes and Noble Books, 2004, p. 171.

"The natural state of human beings is not one of equality but of dependence on more powerful human beings. Economic freedom, including freedom of contract, in the classical liberal sense is one of the luxuries established by social organization."—Richard Posner, *Overcoming Law.* Cambridge: Harvard University Press, 1995, pp. 300–301.

Consider the following questions: Is Holmes correct that the underlying concept of agency is based on the disappearance of the agent's individuality into the principal, so that the agent, from a legal standpoint at least, ceases to exist? If so, is this concept explained by Posner's declaration that the basic human state is one of dependence on more powerful beings? In the agency relationship is the principal always the more powerful of the two individuals? Consider the following agency relationships and explore the question of whether the agent in fact disappears into the principal. Also consider whether the agent or the principal holds more power in these relationships: (1) attorney-client; (2) stock broker-investor; (3) seller-real estate agent; (4) trustor-trustee; (5) CEO-corporation; (6) department store-sales clerk; (7) manager-hotel owner; (8) partner-partner (9) president-college; (10) ward-guardian.

Implied Authority

Implied authority is the agent's authority to perform acts that are necessary or customary to carry out expressly authorized duties. It stems from the reasonable effort of an agent to understand the meaning of the principal's words describing what the agent is to do. Implied authority can be described as *incidental authority* when the acts performed are reasonably necessary to carry out an express authority. For example, an agent might have incidental authority to contract for the repair of the principal's van that broke down while being used to deliver perishable products that the agent had express authority to sell and deliver. Implied authority may be described as *customary authority* when the agent acts in conformity with the general trade or professional practices of the business.

Apparent Authority

Apparent authority is an accountability doctrine whereby a principal, by virtue of words or actions, leads a third party to believe that an agent has authority even though no such authority was intended. Apparent authority is sometimes referred to as *agency by estoppel, apparent agency,* and *ostensible agency.* The principal may make known to the third party in a variety of ways that such authority exists. For instance, it may be generated by making a direct statement to the third party, by permitting someone to have a meaningful business title, by enabling someone to occupy a position of authority, or by allowing someone to perform duties that give a third party reason to believe that the person has the authority to act for the principal. Sometimes apparent authority can even arise because the principal fails to act in some way. For example, apparent authority may be created if the principal terminates an agent's actual authority but fails to give proper notice of that termination to those who are entitled to receive such notice. Such apparent authority is sometimes referred to as **lingering apparent authority.**

Example 33-1

Sabastian Sandoval worked as a purchasing agent for BiblioBuyers, Inc., a used-book company that recycled used textbooks purchased primarily from college professors. Sandoval generally visited professors in their offices, and paid them in cash for their used books. Occasionally, he would take the books and promise a cash payment at his next visit. When he did this, he would give each professor a credit receipt written out on a BiblioBuyers letterhead indicating the title of the books he'd purchased and the total amount the company owed to each individual. Sometimes this amounted only to a few dollars per instructor. However, in some cases it amounted to hundreds of dollars. Later, when Sandoval was discharged by BiblioBuyers, the company did not notify any of the professors on his regular route. Sandoval took advantage of this by visiting those professors on his route, taking their books and giving them credit receipts on BiblioBuyers letterheads. He then took the books and sold them to Alpha-Best-Bet Book Buyers, BiblioBuyers' fiercest competitor. When the professors demanded their money, BiblioBuyers discovered Sandoval's deceit. Because the company had not notified the professors, the company had clothed Sandoval with lingering apparent authority.

The party with whom the agent is dealing must reasonably believe that the agent has authority to so act, must have had no notice of a lack of such authority, and must act or rely upon the agent's appearance of authority. Once the principal clothes an agent with the semblance of authority, the principal cannot deny that the authority exists when another person has relied upon that appearance. The doctrine of apparent authority protects innocent third parties who rely on the impression created by the principal's words, acts, or conduct that appropriate authority has been conferred on the agent.

Although apparent authority is often thought of within the context of contract law, it is also used in tort law. In hospitals, for example, physicians and other health care professionals, who are actually independent contractors, may appear to the patient to be agents of the hospital. Under these circumstances, a hospital might be held liable for the negligence of the health care practitioner. This would occur if the hospital presents itself to the public as a dispenser of health care assistance and if the patient believes that the hospital, rather than a particular professional, is providing that assistance.

> ### A Question of Ethics
>
> Suppose the director of a hospital knows that a physician is incompetent but allows the physician to continue to treat patients at that hospital. Suppose further that only the director knows of the problem and that there is no evidence to prove that the director knew of the physician's incompetence. Would it be ethical for the director to allow the hospital to escape liability in a malpractice suit based on the tort reform provision discussed here? Why or why not?

In some states, apparent agency in hospitals has become the focus of tort reform. In such states, hospitals can avoid clothing independent health care practitioners with apparent authority by posting notices which announce that the practitioners who render care in the hospital are independent contractors rather than hospital employees. The hospital may protect itself further by adding a sentence that specifically states that the hospital is not liable for the actions of such independent contractors, unless those actions are directly controlled by the hospital.

Appointment of Subagents

Agents are appointed by principals because of their assumed fitness to perform some particular job. Since principals rely on the agent's personal skill and integrity, they do not ordinarily give agents the power to delegate someone else to do the job they have agreed to do. Should an agent delegate authority without authorization, the acts of the subagent do not impose any obligation or liability on the principal to third parties. In some instances, the agent is permitted to delegate authority even though the agency agreement does not contain an express power of delegation. Such an intention may be implied from the nature of the employment or custom and usage. A real estate broker, for example, has the implied authority to delegate authority to salespersons. The nature of the business is such that it is presumed that the principal (seller) contemplates that the authority given to the agent (broker) would be exercised through the broker's agents (subagents).

Exceptions to the Delegation of Authority

The purpose of agency cannot be criminal or contrary to public policy. In addition, some acts must be performed in person, not delegated to an agent. Nondelegable acts include, but are not limited to, voting, serving on juries, testifying in court, making a will, and holding

Terms Subagents working for independent contractors are often called *subcontractors*. In construction, for example, a general contractor may hire a subcontractor to install plumbing or electrical systems.

Related Cases The Barrowses entered into the state of marriage by proxy (Barrows was to be away, so an agent stood in for him at the ceremony). When Barrows died, the couple's life insurance company attacked the validity of the marriage. The court ruled that there is a long history of proxy marriages; therefore, the insurance company was liable for the settlement. *Barrows v. U.S.*, 191 F. 2d 92.

public office. However, forms required by law, such as tax returns and license applications, may be executed by an agent provided that the identity of the principal as well as the identity and capacity of the agent are clearly shown.

Quick Quiz 33-1 True or False?

1. Apparent authority is the agent's authority to perform acts that are needed or customary in the performance of the principal's business.

2. Implied authority is generally referred to as agency by estoppel.

3. Apparent authority is never used in tort law.

33-2 The Agent's Obligations to a Principal

The agency relationship between agent and principal establishes rights and obligations that may be expressed in the agreement or merely implied. As noted in Chapter 32, an individual who acts as agent for another has a fiduciary relationship with the principal. This relationship implies the placement of trust and confidence in the agent that the agent will serve the principal's interests before all others. Thus, an agent may not enter any agency transaction in which the agent has a personal interest. An agent must also not take a position in conflict with the interest of the principal.

In compliance with the agency contract and the fiduciary relationship, various obligations are imposed upon the agent. These obligations generally involve the following duties:

- to obey all instructions
- to be loyal to the principal
- to exercise reasonable judgment, prudence, and skill
- to account for money and property received
- to perform work personally
- to communicate fully all facts that affect the subject matter of the agency

Obedience to Instructions

The agent, whether being paid or acting gratuitously, must obey all reasonable and legal instructions issued by the principal that relate to the agency agreement. In obeying the instructions of the principal, the agent is duty-bound to remain within the **scope of authority** (i.e., range of acts authorized by the principal). For example, if the agent were to sell equipment to a third party in violation of the principal's instructions, the agent would be liable for any injury suffered by the principal.

Loyalty to the Principal

An agent may not engage in any activity that would result in a conflict of interest with the business of the principal. This duty of loyalty implies strict and continuing faithfulness to the principal's best interests at all times. Hence, the agent must resist any temptation to use acquired confidential information to advance the agent's own interest at the expense of the principal's.

Example 33-2

Carl Vermeer worked as the chief financial officer for Filodyne Electronics, Inc. In a meeting with Hannah Garrison, the CEO and president of Filodyne, Vermeer learned that Filodyne was about to patent a new nanomachine that would be capable of performing microsurgery on certain individuals in order to repair arterial blockage. Vermeer took this information and offered it to Kenneth Pierce, the president of Global Electronics, Inc., in exchange for a position with Global. In this scenario there is no doubt that Vermeer violated his duty of loyalty to Filodyne and Garrison.

Related Cases The general manager of a corporation, while purchasing supplies for his company, purchased an additional quantity of supplies on his own account and sold them at a profit. The corporation sued and was awarded the proceeds from the sale of the goods. *Michigan Crown Fender Co. v. Welch,* 178 N.W. 684.

Judgment, Prudence, and Skill

Agents imply that they possess the required knowledge, training, and skill to perform and carry out their agency obligations properly with reasonable care and diligence. Unless an agent claims to be an expert, the principal is entitled to expect that the agent has the degree of skill commonly displayed by others employed in similar work. An expert, such as a person in a profession requiring specific education and a special license, must use the expert judgment, prudence, and skill possessed by others who have been admitted to those professions. Whether an expert or not, the agent may be liable to the principal for losses resulting from personal neglect or incompetence.

Many houses are sold through a real estate agent who brings the parties together.

The Duty to Account

The agent has a duty to keep a separate account of the principal's funds. Whatever money the agent receives during and as a result of the agency relationship is held in trust for the principal. An accounting must be given to the principal within a reasonable period of time after money or property is received or disbursed. Money collected by the agent must be held separate from funds belonging to the agent. If deposited in a bank, the money must be deposited in a separate account and so identified that a trust is apparent. Failure to keep such funds separate is known as *commingling,* and the agent may be held personally liable for any resulting losses.

Example 33-3

In Example 33-1 we learned that Sandoval visited college professors and, whenever he found suitable used textbooks, paid the professors in cash for those books. Whenever he made a cash collection, Sandoval would mix the money with his own cash. Unfortunately, when BiblioBuyers asked for an accounting, Sandoval could not remember which part of the cash belonged to him and which part was rightfully the property of BiblioBuyers. When BiblioBuyers asked for all of the cash, which was their right under agency law, Sandoval refused to turn over the cash. This problem with the cash turned out to be the precipitating event that led to his ultimate discharge.

Background Information The Major League Baseball Players Association has an agreement requiring the agents to be certified. The association also limits player-agent contracts to one year.

Terms The word *mingle,* part of *commingle,* means "to mix." Things are *commingled* when they are blended, or mixed, into a whole.

Personal Service

The agency relationship is usually one involving an agreement for personal services. In the absence of authority to do so, an agent may not delegate duties to others unless such duties are purely mechanical in nature and require no particular knowledge, training, skill, or responsibility.

Communicate Information

The agent is duty-bound to keep the principal fully informed of all facts that materially affect the subject matter of the agency and that come to the agent's attention when acting within the agent's scope of authority. The law assumes that if an agent receives either notice or information, it was also communicated to the principal. Therefore, the rights and liabilities of the principal to any third party are the same as if the principal had personally received the notice or information.

Example 33-4

Marcy Magliozzi instructed Barbara Harrison to purchase a particular furnished house on Catawba Island for her. While examining the final contract, Harrison discovered that several thousand books that were in the house would not be considered as part of the "furnishings" that went along with the sale. Despite this, Harrison completed the purchase for Magliozzi. A little later, Magliozzi discovered that the books did not come with the "furnished" house. Magliozzi demanded that the contract be voided. Since in the course of carrying out her duties and before buying the house, Harrison learned that the books were not part of the deal, the law assumes that Magliozzi had the same information. She cannot use the loss of the books as the basis for voiding the contract.

Remedies Available to the Principal

Remedies are always available when an agent fails to observe a duty owed to a principal. For instance, the principal may do one or more of the following:

- terminate the agent's contract of employment
- withhold compensation otherwise due the agent
- recover profit the agent made in violation of agency obligations
- recover money or property gained or held by the agent to which the principal is entitled
- restrain the agent from continuing to breach the agency obligations
- recover damages from the agent for breach of the contract of employment or assessed against the principal for the agent's wrongdoing
- rescind a contract entered into by the agent based on an improper relationship between the agent and the third party

The Opening Case Revisited
"Tarzan and the Agent"

In this situation, Burroughs, the principal, availed himself of two remedies: (1) he terminated Stern's contract of employment and (2) he withheld compensation that was allegedly due to Stern.

Quick Quiz 33-2 True or False?

1. In obeying the orders of a principal, the agent has a duty to stay within the scope of authority granted by the principal.

2. The law assumes that information communicated to the principal is known by the agent.

3. The agent has a duty to keep a separate account of the principal's funds.

33-3 The Principal's Obligations to the Agent

The agreement between a principal and an agent creates the duties the principal owes to the agent. Even when the agency agreement is silent, there are implied obligations that are owed to the agent. Among the principal's actual and implied duties are the following obligations:

- to compensate the agent for work or services performed
- to reimburse the agent for authorized advances and expenses
- to indemnify the agency against liability to third parties
- to cooperate with the performance of the agent's duties

Talking Points

The question of how human rights arise has been a perennial problem among legal philosophers. Two such philosophers, Jeffrie Murphy and Jules Coleman, suggest one answer while Robert Paul Wolff proposes another.

In their book, *Philosophy of Law,* Murphy and Coleman state: "Rights protected by inalienability rules are not transferable. The right to one's freedom from servitude and the right to vote are examples of rights protected by inalienability rules."

In contrast, Wolff writes in his essay "Beyond Tolerance" that: "Those philosophers are therefore deeply mistaken who suppose that the social inheritance is a burden to be cast off, a spell from which we must be awakened. Without that inheritance the individual is nothing— he has no organized core of personality into which his culture has not penetrated."

Murphy and Coleman propose that certain human rights are inalienable, that is, they exist regardless of the social context, while Wolff suggests that the human individual is nothing outside the social context. Which view is correct? How would these approaches to human nature impact on agency rules? Agency appears to preserve individual integrity by permitting individuals to expand the scope of their activities; yet, it also evolves from the idea that the servant is absorbed into the master, and, therefore, ceases to exist separate from the master. Which side of the dichotomy does agency law promote today? Explain.

For a more detailed look at the ideas covered in Talking Points, see: Murphy, Jeffrie G., and Jules L. Coleman. *Philosophy of Law*. Boulder, CO: Westview Press, 1990, p. 198; Wolff, Robert Paul. "Beyond Tolerance." *A Critique of Pure Tolerance*. Boston: Beacon Press, 1969, pp. 18–19.

Background Information Some writers' agents are creating their own compensation by identifying news stories with best-seller potential and recruiting writers and publishers for the project. Agents comb newspapers and magazines for ideas, such as the story of Congressman Mickey Leland's death or Leona Helmsley's arrest for tax evasion and subsequent conviction.

Compensation

The principal is under a duty to pay an agent an agreed amount or the fair value for work or services that the agent performs within the scope of authority or employment, unless the agent agrees to perform gratuitously. In addition, the principal must make salary deductions and payments to the government as are required by law. All states have statutes that provide for the enforcement of the payment of wages and that place penalties on delinquent employers. The agent may not recover compensation for illegal services, even though they were rendered at the request of the principal. The agent may also forfeit rights to compensation when the agent breaches his or her duties to the principal.

Reimbursement

The principal is obligated to reimburse the agent for any reasonable expenses incurred while working on the principal's behalf and within the scope of the agent's authority or employment. The agent cannot recover for expenses due to the agent's own negligence. Recovery is also barred when expenses incurred by an agent are unnecessary or unreasonable in the discharge of the agency.

Indemnification

Agents are entitled to **indemnification** (i.e., payment for loss or damage suffered) if they incur a loss or are damaged as a result of a request made by the principal. The obligation to pay for the agent's personal loss or damage, which may occur in the future or is already suffered, is avoidable if the loss or damage results from an action the agent knew to be illegal or from the agent's negligence. Public policy also requires employers to indemnify employees for personal injury sustained in the course of employment, except for self-inflicted injury or intoxication. State worker's compensation laws hold that the cost of paying for such injury should be a part of the operating expense of the business.

Cooperation with the Agent

The principal, having granted the agent the duty to perform certain tasks, must not interfere with the performance of those tasks. Should the principal make the agent's job difficult or impossible, the principal has breached the duty of cooperation.

Example 33-5

Charles Farnsworth, the CEO and president of Farnsworth Aeronautics, Inc., hired Dale Thornicroft to be a sales representative for the firm. Thornicroft's job was to visit the major airlines on the West Coast in an attempt to sell Farnsworth's new jet engine design. When Thornicroft was hired, she was given a salary plus a substantial commission on each engine sold. She was also given a quota that she had to meet during the first six months of her employment with Farnsworth. She was, however, assured that the West Coast would be her exclusive territory. Within the first month of her employment with Farnsworth, Thornicroft discovered that Farnsworth had another agent on salary who also sold engines on the West Coast. The other agent made it impossible for Thornicroft to meet her quota. Farnsworth had breached his duty of cooperation with Thornicroft because of his interference with what was supposed to be Thornicroft's exclusive right to sell to airline companies on the West Coast.

Remedies Available to the Agent

The remedies of an agent against a principal are based upon the principal's breach of express or implied contract obligations. Where appropriate, the agent has the option of exerting one or more of the agent's rights:

- leave the principal's employ
- recover damages for the principal's breach of contract

- recover the value of services rendered
- obtain reimbursement for payments made for the principal
- secure indemnity for personal liability sustained while performing an authorized act for the principal

---

Quick Quiz 33-3 True or False?

1. An agent may forfeit rights to compensation when the agent breaches his or her duties to the principal.

2. An agent cannot recover expenses from the principal if those expenses are a result of the agent's own negligence.

3. If a principal makes an agent's job difficult or impossible that principal has breached the duty of cooperation.

33-4 Termination of Agency

The agency agreement may be terminated by the acts of one or both parties to the agreement or by operation of the law. When the authority of the agent is terminated, the agent loses the right to act for the principal.

Termination by Act of the Parties

Both principal and agent may terminate an agency relationship by their acts. Most agency relationships are terminated when the parties have satisfied their contractual obligations. The relationship may also be discharged by mutual consent as well as when either the agent or the principal breaches the agency contract.

Fulfillment of Purpose When the purpose for which the agency was created is achieved, the agency is terminated. If an agent is appointed for a specific period of time, the arrival of that time terminates the agency. In short, when the contract is performed, the agency is at an end.

Mutual Agreement The parties to an agency relationship may terminate it at any time by agreement, even before the contract is fully performed.

Revocation or Renunciation The principal or the agent usually has the power (not necessarily the right) at any time to terminate the agency relationship. Acting with or without cause, the principal may terminate the agreement by simply recalling the agent's authority to act (i.e., **revocation**). Even though the principal's act of revocation may be a violation of contract, the agent's authority is terminated. Agents may terminate by simply giving notice to principals that they are quitting (i.e., **renunciation**). Unless the terms of the agency agreement permit termination "at will," agents and principals who end their relationship may be liable for damages resulting from the violation of the contractual promise (see Figure 33-1). Nevertheless, one cannot be forced to work against one's will.

Termination by Operation of Law

The termination of the agency agreement by operation of the law results when significant events make the continuance of the agency impossible or impractical. Termination by

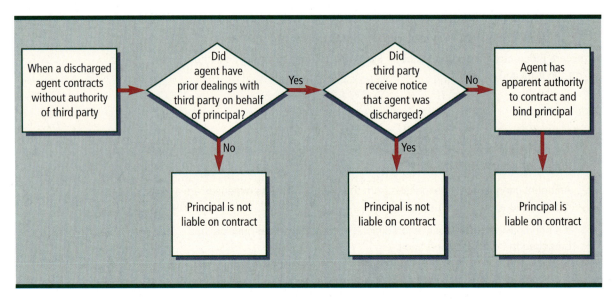

Figure 33-1 This chart indicates how liability is determined after the termination of an agency relationship.

operation of the law occurs in instances of death, insanity, bankruptcy, or impossibility of performance.

Death The death of the principal or agent ordinarily terminates the agency relationship automatically, even without notice. Hence, any agreement made between the agent and a third party is ineffective upon the death of the principal. Although the agent may be liable to third parties for breach of the implied warranty that the agent has authority to act, third parties cannot recover from the estate of the principal because the contract is not binding.

Insanity The insanity of either the principal or the agent usually terminates the authority of the agent. In some states, however, the courts have held that an agent has power to bind a principal who has become insane if the principal has not been legally declared insane and if the third party had no knowledge of the insanity. If the principal is only incapacitated briefly, the agent's authority may be suspended rather than terminated.

Durable Power of Attorney Generally, an agency relationship is terminated upon the incapacity of the principal. However, the trend in many states has been to adopt the **Uniform Durable Power of Attorney Act (UDPA).** Under the UDPA a person can appoint an agent called an "attorney in fact" by signing a written durable power of attorney. A **durable power of attorney** preserves the authority of an agent should the principal become incapacitated. In some cases, the durable power of attorney may even activate the agent's power once the principal is incapacitated. The durable power of attorney should contain the following words: "this power of attorney shall not be affected by subsequent disability or incapacity of the principal" or "this power of attorney shall become effective upon the disability or incapacity of the principal."

Bankruptcy In the event of the bankruptcy of the principal, the agency is ended. All of the principal's ordinary contracts are cancelled, and title to the principal's property passes to a trustee for the benefit of creditors. The bankruptcy of the agent sometimes terminates the agency for the same reasons, but the principal and the agent may continue

Did You Know?

Traditionally there is a difference between a bankruptcy law and an insolvency law. Although both types of laws deal with people who cannot pay their debts, bankruptcy laws are for the benefit of the creditors and are activated by them. In contrast, insolvency laws are for the benefit of the debtor and are set in motion by the debtor.

the relationship if they choose. Usually, the bankruptcy of the agent does not prevent the agent from doing the job in the regular way, provided the agent is not using personal funds.

Impossibility of Performance An agency relationship terminates when it is impossible for the agent to accomplish the purpose of the agency for any reason. Destruction of a house by fire ends the real estate broker's agency to sell the property. A broker authorized to sell a principal's boat loses that authority if the boat is destroyed in a storm. An agent's loss of a license required to conduct the principal's business ends the authority of the agent. A change in the law that causes authorized acts to be illegal terminates the agent's authority. The authority of the agent is also terminated by notice or knowledge of a change in business conditions or values that substantially affects the agent's exercise of authority. For example, an agent hired to sell property at a specified price would have that authority terminated when the value of the property increases substantially because of zoning changes.

Agency Coupled with an Interest

The only exception to the rule that either the principal or the agent may terminate an agency relationship at any time arises in the situation of an agency coupled with an interest. An **agency coupled with an interest** is an agency agreement in which the agent is given an interest in the subject matter of the agency, in addition to the compensation for services rendered to the principal. The concept protects the agent's interest in specific property belonging to the principal. The principal lacks power to revoke agencies of this kind without the consent of the agent.

Example 33-6

James Heilman borrowed $9,000 from the National Security Specialty Bank of Louisville. He put up as security 200 shares of stock in the Actors' Theatre Group of Louisville. Heilman then authorized the bank to sell the shares to satisfy the loan obligation should he default on that loan. In the event that it becomes necessary to sell the stock, the bank serves as Heilman's agent. Heilman may not terminate the agency except by paying off the $9,000 loan (plus interest as per his agreement with the National Security Specialty Bank).

Notice of Termination to Third Parties

The principal has the duty to notify third parties with whom the agent has done business when the agency relationship has been terminated by the act of the parties. The exception to this rule is when the agency is terminated by operation of the law. In such instances, the principal is not required to notify anyone and no subsequent act by the agent will bind the principal.

The type of notice required depends on how the former business relations were conducted. When the third party has given credit to the principal through the agent, the third party is entitled to actual notice of termination of authority. This may be done by regular mail or by telephone. The safest way, however, is by certified mail, because the post office provides a receipt of the notice. A notice in the classified advertisement section in a newspaper of general circulation is sufficient for third parties who have never given credit, but who have had cash transactions with the agent or who know that other persons have dealt with the principal through the agent. The failure to give third parties appropriate notice would make the principal liable on contracts made by a former agent with third parties.

Further Reading *The Power of Attorney Book,* by attorney Denis Clifford (Berkeley, CA: Nolo Press, 1990), is a complete guide to the procedures involved in appointing a third party with power of attorney.

Background Information A real estate broker who goes into bankruptcy will usually lose his or her license. All agency relationships terminate, and the broker can no longer collect a commission.

Teaching Tips The agency coupled with an interest is not a true agency power because it cannot be terminated at will. It may be terminated only as agreed to in the transaction that created it or if the subject matter of the interest is destroyed.

Related Cases When former basketball star Kareem Abdul-Jabbar tried to terminate his contract with his agent Tom Collins, whose mismanagement had led Abdul-Jabbar into financial difficulty, the player's creditors called in their loans to him. As a result, the deals that Collins had made in Abdul-Jabbar's name quickly went bankrupt or sank into debt, causing even more financial devastation.

Quick Quiz 33-4 True or False?

1. The parties to an agency relationship may mutually agree to terminate their agreement at any time.

2. The death of the principal or agent ordinarily terminates the agency relationship automatically.

3. The failure to give third parties appropriate notice would make the principal liable on contracts made by the former agent.

Summary

33-1 An agent's authority may arise expressly from the written or spoken words of the principal to the agent or implied from the agent's reasonable effort to understand the meaning of the principal's words describing what the agent is to do. Apparent authority results from actions by the principal to a third party that give the third party reason to believe that an individual has the authority to act for the principal. Principals do not often give agents the power to delegate authority to subordinates.

33-2 As a result of the fiduciary relationship, the agent owes the principal the duty of obedience to instructions; loyalty; reasonable judgment, prudence, and skill; accounting for agency money and property; personal performance of agency work; and communication of all facts that affect the subject matter of the agency.

33-3 In addition to the duties that the principal owes to the agent under the agency agreement, there are certain implied obligations. These include the duty to compensate the agent, reimburse the agent for authorized expenses incurred, indemnify the agent for losses caused by the agency relationship through no fault of the agent, and comply with the terms of the agency contract.

33-4 An agency agreement generally terminates when its purposes are accomplished. The agency may also terminate at any time by the principal's revocation of the agent's authority or by the agent's renunciation of the agency relationship. If either party dies, becomes insane, goes bankrupt, or ceases to be qualified to act, the agency relationship is terminated by operation of the law. The principal has the duty to notify third parties with whom the agent has done business when the agency relationship has been terminated by acts of the parties. Actual notice is required when the third party has given credit to the principal through the agent. A public notice in a newspaper of general circulation is sufficient for third parties who have never given credit but who have had cash transactions with the agent.

Key Terms

agency coupled with an interest, 631

apparent authority, 622

durable power of attorney, 630

express authority, 621

implied authority, 622

indemnification, 628

lingering apparent authority, 622

renunciation, 629

revocation, 629

scope of authority, 624

Uniform Durable Power of Attorney Act (UDPA), 630

Questions for Review and Discussion

1. What is the difference between express and implied authority?
2. What is apparent authority?
3. What are the consequences of an unauthorized delegation of agency authority?
4. When can an agent legally appoint a subagent?
5. What are the duties of an agent to the principal?
6. What are the remedies available to a principal?
7. What are the duties that a principal has in relation to an agent?
8. What are the remedies of an agent?
9. What are the ways that an agency relationship can be terminated?
10. Who is entitled to notice that an agency has ended?

Investigating the Internet

The most visible examples of agency law in action today occur in sports. As a research assignment, access the journal entitled *Entertainment and Sports Lawyer* and write a report on any article that relates to agents in sports law.

Cases for Analysis

1. Sturgill gave his significant other the authority to write checks that were drawn on his personal checking account. After Sturgill passed away, she continued to write checks that were drawn on his account. The executor of Sturgill's estate objected to this practice, and brought a lawsuit against the bank for continuing to honor the checks. The bank argued that, since it had received no notice of Sturgill's death, it was within its rights when it honored her authority to cash the checks. The executor argued that the death of Sturgill automatically terminated the agency and the bank, therefore, had no right to continue to cash the checks. Who is correct here? If the bank is found liable to the estate, does it have a cause of action against the agent? Explain. *Sturgill v. Virginia Citizens Bank Co.,* 291 S.E.2d 207.

2. Luken drove her car onto a parking lot owned and operated by the Buckeye Parking Corporation. She had been in the habit of using this particular parking lot at least once a week for about two years. The lot had a sign over the entrance that clearly indicated that it was a parking lot. About two dozen cars were in the lot. A young man who appeared to be the parking attendant and who had in his posses-

sion a handful of tickets approached Luken. Luken asked him to park her car, which he agreed to do. He then asked her how long it would be before she returned and she answered that she would be back in about an hour. When she returned, the lot was unattended and she could not find her car. Subsequently, Luken discovered that the apparent attendant had taken her car and had been involved in an accident that extensively damaged the vehicle. Luken sued Buckeye claiming that the corporation had, by its actions, led her to believe that the young man was an attendant in its employ. Therefore, under the theory of apparent authority, she claimed that she deserved to be reimbursed for her loss. Was Luken correct? Explain your response. *Luken v. Buckeye Parking Inc.,* 68 N.E.2d 217 (OH).

3. George Jackson, purchasing agent for Ozan, Inc., using his own funds, purchased computer supplies from Lenwell Office Supply Store at a special discount. Each time Ozan needed additional computer supplies, Jackson took them from his personal stock and charged Ozan the regular price. He recorded the transaction as if the supplies were purchased from an acceptable supplier. He then pocketed the difference. What duties, if any, has

Jackson breached by reselling the supplies to Ozan? Explain.

4. On April 11, Fred Chapman discharged Anna Savant, the manager of his store, the Super Electronic Supply Outlet. On April 12, Chapman called *The Barnard Crossings Chronicle* and had a notice printed to the effect that Savant no longer worked for Super. On that same day, Savant ordered twelve electronic games, two computers, two laser printers, a fax machine, and a car stereo from the Global Electronic Components Corporation. As she had frequently done in the past while acting as manager for Super, she told George Pierce, the owner of Global, to send the bill to Super. Pierce did so. Savant then kept these items for herself. Pierce did not have actual notice of Savant's discharge until April 28, when he saw the notice as he was throwing out some old newspapers. Savant could not be located, so Pierce brought suit against Chapman and Super. Chapman argued that the newspaper notice was sufficient to warn Pierce not to deal with Savant. How would the court rule? Explain.

5. Stahl was having trouble with her Volkswagen. She brought it to the service station of LePage, where it was examined and the trouble was diagnosed. LePage informed Stahl that he would not be able to do the work, but that his employee Donley wanted to take the job on his own and could make use of the garage facilities for this purpose. A new engine was required, and Donley installed the wrong engine. The entire job had to be done over at a cost of hundreds of dollars. Stahl brought suit against LePage. She argued that she should be allowed to recover against LePage for the misdeed of Donley, because Donley had apparent authority to act as LePage's agent. LePage disputed this, arguing that the facts did not warrant a finding of agency under any theory. How did the court find in this dispute? Why? *Stahl v. LePage,* 352 A.2d 682 (VT).

6. Castle Fabrics, Inc., sold fabric to Fortune Manufacturers, Inc. A dispute arose as to the acceptability of the fabric received, and Fortune returned the fabric to Castle for full credit. Castle gave Fortune only partial credit and sued Fortune for recovery of its loss. In court, Fortune showed a credit memorandum from a Castle employee indicating that Fortune would be given full credit for the fabric. Although it was within the regular responsibility of the Castle employee to send the memorandum, on this occasion management had specifically instructed the employee not to send one. Fortune argued that the employee was an agent of Castle and thus chargeable with any mistake the agent made. Castle claimed it was not chargeable with the action of its employee because the employee had disobeyed specific instructions not to send the memorandum. The judgment was for whom and why? *Castle Fabrics, Inc., v. Fortune Furniture Mfrs. Inc.,* 459 F. Supp. 409 (N.D. MS).

7. Lloyd, an attorney, was appointed guardian of Ernest Parker. Two years later he was appointed guardian of Virginia Hockenberry. That same year, he agreed to represent David Isaac in the purchase of a plot of real estate from Debra Taylor. On several occasions Lloyd deposited client settlement checks into his own account. The funds received were therefore commingled with the funds in his personal account. He later used these funds to pay for his student loans, his automobile loan, his insurance, his taxes, his outstanding credit card bills, and his barber. Identify the duties that Lloyd has violated in relation to his principals, Parker, Hockenberry, and Isaac. *Office of Disciplinary Counsel v. Lloyd,* 643 N.E.2d 1086 (OH).

8. Ross needed a grinding mill and consulted Clifton, who on occasion repaired such mills but who did not sell them. Ross and Clifton together selected a mill from a catalog, which Clifton happened to have on hand, that they decided would meet Ross's purposes. Ross instructed Clifton to order the mill they had selected, and Clifton did so in his own name and with his own money. When the mill arrived, Ross refused to accept it, stating that it was too small and would not do the job he intended it to do. Clifton brought suit to recover the amount he had spent. The judgment was for whom and why? *Clifton v. Ross,* 28 S.W. 1085 (AR).

Quick Quiz Answers

33-1	33-2	33-3	33-4
1. F	1. T	1. T	1. T
2. F	2. F	2. T	2. T
3. F	3. T	3. T	3. T

Chapter 34   Employment Law

The Opening Case
"The Enemy of 40 Is 30, Not 50"

As part of a collective bargaining agreement negotiated between General Dynamics and its employees, the company made some significant changes in its health benefits package. One change, which affected workers at facilities in Sterling, Michigan; Lima, Ohio; and Scranton, Pennsylvania, stated that only long-term employees who were over fifty years of age would continue to be offered full health care benefits after retirement. Under the former collective bargaining agreement, all employees over forty were eligible for full benefits after retirement. Several long-term employees between forty and forty-nine cried "foul," arguing that this new provision created a type of "reverse age discrimination" which violated the Age Discrimination in Employment Act (ADEA) which was passed by Congress to protect workers who were forty and older from discrimination. A class action lawsuit was filed in federal district court on behalf of all these employees. The executive branch of the federal government and the Equal Employment Opportunity Commission (EEOC) upheld the viewpoint of the plaintiffs, while the American Association of Retired People (AARP) supported the position offered by the defendant and eventually put forth by the United States Supreme Court. The Supreme Court ruled in favor of the defendant noting that the objective of the ADEA "does not mean to stop an employer from favoring an older employee over a younger one." In interpreting the meaning of the ADEA, the High Court ruled that "(i)n a world where younger is better, talk about discrimination because of age is naturally understood to refer to discrimination against the older. . . . The enemy of 40 is 30, not 50." Does the interpretation of the ADEA offered by the Supreme Court make sense in light of the purpose of the ADEA? What other instances of reverse discrimination have been raised before the court? Since the EEOC supported a point of view that is counter to the ruling of the United States Supreme Court, can that agency pursue to its own position or must it adopt the ruling of the court? As you read Chapter 34, Employment Law, consider whether the Supreme Court has really upheld the spirit of the law as envisioned by Congress.

Chapter Outcomes

1. Explain the doctrine of employment-at-will.
2. Itemize the situations that fall outside employment-at-will.
3. List the wrongful discharge exceptions to employment-at-will.
4. Explain the after acquired evidence rule.

5. Indicate the functions of the Occupational Safety and Health Act.
6. List the functions of the Fair Labor Standards Act.
7. Explain the difference between unemployment insurance and workers' compensation.
8. Identify the major provisions of the Family Medical Leave Act.
9. Distinguish between disparate treatment and disparate impact.
10. Distinguish between business necessity defenses and the defense offered by a bona fide occupational qualification (BFOQ).

For a more detailed look at the events covered in The Opening Case see: Harris, Andrew. "Reverse Age Discrimination Claim Rejected." *The National Law Journal,* March 1, 2004, p. 7.

34-1 The Employment Relationship

An employment relationship may be formed in many ways. It may result from a simple oral agreement between two individuals, or it may be created by a detailed written contract that is finalized after complex negotiations between a union and a corporation. In the United States, the dominant legal doctrine governing most employment relationships is employment-at-will. Many states, however, have come to the conclusion that employment-at-will must be changed to ensure justice for employees. For this reason, the at-will doctrine has been modified by the addition of several wrongful discharge exceptions.

Employment-at-Will

As noted, most jurisdictions in the United States still follow the doctrine of **employment-at-will,** which states that an employer can dismiss an employee at any time for any reason. Under this doctrine, the employer does not even have to give a reason for the firing. The rationale for the employment-at-will doctrine is that both the employer and the employee should be free to terminate the employment relationship at any time. This principle allows both parties to end an unsatisfactory relationship or to take advantage of new opportunities. Unfortunately, the principle can be abused by unscrupulous employers.

Getting Students Involved Ask four students to volunteer to conduct a panel discussion on the pros and cons of employment-at-will. Have two students take the position of the employer and two students take the position of the employee.

Example 34-1

Laura Farragher worked as a cashier for the Gentry Merry-Go-Round of Foods Company, a concessionaire business which worked the fair and festival circuit in Arkansas each summer. Generally, Farragher started work in May at the Memorial Day Festival at the Little Rock Airport and stayed with the company all summer until the Arkansas Horse Show in October held at the state fair grounds. This year, after the Independence Day Festival, Ben Gentry, the owner and operator of Gentry Merry-Go-Round, told Farragher that her services were no longer needed because he wanted his daughter to work to earn tuition for college. Under the doctrine of employment-at-will, Farragher would have no legal recourse. Gentry can discharge her at any time with or without notice, or offering her a reason.

Background Information The origins of the employment-at-will doctrine date to the 1890s when factories claimed they needed to be free to hire and fire at will to operate their businesses profitably. An 1894 case, *Payne v. Western & Atlantic RR* (81 Tenn. 507), established this legal doctrine, and subsequent cases broadened its application to all types of jobs in private industry.

State Variations Indiana, Missouri, Montana, and Oklahoma have statutes requiring an employer to provide discharged employees with written statements about their work history, known as "service letters," within a prescribed period of time. All of these states require that the letters contain an explanation for the employee's discharge.

Collective Bargaining Agreements

An early victory over employment-at-will was won by organized labor. As a result of some hard-fought battles during the 1930s and 1940s, those employees who belong to labor unions today are frequently protected by hiring and firing procedures written into their collective bargaining agreements. A **collective bargaining agreement** is a contract negotiated by the employer and the labor union that covers all issues related to employment. Such agreements prevent the unfair discharge of employees. The employer needs some legitimate, employment-related reason, or just cause, for the release. In general, collective

For a more detailed look at these interpretations of at-will-employment see: Posner, Richard. "Hegel and Employment at Will." In *Overcoming Law*. Cambridge: Harvard University Press, 1995, pp. 300–302.

Talking Points

In his treatise, *"Overcoming Law,"* Richard Posner offers two opposing views on employment-at-will, both of which appear to emerge from the philosophy of Georg Wilhelm Friedrich Hegel. The first he attributes to the legal philosopher, Richard Epstein.

According to Posner's interpretation, Epstein proposes that, "Employment at will is a corollary of freedom of contract, and freedom of contract is a social policy with a host of economic and social justifications, even though nature is not one of them. Employment at will happens to be the logical terminus on the road that begins with slavery and makes intermediate stops at serfdom, indentured servitude, involuntary servitude, and guild restrictions. . . . Hegel himself . . . would have thought employment at will a fine idea."

On the other side of the employment fence is the American legal scholar, Drucilla Cornell who proposes, according to Posner, that, "employment at will should be outlawed. Every employee would be entitled after successful completion of a brief probationary period to retain his or her job for life unless economic adversity required layoffs or an arbitrator or some other neutral adjudicator determined that the employer had good cause to discharge the employee."

Which side of the argument makes the most sense to you? Is employment part of the right to contract which allows both sides to freely enter and leave the agreement or is it something which should bind one side, the employer, for the life of the employee, while allowing the employee to leave at any time, with or without reason or notice? Explain your position thoroughly and thoughtfully.

bargaining contracts also provide a grievance procedure. Under a **grievance procedure,** employees have the right to appeal any employer's decision that they think violates just cause.

Often, economic conditions will force layoffs or plant closings. When such events occur, some or all employees may lose their jobs. Still, most collective bargaining agreements provide a negotiated procedure under which such layoffs occur. In this way, employees are at least guaranteed that the layoffs will be handled in as fair a manner as possible.

Worker Adjustment and Retraining Notification Act

Many employers who contemplate mass layoffs and/or plant closings must comply with the provisions of the Worker Adjustment and Retraining Notification Act (WARN). Under this federal statute, employers with over 100 full time employees must give written notice to a union official sixty days before any plant closing or mass layoff. If the employees are not represented by a union, the advance notice must go directly to all employees who will be affected by the layoff or closing.

Most employers provide a severance package to employees terminated during a reorganization or downsizing.

Written notice is not required if the layoff or closing is caused by a natural disaster, such as a flood or an earthquake. Notice is also not required if the closing is caused by an unpredictable business situation or if the notice might prevent the acquisition of business or capital that the employer is attempting to acquire.

Professional Employment Contracts

Individuals with unique abilities, special talents, or a highly specialized education often have the power to negotiate their own employment contracts. Such individuals would not be affected by employment-at-will. Generally, such people are in demand and can thus be selective in the choice of employers. Professional athletes, established scientists, top business executives, famous entertainers, and well-known artists and writers belong in this category.

Wrongful Discharge

Despite the prevalence of labor unions in this country, most employees are not union members. Also, most workers are not in a position to dictate the terms of their own employment contracts. As a result, most workers are subject to the doctrine of employment-at-will and can, therefore, be dismissed at any time for any reason or for no reason. These employees would have no protection were it not for the exceptions to employment-at-will that the courts have recently created under the heading of wrongful discharge. **Wrongful discharge,** which is also referred to as *unjust dismissal* in some states, gives employees legal grounds for a lawsuit against employers who have dismissed them unfairly. The courts have used several theories to judge the injustice of a dismissal. These theories include public policy tort, intentional inflection of emotional distress, implied contract, promissory estoppel, and implied covenant.

Public Policy Tort   An employee who can prove that his or her discharge somehow violated public policy may recover damages in tort. Upholding public policy is the broad legal principle that says that the courts will not allow anyone to do anything that tends to injure the public at large. For example, in many jurisdictions if an employee is fired for refusing to violate the law, such a discharge would violate public policy. Public policy encourages people to obey the law. Firing someone who wants to obey the law would clearly violate public policy. Similarly, if the firing itself violates the law, public policy will provide a remedy for the employee.

   To succeed in a wrongful discharge lawsuit grounded on the public policy tort exception to employment-at-will, the employee would have to prove the following elements: the existence of clarity, jeopardy, and causation and the lack of an overriding business justification. Each of these elements can be explained in the following way:

1. Clarity requires the existence of a definite public policy, clearly created by the U.S. Constitution, the state constitution, a federal or state statute, an administrative regulation, or a common law principle.

2. Jeopardy requires that the discharge of the employee plainly violates the stated public policy issue.

3. Causation requires that the discharge be induced by actions that are related to the stated public policy issue.

4. The lack of an overriding business justification means that the employer had no legitimate business reason for the discharge of the employee.

   In a wrongful discharge lawsuit based on public policy, the judge is charged with determining whether the first two elements, clarity and jeopardy, exist. This is because those two elements are considered questions of law. If the case is tried before a jury, the jurors, as the triers of fact, would determine the existence of causation and the absence of an overriding business justification. In the absence of a jury, the judge would make this determination.

Complex Adaptation and Public Policy Tort   The interaction of the state legislature and the court system in the development the public policy tort exception to employment-at-will demonstrates how the law works as a complex adaptive system. In this case, the interaction begins with the state legislature that creates a statutory provision or which promotes a state policy that is designed to further a social objective deemed

Teaching Tips   Explain to students that, absent a written employment contract, the practice of giving an employer a notice of two weeks or more before resigning is a traditional professional courtesy and not a legal requirement.

Teaching Tips   Emphasize to students the importance of documentation in proving a wrongful discharge claim by an employee. Both employers and employees should keep detailed records of written and oral statements and actions regarding job performance and the circumstances leading to a firing. It is especially important that there be witnesses to the statements. Discuss with students the best possible method of documenting incidents.

State Variations   The federal government along with all states except Virginia, Oklahoma, and New Jersey have laws that make it illegal for employers to fire or otherwise punish employees for taking time off to serve on juries. California, Illinois, Nebraska, and Ohio require that employers be given reasonable notice that a leave for jury duty will be needed. Most states also make it illegal to fire someone for reporting employers' violations of law ("whistle blowing").

Terms Most people agree that getting *fired* is a consequence of doing something wrong at work. Other terms, such as *dismissal, discharge, layoff, staff cut,* and *downsize* are euphemisms for firing often used by employers to prevent bad community relations, anti-company sentiment among employees, and wrongful discharge lawsuits. To refer to mass firings, some companies have coined such expressions as *reorganizational incentives* and *activity analysis and review*.

Teaching Tips Inform students that employers are also required under WARN to give sixty days notice of staff reduction to the chief local elected official, such as the mayor of the city in which the reduction will take place.

necessary to promote harmony, stability, or justice in the state. The court then intervenes in reaction to an individual case whose facts are intertwined with that policy. The result of the case either promotes or thwarts the legislative objective, prompting or alleviating the need for further legislative action.

Example 34-2

A court order issued by the Eastlake County Court compelled the Halifax Computer Outlet to send a portion of Terry Nugent's wages directly to the county court to pay his child support. State law said that anyone who disobeyed such an order could be fined or imprisoned for contempt of court. The same law also expressly forbids an employer to discharge an employee whose wages are subject to this type of court order. The employer could be fined up to $500 for discharging an employee in such a situation. Halifax discharged Nugent rather than go through the hassle of sending a part of his check to the court. Nugent sued the company for wrongful discharge arguing that his discharge violated public policy because it was a direct and incontrovertible violation of a state statute which expressly outlawed that sort of discharge. The company admitted that it had violated the law, but said that it was immune to a wrongful discharge lawsuit because the worker in question was an at-will employee and the company had already been penalized for breaking the law when the court levied a fine against it. The company said that it was willing to pay the $500 rather than rehire Nugent. Since it had paid the fine, Halifax argued that Nugent could not sue the company because rehiring Nugent and paying him back wages and other damages would amount to a double penalty for the same offense. The court ruled against Halifax stating that it could not permit the company to willfully defy the law because such an action would violate public policy.

Intentional Infliction of Emotional Distress Another tort claim that is being used more frequently in wrongful discharge lawsuits is the intentional infliction of emotional distress. An employee may attempt to recover damages for the intentional infliction of emotional distress if the conduct of the employer in the discharge of the employee caused serious mental and emotional suffering. To succeed in such a lawsuit, the plaintiff must prove that the employer's conduct was extreme, that the employer knew the conduct was extreme and would result in emotional distress, and that the conduct was the proximate cause of serious mental and emotional suffering.

Related Cases When DeMinico was hired by the Monarch Wine Company, he was told his job would be secure and he would only be fired if he stole, cheated, or otherwise did something to harm the company. He was also told he had a job until he retired. Less than ten years later, the company laid DeMinico off in a downsizing effort. DeMinico sued, claiming that the oral assertions amounted to an employment contract for life. The court ruled in Monarch's favor, however, because the oral contract violated the Statute of Frauds. *DeMinico v. Monarch Wine Co.,* 803 F.2d 1097.

Fraud-Related Employment Cases Some states now permit an employee to bring a wrongful discharge based on fraud. The cause of action generally applies only to false promises made by a prospective employer to a possible future employee who relies on those promises to his or her detriment. Often in such a situation the employer induces a potential employee to take a job that the employer knows will last only a limited amount of time, without telling the employee about the short duration of that position. The employer thus exploits the employee for a limited period of time and then discharges the employee. Hiring an employee without informing him or her that the business is ending or that an office, store, or plant is about to close down are circumstances that could provide the basis for employment-related lawsuits based on fraud.

Implied Contract **Implied contract** involves an employment relationship that would have been considered at-will, under normal circumstances, had the employer or an agent of the employer not said, done, written, or printed something that implies otherwise. When examining a case to determine whether the employer has created an implied contract, the court can look at all of the facts involving that employment arrangement. The court can look at oral promises made by the employer, the nature of the employment relationship, the way the parties have dealt with each other in the past, the length of the employment relationship, the customary way the employer handles such situations, and the employer's policies and procedures. To determine the employer's policies and procedures, the court can examine various company documents, including the employee handbook, letters and memos sent to the employee, the employee's evaluation record, as well as any oral promises made by the employer. The creation of the implied contract exception gives employees a fighting chance to have their day in court, a chance which previously did not exist in pure employment-at-will jurisdictions.

Example 34-3

When Cynthia Montalbano went to work for Holmes Enterprises, she was required to read the entire employee handbook and to sign an acknowledgment indicating that she had, in fact, read and understood all of the terms in that manual. One of the procedures involved a progressive disciplinary process which promised that, when employees were to be disciplined for any problem, they would first receive an oral warning, followed by a written warning. Only on the third offense would employees be penalized by a suspension, and only on a fourth offense would an employee be subject to a possible discharge order. The first time Montalbano was absent without permission, she was immediately discharged. When Montalbano filed a wrongful discharge suit against Holmes Enterprises, the company filed a summary judgment motion for dismissal noting that since Montalbano was an at-will employee, the company could discharge her at any time for any reason or for no reason with or without notice. The court would not grant the summary judgment motion because the judge believed that Montalbano had presented a *prima facie* case for the creation of an implied contract. This was established because Holmes had clearly indicated that the handbook was to be considered a part of the employment relationship.

Further Reading *The American Bar Association Guide to Workplace Law* (New York: Three Rivers Press, 1997) offers a detailed but straightforward explanation of the major laws affecting employment. *Fair, Square, and Legal* by Donald H. Weiss (New York: American Management Association, 1995) offers managers valuable advice on legal hiring, managing, and firing practices. For a technical and in-depth study of the state of employment law in the United States see *Employment Law: Cases and Materials* by Mark Rothstein and Lance Liebman (New York: Foundation Press, 1998.)

Many jurisdictions which have recognized the implied contract exception will still allow employers to preserve an employment-at-will arrangement by using a disclaimer. In effect a **disclaimer** says that, regardless of provisions or policies in the employee handbook and regardless of any oral promises to the contrary, an employment-at-will situation still exists between the employer and its employees. A legally effective disclaimer must include the following statements:

1. Neither the employee policy manual nor any other communication to employees is intended to create a contract between the business and its employees.

2. The employer reserves the right to dismiss an employee at any time with or without reason and with or without notice.

3. No one other than the president of the firm (or some other specified executive) can make any oral or written change in this disclaimer.

To be an effective attempt to preserve employment-at-will, a disclaimer must also be written in clear, unequivocal language. Moreover, it must be placed somewhere conspicuous, such as within the opening pages of the employee handbook or on a centrally located bulletin board. Finally, an effective disclaimer must be communicated to the employees or at least acknowledged by them in some way. Even then, a disclaimer might prove to be

Teaching Tips Explain to students that, with the erosion of the employment-at-will doctrine, labor lawyers often recommend putting disclaimer statements on employment application forms and in employee handbooks.

ineffective if the employer has made some sort of specific promise. For instance, if an employer adds a disclaimer to a handbook that also includes a very specific plan for progressive discipline, that employer might still be required to follow that disciplinary plan. Employers who fail to follow their own progressive disciplinary plan may find themselves in the midst of a wrongful discharge lawsuit despite the disclaimer.

State Variations in Handbook Rules

The basic law in relation to employment-at-will, implied contracts, and disclaimers is, with a few exceptions, essentially identical in most jurisdictions, at least in relation to the original presentation of an employment manual to employees. The same is not true about the law when employers make subsequent changes in the employee handbook. Since the law varies from jurisdiction to jurisdiction, this problem can become especially acute for businesses with offices, plants, and/or stores in several states. Nevertheless, a general statement of the law is possible in relation to a situation in which an employer alters an employee manual, after that manual has been established as a part of the employment relationship. The general rule states that when an employer makes changes in an employee manual and the employee continues to work under the new terms, the employee has accepted the new terms, and the continued work by the employee amounts to that employee's consideration.

Some states say that the employee must work for a certain amount of time, such as three weeks, before the continued work is enough to constitute consideration for the changes. Others set no such minimum. Some jurisdictions adhere to the proposition that an implied contract requires a strong message from the employer that he or she intends that the handbook operate as a contract. When this is the case, any and all alterations must be clearly communicated to the employee. This is usually accomplished by having all employees sign a separate form indicating that they have seen the changes. A few states will not permit changes to enter the implied contract if those changes are so drastic that they considerably interfere with an employee's expectations as established by the original working conditions.

Promissory Estoppel

Some courts also use promissory estoppel to support wrongful discharge cases brought in employment-at-will jurisdictions. The facts that support promissory estoppel claims are similar to those which validate an implied contract case, and so the two arguments are often seen in the same case. However, there are differences. A promissory estoppel claim could be raised in a case involving an employee handout because the promises made in the handbook could be used to support promissory estoppel as well as implied contract. However, the existence of a handbook or the presence of written terms within a handbook, memo, letter, e-mail, or some other form of written communication, are not essential to a promissory estoppel case. In fact, a promissory estoppel case could be brought in the absence of any handbook or in a case in which the handbook itself cannot be used to create an implied contract. This distinction occurs because in promissory estoppel the promise, the reliance on that promise, and the injury to the employee matter the most. Promissory estoppel involves four elements.

1. The employer makes a promise.
2. The employer can reasonably expect the employee to rely on the promise.
3. The employee really does rely on the promise and, as a consequence, that employee does something or refrains from doing something.
4. The employee is, in turn, hurt by the action or inaction in reliance on the promise.

Under these circumstances, the employer cannot deny the promise made to the employee, and the doctrine of employment-at-will is unavailable as a defense.

Example 34-4

Bennett worked for Jameson for three years without incident. Unfortunately, on the eve of the beginning of his fourth year, Bennett was arrested for a drug-related felony, allegedly committed during his free time. Sonja Gephardt, Bennett's supervisor, told him in front of several witnesses that, "We have to lay you off now, but the company bosses have promised that you can have your job back at full seniority, once the case is over. They've also promised that you'll get back pay too." When Bennett was acquitted, he attempted to be reinstated as per Gephardt's promise but he was told that he was no longer needed. When Bennett brought a wrongful discharge suit against Jameson, the company filed a summary judgment motion for dismissal noting that, since Bennett was an at-will employee, the company could discharge him at any time for any reason or for no reason with or without notice. The court, however, refused to grant the summary judgment motion because the judge believed that Bennett had presented a *prima facie* case for promissory estoppel. This was established because:

1. Gephardt, representing Jameson, had made a promise to Bennett that his job with full seniority and back pay would be waiting for him after the case was resolved.

2. Gephardt, and therefore Jameson, could have reasonably expected Bennett to rely on the promise.

3. Bennett really did rely on the promise and, as a consequence, did not look for employment elsewhere.

4. Bennett was hurt by not looking for another job because he lost money while he was unemployed and while he sought a new job.

Under the circumstances of this case, the company will not be able to deny the promise that its agent, Gephardt, made to the employee, Bennett, and the doctrine of employment-at-will will be unavailable to it.

Implied Covenant Implied covenant holds that there is an implied promise in any employment relationship that the employer and the employee will be fair and honest with one another. This means that neither party will unfairly or dishonestly cheat the other out of anything due to the other party because of the employment relationship. The existence of an implied covenant has nothing to do with anything that the employer has said, written, or done. The implied covenant exists because the employment relationship exists.

A Question of Ethics

Beth Waid was to receive a 15 percent commission on all sales she made for her employer, the Jian Computer Corporation. Waid sold a $10,000,000 computer system to the Defense Department. To avoid paying $1,500,000 to Waid, Jian fired her, despite her record as a terrific sales person. In an employment-at-will state that did not recognize the implied covenant exception, such a discharge would be legal. However, would such a termination be ethical? Explain.

Getting Students Involved Lead students in a discussion of whether they think the after acquired evidence defense is fair to employees. Alternatively, you may wish to organize the class into debate teams to resolve the following question: Is it fair that an employer can defeat a valid claim for wrongful discharge by finding later evidence that could have been used to fire the employee?

Business Law in the News

Couch Leaves Town Holding Head High

Tim Couch took the high road on his way out of town and refused to criticize the Browns or coach Butch Davis for how they've treated him over the past year and a half.

Couch agreed to a one-year deal with the Green Bay Packers on Monday evening and is expected to sign today. The deal is worth about $1.25 million with a chance to make another $500,000 in incentives.

"I've always tried to handle things in a positive way since I've been in Cleveland, and I don't want to change that now," he said. "I wish things could've turned out differently, but I'm excited about playing for a Super Bowl contender."

Couch said he had no hard feelings against Davis for giving him the impression he was going to re-sign him, then signing Jeff Garcia instead.

"It's coach Davis' football team and he has to do what he thinks is best for the team," Couch said. "I thought for sure when [former team president] Carmen Policy came down to see me in Florida that I was going to be a Cleveland Brown again, but it just didn't work out that way."

Couch said he does wish the Browns would have released him earlier so he could have participated in the busy free-agent market. He was the 20th quarterback to change teams this off-season.

"They knew they weren't going to bring me back once they signed Jeff Garcia, so it's been very frustrating," Couch said. "But I still ended up in Green Bay, which is a great situation for me."

He said he has no ill will against the Browns for banning him from working out at the team facility while he was still under contract. He filed a grievance against the club, but it was dropped when the Browns agreed to release him last week.

"They sent me a letter telling me not to show up because they were worried about me getting hurt," he said. "I didn't think it was right, so I tried to do it anyway and they asked me to leave. I finally decided to come back down to Florida and hired a personal trainer. I've put on 8 pounds, and I'm in the best shape of my life."

Questions for Analysis

1. Would Tim Couch be considered an at-will employee in relation to his former position with the Cleveland Browns? Explain.

2. Did the Cleveland Browns commit any legal violation by not releasing Couch earlier? Explain. Did the team commit any ethical violation? Explain.

3. What was the essence of the grievance that Couch filed against the management of the Cleveland Browns? Explain.

4. If you were representing Couch in his grievance case, what argument would you make to support him? Explain. If you were representing the Cleveland Browns management, what counter-argument would you make? Explain. What counter-counterargument would you make for Couch? Explain.

5. After Couch signed with the Green Bay Packers, did he become an at-will employee? Explain.

After Acquired Evidence Defense

A relatively new defense that employers have successfully used in wrongful discharge cases is called the *after acquired evidence defense.* This defense is applied when an employer uncovers evidence, usually during the discovery process, that reveals that the employer could have legitimately discharged the employee, even if the employee's claims of wrongful discharge prove to be true. The defense is often raised as the grounds for the granting of a summary judgment.

Example 34-5

Frank Handley was discharged from his position as a test pilot for Coastline Aviation, Inc., when he was absent from work on one occasion without notifying his superior. The company's employment manual, which had no disclaimer, indicated that an employee would receive three warnings, one oral and two in writing, for unexcused absences before being suspended. Only after a fourth unexcused absence could an employee be discharged. Handley filed a wrongful discharge suit against Coastline based on a breach of the implied contract created by the promises in the employment manual. During the discovery process, attorney's for Coastline found out that Handley's pilot's license had been suspended several years before he was hired and that Handley had lied about this on his job application. The court ruled that, even though the lack of a license had not been the reason that he was discharged, under the circumstances, since he had falsified his application and since he was not qualified to fly an airplane, which is clearly the function of a test pilot, he would not be entitled to receive any damages.

The after acquired evidence defense has also been used by defendants in discrimination lawsuits. Consequently, the Equal Employment Opportunity Commission has issued a special rule that is to be applied when such a defense is raised. This rule is discussed later in the chapter.

Quick Quiz 34-1 True or False?

1. Employment-at-will has virtually disappeared as a legal doctrine in most states thanks to the development of wrongful discharge.

2. Generally, collective bargaining agreements have eliminated grievance procedures as cumbersome and outdated because of the development of wrongful discharge.

3. Fraud is no longer considered grounds for a lawsuit in any kind of wrongful discharge case.

34-2 Laws Regulating Employment Conditions

Employment conditions can be divided into two distinct areas: the actual physical situation in which employees must work and the compensation received by employees. Moreover, there is a national employment verification system that affects all newly hired employees. The federal government regulates these working conditions to protect workers.

Health and Safety Laws

Various state and federal laws and administrative rules and regulations are designed to reduce preventable hazards to employees in the workplace and to provide for safe and helpful working conditions. On the state level, departments of labor and health may be charged with determining whether an employer is complying with state health and safety laws. On

Related Cases The South Forty restaurant's liquor license was suspended because the owners had failed to comply within thirty days with state health and safety codes. In *Haughland v. Spaeth* (476 N.W.2d 692), the court upheld the suspension. State laws do not allow a retail liquor license to be issued to businesses if the buildings they occupy are in violation of health and safety codes.

the federal level, the Occupational Safety and Health Act assures all workers in a business, in or affecting interstate commerce, a safe and healthful place of employment.

Occupational Safety and Health Administration The Occupational Safety and Health Administration (OSHA), an agency responsible to the Department of Labor, establishes and enforces occupational health and safety standards with which employers must comply. To withstand a court challenge, however, it must be shown that the OSHA standards and regulations reasonably reduce the frequency or the severity of employee injuries or illnesses. Employers are required to keep records of illnesses, injuries, and deaths suffered by employees and to submit requested reports to the secretary of labor.

A corps of OSHA inspectors enforce compliance with its many and varied health and safety regulations. Employees are permitted to request an inspection if they believe that a violation exists. The U.S. Supreme Court has ruled that an OSHA inspector must produce a search warrant if the employer refuses to admit an inspector to the job site voluntarily.

When a violation of a standard is observed, the inspector issues a citation. A citation is a notice commanding the appearance of the employer in a proceeding. Employers may contest citations before the OSHA's Review Commission. If this effort fails, they may seek relief in the U.S. Court of Appeals.

Fair Labor Standards Act

The principal federal law affecting the wages and hours of employees is the Fair Labor Standards Act (FLSA), commonly referred to as the Wage-Hour Law. Frequently amended, the act provides that workers in interstate commerce or in an industry producing goods for sale in interstate commerce, must be paid no less than a specified minimum wage. Further, it specifies that employees cannot work for more than forty hours per week unless they are paid time and a half for overtime. The act prohibits the employment of children under the age of fourteen, and the employment of "oppressive child labor" in any enterprise engaged in commerce or in the production of goods for commerce. Provisions of the FLSA have been duplicated by a number of states to regulate intrastate commerce and industries not covered by the federal law.

Wage and Hour Exceptions and Exemptions The wage and hour provisions of the FLSA permit the employment of learners, apprentices, and messengers at less than the minimum wage. However, the employer must obtain express permission from the Wage and Hour Division of the Department of Labor and is subject to conditions set by it governing wages and hours. Fulltime students are permitted to be employed under the same conditions in retail and service stores outside of school hours.

The wage and hour provisions of the FLSA, with certain exceptions, do not apply to people employed in an executive, administrative, or professional capacity. The exempt workers are generally identified as those who manage other employees. At least 50 percent of their primary duties must be in the performance of office or nonmanual work relating to the operations of the company or in the performance of work requiring scientific or specialized study.

State, local, and federal employees; self-employed persons; and armed forces personnel are exempted from the wage and hour provisions. Also exempted are outside salespeople, employees of certain seasonal amusement or recreational businesses, and employees of small retail or service establishments.

Identity and Employment Eligibility

The federal Immigration Reform Act of 1986 created a national employment verification system that placed responsibility for verification of the identity and employment of all employees on the employer. The act provided that alien workers hired on or before

November 6, 1986, had until May 5, 1988, to seek temporary resident status. Those who do not have documentation of their right to work in this country are not entitled to help from the National Labor Relations Board (NLRB) in labor disputes.

Employers are required to request and examine documentation of identity and employment eligibility of all new hires and rehires, including U.S. citizens, permanent residents, and nonimmigrant visa holders. Job applicants must present original documentation. After the documents are reviewed by the employer, individuals who accept an offer of employment are required to complete and sign an employment eligibility verification form in the presence of a supervisor or a human resource officer.

Teaching Tips Assign a short research paper on the history of the federal immigration Reform and Control Act of 1986. Included should be an explanation of why the law was enacted and what employers and potential employees must do to comply with it. Encourage students to use the Internet for this assignment.

Quick Quiz 34-2 True or False?

1. The Occupational Safety and Health Act is a model law created by the American Law Institute.

2. The minimum wage is set by OSHA.

3. The Immigration Reform Act of 1986 does not affect the job application process.

Business Law in the News
'Sue Your Boss' Law Settles In

At the start of the year, California made it easier and more lucrative for employees to sue employers.

The experiment—the first in the nation—is to see if deputized employees can take over the job of enforcing workplace rules. Plaintiffs' attorneys are starting to file the first of the suits that give the law its teeth, and while no overall statistics are available, so far the flood of lawsuits the business community predicted has not materialized.

For example, an informal survey of Seyfarth Shaw's three West Coast offices—in Los Angeles, San Francisco and Sacramento, Calif.—shows that the Chicago-based firm's sizeable employment law practice is defending a dozen suits that cite the new law, the Labor Code Private Attorneys General Act.

"It's not Chicken Little time," said Brian T. Ashe, a Seyfarth partner who is representing employers in two suits. "But as a proportion of the lawsuits our firm has gotten since Jan.1, it is significant."

Dubbed the "sue your boss bill" and "a hunting license" by opponents, the new law creates a private cause of action to sue over any alleged labor code violations that have not already been addressed by the state labor commissioner.

A litigant can go directly to court, with no waiting to exhaust administrative remedies.

If there is no stated civil penalty for a particular labor code violation, employers can be fined $100 per employee per pay period and $200 for each subsequent violation, in addition to attorney fees and costs. The prevailing employees will receive 25% of these penalties. (Half goes to the state's general fund and the remaining quarter to the state Labor and Workforce Development Agency.)

Streamlined States

Supporters say it was needed because staffing levels for state labor law enforcement agencies have declined over the last decade. Opponents, including the governor, say it makes an already business-hostile climate worse and will drive jobs out of state.

A number of other states have adopted streamlined causes of action for workers in limited areas, such as construction disputes, said Mark Schacht,

(Continued)

Business Law in the News (*Continued*)

deputy director of the California Rural Legal Assistance Foundation, who drafted the legislation.

"What's unique is that this statute is global," noted Schacht.

The statute covers a hot area—wage-and-hour obligations, including overtime and minimum wage laws—as well as employee classification issues, drug and alcohol rehabilitation requirements, state law governing layoffs, public works, occupation safety and health.

Questions for Analysis

1. What cause of action was created by the California "sue your boss" bill? Explain.

2. Why did the California legislature feel it necessary to create the "sue your boss" bill? Explain.

3. What penalties are employers subject to under the bill? Explain. Who receives the proceeds from fines levied against those employers who are found in violation of various employment law provisions? Explain.

4. What areas of employment law are covered by the new California act? Explain.

5. Is the "sue your boss" bill in line with the principles behind employment-at-will? Explain. Would you support or oppose a "sue your boss" bill in your home state? Explain.

34-3 Worker Benefits

The law attempts to protect workers who have left the job because of retirement, injury, or disability. The law also assists workers who have been laid off or discharged. These objectives are accomplished through Social Security, unemployment insurance, and worker's compensation.

Social Security

According to the official Social Security website (www.ssa.gov) the Social Security benefit is mainly financed through a payroll tax on workers and employers.

Federal and state governments participate in programs designed to reduce the financial risk to workers by reason of their unemployment, disability, hospitalization, retirement, or death. The primary federal law covering these risks is the Social Security Act of 1935.

Under the Federal Insurance Contributions Act (FICA), both employers and employees are taxed equally to help pay for the worker's loss of income on retirement. The law provides that the employee's contribution is held back by the employer who then provides a matching contribution. The amount that an employee is assessed is based upon the employee's annual wage base. Each year the annual wage base is raised to accommodate changes that occur because of increases in the cost of living. The Social Security Administration will pay benefits to retired workers who are eligible under the plan. Each retired worker's benefit payments are set by law but are also raised automatically to match cost of living increases.

Unemployment Insurance

The unemployment insurance section of the Social Security Act provides for a joint federal and state system of unemployment insurance. Temporary financial assistance is available to individuals who are unemployed through no fault of their own and who have earned sufficient credits from prior employment. Under the Federal Unemployment Tax Act, each state operates its own unemployment insurance system, subject to conditions established by the federal government. In addition to meeting state requirements regarding length of time employed and amount of wages, former employees must be ready, willing, and able to take suitable full-time employment should it become available. Thus, claimants are ineligible to receive unemployment benefits when they refuse to work without good cause. Good cause for refusing to work must be real not imaginary; substantial, not trivial; and reasonable, not whimsical. For example, a desire to avoid a small cut in pay does not constitute good cause to refuse an employer's offer of employment in a reasonably similar position.

Example 34-6

Regina Pastoria, an administrative assistant with Jacksonville Contractors, was discharged when the firm was downsizing. She registered with the state unemployment agency and asked for unemployment compensation. The interviewing official at the unemployment office told her about an opening for an administrative assistant at the Rayfield Construction Corporation. Pastoria refused the position on the grounds that she needed a short vacation before accepting another job. Pastoria would be ineligible for benefits for any week in which she refused suitable employment without good cause.

In order to recover for work-related injuries under workers' compensation, a worker must be injured on the job. A worker traveling to work, traveling home, or traveling to some other non-work-related destination, cannot recover for injuries. This is also true of

People eligible for unemployment benefits must be willing to accept new job opportunities as jobs become available.

Further Reading For a thorough review of employee benefits, see *Know Your Rights in the Work Place: A Complete Guide for Employees,* by Barbara Kate Repa (Berkeley: Nolo Press, 1994).

Getting Students Involved The average male receives about 25 percent more in U.S. Social Security benefits than the average female. Have students research the inequalities between men and women in the Social Security system. Students should examine the ways in which the system discriminates against women who are divorced, widowed, disabled, or who work at home. Ask students to devise strategies for eliminating these inequities.

(T)he success of vicarious liability statutes and workmen's compensation provisions in the law suggest that in order to secure accident deterrence we need not penalize those at fault (or likely to be at fault) in causing injuries. In the case of workmen's compensation, employers have shown a remarkable facility for improving safety conditions—and thereby reducing the number of accidents—when, regardless of personal culpability, they have been placed in the position of standing to lose in virtue of increased accident costs.

—Jeffrie Murphy and Jules Coleman, *Philosophy of Law.* Boulder, CO: Westview Press, 1990, p. 151.

Did You Know?

One of the earliest forms of public assistance for the poor was instigated in Antwerp in the fourteenth century. Citizens considered deserving of the city's assistance were given identification badges. No one could receive food without the appropriate identification badge.

lunches and breaks when a worker leaves the workplace. The result is different, however, when a worker leaves the work site on a *special mission* for the employer. Then the employee would be eligible to recover if he or she is injured. This would be especially true if the trip involved a business-related lunch that the employee was required to attend away from the job site. Sometimes the distinction between a work-related injury and one that is not related to work is clear. Often, however, this distinction is not obvious. An examination of the surrounding circumstances will help make a determination when a close call must be made. One of the things to look for to make such a determination would be whether, from an objective point of view, the employee believed that he or she was required by the employer to perform the task involved in the injury. An additional piece of evidence would be the location of the injury. If the injury takes place on the job site and under the orders of the employer, for example, then the activities would be work related.

An employee who quits a job without cause or is discharged for misconduct or theft generally does not qualify for unemployment benefits. Most states disqualify workers from receiving benefits if they are on strike because of a labor dispute. Domestic workers, agricultural workers, and state and local government employees are not governed by the federal-state program. Separate federal unemployment programs exist for railroad workers and for federal civilian workers.

Workers' Compensation

Workers' compensation laws are in effect in all states. These statutes compensate covered workers or their dependents for injuries, disease, or death that occurred on the job or as a result of it. One form provides a fund operated only by the state government. Employers pay into a state-controlled fund. When employees suffer injuries, they apply to the state to receive their benefits.

In another form of workers' compensation, companies are required to carry insurance for their workforce, but they have the option of contributing to the state fund or purchasing insurance from a private insurer. In the third form, all employers are required to purchase workers' compensation insurance from private insurers.

Workers' compensation coverage is especially important for employees in hazardous or life-threatening occupations.

Pension Plan Regulation

The Employee Retirement Income Security Act (ERISA) provides needed supervision over employee pension plans that are established by many employers. Under the act, employers must place their pension contributions on behalf of the employees into a pension trust, independent of the employer. Under the rules of vesting, workers are guaranteed the right to receive pension benefits regardless of whether they are working under the plan at the time of retirement. The law requires all pension plans to have minimum vested benefits. All pension plans must provide vested benefits after a worker has been on the job for five years.

Family and Medical Leave Regulation

Under provisions of the federal Family and Medical Leave Act (FMLA), employers who have fifty or more employees at the workplace (or within seventy-five miles of the workplace) must give those employees up to twelve weeks of leave time in a twelve-month period for child, spousal, or parental care, or for the employee's own serious medical condition if that condition necessitates either in-patient treatment or medical care on a continuing basis. The twelve-month period can be calculated based on a calendar year or from the time the leave actually begins. The leave time may be unpaid, but it must not jeopardize the job of the employee. To qualify for the leave time guaranteed by the FLMA, the worker must have been employed by the firm for at least one year and must have worked for 1,250 hours over the twelve-month period before the leave is requested. Employees can draw on the twelve weeks consecutively, at intervals, or as an adjusted work plan. For example, an employee might take a half week of leave time now, and another half week later, or an employee might reduce his or her workweek from five to four days, or a worker might adjust his or her daily work schedule from eight to six hours, and so on.

Employer Responsibilities Both the employee and the employer have responsibilities under the FMLA. For instance, the employer must keep the employee's group health insurance in effect while the employee is on leave. Furthermore, when the employee returns to work, the employer must reinstate the employee to his or her former job, or a job equal to the former job. In addition, the employer must make certain that, upon returning to work, the employee receives the same pay and the same benefits that he or she received before going on leave. Employers are also forbidden to dismiss an employee or to discriminate against a worker who exercises his or her leave rights under the FMLA. Similarly, the employer cannot retaliate against a worker who protests the employer's attempt to bypass the rights granted to employees under this act. Employers are also responsible for informing employees, in writing, when leave time under the FMLA has been activated.

Employee Responsibilities FMLA also imposes certain obligations on employees. For instance, employees are required by law to give notice of their intention to take an FMLA leave whenever they can foresee the need for the leave. This notice must be given to the employer at least thirty days before the employee intends to take the leave. If the need for a leave is unpredictable then the employee must give notice as soon as doing so is practical.

Enforcement of FMLA Rules Employees who believe that their employer has violated FMLA rules can file complaints with the Labor Employment Standards Administration. Moreover, employees who believe that their rights have been violated may file a lawsuit against their employers. Finally, a state statute or a collective bargaining agreement that give employees more comprehensive leave coverage would supersede FMLA.

Further Reading For a study of abuses reported in relation to the FMLA, see an article in the June 14, 2004, issue of *The National Law Journal,* by Frank C. Morris, entitled, "FMLA is exceeding the intentions of Congress." Most of the abuses discussed in the article describe how employees exploit the system.

> ## Quick Quiz 34-3 True or False?
>
> 1. Most states have eliminated Workers' Compensation Laws because they are too expensive to maintain.
>
> 2. Under the Federal Unemployment Tax Act all state unemployment compensation systems were dismantled.
>
> 3. The Family Medical Leave Act provides for twelve weeks of paid leave for all employees in any twelve-month period.

34-4 Equal Employment Opportunity

In recent years, the government has attempted to address the problem of discrimination in the workplace. One integral part of this attempt was the Civil Rights Acts of 1964 and 1991. Other facets of this attempt include the Equal Pay Act of 1963, the Age Discrimination in Employment Act, the Uniformed Services Employment and Reemployment Rights Act, and the Americans with Disabilities Act.

The Equal Pay Act of 1963

Under provisions of the federal Equal Pay Act of 1963, employers must pay women the same amount that they pay men for the same job. The underlying motto of those who support the Equal Pay Act was and is "equal pay for equal work." Such a rule is easy to follow when the work in question is exactly the same. Problems occur when the work done by the women in the workplace is comparable, but not identical, to the work done by the men. To deal with this issue, the courts have ruled that, as long as the work in question requires the same level of effort, ability, and accountability, and is rendered in a comparable work environment, it is considered substantially equal. Substantially equal work requires equal pay. When a worker brings a claim under the Equal Pay Act, she must first establish that the employer does not pay women workers the same as men workers for essentially the same work. The burden then moves to the employer who must show that the different pay rate is based on some sort of nondiscriminatory criterion. Systems based on merit, training, and productivity are acceptable to the court as legitimate reasons for different pay rates. Remedies available under the Equal Pay Act include back wages and punitive damages. Employers might also be ordered to eliminate the unfair pay system. Since 1979, the Equal Pay Act has been administered by the Equal Employment Opportunity Commission (EEOC).

Civil Rights Act of 1964

The Civil Rights Act of 1964 prohibits discrimination based on sex, race, color, national origin, or religion. Employees who believe that they have been discriminated against can file complaints with the Equal Employment Opportunity Commission (EEOC). Moreover, some state governments have equal employment agencies that have been designated as deferral agencies under Title VII. In those states, all discrimination charges filed with the EEOC must be sent by the EEOC to the state equal employment agency. Even so, an employee who has filed such a claim can ask the EEOC, rather than the state agency, to conduct the inquiry. Discrimination claims must be registered with the EEOC no later than 180 days after the prohibited activity. In states with deferral agencies, that deadline is lengthened to 300 days. Discrimination can be committed in one of two ways: disparate treatment and disparate impact.

Background Informa-tion The Civil Rights Act of 1964, as originally introduced in Congress, did not include any mention of discrimination on the basis of sex. Sex discrimination was added at the last minute by conservative southern opponents of the bill who thought that it would be considered so ridiculous that it would kill the entire bill when Congress finally voted on it.

Disparate Treatment Under **disparate treatment,** the employer intentionally discriminates against an individual or a group belonging to a protected class. The protected classes are sex, race, color, religion, or national origin. For instance, a business that advertised for "salesmen" or "saleswomen" rather than "salespersons" would be practicing this type of discrimination. A common misconception exists that this type of brazen discrimination has been eliminated from the workplace. Such is not the case. Even into the 1990s, the United States Supreme Court was still reviewing cases that dealt with companies that continued to discriminate in direct and obvious ways.

Teaching Tips Students may think that quotas for hiring exist under affirmative action programs. However, it is illegal for an employer to specify that he or she is seeking to hire a member of a particular minority or ethnic group in job advertisements, even for the purpose of fulfilling conditions of affirmative action programs.

Example 34-7

Johnson Controls Inc., a battery manufacturer located in Wisconsin, had an employment policy that eliminated women under seventy years of age from performing certain jobs in the making of batteries unless they could produce proof that they were infertile. The company argued that it was just trying to protect its workers, since all the prohibited jobs involved prolonged exposure to lead. The U.S. Supreme Court disagreed and labeled the company's policy as a clear-cut example of sex discrimination.

Businesses have a defense against a charge of disparate treatment, called a *bona fide occupational qualification (BFOQ).* The discrimination may be justified if the employer can prove that the job requirement is a BFOQ. Even so, a BFOQ defense can never be raised to justify racial discrimination. However, a BFOQ defense can work for some forms of sexual discrimination. For example, a requirement that all applicants for a job modeling women's bathing suits be female would be a BFOQ.

Further Reading For a complete overview of employees' rights, including a section on sexual harassment, see *Power on the Job: The Legal Rights of Working People,* by Michael Yates (Boston: South End Press, 1994).

Example 34-8

Could Johnson Controls Inc., in Example 34-8, argue that infertility in a woman is a valid BFOQ? The U.S. Supreme Court said no. A BFOQ must be related to the job performance. Since men and women can both be competent battery makers, excluding one sex or the other from that job cannot be justified.

Disparate Impact In contrast to disparate treatment, disparate impact is a more subtle form of discrimination. Discrimination through **disparate impact** or *adverse impact* occurs when an employer has a policy that on the surface seems neutral, but which has an unequal and unfair impact on the members of one or more of the protected classes. For instance, an employer who requires all employees who work in the warehouse to be six feet tall and to weigh at least 180 pounds may have discriminated against women under the doctrine of disparate impact. Although the criteria seem neutral on the surface, they would exclude women disproportionately and would thus have an unfair impact on them.

Businesses have a defense against a charge of disparate impact known as *business necessity.* A qualification may be permitted despite its disparate impact on a protected class, if the employer can show that the qualification is needed to perform the job. For example, a requirement that all job applicants have a law degree for a job as an attorney might have a disparate impact on one or more of the protected classes. However, since a law degree is needed for the job, it will be allowed. Naturally, the claimant has an opportunity to demonstrate that the challenged practice is not really needed to perform the job in question.

Background Information A total 3,661 complaints of sexual harassment were filed with the Equal Employment Opportunity Commission (EEOC) in 1981. In 1990, the number of annual complaints was 5,964. The EEOC attributed the rise to the Supreme Court's recognition in 1986 that sexual harassment is a form of sex discrimination (*Meritor Savings Bank v. Vinson*, 477 U.S. 57). The EEOC expected additional increases in complaints to follow the 1991 hearings for U.S. Supreme Court nominee Clarence Thomas who was accused of sexually harassing former co-worker Anita Hill while employed at the EEOC. During the first quarter of 1992, immediately after the hearings, 1,244 complaints were filed.

Background Information The Equal Employment Opportunity Commission (EEOC) Guidelines on Discrimination Because of Sex provides: Where employment opportunities or benefits are granted because of an individual's submission to the employer's sexual advances or requests for sexual favors, the employer may be held liable for unlawful sex discrimination against the other person who was qualified for but denied that employment opportunity or benefit.

Sexual Harassment In recent years, the courts have witnessed an increase in the number of **sexual harassment** claims. There is no question that sexual harassment is a type of sexual discrimination, and that it is forbidden by the Civil Rights Act. However, exactly what constitutes sexual harassment is misunderstood by many people. While most people recognize *quid pro quo* harassment, they do not realize that the creation of a hostile work environment also constitutes sexual harassment. ***Quid pro quo* sexual harassment** occurs when a supervisor makes unwelcome sexual advances toward a subordinate or suggests that the subordinate trade sexual favors for preferential treatment. A hostile work environment occurs when misconduct, such as sexually explicit comments, photographs, pictures, cartoons, jokes, posters, or gestures, pervade the workplace to the extent that conditions become distressing, offensive, or hostile. The law also expressly forbids employers to retaliate against employees who file sexual harassment complaints.

Example 34-9

Jarod Wilson, the second shift supervisor at the Binghamton Oil Refinery, frequently insulted Regina Davidson on the basis of her gender. He also made her the object of sexual comments, jokes, and innuendos. In addition, he purchased and distributed pornographic calendars throughout the department. First, Davidson complained to Wilson's supervisor. Later she filed a complaint with the human resources director. No action was taken against Wilson. In fact, after filing the complaint, she was discharged. Davidson's sexual harassment lawsuit would be based on a valid claim that Wilson and the management of the refinery created a hostile work environment. As a part of her lawsuit, Davidson may also argue that the company discharged her in retaliation for her complaint.

Affirmative Action and Reverse Discrimination The term **affirmative action** refers to a practice by which an employer actively pursues a policy that will reduce the effects of past discrimination in the workplace. The term "affirmative," in this context, means to go forth actively, and the word "action" means a definitive plan. Therefore, affirmative action occurs when an employer initiates a definitive plan to eliminate discriminatory practices. Affirmative action is not mandated by the Civil Rights Act of 1964. However, it is not prohibited either. Generally, affirmative action plans come from a court order as the result of a court case. Nothing, however, prevents an employer from pursuing an affirmative action plan voluntarily. An affirmative action declaration might also be issued by the chief executive, as was the case in 1965 when President Johnson issued an Executive Order to eliminate discrimination in businesses holding federal contracts.

Some people are opposed to affirmative action because they see it as a form of reverse discrimination. **Reverse discrimination** is a term that refers to a practice that is designed to eliminate discrimination against the members of a protected class, but which has the opposite effect on other members of that class or on the members of another protected class. The Supreme Court has reacted to such complaints by requiring that affirmative action plans promote a "compelling state interest" and be finely drawn in order to minimize any harm to those workers not included in the plan. To preserve an affirmative action plan, the government must show that the plan is necessary to fight past discriminatory practices, has a specified termination date, and is the only way to reverse the discriminatory practice.

Civil Rights Act of 1991

Congress enacted the Civil Rights Act of 1991 to meet several objectives. One objective involves the doctrine of disparate impact. The second objective involves an expansion of the remedies available under the Civil Rights legislation.

Strengthening Disparate Impact The first goal of the Civil Rights Act of 1991 was to strengthen the doctrine of disparate impact that had been weakened by the U.S. Supreme Court. The act makes it clear that, in disparate impact cases, the employer has the burden of proving that a business necessity exists for the discriminatory practice that is the basis of the complaint. The law also makes it clear that the employer must prove that the hiring or promotion qualification is directly related to the specific job in question rather than to general business needs. The party who files a complaint in a disparate impact case may also be victorious if he or she can show that the same business goal can be reached by using a nondiscriminatory employment practice.

Teaching Tips Advise students that if they send letters to employers or employees about contentious legal issues, they should send them as certified mail because the receiver has to sign for the mail to obtain it. In this way, if necessary, the dates on which the letters were sent and received can be proved.

Compensatory and Punitive Damages A second objective was to expand the availability of compensatory and punitive damages. Prior to the passage of the new act, only victims of racial discrimination could collect compensatory and punitive damages. All other victims of discrimination were limited to collecting back pay only. Under the Civil Rights Act of 1991, compensatory and punitive damages are now available to people who have been discriminated against because of their sex, religion, or national origin. However, Congress set a limit of $300,000 on such damages. Other remedies that are available under Title VII are back pay, reinstatement, and attorney fees.

Other Effects of the Civil Rights Act of 1991 The 1991 Civil Rights Act also added a few other critical provisions designed to reinstate the actual intent of Congress in creating the original statute in 1964. For instance, the new law mandates that American businesses must give U.S. citizens working abroad the same protection against discrimination that they give workers in the United States. In addition, the new act makes it clear that an employment practice is illegal even if only a portion of the practice is discriminatory.

After Acquired Evidence in Relation to Discrimination Cases The EEOC has adopted an approach for discrimination cases in which after acquired evidence reveals that the employer had a legitimate reason for discharging the employee. The rule, which applies only to cases involving the EEOC, states that the commission will not require that the employer rehire the claimant, nor will the commission attempt to recover backpay or compensatory damages that arise after the time that the after acquired evidence was obtained. However, in order not to frustrate the purposes of the Civil Rights Act of 1991, the EEOC will still seek punitive damages in such cases.

Terms The EEOC and the United States Supreme Court accepted this nineteenth-century definition of *race* in the Civil Rights Law of 1866, Section 1981: "any ethnic minority."

Age Discrimination in Employment Act

The Age Discrimination in Employment Act (ADEA) prohibits discrimination on the basis of age. ADEA covers employment agencies, employers of twenty or more employees, and labor unions of more than twenty-five members. This act protects any person aged forty or older from discrimination in hiring, firing, promotion, or other aspect of employment.

Like the Civil Rights Act, the ADEA is administered by the EEOC. Age discrimination claims must be registered with the EEOC no later than 300 days after the prohibited

Teaching Tips Make sure students are aware that an employee's burden to prove age discrimination includes producing the following evidence: The employee 1) was over forty years old; 2) was terminated or demoted; 3) was doing a good enough job to meet the employer's legitimate expectations; and 4) was treated less favorably than those employees under the age of forty.

The Opening Case Revisited
"The Enemy of 40 Is 30, Not 50"

In The Opening Case at the beginning of this chapter in interpreting the meaning of the ADEA, the Supreme Court ruled that "(i)n a world where younger is better, talk about discrimination because of age is naturally understood to refer to discrimination against the older. . . . The enemy of 40 is 30, not 50." This ruling indicates that it is sometimes justifiable for employers to favor some members of a protected class over other members of the same class.

activity. Naturally, if age is a true job qualification, the law does not apply. For instance, if the job involves the modeling of junior miss fashions, it would not be discrimination to hire someone of suitable age to model the clothes. The courts, however, will carefully scrutinize all such requirements and will generally be able to detect those that are merely a pretense covering age discrimination.

Example 34-10

Thomas Taggart, aged fifty-eight, lost his position when the subsidiary he worked for was disbanded by Time, Inc., the parent corporation. All of the employees who were laid off as a result of the closing were promised preferential treatment for other jobs at Time, Inc. Taggart applied for more than thirty of these positions. He was never rehired. Most of the time the reason given for his rejection was that he was overqualified. Taggart brought an age discrimination suit under the ADEA. Time, Inc., argued that Taggart was not rehired because of an overqualification barrier that had nothing to do with his age. The court disagreed. The court ruled that calling Taggart overqualified was just another way of saying he was too old.

In 1990, Congress amended the ADEA in response to a U.S. Supreme Court case that held that the original ADEA did not cover employee benefit plans. The amendment, which is called the Older Workers' Benefit Protection Act (OWBPA), makes it clear that the ADEA forbids discrimination against older workers in the handling of their employee benefit and retirement plans. OWBPA also gives older workers legal recourse if they are forced or tricked into giving up their rights under the ADEA. Usually this occurs when the employee is asked to sign a waiver. A waiver of rights is valid only if it is given freely and without force or coercion. The employer has the job of proving that the waiver is valid if it is introduced as evidence in court.

Uniformed Services Employment and Reemployment Rights Act

Under provisions of the Uniformed Services Employment and Reemployment Rights Act (USERA), an employee who has served in the armed forces and who has successfully completed his or her tour of duty is entitled, upon returning to work, to be reinstated in his or her previous position on the job. Unlike the Civil Rights Act which is controlled by the

EEOC, USERA is administered by the Office of Veterans' Employment and Training Service (VETS). Also unlike the Civil Rights Act, under USERA, employees may file a complaint with VETS or they can take the case directly to court. No statute of limitations is connected to USERA. However, employees are not permitted to hold back on the filing of a case for an unreasonable length of time. Employees who succeed in a case might receive damages, an injunction to prevent their termination, and sometimes, at the discretion of the judge, attorneys' fees.

Americans with Disabilities Act

The Americans with Disabilities Act (ADA) is designed to open the American workplace to this country's disabled citizens. The ADA is divided into several titles. Title I lays out the duties imposed on private-sector employers and Title II covers public services and public transportation. The ADA is administered by the EEOC. The ADA carefully outlines what is considered a disability. It also explains who and what are covered by the act and what practices are specifically forbidden.

Disabilities The ADA defines **disability** as any physical or mental impairment that substantially limits one or more of the major life activities. This definition includes paralysis, blindness, deafness, cancer, mental retardation, learning disabilities, and AIDS among others. Excluded from protection are people with kleptomania, pyromania, or gambling disorders. Nor does the act extend to people who use illegal drugs. The definition of disability also does not include homosexuality or bisexuality. However, since the act forbids discrimination against people who are associated with a particular disability, discrimination against homosexuals, simply because they are more likely to contract AIDS, would also be forbidden.

Activities and Individuals Covered by ADA Discrimination is forbidden in the screening of applicants, in the initial hiring, and in on-the-job treatment. This protection against discrimination also extends to apprenticeship programs, promotions, pay raises and on-the-job training opportunities. Individuals, including not only employees but also applicants for employment, also cannot be segregated or classified because of a disability. The ADA also protects an individual from discrimination because that individual is associated with someone who has a disability. As is true of other situations, a state statute that gives individuals with disabilities more protection than the ADA would supersede the federal statute.

Forbidden Practices ADA forbids discrimination on the basis of a disability if the disabled individual can do the essential functions of the job with "reasonable accommodations." Exactly what would qualify as a reasonable accommodation in a given set of circumstances is, at best, problematical. Nevertheless, the statute does give some guidance in determining the extent of a **reasonable accommodation.** An accommodation will be reasonable if it permits the disabled individual to accomplish the essential functions of the job without imposing an undue hardship on the employer. Factors used in determining whether a proposed accommodation will cause **undue hardship** include the type of accommodation needed, the expense involved in providing the accommodation, the financial ability of the company to provide the necessary accommodation, and the size and nature of the company involved. Because of the innovative nature of the law, and the lack of precedent, the EEOC has decided to follow a case-by-case evaluation of all claims filed by disabled individuals against employers.

Terms "Major life activities," noted in the Americans with Disabilities Act, consist of caring for oneself, performing manual tasks, walking, seeing, hearing, speaking, breathing, learning, and working (475 U.S. 1118).

Getting Students Involved Challenge students to research the standards established by the Americans with Disabilities Act and compare them with the standards of the Rehabilitation Act of 1973, including the amendments of 1974 and 1978.

State Variations Nebraska has one of the most comprehensive state definitions of disabled citizens: "disability shall mean any physical condition, infirmity, malformation, or disfigurement which is caused by bodily injury, birth defect, or illness, including epilepsy or seizure disorder, and which shall include, but not be limited to, any degree of paralysis, amputation, lack of physical coordination, blindness. . . ."

Further Reading For a thorough and up-to-date look at the ADA from the employer's perspective, see *Employer's Guide to the Americans with Disabilities Act,* 2nd Ed., by James G. Frierson (Washington DC: BNA, 1995).

Quick Quiz 34-4 True or False?

1. The term affirmative action refers to a practice by which an employer actively pursues a policy that will reduce the effects of past discrimination in the workplace.

2. American businesses working in other countries need not give U.S. citizens the same protection against discrimination under the Civil Rights Act as those afforded workers in the United States itself.

3. The Uniformed Services Employment and Reemployment Rights Act (USERA) is administered by the EEOC.

Summary

34-1 In the United States, the dominant legal doctrine governing most employment relationships is employment-at-will. This means than an employer can dismiss an employee at any time for any reason. Employees who belong to labor unions today are frequently protected by hiring and firing procedures written into their collective bargaining agreements. Individuals with unique abilities, special talents, or a highly specialized education often have the power to negotiate their own employment contracts and would not be affected by employment-at-will. Most employees would have no protection were it not for the exceptions to employment-at-will that the courts have created under the heading of wrongful discharge. Wrongful discharge gives employees legal grounds for a lawsuit against employers who have dismissed them unfairly. The courts have used several theories to judge the injustice of a dismissal. These include public policy tort, intentional inflection of emotional distress, implied contract, promissory estoppel, and implied covenant.

34-2 OSHA establishes and enforces occupational health and safety standards with which employers must comply. The principal federal law affecting the wages and hours of employees is the Fair Labor Standards Act. The act provides that workers in interstate commerce or in an industry that produces goods for sale in interstate commerce must be paid no less than a specified minimum wage. Further, it specifies that employees cannot work for more than forty hours per week unless they are paid time and a half for overtime and prohibits the employment of children under the age of fourteen, and the employment of oppressive child labor in any enterprise engaged in commerce or in the production of goods for commerce. The federal Immigration Reform Act of 1986 created a national employment verification system that placed on the employer responsibility for verification of the identity and employment of all employees. Employers are required to request and examine documentation of identity and employment eligibility of all new hires and rehires, including U.S. citizens, permanent residents, and nonimmigrant visa holders.

34-3 Federal and state governments participate in programs designed to reduce the financial risk to workers by reason of their unemployment, disability, hospitalization, retirement, and death. The principal federal law covering these risks is the Social Security Act of 1935. The unemployment insurance section of the Social Security Act provides for a joint federal and state system of unemployment insurance. Under the Federal Unemployment Tax Act, each state operates its own unemployment insurance system, subject to conditions established by the federal government. Workers' compensation laws are in effect in all states. These statutes compensate covered workers or their dependents for injuries, disease, or death that occurred on the job or as a result of it. ERISA provides needed supervision over employee pension plans established by many employers. Under the act, employers must place their pension contributions on behalf of the employees into a pension trust, independent of the employer. Under provisions of the Family and Medical Leave Act (FMLA), employers who have fifty or more employees must give those employees up to twelve weeks of leave time for child, spousal, or parental care. This leave time may be unpaid but it must not jeopardize the job of the employee.

34-4 The Equal Pay Act mandates that workers receive equal pay for equal work. The Civil Rights Act of 1964 prohibits discrimination based on sex, race, color, national origin, or religion. Employees who believe they have been discriminated against can file a complaint with the EEOC. Discrimination can be committed in one of two ways: disparate treatment or disparate impact. Sexual harassment is also a type of sexual discrimination, and it is forbidden by the Civil Rights Act. The Civil Rights Act of 1991 was enacted by Congress to strengthen the doctrine of disparate impact and to extend the availability of compensatory and punitive damages. Other steps toward equality in employment include the Age Discrimination in Employment Act, the Uniformed Services Employment and Reemployment Rights Act, and the Americans with Disabilities Act.

Key Terms

affirmative action, 654	employment-at-will, 637	reverse discrimination, 654
collective bargaining agreement, 637	grievance procedure, 638	sexual harassment, 654
disability, 657	implied contract, 640	undue hardship, 657
disclaimer, 641	implied covenant, 643	workers' compensation, 650
disparate impact, 653	*quid pro quo* sexual harassment, 654	wrongful discharge, 639
disparate treatment, 653	reasonable accommodation, 657	

Questions for Review and Discussion

1. What is employment-at-will?
2. What situations fall outside employment-at-will?
3. What theories are offered under wrongful discharge?
4. What is the after acquired evidence rule?
5. What are the functions of the Occupational Safety and Health Act?
6. What are the functions of the Fair Labor Standards Act?
7. What are the differences between unemployment insurance and workers' compensation?
8. What are the major provisions of the Family Medical Leave Act?
9. What is the difference between disparate treatment and disparate impact?
10. What is the difference between the business necessity defense and the defense offered by a bona fide occupational qualification (BFOQ)?

Investigating the Internet

Access the Employment Law Information Network and locate the state employment law index. Find your state and locate a recent article on employment-at-will. Write a report on that article as it relates to developments in your state.

Cases for Analysis

1. Carla McFarland was an associate professor of English literature at Highland College. She was the only single person in her department. Consequently, she was frequently assigned classes late in the evening, on weekends, and during the summer semester. She was also called upon to pick up visiting professors and to serve as their escort and guide during their stays at the college. She was

also given extra duty as adviser to the *The High-land Review,* the college's literary magazine. When McFarland complained about the unequal treatment, she was told that the married professors had family responsibilities that she did not have, which took up much of their time and which prevented them from having the flexibility that she had. Thus, she would continue to carry the extra load. McFarland filed a complaint with the EEOC. Can discrimination based on an employee's status as a single person be considered unlawful under the Civil Rights Act? Explain. Is this a case of disparate impact or disparate treatment? Explain. See Wilson, Robin. "Singular Mistreatment: Unmarried Professors Are Outsiders in the Ozzie and Harriet World of Academe." *The Chronicle of Higher Education,* April 23, 2004, pp. A10–A12.

2. Henderson worked as a chemical engineer for the Wannisky Chemical Corporation. McGuire, Henderson's supervisor, ordered him to remove the labels from several hundred steel drums that had once contained a severely corrosive acid. McGuire told Henderson that they intended to reuse the drums to ship a new chemical fertilizer. Henderson refused to remove the labels because reusing the old drums would violate both state and federal laws. When McGuire told another employee to remove the labels and reuse the drums, Henderson reported the company's activities to the state and federal authorities. Henderson was fired for his refusal to follow orders and for notifying the authorities. In a lawsuit against Wannisky, which legal exception to the employment-at-will doctrine did Henderson use? Explain.

3. Bennerson was employed by the Checker Garage Service Corporation as an auto mechanic. His duties included both assisting mechanics in the garage and making road calls to service vehicles owned and operated by his employer. During his lunch hour, Bennerson used one of his employer's taxi cabs to drive to a restaurant. En route to the restaurant, he was seriously injured when the taxi struck a pole. Bennerson filed a claim before the workers' compensation board. His claim was granted. Checker Garage appealed, arguing among other things that the taxi that Bennerson drove did not "go out of control," but that Bennerson had lost control. Was Checker correct? Explain. *Bennerson v. Checker Garage Service Corporation,* 388 N.Y.S.2d 374 (NY).

4. Nancy Barillaro and Nancy Fotia were employed in the inspection and trimming departments at Elwood Knitting Mills for approximately sixteen years. Barillaro was laid off in September and Fotia in November. Both were offered the option of returning to work in March of the following year as knitting machine operators, but at an 18 percent reduction in pay. Neither accepted the offer. They argued that the offered work would have involved a loss in seniority and a substantial reduction in pay. In addition, Fotia claimed that she was not familiar with the operation of the machine. Barillaro claimed that she was too short to operate the machine. The Pennsylvania Unemployment Compensation Board decided that neither claimant was eligible to receive benefits because they refused offers of suitable work without good cause. Was the board correct in its ruling? Explain. *Barillaro v. Unemployment Compensation Bd. Of Review,* 387 A.2d 1324 (PA).

5. The Wynn Oil Company, which carried out an enormous amount of business with Latin American companies, argued that being male was a bona fide occupational qualification (BFOQ) for the position of sales executive. Wynn contended that, because of certain Latin American customs, the hiring of a woman sales executive would have a serious detrimental effect on the company's business. The contention was challenged in federal court. Will Wynn's argument succeed? Explain. *Fernandez v. Wynn Oil Co.,* 653 F.2d 1273 (9th Cir.).

6. The Spelling Entertainment Group hired actress Hunter Tylo to appear in the television show *Melrose Place.* Her role was to involve the seduction of another character's husband. When Tylo became pregnant she dutifully reported her condition to Spelling. The entertainment company then discharged her, arguing that non-pregnancy was a bona fide occupational qualification (BFOQ) for the role designed for Tylo. Tylo challenged the contention that her condition disqualified her from performing her job. Can non-pregnancy be a BFOQ? Explain. *Tylo v. Superior Court,* 55 Cal. App. 4th 1379 (CA).

7. Rice, an African American woman, was denied employment as a public health representative by the city of St. Louis for lack of a college degree. Failing to obtain relief after filing a complaint with the EEOC charging racial discrimination, she filed a lawsuit in the federal district court. Rice took the position that the degree requirement had a disparate impact on African Americans and was invalid under the Civil Rights Act of 1964. She

pointed out that blacks were only approximately 55 percent as likely as whites in the St. Louis area to have a college degree. Testimony showed that the satisfactory performance of public health representatives required the ability to communicate with others, frequently in an emotional situation, and the ability to speak and write intelligibly. There was also a risk to the public health and safety in the employment of unqualified applicants. Did Rice prevail? Explain. *Rice v. The City of St. Louis,* 607 F.2d 791 (8th Cir).

8. The Commonwealth of Virginia required all applicants for state troopers to be between twenty-one and twenty-nine years old, to be at least 5 feet 9 inches tall, and to weigh at least 156 pounds. The height and weight requirements eliminated 98 percent of the female applicants. The basic employment requirements also made it mandatory that all applicants, including applicants for civilian dispatcher positions, complete and pass written mental ability tests. The tests for dispatcher positions were not valid predictors of job performance. The tests for the trooper positions also were shown not to be predictors of job performance. The United States brought suit, charging that Virginia engaged in a pattern and practice of discrimination against African American applicants for the civilian positions and against both African American and women candidates for the trooper positions. Did the United States prevail? Explain. *United States v. Commonwealth of Virginia,* 620 F.2d 1018 (4th Cir).

9. Shirley Painter was the Chief Deputy Clerk in the Bookkeeping Department of the Civil Division of the Municipal Court of the City of Cleveland. She decided to run for city council and asked for a leave of absence to pursue that goal. At first she was granted the leave. However, two months later she was terminated. Painter brought a wrongful discharge lawsuit against Charles Graley, the assistant personnel director in the municipal court clerk's office. Painter asked to be reinstated. She also asked for back pay and for punitive damages. Her wrongful discharge suit was based on a violation of public policy. She argued that she had appropriate grounds for the suit because her termination violated the state constitution. Graley argued that a plaintiff can bring a wrongful discharge lawsuit based upon public policy only if a statute exists that prohibits the firing in question. Has Painter stated sufficient legal grounds for her wrongful discharge lawsuit? Explain. *Painter v. Graley,* 639 N.E.2d 51 (OH).

Quick Quiz Answers

34-1	34-2	34-3	34-4
1. F	1. F	1. F	1. T
2. F	2. F	2. F	2. F
3. F	3. F	3. F	3. F

Chapter 35 | Labor-Management Relations Law

The Opening Case
"Workers of All Boston, Unite!"

One evening in June, about six weeks before the Democratic National Convention was supposed to open in Boston, a handful of picketers representing Boston's police union showed up at FleetCenter, the site of the convention. The picketers were angry at the lack of progress in the collective bargaining process between the city and the police union. The union, in fact, had accused the city of bargaining in bad faith. The city, in turn, argued that it had already offered the union an 11.9 percent pay raise over four years. In response, the police union pointed to the city's willingness to spend enormous sums of money on paving the streets and renovating the center for the convention, and asked for a 15 percent raise over four years. The city refused and the bargaining process broke down. The goal of the demonstration was to suggest that union workers involved in the renovation project at FleetCenter should not cross the picket line. That night, very few people took notice of this tiny gathering. However, by the next morning, the small number of picketers had grown to over 300. Moreover, the ranks of picketers included not only police officers, but also firefighters, transit workers, janitors, and other public workers, as well as such private sector employees as telephone workers and utilities employees. When workers for a moving company showed up to remove furniture and equipment from the building so that the renovation could begin, they were faced with the massive picket line. Consequently, those workers, who were themselves union members, refused to cross the line and the renovation project was stopped in its tracks. Was this a legitimate exercise of the union's power or was it a move that was unwarranted and illegal? Should union members always honor picket lines by refusing to cross them? What exactly constitutes bad faith during the collective bargaining process? As you read Chapter 35, Labor-Management Relations Law, consider whether the police union or the city held the legally correct hand in this case.

Chapter Outcomes

1. Relate the historical context in which unions developed.
2. Outline the congressional-judicial tug-of-war in union history.
3. List the basic aims of labor unions.
4. Identify the major provision of the Norris-LaGuardia Act.
5. Indicate the primary tenets of the Wagner Act.
6. List the functions of the Taft-Hartley Act.
7. Explain the provisions of the Landrum-Griffin Act.

8. Describe the jurisdiction of the National Labor Relations Board.
9. Identify the possible results of a complaint filed with the NLRB.
10. Distinguish between the public sector's right to strike in the states and at the federal level.

35-1 Labor Law and the Complex Adaptive System

A **labor union** is an organization that acts on behalf of all employees in negotiations with the employer regarding the terms of their employment. It is a lawful assembly which is protected by the first Amendment to the United States Constitution and by federal and state statutes. Americans have always had a love-hate affair with unions. On the one hand, they recognize that the marketplace should be allowed to fluctuate without undue interference from the government. On the other hand, they also acknowledge that businesses, when left unregulated, will often take advantage of that freedom and exploit the labor market. Americans also recognize that people ought to have the right to enter and leave the job market at will. On the other hand, they also recognize that employers hold a great deal of power in the labor market, and are, therefore, grateful when unions create a more level playing field. This seesaw-like relationship is evident in the historical development of the union movement in the United States.

A Complex Adaptive Tug-of-War

The history of union development in the United States affords us one of the most unique examples of how the law operates as a complex adaptive system. In this case, two powerful agents in the legal system, the legislature and the courts, were at odds for a long period of time, and thus played off one another in a lengthy and complicated tug-of-war. While this legal tug-of-war really had no definitive beginning, for the sake of convenience, we can identify the passage of the Sherman Antitrust Act in 1890 as a logical starting point. This statute was designed to break up the great anticompetitive trusts of the nineteenth century. However, the act was also used by big business with the support of the courts to outlaw union activities in a way that had been neither anticipated nor sanctioned by Congress. One of the primary legal tools that the courts used against strikes was the injunction. Big business argued that net effect of a strike was to hurt a company's ability to compete with rival companies. As such, it was an illegal restraint of trade under the Sherman Act. The courts agreed and willingly issued injunctions even when a union simply threatened to strike against a company as a bargaining tactic.

Congress reacted to this example of judicial activism by passing the Clayton Act in 1914. One of the central objectives of the Clayton Act was to hamper the federal courts' ability to issue injunctions to stop union activities. The federal judicial system, however, effectively destroyed the Clayton Act when the Supreme Court created two criteria that allowed the courts to freely issue injunctions to stop labor activities. The first test was the objectives test. Under this test, a court could issue an injunction if it determined that the goal or the objective of a strike was unlawful. Under the second test, the means test, the courts could stop a strike if it was conducted in an unlawful manner. The two tests were easily manipulated by big business so that the courts routinely issued injunctions in ways that had not been foreseen nor intended by Congress. Not to be outdone, Congress reacted to this subterfuge by passing the Norris-LaGuardia Act in 1932. The net effect of the Norris-LaGuardia Act was to completely prohibit the federal courts from issuing injunctions

For a more detailed account of the events outlined in The Opening Case see: Belluck, Pam. "Turbulence Shakes Boston as the Convention Nears." *The New York Times,* July 9, 2004, p. A-14.

John L. Lewis (left), founder of the Congress of Industrial Workers (CIO), and Samuel Gompers (right), founder of the American Federation of Labor (AFL) combined to form the AFL-CIO in 1955. Labor Unions continue to shape the way companies operate.

Background Information Even though union workers still earn more money, have better job security, and receive better benefits than nonunion workers (except in the managerial and professional sectors) union membership has declined steadily in most industrialized nations since 1985. The greatest drop occurred in Central and Eastern Europe which lost 7.8 million members over a ten year period. Nations that saw a rise in membership were Chile, the Philippines, South Africa, South Korea, and Spain.

State Variations In addition to federal agencies, many states have their own state agencies addressing labor issues.

against union-organized strikes. The law also forbids the courts to use injunctions to stop picketing and boycotts organized by unions.

The Objectives of Labor Organization

The Norris-LaGuardia Act was just one step down a long road of labor law development. Later labor laws both promoted the aims of labor unions and helped prevent unions from becoming too powerful. Many different types of unions have developed over the years since the advent of the Norris-LaGuardia Act. Whatever their form, however, labor unions do have several objectives in common. These objectives include (1) to create a seniority system to protect workers' jobs from arbitrary layoffs and replacement with cheaper wage earners; (2) to upgrade worker status through wage and fringe benefit increases; and (3) to sponsor laws that improve social, economic, and political conditions for workers.

Quick Quiz 35-1 True or False?

1. A labor union is an organization that acts on behalf of all employees in negotiations with the employer regarding the terms of their employment.

2. Labor union activity is not protected by the First Amendment.

3. One of the first successful union organizing efforts took place in 1886 when Samuel Gompers organized the Congress of Industrial Workers.

35-2 Major Federal Labor Legislation

After the Norris-LaGuardia Act was passed by Congress in 1932, several tough labor laws were enacted. The three most important legislative enactments are the National Labor Relations Act of 1935 (generally referred to as the Wagner Act); the Labor-Management Relations Act of 1947 (popularly referred to as the Taft-Hartley Act); and the Labor Management Reporting and Disclosure Act of 1958 (often simply called the Landrum-Griffin Act). The first of these was designed to support labor's attempt to organize. The last two were designed to curb some unanticipated problems that accompanied the growth of unions in the United States. (See Table 35-1.)

The Wagner Act

The passage of the National Labor Relations Act in 1935 (commonly known as the Wagner Act) opened the door for the rapid growth of the union movement. It is probably the most significant labor relations statute in that it expressly set forth the unfair labor practices prohibited for both employers and unions.

The Wagner Act gives workers the right to organize by allowing them to form, join, or aid labor unions. It also establishes procedures for representative elections and for collective bargaining. After a union has been chosen to represent the employees of a business, only that union can bargain with management. After the union has been set up at a business, individual workers cannot on their own initiative negotiate with management. The union has the exclusive right to bargain with the management of the business. This is true even if the employees do not agree with how the union is handling a matter. The Wagner Act is also known for the creation of the National Labor Relations Board (NLRB), which hears and

Table 35-1 Federal Laws Governing Labor-Management Relations

Year	Law	Major Provisions
1914	Clayton Act	Exempted union activity from the antitrust laws
1926	Railway Labor Act	Provided for supervision of collective bargaining for railroads and airlines Established the National Mediation Board to conduct union elections and mediate employer-union disputes
1932	Norris-LaGuardia Act	Outlawed yellow-dog contracts Limited the power of federal courts to issue injunctions to halt labor disputes Guaranteed employees the right to organize into unions and to engage in collective bargaining
1935	Wagner Act	Created the National Labor Relations Board (NLRB) Authorized NLRB to conduct representative elections and to determine the bargaining unit Outlawed certain conduct by employers as unfair labor practices Authorized NLRB to hold hearings on unfair labor practice petitions
1947	Taft-Hartley Act	Outlawed certain practices by unions as unfair labor practices Allowed states to legislate right-to-work laws Provided an 80-day cooling-off period in strikes that endangered national health or safety Created a mediation and conciliation service to assist in the settlement of labor disputes
1959	Landrum-Griffin Act	Established a bill of rights for union members Required unions to adopt constitutions and bylaws Required unions to submit annual reports detailing assets, liabilities, payments, and loans Added further provisions to the list of unfair labor practices

rules on charges that unfair labor practices have been committed by employers or by unions.

Various activities are prohibited by the Wagner Act as **unfair labor practices,** that is, improper employment practices by either an employer or union. These activities include the following:

- interference with employees' right to organize
- domination or interference with the formation or administration of any union
- discrimination to encourage or discourage union membership
- discharge for charges filed or testimony given
- refusal to bargain collectively

Interference with Employees' Right to Organize

An employer cannot interfere with employees when they are forming a union, selecting their representatives, voting, striking, picketing, or engaging in any other protected and legal acts. For example, an employer cannot threaten to fire or to discipline a worker for union activity or to reward workers who do not participate in union activities. Threats to eliminate certain benefits or privileges, to close down the business, or to discharge workers for union activity are prohibited.

Further Reading *U.S. Labor Relations Law: Historical Developments* by Benjamin J. Taylor and Fred Witney (Englewood Cliffs: Prentice Hall, 1992) offers a look at the progress made by unions from the U.S. government's suppression to its support.

Talking Points

No two intellectuals appear to be further apart than Adam Smith, the spiritual founder of capitalism, and Karl Marx, the principal architect of communism. Yet, if we read the following two excerpts from their most influential treatises, the two of them appear to be in agreement on at least one point, the propensity of workers to unite in a common cause and to eventually become violent as a result.

"Such combinations, however, are frequently resisted by a contrary defensive combination of the workmen; who sometimes too, without provocation of this kind, combine of their own accord to raise the price of their labour. Their usual pretences are, sometimes the high price of provisions; sometimes the great profit which their masters make by their work. But whether their combinations be offensive or defensive, they are always abundantly heard of. In order to bring the point to a speedy decision, they have always recourse to the loudest clamour, and sometimes to the most shocking violence and outrage."—Adam Smith, *The Wealth of Nations,* p. 71.

"The unceasing improvement of machinery, ever more rapidly developing, makes their livelihood more and more precarious. The collisions between individual workmen and individual bourgeois take more and more the character of collisions between two classes. Thereupon the workers begin to form combinations (trade unions) against the bourgeois; they join together in order to keep up the rate of wages; they form permanent associations in order to provision beforehand for these occasional revolts. Here and there the contest breaks out into riots."—Karl Marx and Frederick Engels, *The Communist Manifesto,* p. 21.

Looking back from a historical perspective, were Marx and Smith correct in their predictions that unionization leads to violence? Is such violence ever justifiable from a moral perspective? If these two philosophers are convinced that unionization leads to violence, at what point do you suppose they part company? Explain.

Example 35-1

In his ten years as a chef at the Imperial National Hotel in Houston, James Kirby might have been fired several times for violating work rules. He frequently refused to follow orders, disobeying direct instructions from his supervisor. When a union began organizing the kitchen service and housekeeping staff, Kirby strongly supported the effort. During the organizing campaign, Kirby apparently acted in an insubordinate manner and was discharged. At a subsequent NLRB hearing, his discharge was found to be tainted. On appeal, the court reasoned that, although Kirby was far from the valued and trusted employee the union claimed he was, the hotel had tolerated his insubordination for ten years. The court held that Kirby's discharge was more the result of his union activities than his work performance and reinstated him with back pay.

Domination or Interference with the Formation or Administration of Any Union An employer cannot form a company-run union for its employees. The purpose of this prohibition is to bar company-owned unions from bowing to the wishes of management. It is also an unfair practice to aid one union over another, place employer spies at union meetings, reward some union officials, or agree with a union that a closed shop will be maintained. A **closed shop** is a work site in which the employer, by agreement, hires only union members in good standing. It is usually lawful, however, to have a provision allowing a union shop in the employment contract. A **union shop** is a place of employment where nonunion workers may be employed for a trial period of not more than thirty days, after which the nonunion workers must join the union or be discharged.

Discrimination to Encourage or Discourage Union Membership

Intentional discrimination by the employer toward an employee to encourage or discourage union membership is an unfair labor practice. Such discrimination may involve assigning an employee to less desirable work or denying an employee the opportunity to participate in overtime work. Also viewed as discriminatory is **constructive discharge;** which occurs when an employee is demoted to a job with lesser pay or authority or poorer working conditions than a previously held job or when the employee is subjected to supervisory harassment. To avoid employee complaints of intentional discrimination, employers must rely on meaningful business reasons when bestowing or denying employment opportunities.

Example 35-2

Teresa Remington was chosen by the union members to serve as their representative in collective bargaining meetings with the Harrisburg Construction Company. After her selection, Remington was harassed by the general manager of her department for trivial matters concerning scheduled lunch breaks and the cleanliness of her locker in the break room. Remington has the right to file a complaint with the NLRB charging constructive discharge due to her union activities.

Discharge for Charges Filed or Testimony Given   It is unlawful for employers to discharge or otherwise discriminate against employees because they file charges or give testimony under the Wagner Act. The courts interpret discrimination under this provision to include discharge, layoff, failure to rehire or recall, and transfer of covered employees.

Refusal to Bargain Collectively   An employer must negotiate with employee representatives over wages, hours, the effects of business changes on employees, grievance procedures, health benefits, seniority systems, dues checkoffs, and vacations.

Issues must be discussed willingly, free of delaying tactics, coercion, or harassment by both sides. The employer has no duty to agree to any union demands, but must meet with employee representatives at reasonable times and places to bargain in good faith. Neither party can bargain about a closed shop contract, politics, religious issues, management functions, or foreign affairs.

The NLRB has no jurisdiction over religious schools, both on labor relations grounds and by virtue of the religion clauses of the First Amendment of the U.S. Constitution. The U.S. Supreme Court has ruled that the requirements of collective bargaining would represent an encroachment upon the freedom of church authorities to shape and direct teaching in accordance with the requirements of their religion.

The Taft-Hartley Act

The Labor-Movement Relations Act of 1947, popularly named the Taft-Hartley Act, established a means to protect employers in collective bargaining and labor organization matters. A detailed list of unfair labor activities that unions as well as employers were forbidden to practice was added to those of the Wagner Act.

Getting Students Involved Ask small groups of students to research labor-management relations in a particular industry and present their information to the class in a panel discussion. Encourage students to look at the history of industries such as mining, transportation, and sports.

Cross-Cultural Notes The International Labor Office (ILO) was established under Part XIII of the Treaty of Versailles. Delegates to the ILO represent various participating nations' employers and workers. American delegates were not formally present at ILO conferences until 1934.

The Opening Case Revisited
"Workers of Boston Unite!"

In The Opening Case at the beginning of this chapter we learned that members of the police union in Boston were joined by firefighters, transit workers, janitors, and other public workers, as well as telephone workers and utilities employees to picket FleetCenter where the Democratic National Convention was scheduled to be held. The picketers were angry at the lack of progress in the collective bargaining process between the city and the police union. The police union had in fact, accused the city of bargaining in bad faith. Bad faith bargaining is a clear violation of the Wagner Act. However, neither the employer nor the union can be accused of bad faith simply for disagreeing with the demands made by the other side. In this case, the city argued that it had offered the union an 11.9 percent pay raise over four years. The police union pointed to the city's willingness to spend enormous sums of money on paving the streets and renovating the center for a one-time event, and asked for a 15 percent raise over four years. The city refused and the bargaining process broke down. Despite this disagreement, it is not likely that an arbitrator would consider either side as acting in bad faith. This difference of opinion simply represents a disagreement on basic terms in the bargaining process.

State Variations Many states have right-to-work laws. Utah has a provision in its state code which says, "the right of persons to work, whether in private employment or for the state, its counties, cities, school districts, or other political subdivisions, shall not be denied or abridged on account of membership or nonmembership in any labor union, labor organization, or any other type of association; and further, that the right to live includes the right to work. The exercise of the right to work must be protected and maintained free from undue restraints and coercion."

Getting Students Involved Have students research the history of anti-union sentiment, reasons for the current decline in union membership, and the effects of automation and globalization on the future of unions. Ask them to write brief reports of their findings.

State Right-to-Work Laws
State laws that prohibit labor-management agreements requiring union membership as a condition of getting or keeping a job are **right-to-work laws.** These laws, in effect, outlaw both the closed shop and the union shop.

Ordinarily, state labor relations laws have not applied to unions and businesses that are involved in interstate commerce and that are governed by federal labor laws. The Taft-Hartley Act, however, has created special rules with regard to state right-to-work laws. It provides that union shop contracts are legal only in states that do not forbid them. As a result, state right-to-work laws, where they exist, are applicable to most unions and businesses. All employees in the **bargaining unit,** i.e., a unit formed for the purpose of collective bargaining, are benefited by the collective bargaining agreement negotiated by the union, even though they have not paid union dues. However, nonunion employees lose all right to vote on union officers or on collective bargaining agreements.

Free Speech Provision
The Taft-Hartley Act includes a free speech provision that allows employers to comment freely on union-organizing activities. The provision states that employers do not commit an unfair labor practice by speaking to employees about unions unless they threaten reprisal or promise some benefit to employees. For instance, an employer might properly inform its employees that they should not vote for a union, but a threat to fire anyone for favoring a union shop would be an unfair labor practice.

Employee Coercion Provision
It is also an unfair labor practice for a labor union to try to coerce employees to join the union, to block the employment of individuals who refuse to support a union, or to encourage an employee to withdraw an unfair labor practice charge.

A union can set rules for its internal operations and can punish any member who refuses to follow them, but it cannot use force, violence, or intimidation against an employee. A union is also not permitted to discipline one of its members without good cause. The union has a duty to represent all of its members on an equal basis.

> ### Example 35-3
>
> Gregory Rogers was a member of the union representing the Raymond Fields Spring Water Company. He learned that another union member was stealing crates of bottled water from the company warehouse and selling them at a reduced rate to concessionaires. He warned the person that the theft would be reported. When informed of the warning, the union representative revoked Rogers's membership and asked the company human resources director to have him discharged. Rogers filed a complaint with the NLRB, charging the union with illegal restraint in the exercise of his legal rights. The NLRB ruled that Rogers's union membership could not be withdrawn and ordered the union to restore it.

Secondary Boycott It is also prohibited for a union to engage in a **secondary boycott.** This is a conspiracy in which a union places pressure on a neutral customer or supplier with whom the union has no dispute in order to cause the neutral entity to cease doing business with the employer with whom the union has a dispute. Under the Taft-Hartley Act provision, it is an unfair labor practice for a union (1) to strike against an employer because another employer uses nonunion employees, (2) to strike against a general contractor to force the contractor to stop dealing with a subcontractor, (3) to ask employees of another company not to load trucks carrying the products of a company the union is striking, or (4) to refuse to work on products made by nonunion employees.

> ### Example 35-4
>
> The Benning Oil Company sold fuel oil to the Monarchy Empire Hotel chain. The oil is shipped on tankers owned by the Metroliner Transport Corporation, whose employees are nonunion. The union representing Benning instructed its members to refuse to ship the fuel oil to the docks where the Metroliner tankers were docked in order to force Benning to stop using a nonunion shipper. This form of secondary boycott is an unfair labor practice because it involved an innocent employer in a union tactic intended to harm another employer.

National Emergency Strikes The Taft-Hartley Act gives the President of the United States special powers to deal with actual or threatened strikes that affect interstate commerce or that endanger the nation's health and safety. On the basis of a board of inquiry's findings, the President can order the attorney general to petition a federal district court to issue an injunction stopping the strike for sixty days. The board of inquiry may then require the union members to vote on the most recent offer within an additional fifteen-day period and to send the results to the attorney general within five days after balloting. When the injunction ends after this eighty-day period, the employees may strike. However, the president can then make legislative recommendations to Congress that would resolve the dispute.

Other Prohibited Union Practices Under other provisions of the Taft-Hartley Act, unions cannot refuse to bargain collectively with an employer and must give notice to the employer of an intention to strike prior to the termination date of a collective bargaining contract.

It is also an unfair labor practice for a labor union to require an employer to keep unneeded employees, to pay employees for not working, or to assign more employees to a given job than are needed (i.e., **featherbedding**).

Terms The word *boycott* was coined during the Irish potato famine of the mid-1800s. Because of crop failures, thousands of farming tenants were unable to pay their rents. Most landlords accepted the partial payments that the tenants offered, but Lord Erne ordered his agent, Captain Boycott, to collect the full amount from his tenants. Boycott's harsh treatment of the farmers induced them to organize and refuse to gather crops or talk with him—in essence, to boycott him.

Related Cases In June of 1992, for the twelfth time since 1963, Congress became involved in the resolution of a labor dispute in the railroad industry. The 1992 dispute involved a two-day strike by railroad mechanics. The strike had a crippling effect on passenger service and nearly every business that depended on railroads for supplies and transportation or goods. Despite opposition from railroad unions, Congress approved an emergency bill signed by the President that imposed a cooling-off period and binding arbitration for the railroads and the railroad unions.

Background Informa-tion Historically, Presidents have intervened in labor disputes for three purposes: to suppress physical vio-lence, to compel continua-tion of production, and to mediate a settlement. A presidential injunction to quell violence was enforced in 1834 when Andrew Jack-son called in federal troops to break up fighting be-tween rival gangs of labor-ers over jurisdiction rights on the Chesapeake & Ohio Canal. Abraham Lincoln was the first President to enforce production when he ordered soldiers to load and unload government ships at New York pier during an 1863 strike of longshore-men. In 1902, Theodore Roosevelt became the first President to use mediation to settle a dispute when he summoned both parties in a mining strike to the White House and induced them to accept binding arbitra-tion by a presidential board.

Another provision of the law prohibits a union from requiring employees who join a union to pay excessively high dues, fees, and related expenses. To determine what is excessive, the courts consider the amounts other unions charge and the employee's wages.

The Landrum-Griffin Act

The Labor Management Reporting and Disclosure Act of 1959, known as the Landrum-Griffin Act, is a tough anticorruption law. It is designed to clean up the corruption and vio-lence that had been uncovered in the internal affairs of unions. The law requires all unions to adopt constitutions and bylaws and to register them with the secretary of labor. In addi-tion, unions are required to submit annual reports detailing assets, liabilities, receipts and sources, payments to union members exceeding $10,000, loans to union members and businesses, and other monies paid out.

Bill of Rights Provision
An important part of the Landrum-Griffin Act is the bill of rights provision for union members. This provision assures all union members of the opportunity to participate in the internal affairs of their union. They are guaranteed the right to vote in union elections, to speak at union meetings, and to receive union financial reports.

Hot-Cargo Agreement
The Landrum-Griffin Act amended the Taft-Hartley Act, making it an unlawful labor practice to become involved in a **hot-cargo contract.** This is an agreement in which an employer voluntarily agrees with a union not to handle, use, or deal in nonunion-produced goods of another employer.

Business Law in the News
Union Leader Abused Power, U.S. Board Says

A federal oversight board has accused the New York area's top Teamsters union official of extensive mis-deeds, among them using business agents to install a roof, deck and skylights at his second home and to take his daughters shopping and to a guru.

The charges, filed last week by the oversight board's chief investigator, could lead to the expulsion of the official, Anthony Rumore, president of Teamsters Joint Council 16, the umbrella group for more than 100,000 area Teamsters.

The chief investigator, Charles M. Carberry, said that Mr. Rumore had improperly used two union busi-ness agents to pick up his two daughters at their Manhattan high schools in the 90's and, several years later, to take one shopping for flowers, rings, dresses and a photographer for her wedding. The board also accused him of using officials to move his belongings to a new home, to take his family's clothes to the cleaners and to take his daughters to yoga classes.

In addition to his post as head of the Joint Coun-cil 16 of the International Brotherhood of Teamsters, Mr. Rumore is president of Local 812, a beverage dri-vers' local with 3,855 members based in Scarsdale, in Westchester County. His salary is $198,000 a year. His wife, Elizabeth, received a salary of $202,500 as director of Local 812's retirement fund; she resigned last January. Her main responsibility had been overseeing the mailing of pension checks.

The oversight board, known as the Independent Review Board, is part of an elaborate federal system that monitors the Teamsters. The charges stated that Mr. Rumore had "breached his fiduciary duties and embezzled Local 812 assets through engaging in a pattern of directing local employees to perform personal services for him and his family."

Mr. Rumore did not return several telephone calls made to Local 812 in Scarsdale and to Joint Council 16 in Manhattan. His lawyer, Thomas

Puccio, who was at a trial yesterday, did not return calls.

Mr. Rumore had told the oversight board's investigators that the personal services that business agents and the union's clerical staff performed for him were voluntary favors. He said that since their hours were flexible, any personal services performed on business days were offset by their union work at other times.

The board's investigator also accused Mr. Rumore of improperly canceling 17 arbitration cases on behalf of fired or suspended workers because he felt that Local 812's members had not contributed enough to his legal defense fund.

Mr. Rumore ran up $88,000 in bills in a legal battle after the oversight board accused him, in late 2002, of improper behavior for inviting a Teamsters leader who had been ousted on corruption charges to speak at a union meeting in Miami Beach. As a result, Mr. Rumore was suspended for two months.

Mr. Rumore has headed the local since 1988, and one union official said his subordinates began providing evidence against him after he squeezed them to contribute to his legal fund.

The 91 pages of charges filed last week describe a union local in which Mr. Rumore reigned supreme. He had union subordinates do everything from setting up a Christmas tree in his Manhattan apartment to driving him and his family to a wedding in Baltimore, according to the charges.

The charges have been sent to the executive board of the International Brotherhood of Teamsters, which represents 1.4 million workers. Its board can punish Mr. Rumore itself or send the case back to the oversight board so it can conduct a hearing.

The oversight board also accused Mr. Rumore of misappropriating union resources by ordering business agents to drive his father, Louis, to medical appointments. That was improper, the board said, because union officials were barred from having any contact with the father.

In 1990, Louis Rumore, who had been Local 812's vice president, resigned from the union after the oversight board accused him of being a member of the Gambino crime family. He was barred from having any contact with Teamsters, except for members of his own family.

In August 2003, Anthony Rumore ordered the union's business agent to concentrate on collecting money for his legal defense fund and to ignore union business, according to the charges. He also shunned the protests of the local's business agents when he canceled the 17 arbitration cases.

"When Local 812 business agents protested the suspension of the arbitrations because some of the members might lose their jobs or continue on suspension," Mr. Carberry wrote, "Mr. Rumore responded with an obscenity."

Questions for Analysis

1. What offenses was the union leader accused of in this article? Explain.

2. What penalties might be levied against the union leader in this case? Explain.

3. What union is involved in this story? Explain.

4. What federal law might cover the type of union activity questioned by federal investigators in this article? Explain.

5. Is it a good idea to have a federal oversight board, like the one outlined in this story, keep an eye on union leadership? Explain. Are such oversight boards ethical? Explain.

Source: Steven Greenhouse. "Union Leader Abused Power, U.S. Board Says," *The New York Times,* May 11, 2004, p. A-23. Copyright © 2004 by The New York Times Co. Reprinted with permission.

Quick Quiz 35-2 True or False?

1. The Wagner Act allowed unions to organize but did not identify any unfair labor practices.

2. Right-to-work laws were outlawed by the Landrum-Griffin Act.

3. The Taft-Hartley Act outlawed secondary boycotts.

35-3 The Collective Bargaining Process

The Taft-Hartley Act established a system for helping labor and management settle their disputes without causing a major disruption in the economy or endangering the public health and safety. Central to this collective bargaining process is the NLRB and the procedures it follows in settling labor-management disputes.

The National Labor Relations Board

The NLRB is a governmental commission that has the exclusive jurisdiction to enforce the Taft-Hartley Act and related laws. It has the power to act when cases are brought before it, but only in cases in which the employer's operation or the labor dispute affects commerce.

Like most government regulatory agencies, the NLRB has investigative, regulatory, administrative, enforcement, and judgmental powers. It can make its own rules of procedure, conduct investigations into unfair labor practice charges, compel individuals to appear with papers relevant to the controversy, hold hearings, and issue orders. Appeal from the five-member board goes first to the appropriate U.S. Court of Appeals and then to the U.S. Supreme Court.

Unfair Labor Practice Procedure

A person, union, or employer can file notice with the NLRB of an alleged unfair labor practice within six months after it occurs. If the charge has merit, a complaint is issued notifying the offending party that a hearing is to be held concerning the charges. Efforts are made through arbitration to resolve the dispute before the hearing date. **Arbitration** involves the submission of the dispute to selected persons and the substitution of their decision for the judgment of the NLRB. If arbitration efforts fail, the hearing is held.

In the event that the complaint is found to be valid, a cease and desist order may be issued, restoring the parties to the state that existed before the unfair practice began. For example, wrongfully discharged employees may be reinstated with or without back pay. Evidence at the hearing that does not support the complaint is dismissed. Either party to the hearing may subsequently appeal the NLRB action to the appropriate U.S. Court of Appeals and then to the Supreme Court.

Mediation   The Taft-Hartley Act encourages labor and management to agree freely on the settlement of disputes. To further this effort to preserve labor peace and to promote prompt settlements, Congress has formed the Federal Mediation and Conciliation Service. This body can act by itself or upon the request of either side to a labor dispute. Its mediation role is to offer nonbinding suggestions for settling the dispute, require the parties to negotiate, and force a vote by employees on an employer's offers.

The Right to Strike in the Public Sector

In the public sector, where the general welfare, safety, health, and morals of the public are involved, the right to strike is restricted. Consequently, strikes by police, firefighters, refuse collectors, air traffic controllers, postal workers, and other public employees who perform vital services are generally illegal, unless specifically authorized by statute.

The U.S. Code states that "an individual may not accept or hold a position in the government of the United States or the government of the District of Columbia if he participates in a strike or asserts the right to strike against the government." The U.S. Supreme

---

Teaching Tips The U.S. Supreme Court has determined that federal courts may resolve labor grievances unless specifically barred by a collective bargaining agreement (CBA). To avoid the intrusion of federal courts in employment disputes, employers can incorporate final, binding, and mandatory arbitration provisions in CBAs to allow unions and individual employees to initiate arbitration.

Background Information A planned merger of the United Auto Workers, the Steelworkers, and the Machinists in the United States may create a mega-union with almost 2 million members. The strike fund of this super-union would exceed $2 billion.

I shall always be a friend of labor, but in any conflict that arises between one particular group, no matter who they may be, and the country as a whole, the welfare of the country comes first.

—Harry S. Truman
   (1884–1972), President
   of the United States,
   1945–1953

In 2003, Chicago was nearly suffocated with trash when garbage haulers went on strike.

Teaching Tips Have students write short research papers on the air traffic controllers' strike during the Reagan Administration. Students should include the reason for the strike and its consequences.

Further Reading For an in-depth look at employment law, see *Employment Law: Cases and Materials* by Mark A. Rothstein and Lance Liebman (New York: Foundation Press, 1998).

Court has affirmed lower court rulings that there is no constitutional right to strike against the federal government. Thus, strikes by federal employees are substantially more than merely unfair labor practices; they are crimes.

Example 35-5

The air traffic controllers, employees of the Federal Aviation Administration, went on strike. The controller's union, the Professional Air Traffic Controllers Organization, demanded that the controllers be removed from the civil service designation that prohibited them from striking. They argued that prohibition of the right to strike was a violation of a fundamental civil liberty. A federal district court ruled that government employees do not have the right to strike because Congress had not given them such a right. The controllers persisted in their strike. As a result, all striking controllers were fired and the union was fined $100,000 an hour for the duration of the strike. The union was subsequently decertified, removing its rights to bargain on behalf of the controllers.

Did You Know?

Union membership in Great Britain surpassed two million at the beginning of the twentieth century. This made the British labor movement the most influential European union movement up to that time in history.

A Question of Ethics

The air traffic controllers in Example 35-6 simply wanted rights that are guaranteed to many similarly situated workers. They argued that prohibition of the right to strike was a violation of a fundamental civil liberty. Nevertheless, the court held that Congress had the authority to deny them that right. Consequently, the firing of the striking air traffic controllers was legal. Now consider whether the firing was ethical. Explain your response.

Quick Quiz 35-3 True or False?

1. There is no appeal permitted after a decision has been rendered by the National Labor Relations Board.

2. If a complaint is found valid under the NLRB procedures, a cease and desist order may be issued restoring the parties to the state that existed before the unfair labor practice began.

3. The United States Supreme Court has repeatedly affirmed that federal employees have a constitutionally protected right to strike.

Summary

35-1   The first federal statute relating to labor was the Clayton Act which attempted to prohibit federal courts from forbidding activities such as picketing and strikes. The Norris-LaGuardia Act specified acts, such as striking, picketing, and boycotting that were not subject to federal injunctions.

35-2   The Wagner Act opened the door for the growth of labor unions. It set forth specific labor practices that were prohibited for employers and unions, established procedures for representative elections and collective bargaining, and created the NLRB. The Taft-Hartley Act outlaws specific conduct by unions as unfair labor practices and provides for an eighty-day cooling off period in strikes that endanger national health or safety. The act also provides a mediation and conciliation service to assist in the settlement of labor disputes. The Landrum-Griffin Act provides a bill of rights for union members, requires unions to report to the secretary of labor, and has added to the list of unfair labor practices.

35-3   The NLRB has exclusive jurisdiction to enforce labor-management relations laws with investigative,

regulatory, administrative, enforcement, and judgment powers. Any person, union, or employer can file notice with the NLRB of an alleged unfair labor practice. If the complaint has merit, a hearing is held before the NLRB. If the complaint is found to be valid, an order may be issued restoring the parties to the state existing prior to the unfair practice. Appeals to NLRB action can be taken to the appropriate U.S. Circuit Court of Appeals and then to the U.S. Supreme Court. The Federal Mediation and Conciliation Service was formed to encourage labor and management to agree freely on the settlement of their disputes. Its mediation role is to offer nonbinding suggestions for settling the dispute, require the parties to negotiate, and force a vote by employees on employers' offers.

In the public sector, the right to strike is restricted. The U.S. Code states that "an individual may not accept or hold a position in the government of the United States or the government of the District of Columbia if he participates in a strike or asserts the right to strike against the government."

Key Terms

arbitration, 672
bargaining unit, 668
closed shop, 666
constructive discharge, 667

featherbedding, 669
hot-cargo contract, 670
labor union, 663
right-to-work laws, 668

secondary boycott, 669
unfair labor practices, 665
union shop, 666

Questions for Review and Discussion

1. In what historical context did unions develop?
2. What was the nature of the congressional-judicial tug-of-war in union history?
3. What are the basic aims of labor unions?
4. What was the major provision of the Norris-LaGuardia Act?
5. What are the primary tenets of the Wagner Act?
6. What are the functions of the Taft-Hartley Act?
7. What are the provisions of the Landrum-Griffin Act?
8. What is the extent of the jurisdiction of the National Labor Relations Board?
9. What possible results can come from filing a complaint with the NLRB?
10. What is the difference between the public sector's right to strike in the states and at the federal level?

Investigating the Internet

Access LaborNet on the Web and write a report on one of the many features found there. These features include news about labor unions, action alerts for labor union members, upcoming labor events, publications, and LaborNet conferences.

Cases for Analysis

1. The union representing employees of the Consolidated Manufacturing Company elected Franco and Allanson to act on their behalf at a collective bargaining session with management. At the session, Franco and Allanson demanded that the new collective bargaining agreement include terms that would require management to hire only union members in good standing. Management disagreed with this proposal. Instead, management offered a term in the agreement that would allow the company to hire nonunion workers for a trial period lasting no more than thirty days. After the thirty-day trial period the nonunion worker would have to join a union. Which of these terms in the proposed collective bargaining agreement would be allowed under federal labor law? Explain. Management also proposed that the employee union be disbanded and replaced by a company-run union. Management argued that the new company-run union would not only be more efficient, but also more economical than the current union. Would this proposal be allowed under federal labor law?

2. An employee was discharged for violation of the company's no-solicitation rule in its factory and offices. The employee had persisted in soliciting union membership on company property during lunch periods. The company argued that its no-solicitation rule would have been enforced not merely against union solicitation but against any solicitation. How would you decide? Why? *Republic Aviation Corp. v. NLRB,* 324 U.S. 793 (U.S. Sup. Ct.).

3. Having advised Exchange Parts Co., that it was conducting an organizational campaign, the union petitioned the NLRB for an election to determine whether it would be certified as the bargaining agent of the company's employees. During the organizational campaign, while the granted certification election was pending, the company announced five additional benefits for the employees, two of which were announced only a few days before the election. In the election, the employees voted against being represented by a union. The union then filed a complaint with the NLRB charging the company with an unfair labor practice because it granted benefits while the campaign was taking place and the election was pending. The union argued that the company's actions interfered with the freedom of choice of the employees to determine whether they wished to be represented by the union. For whom would you decide? Why? *NLRB v. Exchange Parts Co.,* 375 U.S. 405 (U.S. Sup. Ct.).

4. Darlington Manufacturing Co., operated one textile mill that was controlled by Deering Milliken, which operated twenty-seven other such mills. The union began an organizational campaign, which Darlington resisted. The employees filed charges of unfair labor practices with the NLRB. The board found in a subsequent hearing that the different mills controlled by Deering Milliken represented an integrated enterprise, and that the closing of the Darlington mill was due to the antiunion hostility of Deering Milliken. The NLRB ordered Deering Milliken to provide back pay to the workers until they obtained similar work. The court of appeals denied enforcement of the NLRB order, holding that an independent employer has an absolute right to close a business regardless of notice. On review by the U.S. Supreme Court, how should the Court rule on the question of whether an employer has the absolute right to close part of a business, no matter what the reason? Why? *Textile Worker's Union v. Darlington Mfg. Co.,* 380 U.S. 263 (U.S. Sup. Ct.).

5. The NLRB conducted an election among employees of Savair Manufacturing Co., to determine whether the union would represent the employees. During the election, recognition slips were distributed. The employees were told by the union that if they signed the slips before the election they would not have to pay an initiation fee if the union won. At least thirty-five employees signed the slips before the election, which the union won by a vote of 22 to 20. The company refused to bargain with the union, contending that the union, by offering possible benefits to employees for signing the recognition slips, was guilty of an unfair labor practice. Did the practice of the union prevent a fair and free choice of a bargaining representative? Why or why not? *NLRB v. Savair Mfg. Co.,* 414 U.S. 270 (U.S. Sup. Ct.).

6. The Department Store Employees Union (union) was selected by the employees of the Emporium Capwell Company (company) as their exclusive bargaining unit. Charges of discrimination in the workplace were levied against the company through the union. The union followed the grievance procedure as established in the collective bargaining agreement. Some of the employees became dissatisfied with the union's handling of the case. Accordingly, they asked the union to begin to picket the company. Union officials advised these dissatisfied employees that, according to the collective bargaining agreement, the union was bound to follow the established grievance procedure. The employees refused to cooperate with the grievance procedure and demanded that company management deal with them directly to establish an overall antidiscrimination policy. Later the employees also picketed the store. Written notices were given to the picketing employees, telling them that they could be discharged if they repeated the conduct. The employees ignored the notices, and after picketing on the following weekend, were discharged. The employees filed a complaint with the National Labor Relations Board which found that it could not support the employees. The Board believed that such support would challenge the exclusive bargaining power of the union and thereby subvert the statutory intent of Congress. The appeals court hearing the case reversed the Board's findings stating its belief that discrimination cases had a special position and, thus, fell outside the guarantee to the union of exclusive bargaining power. The case was appealed to the United States Supreme Court. Should the Supreme Court uphold the union's exclusive right to engage in collective bargaining with the company? Explain. *Emporium Capwell, Co. v. Western Addition Community Organization,* 420 U.S. 50. (U.S. Sup. Ct.).

Quick Quiz Answers

35-1		35-2		35-3	
1. T		1. F		1. F	
2. F		2. F		2. T	
3. F		3. T		3. F	

Part 7 Case Study

Stephenson v. Litton Systems, Inc.

Court of Appeals for Montgomery County, Ohio 646 N.E.2d 259 (OH)

Summary

Carletta Stephenson, the plaintiff in this case, worked as an employee of Litton Systems, Inc. Over the period of a year, prior to the incident that eventually provoked this lawsuit, Stephenson had seen King, her supervisor, so inebriated after lunch that he could not perform his tasks properly. These incidents had occurred at least once a week. Stephenson also had evidence that King had, on at least one occasion previously, driven home from work under the influence of alcohol. On the day in question, Stephenson again had evidence that King had been drinking heavily at lunch and was, as a result, intoxicated. Fearing that he was about to drive under this condition, Stephenson called that state's hotline for the prevention of drunk driving. On the hotline, she reported her suspicion that King was about to drive in an inebriated condition. The conversation was, of course, tape recorded. In response to Stephenson's call, the police arrived at the restaurant where King had been drinking and questioned the waitress who said that King had not been drinking to excess and was not inebriated. After the officers left the restaurant, the waitress told King that the police had been asking questions about his condition at lunch. Under provisions of the state's Public Records Act, King later obtained a copy of the tape recording of Stephenson's call to the drunk driving hotline. Although Stephenson's identity was protected by law, King recognized her voice on the tape. When Stephenson denied making the call, King had several other employees identify her voice on the tape. King then discharged Stephenson. Stephenson brought this lawsuit alleging that her discharge was a wrongful violation of public policy. She argued that it would be against public policy to allow employers to terminate the employment of workers for attempting to follow the explicit policy of the state in trying to protect the public by keeping drunk drivers off of the road. King and Litton Systems., Inc., brought a summary judgment motion to dismiss the case. The defendants argued that the public policy tort exception to the prevailing doctine of employment-at-will applies only if a firing has violated a statute that specifically forbids the type of employment termination in question. The trial judge granted the motion for summary judgment, and the case was dismissed. Stephenson appealed the dismissal.

The Court's Opinion

Judge Fain

Stephenson's assignment of error is as follows:

   "There are genuine issues of material fact concerning whether or not the appellant was terminated in violation of Ohio public policy."

   The trial court held, based on *Tulloh v. Goodyear Atomic Corporation, supra,* and *Edelman v. Franklin Iron & Metal Corporation* (1993), 87 Ohio App.

3d 406, 622 N.E.2d 411, a decision of this court following *Tulloh,* that there can be no public policy exception to the employment-at-will doctrine without statutory authority.

1. *Tulloh* has been expressly overruled in *Painter v. Graley, supra,* a recent decision by the Ohio Supreme Court. In that case it was held that a public policy exception to the employment-at-will doctrine is not limited to instances in which it has been expressly authorized by statute, but may find support in legislation generally, as well as other sources, including common law. . . . In *Painter,* it was held that public policy exceptions to the employment-at-will doctrine must be clear, and should only sparingly be recognized by the courts. We understand and share the Supreme Court's concern that the conclave of judges should not be allowed to pull "public policy" out of thin air to make the law conform to their individual conceptions of what the law ought to be. A public policy ought to be objectively discernable [sic] from sources outside the judge's individual social or legal philosophy before being permitted to override the settled doctrine of employment-at-will.

    The public policy of this state in favor of keeping drunk drivers off of the streets appears to be both strong and clear. It is not a matter of a conclave of judges announcing to the world a "public policy" invented by them for the purpose of subjecting the citizens of this state to a rule of law that has little or no support outside the minds of the judges. Recent, sweeping enactments by the General Assembly designed to discourage drunk driving are an objective manifestation of the public policy of this state in favor of taking all reasonable steps to eliminate drunk driving.

    The police drunk driving hotline . . . has been well publicized. It is consistent with the reasonable efforts to get drunk drivers off the roads of our state, and manifests an intent to rely upon citizen informants to assist the police in detecting drunk driving.

2. We hold that the public policy in favor of removing drunk drivers from the roads of our state is sufficiently clear, and sufficiently compelling, to override the doctrine of employment-at-will when an employee is discharged because, having a reasonable basis for her suspicions, she has informed the police of the likelihood that her superior at work is going to be driving while intoxicated.

3. Given our holding, there are genuine issues of material fact in this case precluding summary judgment. Litton Systems has controverted many of the facts upon which Stephenson's claim is predicated, including her averment as to the reason why she was discharged. At oral argument, Litton Systems contended that Stephenson had insufficient basis for suspecting that King was under the influence, and that Stephenson had failed to rebut Litton System's averment that she was fired because of her dishonest refusal to acknowledge her voice as the police informant, rather than because she had informed on King.

    We conclude that whether Stephenson had a reasonable basis for her suspicions is, on this record, a jury question. We further conclude that the evidence in the record, including the fact that King obtained a copy of the tape recording of the anonymous informant's call to the police and the fact averred by Stephenson, that she was told that King's drinking habits were none of her concern, would permit a reasonable jury to infer that it was her phone call to the police, not her unwillingness to acknowledge that call, that resulted in her discharge.

    Stephenson's sole Assignment [sic] of error having been sustained, the judgment of the trial court is reversed, and this cause remanded for further proceedings consistent with this opinion.

Questions for Analysis

1. What is a summary judgment motion?
2. Explain the doctine of employment-at-will.
3. Explain the public policy tort exception to employment-at-will.
4. How has the court interpreted the exception to employment-at-will in this case?
5. Is King a servant of Litton Systems, or is he an independent contractor? Would the doctrine of *respondeat superior* apply here if King were to injure someone while driving under the influence of alcohol? Explain.

Business Organization and Regulation

Part Eight

Sole Proprietorships and Partnerships

The Opening Case

"Watt Happened to Boulton!"

Most of the cases in any law book will portray disputes in which one party is dissatisfied with or has been injured by another. It is rare that these cases have happy endings. Such is not the situation in the case of Matthew Boulton and James Watt who, in 1775, formed one of the most lasting and profitable partnerships in the history of Western capitalism. The partnership was successful because it did what partnerships are supposed to do. It traded on the different talents of each partner, thus maximizing their contribution to the partnership and doubling the effectiveness of the overall business. In this case, James Watt, the inventor of an efficient and low-cost steam engine, brought his scientific and engineering expertise to the enterprise, while his counterpart, Matthew Boulton brought his investment capital and his keen business sense to the venture. Watt probably would have eventually succeeded without Boulton and Boulton would have made a comfortable living without Watt. However, together they reached heights that neither would have reached separately. Watt's poor business sense, his empty bank account, and his tentativeness would have postponed the development of his invention indefinitely. Similarly, Boulton's factories would have continued producing goods using waterwheels and horsepower, but the leap to the use of steam as an alternative source of energy helped his fortunes rise to unlimited heights. When the partners did encounter misfortune, as they did in the 1790s when many other firms were deliberately infringing on their patent rights, they closed ranks and won several difficult court battles that vindicated their patent rights. When the partnership finally dissolved in 1800, they had already introduced their sons to the venture and had formed a second partnership involving their offspring and the enterprise continued well into the nineteenth century. As you read about the principles of partnership outlined in Chapter 36, ask yourself whether Boulton and Watt would have thrived as well as they did had they adopted one of the modern business associations that are available to entrepreneurs today.

Chapter Outcomes

1. List the most common forms of business associations.
2. Outline the advantages and disadvantages of a sole proprietorship.
3. Identify the two model acts that govern partnership law.
4. Describe the differences between the aggregate and the entity theories of partnership.

5. Explain the nature of a partnership agreement.

6. Explain when profit sharing does not create a partnership.

7. Explain what constitutes a person in partnership law.

8. Identify the different views of specific partnership property in partnership law.

9. Distinguish between dissociation and dissolution in partnership law.

10. Distinguish between a registered limited liability partnership and a limited partnership.

For a more detailed account of the Watt-Boulton partnership described in The Opening Case see: Gras, N.S.B., and Henrietta Larson. "Boulton and Watt, 1775–1800." In *Casebook in American Business History.* New York: Appleton-Century-Crofts, 1939, pp. 190–209.

36-1 Sole Proprietorships

There are several forms of doing business available to people who are about to enter the economic arena for the first time. Here are some of the most common forms:

- sole proprietorships

- general partnerships

- registered limited liability partnerships

- limited partnerships

- corporations

- limited liability companies

Formation of a Sole Proprietorship

The easiest business organization to form is a **sole proprietorship.** In most cases, business people can initiate a sole proprietorship by simply opening their doors for business. Depending upon the nature, location, and extent of the business, the sole proprietor may have to check on zoning restrictions, licensing laws, and filing requirements. For example, some states require a formal filing if a sole proprietor chooses to use a fictitious name.

Advantages and Disadvantages of a Sole Proprietorship

Perhaps the greatest advantage to a sole proprietorship is that the owner has complete control over the business. Another major advantage is that the owner may keep all of the profits made by the sole proprietorship. A third advantage is that a sole proprietorship is relatively simple to begin and to end.

A major disadvantage to this type of business is that the owner of a sole proprietorship is subject to unlimited liability. For example, the sole proprietor is responsible for all of the debts incurred in running the business. This liability may even extend to the owner's personal assets. Another disadvantage is that the sole proprietorship's existence depends entirely upon the sole proprietor. Finally, owners of sole proprietorships often find it difficult to raise a lot of cash quickly for expansion purposes.

State Variations In Nevada, as in many other states, any person doing business under an assumed or fictitious name which does not show the real name of each person who owns an interest in the business must file with the county clerk in each county in which the business is being conducted a certificate containing required information identifying the persons involved in the business.

Background Information One disadvantage of owning a sole proprietorship is that the sole proprietorship's income is taxed at the sole proprietor's personal income tax rate. Individuals who run very profitable businesses or who have large incomes from other sources must pay taxes at a higher tax rate.

Quick Quiz 36-1 True or False?

1. Businesspeople can form a sole proprietorship only by going through the attorney general's office in the state capital.

2. The greatest advantage of a sole proprietorship is that the owner has complete control over the operation of the business.

3. A major disadvantage of a sole proprietorship is unlimited liability.

36-2 General Partnership Characteristics

Often a sole proprietor will decide to extend his or her business venture by joining with other people to create a partnership. This is what occurred in the case at the opening of the chapter when James Watt and Matthew Boulder pooled their resources to create Watt and Boulder. The law of partnership has integrated principles associated with tort law, contract law, and agency law. However, because of its unique characteristics, it has also developed its own separate and distinct legal principles.

Revised Uniform Partnership Act

One of the most dependable sources of law affecting partnerships has been the National Conference of Commissioners on Uniform State Laws (NCCUSL) which developed the **Uniform Partnership Act (UPA)** in 1914. The UPA was so successful that it was put into practice by every state in the union but one. Only Louisiana, which is devoted to the Napoleonic Code, did not adopt the UPA. Nevertheless, the UPA has been the mainstay of partnership law, in relation to general partnerships, for over 90 years. It does, however, have its limitations and shortcomings. For instance, it never made it clear whether a partnership should be considered an entity with an existence separate from the partners or whether it was in fact simply an aggregate of all of the partners. These problems motivated two agents within the complex adaptive legal system, the NCCUSL and the American Bar Association (ABA) to collaborate in the development of an updated set of rules for partnerships. This new set of rules, which was cleverly dubbed the **Revised Uniform Partnership Act (RUPA),** has been implemented in over half the states. The RUPA will, therefore, be the basis of the discussion for the remainder of this chapter.

Elements of a Partnership

RUPA says that a **partnership** is "an association of two or more persons to carry on as co-owners a business for profit." The RUPA definition emphasizes the two most essential elements of a partnership. First, partnerships must involve at least two persons. As is often the case with legal terms, the term "person" can have multiple meanings. In this case, the term "person" can refer to a flesh and blood individual, a corporation, other partnerships, joint ventures, trusts, estates, and other commercial or legal institutions. Second, a partnership must involve a sharing of profits. This last point is so crucial that the sharing of profits is considered to be *prima facie* evidence for the existence of a partnership. *Prima facie* evidence in this context means that the law presumes, in the absence of evidence to the contrary, that an individual receiving profits is a partner.

Entity and Aggregate Theories

Under the Uniform Partnership Act there was room to dispute whether a partnership should be considered an aggregate or an entity. Under the **entity theory** a partnership exists as an individual person with its own separate identity. This unique, individual entity is separate from the identities of the partners. In contrast, under the **aggregate theory,** the partnership is seen simply as an assembly or a collection of the partners who do business together. RUPA has settled this dispute. Under the RUPA, a partnership is to be considered an entity in most situations. Thus, a partnership is an entity in its ability to own title to property, to sue or to be sued, and to have its own separate bank accounts in its own name. Under the RUPA, partnerships also have continuity of existence. **Continuity of existence** permits a partnership to continue to operate as an entity even after the individual partners are no longer associated with it. In addition, the partners are to be considered agents of the

Teaching Tips Discuss factors, aside from legal ones, that potential partners should consider before going into business together. Have students discuss what characteristics they would look for or expect in a business partner. Stress to students the importance of partner compatibility regarding working styles, ethics, and personal and professional goals.

Terms The word *entity* refers to a being or self-contained existence, while *aggregate* means "the sum of several parts."

Background Information A partnership formed with a specific purpose in mind, such as drilling for oil, is called a *joint venture.* The laws governing partnerships also apply to joint ventures, which are often established informally by people not realizing they create legal relationships.

The Opening Case Revisited

"Watt Happened to Boulton!"

Under the modern rules established by the Revised Uniform Partnership Act, the Watt and Boulton business venture would be considered an entity, rather than an aggregate. Thus, the patent rights lawsuits discussed in the opening case would, today, be brought by the partnership itself, rather than by the partners themselves. Similarly, if any of the alleged patent infringers wanted to sue Watt and Boulton, they could bring that suit against the partnership as an entity.

partnership. RUPA does, however, still consider a partnership to be an aggregate in relation to liability. Thus, even under RUPA partners still have unlimited liability for the obligations of the partnership. It is, however, even possible to avoid this problem if the partners elect to form a registered limited liability partnership. The concept of registered limited liability partnerships is discussed later in the chapter.

Quick Quiz 36-2 True or False?

1. The Revised Uniform Partnership Act has yet to be adopted by any state legislature.
2. Under RUPA a partnership is usually considered to be an aggregate.
3. Under RUPA partners are seen as agents of the partnership.

36-3 Partnership Formation

The problem with a partnership is that it can emerge simply because of the way that two or more parties are doing business with one another. That is why it is essential that businesspeople be aware of their relationships with other businesspeople that they work with on a daily basis (see Table 36-1). Certainly the best way to form a partnership is to enter a contractual relationship by drawing up a partnership agreement. Consequently, we will examine this approach first. However, we will also look at the circumstances that can automatically create a partnership as a matter of law.

Table 36-1 Partnership Formation	
Form	**Definition**
Partnership by contract	Express agreement drawn up by partners Articles of partnership
Partnership by proof of existence	Individuals form partnership because of their method of doing business Sharing of profits is *prima facie* evidence

Formation of a Partnership by Contract

One of the most common ways to form a partnership is by an express agreement between the parties. Although the agreement can be oral, it is generally best to put the terms in writing to prevent misunderstanding and disputes that might arise later in the life of the partnership. The written agreement that establishes a partnership is called a partnership agreement. RUPA is quite specific about the nature of a partnership agreement. In fact, RUPA defines a partnership contract as "the agreement, whether written, oral, or implied, among the partners concerning the partnership, including amendments to the partnership agreement." It is, of course, still possible for the partners to enter agreements subsequent to the creation of a partnership that would not be considered part of the partnership agreement. Thus, partners might enter a loan or a rental agreement that would be separate from the partnership agreement itself.

Both RUPA and UPA are default statutes. This means that the partners are free to enter any type of agreement that they desire. However, if the partners neglect to include something in the agreement or if they are unsure of the interpretation of some point, RUPA (or UPA in those states that still follow it) will "fill in the gaps." It is advisable for a partnership agreement to include the following provisions:

1. The name and duration of the partnership.
2. The names of the partners.
3. The amount of capital that each partner has contributed to the partnership.
4. The character and the extent of the business of the partnership.
5. The way that profits will be divided.
6. The way that loses will be shared.
7. The duties of the partners.
8. Any limitations placed on the partners.
9. A section on salaries, if this is desired.
10. An explanation of the dissolution process, if it is to be different from the process outlined in RUPA.
11. A provision for determining the value of a partner's interest in the partnership.

It is also wise to recall that, although RUPA does not require that a partnership agreement be in writing, the Statute of Frauds does dictate that certain types of contracts, such as those that will take longer than one year to complete must be in writing. Thus, it is best to cross-reference with the Statute of Frauds just to make certain that none of those provisions apply.

Formation of a Partnership by Proof of Existence

The definition of a partnership offered by RUPA establishes the parameters within which a partnership will be formed. The definition states that a business arrangement will be considered a partnership if it involves two or more persons, in association with one another, who are carrying on a business as co-owners for profit. Therefore, to show that a business is operating as a partnership by proof of existence, we must be able to point to three elements: (1) an association of two or more persons (2) who are co-owners of (3) a business for profit.

An Association of Two or More Persons In the case of a partnership, a "person" can be a living flesh and blood individual, a corporation, another partnership, a joint venture, a trust, an estate, or some other commercial enterprise or legal institution. Any two of these persons working together would be sufficient to create an association.

Co-ownership of the Business There are certain signs that will indicate that the parties in a venture are co-owners. One such sign is the existence of management power. Of course, management power by itself is not enough. Employees who are not partners and even independent contractors who have control over certain projects conducted for the business may have management power without being co-owners. Still, the power to make management decisions is a persuasive piece of evidence that is helpful in establishing co-ownership. Co-ownership is also established by the sharing of profits among the partners. However, RUPA also says that certain types of profit sharing, while real enough, will not rise to the level needed to create a partnership. These profit-sharing activities include the following:

1. The repayment of a debt.
2. Wages to an employee.
3. Payments to an independent contractor.
4. Rent payments to a landlord.
5. Annuity payments or health benefit payments to a beneficiary, to a representative, or to a designee of a retired or deceased partner.
6. Interest payments on a loan, even if the level of payments is tied to profit fluctuations.
7. Consideration for the sale of goodwill or for the sale of other property even if the payments are made in installments.

Although the sharing of profits is *prima facie* evidence of the existence of a partnership, parties can receive profits in any of the ways on this list without being saddled with the label of partner.

Example 36-1

Theresa Nagy owned an office building in downtown River City. Richard Thome and George Justice were partners in a mail order business in Lake City called Baseball Collectibles. In order to open a branch office in River City, Thome and Justice leased the office building from Nagy. As part of the agreement, Nagy received $4,650 in rent each month. Later Nagy claims partnership status in Baseball Collectibles, based upon the fact that she received a $4,650 payment from Thome and Justice each month. She characterized these payments as a share of the profits and argued that this share entitled her to be a partner in the firm. Nevertheless, Nagy will not succeed in her claim because the share of the profits she received each month was a fixed rent installment paid to her according to the lease agreement she negotiated with Thome and Justice.

Teaching Tips The concept of the value of goodwill is often difficult for students to grasp. Goodwill is also referred to as the intangible value of the business that is excluded by the balance sheets. It has also been defined as the difference between the net worth and actual value of the business.

Carrying on a Business for Profit Finally, it is not enough for two or more persons to simply be co-owners of property, even if the property does make a profit. The association must also have the goal of running the business together. It is, of course, also essential that the business in question be run for a profit. This means that the venture cannot involve an unincorporated nonprofit venture. It is also unlikely that a solitary profit-making business transaction by itself will be enough to establish a partnership.

Getting Students Involved Have two students act out a partnership-by-estoppel situation using the Opening Case as a model.

Business Law in the News
As Partnership Sours, Parting Is Sweet

The problem: An inexperienced entrepreneur relies on a partner.

After six years, Jennifer Appel was burning out from the demands of her job as a clinical psychologist in New York's schools treating emotionally disturbed children. To unwind, she often baked cakes and desserts for friends.

Ultimately, she and a friend decided to start a business selling their baked treats. Ms. Appel was nervous, but comforted that her partner had food-industry experience, having grown up around her parents' restaurants.

The women started as wholesalers "to get our feet wet," she says, baking in a basement and carrying samples to sales calls. Soon, they had a half dozen clients and Ms. Appel quit her day job.

The bigger step was opening their own shop. With credit cards and a loan, they opened a bakery in the West Village in Manhattan in 1996. "It felt like a breath of fresh air to do something creative and make a living," she says.

Jennifer Appel's partnership failed, but gave her the courage to strike out on her own.

She happily relied on her friend for business expertise. But as time went on Ms. Appel developed her own ideas about running the business. Soon they were barely speaking, with Ms. Appel working days and her partner working nights. They managed to write a cook-book together, communicating mostly by notes and messages. It wasn't many months before the bakery was a success, but the partnership was a flop.

The solution: Ms. Appel began educating herself about business, first reading the "dummies" books, then more sophisticated fare. Her opinions crystallized.

"I don't think you can work idiosyncratically and develop a brand," she says. Their partnership was barely a year old, and Ms. Appel began working with a lawyer to develop a proposal to buy out her partner's interest.

After negotiations, however, it was the partner who acquired Ms. Appel's ownership. It was enough to set her on the path to launch her own bakery. She approached it her methodical way—for instance, sitting in her car to count the people walking by her proposed Midtown site before she signed a lease. She opened the doors of Buttercup Bake Shop in 1999, taking out another loan and charging up the credit cards again. "I came to believe I was capable of doing it myself," she says.

Now with greater confidence, she could execute her own strategy, free to ask questions and impose order. Recently married and with her first child, she investigated franchising as a way to grow "without killing myself."

She threw herself into the details: finding architects, designing a prototype, writing sales materials. "I went slowly," she says. The first franchise just sold—a huge milestone, she says. "I'm glad someone has confidence in me."

The lesson: If a partnership founders, part nicely, and then move on.

Questions for Analysis

1. If no partnership agreement was drawn up in this case, how would you convince a court that Ms. Appel's business was a partnership? Explain.

2. Is the Buttercup Bake Shop a corporation, a partnership, or sole proprietorship? Explain.

3. Did the first bake shop mentioned in the article enter a dissociation or a dissolution? Explain.

4. What elements should have been included in the partnership agreement for the first bake shop? Explain.

5. Were the actions of both partners ethical in this case? Explain.

Source: Paulette Thomas. "As Partnership Sours, Parting Is Sweet," *The Wall Street Journal,* July 6, 2004, p. A-20. Reprinted with permission.

Quick Quiz 36-3 True or False?

1. A partnership can emerge simply because of the way two or more parties are doing business with one another.

2. A "person" can be a living flesh and blood individual, a corporation, another partnership, a joint venture, a trust, an estate, or some other commercial enterprise or legal institution.

3. The sharing of profits is *prima facie* evidence of the existence of a partnership.

36-4 Partnership Property Rights and Duties

Property is an extremely critical element in partnership law, because virtually every decision made by a partner deals with the disposition of partnership property. Decisions involving the use of partnership property, such as machinery, equipment, furniture, and vehicles; decisions regarding the purchase of raw materials; and decisions concerning the sale of finished products, all involve the disposition of property. Even service-oriented partnerships such as shipping firms and restaurants involve the disposition of property in one way or another. This is why partnership duties and rights always involve partnership property. This is also why it is critical to determine whether a given piece of property belongs to the partnership entity, or to an individual partner as his or her personal property. At times it is relatively easy to distinguish between partnership property and property that belongs to individual partners. For instance, the capital contributions of all the partners are considered to be the property of the partnership. **Capital contributions** are sums that are contributed by the partners as permanent investments and that the partners are entitled to have returned when the partnership is dissolved. In contrast, loans or later advances that partners make to the partnership and accumulated but undivided profits belong to the partners on an individual basis. Other forms of partnership property belong only to the partnership in its status as an entity.

Background Information Although courts have differed about at what point a partnership becomes legally binding, if two people seriously discuss a partnership and talk about details such as suppliers, markets, and office space, many courts will recognize their relationship as a binding partnership without written agreement.

Partnership Property

The fact that RUPA has established the existence of a partnership as an entity has alleviated some of the difficulties that were once associated with identifying partnership property. RUPA states that partnership property is any and all property that has been obtained by the partnership itself. For instance, if the property was obtained in the partnership's name, it is partnership property. If the property was obtained by a partner in his or her role as a partner, it is partnership property. If the instrument of title for the property includes the name of the partnership, it is partnership property. Finally, if the instrument of transfer indicates that the property was obtained by a partner in his or her role as a partner or if the partnership is referred to in the instrument, the property belongs to the partnership.

When it is difficult to determine whether a piece of property belongs to the partnership or to a partner, the court may ask the following questions: Has the partnership included the property in its account books? Has the partnership expended its own funds to improve or repair the property? Has the partnership paid taxes on the property? Has the partnership paid other expenses such as maintenance costs for the property? The more of these questions that can be answered in the affirmative, the more likely it is that the property is partnership property.

Specific Partnership Property

Cross-Cultural Notes While American businesses generally use suppliers on a short-term, best-price basis, Japanese businesses tend to establish permanent, loyal relationships with suppliers that endure through economic difficulty as well as success.

Further Reading For a look at practical drafting suggestions for partnerships, see *The Alpha Partnership Kit: Special Book Edition with Removable Forms,* by Kermit Burton (Alpha Publications of America, 1998).

RUPA has made a significant change in the rule in regard to individual pieces of partnership property. Under UPA, the rule was that each partner had a property interest in all specific items of partnership property. Each partner was, therefore, a co-owner of that property. This form of ownership was known as tenancy in partnership. Under UPA, a tenancy in partnership had the following characteristics:

1. A partner had an equal right with all other partners to possess and use specific partnership property for partnership purposes, but not for that partner's personal use.

2. A partner's interest in partnership property could not be assigned (i.e., transferred by sale, mortgage, pledge, or otherwise) to a nonpartner, unless the other partners agreed to the transfer.

3. Partners' rights in partnership property was not subject to attachment (i.e., taking a person's property and bringing it into the custody of the law) for personal debts or claims against the partners themselves.

4. A deceased partner's interest in real property held by the partnership passed to the surviving partners.

5. Partners' rights in specific partnership property was not subject to any allowances or rights to widows, heirs, or next of kin.

Under RUPA all of this has changed. RUPA states that "A partner is not co-owner of partnership property and has no interest in partnership property which can be transferred, either voluntarily or involuntarily." Of course, partners will still be able to use partnership property. However, their right to hold and use such property is limited to partnership purposes. This is a significant change in relation to partnership law; however, it actually brings partnership property rights in relation to individual pieces of partnership property into line with the way property rights operate for other business associations such as corporations.

Interest in the Partnership

Terms A *silent partner* is one whose identity is not revealed to the public. Silent partners have the same liability as the other partners. A *sub-partner* forms an agreement with one member of a partnership to share in that partner's profits.

RUPA establishes that a partner has an interest in the partnership as a firm. That right consists or two parts: (1) a transferable economic interest and (2) a nontransferable interest in management rights.

Transferable Economic Interest The partner's economic interest is his or her share of the profits and losses, and his or her share of the surplus. **Surplus** includes any funds that remain after the partnership has been dissolved and all other debts and prior obligations have been paid. Partners can voluntarily assign their economic interest to another party. The assignee in such an action, however, is not entitled to take part in the management of the partnership. The assignee also cannot gain access to the partnership books or the partnership financial records. Nor can an assignee demand to receive information concerning the transactions of the partnership.

Terms In large partnerships in which some of the partners do not want to be involved in the day-to-day business operations, a managing partner is hired or chosen from among the partners. Sometimes the managing partner is a limited partner whose liability is determined by the contribution he or she makes to the partnership.

Management of the Firm Participation in management decision making is not limited to the partner's proportional share of the firm. Instead, all partners have equal rights in the management of the partnership business. The day-to-day decisions of the firm are decided by a majority vote of the partners. If a vote is split evenly, then the status quo remains. If such deadlocks persist, and the very operation of the business is threatened, it may be time to dissolve the partnership. Occasionally, a unanimous vote is required in a business decision. However, such decisions must involve actions that fall outside the regular, daily operation of the business. Decisions that involve amendments to the partnership agreement also require unanimous consent.

It is, of course, possible for a partner to voluntarily reduce his or her part in management by becoming a silent partner. A **silent partner** is one who does not participate in the day-to-day business of the firm. This is in contrast to a **secret partner,** whose identity and existence are not known outside the firm, but who, nevertheless, can participate in the management of the firm. Some partnerships create their own hierarchy of partners. Thus, a firm may be divided into *junior* and *senior partners* or into *managing* and *nonmanaging partners.*

Partnership Rights and Duties

We have already pinpointed most of the individual rights that partners possess by virtue of their participation in the partnership. These rights include: (1) the right to use partnership property, as long as the property is held and used for partnership purposes; (2) the right to receive the partner's share of the profits (and losses) and his or her share of the surplus; (3) the right to manage the regular day-to-day operation of the partnership business; (4) the right to approve of serious matters outside the ordinary course of business; and (5) the right to approve of amendments to the partnership agreement. In addition, partners have certain enforcement rights, should the need arise to implement the other rights.

Enforcement Rights Under UPA, a partner's enforcement rights are few. In fact, under UPA, partners have only three enforcement rights: (1) the right to see the firm's financial records, (2) the right to compel an accounting, and (3) the right to compel a dissolution of the entire partnership. Under RUPA those enforcement rights are enhanced. The three rights noted above are retained. However, in addition, a partner can sue a partner directly or, under the entity theory, the partnership itself to enforce his or her partnership rights as expressed in RUPA or as granted by the partnership agreement. In such an action, the partner can ask for damages or for an equitable remedy, such as an injunction or specific performance. Of course, the reverse is also true; that is, the partner can also be sued by another partner or by the partnership itself.

Partnership Duties RUPA notes that partners have three critical duties: (1) the duty of loyalty, (2) the duty to obey, and (3) the duty of due care. The first of these three, the duty of loyalty, is based on the fact that the partners are in a fiduciary relationship.

The Duty of Loyalty The duty of loyalty has become of central importance under RUPA. This was not so under UPA, which devoted only a very small amount of space to the topic. Under RUPA, the duty of loyalty includes the following items:

1. To account to the partnership for any property, profits, or benefit that comes from the partner's use of partnership property or from the winding-up process after dissolution.

2. To refrain from dealing with people who may have an interest that is adverse to the best interests of the partnership.

3. To refrain from entering any competition with the partnership in the operation of partnership business.

A partner does, however, retain the right to look after himself or herself during the formation of the partnership because the duty of loyalty does not arise until the partnership entity actually exists.

The Duty to Obey A partner has the duty to follow faithfully all the arrangements made in the partnership agreement. The partner must also honor all decisions made by the partnership, provided those decisions were made following proper protocols. If a partner disobeys the partnership agreement or disregards a decision lawfully made by the other partners, he or she will be liable for any loss that befalls the partnership as a result of that disobedience.

The Duty of Due Care   Basically, the duty of due care means that partners must do their best in the business, based on their talents, education, and abilities. It does not mean that partners must be infallible. On the contrary, the standard recognizes that partners may make mistakes and allows for those mistakes, provided the partner acted with an ordinary level of skill and competence and in the best interests of the partnership.

For a more detailed discussion of Schumpeter's theories see: Sievers, Allen M. *Revolution, Evolution, and the Economic Order* Englewood Cliffs, NJ: Prentice Hall, 1962, p. 41.

Talking Points

One of the premiere economists of the last century was a Harvard professor names Joseph Schumpeter, who wrote a treatise entitled *Capitalism, Socialism, and Democracy,* in which he foretold the ultimate end of the capitalist economic system. Oddly, Schumpeter was himself a confirmed capitalist, and so, when he predicted the end of the capitalist economy, it was without joy or pleasure. In fact, it was more of a warning than a prediction and it was offered with the hope that something could be done to divert the path of destruction. Schumpeter's affection for capitalism is evident in the following passage, penned by Allen M. Sievers in his study, *Revolution, Evolution, and the Economic Order:*
"The capitalist, for one thing, wishes to provide for his family, and indeed capitalism is really not individual-centered but family-centered. Further, the capitalist shares in lesser degree the romantic adventuresomeness which characterized feudal society, or there would be no risky innovation or entrepreneurial exploit. Capitalism also requires a kind of symbiosis with the aristocracy and other non-bourgeois elements to run the state, and this depends on a kind of loyalty by these classes to capitalism. The masses must also be awed by the glamor or prestige of capitalist success in order to submit to the discipline necessary for business production. The business classes themselves must have an *esprit de corps* and a devotion to their way of life, as well as a code of ethics if the contract and property system is to work."
Allen M. Sievers in his study, *Revolution, Evolution, and the Economic Order,* p. 41.

We can distill from this quotation five essential qualities of the capitalist: (1) family-centeredness, (2) a willingness to take risk, (3) loyalty to the capitalist ideal, (4) awe at the success of capitalistic ventures, and (5) a code of ethics that permits the rules of contract and property law to work. Which of the business organizations listed at the beginning of this chapter is best suited to realizing these ideals? Explain.

Quick Quiz 36-4 True or False?

1. Under RUPA, each partner has a property interest in all specific items of partnership property.

2. RUPA states that partnership property is any and all property that has been obtained by the partnership itself.

3. A partner's economic interest in the partnership is nontransferrable.

36-5 Dissociation and Dissolution

One of the objectives of the National Conference of Commissioners on Uniform State Laws and the American Bar Association in the rewriting of UPA and the development of RUPA was to make certain that the new law coincided as much as possible with commercial realities. Under UPA, whenever a partner ceased to be associated with the partnership technically that partnership went through the dissolution process. Under present commercial realities, it no longer made sense for partners to have to deal with the dissolution technicalities when the only thing that was really happening was the buyout of a partner who wanted to leave the firm. Consequently, RUPA now includes two methods by which a partner becomes dissociated with partnership: dissociation and dissolution.

Dissociation of a Partnership

Under RUPA, a **dissociation** takes place whenever a partner is no longer associated with the running of the firm. It is always possible for partners to leave a partnership firm whenever they want to. However, sometimes, a partner leaves the firm wrongfully because he or she does not have the legal right to do so. A partner's right to withdraw from a partnership may depend on whether the partnership is a term partnership or a partnership at will. A **term partnership** is one has been set up to run for a certain set time period or in order to accomplish a task of some sort. A partner who leaves a term partnership before the term expires or before the task is accomplished, has acted wrongfully. A **partnership at will** is one that any partner may leave without liability. RUPA sets up the circumstances under which it is proper to leave a partnership. Some rules affect both types of partnerships; others apply only to partnerships at will. These include (1) a partner's death in either type of partnership; (2) a partner's leave-taking from a partnership at will; (3) a partner's leave-taking from either type of partnership under the rules set up by the partnership agreement; and (4) a partner's leave-taking from either type of partnership, if a court has decided that a partner cannot do what he or she is supposed to do under the partnership agreement.

Dissolution of a Partnership

The **dissolution** of a partnership occurs when a partner ceases to be associated with the partnership and the partnership ends. The dissolution of a partnership can occur in one of three ways: (1) by an action committed by the partners, (2) by operation of law, or (3) by the decree of a court of law.

An Action by the Partners   Whenever a partnership at will exists, that partnership can be dissolved whenever a partner notifies the other partners that he or she intends to leave the firm. Partnerships at will, however, are not dissolved when a partner dies or enters bankruptcy. Whenever a term partnership is involved, RUPA says that there are several ways to dissolve the firm: (1) when the time limit has passed; (2) when the task of the partnership has been accomplished; (3) when there is express agreement among all partners to end the partnership; (4) when a partner dies; (5) when a partner becomes incapacitated; (6) when a partner goes bankrupt; and (7) when a partner produces a wrongful dissociation from the partnership and, within ninety days of that leave-taking, at least half the other partners agree to end the business.

By Operation of Law   Dissolution becomes effective by operation of law if some event occurs that makes it illegal to continue the business of the firm. If, for instance, at some time in the distant future it became illegal to manufacture and sell tobacco products, then a partnership formed to produce and market cigarettes would dissolve by operation of law.

By a Court Order   When a partner has engaged in some sort of wrongdoing and, on those grounds, another partner petitions the court for a dissolution, the court may dissolve the partnership by court order. When a continuation of the business would be economically foolish, the court may dissolve the firm. Finally, when a partner does something that makes it impractical to continue the business with that partner, the court may order the dissolution of the business.

Winding Up the Partnership Business   When a partnership terminates, there must be a winding up of the partnership affairs. This action includes the orderly

Partners may find life together difficult and decide to dissolve the partnership.

sale of the partnership's assets, the payment of creditors, and the distribution, if any, of the remaining surplus to partners according to their profit-sharing rations.

Quick Quiz 36-5 True or False?

1. RUPA includes two methods by which a partner becomes dissociated with a partnership: dissociation and dissolution.

2. A partnership at will is one that any partner may leave without liability.

3. When partnership terminates, there must be a winding up of the partnership affairs.

36-6 Other Forms of Partnership Business

The changing needs of the modern marketplace and the development of new ideas in the law have combined to allow for a new form of partnership, the registered limited liability partnership. Those same forces have also cooperated to update one of the more traditional forms of the partnership business, the limited partnership.

Registered Limited Liability Partnerships

Recent statutory developments in several states have produced a new type of business organization known as the registered limited liability partnership (RLLP or LLP). A **registered limited liability partnership** is a general partnership in all respects except one—liability. In a traditional general partnership, the liability for the torts committed by a partner or an employee of the partnership is joint and several. This means that each partner is liable and may be sued in a separate action or in a joint action. A judgment may be levied against one or more partners. The release of one partner in one action does not necessarily release the others.

The statutes usually require that the registration statement be filed by all of the partners or at least by those partners holding a majority interest in the partnership. LLPs must update their registration statement each year or risk the loss of registration. As far as the tax laws are concerned, LLPs are to be considered as general partnerships.

Once an LLP has been created, partners can no longer be held jointly or severally liable for the torts, wrongful acts, negligence, or misconduct committed by another partner or by any representative of the partnership. Naturally, partners would still be liable for their own wrongful acts and for the wrongful acts committed by other partners or by employees that are under the direct control of that partner.

Limited Partnerships

Limited partnerships are governed by the Revised Uniform Limited Partnership Act (RULPA). The revised act defines a **limited partnership** as "a partnership formed by two or more persons . . . having one or more general partners and one or more limited partners." **General partners** take an active part in the management of the firm and have unlimited liability for the firm's debts. **Limited partners** are nonparticipating investors. They contribute cash, property, or services to the partnership but do not take part in the management of the firm.

A limited partnership is advantageous for both the limited partner and the general partner. The general partner can accumulate additional capital without admitting another general partner who would be entitled to management rights. Thus, the general partner maintains control while strengthening the firm's treasury. The limited partner also benefits because limited partnership means limited liability. **Limited liability** means that the limited partner's nonpartnership property cannot be used to satisfy any debts owed by the partnership. Thus, limited partners receive a return on their investment while risking only that original investment.

Limited partnerships must follow strict filing requirements. Usually a certificate of limited partnership must be filed with the secretary of state's office. The purpose of the certificate is to warn third parties of the limited liability of some partners. However, some state statutes indicate that neither the names of the limited partners nor the amounts of their capital contributions must be included in the certificate. This provision simplifies the formation of a limited partnership because it allows limited partners to remain anonymous.

Failure to file a certificate of limited partnership will deprive a limited partner of limited liability if third parties attempting to hold the limited partner liable did not know that they were dealing with a limited partnership. Moreover, if in the certificate of limited partnership, a limited partner is incorrectly identified as a general partner, then he or she would not have limited partner status. To correct such an error, the limited partner would have to refile an amended certificate of limited partnership or leave the limited partnership altogether. Such drastic actions would be necessary unless the state statute under which the limited partnership was formed allows a limited partner who has been incorrectly named as a general partner to file with the appropriate state office a unilateral **disclaimer of general partner status.** Limited partners must also guard against becoming too involved in the business. A limited partner who exercises too much control over partnership affairs may lose the protective mantle of limited liability. Recently, however, many state legislatures have greatly expanded the types of activities that a limited partner can perform without losing the shelter provided by limited partnership status.

Background Information Limited partnerships were first used in Italy in the twelfth century to give anonymity to clergymen and nobles who were investing capital in various businesses. Limited partnerships spread to France and then to America, first appearing in Louisiana and Florida.

Quick Quiz 36-6 True or False?

1. A registered limited liability partnership is like a general partnership in all respects except liability.

2. In most states, to become a registered limited liability partnership the partners must file with the auditor's office in the county courthouse.

3. Limited partnerships must have at least three limited partners and no general partners.

Summary

36-1 The easiest business organization to form is a sole proprietorship. All that businesspeople have to do is open their doors for business and a sole proprietorship is created. The greatest advantage to a sole proprietorship is that the owner has complete control over the business. The major disadvantage is that the sole proprietor is subject to unlimited liability.

36-2 The Revised Uniform Partnership Act states that a partnership is "an association of two or more persons to carry on as co-owners a business for profit." Under RUPA a partnership is considered an entity, or an individual unit that exists separate from the partners. A partnership is an entity in its ability to own title to property, to sue or to be sued, and to have its own separate bank accounts in its own name. Under RUPA, partnerships also have continuity of existence.

36-3 One of the most common ways to form a partnership is by an express agreement between the parties. It is generally best to put the terms in writing to prevent misunderstanding and disputes that might arise later in the life of the partnership. The written agreement that establishes a partnership is called a partnership agreement. To show that a business is operating as a partnership by proof of existence, three elements must exist: (1) an association of two or more persons (2) who are co-owners of (3) a business for profit.

36-4 Capital contributions are sums that are contributed by the partners as permanent investments and that the partners are entitled to have returned when the partnership is dissolved. Loans or later advances that partners make to the partnership and accumulated but undivided profits belong to the partners on an individual basis. Other forms of partnership property belong only to the partnership in its status as an entity. RUPA states that "A partner is not co-owner of partnership property and has no interest in partnership property which can be transferred, either voluntarily or involuntarily." Partners can use a partnership for partnership purposes. RUPA establishes that a partner has an interest in the partnership as a firm. That right consists of two parts: (1) a transferable economic interest and (2) a nontransferable interest in management rights.

36-5 Under RUPA, a dissociation takes place whenever a partner is no longer associated with the running of the firm. Partners can leave a partnership firm whenever they want. A partner leaves a firm wrongfully if he or she does not have the legal right to do so. The dissolution of a partnership occurs when a partner ceases to be associated with the partnership and the partnership ends. The dissolution of a partnership can occur in one of three ways: (1) by an action committed by the partners, (2) by operation of law, or (3) by the decree of a court of law.

36-6 The changing needs of the modern marketplace and the development of new ideas in the law have combined to allow for a new form of partnership, the registered limited liability partnership. Those same forces have also cooperated to update one of the more traditional forms of the partnership business, the limited partnership.

Key Terms

aggregate theory, 682

capital contribution, 687

continuity of existence, 682

disclaimer of general partner status, 693

dissociation, 691

dissolution, 691

entity theory, 682

general partner, 692

limited liability, 693

limited partner, 692

limited partnership, 692

partnership, 682

partnership at will, 691

registered limited liability partnership, 692

Revised Uniform Partnership Act (RUPA), 682

secret partner, 689

silent partner, 689

sole proprietorship, 681

surplus, 688

term partnership, 691

Uniform Partnership Act (UPA), 682

Questions for Review and Discussion

1. What are the most common forms of business associations?
2. What are the advantages and disadvantages of a sole proprietorship?
3. What are the two model acts that govern partnership law?
4. What are the differences between the aggregate and the entity theories of partnership?

5. What is the nature of a partnership agreement?
6. When does profit sharing not create a partnership?
7. What constitutes a person in partnership law?
8. What are the different views of specific partnership property in partnership law?
9. What is the difference between dissociation and dissolution in partnership law?
10. What is the difference between a registered limited liability partnership and a limited partnership?

Investigating the Internet

The Small Business Administration (SBA) maintains a website which includes an introduction to the SBA as well as information on how to start, finance, and expand a small business. Access this website and write a report on how to start a small business of your own choosing.

Cases for Analysis

1. Kerry Taylor owned a warehouse in the industrial flats of Parke Central City. Yale Roberts and William Hull were partners in a chain of restaurants called Pirate's Seafood Carousel. Roberts and Hull leased Taylor's warehouse for their restaurant. As part of the agreement, Taylor received $7,500 in rent each month. Taylor retained office space on the top floor of the warehouse. She also agreed to allow Roberts and Hull to remodel the rest of the warehouse to meet the needs of their new restaurant. Taylor occasionally offered advice about the remodeling of the warehouse. In addition, after the restaurant opened for business, Taylor frequently signed for shipments that Roberts and Hull had ordered for the restaurant. After five years in this location, and after selling their other restaurants, Roberts and Hull decided to dissolve their partnership. During the winding up process, they were surprised to learn that Taylor claimed that she should receive a share of the surplus cash after the dissolution of the partnership, because she claimed to be a partner in Pirate's Seafood Carousel. Is Taylor correct in her claim? Will Roberts and Hull have to pay her a share of their surplus cash? Explain.

2. When the father of Stephen and Chris Nuss died, the two boys, aged 15 and 12, began to work the family farm. While the boys were still under the age of majority, their mother, Lois, kept the books for the farm. As the boys grew older, they took more and more responsibility in running the farm. They also rented and worked additional acres of farmland. They financed these rental agreements on their own, but their mother cosigned the arrangements. The boys also purchased additional farmland. Again their mother helped in this purchase by cosigning. When Chris decided to leave farming, Stephen paid him $100,000 and, in exchange, Chris signed over the deed to the newly purchased land. Lois was not involved in this transaction. Stephen's farming business grew. He eventually amassed over 1,200 acres. He and his wife, Linda, kept their own financial records and maintained their own checking account for the running of the farm. Stephen's mother was not involved in any of this. However, Stephen continued to pay many of the expenses involved on the original farm where his mother still maintained her residence. Stephen also paid the insurance, maintenance, and repair expenses on all buildings and equipment on the original farm. Since Stephen continued to farm this land, in addition to the land he had subsequently purchased, these payments were always characterized as rent. No other payments went to Stephen's mother. When Stephen died, Linda, his widow and executor, claimed that a partnership existed, and that the farm equipment on the original acreage and original acreage itself belonged to that partnership. Lois argued that no partnership between Stephen and her existed. Is Linda or Lois correct? Did a partnership exist? Explain. *In re Estate of Nuss,* 646 N.E.2d 504 (OH).

3. McCoy and Gugelman borrowed money from State Security Bank for their partnership, Antiques, Etc.

When McCoy and Gugelman failed to pay back the debt, the bank sued them as individuals. At trial, McCoy and Gugelman argued that their partnership, Antiques, Etc., was an entity, not an aggregate, of the partners. Therefore, they concluded, the bank would have to show that the partnership funds were insufficient to answer the judgment before it could proceed against them individually. Are they correct? Why or why not? *Security State Bank v. McCoy,* 361 N.W.2d 514 (NE).

4. Shane ran a liquid fertilizer business. As part of the operation of the business, Shane paid Svoboda a specified amount per acre to spread the fertilizer on his clients' crops. Svoboda's per-acre payments remained steady, despite Shane's profits or losses. Frisch was injured while filling a tank truck that was supposed to haul the fertilizer to Svoboda's tractor. Frisch sued both Shane and Svoboda, claiming that Svoboda was sharing in Shane's profits and was therefore a partner. Was Frisch correct? Explain. *Frisch v. Svobada,* 157 N.W.2d 774 (NE).

5. Summers and Dooley formed a partnership for the purpose of operating a trash collection business.

The business was operated by the two men, and when either was unable to work, the non-working partner provided a replacement at his own expense. Summers approached Dooley and requested that they hire a third worker. Dooley refused. Notwithstanding Dooley's refusal, Summers, on his own initiative, hired a worker. Summers paid the employee out of his own pocket. Dooley, upon discovery that a third person had been hired, objected. He stated that the additional labor was not necessary and refused to allow partnership funds to be used to pay the new employee. After paying out more than $11,000 in wages without any reimbursement from either partnership funds or his partner, Summers brought suit in the Idaho state courts. The trial court held that Summers was not entitled to reimbursement for the wages he had paid the employee. On appeal, did the Supreme Court of Idaho uphold the trial court's decision? Explain. *Summers v. Dooley,* 481 P.2d 318 (ID).

Quick Quiz Answers

36-1	36-2	36-3	36-4	36-5	36-6
1. F	1. F	1. T	1. F	1. T	1. T
2. T	2. F	2. T	2. T	2. T	2. F
3. T	3. T	3. T	3. F	3. T	3. F

Chapter 37 | The Corporate Entity

The Opening Case
"A Preemptive Pump and Dump!"

While checking the records of several companies, officials at the Securities Exchange Commission discovered over two dozen companies that were behind in the filing of financial disclosure statements. This discovery disturbed SEC officials because the SEC saw the possibility that those companies, and others like them, could be used as bait in a series of "pump and dump" schemes. A pump and dump scheme is designed to lure unsuspecting investors into the trap of investing in what is essentially an "empty shell," that is, a poorly financed corporation that appears to be more valuable than it really is. In an unprecedented move, the SEC issued an order that stopped investors from trading in the shares of those companies. The avowed motive for the order was that the companies had not filed disclosure statements with the SEC as required by law. In reality, the SEC had launched a preemptive strike against these companies in an attempt to prevent the initiation of any pump and dump scheme that the owners of those shells might be contemplating. What other situations might arise in which corporate shells are used to cheat investors? Are investors alone at risk, or can such schemes also hurt suppliers and customers? Can the victims of such schemes pierce the veil of the shell and reach the real owners, despite the shield of the corporate structure? Or are they without an effective remedy in court? As you read about corporate evolution in Chapter 37, ask yourself whether the corporate structure is really as foolproof as it first appears.

Chapter Outcomes

1. Describe the evolution of the associative corporativism.
2. Explain the nature of a corporation.
3. List the constitutional rights of a corporation.
4. Distinguish between a close and an S corporation.
5. Describe the differences among a private, a public, and a quasi-public corporation.
6. List the typical elements within the articles of incorporation.
7. Distinguish between the articles of organization and the operating agreement of a limited liability company.
8. Distinguish between a *de jure* and a *de facto* corporation.
9. Identify the objective of piercing the corporate veil.
10. Distinguish between common and preferred stock.

37-1 The Corporation in the Complex Adaptive System

For more details on the alleged "pump and dump" scenario described in The Opening Case see: Bloomberg News. "S.E.C. Acts on Corporate Shells." *The New York Times*, June 9, 2004, p. C-9.

Corporations are a product of capitalism. Capitalism flourished in the United States in the nineteenth century because the American economic system at that time provided the perfect engine for capitalistic progress. Much of this progress occurred because there was an enormous amount of land that needed to be developed in the United States and an influx of energetic immigrants who were willing to improve that land. The corporation grew in response because capitalism needed an efficient way to raise capital to finance land development projects. The corporation of today, however, bears little resemblance to the corporation as it was born in the nineteenth century, and the development of the corporate form of doing business is a vivid example of the complex adaptive system at work.

The Beginnings of Corporativism

A **corporation** is a legal entity created under the authority of a state or federal statute that gives certain individuals the capacity to operate an enterprise. The process of doing business as a self-governing business association, that is, as a corporation, is called **associative corporativism,** or simply, **corporativism.** In the nineteenth century each corporation was individually created by a unique legislative enactment. Each corporation had its own charter which outlined the powers and abilities of that corporation.

For more information on corporate charters in the nineteenth century see: Friedman, Lawrence W. *Law in America: A Short History*. New York: The Modern Library, 2002, pp. 48–49.

For more information on associative corporativism see: Sievers, Allen M. *Revolution, Evolution, and the Economic Order*. Englewood Cliffs, NJ: Prentice Hall, 1962, p. 39.

Corporate Limited Liability

Today one of the most attractive features of the corporate way of doing business is its limited liability. **Limited liability** means that the corporate investors cannot be held personally liable for the debts of the corporation. Thus, the most that an investor can lose is the amount of money used to purchase his or her **shares** of the corporation.

Corporate Entity Status

A corporation exists apart from its owners and is taxed directly on the income it earns. As a legal entity, a corporation can own property and can sue or be sued just as an individual can. Moreover, the existence of a corporation is not affected by the death, incapacity, or bankruptcy of a manager or shareholder.

Background Information In the Roman Empire, corporations were recognized as entities with legal identities separate from those of their individual members. As business organizations grew more powerful, the Roman government created mandates to control and tax these early corporations.

Corporate Constitutional Rights

Under provisions of the U.S. Constitution, a corporation is also considered an artificially created legal person. Within the meaning of Amendment 14, a corporation—like a natural person—may not be deprived of life, liberty, or property without due process of law. Also, a corporation may not be denied equal protection of the laws within the jurisdiction of a state.

Corporate Citizenship

A corporation is considered a citizen both of the state in which it is incorporated and the state where it has its principal place of business. It can also be sued as a citizen of both these states. By virtue of the due process clause of Amendment 14, a state court may also exercise jurisdiction over a noncitizen corporate defendant as long as that corporation has had an appropriate contact with that state. Such contact can include owning property within the state, doing business in the state, or committing a tort within the state.

U.S. Const. Amendment 14 (see page 861)

> ### Quick Quiz 37-1 True or False?
>
> 1. A corporation is a legal entity created by either a state or federal statute authorizing individuals to operate an enterprise.
>
> 2. A corporation may not be deprived of life, liberty, or property without due process of law.
>
> 3. A corporation is considered a citizen of only the state in which it is incorporated.

37-2   Types of Corporate Entities

Corporations may be classified in various ways in order to emphasize a purpose or characteristic. For clarity, this chapter is limited mainly to a discussion of the major kinds of corporations created by statute and authorized by state-granted charters to incorporate.

Private, Public, and Quasi-Public

A **private corporation** is a corporation formed by private persons to accomplish a task best undertaken by an entity that can raise large amounts of capital quickly or that can grant the protection of limited liability. Private corporations can be organized for a profit-making business purpose or for a nonprofit charitable, educational, or scientific purpose. If the corporation is organized for profit-making purposes, those profits may be distributed to the shareholders in the form of dividends. **Dividends** are the net profits, or surplus, set aside for the shareholders. **Shareholders** (or stockholders, as they are also known) are the persons who own units of interest (shares of stock) in a corporation.

Large private corporations generally sell their stock to the public at large and are, therefore, often referred to as public corporations. This designation can be confusing because the term **public corporation** is more properly used to describe a corporation created by the federal, state, or local government for governmental purposes. When used in the latter sense, the term includes incorporated cities, sanitation districts, school districts, transit districts, and so on.

Corporations that are privately organized for profit but also provide a service upon which the public is dependent are generally referred to as **quasi-public corporations.** In most instances, they are public utilities, which provide the public with such essentials as water, gas, and electricity. (Note: Unless specified otherwise, the discussion in this chapter and those that follow will focus on private corporations.)

Domestic, Foreign, and Alien

A corporation is a **domestic corporation** in the state that grants its charter. It is a **foreign corporation** in all other states. The right to do business in other states (subject to reasonable regulation) is granted by the commerce clause of the U.S. Constitution. In order to qualify to do business in another state, a foreign corporation must obtain a certificate of authority by providing information similar to the information provided by a domestic corporation applying for a charter. A **certificate of authority** is a document that grants a foreign corporation permission to do business within another state. A registered office and agent must be maintained within the state upon which service of process (notice of a lawsuit) may be made on behalf of the corporation. An **alien corporation** is one that, though incorporated in a foreign country, is doing business in the United States.

Close and S Corporations

A business corporation may be designated as a **close corporation** when the outstanding shares of stock and managerial control are closely held by fewer than fifty shareholders (often members of the same family) or by one person. State business corporation statutes generally accommodate closely held corporations by allowing them to have a few directors or a sole director and president with no voting shares in the hands of the public.

The Subchapter S Revision Act of 1982 gives small, closely held, business corporations the option of obtaining special tax advantages by becoming an S corporation. An **S corporation** is a corporation in which shareholders have agreed to have the profits (or losses) of the corporation taxed directly to them rather than to the corporation. In this way they avoid double taxation. There are, however, several restrictions on S corporations. These restrictions include limits on the number and types of owners that can be involved in such an entity. Consequently, many individuals now look to limited liability companies to escape double taxation.

Limited Liability Companies

Twenty-five years ago, various state legislatures began to add a new type of business enterprise to the many forms of doing business that are available in the marketplace today. This enterprise, the **limited liability company (LLC),** is now available in all fifty states. An LLC is best thought of as a cross between a partnership and a corporation. Like a corporation the LLC offers the protection of limited liability to its owners. However, unlike a corporation, the LLC's tax liability flows through the LLC and to the owners. In this way an LLC, like a partnership and an S corporation, escapes the double taxation penalty that falls upon corporate entities.

LLCs are statutory, which means that they may come into existence only if the owners follow the precise steps laid out in the state code by the state legislature. The owners of an LLC are called members. The people who run the LLC are called managers. Later in this chapter the formation details of an LLC are discussed. Chapter 38 includes a discussion of the duties and the responsibilities of the members and the managers of an LLC.

Quick Quiz 37-2 True or False?

1. A private corporation is one that is formed under the authority of a state statute to perform a governmental function.

2. A certificate of authority is issued only to S corporations which have passed the test of associative liability.

3. Limited liability companies have been outlawed in most states because they limit the tax revenue that is due to the government.

37-3 Corporate Formation

A corporation may be incorporated in any state that has a general incorporation statute. Keep in mind that corporations are also subject to court decisions and to the state constitution. Federal agencies such as the Securities and Exchange Commission (SEC) also regulate corporate activity. A proper understanding of effective corporate formation necessitates an examination of promoters, the articles of incorporation, the corporate name, the approval of the articles, and commencement of business. Figure 37-1 illustrates the steps of the incorporation process.

Teaching Tips Certification of authority is obtained by filling out an application, along with other required documents, and submitting them with the Secretary of State. It is important for the applying corporation to consult the Secretary of State to ensure that all statutes are being followed.

Terms An S corporation is sometimes called a *pseudo-corporation.*

Getting Students Involved Write descriptions of the missions and purposes of several imaginary corporations that are in the process of being formed. Assign a different corporation to each group of five students. Each student should represent a type of corporation: public, private, quasi-public, close, S, or LLC. Each student should try to persuade fellow group members that the classification he or she represents is the best for their corporation. Group members should then vote on the classification they think is best.

Did You Know?

The first state statute authorizing the creation of limited liability companies in the United States was passed in Wyoming in 1977.

[A corporation is] an ingenious device for obtaining individual profit without individual responsibility.

—Ambrose Bierce (1842–1914), American author

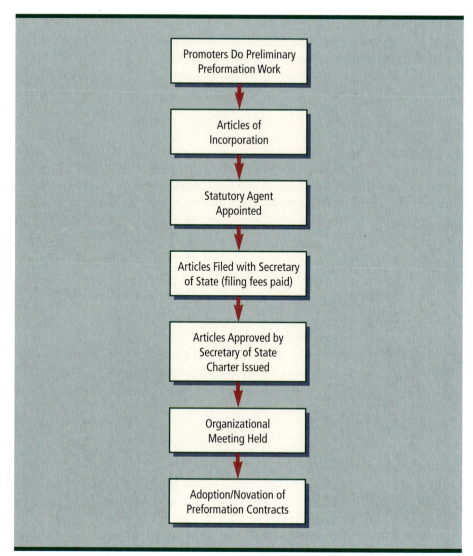

```
┌─────────────────────────┐
│  Promoters Do Preliminary│
│     Preformation Work    │
└─────────────────────────┘
            ↓
┌─────────────────────────┐
│       Articles of        │
│      Incorporation       │
└─────────────────────────┘
            ↓
┌─────────────────────────┐
│     Statutory Agent      │
│        Appointed         │
└─────────────────────────┘
            ↓
┌─────────────────────────┐
│ Articles Filed with Secretary│
│  of State (filing fees paid) │
└─────────────────────────┘
            ↓
┌─────────────────────────┐
│   Articles Approved by   │
│    Secretary of State    │
│      Charter Issued      │
└─────────────────────────┘
            ↓
┌─────────────────────────┐
│      Organizational      │
│      Meeting Held        │
└─────────────────────────┘
            ↓
┌─────────────────────────┐
│   Adoption/Novation of   │
│   Preformation Contracts │
└─────────────────────────┘
```

Figure 37-1   This chart shows the steps in the incorporation process.

Promoters

The people who want to begin a new corporation or who want to incorporate an existing business are called **promoters.** These people do the actual day-to-day work involved in the incorporation process. **Incorporators** are the people who actually sign the articles of incorporation and submit them to the appropriate state officials. The promoters may also be the incorporators who later may become shareholders and directors of the corporation. Promoters occupy a fiduciary relationship with the nonexistent corporation and its future shareholders. This means that the promoter must act in the best interests of the new corporation and its shareholders. The promoter must be honest and loyal and must fully reveal all information about any contracts made for the corporation.

Preformation Contracts Often, promoters will have to enter contracts for the unborn corporation. For example, it may be necessary to lease office and warehouse space, purchase equipment, and hire employees as preliminary steps in preparing the way for the new corporation. A corporation is not bound by any of the promoter's contracts unless it adopts those contracts. Adoption occurs expressly if the directors pass a resolution agreeing to be bound by a contract. Adoption can also occur impliedly if the corporation accepts the benefits of a contract or makes any payments called for by the agreement.

Novation Even after adoption of the contracts, promoters are still potentially liable under the preincorporation contracts. One way for promoters to escape potential liability is to have the corporation and the third party agree to release them. The agreement releasing a promoter is known as a **novation.** The promoter may also include an automatic release clause in all contracts negotiated for the unborn corporation. However, the release clause must do more than simply include the corporation as a party to the contract. It must also specifically release the promoters from liability.

Further Reading *How to Form Your Own California Corporation,* by Anthony Mancuso (Berkeley, CA: Nolo Press, 1998), includes instructions, forms, and text information for small businessowners who want to incorporate. The book is also issued in editions for Florida, Texas, and New York.

A Question of Ethics

Frank Klesner served as a promoter for the formation of a corporation which eventually came to be known as Aerospin, Inc. The Board of Directors of Aerospin, Inc. held an initial organization meeting at which they were asked to ratify several contracts that Klesner had made on behalf of the corporation before the corporation had actually been formed. One of the contracts involved the purchase of an office building in downtown Billings, Montana. Rudy Lawnbridge, one of the directors, knew of an office building that Aerospin, Inc. could get for much less than the price paid for the building purchased by Klesner. Lawnbridge knew that, since the contract for the Billings building did not include a release clause, Aerospin, Inc. did not have to adopt the contract. Legally Lawnbridge is correct, but is it ethical for the board of Aerospin, Inc. to abandon Klesner in this manner? Explain.

Articles of Incorporation

The **articles of incorporation** are the written application to the state for permission to incorporate. This written application is prepared by the corporation's incorporators. The articles, together with the status of incorporation, represent the legal boundaries within which a corporation must conduct its business. Some state incorporation statutes are very strict, requiring detailed information in the articles of incorporation. Typically this information includes the following:

- the corporation's name
- the duration of the corporation
- the purpose(s) of the corporation
- the number and classes of shares
- the shareholders' rights in relation to shares, classes of shares, and special shares
- the shareholders' right to buy new shares
- the addresses of its original registered (statutory) office and its original registered (statutory) agent
- the number of directors plus the names and addresses of the initial directors
- each incorporator's name and address

Other states have simplified this list somewhat, requiring only the name of the corporation, the number of shares originally authorized, the address of the original registered

Teaching Tips To facilitate discussion of this section, obtain the form for a certificate of incorporation and for the appointment of a statutory agent from your local secretary of state's office. Distribute the copies to the class.

Teaching Tips Using the certificate-of-incorporation form as a starting point, create a hypothetical situation that would require students to complete the form. Remember to include the name of the corporation, principal office location, authorized capital stock, and names and addresses of the incorporators.

State Variations In Delaware, a professional corporation which has only one shareholder need have only one director who must be the shareholder and must serve as the president of the corporation.

(statutory) office, the address of the original registered agent, and the incorporators' names and addresses.

The Corporate Name

One of the first steps in forming a corporation is to choose a corporate name. Usually, the words or an abbreviation of the words *corporation, company,* or *incorporated* must appear somewhere in the corporate name. Also, the corporation cannot choose a name that some other corporation already uses or a name that would confuse the new corporation with one already in existence. Even in situations in which a specific state statute does not prohibit the use of similar names, the court will prevent such duplication if confusion or unfair competition results.

Often the secretary of state's office can tell promoters whether a name has been taken. It is also possible to reserve a name. Usually, there is a small fee for this service. Promoters also make certain that they check the availability of a corporate name, not only in the state of incorporation, but also in any state within which they plan to have the corporation do business.

Approval of Articles

After the articles of incorporation are submitted to the state, the appropriate state officer, often the secretary of state, will examine them to make certain that they meet all legal requirements. The secretary of state will also make certain that all filing fees have been paid and that a registered or statutory office and a registered or statutory agent have been appointed. The registered or **statutory agent** is an individual who is designated to receive service of process when a lawsuit is filed against the corporation. Once satisfied that all legal formalities have been met, the secretary of state will issue the corporation's charter, or certificate of incorporation. The charter, or **certificate of incorporation,** is the corporation's official authorization to do business in the state. After the charter is issued, the corporation then becomes a fully and legally incorporated entity. The work of the promoters and incorporators ends, unless they become directors or officers of the corporation.

Commencement of the Business

Most state statutes provide that the first order of business upon incorporation is the holding of an organizational meeting. Some states require that the meeting be run by the initial directors designated in the articles. In contrast, those states that do not require the naming of directors in the articles, allow the organizational meeting to be run by the incorporators. Nevertheless, the first order of business at an incorporator-run meeting is to elect the directors.

In addition to the appointment of the first directors, the adoption of bylaws, or regulations, also occurs at the organizational meeting. **Bylaws** or regulations are the rules that guide the corporation's day-to-day internal affairs. Bylaw provisions usually stipulate the time and place of shareholders' and directors' meetings, quorum requirements, qualifications and duties of directors and officers, and procedures for filling board vacancies.

Formation of a Limited Liability Company

Like a corporation, a limited liability company requires only one person to incorporate. However, the term "person" is liberally defined to include not only people, but also corporations and other legal entities, such as partnerships, limited partnerships, trusts, estates, and so on. The term "person" can even include another LLC. Since not all states recognize the tax advantage usually granted to limited liability companies, it is wise for individuals contemplating the formation of an LLC to check the legal status of such entities in all of the states in which they intend to do business.

Talking Points

One of the central problems of the law is the question of justice. How do jurists know when a decision is just? Is there some sort of internal voice of human nature that tells them they are doing the right thing? Or does the standard for judgment emerge from within the social system. Is it experience, education, or intuition that forms the seat of judgment in these matters? This is the issue that is placed before us by Arnold Brecht in his essay, "Relative and Absolute Justice." Brecht describes this ethical-legal battle in the following way: "What is just, what is unjust? . . . In examinations of these old questions a modern school of relativity has evolved during the last three or four decades, in this and other fields of the social sciences. This school has advanced the doctrine that justice, the idea or feeling of justice (or, as some would say, the idea of right, or the ends of law and justice) are conceptions or phenomena of a relative character, because postulates of justice cannot be ascertained apart from the system of values accepted in a certain period and locality by a certain person or group of persons. Especially will these postulates vary according to whether one regard(s) the individual or the group as the highest value."—Arnold Brecht in his study, "Relative and Absolute Justice," pp. 21–22.

Over the last century, progress has led to pollution, energy shortages, unemployment, new diseases, and, perhaps worst of all, preemptive war. In this context, is progress as highly valued in the twenty-first century as it was in the nineteenth? Which value system is correct? Does such a question even make sense in a system of relative justice? Do you believe in the concept of relative justice or the principle of absolute justice? Explain your answers to each of these questions.

For more information on Brecht's views see: Brecht, Arnold. "Relative and Absolute Justice." In *The Political Philosophy of Arnold Brecht*. Edited by Morris D. Forkosch. New York: Exposition Press, 1954, pp. 21–22.

The Articles of Organization The **articles of organization** are the written application to the state for permission to form a limited liability company. These articles must include the name of the LLC, the duration of the LLC, and the address where the LLC's operating agreement and bylaws are to be kept. If neither the articles nor the operating agreement, as discussed below, include a duration statement, then some state statutes set an automatic duration period, generally of thirty years. In contrast, in the absence of a duration statement, other state statutes set an unlimited duration.

The name of the LLC must include the term "Limited Liability Company," or those words abbreviated followed by the word "Limited," or the abbreviation "Ltd." In addition, the name of the LLC must not be the same as the name of another LLC or of a corporation.

However, a problem may arise when a general partnership is transformed into an LLC. An existing general partnership may discover that it has been using a name that is reserved for a corporation or for an already existing LLC. This will mean changing the name of the existing partnership before it becomes an LLC. Such a change can be bothersome and complicated, not to mention expensive. The only other alternatives in such a situation would be to acquire authorization to use the common name, or to abandon the effort to form an LLC.

In addition, a statutory agent for the service of process must be named at the time that the articles are filed in the office of the secretary of state. Finally, proper filing fees must also be paid. Such fees are generally not exorbitant.

State Variations New York law prohibits corporations from using words or phrases that might suggest government affiliations or otherwise mislead the public about a business's purpose. Examples of such forbidden words are *annuity, benefit, state police, doctor, urban development, casualty, and mortgage.*

The Operating Agreement It is also beneficial for the members of an LLC to draw up an **operating agreement.** Such an agreement, though not required by law in all states, is still very helpful in establishing the bylaws of the LLC, which outline the structure and operation of an LLC. Typically the articles of organization include formation provisions, operating provisions, the nature of the business to be conducted by the LLC, distribution of profits and losses, the powers of the managers, voting rights of the members, admission and withdrawal procedures, provisions regarding the transfer of a member's interest in the LLC, and provisions involving the termination of the LLC, among

Cross-Cultural Notes Other countries besides the United States have adopted forms of the limited liability company. In Germany an LLC is known as "Gessellschaft mit beschrenkter Haftung" ("GmbH"). In Latin America it is referred to as "Limitada."

others. Provisions not covered by the operating agreement are determined by the statute authorizing the creation of LLCs in that state.

Oral Modifications of the Operating Agreement Some state LLC statutes specify that operating agreements can be oral. Under such a provision, certain procedures may inadvertently be added to the operating relationship between the members simply because of a conversation among those members. For this reason, operating agreements should be written even if state law does not require a writing. Moreover, it is wise to add a provision to the written operating agreement which states that there can be no oral modifications to that agreement. Fortunately, even those statutes which allow oral additions to the operating agreement specify that certain things, such as an agreement to make a capital contribution to the LLC, must be in writing to be binding on the members.

Taxation of an LLC Under Internal Revenue Service (IRS) regulations, the status of a business under state law is not the determining factor in establishing whether a firm, such as an LLC, should be taxed as a partnership or a corporation. Rather, the tax status of such an entity depends upon an election made by the owners of that entity. Under the regulations, an entity with two or more members can elect to be treated for tax purposes as an association or as a partnership. An entity owned by one person can elect either association status or a status that will, in effect, hold that the owner and the entity are identical. Election as an association in either situation means that the entity will be taxed as a corporation. The other choice will avoid the corporate tax status.

Quick Quiz 37-3 True or False?

1. An agreement which releases a promoter is called a novation.
2. Bylaws are the rules that guide the corporation's day-to-day internal affairs.
3. Operating agreements for LLCs are required in all states.

37-4 Defective Incorporation

For various liability reasons, the courts may be called upon to decide whether a business entity is a *de jure* corporation, a *de facto* corporation, or a corporation by estoppel.

De Jure Corporation

A corporation whose existence is the result of the incorporators having fully or substantially complied with the relevant corporation statutes is a *__de jure__ corporation.* Its status as a corporation cannot be challenged by private citizens or the state.

De Facto Corporation

Sometimes an error is made in the incorporation process. When this occurs, the corporation does not exist legally. Nevertheless, as long as the following conditions have been met, a *__de facto__ corporation* (a corporation in fact) will exist:

1. A valid state incorporation statute must be in effect.
2. The parties must have made a *bona fide* (good faith) attempt to follow the statute's requirements for incorporation.
3. The business must have acted as if it were a corporation.

Usually, if only some minor requirement has been left unsatisfied, the court will hold that there has been a good faith attempt to incorporate. Only the state can directly challenge the existence of a *de facto* corporation. Thus, a *de facto* corporation has the same rights, privileges, and duties as a *de jure* corporation as far as anyone other than the state is concerned.

Example 37-1

Illya Roosevelt, Barry Kennedy, and Sam Hoover hired Nancy Lincoln, a financial planner, to file incorporation papers for their new corporation, Executive Power, Inc. Unfortunately, Lincoln filed an incomplete set of papers that failed to comply with the state's legal requirements. Nevertheless, Executive Power acted as if it were a corporation establishing a corporate headquarters and several offices in Montana. When one of Executive Power's delivery drivers ran a red light and collided with Allen Johnson, he filed a lawsuit against Executive Power. When Linda Adams, Johnson's attorney, went through discovery, she uncovered the fact that Executive Power had never really been incorporated. She then amended her complaint to name Roosevelt, Kennedy, and Hoover as plaintiffs indicating that, since no corporation existed, the three of them were personally liable. Because Roosevelt, Kennedy, and Hoover had made a good faith attempt to incorporate under an existing incorporation statute, and because they had exercised corporate power, the corporate law doctrine of *de facto* corporation would protect them from personal liability.

Corporation by Estoppel

In some states, if a group of people act as if they are a corporation when in fact and in law they are not, any parties who have accepted that counterfeit corporation's existence will not be allowed to deny that acceptance. Similarly, individuals who acted as if they were a corporation will not be able to deny that the corporation exists. This doctrine has been labeled **corporation by estoppel.** Corporation by estoppel does not create a real corporation. Instead, it is a legal fiction used by the courts on a case-by-case basis to prevent injustice. Generally, it is applied in contract cases rather than in tort cases.

Teaching Tips The Model Business Corporation Act § 2.04 abolishes incorporation by estoppel by explicitly imposing liability on parties who purport to act on behalf of a corporation without incorporating. How does holding the parties personally liable change the law with respect to estoppel?

Quick Quiz 37-4 True or False?

1. The legal status of a *de jure* corporation cannot be challenged by private citizens or the state.

2. The doctrine of the *de facto* corporation requires that there be a *bona fide* attempt to incorporate under an existing incorporation statute and an exercise of corporate power.

3. Corporation by estoppel does not create a real corporation.

37-5 Piercing the Corporate Veil

Sometimes the court will disregard corporate status to impose personal liability on those who have used the corporation to commit fraud or crimes or to harm the public. In such cases, the court will **pierce the corporate veil** and hold the wrongdoers (usually the controlling shareholders) personally liable for activities committed in the corporation's name. The shareholders of close corporations are more likely to fall victim to piercing the corporate veil than the shareholders of large corporations. This is because the shareholders of a close corporation are usually also the directors and officers of the corporation and thus may neglect to follow the corporate formalities required by statute, and/or may fail to keep corporate property and business separate from their personal property and business.

Example 37-2

For twelve years Laurie Bostic ran the Jamestown Beauty and Tanning Salon by herself. On advice from her financial planner, she decided to incorporate. She named herself president and chairperson of the board. She was also the sole shareholder. Despite the incorporation of Jamestown, Bostic continued to run her salon as if it were a sole proprietorship. She failed to keep a separate bank account for the salon and usually simply commingled her personal funds with funds that actually belonged to the corporation. She also used all of the property in the salon as her own personal property. She held no directors' meetings and kept no corporate records. When she was sued by a creditor, the court allowed that creditor to pierce the corporate veil and hold Bostic personally liable. Bostic had failed to maintain a distinction between herself and the corporation so that, even though on paper in the secretary of state's office, they appeared to be different, in reality, they were not.

Veil piercing by the courts is less likely to occur with an LLC because corporate formalities are not required by law for LLCs as they are with a corporation. On the other hand, in many states, the shareholders of a small corporation can enter a close corporation agreement which would allow them to escape the need to follow many corporate formalities.

Large corporations can also fall victim to piercing the corporate veil if they set up subsidiaries, completely control those subsidiaries, and then commit some fraud through the subsidiary. In such cases, however, it is the parent corporation, rather than the individual shareholders, that the courts will hold liable.

The test used to determine whether the corporate veil should be pierced to reach the parent corporation is called the *instrumentality test*. This test requires that the parent corporation so dominate the subsidiary that the subsidiary has become a "mere instrumentality of the parent." In this situation, the courts will allow the veil of the instrumentality to be pierced to reach the dominant corporation and to hold that corporation liable for any harm

---

The Opening Case Revisited
"A Preemptive Pump and Dump!"

In The Opening Case, the SEC issued an order that stopped investors from trading in the shares of over two dozen companies. In doing this, the SEC had launched a preemptive strike against those companies in an attempt to prevent the initiation of any pump and dump scheme that the owners of those shells might be contemplating. In essence, the SEC was declaring that it suspected that each of these corporate shells was merely an instrumentality of its owners that could be used at any time to perpetrate a fraud on unsuspecting investors.

that has been committed through the instrumentality. The courts, however, do not engage in such veil piercing lightly. Still, while the courts respect the separate corporate identity of most subsidiaries, they cannot allow a subsidiary to be used by the parent so that the parent can escape liability. This is especially true if the instrumentality was set up in the first place to commit fraud. When a corporation is set up as a mere instrumentality of a parent, it is sometimes referred to as a **dummy corporation** or as a **corporate shell.**

Quick Quiz 37-5 True or False?

1. Most courts have decided that the practice of corporate veil piercing is actually a form of corporation by estoppel.

2. Large corporations are never subject to veil piercing.

3. The standard used to determine whether the corporate veil should be pierced to reach the parent corporation is called the instrumentality test.

37-6 Corporate Financing

Corporate financing begins when the original investments are made to set up the corporation. Once the corporation is operating, additional corporate financing may be obtained from earnings, loans, and the issuance of additional shares of stock. The issuing and selling of shares of stock in order to raise capital is known as *equity financing,* and the equity securities give their owners a legal interest in the assets, earnings, and control of the corporation. The part of corporation's net profits or surplus that is set aside for the shareholders is known as dividends.

Classes of Corporate Stock

The number of shares and classes of stock that a corporation is authorized to issue are established in its certificate of incorporation. A shareholder who purchases corporate stock invests money or property in the corporation and receives a stock certificate. A **stock certificate** is written evidence of ownership of a unit of interest in the corporation.

Dividends

The most common type of dividend is the **cash dividend,** declared and paid out of current corporate earnings or accumulated surplus at regular intervals. A corporation's board of directors has the sole authority to determine the amount, time, place, and manner of dividend payment. Typically, the directors' declaration of a dividend sets a cutoff date—the date by which a shareholder must hold corporate stock of record in order to receive payment. In a few instances, a distribution of earnings is made in shares of capital stock. This is called a **stock dividend.**

Common Stock The most usual type of corporate stock is **common stock.** Common stock carries with it all the risks of the business, inasmuch as it does not guarantee its holder the right to profits. The shareholder is usually entitled to one vote for each share of stock held. The holders of common stock are paid dividends when the corporation elects to make such a distribution. Holders of common stock risk whatever they invest.

Preferred Stock Those classes of stock that have rights or preferences over other classes of stock are known as **preferred stock.** These preferences generally involve the payment of dividends and/or the distribution of assets on the dissolution of the corporation. Preferred stock may be either cumulative or noncumulative. Generally, dividends on cumulative preferred stock are paid every year. However, if the dividends are not paid in one year, they will be paid in later years if any dividends at all are paid by the corporation. Dividends on noncumulative preferred stock are also usually paid each year. However, with noncumulative preferred stock, dividends that are not paid in one year are lost forever.

Cross-Cultural Notes
The requirements for issuing stocks on the Tokyo Stock Exchange (TSE) are stringent. The TSE requires three years of audited financial statements and certain levels of sales and capital before accepting an initial public offering.

Stock Valuation **Par value** is the value that is placed on the shares of stock at incorporation. This value, which is the same for each share of stock of the same issue, is stated on the corporation's certificate of incorporation. In the case of par value shares, the amount of the capital stock or stated capital is the total par value of all the issued stock.

The practice of placing a par value on a share of stock has been criticized as misleading. Uninformed buyers often interpret par value printed on the face of the certificate as the actual market value of the shares. To correct this condition, all states have authorized the issuance of no par value stock. *No par value stock* is corporate stock that is issued without any stated price. The advantage of stock without par value has been outlined in a Delaware court ruling.

Quick Quiz 37-6 True or False?

1. Corporate financing cannot begin until six months after the certificate of incorporation has been issued.

2. The most common type of dividend is the stock dividend.

3. The practice of placing a par value on a share of stock has been approved of and is now mandated by the American Federated Banking Commission.

Summary

37-1   The process of doing business as a self-governing business association, that is, as a corporation, is called associative corporativism, or simply, corporativism. A corporation is a legal entity (also referred to as a legal person) the creation of which is empowered by a state or a federal statute authorizing individuals to operate an enterprise. A corporation is a legal person and, therefore, has certain constitutional rights such as the right to equal protection of the law and the right not to be deprived of property without due process. Corporations also have dual citizenship. They are citizens of the state in which they are incorporated and in which they have their principal place of business.

37-2   Corporations can be classified in many ways, including private, public, and quasi-public corporations;

domestic and foreign corporations; and close and S corporations. The limited liability company offers the protection of limited liability but allows tax liability to flow through the LLC and to its owners.

37-3   A corporation can be incorporated in any state that has a general incorporation statute. The people who actually start the corporation are the promoters. Promoters are liable on preformation contracts until those contracts are adopted by the corporation. The articles of incorporation are drawn up by the corporation's incorporators. After reviewing the articles of incorporation, the secretary of state will issue a corporate charter, and the corporation becomes a legally incorporated entity. The members of a limited liability company must also follow precise formation procedures.

37-4   A *de jure* corporation is a legally formed corporation. Two doctrines, *de facto* corporation and corporation by estoppel, have been developed to deal with the problem of defective incorporation. A *de facto* corporation exists if there has been a good faith attempt to comply with an existing incorporation statute and an exercise of corporate power. The doctrine of corporation by estoppel prevents later denial of corporate existence by parties willing to deal with an entity as if it were a corporation.

37-5   Under the doctrine of piercing the corporate veil, courts can refuse to recognize a legally formed corporation to prevent injustice and to impose personal liability on the wrongdoers.

37-6   Corporate financing begins when the incorporators give money to set up the business. Subsequent financing takes many forms. The issuing and selling of shares of stock to raise capital is called equity financing. The two most popular classes of stock are common stock and preferred stock. Stock can also be par value or no par value stock. Dividends can be issued as cash or as stock.

Key Terms

alien corporation, 700

articles of incorporation, 703

articles of organization, 705

associative corporativism, 699

bylaws, 704

cash dividend, 709

certificate of authority, 700

certificate of incorporation, 704

close corporation, 701

common stock, 709

corporate shell, 709

corporation, 699

corporation by estoppel, 707

corporativism, 699

de facto corporation, 706

de jure corporation, 706

dividends, 700

domestic corporation, 700

dummy corporation, 709

foreign corporation, 700

incorporators, 702

limited liability, 699

limited liability company (LLC), 701

novation, 703

operating agreement, 705

par value, 710

pierce the corporate veil, 707

preferred stock, 709

private corporation, 700

promoters, 702

public corporation, 700

quasi-public corporation, 700

S corporation, 701

share, 699

shareholders, 700

statutory agent, 704

stock certificate, 709

stock dividend, 709

Questions for Review and Discussion

1. How did the concept of corporativism evolve?
2. What is the nature of a corporation?
3. What are the constitutional rights of a corporation?
4. What is the difference between a close and an S corporation?
5. What are the differences among a private, a public, and a quasi-public corporation?
6. What are the typical elements within the articles of incorporation?
7. What is the difference between the articles of organization and the operating agreement of a limited liability company?
8. What is the difference between a *de jure* and a *de facto* corporation?
9. What is the objective of piercing the corporate veil?
10. What is the difference between common and preferred stock?

Investigating the Internet

Access Hoover's Online website and write a report on a corporation found as part of the list of Hoover's "Companies A-Z." Since much of the information on this site is brief and to the point, it might be a good idea to write a report which compares and contrasts several similarly situated companies.

Cases for Analysis

1. The Aerenthal Financial Loan Corporation lent $578,000 to Raymond Viviani and secured the loan with a mortgage on Viviani's ski lodge which was located south of Burlington, Vermont. Vermont decided to build a new state highway along a route that cut right through Viviani's lodge. Viviani contested the state's decision and attempted to get the highway rerouted. After several months of unsuccessful battles with the state, Viviani decided to settle for the offer from the government. The state then paid Viviani the market value for the property. Unfortunately, the state failed to notify Aerenthal Financial Loan Corporation about the transaction. When Aerenthal discovered that it had not been notified, it filed a formal protest with the state. The state sent its apologies, but argued that Aerenthal had no right to be notified about what was essentially a contractual matter between Viviani and the government. Aerenthal disagreed arguing that the government had violated its constitutional right not to be deprived of property without due process of law. The state responded by noting that under the state constitution it had operated properly and Aerenthal was not entitled to due process. Who is correct here? Explain.

2. General Housing Assistance was incorporated as a nonprofit organization that provides low-cost housing for families who have been economically dislocated because of the downsizing of a company or the outsourcing of jobs. One year after the formation of General Housing Assistance, General Mutual Housing Assistance was incorporated in the same state. General Mutual Housing Assistance sold housing shares in condominiums to subscribers. General Mutual ran an aggressive, often obnoxious advertising campaign. After this campaign, General Housing found that people

were confusing the two entities. The resulting mix-up damaged General Housing Assistance's image and threatened its charitable funding sources. Consequently, it filed suit to stop General Mutual from using the name because of the confusion between the two entities. Are the names similar enough to cause the court to order General Mutual to change its name? Explain.

3. Through Langham Engineering, Michael Langham marketed his invention, the cross-slope monitor (CSM), as an accessory to John Deere equipment. He had a plan to expand his business to include the CSM as an accessory to Caterpillar Tractor (CAT) equipment. To do this, Langham and Clark Balderson of Balderson, Inc., entered a preincorporation agreement (PIA) in which Langham agreed to contribute his technical abilities, and Balderson agreed to contribute his leadership capabilities to manufacture and market the CSM to CAT. No release clause was included in the PIA. The resulting corporation was named Illinois Controls, Inc. Balderson was designated the president and chairman of the board and Langham was named vice president. Over the next two years, Balderson failed to train and motivate the sales staff as to the proper techniques for selling the CSM to CAT dealers. Balderson also neglected to arrange demonstrations and consignment sales, failed to employ properly trained personnel, and disregarded the need to develop, print, and distribute installation manuals for the CSM. Finally, Balderson set up another corporation named the Dymax Corporation, which dealt with CAT's competitors, thereby undermining Illinois Control's relationship with CAT. As a result, Illinois Controls was forced to shut down operations. Langham sued Balderson personally for the losses that he incurred as a result of Balderson's

failure to meet his obligations as outlined in the PIA. Balderson argued that the PIA was a promoter's contract and that the corporation had adopted it. Therefore, Illinois Controls should be held liable. Was Balderson correct? Explain. *Illinois Controls, Inc., v. Langham,* 639 N.E.2d 771 (OH).

4. Harry and Kay Robinson of New York purchased a new Audi automobile from World Wide Volkswagen (WWV) in New York. After having an accident in Oklahoma, they brought a product liability action against WWV. The case was brought to court in Oklahoma. The Robinsons claimed that the injuries they suffered were caused by the defective design and placement of their automobile's gas tank and fuel system. WWV, which was incorporated in New York and did business there, contended that the Robinsons could not sue WWV in Oklahoma because it was not a citizen of Oklahoma. WWV further contended that it performed no services, owned no property, and closed no sales in Oklahoma. It solicited no business in Oklahoma either through salespersons or through advertising. It also did not indirectly through others serve or seek to serve the Oklahoma market. Did the Oklahoma state court have jurisdiction over WWV? Explain. *World Wide Volkswagen Corporation v. Woodson,* 100 S.Ct. 559 (U.S. Sup. Ct.).

5. Spence was a promoter in the incorporation of a new business. The new corporation had not yet been formed when he bought Huffman's employment agency to serve as the nucleus of that corporation. Eventually, the corporation was formed, but it never generated enough cash to pay Huffman for the employment agency. Huffman sued Spence, attempting to hold him personally liable for the amount due. Spence claimed that the corporation was liable and that his personal assets were not a property target of the suit. Was Spence correct? Explain. *Spence v. Huffman,* 486 P.2d 211 (AZ).

6. MBI filed its original articles of incorporation under the name Montana Public Employees Benefit Services Co., Inc. After filing the articles, the corporation entered a contract with the Montana Department of Administration. Under the contract, the new corporation would have exclusive administrative control over Montana's public employee deferred-payment pension plan. The articles were not approved by the secretary of state who requested a name change. After the corporation's name was changed to MBI, the charter was issued

and the corporation became a legal entity. The Montana Association of Underwriters, a private corporation that wanted a share in administering the state pension plan, challenged the validity of the contract, arguing that at the time the contract was signed, MBI did not legally exist. Was the Montana Association of Underwriters correct? Explain. *Montana Association of Underwriters v. Department of Administration and MBI,* 563 P.2d 577 (MT).

7. Lamas Company, Inc., was incorporated in Georgia. Baldwin negotiated with Lamas, sole owner of Lamas Company, Inc., to finish some electrical work on a construction site. When Baldwin was dissatisfied with the work, he decided to sue. Unfortunately, the statute of limitations ran out before he could sue Lamas Company, Inc., and so he sued Lamas individually. Baldwin argued that he had dealt only with Lamas, that he did not know Lamas was an agent of the company, that Lamas did not tell him about the company, and that he understood the contract to be with Lamas individually. Lamas pointed out that Baldwin made out and sent checks directly to Lamas Company, Inc., and that Lamas Company, Inc., always appeared as the payee on those checks. Lamas claimed that this evidence alone would be enough to stop Baldwin from denying that he had dealt with Lamas Company, Inc. The trial court rendered judgment against Lamas. On appeal, did the appellate court reverse? Explain. *Lamas v. Baldwin,* 230 S.E.2d 13 (GA).

8. Boafo was allegedly injured while giving birth at Parkway Regional Hospital. Boafo sued both Parkway Regional and Hospital Corporation of America (HCA), asking the court to pierce the corporate veil to reach HCA, which Boafo claimed was a parent company. Boafo showed that the two corporations shared the same offices, that they purchased hospital equipment together, that HCA owned 100 percent of Parkway stock, that major financing for Parkway was performed by HCA through a national accounting system, and that Parkway was insured by another wholly owned subsidiary of HCA. In answer, HCA emphasized that Parkway handled its own daily financing, that it was free to negotiate and enter its own contracts, that it had an adequate amount of money in its treasury, and that it was not formed to promote fraud, conceal crime, or evade legal liability. The trial court granted summary judgment, dismissing the claim against HCA. Did the appellate court

uphold the trial court's ruling? Explain. *Boafo v. Hospital Corporation of America,* 338 S.E.2d 477 (GA).

9. The Northeastern Corporate Institute of Technology (NCIT), a profit oriented corporation engaged in nuclear research projects, owned and operated an experimental station in a remote region of Alaska. The Alaskan Chemical Disposal Corporation, a subsidiary of NCIT, disposed of all chemical and nuclear waste products produced by NCIT's experimental station. On a routine disposal route, an Alaskan Chemical Disposal transport convoy collided with a North Coast moving van. The lead truck in the convoy spilled chemical waste into a lake owned by Kenneth Ridgeway. Ridgeway sued both NCIT and Alaskan Chemical Disposal. NCIT argued that the disposal of NCIT's chemical was the sole responsibility of Alaskan Chemical Disposal, which it characterized as an independent contractor. Ridgeway's attorney, however, had discovered that Alaskan Chemical Disposal had no business other than providing waste disposal services to NCIT. The attorney also discovered that Alaskan Chemical Disposal was listed as a division of NCIT, was financed by NCIT, and shared the same board of directors and officers as NCIT. Moreover, the attorney found out that Alaskan Chemical Disposal was badly undercapitalized. In addition, all decisions in the running of Alaskan Chemical Disposal were made by NCIT. In light of all of this evidence, Ridgeway's attorney began to suspect that Alaskan Chemical Disposal might have been formed to allow NCIT to escape liability in just this type of situation. Will Ridgeway be allowed to maintain its suit against NCIT? Explain.

Quick Quiz Answers

37-1	37-2	37-3	37-4	37-5	37-6
1. T	1. F	1. T	1. T	1. F	1. F
2. T	2. F	2. T	2. T	2. F	2. F
3. F	3. F	3. F	3. T	3. T	3. F

Chapter 38 Corporate Governance

The Opening Case
"The Shareholder's Dilemma"

Victor Vasily, a minority shareholder in Harrington Industries, Inc., was upset with the management of the corporation because they had decided to shut down a factory that had been operating for years in his hometown of Ontario, Indiana. He was also concerned that management had decided to spend over 14 million dollars in an attempt to become a state-of-the art facility in the research and development of nanotechnology. Vasily was certain that the funds would not be spent properly and that a great deal of the money would be wasted pursuing what he referred to as "science fiction nonsense." He was also concerned that the experiments in nanotechnology would be dangerous and expensive. Finally, Vasily opposed the firing of a long time vice-president of development who shared his views on the dangerous foray that Harrington Industries was about to take into nanotechnology research. What options does Vasily have, assuming that he is unable or unwilling to sell his shares and abandon Harrington Industries altogether? Can he increase his voting power without purchasing more shares? Could he use cumulative voting if he wanted to? What about a voting trust? Can he do that alone or would he need other shareholders to help him in that endeavor? Is a pooling agreement an option in this case? What are the rules surrounding a proxy solicitation venture? Can Vasily file a shareholder proposal with the directors? If he does file a shareholder proposal, does the board have to present his proposal to the rest of the shareholders? What about a shareholder lawsuit? Can Vasily file a direct suit against the directors of the corporation? Can he file a derivative suit? What rules govern the filing of both types of lawsuits? These and other issues like them are addressed in this chapter on corporate governance.

Chapter Outcomes

1. Explain the central dilemma of corporate governance.
2. Describe the functions of directors, officers, and shareholders.
3. List the five theories of corporate governance.
4. Describe cumulative voting and proxy solicitation.
5. Distinguish between voting trusts and pooling agreements.
6. Explain shareholder proposals.
7. Contrast shareholder direct suits with shareholder derivative suits.
8. Contrast the business judgment rule with the fairness rule.
9. List the rights that belong to shareholders.
10. Explain the management of a limited liability company.

38-1 Management of the Corporation

Most state incorporation statutes provide that a corporation's business affairs are to be managed under the direction of a board of directors. The board of directors establishes broad policies, and the officers and other employees implement those policies. How to keep the role of the board separate from that of executive management is related to the challenge of how best to organize the board and select its members. The issues are even more complex today because a single individual often functions as both a director and an officer. Nevertheless, the two roles have distinct functions and should be examined separately.

Board of Directors

The business affairs of a corporation are managed by a board of directors elected by the shareholders. The board's responsibility is to take whatever actions are appropriate, in keeping with the corporation's rules and regulations, to further the corporation's business. Individual board members are supposed to use their own judgment in the corporate decision-making process.

Qualifications of Directors State law and corporate rules set up the qualifications that a person must have to be a corporate director. Unless prohibited by the corporation's certificate of incorporation, membership on the board of directors can be extended to anyone, including aliens, minors, and nonshareholders. Often the certificate stipulates that at least one director is a state resident and at least one is a shareholder.

Time Commitment of Directors Directors are elected at the annual meeting of the shareholders. Generally, directors hold office for one or two years. The number of directors on the board varies between eight and twelve. Usually, several directors are elected as a group to maintain continuity; this procedure permits one-third of the board to be elected annually. The basic time commitment for a director is approximately thirty days per year, but depending upon need, availability, and interest, it can be forty, sixty, eighty, or even more days. Naturally, directors can resign from the board. However, many states require a handwritten notice of the director's resignation to the corporation.

Meetings of Directors The directors of most large corporations meet on a regular basis at a precise time and place of their choosing. The directors of many smaller corporations meet only when specific items are to be considered. Some states allow small corporations having fewer than fifty shareholders to eliminate the board of directors entirely, as long as someone is assigned the duties that the board would have performed.

Directors are not entitled to be notified about regular board meetings unless notice is required by the corporation's bylaws. (The bylaws, or regulations of a corporation, determine how that corporation will operate.) However, directors must be notified of special meetings of the board. For example, a special meeting of the directors might be called to decide whether the corporation should institute a lawsuit. If any director is not notified of a special meeting, all actions taken at the meeting are void. A director may not specify another person to vote in her or his place. The quorum, or minimum number of directors necessary to conduct business, is usually one more than half of the total number of directors. Bylaws may require more than a quorum, perhaps 70 percent of the directors, to conduct certain types of business. This supermajority might be needed, for instance, to remove a director or to sell a significant portion of the business. Generally, though, the actions of a quorum constitute the official actions of the board.

Background Information A corporation's board of directors usually has the right to hire officers of the corporation, determine corporate policy, and authorize loans, real estate purchases, and pension plans.

State Variations Under Nevada law, the president of any loan association or lending institution must have at least ten years of experience working in a financial institution.

Background Information Most corporations need at least three directors. When all of the shares are held by fewer than three people, there can be fewer than three directors as long as they are not fewer than the number of shareholders.

Teaching Tips Inform students that boards of directors traditionally take formal action by vote. Each member has one vote; and a director may not vote by proxy.

Terms The term *quorum*, which comes from Latin, first appeared in Middle English in reference to justices of the peace whose presence was necessary to constitute a court. Today, *quorum's* meaning has broadened, referring to those who must be present before any business is conducted.

> ## Example 38-1
>
> The board of directors of Barber Enterprises, Inc. consisted of seven persons. At a properly called meeting, one of the directors presented a motion calling for a stock-option purchase plan for Barber's president, vice presidents, secretary, and treasurer. Five directors attended the meeting. This constituted a quorum. Three of the five voted for the plan. This vote would constitute an official act by the board.

Officers of the Corporation

Directors are not expected to spend all of their time and energy managing the corporation. They have the authority to appoint officers and agents to run the day-to-day affairs of the corporation. By statute, the usual officers are a president, several vice presidents, a secretary, and a treasurer. Other officers, such as a comptroller, cashier, and general counsel, are often provided. The bylaws of the corporation describe the duties of each officer. Officers have the authority of general agents for the operation of the normal business of the corporation. They, in turn, delegate duties to various department heads. Although the roles of directors and officers differ, they are frequently assumed by the same people. An individual may be both chief executive officer and chairman of the board of the same corporation. Directors and officers can also be shareholders in the corporation.

> ## Quick Quiz 38-1 True or False?
>
> 1. The business affairs of a corporation are managed by a board of directors elected by the shareholders.
>
> 2. Membership on a board of directors can never be extended to aliens, minors, or nonshareholders.
>
> 3. Directors have authority to appoint officers and agents to run the day-to-day affairs of the corporation.

38-2 Issues in Corporate Governance

Under the original concept of a corporation, the shareholders are the primary reason that a corporation exists. This image, has, nevertheless, evolved over the years, so the shareholders often take a back seat to consumers, employees, environmentalists, politicians, social science engineers, and economists. This is why the corporate landscape has come to resemble a battlefield in recent years. There are those who believe that the battle is a good thing because it helps make corporations more responsible. There are others, however, who believe that the battle has weakened, and in some cases, completely dismantled, corporate power. Which side has correctly diagnosed the problem remains to be seen. For the present, we can examine five different points of view on how a corporation ought to be governed. These include special interest group control, governmental control, independent director control, managerial control, and shareholder democratic control.

Theories of Corporate Governance

As noted above, five theories have been put forth by legal scholars and business experts concerning how corporations should be managed. These theories are special interest group control, governmental control, independent director control, managerial control, and share-holder democracy.

Special Interest Group Control

Special interest group control is based upon the fact that corporate decision making impacts upon more individuals and groups than just the shareholders and the managers of the corporation. The people who support special interest group control argue that many corporate decisions, such as a decision to open or close a factory, affect the community through its consumers, suppliers, employees, and community neighbors. Consequently, all of these groups and more should be represented on the boards of directors of all major corporations. Individuals who support special interest group control would like to see representatives from the employees' unions, from consumer protection organizations, and from environmental protection groups on these boards. Opponents of the theory point out the impracticality of this approach to corporate management.

Governmental Control

Support for the **governmental control** theory of corporate management is based upon the belief that because corporate decision making impacts upon more individuals and groups than just the shareholders and the managers, those corporate decisions should be made by an impartial group of corporate outsiders. Usually, the corporate outsiders named are government officials. These specially educated government officials would make corporate decisions in an objective manner, based upon the needs of the entire society and the economy as a whole. Opponents of this theory label such an approach socialistic and point to the relatively poor record of many socialist economies as evidence of the impracticality of this approach.

Independent Director Control

A third theory of corporate control involves the establishment of independent directors. Those theorists who support the use of independent directors argue that the most effective way to ensure that corporate decisions are made in the best interests of those affected is to make certain that the decision makers themselves are not affected by those decisions. Some groups have already implemented requirements to ensure the addition of independent directors to the boards of many corporations. For instance, both the New York Stock Exchange and the Nasdaq Stock Market require companies to have boards that consist of a majority of independent directors. **Independent directors** are defined as directors who have no family members employed by the corporation, who are not themselves employed by the corporation, or, if they were at one time employed by the corporation, have not been on the staff for at least three years. There is, of course, an "opt out" rule that permits some corporations to sidestep the independent directors' rule if they are a "controlled" company. A **controlled company** is one that has more than half its voting power concentrated in one person, or a small group of persons, who always vote together. The "opt out" provision is designed to give parent companies which are already controlled by independent boards, a technique for eliminating a duplication of the independence restriction in their subsidiaries.

Managerial Control

The fourth approach to corporate governance is **managerial control.** Those who favor managerial control point out that the officers and the directors of a corporation are in the best position for judging not only the needs of the corporation but also the needs of the community and the needs of society at large. Individuals who favor managerial control would insulate the managers from shareholders by limiting the shareholders' power to vote and by making it difficult for shareholders to sue managers. Opponents of managerial control argue that corporate managers may tend to be self-interested and may, as a result, make relatively short-sighted decisions.

Shareholder Democracy

Individuals who favor **shareholder democracy,** or **corporate democracy** as it is also known, believe that the shareholders have the right to run the corporation because without their money the corporation would not be able to survive. As the real owners of the corporation, the shareholders have a right to say how their money and their property should be used. Supporters of shareholder democracy would make management more responsive to shareholders by giving shareholders greater voting control and by making it easier for them to take managers to court. Opponents of this theory point out that most shareholders are removed from the center of corporate activity and therefore cannot make the same type of informed decisions that the managers can make. Today there is a delicate balance between the theories of managerial control and shareholder democracy. Therefore, the chapter will focus on the battle between these two positions as it examines the subject of corporate control. The two most significant areas of this conflict lie in shareholder voting control and shareholder lawsuits. Shareholders can influence corporate decision making through their voting powers and through their right to initiate a lawsuit against managers (see Table 38-1).

Shareholder Voting Control

Shareholders usually receive one vote per share of common stock held. Shareholders who are dissatisfied with management can attempt to buy more shares to increase their voting power. With this increased voting power, the dissatisfied or dissident shareholders can influence the election of the board of directors. However, shareholders are not always able to buy more shares of the corporation, either because they cannot afford them or because the other shareholders are not willing to sell. In such cases, shareholders can resort to one of the other voting methods available:

- cumulative voting
- proxy solicitation
- voting trusts
- pooling agreements
- shareholder proposals
- shareholder nominations
- unanimous voting restrictions

Cumulative Voting Ordinarily, each share of common stock is worth one vote. Therefore, only a majority of shareholders can elect directors of the corporation. To give minority shareholders an opportunity to elect one or more directors, some states permit **cumulative voting.** This system allows shareholders to multiply the number of their voting

Table 38-1 Shareholder Control	
Votes and Lawsuits	**Explanation**
Voting control:	
Cumulative voting	Each share of stock has as many votes as there are directors to be elected
Proxy voting	The right to vote another shareholder's stock
Voting trusts	An agreement among shareholders to transfer their voting rights to a trustee
Pooling agreements	Shareholders join together in a temporary arrangement, agreeing to vote the same way on a particular issue
Shareholder proposals	A suggestion about a broad company policy or procedure submitted by a shareholder and included in management's proxy solicitation
Shareholder suits:	
Direct suit	A suit brought by shareholders who have been deprived of a right
Derivative suit	A suit brought by shareholders based on an injury to the corporation

shares by the number of directors to be elected. All these votes may be cast for one candidate or distributed among several candidates. This procedure allows minority shareholders an opportunity to be represented on the board of directors.

State Variations In Tennessee, the failure to hold the annual meeting does not affect the validity of any corporate action.

Example 38-2

Beth General, James Garrett, Ken Collins, and Heather Gilliam were presented to the shareholders as candidates for the board of directors of Shopton Enterprises, Inc. Three of the four were to be chosen. Since cumulative voting was authorized, the minority shareholders cast all their weighted votes for Gilliam, who had promised to represent the minority voice in corporate affairs. Had the minority voters been allowed only one vote for each share instead of three, they might have failed in their effort to elect a favored director.

Proxy Voting
A **proxy** is the authority given to one shareholder to cast another shareholder's votes. **Proxy solicitation** is the process by which one shareholder asks another for his or her voting right. Proxy solicitation also refers to the actual document that is used to request the right to vote the other shareholders' votes. The minority shareholder's voting power increases as the number of proxies held rises. Since majority shareholders, including management, can also solicit proxies, a struggle between the two groups, known as a **proxy contest,** often results. Proxy contests involving large publicly held corporations are closely regulated by the Securities and Exchange Commission (SEC). This regulation is examined in Chapter 39.

Voting Trusts
A **voting trust** is an agreement among shareholders to transfer their voting rights to a trustee. A **trustee** is a person who is entrusted with the management and control of another's property or the rights associated with that property. Sometimes, the trustee is one of the shareholders; at other times the trustee is an outsider. The trustee votes those shares at the annual shareholders' meeting at the direction of the shareholders. Shareholders surrender only their voting rights. All other rights, including the right to receive profits,

Background Information States often use the following criteria to identify a true voting trust: There is a grant of voting rights for an indefinite period of time; the acquisition of voting control of the corporation is the common purpose of the shareholders to the trust; the voting rights are separated from the other attributes of stock ownership.

Stockholders exercise their control through votes at annual meetings and through proxies.

remain with them. Generally, once a voting trust has been created, it cannot be ended until the specified time period has run its course. However, state statutes usually place a maximum time limit on the duration of a voting trust. Most state time limits run from ten to twenty-one years. Voting trusts must be in writing and must be filed with the corporation.

Pooling Agreements   Sometimes, shareholders join together in a temporary arrangement agreeing to vote the same way on a particular issue. Such agreements are known as **pooling agreements,** shareholder agreements, or voting agreements. They differ from proxies and voting trusts because the shareholders retain control of their own votes. In this sense, pooling agreements are also the weakest voting arrangement because shareholders can change their votes at the last minute. If a member of a pooling agreement changes her or his vote, however, the other members may bring a lawsuit against the shareholder who broke the agreement. In general, pooling agreements are interpreted by the court under principles of contract law.

Shareholder Proposals   Another alternative allows shareholders to influence corporate affairs, even if they cannot engage in cumulative voting, solicit proxies, create a voting trust, or join in a pooling agreement. Under SEC guidelines, shareholders of large, publicly owned corporations can compel management to include their proposals in management's proxy solicitation prior to the next shareholder meeting. A **shareholder proposal,** then, is a suggestion about a broad company policy or procedure that is submitted by a shareholder. The proposal cannot be about the ordinary business operation of the corporation. It must concern something that affects all shareholders. A proposal to hire or fire a particular employee would not qualify, whereas a proposal to amend the corporate charter would.

To qualify as a valid shareholder proposal under SEC rules, the proposal must be no more than 500 words long and must be submitted to management at least 120 days before the shareholders' meeting. In addition, the shareholder must own at least 1 percent or

Business Law in the News
Less Laissez-Faire In Delaware?

When Shareholders sued four Oracle Corp. directors in 2001 alleging insider trading, the company's board promptly appointed two outside directors to investigate. The duo cleared the directors, including Chairman and CEO Lawrence J. Ellison, and asked Delaware's Chancery Court to toss out the lawsuit. That normally would have ended the matter in Corporate America's home court, where judges have traditionally deferred to the wisdom of board members and independent directors.

But Judge Leo E. Strine Jr. was disturbed by the web of social and philanthropic ties between the investigators and the directors they were probing. The two specially appointed outsiders were professors at Stanford University—employer of one of the defendant directors, alma mater of another, and recipient of $300,000 in Oracle donations and a $10 million gift from Ellison's own foundation. "This was a social

atmosphere painted in too much vivid Stanford Cardinal red for the [committee] members to have reasonably ignored it," Strine wrote in his June, 2003, opinion. Ruling that the outside directors weren't independent, he allowed shareholders to pursue their suit.

Clearly, aftershocks of the recent wave of corporate scandals are finally hitting Wilmington. In the wake of reforms by Congress, the Securities & Exchange Commission, and the major stock exchanges, Delaware's Chancery Court, too, is tightening the screws on Corporate America. The five-judge court, long pilloried as pro-management, is allowing shareholder suits it would have tossed out in years past. In a handful of high-profile cases over the past 18 months, Delaware judges have sided with shareholders on issues from exorbitant CEO pay to director independence (table). "This signals a new ball game on Delaware's part," says Charles M. Elson, a

University of Delaware governance expert. "The old regime of 'management can do what it wants' is over."

A Tiny State's Big Clout

The consequences could be profound. Internal business dealings are largely governed by state law, and tiny Delaware dominates the field. More than half of all publicly traded companies are incorporated in the state, making Delaware jurisprudence virtually the national corporate law. Rulings there demanding greater corporate accountability ultimately could do more to improve boardroom behavior than the Sarbanes-Oxley Act or many of the reforms approved by the SEC.

Traditionally, Delaware has given companies a wide berth under the so-called business judgment rule, which holds that courts won't second-guess boards as long as directors act reasonably and in good faith. That has made it hard for governance critics to successfully challenge board decisions. Now, the scope of the rule is being narrowed.

Consider the issue of CEO pay. Judge William B. Chandler III last May refused to dismiss a shareholder lawsuit that challenged Walt Disney Co.'s $140 million severance payment to former President Michael Ovitz. "The facts belie any assertion that [Disney directors] exercised *any* business judgment or made *any* good faith attempt to fulfill the fiduciary duties they owed to Disney and its shareholders," Chandler wrote.

In another decision in January that put independence under a microscope, Chandler ruled that certain eBay Inc., outside directors weren't disinterested, because they held huge option grants that would not vest unless they were reelected. That effectively undermined their ability to decide whether to pursue shareholder claims that eBay's investment bank, Goldman Sachs & Co., bribed company insiders with hot stock offerings. Chandler also castigated eBay officials for pocketing the initial public offerings, which could be considered a gratuity that belonged to the company.

"Gimlet-Eyed Skepticism"

Why are Delaware judges putting boards in the hot seat? In part, they're simply reacting to the corporate crime wave. Judges insist they're not reinterpreting the law but reacting to new trends, such as the astronomical sums now lavished on CEOs. "There will continue to be gimlet-eyed skepticism by stockholders of compensation unless boards demonstrate that they're taking a businesslike approach," says Strine in an interview with *BusinessWeek.* "And if [stockholders] can show that there is no rational business reason for the level of pay, under traditional standards they have a claim."

So far, the shift in rulings from the bench hasn't deterred companies from flocking to Delaware. While other states have attempted to lure corporations with special business courts, they still lack the vast body of legal precedent that exists in Delaware. In 2003, 68% of the 73 companies that went public incorporated there, say state officials.

And surely, clubby Delaware—where lawyers and judges regularly cross paths lunching at Libby's, a Wilmington greasy spoon—is no hotbed of reform. The state's dependence on the corporate law industry is likely to deter radical moves. Franchise taxes and fees generate about a third of state revenues. But there's no mistaking the signals. "The court is sending a message that it wants boards to be more engaged," says former judge William T. Allen, director of New York University's Center for Law & Business. That's good news for shareholders in all 50 states.

Questions for Analysis

1. Why do so many corporate lawsuits occur in the state of Delaware?

2. Traditionally how has the Delaware Court treated the business judgment rule? What has been the result of this treatment? Explain. How has this traditional treatment of the rule been altered recently? Explain.

3. Why has the Delaware Court changed its attitude toward the business judgment rule? Explain.

4. Has this change in judicial attitude altered the movement of corporations to Delaware? Why or why not?

5. What may prevent any more radical changes in corporate law in Delaware? Explain.

Source: Amy Borrust. "Less Laissez-Faire In Delaware," *BusinessWeek,* March 22, 2004, pp. 80, 82.

$1,000 in market value of the voting stock of the corporation and may submit only one proposal at a time. Even then, managers can reject the proposal if they feel that it does not qualify as a valid shareholder proposal under a lengthy list of disqualifying characteristics cataloged by the SEC. Included on this list are proposals that are personal grievances and those that are beyond the corporation's power.

For more detail on the ideas discussed in this segment of Talking Points see: Lekachman, Robert. "The Analysis of Capitalism." In *A History of Economic Ideas.* New York: McGraw-Hill, 1959, pp. 398–399; Sievers, Allen M. "Schumpeter and His Work" and "Schumpeter the Conservative." In *Revolution, Evolution, and the Economic Order.* Englewood Cliffs, NJ: Prentice Hall, 1962, pp. 26–58.

Talking Points

Corporate risk takers will be successful only if they can avoid the inclination to move from a simple, practical operation to one that is strangled by unnecessarily formal procedures. This is the issue that is placed before us by Robert Lekachman in his essay, "The Analysis of Capitalism." In this essay, Lekachman describes the economic philosophy of Joseph Alois Schumpeter in the following way:

"Schumpeter identified four major changes in capitalism, all of them by-products of success. Increasingly, corporate bureaucracy had substituted itself for the entrepreneur. This was the most important change. Invention had become a social process, the product of group research supported and controlled in great laboratories, administered by large corporations. . . . With the replacement of the entrepreneur by the salaried employee, the organization man, the dynamic of capitalism vanished. For the salaried administrator will work just as readily for the state after industry has been nationalized. He may scarcely know the difference."—Robert Lekachman in his study, "The Analysis of Capitalism," pp. 398–399.

Is Schumpeter correct that the ultimate future of corporate governance is corporate bureaucracy? If Schumpeter is correct is this necessarily a bad thing? Can you think of situations in which corporate bureaucracy might be a good thing, that is, when it might actually fuel progress rather than hamper it? Or is bureaucracy always destructive? Explain your answers to each of these questions.

Example 38-3

The shareholders of The Boeing Company were asked to vote on a shareholder proposal that recommended that the Board of Directors institute a committee to look into the possibility of establishing a set of guidelines for the handling of military contracts. Such a proposal met the substantive requirements of SEC rules, in that it involves a suggestion about a broad company policy rather than the ordinary business operation of the corporation. Moreover, the action proposed by the shareholders did not involve a personal grievance and was clearly within the corporation's power to implement.

When a shareholder proposal appears on a ballot, it is generally accompanied by supporting and opposing arguments. The supporting arguments are presented by the shareholder or shareholders who authored the proposal while the opposing arguments are offered by corporate management. Usually shareholders can expect management to oppose most of their proposals because, if the managers supported a particular proposal, the shareholders would not have had to submit the proposal in the first place.

Example 38-4

In the shareholder proposal mentioned in Example 38-3, the shareholders argued that all people have a duty to promote peace and justice and that, as a part of this social duty, individuals must scrutinize and evaluate the ethical nature of corporate activities. Accordingly, the shareholders suggested that their proposed ethics committee look at several issues including the consequences of making military contracts with repressive governments, the effects of military contracts on geopolitical stability, and the repercussions that may flow from technology transfer contracts. In opposition, management said that the corporation already complies with all federal laws and regulations in regard to the sale and export of military equipment. Moreover, the Audit Committee of the Board of Directors supervises the work of the Ethics and Conduct Office, which has ethics advisors working within the corporation.

A Question of Ethics

After reading the two positions in the Boeing situation, explain which of the two points of view you find to be the more ethical attitude. Refer to Chapter 1, "Ethics," as you formulate a defense for the stand that you have adopted.

Shareholder Nominations Another way to increase the voting power of shareholders is to augment their ability to elect a director or directors who will represent their point of view in crucial issues facing the company. Several ways to do this include enacting state statutes, altering SEC rules, or changing stock exchange regulations so that certain events will trigger the ability of shareholders to elect board members. One such triggering event might be coupled with a shareholder proposal to permit shareholders to nominate their own directors. The rules might permit this nomination process to go forward as long as 50 percent of the votes cast (not 50 percent of the available votes, but 50 percent of those votes which are actually used in an election) support such a proposal. Another triggering event might be the ability of the minority shareholders to reach a 35 percent to 50 percent (depending on how the rule is worded) margin of voters who block the election of a management-nominated board candidate. Should either of these events occur, the minority shareholders would be permitted to place their own director on the next ballot at the expense of the corporation.

Unanimous Voting Restrictions An additional approach to strengthening the power of the shareholders involves a change in the corporate bylaws that makes it more difficult for the board to approve crucial issues that affect the fate of the corporation. The new voting bylaws would require unanimous agreement among all directors when the issue before the board involves a critical matter such as a merger, the sale of corporate assets, or a large increase in the salary of a top officer. Under current bylaws, one director with one vote on a board of twelve is of little consequence. However, under the revised regulations requiring the unanimous approval of the board when major issues are decided, a single board member would have the power to block any material change contemplated by the rest of the board. The fact that a single director would have the power to stop major changes in corporate structure and policy might encourage minority shareholders to join forces in a campaign to elect their own director to the board.

Combinations While each of these voting techniques is discussed separately, in practice they can be combined to increase shareholder voting power. For example, a group of minority shareholders could enter a pooling agreement in which they all agree to cast their cumulative votes for a single board candidate. It is even possible for one of the voting techniques to be used to institute another of those techniques.

Example 38-5

A second shareholder proposal on the ballot at the Boeing shareholders' meeting mentioned in Example 38-3 asked shareholders to institute cumulative voting at Boeing. Supporters stated that cumulative voting would help establish a wide range of diversity within the board of directors. Moreover, cumulative voting would encourage the election of independent directors with the expertise needed to pull the corporation out of its downward spiral. Management, on the other hand, argued against the proposal noting that cumulative voting would curtail the effectiveness of the board of directors. In addition, the election of a director who must represent the views of the minority shareholders would undermine the duty that directors have to represent all shareholders equally.

Shareholder Lawsuits

The battle between management and dissident shareholders may also be waged on a front other than the annual shareholders' meeting. That front is the courtroom. Shareholders can sue management to compel a change in direction or to force management to overturn a decision. The two types of suits available to shareholders are direct suits and derivative suits.

Direct Suits A **direct suit** is brought by shareholders who have been deprived of a right that belongs to them as shareholders. These rights include the right to vote, the right to receive dividends, the right to transfer shares, the right to purchase newly issued stock, and the right to examine corporate books and records. If shareholders have been denied any of these rights, they can bring a direct suit to make up for any loss they have suffered.

Derivative Suits A **derivative suit** allows shareholders to sue corporate management on behalf of the corporation. Unlike a direct suit, a derivative suit is not based on a direct injury to a shareholder. Instead, the injury is to the corporation. The shareholders' right to sue is *derived* from the corporate injury. Shareholders who bring a successful derivative suit are entitled to recover attorney fees.

To bring a derivative suit, shareholders must meet certain prerequisites. One prerequisite is the exhaustion of internal remedies. Before bringing suit, the shareholder must attempt to solve the problem by communicating with the board of directors and with other shareholders. In their original complaint commencing the derivative action, the shareholders must state the steps that they took to exhaust all internal remedies. If the shareholders have not exhausted internal remedies and still insist on bringing the lawsuit, the court will dismiss the case and deny any request from the shareholders for the payment of attorney fees.

In order to bring a derivative suit, a shareholder must also own stock at the time of the injury and at the time of the suit. This is known as the **rule of contemporary ownership.** Frequently, state corporate laws also require derivative suit plaintiffs to pay a security deposit to cover the corporation's potential expenses in defending the derivative suits. All of these requirements make it difficult for a shareholder to bring a derivative lawsuit.

Related Cases A minority shareholder brought direct action against a corporation to enforce its right to obtain financial statements and inspect its corporate records. The court found in the corporation's favor, stating that it could reasonably infer that the stockholder's true purpose for the inspection demand was to obtain competitive advantage over the corporation. *Advance Concrete Form v. Accuform, Inc.,* 462 N.W.2d 27.

State Variations Under California laws governing nonprofit corporations, a court can assign a plaintiff to pay a bond of not more than $50,000 to cover the expenses of a derivative lawsuit.

The Opening Case Revisited
"The Shareholder's Dilemma"

Obstacles to a Derivative Suit Before Vasily could bring a derivative suit to challenge management's decisions, he would have to attempt to solve the problem by communicating with the board of directors and with other shareholders. In addition, he would be required to own stock when the suit was commenced and to retain that stock for the duration of the suit. Finally, depending on state law, he might have to pay a security deposit to cover the corporation's potential expenses.

Quick Quiz 38-2 True or False?

1. Under the original concept of the corporation, the shareholders are the primary reason that a corporation exists.

2. Pooling agreements have been outlawed in all states.

3. A controlled company is one that has more than half its voting power concentrated in one person, or a small group of persons, who always vote together.

38-3 Governance Responsibilities

When the court hears a case challenging a manager's decision, it will turn to one of two rules in judging that conduct: the business judgment rule or the fairness rule (see Table 38-2).

The Business Judgment Rule

Under the **business judgment rule,** the court will not interfere with most business decisions. The rule protects managers who act with due care and in good faith, as long as their decisions are lawful and in the best interests of the corporation. The rule results from the common sense belief that, based on their education, experience, and knowledge, managers are in the best position to run the corporation. In contrast, shareholders and judges are far removed from the day-to-day operation of the business and should not be allowed to second-guess most management decisions. Protecting directors and officers in this way

Background Information The American Law Institute Principles states: "A director or officer who makes a business judgment in good faith fulfills the duty if the director or officer is not interested in the subject of the business judgment; is informed with respect to the subject of the business judgment to the extent . . . appropriate under the circumstances; and rationally believes that the business judgment is in the best interest of the corporation."

Table 38-2 Management Responsibilities

Rule	Situation	Explanation
Business judgment rule	Manager does not profit from decision	The decision stands if it is made (1) in good faith, (2) with due care within the law, and (3) in corporation's best interests.
Fairness rule	Manager profits from decision	The decision must be fair to the corporation because managers must remain loyal to the corporation.

encourages people to become corporate managers and reassures them that they will be protected when making difficult business decisions. The business judgment rule emerges from the duty of due diligence that a manager owes to the corporation. The **duty of due diligence** comes in three parts. It says that, when acting on behalf of the corporation, a manager must act (1) in good faith, (2) using the same level of care that an ordinarily prudent individual would use in a comparable situation, and (3) in the reasonable belief that the best interests of the company are being met.

Example 38-6

Donald Young was chair of the board and chief executive officer of the Sterling Software Corporation. On September 9, a Connecticut software company went on the market for $590 million. The Connecticut company appeared to be a guaranteed money-maker. In considering the plant's purchase, Young had to act before September 12. After careful examination of the plant's financial records, consultation with the corporation's legal and financial experts, and a detailed study of the marketplace, Young decided to buy. According to the business judgment rule, if the Connecticut software company proves to be an unprofitable investment, Young will be protected because he acted (1) with due care, (2) in good faith, (3) within the law, and (4) in the best interests of the corporation.

The Fairness Rule

The business judgment rule assumes that managers do not personally profit from business decisions. If managers do profit, then the decision is suspect, because all managers owe a **duty of loyalty** to the corporation. To fulfill this duty, managers must place the corporation's interests above their own. When managers enter contracts with the corporation or when they are on the boards of two corporations that do business with each other, a different standard is used to judge their conduct. This standard, known as the **fairness rule,** requires managers to be fair to the corporation when they personally benefit from their business decisions. Managers who benefit from their own decisions are said to be self-dealing. The fairness rule does not automatically declare managers disloyal if they profit from a corporate decision. Rather, it allows the court to examine the decision to determine its basic fairness to the corporation. How to measure fairness is, at best, problematical. At a minimum, it requires corporate managers to disclose all crucial information when they enter contracts with the corporation.

Example 38-7

Amy Myers was chair of the board of the Ural-Orenburg Shipping Corporation. The corporation leased a shipping depot from Denikin, Inc. Myers was also the majority shareholder and CEO of Denikin. Before finalizing the lease agreement, Myers revealed her relationship with Denikin to the other board members of Ural-Orenburg. The rental rate for the warehouse was in keeping with current market rates. Consequently, if the lease were challenged by shareholders of either corporation, a court, using the fairness rule, would uphold its validity.

Two rules that are offshoots of the fairness rule and the duty of loyalty are the insider trading rule and the corporate opportunity doctrine. Both rules give specific ways to measure a corporate manager's fairness in certain types of situations.

The Insider Trading Rule Because of their role in corporate affairs, directors and officers often possess inside information. **Inside information** is material, nonpublic, factual data that can be used to buy or sell securities at a profit. Directors, officers, and other key individuals in a corporation, such as major shareholders, who are not directors or officers, qualify as insiders. In fact, under current SEC rules any individual who holds such information including corporate employees, such as administrative assistants, researchers, public relations executives, human resource personnel, marketing directors, and so on, can be insiders. Even nonemployees such as financial planners, accountants, auditors, and attorneys, who, by virtue of their contact with a company have material nonpublic data about the company's stock, can be insiders. In fact, even corporate "outsiders," such as spouses, family members, and friends, may be considered insiders if they receive corporate information about corporate stock without being involved in any actual business need to have the information. Such "outside" insiders are generally referred to as **tippees.** Nevertheless, the most common actual corporate insiders are directors and officers.

Inside information clearly gives directors and officers an advantage over corporate outsiders in the buying and selling of stock. This advantage must not be abused when dealing with the corporation, or with individuals outside the corporation. Corporate managers act unfairly when they use their inside information to either cheat the corporation or take unfair advantage of corporate outsiders. Such transactions, which are referred to as **insider trading,** are forbidden by law. According to the **insider trading rule,** when managers possess important inside information, they are obligated to reveal that information before trading on it themselves. The rule also states that when inside information is revealed, the managers must use that information when trading with the corporation or with those outside the corporation.

The Corporate Opportunity Doctrine As noted earlier, along with the duty of due diligence and the duty of actual authority (see below), corporate managers also owe a duty of loyalty to the corporation. The duty of loyalty requires that corporate managers place the corporation's well-being ahead of their own interests. One offshoot of this duty is the idea of the corporate opportunity doctrine. The **corporate opportunity doctrine** states that corporate managers cannot take a corporate business opportunity for themselves if they know that the corporation would be interested in that opportunity as well. Before taking such an opportunity, a manager must first offer it to the corporation by informing other managers and shareholders. If the corporation rejects the opportunity then the manager is free to take that opportunity.

The Actual Authority Rule

Corporate managers are also held to a third duty, that is, the duty to act within actual authority. The authority spoken of here includes those powers that have been granted to managers by virtue of their position within the corporation. The duties of the directors and officers of the corporation are outlined in the appropriate state statutes, in the article of incorporation, in the regulations issued by government bodies such as the SEC, in relevant case law, and in the bylaws of the company. The **actual authority rule** states that a manager may be held liable if he or she exceeds his or her authority and the corporation is harmed as a result. Some states say that the managers will be liable for any violation of the limits of their authority on the basis of absolute or strict liability; some jurisdictions will consider the managers responsible only if the violation results in negligent or intentional conduct. This duty is also sometimes referred to as the **duty of obedience.** It is, of course, possible for a vote of the board or of the shareholders to approve a previously unauthorized act by a manager. This is known as the process of **ratification.**

Efforts to Limit Liability Corporate managers have come under very close scrutiny by regulators and by the courts in recent years. As a result, many otherwise well-qualified individuals have avoided serving as corporate managers in general but, in particular, as corporate directors. To counteract this trend, some states have enacted legislation that is designed to help protect the good faith and due diligent activities of such managers. These legislative enactments take three forms: (1) voluntary protective measures, (2) automatic protective measures, and (3) protective measures that limit the amount of damages that can be recovered against directors. A voluntary protective measure is one that permits corporate shareholders to fashion their bylaws so as to limit or eliminate the liability of directors for decisions made in carrying out their duties. Such measures would allow recovery of damages only if the director deliberately broke the law, deliberately violated the duty of loyalty, deliberately violated the duty of good faith, or improperly benefited from the transaction in question. Automatic protective measures grant the same type of immunity by state law, regardless of the action or inaction of corporate shareholders. The final measure would allow lawsuits against managers even in the cases noted above, but would place a cap on the amount of money damages that can be recovered against directors.

Efforts to Increase Responsibility

At the same time that the state governments are attempting to ease the liability of directors, the federal government has enacted efforts to increase director responsibilities for catching and stopping the wrongdoing of others within the corporation. One such measure is the **Sarbanes-Oxley Act,** which places an affirmative duty on the directors of publicly traded corporations to monitor whether their corporation is conforming to all legal requirements. A second measure involves the **United States Sentencing Commission,** which has issued a set of rules that control the discretion of the federal courts in issuing fines against corporations found guilty of criminal activities. Under the new rules, if the directors of a corporation did not do their best to discover and stop illegal activities, the court can place very severe penalties on the corporation, once it has been found guilty of those violations. The idea behind the new rules is to force directors to pay more attention to what is going on within their own companies, especially in relation to crime-stopping activities.

The new rules have led some legal commentators to suggest a series of steps that corporate directors should take when faced with suspected wrongdoing within their company. Seven steps are recommended: (1) once a legal violation has been uncovered (or even suspected) the activity must cease instantly; (2) any and all consequences that have flowed from the violation should be uncovered and stopped immediately; (3) any attempt to engage in a cover-up, in fact, any actions that can be remotely perceived as a cover-up must be avoided religiously; (4) notification of the violation must be made to the proper authorities; (5) investigations must be made to uncover any similar or related activities that may be illegal; (6) the cause or causes of the legal violations must be determined; (7) an action plan must be created and executed to punish the violators and to prevent any future violations.

For more information on the responsibilities of directors to stop wrongdoing in their corporations see: Henry, David. "Governance: Will Directors Morph into Corporate Constables?" *BusinessWeek,* June 14, 2004, p. 38.

For more detail on the steps that corporate directors should take when facing wrongdoing in their corporations see: Cooper, Richard. "Business Crime: Handling Violations." *The National Law Journal,* July 5, 2004, p. 11.

Quick Quiz 38-3 True or False?

1. The business judgment rule states that a manager's decision will stand as long as it was legal, was made with due care and in good faith, and was made in the best interests of the corporation.

2. The fairness rule states that a decision made by a manager will stand if it is fair to the corporation.

3. The business judgment rule is used by the courts when the manager is disinterested, that is, he or she is not personally gaining from the decision.

38-4 Shareholder Rights

In addition to their voting rights and their right to sue, shareholders are entitled to examine certain corporate records, to share in dividends, to transfer shares of stock, and to buy newly issued stock.

Right to Examine Corporate Records

A shareholder's right by statute to inspect the records of the corporation is usually limited to inspections for proper purposes at an appropriate time and place. Idle curiosity and an intent that unreasonably interferes with or embarrasses corporate management would prompt officers or directors to refuse shareholders' requests to examine corporate accounts, minutes, and records. When the purpose of inspection is proper, it may be enforced by a court order.

Background Information Before Microsoft Corporation went public in 1986, its employees were given an option to buy company stock at one dollar a share. A year after the stocks were offered to the public, prices reached $90 a share, making millionaires out of many of the original employee investors.

Right to Share in Dividends

Shareholders have the right to share in dividends after they have been declared by the board of directors. Once declared, a dividend becomes a debt of the corporation and enforceable by law, as is any other debt. However, shareholders cannot force the directors to declare a dividend unless the directors are not acting in good faith in refusing to do so. Courts are not inclined to order directors to meet and declare a dividend if the court must substitute its own business judgment for that of the directors.

Right to Transfer Shares of Stock

Shareholders have the right to sell or transfer their shares of stock. The person to whom stock shares are transferred has the right to have the stock transfer entered on the corporate books. The transferee becomes a **shareholder of record** and is entitled to vote, receive dividends, and enjoy all other shareholder privileges.

Background Information In early corporate history, the preemptive right was regarded as so basic that it was assumed to exist in most situations unless there was a contrary express provision. Today, however, the preemptive right is no longer considered basic in most jurisdictions, because the cost of preemptive rights may frequently exceed their benefits. Now, no preemptive rights exist unless explicitly stated in the contract.

Preemptive Rights

Unless the right is denied or limited by the corporate charter or by state law, shareholders have the right to purchase a proportionate share of every new offering of stock by the corporation. This is known as the shareholder's **preemptive right.** Preemptive rights are more prevalent in small, closely held corporations than in large, publicly owned corporations. This right prevents management from depriving shareholders of their proportionate control of a corporation simply by increasing the number of shares in the corporation.

Quick Quiz 38-4 True or False?

1. Assuming a request by a shareholder to inspect the corporate books is a proper one, the courts will enforce that request.

2. Today the courts will readily substitute their own judgment and declare a dividend on corporate stock even when the directors of the corporation have voted against such a move.

3. Preemptive rights are more common in large publicly held corporations than in small closely held corporations.

38-5 Governance of a Limited Liability Company

The members of a limited liability company can choose to manage the business themselves or they can hire outside management. An LLC that is run by the members themselves is called a member-managed LLC, while one that is operated by outside managers is referred to as a manager-managed LLC.

Member-Managed LLCs

If the managers choose to run the LLC on their own, then management rights are apportioned among the members, according to the capital contributions made by each member to the LLC. Like the partners in a general partnership, the members of the LLC act as agents of the LLC. Accordingly, whenever a member performs a function within that member's apparent authority, the LLC will be bound by that action. However, as is true of a partnership, there are some actions that fall outside the member's apparent authority. These include but are not limited to disposing of the firm's goodwill and submitting a claim of the LLC to arbitration. Naturally, the operating agreement can alter any of these statutory provisions.

Manager-Managed LLCs

If the members hire outside managers, then the LLC is run like a corporation. In the absence of an operating agreement, a single manager operates much like the CEO of a corporation, while a group of managers acts as a board of directors. Nevertheless, regardless of the number of managers involved in an LLC, both the business judgment rule and the fairness rule apply to their decisions in the same way that those rules apply to the directors of a corporation.

Fiduciary Duties

Regardless of whether the members or the managers ultimately run the LLC, both groups have a fiduciary duty to the LLC and to its members. Nevertheless, as noted in the last chapter, it would be wise to outline specific management duties in the written operating agreement.

Quick Quiz 38-5 True or False?

1. The members of an LLC have no choice in the matter of who will manage their firm.

2. An operating agreement established by the LLC is not permitted to alter statutory provisions regarding governance in any way.

3. Regardless of whether the members or the managers ultimately run the LLC, fiduciary duties have been suspended by provisions outlined in the latest version of the Uniform Limited Liability Company Act.

Summary

38-1 The business affairs of a corporation are managed by a board of directors elected by the shareholders. The directors have the authority to appoint officers and agents to run the day-to-day affairs of the corporation.

38-2 Five theories have been put forth by legal scholars and business experts concerning how corporations should be managed. These theories are special interest group control, governmental control, independent director control, managerial control, and shareholder democracy. Shareholders can increase their voting power by purchasing additional stock. If they cannot purchase additional stock, they may use another device to increase their voting power, cumulative voting, proxies, voting trusts, pooling agreements, and shareholder proposals, shareholder nominations, unanimous voting restrictions. Shareholders can also sue the corporation. Direct suits are brought by shareholders to protect their own rights. Derivative suits are brought by shareholders when they feel that the corporation has been damaged by a management decision.

38-3   Under the business judgment rule, the court will not interfere with most management decisions as long as those decisions are made with due care, in good faith, within the law, and in the best interests of the

corporation. If the manager profits personally from a business decision, then the court will use the fairness rule to judge the manager's conduct.

38-4   Shareholder rights include the right to examine corporate records, the right to share dividends, the right to transfer shares of stock, and the right to buy newly issued stock.

38-5   The members of a limited liability company can choose to manage the business themselves or they can hire outside management. Regardless of whether the members or the managers ultimately run the LLC, both groups have a fiduciary duty to the LLC and to the members of the LLC. Nevertheless, it would be wise to outline specific management duties in the operating agreement.

Key Terms

actual authority rule, 729

business judgment rule, 727

controlled company, 719

corporate democracy, 719

corporate opportunity doctrine, 729

cumulative voting, 720

derivative suit, 726

direct suit, 726

duty of due diligence, 728

duty of loyalty, 728

duty of obedience, 729

fairness rule, 728

governmental control, 719

independent director, 719

independent director control, 719

inside information, 729

insider trading, 729

insider trading rule, 729

managerial control, 719

pooling agreement, 722

preemptive rights, 731

proxy, 721

proxy contest, 721

proxy solicitation, 721

ratification, 729

rule of contemporary ownership, 726

Sarbanes-Oxley Act, 730

shareholder democracy, 719

shareholder of record, 731

shareholder proposal, 722

special interest group control, 719

tippee, 729

trustee, 721

United States Sentencing Commission, 730

voting trust, 721

Questions for Review and Discussion

1. What is the central dilemma of corporate governance?
2. What are the functions of directors, officers, and shareholders?
3. What are the five theories of corporate governance?
4. What is the difference between cumulative voting and proxy solicitation?
5. What is the difference between a voting trust and a pooling agreement?
6. What is a shareholder proposal?
7. What is the difference between a shareholder direct suit and a shareholder derivative suit?
8. What is the difference between the business judgment rule and the fairness rule?
9. What are the rights that belong to shareholders?
10. How does the management of a limited liability company operate?

Investigating the Internet

Facts about limited liability companies can be found by accessing Limited Liability Companies on the Lectric Law Library website. Access this website and write a report on the creation and operation of LLCs. As an alternative assignment, write a report on the innovative uses of an LLC.

Cases for Analysis

1. United Missionary Baptist Church, a not-for-profit corporation, held an election for the new church pastor. Several members of the church were dissatisfied with the results of the election and with the procedures that were followed during the election. They claimed that the inclusion of absentee balloting violated the church's constitution. Without making any parliamentary moves to correct the alleged misapplication of the constitution, and despite the fact that they had used their own absentee ballots during the election, these unhappy members brought a derivative lawsuit, asking the court to compel the church to follow its own constitution. The suit was dismissed. However, the members who brought the lawsuit claimed that, since the lawsuit was a derivative action, they were entitled to attorney's fees, just as the shareholders of a profit corporation were entitled to attorney's fees. The court agreed that the same rules that apply to profit corporations in derivative actions apply to derivative suits brought for nonprofit corporations. However, the court still refused to grant the request for attorney's fees. Why? *Russell v. United Missionary Baptist Church,* 637 N.E.2d 82 (OH).

2. The bylaws of Jameson Enterprises, Inc., required a 70 percent supermajority to establish a quorum sufficient to hold a meeting to remove a director from the board. The bylaws also designated a meeting with such a purpose as a special meeting. The board consisted of ten directors. Six showed up at the meeting. Of the four who failed to attend, three were in Europe. The fourth, Weinberger, was not notified of the meeting because he was the one to be removed. The six directors attending the meeting first voted to change the bylaws to require only 60 percent of the directors to establish a quorum sufficient to hold a special meeting. The six directors then unanimously voted to remove Weinberger. When Weinberger found out about the

meeting, he objected to the vote and claimed that the entire procedure was void. Was Weinberger correct? Explain.

3. Smith, a shareholder, filed suit against the board of directors of a corporation in which he had owned stock. Smith claimed that he and other shareholders had not received top dollar for their shares when their corporation had merged with another. Consequently, they sought either a reversal of the merger or payment from the directors to make up for their losses. The directors, Smith argued, had violated their duty of due care because they based their decision on a twenty-minute speech by the CEO. Also, the directors had not even looked at the merger documents, let alone studied them. Further, the directors had not sought any independent evaluation by outside experts. For their part, the directors argued that since their decision was made in good faith and was legal, they were protected by the business judgment rule. Were the directors correct? *Smith v. VanGorkon,* 488 A.2d 858 (DE).

4. Donald Lewis was a shareholder in S.L.&E., Inc., a corporation that owned land and a complex of buildings in Rochester, New York. The land and buildings were leased to LGT, a tire manufacturer. Donald's brothers were shareholders and directors of both S.L.&E. and LGT. Donald had no financial or managerial interest in LGT. S.L.&E. leased the land to LGT at a rate that Donald considered damaging to S.L.&E. He pointed out that S.L.&E. collected only $14,000 per year in rent from LGT while paying out $11,000 in taxes. This, he argued, meant that S.L.&E. could never be a profit-making corporation. Should the directors of LGT and S.L.&E. be judged by the business judgment rule or the fairness rule? Explain. *Lewis v. S.L.&E., Inc.,* 629 F.2d 764 (2nd Cir.).

5. Jackson set up a trust for his seven children. Most of the assets in the trust consisted of stock in the

two newspapers owned and run by Jackson. Over the course of eighteen years, Jackson transferred all but two shares of voting stock in the newspapers. The trustee of the trust was given full power to manage the assets in the fund and to sell or otherwise dispose of the newspaper stock. State law places a strict ten-year limit on voting trusts. The plaintiffs claimed that the trust, which had lasted eighteen years, was no longer valid, having passed the ten-year limit eight years before. The defendants claimed that the ten-year limit did not apply to this trust. Were the defendants correct? Explain. *Jackson v. Jackson,* 402 A.2d 893 (CT).

6. Klinicki and Lundgren incorporated to form an air taxi service known as Berlinair, Inc. Each of them owned one-third interest in the corporation. The final third was owned by Lelco, Inc., a company owned by Lundgren. In his capacity as president of Berlinair, Lundgren learned that the Berlinair Flug Ring (BFR), a business association of Berlin's travel agents, was looking for an air charter service. Lundgren incorporated a new corporate entity called Air Berlin Charter (ABC). ABC then negotiated an air charter contract with BFR. Klinicki brought suit, demanding that Lundgren reimburse Berlinair for any profits made by ABC on the BFR contract. Was this a direct or derivative suit? Explain. Should the business judgment rule or the fairness rule be used by the court to measure Lundgren's performance? Explain. Who should have won the suit? Defend your choice. *Klinicki v. Lundgren,* 695 P.2d 906 (OR).

7. Naquin, Dubois, and Hoffpauir incorporated to form Air Engineered Systems and Services, Inc. Dubois became president and Hoffpauir became secretary-treasurer. Naquin was employed by the company. Conflicts between the three caused a breakdown in the working relationship. Dubois and Hoffpauir offered Naquin $2,000 a month for ten years for his share of the business if he would sign a non-competition agreement. Naquin refused to sell until he could examine the corporate records. Dubois and Hoffpauir refused to allow Naquin to see the books until he signed the non-competition agreement. Could Dubois and Hoffpauir attach such a condition to Naquin's request? Explain. *Naquin v. Air Engineered Systems and Services, Inc.,* 463 So.2d 992 (LA).

8. Snodgrass, a minority shareholder in the 21st Century Broadcasting Network, Inc., was dissatisfied with management's decision to cancel several long running news shows and replace them with several sitcoms and talk shows. She was also disturbed that management had decided to discharge several editorial writers and newscasters, including one who had recently won a major award for investigative journalism. Finally, she believed that a change in policy that would phase out foreign broadcast efforts would eventually cost the company an enormous amount of money. Assuming that Snodgrass does not want to sue the corporation, what options does she have if she wants to increase her influence over the board of directors of 21st Century Broadcasting Network, Inc.? Explain.

9. Keith Harris, a shareholder of Fastway Airlines, Inc., discovered that Donald Fleure, chief executive officer of Fastway, had sold some of his own land to the corporation at what Harris believed to be excessive prices. Can Harris bring a direct or a derivative suit in this situation? Explain. Would the fairness rule or the business judgment rule be used to evaluate the activities of Fleure? Explain.

Quick Quiz Answers

38-1	38-2	38-3	38-4	38-5
1. T	1. T	1. T	1. T	1. F
2. F	2. F	2. T	2. F	2. F
3. T	3. T	3. T	3. F	3. F

Chapter 39

Government Regulation of Corporate Business

The Opening Case

"Anti-Antitrust Law in the Foreign Marketplace"

Five foreign drug manufacturers filed a lawsuit in a United States District Court in Washington, DC, against several large American pharmaceutical corporations. The class action lawsuit alleged that the pharmaceutical companies had been involved in a long-term systematic scheme to illegally increase the cost of vitamins within the global marketplace. The action was alleged to be in direct violation of the Sherman Antitrust Act, a federal law that is designed to prevent a wide variety of practices each of which somehow impairs competition within the economic system. The plaintiffs were eager to file under the Sherman Antitrust Act because the statute provides successful plaintiffs with three times the amount of damages awarded by the jury. The Sherman Act was also attractive to the plaintiffs because price-fixing is specifically outlawed by the statute. In fact, price-fixing is so destructive a practice that, under the act, it is considered a *per se* violation. Per se violations are practices that are so contrary to antitrust policy that harm is presumed and the practice is prohibited on its face. The plaintiffs were also encouraged in the case because the defendants had already settled several domestic civil cases for over $2 billion and had admitted guilt in a criminal antitrust case that had resulted in over $900 million in fines. Despite all of this, the plaintiffs still lost the case and went away empty handed. The plaintiffs failed in their suit because they ran afoul of another federal law, the Foreign Trade Antitrust Improvements Act (FTAIA). The FTAIA mandates that the extraterritorial activities of American companies are not subject to American antitrust law. Some people defend the FTAIA as a way to protect American companies by permitting them to compete equally with their counterparts in foreign markets. Others see the FTAIA as a way to allow big American corporations to sidestep antitrust regulations. As you read Chapter 39, consider both sides of this argument and try to reconcile these two antitrust statutes as best you can.

Chapter Outcomes

1. Explain the development of the federal government's power to regulate business.
2. Describe the source of state power to regulate business.
3. Explain how the Securities Exchange Commission prevents unfair practices.

4. Contrast per se antitrust violations with rule of reason violations.
5. Define the various techniques of corporate expansion.
6. Contrast the interest of the Securities Exchange Commission with that of the Federal Trade Commission in corporate expansion.
7. Contrast the role of the Environmental Protection Agency with that of the Federal Energy Regulatory Commission.
8. Identify the rights that are guaranteed to workers under the Employee Retirement Income Security Act and the Worker Adjustment and Retraining Notification Act.
9. Identify the two ways that a corporation may undergo dissolution.
10. Explain the circumstances under which a limited liability company may undergo dissolution.

For more details on the facts outlined in The Opening Case see: McDavid, Janet L., and Shane Anderson. "Antitrust Law: The 'Empagran' Decision." *The National Law Journal,* July 12, 2004, p. 12.

39-1 Business and the Constitution

Despite the beliefs of many theorists, it is not possible to separate the world of the law from the world of economics. In the real world, the two systems interact with one another in such a way that they become, at times, one single system, the **juris-economic system.**

The Commerce Clause of the Constitution

Sometimes the law must adapt to economic realities. This is seen in the way the law adjusted to economic realities in order to give the federal courts the power to regulate economic activity. The process worked something like this. The **Commerce Clause** is found in Article I, Section 8, Clause 3 of the Constitution. Clause 3 states that "Congress shall have the Power . . . To regulate Commerce with foreign nations, and among the several States." At first the courts interpreted this to mean that the federal courts could only regulate commercial activity if the activity passed between two or more states.

U.S. Const. Article I (see page 856)

However, changing economic needs demanded a revision of this narrowly drawn interpretation. The federal government, which had entered the land-granting business, had determined that it needed a way to enforce the distribution of this land. To meet this and other related economic needs, the Supreme Court in an 1824 case, *Gibbons v. Ogden,* held that any commercial activity that affected commerce among the states could be regulated by the federal government. This included the activity that occurred within a single state, so long as that completely in-state activity affected interstate commerce. The extent of this interpretation was not felt until 1942, when in the case of *Wickard v. Filburn,* the Supreme Court upheld the doctrine so thoroughly, that a farmer's production of wheat for use only on his own farm was held to impact interstate commerce. The court reasoned that if the farmer used his own wheat he would not buy wheat in interstate commerce thus weakening the entire interstate market. The justices emphasized that it was the cumulative effect of many such farmers that concerned them, rather than the effect of a single farmer.

Law is not a profession at all, but rather a business service station and repair shop.

—Adlai E. Stevenson (1990–1965), American politician

Terms The word *business* comes from the medieval term *bisiznis,* indicating a state of being busy. By 1700, as commercial activity increased, *business* became associated with a particular kind of activity—the buying and selling of goods.

The Internal Balancing Act of the Juris-Economic System

Several dynamic factors work together in the juris-economic system to make this type of revolutionary adjustment to the realities of the marketplace palatable to the culture as a whole. These factors include (1) the need to reason by analogy in the common law system, (2) the desire to balance individual justice with regulatory justice, and (3) the inclination on the part of jurists to control legal change so that the revolutionary process is almost imperceptible from case to case.

Reasoning by Analogy

Whenever a judge must decide a case, he or she is faced with a conflict that involves real people embroiled in a series of real events. In such cases the judge must make a decision based on precedent. When a judge applies the law of an old case to the facts of the new case, the match between the two is rarely exact. This means that the judge must reason by analogy. Reasoning by analogy gives the judge a certain degree of flexibility. Generally, if there is a deviation from precedent the judge will justify this slight change in the law by explaining how the present case can be distinguished from the past case.

Balancing Individual and Regulatory Justice

The inclination to reason by analogy is driven by the perceived need to balance individual justice with regulatory justice. **Individual justice** is the justice that is meted out to the people in the case that is before the judge. It is important that the parties in the case feel that the judge has entered a fair ruling that is tailor-made to their situation. On the other hand, the judge must also promote regulatory justice. **Regulatory justice** is a fair and balanced interpretation of the law that evolves from and is consistent with previous law. When a judge deviates too much from regulatory justice he or she risks a political upheaval. As a result, in most cases, the judge balances the two goals and creates a new ruling that is in line with regulatory justice but which fine-tunes the rule enough to fit this particular case, thus introducing a small measure of change into the system.

Controlling Legal Change

What results from the judge's need to reason from analogy and his or her desire to balance individual justice with regulatory justice is a system that promotes change at a slow and measured rate. This is why it is possible for the juris-economic system to adjust legal rules to changing economic realities. The parties to the case welcome change because it reassures them that the law is flexible enough to deal with their individual problems. Other jurists welcome the new precedent as an added weapon to their arsenal of past cases. Legislators welcome the new case as long as it offers a change that is so small it manages to preserve the juris-economic status quo.

For a more detailed discussion of the internal balancing act of the juris-economic system, see: Brion, Denis J. "The Chaotic Indeterminacy of Tort Law: Between Formalism and Nihilism." In *Radical Philosophy of Law: Contemporary Challenges to Mainstream Legal Theory.* Edited by David S. Caudill and Steven Jay Gold. Atlantic Highlands, N.J.: Humanities Press, 1995, pp. 193–198; Murphy, Jeffrie G., and Jules L. Coleman. *Philosophy of Law: An Introduction to Jurisprudence.* Boulder, CO: Westview Press, 1990, p. 10.

Example 39-1

The Lafayette Nuclear Research and Development Corporation owned and operated DeBroglie Plutonium Processing Plant, Inc. Both corporations were based in Louisiana. DeBroglie supplied Lafayette with about 25 percent of its plutonium needs, and did no other plutonium business with anyone. The other 75 percent of Lafayette's plutonium came from one in-state producer and two out-of-state suppliers. When the federal government imposed new safety regulations on all plutonium processing plants, DeBroglie argued that the regulations did not apply to it since its business was totally within the borders of Louisiana. The court disagreed. The court said that the fact that 25 percent of Lafayette's plutonium was purchased from DeBroglie meant that Lafayette did not buy that 25 percent from other corporations, including the two corporations from outside Louisiana. Since the two corporations outside Louisiana could have sold more plutonium to Lafayette had DeBroglie not sold its plutonium to Lafayette, DeBroglie's business was affecting interstate commerce, and could, therefore, be regulated by Congress.

A Question of Ethics

The Framers of the U.S. Constitution clearly wanted to limit the legislative power of the central national government. They made this fact quite clear by enumerating the powers that Congress would possess and by specifically starting Article I of the Constitution with the following words, "All legislative Powers herein granted shall be vested in a Congress of the United States." Now reread Example 39-1. In that case, the court allowed Congress to regulate DeBroglie, a corporation which did business totally within a single state. Is it ethical for the courts, in their interpretation of the Commerce Clause, to ignore the deliberate attempt by the Framers to limit Congressional power to the regulation of commerce "among the several states" and to extend that power, allowing Congress to regulate a commercial activity that takes place completely within one state? Explain.

State Regulatory Power

In contrast, to the convoluted and indirect way that the juris-economic system developed federal commerce power, the system had no problem accommodating state economic power. This is because the states automatically have the power to regulate economic activities. This power comes from a state's police power. **Police power** is the state's authority to restrict private rights in order to promote and maintain public health, safety, welfare, and morals. A state has police power simply by virtue of its existence as a legitimate governmental authority. Today we take for granted that all business activity, even that of the sole proprietor, is subject to state regulation. The state government and the various subdivisions of the state government, from countries to cities to zoning districts, all play a role in this regulatory process.

State Variations In Florida, any corporation failing to file an annual report is not permitted to maintain or defend any action in Florida, until such report is filed and all fees and taxes are paid, and shall be subject to dissolution and cancellation of its certificate to do business in Florida.

Quick Quiz 39-1 True or False?

1. The world of the law and the world of economics often interact with one another in such a way that the two become, at times, one single system, the juris-economic system.

2. Police power is the state's authority to restrict private rights in order to promote and maintain public health, safety, welfare, and morals.

3. The Contracts Clause is found in Article I, Section 8, Clause 3 of the Constitution.

39-2 Securities Regulation

Two pieces of federal legislation that affect business are the Securities Act of 1933 and the Securities Exchange Act of 1934 (See Table 39-1). The primary purpose of these acts is to protect business investors by making certain that they are informed about the securities they purchase. The independent regulatory agency that carries out this function is the Securities and Exchange Commission (SEC). The SEC regulates the issuance of securities by corporations and partnerships. A **security** has been defined as a money investment that expects a return solely because of another person's efforts. As the following case demonstrates, a security is a security even if it is called something else.

Did You Know?

Since the Constitution was ratified, over 10,000 amendments have been proposed by Congress. Despite all this activity, only twenty-seven amendments have been ratified.

Table 39-1 Securities and Antitrust Regulations

Regulation	Explanation
Securities regulation:	
Securities Act of 1933	Regulates the issuance of new securities
Securities Exchange Act of 1934	Established the Securities and Exchange Commission; act deals with subsequent trading in securities
Antitrust regulations:	
Sherman Antitrust Act	Prohibits contracts, combinations in restraint of trade; also prohibits monopolies, attempts to monopolize, and conspires to monopolize
Clayton Act	Prohibits specific practices such as tying agreements and interlocking directorates
Robinson-Patman Act	Deals with product pricing, advertising, and promotional allowances
Federal Trade Commission Act	Established the Federal Trade Commission

About the Law

While the shareholders of a corporation are the actual owners of the corporation, they are not agents of the corporation unlike the directors and the officers, and therefore, cannot commit the corporation to any contractual arrangements.

Background Information Although Herbert Hoover and Franklin Roosevelt differed on many issues, they agreed that unregulated speculation in securities was one of the causes of the Stock Market Crash of 1929 and the following Great Depression.

Example 39-2

Osgood Minerals, Inc., had to raise an enormous amount of capital quickly. One of the directors devised a scheme whereby Osgood would sell to investors parcels of land owned by the corporation and used for mining purposes. In return, the investors would be entitled to a return on their investment. The return would be calculated in relation to the amount of land owned by each investor. To avoid having to comply with SEC regulations, Osgood labeled each sale a land contract, rather than a security. Since the sales were land contracts, Osgood argued, it did not have to follow SEC regulations. The SEC disagreed and brought suit to stop the sale of unregulated securities. The court held that since each investor's profits would be derived solely from the efforts of others, the investments were securities and were, therefore, subject to SEC regulations.

Securities Act of 1933

The Securities Act of 1933 regulates the issuance of new securities by corporations and partnerships. Offers of securities by mail or through interstate or foreign commerce must be registered with the SEC. A registration statement and a prospectus must be filed with the SEC. A **registration statement** contains detailed information about the corporation, including data about its management, capitalization, and financial condition. A **prospectus** contains much of the same information but in a condensed and simplified form. The registration statement is designed for the experts at the SEC, whereas the prospectus is designed for potential investors.

Securities Exchange Act of 1934

The Securities Exchange Act of 1934, which actually established the SEC, deals with the subsequent trading in securities. It requires periodic reports of financial information concerning registered securities, and it prohibits manipulative and deceptive actions in the sale and purchase of securities. The act prohibits insiders, including officers and directors, from realizing profit from any purchase and sale of securities within any period of less than six months. The courts have held that insiders are not permitted to trade on information until that information has been made available to the public.

The primary role of the Securities and Exchange Commission is to inform investors about the securities they purchase.

Further Reading Joel Seligman's *The Transformation of Wall Street, A History of the Securities and Exchange Commission and Modern Corporate Finance* (Boston: Houghton-Mifflin, 1995) describes the commission's birth and growth, its leaders, and its lasting effects on corporate finance.

Under the 1934 act, shareholders, including majority shareholders, who solicit proxies (see Chapter 38) must also follow strict reporting requirements. The SEC requires a written proxy solicitation to include the identity of the individual or individuals seeking the proxy, any potential conflicts of interest, and specific information about any corporate changes to be voted on. When management solicits proxies, the solicitation must also include information concerning management salaries. The SEC regulations also state quite specifically that all material information must be stated in readable language and be displayed prominently, rather than buried in small type somewhere in the back of the document. The regulations also explicitly forbid false or misleading information.

> ### Quick Quiz 39-2 True or False?
>
> 1. The Securities Exchange Commission regulates the issuance of securities by corporations and partnerships.
>
> 2. The Securities Exchange Act of 1934 actually established the Securities Exchange Commission.
>
> 3. Under the Securities Exchange Act of 1934 majority shareholders are exempt from proxy solicitation reporting requirements.

39-3 Antitrust Regulation

Both the federal government and the states have antitrust laws to preserve the values of competition and to discourage monopolies. A **monopoly** is the exclusive control of a market by a business enterprise. At the federal level, the four principal antitrust statutes are the Sherman Antitrust Act, the Clayton Act, the Robinson-Patman Act, and the Federal Trade Commission Act.

Sherman Antitrust Act

The Sherman Antitrust Act (1890) prohibits contracts, combinations, and conspiracies in restraint of trade. It also prohibits monopolization, attempts to monopolize, and combinations or conspiracies to monopolize any part of interstate or foreign commerce. Violations of the Sherman Antitrust Act must involve at least two people acting together.

Getting Students Involved Invite students to research and report on one of the "robber barons" of the late nineteenth century, such as J.P. Morgan, Andrew Carnegie, or John D. Rockefeller, whose huge trusts and monopolies led to a call for antitrust laws.

Per Se Violations   Some restraint-of-trade practices are so serious that they are prohibited whether or not they harm anyone. These practices are labeled **per se violations,** which means that the practice is so contrary to antitrust policy that harm is presumed and the practice is prohibited. For example, price fixing is inherently unreasonable and is, therefore, considered a per se violation. An agreement between competitors to divide territories among themselves to minimize competition would also be unlawful. This is true even if the agreement helps the parties to compete against other parties outside the agreement. Similar unlawful activities include agreements among competitors to stop competing with one another in prices, customers, or products.

Rule-of-Reason Standard   If an alleged antitrust practice is not considered a per se violation, then the courts will judge the legality of that practice with the rule-of-reason approach. The **rule-of-reason standard** will stop certain practices only if they are an unreasonable restriction of competition. As a result, some practices that, in fact, limit competition may be legal. To determine if an anticompetitive practice is legal, the court considers such facts as the history of the restraint, the harm that results, the reason for the practice, and the purpose to be attained.

Post-Sherman Antitrust Legislation

Three principal antitrust statues made the Sherman Act more specific and, as a result, more effective. The Clayton Act of 1914, the Robinson-Patman Act of 1936, *the Foreign Trade Antitrust Improvements Act,* and the Federal Trade Commission Act of 1914 sought to prevent practices that reduced competition or that favored the creation of monopolies.

Clayton Act   Congress passed the Clayton Act to police specific business practices that could be used to create a monopoly. One practice outlawed by the act is the tying agreement. A **tying agreement** occurs when one party refuses to sell a product unless the buyer also purchases another product tied to the first product. The issue is the effect of the tie-in on the seller's competitors.

Interlocking directorates are also outlawed by the Clayton Act. **Interlocking directorates** occur when individuals serve as directors of two corporations that are competitors. This provision is not entirely foolproof, however, because banks and common carriers are exempt. To fall under this part of the Clayton Act, at least one of the corporations must have an aggregate worth (capital, surplus, and individual profits) more than $1 million.

Related Cases Warner-Lambert, the makers of Listerine mouthwash, advertised that its product prevents, cures, or alleviates the common cold. The FTC issued an order for Warner-Lambert to cease and desist from advertising these claims, since there was no medical basis for them. Warner-Lambert appealed and the court affirmed the order, also requiring that future advertisements disclaim the prior assertions. *Warner-Lambert v. FTC,* 562 F.2d 749.

Robinson-Patman Act   The Robinson-Patman Act deals with product pricing, advertising, and promotional allowances. It specifically prohibits a seller from charging different prices to different customers for the same product when such differences might injure competition. However, nothing in the law is intended to prevent price differences due to cost of manufacture, sale, delivery, or bulk purchases.

Federal Trade Commission Act   In addition to establishing the Federal Trade Commission (FTC), the Federal Trade Commission Act, as amended, declared that "unfair methods of competition, and unfair or deceptive practices in or affecting commerce are hereby declared unlawful." The act did not name specific unfair methods of competition. Instead, it has allowed the courts and the FTC to determine those unfair practices.

The Federal Trade Commission Act was amended by the Wheeler-Lea Act and amendments in 1938 and 1975. This legislation authorized the FTC to act against unfair or deceptive acts without first proving the existence of anti-competitive behavior. The FTC was also granted the power to challenge false advertising of food, drugs, and cosmetics regardless of the advertiser's knowledge of the advertisement's truth or falsity.

The Foreign Trade Antitrust Improvements Act (FTAIA) Another antitrust measure passed by Congress is the Foreign Trade Antitrust Improvements Act (FTAIA). Unlike the other antitrust provisions supported by Congress the FTAIA is designed to circumvent some of the restrictions placed on American companies by the Sherman Antitrust Act. The objective of the FTAIA is to permit American companies operating in foreign markets to have a fighting chance against foreign competitors who are not subject to the strict antimonopoly provisions of the act. Under terms of the bill, if an American company is operating totally in a foreign market, that company is not subject to American antitrust law.

Antitrust Revisionism

In recent years, Congress has paid close attention to developments in antitrust law, and has, as a result, inaugurated a congressional think tank known as the **United States Antitrust Modernization Committee.** Four members of this twelve-member bipartisan group are appointed by the President, while the remaining eight are appointed by Congress. The stated objective of the group is to examine antitrust law and to report recommendations on how to modernize the law. The group must hold public hearings, attended by those constituents who are affected by the law. Those parties affected include large corporations, consumer advocate groups, and government regulators. Many large corporations favor several proposed reforms including the elimination, or at least, the streamlining of the list of per se violations now outlawed by the act. Another reform promoted by the companies is the elimination of triple damage awards that are now permitted under law. A final reform favored by the corporations is the elimination of the Robinson-Patman Act which deals with product advertising, pricing practices, and promotional allowances.

In contrast, consumer advocates want to make it easier for plaintiffs to bring antitrust lawsuits against certain types of defendants, but especially against manufacturers. Plaintiffs frequently complain that retailers rarely bring antitrust claims against manufacturers, because retailers can avoid the effects of any antitrust scheme, such as a price-fixing

For more detailed information on the United States Antitrust Modernization Committee see: Bobelian, Michael. "Antitrust: Group Aims to Update Antitrust Law." *The National Law Journal,* July 12, 2004, p. 8.

The Opening Case Revisited
"Anti-Antitrust Law in the Foreign Marketplace"

In The Opening Case, the plaintiffs failed in their suit because the Foreign Trade Antitrust Improvements Act mandates that extraterritorial activities of a company are not subject to American antitrust law. The FTAIA was designed by Congress as a way to protect American companies by permitting them to compete equally with their counterparts in foreign markets.

conspiracy, by passing the increased cost of doing business on to the consumers. The consumers, who under current rules are frequently barred from bringing lawsuits against manufacturers, have no recourse other than to pay the higher prices. For this reason, consumer advocate groups favor making it easier for plaintiffs to file class action lawsuits against all manufacturing firms that violate antitrust law but especially against those large cartels that are the worst offenders. Finally, state and local regulators would also like to see changes in the law. These regulators favor changes that would transfer more antitrust enforcement authority from the federal government to the states.

Quick Quiz 39-3 True or False?

1. Price-fixing is an example of a rule of reason practice under the Sherman Antitrust Act.

2. Per se violations must involve actual harm to be actionable under the Sherman Antitrust Act.

3. The Robinson-Patman Act has been repealed by the United States Antitrust Modernization Committee.

39-4 Regulation of Corporate Expansion

Teaching Tips List the various methods of corporate expansion—merger, consolidation, asset acquisition, and stock acquisition—on the board. Have students explain each technique and ask them to help you create a list of the advantages and disadvantages of each. Finally, have students evaluate which technique is the most effective and which is the least effective.

No other area of corporate activity has been scrutinized by the government more closely in recent years than the area of corporate expansion (See Table 39-2). As previously noted, the two governmental agencies that regulate this activity are the SEC and the FTC. The two commissions have different interests in the expansion process. The SEC is concerned with regulating the expansion itself, while the FTC is more concerned with the effects of that expansion.

Expansion Techniques and Securities Law

All corporations change in size. Some grow and expand while others shrink until they dissolve completely or are absorbed by a larger, more successful enterprise. Like all other corporate activities, corporate expansions are looked at very closely by government. The

Table 39-2 Securities Law and Corporate Expansion

Technique	Explanation	Regulation
Merger and consolidation	In a merger, one company is absorbed by another; in a consolidation, two companies join and a new company results.	Most antifraud provisions of the SEC apply here.
Asset acquisition	One corporation buys all the property of another.	Antifraud provisions of the SEC apply here if a proxy solicitation is involved or if insider information is used to profit from the sale.
Stock acquisition (takeover)	One corporation (suitor) makes a tender offer to the shareholders of another corporation (target).	Whenever a suitor makes an offer to acquire more than 5 percent of the target, the suitor must file with the SEC.

primary expansion techniques include merger, consolidation, asset acquisition, and stock acquisition (takeover).

Merger and Consolidation

Traditionally, a **merger** involves two corporations, one of which is absorbed by the other. One of the two corporations continues to carry on business under its original name, and the other simply disappears into the first. In contrast, in a **consolidation** both companies disappear and a new company carries on the business under a new name. Today, most legal scholars do not make any distinction between merger and consolidation. In fact, many state incorporation statutes today make no reference to consolidation, preferring the term *merger* instead. A merger requires advance approval from the boards and shareholders of both corporations. In general, a two-thirds majority vote of the shareholders will be required before a merger can be approved, although some states require a super majority of four-fifths. Shareholders who dissent are entitled to be paid for their stock if they do not wish to be a part of the merger. Written notice of a dissent is required so that the cost of purchasing the dissenter's stock can be figured as a part of the expense involved in the merger.

Most antifraud provisions of the SEC apply to the merger process. Often the merger vote will be preceded by a proxy solicitation battle. All material facts about the merger must be included in the proxy solicitation. In addition, the solicitation must not contain any false or misleading information. Similarly, the SEC prohibits insiders who know of merger plans to take advantage of that knowledge to profit personally before the knowledge is revealed to the public.

Some state statutes apply different rules to a merger that involves a limited liability company (LLC). Under some state statutes, a merger involving an LLC requires the unanimous approval of the members rather than the two thirds majority required of corporations. On the other hand, as is true in other circumstances, the operating agreement of an LLC could cancel this unanimous vote requirement. If the operating agreement specifies that a merger vote could be approved by less than a unanimous vote, then many states give those members who are opposed to the merger the right to withdraw from the LLC and to receive the cash value of their investment. However, once again, the operating agreement can alter this statutory right.

Asset Acquisition

In an **asset acquisition,** one corporation purchases all the property of a second corporation. However, as in the case of mergers, SEC antifraud regulations can be applied to asset acquisitions if a proxy solicitation process is involved or if insider information is used to profit from the sale. Asset acquisition is easy and efficient because the only formality required is approval by the directors and shareholders of the corporation that is selling its assets. A second advantage is that the buyer need not purchase all of the assets of the seller. The buyer may choose to purchase some assets while rejecting others.

Another advantage of asset acquisition is that, in general, no debts or other liabilities are transferred from seller to buyer. There are exceptions to this rule, however. In certain situations the debts of the selling corporation will transfer to the buying corporation. For instance, if the buyer is simply a continuation of the selling corporation, the buyer will not escape the liabilities of the seller. Similarly, if the sale is structured fraudulently to escape the liabilities of the selling corporation, the debts will transfer to the buyer. It is also possible for the buyer to either expressly or implicitly assume the debts and liabilities of the seller. Finally, if, despite its label as an asset acquisition, the sale is actually a merger, the liabilities will transfer to the buyer.

Stock Acquisition

Stock acquisitions are also known as *takeovers*. In a **takeover bid,** one corporation, the **suitor,** offers to buy the voting stock of another corporation, the **target.** A successful takeover occurs once the suitor has purchased enough voting stock to control the target. One advantage of the stock acquisition process is that it sidesteps the

Background Informa-tion Because it is nearly impossible to gain 100 percent ownership of a company by stock purchase alone, nearly all acquisitions of public companies are accomplished by mergers alone or in combination with stock purchases.

Further Reading For a technical and up-to-date look at expanding businesses, see *Mergers and Acquisitions from A to Z: Strategic and Practical Guidance for Small and Middle Market Buyers and Sellers* by Andrew J. Shermon (New York: Amacom Publishing, 1998).

For the source of the ideas discussed in this segment of Talking Points see: Posner, Richard. *Overcoming Law.* Cambridge, MA: Harvard University Press, 1995, pp. 411–413.

Talking Points

In his treatise, *Overcoming Law,* the legal scholar, Richard Posner, spends a great deal of time exploring the relationship between economics and the law. In doing so, he focuses on the ideas of two economists, Ronald Coase, who won the Nobel Memorial Prize for Economic Sciences in 1991, and George Stigler, the author of *The Citizen and the State: Essays on Regulation.* Posner explains their points of view in the following way:

"The Swedish Academy had also emphasized **Stigler's** theory of regulation . . . as 'treating *political behavior as utility-maximizing* [and] *political parties as firms supplying regulation,* with *what is supplied being what is wanted by those groups* (or coalitions) which are able to outbid others in the political markets.'"—Posner, *Overcoming Law,* pp. 411–412 (italics added).

"These terms, and the vast bodies of formal theory that have grown up around them, assume a *fragility of markets* and the *robustness of government,* whereas **Coase** believes that careful observation of markets and government discloses the *robustness of markets* and the *fragility of government.*"—Posner, *Overcoming Law,* p. 413 (italics added).

Of the two economists, which one would appear to support government regulation? Summarize the theory of that economist. What is the major objection that the other economist has for opposing government intervention? Which view supports the idea that the juris-economic system is a flexible and responsive system? Explain your answers to each of these questions.

Getting Students Involved Have students investigate and define some of the terminology associated with mergers and acquisitions, including *tender offers, poison pills, doomsday strategies, lockups, no-shop agreements, arbitrage, stakeholder, greenmail, sharkrepellents, corporate raiders, leverage buyouts, white knights, turnabouts, veto stock, accelerated loans, supermajority, voting rights,* and *golden parachutes.*

board of directors. The acquiring corporation deals directly with the shareholders. Usually, the shareholders are motivated to sell because the acquiring company has made an offer that is above the current market price of the stock.

At times, corporations are targeted by unfriendly suitors. An **unfriendly suitor,** also known as a **hostile bidder,** is one which intends to change management and shake up the corporation after the takeover. To avoid being taken over by a hostile bidder the management of a corporation can institute both post-offer and pre-offer tactics. Post-offer tactics include, but are not limited to, public relations initiatives, greenmail, the white knight gambit, and lockup agreements. In contrast, pre-offer tactics could involve supermajority voting and accelerated loans, among others.

Post-Offer Techniques Probably the least problematic post-offer technique is the public relations initiative. Such an initiative is aimed at convincing shareholders that it is in their best interests not to sell their shares to the hostile bidder. News releases, advertisements, press conferences, and even personal letters would attempt to convince shareholders that present management should be retained. The difficulty with this approach is that many arguments pale into insignificance when placed alongside a bid that is high above the current market price of the stock.

Sometimes the most effective way for a target to shake off a bidder's hostile suit is to offer the bidder **greenmail.** A corporation which activates the greenmail defense has offered to buy that portion of the target's stock which the bidder already owns. Naturally, such an approach will work only if the target's offer is significantly higher than the amount that the bidder paid for the stock in the first place. Such an approach is disfavored because it robs the shareholders of the opportunity to make a profit by selling their shares and may seriously devalue the target's remaining stock, thereby victimizing the shareholders a second time.

Another post-offer technique that can be used by the target company is the white knight gambit. To implement this tactic, the target invites another suitor to outbid the hostile bidder. The second suitor is known as a **friendly suitor** or a **white knight** because the invited suitor agrees that it will retain existing management. The white knight also frequently agrees not to disrupt the smooth running of the target by selling off key assets, closing down plants, or laying off employees. A takeover battle usually follows. The winner is generally the suitor who can offer the highest price for the target's outstanding stock.

A fourth post-offer technique is the **lockup agreement.** A lockup agreement might be used by target management if the target owns an irreplaceable piece of property, the sale of which would seriously devalue the overall worth of the target. Such property might include rich timberland or an extremely productive coal mine. Provided that the sale of that property does not deplete virtually all the assets of the target, management could enter a contract with a white knight, giving the knight an option to buy that valuable piece of property should the hostile bidder gain control of the target corporation. The idea is to discourage the hostile bidder from buying the now devalued target.

Pre-Offer Techniques Sometimes post-offer techniques are instituted too late to prevent takeover. For this reason, many corporations plan ahead by instituting certain pre-offer measures even before any unfriendly suitors have appeared on the horizon. For example, a corporation could institute a supermajority provision into its bylaws that would require a 90 percent affirmative vote by all shareholders for the approval of any merger. Such a move would mean that any suitor would have to acquire 90 percent of the stock of the target in order to assure a takeover. A back-up provision requiring a supermajority to change the supermajority bylaws would also be necessary to ensure that the suitor does not simply take 51 percent of the target and then use that majority control to eliminate the supermajority merger vote provision.

An additional pre-offer technique involves the corporation in a series of accelerated loans. Under the provisions of an accelerated loan program, all major loans taken out by the corporation are due in full immediately upon the takeover of the target by an unfriendly suitor. The plan is to place the suitor in a precarious financial position because, once the target has been acquired, the suitor would be forced to pay off a series of expensive loans, thus straining the treasury of the target. The accelerated loan gambit is often unsuccessful because the financial institutions which made the loans are often willing to renegotiate the terms of the accelerated loans with the target's new owner in order to avoid getting a poor return on their investments.

Takeover Bids and the SEC Takeover bids are closely scrutinized by the SEC. Under recent amendments to federal securities law, whenever a suitor makes an offer to acquire more than 5 percent of a target, that suitor must file a statement with the SEC. The statement must indicate: (1) where the money for the takeover originates, (2) why the suitor is buying the stock, and (3) how much of the target the suitor already owns. These procedures are designed to let shareholders know the identity and intention of a takeover bidder. Bidders who falsify any information on their statement may find their takeover bid stopped by a court order.

Expansion Effects and Antitrust Law

Antitrust law does not focus on corporate expansion techniques. Instead, it looks at how an expansion attempt will affect competition in the marketplace (see Table 39-3). Section 7 of the Clayton Act forbids any corporate expansion if that expansion sets up a monopoly or otherwise hurts competition. The Clayton Act applies to horizontal, vertical, or conglomerate expansion attempts.

Expansion Attempts Because **horizontal expansion** occurs between companies that are involved in the same business, such attempts often result in monopolies. Consequently, horizontal expansion schemes are closely scrutinized by the FTC and are more likely to be labeled illegal. A **vertical expansion** occurs between companies that were in a customer-supplier relationship. If a manufacturer of designer jeans were to buy a chain of department stores that carried its jeans, a vertical expansion would result. A **conglomerate expansion**

Related Cases In North Carolina, Food Town Stores and Lowe's Food Stores planned to merge. The Federal Trade Commission sued to stop the merger, claiming that the new corporation would violate the Clayton Act. The FTC's protest included concern that the merger would eliminate competition between Food Town and Lowe's in six cities, would increase concentration in these markets, would eliminate potential competition in other markets, and would increase barriers to entry into the local food business. The court granted the FTC's injunction to block the merger. *FTC v. Food Town Stores, Inc.,* 539 F.2d 1339.

Table 39-3 Antitrust Law and Corporate Expansion

Technique	Explanation	Regulation
Horizontal expansion	Occurs between companies that are involved in the same business	Closely scrutinized by the FTC because of the likelihood of a monopoly
Vertical expansion	Occurs between companies that are in a customer-supplier relationship	Less likelihood of monopoly, therefore less FTC scrutiny
Conglomerate expansion	Occurs between two companies that are not in competition with each other	Least likelihood of monopoly, therefore least FTC scrutiny

joins two companies that were not in competition with one another either because they dealt in different products or services or because they operated in different geographical areas.

Hart-Scott-Rodino Antitrust Act Like the SEC, the FTC has a chance to step into expansion situations even before they become an established fact. This opportunity is provided by the Hart-Scott-Rodino Antitrust Act. Hart-Scott-Rodino is designed to police any expansion attempts that might harm competition in the marketplace. The act requires corporations that are setting up an expansion attempt to notify the FTC before the deal is completed. This advance notice allows the FTC to investigate the anticompetitive effects of the planned expansion. Should the FTC decide that the expansion will hurt competition, it can go to court and ask for an injunction to prevent the expansion.

Quick Quiz 39-4 True or False?

1. Most antifraud provisions of the Securities Exchange Commission apply to the merger process.
2. Greenmail is the least effective antihostile takeover technique.
3. The Hart-Scott-Rodino Act is designed to police any expansion attempts that might harm competition in the marketplace.

39-5 Other Forms of Regulation

Corporations are regulated by the government in a variety of ways that extend beyond their involvement in the securities market, the antitrust arena, and the corporate expansion game. Many of these controls have been discussed in earlier chapters, including labor regulations in Chapter 34, bankruptcy and debt adjustment in Chapter 31, commerce regulation in Chapter 21, and consumer protection regulation in Chapter 19. Three areas of regulation as yet unmentioned are energy regulation, environmental protection, and employment regulation.

Energy Regulation

The Arab Oil embargo of 1973 and the subsequent energy crisis focused national attention on the power industry. In answer to these concerns, Congress created the Department of Energy and the Federal Energy Regulatory Commission. National concern with the problems of nuclear energy has also recently focused attention on the Nuclear Regulatory Commission.

AOL CEO Steve Case (left) and Gerald Levin, CEO of Time Warner, announce the merger of their companies.

Federal Energy Regulatory Commission The Federal Energy Regulatory Commission (FERC) is responsible for regulating the transportation and the wholesale price of natural gas and electricity sold for use in interstate commerce. State utility commissioners regulate intrastate prices. Rates are calculated to allow companies a specific rate of return on investments (earnings divided by total assets), which they may not exceed. When utilities are confronted with increased costs due to higher fuel prices, they can apply to the commission for permission to pass these increased costs on to customers through fuel adjustment charges.

Nuclear Regulatory Commission Mandated by the Energy Reorganization Act, the Nuclear Regulatory Commission (NRC) is responsible for the licensing, construction, and operation of nuclear reactors. It is also responsible for regulating the possession, use, transportation, handling, and disposal of nuclear material. The NRC develops and implements rules and regulations governing licensed unclear activities.

Environmental Protection Regulation

The Environmental Protection Agency (EPA) is an independent agency in the executive branch of the federal government. It was created to carry out the provisions of the National Environmental Policy Act and other major environmental laws and executive orders dealing with air, water, solid waste, toxic substance, and noise pollution.

National Environmental Policy Act The purpose of the 1969 National Environmental Policy Act is to establish a national policy that will combat pollution and improve the environment. The legislation encourages efforts that prevent or eliminate damage to the environment and that stimulate the health and welfare of the public. The act requires a detailed statement of environmental consequences in every recommendation or proposal for legislation and other major federal actions significantly affecting the quality of the human environment. These environmental impact statements describe in detail the expected adverse environmental consequences of a proposed action. The alternatives to the action are also described.

Environmental Protection Agency All major antipollution programs dealing with air, noise, solid wastes, toxic substances, and pesticides were placed under the

Related Cases The Babcox and Wilcox Company, a supplier of nuclear fuel, and Allied-General Nuclear Services, a nuclear service company, entered into an agreement in which Allied-General would reprocess fuel used by Babcox and Wilcox. However, when the construction of Allied-General's nuclear facility was completed, the Nuclear Regulatory Commission denied it an operating license. In *The Babcox and Wilcox Company v. Allied-General Nuclear Services* (161 A.D.2D 350), the court ruled that the defendant showed good faith in trying to overturn the government's ruling, so the defendant was not liable for breach of contract.

Teaching Tips Inform students that the Occupational Safety and Health Administration (OSHA), which monitors worker safety, concentrates on the use of potentially hazardous products, and the EPA, which monitors environmental consequences, focuses on the disposal of potentially hazardous products. The responsibilities of the two organizations are likely to overlap more in the future, particularly in the development of programs to manage newly created chemicals.

The Environmental Protection Agency exercises significant regulatory power over U.S. businesses.

Further Reading For an excellent study of corporate crimes involving finances, OSHA, and the environment, see *Corporate Crime: Contemporary Debate,* edited by Frank Pierce and Laureen Snider (Toronto: University of Toronto Press, 1995).

Did You Know?

According to some experts, implementing the Environmental Protection Agency's regulations costs state and local governments in excess of $40 billion every year.

---

administrative control of the EPA in 1970. The EPA's primary responsibilities are to conduct research on all aspects of pollution, set and enforce pollution control standards, monitor programs to determine whether pollution abatement standards are being met, and administer grants to assist states in controlling pollution.

The EPA has the power to enforce the standards and programs it initiates. It encourages voluntary compliance by industry and communities and supports state and local governments' efforts to conduct enforcement actions of their own. When such efforts fail, the EPA conducts enforcement proceedings. Often the EPA must act against companies that pollute the environment, even if the pollution activity is unintentional. For example, the Federal Water Pollution Control Act forbids "any addition of any pollutants to navigable waters from any source." The courts have interpreted this broad prohibition to include even accidental pollution, because to hold otherwise would weaken the statute.

Employment Protection Regulation

In Chapters 34 and 35, employment law and labor-management relations law were both discussed at length. However, this is not the extent of the law regarding employment matters. The law has taken several steps to protect employees who are affected by the sale, merger, or closing of a business. Two key pieces of legislation in this regard are the Employee Retirement Income Security Act (ERISA) and the Worker Adjustment and Retraining Notification Act (WARN).

Employee Retirement Income Security Act As noted in Chapter 34, ERISA employers must place their pension contributions into a pension trust on behalf of their employees, independent of the employer. Under the rules of vesting detailed in the statute, workers are guaranteed the right to receive their pension benefits regardless of whether they are working under the plan at the time of retirement. However, what happens if a business is sold or merges with another business? The answer to this question depends on whether the sale is a stock acquisition or an asset acquisition.

If the sale is a stock acquisition, in most cases the employee benefit plan is assumed by the purchasing corporation. On the other hand, if the sale involves an asset acquisition, then the buyer may or may not adopt the plan. The purchasing corporation may also elect to assume the plan after it has amended the plan to its satisfaction. Another alternative is for the purchaser to adopt an entirely new employee benefit plan that is similar but not identical to the plan of the selling corporation. Whatever the case, it is incumbent upon the purchaser to examine all pertinent records regarding the seller's employee benefit plan. These records include but are not limited to the annual report that is given to all participants in the plan, all insurance and annuity contracts, all Internal Revenue Service forms associated with the benefit plan, as well as the writing that describes the plan.

Worker Adjustment and Retraining Notification Act If the sale of a business involves a plant closing or a mass layoff, then provisions of the Worker Adjustment and Retraining Notification Act (WARN) must be considered. WARN requires employers with at least 100 full-time employees to give those employees sixty days notice before all plant closings and mass layoffs. The notice must be in writing and must be given to every affected worker unless the workers are represented by a union, in which case the notice must be given to a representative of the union. WARN also requires that written notice of all plant closings and mass layoffs be given to the highest elected official of the local political subdivision in which the layoff or closing will happen. WARN's provisions do not apply if a state statute or a collective bargaining agreement requires a longer period of advance notice.

Quick Quiz 39-5 True or False?

1. The Arab Oil Embargo of 1973 and the subsequent energy crisis focused national attention on environmental protection and resulted in the establishment of the Environmental Protection Agency.

2. The Nuclear Regulatory Commission replaced the Federal Energy Regulatory Commission.

3. The Worker Adjustment and Retraining Notification Act repealed the Employee Retirement Income Security Act.

Government can easily exist without law, but law cannot exist without government.

—Bertrand Russell (1872–1970), British mathematician and philosopher

39-6 The Government and Corporate Dissolution

Just as the government is involved in the birth and the growth (expansion) of a corporation, it is also involved in its death, or dissolution. Whether a corporation ends involuntarily or voluntarily, the government is somehow involved.

Involuntary Dissolution

If a corporation has repeatedly conducted business in an unlawful manner, the secretary of state can ask the state attorney general to bring a *quo warranto* action against that corporation. Under a *quo warranto* proceeding, the state revokes the corporation's charter. Common examples of illegal actions forming the grounds for revocation include a failure to file annual reports, a failure to pay franchise taxes, or a failure to maintain a registered or statutory agent for service of process. Corporations formed fraudulently and those exceeding their authority may also be subject to a *quo warranto* proceeding.

Courts have the power to liquidate the assets of a corporation when an action is brought by a shareholder. Grounds for involuntary dissolution at the request of a shareholder include the following:

- evidence of illegal, oppressive, or fraudulent acts
- a misapplication or waste of corporate assets
- a deadlock of directors that threatens irreparable harm
- evidence that a dissolution is necessary to protect the rights of the complaining shareholder

Voluntary Dissolution

Since the government grants corporate charters and regulates corporate activity, it must be informed when a corporation voluntarily dissolves. A corporation can be dissolved voluntarily by the unanimous approval of the shareholders or by a positive vote of the directors with the approval of two-thirds of the shareholders. Once the decision to dissolve has been approved, a statement of intent must be filed with the state government. The corporation will then cease business and notify creditors (by certified mail) and the public (by publication). After all claims have been received, corporate assets will be used first to pay creditors, with the surplus going to shareholders. If the existing assets cannot meet all claims, a receiver may be called in to handle matters. A *receiver* is a person appointed by law to hold property subject to diverse claims. The receiver would divide assets fairly among creditors. Following the distribution of all assets, the corporation must prepare articles of dissolution and present them to the secretary of state.

39-7 Dissolution of a Limited Liability Company

Because limited liability companies are created by state statutory law, the dissolution of a limited liability company is also regulated by state statutory law. Most state LLC statutes outline the circumstances that will trigger the dissolution of an LLC.

Circumstances of Dissolution

State Variations A Nebraska statute allows a surviving member of a limited liability company to "rescue" the LLC after a member's death by admitting a new member and then voting to continue the business.

The dissolution of an LLC can be initiated by the unanimous agreement of all of its members. Similarly, the dissolution can be triggered by the expulsion, bankruptcy, or withdrawal of a member. However, many state statutes now declare that in both member-managed and manager-managed LLCs a member may not leave the LLC unless such a departure is authorized by the operating agreement. Naturally, the articles of organization or the operating agreement can also specify other events that would cause a dissolution. Some state statutes also assert that the death of a member does not trigger a dissolution. Instead the death of a member is classified as a disassociation.

Effects of Dissolution

As is true with a partnership, a limited liability company does not stop business immediately upon the dissolution event. Dissolution must be distinguished from the winding up of the LLC, which effectively puts it out of business. Winding up involves completing all of the business of the LLC and selling its property to satisfy all of the debts of the firm. As is the case with the dissolution of a partnership, the dissolution of an LLC need not be followed by a winding up of the LLC. If all of the remaining members of the LLC want to continue the LLC they may do so. It is also possible for the operating agreement to specify that the vote to continue need not be unanimous among the remaining members. The operating agreement should also indicate that the LLC will dissolve when the number of members within the LLC falls below the number required by state law.

Summary

39-1 The federal government, the state government, and various subdivisions of the state government all play a role in the regulation of business. The state government and it subdivisions all come by their power along traditional lines. The regulatory power of the state government is based on the state's police power. Police power is the state's authority to restrict private rights in order to promote and maintain public health, safety, welfare, and morals. A state has police power simply by virtue of its existence as a legitimate governmental authority. The federal government, however, has no inherent police power, because it is a government of limited powers. The federal government exercises power over commercial activities through the Commerce Clause of the Constitution (Article I, Section 8, Clause 3).

39-2 The primary objective of the Securities Act of 1933 and the Securities Exchange Act of 1934 is to protect investors by informing them about the securities they purchase. The Securities and Exchange Commission carries out this objective.

39-3 To preserve the value of competition and to discourage monopolies, the government has enacted several antitrust statutes. The Sherman Antitrust Act prohibits contracts, combinations, and conspiracies in restraint of trade. The Clayton Act, the Robinson-Patman Act, the Foreign Trade Improvements Act, and the Federal Trade Commission Act make the Sherman Antitrust Act more specific and more effective.

39-4 While both securities law and antitrust law are concerned with monopolies, they have different areas of concern. Securities law is concerned with regulating corporate expansion techniques including mergers, consolidations, asset acquisitions, and stock acquisition. Antitrust law is concerned with how corporate expansion affects competition in the marketplace. Antitrust law applies to horizontal, vertical, or conglomerate expansion attempts.

39-5 Through the Federal Energy Regulatory Commission and the Nuclear Regulatory Commission, the government regulates businesses involved in energy production. By means of the Environmental Protection Agency, the government also regulates business that pollute the environment.

39-6 Corporations can dissolve involuntarily or voluntarily. A corporation that has repeatedly conducted business in an unlawful manner may be subject to involuntary dissolution by the state. A corporation can be voluntarily dissolved by unanimous approval of the shareholders or by a positive vote of the directors with the approval of two-thirds of the shareholders. The government is involved in both involuntary and voluntary dissolution.

39-7 Since limited liability companies are created by state statutory law, the dissolution of a limited liability company is also regulated by state statutory law. Most state LLC statutes outline the circumstances that will trigger the dissolution of an LLC.

Key Terms

asset acquisition, 745
Commerce Clause, 737
conglomerate expansion, 747
consolidation, 745
friendly suitor, 746
greenmail, 746
horizontal expansion, 747
hostile bidder, 746
individual justice, 738
interlocking directorates, 742
juris-economic system, 737

lockup agreement, 747
merger, 745
monopoly, 741
per se violation, 742
police power, 739
prospectus, 740
registration statement, 740
regulatory justice, 738
rule-of-reason standard, 742
security, 739
stock acquisition, 745

suitor, 745
takeover bid, 745
target, 745
tying agreement, 742
unfriendly suitor, 746
United States Antitrust Modernization Committee, 743
vertical expansion, 747
white knight, 746

Questions for Review and Discussion

1. What is the source of the federal power to regulate business?
2. What is the source of state power to regulate business?
3. How does the Securities Exchange Commission prevent unfair practices?
4. How do per se antitrust violations differ from rule of reason violations?
5. What are the various techniques of corporate expansion?
6. How does the interest of the Securities Exchange Commission in corporate expansion differ from that of the Federal Trade Commission?
7. How does the role of the Environmental Protection Agency compare with that of the Federal Energy Regulatory Commission?
8. What are the rights that are guaranteed to workers under the Employee Retirement Income Security Act and the Worker Adjustment and Retraining Notification Act?
9. What are the two ways that a corporation may undergo dissolution?
10. What are the circumstances under which a limited liability company may undergo dissolution?

Investigating the Internet

Access the Securities and Exchange Commission's home page and write a paper about the creation and organization of the SEC.

Cases for Analysis

1. Filburn, a farm owner in Ohio, raised winter wheat primarily to feed his livestock and poultry and to make flour for home use. Under the provisions of the Agricultural Adjustment Act, Filburn was given notice of a wheat acreage and yield allotment. Filburn, however, sowed more acreage and harvested more wheat than he was allowed. As a result, the government fined him $117.11. Filburn sued the government to prevent it from collecting the fine. He argued that the production and consumption of wheat on his own land for his own purposes are outside the reach of Congress because, at most, this activity had an indirect effect upon interstate commerce. Was Filburn correct? Explain. *Wickard v. Filburn,* 63 S.Ct. 82 (U.S. Sup. Ct.).

2. The W. J. Howey Co., owned a large citrus grove in Florida. The citrus grove was serviced by Howey-in-the-Hills, Inc., a corporation owned and operated by the same people who ran the Howey Co. When the Howey Co., needed money, it sold tracts of land in the grove. Each buyer had

to purchase both land from the Howey Co., and a service contract from Howey-in-the-Hills. The purchasers had no right to enter the land or to market the crop. All cultivating and marketing was done by the service company. Most of the buyers were from out of state. In return for their purchase, they received a share of the profits after the crops were harvested and sold. The SEC brought suit against both companies, arguing that the land and service contracts were actually securities that should have been registered with the commission. Was the SEC correct? Explain. *Securities and Exchange Commission v. W. J. Howey Co.,* 66 S.Ct. 1100 (U.S. Sup. Ct.).

3. Topco Associates, Inc., is a cooperative association of small and medium-sized regional supermarket chains. Each of its member chains operates independently. All members are required to operate under exclusive territorial licenses issued by Topco. These licenses provide that members will sell Topco-controlled brands only within the

marketing territory given them. The government filed suit in federal district court. It argued that this scheme of dividing markets among competing chains violated the Sherman Antitrust Act because it prohibited competition in Topco-brand products among grocery chains engaged in retail operations. Topco defended by arguing that the association actually increased competition between the smaller and the larger chains. Was Topco correct? Defend your answer. *United States v. Topco Associates, Inc.,* 92 S.Ct. 1126 (U.S. Sup. Ct.).

4. Enstrom purchased an aircraft from the Interceptor Corporation. When the aircraft crashed due to a design defect, Enstrom sued Interceptor. However, when Enstrom found out that Interceptor's assets had been purchased by the Interceptor Company (IC), it asked the court to join IC as a new defendant. IC argued that it was a different corporation involved in a different business. IC further argued that it had simply purchased the assets of Interceptor and was now involved in selling those assets, like the aircraft, to other buyers, like Enstrom. IC concluded that it was, therefore, not liable to Enstrom. Was IC correct? Why or why not? *R. J. Enstrom Corporation v. Interceptor Corporation,* 555 F.2d 277 (10th Cir.).

5. Earth Sciences, Inc., conducted gold-leaching operations in Colorado. The process involved spraying gold ore with a toxic substance. To prevent pollution, Earth Sciences had installed a reserve sump to catch any toxic runoff. An unexpected early thaw melted a snowbank, covering the ore heap. As a result, the reserve sump overflowed, dumping toxic waste into the Rito Seco Creek. The United States brought suit, alleging that Earth Sciences had violated pollution laws. Earth Sciences argued that it should not be held liable for an unintentional pollution accident. Was Earth Sciences correct? Explain. *United States v. Earth Sciences, Inc.,* 559 F.2d 368 (10th Cir.).

6. C. E. Stumpf & Sons, Inc., was formed to conduct a masonry and general contracting business. The corporation was owned in equal shares by Stumpf and his two sons, who had previously operated the same business as partners. Hostility between the two sons grew so extreme that one, Donald, ended contact with his family and was allowed no say in the operation of the business. After Donald's withdrawal from the business, he received no salary, dividends, or other revenue from the company. He brought suit seeking involuntary dissolution of the corporation. Should the court of appeals of California uphold the trial court's dissolution order? Why or why not? *Stumpf v. C. E. Stumpf & Sons, Inc.,* 120 Cal. Rptr. 671 (CA).

7. Image Technical Services, Inc. (ITS), an independent service organization (ISO), provides services for companies with copying machines made by the Eastman Kodak Co. In response to such competition, Kodak tied the sale of any of its parts to an agreement not to contract for services from any ISO. Under the terms of such an agreement, a customer who wished to buy Kodak parts had to agree not to purchase service from an ISO. ITS brought a lawsuit against Kodak under the Sherman Antitrust Act. In the suit, ITS alleged that such arrangements amounted to the type of tying agreement that was specifically outlawed by the Sherman Act. Kodak filed a motion for a summary judgment arguing that the purchase of parts and the service of the machines with those parts did not represent the purchase of two separate products. Kodak concluded that it was, therefore, entitled to a judgment as a matter of law. Should the Court grant the summary judgment motion or is there enough evidence of a tying agreement here to allow the matter to proceed to trial? Explain. *Eastman Kodak Co. v. Image Technical Services, Inc., et al.,* 504 U.S. 451 (U.S. Sup. Ct.).

Quick Quiz Answers

39-1	39-2	39-3	39-4	39-5	39-6
1. T	1. T	1. F	1. T	1. F	1. F
2. T	2. T	2. F	2. F	2. F	2. F
3. F	3. F	3. F	3. T	3. F	3. F

39-7
1. F
2. T
3. T

Part 8 Case Study

Gries Sports Enterprises, Inc. v. Cleveland Browns Football Co., Inc.
Supreme Court of Ohio
496 N.E.2d 959

Summary

Arthur Modell, president, CEO, and a director of the Cleveland Browns Football Co., Inc., (Browns) owned 53 percent of that corporation. Other members of the board at that time included: Pat Modell, Modell's wife; James Bailey, who was also chief counsel for and an employee of the Browns; James Berick, who was outside counsel representing the corporation and a Browns shareholder; Richard Cole; and Nate Wallack, who was also an employee of the Browns. The final member of the board of directors was Robert Gries, who owned 43 percent of the Browns and who also owned Gries Sports Enterprises, Inc. (GSE). Modell also owned 80 percent of the Cleveland Stadium Corporation (CSC), which leased Cleveland Stadium from the city and which then subleased the Stadium to the Browns and the Cleveland Indians. Other shareholders of CSC included Berick, Bailey, Cole, Wallack, Gries, and GSE. Modell was also president of CSC and Bailey was both secretary and general counsel of that corporation.

CSC purchased 190 acres of land in Strongsville, Ohio, from Modell for $3,000,000 in cash and a promissory note for $1,000,000. Although Modell later canceled the $1,000,000 note, CSC still had debts exceeding $4,000,000. Modell decided that it would be expedient for the Browns to purchase CSC. Accordingly, he had CSC appraised by the brokerage and investment banking firm of McDonald and Company. Modell and Bailey, along with Michael Poplar, chief financial officer of CSC, determined that the Browns should pay $6,000,000 for the purchase of CSC. After this decision had been made, Modell, Bailey Berick, and Poplar told Gries and Cole that CSC would be purchased by the Browns for $6,000,000. The purchase plan involved a payment of $120 per share of CSC to the minority shareholders among whom were Berick, Bailey, Wallack, and Cole. Modell, the majority shareholder in CSC was to receive a payment of $4,800,000 for his shares.

Subsequently, Gries did his own investigation into the value of CSC and concluded that Modell, Bailey, and Poplar had seriously overvalued the worth of that corporation. When the board met to consider the purchase, Modell made a presentation in support of the plan and Gries explained his opposition. When the matter came to a vote, Bailey, Berick, Cole, and Wallack all voted for the plan. Neither Arthur nor Pat Modell participated in the vote and Gries voted against the transaction. The following day, Gries filed a derivative lawsuit, the objective of which was to compel a reversal of the decision to purchase CSC. Gries stated that the transaction was unfair to the corporation in that CSC was worth only $2,000,000 at the time that the Browns purchased it for $6,000,000. Gries argued that the fairness rule rather than the business judgment rule should be used to evaluate the directors' conduct because the directors who voted for the purchase were either "interested" directors due to their stock ownership or they were dominated by Modell and had simply "rubber stamped" his decision.

Moreover, Gries contended that the over valuation of CSC was prompted by Modell's need to secure the money to pay off outstanding debts to several banks. Modell and the other directors argued that the decision to buy CSC should be evaluated by the business judgment rule. The trial court agreed with Gries but the appeals court reversed that decision. The case then went to the Ohio Supreme Court.

The Court's Opinion

Justice Wise

The appellees-directors herein claim that they are protected by the presumption of good faith and fair dealing that arises from the business judgment and, therefore, they do not have the burden of proving that their decision to purchase CSC was intrinsically fair to the Browns' minority shareholders.

The issue before us, then, centers on the applicability of the business judgment rule. The business judgment rule is a principle of corporate governance that has been part of the common law for at least one hundred fifty years. It has traditionally operated as a shield to protect directors from liability for their decisions. If the directors are entitled to the protection of the rule, then the courts should not interfere with or second-guess their decisions. If the directors are not entitled to the protection of the rule then the courts scrutinize the decision as to its intrinsic fairness to the corporation and the corporation's minority shareholders. . . . A party challenging a board of directors' decision bears the burden of rebutting the presumption that the decision was a proper exercise of the business judgment of the board. . . .

In a stockholders' derivative action challenging the fairness of a transaction approved by a majority of directors of a corporation a director must be (1) disinterested, (2) independent, and (3) informed in order to claim benefit of the business judgment rule. If a director fails to pass muster as to any one of these three, he is not entitled to the business judgment presumption. This does not mean that the director's decision is necessarily wrong; it only removes the protection provided by the business judgment presumption. Once this presumption is removed, the court must then inquire into the fairness of the director's decision.

(A) a director is interested if (1) he appears on both sides of the transaction or (2) he has or expects to derive a personal financial benefit not equally received by the stockholders; (B) a director is independent if his decision is based on the corporate merits of the subject before the board rather than extraneous considerations or influences; a director is not independent when he is dominated by or beholden to another person through personal or other relationship; and (C) a director is informed if he makes a reasonable effort to become familiar with the relevant and reasonably available facts prior to making a business judgment.

Browns' directors Modell, Gries, Bailey, Berick, Cole, and Wallack, were all stockholders in CSC. Modell was the fifty-three percent majority stockholder in the Browns and the eighty percent majority stockholder in CSC (one hundred percent after March 2, 1982). (These facts convinced the court that the directors were interested in the challenged decision and were, therefore, not entitled to the protection of the business judgment rule. The court then went on to apply the fairness rule to the purchase of CSC by the Browns.)

(W)hen the transaction ". . . involves insiders dealing with their corporation the test of validity of the transaction is fairness. That our courts have frequently so held is without question. . . . the substance of our decisions that 'when the persons, be they stockholders or directors, who control the making of a transaction and the fixing of its terms, are on both sides, then the presumption and deference to sound business judgment are no longer present.'"

In the instant case, no arms length negotiations as to price, terms, the elements to be included (or not to be included), or any other aspect of the proposed acquisition ever took place between the Browns and CSC. The $6,000,000 price was arrived at by Messrs. AMA (Modell), Bailey and Poplar . . . prior to any disclosure to plaintiffs of the possibility of such an acquisition, and never changed despite plaintiff's objections and despite the valuations furnished the defendants by plaintiffs. The manner in which the subject transaction was initiated, structured and disclosed to plaintiffs therefore did not satisfy the reasonable concept of fair dealing. . . .

The judgment of the court of appeals is reversed, and the judgment of the trial court is reinstated.

Judgment reversed.

Questions for Analysis

1. Which party had the burden of proof in this case?

2. According to the court's opinion, what factors should be taken into consideration in determining whether a director has an interest in a transaction that is challenged by a shareholder in a derivative lawsuit?

3. According to the court's opinion, when is a director independent and under what circumstances does the director lose that independence?

4. What circumstances does the court say will make a director informed?

5. When the business judgment rule cannot be used, as occurred in this case, what standard is applied by the court to determine whether to reverse a challenged decision made by the directors?

6. Did the court consider the purchase of the Cleveland Stadium Corporation by the Cleveland Browns to be fair to the corporation and the minority shareholders in this case? Why or why not?

Emerging Trends and Issues

Part Nine

Professional Liability

The Opening Case
"A Nontraditional Duty to Inform"

The belief that physicians have a duty to inform their patients about medical problems is unquestioned in the law. In fact, the existence of a legal duty between the physician and the patient is so well-established that the element of duty is rarely at issue in a malpractice lawsuit. Of course, most legal questions involving a physician's duty have presupposed the existence of a traditional relationship between the patient and the physician. However, the world of modern medicine has created many nontraditional relationships which can lead to new and challenging nontraditional problems. This is exactly what happened to Arnold Franklin, a student in Bostic, Nevada, when he underwent a physical examination after applying for admission to Salisbury University. Franklin's blood tests and x-rays were evaluated by Dr. Samuel Tillich, a diagnostician who worked for Zimmerman Laboratories. Dr. Tillich, who never had any personal contact with Franklin, noted that Franklin's white blood cell count was very low. Consequently, Dr. Tillich recommended another evaluation. Dr. Tillich filed his report with Salisbury University and, for some unknown reason, the reporting process ended there. Neither Dr. Tillich nor the university notified Franklin who, by the way, was admitted to the university. Twelve months after this, Franklin was diagnosed with leukemia. Later, to Dr. Tillich's surprise, he found himself a defendant in a medical malpractice case. Franklin's attorneys alleged that Dr. Tillich owed a duty to Franklin which he had violated by not informing him about the results of his blood test. Dr. Tillich's attorney confidently argued that, since there was no traditional patient-physician relationship between Dr. Tillich and Franklin, there could be no duty on the part of Dr. Tillich to report directly to Franklin. That duty, the attorney argued, fell squarely on the university's shoulders not the diagnostician's. Franklin's attorney disagreed and argued quite convincingly that it was unreasonable to say that a physician who knows about a life-threatening problem, and who knows how to reach the patient, has no duty to inform that patient of the problem. The court agreed with the plaintiff's attorney and ruled that, even though Franklin and Tillich had a nontraditional relationship, the diagnostician had a duty to inform him of the problem. The court emphasized the fact that no other physician was involved in the transaction and that the diagnostician clearly knew how to contact Franklin. As you read Chapter 40, consider both sides of this argument and try to reconcile these points of view as best you can.

Chapter Outcomes

1. Distinguish between a certified public accountant and a public accountant.
2. Identify the types of auditing opinions that can be issued by auditors.
3. Differentiate between generally accepted accounting principles and generally accepted auditing standards.
4. Indicate the duties that accountants owe to their clients.
5. Outline the registration requirements imposed on architects by the state.
6. Identify the duties that an architect owes to his or her clients.
7. Determine the duties that an attorney owes to his or her clients.
8. State the standard of care used to judge health care professionals.
9. Contrast the locality rule with the national standard in determining a health care provider's liability.
10. Explain the circumstances under which hospitals can be held liable for the torts of independent contractor physicians.

For a case that outline facts similar to those in The Opening Case see: Landau, Joel. "Doctor's Obligation Is Broadened: Responsibilities Can Go Beyond Traditional Doctor-Patent Relation." *The National Law Journal,* August 2, 2004, p. 11; *Stanley v. McCarver,* No. CV-03-099-PR.

40-1 The Liability of Accountants

As we've seen in the commercial world, the legal system and the economic culture interact with one another in such a way that they become, at times, one single system, the juris-economic system. In the last chapter, we also examined how the juris-economic system acts as another aspect of the complex adaptive system of the law. Now we turn our attention to one of the key players in the juris-economic system, the accountant.

The Regulation of Accounting

Accountants, like all professionals, must meet certain basic standards that are defined by the nature of their profession. A **professional** is a person who can perform a highly specialized task because of special abilities, education, experience, and knowledge. Often the term professional is reserved for those individuals who perform a service for the public good. An **accountant** is a professional who can plan, direct, and evaluate a client's financial affairs. Although many accountants are charged with keeping a client's financial records, their responsibilities often go far beyond such routine tasks. Moreover, the nature of accounting means that an accountant's activities may have an impact on investors who exist outside the accountant's inner circle of clients. For these reasons, among others, accountants are regulated by the government. The federal government's power to regulate business, in general, and accounting, in particular, emerges from the Commerce Clause of the Constitution. The regulation of accounting by the state is part of the state's police power. The state's police power permits the state to regulate various activities in order to promote the general health, safety, welfare, and morals of the people.

Accountant Registration

The regulation of accounting is part of the state's police power. The state's police power allows the state government to regulate various activities in order to promote the general health, safety, welfare, and morals of its citizens.

Types of Accountants

There are many different types of accountants. Some accountants work only for one employer. British Petroleum, for example, employs hundreds of accountants to chart the financial fortunes of the corporation. Other accountants hire themselves out to work for a wide variety of different clients. Such accountants generally belong to two categories: certified public accountants and public accountants.

Background Information The fear of being sued has generated interest in overseas asset protection trusts (APTs) among some wealthy professionals, including doctors, accountants, lawyers, and property developers. Through an APT, an individual can sign over official ownership of assets to a trust manager, while retaining ultimate control of the assets. The advantage of this arrangement is that if people with APTs are sued, they cannot lose their assets because the assets are technically no longer theirs in the eyes of the law.

State Variations In Nebraska, no partnership or limited liability company may use the title or designation, "Certified Public Account" or "CPA," unless such partnership or limited liability company is registered with the state and is issued a permit which is not revoked or suspended.

Related Cases A Mississippi statute restricting the preparation of tax returns for compensation to CPAs was held void as an unconstitutional exercise of police powers in *Moore v. Grillis,* 39 So.2d 505.

Certified public accountants (CPAs) have met certain age, character, education, experience, and testing requirements. These requirements are generally established by the state. For example, the state government may require CPAs to be at least eighteen years old and of good moral character. The state may also require a bachelor's degree, two years of experience, and a passing score on a written examination that covers accounting, auditing, and other related subject areas.

Public accountants (PAs) are accountants who work for a variety of clients but are not certified. Frequently, states will not allow individuals to call themselves public accountants unless they have met certain requirements that are not as strict as the requirements for CPAs.

The Effect of State Registration State registration requirements are designed to shield citizens against people who practice accounting without the education or experience necessary to do a competent job. The state cannot, however, prevent someone from practicing accounting as a profession. The state can only stop such individuals from calling themselves CPAs, PAs, or any other title that might mislead a client into thinking the nonregistered accountant is registered.

Accounting and Auditing

Accountants perform a number of functions for their clients. They may balance accounts, reconcile bank records with account books, handle the payroll, fill out income tax returns, and handle other tax matters. Another important job that falls to the accountant is the task of auditing.

Auditing An **audit** is an examination of the financial records of an organization to determine whether those records are a fair representation of the actual financial health of the institution. To be effective an audit is usually conducted by an outside, independent auditor. An **auditor** is an accountant who conducts an audit. The dilemma that auditors face is that they are responsible at two levels of accountability. Traditionally auditors are hired by and work for the organization which is being audited. This is the first level of accountability. At the second level of accountability, auditors are responsible to the investors, lenders, shareholders, and others who rely on the financial statements made by those auditors. Idealistically, auditors ought to be loyal to both groups of individuals. Realistically, auditors do not always overlook the fact that the organization is the one that hired them and that makes out their paycheck. As a result, there is a tendency, probably unconscious in most cases, to help the organization rather than the outside investors.

Example 40-1

Enron Corporation, a global energy management company, engaged in a series of questionable practices that resulted in the company filing for bankruptcy. The bankruptcy was investigated by federal regulators who were curious about a number of irregularities in the company's overstated value, in the unusually high earnings of its top executives, and in a series of dubious accounting procedures that had been conducted by the firm of Arthur Andersen, the corporation's auditors. Ostensibly, auditors are supposed to be loyal to both the organization and those who invest in the company including not only present shareholders, but also future investors as well. Even if it were possible to argue that the accounting procedures engaged in by the company were appropriate, Arthur Andersen employees apparently crossed the line when they engaged in the alleged shredding of documents related to Enron's financial health (or lack thereof). The fact that Enron may have employed about 150 Andersen workers, and paid the accounting firm $23 million annually for auditing services and $29 million each year for advice and consultation support, may have played a role in the alleged decision to shred those crucial documents. It might have been wiser for the Arthur Andersen employees at Enron to remember that an auditor does not guarantee an institution's financial health. Rather, the auditor renders an opinion as to the fairness and accuracy of the financial statements issued by the institution. Auditors also check to see if an institution has followed generally accepted accounting principles. Moreover, in fashioning their audit, auditors must follow generally accepted auditing standards.

Accounting Principles An independent group known as the Financial Accounting Standards Board (FASB) has established **generally accepted accounting principles (GAAP).** The rules established by the FASB are followed by the American Institute of Certified Public Accountants (AICPA). The rules outline the procedures that accountants must use in accumulating financial data and in preparing financial statements. In general, the procedures facilitate the preparation of reports that are useful, understandable, reliable, verifiable, and comparable.

Auditing Standards The Auditing Standards Board of the AICPA has set up **generally accepted auditing standards (GAAS).** These auditing standards measure the quality of the performance of the auditing procedures. In short, the auditing standards explain how an auditor can determine whether proper accounting procedures have been used. There are ten auditing standards. Three of these relate to the auditors, three relate to their work in the field, and four relate to the opinions that they issue.

Types of Opinions An auditor's opinions may be unqualified or qualified. When auditors conclude that the financial records of the company are an accurate reflection of the company's financial status, they will issue an **unqualified opinion.** When auditors issue a **qualified opinion,** they are saying that the books represent the company's financial health as of a given date. However, auditors may qualify the opinion in one of two ways. One type of qualified opinion is the "subject to" opinion. In this case, auditors state that the books represent the company's financial health subject to some uncertainty, such as a pending lawsuit, which may affect the company in the future. The second type of qualified opinion is an "except for" opinion. Such an opinion indicates that the financial statements are an accurate reflection of the company's financial health except for some minor deviation from GAAP, not serious enough to warrant an adverse opinion.

Auditors may also issue adverse opinions and disclaimers. An **adverse opinion** is rendered when the deviations from GAAP are so serious that an unqualified

Accountants can be an excellent source of advice about a client's financial matters.

opinion is impossible and a qualified opinion is not justified. An adverse opinion would be rendered in the following cases:

- The financial statements do not fairly present the financial health of the organization.
- Generally accepted accounting principles are consistently ignored.
- Financial information has not been adequately disclosed.
- There are major uncertainties that could have a serious impact on the organization and the auditor disagrees with management's presentation of those uncertainties.

A **disclaimer** declares that the auditor has decided not to give any opinion on the company's financial records. This situation generally occurs because the auditor has not had enough time to examine the books properly or was denied access to crucial records. An auditor might also issue a disclaimer if the books indicate that the organization exercised no control over the accounting process.

The Sarbanes-Oxley Act

In response to some of the difficulties that can be traced to the dual identity that auditors must assume, Congress enacted the **Sarbanes-Oxley Act.** Although the Sarbanes-Oxley bill has many targets, one of the most crucial is to restore the confidence of the investment community. This is extremely important because that confidence has been shattered recently by the scandals surrounding Arthur Andersen and Enron, and the problems that have been associated with the uncertainty of stock market trading. One of the most important parts of the new act was the creation of the **Public Company Accounting Oversight Board (PCAOB).** This new regulatory agency is charged with the task of making certain that correct, unbiased, and comprehensive data find their way to potential investors, so that they can make informed decisions about investment opportunities. To accomplish this task, Congress has given the board responsibility for the supervision of public accounting firms. With this power comes the ability to set up practical instructions for auditing procedures, and philosophical canons for the ethical values that such firms must follow. In order to give the new federal board proper authority, the act requires the registration of all public accounting firms that are involved in auditing publicly traded corporations. The board then has the authority to inspect those companies and their procedures on a regularly established schedule. The board consists of five members, only two of which are permitted to be certified public accountants. The hope is that this approach will keep the agency objective and unbiased as it evaluates both the accounting firms and the procedures under which they operate.

The Sarbanes-Oxley Act has also enacted several additional features. For example, the act specifically prohibits conflicts of interest that might arise when former auditors are hired by a company, when that company is still being audited by the same firm that once employed the former auditor. The prohibition lasts for one year and covers only the uppermost management positions of the audited company. Sarbanes-Oxley also requires that corporate audit committees receive timely and comprehensive reports from the accounting firm that is auditing the company. Alternative approaches to the way that financial data is packaged must be included in these regular reporting sessions. Under provisions of the new act, Congress has also ordered a probe into the recent merging of the Big Eight accounting firms into the Big Four. The aim of the probe is to find out what led to the mergers, what fallout will result from the new configuration, and what ways exist to improve the competitive atmosphere in the accounting profession.

Background Information Eighty percent of all CPAs in the United States are members of the AICPA and thus are subject to its discipline standards. Since 1975, the AICPA has jointly operated ethics enforcement with the state societies of CPAs.

Ethical Rules of Accountants   The AICPA has also established a **Code of Professional Ethics,** which outlines rules that govern the ethical conduct of accountants. These rules are frequently used by the courts to determine whether an accountant has breached a duty to the client in nontechnical matters not covered by GAAP and GAAS. For

Business Law in the News
Sarbanes-Oxley: The Pain Ahead

Compliance with Sarbanes-Oxley (sometimes called SOX or SarbOX) section 404 has been far more burdensome than anyone expected—so much so that the United States government has extended the deadline twice. The good news is that most companies either are in compliance (even if they do not have a formal auditor sign-off) or will be when the rule kicks in for calendar year filers at the end of 2004. The bad news is that the ongoing burden of 404 compliance will continue. Some companies (maybe 10–20%) will have either "material weakness" or a "significant deficiency" noted by their auditor. Ventana Research expects at least half of these companies will restructure their control processes within the first two years to make them more efficient. We advise companies to begin assessing the changes they must make in their IT assets to fully support changes in the financial controls environment.

For publicly traded companies in the US, the good news is Sarbanes-Oxley section 404 compliance efforts are either completed or coming to a close. The bad news is the process has turned out to be substantially more difficult, time consuming and expensive than the U.S. government forecasted when it passed the law in 2002 (no surprise here). It also was much more of an issue than corporations anticipated. In a recent survey of its membership, Finance Executives International (FEI) found that first year compliance costs for section 404 averaged $1.9 million, including an additional $509,000 in auditing expenses and $700,000 in IT consulting and software. The effort has cost the companies an average of 12,000 hours of internal time (i.e., about seven "full-time equivalent" years). For the largest companies (revenues in excess of $5 billion), FEI found an even greater burden. Initial year expenses were $4.7 million, including 35,000 hours (i.e., 20 FTE-years) of internal time.

The worse news is there will still be more to do. Some companies will not meet initial compliance requirements, and Ventana Research expects even more will find it necessary to restructure their financial controls within the first two audit cycles, even if they comply, to make the process more efficient.

Early in 2005, we will find out just how well publicly traded companies have prepared for Sarbanes-Oxley section 404. Some auditors believe that 10–20% of companies covered by the Act will fail to comply fully in the first year. They expect a minority of these will receive a finding of a "material weakness" while the rest will have a "significant deficiency" in their internal controls noted in their audit letter. A "material weakness" is the more severe condition, as it will prevent management from attesting that internal controls are effective. Even if there is no material weakness, auditors must note any finding of a "significant deficiency" because a set of these might create a "material weakness." We also expect on average auditors will be far more lenient in their first pass, and will raise the bar in successive years, so the standards will be uniformly more demanding in subsequent annual audits.

Discussions with auditors point to another problem. In their haste to achieve compliance with Sarbanes-Oxley section 404 finance organizations (understandably) have taken short-cuts that must be rectified in 2005 and 2006. Many have taken a bottoms-up, granular approach, identifying more points of control than they should. This makes ongoing compliance more complicated, time consuming, and therefore expensive than it ought to be. We expect a large percentage of public companies will need to redesign their controls and effectiveness tests—some significantly—to make periodic testing more efficient.

Moreover, even companies that have adequate and efficient controls may not have a truly mature control environment (as defined by the COSO methodology). Ventana Research finds that investments in creating a mature control environment pay off quickly because they greatly enhance the effectiveness of finance functions and over time substantially reduce ongoing costs. We advise all companies to assess how they can leverage existing and new IT systems to make the compliance process more efficient and achieve a mature control environment.

(Continued)

Business Law in the News *(Continued)*

Assessment

We advise clients to find ways to automate the testing and documentation processes to find ways ahead of time to cut the resources they will devote to achieving ongoing compliance with sections 404 and 302. Finance people generally do not automatically consider how IT can improve efficiency, and ongoing compliance is no exception. According to The Working Council for Chief Financial Officers, three-quarters of public companies they surveyed have no plans to purchase any new software to manage their compliance testing process beyond the applications used for initial testing. When the initial 404 project becomes a process, we assert that companies must rethink how they manage it.

Ventana Research recommends finance groups investigate using content management software to automate the documentation process, ensure that their reporting systems are adequate for reliably capturing not just financial information but information about processes, and determine if their transactions recording systems (e.g., ERP) should be revamped to improve efficiency (e.g., consolidating instances).

Questions for Review and Discussion

1. What is the good news in relation to the Sarbanes-Oxley reporting deadlines? Explain. What is the bad news? Explain.

2. What is the difference between a "material weakness" and a "significant deficiency"? Explain.

3. What additional problems have appeared as financial institutions have been hastily attempting to meet the Sarbanes-Oxley requirements? Explain.

4. What advice does the author give to companies that are involved in attempts to comply with Sarbanes-Oxley?

5. Will auditors be strict or lenient in a company's first attempt to comply with Sarbanes-Oxley? Is this good, bad, or neutral? Explain.

Source: Robert D. Kugel. "Sarbanes-Oxley: The Pain Ahead." Sales Masters World, October 5, 2004. http://www.sales-masters-world.com. © 2004 Ventana Research. Ventana Research is the preeminent Performance Management research and advisory services firm helping clients leverage technology and business processes to improve efficiency and effectiveness throughout their organizations. Visit Ventana Research at http://www.ventanaresearch.com/index.php

example, the AICPA's code has established that accountants owe their clients a duty of confidentiality even after the relationship has terminated. In this regard, an accountant cannot reveal information about a client's business to anyone outside of the accountant-client relationship unless authorized to do so by the client. Although this privilege does not extend to a court's request for information, it does cover most other situations. The ethical code also encompasses contingent fees, the independence of the auditor, promotional practices, operational practices, and quality reviews by the peers.

Neglect of duty does not cease by repetition to be neglect of duty.

—Lord Thomas J. C. Tomlin (1736–1812). British jurist

Getting Students Involved Have students review the definition of a fiduciary relationship (see Chapter 8). Remind them that the relationship between an accountant and a client is a fiduciary relationship. Then discuss why the statements of persons in a fiduciary relationship are actionable.

Duties Owed by the Accountant to the Client

A client often hires an accountant to take care of all the client's financial affairs. Therefore, the client and the accountant have a contractual arrangement. If an accountant fails to fulfill the terms of the contract, the client could bring a breach of contract suit against the accountant. For this reason it is very important that the terms of the contract include express duties which outline the task of the accountant and the time limits, if any, within which the tasks must be performed. Naturally, there are also implied duties that are included in any contract between an accountant and the client. These implied duties arise simply because the relationship exists. Thus, the accountant's agreement to work for the client implies an agreement to use the appropriate level of skill and due care that would be expected of any similarly situated accountant. An accountant might also be liable to clients under common law for negligence and fraud.

Talking Points

The passage of the Sarbanes-Oxley Act has caused a great deal of furor and consternation among companies that must comply with its strict reporting requirements as well as among the accounting and auditing firms that must carry out the actual financial analyses of such companies. Some experts see the changes brought by the Sarbanes-Oxley Act as a chance to make things better by improving internal operations and boosting investor confidence. Others see these changes as additional requirements imposed as a punishment on an entire industry as the result of the malfeasance of a few bad apples. These two points of view are expressed in the following ways.

In a speech before the National Press Club on July 30, 2003, Securities and Exchange Chairman William Donaldson remarked, "Simply complying with the rules is not enough. They should, as I have said before, make this approach part of their companies' DNA. For companies that take this approach, most of the major concerns about compliance disappear. Moreover, if companies view the new laws as opportunities—opportunities to improve internal controls, improve the performance of the board, and improve their public reporting—they will ultimately be better run, more transparent, and therefore more attractive to investors."

In contrast, in a publication entitled, *Taking Control: A Guide to Compliance with Section 404 of the Sarbanes-Oxley Act of 2002,* representatives of the financial consulting firm of Deloitte & Touche LLP, state that, "Few will publicly admit it but many have come to view the Sarbanes-Oxley Act of 2002 as an unwelcome requirement. Cost, effort and energy poured into complying with new regulations, all caused by a tiny minority of unethical individuals. Most will agree that the law was needed to restore investor confidence. But few will acknowledge that they themselves need it. Or can benefit from it. This is someone else's problem—and, like schoolyard justice, the whole class gets punished."

Which of these two views do you think is the most accurate view of the situation? Will companies and auditors alike welcome the changes introduced by Sarbanes-Oxley or will they try to get around the law? Explain. Does the analogy of "school yard justice" accurately describe the wide target area hit by Sarbanes-Oxley? Why or why not?

A Question of Ethics

Samuel Sorrell works as a CPA for the accounting firm of Morris, Miller, and Kierns. He has just completed an audit of the Randall-Cassidy Sports Wear Corporation. The audit revealed that Randall-Cassidy is in serious financial difficulty. Moreover, Sorrell feels obligated to issue an adverse opinion because Randall-Cassidy's financial statements do not fairly reflect the financial status of the corporation, generally accepted accounting principles have not been followed properly, and major uncertainties about the sportswear market could cause a serious slump in corporate sales. Sorrell learns that Thomas Keifer, the CEO of Randall-Cassidy, plans to make a presentation to a group of potential investors. The presentation contains figures that are technically accurate, but which will actually mislead the investors as to the true financial state of the corporation. Ethically what should Sorrell do now? Would your answer change if one of the investors directly asked Sorrell about the company's financial condition? Why or why not?

Negligence/Malpractice The client has the right to expect the accountant to do a good job in whatever task has been assigned. From this right arises the accountant's duty of due care. The duty of due care means that the accountant must perform the job with the same skill and competence that a reasonable accounting professional would use in the same situation. **Negligence** or **malpractice** occurs whenever an accountant fails to meet his or her duty of due care. Although the term malpractice is usually reserved for health care professionals and attorneys, it could also be applied to any form of professional negligence. How the reasonable accounting professional would handle a given situation, and thus avoid a charge of malpractice, would be determined by reference to GAAS or GAAP.

Whenever accountants ignore the rules established by GAAS and GAAP, they do so at their own risk. It is fairly certain that ignoring or remaining ignorant of these principles and procedures is a one-way ticket to a malpractice suit, and there is little question that, under such circumstances, the accountant would be found liable for negligence. Unfortunately, the opposite precept is not always true; that is, just because an accountant follows the GAAS or the GAAP guidelines does not automatically lead to his or her vindication in a court of law. It is always possible that an accountant can follow the proper principles and procedures, yet still make other errors that lead to liability. Thus, an accountant might follow GAAS, yet file a return after a required deadline, or the accountant might make a calculation error, or might send the forms to the wrong agency, and so on.

Fraud Accountants must perform their duties with the best interests of the client in mind. If an accountant *deliberately* misrepresents the client's financial condition or in some way *deliberately* falsifies a statement or an auditing report, that accountant may be liable to the client for fraud. Accountants may also be liable for fraud if they compile a financial report or conduct an audit recklessly. To make a proper case for fraud, it is not enough for the plaintiff to show that the accountant deliberately or recklessly attempted to falsify records and statements. In addition, the plaintiff must demonstrate that he or she actually relied on the false statements or reports. The extra effort is worth it, however, because, if the plaintiff succeeds in proving that he or she was defrauded by the accountant, that plaintiff can ask for and will often be awarded punitive damages.

Background Information The AICPA frequently files *amicus curiae* (friend of the court) briefs in cases regarding accounting liability. For example, some briefs point out errors in the foreseeability standard for third parties. The institute promotes the privity doctrine, which holds that an accountant is liable to a nonclient third party for negligence only if the accountant knew and intended that his or her work product would be used by the third party for a specific purpose.

The Accountant's Liability to Third Parties

Under common law, an accountant can be held liable to some third parties who are damaged by a negligently prepared financial statement. Accountants are also liable to some third parties if they deliberately make fraudulent statements.

Negligence/Malpractice The right to bring suit for a negligently prepared financial statement will always extend to actually named third parties. Most states also extend this right to any limited classes of specifically foreseen third parties. A few states extend the right to bring suit protection to reasonably foreseeable classes of third parties (see Table 40-1).

Table 40-1 Accountants' Liability to Third Parties Under Common Law

Liability Theory	Explanation
Actually named third parties	When accountants prepare financial statements knowing that the client will show the statement to a named third party, then those accountants will be liable to that known third party if through their negligence the third party is injured. Only a few states limit recovery to actually named third parties.
Specifically foreseen third parties	Accountants may also be liable to certain third parties for negligently prepared financial statements if those third parties are members of a limited class that is specifically foreseen when the financial statement is drawn up. Most states follow this theory.
Reasonably foreseeable third parties	Accountants may also be liable for negligently prepared financial statements, if those third parties can be reasonably foreseen as recipients of the statements. Only a few states extend recovery this far.

Actually Named Third Parties If an accountant prepares a financial statement with the actual knowledge that the client is going to show the statement to a particular third party, then the accountant is clearly liable to that *known* third party. If, for example, the client tells the accountant that the statement is for Mr. X, then Mr. X can recover if he suffers actual financial loss due to the accountant's negligence.

Specifically Foreseen Third Parties Most states have extended this rule even further, holding that accountants are also liable to any limited class of third parties that is specifically foreseen when the financial statement is drawn up. Thus, an accountant who prepares a financial statement knowing that the client intends to show it to investors would be liable to any investor in that same class of specifically foreseen third parties. To recover from the accountant, the investors would have to rely on the statements and would have to suffer financial loss.

State Variations Louisiana, Michigan, and Missouri are some of the states that have adopted Restatement (Second) of Torts section 552, whereby negligent accountants are liable to specifically foreseen and limited classes of persons for identifiable transactions.

Reasonably Foreseeable Third Parties Some courts have become very strict in holding accountants liable to third parties. These jurisdictions have adopted a test that depends on whether the plaintiff in the case was foreseeable as a possible recipient of the accountant's report. For instance, if it is reasonable for the accountant to foresee that the financial statement will be shown to bankers, suppliers, and potential investors, then the accountant is liable to anyone of these reasonably foreseeable classes of individuals. This would be true even if the class was not specifically mentioned when the accountant was hired by the client. This is the strictest of the three tests that the courts have adopted for determining the extent of an accountant's liability to third parties in negligence cases.

Fraud Since fraud involves a deliberate deception, the courts have no difficulty extending protection to a wide class of third parties. Thus, an accountant who prepares a fraudulent financial statement is liable to anyone who can be reasonably foreseen as relying on that statement.

Example 40-2

Isaac Berryman brought suit against the accounting firm of Dowling, Krueger, and McBride when it failed to detect the poor financial condition of New Design Software, Inc. Berryman was an investor who lost his life savings when New Design collapsed. The accountants argued that Berryman could not sue them because New Design, not Berryman, was their client. Under the named third-parties test, the accountants would be correct because Berryman was not actually named as a recipient of the financial reports prepared by the accountants. However, under the specifically foreseen rule, the accountants would be wrong because Berryman is a member of a limited class of third parties that was specifically foreseen as a recipient of the information. Significantly, if Berryman could show fraud it would not matter whether he was actually named as a recipient or simply the member of a specifically foreseen class. If fraud is involved, anyone who can be reasonably foreseen as a recipient of those reports could hold Dowling, Krueger, and McBride liable for any actual loss caused by reliance on those reports.

An Accountant's Statutory Liability

Accountants may also be sued for violating statutory laws governing their activities. Such suits can arise under the Securities Act of 1933, the Securities Exchange Act of 1934, and various state laws.

Securities Act of 1933 Under the Securities Act of 1933, the first time a corporation issues stock for sale it must file a registration statement (see Chapter 39). Such statements are prepared by accountants. The 1933 act allows purchasers who have lost money after buying corporate stock based on misleading or false registration statements to sue the accountants who prepared the statements. To succeed in such a lawsuit, the plaintiff must show that the registration statement included a false or misleading statement about a material matter and that he or she suffered a measurable financial setback as a result of relying on that statement. However, the accountant does have a defense in such cases. Usually, if the accountant can show that he or she used due diligence in preparing the report, he or she will escape liability. Due diligence is generally demonstrated by reference to the proper application of the GAAS and GAAP standards. However, the accountant will also have to show that he or she committed no additional negligent actions and made no other avoidable mistakes.

Securities and Exchange Act of 1934 A second federal law, the Securities and Exchange Act of 1934, also contains some provisions that affect accountants. These provisions are designed to prevent the fraudulent filing of various documents with the SEC and the fraudulent manipulation of the securities market. Both acts also contain provisions that impose criminal liability on accountants in some situations.

State Statutes In addition to these federal statutes, most states have enacted similar statutes regulating the activities of accounts as they relate to the sale of stock. State statutes that regulate the sale of stock are frequently referred to as blue sky laws because they are set up to stop the sale of securities that are as empty as several feet of blue sky.

Quick Quiz 40-1 True or False?

1. An accountant is a professional who can plan, direct, and evaluate a client's financial affairs.

2. An auditor's report and the accompanying financial statements will always guarantee an institution's financial health.

3. Whenever certified public accountants ignore the rules established by GAAS and GAAP, they do so with little or no risk, because of their certified status.

40-2 The Liability of Architects and Attorneys

In addition to accountants, two other frequently contracted business professionals are architects and attorneys. Both are regulated by the states and both must follow certain clearly stated duties.

The Liability of Architects

An architect is a professional who plans the construction or alteration of a variety of structures from small, single-family dwellings to enormous skyscrapers. Generally, architects do not actually construct the building. However, they may often manage the construction according to their detailed plans.

State Regulation   Under its police power, the state can regulate the conduct of architects. States often establish an agency that makes the rules that architects must follow to be officially recognized as professionals in their field of expertise. The state will usually establish age, character, education, experience, and testing requirements. Often a state will maintain a list of all architects officially registered as having met all of these legal requirements.

Duties of the Architect   Like any other professional, an architect owes a duty to exercise due care and skill in carrying out professional duties. This standard of care requires the architect to use the same methods, techniques, and procedures that any architect of ordinary skill would use in a similar situation. The standard does not demand that the architect's design be perfect or that the execution of the design be faultless. Architects can make mistakes, as long as those mistakes do not result from a failure to use appropriate skill and good judgment according to accepted professional standards.

Contractual Liability   Sometimes the final version of a building differs from the original plan at the time the contract was made. If the deviation is actually an error caused by the architect's failure to use due care and skill, then the architect may have to reimburse the client for any extra money spent to correct the error. This is known as the **cost of repair rule.** A different rule is followed if the design is so defective that the structure is unusable for its originally intended purpose. In such situations, the court may declare that the architect owes the client the difference between the market value of the building as it stands and the market value of the intended structure.

Tort Liability   Unlike mistakes made by accountants, errors made by architects may injure people or damage property. If the architect has failed to exercise the appropriate standard of care and if, as a result, property is damaged or people are injured, then the architect may have to compensate the victims. Note, however, that the architect's mistake must cause injury or damage.

Related Cases Kangas sued the builder and the architect for a myriad of problems in the construction of his new house. One of the problems was that the basement was poured four inches too high. The court found the defects to be a willful violation of the building contract and awarded damages of $20,000. The court further rejected the builder's claim for a $7,500 award based on diminution of the value of the house. *Kangas v. Trust,* 441 N.E.2d 1271.

State Variations Most states have a ten-year statute of limitations for architecture negligence lawsuits. Arkansas, Florida, and Iowa have the longest—fifteen years.

Example 40-3

Architects Lefkowitz and Rudman were hired to plan the new Convention Center to be located in Las Vegas. Rudman failed to check the stress specs on a balcony on the second level of the convention center's main exhibition floor. Had he made the check, his inspection would have revealed that an error had been made that could cause the balcony to collapse under its own weight. The construction firm of McMahon-Fulton, Inc., ignored the Lefkowitz-Rudman specs and used their own plans. However, the McMahon-Fulton plan contained the same error that the architects' plan had contained. On the night that the convention center opened, the balcony suffered a partial collapse that injured several people. Because the contractor had ignored the Lefkowitz-Rudman Plan, the architects were not held liable, despite their error.

The Liability of Attorneys

Next to the accountant, one of the most sought-after professionals by a business person is the attorney. An attorney is a professional because of expert knowledge, ability, and education in interpreting and applying the law. Attorneys advise their clients in a variety of different ways, all of which require good faith, loyalty, and the exercise of due care.

State Regulation of Attorneys   Like accountants and architects, attorneys are regulated by the state's police power. Also like accountants and architects, attorneys are

Background Information The American Bar Association has over 370,000 members, spends more than $100 million annually, and supports an administrative staff of 700 employees.

Talking Points

In his essay, "The Chaotic Indeterminacy of Tort Law: Between Formalism and Nihilism," Denis J.Brion, professor of law at Washington and Lee University School of Law, explains that two very distinct interpretations of the law have existed side by side for a number of years. He calls one of these two theories formalism and the other nihilism. Brion explains the two theories in the following way:

In "'Legal Formalism: On the Immanent Rationality of the Law,' Ernest Weinrib offers . . . the idea that the law can be described in terms of . . . its 'inner coherence.' He argues that the law is altogether distinct from politics and that it can only be understood from within itself. The function of judges is to 'make transactions and distributions' in the social world conform to the 'latent entity' of the law. The function of legal scholars is to make explicit the internal coherence and intelligibility of the law."

"In *The Disorder of Law: A Critique of Legal Theory,* Charles Sampford sets out to criticize various theories of law that seek to describe it as systematic. His principal thesis is that society itself is without system—his term is the 'social melee'—and that the law, as an integral part of society, is correspondingly disordered—the 'legal melee.' He concludes that, because of this disorder, the impact of legal doctrine on social and individual practices is strongly attenuated."

Of the two theorists, which one has the more accurate view of the legal system? Which view supports the idea that the juris-economic system is a flexible and responsive system? Explain your answers to each of these questions. A third alternative is offered by Lawrence Friedman in his treatise, *Law in America.* The law, Friedman says, is not a separate autonomous system. Rather, the law "is, essentially, a product of society; and as society changes, so does the legal system. Feudal societies have feudal legal systems; socialist societies have socialist systems; tribal societies have tribal systems; capitalist societies have capitalist legal systems. How could it be otherwise?" Of the three theorists, which one reflects your own personal view? Which view is supported by the evidence in this chapter concerning the regulation of the legal profession? Explain your answers.

The sources for this segment of Talking Points are: Brion, Denis J. "The Chaotic Indeterminacy of Tort Law: Between Formalism and Nihilism." In *Radical Philosophy of Law.* Atlantic Highlands, NJ: Humanities Press, 1995, p. 179; Friedman, Lawrence. *Law in America: A Short History.* New York: The Modern Library, 2002, p. 18; Sampford, Charles. *The Disorder of Law: A Critique of Legal Theory.* New York: Basil Blackwell, 1989. Weinrib, Ernest. "Legal Formalism: On the Immanent Rationality of the Law." *Yale Law Journal* 97 (1988): 949.

normally required to be of a certain age (usually eighteen), and to be of good moral character. They are required to possess a certain educational background and to pass a special examination, demonstrating minimum competency. Unlike architects and accountants, attorneys often do not have any experience requirements. This is because architects and accountants usually are required to have only a bachelor's degree, whereas attorneys obtain an advanced degree in law. This extra education often takes three to four years beyond the bachelor's degree. The experience requirement of architects and accountants frequently amounts to two years.

Ethical Rules of Attorneys

The American Bar Association has also established a Model Code of Professional Responsibility, which outlines rules that govern the ethical conduct of attorneys. These rules are frequently used by the courts to determine whether an attorney has breached a duty to the client in matters that do not involve the interpretation or application of the law. Many states have adopted the Model Code of Professional Responsibility and have incorporated it into their standards for judging the ethical conduct of attorneys licensed to practice law in those states. The code is divided into three types of guidelines: the nine canons, the ethical considerations, and the disciplinary rules. The canons describe how an ethical attorney should behave. The ethical considerations outline how to interpret the canons, while the disciplinary rules set down specific activities that attorneys are required to perform.

Negligence/Malpractice

An attorney has the duty to represent clients with good faith, loyalty, and due care. An attorney who does not fulfill these duties may be liable for malpractice. Usually, however, an attorney is not liable to a third party who is not a client.

Duties of the Attorney When a client hires an attorney, the client has the right to expect the attorney to act in *good faith,* which means that the attorney's duty is to act in the best interests of the client. In the absence of such good faith conduct, the attorney may face a lawsuit brought by the client and disciplinary action brought by the state.

An attorney also has a duty of *loyalty* to protect the client and to make certain that the client receives advice and representation that is free of conflicting interests. Thus, an attorney cannot represent two clients on opposite sides of the same dispute, unless both sides have been completely informed of the dual representation and consent to it. Similarly, an attorney violates the duty of loyalty if advantage is taken of the client for personal profit.

Like all other professionals, an attorney owes a duty of *due care* to clients. This means that in giving legal advice, negotiating claims, litigating suits, making out wills, negotiating divorce settlements, and performing any number of other legal tasks, an attorney must exercise the same skill and care that would be expected of other attorneys in the same situation.

Steps in a Legal Malpractice Case

In order for a plaintiff to succeed in a malpractice case against an attorney, that plaintiff must demonstrate the existence of four specifically drawn elements. First, the plaintiff must show that the attorney owed a duty to that plaintiff. Generally, this is not a problem because when the client consults the attorney a contract is created under which the attorney assumes the duty to represent that client with the appropriate level of care. The question of duty can arise, however, when there is a factual discrepancy over whether the client actually hired the attorney to represent him or her. Thus, the duty clearly arises when the client comes to the attorney's office and specifically asks the attorney to help him or her deal with a legal problem. In contrast, if a student were to ask a law professor a hypothetical question during a class discussion, then no duty has arisen because there is no client-attorney relationship created in such a situation.

Second, the attorney must have breached the duty that is owed to the client. The attorney's duty is measured by his or her compliance with a standard that holds that an attorney must represent a client in a way that demonstrates enthusiasm and dedication to the client's best interests. The attorney cannot, however, file claims or advance arguments that have no realistic chance of succeeding or that are not firmly grounded in acceptable legal principles. The attorney must act as a reasonable professional would under the same circumstances. This standard does not mean that attorneys are not permitted to make mistakes. On the contrary, mistakes are tolerated as an inevitable part of the legal profession, just as a long as they do not result from carelessness, inattention, laziness, or ignorance. Third, the plaintiff must show that the attorney's questionable behavior caused the resulting harm to the plaintiff. Moreover, it is not enough that there is a factual connection between the behavior and the injury. There must also be a legal connection between the two. Such a legal connection requires foreseeability. Finally, the plaintiff must show that he or she suffered actual harm as a result of the attorney's breach of duty.

Because attorneys are professionals and because the intricacies of the law are often mystifying to the lay person, the law requires that the elements of malpractice be supported by expert testimony. Expert testimony can only be overlooked when the relationship between the injury suffered by the client and the behavior by the attorney are so obviously connected that the experience of the plaintiff is within the everyday experience of the jury. As we shall see, a very similar, in fact, an almost identical standard is used to guide the question of whether expert testimony is needed in the case of malpractice claims that are filed against health care professionals.

Third-Party Liability In contrast to accountants and architects, attorneys are rarely held liable to third parties because the attorney's responsibilities are tied closely with the interests of that client and that client alone.

> ### Example 40-4
>
> William Zafris hired the Brooks Construction Company to replace the windows on his back patio. Four days after the job was finished, the windows began to crack. When Zafris called Brooks, the company refused to take any responsibility. Unable to get any satisfaction through normal channels, Zafris contacted Sarah Montgomery, a local attorney. Montgomery advised Zafris not to pay Brooks pending a resolution of the dispute. Eventually the matter was settled in Brooks's favor. Brooks then sued Montgomery for advising Zafris not to pay his bill. The court ruled that Brooks could not hold Montgomery liable for the advice she had given Zafris, even though that advice had proved to be incorrect, because she had acted in good faith and with due care.

Court-Driven Protection As we've seen, attorneys who are negligent can be the target of a civil suit brought by a wronged client. There are other safeguards within the legal system, however, which are designed to make certain that attorneys do not file phony lawsuits, promote unwarranted legal arguments, conduct unnecessary investigations, file unjustifiable motions, or make allegations that lack evidentiary support. The Federal Rules of Civil Procedure, for example, include a rule which specifically forbids such objectionable conduct and which imposes severe penalties should the rule be broken. Many states have similar civil rules that are designed to deter unprofessional conduct on the part of unscrupulous attorneys. Penalties can include a payment of money to the court or to the other party. These payments may even include attorneys' fees in appropriate cases.

Quick Quiz 40-2 True or False?

1. An architect is a professional who plans the construction or alteration of a variety of structures from single-family dwellings to enormous skyscrapers.

2. In order for a plaintiff to fail in a malpractice case against an attorney, that attorney must disprove the existence of all four elements of malpractice.

3. Because attorneys are professionals and because the intricacies of the law are often mystifying to the lay person, the law requires that the elements of malpractice be supported by expert testimony.

40-3 The Liability of Health Care Providers

Teaching Tips Assign a short research paper on the legal requirements for becoming a health care professional in your state. Students may choose a specialty from any of the health care professions.

Health care providers are professionals who possess the specialized knowledge, abilities, education, and experience that make it possible for them to answer some aspect of a patient's health care needs. Some business people must deal with health care providers on a daily basis. Such contact is routine for hospital administrators, risk-management experts, pharmaceutical salespeople, hospital accountants, insurance adjusters, and biomedical equipment salespeople. Even individuals who do not deal regularly with health care providers in the business world may one day have to deal with them as patients. Knowledge of the liability of such professionals may be helpful in these situations.

The Professional Status of Health Care Providers

It should be obvious that physicians are professionals, since they must possess the specialized knowledge, abilities, education, and experience needed to perform their jobs. However, dentists, podiatrists, chiropractors, nurses, nurse practitioners, nurse technicians, radiologic technologists, respiratory therapists, and laboratory technicians are also considered health care professionals. All these professions are regulated by the state. In addition, most are regulated by independent professional organizations such as the American Society of Clinical Pathologists.

The Health Care Standard of Care

Unlike accountants, architects, and attorneys, health care professionals frequently must physically touch their patients. This physical touching can involve routine tests and examinations as well as dangerous and painful procedures. To avoid liability for the intentional tort of battery, health care providers must frequently obtain the patient's written consent. In addition to intentional torts, health care providers might be vulnerable to charges of negligence if they do not follow the appropriate standard of care.

Consent Patients who undergo tests and treatment have the right to know about those procedures and have the right to refuse to undergo them if they so desire. These rights impose a duty on the health care professional to seek the patient's consent. Consent takes two forms: general consent and informed consent.

Upon entering a hospital, a patient automatically gives **general consent** for the routine tests and procedures that are needed for diagnosis and treatment. Although such consent is implied in the situation, many hospitals require patients to sign general consent forms (see Figure 40-1).

When a diagnostic test or a procedure will be dangerous or painful, the treating physician must obtain the patient's **informed consent.** For this type of consent, the physician must tell the patient in advance about the procedure and the risks involved. Informed consent must be in writing on a form that is signed by the patient and witnessed by a third party. Generally, a written consent form is considered valid by the court and precludes any suit based on battery unless the patient can prove a lack of understanding of the information on the form or a deliberate misrepresentation as to its content.

Related Cases Dr. Thomas advised Truman to get a Pap smear but did not warn her of the dangers of failure to have the test. The patient eventually developed cervical cancer and died. Truman's husband brought a wrongful death action against the doctor, arguing that he had failed to disclose all the risks of not having the test. In *Truman v. Thomas* (611 P.2d 902), the California Supreme Court held that the doctor should have given the patient all "information material to her decision." However, the court remanded the case to the trial level so that a jury could determine whether the consequences of failure to have a Pap smear were so well known that the doctor had no general duty to disclose the risks to all patients.

The Opening Case Revisited

"A Nontraditional Duty to Inform"

In The Opening Case at the beginning of this chapter, the court broke new legal ground extending the concept of medical duty to cover cases in which a physician knows that the patient is seeing no other physician and in which that physician can easily contact the patient directly.

Background Information Stephen Smith, one of the leaders of nineteenth-century American medicine, stated in 1860 that it was ludicrous "in our time when communication is so rapid, and books and periodicals are so abundant and cheap," for a doctor to plead ignorance of generally recognized medical knowledge.

CONSENT UPON ADMISSION TO HOSPITAL

Patient _____ Date _____ a.m. _____ p.m. _____

(or _____ for _____)
knowing that I, or the patient (am) (is) suffering from an illness requiring hospital care do hereby
voluntarily consent to such hospital care requiring an operation, diagnostic tests or therapeutic
treatment by Dr. _____ , his/her
assistant or his/her designee or as necessary according to his/her judgment.

I also recognize that during the course of my operation, tests, or therapy unforeseen conditions may
necessitate additional or different procedures and I am aware that inasmuch as the practice of
medicine and surgery is not an exact science, there have been no guarantees made to me as the
result of treatments or examinations to be performed in this hospital.

I have read the above statements and I certify that I understand them.

_____   _____
Witness   Signature of Patient

Figure 40-1 Many hospitals today require patients to sign general consent forms like this one upon admission.

Negligence In order for a patient to succeed in a negligence case against a health care professional, the patient must show that the four elements of negligence exist in the case. First, the patient must demonstrate that the health care provider owed a duty to that patient. Usually, the question of duty is not at issue in such cases. However, the question will arise whenever the relationship between the patient and the health care provider is not clear-cut or obvious. In such cases, the court may be asked to determine whether the health care provider owed a duty to the plaintiff.

After establishing the existence of a duty between the health care provider and the patient, the plaintiff must show that the health care professional breached that duty. The health care professional's duty is measured by his or her compliance with a standard of care. The health care provider must act with the same level of skill, care, and knowledge that any reasonable health care provider would display in a similar situation. Determining how a reasonable health care provider would act in a given situation can be determined in several ways. One way is to refer to the hospital's policy and procedure manual. When professionals follow the standard policies and procedures as written in the manual, they are performing as any reasonable professional would, unless the procedure in the manual can be shown to be out of date, incompetently written, or incomplete in some way.

If a hospital's manual does not address a situation, if the manual is outdated, if the procedure is incompetently written, or if the steps in the procedure are incomplete, the court may judge the performance by going outside the hospital and looking at the manuals or the procedures used at other hospitals. At one time, the courts used a rule that was referred to as the **locality rule.** This rule judges a health care provider's behavior on the basis of how other health care professionals in a similar locality would act. Thus, rural physicians were compared to other rural physicians, urban physicians with other urban physicians, and so on. Today, most courts use another rule called the **national rule** or the **national standard.** With the advent of continuing education requirements and with the presence of mass communication, online continuing education programs, and the like, the courts have decided that there is rarely any good reason for a health care professional to be unaware of the development of medical trends on a national, or, at times, even an international basis.

Causation in a Malpractice Suit A crucial element in any malpractice case is the issue of causation. In such a case, the plaintiff must prove not only that the defendant's conduct did not conform to acceptable medical practices, but also that this failure to follow acceptable procedures was the cause of the plaintiff's injury. Much of the difficulty in supplying this proof arises because the fact finder in a malpractice case must attempt to understand medical evidence that is frequently beyond his or her experience.

Expert Testimony Since many of the tasks performed by the health care provider are highly specialized, determining how the professional should act often requires expert testimony. However, expert testimony is not required if the action under examination is within the common knowledge of all people.

Further Reading For an interesting look at the medical malpractice problem from an author who is both an attorney and a doctor, see *Lethal Medicine: The Epidemic of Medical Malpractice Today,* by Harvey F. Wachsman, M.D., J.D. (New York: Henry Holt and Company, 1993).

Example 40-5

Nurse Noel Grady was called away from Kurt Yarborough's room by another nurse. Yarborough was sedated, but restless. He was thrashing about and had attempted to leave the bed several times. Despite this, Grady left him alone, failing to raise the siderails or restrain Yarborough in any way. While Grady was absent, Yarborough tried to get out of bed. He fell and broke his leg. At Grady's negligence trial, the judge ruled that no expert testimony was needed to measure Grady's standard of care. The judge felt that the issue of whether a sedated and restless patient should be left unsupervised and unrestrained was well within the common knowledge of the jurors.

Medical Records and the Patient's Rights

In recent years, concerns about privacy matters have come to the forefront of the law. In no area of the law is this truer than in health care law. Physicians once effectively guarded the secrecy of their files by arguing that patients were apt to misinterpret or misunderstand notations made in medical jargon or hospital shorthand. These arguments are no longer acceptable. In fact, to ensure the patient's right to see his or her records Congress passed the **Health Insurance Portability and Accountability Act (HIPAA).** Under HIPAA, Congress has ensured that patients have the right to see their medical records and parents have the right to see the medical records of their children. The act also gives both groups the right to obtain duplicates of the records. There are, of course, exceptions to this rule. For instance, records that result from psychotherapy sessions receive a higher level of protection under the act. Patients are permitted to see such records only if the patient has the physician's permission. Even with permission, the patient must look through the records along with the physician. These extra limitations are placed on psychotherapy records because they are seen as somewhat emotional and open to a wide variety of false impressions.

You have the right to see your medical records because of the Health Insurance Portability and Accountability Act (HIPAA).

Quick Quiz 40-3 True or False?

1. In order for a patient to succeed in a negligence case against a health care professional, the patient must show that the four elements of negligence exist in the case.

2. Today, most courts use a rule called the national rule or the national standard to make judgments in relation to the standard of care for health care providers in negligence cases.

3. To ensure the patient's right to see his or her records, the American Law Institute and the American Bar Association collaborated to create a model act called the Health Insurance Portability and Accountability Act (HIPAA).

40-4 Hospital Liability

Hospitals can be held liable for the negligence of a physician, even if that physician is not an employee of the hospital. Hospitals routinely grant physicians, who are not employed by the hospital, the privilege to treat their patients at that hospital. The granting of such **staff privileges** can be troublesome for the hospital if the staff physician becomes the defendant in a malpractice lawsuit. This is because the patient frequently sues not only the physician, but also the hospital. Two legal theories which have been used successfully to add the hospital to the list of defendants in a malpractice lawsuit are ostensible authority and negligent credentialing.

Ostensible Authority and Hospital Liability

Ostensible authority, which is also known as agency by estoppel and apparent authority, has been successfully used by plaintiffs to hold the hospital, as well as the physician, liable for malpractice. **Ostensible authority** is created when a hospital presents itself to the public-at-large as a provider of health care services and in some way leads the patient to believe that a physician with staff privileges is an employee of the hospital. This can be shown if the hospital allows the physician to wear a hospital identification tag, to use hospital equipment, to dispense medication at the hospital, to issue orders to hospital employees, and so on. Under such circumstances, the courts have been willing to hold that, since it is reasonable to believe that these representations would lead the patient to the conclusion that the physician is an employee of the hospital, the patient can add the hospital to the malpractice suit as a defendant.

Negligent Credentialing by Hospital Authorities

Negligent credentialing occurs if the hospital has retained a physician that the governing body of the hospital knew or should have known was incompetent. Another form of negligent credentialing occurs if a previously competent physician with staff privileges loses that competence and the hospital governing body knows or should have known about the changed circumstances and takes no remedial action. This form of negligent credentialing is sometimes referred to as **negligent retention.** In either situation, a patient injured by the malpractice of the incompetent physician can also hold the hospital liable.

Tort Reform and Litigation

In recent years, some states have attempted to lessen the burden placed on hospitals by ostensible authority and negligent credentialing. This movement has been motivated by the belief that such lawsuits frequently pull the hospital into a lawsuit unjustly. To alleviate this injustice, the tort reform provisions often place the burden of proof on the plaintiff to prove both ostensible authority and negligent credentialing.

For instance, in the area of ostensible authority, some states say that the plaintiff must prove that the hospital held itself out to the public at large as a provider of health care services and that the hospital gave no notice that nonemployee staff physicians, rather than hospital employees, would render services to the patient. Moreover, these statutes also allow the hospital to escape liability by posting notices that inform patients of the independent status of staff physicians. In states which have established such a statutory protection for hospitals, a patient can hold a hospital which posts such notices liable only if the hospital directed the negligent actions that injured the patient.

In negligent credentialing, some states have created a rebuttable presumption that says a hospital is presumed to have properly credentialed staff physicians if the hospital is accredited by the Joint Commission of Accreditation of Health Care Organizations. If the hospital can show that it is accredited, then the burden of proof shifts to the plaintiff to show that the hospital did not follow the credentialing procedures of the Joint Commission, that the hospital knew or should have known of the physician's incompetence and did nothing to limit the physician's privileges, or that the credentialing process did not apply to this hospital, this physician, or the type of case that formed the basis for the lawsuit.

Quick Quiz 40-4 True or False?

1. A hospital can never be held liable for the torts of a physician unless that physician is an employee of that hospital.

2. Ostensible authority applies only to hospitals in large urban areas.

3. Negligent credentialing and negligent retention have been outlawed under the Restatement (Second) of Torts.

Summary

40-1 Accountants are business professionals who can plan, direct, and evaluate the complex financial affairs of their clients. The most common types of accountants are certified public accountants and public accountants. Accountants must follow generally accepted accounting principles. Auditors must follow generally accepted auditing standards. They must also follow the Code of Professional Ethics of the AICPA. Accountants may be liable to both their clients and to third parties.

40-2 Architects and attorneys are considered professionals and are regulated by the state. Architects may find themselves liable to clients and to third parties, whereas attorneys are generally responsible to their clients alone. Both architects and attorneys must exercise due care and skill in carrying out their professional duties.

40-3 The term *health care provider* includes not only physicians but also dentists, chiropractors, podiatrists, nurses, nurse practitioners, nurse technicians, radiologic technologists, respiratory therapists, and laboratory technicians. Like other professionals, the health care provider must act with the same skill, care, and level of knowledge that a reasonable health care professional would display in a similar situation.

40-4 Hospitals can be held liable for the negligence of a physician, even if that physician is not an employee of the hospital. The granting of such staff privileges can be troublesome for the hospital if the staff physician becomes the defendant in a malpractice lawsuit, because the patient can sue both the physician and the hospital. Two legal theories which have been used successfully to add the hospital to the list of defendants in a malpractice lawsuit are ostensible authority and negligent credentialing.

Key Terms

accountant, 761
adverse opinion, 763
audit, 762
auditor, 762
certified public accountant, 762
Code of Professional Ethics, 764
cost of repair rule, 771
disclaimer, 764
general consent, 775
generally accepted accounting principles (GAAP), 763
generally accepted auditing standards (GAAS), 763
Health Insurance Portability and Accountability Act (HIPAA), 777
informed consent, 775
locality rule, 777
malpractice, 767
national rule, 777
national standard, 777
negligence, 767
negligent credentialing, 779
negligent retention, 779
ostensible authority, 778
professional, 761
public accountant, 762
Public Company Accountability Oversight Board (PCAOB), 764
qualified opinion, 763
Sarbanes-Oxley Act, 764
staff privileges, 778
unqualified opinion, 763

Questions for Review and Discussion

1. What is the difference between a certified public accountant and a public accountant?
2. What are the various types of auditing opinions that can be issued by auditors?
3. What is the difference between generally accepted accounting principles and generally accepted auditing standards?
4. What duties do accountants owe to their clients?

5. What are the registration requirements imposed on architects?
6. What are the duties that an architect owes to his or her clients?
7. What are the duties that an attorney owes to his or her clients?
8. What is the standard of care used to judge health care professionals?

9. What is the difference between the locality rule and the national standard in determining a health care provider's liability?
10. What are the circumstances under which hospitals can be held liable for the torts of independent contractor physicians?

Investigating the Internet

Access the American Legal Ethics Library website and write a paper about the professional code of conduct that binds the attorneys in your state. As an alternative assignment, write a report about the most interesting article that you find archived at this website.

Cases for Analysis

1. Fred Stern and Company applied to the Ultramares Loan Corporation for a credit advance in support of its import business. As was its custom, Ultramares asked Stern for a detailed financial statement that included an audited balance sheet. Stern agreed and supplied Ultramares with a report from its auditors, Touche, Niven, and Company. When Stern went to Touche, Niven, and Company, the import corporation did not reveal to the accounting firm that Ultramares would see the report. The only thing that the importers told the auditors was that the report would be shown to some possible creditors. Touche, Niven, and Company filed an audit report which stated that Stern had a net worth of $1 million. Satisfied with the statement, Ultramares loaned the money to Stern. The report turned out to be completely false. Fred Stern and Company was not only worth less than $1 million; it was actually completely worthless. The auditors had filed the erroneous report because Stern had shown them a phony set of books that misrepresented the company's value. The importer, of course, could not hope to pay Ultramares back for the money it had borrowed and so the loan company went after someone who actually had enough money to make up for their loss, and that was the accounting firm of

   Touche, Niven, and Company. The firm argued that the report had been prepared for Stern, and since they had no knowledge that Ultramares would see the report they could not be liable to the loan company. Apply each of the standards used to evaluate an accounting firm's liability to third parties and report on the results for each test in this case. *Ultramares Corp. v. Touche*, 255 N.Y. 70, 174 N.E. 441.

2. The Consolidata Services Company (CDS) was established to provide small businesses with payroll services. All CDS clients were required to provide CDS with an advance deposit equal to the amount of one payroll. When CDS got into a cash flow problem, it tapped into some of this deposit money to cover its own debts. Eventually, the accounting firm of Alexander Grant, which had been hired by CDS to advise it on taxes and on other financial matters, discovered that the deposit account was $150,000 short. CDS assured Grant that it was devising a plan to cover the missing $150,000. Accordingly, CDS asked Grant not to reveal the deficit. Nevertheless, Grant informed several of its own clients using the CDS payroll services and other nonclients of CDS's problem. Was Alexander Grant correct in revealing the information? What guidelines did the court use to answer this question? Explain.

Wagenheim v. Alexander Grant and Co., 482 N.E.2d 955 (OH).

3. Burke, an energy tycoon, hired the accounting firm of Arthur Young and Company to audit several of his operations. The SEC brought an action against Burke for fraud and for failure to meet certain SEC reporting requirements. The SEC also named Arthur Young as a defendant, claiming that the accounting firm should have discovered the fraud. Arthur Young argued that it had followed GAAS when it had audited Burke. The accounting firm concluded that this strict adherence to GAAS immunized it from liability under securities law. The SEC argued that Arthur Young should have done more to discover the fraud than what was required under GAAS. Was the SEC correct? Explain. *Securities and Exchange Commission v. Arthur Young and Company,* 590 F.2d 785 (9th Cir.).

4. Hutchins and O'Neil, as general partners in the Haddon View Investment Co., became limited partners in Car Wash Investments. The general partner in Car Wash was the Minit Man Development Company. Coopers and Lybrand were accountants who handled the accounting work for both Minit Man and Car Wash. They performed audits and prepared financial statements that allegedly revealed two healthy companies. Nevertheless, both Car Wash and Minit Man went out of business. As a result, Hutchins and O'Neil lost a total of $252,000. They sued Coopers and Lybrand alleging malpractice, breach of contract, concealment, fraud, and deceit in the accountants' work for Car Wash and Minit Man. Coopers and Lybrand argued that Hutchins and O'Neil could not sue them because Car Wash and Minit Man were their clients, not Hutchins and O'Neil. Were the accountants correct? *Haddon View Investment Co. v. Coopers and Lybrand,* 436 N.E.2d 212 (OH).

5. Bainbridge hired the architectural firm of Seymour, Shaefer, and Lashutke to draw up plans for the alteration of Bainbridge's office building in Albuquerque, New Mexico. The plans called for the removal of the paneling in parts of the building and its replacement with Maxwell-Plus, a new, more durable material. Maxwell-Plus was specifically recommended by the architects as the best product on the market. From the beginning, the contractor had difficulty with the installation of Maxwell-Plus. In addition, two months after the work was completed, the new paneling began to deteriorate rapidly. Investigation indicated that Seymour, Shaefer, and Lashutke had failed to consider the dry, arid climate of Albuquerque for which Maxwell-Plus was totally unsuitable. Bainbridge had to have the paneling replaced at a cost of $122,532. Subsequently, he sued the architects. Seymour, Shaefer, and Lashutke argued that they were not liable to Bainbridge because the total value of the building had not been altered by their alleged error. Were the architects correct? Explain.

6. Craybaugh worked as a research scientist for National Research Industries, Inc. While conducting a field experiment involving a new solar energy converter, something went amiss and the converter exploded, injuring several bystanders. Craybaugh was also injured. While being treated in the company infirmary, several attorneys from National's legal department arrived on the scene, told Craybaugh they were representing her, and took her confidential statement. They later turned the statement over to the district attorney, and Craybaugh ended up facing criminal charges. Craybaugh and her mother joined as plaintiffs in a suit against the attorneys in the legal department. What duty or duties may have been violated by the attorneys? Was the mother a proper party in this lawsuit? Why or why not?

7. Malcolm was a physician who ran a small private practice in Harrison, Kansas. One evening the Sandersons brought their young daughter in for treatment of what they thought was a minor throat infection. Dr. Malcolm treated her with a standard antibiotic and sent the child home. What neither Dr. Malcolm nor the Sandersons knew was that the child had contracted a rare and often fatal blood disease. The disease, Seballian Syndrome, could only be treated with a new antibiotic called Veritrium. Had the Sanderson child been treated with Veritrium in a timely manner, her illness would have been short lived and she would have suffered no permanent damage. As it was, the inaccurate diagnosis and the ill advised treatment initiated by Dr. Malcolm actually made the child worse and almost caused her untimely death. Although the child eventually recovered, her hearing was permanently damaged. The Sandersons initiated a malpractice suit against Dr. Malcolm. The doctor argued that, because of her location in

the remote section of Kansas, she should not be expected to be as up to date on modern techniques as physicians who practice in large metropolitan areas. Furthermore, she argued that she could not have known about the new treatment and should, therefore, not be held liable. Is the physician correct? Explain.

Chapter 41

Substantive and Procedural Cyberlaw

The Opening Case

"A Cyberinvasion of Privacy"

Sometimes in the strange cyberspace of the electronic matrix, it is difficult to know who is the victim and who is the architect of a tort. This was the situation that faced the court in the following case. This unusual case began when a married couple, whom we will call the Carraways, of West Bay Peninsula realized that they had been victimized by an anonymous e-mail that depicted them in less than admirable terms. The e-mail had an address of CarrawayBay, which made it clear that Mr. and Mrs. Carraway had been targeted because they held title to a number of different residences on the peninsula. The couple believed that they had been the victims of several intentional torts including identity theft, emotional distress, and false light. What was especially vexing was that they had no idea who their tormentor was. Nevertheless, they were permitted to proceed with the lawsuit and, in their pleadings, referred to the defendant as "Jane or John Doe." The plaintiffs moved forward quickly and asked the court to order the Internet service provider (ISP) to reveal the identity of Jane or John Doe. The court agreed that the ISP had to reveal the defendant's identity and issued an order compelling the ISP to comply with the identity request. Attorneys for the defense refused to reveal John or Jane Doe's identity and appealed to the Maine Supreme Judicial Court. The defendant argued that his or her identity is protected by the right to privacy. Moreover, the defense characterized the main issue in the case as freedom of speech. In response, the plaintiffs pointed to the standard contract issued by the ISP which contains a waiver that notifies all subscribers that such identity revelations may, at times, be necessary. This waiver, they say, makes it clear that the defendant has no particular privacy claim and no exclusive immunity from a tort claim like the one they filed. As you read Chapter 41, consider both sides of this argument and try to reconcile these points of difference by determining whose privacy has actually been invaded here.

Chapter Outcomes

1. Define the key terms involved in cyberlaw.
2. Explain the nature of cybertrespass.
3. List those cybercrimes that are committed with a computer and those that are committed against computers.
4. Describe the nature of a cybertort.

5. Distinguish between cyberdefamation and cyberinvasion of privacy.
6. List those statutes that are involved in cybercontract law.
7. Describe the nature of the cybercourt network.
8. Explain what cybermanagement software can improve the practice of law.
9. Judge when trade secret protection will be provided for a computer program.
10. Judge when patent protection can be obtained for a computer program.

For a case involving facts similar to those in The Opening Case see: McAree, Dee. "Civil Case to Test Privacy Shield on Internet." *The National Law Journal,* July 14, 2004, p. 4.

41-1 The Basics of Cyberlaw

Computers have become an integral part of our lives and the law has been forced to deal with this reality. The area of law that concerns computers and their related difficulties is known as **cyberlaw.** Cyberlaw is so new that it still has a variety of different names. Legal experts refer to it variously as **electronic law, e-law,** and **computer law.** A decade ago there was no such thing cyberlaw. Instead, the law governing computers was a mis-matched hodgepodge of principles, doctrines, and theories, loosely hammered together from other legal disciplines. Today, although cyberlaw is not yet completely autonomous, it has, nevertheless, begun to develop its own rules, statutes, and precedents. Thus, it is becoming more and more common to talk about cyberlaw as if it were *sui generis,* that is, a law unto itself. Even though cyberlaw has a long way to go before it is officially *sui generis,* it can still be thought of today as having its own identity.

The Development of Cyberlaw

The juris-economic system has had to deal with developments in cyberlaw for five decades. To appreciate these developments, we will first explore the terms and concepts associated with computers and cyberlaw. We will then look at how cyberlaw has developed its own principles and doctrines within criminal law, tort law, and contract law. After exploring these three disciplines, we will look inside the day-to-day operation of the law to see how computers have affected courts and law offices. Finally, we will examine the legal princi-ples which govern the ownership of computer programs. Once we understand ownership rights we will discuss how those rights can be retained and how they can be transferred without running afoul of the law.

Computer Hardware

The term **computer hardware** refers to the actual device known as a computer and its components. The keyboard, screen, disk drive, and printer, for example, would all be con-sidered computer hardware. If a legal question involves hardware, the answer is usually rather straightforward since computer hardware is essentially electronic equipment. Con-sequently, a contract for the purchase of a laser printer for use with a personal computer is much the same as a contract for the purchase of a VCR for use with a television set and is governed by the UCC.

Computer Software

The term **computer software** refers to the card, tape, disk, or silicon chip that contains the computer program. The **computer program** consists of the instructions that tell the hardware what to do and when to do it. Computer programs often are based upon mathe-matical algorithms. An **algorithm** is a series of steps that, if followed properly, will reach a desired goal. When hardware and software are sold together the combination is called a **computer package.**

In 1952 computer giant IBM introduced its IBM701, which was the company's first production computer.

Computer Firmware Often computer software can be used with many different computers. Sometimes, however, it is written to be used with only one type or brand of computer. If fact, the program may be implanted in a microchip within a specific computer itself. In such a case, the software is called **computer firmware.**

Source Code and Object Code A computer program is written by a computer programmer who uses a programming language to create a source code. A **source code** is a set of instructions that tells the computer what to do or how to perform a particular task. A source code can be read and used by another computer programmer provided that the programmer understands the programming language. For this reason, establishing the legal ownership of a source code is extremely important. In contrast to the source code, the **object code** is the program after it has been translated by the computer into a language that only the computer can comprehend.

Teaching Tips Inform students that the source code serves two main functions. First, it can be treated as comparable to text material by virtue of the fact that it can be printed out, read and studied, and loaded into a computer's memory, just as documents are loaded into word processing equipment. Secondly, the code can be used to cause a computer to execute the program by the source code being compiled. The compiler translates the source code into an object code.

Example 41-1

Northeast Center for Technological Creativity (NCTC) is in the process of negotiating a contract with The Cuyahoga Computer Center (Tri-C) for the installation of a new computer at NCTC's main research center in Olentangy, Pennsylvania. During the last stage of the negotiations, Dr. Nathan Ellsworth, the president of NCTC asks for a copy of the source code for the new computer system. Jennifer Ward, the CEO of Tri-C, refuses to release the source code. Dr. Ellsworth wants a copy of the source code so that his computer programmers can re-program the system, if, for some reason, Tri-C is no longer able to do so. Ms. Ward is reluctant to release a copy of the code because her company uses the same code to program other systems. The source code is, therefore, the heart and soul of much of her business. Thus, her reluctance to reveal the source code is understandable.

Screen Displays The **screen display** is the audiovisual configuration that appears on the screen of the computer monitor. Most computer users are more familiar with a program's screen display than with any other aspect of the program. For this reason, identifying the ownership of a screen display is often at the heart of many legal disputes involving computer programs.

Databases A **database** is the compilation of information in a form that can be understood and used by a computer. Over the last two decades, the use of databases at home and in the workplace has become more and more prevalent. Databases can be invaluable multipurpose tools. For example, they can be used to find books in a library, to locate cases in a particular area of the law, or to determine the availability of a product in the marketplace. It is understandable that such a valuable resource might be at the heart of many legal disputes.

Teaching Tips Have students list the variety of computer databases that are especially useful to them in their academic careers.

Quick Quiz 41-1 True or False?

1. Computer software refers to the card, tape, disk, or silicon chip that contains the computer program.

2. The screen display is the audiovisual configuration that appears on the screen of the computer monitor.

3. Cyberlaw can presently be considered totally *sui generis*.

41-2 Cybercrimes

The term cybercrime is not yet a part of our everyday vocabulary. However, the increased attention that politicians, the media, and law enforcement agencies have given to crimes against computers and to those committed by using computers means that most people are aware of this type of criminal activity, even if they do not know what to call it. A cursory glance at any newspaper or newsmagazine will reveal articles, columns, editorials, and letters to the editor that touch on a wide variety of computer issues on a daily basis. To initiate an exploration of cybercrime, it is best to begin by defining a few essential terms.

Cybercrimes and Cybertrespass

Because of the multijurisdictional nature of the American legal system, there is no single way to deal with cybercrime. It is safe to begin, however, by noting that a **cybercrime** is any criminal activity that is associated with a computer. This includes crimes that are committed by using a computer, such as cyberblackmail, and crimes that are committed against a computer, such as cyberterrorism or computergerm warfare. Some states have dealt with the problem of defining cybercrimes by simply folding the traditional criminal code into the cybercrime lexicon. This approach is termed cybertrespass. **Cybertrespass** is the use of a computer or other electronic device as an instrumentality to commit any crime defined within the conventional criminal code. In any jurisdiction using the cybertrespass approach, there is no need to have a separate definition for a crime like cyberextortion. The cybertrespass statute simply assumes that, if extortion is committed using a computer, then the rules, the definitions, and the penalties associated with extortion by nonelectronic means apply to extortion committed by computer.

Cybercrimes Executed with Computers

The second way to deal with cybercrime is to create individual crimes associated directly with the computer. While this technique is time consuming and difficult, some jurists prefer it over the cybertrespass approach because criminal law must involve narrowly drawn and specifically written statutes. This is because some crimes are punishable by imprisonment and others by death. Specificity and exactness are also required in criminal law because the accused has the right to know exactly what behavior is prohibited by the criminal code. For this reason we find that some states have added crimes to their criminal codes that heretofore existed only in law review articles. Such innovative crimes include cyberextortion, cyberstalking, cyberspoofing, and cyberpiracy.

Cyberextortion   **Cyberextortion** or **cyberblackmail,** as it is sometimes called, can happen when a hacker gains access to the computer records of an individual, a business firm, or some other type of organization and uncovers some illegal, reckless, negligent, unethical, or embarrassing conduct that would damage the image or the financial status of that individual, company, or institution. Often the hacker then contacts the victim and threatens to reveal the damaging information unless he or she receives a payoff of some sort. A talented but unprincipled hacker could make an enormous amount of money from those people and institutions willing to meet his or her unscrupulous demands. Computer users who spend a great deal of time in chatrooms are especially susceptible to the tricks of the cyberblackmailer. Cyberblackmailers will gain the confidence of a fellow chatroom regular and then elicit private information that can be used to extort money from the victim. Cyberblackmailers might also demand payments from a business to prevent the hacker from shutting down the company's computer system and thus effectively destroying the ability of that firm to do business.

Cyberstalking   Cyberstalking is closely associated with cyberblackmail. Cyberstalking sometimes comes before, after, or during the cyberblackmail process. **Cyberstalking** involves targeting vulnerable individuals by tracking their computer transactions, personal records, and communication habits and then using those transactions, records, and habits to victimize the innocent party. Again, chatroom regulars are the target of choice for the cyberstalker who acts as the victim's confidant, and then arranges a face-to-face meeting with the victim in order to take advantage of the victim in some way.

Cyberspoofing   Although cyberspoofing may sound harmless, it is actually a very serious crime. In **cyberspoofing,** the perpetrator uses a computer to assume another computer user's identity to carry out a crime. A simple form of cyberspoofing involves adopting the identity of an e-mailer in order to defraud recipients of the original e-mailer's e-mail. Another type of cyberspoofing involves creating a phony website to obtain credit card numbers, debit card numbers, passwords, and other confidential information to commit a wide variety of crimes such as investment fraud, credit card fraud, pyramid schemes, and so on. Sometimes cyberspoofers create their own websites. More often, however, they find a way to divert consumers from a legitimate website to one with a similar name or address. The cyberspoofer can then promise to send merchandise that appears on the genuine website while confiscating the funds used to "buy" the actual merchandise. Another form of cyberspoofing involves online auction houses such as eBay. While most auction house sellers and buyers are legitimate, some are not. Phony sellers can promise merchandise that they never deliver. Some cyberspoofers may actually bid on their own phony items, thus raising the final bid on items that are never sent to the auction winner. Another cyberspoofing method involves sending out phony e-mails that solicit buyers and, in the process, obtain credit card information, account numbers, passwords, and the like. This last technique, for obvious reasons, is called **phishing.**

Cyberpiracy   The crime of **cyberpiracy** involves using a computer or other electronic device to create at least one, but usually more than one, illegal duplicate of data stored in a digital format. The copied data can include, but are not strictly limited to software. The downloading or transmission of unauthorized copies over the Internet or within an intranet would also be considered cyberpiracy. Stripped down to its simplest form, cyberpiracy is nothing more than theft. The fact that cyberpiracy is the theft of intellectual property rather than the theft of money or goods probably makes it more, rather than less, reprehensible.

Cybercrimes That Focus on Computers

Another way to deal with cybercrime is to single out those crimes that target computers in order to disable the entire system that they operate or to steal secret information or data stored within the system. Sometimes the data are stolen and then the original computer's memory is erased. This makes the stolen data that much more important to the innocent computer user. Crimes that target computers include cyberterrorism, identity theft, cybervandalism, and cybergerm warfare.

Cyberterrorism   An act of **cyberterrorism** includes operating a computer to disrupt or destroy one or more of the critical elements of the national electronic infrastructure. These elements include the national or a regional power grid, the air traffic control system, any urban water or sanitation system, ground transportation systems such as a railroad or a subway system, the national stock markets, the national weather service, the postal service, the banking system, a harbor system, and/or the national defense system. Cyberterrorists can use any number of techniques to enter and disrupt these systems. Cyberterrorists might, for instance, send a virus into a vital computer network that causes the entire infrastructure to collapse. Or hackers might enter a single system to establish false websites, to misdirect or falsify e-mails, to destroy data streams, to disrupt calendaring programs, to erase stored data, or to vandalize Internet service providers. Hackers might also enter a system to destroy a website so that legitimate users can no longer access that site. The banking system and the stock market are obvious targets for such attacks. Cyberterrorists might also seek out crucial corporate electronic systems for attack in order to shut down vital national industries.

Identity Theft   In **identity theft** the cybercriminal, using one of the techniques noted previously, steals credit card information, financial and personal data, passwords, access code numbers, and debit card information. The cybercriminal then uses this stolen information to impersonate the innocent party. Using this technique, the identity thief can clean out bank accounts, run up credit card transactions, divert cash transfers, and generally disrupt the financial and the personal life of the victim. What is especially insidious about identity theft is that it sometimes takes the victim months or even years to reestablish his or her own credit, employment, housing, and personal history with banks, credit unions, department stores, credit card companies, schools, and even the government itself. The damage done by identity theft can, therefore, last far beyond the immediate monetary loss in such transgressions. Often overlooked in identity theft is the fact that the innocent party is not the only victim. Those banking institutions, credit card companies, and department stores involved in the theft are also victims, because they can literally be left "holding the bag."

Cybervandalism   Gifted but unprincipled cybervandals can disrupt a computer system so thoroughly that an entire website crashes, or is so totally paralyzed that the legitimate owner of the website can no longer function properly. This type of operation is referred to as **cybervandalism.** Sometimes cybervandalism is implemented to undermine the operation of a business as revenge for real or imaginary transgressions, to exercise

Business Law in the News

Identity Thief May Not Be a Stranger

A California small-business owner used an employee's work records to ring up about $3,000 at department stores and on home-delivery gourmet meals. A father used his disabled son's Social Security number to get a credit card. Another son used his elderly father's identification numbers, knowing the father wouldn't turn him in because he relied on the son to help take care of him. A bitter ex-husband posted his former wife's Social Security number and other information on a Web site.

Plenty of identity thieves are closely connected to their victims. They represent a fraction of the 27.3 million identity theft cases the Federal Trade Commission has counted in the last five years.

For the victims, the crime cuts far deeper when the perpetrator is someone they know, or even love. In addition to clearing up financial records and credit histories, they have the added burdens of deciding whether to turn the person in to authorities or handle the rift within a circle of friends or family.

"We were friends and had even gone on vacations together," said one Chicago-area identity-theft victim who suspects his friend stole his identification information while he worked for the friend's business, and then used it with another friend to spend thousands of dollars at home improvement stores. The second friend's court case in the matter is pending. "I have a good, core group of friends now," but trusting anyone is difficult, he said.

Linda Foley experienced a similar fraud nearly seven years ago. Looking for work after moving to San Diego, she approached a magazine publisher about doing some sales and writing work as a contractor.

A job and a friendship blossomed between the women, but just a few months later, Citibank was on the phone asking Foley about an address change on a credit card.

"She had applied for a card with me as the primary and her as the secondary user and then had the billing address changed to a P.O. box where we worked," said Foley, who founded the Identity Theft Resource Center because of her experience.

The center serves as an information clearinghouse and offers tips to victims on getting their lives back in order.

Identity-theft experts at financial institutions say it's rare to find family members willing to proceed with a case when they discover the perpetrator is a relative.

"We try to tell people that unless they are willing to follow through [with prosecution], the thieves are going to continue to get away with the behavior," said Mary Biron, vice president of corporate investigations and loss prevention for Harris Bank in Chicago. Foley counsels victims to think of theft just like a gambling or drug addiction.

"If you don't stop them, you're enabling them just like a drinker, gambler or a drug user," she said. "You have the ability to stop them from hurting innocent people because once they've used up a family member's credit, they will turn to the outside."

Experts advise that, in addition to turning in the perpetrator and filing a police report, victims should consider putting passwords on any accounts that will allow them.

"All of that helps the healing process," said Judith Collins, an identity theft expert at Michigan State University. "Even if it's someone you know, you have to do the practical things. But it certainly is tough love."

Questions for Analysis

1. What are the situations outlined in the story that detail identity theft among friends and family members? Explain.

2. What is especially insidious about identity theft when it involves a friend or family member? Explain.

3. What is the other class of crimes that identity theft can be listed as? Explain.

4. What advice does the article offer for dealing with identity theft? Explain.

5. What is the Identity Theft Resource Center?

power, or to injure the owner of a business. Unlike cyberterrorism, which often has a political end, and cyberextortion and cyberspoofing, which have financial goals, cybervandalism, like other forms of vandalism, is often performed on a dare, to gain attention, or just to show that the cybervandals can get away with it.

Cybergerm Warfare When perpetrators use viruses to enter and destroy a computer system, they are engaged in **cybergerm warfare.** Clearly, viruses can be utilized to attack a computer system in order to commit several of the cybercrimes explained previously. A cyberextortionist can, for example, threaten to unleash a virus that might cripple a company's computer system unless that company pays a certain sum of money to the cybercriminal. In effect, the cyberextortionist is using the virus to extract a ransom from the business. Likewise, a cyberterrorist or a cybervandal could employ a virus to upset a computer system for psychological motives or for political reasons. However, unleashing a virus into a system for no reason other than personal viciousness can also be a cybercrime. Viruses are especially destructive because they are often undetectable until the damage had been done. Viruses are also especially treacherous because they can affect a single computer, a business intranet, or even the entire Internet itself.

Quick Quiz 41-2 True or False?

1. Cybertrespass is the use of a computer or other electronic device as an instrumentality to victimize in terms of any crime as defined within the conventional criminal code.

2. Phishing involves sending out phony e-mails that solicit buyers and, in the process, obtain credit card information, account numbers, and passwords.

3. Cyberblackmail includes operating a computer to disrupt or destroy one or more of the critical elements of the national electronic infrastructure.

41-3 Cybertorts

The rapid development of computer science has changed the operation of the juris-economic system in many ways, from the way we communicate to the way we conduct ourselves in the marketplace. Computers and their technological cousins, the mobile phone, the videocam, the fax machine, and the phonecam have made our lives more convenient, more efficient, and, in many situations, easier. However, these innovations have also inspired the villainous among us to create new and different tactics for committing torts. The term cybertort has been coined to cover those torts which either use or target a computer.

The Basics of Cybertort Law

A tort is a private wrong that injures another party. Generally, such injuries involve bodily harm, emotional suffering, property damage, and/or the ruin of the victim's reputation. The objective of tort law is to compensate the victim for the harm that is caused by the tortfeasor. The tortfeasor is the one who commits a tort. In cyberlaw, cybertorts are different from most other torts because they are always somehow entangled with information. A **cybertort,** then, can be described as the invasion, distortion, theft, falsification, destruction, misuse, deletion, or exploitation of data stored in or associated with an electronic mechanism including desktop PCs, laptops, mobile phones, phonecams, videocams, personal digital assistants (PDAs), mainframes, and home computers that are isolated or that are integrated into an intranet or the Internet. It would be highly unusual for a cybertort to involve a physical injury to the victim. However, it can often happen that the victim's reputation is damaged because of a false report distributed via e-mail, that the victim's emotional health is disturbed because of an invasion of his or her privacy, or that the innocent party's financial condition is disrupted because his or her identity has been confiscated. The focus here will be on two intentional torts: cyberdefamation and cyberinvasion of property.

Cyberdefamation

Like all forms of defamation, cyberdefamation is the communication of false and destructive data about a person that harms that person's reputation. The essential difference between defamation and cyberdefamation is that, in **cyberdefamation,** the false and destructive information is transmitted by an electronic device. What is most interesting about cyberdefamation is that, in most cases, the courts have limited, rather than expanded, liability for defamation using a computer. Such was not always the case. When the courts first faced these issues, they usually ruled in favor of the victim. For instance, in the now famous Prodigy case, the court easily extended liability for defamation from the instigating party to the Prodigy Service Company, the firm which had set up and which controlled the defendant's Internet service.

This case, however, represented only the first volley fired in the battle over cyberdefamation. The second round was fired by Congress, which passed the Communications Decency Act (CDA). One of the express objectives of the CDA is to protect ISPs from future defamation lawsuits for false statements posted by other individuals on the Net. Still, the law by itself has not halted the proliferation of cyberdefamation lawsuits which attempt to hold ISPs liable for defamatory statements. In one especially telling case, America Online was found not responsible for defamation even though the plaintiff clearly demonstrated that the provider knew about the defamatory nature of a posting and had not removed the posting with proper haste. In addition, the protection granted to ISPs has gone beyond protecting those who post defamatory comments. The courts have also decided that ISPs are not responsible when hackers introduce viruses into a computer system, when piracy is permitted to occur on the Net, and when an invasion of privacy takes place via the ISP's link.

Cyberinvasion of Privacy

A **cyberinvasion of privacy** results from an unwelcome and unwanted intrusion into the private matters of an individual when the intrusion is carried out or sustained by an electronic device. Since computer science is itself in a constant state of change, it should not be a surprise to discover that the principles of cyberlaw, as they relate to privacy, are also in a highly unsettled state. Nevertheless, there are still some general points that can be made in relation to cyberinvasion of privacy. The first of these points explores the principles of privacy.

Principles of Privacy   The right to privacy is not explicitly mentioned in the United States Constitution. Nevertheless, the law has long recognized the existence of a right to privacy in both common law and constitutional law.

Revelation of Private Computer Records   Today, the revelation of private records often involves an invasion into information that is stored in a computer file. Most invasions that affect private records involve employees who, because of their jobs, work

The Opening Case Revisited
"A Cyberinvasion of Privacy"

In the case featured at the beginning of this chapter, the plaintiffs asked the court to force the ISP to reveal the name of the defendant in the lawsuit. The court agreed and issued an order compelling the ISP to reveal the name. The ISP, however, realizing that the law in this area is still highly unsettled, continued to resist. The ISP's chief argument was that its customers have a right to privacy. The ISP, therefore, has no authority to violate that right, and neither does the court. Whether the ISP will succeed in this argument remains to be seen.

closely with confidential files, such as medical records, financial records, scholastic records, and employment records. A failure to protect such records, whether they are stored in a computer or on paper, can result in an invasion of privacy lawsuit. Nevertheless, some courts have held that records stored as data in a computer require a degree of protection that is higher than the protection given to paper records because paper records can be hidden away or locked in a filing cabinet, while computer records are easy to retrieve, compile, and disseminate. Still, not every claim of a computer-related invasion of privacy automatically translates into a successful lawsuit. The law is still unsettled in several key areas, not the least of which is the question of whether Internet service providers are permitted to protect the privacy rights of their subscribers.

Private Privacy versus Public Privacy

Most of the time **private information** or **private-private information,** as it is sometimes called, includes reports on personal matters, family relationships, sexual habits, employment records, medical data, and financial records. The dispute in The Opening Case, however, highlights another issue in the law, the difference between **private privacy** and **public privacy.** The law is familiar with private privacy concerns over matters such as health concerns, sexual preferences, family matters, and so on. However, the computer age has given rise to another privacy concern; that is, the concern over the publication of what is essentially public information, or what has been termed public privacy matters. Some jurists and many private citizens are convinced that computer records require a higher degree of protection than paper records because paper records can be hidden in a drawer or locked in a safe, while computer records are easy to locate, retrieve, compile, and disseminate.

A very vivid example of the belief in the right to protect public-private matters occurred in the 1990s, when a company called Lotus Development suggested putting together a CD-ROM that would list over 120 million Americans. The proposed list would include the individuals' names, addresses, phone numbers, marital status, age, educational background, income, buying habits, employment status, and so on. All of the information that would have been included on the CD was essentially "public" information, easily obtained by examining public records. Yet, there was a huge outcry from the public against the plan. The cry was so loud and so strong that Lotus never issued the CD-ROM package. The lesson to be learned from the Lotus case is that the computer age has given rise to new privacy concerns about how public-private matters are stored and disseminated. The public privacy principle is based on two suppositions: (1) privacy rules must be applied to some public information or at least to the way information is compiled, stored, retrieved, and disseminated; and (2) there is a substantial difference between isolated bits of public information and the compilation of that same information in a database that can be easily stored, retrieved, and disseminated by businesses, educational institutions, and the government.

Data Mining of Public-Private Information

Data mining occurs when an individual associates two or more pieces of public information to create information that the victim considers private, despite the public nature of the data from which the private information is obtained. The issue here is whether mining the public information to uncover private matters is a violation of the individual's right to privacy. Some commentators have argued that an individual's privacy is invaded if, in obtaining the individually separate pieces of public information, the alleged tortfeasor ignores or bypasses the victim's consent and produces a piece of hybrid information, information referred to as **public-private information,** that embarrasses, disturbs, or financially injures the innocent party. In such a situation, these commentators argue that the innocent party ought to have a cause of action against the data miner, at least to the extent that the innocent party can show harm.

Example 41-2

George Filmore was an avid biker who regularly rode his bicycle into town to do his daily errands. One of those errands involved stopping off at the ATM outside a local branch of the Buckeye National Bank. The ATM contained a video camera that photographed individuals as they activated the computerized system. Shortly after one of his usual stops at the ATM, Filmore discovered that he was being inundated with advertisements, telemarketing phone calls, and e-mail spam, selling a wide variety of products for bikers. Eventually, Filmore discovered that one of the bank's subsidiaries owned and operated a sports equipment company that regularly accessed the videos produced at the ATMs around the country and used the information to target potential buyers. This particular instance of data mining may not have financially hurt Filmore, but it did annoy him enough for him to send a nasty letter of protest to the bank, to close all of his accounts, and to move his money into a bank which assured him they did not routinely data mine their customers.

In the Filmore case in Example 41-2, the various pieces of information that the bank mined included Filmore's address, phone number, e-mail address, bank account balance, and his hobby as a bicyclist. Arguably, all of these pieces of information taken individually are public. The privacy rights emerge because the public pieces of information have been mined to produce a valuable piece of public-private information that was exploited by the bank and its subsidiary without Filmore's approval and in a way that enraged him. Unfortunately, there is little case law concerning public-privacy rights. Moreover, the law that does exist today militates against the firm establishment of a public-privacy right, at least at the present time.

Statutory Protections and Violations of Privacy

Despite appearances to the contrary, the government has not been totally oblivious to the computerized trafficking in public-private and private-private information that has occurred in recent years. In fact, the government has enacted several statutes to deal with certain aspects of these privacy invasions. These acts include the Fair Credit Reporting Act, the Right to Financial Privacy Act, the Electronic Communications Privacy Act, and the Driver's Privacy Protection Act. As is usually the case, however, the government has also found new ways to violate the privacy rights of its citizens. Perhaps the most controversial federal law responsible for many of these potential violations is the USA PATRIOT Act.

The Fair Credit Reporting Act The Fair Credit Reporting Act (see Chapter 19) involves records kept by credit bureaus, most of which now use computers to store data on consumers. Credit reports, by their very nature, include information that can be issued to businesses, insurance companies, banks, and employers. Under the act, credit bureaus must inform people about the nature of the information that is in their files. The act also gives people the right to change any inaccurate information found in their files. In addition, the credit bureau is responsible for sending notices to businesses and others who have received reports containing inaccurate data.

The Right to Financial Privacy Act The Right to Financial Privacy Act forbids financial institutions from opening customer records, most of which are kept on computer files, to the government without appropriate authorization from the customer or without an official court order of some sort. In addition, if the government does ask for a client's financial information, the institution must inform the client about the invasion of his or her records. The client then has the right to contest the intrusion as an unwarranted violation of his or her privacy rights. Naturally, none of this actually stops either the government or the financial institution itself from investigating allegations of wrongdoing on the part of the client.

The Electronic Communications Privacy Act The Electronic Communications Privacy Act was designed to add additional electronic communication techniques, such as e-mail transmissions, to the list of illegal wire-tapping prohibitions. Unfortunately, a number of exceptions to this general rule were also added to the statute, allowing employers to monitor the e-mail transmissions of their employees. One of these exceptions permits an employer to monitor the e-mail transmissions of employees if those employees consent to the surveillance. Another exception allows surveillance if the e-mail transmissions are carried out in the ordinary course of business.

The Driver's Privacy Protection Act The Driver's Privacy Protection Act was added to the Violent Crime Control and Law Enforcement Act of 1994. The goal of the statute was to give drivers the opportunity to pass up the "opportunity" to be placed on any lists that the motor vehicle bureau might distribute to businesses and other governmental agencies. The creation of such lists is an example of the type of data mining that has come to the attention of jurists as a new way to violate the privacy rights of American citizens.

The USA PATRIOT Act One of the most far-reaching attempts by the federal government to expand its surveillance power was the passage of a federal statute entitled the Uniting and Strengthening America by Providing Appropriate Tools Required to Intercept and Obstruct Terrorism Act. Often referred to as the USA PATRIOT Act, or simply as the Patriot Act, this statute involves several stipulations that encourage federal law enforcement organizations, including the Federal Bureau of Investigation and the Secret Service, to undertake surveillance projects that involve communication transmissions by wire, voice, and other electronic means. This would include transmissions via computer lines using the Internet and e-mail capabilities. The statute also alters other federal laws including two of the laws mentioned above, the Fair Credit Reporting Act and the Right to Financial Privacy Act. Under the USA PATRIOT Act, for example, the Fair Credit Reporting Act requires consumer reporting agencies to turn over to the federal government

For the sources of this segment of Talking Points see: Posner, Richard. "The Face We Present to the World." In *Overcoming Law.* Cambridge, MA: Harvard University Press, 1995, pp. 531–551; Introna, Lucas D. "Workplace Surveillance, Privacy, and Distributive Justice." In *Readings in Cyberethics.* Edited by Richard A. Spinello and Herman T. Tavani. Boston: Jones and Bartlett Publishers, 2004, pp. 476–487.

Talking Points

In his essay, "The Face We Present to the World," Richard Posner, chief justice for the Appeals Court of the United States Seventh Circuit, argues that the right to privacy is just a fancy way for people to cover up the truth and thus present a false face to those with whom they deal. Posner contends that if the false image that one presents in the marketplace fools people who have trusted that individual, then that false image must be destroyed.

Lucas D. Introna, reader in the Center for the Study of Technology and Organization, Lancaster University, UK, has interpreted Posner's position in the following way, "Posner, (1978) tend(s) to see the need for privacy as a way of hiding or covering up what ought to be exposed for scrutiny. He argues that exposure through surveillance would provide a more solid basis for social interaction because participants will be able to discern the facts of the matter for themselves. Privacy, for him, creates opportunities for hiding information that could render many social interactions 'fraudulent.' To interact with someone without providing that person with all information would be to socially defraud that person, or so he argues. This is a very compelling argument."

In contrast, in his article "Workplace Surveillance, Privacy, and Distributive Justice," Introna argues that employees are "rightly concerned that the employer will have only 'part of the picture,' and that they may be reduced, in subsequent judgments, to that 'part of the picture' alone. They are also concerned that employers will apply inappropriate values when judging this 'part of the picture.' More than this, they will also be concerned by the fact that employers may implicitly and unbeknowingly bring into play a whole lot of other 'parts' of the picture that ought not to be considered in that *particular* context."

Of the two positions, which one has the more accurate view of the results of workplace surveillance? Of the two legal theorists, which one reflects your own personal view? Which view is supported by the evidence in this chapter concerning the right of privacy? Explain your answers.

a consumer's records if a government agency says that those records *could* be related to an intelligence operation conducted by the government against suspected terrorist activities. Furthermore, the USA PATRIOT Act allows the FBI to compel libraries to turn over library circulation reports, information on library patrons, and records on patron Internet use. Fortunately, under terms of the original USA PATRIOT Act, many of the law's provisions on intelligence gathering and law enforcement were set to expire in 2005. Nevertheless, it would be good to check on the status of the act to see whether Congress renewed it or any part of it before the deadline.

Privacy and the European Union

American courts have called upon both the common law tradition and the United States Constitution to create a new right to privacy. The courts, Congress, and various state legislatures have then defended that right in a variety of creative ways. In contrast, the Europeans have simply admitted that privacy is an inherently fragile concept that will be invaded by computers no matter what they try to do about it. Perhaps the most visible weapon against cyberinvasion in the European arsenal is the European Data Protection Directive, which assures the citizens of Europe that they will enjoy certain protections should they engage in commerce on the Internet. Among the protections granted to cyberconsumers in Europe are the ability to obtain any computer data stored on them, the opportunity to adjust any incorrect data, the authority to prevent some people from using certain types of data, and the chance to demand certain remedies for any unlawful activities that impact on their own stored data. The EU privacy directive also prevents European firms from dealing in businesses in countries that do not grant similar protections. This prohibition is problematic to American firms because the United States currently has no such guarantees.

> ## Quick Quiz 41-3 True or False?
>
> 1. Cybertorts are different from most other torts because they are always somehow entangled with information.
>
> 2. The right to privacy is explicitly mentioned in Article VIII of the United States Constitution.
>
> 3. Data mining occurs when an individual associates two or more pieces of public information to create information that the victim considers private, despite the public nature of the data from which the private information is obtained.

41-4 Cybercontract Law

Cybercommerce, electronic commerce, or **e-commerce** involves the process of transacting business by electronic means. Cybercommerce can involve purchasing products by using electronic credit and debit cards, extracting money from a checking account at the local ATM, transferring funds electronically from one financial institution to another, and buying and selling merchandise on the Internet. All of these new electronic techniques of carrying on business have led to changes in the law. The most important cybercommercial statutes in this regard are the federal E-Sign Act, the Uniform Electronics Transactions Act, and the Uniform Computer Information Transactions Act.

The E-Sign Act

The **E-Sign Act** was instigated by Congress as a way to make sure that any cybercommercial document is given the same credibility that its paper equivalent would receive. Briefly then, the E-Sign Act guarantees that any cybercontract created on the Internet or by e-mail will be considered completely legal, just so long as the parties to the contract have agreed that electronic signatures will be used by all parties to the agreement. So long as the cyber-agreement can be duplicated and kept within a computer, it will be afforded the same validity as its paper counterpart. The statute clearly applies to the sale of goods contracts, as covered by Article 2, and leases, as covered by Article 2A, of the Uniform Commercial Code. Some documents are intentionally excluded from the federal law. These include records of court proceedings, wills, health insurance cancellations, foreclosure notices, prenuptial agreements, eviction notices, and divorce agreements.

The Uniform Electronic Transactions Act

Like the E-Sign Act, the Uniform Electronic Transactions Act (UETA) makes certain that cyberdocuments and paper documents receive identical treatment in the marketplace. The act is concerned, therefore, with the similarities among, rather than the differences between, paper and electronic documents. Once the parties to a cybercontract have willfully entered an agreement using electronic means, the agreement will be just as valid as a similar one that is negotiated outside the Web and is subsequently reduced to paper. The law also makes it clear that, if another statute such as the Statute of Frauds requires a writing and a signature, then the electronic record and the electronic signature will meet that requirement. Under the UETA, an electronic signature is defined as "an electronic sound, symbol, or process attached to or associated with a record and executed or adopted by a person with intent to sign the record."

UETA 2 (8)

The Uniform Computer Information Transactions Act (UCITA)

The Uniform Computer Information Transactions Act (UCITA) handles such diverse agreements as: database contracts, software licensing agreements, customized software formulation, and the rights associated with multimedia packages. The new act does manage to respond to concerns involved in the making of any Internet-related contract. Despite the apparent strength of UCITA, it must be remembered that it is a **default statute.** As a result, under UCITA, the parties to a cybercontract are granted the freedom to indicate what they want when they enter into an agreement. It is only when the parties to a cybercontract have overlooked some term, condition, clause, practice, or procedure, that they are compelled to look at the provisions of the uniform statute.

Quick Quiz 41-4 True or False?

1. The E-Sign Act was instigated by the ALI as a way to make sure that any cybercommercial document is given the same credibility that its paper equivalent has received for centuries.

2. The UETA makes certain that cyberdocuments and paper documents receive different treatments in the marketplace.

3. The UCITA is a default statute.

41-5 Cyberprocedure

Thus far our study has examined how changes in computer technology have affected substantive law. Computers, however, also affect how the law operates on a procedural level. Judges, lawyers, and paralegals have discovered that many familiar tasks have been made easier, more efficient, and more economical by the introduction of computer technology into courtrooms and law offices. Many jurisdictions have decided to establish standards and guidelines for the addition of technology into the running of the court system. These standards set down general principles to deal with such diverse problems as instituting a universal case-numbering system, establishing a shared document filing process, initiating a common procedure for pretrial discovery, and so on.

The Cybercourt Network

Some jurisdictions have taken steps toward the establishment of a universal cybercourt network in their home state. In such a system, all courts throughout the state would transmit their case results to a central computerized depository that would store the reports and categorize them automatically on the basis of certain key terms. The process results in a master database that shows how cases are related to one another throughout the entire state. Cases can be organized according to shared legal principles, similar fact patterns, similar procedures, identical filings by multiple law firms, similar results in widely diverse actions, and similar statutory, regulatory, common law, and constitutional references. Local courts would not lose control over their own cases, however. Still, the cybercourt network could create an infrastructure that would promote a more efficient sharing of cases and the opinions issued in those cases.

A statewide cybercourt network could also work toward a common method for filing pleadings and other documents electronically, by fax machine, or both. Procedures could be established by each local court so long as those procedures fell within certain minimum guidelines established at the state level. A central state committee could also work toward answering certain questions that would need uniform answers throughout the jurisdiction. Thus, it would be necessary, for example, to have a common response to the question of timing in the filing of documents with the courts. Another task that can be more easily accomplished with the addition of computers into the state court system is the establishment of a common case numbering system throughout an entire state. The goal of such a project would be to create a streamlined system to make filing and research as user friendly as possible and to standardize the interlocking aspects of the statewide system. Ultimately, it would be best if a national system could be established that crossed state boundaries and standardized filing procedures, numbering systems, and discovery procedures that now differ on a state-by-state basis.

Cybermanagement of Legal Procedure

The introduction of computers into law firms can also help make the practice of law more efficient and more effective. Several software packages are available on the market today that can help lawyers and paralegals manage law office operations. Specifically, case management software programs can help attorneys keep close tabs on such items as daily, weekly, and monthly calendars; task lists of work to be accomplished; and address books that keep track of clients, colleagues, judges, expert witnesses, factual witnesses, and adversaries. Case management software programs can combine these tasks in a centralized computer file that can be accessed by the attorney at any time from any local or remote computer station. The software can help attorneys perform a number of diverse tasks efficiently, effectively, and economically. Included in these tasks would be such things as investigating and tracking new and potential clients; managing forms and templates for filing; creating a firmwide address book; tracking contacts with clients, judges, witnesses, and opponents; synchronizing the efforts of each member of a firm; managing deadlines and statutes of limitation dates; capturing billable hours in a uniform and practical manner; and cataloging documents, photos, correspondence, pleadings, and so on, all in one place.

Contemporary Cyberdiscovery Techniques

The introduction of computers into the legal environment has also had a profound effect on the way that discovery is conducted. Discovery is a step in the litigation process during which each side of a dispute attempts to uncover all evidence that is relevant to the lawsuit. Computer technology impacts on discovery in two ways. First, the discovery process itself can be enhanced through the use of computers and their electronic cousins, the phonecam, the PDA, the mobile phone, the video recorder, the fax machine, and so on. Second, the discovery process must also now take into account the fact that an enormous amount of discoverable evidence may be stored in computers. This includes e-mail files, stored databases, and calendaring software, to name a few.

The Discovery Process Itself The discovery process permits the use of a number of tools and techniques including depositions, interrogatories, requests for real evidence, requests for physical and mental examinations, and requests for admissions. Of these, the deposition lends itself to a number of computer-related enhancements. Thus, for example, depositions can now be conducted on the phone and on the Internet. Moreover, it is also possible to use recording equipment to preserve a deposition in both audio and video form. It is even becoming common today to see judges permit the use of recordings of depositions in open court when witnesses are not physically available to testify at trial. Lawyers have also made increased use of videoconferencing and Web conferencing during the discovery phase of a lawsuit. A **videoconference** allows any number of people at geographically separate locations to discuss the details of a case live and in real time. A **Web conference** is similar to a videoconference but it is carried out online via the Internet using personal computers. This approach is less complicated and generally more efficient because it cuts down on the complexity of the process. Because interrogatories involve specific questions that require detailed answers, videoconferencing and Web conferencing can also be of help in that process.

Discoverable Evidence and Computer Retrieval

Discoverable Evidence and Computer Retrieval In addition to using electronic tools to conduct discovery, attorneys must also be prepared to take into account the fact that, in the modern business office, a substantial quantity of discoverable information is collected and saved in computers. These stored files may include e-mail files, stored databases, Internet search records, intranet or portal records, and calendaring software, to name a few. In order to conduct a fruitful search of computer records an attorney must be aware that such cyberevidence may fall into one or more of the following three categories: (1) a class of cyberevidence derived from the system's configuration, (2) a category of cyberevidence derived from the character of the evidence itself, and (3) a grouping of cyberevidence derived from how it is kept in the computer network under examination.

First, cyberevidence can be categorized on the basis of the configuration of the computer system itself. This means that an attorney must understand the nature and the extent of the computer system being used not only in the opposing party's office, but also in the offices of all significant witnesses. As discovery is conducted, the attorney must keep in mind that the word "computer" can be interpreted to include laptops, the mainframe, desktop personal computers, home computers, phonecams, PDAs, and mobile phones. Second, cyberevidence can be distinguished by the character of the evidence. This means that the attorney must be aware that cyberevidence can be found not only in a variety of physical places, but also in cyberspace. Attorneys should, therefore, routinely investigate the other party's e-mail records, Internet search records, fax machine logs, and copier logs. In addition, computer-related technology should also be investigated.

Finally, it is crucial for an attorney to recall that cyberevidence is also categorized on the basis of how it is kept in the computer. Thus, the attorney must remember that the data can be classified as active, inactive, backup, extant, and paper. **Active data** concern information being used now. Active data are, therefore, easy to retrieve because they are used on a daily basis. **Inactive data** concern information that is easily retrievable because it is still located somewhere in the computer's memory and has not yet been deleted. **Backup data** are data that have been duplicated for safe keeping. Such data are kept on disks or stored in the hardware of a second computer, removed in location from the first for safety. **Extant data** are information that is difficult to retrieve because it is hidden in the computer system. Finally, **paper data** are information that has been printed out in hard copy for filing in a conventional way.

Quick Quiz 41-5 True or False?

1. Computers affect how the law operates on a substantive level but do not really affect substantive law.

2. Some jurisdictions have taken steps toward the establishment of a universal cybercourt network in their home state.

3. The National Center for State Courts has established a uniform method for filing documents in court.

41-6 Intellectual Property Rights and Cyberprotection Law

Cybernetic technology has made personal computers in the home, office, factory, and store almost as indispensable as the telephone. Consequently, it has become imperative to protect the ownership of computer programs. Ownership can be protected in the law in three ways: establishing trade secret status, securing a copyright, or obtaining a patent.

Trade Secret Protection

A **trade secret** is a plan, process, device, procedure, formula, pattern, compilation, technique, program, design, method, or improvement that is used in a business and that is disclosed only to those employees who need to know it to do their jobs. The Uniform Trade Secrets Act sets up two conditions that must be met in order for a plan, process, program, and so on to gain trade secret status. First, the plan, process, program, and so on, must gain financial worth simply because it is a secret and cannot be applied by others who might use it to compete with the owner of the secret. Second, the alleged secret must be the subject of reasonable attempts to protect it from those who would use it in a way that would financially hurt the owner of the secret.

Establishing Trade Secret Status   The right to characterize a computer program as a trade secret depends on the way the owners of the program treat it in relation to other people. In general, the easier it is for people to gain access to the program, the less likely it is that the program will be considered a secret should the matter be contested in court. Therefore, to protect trade secret status, the owners of a program must make certain that the program is treated as a secret from the very beginning. The goal is to grant access to the secret only to those people who need to know it in order to carry out their duties in the ordinary course of business. Steps that can be taken to increase the likelihood that a court will rule that a program is a trade secret include the following: (1) label the program as a secret in all documents related to the program, (2) limit employee access to the program on a need-to-know basis, (3) maintain tight security in the business in general but especially in any area where the program is required to be out in the open for business purposes, (4) keep the program and all related material under lock and key when it is not in use, (5) require employees who work with the program to sign secrecy agreements, (6) require customers who purchase the use of the program to sign licensing agreements, and (7) be especially vigilant in limiting any access to the program by competitors.

Computer Programs Denied Trade Secret Status   Computer programs that have been transferred to software and then placed on the open market for wide distribution cannot claim trade secret status. Software that is widely distributed can be easily copied. Thus, it becomes difficult to demonstrate that the company has taken extensive measures to protect the information on the software. Moreover, since the purpose of placing the software on the open market is to sell it to as many people as possible, the seller must make the software readily available in bookstores and video outlets. This availability on the open market defeats the whole trade secret concept.

Computer Programs Granted Trade Secret Status   Trade secret status is available to companies that distribute their software on a limited, highly selective basis. For example, a computer company that produces and sells a program used to control the distribution of drugs by pharmaceutical firms might be able to call that program a trade secret. Such a company would not actually sell the program to the pharmaceutical firm, but would instead allow the firm to use the program via a licensing agreement. A **licensing agreement** is made when the producer of a product, in this case a computer program, allows a purchaser to use the product only if the purchaser agrees to respect the producer's desire for secrecy. In this situation, in order to use the program the pharmaceutical company would have to agree to respect the computer company's desire for secrecy. In this type of highly selective, strictly controlled transaction, trade secret status works.

State Statutory Trade Secret Protection A number of states have enacted trade secret statutes designed to protect trade secrets within the state's borders. Many of these statutes are patterned after the **Uniform Trade Secrets Act** written by the National Conference of Commissioners on Uniform State Laws. Typically, these statutes will define a trade secret, will describe transgressions of the act, and will provide for both damages and injunctive relief when there has been a trade secret infringement. The statutes also generally include a statute of limitations, typically about four years, and will indicate that a continuing use of a trade secret is a single rather than a series of transgressions. Some state statutes also allow for attorney's fees.

The Economic Espionage Act The federal government also entered the trade secret arena with the passage of the **Economic Espionage Act** of 1996. The espionage act does not provide for any civil actions but, instead, outlines criminal sanctions for the theft of trade secrets and for the use of fraud to obtain trade secrets. Individuals convicted under the statute can face up to ten years of imprisonment and fines that can reach as much as $500,000. The statute forbids the theft of trade secrets for distribution to a foreign government, to an agent of a foreign government, or for economic gain that does not benefit the actual owner of the trade secret.

Copyright Protection

A **copyright** is an intangible property right that is granted to authors of literary, artistic, and musical compositions. A copyright means that the owner has the exclusive right to reproduce, publish, and sell his or her work in a fixed tangible medium of expression. Since a computer program is a fixed medium of expression, it is subject to copyright protection. The federal Copyright Act specifically lists the following as works that are subject to copyright protection: literary works, dramatic works, musical works, pantomimes, pictorial works, sculptures, graphic works, motion pictures, audiovisual works, sound recordings, architectural works, and choreographic works. Computer programs are also specifically covered by the Copyright Act of 1980, which includes computer programs in the category of "writings" or "literary" works to which exclusive rights can be granted.

The juris-economic system has responded to the rapid changes that have occurred in cybertechnology. In fact, many of the recent alterations in law were specifically designed to keep abreast of the effects of cybercommunication on copyright privileges. Despite this effort, the high-speed, global, interactive nature of the Internet has caused unforeseen problems in copyright law. For example, cybertechnology now makes it possible for a single copy of a computer program, or one individual copy of a literary work, to be made available to millions of computer users simply by placing that single copy on a website that is accessible to other users. This advance in cybertechnology may have been predictable to cybernecticists, but it went virtually unnoticed for quite some time by jurists and legislators. Nevertheless, despite the unpredictability of the problem, the law, as a complex adaptive system, did adapt to the problem and has provided a few solutions.

The No Electronic Theft Act One such solution came from Congress in the form of the **No Electronic Theft Act (NET Act)** of 1997, a federal law which granted limited immunity to individuals who duplicate copyrighted works on the Internet, as long as those users do not profit from the copying process. The statute does not simply grant immunity to infringers, however. Instead, it imposes criminal penalties for the violation of certain provisions. Specifically, it makes it illegal to create a duplication (including an electronic duplication) of a copyrighted work for commercial profit or private financial gain by copying or handing out one or more copies of one or more copyrighted productions within a single 180-day period, if the productions in question have a complete retail value of over $1,000. Penalties can include fines of up to $100,000 and imprisonment of up to ten years.

The Digital Millennium Copyright Act To defend their copyright privileges, copyright holders developed cyberprotection programs that would prevent users from duplicating their copyrighted works. Thus, the copyright owner of a film or television show would place a protective program on a DVD that would prevent users from creating a copy of that film or television show from the DVD. Not to be outdone, cyberinfringers then created software that would allow a user to side step the protective program and create a duplicate of the scrambled work. In response to this technological tug-of-war, Congress passed the **Digital Millennium Copyright Act (DMCA)** of 1998. The DMCA is designed to combat those technological advances that permit users to override protection systems. The law makes it illegal to use technological means to bypass or override programs designed to prevent gaining access to a copyrighted work. Another provision of the DMCA makes it illegal to use any means to circumvent a program intended to frustrate the copying of a copyrighted work. First-time offenders can be fined up to $500,000 and imprisoned for up to five years. Second offenders can be fined up to $1 million and can receive a prison sentence that can reach as high as ten years.

The World Intellectual Property Organization It would be unfair and incomplete to close the discussion of the Digital Millennium Copyright Act without mentioning its connection to the **World Intellectual Property Organization (WIPO).** WIPO, which is a part of the United Nations, supported the development of two international treaties that were specifically designed to deal with cybercopyright problems. Two separate but closely related treaties resulted from the efforts of the WIPO. The first treaty is known as the **World Intellectual Property Organization Copyright Treaty.** This treaty guarantees that copyright holders will be allowed to use the Internet to post their works with full copyright protection. The second WIPO treaty, the **World Intellectual Property Organization Phonograms Treaty,** gives copyright holders the right to copy, publish, and distribute their works in any way, including the making of video copies, audio copies, and encrypted copies. The DMCA was written to implement provisions of these treaties into law in the United States.

Peer-to-Peer Network Problems Cybertechnology has generally managed to stay several steps ahead of developments in the juris-economic system. It seems as though each problem that is solved by the juris-economic system leads to a new, heretofore unanticipated problem. Such was the case with developments in file-sharing technology. One file-sharing development that caused a great deal of concern among copyright holders was a system known as **peer-to-peer (P2P) networking.** P2P networking involved connections among personal computers joined to the same interconnected network. This technique eliminated the need to go through a core Web server. It also permitted the users to access and download files that are located on other personal computers on the same network. While peer-to-peer systems have many legitimate purposes, they are also open to abuse. One abuse involved the downloading of music files. Copyright owners felt threatened by the use of these interconnected peer-to-peer systems to download music files. To vindicate their rights, a number of firms in the music industry joined together in a lawsuit. Their target was a company named Napster, Inc., which ran a file-sharing network. Napster was accused of copyright infringement by providing a network that facilitated the downloading of music files. Napster provided the software, known as MusicShare, that permitted the members of its system to download duplicates of music files via the Internet, and aided members by providing them with technical support whenever it was needed. The court ruled that Napster was liable for infringement even though it did not directly infringe itself, because it clearly aided the illegal and abusive infringement activities of the members of its network.

Business Law in the News
How the Supreme Court May Have Already Saved Napster

An extremely interesting article by Anupam Chander of FindLaw.com illuminates a concept of law called eminent domain and how a recent Supreme Court decision could use it to bring back Napster in its original form. It's a must read for anyone who has any interest in how we will access digital music in the future.

The logic is as follows. Last month, the Supreme Court ruled in a case *New York Times v. Tasini* for freelancers whose pre-Net works were entered into electronic databases and made available online without their permission and without any compensation. The court ruled that when Tasini authorized his work to be published in the paper this right did not include the right to republish his work in electronic form. That right still stayed with him.

Somewhat. The court also realized that the manpower needed for the Times to secure the permissions from thousands of freelancers over hundreds of thousands of legacy articles would be daunting if not impractical. Furthermore, as a complete entity, that database online provides a useful and important service for that benefits the general public. When something benefits the general public, the law can give it extra consideration.

As Chander later pointed out, the court feared that "holes in history" could be created if important works could be removed from these electronic databases. Since the goal here is the good of the general public, the courts and legislators have a duty to insure this intellectual property be made available to the public and can coerce a contractual agreement. This could be accomplished by mutual negotiations or, if that should fail, compulsory licensing.

What does this have to do with Napster?

Like the NY Times online, Napster is an electronic database. It contains copyrighted material it did not pay for and also has been sued to remove said material. Unlike the Times, Napster was shut down by the lower courts and told it MUST get permissions from every single copyright holder.

As Chander points out, this ruling essentially put all the cards in the hands of the record companies who established the bulk of these rights and have little interest in licensing their works to Napster. They have ultimate control and through their lobby the Recording Industry Association of America (RIAA) monopoly power.

Compulsory licenses avoid the abuses of monopoly power according to Chander. Napster will now go into district court, using the Supreme Court's ruling to claim its database serves the public good by providing easy access to a wide variety of material.

Music, like the written word, is part of our times and culture. They represent the mood of an era just as equally as a news commentary on a historical event. If thoughts on World War II can invoke a sound track of Big Band era music, then Napster's claim that it serves the general public is both plausible and viable. Napster can therefore force the court to grant compulsory licensing, licensing that will allow users to trade ALL music available as they did before Judge Patel's ruling a few months back.

This also means that Napster will have to pay for all the files traded and that means the user will have to pay for Napster. Napster is already converting to a subscription service, but with restrictions that put serious doubt on it becoming a viable pay service. Compulsory licensing removes those restrictions.

With compulsory licensing the songwriters get paid, the music publishers get paid and the record companies get paid. The artists won't get paid unless they prevent the record companies from collecting their check in their name. Call it creative accounting, a subject that has been covered by hundreds of news articles since the Napster debate began, but also goes beyond the sphere of Napster.

Questions for Analysis

1. What controversy was at the heart of *New York Times v. Tasini?* How did the Supreme Court rule in the Tasini case? Explain.

2. What creative solution did the Supreme Court offer in *New York Times v. Tasini* that might benefit the public's right to have an in-depth record of important historic events? Explain.

3. What controversy was involved in the Napster case? Why are music based copyright lawsuits more complicated than literary based copyright lawsuits? Explain. How did the court rule in the NAPSTER case?

4. How might the Court's concept of compulsory licensing help NAPSTER? Explain.

5. Who in the music industry stands to benefit the most from the Supreme Court's ruling in *New York Times v. Tasini?* Explain.

Source: Richard Menta. "How the Supreme Court May Have Already Saved Napster." *MP3 newswire.net,* July 31, 2001, http://www.mp3newsire.net/2001/tasini.html.

Patent Protection

A *patent* is a property right granted by the federal government to an inventor. A patent gives the inventor the exclusive right to make, use, and sell that invention for a period of years. A patent differs from both a trade secret and a copyright. A patent is, in effect, a deal with the government. The inventor reveals the details of the invention in the patent application. In exchange the inventor receives a guarantee from the government that it will protect the inventor's exclusive right to produce and profit from that invention for a specified period of time. In contrast, a trade secret is not revealed in any way in the open marketplace; the holder of the trade secret receives no guaranteed protection from the government. A copyright differs from a patent in that a copyright protects only the expression of an idea, while a patent protects the idea itself.

The Patent Application Process Unlike a copyright application process, which involves the use of preprinted forms provided by the Copyright Office, each patent application requires the creation of a unique technical document. The document is then filed with the Patent Office. To qualify for a patent, an invention must meet three requirements. First, the invention must fall within the limits defined by the statute as "patentable subject matter." Second, the invention must consist of some nonobvious, new, and useful feature not known or understood before the invention of this particular device. Third, the patent application must be so specific that individuals who are educated and experienced in the field can create the device on their own.

Patentable Subject Matter The law states that in order for the subject of a patent application to be patentable it must be a "process, machine, manufacturer or composition of matter." In contrast, such things as laws of nature, natural phenomena, and abstract ideas cannot be patented. Neither mathematical formulas nor mathematical algorithms are patentable because they are actually laws of nature. Recall that an algorithm is a series of steps that, if followed properly, will reach a desired goal. Since many computer software programs are based on mathematical algorithms, problems arose when inventors first attempted to patent computer software. In fact, when patent applications for computer software programs began to appear in the Patent Office in the 1970s, most software programs were eventually found to be unpatentable. However, during the 1980s and the 1990s, the trend reversed itself. Today, more than 80 percent of all patent claims involving computers have been upheld, including those involving software alone. However, the law in this area

Background Information Some people choose not to obtain patents for computer programs for several reasons. First, laws regarding computer patentability are still developing so patents obtained now may become obsolete as new laws are passed. Second, patents are expensive and time consuming, so an invention may be obsolete by the time a patent is issued. Third, patents are frequently held invalid when litigated. Fourth, patents are incompatible with trade secret protection. Nevertheless, patents offer the broadest type of legal protection and should be acquired if software (1) has high commercial value, (2) will be used for at least five years, and (3) is used with specific hardware.

remains somewhat unclear. Fortunately, some general guidelines can be laid down. For example, if a software program is only one part of a larger, more conventional process, then the courts will allow patent protection for the whole process.

Example 41-3

Engineers at Ramirez-Lofton, Inc., developed a new process for mass producing shatter-proof glass products. The new process allowed Ramirez-Lofton to produce a better-quality glass at about half the cost of its closest competitors. Part of the company's success was due to the use of lasers in the process. However, the lasers had to be timed so precisely that each one was controlled by a computer following the directions of a computer program. This portion of the process was only about one-fourth of the entire operation, the rest of which was relatively conventional. The patent examiner denied Ramirez-Lofton's patent application because part of the process involved an unpatentable computer program. A federal court reversed the refusal because the process itself was new and could be patented. The use of the program was only one part of that process.

However, if the software stands alone, the question of whether the patent application will be granted is more difficult. The Court of Appeals for the Federal Circuit has addressed the issue in several cases and tends to affirm such patent applications. The appellate court generally upholds the patentability of software despite the fact that it is based upon a mathematical algorithm, because the software actually changes the operation of the computer. Thus, the software can be viewed either as a process or as a change in the physical nature of the computer itself.

Example 41-4

Spacetime Computer Products Inc. developed SpaceTimeSatelliteSpin, a software program that allowed the user to overlay on a computer screen all available trajectories for any planned satellite launch, while simultaneously displaying all changes in the data relating to each pictured trajectory. Such a program would be invaluable to engineers as they planned the launch of future satellite missions. The patent examiner refused to issue a patent arguing that the program was simply the expression of a mathematical algorithm. The Board of Patent Appeals supported the examiner's position. The Court of Appeals for the Federal Circuit, however, reversed the decision stating that, in effect, the program transformed an ordinary all purpose computer into a specialized computer. Thus, the all purpose computer had, in effect, become a new computer capable of performing a new function following the commands of the software program. Thus, SpaceTimeSatelliteSpin can be viewed either as a process creating a change or as an alteration in the physical nature of the computer itself.

In 1996, the U.S. Patent and Trademark Office established a set of guidelines for Computer Related Inventions. The objective of the guidelines is to help eliminate ambiguity in the law regarding the patentability of software.

The speed of today's computers makes cybercommerce fast and nearly effortless.

Until recently a **business system** was also considered to be unpatentable because it was not a "process, machine, manufacturer, or composition of matter." However, in a recent court case a computer system for analyzing information concerning a group of mutual funds was declared patentable by a federal court. This decision actually culminated a slow erosion of the business systems category of unpatentable subjects. Even so, the computerized business system must still consist of some nonobvious, new, and useful feature not known or understood before the invention of this system. It must also be so specific that individuals who are educated and experienced in the field can recreate the system on their own.

Usefulness, Novelty, and Nonobviousness
The objective of patent law is to encourage inventiveness and to promote progress for the benefit of all society. Thus, a device, to be patentable, must be useful. For this reason, many processes involving computer programs would pass the usefulness test. Passing the usefulness test alone, however, is not enough to qualify for a patent. The new invention must also be novel and nonobvious. To pass the novelty test, the new device or process must be original. Copying someone else's innovation, even unintentionally, will disqualify an invention from patent eligibility. Similarly, to pass the nonobviousness test, the changes or improvements must not be obvious to a person of ordinary skill in the field. If the changes are obvious, then a patent will not be issued.

Specificity in the Application
Federal law states that a patent application must describe the nature of the invention in "full, clear, concise, and exact terms." In fact, the application must be so clear that an individual educated and experienced in that field can recreate the invention without having to engage in an extensive trial and error period. This requirement causes some difficulty in computer software patent applications, because the surest way to guarantee that someone else will be able to re-create the invention is to provide the source code in the patent application. However, many inventors are reluctant to include the source code because such codes often contain trade secrets that they are unwilling to dump onto the public domain. The usual compromise is to include in the patent application either a flowchart or some other visual diagram that reveals the details of the process.

Summary

41-1 The area of law that concerns computers and their related difficulties is known as cyberlaw. Cyberlaw is so new that it still has a variety of different names. Legal experts refer to it variously as electronic law, e-law, and computer law. Other terms that are crucial to grasp in relation to computers are source code, object code, screen display, and database. A source code is a set of instructions that tells a computer what to do. The object code is the program after it has been translated into computer language. A screen display is the audiovisual configuration that appears on the screen of the monitor. The database is the compilation of information in a form that can be understood by the computer.

41-2 A cybercrime is any criminal activity that is associated with a computer, including crimes that are committed by using a computer, such as cyberblackmail, and crimes that are committed against a computer, such as cyberterrorism or computergerm warfare. Some states have dealt with the problem of defining cybercrimes by simply folding the traditional criminal code into the cybercrime lexicon. This approach is termed cybertrespass. Cybertrespass is the use of a computer or other electronic device as an instrumentality of any crime as defined within the conventional criminal code. Cybertrespass also includes crimes that target computers as victims.

41-3 A cybertort is the invasion, distortion, theft, falsification, destruction, misuse, deletion, or exploitation of data stored in or associated with an electronic mechanism including desktop PCs, laptops, mobile phones, phonecams, videocams, personal digital assistants (PDAs), mainframes, and home computers that are isolated or that are integrated into an intranet or the Internet. Generally, when a cybertort has been commit-

ted the victim complains of one or more of the following injuries: The victim's reputation has been damaged because of a false report distributed via e-mail or some other electronic text-messaging technique, the victim's emotional health is disturbed because of an invasion of his or her privacy, or the innocent party's financial condition has been disrupted because his or her identity has been confiscated via computer. The focus in this chapter is on two cybertorts: cyberdefamation and cyberinvasion of privacy.

41-4 New electronic techniques of carrying on business have led to changes in the law. The most important cybercommercial statutes in this regard are the federal E-Sign Act, the Uniform Electronics Transfer Act, and the Uniform Computer Information Act.

41-5 Computers have affected how the law operates on a procedural level. Judges, lawyers, and paralegals, have discovered that many familiar tasks have been made easier, more efficient, and more economical by the introduction of computer technology into courtrooms and law offices. Some jurisdictions have taken steps toward the establishment of a universal cybercourt network in their home state. In such a system, all courts throughout the state would transmit their case results to a central computerized depository that would store the reports and categorize them automatically on the basis of certain key terms. The introduction of computers into law firms can also help make the practice of law more efficient and more effective.

41-6 Ownership rights in computer programs and computer software can be protected by trade secrets, copyrights, and patents. A trade secret is a plan, process, or device used in a business and known only to employees who need to know the secret to do their jobs. A program can be protected by a trade secret only if its distribution is tightly controlled. Copyrights are intangible property rights that are granted to authors of literary, artistic, and musical productions. Computer programs can be copyrighted. A patent is a property right that is granted by the federal government to an inventor. A computer program that is part of a larger, more conventional process can be patented.

Key Terms

active data, 800
algorithm, 785
backup data, 800
business system, 807
computer firmware, 786
computer hardware, 785
computer law, 785
computer package, 785
computer program, 785
computer software, 785
copyright, 802
cyberblackmail, 788
cybercommerce, 797
cybercrime, 787
cyberdefamation, 792
cyberextortion, 788
cybergerm warfare, 791
cyberinvasion of privacy, 792
cyberlaw, 785
cyberpiracy, 789
cyberspoofing, 788
cyberstalking, 788

cyberterrorism, 789
cybertort, 791
cybertrespass, 787
cybervandalism, 789
database, 787
data mining, 794
default statute, 798
Digital Millennium Copyright Act (DMCA), 803
e-commerce, 797
Economic Espionage Act, 802
e-law, 785
electronic commerce, 797
electronic law, 785
E-Sign Act, 797
extant data, 800
identity theft, 789
inactive data, 800
licensing agreement, 802
No Electronic Theft Act (NET Act), 802
object code, 786

paper data, 800
peer-to-peer (P2P) networking, 803
phishing, 788
private information, 793
private privacy, 793
private-private information, 793
public privacy, 793
public-private information, 794
screen display, 787
source code, 786
trade secret, 801
Uniform Trade Secrets Act, 802
videoconference, 800
Web conference, 800
World Intellectual Property Organization (WIPO), 803
World Intellectual Property Organization Copyright Treaty, 803
World Intellectual Property Organization Phonograms Treaty, 803

Questions for Review and Discussion

1. What are the key terms involved in cyberlaw?
2. What is the nature of cybertrespass?
3. What cybercrimes can be committed with a computer and what cybercrimes can be committed against a computer?
4. What is the nature of a cybertort?
5. What is the difference between cyberdefamation and cyberinvasion of privacy?
6. What statutes are involved in cybercontract law?
7. What is the nature of the cybercourt network?
8. How can cybermanagement software improve the practice of law?
9. When will trade secret protection be provided for a computer program?
10. When can patent protection be obtained for a computer program?

Investigating the Internet

Access the Computer Professionals for Social Responsibility website and write a paper about one of the "Recent News" items that you find there.

Cases for Analysis

1. Officials at Semco, Inc., believed that some of their company's most important computer files, which they characterized as trade secrets, had been appropriated by Terry Hildreth, a former vice president of Semco. Semco officials accused Hildreth of using these programs in running his new limited liability company, Hildreth Manufacturing, LLC. Semco engaged in a series of harassing tactics designed to stop Hildreth's use of the alleged trade secrets. To protect himself and his new firm, Hildreth brought a lawsuit asking for a declaratory judgment that no trade secrets had been taken, despite Semco's allegations to the contrary. Semco then brought a second lawsuit alleging, among other things, that trade secrets had, indeed, been misappropriated by Hildreth. After the suits were decided in favor of Hildreth, the results were appealed. During both suits the following facts came to light. Material that described the manufacturing steps that Semco now claimed were trade secrets had been routinely made available to vendors. Semco also regularly provided information about its "secret" manufacturing processes to people outside the company. Semco did not require employees to file nondisclosure or secrecy agreements. Visitors were not screened, the building was locked only after regular business hours, and the plant was open for public tours. On the basis of these facts, how should the appeals court rule on the issue of trade secrets? Explain. *Hildreth Mfg., LLC. v. Semco, Inc.,* 151 Ohio App. 3d 693.

2. Parrish and Chlarson worked for J&K Computer Systems, Inc. Parrish was a computer programmer and Chlarson was a trainee. In his capacity as programmer, Parrish wrote an accounts receivable program. Customers of J&K were granted licenses to use the program. A label on the program noted that it was J&K's property and that it could not be used without authorization under a licensing agreement. Parrish, Chlarson, and all other J&K employees were informed that the program was a secret. Nevertheless, Parrish copied it, left J&K's employ, and, along with Chlarson, opened a business similar to J&K. Parrish and Chlarson then sold the copied program to various customers. When J&K sued, Parrish and Chlarson argued that the fact that J&K had revealed the program to their customers meant it was no longer a trade secret. Were Parrish and Chlarson correct? Explain. *J&K Computer Systems, Inc., v. Parrish,* 642 P.2d 732 (UT).

3. Diehr and Latton applied for a patent to protect their development of a new process for molding raw, uncured synthetic rubber into cured products. Diehr and Latton argued that their unique contribution was to measure the temperature inside the mold and to feed that temperature into a computer that was programmed to calculate the exact time needed for the curing process. The computer would then activate a mechanism to open the mold. The process, as conceived by Diehr and Latton, eliminated the guesswork as to measuring the length of time for the mold to remain closed. The patent office denied the patent because it used a computer program in the process. The office said that the program was essentially a mathematical idea and was, therefore, unpatentable. Diehr and Latton argued that the mere fact that a computer program was used as part of a process does not mean that the whole process would be unpatentable. Were Diehr and Latton correct? Why or why not? *Diamond v. Diehr,* 101 S.Ct. 1048 (U.S. Sup. Ct.).

4. Hiroyuki Iwahashi, Yoshiki Nishioka, and Mitsuhiro Hakaridani applied for a patent for an autocorrelation unit for use in computers for pattern recognition, in this case to aid in voice

recognition. To achieve this type of pattern recognition, computers must perform a lengthy multiplication cycle that requires intricate circuitry and a costly multiplier unit. The computer hardware involved in this process is also large and cumbersome. The purpose of the new invention is to streamline the multiplication cycle. The elimination of the multiplier and the intricate circuitry is made possible by an algorithm that allows the computer to obtain the needed result by detouring the time-consuming multiplication cycle and using instead the electronic equivalent of a multiplication table. The United States Patent and Trademark Office rejected the patent application and the Board of Patent Appeals and Interferences upheld that decision. Both concluded that the alleged invention was nothing more than an algorithm, and could not, therefore, be patented. The inventors appealed the decision, arguing that the algorithm is simply part of an apparatus that alters the operation of a computer and is therefore subject to patentability. Can a patent be rejected based solely on the argument that the invention involves an algorithm? Explain. *In re Iwahashi,* 888 F.2d 1370 (Fed. Cir.).

5. Stern Electronics, Inc., entered a licensing agreement with Konami Industry Co., Ltd., granting Stern exclusive rights to market the video game Scramble in the United States. Omni Video Games, Inc., wrote a new program that duplicated the sights and sounds of Scramble. Stern sued Omni in federal court asking for an injunction to prevent Omni from marketing their knockoff of Scramble. Omni argued that Stern could not get a copyright for the Scramble audiovisual display because every time a player plays the game, the display is different. The display is not fixed in a tangible medium as required by law. Since Omni had written its own program, Stern could not stop it from marketing the duplicate Scramble games. Was Omni correct? Explain. *Stern Electronics, Inc., v. Kaufman and Omni Video Games, Inc.,* 669 F.2d 852 (2nd Cir.).

Quick Quiz Answers

41-1	41-2	41-3	41-4	41-5	41-6
1. T	1. T	1. T	1. F	1. F	1. T
2. T	2. T	2. F	2. F	2. T	2. T
3. F	3. F	3. T	3. T	3. T	3. F

Chapter 42

Alternative Dispute Resolution

The Opening Case

"Arbitrating the Power of Arbitration"

When one of Westcot Insurance Company's clients was involved in an accident on his farm, he filed a claim with the company which paid him a settlement of $50,000. Later the client discovered that he had been denied the chance to increase his coverage to $200,000. This discovery disturbed him because Westcot had allowed his ex-wife to expand her coverage to the new limit of $200,000 and had not consulted him, although the company had apparently had the opportunity to do so. Feeling cheated, he asked for the missing $150,000 and, predictably, Westcot said, "no." The company brought suit for a judgment that would declare that it owed the client no more than the $50,000 that he already had in hand. The client pointed to an arbitration clause in his policy. The court said that the policy did, indeed, guarantee an arbitration hearing and told the parties to settle their differences in that way. An arbitration hearing was held and the arbitrators decided in the client's favor. So far the process had worked the way it was supposed to work. Then the unexpected happened. Westcot appealed the arbitrator's decision to the federal court that had heard the case in the first instance. The appeal was based on the fact that the client had argued that his policy was "contrary to legislative mandate or public policy." The judge said that the client's claim in the case gave the court the authority to review the arbitrator's decision. Accordingly, the judge ruled in favor of the insurance provider stating that the company had not been obligated to make the client an offer of increased coverage. So, it appears in this case, that the arbitration clause in the insurance agreement did not work the way it was supposed to work, or at least not the way that the client had expected it to work. As you read Chapter 42, consider this case and ask yourself whether ADR is as foolproof and effective as its supporters contend.

Chapter Outcomes

1. Discuss the shortcomings of litigation.
2. List the advantages and disadvantages of ADR.
3. Identify the advantages of mediation.
4. Explain the nature of an arbitration hearing.
5. Outline the med-arb process.
6. Relate the role of an early neutral evaluator.
7. Describe the process of running a summary judgment trial.

8. Determine the advantages of a private civil trial.
9. Clarify the private options available under ADR.
10. Specify the governmental options available under ADR.

42-1 A Primer on Alternative Dispute Resolution

As we have seen at various points throughout this text, the law operates as a complex adaptive system that must adjust to rapid, unpredictable alterations in the socioeconomic-cultural context. Sometimes the juris-economic system must make internal, self-adapting changes in order to correct mistakes or to redefine the mission of the system. A case in point involves the problems that have arisen within the litigation process. Litigation is the process of bringing a case to court to enforce a right. The people involved in litigation are called litigants. Litigation has always been a part of the American legal system. Lately, however, things have begun to change. The extensive backlog in many courts and the perceived injustice of many verdicts have led many people to seek alternative dispute resolution techniques to redress their grievances. **Alternative dispute resolution (ADR)** occurs whenever individuals attempt to resolve disagreements by stepping outside the usual adversarial system and applying creative settlement techniques, many of which have fact finding and the discovery of truth as their goals.

Problems with Litigation

Many people choose a dispute resolution process that sidesteps the adversarial approach of civil litigation because they believe that it is the best way to achieve justice. Part of this belief is based on the suspicion that, with the adversarial approach, victory often depends not on who is in the right, but on which advocate is the better tactician. Unfortunately, the best tactician is often one of the most expensive advocates available, which can mean that justice often goes to those who can afford it. For this reason, many people seek an alternative that is less costly to both sides.

Litigation can also be expensive because of the initial steps that lead to the filing of a lawsuit. For instance, before an attorney can file a medical malpractice lawsuit, he or she must obtain the client's medical records. This means paying an initial copying fee, which can amount to hundreds or even thousands of dollars. The attorney must then hire an expert to evaluate the records to determine whether the information in the records indicates that the client has a viable claim. Again this expense can run into hundreds or thousands of dollars. All these expenses are encountered before the attorney even knows that a claim actually exists.

In addition to being expensive, litigation can also be time consuming. The initial steps after the filing of a complaint can delay progress on a lawsuit for many months. For instance, should the defendant's motion for dismissal be granted by the court, a lengthy and time-consuming appeal process may ensue. In some cases, the appeal could even find its way to the highest court in the jurisdiction. In such a case, if the highest court reverses the lower court's dismissal of the action, the case quite literally returns to the starting line. Another time-consuming step in litigation is the process of discovery. Taking depositions,

For a case involving facts similar to those outlined in The Opening Case see: Hechler, David. "Arbitration Not Such a Sure Thing?" *The National Law Journal,* May 3, 2004, p. 1; *Hartford Ins. Co. of the Midwest v. Green,* No. 03-3368 (E.D. Pa.).

Teaching Tips Before discussing the pros and cons of adversarial litigation, have the students form teams of 3-4 learners each. The teams should be assigned the task of defining the adversarial system and of developing a list of advantages and disadvantages for that system.

State Variations Many state legislatures have enacted alternative dispute resolution programs. Colorado, for example, encourages or mandates ADR in specific subject areas, such as domestic relations and worker's compensation.

Litigation is adversarial in nature. Alternative dispute resolution techniques focus more on fact finding.

answering interrogatories, filing, and responding to requests for real evidence and handling requests for mental or physical examinations can tie up a lawsuit for months.

Moreover, some jurisdictions require litigants to submit to case management hearings and settlement hearings before they can secure a trial date. Even when a court date is secured, many court dockets, especially those in large urban areas, are backed up for months, even years, which often means that the parties to a lawsuit must wait for long periods of time before having their day in court. Even once a trial has occurred and a decision rendered, recovery can be delayed as the parties enter a second phase of the lawsuit, the execution of the judgment phase. This process involves its own complex set of procedures which, like the actual lawsuit, can cause expensive and time consuming delays.

The ADR Option

ADR can provide an economical and efficient alternative to litigation. Depending upon the ADR technique employed, the time involved in settling a dispute can be shortened considerably and the expenses lowered significantly. Arbitration and mediation, for example, can be scheduled quickly, even before a lawsuit is filed. When scheduling either a mediation or an arbitration session, the parties need not consult the court's dockets or worry about any preliminary requirements, such as a case management conference. Moreover, even if the arbitration or mediation session does not end the dispute, it can save time by narrowing the issues or providing an evaluation of the strength of each side's case. The arbitration or medication session may also, in some cases, provide a short cut to discovery, thus saving time and lowering expenses.

Other ADR approaches, such as early neutral evaluation (ENE), can save money and time by providing an open and honest assessment of not only the issues at stake in the case, buy also the range of damages that would be available, should the outcome of the case demand a remedy of some sort. Summary jury trials, private trials, and mini-trials can all be inexpensive and quick because they can be scheduled without regard to the court's docket and because they can be held without the expenses involved in hiring expert witnesses and providing travel and hotel accommodations for those witnesses. The cost and time involved in lengthy discovery processes can also be avoided by selecting any one of these ADR techniques.

Private proactive ADR techniques such as drafting contract clauses and entering partnering agreements can help to make litigation unnecessary from the outset. The idea behind the proactive ADR approach is to anticipate and deal with disputes before they occur. By providing a solution to problems before those problems arise, proactive ADR eliminates the uncertainty and risk inherent within the litigation process.

Shortcomings of ADR

ADR is not without problems. On the contrary, some critics of the alternative dispute resolution process have pointed out that the private administration of justice hampers the development of the law. Since many ADR techniques completely sidestep the courts, many critical social issues may never reach the judicial system, causing gaps in the evolution of case law and the progression of legislation. Another criticism of ADR involves its limited scope. Some legal conflicts, notably employment, contract, and tort cases, are especially well suited for ADR. However, other legal problems, primarily those involving constitutional law, civil rights, and criminal law, could never be brought before an ADR panel.

Other difficulties associated with ADR have also appeared in recent years. One problem is that ADR does not always save time and money the way it is supposed to. Typically, two of the advantages that supporters of ADR promote are the idea that ADR is less expensive and less time consuming because little discovery is involved in the process and because attorneys do not file long and complicated motions. Although this argument sounds good in theory, it does not always play out in reality. Unfortunately, sometimes a case may actually take longer to resolve because there is no discovery or motion practice involved. Part of the delay is due to the fact that discovery and motion practice often help attorneys focus on the most crucial issues in a case. Also discovery will sometimes reveal that it is necessary to settle a case rather than proceeding to trial. When there is no discovery or motion practice the issues remain wide open. This means that attorneys must anticipate all the possible moves that their opponents might take. The lack of discovery also means that the small flaws in an argument may not be revealed and a case that would have been settled during a conventional lawsuit might drag on in arbitration.

On the other hand, ADR is not intended as a replacement for the legal system. Rather it is intended to provide potential litigants with a wider variety of choices when they are facing a legal dispute. As noted above, because of the delays and the expense involved in litigation, many people would like to avoid that route altogether. Others would like to find a way to streamline the litigation process, so that, should the need for a trial finally present itself, the preliminary steps can be administered as painlessly as possible. With these facts in mind, we will proceed with an examination of ADR techniques.

State Variations Over thirty states have some type of victim/offender reconciliation program which brings the parties together in a search for restitution outside the court system.

Quick Quiz 42-1 True or False?

1. Adversarial litigation has only recently become a part of the American legal system.

2. Two of the advantages that supporters of ADR promote are the ideas that ADR is less expensive and less time consuming than litigation.

3. ADR is not intended as a replacement for the legal system.

42-2 ADR Techniques

There are numerous ADR techniques that can be invoked once a dispute has arisen between parties. These include but are not limited to mediation, arbitration, med-arb, early neutral evaluation, summary jury trials, private civil trials, and mini-trials.

Mediation

As a first step in the resolution of a dispute, the parties sometimes invite a third party to help find the solution. This is called **mediation.** The third party is called the **mediator.** The job of a mediator is to convince the contending parties to adjust or to settle their dispute. The mediator will try to persuade the parties to reach some sort of compromise but cannot decide what the parties will do.

Mediation is often more successful than litigation, because, in mediation, the parties remain involved in the settlement of the dispute. Unlike litigation, which is decided by a judge or a jury, a mediation session is in the hands of the parties. The mediator does not decide the disagreement. Rather, he or she serves as an intermediary who attempts to understand what brought the parties into disagreement and what issues lie at the heart of the disagreement. The mediator does not act as a therapist, a judge, or an advocate. Rather, he or she acts as an impartial outsider who can serve as a source of ideas and can suggest solutions that will please all the parties involved in the dispute. Often the mediator can cut to the center of a dispute in objective ways that are unavailable to the parties themselves.

Did You Know?

When mediation is used to settle cases of sexual harassment in the workplace, eighty-five percent of those cases are resolved successfully without having to go to court.

Example 42-1

Bruce Langton brought suit against David Winchester in small claims court after Winchester's daughter, Jackie, backed her car into Langton's truck causing extensive damage to the front end of the vehicle. Langton wanted damages in the amount of $4,000. Langton's sister-in-law, Wendy Miller, suggested that the parties hire a mediator to try to reach a settlement. During the mediation session, the mediator saw that the real issue was the fact that Langton's truck was still damaged. Winchester's brother, who owned and operated an auto body shop, agreed to fix Langton's truck at no cost. This solution satisfied both parties. Langton had his truck fixed and Winchester suffered no out-of-pocket expenses.

Arbitration

Sometimes the parties to a dispute invite a third party or parties to actually settle their dispute. This procedure is known as **arbitration.** The third party is called an **arbitrator.** The procedures involved in arbitration are generally more flexible than those followed in a lawsuit. The rules are either set by law or are agreed to by an arbitration agreement. The hearing may be relaxed, with the arbitrator or arbitrators receiving informal testimony from the parties, or it may be rigidly controlled, with the arbitrator or arbitrators following strict rules of evidence and requiring lengthy explanations. The parties may agree in advance to be bound by the arbitrator's decision. If they do not so agree, the arbitrator's decision can be appealed in court.

Some states require arbitration prior to trial in certain cases. Required arbitration is called *mandatory arbitration.* Some litigants have challenged government imposed mandatory arbitration as an unconstitutional deprivation of their right to a trial by jury and to equal protection under the law. Most states faced with this question have disagreed with these arguments as long as the governmentally mandated arbitration requirement does not replace the jury trial, and as long as the motives for establishing mandatory arbitration are reasonable.

An arbitration hearing can be planned and executed by the parties themselves. Generally, this means that the parties set the ground rules for choosing the arbitrator or arbitrators,

The Opening Case Revisited
"Arbitrating the Power of Arbitration"

In the case at the beginning of this chapter, the order entered by the arbitrators in the Westcot Insurance case was sent to the court on appeal. The appeal was based on the fact that the client had argued that some of the elements in his insurance policy were "contrary to legislative mandate or public policy." The same judge who had earlier ruled that the case had to go to arbitration because of the terms of the policy, now ruled that the client's legal argument in the case gave him the authority to review the arbitrator's decision. Accordingly, he ruled in favor of the insurance provider stating that the company had not been obligated to make the client an offer of increased coverage.

for conducting discovery, for presenting evidence, for determining the outcome, and for enforcing the reward. In addition, details such as setting the time and the place of the hearing, filling vacancies on the arbitration panel, recording the proceedings, handling objections, granting time extensions, and so on, must also be agreed upon. Because of the intricacies of such a process, many individuals who select arbitration prefer to use professional arbitration organizations such as the American Arbitration Association to handle the details of their arbitration proceeding.

Arbitration has certain advantages over litigation. As noted above, arbitration is frequently less expensive and more efficient than litigation. In addition, arbitration can also involve arbitrators specifically chosen because of their expertise in a given field. Thus, rather than having to educate a judge or jury by calling in expert witnesses, the parties can concentrate on presenting the facts to the arbitrators who then apply their expertise to come to a final decision.

Like most forms of ADR, arbitration is not without its difficulties. One shortcoming is the fact that an arbitration hearing is run much like a trial but without the safeguards and assurances that come with the rules of civil procedure, discovery, and motion practice. This may actually extend the time involved in an arbitration hearing because attorneys and negotiators must prepare a wide variety of legal arguments, some of which might have been eliminated during motion practice. Discovery also sometimes reveals facts that lead the parties into settlement negotiations that might not otherwise take place. Moreover, the wide discretion that is usually granted to arbitrators has, in some cases, led to unreasonable decisions and unjustifiable awards. Sometimes the decision made by an arbitrator comes under the review of the courts, which may result in a reversal of the arbitration order and thus frustrate the whole object of entering arbitration in the first place.

Some of these difficulties can be overcome by stipulating that an arbitration award cannot be reversed by the courts except to correct a violation of the arbitration agreement itself. The difficulties associated with the limitations on discovery can be solved by liberalizing the discovery process in arbitration, without going to the extremes represented by the way that discovery is conducted in litigation. Other problems can be solved by stipulating that arbitrators must conduct the hearing according to a predetermined set of rules and by insisting that they place the reasoning behind their decisions in writing.

Med-Arb

An increasingly popular form of ADR combines the best aspects of both mediation and arbitration. Under this combined approach, known as **med-arb,** the parties first submit their dispute to a mediation session. If the dispute is settled via mediation, then all of the parties can leave satisfied. If, however, some matters are left undecided, the parties can move on to an arbitration hearing. During the hearing, the undecided issues would be placed before an arbitrator or arbitrators for final deliberation.

Early Neutral Evaluation

The **early neutral evaluation (ENE)** process is similar to that of a settlement hearing. At the outset of an ENE process, an independent, objective evaluator is provided with an overview of the facts involved in the dispute and a summary of the legal arguments upon which each side has built his or her case. The evaluator, after examining the facts, the case, and the law renders an impartial assessment of the legal rights of each party and a determination of the amount of the award that should be rendered, if any. The parties can use this impartial evaluation to either settle the case or to proceed to trial. Even if the ENE does not result in a final decision it can be used to shape the issues, to plan discovery, and to guide any research that the attorneys must conduct as the case proceeds to trial.

Background Information The American Arbitration Association was founded in 1926. It now has ADR employment plans in place that cover over 3,000,000 workers.

Further Reading Other journals published by the American Arbitration Association include: *Dispute Resolution Journal, Dispute Resolution Times, ADR Currents, Summary of Arbitration Awards, Labor Arbitration in Government* and the *New York State No-Fault/SUM Arbitration Reporter.*

Further Reading The American Arbitration Association also publishes a quarterly newsletter entitled *Punch List.* This newsletter is specifically designed to focus on ADR procedures that affect the construction industry. The newsletter includes cases, articles, and interviews.

Background Information When the parties to a dispute agree to submit their case to binding arbitration, they will be bound by the decision of the arbitrators. Such awards are governed by the Federal Arbitration Act and cannot be vacated unless there is fraud or misconduct on the part of the arbitrators. Many states have also adopted the Uniform Arbitration Act which might also govern such awards.

Business Law in the News
Arbitration Clause Risks

In the past several decades, arbitration clauses in commercial contracts have gained favor in the business community. They are viewed as devices to expedite and reduce the costs of litigation and to avoid the risk of excessive judgments. Businesses would be wise to take a second look.

Surprisingly, in light of the widespread use of arbitration clauses, there are no reliable statistical data to support the assumptions underlying the business community's decision to embrace the concept, and logic and individual case studies strongly suggest that the supposed benefits of arbitration do not outweigh the risks.

The belief that arbitration will significantly reduce the length and cost of litigation often proves illusory. In the first place, arbitration often generates its own litigation. Parties often mount judicial challenges at both ends of the process. Moreover, lawyers who participate in arbitration of major commercial cases often quickly learn that the arbitration proceeding itself is neither fast nor cheap. Judges, constrained by crowded dockets and, at the state level, limited courtroom availability, utilize rules of practice to streamline cases. Arbitrators, not faced with such constraints, have no incentive to set limits that reduce length or complexity of the proceeding. Two recent cases illustrate the point.

The primary basis for the assumption that arbitration will be shorter than litigation is the limited discovery and motion practice available in arbitration. In fact, this can have the opposite effect. Motion practice defines and crystallizes the issues. Discovery provides a window into the opposition's case and avoids surprises. Together, they increase the chance of settlement and enable a lawyer to craft a precisely developed case with confidence that there will be no lurking traps. Without motion practice and discovery, the lawyer must spend the time and money to prepare for every conceivable eventuality, and the incentive to settle that comes with knowledge of the opposition's case is absent.

The belief that arbitration is likely to result in lower awards than a trial makes no sense. If the fear is of runaway jury verdicts, a clause waiving jury trial can be included in the contract. Nor is there reason to assume that arbitrators, often retired judges, will tend toward lower awards than judges. The $27 million award in *Sawtelle* and $42 million award in *Engel,* among others, should disabuse anyone of that idea. It is likely that the perception that arbitration produces smaller recoveries is generated by the relatively smaller amounts awarded on average by securities exchange panels.

Those results have been attributed to a number of factors unique to such panels that would not suggest elements indicative of arbitrators in general. Even before such panels, however, there is no guarantee of a low award. Despite the small number of such arbitrations annually compared to dispute resolution in general, barely a year passes without at least one six- or seven-figure award. (Examples include a 2000 Pacific Stock Exchange $3.9 million award, a 2001 National Futures Association $43 million award, a 2002 private arbitration panel $7.7 million award, a 2002 National Association of Securities Dealers $7.3 million award and a 2003 NASD $27 million award.)

Arbitration's questionable promise of fast and cheap dispute resolution comes at a high price. Once made, the contractual election to arbitrate cannot unilaterally be undone, and the client sacrifices fundamental protections against arbitrary and unfair treatment.

Questions for Analysis

1. What causes some of the problems associated with arbitration clauses when those clauses are actually activated by the parties involved in a dispute? Explain.

2. What are the objectives that discovery and motion practice are designed to meet during a conventional lawsuit? Explain.

3. What effect does the elimination of discovery and motion practice have on the arbitration process? Explain.

4. Does arbitration always result in awards that are lower than those rendered in jury trials? Explain.

5. According to the author, what is the "high price" paid by parties once they enter arbitration? Explain.

Source: Barry Richards. "Arbitration Clause Risks." *The National Law Journal,* June 14, 2004, p. 15. Reprinted with permission from the June 14, 2004 edition of The National Law Journal. Copyright © 2004 ALM Properties, Inc. All rights reserved. Further duplication without permission is prohibited.

Summary Jury Trials

A **summary jury trial** is a shortened version of a trial conducted in less than a day before an actual jury which then renders a verdict in the case. The verdict is advisory only. However, the summary jury process offers litigants an opportunity to see how an actual jury would react to the facts of the case as well as to the legal arguments that will be made by both sides at the actual trial. On the day of the summary jury trial, lawyers from both sides present an abbreviated version of the case to an actual jury. The presentations are simplified so as to focus on only the essential facts and the applicable law. In this way, the summary jury trial eliminates much of the repetition and redundancy that occurs during a "real" trial and allows the judge and jury to focus on the essentials of the case.

As noted above, the ultimate objective of a summary jury trial is to help both sides evaluate the effectiveness of their arguments in front of a judge and jury. This in turn helps the attorneys to shape the issues and to select the positions that are most advantageous to their case. This knowledge is enhanced by the fact that, after the trial, each side has the opportunity to interview the jurors to see why they reacted as they did.

The success or failure of a summary jury trial depends upon several factors. First, it is absolutely necessary for the attorneys involved to select a case that is appropriate for the summary jury trial format. Only those cases which involve a bona fide dispute as to the facts or authentic questions of law should be considered for a summary jury trial. Second, advanced planning is necessary to ensure a successful summary jury trial. The judge must be consulted, issues should be settled, the facts should be composed properly, the jury instructions should be determined, and an absolute date and time established before the trial begins.

Third, during the actual trial, strict controls and ironclad time limits must be imposed upon the parties. For instance, opening statements should last no more than twenty minutes. Both sides should have no more than one hour for the presentation of their case in chief and thirty minutes for their rebuttal. The closing arguments should also be limited to no more than twenty minutes. Finally, a conference should be held after the trial during which the parties have the opportunity to discuss an immediate settlement. Such a conference should be held after the jury has been polled so that their input can be factored into the settlement discussion.

Related Cases For a case involving arbitrator misconduct see: *M & C Corporation v. Erwin Behr GambH & Co.*, 91 F.3d 26 (6th Cir.).

Further Reading The American Arbitration Association publishes a number of diverse journals all of which are available to members of that organization. One journal of special interest to educators is *Arbitration in Schools* which is published monthly.

Background Information One of the first summary jury trials in federal court involved a product liability case. The case focused on an allegedly defective football helmet. The summary jury trial, which was held in 1980, led to a settlement of the case.

Example 42-2

When Ashley Utalizar was discharged from her job with Solarpower Industries Inc., she was certain that the dismissal had been in direct violation of an implied contract that had been created by Solarpower's employee policy manual. When she brought a lawsuit against Solarpower, both parties decided to hold a summary jury trial. After the trial was held, both sides participated in a posttrial settlement conference. The results of the jury poll indicated that, although the jury had decided in favor of Utalizar, they were unable to agree on the amount of damages that should be awarded to her. As a result, both Solarpower and Utalizar decided that it would be in their best interests to settle the case immediately. The attorneys for Solarpower agreed to the settlement because they saw that the jury was sympathetic to Utalizar, while Utalizar's attorneys agreed that they could not be certain that Utalizar would receive an adequate award if the jury were permitted to decide the amount of damages.

Since one reason for holding a summary jury trial is to determine how a judge and/or the jury will react to the facts and the legal arguments, it is often helpful to have observers available to gauge how the judge and the jurors react to the various points made by both sides. The observers, who are often students recruited from local law schools and paralegal institutes, will record the reactions of the judge and the jurors during the trial. As an alternative, the entire trial can be audiotaped or videotaped, so that reactions can be recorded after the fact.

Private Civil Trials

Background Information One private firm that will arrange private jury trials is known as Judicial Alternatives of Ohio, Inc. The firm is located in Columbus, Ohio.

Some states now permit the parties to a lawsuit to voluntarily have their cases tried in a private civil trial. **Private civil trials** are run according to the same rules of procedure and evidence as trials held under the official auspices of the court. The difference is that, in a private trial, the parties can hold the trial at a time and a place of their own choosing. In addition, the choice of the judge is also up to the parties. Often the parties will select a retired judge to preside over their private trial. Decisions rendered by a judge in a private civil trial are just as binding as those made by judges on the official court docket. Moreover, private trial decisions can also be appealed in the same way that public decisions are appealed.

The fact that the parties to a private civil trial are operating outside the official system means that they can be sure that the trial will be held as arranged. Private civil trials are not postponed nor are they interrupted because the court has more pressing duties to perform. Because of this fact, the trial receives the undivided attention of the judge who is not sidetracked by the need to attend to other matters such as the sentencing of criminal defendants. Intricate, lengthy civil cases are ideally suited for the private civil trial alternative because, in such cases, time is money. Consequently, the shorter the trial, the less expensive the final bill facing the client.

In recent years some private firms have appeared which specialize in setting up private civil trials. Such firms will make most of the arrangements for the litigants. These arrangements include securing a judge, providing the place for the trial, and providing all necessary administrative support. These firms can also provide a jury for the trial. Jurors for private trials are generally selected from a pool of individuals who have recently served on a jury in an official trial. This is done so that the jurors at the private civil trial are well acquainted with the trial procedures.

Quick Quiz 42-2 True or False?

1. The job of a mediator is to convince the contending parties to adjust or settle their dispute.

2. Some states require arbitration prior to trial in certain cases.

3. The early neutral evaluator process is similar to that of a settlement hearing.

42-3 Proactive ADR

All of the ADR techniques discussed thus far are invoked after a dispute has arisen. Since ADR has become so popular in recent years, some business people are taking a proactive approach to the situation by agreeing in advance to submit to one of the alternative dispute resolution tools should a disagreement between the parties arise at a later date. These proactive ADR techniques include, but are not limited to, partnering, ADR contract clauses, settlement week, negotiated rule making, and the science court proposal.

Partnering

The establishment of supportive relationships among the parties to a contract is the objective of the partnering process. Generally, partnering is best used when a contract involves complex interrelationships among a wide variety of different parties. Construction agreements are ideally suited to partnering arrangements. This is because construction contracts involve contractors and subcontractors all of whom must perform in a cooperative manner in order to fulfill a contract which often takes a long period of time to complete.

Partnering attempts to deter the disorder that can arise during a dispute by drawing up certain ground rules that all the parties agree to observe. The entire process begins with a meeting held after the contract has been finalized but before the project has begun. The meeting is held at a location that is unrelated to the business of any party to the contract. In this way, the process can procede in an uninterrupted fashion.

Moreover, the meeting should be directed by an objective third party whose job it is to help create an atmosphere of trust among the parties to the contract. The parties attempt to anticipate problems that may arise during the project as well as potential solutions to those problems. The parties agree to address all problems when they arise and to look for solutions that will mutually benefit all those involved in the project. Ultimately, the goal is to maximize efficiency, ensure safety, and to maximize profit by minimizing expenses, especially those that arise from cost overruns.

The parties agree to handle problems according to some ADR technique rather than by litigation. Finally, they agree to deal with one another in a fair manner within the confines of their legal relationships.

A Question of Ethics

Andrew Zapior, the president and CEO of Zapior Industries, and Oliver McMurray, the president of Georgetown Construction, have just finalized a contract for the construction of Zapior's new research facility in Cincinnati, Ohio. In order to minimize the problems that may arise, they agree to enter a partnering arrangement. At the end of the three day meeting, the parties draw up an agreement, one clause of which states that they will submit any claim to mediation. In the third month of the contract one of Georgetown's suppliers goes on strike, delaying an important shipment of material to the construction site. Zapior demands that McMurray and Georgetown find a different supplier. McMurray, who has done business with this supplier for twenty years, resists the suggestion and calls for a mediation session. Zapior, refuses to comply stating that there is no need to delay the project in order to maintain a contractual relationship with a supplier who can easily be replaced. Analyze the ethical stand taken by McMurray. Now do the same for Zapior. Which stand do you find easier to support? Explain.

ADR Contract Clauses

Like partnering, the drafting of ADR contract clauses is a proactive attempt to ensure that litigation will be avoided should a dispute arise. Unlike partnering, which is best suited to long-term construction contracts, ADR clauses can be included in just about any contract. An **ADR contract clause** will specify that the parties to the agreement have promised to use an alternative dispute resolution technique when a disagreement arises rather than litigating the issue.

ADR clauses can take many shapes and forms. It is possible, for instance, to insert a clause that states merely that the parties have the option of using an ADR technique. Such a clause is weak, at best, serving only to remind the parties that they do not have to sue one another to gain satisfaction. One step beyond the optional clause in the compulsory clause. This clause states that the parties are required to submit all claims that arise under the contract to an ADR technique, most often mediation or arbitration, before filing a lawsuit. The final type of clause would require the parties to submit any claim to binding arbitration. This is the strictest type of ADR clause because it forces the parties to abide by the decision of the arbitrator.

Regardless of the type of clause used by the parties, the language should include certain standard provisions. For instance, the clause should specify the types of disagreements that will be submitted to ADR, the ADR technique or techniques that can be used, the scope of discovery allowed, the substantive law and the procedural rules that will be followed in the proceeding, the remedies that will be authorized, the grounds for and the procedure to follow in an appeal, and the methods on enforcing an award. The failure to follow provisions specified in an ADR clause may be grounds for the court to revoke a ruling made by an arbitrator.

ADR clauses have several advantages. They are especially helpful when two or more parties have embarked on an extended affiliation that may involve numerous contracts. ADR clauses clearly establish a reliable and predictable method of dealing with disputes that will inevitably arise whenever two parties are involved in a lengthy association with one another. ADR clauses are also very beneficial to those parties with the weakest position within a contractual relationship. Often, when a dispute does arise, the more powerful party will threaten litigation, secure in the knowledge that he or she can afford a lawsuit more easily than the weaker party. ADR clauses eliminate this leverage point.

Example 42-3

Audrey Kemmelman, a freelance photographer, entered a work for hire agreement with The Daily Montgomery Central Times Corporation. During the negotiation stages, Kemmelman asked that an ADR clause be added to the contract that would compel the signatories to submit any claim to ADR. The clause stated that, in the event of any dispute, the signatories to the contract would first discuss the points of conflict informally. If after thirty days no satisfactory solution had been reached, the signatories agreed to submit the problem to the American Arbitration Association, which would assist in selecting an objective moderator who would help the signatories decide on an appropriate ADR method. This ADR clause would benefit Kemmelman because, as the weaker party, she might not have the resources to finance a lengthy and expensive lawsuit.

Because the parties to an ADR clause are agreeing, at least initially, to forgo the right to litigate any claims that arise among them, the courts prefer that such clauses be clear and precise. Clauses that are drafted in imprecise and ambiguous language may be struck down by the court as invalid. If the parties intend to submit all the claims arising out of their contractual relationship to ADR, then they should spell that out as precisely and completely as possible. Otherwise a party who, at a later date, wishes to invoke the clause, may find that the court is reluctant to support that position. When writing an ADR contract clause, it is best to use standard expressions that the court will recognize. Clauses that say that the parties agree to use ADR for "any controversy or claim arising out of or relating to the agreement" will convince the court to enforce the clause for most disputes between the parties. Anything less, may meet with judicial resistance.

Talking Points

Many Americans have a somewhat distorted view of the original Framers of the United States Constitution, envisioning all of them as sharing the same basic view of human nature, God, and good government. Moreover, this vision sees all of the Framers as sharing a dedicated and unwavering faith in a pure democratic state that gives all of the power to the people. As appealing and comforting as this view is, it is, nevertheless, essentially wrong.

John Adams, for example, is one of the Framers who favored establishing a government that would be ruled by a natural elite, as happens in a monarchy or an aristocracy. Apparently, Adams believed that because of their physical, intellectual, and moral genius, this elite group of citizens would be best suited to rule the rest of the people. Adams writes, "(w)hen superior genius gives greater influence in society than is possessed by inferior genius, or a mediocrity of genius, that is, than by the ordinary level of men, this superior influence I call natural aristocracy. . . . While I admit the existence of democracy, notwithstanding its instability, you (Taylor) must acknowledge the existence of natural aristocracy, notwithstanding its fluctuations." (p. 239)

John Taylor, a lawyer, scholar, senator, and one of the most vocal supporters of American representative democracy, countered this idea when he wrote, "Monarchy and aristocracy, have the strongest tendency of any conceivable human situation, to excite the evil moral quality, or propensity, of injuring others for our own benefit, both by the magnitude of the temptation, and the power of reaching it. . . . These forms of government are therefore founded in the evil moral qualities of man, and it is unnatural that evil moral qualities, should produce good moral effects." (p. 221)

Of the two positions, which would support the idea promoted by ADR that the people involved in disputes are best suited to determine the method for solving those disputes? Which would support the idea that a special elite class of jurists and litigators should be entrusted with the task of solving legal disputes through the traditional legal process of litigation? Which of the two positions do you prefer? Explain.

For the sources referred to in this segment of Talking Points see: Taylor, John. "An Inquiry into the Principles and Policy of the Government of the United States" (pp. 213–231) and Adams, John. "Letters to John Taylor" (pp. 231–246). Both in *Philosophy in America*. Edited by Paul Russell Anderson and Max Harold Fisch. New York: Appleton-Century-Crofts, 1939.

Settlement Week

Another proactive ADR technique is one that has been initiated by the court system itself. Some states have provided a proactive ADR technique known as settlement week. During **settlement week** a court's docket is cleared of all business, except for settlement hearings. Prior to the opening of settlement week, all attorneys with cases pending before the court are asked to choose which of those cases might be best handled by a mediator. Judges are also permitted to nominate cases for mediation during settlement week. Also before the opening of settlement week, a list of volunteer mediators is complied. Cases are then matched with mediators and a schedule is established. Attorneys are required to be present for the mediation session.

A mediation session is then held for each case. Following each session, the mediator is required to file a report with the court stipulating the results of the session and asking for the judge's approval. Occasionally, some cases, chiefly those that do not involve determining liability, are submitted to an arbitration panel rather than to a single mediator. In such a situation, the plaintiff chooses one of the arbitrators, the defendant chooses one, and the court names the final one. Not all cases scheduled for settlement week are actually resolved during that time. However, the technique is an effective way to lighten the court's docket and is becoming more and more popular.

Getting Students Involved One state trial court that has a very successful record with settlement week is the Delaware County Court of Common Pleas. Have students write to the court at 91 North Sandusky Street, Delaware, Ohio for details of the process.

Negotiated Rule Making

Certain governmental agencies have also become involved in proactive ADR through negotiated rule making. In **negotiated rule making,** which is sometimes referred to as **reg-neg,** an agency which is about to create a new rule or revise existing rules enters into a cooperative process by which all parties affected by the rule have a chance to shape the

Further Reading For a comprehensive introduction to the negotiated rule making process see "Working Together for Better Regulations," by David Pritzker. The article appeared in the volume 5, issue 2 of *Natural Resources and the Environment*.

Terms The objective outsider who is trained in facilitating the early stages of the negotiated rule making process is called a **convenor.** The preliminary steps in the negotiated rule making process are collectively referred to as **convening.** The convenor must issue a report to the agency involved in the negotiated rule making process before the actual rule making process can begin.

final form that the rule will take. A working team is established which consists of representatives of the affected groups, including the agency issuing the rule. One member of the team is an objective outsider trained in the art of facilitating such discussions. The objective of negotiated rule making, of course, is to avoid disputes before they have a chance to blossom forth.

All representatives have the opportunity to present their point of view in relation to the proposed rule. Discussions follow during which all of these issues are examined. Eventually, the team is expected to formulate a rule that reflects a consensus of the representatives. This consensus does not necessarily mean that all parts of the rule are enthusiastically embraced by all of the representatives. Rather, it means that all of the parties agree that they have fashioned a rule that everyone on the rule making team can live with. The text of the proposed rule in then submitted to the rule making agency. The success of the process depends upon the willingness of the members of the team to work in a cooperative fashion and upon the willingness of the agency to accept the results of the team's deliberations.

Despite its advantages, negotiated rule making cannot be used in all situations. Certain subject areas are more fitting than others. A suitable subject area for reg-neg would be one that will ultimately affect a wide range of individuals and institutions, is both complicated and controversial, and would meet with resistance if those individuals and institutions affected did not have a hand in shaping the rule. Reg-neg is also a wise course of action when the subject area affected involves nuances that fall outside the expertise of the agency representatives.

Example 42-4

The Ohio Environmental Protection Agency (OEPA) was charged with the task of drafting a series of rules to implement the Great Lakes Initiative. Rather than simply writing the rules and placing them before the affected parties, the OEPA decided to take a negotiated rule making approach. Consequently, it created the Great Lakes Initiative External Advisory Group (EAG). The EAG was composed of representatives from the agency itself, from the regulated industry, and from environmental groups. The team engaged in eight months of intense negotiations. These negotiations followed a precisely planned series of steps carried out under the watchful eyes of professional facilitators. The EAG reached a firm consensus on most of the issues that arose during the negotiations. Consequently, the Joint Committee on Agency Rule Review of the Ohio General Assembly adopted a set of rules to implement the Great Lakes Initiative in a relatively harmonious atmosphere and with almost no conflict. This is an extremely successful example of reg-neg in action.

The Science Court Proposal

Teaching Tips To get students involved in a lively discussion of the science court concept have them read, discuss, and write a report on the novel *Brothers* by Ben Bova (New York: Bantam Books, 1996).

A final way that the government could get involved in ADR involves the proposed establishment of a national science court. The proposed **science court** would act as a forum for disputes involving scientific and technological controversies. Individuals and institutions with concerns about certain scientific activities, such as genetic engineering, nuclear energy research, and so on, might ask the court to act as an impartial arbitrator in the evaluation of those concerns. The judges on the science court would be scientists educated in the areas under investigation, thus allowing them to use their expertise in deciding cases.

Supporters of the establishment of a science court argue that a panel of objective judges with scientific backgrounds would provide a neutral body capable of making unbiased, well-informed, decisions. Moreover, the science court would not necessarily provide the last word in any case held under its jurisdiction. An appeal stage would be a part of the process. Finally, the decision-making process involved in science related controversies would be centralized by the science court, thus providing a forum that many individuals could take advantage of.

Critics of the science court proposal argue that a panel made up of objective judges with scientific backgrounds would be almost impossible to convene. Moreover, critics point out that the science court would represent an additional level of bureaucratic red tape. In addition, critics point out that such a forum could rapidly become buried under an avalanche of claims, many of which would be a frivolous waste of the court's time. Finally, some critics argue that, since the issues placed before a science court would be highly controversial, the entire process could be plagued with political considerations that would threaten the legitimacy of the entire process.

Further Reading For another view on the effectiveness of the proposed science court see: *Lifting the Scientific Veil: Science Appreciation for the Nonscientist* by Paul Sukys (Lanham, Maryland: Rowman and Littlefield, 1999).

Example 42-5

Two power co-ops, the Cooperative Power Association and the United Power Association, planned to construct a system of high-voltage power lines across farmland located in Minnesota. The farm owners objected to the way in which their land was appropriated for the project by the government and the co-ops. The farmers also objected to the planned location of the power lines because they would interfere with their ability to farm the land properly. The governor of Minnesota called for the creation of a science court to resolve the dispute. Unfortunately, the situation rapidly became politicized. The co-ops, which had received a green light for the project from conventional authorities, refused to cooperate with the science court unless they were allowed to continue building the power lines during the science court's deliberations. The farmers argued that the purpose for calling the science court in the first place would be undermined if the construction of the power lines was allowed to continue. Moreover, the farmers wanted an extended set of issues placed before the court, including the possible rerouting of the lines and the consideration of alternative power sources. The co-ops, on the other hand, wanted the issues narrowed to an examination of any health problems associated with the power lines. Ultimately, the governor was compelled to withdraw his science court proposal because it caused more political problems than it had solved.

The Minnesota experience taught certain valuable lessons about the establishment of a science court. First, a science court will not succeed unless it has the power to compel the parties to submit to its authority. In the Minnesota case, for instance, the co-ops saw no reason to cooperate with a voluntary court because their project had already been approved by conventional authorities. Secondly, a successful science court must have the power to halt work done on any project that is the focus of the court's investigation. Otherwise, the court's entire process becomes an exercise in futility. Finally, a successful science court will ensure that all sides have the opportunity to present their views on all issues facing the court. Permitting certain parties to speak on certain issues while denying the same right to others can destroy the credibility of the court and of those involved in its creation and operation.

Further Reading For an in-depth account of the Minnesota science court incident see *Powerline: The First Battle in America's Energy War* by Barry Casper and Paul Wellstone (Amherst: University of Massachusetts Press, 1981) and "Science Court on Trial in Minnesota" also by Barry Casper and Paul Wellstone in *Science in Context: Readings in the Sociology of Science* (Cambridge: The MIT Press, 1982).

Quick Quiz 42-3 True or False?

1. The partnering process begins with a meeting held after a contract has been finalized but before the project has begun.

2. In negotiated rule making a government agency creates a new set of regulations without the troublesome, time-consuming, expensive, and difficult step of getting input from its constituency, thus streamlining the process, saving money, and eliminating controversy.

3. The proposed science court would act as a forum for disputes involving scientific and technological controversies.

Summary

42-1 Litigation has always been a part of the American legal system. Lately, however, things have begun to change. The extensive backlog in many court systems and the perceived injustice of many verdicts have led many people to seek other methods to redress their grievances. These other methods are often grouped under the heading of alternative dispute resolutions (ADR). Alternative dispute resolution (ADR) occurs whenever individuals attempt to resolve a disagreement by stepping outside the usual adversarial system and applying certain creative settlement techniques, many of which have fact finding and the discovery of truth as their goal.

42-2 There are many different ADR techniques that can be invoked once a dispute has arisen between parties. These include but are not limited to mediation, arbitration, med-arb, early neutral evaluation, summary jury trials, private civil trials, and mini-trials.

42-3 Since ADR has become so popular in recent years, some business people are taking a proactive approach to the situation by agreeing in advance to submit to one of the alternative dispute resolution tools should a disagreement between the parties arise at a later date. These proactive ADR techniques include, but are not limited to partnering, ADR contract clauses, settlement week, negotiated rule making, and the science court proposal.

Key Terms

ADR contract clause, 821
alternative dispute resolution (ADR), 813
arbitration, 816
arbitrator, 816

early neutral evaluation (ENE), 817
med-arb, 817
mediation, 815
mediator, 815
negotiated rule making, 823

private civil trial, 820
reg-neg, 823
science court, 824
settlement week, 823
summary jury trial, 819

Questions for Review and Discussion

1. What are the shortcomings of litigation?
2. What are the advantages and disadvantages of ADR?
3. What are the advantages of mediation?
4. What is the nature of an arbitration hearing?
5. What happens during the med-arb process?

6. What is the role of an early neutral evaluator?

7. What happens in the running of a summary judgment trial?

8. What are the advantages of a private civil trial?

9. What are the private options available under ADR?

10. What are the governmental options available under ADR?

Investigating the Internet

Access the website of BusinessLaw.gov and write a short report about the International Center for Dispute Resolution (ICDR).

Cases for Analysis

1. The Beattys sued the Akron City Hospital and Dr. Walker in state court. They claimed that Dr. Walker had performed an operation on Mrs. Beatty without her consent. Under state law, the case was submitted for mandatory arbitration before trial. The Beattys lost the arbitration hearing. The case then went to trial. At the trial the hospital asked the court to allow the results of the arbitration hearing into evidence. The Beattys attempted to block the submission of the arbitration results. They argued that the mandatory arbitration of such claims is an unconstitutional deprivation of their right to an impartial jury trial and an unconstitutional violation of their right to equal protection of the law. Are the Beattys correct? Explain. *Beatty v. Akron City Hospital,* 424 N.E.2d 586.

2. An ADR clause inserted into a contract between the parties stated that any dispute that arose as a result of the contract would be submitted to arbitration. In addition, the clause specified that the arbitrator of such a dispute would render a decision that included both findings of fact and findings of law. The arbitrator failed to follow that provision when the decision was rendered. Would the failure of the arbitrator to make findings of fact and findings of law as required by the ADR clause in the settlement of a dispute be grounds for the court to revoke the arbitrator's ruling? Explain. *Western Empire Ins. Co. v. Jefferies & Co.,* 958 F.2d 258 (9th Cir.).

3. In a case involving an ADR clause, the parties to a contract disagreed as to whether the clause required them to submit a dispute over a trade secret problem to arbitration. The clause required the parties to submit "any controversy or claim arising out of the agreement" to arbitration. Strictly speaking, the trade secret controversy did not arise "out of" the agreement. On the other hand, it was clear that the trade secret dispute was related to the agreement. The trial court held that the language of the ADR clause was too narrow and that, since the trade secret dispute did not arise out of the controversy, the parties were not required to send it to arbitration. Should the appellate court overrule the trial court's decision rejecting the requirement that the parties arbitrate the trade secret dispute? Explain your response. *Tracer Research Corp. v. National Environmental Services, Co.,* 42 F.3d 1292 (9th Cir.)

4. In the early 1990s, serious concerns about the dangers associated with genetic engineering arose after an incident that concerned the use of certain genetically altered mice in experiments involving a highly infectious disease. In the wake of these concerns, the National Institute of Allergy and Infectious Diseases held a conference to discuss the level of safety that should be followed in laboratories involved in such research. Those involved in the conference included the researchers themselves, certain biosafety experts, representives from organizations involved in or planning to be involved in similar research, and governmental representatives from the Center for Disease Control, the National Institutes of Health, and the Food and Drug Administration. Would this type of situation be appropriate for a reg-neg approach?

Explain. Might a science court handle this type of situation even better than an agency's reg-neg procedure? Explain.

5. Andrei Kerensky, CEO of the Malenkov Electronic Surveillance Corporation, entered negotiations with Thomas John King, president and chair of the board for Beckett Industries, Inc., the purpose of which was to develop a new security system for Beckett. The system would use a newly designed security system based upon a new laser electronic coding system developed by engineers at Malenkov. King and Kerensky finalized the deal and the security system was installed at Beckett. After Malenkov's engineers installed the system, security personnel and engineering technicians at Beckett made some subtle alterations in the system's computerized control system. Shortly thereafter, the entire system crashed. When Malenkov's bill was not paid, Kerensky went to see King at Beckett's corporate headquarters. During a short encounter, King informed Kerensky that Beckett was not going to pay Kerensky and Malenkov because the system had crashed. King argued that Malenkov's engineers were responsible for the breakdown, while Kerensky insisted that the modifications made by the engineers at Beckett were at fault because of their unauthorized and incompetently rendered modifications to the system. Kerensky wants to sue King and Beckett but is hesitant to do so because the primary factual issues in the case focus on the engineering modifications. Consequently, he is apprehensive about his belief that a judge and jury will be lost by the technical jargon that may be used at trial. What alternatives are available to Kerensky?

Quick Quiz Answers

42-1	42-2	42-3
1. F	1. T	1. T
2. T	2. T	2. F
3. T	3. T	3. T

Chapter 43 International Law

The Opening Case
"The Changing International Community"

When the funeral of Edward IV of England was held in May 1910, the citizens of London who witnessed the exhibition of royalty at the ceremony did not realize that they were also looking at the passing of the old world. In attendance at the funeral were nine kings, including George V, the new King of England; King Frederick of Denmark; King George of the Hellenes; King Haakon of Norway; King Albert of Belgium; King Ferdinand of Bulgaria; King Alfonso of Spain; King Manuel of Portugal; and Kaiser Wilhelm of Germany. In addition there were five heirs apparent to a variety of thrones, seven queens, and forty or more other members of the royal families of Europe, most of whom were related to one another. Today, such a scene is unimaginable to us. We are separated from this spectacle not only by a century of time, but also by two world wars; two international organizations, The League of Nations and the United Nations; a Cold War; nuclear weapons; the Nuremburg War Crimes Trials; several reconfigurations of the European map; the collapse of Western colonialism; the rise and fall of the Soviet Union; an energy crisis; the advent of international terrorism; and the ascendancy of the European Union. Throughout all this turmoil there has been one beacon that has led the way, a beacon which, while it has dimmed from time to time, has never been extinguished. That ever-present beacon is the law. Even in the darkest hours of the last century, people have evoked the rule of law to make things right again. From the establishment of the United Nations to the advent of the Nuremberg Trials; from the horrors of World War II to the establishment of the Geneva Conventions; from the brinkmanship of the Cuban Missile Crisis to the fall of the Berlin Wall; from the tragedy of 9/11 to the establishment of a new Iraqi constitution, the law is called upon to condemn, to justify, to oppose, and to defend international actions. As you read Chapter 43, consider these facts and ask yourself what the international community would be like without any law at all.

Chapter Outcomes

1. Differentiate between national and international standards.
2. List the criteria for a just war.
3. Explain the jurisdiction of the International Court of Justice.
4. Describe the mission of the International Criminal Court.
5. Identify the main goal of UNCITRAL.
6. State the differences between the UCC and the CISG.

7. Outline the structure of the World Trade Organization.
8. Relate the objectives of the Dispute Settlement Understanding.
9. Determine the major purpose of NAFTA.
10. Clarify the goals of the European Union.

43-1 International and National Standards

This chapter will explore some critical issues involving international law. It will focus not only on the business aspects of international law but also on some of the more basic issues of substantive and procedural law. These issues include the diversity of legal perspectives, the function of the United Nations in the areas of international law and international trade, the purpose of the General Agreement on Tariffs and Trade (GATT), the mission of the World Trade Organization (WTO), the task of comprehensive trade coalitions such as the North American Free Trade Agreement (NAFTA) and the impact of the European Union on international business. The proper framework for this study must begin with an examination of the different legal perspectives apparent on the international scene today. One of the first things that we must understand and appreciate as we approach any study of international law is the fact that many countries in the world do not have the same view of the law as we do in the United States. Two common areas of disagreement are (1) the belief that the adversarial system is the best procedure for courts to follow and (2) the position that the Rule of Law as a governing principle is absolutely inviolable.

Law and the Adversarial System

The American view of the law is not always in harmony with the view of many other people in the international community. The typical American point of view is that the law is the champion of order and stability within society. The law, it is argued, provides society with rules and procedures that effectively control the competitive and aggressive urges of human nature. In the American legal process, one essential focus of control over this competitive urge is the **adversarial system.** Through the adversarial system, the law gives society an orderly and effective way to settle disputes. Each side in a dispute has its champion, the attorney of record, who goes into battle against the other side's champion. The battle, a civil lawsuit or a criminal prosecution, ensues with victory going to the champion who persuades the judge or the jury of the justice of his or her case.

Although many citizens of the United States are reluctant to admit it, the American adversarial view of the law is not one that is shared by all the people of the world. Other systems exist which emphasize techniques and procedures that are foreign to the American legal system. One such system, the continental system, is based on a fact-finding approach rather than the adversarial approach. In the fact-finding system, the major objective of a trial is to uncover the truth. Many people find this approach to be preferable to the adversarial system, which has victory as its primary objective. Supporters of the fact-finding approach would point out that a victory in an adversarial procedure is often sought at the cost of the truth.

Also essential to the adversarial system is the underlying belief that each individual should have access to the judicial process. This is why the U.S. Constitution guarantees the accused in a criminal case the right to remain silent and the right to be represented by an attorney when being questioned by the authorities. This is also why the Constitution guarantees that all statements coerced from a defendant after that defendant has expressed a desire for counsel, are inadmissible at trial. In a fact-finding continental system, this protection is not guaranteed and statements coerced from defendants who are without legal representation may be used against the defendant at trial.

For a more detailed account of the scene depicted in The Opening Case see: Tuchman, Barbara. "A Funeral." In *The Guns of August.* New York: Dell Publishing, 1970, pp. 15–17; Strachan, Hew. "To Arms." In *The First World War.* New York: Viking, 2003, p. 5.

Getting Students Involved In order to prepare students for the chapter, lead them in a discussion about recent global changes that have brought about a greater need for international law and international trade. You may wish to have students research specific areas of the world and report on the recent changes that have occurred in those areas. For example, students could report on the changes in government in Eastern Europe, the transfer of government in Hong Kong, and the growing economic strength in certain Asian countries.

Teaching Tips The theory behind the adversarial system is that if both sides are ably represented in the lawsuit, then the jury will reach a fair verdict based upon the truth. Have students list examples of recent court cases in which it appears the adversarial system failed. Ask students to cite the particulars in each case without which the trial would have met with success.

Background Informa-tion A situation in which continental law, which is practiced in many Western European countries, and common law diverge is in the decision-making pro-cess of the International Court of Justice. The rules of the ICJ allow a judge to add his or her own opinion into the majority decision. This right to append indi-vidual opinions is unknown in continental law, but is frequently used in common law jurisdictions with dis-senting judicial opinions.

Example 43-1

As discussed later in the chapter, the International Court of Justice (ICJ) of the United Nations has limited jurisdiction. One limit applies to the parties permitted to present a case to the Court. The Charter of the United Nations provides that "Only States may be parties in cases before the Court." These "states" include nations that are members of the UN and nations that elect to submit themselves to the jurisdiction of the Court. Private individuals, however, may not bring a case before the ICJ. Such limited access to the Court may be required simply because of the large number of people who might bring cases before the ICJ. Nevertheless, this restriction upon the accessibility of the Court is seen by some as an unnecessary limitation upon the adversarial system.

Different legal philosophies like these can make the resolution of international disputes difficult, and may interfere with such basic decisions as the choice of forums. In fact, the inability to agree on the appropriate dispute resolution technique may interfere with, and at times even prevent, the negotiation of key international agreements. Moreover, even when such agreements have been negotiated, the inability to accept a nonadversarial approach may prevent some parties from recognizing the validity of any decree handed down by any international organization, such as the International Court of Justice.

The Supremacy of the Rule of Law

Teaching Tips Ask stu-dents to review the reasons why the Founding Fathers insisted on separating the judicial branch from the legislative and executive branches of government. What type of system were they used to serving under? Why was that system no longer desirable?

Another prevalent American idea that differs from the point of view held in many other countries is the conviction that the rule of law is supreme. This belief in the supremacy of law is rooted in the fact that, in the American system, each branch of the government is subject to a system of checks and balances. Under this system, the activities of the leg-islative and executive branches of the government are subject to review by the judicial branch. Similarly under this view, the jobs of interpreting the law and making final deci-sions on the constitutionality of the law are up to the courts, rather than some legislative or administrative body. In contrast, in some other countries, the court system is not inde-pendent but exists as a part of the executive or the legislative branches. Moreover, gov-ernments that are based on civil law rather than common law tend to insulate the executive and legislative branches from the courts. Thus, decisions as to the constitutionality of various legislative acts or administrative decisions may be placed within the jurisdiction of nonjudicial bodies.

Terms The word *jurisdic-tion* comes from the Latin *juristictio*, which means "administration of the law." The meaning of the word has become more specific, and it is now defined as "the authority or power of a court or tribunal to hear a particular case or dispute."

Example 43-2

In France, the courts do not have the power or authority to determine the constitu-tionality of any law. Instead, a constitutional council, created under the French constitution, has the power to determine questions of constitutionality. Unlike the courts in this country, which can answer questions of constitutionality only if they are embedded within the facts of a case, the constitutional council can deal directly with the issue of the constitutionality of a law outside the confines of a case. The consti-tutional council consists of nine associates who serve nine-year terms. Also seated on the council are all former presidents of France.

National and International Law

Despite the importance of focusing on international law and the laws of other countries, businesses involved in international trade must always first focus on the laws of their own nation. Sometimes a national law will reach into the jurisdiction of a foreign country. Although such instances are rare, they may occur when one or more of the parties to a lawsuit are citizens of the country attempting to exercise jurisdiction and when the foreign activity somehow affects the welfare of that country.

Example 43-3

Steele, a citizen of the United States, bought component parts for watches in Switzerland and the United States. He took those parts to Mexico where he constructed the watches, stamped them with the name Bulova, and sold them. None of the watches were imported into the United States, and Steele had a Mexican registration that allowed him to use the trade name Bulova. Nevertheless, Bulova brought a lawsuit against Steele in U.S. district court. The suit was brought under the Lanham Act, a U.S. statute that seeks to protect trademark owners from infringement and counterfeit copying in foreign marketplaces. The court decided that Steele's activities did, in fact, violate the Lanham Act.

Related Cases A French corporation shipped goods to AMCO Transworld, Inc., a company based in Texas. Upon inspection, AMCO discovered that the goods were damaged, and consequently filed suit in U.S. court. The French corporation moved to dismiss the case because of lack of jurisdiction. The court granted the dismissal on the grounds that the French corporation never purposely availed itself of the privilege of conducting activities in Texas. It had never maintained an agent in Texas. Neither had it maintained a business, stationed any employees, nor performed any business in the state. *AMCO Transworld, Inc. v. M/V Bambi*, 257 F. Supp. 215.

The district court in Example 43-3 noted that Steele's actions affected U.S. commerce even though the watches were sold only in Mexico. This was because the component parts were purchased within the United States, because Steele was an American citizen, and because many of the counterfeit watches eventually found their way into the U.S. marketplace. Even in such situations, however, a conflict between the law of the United States and the law of the foreign jurisdiction involved in the lawsuit must be avoided. Such a conflict could have occurred in Example 43-3 because of Steele's registration of the Bulova name under Mexican law. The court did not reach the issue of Steele's Mexican registration, however, because by the time the case had reached the appellate court, the Mexican government had withdrawn that registration. Still, this potential conflict of law could have affected the outcome of the lawsuit.

Despite the need to focus on national law, businesses in international trade must also be familiar with international law. Consequently, for purposes of developing a working knowledge of the stage upon which international commerce takes place, this chapter will explore three key areas of international law: international law and war, international law and the United Nations, and international law, finance, and trade.

Getting Students Involved Ask students to work in small groups to research recent cases in which U.S. businesses have challenged foreign businesses in U.S. courts. Have them prepare a synopsis of each case, along with summary comments concerning the case and international law.

Quick Quiz 43-1 True or False?

1. In the adversarial system of law each side is represented by a lawyer who seeks to uncover the truth regardless of the consequences.

2. Since all national legal systems are essentially the same, there are few international disputes that cannot be resolved by following the universal law.

3. The idea that the rule of law is supreme is a global principle held by all countries.

43-2 International Law and War

Karl von Clausewitz, a nineteenth-century Prussian soldier and political scientist, is credited with one of the most often-quoted definitions of war. "War," Clausewitz claims, "is a continuation of politics by other means." In today's world of complex multinational corporations, delicate international relationships, and instantaneous Internet transactions, Clausewitz might have added that war is also the continuation of international business by other means. As we have seen recently, international business can be affected profoundly by war, but especially when it is an unpopular war that lacks international legal authorization, and when it results in a protracted campaign of attrition that drags on for months with no clear goals and with no end in sight. Such a situation can increase costs, cause shortages of raw materials, endanger shipping, and render the execution of a contract commercially impracticable, if not impossible to perform. This may be true even if the parties to a war are not citizens of the nations that are at war. Some of these problems can be solved by the internal law of a particular nation-state.

Example 43-4

The Transatlantic Financing Corporation operated the *S.S. Christos,* a cargo ship carrying wheat from Texas to Iran for the United States government. While the *S.S. Christos* was en route to Iran, Israel invaded Egypt. Two days later, France and Great Britain invaded the Suez Canal Zone. The invasion and subsequent closing of the Suez Canal made it impossible for the *S.S.Christos* to use the canal. A 3,000-mile detour around the southern coast of Africa cost Transatlantic an unexpected $44,000 above the original estimated cost of $305,842.92. When the United States government refused to pay the additional amount, the company brought a lawsuit. Although the United States and Transatlantic were not directly involved in the Suez hostilities, their contract had been affected by the conflict. Nevertheless, the federal court did not allow Transatlantic to recover the additional payment from the government of the United States. The court's decision was based on a traditional rule of contract law in the United States. The court declared, "While it may be an overstatement to say that increased cost and difficulty of performance never constitute impracticability, to justify relief there must be more of a variation between the expected costs and the cost of performing by an available alternative than is present in this case."

The lesson to be learned from this case is a simple one. When entering a contract that impacts upon the international marketplace, it is wise for all parties to be aware of international conditions in all areas of the globe that may affect the contract. This approach is crucial because courts in the United States will take into account the foreseeability of any international crisis, including not only war, but also war-related events, such as blockades, quarantines, and border closings. If the court deems that the international crisis was foreseeable, the loss suffered by the parties affected by the crisis will not be offset by the court.

The Just War Theory

One central question that cannot be answered solely by the law of a single national state is whether a war is just. Ethical and legal philosophers in the West have developed criteria for determining when a war can be considered legally and morally correct. This theory, termed the **just war theory,** has been invoked for defending and for questioning the morality of

Talking Points

In 1910 two very different, yet equally popular views on the prospect of future wars existed on both sides of the Atlantic. One of these views was represented by a book by Norman Angell entitled *The Illusion of War.* War, Angell argued, had become an untenable option because of the financial interdependence of the global community. Any war would have such devastating consequences that nations could no longer afford to engage in any sort of armed conflict.

In support of this view, Viscount Escher, chairman of the British War Committee, who had been appointed to restructure the British army, contended that, a combination of factors including "commercial disaster, financial ruin, and individual suffering" made war in the twentieth century "more difficult and improbable" than ever before in the history of civilization.

The opposite view was represented by a German general named Friedrich von Bernhardi who, in a work entitled *Germany and the Next War,* argued that war was inevitable. In fact, war, Bernhardi argued, was a consequence of natural law. Bernhardi insisted that war was a "biological necessity." War is actually the human expression of "the struggle for existence." Nations, Bernhardi wrote, must move forward or fall into decay. He concluded that, among nation-states, "there can be no standing still."

Of the two positions, which has been supported by the weight of world history in the twentieth century? Which view continues to be popular in the twenty-first century? Which view seems to have been adopted by the international community? Which view seems to be supported by most Americans? Which view seems to be in line with American political and military policy in the twenty-first century? Which view is morally correct? Explain.

For a more detailed discussion of the ideas found in this segment of Talking Points see: Tuchman, Barbara. "A Funeral." In *The Guns of August.* New York: Dell Publishing, 1970, pp. 24–25.

many armed conflicts. In its traditional form the theory focuses on two main areas. First, it establishes the criteria that would justify going to war. Second, it institutes criteria for the proper conduct of a war that is already in progress. A third modern area of justifiability adds a set of criteria that establish the rules of conduct that must be followed after a war ends.

Criteria for Going to War   The just war theory endorses six criteria for deciding on whether a war can be morally justifiable. These criteria include the following: (1) just cause, (2) right intention, (3) competent authority, (4) probability of success, (5) proportionality, and (6) last resort. The first criterion, **just cause,** says that to be morally permissible, a war must be waged for honorable motives. Included among these motives are self-defense and the defense of a fellow sovereign nation that has been targeted by an aggressor, and has been unable to properly defend itself. The second criterion, **right intention** declares that a war must be waged only if the combatant has the correct objective. For instance, a war that is fought for the liberation of a nation unjustly invaded and subjugated by an aggressor would not be based on a proper objective. The difference between the first and the second criteria is the difference between an objective justification for war and the subjective intent of the actual combatants. A war may have an objectively justifiable cause and yet be fought for the wrong reasons. This could happen, for instance, if one country goes to the defense of another country, but uses that defensive campaign as a pretext to destroy the government and subjugate the civilian population of the aggressor nation.

For an extensive treatment of the just war theory in the twenty-first century see: *Just War Against Terrorism* by Jean Bethke Elshtain (New York: Basic Books 2003).

The third criterion, **competent authority,** states that war can be declared and run only by legitimately recognized governmental agencies. This does not mean, however, as some people have suggested, that the United Nations must declare a war in order for that war to have been declared by competent authority. In fact from a legal perspective, the UN cannot declare war. The UN Charter is founded on the belief that all member nations maintain their sovereign authority. This includes the authority to declare war. The fourth criterion, **probability of success,** declares that at the outset of a war there must be a reasonable chance that the war will be successful; a suicidal war would fall outside this criterion. Fifth, **proportionality,** holds that the good advanced by the war must exceed the negative consequences of entering the conflict. Thus, a war fought over an imaginary diplomatic insult must be considered unjust, because the objective of vindicating a spurious affront to national honor is not proportional to the death and destruction caused by war. Finally, the criterion of **last resort** means that a war can be fought only after all other means for the resolution of the dispute have been tried and have failed. If both nations still have diplomatic options available for ending the crisis in a nonviolent way; if an international organization, such as the United Nations, is still willing to explore a negotiated settlement; or if time still exists to pursue a nonviolent solution, war cannot be waged as a solution to the conflict and, if one side insists on declaring war, then that war will be an unjust conflict. However, the fact that all options have not been implemented is not decisive. What matters is that the nation which began the war gave authentic consideration to each available option, short of war.

Criteria for the Proper Conduct of War It is not enough to advocate a set of ethical and legal criteria for entering war and to ignore the criteria for conducting the war or for conduct that must be followed after the end of a war. For this reason, many modern, legal, and moral theorists suggest several additional criteria that should guide conduct during a war and behavior after a war. The first of the criteria for conducting a war requires that the warring factions use only those military means that are proportional to the ends that they wish to achieve. Thus, since it was possible for the international coalition to subdue and eject the invading Iraqi army from Kuwait in Gulf War I by using conventional weapons, the use of nuclear weapons would have been considered a disproportionate tactic. The second criterion states that the war must be fought with discrimination. This means that only combatants should be targeted in the war and that civilians must be kept out of harm's way.

Criteria for Proper Postwar Conduct Three just war principles have been established for gauging the morality of conduct following the cessation of hostilities. The first of these principles is the principle of repentance. The **principle of repentance** calls for a genuine expression of remorse by the combatants for the death and the destruction caused by war. Conduct that expresses either joy or satisfaction at the death of enemy combatants, even combatants involved in a war of aggression, would violate this principle. The second criterion, the **principle of honorable surrender,** requires the victor in a war to accept the surrender of the enemy and to treat the defeated combatants with dignity and respect. Refusing a genuine offer of surrender, violating that surrender after it has been implemented, or mistreating enemy combatants after surrender, would all be violations of this principle. Actions that are motivated by revenge or retribution would also violate the principle of honorable surrender. Conduct that injures or humiliates prisoners of war would also breach this standard of behavior. Finally, the **principle of restoration** requires that the victor in a conflict act responsibly in rebuilding the defeated nation's physical environment, economy, and governmental structure.

The Strategy of Preemptive War

A nation starts a **preemptive war** to stop another nation's imminent attack on the first nation. A preemptive war is not the same as a preventative war, although the terms are often used as synonyms. A preemptive war is waged to stop an attack before it can begin. In contrast, a nation begins a **preventative war** to stop another nation from reaching a point at which it is capable of attacking the first nation. The doctrine adopted by the United States in 2002 was a doctrine of preemptive war, not one of preventative war. The concept of preemptive war goes back five hundred years to Thomas More who in his work *Utopia*, noted that it would be wise to preemptively attack a force that was about to attack you.

In the United States, two major military figures, General Leslie Groves, the head of The Manhattan Project that developed the atomic bomb during World War II, and General Curtis LeMay, former commander of the Strategic Air Command (SAC), advocated preemptive war against the Soviet Union. Moreover, in the 1950s, the Joint Chiefs of Staff commissioned a study which also recommended a preemptive strike against the Soviet Union. In all of these cases, cooler heads prevailed and preemptive war was not, at that time, advocated as a strategic policy of the United States.

Times have changed, however, and preemptive war has become an active strategic policy of the United States, and was, in fact, the primary stated motivation for the invasion of Iraq in 2003. While it is difficult to pinpoint the exact moment of this shift in policy, the move toward preemptive war as the national policy of the United States seems to have come less than three months after September 11, 2001, when, in the aftermath of the attacks on the World Trade Center and the Pentagon, President George W. Bush asked Secretary of Defense, Donald Rumsfeld about war plans for an attack against Iraq. Evidence indicates that President Bush had similar strategic planning discussions with Vice President Richard Cheney and National Security Advisor Condoleezza Rice. Nevertheless, the first conscious public declaration of this change in policy was made in a presidential address to the graduating class of West Point on June 1, 2002.

Sources: Several accounts of the events leading to the 2003 preemptive war against Iraq can be found in the following books: *Winning Modern Wars: Iraq, Terrorism and the American Empire* by Wesley K. Clark (New York: Public Affairs 2004); *America Alone: The Neo-Conservatives and the Global Order* by Stefan Halper and Jonathan Clarke. (Cambridge: Cambridge University Press, 2001).

Preemptive War and the Just War Theory

The just war theory is designed to help individuals and governments make judgments about the justifiability of particular wars, rather than about the morality of war in general. Indeed, the very existence of a just war theory presumes that some wars are, in fact, justifiable. Therefore, it is difficult to characterize the morality of a war-making strategy, such as the strategy of preemptive war, without reference to the war's actual historical context. Nevertheless, all preemptive wars share certain characteristics that make it possible to judge such wars under the theory. First, preemptive wars rarely pass the requirement of last resort. This is because preemptive wars by definition are never a last resort and, therefore, can rarely be justifiable under that criterion. Second, it is doubtful that a war that is designed to prevent the future actions of an adversary can be proven to outweigh the negative consequences of an actual conflict. Since the actions contemplated by the enemy never actually take place, they can never be weighed accurately against the actions that actually do take place in a war. Thus, preemptive wars often fail the test of proportionality. Finally, since preemptive wars are always based on preventing future events rather than on dealing with events that have actually taken place, it is much too easy to conjure up a pretext that will allow a nation to go to war against another sovereign state. Such an abuse of power is precisely what the just war theory is designed to prevent. Thus, preemptive wars also often fail the initial just cause test.

Of course, very few philosophical arguments are as clear-cut as the case against preemptive war seems at first. A case can certainly be made that preemptive wars do not automatically fail the first test of just case. To automatically classify preemptive war as unjust is to ignore the fact that a nation may have a valid reason for entering such a conflict. If, for example, one nation repeatedly commits a wide variety of human rights violations, especially violations that involve indiscriminate attacks on innocent victims, other nations may be justified in coming to the aid of such innocent victims. In fact, a nation that ignores evidence that a rogue state has repeatedly victimized its own people may be morally culpable for failing to act against that rogue state. Similarly, the argument that proportionality can never be judged when the wrong prevented is a future event fails to consider that the best judge of future behavior is usually past behavior. Thus, few reasons exist to believe that a nation that has consistently victimized innocent people in

Business Law in the News
U.S. Disputed Protected Status Of Iraq Inmates

Presented last fall with a detailed catalog of abuses at Abu Ghraib prison, the American military responded on Dec. 24 with a confidential letter asserting that many Iraqi prisoners were not entitled to the full protections of the Geneva Conventions.

The letter emphasized the "military necessity" of isolating some inmates at the prison for interrogation because of their "significant intelligence value," and said that prisoners held as security risks could legally be treated differently from prisoners of war or ordinary criminals.

But the military insisted that there were "clear procedures governing interrogation to ensure approaches do not amount to inhumane treatment."

In recent public statements, Bush administration officials have said that the Geneva Conventions were "fully applicable" in Iraq. That has put American-run prisons in Iraq in a different category from those in Afghanistan and in Guantánamo Bay, Cuba, where members of Al Qaeda and the Taliban have been declared unlawful combatants not eligible for protection. However, the Dec. 24 letter appears to undermine administration assertions of the conventions' broad application in Iraq.

The International Committee of the Red Cross had reported in November that its staff, in a series of visits to Abu Ghraib in October, had "documented and witnessed" ill treatment that "included deliberate physical violence" as well as verbal abuse, forced nudity and prolonged handcuffing in uncomfortable positions.

In congressional testimony last week, Lt. Gen. Lance Smith, the deputy commander of American forces in the Middle East, asserted that the Dec. 24 response demonstrated that the military had fully addressed the Red Cross complaints.

But the three-page response, drafted by American military lawyers, did not address many of the specific concerns cited by the Red Cross, whose main recommendations included improving the treatment of prisoners held for interrogation.

Instead, much of the military's reply is devoted to presenting a legal justification for the treatment of a broad category of Iraqi prisoners, including hundreds identified by the United States as "security detainees" in a cellblock at Abu Ghraib and in another facility known as Camp Cropper on the outskirts of the Baghdad airport, where the Red Cross had also found abuses.

Prisoners of war are given comprehensive protections under the Third Geneva Convention, while civilian prisoners are granted considerable protection under the Fourth Convention.

But under the argument advanced by the military, Iraqi prisoners who are deemed security risks can be denied the right to communicate with others, and perhaps other rights and privileges, at least until the overall security situation in Iraq improves.

The military's rationale relied on a legal exemption within the Fourth Geneva Convention.

"While the armed conflict continues, and where 'absolute military security so requires,' security detainees will not obtain full GC protection as recognized in GCIV/5, although such protection will be afforded as soon as the security situation in Iraq allows it," the letter says, using abbreviations to refer to the Article 5 of the Fourth Geneva Convention.

That brief provision opens what is, in effect, a narrow, three-paragraph loophole in the 1949 convention.

The Red Cross's standing commentary on the provision calls it "an important and regrettable concession to State expediency." It was drafted, during intense debate and in inconsistent French and English versions, to address the treatment of spies and saboteurs.

"What is most to be feared is that widespread application of the Article may eventually lead to the existence of a category of civilian internees who do not receive the normal treatment laid down by the Convention but are detained under conditions which are almost impossible to check," says the Red Cross commentary, which is posted on its Web site. "It must be emphasized most strongly, therefore, that Article 5 can only be applied in individual cases of an exceptional nature."

An authority on the laws of war, Prof. Scott L. Silliman of Duke University, said that the assertions in the military's letter, signed by Brig. Gen. Janis Karpinski of the Army, were highly questionable and that the military lawyers who drafted it may have misconstrued the law.

The category in which prisoners may be excluded from the protections of the Geneva Conventions that General Karpinski cites, Professor Silliman said, are for people who can be shown to be a continuing threat to the occupying force, not people who might have valuable intelligence.

"They may be high value assets but that does not necessarily make them security risks," he said. The provision cited by General Karpinski provides that the protections could be suspended for people suspected of "activities hostile to the security" of a warring state or an occupying power.

In testimony last week on Capitol Hill, Col. Marc Warren, a top American military lawyer in Iraq, defended harsh techniques available to American interrogators there as not being in violation of the Geneva Conventions. He said the conventions should be read in light of "various legal treatises and interpretations of coercion as applied to security internees."

Until now, the only known element of the Dec. 24 letter had been a provision described by a senior Army officer as having asserted that the Red Cross should not seek in the future to conduct no-notice inspections in the cellblock where the worst abuses took place.

Questions for Analysis

1. Which of the Geneva Conventions was used to justify the argument that certain Iraqi prisoners could be legally denied the protection of those conventions? Does this convention apply to prisoners of war or to civilian prisoners held during an occupation?

2. Are the arguments presented by the military in the December letter supported or contradicted by statements made by the American administration? Explain.

3. Does the interpretation of the Geneva Conventions as outlined by the military officials in the December letter follow the rules of interpretation established by the U.S. courts? Explain.

4. Does the interpretation of the Geneva Conventions as outlined by military officials in the December letter support the underlying objectives of the Geneva Conventions or is it simply a loophole to allow mistreatment of prisoners? What dangers could result from the acceptance of the military's interpretation of the conventions? Explain.

5. What motivated the authors of the Geneva Conventions to include Article V in those conventions? Was it a good idea to include Article V or would it have been wiser to exclude the provision altogether? Explain.

the past will change its policy in the future. Finally, the point at which a war becomes a last resort often depends on a number of factors, many of which are highly problematic. In gauging whether a war really was waged as a last resort, the fact that other options were not tried is not evidence that the war was not a last resort. It is generally enough that the other alternatives were authentically considered as viable options. If, after serious consideration, pursuing such alternatives seemed foolish at best and dangerous at worst the preemptive war may have been justified.

Substantive and Procedural Issues

Most of these just war requirements were established before the advent of contemporary warfare. In the modern age, the face of war has changed. Along with these changes have come alterations in the conduct of war, including ways of dealing with prisoners of war, occupation forces, and war crimes.

Substantive Legal Changes Following World War II in 1949, a major effort involving most of the nations of the world and sponsored by the American Red Cross was held in Geneva, Switzerland, to address the issues of prisoners of war, occupation forces, and war crimes. Out of this series of international meetings came the **Geneva Conventions.** These conventions attempt to deal with many of the problems brought on by the nature of warfare in the modern era. For instance, the first, second, and third conventions are concerned with prisoners of war, and the fourth convention deals with occupation forces.

Procedural and Analytical Problems   Substantive changes in the law of war and international relations, such as the Geneva Conventions, are frequently complicated by procedural and analytical questions. The mere fact that a convention has been written and adopted does not always mean that it will be applied properly and consistently by the nations that signed the convention. Analytical questions nearly always plague any court that is faced with the application of an international agreement. To facilitate this analytical process, the U.S. courts have established some guidelines for the interpretation of international agreements such as the Geneva Conventions.

For instance, in determining the applicability of such international pacts, the courts will first look at the literal language of the agreement, especially any definitions contained within the agreement. Second, the court will examine any supporting documentation, such as the Red Cross Commentaries in the case of the Geneva Conventions, for assistance in interpretation of the settlement. Finally, the U.S. courts will take a liberal view in the interpretation of such agreements. This means that the court will broadly and openly interpret the convention to include as many cases and situations as are justly warranted.

Quick Quiz 43-2 True or False?

1. One central question that cannot be answered solely by the law of a single national state is whether a war is just.

2. The just war theory was developed in the twenty-first century to deal with problems of modern warfare.

3. The Geneva Conventions attempt to establish rules involving occupation forces and prisoners of war.

43-3 International Law and the United Nations

As World War II drew to a close, representatives of fifty nations met in San Francisco to work out details in the formation of the United Nations. At that meeting, which was called the United Nations Conference on International Organization, fifty nations adopted a charter that, on June 26, 1945, established the United Nations. The stated purposes of the United Nations are to advance human rights, to end war, to enhance human achievement, to support peaceful international coalitions, and to promote truth, justice, and the rule of law. The promotion of international law has taken many forms within the structure of the United Nations, including the International Court of Justice, the International Criminal Court, the UN Commission on International Trade Law, and the UN Convention on Contracts for the International Sale of Goods.

The Structure of the United Nations

The United Nations is an enormous, complicated organization that is made up of many agencies, organizations, courts, and commissions. The three major governing bodies are the Secretary General, the General Assembly, and the Security Council. The **Secretary General** is the chief administrator of the United Nations. He or she heads up the **Secretariat,** which is the administrative bureaucracy of the UN. The Secretary General also takes a leading role in promoting world peace. The Security Council recommends a candidate for the position of Secretary General, but the General Assembly votes that person into office. The **General Assembly** is made up of all the member nations of the UN. Each nation has one vote on resolutions and other matters presented to the assembly. The UN **Security Council** deals with crises that involve threats to international peace. The Council consists of fifteen members. Five of these members hold permanent seats. The permanent members are China, France, Russia, the United Kingdom, and the United States. The General Assembly elects the remaining ten members for two-year terms.

The International Court of Justice

One of the principal vehicles for the establishment of international law and justice is the **International Court of Justice (ICJ).** The ICJ, which is situated at the Hague in the Netherlands, was established under provisions within the UN Charter. Key features of the court include its structure and its jurisdiction.

The Structure of the ICJ The ICJ is made up of fifteen judges. The Security Council and the General Assembly of the United Nations are jointly responsible for electing these judges, each of whom serves a nine-year term. All of the judges are also eligible for reelection. To ensure as much impartiality as possible, the UN Charter also specifies that no two judges can be citizens of the same country and that the judges may not have any additional employment while they sit on the Court. Ideally, the judges on the Court are chosen because of their legal qualifications. Every attempt is also made to ensure that the judges exemplify the foremost legal institutions in the world. When a nation is involved in a case presented to the ICJ, that nation is permitted to appoint a single judge to the court on a temporary basis.

Standing Within the ICJ Only sovereign nations have legal standing to initiate a case before the ICJ. Included within this category are nations that are member states within the United Nations. Nations that are not member states, however, may also have cases heard before the Court. Questions on the legal standing of nonmember states are left up to the determination of the General Assembly and the Security Council.

Subject Matter Jurisdiction in the ICJ Subject matter jurisdiction in the ICJ is outlined within the UN Charter. This jurisdiction includes legal questions specifically referred to within the charter as well as any legal question raised by a member nation before the court. Such legal questions may involve the interpretation of treaties and international conventions. Unlike the courts of the United States, which can render opinions only when faced with an actual case, the ICJ is permitted to issue advisory opinions when requested by the General Assembly, the Security Council, or other authorized agencies within the structure of the United Nations.

Teaching Tips Inform students that before the International Court of Justice (ICJ) can hear a contentious case, all of the parties to the proceedings must have recognized the court's jurisdiction.

Background Information Judges who sit on the ICJ are coming more and more from the ranks of government officials. Many have served as representatives of their governments in United Nations meetings or other international conferences.

The United Nations Headquarters in New York.

Example 43-5

One source of advisory opinions concerns the question of how the corporate body of the United Nations relates to individual member nations. For instance, in 1949 the General Assembly solicited an advisory opinion from the ICJ concerning the assassination of a UN mediator. The mediator had been killed on a mission to Palestine. The issue before the court was whether the United Nations could hold a member state liable for any harm that befell an agent of the United Nations. The Court found that the United Nations did indeed have that capacity.

The International Criminal Court

In order to deal with crimes against humanity, an official **International Criminal Court (ICC)** was established by the United Nations in 1998. The objective of the new court is to preside over trials involving genocide, war crimes, and other human rights violations. The International Criminal Court itself and its prison are physically situated in the Hague along with the International Court of Justice. A defendant placed on trial before the ICC has the right to an attorney and the right to present evidence on his or her own behalf. One major drawback of the court is that it has very limited authority. Specifically, it can hear only cases that involve the citizens of those countries that ratified the original treaty that created the court. Several major countries, including the United States, have not ratified the treaty, which places their citizens outside the court's jurisdiction.

The Opening Case Revisited
"The Changing International Community"

In the case at the opening of the chapter, we saw that the world has changed drastically since the funeral of Edward IV of England in 1910 when most European nations were ruled by the members of the same royal family. In those days there was no overall international organization to mediate international disputes. Instead, international relations were carried out by a professional class of diplomats who were educated on the job in embassies and consulates around the globe. There was no school for diplomats, nor was there any international forum for debate. There were, of course, attempts to create international organizations. One such effort was engineered by Tsar Nicholas II of Russia in 1899 when he convened an international conference, the goal of which was to create an international court to negotiate the settlement of international disagreements. The court was designed to operate as a cross between today's International Court of Justice and the UN Security Council. Disputes between nations were to be settled by arbitration, which is why the organization was also referred to as the Court of Arbitration. Unfortunately, there was one central flaw to the plan and that was that the court would only be conducted on a voluntary basis. In this way, as we shall see shortly, it actually operated much like the International Criminal Court.

The UN Commission on International Trade Law

In 1996, the General Assembly of the United Nations authorized the creation of the **UN Commission on International Trade Law (UNCITRAL).** The commission consists of thirty-six nations chosen to represent the primary social, economic, legal, and geographical areas of the globe. The goal of the commission is to cultivate the organization and integration of international law in relation to international trade. To this end, the commission coordinates the activities of institutions involved in international trade, encourages continued commitment to current treaties and conventions, and constructs new agreements for the community of international trade.

The UN Convention on Contracts for the International Sale of Goods

One of these agreements is the **UN Convention on Contracts for the International Sale of Goods (CISG).** This agreement became effective in 1988. It applies only to sales between businesses located in different countries. The agreement specifically excludes contracts involving goods purchased for use by individuals or families. The CISG affects the formation of an international trade contract as well as the rights and duties that arise under such contracts. However, it deals neither with the validity of such contracts, nor with the liability of the seller for harm caused by the goods. Application of the CISG is limited to businesses that are located in countries that have ratified the agreement or to businesses that create contracts that expressly stipulate that the CISG will apply to the agreement.

The CISG governs contracts for goods within the international community in much the same way that the Uniform Commercial Code (UCC) applies to sale of goods contracts within the United States. There are some significant differences, however. For example, the UCC applies to contracts between merchants and also to those that involve nonmerchants. The CISG, in contrast, involves only contracts between merchants. The UCC also involves not only sale of goods contracts, but also other commercial agreements, such as leases. The CISG, in contrast, applies only to sale of goods contracts. Also, the UCC has modified the traditional mirror image rule to overcome problems caused by the battle of the forms. The CISG still applies the mirror image rule to the acceptance of a contractual offer. Finally, the UCC has a provision that says that any contract for sale of goods valued at over $500 must be in writing to be enforceable. CISG has no such provision.

Additional UN Economic Agencies

The efforts extended by the United Nations to monitor and regulate economic conditions in the global marketplace are evident in the existence of a number of organizations, each of which has its own mission in the financial structure of the worldwide economy. These agencies include global councils and conferences such as the Economic and Social Council (ECOSOC) and the UN Conference on Trade and Development (UNCTAD), and regional agencies such as the Economic Commission for Africa and the Economic Commission for Europe. Other agencies include the International Labor Organization, the World Health Organization, the United Nations Educational, Scientific, and Cultural Organization (UNESCO), the World International Property Organization (WIPO), and the Food and Agriculture Organization. Each organization makes assessments and enters judgments that have an impact on how international business is conducted. One such organization that has special significance in this regard is the Division for Science and Technology of UNCTAD.

The Division for Science and Technology of UNCTAD

The **Division for Science and Technology** was created in response to recommendations made by the eighth conference of UNCTAD and the Ad Hoc Working Group of the International Commission on Science and Technology. Both of these groups saw the need to improve the international sharing of science and technology among governments, businesses, and educational institutions, especially all sharing that exists between developed and developing nations. The Division of Science and Technology was created to coordinate the activities of several agencies that had previously been charged with handling issues of international cooperation in the sharing of science and technology for economic development. Many experts see this as a step in the right direction, but urge a more unified response in this regard.

The Economic Security Council

The Commission on Global Governance, a twenty-six member international organization, has suggested streamlining the surveillance of international economic efforts under the auspices of an **Economic Security Council (ESC).** The ESC would be a single, unified international agency under the management of the United Nations that would monitor the economic activities of the member nations of the UN. The ESC would evaluate the state of the international economy and implement long-term strategic planning to promote sustainable development throughout the planet. The ESC would not take the place of existing international agencies, such as the Economic and Social Council and the UN Conference on Trade and Development, but would coordinate their efforts in an efficient, effective, and economic manner.

Quick Quiz 43-3 True or False?

1. The Secretary General is the chief administrator of the United Nations.

2. When a nation is involved in a case presented to the ICJ, that nation must voluntarily eliminate any judge on the panel that is a citizen of that nation.

3. The UCC and the CISG are identical in every way.

43-4 International Law, Finance, and Trade

Not everyone who wants to enter a local business transaction has the ready cash to do so. This hurdle, however, does not necessarily prevent them from looking for ways to expand their financial base. Therefore, by their very nature, business transactions often involve buying on credit, borrowing money, and investing in risky ventures designed to make a fast profit. The same thing can be said about international business transactions. In order to deal with issues of finance and trade on a worldwide scale, several international organizations and agreements have emerged that are designed to make global dealings work as smoothly as local ones.

The International Monetary Fund and the World Bank

Two organizations that emerged in the aftermath of the Great Depression and the Second World War were the International Monetary Fund and the World Bank. Both institutions came out of a series of meetings held in Bretton Woods, New Hampshire, in the final months of World War II. The **International Monetary Fund (IMF)** is designed to serve as a way for financially strapped nations to secure loans that will help them engage in programs of sustainable economic growth and development. The IMF has 184 members, each of which has pledged to act responsibly in the pursuit of economic and developmental goals.

The **World Bank** has a mission that is quite similar to the mission of the IMF. The difference is that the IMF is dedicated to helping all nations, developed, developing, and undeveloped, with fiscal problems, while the World Bank works exclusively with the poorest nations in the international community. Even this mission is split between the two arms of the World Bank. The International Bank for Reconstruction and Development (IBRD) handles more conventional loans based on normal market provisions, while the International Development Association (IDA) handles loans to the world's most economically challenged nations.

Teaching Tips Present the students with these questions: Why should the United States feel the need to trade with other nations when so much can be grown and manufactured right in our own country? Do other countries need us as trading partners more than we need them?

The World Trade Organization

After the end of the Second World War, the primary trading nations of the international community met to work out the details of a major trade agreement. The agreement, which was named the **General Agreement on Tariffs and Trade (GATT),** had as part of its original plan, the creation of an International Trade Organization (ITO). Although the ITO was never established, GATT continued to function, frequently holding international conferences on the formation and execution of international trade law. The eighth conference, which came to be known as the Uruguay Round Agreements, resulted in the creation of the **World Trade Organization (WTO).**

The Structure of the World Trade Organization The World Trade Organization was designed to serve as the corporate nucleus for the management of international trade relationships. As such, the WTO replaced GATT as the focus of world trade

Teaching Tips Invite a representative of an international trade organization or a public relations representative from a multinational corporation to speak to the class about world trade.

World Trade Organization summits are regularly the target of protesters.

talks. However, all agreements, treaties, and trade obligations created under GATT have been included in the WTO and thus remain in force. The structure of the WTO involves three levels, the Ministerial Conference, the General Council, and the Secretariat. The power to make key determinations under the authority of multinational trade agreements falls to the Ministerial Conference, which meets every two years. The responsibilities of the Ministerial Conference pass to the General Council whenever the Ministerial Conference is not assembled. Finally, the Secretariat, which is headed by a Director General, is responsible for the administration of the WTO.

The World Trade Organization Principles The WTO has established certain overall principles that regulate how member nations must treat one another in the world of international trade. The first principle, the **national treatment principle,** states that WTO nations must apply the same standards to imports that they apply to domestic goods. The second principle, the **most-favored nation principle,** maintains that all member nations must apply the same privileges, advantages, and benefits to all other member nations in relation to similar imports. The third principle, the **tariff-based principle,** asserts that the only way that member nations can regulate the imports of other nations is through tariffs. This rule eliminates the use of more drastic techniques such as boycotts, quotas, and quantitative limits.

The Dispute Settlement Board The **Dispute Settlement Board (DSB)** of the WTO was established to provide a forum for the settlement of trade disputes among member nations. The DSB follows a commonly adopted procedure known as the **Dispute Settlement Understanding (DSU).** All member nations can be held accountable under DSU regulations. According to those regulations, only member nations have standing to initiate a case. The DSU implements a number of measures designed to improve the way that quarrels are handled. For instance the DSU has set up a series of precise time limits for the stages in a trade conflict. The DSU ensures that a network of comprehensive guidelines is consistently followed in all such controversies. The DSU also allows effective retaliatory measures that can be implemented by one nation against another if the offending nation refuses to adhere to a decision rendered under the DSU.

Example 43-6

Germany and Korea were involved in a dispute concerning trade in electronic appliances and automobiles. Korea claimed that in violation of trade agreements, Germany imposed a tariff on certain electronic appliances manufactured in Korea and imported to Germany. Korea followed proper DSU procedures and received a ruling from a panel that was supported by an appellate board. The ruling indicated that Germany had indeed violated the agreement. The WTO could not directly sanction Germany. Instead, it allowed Korea to impose an enormous tariff on luxury and sports model automobiles imported from Germany to Korea. This form of sanction is known as retaliation.

The North American Free Trade Agreement

The United States and many other similarly situated nations have entered comprehensive trade coalitions designed to open their borders to the free flow of international trade. The most famous of these comprehensive coalitions is the **North American Free Trade Agreement (NAFTA).** NAFTA is a trading coalition that includes the United States, Canada, and Mexico. The goal of the coalition is to establish a trading market in North America free from the burdens imposed by internal tariff barriers. Thus, each country within the agreement can take advantage of this free market by importing those goods that it cannot produce itself in exchange for the tariff-free exportation of the goods that it can produce.

The European Union

One of the most significant events to impact international law and commerce lately was the inauguration of the **European Union (EU).** The creation of the European Union, the attempt to formulate a common European economic policy, and the introduction of a common currency for most of Europe may transform the EU into a major competitor with the power to challenge American business interests in the global marketplace. Moreover, since many businesses within the EU have embraced cybercommerce, American firms may also face unique challenges in that arena.

The Introduction of the Euro In order to adopt the **euro,** Europe's common currency, a country must first belong to the European Union. Membership in the EU alone, however, is not enough to allow a nation to adopt the euro. In addition, a nation must have a stable inflation rate, a history of interest rate convergence that falls within certain guidelines, and a pattern of fiscal responsibility. Of those nations which have qualified, eleven, including Austria, Belgium, France, Germany, Ireland, Italy, Luxembourg, Netherlands, and Spain elected to join the effort. Several nations including the United Kingdom, Denmark, and Sweden, opted out of the program. The use of the euro is designed to lower costs by eliminating the need to change currencies when firms in the member states deal with one another across national boundaries.

The euro—the common currency for the EU member states—replaced many of the different currencies across the European Union in January 2002.

Cybercommerce and the European Union The EU has been active in the development of cybercommerce directives in order to head off proposed legislative initiatives in the individual member nations. Such individualized rules would complicate the rules of European cybercommerce and defeat the purpose of a unified EU economic policy. One example of a unified directive is the Data Protection Directive. This directive assures all citizens of Europe that they will enjoy certain definitive privacy rights when they engage in cybercommerce.

A Question of Ethics

At what point should the commitment to a multinational coalition such as the European Union give way to individual national loyalties? Suppose, for example, that a majority of the member states of the EU voted to impose economic sanctions on one of its own members. Would businesses that are incorporated within the sanctioned state be required to go along with the EU action or would they be permitted to remain loyal to their home nation? What if the action imposed by the EU against one of its own members was political or military rather than economic? Would that change your answer? Explain.

Among the rights held by consumers in Europe are the right to obtain any computer data stored on them, the right to adjust any incorrect data, the right to deny another party the use of computer data, and the right to a legal remedy for any unlawful activities in relation to computer data. Another EU directive that affects cybercommerce is the Directive on the Protection of Consumers in Respect of Distance Contracts (ECD). This directive gives specifically enumerated privileges to consumers who deal with companies selling goods and services within the EU by electronic means. The ECD allows consumers to cancel any cybercommerce transaction without penalty within seven working days.

Quick Quiz 43-4 True or False?

1. Two organizations that emerged in the aftermath of the Great Depression and the Second World War were the International Monetary Fund and the World Bank.

2. None of the agreements, treaties, or trade obligations created under GATT have been included in the WTO.

3. NAFTA is a trading coalition that includes the United States, the United Kingdom, and Greenland.

Summary

43-1 Many countries in the world do not share the same view of law as the United States. Two common areas of disagreement are the belief that the adversarial system is the best procedure for courts to follow and the position that the rule of law is absolutely inviolable.

43-2 War has many significant effects upon the transaction of business in the international marketplace. One of the key questions concerning the nature of war as it relates to international business is whether the war is just. Ethical and legal philosophers in the West have developed criteria for determining when a war can be considered legally and morally correct. This theory is termed the just war theory.

43-3 The stated purposes of the United Nations are to advance human rights, to end war, to enhance human achievement, to support peaceful international coalitions, and to promote international fidelity to truth, justice, and the rule of law. The promotion of international law has taken many forms within the structure of the United Nations, including the International Court of Justice, the International Criminal Court, the UN Commission on International Trade Law, and the UN Convention on Contracts for the International Sale of Goods.

43-4 In order to deal with issues of finance and trade on a worldwide scale, several international organizations and agreements have emerged that are designed to make global dealings work as smoothly as local ones. These include the International Monetary Fund and the World Bank, The World Trade Organization, The North American Free Trade Agreement, and The European Union.

Key Terms

adversarial system, 831

competent authority, 835

Dispute Settlement Board (DSB), 846

Dispute Settlement Understanding (DSU), 846

Division for Science and Technology, 844

Economic Security Council (ESC), 844

euro, 847

European Union (EU), 847

General Agreement on Tariffs and Trade (GATT), 845

General Assembly, 841

Geneva Conventions, 840

International Court of Justice (ICJ), 841

International Criminal Court (ICC), 842

International Monetary Fund (IMF), 845

just cause, 835

just war theory, 834

most-favored nation principle, 846

last resort, 836

national treatment principle, 846

North American Free Trade Agreement (NAFTA), 846

preemptive war, 836

preventative war, 836

principle of honorable surrender, 836

principle of repentance, 836

principle of restoration, 836

probability of success, 835

proportionality, 835

right intention, 835

Secretariat, 841

Secretary General, 841

Security Council, 841

tariff-based principle, 846

UN Commission on International Trade Law (UNCITRAL), 843

UN Convention on Contracts for the International Sale of Goods (CISG), 843

World Bank, 845

World Trade Organization (WTO), 845

Questions for Review and Discussion

1. What are the differences between national and international standards?
2. What are the criteria for a just war?
3. What is the extent of the jurisdiction of the International Court of Justice?
4. What is the mission of International Criminal Court?
5. What is the main goal of UNCITRAL?
6. What are the differences between the UCC and the CISG?
7. What is the structure of the World Trade Organization?
8. What are the objectives of the Dispute Settlement Understanding?
9. What is the major purpose of NAFTA?
10. What is the European Union?

Investigating the Internet

Access the website of the United Nations Commission on International Trade Law and write a brief paper on the basic structure, membership, and operation of the agency.

Cases for Analysis

1. Initially, after Saddam Hussein was captured by American forces in the aftermath of the American invasion of Iraq, he was supposed to be placed on trial in Iraq. The trial was to be held under the jurisdiction of a tribunal of judges who had the authority to conduct an independent preliminary investigation in order to find out as many facts as they could before the trial was to begin. Moreover, the judges themselves were responsible for filing the charges against Hussein. This means that the defendant is not presumed innocent by the judges once the trial begins. Does this trial system resemble the American adversarial process or the procedure used in the continental system? Explain.

2. Saddam Hussein was accused of many crimes. One of those crimes was the invasion of Kuwait. Allegedly the authorities questioned Hussein without permitting him to have any type of proper legal representation. At one point during the questioning, Hussein is alleged to have stated that he invaded Kuwait to forestall a rebellion among his own military. Would such an admission be admissible as evidence in an American court during a criminal trial? Would such an admission be permitted as evidence in a continental-style court? Explain.

3. During the American occupation of Iraq, lawyers from the Justice Department, the Defense Department, and the White House counsel's office wrote a memo that allegedly defended the use of torture by American interrogators in the questioning of prisoners at Guantanamo Bay. One of the arguments that the lawyers made in the memo was that inflicting pain on a detainee could be justified as long as it was not "severe" and was inflicted by necessity. The guidelines in the memo said that inflicting pain would be constitutionally permissible as a necessity (1) if it were done outside the United States, (2) if the subject was an actually identified enemy combatant, and (3) if the questioning involved an attack planned by the enemy. Taking into account the spirit of the Geneva Conventions as well as the United States courts' intent to liberally construe the Geneva Conventions, explain whether the conclusions in this memo appear to be in line with those conventions.

4. After General Manuel Noriega had come under the authority of the United States forces following the invasion of Panama, his attorneys argued that he should be treated as a prisoner of war (POW) under the Geneva Conventions. The United States government agreed to treat Noriega as a POW but refused to give him official POW status. Noriega's attorneys argued that this treatment as POW could at any time be withdrawn by the government. They asked the court to declare their client a POW under the Geneva Conventions. The government argued that the events in Panama were considered hostilities rather than a war. Consequently, the government pointed out, Noriega could not be a POW. Article II of Geneva Convention III states that "the present convention shall apply to all cases of declared war and of any other armed conflict which may arise between two or more of the High Contracting Parties, even if the state of war is not recognized by one of them." Moreover, the

International Red Cross Commentary on Convention III says, "Any difference between two states leading to the intervention of the armed forces is an armed conflict within the meaning of Article II." Finally, Article IV of the Convention defines POWs as "persons belonging to one of the following categories, who have fallen into the power of the enemy: (1) members of the armed forces of a Party to the conflict. . . ." Taking all of this into account, as well as the United States courts' intent to liberally construe the Geneva Conventions, should the court declare Noriega a POW? Explain. *United States of America v. Manuel Antonio Noriega,* 808 F. Supp. 791 (S.D. FL.)

5. American Rice, Inc., a U.S. corporation, sold its goods in Saudi Arabia under the trade name of ABU BINT, which means "of the girl." Another American corporation, the Arkansas Rice Growers Cooperative Association, marketed similar products in Saudi Arabia using the name BINT ALARAB, which in English means "Gulf Girl." American Rice sued Arkansas in federal district court under the Lanham Act, alleging an infringement by Arkansas of American Rice's exclusive trademark. None of the Arkansas rice products that American Rice complained of had entered any market within the United States. Arkansas argued that the federal district court had no extra territorial power to mediate this international trade dispute. Was Arkansas correct? Explain. *American Rice, Inc., v. Arkansas Rice Growers Coop. Ass'n.,* 701 F.2d 414 (5th Cir.).

6. Gulf Oil Corporation and Eastern Air Lines entered a contract under the terms of which Gulf Oil was obligated to supply Eastern with jet fuel according to an established pricing system. In 1973, the Organization for Petroleum Exporting Countries (OPEC), established an oil embargo that precipitated the now famous energy crisis of the 1970s. As a result of the oil embargo and the energy crisis, the price of crude oil skyrocketed. Gulf Oil asked Eastern to consent to a price increase over the price agreed to under the original contract. Eastern refused to comply with the increase. Gulf Oil then vowed to stop all jet fuel shipments to Eastern unless Eastern would reconsider its refusal to go along with the price increase. Eastern filed a lawsuit in federal district court alleging a breach of contract on Gulf Oil's part. Did the American court have jurisdiction over an exclusively American contract affected by an international incident, such as the 1973 oil embargo?

Did the court agree that Gulf breached its contract with Eastern Airlines? Explain. *Eastern Air Line, Inc., v. Gulf Oil Corporation,* 415 F. Supp. 429 (S.D. FL).

7. Kenneth Armstrong, an American citizen, purchased the component parts of computers in Germany, Japan, and the United States. He took those parts to Bolivia where he constructed the computers, stamped them with the name Starlight Computers, and sold them. Armstrong had a Bolivian registration that allowed him to use the trade name Starlight. While none of the computers were imported into the United States by Armstrong, many of the counterfeit computers eventually found their way into the United States' marketplace. Starlight Computers, Inc., an American corporation, brought a lawsuit against Armstrong in United States District Court, under the Lanham Act. Armstrong moved for a dismissal of the case, arguing that the American court did not have the authority to enforce the Lanham Act against his Bolivian operation. Is Armstrong correct? Explain.

8. France and Japan are involved in a dispute concerning trade in aircraft parts. France claims that in violation of certain trade agreements, Japan is imposing a tariff on certain types of aircraft parts that are manufactured in France and imported to Japan. France follows proper DSU procedures and receives a ruling from a panel that is supported by an appellate board. The ruling indicates that Japan has, indeed, violated the agreement. France asks the WTO to apply punitive sanctions directly against Japan. Will France's request be granted? Explain.

9. Helga Godel, a German citizen, placed an order for certain software items from Pascal Enterprises, a French firm. On the same day she ordered a silverware set from Silverwings Ltd., an Austrian company. When Godel received the package from Pascal, she unwrapped the software and attempted to download the program into her computer. When she accessed the program, however, she found that, although the program worked well, it was not what she had expected. Later that day she received the silverware set. Again she was dissatisfied, this time with the quality of the product. As a European E-consumer what rights does Godel have under the EU Directive on the Protection of Consumers in Respect of Distance Contracts? Explain.

Quick Quiz Answers

43-1	1. F	43-2	1. T	43-3	1. T	43-4	1. T
	2. F		2. F		2. F		2. F
	3. F		3. T		3. F		3. F

Part 9 Case Study

New York Times v. Tasini
533 U.S. 483 (2001)

Summary

Jonathan Tasini worked as a freelance writer, regularly contributing pieces to the *New York Times* and *Newsday.* He was joined in this lawsuit by Margot Mifflin and Mary Kay Blakely both of whom also contributed articles to the *Times* and by Barbara Garson, Sonia Jaffe Robbins, and David S. Whitford all of whom wrote articles for *Newsday.* Whitford also wrote an article for *Sports Illustrated,* which is owned and operated by Time, Inc. The authors retained the copyright privileges to their individual articles while the publishers owned the copyrights to the actual publications. The agreements made between the authors and the publishers were drafted at a time when it was not common to post articles on the web. The authors were therefore surprised to discover that the publishers had made arrangements to have their articles posted on the web without their permission and without compensation.

The publishers had made a deal with LEXIS/NEXIS which is a company that publishes a computerized database on the web called NEXIS. The articles on NEXIS can be accessed in a variety of ways by a computer user. For instance, a computer user may search for the article by subject, by author, or by title. The article can be viewed on the screen, downloaded, or reproduced in paper format. The articles are accessed as stand alone items divorced from the context in which they appeared when they were first printed. All photographs and headlines that appeared with the articles when in print do not appear on the database. Surrounding articles are also notably absent from the computerized compilation.

The *New York Times* had a second licensing agreement with two additional secondary publishers, University Microfilms International which reproduced articles from the *Times* on CD-ROM, and General Periodicals OnDisc (GPO). GPO had a license to reproduce articles from the *Times' Sunday Magazine* and the *Times Sunday Book Review* magazine. These two companies also reproduced only the articles themselves and none of the surrounding matter that appeared with the articles when they were originally published. Computer users can search the CD-ROM products in much the same way that they search the LEXIS/NEXIS database.

The authors brought suit against The New York Times Company and the other publishers in United States District Court for the Southern District of New York alleging that their copyright privileges had been violated by the publishers. They asked the court for an injunction to stop the publication of their articles on the web and in the CD-ROM format without their permission. They also asked for a judgment declaring their rights to the copyrighted articles. Finally, they asked for an appropriate level of damages. The publishers filed a summary judgment motion, arguing that they held a copyright to the original periodical in which the articles appeared. They pointed to Section 201 [c] of the Copyright Act which permits the owner of a publication to publish a revision of an original publication containing articles like the ones in question. The publishers concluded that their licensing of the article to NEXIS and the other publishers was simply an exercise of their right to reprint such revisions.

The District Court agreed and granted the summary judgment motion. In doing so, the court noted that, as long as all of the articles in a given issue were licensed to the online and CD-ROM publishers, the spirit of the statute had been met. The authors were dissatisfied with this decision and appealed to the Second Circuit Court of Appeals. The Second Circuit reversed the lower court's decision. The Second Circuit concluded that section 201 [c] permitted the publishers to reprint a revision of an entire issue of a newspaper or magazine, but did not permit them to sell off paper copies of the individual articles one by one. Since the publishers could not do this with the paper copies of the articles, they could also not do the same thing electronically. The publishers were dissatisfied and asked the Supreme Court to hear the case. The Supreme Court agreed.

Opinion of the Court

Justice Ginsburg delivered the opinion of the Court.

This copyright case concerns the rights of freelance authors and a presumptive privilege of their publishers. The litigation was initiated by six freelance authors and relates to articles they contributed to three print periodicals (two newspapers and one magazine). Under agreements with the periodicals' publishers, but without the freelancers' consent, two computer database companies placed copies of the freelancers' articles—along with all other articles from the periodicals in which the freelancers' work appeared—into three databases. Whether written by a freelancer or staff member, each article is presented to, and retrievable by, the user in isolation, clear of the context the original print publication presented.

The freelance authors' complaint alleged that their copyrights had been infringed by the inclusion of their articles in the databases. The publishers, in response, relied on the privilege of reproduction and distribution accorded them by §201(c) of the Copyright Act.

We granted certiorari to determine whether the copying of the Authors' Articles in the Databases is privileged by 17 U.S.C. §201(c). 531 U.S. 978 (2000). Like the Court of Appeals, we conclude that the §201(c) privilege does not override the Authors' copyrights, for the Databases do not reproduce and distribute the Articles as part of a collective work privileged by §201(c). Accordingly, and again like the Court of Appeals, we find it unnecessary to determine whether the privilege is transferable.

II

Under the Copyright Act, as amended in 1976, "[c]opyright protection subsists . . . in original works of authorship fixed in any tangible medium of expression . . . from which they can be perceived, reproduced, or otherwise communicated." 17 U.S.C. §102(a). When, as in this case, a freelance author has contributed an article to a "collective work" such as a newspaper or magazine, see §101 (defining "collective work"), the statute recognizes two distinct copyrighted works: "Copyright in *each separate contribution to a collective work* is distinct from copyright in *the collective work as a whole* . . . ." §201(c) (emphasis added). Copyright in the separate contribution "vests initially in the author of the contribution" (here, the freelancer). *Ibid.* Copyright in the collective work vests in the collective author (here, the newspaper or magazine publisher) and extends only to the creative material contributed by that author, not to "the preexisting material employed in the work," §103(b). See also *Feist Publications, Inc. v. Rural Telephone Service Co.,* 499 U.S. 340, 358 (1991) (copyright in "compilation"—a term that includes "collective works," 17 U.S.C. §101—is limited to the compiler's original "selection, coordination, and arrangement").

Section 201(c) both describes and circumscribes the "privilege" a publisher acquires regarding an author's contribution to a collective work:

> "In the absence of an express transfer of the copyright or of any rights under it, the owner of copyright in the collective work is presumed to have acquired *only* the privilege of reproducing and distributing the contribution as part of that particular collective work, any revision of that collective work, and any later collective work in the same series." (Emphasis added.)

A newspaper or magazine publisher is thus privileged to reproduce or distribute an article contributed by a freelance author, absent a contract otherwise providing, only "as part of" any (or all) of three categories of collective works: (a) "that collective work" to which the author contributed her work, (b) "any revision of that collective work," or (c) "any later collective work in the same series." In accord with Congress' prescription, a "publishing company could reprint a contribution from one issue in a later issue of its magazine, and could reprint an article from a 1980 edition of an encyclopedia in a 1990 revision of it; the publisher could not revise the contribution itself or include it in a new anthology or an entirely different magazine or other collective work." H. R. Rep. 122–123.

Essentially, §201(c) adjusts a publisher's copyright in its collective work to accommodate a freelancer's copyright in her contribution. If there is demand for a freelance article standing alone or in a new collection, the Copyright Act allows the freelancer to benefit from that demand; after authorizing initial publication, the freelancer may also sell the article to others.

III

In the instant case, the Authors wrote several Articles and gave the Print Publishers permission to publish the Articles in certain newspapers and magazines. It is undisputed that the Authors hold copyrights and, therefore, exclusive rights in the Articles.

Against the Authors' charge of infringement, the Publishers do not here contend the Authors entered into an agreement authorizing reproduction of the Articles in the Databases.

The Publishers press an analogy between the Databases, on the one hand, and microfilm and microfiche, on the other. We find the analogy wanting. Microforms typically contain continuous photographic reproductions of a periodical in the medium of miniaturized film. Accordingly, articles appear on the microforms, writ very small, in precisely the position in which the articles appeared in the newspaper.

IV

The Publishers warn that a ruling for the Authors will have "devastating" consequences. Brief for Petitioners 49. The Databases, the Publishers note, provide easy access to complete newspaper texts going back decades. A ruling for the Authors, the Publishers suggest, will punch gaping holes in the electronic record of history. The Publishers' concerns are echoed by several historians, see Brief for Ken Burns et al. as *Amici Curiae,* but discounted by several other historians, see Brief for Ellen Schrecker et al. as *Amici Curiae;* Brief for Authors' Guild, Jacques Barzun et al. as *Amici Curiae*.

Notwithstanding the dire predictions from some quarters, it hardly follows from today's decision that an injunction against the inclusion of these Articles in the Databases (much less all freelance articles in any databases) must issue. The parties (Authors and Publishers) may enter into an agreement allowing continued electronic reproduction of the Authors' works; they, and if necessary the courts and Congress, may draw on numerous models for distributing copyrighted works and remunerating authors for their distribution.

In any event, speculation about future harms is no basis for this Court to shrink authorial rights Congress established in §201(c). Agreeing with the Court of Appeals that the Publishers are liable for infringement, we leave remedial issues open for initial airing and decision in the District Court.

We conclude that the Electronic Publishers infringed the Authors' copyrights by reproducing and distributing the Articles in a manner not authorized by the Authors and not privileged by §201(c). We further conclude that the Print Publishers infringed the Authors' copyrights by authorizing the Electronic Publishers to place the Articles in the Databases and by aiding the Electronic Publishers in that endeavor. We therefore affirm the judgment of the Court of Appeals.

It is so ordered.

Questions for Analysis

1. What are the central rights at issue in this case? Why did the Supreme Court agree to hear this case? Explain.

2. What rights did Congress attempt to balance with the provisions of Section 201[3] of the Copyright Act?

3. Why did the Court reject the publishers' microform analogy? Explain.

4. What "devastating" consequences did the publishers predict would occur if the Supreme Court ruled for the authors in this case? Explain.

5. What avenue of approach did the Court suggest to escape the predictions of the publishers? Could this ruling affect the results of the Napster case? Explain.

Appendix A

The Constitution of the United States

Preamble

We the People of the United States, in Order to form a more perfect Union, establish Justice, insure domestic Tranquility, provide for the common defence, promote the general Welfare, and secure the Blessings of Liberty to ourselves and our Posterity, do ordain and establish this Constitution for the United States of America.

Article I

Section 1. All legislative Powers herein granted shall be vested in a Congress of the United States, which shall consist of a Senate and House of Representatives.

Section 2. [1] The House of Representatives shall be composed of Members chosen every second Year by the People of the several States, and the Electors in each State shall have the Qualifications requisite for Electors of the most numerous Branch of the State Legislature.

[2] No Person shall be a Representative who shall not have attained to the Age of twenty-five Years, and been seven Years a Citizen of the United States, and who shall not, when elected, be an Inhabitant of that State in which he shall be chosen.

[3] Representatives and direct Taxes shall be apportioned among the several States which may be included within this Union, according to their respective Numbers, which shall be determined by adding to the whole Number of free Persons, including those bound to Service for a Term of Years, and excluding Indians not taxed, three fifths of all other Persons. The actual Enumeration shall be made within three Years after the first Meeting of the Congress of the United States, and within every subsequent Term of ten Years, in such Manner as they shall by Law direct. The Number of Representatives shall not exceed one for every thirty Thousand, but each State shall have at Least one Representative; and until such enumeration shall be made, the State of New Hampshire shall be entitled to chuse three, Massachusetts eight, Rhode Island and Providence Plantations one, Connecticut five, New York six, New Jersey four, Pennsylvania eight, Delaware one, Maryland six, Virginia ten, North Carolina five, South Carolina five, and Georgia three.

[4] When vacancies happen in the Representation from any State, the Executive Authority thereof shall issue Writs of Election to fill such Vacancies.

[5] The House of Representatives shall chuse their Speaker and other Officers; and shall have the sole Power of Impeachment.

Section 3. [1] The Senate of the United States shall be composed of two Senators from each State, chosen by the Legislature thereof, for six Years; and each Senator shall have one Vote.

[2] Immediately after they shall be assembled in Consequence of the first Election, they shall be divided as equally as may be into three Classes. The Seats of the Senators of the first Class shall be vacated at the Expiration of the Second Year, of the second Class at the Expiration of the fourth Year, and of the third Class at the Expiration of the sixth Year, so that one third may be chosen every second Year; and if Vacancies happen by Resignation, or otherwise, during the Recess of the Legislature of any State, the Executive thereof may make temporary Appointments until the next Meeting of the Legislature, which shall then fill such Vacancies.

[3] No Person shall be a Senator who shall not have attained to the Age of thirty Years, and been nine Years a Citizen of the United States, and who shall not, when elected, be an Inhabitant of that State for which he shall be chosen.

[4] The Vice President of the United States shall be President of the Senate, but shall have no Vote, unless they be equally divided.

[5] The Senate shall chuse their other Officers, and also a President pro tempore, in the Absence of the Vice President, or when he shall exercise the Office of President of the United States.

[6] The Senate shall have the sole Power to try all Impeachments. When sitting for that Purpose, they shall be on Oath or Affirmation. When the President of the United States is tried, the Chief Justice shall preside: And no Person shall be convicted without the Concurrence of two thirds of the Members present.

[7] Judgment in Cases of Impeachment shall not extend further than to removal from Office, and disqualification to hold and enjoy any Office of honor, Trust, or Profit under the United States: but the Party convicted shall nevertheless be liable and subject to Indictment, Trial, Judgment, and Punishment, according to Law.

Section 4. [1] The Times, Places and Manner of holding elections for Senators and Representatives, shall be prescribed in each State by the Legislature thereof; but the Congress may at any time by Law make or alter such Regulations, except as to the Places of chusing Senators.

[2] The Congress shall assemble at least once in every Year, and such Meeting shall be on the first Monday in December, unless they shall by Law appoint a different Day.

Section 5. [1] Each House shall be the Judge of the Elections, Returns, and Qualifications of its own Members, and a Majority of each shall constitute a Quorum to do Business; but a smaller Number may adjourn from day to day, and may be authorized to compel the Attendance of absent Members, in such Manner, and under such Penalties as each House may provide.

[2] Each House may determine the Rules of its Proceedings, punish its Members for disorderly Behavior, and, with the Concurrence of two thirds, expel a Member.

[3] Each House shall keep a Journal of its Proceedings, and from time to time publish the same, excepting such parts as may in their Judgment require Secrecy; and the Yeas and Nays of the Members of either House on any question shall, at the Desire of one fifth of those Present, be entered on the Journal.

[4] Neither House, during the Session of Congress, shall, without the Consent of the other, adjourn for more than three days, nor to any other Place than that in which the two Houses shall be sitting.

Section 6. **[1]** The Senators and Representatives shall receive a Compensation for their Services, to be ascertained by Law, and paid out of the Treasury of the United States. They shall in all Cases, except Treason, Felony and Breach of the Peace, be privileged from Arrest during their Attendance at the Session of their respective Houses, and in going to and returning from the same; and for any Speech of Debate in either House, they shall not be questioned in any other Place.

[2] No Senator or Representative shall, during the Time for which he was elected, be appointed to any civil Office under the Authority of the United States, which shall have been created, or the Emoluments whereof shall have been increased during such time; and no Person holding any Office under the United States, shall be a Member of either House during his Continuance in Office.

Section 7. **[1]** All Bills for raising Revenue shall originate in the House of Representatives; but the Senate may propose or concur with Amendments as on other Bills.

[2] Every Bill which shall have passed the House of Representatives and the Senate, shall, before it becomes a Law, be presented to the President of the United States; If he approve he shall sign it, but if not he shall return it, with his Objections to the House in which it shall have originated, who shall enter the Objections at large on their Journal, and proceed to reconsider it. If after such Reconsideration two thirds of that House shall agree to pass the Bill, it shall be sent together with the Objections, to the other House, by which it shall likewise be reconsidered, and if approved by two thirds of that House, it shall become a Law. But in all such Cases the Votes of both Houses shall be determined by yeas and Nays, and the Names of the Persons voting for and against the Bill shall be entered on the Journal of each House respectively. If any Bill shall not be returned by the President within ten Days (Sundays excepted) after it shall have been presented to him, the Same shall be a Law, in like Manner as if he had signed it, unless the Congress by their Adjournment prevent its Return in which Case it shall not be a Law.

[3] Every Order, Resolution, or Vote, to Which the Concurrence of the Senate and House of Representatives may be necessary (except on a question of Adjournment) shall be presented to the President of the United States; and before the Same shall take Effect, shall be approved by him, or being disapproved by him, shall be repassed by two thirds of the Senate and House of Representatives, according to the Rules and Limitations prescribed in the Case of a Bill.

Section 8. **[1]** The Congress shall have Power To lay and collect Taxes, Duties, Imposts and Excises, to pay the Debts and provide for the common Defence and general Welfare of the United States; but all Duties, Imposts and Excises shall be uniform throughout the United States;

[2] To borrow money on the credit of the United States;

[3] To regulate Commerce with foreign Nations, and among the several States, and with the Indian Tribes;

[4] To establish an uniform Rule of Naturalization, and uniform laws on the subject of Bankruptcies throughout the United States;

[5] To coin Money, regulate the Value thereof, and of foreign Coin, and fix the Standard of Weights and Measures;

[6] To provide for the Punishment of counterfeiting the Securities and current Coin of the United States;

[7] To Establish Post Offices and Post Roads;

[8] To promote the Progress of Science and useful Arts, by securing for limited Times to Authors and Inventors the exclusive Right to their respective Writings and Discoveries;

[9] To constitute Tribunals inferior to the supreme Court;

[10] To define and punish Piracies and Felonies committed on the high Seas, and Offenses against the Law of Nations;

[11] To declare War, grant Letters of Marque and Reprisal, and make Rules concerning Captures on Land and Water;

[12] To raise and support Armies, but no Appropriation of Money to that Use shall be for a longer Term than two Years;

[13] To provide and maintain a Navy;

[14] To make Rules for the Government and Regulation of the land and naval Forces;

[15] To provide for calling forth the Militia to execute the Laws of the Union, suppress Insurrections and repel Invasions;

[16] To provide for organizing, arming, and disciplining, the Militia, and for governing such Part of them as may be employed in the Service of the United States, reserving to the States respectively, the Appointment of the Officers, and the Authority of training the Militia according to the discipline prescribed by Congress;

[17] To exercise exclusive Legislation in all Cases whatsoever, over such District (not exceeding ten Miles square) as may, by Cession of particular States, and the Acceptance of Congress, become the Seat of the Government of the United States, and to exercise like Authority over all Places purchased by the Consent of the Legislature of the State in which the Same shall be, for the Erection of Forts, Magazines, Arsenals, dock-Yards and other needful Buildings;—And

[18] To make all Laws which shall be necessary and proper for carrying into Execution the foregoing Powers, and all other Powers vested by this Constitution in the Government of the United States, or in any Department or Officer thereof.

Section 9. [1] The Migration or Importation of Such Persons as any of the States now existing shall think proper to admit, shall not be prohibited by the Congress prior to the Year one thousand eight hundred and eight, but a Tax or duty may be imposed on such Importation, not exceeding ten dollars for each Person.

[2] The privilege of the Writ of Habeas Corpus shall not be suspended, unless when in Cases of Rebellion or Invasion the public Safety may require it.

[3] No Bill of Attainder or ex post facto Law shall be passed.

[4] No Capitation, or other direct, Tax shall be laid, unless in Proportion to the Census or Enumeration herein before directed to be taken.

[5] No Tax or Duty shall be laid on Articles exported from any State.

[6] No Preference shall be given by any Regulation of Commerce or Revenue to the Ports of one State over those of another: nor shall Vessels bound to, or from, one State be obliged to enter, clear, or pay Duties in another.

[7] No money shall be drawn from the Treasury, but in Consequence of Appropriations made by Law; and a regular Statement and Account of the Receipts and Expenditures of all public Money shall be published from time to time.

[8] No Title of Nobility shall be granted by the United States: And no Person holding any Office of Profit or Trust under them, shall, without the Consent of the Congress, accept of any present, Emolument, Office, or Title, of any kind whatever, from any King, Prince, or foreign State.

Section 10. [1] No State shall enter into any Treaty, Alliance, or confederation; grant Letters of Marque and Reprisal; coin Money; emit Bills of Credit; make any Thing but gold and silver Coin a Tender in Payment of Debts; pass any Bill of Attainder, ex post facto Law, or Law impairing the Obligation of Contracts, or grant any Title of Nobility.

[2] No State shall, without the Consent of the Congress, lay any Imposts or Duties on Imports or Exports, except what may be absolutely necessary for executing its inspection Laws: and the net Produce of all Duties and Imposts, laid by any State on Imports or Exports, shall be for the Use of the Treasury of the United States; and all such Laws shall be subject to the Revision and Control of the Congress.

[3] No State shall, without the Consent of Congress, lay any Duty of Tonnage, keep Troops, or Ships of War in time of Peace, enter into any Agreement or Compact with another State, or with a foreign Power, or engage in War, unless actually invaded, or in such imminent Danger as will not admit of delay.

Article II

Section 1. [1] The executive Power shall be vested in a President of the United States of America. He shall hold his Office during the Term of four Years, and, together with the Vice President, chosen for the same Term, be elected, as follows:

[2] Each State shall appoint, in such Manner as the Legislature thereof may direct, a Number of Electors, equal to the whole Number of Senators and Representatives to which the State may be entitled in the Congress; but no Senator or Representative, or Person holding an Office of Trust or Profit under the United States, shall be appointed an Elector.

[3] The Electors shall meet in their respective States, and vote by Ballot for two Persons, of whom one at least shall not be an Inhabitant of the same State with themselves. And they shall make a List of all the Persons voted for, and of the Number of Votes for each; which List they shall sign and certify, and transmit sealed to the Seat of the Government of the United States, directed to the President of the Senate. The President of the Senate shall, in the Presence of the Senate and House of Representatives, open all the Certificates, and the Votes shall then be counted. The Person having the greatest Number of Votes shall be the President, if such Number be a Majority of the whole Number of Electors appointed; and if there be more than one who have such Majority, and have an equal Number of Votes, then the House of Representatives shall immediately chuse by Ballot one of them for President; and if no Person have a Majority, then from the five highest on the List the said House shall in like Manner chuse the President. But in chusing the President, the Votes shall be taken by States the Representation from each State having one Vote; A quorum for this Purpose shall consist of a Member or Members from two thirds of the States, and a Majority of all the States shall be necessary to a Choice. In every Case, after the Choice of the President, the Person having the greater Number of Votes of the Electors shall be the Vice President. But if there shall remain two or more who have equal Votes, the Senate shall chuse from them by Ballot the Vice President.

[4] The Congress may determine the Time of chusing the Electors, and the Day on which they shall give their Votes; which Day shall be the same throughout the United States.

[5] No person except a natural born Citizen, or a Citizen of the United States, at the time of the Adoption of this Constitution, shall be eligible to the Office of President; neither shall any Person be eligible to that Office who shall not have attained to the Age of thirty-five Years, and been fourteen Years a Resident within the United States.

[6] In case of the removal of the President from Office, or of his Death, Resignation or Inability to discharge the Powers and Duties of the said Office, the Same shall devolve on the Vice President, and the Congress may by Law provide for the Case of Removal, Death, Resignation or Inability, both of the President and Vice President, declaring what Officer shall then act as President, and such Officer shall act accordingly, until the Disability be removed, or a President shall be elected.

[7] The President shall, at stated Times, receive for his Services, a Compensation, which shall neither be increased nor diminished during the Period for which he shall have been elected, and he shall not receive within that Period any other Emolument from the United States, or any of them.

[8] Before he enter on the Execution of his Office, he shall take the following Oath or Affirmation: "I do solemnly swear (or affirm) that I will faithfully execute the Office of

President of the United States, and will to the best of my Ability, preserve, protect, and defend the Constitution of the United States."

Section 2. [1] The President shall be Commander in Chief of the Army and Navy of the United States, and of the militia of the several States, when called into the actual Service of the United States; he may require the Opinion, in writing, of the principal Officer in each of the Executive Departments, upon any subject relating to the Duties of their respective Offices, and he shall have Power to grant Reprieves and Pardons for Offenses against the United States, except in Cases of Impeachment.

[2] He shall have Power, by and with the Advice and Consent of the Senate to make Treaties, provided two thirds of the Senators present concur; and he shall nominate, and by and with the Advice and Consent of the Senate, shall appoint Ambassadors, other public Ministers and Consuls, Judges of the supreme Court, and all other Officers of the United States, whose Appointments are not herein otherwise provided for, and which shall be established by Law; but the Congress may by Law vest the Appointment of such inferior Officers, as they think proper, in the President alone, in the Courts of Law, or in the Heads of Departments.

[3] The President shall have Power to fill up all Vacancies that may happen during the Recess of the Senate, by granting commissions which shall expire at the End of their next Session.

Section 3. He shall from time to time give to the Congress Information of the State of the Union, and recommend to their Consideration such Measures as he shall judge necessary and expedient; he may, on extraordinary Occasions, convene both Houses, or either of them, and in Case of Disagreement between them, with Respect to the Time of Adjournment, he may adjourn them to such Time as he shall think proper; he shall receive Ambassadors and other public Ministers; he shall take Care that the Laws be faithfully executed, and shall commission all the Officers of the United States.

Section 4. The President, Vice President and all civil Officers of the United States, shall be removed from Office on Impeachment for, and Conviction of, Treason, Bribery, or other high Crimes and Misdemeanors.

Article III

Section 1. The judicial Power of the United States, shall be vested in one supreme Court, and in such inferior Courts as the Congress may from time to time ordain and establish. The Judges, both of the supreme and inferior Courts, shall hold their Offices during good Behaviour, and shall, at stated Times, receive for their Services a Compensation, which shall not be diminished during their Continuance in Office.

Section 2. [1] The judicial Power shall extend to all Cases, in Law and Equity, arising under this Constitution, the Laws of the United States, and Treaties made, or which shall be made, under their Authority;—to all Cases affecting Ambassadors, other public Ministers and Consuls;—to all Cases of admiralty and maritime Jurisdiction;—to Controversies to which the United States shall be a Party;—between a State and Citizens of another State; between Citizens of different States;—between Citizens of the same State claiming Lands under the Grants of different States, and between a State, or the Citizens thereof, and foreign States, Citizens or Subjects.

[2] In all Cases affecting Ambassadors, other public Ministers and Consuls, and those in which a State shall be a Party, the supreme Court shall have original Jurisdiction, In all the other Cases before mentioned, the supreme Court shall have appellate Jurisdiction, both as to Law and Fact, with such Exceptions, and under such Regulations as the Congress shall make.

[3] The trial of all Crimes, except in Cases of Impeachment, shall be by Jury; and such Trial shall be held in the State where the said Crimes shall have been committed; but when not committed within any State, the Trial shall be at such Place or Places as the Congress may by Law have directed.

Section 3. [1] Treason against the United States, shall consist only in levying War against them, or, in adhering to their Enemies, giving them Aid and Comfort. No Person shall be convicted of Treason unless on the Testimony of two Witnesses to the same overt Act, or on Confession in open Court.

[2] The Congress shall have Power to declare the Punishment of Treason, but no Attainder of Treason shall work Corruption of Blood, or Forfeiture except during the Life of the Person attainted.

Article IV

Section 1. Full Faith and Credit shall be given in each State to the public Acts, Records, and judicial Proceedings of every other State. And the Congress may by general Laws prescribe the Manner in which such Acts, Records and Proceedings shall be proved, and the Effect thereof.

Section 2. [1] The Citizens of each State shall be entitled to all Privileges and Immunities of Citizens in the several States.

[2] A Person charged in any State with Treason, Felony, or other Crime, who shall flee from Justice, and be found in another State, shall on demand of the executive Authority of the State from which he fled, be delivered up, to be removed to the State having Jurisdiction of the Crime.

[3] No Person held to Service or Labour in one State, under the Laws thereof, escaping into another, shall, in Consequence of any Law or Regulation therein, be discharged from such Service or Labour, but shall be delivered up on Claim of the Party to whom such Service or Labour may be due.

Section 3. [1] New States may be admitted by the Congress into this Union; but no new State shall be formed or erected within the Jurisdiction of any other State; nor any State be formed by the Junction of two or more States, or Parts of States, without the Consent of the Legislatures of the States concerned as well as of the Congress.

[2] The Congress shall have Power to dispose of and make all needful Rules and Regulations respecting the Territory or other Property belonging to the United States; and nothing in this Constitution shall be so construed as to Prejudice any Claims of the United States, or of any particular State.

Section 4. The United States shall guarantee to every State in this Union a Republican Form of Government, and shall protect each of them against Invasion; and on Application of the Legislature, or of the Executive (when the Legislature cannot be convened) against domestic Violence.

Article V

The Congress, whenever two thirds of both Houses shall deem it necessary, shall propose Amendments to this Constitution, or, on the Application of the Legislatures of two thirds of the several States, shall call a Convention for proposing Amendments, which, in either case, shall be valid to all Intents and Purposes, as part of this Constitution, when ratified by the Legislatures of three fourths of the several States, or by Conventions in three fourths thereof, as the one or the other Mode of Ratification may be proposed by the Congress; Provided that no Amendment which may be made prior to the Year One thousand eight hundred and eight shall in any Manner affect the first and fourth Clauses in the Ninth Section of the first Article; and that no State, without its Consent, shall be deprived of its equal Suffrage in the Senate.

Article VI

[1] All Debts contracted and Engagements entered into, before the Adoption of this Constitution shall be as valid against the United States under this Constitution, as under the Confederation.

[2] This Constitution, and the Laws of the United States which shall be made in Pursuance thereof; and all Treaties made, or which shall be made, under the Authority of the United States, shall be the supreme Law of the Land; and the Judges in every State shall be bound thereby, any Thing in the Constitution or Laws of any State to the Contrary notwithstanding.

[3] The Senators and Representatives before mentioned, and the Members of the several State Legislatures, and all executive and judicial Officers, both of the United States and of the several States, shall be bound by Oath or Affirmation, to support this Constitution; but no religious Test shall ever be required as a Qualification to any Office or public Trust under the United States.

Article VII

The Ratification of the Conventions of nine States shall be sufficient for the Establishment of this Constitution between the States so ratifying the Same.

Amendments

Articles in addition to, and in amendment of, the Constitution of the United States of America, proposed by Congress, *and ratified by the Legislatures of the several States pursuant to the Fifth Article of the original Constitution.*

Amendment 1 [1791]

Congress shall make no law respecting an establishment of religion, or prohibiting the free exercise thereof; or abridging the freedom of speech, or of the press; or the right of the people peaceably to assemble, and to petition the Government for a redress of grievances.

Amendment 2 [1791]

A well regulated Militia, being necessary to the security of a free State, the right of the people to keep and bear Arms, shall not be infringed.

Amendment 3 [1791]

No Soldier shall, in time of peace be quartered in any house, without the consent of the Owner, nor in time of war, but in a manner to be prescribed by law.

Amendment 4 [1791]

The right of the people to be secure in their persons, houses, papers, and effects, against unreasonable searches and seizures, shall not be violated, and no Warrants shall issue, but upon probable cause, supported by Oath or affirmation, and particularly describing the place to be searched, and the persons or things to be seized.

Amendment 5 [1791]

No person shall be held to answer for a capital, or other infamous crime, unless on a presentment or indictment of a Grand Jury, except in cases arising in the land or naval forces, or in the Militia, when in actual service in time of War or public danger; nor shall any person be subject for the same offence to be twice put in jeopardy of life or limb; nor shall be compelled in any criminal case to be a witness against himself, nor be deprived of life, liberty, or property, without due process of law; nor shall private property be taken for public use, without just compensation.

Amendment 6 [1791]

In all criminal prosecutions, the accused shall enjoy the right to a speedy and public trial, by an impartial jury of the State and district wherein the crime shall have been committed, which district shall have been previously ascertained by law, and to be informed of the nature and cause of the accusation; to be confronted with the witnesses against him; to have compulsory process for obtaining witnesses in his favor, and to have the Assistance of Counsel for his defence.

Amendment 7 [1791]

In Suits at common law, where the value in controversy shall exceed twenty dollars, the right of trial by jury shall be preserved, and no fact tried by jury, shall be otherwise re-examined in any Court of the United States, than according to the rules of common law.

Amendment 8 [1791]

Excessive bail shall not be required, nor excessive fines imposed, nor cruel and unusual punishments inflicted.

Amendment 9 [1791]

The enumeration in the Constitution, of certain rights, shall not be construed to deny or disparage others retained by the people.

Amendment 10 [1791]

The powers not delegated to the United States by the Constitution, nor prohibited by it to the States, are reserved to the States respectively, or to the people.

Amendment 11 [1798]

The Judicial power of the United States shall not be construed to extend to any suit in law or equity, commenced or prosecuted against one of the United States by Citizens of another State, or by Citizens or Subjects of any Foreign State.

Amendment 12 [1804]

The Electors shall meet in their respective states and vote by ballot for President and Vice President, one of whom, at least, shall not be an inhabitant of the same state with themselves; they shall name in their ballots the person voted for as President, and in distinct ballots the person voted for as Vice President, and they shall make distinct lists of all persons voted for as President, and of all persons voted for as Vice President, and of the number of votes for each, which lists they shall sign and certify, and transmit sealed to the seat of the government of the United States, directed to the President of the Senate;—The President of the Senate shall, in the presence of the Senate and House of Representatives, open all the certificates and the votes shall then be counted;—The person having the greatest number of votes for President, shall be the President, if such number be a majority of the whole number of Electors appointed; and if no person have such majority, then from the persons having the highest numbers not exceeding three on the list of those voted for as President, the House of Representatives shall choose immediately, by ballot, the President. But in choosing the President, the votes shall be taken by states, the representation from each state having one vote; a quorum for this purpose shall consist of a member or members from two thirds of the states, and a majority of all states shall be necessary to a choice. And if the House of Representatives shall not choose a President whenever the right of choice shall devolve upon them before the fourth day of March next following, then the Vice President shall act as President, as in the case of the death

or other constitutional disability of the President.—The person having the greatest number of votes as Vice President, shall be the Vice President, if such number be a majority of the whole number of Electors appointed, and if no person have a majority, then from the two highest numbers on the list, the Senate shall choose the Vice President; a quorum for the purpose shall consist of two thirds of the whole number of Senators, and a majority of the whole number shall be necessary to a choice. But no person constitutionally ineligible to the office of President shall be eligible to that of Vice President of the United States.

Amendment 13 [1865]

Section 1. Neither slavery nor involuntary servitude, except as a punishment for crime whereof the party shall have been duly convicted, shall exist within the United States, or any place subject to their jurisdiction.

Section 2. Congress shall have power to enforce this article by appropriate legislation.

Amendment 14 [1868]

Section 1. All persons born or naturalized in the United States, and subject to the jurisdiction thereof, are citizens of the United States and of the State wherein they reside. No State shall make or enforce any law which shall abridge the privileges or immunities of citizens of the United States; nor shall any State deprive any person of life, liberty, or property, without due process of law; nor deny to any person within its jurisdiction the equal protection of the laws.

Section 2. Representatives shall be apportioned among the several States according to their respective numbers, counting the whole number of persons in each State, excluding Indians not taxed. But when the right to vote at any election for the choice of electors for President and Vice President of the United States, Representatives in Congress, the Executive and Judicial officers of a State, or the members of the Legislature thereof, is denied to any of the male inhabitants of such State, being twenty-one years of age, and citizens of the United States, or in any way abridged, except for participation in rebellion, or other crime, the basis of representation therein shall be reduced in the proportion which the number of such male citizens shall bear to the whole number of male citizens twenty-one years of age in such State.

Section 3. No person shall be a Senator or Representative in Congress, or elector of President and Vice President, or hold any office, civil or military, under the United States, or under any State, who having previously taken an oath, as a member of Congress, or as an officer of the United States, or as a member of any State legislature, or as an executive or judicial officer of any State, to support the Constitution of the United States, shall have engaged in insurrection or rebellion against the same, or given aid or comfort to the enemies thereof. But Congress may by a vote of two thirds of each House, remove such disability.

Section 4. The validity of the public debt of the United States, authorized by law, including debts incurred for payment of pensions and bounties for services in suppressing insurrection or rebellion, shall not be questioned. But neither the United States nor any State shall assume or pay any debt or obligation incurred in aid of insurrection or rebellion against the United States, or any claim for the loss or emancipation of any slave; but all such debts, obligations and claims shall be held illegal and void.

Section 5. The Congress shall have power to enforce, by appropriate legislation, the provisions of this article.

Amendment 15 [1870]

Section 1. The right of citizens of the United States to vote shall not be denied or abridged by the United States or by any State on account of race, color, or previous condition of servitude.

Section 2. The Congress shall have power to enforce this article by appropriate legislation.

Amendment 16 [1913]

The Congress shall have power to lay and collect taxes on incomes, from whatever source derived, without apportionment among the several States, and without regard to any census or enumeration.

Amendment 17 [1913]

[1] The Senate of the United States shall be composed of two Senators from each State, elected by the people thereof, for six years; and each Senator shall have one vote. The electors in each State shall have the qualifications requisite for electors of the most numerous branch of the State legislatures.

[2] When vacancies happen in the representation of any State in the Senate, the executive authority of such State shall issue writs of election to fill such vacancies: *Provided,* That the legislature of any State may empower the executive thereof to make temporary appointments until the people fill the vacancies by election as the legislature may direct.

[3] This amendment shall not be so construed as to affect the election or term of any Senator chosen before it becomes valid as part of the Constitution.

Amendment 18 [1919]

Section 1. After one year from the ratification of this article the manufacture, sale, or transportation of intoxicating liquors within, the importation thereof into, or the exportation thereof from the United States and all territory subject to the jurisdiction thereof for beverage purposes is hereby prohibited.

Section 2. The Congress and the several States shall have concurrent power to enforce this article by appropriate legislation.

Section 3. This article shall be inoperative unless it shall have been ratified as an amendment to the Constitution by the legislatures of the several States, as provided in the Constitution, within seven years from the date of the submission hereof to the States by the Congress.

Amendment 19 [1920]

[1] The right of citizens of the United States to vote shall not be denied or abridged by the United States or by any State on account of sex.

[2] Congress shall have power to enforce this article by appropriate legislation.

Amendment 20 [1933]

Section 1. The terms of the President and Vice President shall end at noon on the twentieth day of January, and the terms of Senators and Representatives at noon on the third day of January, of the years in which such terms would have ended if this article had not been ratified; and the terms of their successors shall then begin.

Section 2. The Congress shall assemble at least once in every year, and such meeting shall begin at noon on the third day of January, unless they shall by law appoint a different day.

Section 3. If, at the time fixed for the beginning of the term of the President, the President elect shall have died, the Vice President elect shall become President. If the President shall not have been chosen before the time fixed for the beginning of his term, or if the President elect shall have failed to qualify, then the Vice President elect shall act as President until a President shall have qualified; and the Congress may by law provide for the case wherein neither a President elect nor a Vice President elect shall have qualified, declaring who shall then act as President, or the manner in which one who is to act shall be selected, and such person shall act accordingly until a President or Vice President shall have qualified.

Section 4. The Congress may by law provide for the case of the death of any of the persons from whom the House of Representatives may choose a President whenever the right of choice shall have devolved upon them, and for the case of the death of any of the persons from whom the Senate may choose a Vice President whenever the right of choice shall have devolved upon them.

Section 5. Sections 1 and 2 shall take effect on the fifteenth day of October following the ratification of this article.

Section 6. This article shall be inoperative unless it shall have been ratified as an amendment to the Constitution by the legislatures of three fourths of the several States within seven years from the date of its submission.

Amendment 21 [1933]

Section 1. The eighteenth article of amendment to the Constitution of the United States is hereby repealed.

Section 2. The transportation or importation into any State, Territory, or possession of the United States for delivery or use therein of intoxicating liquors, in violation of the laws therefore, is hereby prohibited.

Section 3. This article shall be inoperative unless it shall have been ratified as an amendment to the Constitution by conventions in the several States, as provided in the Constitution, within seven years from the date of the submission hereof to the States by the Congress.

Amendment 22 [1951]

Section 1. No person shall be elected to the office of the President more than twice, and no person who has held the office of President, or acted as President, for more than two years of a term to which some other person was elected President shall be elected to the office of President more than once. But this Article shall not apply to any person holding the office of President when this Article was proposed by the Congress, and shall not prevent any person who may be holding the office of President, or acting as President, during the term within which this Article becomes operative from holding the office of President or acting as President during the remainder of such term.

Section 2. This article shall be inoperative unless it shall have been ratified as an amendment to the Constitution by the legislatures of three fourths of the several States within seven years from the date of its submission to the States by the Congress.

Amendment 23 [1961]

Section 1. The District constituting the seat of Government of the United States shall appoint in such manner as the Congress may direct:

A number of electors of President and Vice President equal to the whole number of Senators and Representatives in Congress to which the District would be entitled if it were a State, but in no event more than the least populous state; they shall be in addition to those appointed by the states, but they shall be considered, for the purposes of the election of President and Vice President, to be electors appointed by a state; and they shall meet in the District and perform such duties as provided by the twelfth article of amendment.

Section 2. The Congress shall have power to enforce this article by appropriate legislation.

Amendment 24 [1964]

Section 1. The right of citizens of the United States to vote in any primary or other election for President or Vice President, for electors for President or Vice President, or for Senator or Representative in Congress, shall not be denied or abridged by the United States, or any State by reason of failure to pay any poll tax or other tax.

Section 2. The Congress shall have power to enforce this article by appropriate legislation.

Amendment 25 [1967]

Section 1. In case of the removal of the President from office or of his death or resignation, the Vice President shall become President.

Section 2. Whenever there is a vacancy in the office of the Vice President, the President shall nominate a Vice President who shall take office upon confirmation by a majority vote of both Houses of Congress.

Section 3. Whenever the President transmits to the President pro tempore of the Senate and the Speaker of the House of Representatives his written declaration that he is unable to discharge the powers and duties of his office, and until he transmits to them a written declaration to the contrary, such powers and duties shall be discharged by the Vice President as Acting President.

Section 4. Whenever the Vice President and a majority of either the principal officers of the executive departments or of such other body as Congress may by law provide, transmit to the President pro tempore of the Senate and the Speaker of the House of Representatives their written declaration that the President is unable to discharge the powers and duties of his office, the Vice President shall immediately assume the powers and duties of the office as Acting President.

Thereafter, when the President transmits to the President pro tempore of the Senate and the Speaker of the House of Representatives his written declaration that no inability exists, he shall resume the powers and duties of his office unless the Vice President and a majority of either the principal officers of the executive department or of such other body as Congress may by law provide, transmit within four days to the President pro tempore of the Senate and the Speaker of the House of Representatives their written declaration and the President is unable to discharge the powers and duties of his office. Thereupon Congress shall decide the issue, assembling within forty-eight hours for that purpose if not in session. If the Congress, within twenty-one days after receipt of the latter written declaration, or, if Congress is not in session, within twenty-one days after Congress is required to assemble, determines by two thirds vote of both Houses that the President is unable to discharge the powers and duties of his office, the Vice President shall continue to discharge the same as Acting President; otherwise, the President shall resume the powers and duties of his office.

Amendment 26 [1971]

Section 1. The right of citizens of the United States, who are eighteen years of age or older, to vote shall not be denied or abridged by the United States or by any State on account of age.

Section 2. The Congress shall have power to enforce this article by appropriate legislation.

Amendment 27 [1992]

No law varying the compensation for the services of Senators and Representatives shall take effect, until an election of Representatives shall have intervened.

Appendix B

Uniform Commercial Code (Articles 1, 2, 2a, and 3)

Article 1: General Provisions

Part 1: Short Title, Construction, Application and Subject Matter of the Act

§1-101. Short Title. This act shall be known and may be cited as Uniform Commercial Code.

§1-102. Purposes; Rules of Construction; Variation by Agreement.

(1) This Act shall be liberally construed and applied to promote its underlying purposes and policies.

(2) Underlying purposes and policies of this Act are
    (a) to simplify, clarify and modernize the law governing commercial transactions;
    (b) to permit the continued expansion of commercial practices through custom, usage and agreement of the parties;
    (c) to make uniform the law among the various jurisdictions.

(3) The effect of provisions of this Act may be varied by agreement, except as otherwise provided in this Act and except that the obligations of good faith, diligence, reasonableness and care prescribed by this Act may not be disclaimed by agreement but the parties may by agreement determine the standards by which the performance of such obligations is to be measured if such standards are not manifestly unreasonable.

(4) The presence in certain provisions of this Act of the words "unless otherwise agreed" or words of similar import does not imply that the effect of other provisions may not be varied by agreement under subsection (3).

(5) In this Act unless the context otherwise requires
    (a) words in the singular number include the plural, and in the plural include the singular;
    (b) words of the masculine gender include the feminine and the neuter, and when the sense so indicates words of the neuter gender may refer to any gender.

§1-103. Supplementary General Principles of Law Applicable.

Unless displaced by the particular provisions of this Act, the principles of law and equity, including the law merchant and the law relative to capacity to contract, principal and agent, estoppel, fraud, misrepresentation, duress, coercion, mistake, bankruptcy or other validating or invalidating cause shall supplement its provisions.

§1-104. Construction Against Implicity Repeal. This Act being a general act intended as a unified coverage of its subject matter, no part of it shall be deemed to be impliedly repealed by subsequent legislation if such construction can reasonably be avoided.

§1-105. Territorial Application of the Act; Parties' Power to Choose Applicable Law.

(1) Except as provided hereafter in this section, when a transaction bears a reasonable relation to this state and also to another state or nation the parties may agree that the law either of this state or of such other state or nation shall govern their rights and duties. Failing such agreement this Act applies to transactions bearing an appropriate relation to this state.

(2) Where one of the following provisions of this Act specifies the applicable law, that provision governs and a contrary agreement is effective only to the extent permitted by the law (including the conflict of laws rules) so specified:
    Rights of creditors against sold goods. Section 2-402.
    Applicability of the Article on Leases. Sections 2A-105 and 2A-106.
    Applicability of the Article on Bank Deposits and Collections. Section 4-102.
    Bulk transfers subject to the Article on Bulk Transfers. Section 6-102.
    Applicability of the Article on Investment Securities. Section 8-106.
    Perfection provisions of the Article on Secured Transactions. Section 9-103.

§1-106. Remedies to Be Liberally Administered.

(1) The remedies provided by this Act shall be liberally administered to the end that the aggrieved party may be put in as good a position as if the other party had fully performed but neither consequential or special nor penal damages may be had except as specifically provided in this Act or by other rule of law.

(2) Any right or obligation declared by this Act is enforceable by action unless the provision declaring it specifies a different and limited effect.

§1-107. Waiver or Renunciation of Claim or Right After Breach.

Any claim or right arising out of an alleged breach can be discharged in whole or in part without consideration by a written waiver or renunciation signed and delivered by the aggrieved party.

§1-108. Severability. If any provision or clause of this Act or application thereof to any person or circumstances is held invalid, such invalidity shall not affect other provisions or applications of the Act which can be given effect without the invalid provision or application, and to this end the provisions of this Act are declared to be severable.

§1-109. Section Captions. Section captions are parts of this Act.

Part 2: General Definitions and Principles of Interpretation

§1-201. General Definitions. Subject to additional definitions contained in the subsequent Articles of this Act which are applicable to specific Articles or Parts thereof, and unless the context otherwise requires, in this Act.

(1) "Action" in the sense of a judicial proceeding includes recoupment, counterclaim, set-off, suit in equity and any other proceedings in which rights are determined.

(2) "Aggrieved party" means a party entitled to resort to a remedy.

(3) "Agreement" means the bargain of the parties in fact as found in their language or by implication from other circumstances including course of dealing or usage of trade or course of performance as provided in this Act (Sections 1-205 and 2-208). Whether an agreement has legal consequences is determined by the provisions of this Act, if applicable; otherwise by the law of contracts (Section 1-103). (Compare "Contract".)

(4) "Bank" means any person engaged in the business of banking.

(5) "Bearer" means the person in possession of an instrument, document of title, or certificated security payable to bearer or indorsed in blank.

(6) "Bill of lading" means a document evidencing the receipt of goods for shipment issued by a person engaged in the business of transporting or forwarding goods, and includes an airbill. "Airbill" means a document serving for air transportation as a bill of lading does for marine or rail transportation, and includes an air consignment note or air waybill.

(7) "Branch" includes a separately incorporated foreign branch of a bank.

(8) "Burden of establishing" a fact means the burden of persuading the triers of fact that the existence of the fact is more probable than its non-existence.

(9) "Buyer in ordinary course of business" means a person who in good faith and without knowledge that the sale to him is in violation of the ownership rights or security interest of a third party in the goods buys in ordinary course from a person in the business of selling goods of that kind but does not include a pawnbroker. All persons who sell minerals or the like (including oil and gas) at wellhead or minehead shall be deemed to be persons in the business of selling goods of that kind. "Buying" may be for cash or by exchange of other property or on secured or unsecured credit and includes receiving goods or documents of title under a preexisting contract for sale but does not include a transfer in bulk or as security for or in total or partial satisfaction of a money debt.

(10) "Conspicuous": A term or clause is conspicuous when it is so written that a reasonable person against whom it is to operate ought to have noticed it. A printed heading in capitals (as: NON-NEGOTIABLE BILL OF LADING) is conspicuous. Language in the body of a form is "conspicuous" if it is in larger or other contrasting type or color. But in a telegram any stated term is "conspicuous". Whether a term or clause is "conspicuous" or not is for decision by the court.

(11) "Contract" means the total legal obligation which results from the parties' agreement as affected by this Act and any other applicable rules of law. (Compare "Agreement".)

(12) "Creditor" includes a general creditor, a secured creditor, a lien creditor and any representative of creditors, including an assignee for the benefit of creditors, a trustee in bankruptcy, a receiver in equity and an executor or administrator of an insolvent debtor's or assignor's estate.

(13) "Defendant" includes a person in the position of defendant in a cross-action or counterclaim.

(14) "Delivery" with respect to instruments, documents of title, chattel paper or certificated securities means voluntary transfer of possession.

(15) "Document of title" includes bill of lading, dock warrant, dock receipt, warehouse receipt or order for the delivery of goods, and also any other document which in the regular course of business or financing is treated as adequately evidencing that the person in possession of it is entitled to receive, hold and dispose of the document and the goods it covers. To be a document of title a document must purport to be issued by or addressed to a bailee and purport to cover goods in the bailee's possession which are either identified or are fungible portions of an identified mass.

(16) "Fault" means wrongful act, omission or breach.

(17) "Fungible" with respect to goods or securities means goods or securities of which any unit is, by nature or usage of trade, the equivalent of any other like unit. Goods which are not fungible shall be deemed fungible for the purposes of this Act to the extent that under a particular agreement or document unlike units are treated as equivalents.

(18) "Genuine" means free of forgery or counterfeiting.

(19) "Good faith" means honesty in fact in the conduct or transaction concerned.

(20) "Holder" means a person who is in possession of a document of title or a certificated instrument or an investment security drawn, issued or indorsed to him or to his order or to bearer or in blank.

(21) To "honor" is to pay or to accept and pay, or where a credit so engages to purchase or discount a draft complying with the terms of the credit.

(22) "Insolvency proceedings" includes any assignment for the benefit of creditors or other proceedings intended to liquidate or rehabilitate the estate of the person involved.

(23) A person is "insolvent" who either has ceased to pay his debts in the ordinary course of business or cannot pay his debts as they become due or is insolvent within the meaning of the federal bankruptcy law.

(24) "Money" means a medium of exchange authorized or adopted by a domestic or foreign government as part of its currency.

(25) A person has "notice" of a fact when
    (a) he has actual knowledge of it; or
    (b) he has received a notice or notification of it; or
    (c) from all the facts and circumstances known to him at the time in question he has reason to know that it exists.

A person "knows" or has "knowledge" of a fact when he has actual knowledge of it. "Discover" or "learn" or a word or phrase of similar import refers to knowledge rather than to reason to know. The time and circumstances under which a notice or notification may cease to be effective are not determined by this Act.

(26) A person "notifies" or "gives" a notice or notification to another by taking such steps as may be reasonably required to inform the other in ordinary course whether or not such other actually comes to know of it. A person "receives" a notice or notification when
    (a) it comes to his attention; or
    (b) it is duly delivered at the place of business through which the contract was made or at any other place held out by him as the place for receipt of such communications.

(27) Notice, knowledge or a notice or notification received by an organization is effective for a particular transaction from the time when it is brought to the attention of the individual conducting that transaction, and in any event from the time when it would have been brought to his attention if the organization had exercised due diligence. An organization exercises due diligence if it maintains reasonable routines for communicating significant information to the person conducting the transaction and there is reasonable compliance with the routines. Due diligence does not require an individual acting for the organization to communicate information unless such communication is part of his regular duties or unless he has reason to know of the transaction and that the transaction would be materially affected by the information.

(28) "Organization" includes a corporation, government or governmental subdivision or agency, business trust, estate, trust, partnership or association, two or more persons having a joint or common interest or any other legal or commercial entity.

(29) "Party", as distinct from "third party", means a person who has engaged in a transaction or made an agreement within this Act.

(30) "Person" includes an individual or an organization (See Section 1-102).

(31) "Presumption" or "presumed" means that the trier of fact must find the existence of the fact presumed unless and until evidence is introduced which would support a finding of its non-existence.

(32) "Purchase" includes taking by sale, discount, negotiation, mortgage, pledge, lien, issue or re-issue, gift or any other voluntary transaction creating an interest in property.

(33) "Purchaser" means a person who takes by purchase.

(34) "Remedy" means any remedial right to which an aggrieved party is entitled with or without resort to a tribunal.

(35) "Representative" includes as agent, an officer of a corporation or association, and a trustee, executor or administrator of an estate, or any other person empowered to act for another.

(36) "Rights" includes remedies.

(37) "Security interest" means an interest in personal property or fixtures which secures payment or performance of an obligation. The retention or reservation of title by a seller of goods notwithstanding shipment or delivery to the buyer (Section 2-401) is limited in effect to a reservation of a "security interest". The term also includes any interest of a buyer of accounts or chattel paper which is subject to Article 9. The special property interest of a buyer of goods on identification of those goods to a contract for sale under Section 2-401 is not a "security interest", but a buyer may also acquire a "security interest" by complying with Article 9. Unless a consignment is intended as security, reservation of title thereunder is not a "security interest", but a consignment in any event is subject to the provisions on consignment sales (Section 2-326).

Whether a transaction creates a lease or security interest is determined by the facts of each case; however, a transaction creates a security interest if the consideration the lessee is to pay the lessor for the right to possession and use of the goods is an obligation for the term of the lease not subject to termination by the lessee, and
    (a) the original term of the lease is equal to or greater than the remaining economic life of the goods,
    (b) the lessee is bound to renew the lease for the remaining economic life of the goods or is bound to become the owner of the goods,
    (c) the lessee has an option to renew the lease for the remaining economic life of the goods for no

additional consideration or nominal additional consideration upon compliance with the lease agreement, or

(d) the lessee has an option to become the owner of the goods for no additional consideration or nominal additional consideration upon compliance with the lease agreement.

A transaction does not create a security interest merely because it provides that

(a) the present value of the consideration the lessee is obligated to pay the lessor for the right to possession and use of the goods is substantially equal to or is greater than the fair market value of the goods at the time the lease is entered into,

(b) the lessee assumes risk of loss of the goods, or agrees to pay taxes, insurance, filing, recording or registration fees, or service or maintenance costs with respect to the goods,

(c) the lessee has an option to renew the lease or to become the owner of the goods,

(d) the lessee has an option to renew the lease for a fixed rent that is equal to or greater than the reasonably predictable fair market rent for the use of the goods for the term of the renewal at the time the option is to be performed, or

(e) the lessee has an option to become the owner of the goods for a fixed price that is equal to or greater than the reasonably predictable fair market value of the goods at the time the option is to be performed.

For purposes of this subsection (37):

(x) Additional consideration is not nominal if (i) when the option to renew the lease is granted to the lessee the rent is stated to be the fair market rent for the use of the goods for the term of the renewal determined at the time the option is to be performed, or (ii) when the option to become the owner of the goods is granted to the lessee the price is stated to be the fair market value of the goods determined at the time the option is to be performed. Additional consideration is nominal if it is less than the lessee's reasonably predictable cost of performing under the lease agreement if the option is not exercised;

(y) "Reasonably predictable" and "remaining economic life of the goods" are to be determined with reference to the facts and circumstances at the time the transaction is entered into; and

(z) "Present value" means the amount as of a date certain of one or more sums payable in the future, discounted to the date certain. The discount is determined by the interest rate specified by the parties if the rate is not manifestly unreasonable at the time the transaction is entered into; otherwise, the discount is determined by a commercially reasonable rate that takes into account the facts and circumstances of

each case at the time the transaction was entered into.

(38) "Send" in connection with any writing or notice means to deposit in the mail or deliver for transmission by any other usual means of communication with postage or cost of transmission provided for and properly addressed and in the case of an instrument to an address specified thereon or otherwise agreed, or if there be none to any address reasonable under the circumstances. The receipt of any writing or notice within the time at which it would have arrived if properly sent has the effect of a proper sending.

(39) "Signed" includes any symbol executed or adopted by a party with present intention to authenticate a writing.

(40) "Surety" includes guarantor.

(41) "Telegram" includes a message transmitted by radio, teletype, cable, any mechanical method of transmission or the like.

(42) "Term" means that portion of an agreement which relates to a particular matter.

(43) "Unauthorized" signature or indorsement means one made without actual, implied or apparent authority and includes a forgery.

(44) "Value". Except as otherwise provided with respect to negotiable instruments and bank collections (Sections 3-303, 4-208 and 4-209) a person gives "value" for rights if he acquires them

(a) in return for a binding commitment to extend credit or for the extension of immediately available credit whether or not drawn upon and whether or not a chargeback is provided for in the event of difficulties in collection; or

(b) as security for or in total or partial satisfaction of a pre-existing claim; or

(c) by accepting delivery pursuant to a pre-existing contract for purchase; or

(d) generally, in return for any consideration sufficient to support a simple contract.

(45) "Warehouse receipt" means a receipt issued by a person engaged in the business of storing goods for hire.

(46) "Written" or "writing" includes printing, typewriting or any other intentional reduction to tangible form. As amended 1962 and 1972.

§1-201. General Definitions *(1977 Amendments).* Subject to additional definitions contained in the subsequent Articles of this Act which are applicable to specific Articles or Parts thereof, and unless the context otherwise requires, in the Act:

* * *

(5) "Bearer" means the person in possession of an instrument, document of title or certificated security payable to bearer or indorsed in blank.

* * *

(14) "Delivery" with respect to instruments, documents of title chattel paper or certificated securities means voluntary transfer of possession.

* * *

(20) "Holder" means a person who is in possession of a document of title or an instrument or a certificated investment security drawn, issued or indorsed to him or his order or to bearer or in blank.

* * *

§1-202. Prima Facie Evidence by Third Party Documents.

A document in due form purporting to be a bill of lading, policy or certificate of insurance, official weigher's or inspector's certificate, consular invoice or any other document authorized or required by the contract to be issued by a third party shall be prima facie evidence of its own authenticity and genuineness and of the facts stated in the document by the third party.

§1-203. Obligation of Good Faith.
Every contract or duty within this Act imposes an obligation of good faith in its performance or enforcement.

§1-204. Time; Reasonable Time; "Seasonably".
(1) Whenever this Act requires any action to be taken within a reasonable time, any time which is not manifestly unreasonable may be fixed by agreement.
(2) What is a reasonable time for taking any action depends on the nature, purpose and circumstances of such action.
(3) An action is taken "seasonably" when it is taken at or within the time agreed or if no time is agreed at or within a reasonable time.

§1-205. Course of Dealing and Usage of Trade.
(1) A course of dealing is a sequence of previous conduct between the parties to a particular transaction which is fairly to be regarded as establishing a common basis of understanding for interpreting their expressions and other conduct.
(2) A usage of trade is any practice or method of dealing having such regularity of observance in a place, vocation or trade as to justify an expectation that it will be observed with respect to the transaction in question. The existence and scope of such a usage are to be proved as facts. If it is established that such a usage is embodied in a written trade code or similar writing the interpretation of the writing is for the court.
(3) A course of dealing between parties and any usage of trade in the vocation or trade in which they are engaged or of which they are or should be aware give particular meaning to and supplement or qualify terms of an agreement.
(4) The express terms of an agreement and an applicable course of dealing or usage of trade shall be construed wherever reasonable as consistent with each other; but when such construction is unreasonable express terms control both course of dealing and usage of trade and course of dealing controls usage of trade.
(5) An applicable usage of trade in the place where any part of performance is to occur shall be used in interpreting the agreement as to that part of the performance.
(6) Evidence of a relevant usage of trade offered by one party is not admissible unless and until he has given the other party such notice as the court finds sufficient to prevent unfair surprise to the latter.

§1-206. Statute of Frauds for Kinds of Personal Property not Otherwise Covered.
(1) Except in the cases described in subsection (2) of this section a contract for the sale of personal property is not enforceable by way of action or defense beyond five thousand dollars in amount or value of remedy unless there is some writing which indicates that a contract for sale has been made between the parties at a defined or stated price, reasonably identifies the subject matter and is signed by the party against whom enforcement is sought or by his authorized agent.
(2) Subsection (1) of this section does not apply to contracts for the sale of goods (Section 2-201) nor of securities (Section 8-319) nor to security agreements (Section 9-203).

§1-207. Performance or Acceptance Under Reservation of Rights.
A party who with explicit reservation of rights performs or promises performance or assents to performance in a manner demanded or offered by the other party does not thereby prejudice the rights reserved. Such words as "without prejudice", "under protest" or the like are sufficient.

§1-208. Option to Accelerate at Will.
A term providing that one party or his successor in interest may accelerate payment or performance or require collateral or additional collateral "at will" or "when he deems himself insecure" or in words of similar import shall be construed to mean that he shall have power to do so only if he in good faith believes that the prospect of payment or performance is impaired. The burden of establishing lack of good faith is on the party against whom the power has been exercised.

§1-209. Subordinated Obligations.
An obligation may be issued as subordinated to payment of another obligation of the person obligated, or a creditor may subordinate his right to payment of an obligation by agreement with either the person obligated or another creditor of the person obligated. Such a subordination does not create a security interest as against either the common debtor or a subordinated

creditor. This section shall be construed as declaring the law as it existed prior to the enactment of this section and not as modifying it. Added 1966.

   Note: *This new section is proposed as an optional provision to make it clear that a subordination agreement does not create a security interest unless so intended.*

Article 2: Sales

Part 1: Short Title, General Construction and Subject Matter

§2-101. Short Title. This Article shall be known and may be cited as Uniform Commercial Code—Sales.

§2-102. Scope; Certain Security and Other Transactions Excluded from this Article.
Unless the context otherwise requires, this Article applies to transactions in goods; it does not apply to any transaction which although in the form of an unconditional contract to sell or present sale is intended to operate only as a security transaction nor does this Article impair or repeal any statute regulating sales to consumers, farmers or other specified classes of buyers.

§2-103. Definitions and Index of Definitions.
(1) In this Article unless the context otherwise requires
   (a) "Buyer" means a person who buys or contracts to buy goods.
   (b) "Good faith" in the case of a merchant means honesty in fact and the observance of reasonable commercial standards of fair dealing in the trade.
   (c) "Receipt" of goods means taking physical possession of them.
   (d) "Seller" means a person who sells or contracts to sell goods.
(2) Other definitions applying to this Article or to specified Parts thereof, and the sections in which they appear are:
   "Acceptance". Section 2-606.
   "Banker's credit". Section 2-325.
   "Between merchants". Section 2-104.
   "Cancellation". Section 2-106(4).
   "Commercial unit". Section 2-105.
   "Confirmed credit". Section 2-325.
   "Conforming to contract". Section 2-106.
   "Contract for sale". Section 2-106.
   "Cover". Section 2-712.
   "Entrusting". Section 2-403.
   "Financing agency". Section 2-104.
   "Future goods". Section 2-105.
   "Goods". Section 2-105.
   "Identification". Section 2-501.
   "Installment contract". Section 2-612.
   "Letter of Credit". Section 2-325.
   "Lot". Section 2-105.
   "Merchant". Section 2-104.
   "Overseas". Section 2-323.
   "Person in position of seller". Section 2-707.
   "Present sale". Section 2-106.
   "Sale". Section 2-106.
   "Sale on approval". Section 2-326.
   "Sale or return". Section 2-326.
   "Termination". Section 2-106.
(3) The following definitions in other Articles apply to this Article:
   "Check". Section 3-104.
   "Consignee". Section 7-102.
   "Consignor". Section 7-102.
   "Consumer goods". Section 9-109.
   "Dishonor". Section 3-507.
   "Draft". Section 3-104.
(4) In addition Article 1 contains general definitions and principles of construction and interpretation applicable throughout this article.

§2-104. Definitions: "Merchant"; "Between Merchants"; "Financing Agency".
(1) "Merchant" means a person who deals in goods of the kind or otherwise by his occupation holds himself out as having knowledge or skill peculiar to the practices or goods involved in the transaction or to whom such knowledge or skill may be attributed by his employment of an agent or broker or other intermediary who by his occupation holds himself out as having such knowledge or skill.
(2) "Financing agency" means a bank, finance company or other person who in the ordinary course of business makes advances against goods or documents of title or who by arrangement with either the seller or the buyer intervenes in ordinary course to make or collect payment due or claimed under the contract for sale, as by purchasing or paying the seller's draft or making advances against it or by merely taking it for collection whether or not documents of title accompany the draft. "Financing agency" includes also a bank or other person who similarly intervenes between persons who are in the position of seller and buyer in respect of the goods (Section 2-707).
(3) "Between merchants" means in any transaction with respect to which both parties are chargeable with the knowledge or skill of merchants.

§2-105. Definitions: Transferability; "Goods"; "Future" Goods; "Lot"; "Commercial Unit".
(1) "Goods" means all things (including specially manufactured goods) which are movable at the time of identification to the contract for sale other than the money in which the price is to be paid, investment securities (Article 8) and things in action. "Goods" also includes the unborn young of animals and growing crops and other identified things attached to realty as described in the section on goods to be severed from realty (Section 2-107).

(2) Goods must be both existing and identified before any interest in them can pass. Goods which are not both existing and identified are "future" goods. A purported present sale of future goods or of any interest therein operates as a contract to sell.

(3) There may be a sale of a part interest in existing identified goods.

(4) An undivided share in an identified bulk of fungible goods is sufficiently identified to be sold although the quantity of the bulk is not determined. Any agreed proportion of such a bulk or any quantity thereof agreed upon by number, weight or other measure may to the extent of the seller's interest in the bulk be sold to the buyer who then becomes an owner in common.

(5) "Lot" means a parcel or a single article which is the subject matter of a separate sale or delivery, whether or not it is sufficient to perform the contract.

(6) "Commercial unit" means such a unit of goods as by commercial usage is a single whole for purposes of sale and division of which materially impairs its character or value on the market or in use. A commercial unit may be a single article (as a machine) or a set of articles (as a suite of furniture or an assortment of sizes) or a quantity (as a bale, gross, or carload) or any other unit treated in use or in the relevant market as a single whole.

§2-106. Definitions: "Contract"; "Agreement"; "Contract for Sale"; "Sale"; "Present Sale"; "Conforming" to Contract; "Termination"; "Cancellation".

(1) In this Article unless the context otherwise requires "contract" and "agreement" are limited to those relating to the present or future sale of goods. "Contract for sale" includes both a present sale of goods and a contract to sell goods at a future time. A "sale" consists in the passing of title from the seller to the buyer for a price (Section 2-401). A "present sale" means a sale which is accomplished by the making of the contract.

(2) Goods or conduct including any part of a performance are "conforming" or conform to the contract when they are in accordance with the obligations under the contract.

(3) "Termination" occurs when either party pursuant to a power created by agreement or law puts an end to the contract otherwise than for its breach. On "termination" all obligations which are still executory on both sides are discharged but any right based on prior breach or performance survives.

(4) "Cancellation" occurs when either party puts an end to the contract for breach by the other and its effect is the same as that of "termination" except that the cancelling party also retains any remedy for breach of the whole contract or any unperformed balance.

§2-107. Goods to Be Severed from Realty: Recording.

(1) A contract for the sale of minerals or the like (including oil and gas) or a structure or its materials to be removed from realty is a contract for the sale of goods within this Article if they are to be severed by the seller but until severance a purported present sale thereof which is not effective as a transfer of an interest in land is effective only as a contract to sell.

(2) A contract for the sale apart from the land of growing crops or other things attached to realty and capable of severance without material harm thereto but not described in subsection (1) or of timber to be cut is a contract for the sale of goods within this Article whether the subject matter is to be severed by the buyer or by the seller even though it forms part of the realty at the time of contracting, and the parties can by identification effect a present sale before severance.

(3) The provisions of this section are subject to any third party rights provided by the law relating to realty records, and the contract for sale may be executed and recorded as a document transferring an interest in land and shall then constitute notice to third parties of the buyer's rights under the contract for sale.

Part 2: Form, Formation and Readjustment of Contract

§2-201. Formal Requirements; Statute of Frauds.

(1) Except as otherwise provided in this section a contract for the sale of goods for the price of $500 or more is not enforceable by way of action or defense unless there is some writing sufficient to indicate that a contract for sale has been made between the parties and signed by the party against whom enforcement is sought or by his authorized agent or broker. A writing is not insufficient because it omits or incorrectly states a term agreed upon but the contract is not enforceable under this paragraph beyond the quantity of goods shown in such writing.

(2) Between merchants if within a reasonable time a writing in confirmation of the contract and sufficient against the sender is received and the party receiving it has reason to know its contents, it satisfies the requirements of subsection (1) against such party unless written notice of objection to its contents is given within ten days after it is received.

(3) A contract which does not satisfy the requirements of subsection (1) but which is valid in other respects is enforceable

(a) if the goods are to be specially manufactured for the buyer and are not suitable for sale to others in the ordinary course of the seller's business and the seller, before notice of repudiation is received and under circumstances which reasonably indicate that the goods are for the buyer, has made either a substantial beginning of their manufacture of commitments for their procurement; or

(b) if the party against whom enforcement is sought admits in his pleading, testimony or otherwise in court that a contract for sale was made, but the contract is not enforceable under this provision beyond the quantity of goods admitted; or

(c) with respect to goods for which payment has been made and accepted or which have been received and accepted (Section 2-606).

§2-202. Final Written Expression: Parol or Extrinsic Evidence.

Terms with respect to which the confirmatory memoranda of the parties agree or which are otherwise set forth in a writing intended by the parties as a final expression of their agreement with respect to such terms as are included therein may not be contradicted by evidence of any prior agreement or of a contemporaneous oral agreement but may be explained or supplemented

(a) by course of dealing or usage of trade (Section 1-205) or by course of performance (Section 2-208); and

(b) by evidence of consistent additional terms unless the court finds the writing to have been intended also as a complete and exclusive statement of the terms of the agreement.

§2-203. Seals Inoperative.
The affixing of a seal to a writing evidencing a contract for sale or an offer to buy or sell goods does not constitute the writing a sealed instrument and the law with respect to sealed instruments does not apply to such a contract or offer.

§2-204. Formation in General.

(1) A contract for sale of goods may be made in any manner sufficient to show agreement, including conduct by both parties which recognizes the existence of such a contract.

(2) An agreement sufficient to constitute a contract for sale may be found even though the moment of its making is undetermined.

(3) Even though one or more terms are left open a contract for sale does not fail for indefiniteness if the parties have intended to make a contract and there is a reasonably certain basis for giving an appropriate remedy.

§2-205. Firm Offers.
An offer by a merchant to buy or sell goods in a signed writing which by its terms gives assurance that it will be held open is not revocable, for lack of consideration, during the time stated or if no time is stated for a reasonable time, but in no event may such period of irrevocability exceed three months; but any such term of assurance on a form supplied by the offeree must be separately signed by the offeror.

§2-206. Offer and Acceptance in Formation of Contract.

(1) Unless otherwise unambiguously indicated by the language or circumstances

(a) an offer to make a contract shall be construed as inviting acceptance in any manner and by any medium reasonable in the circumstances;

(b) an order or other offer to buy goods for prompt or current shipment shall be construed as inviting acceptance either by a prompt promise to ship or by the prompt or current shipment of conforming or nonconforming goods, but such a shipment of nonconforming goods does not constitute an acceptance if the seller seasonably notifies the buyer that the shipment is offered only as an accommodation to the buyer.

(2) Where the beginning of a requested performance is a reasonable mode of acceptance an offeror who is not notified of acceptance within a reasonable time may treat the offer as having lapsed before acceptance.

§2-207. Additional Terms in Acceptance or Confirmation.

(1) A definite and seasonable expression of acceptance or a written confirmation which is sent within a reasonable time operates as an acceptance even though it states terms additional to or different from those offered or agreed upon, unless acceptance is expressly made conditional on assent to the additional or different terms.

(2) The additional terms are to be construed as proposals for addition to the contract. Between merchants such terms become part of the contract unless

(a) the offer expressly limits acceptance to the terms of the offer;

(b) they materially alter it; or

(c) notification of objection to them has already been given or is given within a reasonable time after notice of them is received.

(3) Conduct by both parties which recognizes the existence of a contract is sufficient to establish a contract for sale although the writings of the parties do not otherwise establish a contract. In such case the terms of the particular contract consist of those terms on which the writings of the parties agree, together with any supplementary terms incorporated under any other provisions of this Act.

§2-208. Course of Performance or Practical Construction.

(1) Where the contract for sale involves repeated occasions for performance by either party with knowledge of the nature of the performance and opportunity for objection to it by the other, any course of performance accepted or acquiesced in without objection shall be relevant to determine the meaning of the agreement.

(2) The express terms of the agreement and any such course of performance, as well as any course of dealing and usage of trade, shall be construed whenever reasonable as consistent with each other; but when such construction is unreasonable, express terms shall

control course of performance and course of performance shall control both course of dealing and usage of trade (Section 1-205).

(3) Subject to the provisions of the next section on modification and waiver, such course of performance shall be relevant to show a waiver or modification of any term inconsistent with such course of performance.

§2-209. Modification, Rescission and Waiver.

(1) An agreement modifying a contract within this Article needs no consideration to be binding.

(2) A signed agreement which excludes modification or recission except by a signed writing cannot be otherwise modified or rescinded, but except as between merchants such a requirement on a form supplied by the merchant must be separately signed by the other party.

(3) The requirements of the statute of frauds section of this Article (Section 2-201) must be satisfied if the contract as modified is within its provisions.

(4) Although an attempt at modification or rescission does not satisfy the requirements of subsection (2) or (3) it can operate as a waiver.

(5) A party who has made a waiver affecting an executory portion of the contract may retract the waiver by reasonable notification received by the other party that strict performance will be required of any term waived, unless the retraction would be unjust in view of a material change of position in reliance on the waiver.

§2-210. Delegation of Performance; Assignment of Rights.

(1) A party may perform his duty through a delegate unless otherwise agreed or unless the other party has a substantial interest in having his original promisor perform or control the acts required by the contract. No delegation of performance relieves the party delegating of any duty to perform or any liability for breach.

(2) Unless otherwise agreed all rights of either seller or buyer can be assigned except where the assignment would materially change the duty of the other party, or increase materially the burden or risk imposed on him by his contract, or impair materially his chance of obtaining return performance. A right to damages for breach of the whole contract or a right arising out of the assignor's due performance of his entire obligation can be assigned despite agreement otherwise.

(3) Unless the circumstances indicate the contrary a prohibition of assignment of "the contract" is to be construed as barring only the delegation to the assignee of the assignor's performance.

(4) An assignment of "the contract" or of "all my rights under the contract" or an assignment in similar general terms is an assignment of rights and unless the language or the circumstances (as in an assignment for security) indicate the contrary, it is a delegation of performance of the duties of the assignor and its acceptance by the assignee constitutes a promise by him to perform those duties. This promise is enforceable by either the assignor or the other party to the original contract.

(5) The other party may treat any assignment which delegates performance as creating reasonable grounds for insecurity and may without prejudice to his rights against the assignor demand assurances from the assignee (Section 2-609).

Part 3: General Obligation and Construction of Contract

§2-301. General Obligations of Parties.
The obligation of the seller is to transfer and deliver and that of the buyer is to accept and pay in accordance with the contract.

§2-302. Unconscionable Contract or Clause.

(1) If the court as a matter of law finds the contract or any clause of the contract to have been unconscionable at the time it was made the court may refuse to enforce the contract, or it may enforce the remainder of the contract without the unconscionable clause, or it may so limit the application of any unconscionable clause as to avoid any unconscionable result.

(2) When it is claimed or appears to the court that the contract or any clause thereof may be unconscionable the parties shall be afforded a reasonable opportunity to present evidence as to its commercial setting, purpose and effect to aid the court in making the determination.

§2-303. Allocation or Division of Risks.
Where this Article allocates a risk or a burden as between the parties "unless otherwise agreed", the agreement may not only shift the allocation but may also divide the risk or burden.

§2-304. Price Payable in Money, Goods, Realty or Otherwise.

(1) The price can be made payable in money or otherwise. If it is payable in whole or in part in goods each party is a seller of the goods which he is to transfer.

(2) Even though all or part of the price is payable in an interest in realty the transfer of the goods and the seller's obligations with reference to them are subject to this Article, but not the transfer of the interest in realty or the transferor's obligations in connection therewith.

§2-305. Open Price Term.

(1) The parties if they so intend can conclude a contract for sale even though the price is not settled. In such a case the price is a reasonable price at the time for delivery if
  (a) nothing is said as to price; or
  (b) the price is left to be agreed by the parties and they fail to agree; or

(c) the price is to be fixed in terms of some agreed market or other standard as set or recorded by a third person or agency and it is not so set or recorded.

(2) A price to be fixed by the seller or by the buyer means a price for him to fix in good faith.

(3) When a price left to be fixed otherwise than by agreement of the parties fails to be fixed through fault of one party the other may at his option treat the contract as cancelled or himself fix a reasonable price.

(4) Where, however, the parties intend not to be bound unless the price be fixed or agreed and it is not fixed or agreed there is no contract. In such a case the buyer must return any goods already received or if unable so to do must pay their reasonable value at the time of delivery and the seller must return any portion of the price paid on account.

§2-306. Output, Requirements and Exclusive Dealings.

(1) A term which measures the quantity by the output of the seller or the requirements of the buyer means such actual output or requirements as may occur in good faith, except that no quantity unreasonably disproportionate to any stated estimate or in the absence of a stated estimate to any normal or otherwise comparable prior output or requirements may be tendered or demanded.

(2) A lawful agreement by either the seller or the buyer for exclusive dealing in the kind of goods concerned imposes unless otherwise agreed an obligation by the seller to use best efforts to supply the goods and by the buyer to use best efforts to promote their sale.

§2-307. Delivery in Single Lot or Several Lots.

Unless otherwise agreed all goods called for by a contract for sale must be tendered in a single delivery and payment is due only on such tender but where the circumstances give either party the right to make or demand delivery in lots the price if it can be apportioned may be demanded for each lot.

§2-308. Absence of Specified Place for Delivery.

Unless otherwise agreed
(a) the place for delivery of goods is the seller's place of business or if he has none his residence; but
(b) in a contract for sale of identified goods which to the knowledge of the parties at the time of contracting are in some other place, that place is the place for their delivery; and
(c) documents of title may be delivered through customary banking channels.

§2-309. Absence of Specific Time Provisions; Notice of Termination.

(1) The time for shipment or delivery or any other action under a contract if not provided in this Article or agreed upon shall be a reasonable time.

(2) Where the contract provides for successive performances but is indefinite in duration it is valid for a reasonable time but unless otherwise agreed may be terminated at any time by either party.

(3) Termination of a contract by one party except on the happening of an agreed event requires that reasonable notification be received by the other party and in agreement dispensing with notification is invalid if its operation would be unconscionable.

§2-310. Open Time for Payment or Running of Credit; Authority to Ship Under Reservation.

Unless otherwise agreed
(a) payment is due at the time and place at which the buyer is to receive the goods even though the place of shipment is the place of delivery; and
(b) if the seller is authorized to send the goods he may ship them under reservation, and may tender the documents of title, but the buyer may inspect the goods after their arrival before payment is due unless such inspection is inconsistent with the terms of the contract (Section 2-513); and
(c) if delivery is authorized and made by way of documents of title otherwise than by subsection (b) then payment is due at the time and place at which the buyer is to receive the documents regardless of where the goods are to be received; and
(d) where the seller is required or authorized to ship the goods on credit the credit period runs from the time of shipment but post-dating the invoice or delaying its dispatch will correspondingly delay the starting of the credit period.

§2-311. Options and Cooperation Respecting Performance.

(1) An agreement for sale which is otherwise sufficiently definite (subsection (3) of Section 2-204) to be a contract is not made invalid by the fact that it leaves particulars of performance to be specified by one of the parties. Any such specification must be made in good faith and within limits set by commercial reasonableness.

(2) Unless otherwise agreed specifications relating to assortment of the goods are at the buyer's option and except as otherwise provided in subsections (1)(c) and (3) of Section 2-319 specifications or arrangements relating to shipment are at the seller's options.

(3) Where such specifications would materially affect the other party's performance but is not seasonably made or where one party's cooperation is necessary to the agreed performance of the other but is not seasonably forthcoming, the other party
(a) is excused for any resulting delay in his own performance; and
(b) may also either proceed to perform in any reasonable manner or after the time for a material

part of his own performance treat the failure to specify or to cooperate as a breach by failure to deliver or accept the goods.

§2-312. Warranty of Title and Against Infringement; Buyer's Obligation Against Infringement.

(1) Subject to subsection (2) there is in a contract for sale a warranty by the seller that
  (a) the title conveyed shall be good, and its transfer rightful; and
  (b) the goods shall be delivered free from any security interest or other lien or encumbrance of which the buyer at the time of contracting has no knowledge.
(2) A warranty under subsection (2) will be excluded or modified only by specific language or by circumstances which give the buyer reason to know that the person selling does not claim title in himself or that he is purporting to sell only such right or title as he or a third person may have.
(3) Unless otherwise agreed a seller who is a merchant regularly dealing in goods of the kind warrants that the goods shall be delivered free of the rightful claim of any third person by way of infringement or the like but a buyer who furnishes specifications to the seller must hold the seller harmless against any such claim which arises out of compliance with the specifications.

§2-313. Express Warranties by Affirmation, Promise, Description, Sample.

(1) Express warranties by the seller are created as follows:
  (a) Any affirmation of fact or promise made by the seller to the buyer which relates to the goods and becomes part of the basis of the bargain creates an express warranty that the goods shall conform to the affirmation or promise.
  (b) Any description of the goods which is made part of the basis of the bargain creates an express warranty that the goods shall conform to the description.
  (c) Any sample or model which is made part of the basis of the bargain creates an express warranty that the whole of the goods shall conform to the sample or model.
(2) It is not necessary to the creation of an express warranty that the seller use formal words such as "warrant" or "guarantee" or that he have a specific intention to make a warranty, but an affirmation merely of the value of the goods or a statement purporting to be merely the seller's opinion or commendation of the goods does not create a warranty.

§2-314. Implied Warranty: Merchantability; Usage of Trade.

(1) Unless excluded or modified (Section 2-316), a warranty that the goods shall be merchantable is implied in a contract for their sale if the seller is a merchant with respect to goods of that kind. Under this section the serving for value of food or drink to be consumed either on the premises or elsewhere is a sale.
(2) Goods to be merchantable must be at least such as
  (a) pass without objection in the trade under the contract description; and
  (b) in the case of fungible goods, are of fair average quality within the description; and
  (c) are fit for the ordinary purposes for which such goods are used; and
  (d) run, within the variations permitted by the agreement, of even kind, quality and quantity within each unit and among all units involved; and
  (e) are adquately contained, packaged and labeled as the agreement may require; and
  (f) conform to the promises or affirmations of fact made or the container or label if any.
(3) Unless excluded or modified (Section 2-316) other implied warranties may arise from course of dealing or usage of trade.

§2-315. Implied Warranty: Fitness for Particular Purpose.

Where the seller at the time of contracting has reason to know any particular purpose for which the goods are required and that the buyer is relying on the seller's skill or judgment to select or furnish suitable goods, there is unless excluded or modified under the next section an implied warranty that the goods shall be fit for such purpose.

§2-316. Exclusion or Modification of Warranties.

(1) Words or conduct relevant to the creation of an express warranty and words or conduct tending to negate or limit warranty shall be construed wherever reasonable as consistent with each other; but subject to the provisions of this Article on parol or extrinsic evidence (Section 2-202) negation or limitation is inoperative to the extent that such construction is unreasonable.
(2) Subject to subsection (3), to exclude or modify the implied warranty of merchantability or any part of it the language must mention merchantability and in case of a writing must be conspicious, and to exclude or modify any implied warranty of fitness the exclusion must be by a writing and conspicuous.
Language to exclude all implied warranties of fitness is sufficient if it states, for example, that "There are no warranties which extend beyond the description on the face hereof".
(3) Notwithstanding subsection (2)
  (a) unless the circumstances indicate otherwise, all implied warranties are excluded by expressions like "as is", "with all faults" or other language which in common understanding calls the buyer's attention to the exclusion of warranties and makes plain that there is no implied warranty; and
  (b) when the buyer before entering into the contract has examined the goods or the sample or model

as fully as he desired or has refused to examine the goods there is no implied warranty with regard to defects which an examination ought in the circumstances to have revealed to him; and

(c) an implied warranty can also be excluded or modified by course of dealing or course of performance or usage of trade.

(4) Remedies for breach of warranty can be limited in accordance with the provisions of this Article on liquidation or limitation of damages and on contractual modification of remedy (Sections 2-718 and 2-719).

§2-317. Cumulation and Conflict of Warranties Express or Implied.

Warranties whether express or implied shall be construed as consistent with each other and as cumulative but if such construction is unreasonable the intention of the parties shall determine which warranty is dominant. In ascertaining that intention the following rules apply:

(a) Exact or technical specifications displace an inconsistent sample or model or general language of description.

(b) A sample from an existing bulk displaces inconsistent general language of description.

(c) Express warranties displace inconsistent implied warranties other than an implied warranty of fitness for a particular purpose.

§2-318. Third Party Beneficiaries of Warranties Express or Implied.

Note: *If this Act is introduced in the Congress of the United States this section should be omitted. (States to select one alternative.)*

Alternative A—A seller's warranty whether express or implied extends to any natural person who is in the family or household of his buyer or who is a guest in his home if it is reasonable to expect that such person may use, consume or be affected by the goods and who is injured in person by breach of the warranty. A seller may not exclude or limit the operation of this section.

Alternative B—A seller's warranty whether express or implied extends to any natural person who may reasonably be expected to use, consume or be affected by the goods and who is injured in person by breach of the warranty. A seller may not exclude or limit the operation of this section.

Alternative C—A seller's warranty whether express or implied extends to any person who may reasonably be expected to use, consume or be affected by the goods and who is injured by breach of the warranty. A seller may not exclude or limit the operation of this section with respect to injury to the person of an individual to whom the warranty extends. As amended 1966.

§2-319. F.O.B. and F.A.S. Terms.

(1) Unless otherwise agreed the term F.O.B. (which means "free on board") at a named place, even though used only in connection with the stated price, is a delivery term under which

(a) when the term is F.O.B. the place of shipment, the seller must at that place ship the goods in the manner provided in this Article (Section 2-504) and bear the expense and risk of putting them into the possession of the carrier; or

(b) when the term is F.O.B. the place of destination, the seller must at his own expense and risk transport the goods to that place and there tender delivery of them in the manner provided in this Article (Section 2-503);

(c) when under either (a) or (b) the term is also F.O.B. vessel, car or other vehicle, the seller must in addition at his own expense and risk load the goods on board. If the term is F.O.B. vessel the buyer must name the vessel and in an appropriate case the seller must comply with the provisions of this Article on the form of bill of lading (Section 2-323).

(2) Unless otherwise agreed the term F.A.S. vessel (which means "free alongside") at a named port, even though used only in connection with the stated price, is a delivery term under which the seller must

(a) at his own expense and risk deliver the goods alongside the vessel in the manner usual in that port or on a dock designated and provided by the buyer; and

(b) obtain and tender a receipt for the goods in exchange for which the carrier is under a duty to issue a bill of lading.

(3) Unless otherwise agreed in any case falling within subsection (1)(a) or (c) or subsection (2) the buyer must seasonably give any needed instructions for making delivery, including when the term is F.A.S. or F.O.B. the loading berth of the vessel and in an appropriate case its name and sailing date. The seller may treat the failure of needed instructions as a failure of cooperation under this Article (Section 2-311). He may also at his option move the goods in any reasonable manner preparatory to delivery or shipment.

(4) Under the term F.O.B. vessel or F.A.S. unless otherwise agreed the buyer must make payment against tender of the required documents and the seller may not tender nor the buyer demand delivery of the goods in substitution for the documents.

§2-320. C.I.F. and C.&F. Terms.

(1) The term C.I.F. means that the price includes in a lump sum the cost of the goods and the insurance and freight to the named destination. The term C.&F. or C.F. means that the price so includes cost and freight to the named destination.

(2) Unless otherwise agreed and even though used only in connection with the stated price and destination, the term C.I.F. destination or its equivalent requires the seller at his own expense and risk to

(a) put the goods into the possession of a carrier at the port for shipment and obtain a negotiable bill or bills of lading covering the entire transportation to the named destination; and

(b) load the goods and obtain a receipt from the carrier (which may be contained in the bill of lading) showing that the freight has been paid or provided for; and

(c) obtain a policy or certificate of insurance, including any war risk insurance, of a kind and on terms then current at the port of shipment in the usual amount, in the currency of the contract, shown to cover the same goods covered by the bill of lading and providing for payment of loss to the order of the buyer or for the account of whom it may concern; but the seller may add to the price the amount of the premium for any such war risk insurance; and

(d) prepare an invoice of the goods and procure any other documents required to effect shipment or to comply with the contract; and

(e) forward and tender with commercial promptness all the documents in due form and with any indorsement necessary to perfect the buyer's rights.

(3) Unless otherwise agreed the term C.&F. or its equivalent has the same effect and imposes upon the seller the same obligations and risks as a C.I.F. term except the obligation as to insurance.

(4) Under the term C.I.F. or C.&F. unless otherwise agreed the buyer must make payment against tender of the required documents and the seller may not tender nor the buyer demand delivery of the goods in substitution for the documents.

§2-321. C.I.F. or C.&F.; "Net Landed Weights"; "Payment on Arrival"; Warranty of Condition on Arrival.

Under a contract containing a term C.I.F. or C.&F.

(1) Where the price is based on or is to be adjusted according to "net landed weights", "delivered weights", "out turn" quantity or quality or the like, unless otherwise agreed the seller must reasonably estimate the price. The payment due on tender of the documents called for by the contract is the amount so estimated, but after final adjustment of the price a settlement must be made with commercial promptness.

(2) An agreement described in subsection (1) or any warranty of quality or condition of the goods on arrival places upon the seller the risk of ordinary deterioration, shrinkage and the like in transportation but has no effect on the place or time of identification to the contract for sale or delivery or on the passing of the risk of loss.

(3) Unless otherwise agreed where the contract provides for payment on or after arrival of the goods the seller must before payment allow such preliminary inspection as is feasible; but if the goods are lost delivery of the documents and payment are due when the goods should have arrived.

§2-322. Delivery "Ex-Ship".

(1) Unless otherwise agreed a term for delivery of goods "ex-ship" (which means from the carrying vessel) or in equivalent language is not restricted to a particular ship and requires delivery from a ship which has reached a place at the named port of destination where goods of the kind are usually discharged.

(2) Under such a term unless otherwise agreed

(a) the seller must discharge all liens arising out of the carriage and furnish the buyer with a direction which puts the carrier under a duty to deliver the goods; and

(b) the risk of loss does not pass to the buyer until the goods leave the ship's tackle or are otherwise properly unloaded.

§2-323. Form of Bill of Lading Required in Overseas Shipment; "Overseas".

(1) Where the contract contemplates overseas shipment and contains a term C.I.F. or C.&F. or F.O.B. vessel the seller unless otherwise agreed must obtain a negotiable bill of lading stating that the goods have been loaded on board or, in the case of a term C.I.F. or C.&F., received for shipment.

(2) Where in a case within subsection (1) a bill of lading has been issued in a set of parts, unless otherwise agreed if the documents are not to be sent from abroad the buyer may demand tender of the full set; otherwise only one part of the bill of lading need be tendered. Even if the agreement expressly requires a full set

(a) due tender of a single part is acceptable within the provisions of this Article on cure of improper delivery (subsection (1) of Section 2-508); and

(b) even though the full set is demanded, if the documents are sent from abroad the person tendering an incomplete set may nevertheless require payment upon furnishing an indemnity which the buyer in good faith deems adequate.

(3) A shipment by water or by air on a contract contemplating such shipment is "overseas" insofar as by usage of trade or agreement it is subject to the commercial, financing or shipping practices characteristic of international deep water commerce.

§2-324. "No Arrival, No Sale" Term.
Under a term "no arrival, no sale" or terms of like meaning, unless otherwise agreed,

(a) the seller must properly ship conforming goods and if they arrive by any means he must tender them on arrival but he assumes no obligation that the goods will arrive unless he has caused the nonarrival; and

(b) where without fault of the seller the goods are in part lost or have so deteriorated as no longer to conform to the contract or arrive after the contract time, the buyer may proceed as if there had been casualty to identified goods (Section 2-613).

§2-325. "Letter of Credit" Term; "Confirmed Credit".

(1) Failure of the buyer seasonably to furnish an agreed letter of credit is a breach of the contract for sale.

(2) The delivery to seller of a proper letter of credit suspends the buyer's obligation to pay. If the letter of credit is dishonored, the seller may on seasonable notification to the buyer require payment directly from him.

(3) Unless otherwise agreed the term "letter of credit" or "banker's credit" in a contract for sale means an irrevocable credit issued by a financing agency of good repute and, where the shipment is overseas, of good international repute. The term "confirmed credit" means that the credit must also carry the direct obligation of such an agency which does business in the seller's financial market.

§2-326. Sale on Approval and Sale or Return; Consignment Sales and Rights of Creditors.

(1) Unless otherwise agreed, if delivered goods may be returned by the buyer even though they conform to the contract, the transaction is
   (a) a "sale on approval" if the goods are delivered primarily for use, and
   (b) a "sale or return" if the goods are delivered primarily for resale.

(2) Except as provided in subsection (3), goods held on approval are not subject to the claims of the buyer's creditors until acceptance; goods held on sale or return are subject to such claims while in the buyer's possession.

(3) Where goods are delivered to a person for sale and such person maintains a place of business at which he deals in goods of the kind involved, under a name other than the name of the person making delivery, then with respect to claims of creditors of the person conducting the business the goods are deemed to be on sale or return. The provisions of this subsection are applicable even though an agreement purports to reserve title to the person making delivery until payment or resale or uses such words as "on consignment" or "on memorandum". However, this subsection is not applicable if the person making delivery
   (a) complies with an applicable law providing for a consignor's interest or the like to be evidenced by a sign, or
   (b) establishes that the person conducting the business is generally known by his creditors to be substantially engaged in selling the goods of others, or
   (c) complies with the filing provisions of the Article on Secured Transactions (Article 9).

(4) Any "or return" term of a contract for sale is to be treated as a separate contract for sale within the statute of frauds section of this Article (Section 2-201) and as contradicting the sale aspect of the contract within the provisions of this Article on parol or extrinsic evidence (Section 2-202).

§2-327. Special Incidents of Sale on Approval and Sale or Return.

(1) Under a sale on approval unless otherwise agreed
   (a) although the goods are identified to the contract the risk of loss and the title do not pass to the buyer until acceptance; and
   (b) use of the goods consistent with the purpose of trial is not acceptance but failure seasonably to notify the seller of election to return the goods is acceptance, and if the goods conform to the contract acceptance of any part is acceptance of the whole; and
   (c) after due notification of election to return, the return is at the seller's risk and expense but a merchant buyer must follow any reasonable instructions.

(2) Under a sale or return unless otherwise agreed
   (a) the option to return extends to the whole or any commercial unit of the goods while in substantially their original condition, but must be exercised seasonably; and
   (b) the return is at the buyer's risk and expense.

§2-328. Sale by Auction.

(1) In a sale by auction if goods are put up in lots each lot is the subject of a separate sale.

(2) A sale by auction is complete when the auctioneer so announces by the fall of the hammer or in other customary manner. Where a bid is made while the hammer is falling in acceptance of a prior bid the auctioneer may in his discretion reopen the bidding or declare the goods sold under the bid on which the hammer was falling.

(3) Such a sale is with reserve unless the goods are in explicit terms put up without reserve. In an auction with reserve, the auctioneer may withdraw the goods at any time until he announces completion of the sale. In an auction without reserve, after the auctioneer calls for bids on an article or lot, that article or lot cannot be withdrawn unless no bid is made within a reasonable time. In either case a bidder may retract his bid until the auctioneer's announcement of completion of the sale, but a bidder's retraction does not revive any previous bid.

(4) If the auctioneer knowingly receives a bid on the seller's behalf or the seller makes or procures such a bid, and notice has not been given that liberty for such bidding is reserved, the buyer may at his option avoid the sale or take the goods at the price of the last good faith bid prior to the completion of the sale. This subsection shall not apply to any bid at a forced sale.

Part 4: Title, Creditors and Good Faith Purchasers

§2-401. Passing of Title; Reservation for Security; Limited Application of this Section.

Each provision of this Article with regard to the rights, obligations and remedies of the seller, the buyer, purchasers or other third parties applies irrespective of title to the goods except where the provision refers to such title. Insofar as situations are not covered by the other provisions of this Article and matters concerning title become material the following rules apply:

(1) Title to goods cannot pass under a contract for sale prior to their identification to the contract (Section 2-501), and unless otherwise explicitly agreed the buyer acquires by their identification a special property as limited by this Act. Any retention or reservation by the seller of the title (property) in goods shipped or delivered to the buyer is limited in effect to a reservation of a security interest. Subject to these provisions and to the provisions of the Article on Secured Transactions (Article 9), title to goods passes from the seller to the buyer in any manner and on any conditions explicitly agreed on by the parties.

(2) Unless otherwise explicitly agreed title passes to the buyer at the time and place at which the seller completes his performances with reference to the physical delivery of the goods, despite any reservation of a security interest and even though a document of title is to be delivered at a different time or place; and in particular and despite any reservation of a security interest by the bill of lading

  (a) if the contract requires or authorizes the seller to send the goods to the buyer but does not require him to deliver them at destination, title passes to the buyer at the time and place of shipment; but

  (b) if the contract requires delivery at destination, title passes on tender there.

(3) Unless otherwise explicitly agreed where delivery is to be made without moving the goods,

  (a) if the seller is to deliver a document of title, title passes at the time when and the place where he delivers such documents; or

  (b) if the goods are at the time of contracting already identified and no documents are to be delivered, title passes at the time and place of contracting.

(4) A rejection or other refusal by the buyer to receive or retain the goods, whether or not justified, or a justified revocation of acceptance revests title to the goods in the seller. Such revesting occurs by operation of law and is not a "sale".

§2-402. Rights of Seller's Creditors Against Sold Goods.

(1) Except as provided in subsections (2) and (3), rights of unsecured creditors of the seller with respect to goods which have been identified to a contract for sale are subject to the buyer's rights to recover the goods under this Article (Sections 2-502 and 2-716).

(2) A creditor of the seller may treat a sale or an identification of goods to a contract for sale as void if as against him a retention of possession by the seller is fraudulent under any rule of law of the state where the goods are situated, except that retention of possession in good faith and current course of trade by a merchant-seller for a commercially reasonable time after a sale or identification is not fraudulent.

(3) Nothing in this Article shall be deemed to impair the rights of creditors of the seller

  (a) under the provisions of the Article on Secured Transactions (Article 9); or

  (b) where identification to the contract or delivery is made not in current course of trade but in satisfaction of or as security for a pre-existing claim for money, security or the like and is made under circumstances which under any rule of law of the state where the goods are situated would apart from this Article constitute the transaction a fraudulent transfer or voidable preference.

§2-403. Power to Transfer; Good Faith Purchase of Goods; "Entrusting".

(1) A purchaser of goods acquires all title which his transferor had or had power to transfer except that a purchaser of a limited interest acquires rights only to the extent of the interest purchased. A person with voidable title has power to transfer a good title to a good faith purchaser for value. When goods have been delivered under a transaction of purchase the purchaser had such power even though

  (a) the transferor was deceived as to the identity of the purchaser, or

  (b) the delivery was in exchange for a check which is later dishonored, or

  (c) it was agreed that the transaction was to be a "cash sale", or

  (d) the delivery was procured through fraud punishable as larcenous under the criminal law.

(2) Any entrusting of possession of goods to a merchant who deals in goods of that kind gives him power to transfer all rights of the entruster to a buyer in ordinary course of business.

(3) "Entrusting" includes any delivery and any acquiescence in retention of possession regardless of any condition expressed between the parties to the delivery or acquiescence and regardless of whether the procurement of the entrusting or the possessor's disposition of the goods have been such as to be larcenous under the criminal law.

(4) The rights of other purchasers of goods and of lien creditors are governed by the Articles on Secured Transactions (Article 9), Bulk Transfers (Article 6) and Documents of Title (Article 7).

Part 5: Performance

§2-501. Insurable Interest in Goods; Manner of Identification of Goods.

(1) The buyer obtains a special property and an insurable interest in goods by identification of existing goods as goods to which the contract refers even though the goods so identified are non-conforming and he has an option to return or reject them. Such

identification can be made at any time and in any manner explicitly agreed to by the parties. In the absence of explicit agreement identification occurs
  (a) when the contract is made if it is for the sale of goods already existing and identified;
  (b) if the contract is for the sale of future goods other than those described in paragraph (c), when goods are shipped, marked or otherwise designated by the seller as goods to which the contract refers;
  (c) when the crops are planted or otherwise become growing crops or the young are conceived if the contract is for the sale of unborn young to be born within twelve months after contracting or for the sale of crops to be harvested within twelve months or the next normal harvest season after contracting, whichever is longer.
(2) The seller retains an insurable interest in goods so long as title to or any security interest in the goods remains in him and where the identification is by the seller alone he may until default or insolvency or notification to the buyer that the identification is final substitute other goods for those identified.
(3) Nothing in this section impairs any insurable interest recognized under any other statute or rule of law.

§2-502. Buyer's Right to Goods on Seller's Insolvency.
(1) Subject to subsection (2) and even though the goods have not been shipped a buyer who has paid a part or all of the price of goods in which he has a special property under the provisions of the immediately preceding section may on making and keeping good a tender of any unpaid portion or their price recover them from the seller if the seller becomes insolvent within ten days after receipt of the first installment on their price.
(2) If the identification creating his special property has been made by the buyer he acquires the right to recover the goods only if they conform to the contract for sale.

§2-503. Manner of Seller's Tender of Delivery.
(1) Tender of delivery requires that the seller put and hold conforming goods at the buyer's disposition and give the buyer any notification reasonably necessary to enable him to take delivery. The manner, time and place for tender are determined by the agreement and this Article, and in particular
  (a) tender must be at a reasonable hour, and if it is of goods they must be kept available for the period reasonably necessary to enable the buyer to take possession; but
  (b) unless otherwise agreed the buyer must furnish facilities reasonably suited to the receipt of the goods.
(2) Where the case is within the next section respecting shipment tender requires that the seller comply with its provisions.

(3) Where the seller is required to deliver at a particular destination tender requires that he comply with subsection (1) and also in any appropriate case tender documents as described in subsections (4) and (5) of this section.
(4) Where goods are in the possession of a bailee and are to be delivered without being moved
  (a) tender requires that the seller either tender a negotiable document of title covering such goods or procure acknowledgement by the bailee of the buyer's right to possession of the goods; but
  (b) tender to the buyer of a non-negotiable document of title or of a written direction to the bailee to deliver is sufficient tender unless the buyer seasonably objects, and receipt by the bailee of notification of the buyer's rights fixes those rights as against the bailee and all third persons; but risk of loss of the goods and of any failure by the bailee to honor the non-negotiable document of title or to obey the direction remains on the seller until the buyer has had a reasonable time to present the document or direction, and a refusal by the bailee to honor the document or to obey the direction defeats the tender.
(5) Where the contract requires the seller to deliver documents
  (a) he must tender all such documents in correct form, except as provided in this Article with respect to bills of lading in a set (subsection (2) of Section 2-323); and
  (b) tender through customary banking channels is sufficient and dishonor of a draft accompanying the documents constitutes non-acceptance or rejection.

§2-504. Shipment by Seller.
Where the seller is required or authorized to send the goods to the buyer and the contract does not require him to deliver them at a particular destination, then unless otherwise agreed he must
  (a) put the goods in the possession of such a carrier and make such a contract for their transportation as may be reasonable having regard to the nature of the goods and other circumstances of the case; and
  (b) obtain and promptly deliver or tender in due form any document necessary to enable the buyer to obtain possession of the goods or otherwise required by the agreement or by usage of trade; and
  (c) promptly notify the buyer of the shipment.
Failure to notify the buyer under paragraph (c) or to make a proper contract under paragraph (a) is a ground for rejection only if material delay or loss ensues.

§2-505. Seller's Shipment Under Reservation.
(1) Where the seller has identified goods to the contract by or before shipment:
  (a) his procurement of a negotiable bill of lading to his own order or otherwise reserves in him a security interest in the goods. His procurement of

the bill to the order of a financing agency or of the buyer indicates in addition only the seller's expectation of transferring that interest to the person named.

(b) a non-negotiable bill of lading to himself or his nominee reserves possession of the goods as security but except in a case of conditional delivery (subsection (2) of Section 2-507) a non-negotiable bill of lading naming the buyer as consignee reserves no security interest even though the seller retains possession of the bill of lading.

(2) When shipment by the seller with reservation of a security interest is in violation of the contract for sale it constitutes an improper contract for transportation within the preceding section but impairs neither the rights given to the buyer by shipment and identification of the goods, to the contract nor the seller's powers as a holder of a negotiable document.

§2-506. Rights of Financing Agency.

(1) A financing agency by paying or purchasing for value a draft which relates to a shipment of goods acquires to the extent of the payment or purchase and in addition to its own rights under the draft and any document of title securing it any rights of the shipper in the goods including the right to stop delivery and the shipper's right to have the draft honored by the buyer.

(2) The right to reimbursement of a financing agency which has in good faith honored or purchased the draft under commitment to or authority from the buyer is not impaired by subsequent discovery of defects with reference to any relevant document which was apparently regular on its face.

§2-507. Effect of Seller's Tender; Delivery on Condition.

(1) Tender of delivery is a condition to the buyer's duty to accept the goods and, unless otherwise agreed, to his duty to pay for them. Tender entitles the seller to acceptance of the goods and to payment according to the contract.

(2) Where payment is due and demanded on the delivery to the buyer of goods or documents of title, his right as against the seller to retain or dispose of them is conditional upon his making the payment due.

§2-508. Cure by Seller of Improper Tender or Delivery; Replacement.

(1) Where any tender or delivery by the seller is rejected because non-conforming and the time for performance has not yet expired, the seller may seasonably notify the buyer of his intention to cure and may then within the contract time make a conforming delivery.

(2) Where the buyer rejects a non-conforming tender which the seller had reasonable grounds to believe would be acceptable with or without money allowance the seller may if he seasonably notifies the buyer have a further reasonable time to substitute a conforming tender.

§2-509. Risk of Loss in the Absence of Breach.

(1) Where the contract requires or authorizes the seller to ship the goods by carrier

(a) if it does not require him to deliver them at a particular destination, the risk of loss passes to the buyer when the goods are duly delivered to the carrier even though the shipment is under reservation (Section 2-505); but

(b) if it does require him to deliver them at a particular destination and the goods are there duly tendered while in the possession of the carrier, the risk of loss passes to the buyer when the goods are there duly so tendered as to enable the buyer to take delivery.

(2) Where the goods are held by a bailee to be delivered without being moved, the risk of loss passes to the buyer

(a) on his receipt of a negotiable document of title covering the goods; or

(b) on acknowledgment by the bailee of the buyer's right to possession of the goods; or

(c) after his receipt of a non-negotiable document of title or other written direction to deliver as provided in subsection (4)(b) of Section 2-503.

(3) In any case not within subsection (1) or (2), the risk of loss passes to the buyer on his receipt of the goods if the seller is a merchant; otherwise the risk passes to the buyer on tender of delivery.

(4) The provisions of this section are subject to contrary agreement of the parties and to the provisions of this Article on sale on approval (Section 2-327) and on effect of breach on risk of loss (Section 2-510).

§2-510. Effect of Breach on Risk of Loss.

(1) Where a tender or delivery of goods so fails to conform to the contract as to give a right of rejection the risk of their loss remains on the seller until cure or acceptance.

(2) Where the buyer rightfully revokes acceptance he may to the extent of any deficiency in his effective insurance coverage treat the risk of loss as having rested on the seller from the beginning.

(3) Where the buyer as to conforming goods already identified to the contract for sale repudiates or is otherwise in breach before risk of their loss has passed to him, the seller may to the extent of any deficiency in his effective insurance coverage treat the risk of loss as resting on the buyer for a commercially reasonable time.

§2-511. Tender of Payment by Buyer; Payment by Check.

(1) Unless otherwise agreed tender of payment is a condition to the seller's duty to tender and complete any delivery.

(2) Tender of payment is sufficient when made by any means or in any manner current in the ordinary course of business unless the seller demands payment in legal tender and gives any extension of time reasonably necessary to procure it.

(3) Subject to the provisions of this Act on the effect of an instrument of an obligation (Section 3-802), payment by check is conditional and is defeated as between the parties by dishonor of the check on due presentment.

§2-512. Payment by Buyer Before Inspection.

(1) Where the contract requires payment before inspection non-conformity of the goods does not excuse the buyer from so making payment unless
    (a) the non-conformity appears without inspection; or
    (b) despite tender of the required documents the circumstances would justify injunction against honor under the provisions of this Act (Section 5-114).

(2) Payment pursuant to subsection (1) does not constitute an acceptance of goods or impair the buyer's right to inspect or any of his remedies.

§2-513. Buyer's Right to Inspection of Goods.

(1) Unless otherwise agreed and subject to subsection (3), where goods are tendered or delivered or identified to the contract for sale, the buyer has a right before payment or acceptance to inspect them at any reasonable place and time and in any reasonable manner. When the seller is required or authorized to send the goods to the buyer, the inspection may be after their arrival.

(2) Expenses of inspection must be borne by the buyer but may be recovered from the seller if the goods do not conform and are rejected.

(3) Unless otherwise agreed and subject to the provisions of this Article on C.I.F. contracts (subsection (3) of Section 3-221), the buyer is not entitled to inspect the goods before payment of the price when the contract provides
    (a) for delivery "C.O.D." or on other like terms; or
    (b) for payment against documents of title, except where such payment is due only after the goods are to become available for inspection.

(4) A place or method of inspection fixed by the parties is presumed to be exclusive but unless otherwise expressly agreed it does not postpone identification or shift the place for delivery or for passing the risk of loss. If compliance becomes impossible, inspection shall be as provided in this section unless the place or method fixed was clearly intended as an indispensable condition failure of which avoids the contract.

§2-514. When Documents Deliverable on Acceptance; When on Payment.

Unless otherwise agreed documents against which a draft is drawn are to be delivered to the drawee on acceptance of the draft if it is payable more than three days after presentment; otherwise, only on payment.

§2-515. Preserving Evidence of Goods in Dispute.

In furtherance of the adjustment of any claim or dispute
(a) either party on reasonable notification to the other and for the purpose of ascertaining the facts and preserving evidence has the right to inspect, test and sample the goods including such of them as may be in the possession or control of the other; and
(b) the parties may agree to a third party inspection or survey to determine the conformity or condition of the goods and may agree that the findings shall be binding upon them in any subsequent litigation or adjustment.

Part 6: Breach, Repudiation and Excuse

§2-601. Buyer's Rights on Improper Delivery. Subject to the provisions of this Article on breach in installment contracts (Section 2-612) and unless otherwise agreed under the sections on contractual limitations of remedy (Sections 2-718 and 2-719), if the goods or the tender of delivery fail in any respect to conform to the contract, the buyer may
(a) reject the whole; or
(b) accept the whole; or
(c) accept any commercial unit or units and reject the rest.

§2-602. Manner and Effect of Rightful Rejection.

(1) Rejection of goods must be within a reasonable time after their delivery or tender. It is ineffective unless the buyer seasonably notifies the seller.
(2) Subject to the provisions of the two following sections on rejected goods (Sections 2-603 and 2-604)
    (a) after rejection any exercise of ownership by the buyer with respect to any commercial unit is wrongful as against the seller; and
    (b) if the buyer has before rejection taken physical possession of goods in which he does not have a security interest under the provisions of this Article (subsection (3) of Section 2-711), he is under a duty after rejection to hold them with reasonable care at the seller's disposition for a time sufficient to permit the seller to remove them; but
    (c) the buyer has no further obligations with regard to goods rightfully rejected.
(3) The seller's rights with respect to goods wrongfully rejected are governed by the provisions of this Article on Seller's remedies in general (Section 2-703).

§2-603. Merchant Buyer's Duties as to Rightfully Rejected Goods.

(1) Subject to any security interest in the buyer (subsection (3) of Section 2-711), when the seller has no agent or place of business at the market of rejection a merchant buyer is under a duty after rejection of goods in his possession or control to follow any reasonable instructions received from the seller with respect to the goods and in the absence of such instructions to make reasonable efforts to sell them for the seller's account if they are perishable or

threaten to decline in value speedily. Instructions are not reasonable if on demand indemnity for expenses is not forthcoming.

(2) When the buyer sells goods under subsection (1), he is entitled to reimbursement from the seller or out of the proceeds for reasonable expenses of caring for and selling them, and if the expenses include no selling commission then to such commission as is usual in the trade or if there is none to a reasonable sum not exceeding ten percent on the gross proceeds.

(3) In complying with this section the buyer is held only to good faith and good faith conduct hereunder is neither acceptance nor conversion nor the basis of an action for damages.

§2-604. Buyer's Options as to Salvage of Rightfully Rejected Goods.

Subject to the provisions of the immediately preceding section on perishables if the seller gives no instructions within a reasonable time after notification of rejection the buyer may store the rejected goods for the seller's account or reship them to him or resell them for the seller's account with reimbursement as provided in the preceding section. Such action is not acceptance or conversion.

§2-605. Waiver of Buyer's Objections by Failure to Particularize.

(1) The buyer's failure to state in connection with rejection a particular defect which is ascertainable by reasonable inspection precludes him from relying on the unstated defect to justify rejection or to establish breach

   (a) where the seller could have cured it if stated seasonably; or

   (b) between merchants when the seller has after rejection made a request in writing for a full and final written statement of all defects on which the buyer proposes to rely.

(2) Payment against documents made without reservation of rights precludes recovery of the payment for defects apparent on the face of the documents.

§2-606. What Constitutes Acceptance of Goods.

(1) Acceptance of goods occurs when the buyer

   (a) after a reasonable opportunity to inspect the goods signifies to the seller that the goods are conforming or that he will take or retain them in spite of their non-conformity; or

   (b) fails to make an effective rejection (subsection (1) of Section 2-602), but such acceptance does not occur until the buyer has had a reasonable opportunity to inspect them; or

   (c) does any act inconsistent with the seller's ownership; but if such act is wrongful as against the seller it is an acceptance only if ratified by him.

(2) Acceptance of a part of any commercial unit is acceptance of that entire unit.

§2-607. Effect of Acceptance; Notice of Breach; Burden of Establishing Breach After Acceptance; Notice of Claim or Litigation to Person Answerable Over.

(1) The buyer must pay at the contract rate for any goods accepted.

(2) Acceptance of goods by the buyer precludes rejection of the goods accepted and if made with knowledge of a non-conformity cannot be revoked because of it unless the acceptance was on the reasonable assumption that the non-conformity would be seasonably cured but acceptance does not of itself impair any other remedy provided by this Article for non-conformity.

(3) Where a tender has been accepted

   (a) the buyer must within a reasonable time after he discovers or should have discovered any breach notify the seller of breach or be barred from any remedy; and

   (b) if the claim is one for infringement or the like (subsection (3) of Section 2-312) and the buyer is sued as a result of such a breach he must so notify the seller within a reasonable time after he receives notice of the litigation or be barred from any remedy over for liability established by the litigation.

(4) The burden is on the buyer to establish any breach with respect to the goods accepted.

(5) Where the buyer is sued for breach of a warranty or other obligation for which his seller is answerable over

   (a) he may give his seller written notice of the litigation. If the notice states that the seller may come in and defend and that if the seller does not do so he will be bound in any action against him by his buyer by any determination of fact common to the two litigations, then unless the seller after seasonable receipt of the notice does come in and defend he is so bound; or

   (b) if the claim is one for infringement or the like (subsection (3) of Section 2-312) the original seller may demand in writing that his buyer turn over to him control of the litigation including settlement or else be barred from any remedy over and if he also agrees to bear all expense and to satisfy any adverse judgment, then unless the buyer after seasonable receipt of the demand does turn over control the buyer is so barred.

(6) The provisions of subsections (3), (4) and (5) apply to any obligation of a buyer to hold the seller harmless against infringement or the like (subsection (3) of Section 2-312).

§2-608. Revocation of Acceptance in Whole or in Part.

(1) The buyer may revoke his acceptance of a lot or commercial unit whose non-conformity substantially impairs its value to him if he has accepted it

(a) on the reasonable assumption that its non-conformity would be cured and it has not been seasonably cured; or

(b) without discovery of such non-conformity if his acceptance was reasonably induced either by the difficulty of discovery before acceptance or by the seller's assurances.

(2) Revocation of acceptance must occur within a reasonable time after the buyer discovers or should have discovered the ground for it and before any substantial change in condition of the goods which is not caused by their own defects. It is not effective until the buyer notifies the seller of it.

(3) A buyer who so revokes has the same rights and duties with regard to the goods involved as if he had rejected them.

§2-609. Right to Adequate Assurance of Performance.

(1) A contract for sale imposes an obligation on each party that the other's expectation of receiving due performance will not be impaired. When reasonable grounds for insecurity arise with respect to the performance of either party the other may in writing demand adequate assurance of due performance and until he receives such assurance may if commercially reasonable suspend any performance for which he has not already received the agreed return.

(2) Between merchants the reasonableness of grounds for insecurity and the adequacy of any assurance offered shall be determined according to commercial standards.

(3) Acceptance of any improper delivery or payment does not prejudice the aggrieved party's right to demand adequate assurance of future performance.

(4) After receipt of a justified demand failure to provide within a reasonable time not exceeding thirty days such assurance of due performance as is adequate under the circumstances of the particular case is a repudiation of the contract.

§2-610. Anticipatory Repudiation.
When either party repudiates the contract with respect to a performance not yet due the loss of which will substantially impair the value of the contract to the other, the aggrieved party may

(a) for a commercially reasonable time await performance by the repudiating party; or

(b) resort to any remedy for breach (Section 2-703 or Section 2-711), even though he has notified the repudiating party that he would await the latter's performance and has urged retraction; and

(c) in either case suspend his own performance or proceed in accordance with the provisions of this Article on the seller's right to identify goods to the contract notwithstanding breach or to salvage unfinished goods (Section 2-704).

§2-611. Retraction of Anticipatory Repudiation.

(1) Until the repudiating party's next performance is due he can retract his repudiation unless the aggrieved party has since the repudiation cancelled or materially changed his position or otherwise indicated that he considers the repudiation final.

(2) Retraction may be by any method which clearly indicates to the aggrieved party that the repudiating party intends to perform, but must include any assurance justifiably demanded under the provisions of this Article (Section 2-609).

(3) Retraction reinstates the repudiating party's rights under the contract with due excuse and allowance to the aggrieved party for any delay occasioned by the repudiation.

§2-612. "Installment Contract"; Breach.

(1) An "installment contract" is one which requires or authorizes the delivery of goods in separate lots to be separately accepted, even though the contract contains a clause "each delivery is a separate contract" or its equivalent.

(2) The buyer may reject any installment which is non-conforming if the non-conformity substantially impairs the value of that installment and cannot be cured or if the non-conformity is a defect in the required documents, but if the non-conformity does not fall within subsection (3) and the seller gives adequate assurance of its cure the buyer must accept that installment.

(3) Whenever non-conformity or default with respect to one or more installments substantially impairs the value of the whole contract there is a breach of the whole. But the aggrieved party reinstates the contract if he accepts a non-conforming installment without seasonably notifying of cancellation or if he brings an action with respect only to past installments or demands performance as to future installments.

§2-613. Casualty to Identified Goods.
Where the contract requires for its performance goods identified when the contract is made, and the goods suffer casualty without fault of either party before the risk of loss passes to the buyer, or in a proper case under a "no arrival, no sale" term (Section 2-324) then

(a) if the loss is total the contract is avoided; and

(b) if the loss is partial or the goods have so deteriorated as no longer to conform to the contract the buyer may nevertheless demand inspection and at his option either treat the contract as avoided or accept the goods with due allowance from the contract price for the deterioration or the deficiency in quantity but without further right against the seller.

§2-614. Substituted Performance.

(1) Where without fault of either party the agreed berthing, loading, or unloading facilities fail or an agreed type of carrier becomes unavailable or the agreed manner of delivery otherwise becomes commercially impracticable but a commercially

reasonable substitute is available, such substitute performance must be tendered and accepted.

(2) If the agreed means or manner of payment fails because of domestic or foreign governmental regulation, the seller may withhold or stop delivery unless the buyer provides a means or manner of payment which is commercially a substantial equivalent. If delivery has already been taken, payment by the means or in the manner provided by the regulation discharges the buyer's obligation unless the regulation is discriminatory, oppressive or predatory.

§2-615. Excuse by Failure of Presupposed Conditions.

Except so far as a seller may have assumed a greater obligation and subject to the preceding section on substituted performance:

(a) Delay in delivery or non-delivery in whole or in part by a seller who complies with paragraphs (b) and (c) is not a breach of his duty under a contract for sale if performance as agreed has been made impracticable by the occurrence of a contingency the non-occurrence of which was a basic assumption on which the contract was made or by compliance in good faith with any applicable foreign or domestic governmental regulation or order whether or not it later proves to be invalid.

(b) Where the causes mentioned in paragraph (a) affect only a part of the seller's capacity to perform, he must allocate production and deliveries among his customers but may at his option include regular customers not then under contract as well as his own requirements for further manufacture. He may so allocate in any manner which is fair and reasonable.

(c) The seller must notify the buyer seasonably that there will be delay or non-delivery and, when allocation is required under paragraph (b), of the estimated quota thus made available for the buyer.

§2-616. Procedure on Notice Claiming Excuse.

(1) When the buyer receives notification of a material or indefinite delay or an allocation justified under the preceding section he may by written notification to the seller as to any delivery concerned, and where the prospective deficiency substantially impairs the value of the whole contract under the provisions of this Article relating to breach of installment contracts (Section 2-612), then also as to the whole,
   (a) terminate and thereby discharge any unexecuted portion of the contract; or
   (b) modify the contract by agreeing to take his available quota in substitution.

(2) If after receipt of such notification from the seller the buyer fails so to modify the contract within a reasonable time not exceeding thirty days the contract lapses with respect to any deliveries affected.

(3) The provisions of this section may not be negated by agreement except in so far as the seller has assumed a greater obligation under the preceding section.

Part 7: Remedies

§2-701. Remedies for Breach of Collateral Contracts not Impaired.

Remedies for breach of any obligation or promise collateral or ancillary to a contract for sale are not impaired by the provisions of this Article.

§2-702. Seller's on Discovery of Buyer's Insolvency.

(1) Where the seller discovers the buyer to be insolvent he may refuse delivery except for cash including payment for all goods theretofore delivered under the contract, and stop delivery under this Article (Section 2-705).

(2) Where the seller discovers that the buyer has received goods on credit while insolvent he may reclaim the goods upon demand made within ten days after the receipt, but if misrepresentation of solvency has been made to the particular seller in writing within three months before delivery the ten-day limitation does not apply. Except as provided in this subsection the seller may not base a right to reclaim goods on the buyer's fraudulent or innocent misrepresentation of solvency or of intent to pay.

(3) The seller's right to reclaim under subsection (2) is subject to the rights of a buyer in ordinary course or other good faith purchaser under this Article (Section 2-403). Successful reclamation of goods excludes all other remedies with respect to them. As amended 1966.

§2-703. Seller's Remedies in General.
Where the buyer wrongfully rejects or revokes acceptance of goods, or fails to make a payment due on or before delivery or repudiates with respect to a part or the whole, then with respect to any goods directly affected and, if the breach is of the whole contract (Section 2-612), then also with respect to the whole undelivered balance the aggrieved seller may
(a) withhold delivery of such goods;
(b) stop delivery by any bailee as hereafter provided (Section 2-705);
(c) proceed under the next section respecting goods still unidentified to the contract;
(d) resell and recover damages as hereafter provided (Section 2-706);
(e) recover damages for non-acceptance (Section 2-708) or in a proper case the price (Section 2-709); or
(f) cancel.

§2-704. Seller's Right to Identify Goods to the Contract Notwithstanding Breach or to Salvage Unfinished Goods.

(1) An aggrieved seller under the preceding section may
   (a) identify to the contract conforming goods not already identified if at the time he learned of the breach they are in his possession or control; or
   (b) treat as the subject of resale goods which have demonstrably been intended for the particular contract even though those goods are unfinished.

(2) Where the goods are unfinished an aggrieved seller may in the exercise of reasonable commercial judgment for the purposes of avoiding loss and of effective realization either complete the manufacture and wholly identify the goods to the contract or cease manufacture and resell for scrap or salvage value or proceed in any other reasonable manner.

§2-705. Seller's Stoppage of Delivery in Transit or Otherwise.

(1) The seller may stop delivery of goods in the possession of a carrier or other bailee when he discovers the buyer to be insolvent (Section 2-702) and may stop delivery of carload, truckload, planeload or larger shipments of express or freight when the buyer repudiates or fails to make a payment due before delivery or if for any other reason the seller has a right to withhold or reclaim the goods.

(2) As against such buyer the seller may stop delivery until
    (a) receipt of the goods by the buyer; or
    (b) acknowledgement to the buyer or by any bailee of the goods except a carrier that the bailee holds the goods for the buyer; or
    (c) such acknowledgement to the buyer by a carrier by reshipment or as warehouseman; or
    (d) negotiation to the buyer of any negotiable document of title covering the goods.

(3) (a) To stop delivery the seller must so notify as to enable the bailee by reasonable diligence to prevent delivery of the goods.
    (b) After such notification the bailee must hold and deliver the goods according to the directions of the seller but the seller is liable to the bailee for any ensuing charges or damages.
    (c) If a negotiable document of title has been issued for goods the bailee is not obliged to obey a notification to stop until surrender of the document.
    (d) A carrier who has issued a non-negotiable bill of lading is not obliged to obey a notification to stop received from a person other than the consignor.

§2-706. Seller's Resale Including Contract for Resale.

(1) Under the conditions stated in Section 2-703 on seller's remedies, the seller may resell the goods concerned or the undelivered balance thereof. Where the resale is made in good faith and in a commercially reasonable manner the seller may recover the difference between the resale price and the contract price together with any incidental damages allowed under the provisions of this Article (Section 2-710), but less expenses saved in consequence of the buyer's breach.

(2) Except as otherwise provided in subsection (3) or unless otherwise agreed resale may be at public or private sale including sale by way of one or more contracts to sell or of identification to an existing contract of the seller. Sale may be as a unit or in parcels and at any time and place and on any terms but every aspect of the sale including the method, manner, time, place and terms must be commercially reasonable. The resale must be reasonably identified as referring to the broken contract, but it is not necessary that the goods be in existence or that any or all of them have been identified to the contract before the breach.

(3) Where the resale is at private sale the seller must give the buyer reasonable notification of his intention to resell.

(4) Where the resale is at public sale
    (a) Only identified goods can be sold except where there is a recognized market for a public sale of futures in goods of the kind; and
    (b) it must be made at a usual place or market for public sale if one is reasonably available and except in the case of goods which are perishable or threaten to decline in value speedily the seller must give the buyer reasonable notice of the time and place of the resale; and
    (c) if the goods are not to be within the view of those attending the sale the notification of sale must state the place where the goods are located and provide for their reasonable inspection by prospective bidders; and
    (d) the seller may buy.

(5) A purchaser who buys in good faith at a resale takes the goods free of any rights of the original buyer even though the seller fails to comply with one or more of the requirements of this section.

(6) The seller is not accountable to the buyer for any profit made on any resale. A person in the position of a seller (Section 2-707) or a buyer who has rightfully rejected or justifiably revoked acceptance must account for any excess over the amount of his security interest, as hereinafter defined (subsection (3) of Section 2-711).

§2-707. "Person in the Position of a Seller".

(1) A "person in the position of a seller" includes as against a principal an agent who has paid or become responsible for the price of goods on behalf of his principal or anyone who otherwise holds a security interest or other right in goods similar to that of a seller.

(2) A person in the position of a seller may as provided in this Article withhold or stop delivery (Section 2-705) and resell (Section 2-706) and recover incidental damages (Section 2-710).

§2-708. Seller's Damages for Non-Acceptance or Repudiation.

(1) Subject to subsection (2) and to the provisions of this Article with respect to proof of market price (Section 2-723), the measure of damages for non-acceptance or repudiation by the buyer is the difference between the market price at the time and place for tender and the unpaid contract price together with any incidental damages provided in this Article (Section 2-710), but less expenses saved in consequence of the buyer's breach.

(2) If the measure of damages provided in subsection (1) is inadequate to put the seller in as good a position as performance would have done then the measure of damages is the profit (including reasonable overhead) which the seller would have made from full performance by the buyer, together with any incidental damages provided in this Article (Section 2-710), due allowance for costs reasonably incurred and due credit for payments or proceeds of resale.

§2-709. Action for the Price.

(1) When the buyer fails to pay the price as it becomes due the seller may recover, together with any incidental damages under the next section, the price
  (a) of goods accepted or of conforming goods lost or damaged within a commercially reasonable time after risk of their loss has passed to the buyer; and
  (b) of goods identified to the contract if the seller is unable after reasonable effort to resell them at a reasonable price or the circumstances reasonably indicate that such effort will be unavailing.

(2) Where the seller sues for the price he must hold for the buyer any goods which have been identified to the contract and are still in his control except that if resale becomes possible he may resell them at any time prior to the collection of the judgment. The net proceeds of any such resale must be credited to the buyer and payment of the judgment entitles him to any goods not resold.

(3) After the buyer has wrongfully rejected or revoked acceptance of the goods has failed to make a payment due or has repudiated (Section 2-610), a seller who is held not entitled to the price under this section shall nevertheless be awarded damages for non-acceptance under the preceding section.

§2-710. Seller's Incidental Damages.

Incidental damages to an aggrieved seller include any commercially reasonable charges, expenses or commissions incurred in stopping delivery, in the transportation, care and custody of goods after the buyer's breach, in connection with return or resale of the goods or otherwise resulting from the breach.

§2-711. Buyer's Remedies in General; Buyer's Security Interest in Rejected Goods.

(1) When the seller fails to make delivery or repudiates or the buyer rightfully rejects or justifiably revokes acceptance then with respect to any goods involved, and with respect to the whole if the breach goes to the whole contract (Section 2-612), the buyer may cancel and whether or not he has done so may in addition to recovering so much of the price as has been paid
  (a) "cover" and have damages under the next section as to all the goods affected whether or not they have been identified to the contract; or
  (b) recover damages for non-delivery as provided in this Article (Section 2-713).

(2) Where the seller fails to deliver or repudiates the buyer may also
  (a) if the goods have been identified recover them as provided in this Article (Section 2-502); or
  (b) in a proper case obtain specific performance or replevy the goods as provided in this Article (Section 2-716).

(3) On rightful rejection or justifiable revocation of acceptance a buyer has a security interest in goods in his possession or control for any payments made on their price and any expenses reasonably incurred in their inspection, receipt, transportation, care and custody and may hold such goods and resell them in like manner as an aggrieved seller (Section 2-706).

§2-712. "Cover"; Buyer's Procurement of Substitute Goods.

(1) After a breach within the preceding section the buyer may "cover" by making in good faith and without unreasonable delay any reasonable purchase of or contract to purchase goods in substitution for those due from the seller.

(2) The buyer may recover from the seller as damages the difference between the cost of cover and the contract price together with any incidental or consequential damages as hereinafter defined (Section 2-715), but less expenses saved in consequence of the seller's breach.

(3) Failure of the buyer to effect cover within this section does not ban him from any other remedy.

§2-713. Buyer's Damages for Non-Delivery or Repudiation.

(1) Subject to the provisions of this Article with respect to proof of market price (Section 2-723), the measure of damages for non-delivery or repudiation by the seller is the difference between the market price at the time when the buyer learned of the breach and the contract price together with any incidental and consequential damages provided in this Article (Section 2-715), but less expenses saved in consequence of the seller's breach.

(2) Market price is to be determined as of the place for tender or, in cases of rejection after arrival or revocation of acceptance as of the place of arrival.

§2-714. Buyer's Damages for Breach in Regard to Accepted Goods.

(1) Where the buyer has accepted goods and given notification (subsection (3) Section 2-607) he may recover as damages for any non-conformity of tender the loss resulting in the ordinary course of events from the seller's breach as determined in any manner which is reasonable.

(2) The measure of damages for breach of warranty is the difference at the time and place of acceptance between the value of the goods accepted and the value they would have had if they had been as warranted,

unless special circumstances show proximate damages of a different amount.

(3) In a proper case any incidental and consequential damages under the next section may also be recovered.

§2-715. Buyer's Incidental and Consequential Damages.

(1) Incidental damages resulting from the seller's breach include expenses reasonably incurred in inspection, receipt, transportation and care and custody of goods rightfully rejected, any commercially reasonable charges, expenses or commissions in connection with effecting cover and any other reasonable expense incident to the delay or other breach.

(2) Consequential damages resulting from the seller's breach include
(a) any loss resulting from general or particular requirements and needs of which the seller at the time of contracting had reason to know and which could not reasonably be prevented by cover or otherwise; and
(b) injury to person or property proximately resulting from any breach of warranty.

§2-716. Buyer's Right to Specific Performance or Replevin.

(1) Specific performance may be decreed where the goods are unique or in other proper circumstances.

(2) The decree for specific performance may include such terms and conditions as to payment of the price, damages, or other relief as the court may deem just.

(3) The buyer has a right of replevin for goods identified to the contract if after reasonable effort he is unable to effect cover for such goods or the circumstances reasonably indicate that such effort will be unavailing or if the goods have been shipped under reservation and satisfaction of the security interest in them has been made or tendered.

§2-717. Deduction of Damages From the Price.

The buyer on notifying the seller of his intention to do so may deduct all or any part of the damages resulting from any breach of the contact from any part of the price still due under the same contract.

§2-718. Liquidation or Limitation of Damages; Deposits.

(1) Damages for breach by either party may be liquidated in the agreement but only at an amount which is reasonable in the light of the anticipated or actual harm caused by the breach, the difficulties of proof of loss, and the inconvenience or non-feasibility of otherwise obtaining an adequate remedy. A term fixing unreasonably large liquidated damages is void as a penalty.

(2) Where the seller justifiably withholds delivery of goods because of the buyer's breach, the buyer is entitled to restitution of any amount by which the sum of his payments exceeds

(a) the amount to which the seller is entitled by virtue of terms liquidating the seller's damages in accordance with subsection (1), or
(b) in the absence of such terms, twenty percent of the value of the total performance for which the buyer is obligated under the contract or $500, whichever is smaller.

(3) The buyer's right to restitution under subsection (2) is subject to offset to the extent that the seller establishes
(a) a right to recover damages under the provisions of this Article other than subsection (1), and
(b) the amount or value of any benefits received by the buyer directly or indirectly by reason of the contract.

(4) Where a seller has received payment in goods their reasonable value or the proceeds of their resale shall be treated as payments for the purposes of subsection (2); but if the seller has notice of the buyer's breach before reselling goods received in part performance, his resale is subject to the conditions laid down in this Article on resale by an aggrieved seller (Section 2-706).

§2-719. Contractual Modification or Limitation of Remedy.

(1) Subject to the provisions of subsections (2) and (3) of this section and of the preceding section on liquidation and limitation of damages,
(a) the agreement may provide for remedies in addition to or in substitution for those provided in this Article and may limit or alter the measure of damages recoverable under this Article, as by limiting the buyer's remedies to return of the goods and repayment of the price or to repair and replacement of non-conforming goods or parts; and
(b) resort to a remedy as provided is optional unless the remedy is expressly agreed to be exclusive, in which case it is the sole remedy.

(2) Where circumstances cause an exclusive or limited remedy to fail of its essential purpose, remedy may be had as provided in this Act.

(3) Consequential damages may be limited or excluded unless the limitation or exclusion is unconscionable. Limitation of consequential damages for injury to the person in the case of consumer goods is prima facie unconscionable but limitation of damages where the loss is commercial is not.

§2-720. Effect of "Cancellation" or "Rescission" on Claims for Antecedent Breach.

Unless the contrary intention clearly appears, expressions of "cancellation" or "rescission" of the contract or the like shall not be construed as a renunciation or discharge of any claim in damages for an antecedent breach.

§2-721. Remedies for Fraud.

Remedies for material misrepresentation or fraud include all remedies available under this Article for non-fraudulent breach. Neither rescission or a claim for rescission of the contract for sale nor rejection or return of the goods shall bar or be deemed inconsistent with a claim for damage or other remedy.

§2-722. Who Can Sue Third Parties for Injury to Goods.

Where a third party so deals with goods which have been identified to a contract for sale as to cause actionable injury to a party to that contract

(a) right of action against the third party is in either party to the contract for sale who has title to or a security interest or a special property or an insurable interest in the goods; and if the goods have been destroyed or converted a right of action is also in the party who either bore the risk of loss under the contract for sale or has since the injury assumed that risk as against the other;

(b) if at the time of the injury the party plaintiff did not bear the risk of loss as against the other party to the contract for sale and there is no arrangement between them for disposition of the recovery, his suit or settlement is, subject to his own interest, as a fiduciary for the other party to the contract; and

(c) either party may with the consent of the other sue for the benefit of whom it may concern.

§2-723. Proof of Market Price: Time and Place.

(1) If an action based on anticipatory repudiation comes to trial before the time for performance with respect to some or all of the goods, any damages based on market price (Sections 2-708 or Sections 2-713) shall be determined according to the price of such goods prevailing at the time when the aggrieved party learned of the repudiation.

(2) If evidence of a price prevailing at the times or places described in this Article is not readily available the price prevailing within any reasonable time before or after the time described or at any other place which in commercial judgment or under usage of trade would serve as a reasonable substitute for the one described may be used, making any proper allowance for the cost of transporting the goods to or from such other place.

(3) Evidence of a relevant price prevailing at a time or place other than the one described in this Article offered by one party is not admissible unless and until he has given the other party such notice as the court finds sufficient to prevent unfair surprise.

§2-724. Admissibility of Market Quotations. Whenever the prevailing price or value of any goods regularly bought and sold in any established commodity market is in issue, reports in official publication or trade journals or in newspapers or periodicals of general circulation published as the reports of such market shall be admissible in evidence. The circumstances of the preparation of such a report may be shown to affect its weight but not its admissibility.

§2-725. Statute of Limitations in Contracts for Sale.

(1) An action for breach of any contract for sale must be commenced within four years after the cause of action has accrued. By the original agreement the parties may reduce the period of limitation to not less than one year but may not extend it.

(2) A cause of action accrues when the breach occurs, regardless of the aggrieved party's lack of knowledge of the breach. A breach of warranty occurs when tender of delivery is made, except that where a warranty explicitly extends to future performance of the goods and discovery of the breach must await the time of such performance the cause of action accrues when the breach is or should have been discovered.

(3) Where an action commenced within the time limited by subsection (1) is so terminated as to leave available a remedy by another action for the same breach such other action may be commenced after the expiration of the time limited and within six months after the termination of the first action unless the termination resulted from voluntary discontinuance or from dismissal for failure or neglect to prosecute.

(4) This section does not alter the law on tolling of the statute of limitations nor does it apply to causes of action which have accrued before this Act becomes effective.

Article 2A—Leases (Revised 1990)

Part 1: General Provisions

§2A-101. Short Title.—This Article shall be known and may be cited as the Uniform Commercial Code—Leases.

§2A-102. Scope.—This Article applies to any transaction, regardless of form, that creates a lease.

§2A-103. Definitions and Index of Definitions.—

(1) In this Article unless the context otherwise requires:

(a) "Buyer in ordinary course of business" means a person who in good faith and without knowledge that the sale to him [or her] is in violation of the ownership rights or security interest or leasehold interest of a third party in the goods, buys in ordinary course from a person in the business of selling goods of that kind but does not include a pawnbroker. "Buying" may be for cash or by exchange of other property or on secured or unsecured credit and includes receiving goods or documents of title under a pre-existing contract for sale but does not include a transfer in bulk or as security for or in total or partial satisfaction of a money debt.

(b) "Cancellation" occurs when either party puts an end to the lease contract for default by the other party.

(c) "Commercial unit" means such a unit of goods as by commercial usage is a single whole for purposes of lease and division of which materially impairs its character or value on the market or in use. A commercial unit may be a single article, as a machine, or a set of articles, as a suite of furniture or a line of machinery, or a quantity, as a gross or carload, or any other unit treated in use or in the relevant market as a single whole.

(d) "Conforming" goods or performance under a lease contract means goods or performance that are in accordance with the obligations under the lease contract.

(e) "Consumer lease" means a lease that a lessor regularly engaged in the business of leasing or selling makes to a lessee who is an individual and who takes under the lease primarily for a personal, family, or household purpose [if the total payments to be made under the lease contract, excluding payments for options to renew or buy, do not exceed $(WOL)].

(f) "Fault" means wrongful act, omission, breach, or default.

(g) "Finance lease" means a lease with respect to which:

(i) the lessor does not select, manufacture, or supply the goods;

(ii) the lessor acquires the goods or the right to possession and use of the goods in connection with the lease; and

(iii) one of the following occurs:

(A) the lessee receives a copy of the contract by which the lessor acquired the goods or the right to possession and use of the goods before signing the lease contract;

(B) the lessee's approval of the contract by which the lessor acquired the goods or the right to possession and use of the goods is a condition to effectiveness of the lease contract;

(C) the lessee, before signing the lease contract, receives an accurate and complete statement designating the promises and warranties, and any disclaimers of warranties, limitations or modifications of remedies, or liquidated damages, including those of a third party, such as the manufacturer of the goods, provided to the lessor by the person supplying the goods in connection with or as part of the contract by which the lessor acquired the goods or the right to possession and use of the goods; or

(D) if the lease is not a consumer lease, the lessor, before the lessee signs the lease contract, informs the lessee in writing (a) of the identity of the person supplying the goods to the lessor, unless the lessee has selected that person and directed the lessor to acquire the goods or the right to possession and use of the goods from that person, (b) that the lessee is entitled under this Article to the promises and warranties, including those of any third party, provided to the lessor by the person supplying the goods in connection with or as part of the contract by which the lessor acquired the goods or the right to possession and use of the goods, and (c) that the lessee may communicate with the person supplying the goods to the lessor and receive an accurate and complete statement of those promises and warranties, including any disclaimers and limitations of them or of remedies.

(h) "Goods" means all things that are movable at the time of identification to the lease contract, or are fixtures (Section 2A-309), but the term does not include money, documents, instruments, accounts, chattel paper, general intangibles, or minerals or the like, including oil and gas, before extraction. The term also includes the unborn young of animals.

(i) "Installment lease contract" means a lease contract that authorizes or requires the delivery of goods in separate lots to be separately accepted, even though the lease contract contains a clause "each delivery is a separate lease" or its equivalent.

(j) "Lease" means a transfer of the right to possession and use of goods for a term in return for consideration, but a sale, including a sale on approval or a sale or return, or retention or creation of a security interest is not a lease. Unless the context clearly indicates otherwise, the term includes a sublease.

(k) "Lease agreement" means the bargain, with respect to the lease, of the lessor and the lessee in fact as found in their language or by implication from other circumstances including course of dealing or usage of trade or course of performance as provided in this Article. Unless the context clearly indicates otherwise, the term includes a sublease agreement.

(l) "Lease contract" means the total legal obligation that results from the lease agreement as affected by this Article and any other applicable rules of law. Unless the context clearly indicates otherwise, the term includes a sublease contract.

(m) "Leasehold interest" means the interest of the lessor or the lessee under a lease contract.

(n) "Lessee" means a person who acquires the right to possession and use of goods under a lease. Unless the context clearly indicates otherwise, the term includes a sublessee.

(o) "Lessee in ordinary course of business" means a person who in good faith and without knowledge that the lease to him [or her] is in violation of the ownership rights or security interest or leasehold interest of a third party in the goods leases in ordinary course from a person in the business of selling or leasing goods of that kind but does not include a pawnbroker. "Leasing" may be for cash or by exchange of other property or on secured or unsecured credit and includes receiving goods or documents of title under a pre-existing lease contract but does not include a transfer in bulk or as security for or in total or partial satisfaction of a money debt.

(p) "Lessor" means a person who transfers the right to possession and use of goods under a lease. Unless the context clearly indicates otherwise, the term includes a sublessor.

(q) "Lessor's residual interest" means the lessor's interest in the goods after expiration, termination, or cancellation of the lease contract.

(r) "Lien" means a charge against or interest in goods to secure payment of a debt or performance of an obligation, but the term does not include a security interest.

(s) "Lot" means a parcel or a single article that is the subject matter of a separate lease or delivery, whether or not it is sufficient to perform the lease contract.

(t) "Merchant lessee" means a lessee that is a merchant with respect to goods of the kind subject to the lease.

(u) "Present value" means the amount as of a date certain of one or more sums payable in the future, discounted to the date certain. The discount is determined by the interest rate specified by the parties if the rate was not manifestly unreasonable at the time the transaction was entered into; otherwise, the discount is determined by a commercially reasonable rate that takes into account the facts and circumstances of each case at the time the transaction was entered into.

(v) "Purchase" includes taking by sale, lease, mortgage, security interest, pledge, gift, or any other voluntary transaction creating an interest in goods.

(w) "Sublease" means a lease of goods the right to possession and use of which was acquired by the lessor as a lessee under an existing lease.

(x) "Supplier" means a person from whom a lessor buys or leases goods to be leased under a finance lease.

(y) "Supply contract" means a contract under which a lessor buys or leases goods to be leased.

(z) "Termination" occurs when either party pursuant to a power created by agreement or law puts an end to the lease contract otherwise than for default.

(2) Other definitions applying to this Article and the sections in which they appear are:
"Accessions". Section 2A-310(1).
"Construction mortgage". Section 2A-309(1)(d).
"Encumbrance". Section 2A-309(1)(e).
"Fixtures". Section 2A-309(1)(a).
"Fixture filing". Section 2A-309(1)(b).
"Purchase money lease". Section 2A-309(1)(c).

(3) The following definitions in other Articles apply to this Article:
"Account". Section 9-106.
"Between merchants". Section 2-104(3).
"Buyer". Section 2-103(1)(a).
"Chattel paper". Section 9-105(1)(b).
"Consumer goods". Section 9-109(1).
"Document". Section 9-105(1)(f).
"Entrusting". Section 2-403(3).
"General intangibles". Section 9-106.
"Good faith". Section 2-103(1)(b).
"Instrument". Section 9-105(1)(i).
"Merchant". Section 2-104(1).
"Mortgage". Section 9-105(1)(j).
"Pursuant to commitment". Section 9-105(1)(k).
"Receipt". Section 2-103(1)(c).
"Sale". Section 2-106(1).
"Sale on approval". Section 2-326.
"Sale or return". Section 2-326.
"Seller". Section 2-103(1)(d).

(4) In addition, Article 1 contains general definitions and principles of construction and interpretation applicable throughout this Article. As amended in 1990.

§2A-104. Leases Subject to Other Law.—

(1) A lease, although subject to this Article, is also subject to any applicable:
  (a) certificate of title statute of this State: (list any certificate of title statutes covering automobiles, trailers, mobile homes, boats, farm tractors, and the like);
  (b) certificate of title statute of another jurisdiction (Section 2A-105); or
  (c) consumer protection statute of this State, or final consumer protection decision of a court of this State existing on the effective date of this Article.

(2) In case of conflict between this Article, other than Sections 2A-105, 2A-304(3), and 2A-305(3), and a statute or decision referred to in subsection (1), the statute or decision controls.

(3) Failure to comply with an applicable law has only the effect specified therein.

§2A-105. Territorial Application of Article to Goods Covered by Certificate of Title.—

Subject to the provisions of Sections 2A-304(3) and 2A-305(3), with respect to goods covered by a certificate of title issued under a statute of this State or of another jurisdiction, compliance and the effect of compliance or noncompliance with a certificate of title statute are governed by the law (including the conflict of laws rules) of the jurisdiction issuing the certificate until the earlier of (a) surrender of the certificate, or (b) four months after the goods are removed from that jurisdiction and thereafter until a new certificate of title is issued by another jurisdiction.

§2A-106. Limitation on Power of Parties to Consumer Lease to Choose Applicable Law and Judicial Forum.—

(1) If the law chosen by the parties to a consumer lease is that of a jurisdiction other than a jurisdiction in which the lessee resides at the time the lease agreement becomes enforceable or within 30 days thereafter or in which the goods are to be used, the choice is not enforceable.

(2) If the judicial forum chosen by the parties to a consumer lease is a forum that would not otherwise have jurisdiction over the lessee, the choice is not enforceable.

§2A-107. Waiver or Renunciation of Claim or Right After Default.—

Any claim or right arising out of an alleged default or breach of warranty may be discharged in whole or in part without consideration by a written waiver or renunciation signed and delivered by the aggrieved party.

§2A-108. Unconscionability.—

(1) If the court as a matter of law finds a lease contract or any clause of a lease contract to have been unconscionable at the time it was made the court may refuse to enforce the lease contract, or it may enforce the remainder of the lease contract without the unconscionable clause, or it may so limit the application of any unconscionable clause as to avoid any unconscionable result.

(2) With respect to a consumer lease, if the court as a matter of law finds that a lease contract or any clause of a lease contract has been induced by unconscionable conduct or that unconscionable conduct has occurred in the collection of a claim arising from a lease contract, the court may grant appropriate relief.

(3) Before making a finding of unconscionability under subsection (1) or (2), the court, on its own motion or that of a party, shall afford the parties a reasonable opportunity to present evidence as to the setting, purpose, and effect of the lease contract or clause thereof, or of the conduct.

(4) In an action in which the lessee claims unconscionability with respect to a consumer lease:
    (a) If the court finds unconscionability under subsection (1) or (2), the court shall award reasonable attorney's fees to the lessee.
    (b) If the court does not find unconscionability and the lessee claiming unconscionability has brought or maintained an action he [or she] knew to be groundless, the court shall award reasonable attorney's fees to the party against whom the claim is made.

(c) In determining attorney's fees, the amount of the recovery on behalf of the claimant under subsections (1) and (2) is not controlling.

§2A-109. Option to Accelerate at Will.—

(1) A term providing that one party or his [or her] successor in interest may accelerate payment or performance or require collateral or additional collateral "at will" or "when he [or she] deems himself [or herself] insecure" or in words of similar import must be construed to mean that he [or she] has power to do so only if he [or she] in good faith believes that the prospect of payment or performance is impaired.

(2) With respect to a consumer lease, the burden of establishing good faith under subsection (1) is on the party who exercised the power; otherwise the burden of establishing lack of good faith is on the party against whom the power has been exercised.

Part 2: Formation and Construction of Lease Contract

§2A-201. Statute of Frauds.—

(1) A lease contract is not enforceable by way of action or defense unless:
    (a) the total payments to be made under the lease contract, excluding payments for options to renew or buy, are less than $1,000; or
    (b) there is a writing, signed by the party against whom enforcement is sought or by that party's authorized agent, sufficient to indicate that a lease contract has been made between the parties and to describe the goods leased and the lease term.

(2) Any description of leased goods or of the lease term is sufficient and satisfies subsection (1)(b), whether or not it is specific, if it reasonably identifies what is described.

(3) A writing is not insufficient because it omits or incorrectly states a term agreed upon, but the lease contract is not enforceable under subsection (1)(b) beyond the lease term and the quantity of goods shown in the writing.

(4) A lease contract that does not satisfy the requirements of subsection (1), but which is valid in other respects, is enforceable:
    (a) if the goods are to be specifically manufactured or obtained for the lessee and are not suitable for lease or sale to others in the ordinary course of the lessor's business, and the lessor, before notice of repudiation is received and under circumstances that reasonably indicate that the goods are for the lessee, has made either a substantial beginning of their manufacture or commitments for their procurement;
    (b) if the party against whom enforcement is sought admits in that party's pleading, testimony or otherwise in court that: a lease contract was made, but

the lease contract is not enforceable under this provision beyond the quantity of goods admitted; or

(c) with respect to goods that have been received and accepted by the lessee.

(5) The lease term under a lease contract referred to in subsection (4) is:

(a) if there is a writing signed by the party against whom enforcement is sought or by that party's authorized agent specifying the lease term, the term so specified;

(b) if the party against whom enforcement is sought admits in that party's pleading, testimony, or otherwise in court a lease term, the term so admitted; or

(c) a reasonable lease term.

§2A-202. Final Written Expression: Parol or Extrinsic Evidence.—

Terms with respect to which the confirmatory memoranda of the parties agree or which are otherwise set forth in a writing intended by the parties as a final expression of their agreement with respect to such terms as are included therein may not be contradicted by evidence of any prior agreement or of a contemporaneous oral agreement but may be explained or supplemented:

(a) by course of dealing or usage of trade or by course of performance; and

(b) by evidence of consistent additional terms unless the court finds the writing to have been intended also as a complete and exclusive statement of the terms of the agreement.

§2A-203. Seals Inoperative.—The affixing of a seal to a writing evidencing a lease contract or an offer to enter into a lease contract does not render the writing a sealed instrument and the law with respect to sealed instruments does not apply to the lease contract or offer.

§2A-204. Formation in General.—

(1) A lease contract may be made in any manner sufficient to show agreement, including conduct by both parties which recognizes the existence of a lease contract.

(2) An agreement sufficient to constitute a lease contract may be found although the moment of its making is undetermined.

(3) Although one or more terms are left open, a lease contract does not fail for indefiniteness if the parties have intended to make a lease contract and there is a reasonably certain basis for giving an appropriate remedy.

§2A-205. Firm Offers.—An offer by a merchant to lease goods to or from another person in a signed writing that by its terms gives assurance it will be held open is not revocable, for lack of consideration, during the time stated or, if no time is stated, for a reasonable time, but in no event may the period of irrevocability exceed 3 months. Any such term of assurance on a form supplied by the offeree must be separately signed by the offeror.

§2A-206. Offer and Acceptance in Formation of Lease Contract.—

(1) Unless otherwise unambiguously indicated by the language or circumstances, an offer to make a lease contract must be construed as inviting acceptance in any manner and by any medium reasonable in the circumstances.

(2) If the beginning of a requested performance is a reasonable mode of acceptance, an offeror who is not notified of acceptance within a reasonable time may treat the offer as having lapsed before acceptance.

§2A-207. Course of Performance or Practical Construction.—

(1) If a lease contract involves repeated occasions for performance by either party with knowledge of the nature of the performance and opportunity for objection to it by the other, any course of performance accepted or acquiesced in without objection is relevant to determine the meaning of the lease agreement.

(2) The express terms of a lease agreement and any course of performance, as well as any course of dealing and usage of trade, must be construed whenever reasonable as consistent with each other; but if that construction is unreasonable, express terms control course of performance, course of performance controls both course of dealing and usage of trade, and course of dealing controls usage of trade.

(3) Subject to the provisions of Section 2A-208 on modification and waiver, course of performance is relevant to show a waiver or modification of any term inconsistent with the course of performance.

§2A-208. Modification, Rescission and Waiver.—

(1) An agreement modifying a lease contract needs no consideration to be binding.

(2) A signed lease agreement that excludes modification or rescission except by a signed writing may not be otherwise modified or rescinded, but, except as between merchants, such a requirement on a form supplied by a merchant must be separately signed by the other party.

(3) Although an attempt at modification or rescission does not satisfy the requirements of subsection (2), it may operate as a waiver.

(4) A party who has made a waiver affecting an executory portion of a lease contract may retract the waiver by reasonable notification received by the other party that strict performance will be required of any term waived, unless the retraction would be unjust in view of a material change of position in reliance on the waiver.

§2A-209. Lessee Under Finance Lease as Beneficiary of Supply Contract.—

(1) The benefit of a supplier's promises to the lessor under the supply contract and of all warranties, whether

express or implied, including those of any third party provided in connection with or as part of the supply contract, extends to the lessee to the extent of the lessee's leasehold interest under a finance lease related to the supply contract, but is subject to the terms of the warranty and of the supply contract and all defenses or claims arising therefrom.

(2) The extension of the benefit of a supplier's promises and of warranties to the lessee (Section 2A-209(1)) does not: (i) modify the rights and obligations of the parties to the supply contract, whether arising therefrom or otherwise, or (ii) impose any duty or liability under the supply contract on the lessee.

(3) Any modification or rescission of the supply contract by the supplier and the lessor is effective between the supplier and the lessee unless, before the modification or rescission, the supplier has received notice that the lessee has entered into a finance lease related to the supply contract. If the modification or rescission is effective between the supplier and the lessee, the lessor is deemed to have assumed, in addition to the obligations of the lessor to the lessee under the lease contract, promises of the supplier to the lessor and warranties that were so modified or rescinded as they existed and were available to the lessee before modification or rescission.

(4) In addition to the extension of the benefit of the supplier's promises and of warranties to the lessee under subsection (1), the lessee retains all rights that the lessee may have against the supplier which arise from an agreement between the lessee and the supplier or under other law.

§2A-210. Express Warranties.—

(1) Express warranties by the lessor are created as follows:
   (a) Any affirmation of fact or promise made by the lessor to the lessee which relates to the goods and becomes part of the basis of the bargain creates an express warranty that the goods will conform to the affirmation or promise.
   (b) Any description of the goods which is made part of the basis of the bargain creates an express warranty that the goods will conform to the description.
   (c) Any sample or model that is made part of the basis of the bargain creates an express warranty that the whole of the goods will conform to the sample or model.

(2) It is not necessary to the creation of an express warranty that the lessor use formal words, such as "warrant" or "guarantee", or that the lessor have a specific intention to make a warranty, but an affirmation merely of the value of the goods or a statement purporting to be merely the lessor's opinion or commendation of the goods does not create a warranty.

§2A-211. Warranties Against Interference and Against Infringement; Lessee's Obligation Against Infringement.—

(1) There is in a lease contract a warranty that for the lease term no person holds a claim to or interest in the goods that arose from an act or omission of the lessor, other than a claim by way of infringement or the like, which will interfere with the lessee's enjoyment of its leasehold interest.

(2) Except in a finance lease there is in a lease contract by a lessor who is a merchant regularly dealing in goods of the kind a warranty that the goods are delivered free of the rightful claim of any person by way of infringement or the like.

(3) A lessee who furnishes specifications to a lessor or a supplier shall hold the lessor and the supplier harmless against any claim by way of infringement or the like that arises out of compliance with the specifications.

§2A-212. Implied Warranty of Merchantability.—

(1) Except in a finance lease, a warranty that the goods will be merchantable is implied in a lease contract if the lessor is a merchant with respect to goods of that kind.

(2) Goods to be merchantable must be at least such as
   (a) pass without objection in the trade under the description in the lease agreement;
   (b) in the case of fungible goods, are of fair average quality within the description;
   (c) are fit for the ordinary purposes for which goods of that type are used;
   (d) run, within the variation permitted by the lease agreement, of even kind, quality, and quantity within each unit and among all units involved;
   (e) are adequately contained, packaged, and labeled as the lease agreement may require; and
   (f) conform to any promises or affirmations of fact made on the container or label.

(3) Other implied warranties may arise from course of dealing or usage of trade.

§2A-213. Implied Warranty of Fitness for Particular Purpose.—

Except in a finance lease, if the lessor at the time the lease contract is made has reason to know of any particular purpose for which the goods are required and that the lessee is relying on the lessor's skill or judgment to select or furnish suitable goods, there is in the lease contract an implied warranty that the goods will be fit for that purpose.

§2A-214. Exclusion or Modification of Warranties.—

(1) Words or conduct relevant to the creation of an express warranty and words or conduct tending to negate or limit a warranty must be construed wherever reasonable as consistent with each other; but, subject to the provisions of Section 2A-202 on parol or extrinsic evidence, negation or limitation is inoperative to the extent that the construction is unreasonable.

(2) Subject to subsection (3), to exclude or modify the implied warranty of merchantability or any part of it the language must mention "merchantability", be by a writing, and be conspicuous. Subject to subsection (3), to exclude or modify any implied warranty of fitness the exclusion must be by a writing and be conspicuous. Language to exclude all implied warranties of fitness is sufficient if it is in writing, is conspicuous and states, for example, "There is no warranty that the goods will be fit for a particular purpose".

(3) Notwithstanding subsection (2), but subject to subsection (4),

(a) unless the circumstances indicate otherwise, all implied warranties are excluded by expressions like "as is", or "with all faults", or by other language that in common understanding calls the lessee's attention to the exclusion of warranties and makes plain that there is no implied warranty, if in writing and conspicuous;

(b) if the lessee before entering into the lease contract has examined the goods or the sample or model as fully as desired or has refused to examine the goods, there is no implied warranty with regard to defects that an examination ought in the circumstances to have revealed; and

(c) an implied warranty may also be excluded or modified by course of dealing, course of performance, or usage of trade.

(4) To exclude or modify a warranty against interference or against infringement (Section 2A-211) or any part of it, the language must be specific, be by a writing, and be conspicuous, unless the circumstances, including course of performance, course of dealing, or usage of trade, give the lessee reason to know that the goods are being leased subject to a claim or interest of any person.

§2A-215. Cumulation and Conflict of Warranties Express or Implied.—

Warranties, whether express or implied, must be construed as consistent with each other and as cumulative, but if that construction is unreasonable, the intention of the parties determines which warranty is dominant. In ascertaining that intention the following rules apply:

(a) Exact or technical specifications displace an inconsistent sample or model or general language of description.

(b) A sample from an existing bulk displaces inconsistent general language of description.

(c) Express warranties displace inconsistent implied warranties other than an implied warranty of fitness for a particular purpose.

§2A-216. Third-Party Beneficiaries of Express and Implied Warranties.—

Alternative A—A warranty to or for the benefit of a lessee under this Article, whether express or implied, extends to any natural person who is in the family or household of the lessee or who is a guest in the lessee's home if it is reasonable to expect that such person may use, consume, or be affected by the goods and who is injured in person by breach of the warranty. This section does not displace principles of law and equity that extend a warranty to or for the benefit of a lessee to other persons. The operation of this section may not be excluded, modified, or limited, but an exclusion, modification, or limitation of the warranty, including any with respect to rights and remedies, effective against the lessee is also effective against any beneficiary designated under this section.

Alternative B—A warranty to or for the benefit of a lessee under this Article, whether express or implied, extends to any natural person who may reasonably be expected to use, consume, or be affected by the goods and who is injured in person by breach of the warranty. This section does not displace principles of law and equity that extend a warranty to or for the benefit of a lessee to other persons. The operation of this section may not be excluded, modified, or limited, but an exclusion, modification, or limitation of the warranty, including any with respect to rights and remedies, effective against the lessee is also effective against the beneficiary designated under this section.

Alternative C—A warranty to or for the benefit of a lessee under this Article, whether express or implied, extends to any person who may reasonably be expected to use, consume, or be affected by the goods and who is injured by breach of the warranty. The operation of this section may not be excluded, modified, or limited with respect to injury to the person of an individual to whom the warranty extends, but an exclusion, modification, or limitation of the warranty, including any with respect to rights and remedies, effective against the lessee is also effective against the beneficiary designated under this section.

§2A-217. Identification.—

Identification of goods as goods to which a lease contract refers may be made at any time and in any manner explicitly agreed to by the parties. In the absence of explicit agreement, identification occurs:

(a) when the lease contract is made if the lease contract is for a lease of goods that are existing and identified;

(b) when the goods are shipped, marked, or otherwise designated by the lessor as goods to which the lease contract refers, if the lease contract is for a lease of goods that are not existing and identified; or

(c) when the young are conceived, if the lease contract is for a lease of unborn young of animals.

§2A-218. Insurance and Proceeds.—

(1) A lessee obtains an insurable interest when existing goods are identified to the lease contract even though the goods identified are nonconforming and the lessee has an option to reject them.

(2) If a lessee has an insurable interest only by reason of the lessor's identification of the goods, the lessor, until default or insolvency or notification to the lessee that identification is final, may substitute other goods for those identified.

(3) Notwithstanding a lessee's insurable interest under subsections (1) and (2), the lessor retains an insurable interest until an option to buy has been exercised by the lessee and risk of loss has passed to the lessee.

(4) Nothing in this section impairs any insurable interest recognized under any other statute or rule of law.

(5) The parties by agreement may determine that one or more parties have an obligation to obtain and pay for insurance covering the goods and by agreement may determine the beneficiary of the proceeds of the insurance.

§2A-219. Risk of Loss.—

(1) Except in the case of a finance lease, risk of loss is retained by the lessor and does not pass to the lessee. In the case of a finance lease, risk of loss passes to the lessee.

(2) Subject to the provisions of this Article on the effect of default on risk of loss (Section 2A-220), if risk of loss is to pass to the lessee and the time of passage is not stated, the following rules apply:

  (a) If the lease contract requires or authorizes the goods to be shipped by carrier (i) and it does not require delivery at a particular destination, the risk of loss passes to the lessee when the goods are duly delivered to the carrier; but (ii) if it does require delivery at a particular destination and the goods are there duly tendered while in the possession of the carrier, the risk of loss passes to the lessee when the goods are there duly so tendered as to enable the lessee to take delivery.

  (b) If the goods are held by a bailee to be delivered without being moved, the risk of loss passes to the lessee on acknowledgment by the bailee of the lessee's right to possession of the goods.

  (c) In any case not within subsection (a) or (b), the risk of loss passes to the lessee on the lessee's receipt of the goods if the lessor, or, in the case of a finance lease, the supplier, is a merchant; otherwise the risk passes to the lessee on tender of delivery.

§2A-220. Effect of Default on Risk of Loss.—

(1) Where risk of loss is to pass to the lessee and the time of passage is not stated:

  (a) If a tender or delivery of goods so fails to conform to the lease contract as to give a right of rejection, the risk of their loss remains with the lessor, or, in the case of a finance lease, the supplier, until cure or acceptance.

  (b) If the lessee rightfully revokes acceptance, he [or she], to the extent of any deficiency in his [or her] effective insurance coverage, may treat the risk of loss as having remained with the lessor from the beginning.

(2) Whether or not risk of loss is to pass to the lessee, if the lessee as to conforming goods already identified to a lease contract repudiates or is otherwise in default under the lease contract, the lessor, or, in the case of a finance lease, the supplier, to the extent of any deficiency in his [or her] effective insurance coverage may treat the risk of loss as resting on the lessee for a commercially reasonable time.

§2A-221. Casualty to Identified Goods.—If a lease contract requires goods identified when the lease contract is made, and the goods suffer casualty without fault of the lessee, the lessor or the supplier before delivery, or the goods suffer casualty before risk of loss passes to the lessee pursuant to the lease agreement or Section 2A-219, then:

(a) if the loss is total, the lease contract is avoided; and

(b) if the loss is partial or the goods have so deteriorated as to no longer conform to the lease contract, the lessee may nevertheless demand inspection and at his [or her] option either treat the lease contract as avoided or, except in a finance lease that is not a consumer lease, accept the goods with due allowance from the rent payable for the balance of the lease term for the deterioration or the deficiency in quantity but without further right against the lessor.

Part 3: Effect of Lease Contract

§2A-301. Enforceability of Lease Contract.—Except as otherwise provided in this Article, a lease contract is effective and enforceable according to its terms between the parties, against purchasers of the goods and against creditors of the parties.

§2A-302. Title to and Possession of Goods.—Except as otherwise provided in this Article, each provision of this Article applies whether the lessor or a third party has title to the goods, and whether the lessor, the lessee, or a third party has possession of the goods, notwithstanding any statute or rule of law that possession or the absence of possession is fraudulent.

§2A-303. Alienability of Party's Interest Under Lease Contract or of Lessor's Residual Interest in Goods; Delegation of Performance; Transfer of Rights.—

(1) As used in this section, "creation of a security interest" includes the sale of a lease contract that is subject to Article 9, Secured Transactions, by reason of Section 9-102(1)(b).

(2) Except as provided in subsections (3) and (4), a provision in a lease agreement which (i) prohibits the voluntary or involuntary transfer, including a transfer by sale, sublease, creation or enforcement of a security interest, or attachment, levy, or other judicial process, of an interest of a party under the lease contract or of the lessor's residual interest in the goods, or (ii) makes such a transfer an event of default, gives rise to the rights and remedies

provided in subsection (5), but a transfer that is prohibited or is an event of default under the lease agreement is otherwise effective.

(3) A provision in a lease agreement which (i) prohibits the creation or enforcement of a security interest in an interest of a party under the lease contract or in the lessor's residual interest in the goods, or (ii) makes such a transfer an event of default, is not enforceable unless, and then only to the extent that, there is an actual transfer by the lessee of the lessee's right of possession or use of the goods in violation of the provision or an actual delegation of a material performance of either party to the lease contract in violation of the provision. Neither the granting nor the enforcement of a security interest in (i) the lessor's interest under the lease contract or (ii) the lessor's residual interest in the goods is a transfer that materially impairs the prospect of obtaining return performance by, materially changes the duty of, or materially increases the burden or risk imposed on, the lessee within the purview of subsection (5) unless, and then only to the extent that, there is an actual delegation of a material performance of the lessor.

(4) A provision in a lease agreement which (i) prohibits a transfer of a right to damages for default with respect to the whole lease contract or of a right to payment arising out of the transferor's due performance of the transferor's entire obligation, or (ii) makes such a transfer an event of default, is not enforceable, and such a transfer is not a transfer that materially impairs the prospect of obtaining return performance by, materially changes the duty of, or materially increases the burden or risk imposed on, the other party to the lease contract within the purview of subsection (5).

(5) Subject to subsections (3) and (4):

(a) if a transfer is made which is made an event of default under a lease agreement, the party to the lease contract not making the transfer, unless that party waives the default or otherwise agrees, has the rights and remedies described in Section 2A-501(2);

(b) if paragraph (a) is not applicable and if a transfer is made that (i) is prohibited under a lease agreement or (ii) materially impairs the prospect of obtaining return performance by, materially changes the duty of, or materially increases the burden or risk imposed on, the other party to the lease contract, unless the party not making the transfer agrees at any time to the transfer in the lease contract or otherwise, then, except as limited by contract, (i) the transferor is liable to the party not making the transfer for damages caused by the transfer to the extent that the damages could not reasonably be prevented by the party not making the transfer and (ii) a court having jurisdiction may grant other appropriate relief, including cancellation of the lease contract or an injunction against the transfer.

(6) A transfer of "the lease" or of "all my rights under the lease", or a transfer in similar general terms, is a transfer of rights and, unless the language or the circumstances, as in a transfer for security, indicate the contrary, the transfer is a delegation of duties by the transferor to the transferee. Acceptance by the transferee constitutes a promise by the transferee to perform those duties. The promise is enforceable by either the transferor or the other party to the lease contract.

(7) Unless otherwise agreed by the lessor and the lessee, a delegation of performance does not relieve the transferor as against the other party of any duty to perform or of any liability for default.

(8) In a consumer lease, to prohibit the transfer of an interest of a party under the lease contract or to make a transfer an event of default, the language must be specific, by a writing, and conspicuous.

§2A-304. Subsequent Lease of Goods by Lessor.—

(1) Subject to Section 2A-303, a subsequent lessee from a lessor of goods under an existing lease contract obtains, to the extent of the leasehold interest transferred, the leasehold interest in the goods that the lessor had or had power to transfer, and except as provided in subsection (2) and Section 2A-527(4), takes subject to the existing lease contract. A lessor with voidable title has power to transfer a good leasehold interest to a good faith subsequent lessee for value, but only to the extent set forth in the preceding sentence. If goods have been delivered under a transaction of purchase, the lessor has that power even though:

(a) the lessor's transferor was deceived as to the identity of the lessor;

(b) the delivery was in exchange for a check which is later dishonored;

(c) it was agreed that the transaction was to be a "cash sale"; or

(d) the delivery was procured through fraud punishable as larcenous under the criminal law.

(2) A subsequent lessee in the ordinary course of business from a lessor who is a merchant dealing in goods of that kind to whom the goods were entrusted by the existing lessee of that lessor before the interest of the subsequent lessee became enforceable against that lessor obtains, to the extent of the leasehold interest transferred, all of that lessor's and the existing lessee's rights to the goods, and takes free of the existing lease contract.

(3) A subsequent lessee from the lessor of goods that are subject to an existing lease contract and are covered by a certificate of title issued under a statute of this State or of another jurisdiction takes no greater rights than those provided both by this section and by the certificate of title statute.

§2A-305. Sale or Sublease of Goods by Lessee.—

(1) Subject to the provisions of Section 2A-303, a buyer or sublessee from the lessee of goods under an existing

lease contract obtains, to the extent of the interest transferred, the leasehold interest in the goods that the lessee had or had power to transfer, and except as provided in subsection (2) and Section 2A-511(4), takes subject to the existing lease contract. A lessee with a voidable leasehold interest has power to transfer a good leasehold interest to a good faith buyer for value or a good faith sublessee for value, but only to the extent set forth in the preceding sentence. When goods have been delivered under a transaction of lease the lessee has that power even though:

(a) the lessor was deceived as to the identity of the lessee;

(b) the delivery was in exchange for a check which is later dishonored; or

(c) the delivery was procured through fraud punishable as larcenous under the criminal law.

(2) A buyer in the ordinary course of business or a sublessee in the ordinary course of business from a lessee who is a merchant dealing in goods of that kind to whom the goods were entrusted by the lessor obtains, to the extent of the interest transferred, all of the lessor's and lessee's rights to the goods, and takes free of the existing lease contract.

(3) A buyer or sublessee from the lessee of goods that are subject to an existing lease contract and are covered by a certificate of title issued under a statute of this State or of another jurisdiction takes no greater rights than those provided both by this section and by the certificate of title statute.

§2A-306. Priority of Certain Liens Arising by Operation of Law.—

If a person in the ordinary course of his [or her] business furnishes services or materials with respect to goods subject to a lease contract, a lien upon those goods in the possession of that person given by statute or rule of law for those materials or services takes priority over any interest of the lessor or lessee under the lease contract or this Article unless the lien is created by statute and the statute provides otherwise or unless the lien is created by rule of law and the rule of law provides otherwise.

§2A-307. Priority of Liens Arising by Attachment or Levy on, Security Interests in, and Other Claims to Goods.—

(1) Except as otherwise provided in Section 2A-306, a creditor of a lessee takes subject to the lease contract.

(2) Except as otherwise provided in subsections (3) and (4) and in Sections 2A-306 and 2A-308, a creditor of a lessor takes subject to the lease contract unless:

(a) the creditor holds a lien that attached to the goods before the lease contract became enforceable,

(b) the creditor holds a security interest in the goods and the lessee did not give value and receive delivery of the goods without knowledge of the security interest; or

(c) the creditor holds a security interest in the goods which was perfected (Section 9-303) before the lease contract became enforceable.

(3) A lessee in the ordinary course of business takes the leasehold interest free of a security interest in the goods created by the lessor even though the security interest is perfected (Section 9-303) and the lessee knows of its existence.

(4) A lessee other than a lessee in the ordinary course of business takes the leasehold interest free of a security interest to the extent that it secures future advances made after the secured party acquires knowledge of the lease or more than 45 days after the lease contract becomes enforceable, whichever first occurs, unless the future advances are made pursuant to a commitment entered into without knowledge of the lease and before the expiration of the 45-day period.

§2A-308. Special Rights of Creditors.—

(1) A creditor of a lessor in possession of goods subject to a lease contract may treat the lease contract as void if as against the creditor retention of possession by the lessor is fraudulent under any statute or rule of law, but retention of possession in good faith and current course of trade by the lessor for a commercially reasonable time after the lease contract becomes enforceable is not fraudulent.

(2) Nothing in this Article impairs the rights of creditors of a lessor if the lease contract (a) becomes enforceable, not in current course of trade but in satisfaction of or as security for a pre-existing claim for money, security, or the like, and (b) is made under circumstances which under any statute or rule of law apart from this Article would constitute the transaction a fraudulent transfer or voidable preference.

(3) A creditor of a seller may treat a sale or an identification of goods to a contract for sale as void if as against the creditor retention of possession by the seller is fraudulent under any statute or rule of law, but retention of possession of the goods pursuant to a lease contract entered into by the seller as lessee and the buyer as lessor in connection with the sale or identification of the goods is not fraudulent if the buyer bought for value and in good faith.

§2A-309. Lessor's and Lessee's Rights When Goods Become Fixtures.—

(1) In this section:

(a) goods are "fixtures" when they become so related to particular real estate that an interest in them arises under real estate law;

(b) a "fixture filing" is the filing, in the office where a mortgage on the real estate would be filed or recorded, of a financing statement covering goods that are or are to become fixtures and conforming to the requirements of Section 9-402(5);

(c) a lease is a "purchase money lease" unless the lessee has possession or use of the goods or the right to possession or use of the goods before the lease agreement is enforceable;

(d) a mortgage is a "construction mortgage" to the extent it secures an obligation incurred for the construction of an improvement on land including the acquisition cost of the land, if the recorded writing so indicates; and

(e) "encumbrance" includes real estate mortgages and other liens on real estate and all other rights in real estate that are not ownership interests.

(2) Under this Article a lease may be of goods that are fixtures or may continue in goods that become fixtures, but no lease exists under this Article of ordinary building materials incorporated into an improvement on land.

(3) This Article does not prevent creation of a lease of fixtures pursuant to real estate law.

(4) The perfected interest of a lessor of fixtures has priority over a conflicting interest of an encumbrancer or owner of the real estate if:

(a) the lease is a purchase money lease, the conflicting interest of the encumbrancer or owner arises before the goods become fixtures, the interest of the lessor is perfected by a fixture filing before the goods become fixtures or within ten days thereafter, and the lessee has an interest of record in the real estate or is in possession of the real estate; or

(b) the interest of the lessor is perfected by a fixture filing before the interest of the encumbrancer or owner is of record, the lessor's interest has priority over any conflicting interest of a predecessor in title of the encumbrancer or owner, and the lessee has an interest of record in the real estate or is in possession of the real estate.

(5) The interest of a lessor of fixtures, whether or not perfected, has priority over the conflicting interest of an encumbrancer or owner of the real estate if:

(a) the fixtures are readily removable factory or office machines, readily removable equipment that is not primarily used or leased for use in the operation of the real estate, or readily removable replacements of domestic appliances that are goods subject to a consumer lease, and before the goods become fixtures the lease contract is enforceable; or

(b) the conflicting interest is a lien on the real estate obtained by legal or equitable proceedings after the lease contract is enforceable; or

(c) the encumbrancer or owner has consented in writing to the lease or has disclaimed an interest in the goods as fixtures; or

(d) the lessee has a right to remove the goods as against the encumbrancer or owner. If the lessee's right to remove terminates, the priority of the interest of the lessor continues for a reasonable time.

(6) Notwithstanding subsection (4)(a) but otherwise subject to subsections (4) and (5), the interest of a lessor of fixtures, including the lessor's residual interest, is subordinate to the conflicting interest of an encumbrancer of the real estate under a construction mortgage recorded before the goods become fixtures if the goods become fixtures before the completion of the construction. To the extent given to refinance a construction mortgage, the conflicting interest of an encumbrancer of the real estate under a mortgage has this priority to the same extent as the encumbrancer of the real estate under the construction mortgage.

(7) In cases not within the preceding-subsections, priority between the interest of a lessor of fixtures, including the lessor's residual interest, and the conflicting interest of an encumbrancer or owner of the real estate who is not the lessee is determined by the priority rules governing conflicting interests in real estate.

(8) If the interest of a lessor of fixtures, including the lessor's residual interest, has priority over all conflicting interests of all owners and encumbrancers of the real estate, the lessor or the lessee may (i) on default, expiration, termination, or cancellation of the lease agreement but subject to the lease agreement and this Article, or (ii) if necessary to enforce other rights and remedies of the lessor or lessee under this Article, remove the goods from the real estate, free and clear of all conflicting interests of all owners and encumbrancers of the real estate, but the lessor or lessee must reimburse any encumbrancer or owner of the real estate who is not the lessee and who has not otherwise agreed for the cost of repair of any physical injury, but not for any diminution in value of the real estate caused by the absence of the goods removed or by any necessity of replacing them. A person entitled to reimbursement may refuse permission to remove until the party seeking removal gives adequate security for the performance of this obligation.

(9) Even though the lease agreement does not create a security interest, the interest of a lessor of fixtures, including the lessor's residual interest, is perfected by filing a financing statement as a fixture filing for leased goods that are or are to become fixtures in accordance with the relevant provisions of the Article on Secured Transactions (Article 9).

§2A-310. Lessor's and Lessee's Rights When Goods Become Accessions.—

(1) Goods are "accessions" when they are installed in or affixed to other goods.

(2) The interest of a lessor or a lessee under a lease contract entered into before the goods became accessions is superior to all interests in the whole except as stated in subsection (4).

(3) The interest of a lessor or a lessee under a lease contract entered into at the time or after the goods became accessions is superior to all subsequently acquired

interests in the whole except as stated in subsection (4) but is subordinate to interests in the whole existing at the time the lease contract was made unless the holders of such interests in the whole have in writing consented to the lease or disclaimed an interest in the goods as part of the whole.

(4) The interest of a lessor or a lessee under a lease contract described in subsection (2) or (3) is subordinate to the interest of
   (a) a buyer in the ordinary course of business or a lessee in the ordinary course of business of any interest in the whole acquired after the goods became accessions; or
   (b) a creditor with a security interest in the whole perfected before the lease contract was made to the extent that the creditor makes subsequent advances without knowledge of the lease contract.

(5) When under subsections (2) or (3) and (4) a lessor or a lessee of accessions holds an interest that is superior to all interests in the whole, the lessor or the lessee may (a) on default, expiration, termination, or cancellation of the lease contract by the other party but subject to the provisions of the lease contract and this Article, or (b) if necessary to enforce his [or her] other rights and remedies under this Article, remove the goods from the whole, free and clear of all interests in the whole, but he [or she] must reimburse any holder of an interest in the whole who is not the lessee and who has not otherwise agreed for the cost of repair of any physical injury but not for any diminution in value of the whole caused by the absence of the goods removed or by any necessity for replacing them. A person entitled to reimbursement may refuse permission to remove until the party seeking removal gives adequate security for the performance of this obligation.

§2A-311. Priority Subject to Subordination. Nothing in this Article prevents subordination by agreement by any person entitled to priority.

Part 4: Performance of Lease Contract: Repudiated, Substituted and Excused

§2A-401. Insecurity: Adequate Assurance of Performance.—

(1) A lease contract imposes an obligation on each party that the other's expectation of receiving due performance will not be impaired.

(2) If reasonable grounds for insecurity arise with respect to the performance of either party, the insecure party may demand in writing adequate assurance of due performance. Until the insecure party receives that assurance, if commercially reasonable the insecure party may suspend any performance for which he [or she] has not already received the agreed return.

(3) A repudiation of the lease contract occurs if assurance of due performance adequate under the circumstances of the particular case is not provided to the insecure party within a reasonable time, not to exceed 30 days after receipt of a demand by the other party.

(4) Between merchants, the reasonableness of grounds for insecurity and the adequacy of any assurance offered must be determined according to commercial standards.

(5) Acceptance of any nonconforming delivery or payment does not prejudice the aggrieved party's right to demand adequate assurance of future performance.

§2A-402. Anticipatory Repudiation.—If either party repudiates a lease contract with respect to a performance not yet due under the lease contract, the loss of which performance will substantially impair the value of the lease contract to the other, the aggrieved party may:

(a) for a commercially reasonable time, await retraction of repudiation and performance by the repudiating party;

(b) make demand pursuant to Section 2A-401 and await assurance of future performance adequate under the circumstances of the particular case; or

(c) resort to any right or remedy upon default under the lease contract or this Article, even though the aggrieved party has notified the repudiating party that the aggrieved party would await the repudiating party's performance and assurance and has urged retraction. In addition, whether or not the aggrieved party is pursuing one of the foregoing remedies, the aggrieved party may suspend performance or, if the aggrieved party is the lessor, proceed in accordance with the provisions of this Article on the lessor's right to identify goods to the lease contract notwithstanding default or to salvage unfinished goods (Section 2A-524).

§2A-403. Retraction of Anticipatory Repudiation.—

(1) Until the repudiating party's next performance is due, the repudiating party can retract the repudiation unless, since the repudiation, the aggrieved party has cancelled the lease contract or materially changed the aggrieved party's position or otherwise indicated that the aggrieved party considers the repudiation final.

(2) Retraction may be by any method that clearly indicates to the aggrieved party that the repudiating party intends to perform under the lease contract and includes any assurance demanded under Section 2A-401.

(3) Retraction reinstates a repudiating party's rights under a lease contract with due excuse and allowance to the aggrieved party for any delay occasioned by the repudiation.

§2A-404. Substituted Performance.—

(1) If without fault of the lessee, the lessor and the supplier, the agreed berthing, loading, or unloading facilities fail or the agreed type of carrier becomes unavailable the agreed manner of delivery otherwise

becomes commercially impracticable, but a commercially reasonable substitute is available, the substitute performance must be tendered and accepted.

(2) If the agreed means or manner of payment fails because of domestic or foreign governmental regulation:

(a) the lessor may withhold or stop delivery or cause the supplier to withhold or stop delivery unless the lessee provides a means or manner of payment that is commercially a substantial equivalent; and

(b) if delivery has already been taken, payment by the means or in the manner provided by the regulation discharges the lessee's obligation unless the regulation is discriminatory, oppressive, or predatory.

§2A-405. Excused Performance.—Subject to Section 2A-404 on substituted performance, the following rules apply:

(a) Delay in delivery or nondelivery in whole or in part by a lessor or a supplier who complies with paragraphs (b) and (c) is not a default under the lease contract if performance as agreed has been made impracticable by the occurrence of a contingency the nonoccurrence of which was a basic assumption on which the lease contract was made or by compliance in good faith with any applicable foreign or domestic governmental regulation or order, whether or not the regulation or order later proves to be invalid.

(b) If the causes mentioned in paragraph (a) affect only part of the lessor's or the supplier's capacity to perform, he [or she] shall allocate production and deliveries among his [or her] customers but at his [or her] option may include regular customers not then under contract for sale or lease as well as his [or her] own requirements for further manufacture. He [or she] may so allocate in any manner that is fair and reasonable.

(c) The lessor seasonably shall notify the lessee and in the case of a finance lease the supplier seasonably shall notify the lessor and the lessee, if known, that there will be delay or nondelivery and, if allocation is required under paragraph (b), of the estimated quota thus made available for the lessee.

§2A-406. Procedure on Excused Performance.—

(1) If the lessee receives notification of a material or indefinite delay or an allocation justified under Section 2A-405, the lessee may by written notification to the lessor as to any goods involved, and with respect to all of the goods if under an installment lease contract the value of the whole lease contract is substantially impaired (Section 2A-510):

(a) terminate the lease contract (Section 2A-505(2)); or

(b) except in a finance lease that is not a consumer lease, modify the lease contract by accepting the available quota in substitution, with due allowance from the rent payable for the balance of the lease term for the deficiency but without further right against the lessor.

(2) If, after receipt of a notification from the lessor under Section 2A-405, the lessee fails so to modify the lease agreement within a reasonable time not exceeding 30 days, the lease contract lapses with respect to any deliveries affected.

§2A-407. Irrevocable Promises: Finance Leases.—

(1) In the case of a finance lease that is not a consumer lease the lessee's promises under the lease contract become irrevocable and independent upon the lessee's acceptance of the goods.

(2) A promise that has become irrevocable and independent under subsection (1):

(a) is effective and enforceable between the parties, and by or against third parties including assignees of the parties; and

(b) is not subject to cancellation, termination, modification, repudiation, excuse, or substitution without the consent of the party to whom the promise runs.

(3) This section does not affect the validity under any other law of a covenant in any lease contract making the lessee's promises irrevocable and independent upon the lessee's acceptance of the goods.

Part 5: Default

A. In General

§2A-501. Default: Procedure.—

(1) Whether the lessor or the lessee is in default under a lease contract is determined by the lease agreement and this Article.

(2) If the lessor or the lessee is in default under the lease contract, the party seeking enforcement has rights and remedies as provided in this Article and, except as limited by this Article, as provided in the lease agreement.

(3) If the lessor or the lessee is in default under the lease contract, the party seeking enforcement may reduce the party's claim to judgment, or otherwise enforce the lease contract by self-help or any available judicial procedure or nonjudicial procedure, including administrative proceeding, arbitration, or the like, in accordance with this Article.

(4) Except as otherwise provided in Section 1-106(1) or this Article or the lease agreement, the rights and remedies referred to in subsections (2) and (3) are cumulative.

(5) If the lease agreement covers both real property and goods, the party seeking enforcement may proceed under this Part as to the goods, or under other applicable law as to both the real property and the goods in accordance with that party's rights and remedies in respect of the real property, in which case this Part does not apply.

§2A-502. Notice After Default.—Except as otherwise provided in this Article or the lease agreement, the lessor or lessee in default under the lease contract is not entitled to notice of default or notice of enforcement from the other party to the lease agreement.

§2A-503. Modification or Impairment of Rights and Remedies.—

(1) Except as otherwise provided in this Article, the lease agreement may include rights and remedies for default in addition to or in substitution for those provided in this Article and may limit or alter the measure of damages recoverable under this Article.

(2) Resort to a remedy provided under this Article or in the lease agreement is optional unless the remedy is expressly agreed to be exclusive. If circumstances cause an exclusive or limited remedy to fail of its essential purpose, or provision for an exclusive remedy is unconscionable, remedy may be had as provided in this Article.

(3) Consequential damages may be liquidated under Section 2A-504, or may otherwise be limited, altered, or excluded unless the limitation, alteration, or exclusion is unconscionable. Limitation, alteration, or exclusion of consequential damages for injury to the person in the case of consumer goods is prima facie unconscionable but limitation, alteration, or exclusion of damages where the loss is commercial is not prima facie unconscionable.

(4) Rights and remedies on default by the lessor or the lessee with respect to any obligation or promise collateral or ancillary to the lease contract are not impaired by this Article.

§2A-504. Liquidation of Damages.—

(1) Damages payable by either party for default, or any other act or omission, including indemnity for loss or diminution of anticipated tax benefits or loss or damage to lessor's residual interest, may be liquidated in the lease agreement but only at an amount or by a formula that is reasonable in light of the then anticipated harm caused by the default or other act or omission.

(2) If the lease agreement provides for liquidation of damages, and such provision does not comply with subsection (1), or such provision is an exclusive or limited remedy that circumstances cause to fail of its essential purpose, remedy may be had as provided in this Article.

(3) If the lessor justifiably withholds or stops delivery of goods because of the lessee's default or insolvency (Section 2A-525 or 2A-526), the lessee is entitled to restitution of any amount by which the sum of his [or her] payments exceeds:

    (a) the amount to which the lessor is entitled by virtue of terms liquidating the lessor's damages in accordance with subsection (1); or

    (b) in the absence of those terms, 20 percent of the then present value of the total rent the lessee was obligated to pay for the balance of the lease term, or, in the case of a consumer lease, the lesser of such amount or $500.

(4) A lessee's right to restitution under subsection (3) is subject to offset to the extent the lessor establishes:

    (a) a right to recover damages under the provisions of this Article other than subsection (1); and

    (b) the amount or value of any benefits received by the lessee directly or indirectly by reason of the lease contract.

§2A-505. Cancellation and Termination and Effect of Cancellation, Termination, Rescission, or Fraud on Rights and Remedies.—

(1) On cancellation of the lease contract, all obligations that are still executory on both sides are discharged, but any right based on prior default or performance survives, and the cancelling party also retains any remedy for default of the whole lease contract or any unperformed balance.

(2) On termination of the lease contract, all obligations that are still executory on both sides are discharged but any right based on prior default or performance survives.

(3) Unless the contrary intention clearly appears, expressions of "cancellation", "rescission", or the like of the lease contract may not be construed as a renunciation or discharge of any claim in damages for an antecedent default.

(4) Rights and remedies for material misrepresentation or fraud include all rights and remedies available under this Article for default.

(5) Neither rescission nor a claim for rescission of the lease contract nor rejection or return of the goods may bar or be deemed inconsistent with a claim for damages or other right or remedy.

§2A-506. Statute of Limitations.—

(1) An action for default under a lease contract, including breach of warranty or indemnity, must be commenced within 4 years after the cause of action accrued. By the original lease contract the parties may reduce the period of limitation to not less than one year.

(2) A cause of action for default accrues when the act or omission on which the default or breach of warranty is based is or should have been discovered by the aggrieved party, or when the default occurs, whichever is later. A cause of action for indemnity accrues when the act or omission on which the claim for indemnity is based is or should have been discovered by the indemnified party, whichever is later.

(3) If an action commenced within the time limited by subsection (1) is so terminated as to leave available a remedy by another action for the same default or

breach of warranty or indemnity, the other action may be commenced after the expiration of the time limited and within 6 months after the termination of the first action unless the termination resulted from voluntary discontinuance or from dismissal for failure or neglect to prosecute.

(4) This section does not alter the law on tolling of the statute of limitations nor does it apply to causes of action that have accrued before this Article becomes effective.

§2A-507. Proof of Market Rent: Time and Place.—

(1) Damages based on market rent (Section 2A-519 or 2A-528) are determined according to the rent for the use of the goods concerned for a lease term identical to the remaining lease term of the original lease agreement and prevailing at the times specified in Sections 2A-519 and 2A-528.

(2) If evidence of rent for the use of the goods concerned for a lease term identical to the remaining lease term of the original lease agreement and prevailing at the times or places described in this Article is not readily available, the rent prevailing within any reasonable time before or after the time described or at any other place or for a different lease term which in commercial judgment or under usage of trade would serve as a reasonable substitute for the one described may be used, making any proper allowance for the difference, including the cost of transporting the goods to or from the other place.

(3) Evidence of a relevant rent prevailing at a time or place or for a lease term other than the one described in this Article offered by one party is not admissible unless and until he [or she] has given the other party notice the court finds sufficient to prevent unfair surprise.

(4) If the prevailing rent, or value of any goods regularly leased in any established market is in issue, reports in official publications or trade journals or in newspapers or periodicals of general circulation published as the reports of that market are admissible in evidence. The circumstances of the preparation of the report may be shown to affect its weight but not its admissibility.

B. Default by Lessor

§2A-508. Lessee's Remedies.—

(1) If a lessor fails to deliver the goods in conformity to the lease contract (Section 2A-509) or repudiates the lease contract (Section 2A-402), or a lessee rightfully rejects the goods (Section 2A-509) or justifiably revokes acceptance of the goods (Section 2A-517), then with respect to any goods involved, and with respect to all of the goods if under an installment lease contract the value of the whole lease contract is substantially impaired (Section 2A-510), the lessor is in default under the lease contract and the lessee may:

(a) cancel the lease contract (Section 2A-505(1));
(b) recover so much of the rent and security as has been paid and is just under the circumstances;
(c) cover and recover damages as to all goods affected whether or not they have been identified to the lease contract (Sections 2A-518 and 2A-520), or recover damages for nondelivery (Sections 2A-519 and 2A-520);
(d) exercise any other rights or pursue any other remedies provided in the lease contract.

(2) If a lessor fails to deliver the goods in conformity to the lease contract or repudiates the lease contract, the lessee may also:
(a) if the goods have been identified, recover them (Section 2A-522); or
(b) in a proper case, obtain specific performance or replevy the goods (Section 2A-521).

(3) If a lessor is otherwise in default under a lease contract, the lessee may exercise the rights and pursue the remedies provided in the lease contract, which may include a right to cancel the lease, and in Section 2A-519(3).

(4) If a lessor has breached a warranty, whether express or implied, the lessee may recover damages (Section 2A-519(4)).

(5) On rightful rejection or justifiable revocation of acceptance, a lessee has a security interest in goods in the lessee's possession or control for any rent and security that has been paid and any expenses reasonably incurred in their inspection, receipt, transportation, and care and custody and may hold those goods and dispose of them in good faith and in a commercially reasonable manner, subject to Section 2A-527(5).

(6) Subject to the provisions of Section 2A-407, a lessee, on notifying the lessor of the lessee's intention to do so, may deduct all or any part of the damages resulting from any default under the lease contract from any part of the rent still due under the same lease contract.

§2A-509. Lessee's Rights on Improper Delivery; Rightful Rejection.—

(1) Subject to the provisions of Section 2A-510 on default in installment lease contracts, if the goods or the tender or delivery fail in any respect to conform to the lease contract, the lessee may reject or accept the goods or accept any commercial unit or units and reject the rest of the goods.

(2) Rejection of goods is ineffective unless it is within a reasonable time after tender or delivery of the goods and the lessee seasonably notifies the lessor.

§2A-510. Installment Lease Contracts: Rejection and Default.—

(1) Under an installment lease contract a lessee may reject any delivery that is nonconforming if the nonconformity substantially impairs the value of that delivery and cannot be cured or the nonconformity is a defect in the required documents; but if the

nonconformity does not fall within subsection (2) and the lessor or the supplier gives adequate assurance of its cure, the lessee must accept that delivery.

(2) Whenever nonconformity or default with respect to one or more deliveries substantially impairs the value of the installment lease contract as a whole there is a default with respect to the whole. But, the aggrieved party reinstates the installment lease contract as a whole if the aggrieved party accepts a nonconforming delivery without seasonably notifying of cancellation or brings an action with respect only to past deliveries or demands performance as to future deliveries.

§2A-511. Merchant Lessee's Duties as to Rightfully Rejected Goods.—

(1) Subject to any security interest of a lessee (Section 2A-508(5)), if a lessor or a supplier has no agent or place of business at the market of rejection, a merchant lessee, after rejection of goods in his [or her] possession or control, shall follow any reasonable instructions received from the lessor or the supplier with respect to the goods. In the absence of those instructions, a merchant lessee shall make reasonable efforts to sell, lease, or otherwise dispose of the goods for the lessor's account if they threaten to decline in value speedily. Instructions are not reasonable if on demand indemnity for expenses is not forthcoming.

(2) If a merchant lessee (subsection (1)) or any other lessee (Section 2A-512) disposes of goods, he [or she] is entitled to reimbursement either from the lessor or the supplier or out of the proceeds for reasonable expenses of caring for and disposing of the goods and, if the expenses include no disposition commission, to such commission as is usual in the trade, or if there is none, to a reasonable sum not exceeding 10 percent of the gross proceeds.

(3) In complying with this section or Section 2A-512, the lessee is held only to good faith. Good faith conduct hereunder is neither acceptance or conversion nor the basis of an action for damages.

(4) A purchaser who purchases in good faith from a lessee pursuant to this section or Section 2A-512 takes the goods free of any rights of the lessor and the supplier even though the lessee fails to comply with one or more of the requirements of this Article.

§2A-512. Lessee's Duties as to Rightfully Rejected Goods.—

(1) Except as otherwise provided with respect to goods that threaten to decline in value speedily (Section 2A-511) and subject to any security interest of a lessee (Section 2A-508(5)):

  (a) the lessee, after rejection of goods in the lessee's possession, shall hold them with reasonable care at the lessor's or the supplier's disposition for a reasonable time after the lessee's seasonable notification of rejection;

  (b) if the lessor or the supplier gives no instructions within a reasonable time after notification of rejection, the lessee may store the rejected goods for the lessor's or the supplier's account or ship them to the lessor or the supplier or dispose of them for the lessor's or the supplier's account with reimbursement in the manner provided in Section 2A-511; but

  (c) the lessee has no further obligations with regard to goods rightfully rejected.

(2) Action by the lessee pursuant to subsection (1) is not acceptance or conversion.

§2A-513. Cure by Lessor of Improper Tender or Delivery; Replacement.—

(1) If any tender or delivery by the lessor or the supplier is rejected because nonconforming and the time for performance has not yet expired, the lessor or the supplier may seasonably notify the lessee of the lessor's or the supplier's intention to cure and may then make a conforming delivery within the time provided in the lease contract.

(2) If the lessee rejects a nonconforming tender that the lessor or the supplier had reasonable grounds to believe would be acceptable with or without money allowance, the lessor or the supplier may have a further reasonable time to substitute a conforming tender if he [or she] seasonably notifies the lessee.

§2A-514. Waiver of Lessee's Objections.—

(1) In rejecting goods, a lessee's failure to state a particular defect that is ascertainable by reasonable inspection precludes the lessee from relying on the defect to justify rejection or to establish default:

  (a) if, stated seasonably, the lessor or the supplier could have cured it (Section 2A-513); or

  (b) between merchants if the lessor or the supplier after rejection has made a request in writing for a full and final written statement of all defects on which the lessee proposes to rely.

(2) A lessee's failure to reserve rights when paying rent or other consideration against documents precludes recovery of the payment for defects apparent on the face of the documents.

§2A-515. Acceptance of Goods.—

(1) Acceptance of goods occurs after the lessee has had a reasonable opportunity to inspect the goods and

  (a) the lessee signifies or acts with respect to the goods in a manner that signifies to the lessor or the supplier that the goods are conforming or that the lessee will take or retain them in spite of their nonconformity; or

  (b) the lessee fails to make an effective rejection of the goods (Section 2A-509(2)).

(2) Acceptance of a part of any commercial unit is acceptance of that entire unit.

§2A-516. Effect of Acceptance of Goods; Notice of Default; Burden of Establishing Default After Acceptance; Notice of Claim or Litigation to Person Answerable Over.—

(1) A lessee must pay rent for any goods accepted in accordance with the lease contract, with due allowance for goods rightfully rejected or not delivered.

(2) A lessee's acceptance of goods precludes rejection of the goods accepted. In the case of a finance lease, if made with knowledge of a nonconformity, acceptance cannot be revoked because of it. In any other case, if made with knowledge of a nonconformity, acceptance cannot be revoked because of it unless the acceptance was on the reasonable assumption that the nonconformity would be seasonably cured. Acceptance does not of itself impair any other remedy provided by this Article or the lease agreement for nonconformity.

(3) If a tender has been accepted:
   (a) within a reasonable time after the lessee discovers or should have discovered any default, the lessee shall notify the lessor and the supplier, if any, or be barred from any remedy against the party not notified;
   (b) except in the case of a consumer lease, within a reasonable time after the lessee receives notice of litigation for infringement or the like (Section 2A-211) the lessee shall notify the lessor or be barred from any remedy over for liability established by the litigation; and
   (c) the burden is on the lessee to establish any default.

(4) If a lessee is sued for breach of a warranty or other obligation for which a lessor or a supplier is answerable over the following apply:
   (a) The lessee may give the lessor or the supplier, or both, written notice of the litigation. If the notice states that the person notified may come in and defend and that if the person notified does not do so that person will be bound in any action against that person by the lessee by any determination of fact common to the two litigations, then unless the person notified after seasonable receipt of the notice does come in and defend that person is so bound.
   (b) The lessor or the supplier may demand in writing that the lessee turn over control of the litigation including settlement if the claim is one for infringement or the like (Section 2A-211) or else be barred from any remedy over. If the demand states that the lessor or the supplier agrees to bear all expense and to satisfy any adverse judgment, then unless the lessee after seasonable receipt of the demand does turn over control the lessee is so barred.

(5) Subsections (3) and (4) apply to any obligation of a lessee to hold the lessor or the supplier harmless against the infringement or the like (Section 2A-211).

§2A-517. Revocation of Acceptance of Goods.—

(1) A lessee may revoke acceptance of a lot or commercial unit whose nonconformity substantially impairs its value to the lessee if the lessee has accepted it:
   (a) except in the case of a finance lease, on the reasonable assumption that its nonconformity would be cured and it has not been seasonably cured; or
   (b) without discovery of the nonconformity if the lessee's acceptance was reasonably induced either by the lessor's assurances or, except in the case of a finance lease, by the difficulty of discovery before acceptance.

(2) Except in the case of a finance lease that is not a consumer lease, a lessee may revoke acceptance of a lot or commercial unit if the lessor defaults under the lease contract and the default substantially impairs the value of that lot or commercial unit to the lessee.

(3) If the lease agreement so provides, the lessee may revoke acceptance of a lot or commercial unit because of other defaults by the lessor.

(4) Revocation of acceptance must occur within a reasonable time after the lessee discovers or should have discovered the ground for it and before any substantial change in condition of the goods which is not caused by the nonconformity. Revocation is not effective until the lessee notifies the lessor.

(5) A lessee who so revokes has the same rights and duties with regard to the goods involved as if the lessee had rejected them.

§2A-518. Cover; Substitute Goods.—

(1) After a default by a lessor under the lease contract of the type described in Section 2A-508(1), or, if agreed, after other default by the lessor, the lessee may cover by making any purchase or lease of or contract to purchase or lease goods in substitution for those due from the lessor.

(2) Except as otherwise provided with respect to damages liquidated in the lease agreement (Section 2A-504) or otherwise determined pursuant to agreement of the parties (Sections 1-102(3) and 2A-503), if a lessee's cover is by a lease agreement substantially similar to the original lease agreement and the new lease agreement is made in good faith and in a commercially reasonable manner, the lessee may recover from the lessor as damages (i) the present value, as of the date of the commencement of the term of the new lease agreement, of the rent under the new lease agreement applicable to that period of the new lease term which is comparable to the then remaining term of the original lease agreement minus the present value as of the same date of the total rent for the then remaining lease term of the original lease agreement, and (ii) any incidental or consequential damages, less expenses saved in consequence of the lessor's default.

(3) If a lessee's cover is by lease agreement that for any reason does not qualify for treatment under subsection (2), or is by purchase or otherwise, the lessee may recover from the lessor as if the lessee had elected not to cover and Section 2A-519 governs.

§2A-519. Lessee's Damages for Non-Delivery, Repudiation, Default, and Breach of Warranty in Regard to Accepted Goods.—

(1) Except as otherwise provided with respect to damages liquidated in the lease agreement (Section 2A-504) or otherwise determined pursuant to agreement of the parties (Sections 1-102(3) and 2A-503), if the lessee elects not to cover or a lessee elects to cover and the cover is by lease agreement that for any reason does not qualify for treatment under Section 2A-518(2), or is by purchase or otherwise, the measure of damages for non-delivery or repudiation by the lessor or for rejection or revocation of acceptance by the lessee is the present value, as of the date of the default, of the then market rent minus the present value as of the same date of the original rent, computed for the remaining lease term of the original lease agreement, together with incidental and consequential damages, less expenses saved in consequence of the lessor's default.

(2) Market rent is to be determined as of the place for tender or, in cases of rejection after arrival or revocation of acceptance, as of the place of arrival.

(3) Except as otherwise agreed, if the lessee has accepted goods and given notification (Section 2A-516(3)), the measure of damages for non-conforming tender or delivery or other default by a lessor is the loss resulting in the ordinary course of events from the lessor's default as determined in any manner that is reasonable together with incidental and consequential damages, less expenses saved in consequence of the lessor's default.

(4) Except as otherwise agreed, the measure of damages for breach of warranty is the present value at the time and place of acceptance of the difference between the value of the use of the goods accepted and the value if they had been as warranted for the lease term, unless special circumstances show proximate damages of a different amount, together with incidental and consequential damages, less expenses saved in consequence of the lessor's default or breach of warranty.

§2A-520. Lessee's Incidental and Consequential Damages.—

(1) Incidental damages resulting from a lessor's default include expenses reasonably incurred in inspection, receipt, transportation, and care and custody of goods rightfully rejected or goods the acceptance of which is justifiably revoked, any commercially reasonable charges, expenses or commissions in connection with effecting cover, and any other reasonable expense incident to the default.

(2) Consequential damages resulting from a lessor's default include:
   (a) any loss resulting from general or particular requirements and needs of which the lessor at the time of contracting had reason to know and which could not reasonably be prevented by cover or otherwise; and
   (b) injury to person or property proximately resulting from any breach of warranty.

§2A-521. Lessee's Right to Specific Performance or Replevin.—

(1) Specific performance may be decreed if the goods are unique or in other proper circumstances.

(2) A decree for specific performance may include any terms and conditions as to payment of the rent, damages, or other relief that the court deems just.

(3) A lessee has a right of replevin, detinue, sequestration, claim and delivery, or the like for goods identified to the lease contract if after reasonable effort the lessee is unable to effect cover for those goods or the circumstances reasonably indicate that the effort will be unavailing.

§2A-522. Lessee's Right to Goods on Lessor's Insolvency.—

(1) Subject to subsection (2) and even though the goods have not been shipped, a lessee who has paid a part or all of the rent and security for goods identified to a lease contract (Section 2A-217) on making and keeping good a tender of any unpaid portion of the rent and security due under the lease contract may recover the goods identified from the lessor if the lessor becomes insolvent within 10 days after receipt of the first installment of rent and security.

(2) A lessee acquires the right to recover goods identified to a lease contract only if they conform to the lease contract.

C. Default by Lessee

§2A-523. Lessor's Remedies.—

(1) If a lessee wrongfully rejects or revokes acceptance of goods or fails to make a payment when due or repudiates with respect to a part or the whole, then, with respect to any goods involved, and with respect to all of the goods if under an installment lease contract the value of the whole lease contract is substantially impaired (Section 2A-510), the lessee is in default under the lease contract and the lessor may:
   (a) cancel the lease contract (Section 2A-505(1));
   (b) proceed respecting goods not identified to the lease contract (Section 2A-524);
   (c) withhold delivery of the goods and take possession of goods previously delivered (Section 2A-525);

(d) stop delivery of the goods by any bailee (Section 2A-526);

(e) dispose of the goods and recover damages (Section 2A-527), or retain the goods and recover damages (Section 2A-528), or in a proper case recover rent (Section 2A-529);

(f) exercise any other rights or pursue any other remedies provided in the lease contract.

(2) If a lessor does not fully exercise a right or obtain a remedy to which the lessor is entitled under subsection (1), the lessor may recover the loss resulting in the ordinary course of events from the lessee's default as determined in any reasonable manner together with incidental damages, less expenses saved in consequence of the lessee's default.

(3) If a lessee is otherwise in default under a lease contract, the lessor may exercise the rights and pursue the remedies provided in the lease contract, which may include a right to cancel the lease. In addition, unless otherwise provided in the lease contract:

(a) if the default substantially impairs the value of the lease contract to the lessor, the lessor may exercise the rights and pursue and remedies provided in subsections (1) or (2); or

(b) if the default does not substantially impair the value of the lease contract to the lessor, the lessor may recover as provided in subsection (2).

§2A-524. Lessor's Right to Identify Goods to Lease Contract.—

(1) A lessor aggrieved under Section 2A-523(1) may:

(a) identify to the lease contract conforming goods not already identified if at the time the lessor learned of the default they were in the lessor's or the supplier's possession or control; and

(b) dispose of goods (Section 2A-527(1)) that demonstrably have been intended for the particular lease contract even though those goods are unfinished.

(2) If the goods are unfinished, in the exercise of reasonable commercial judgment for the purposes of avoiding loss and of effective realization, an aggrieved lessor or the supplier may either complete manufacture and wholly identify the goods to the lease contract or cease manufacture and lease, sell, or otherwise dispose of the goods for scrap or salvage value or proceed in any other reasonable manner.

§2A-525. Lessor's Right to Possession of Goods.—

(1) If a lessor discovers the lessee to be insolvent, the lessor may refuse to deliver the goods.

(2) After a default by the lessee under the lease contract of the type described in Section 2A-523(1) or 2A-523(3)(a) or, if agreed, after other default by the lessee, the lessor has the right to take possession of the goods. If the lease contract so provides, the lessor may require the lessee to assemble the goods and make them available to the lessor at a place to be designated by the lessor which is reason-

ably convenient to both parties. Without removal, the lessor may render unusable any goods employed in trade or business, and may dispose of goods on the lessee's premises (Section 2A-527).

(3) The lessor may proceed under subsection (2) without judicial process if it can be done without breach of the peace or the lessor may proceed by action.

§2A-526. Lessor's Stoppage of Delivery in Transit or Otherwise.—

(1) A lessor may stop delivery of goods in the possession of a carrier or other bailee if the lessor discovers the lessee to be insolvent and may stop delivery of carload, truckload, planeload, or larger shipments of express or freight if the lessee repudiates or fails to make a payment due before delivery, whether for rent, security or otherwise under the lease contract, or for any other reason the lessor has a right to withhold or take possession of the goods.

(2) In pursuing its remedies under subsection (1), the lessor may stop delivery until

(a) receipt of the goods by the lessee;

(b) acknowledgment to the lessee by any bailee of the goods, except a carrier, that the bailee holds the goods for the lessee; or

(c) such an acknowledgment to the lessee by a carrier via reshipment or as warehouseman.

(3) (a) To stop delivery, a lessor shall so notify as to enable the bailee by reasonable diligence to prevent delivery of the goods.

(b) After notification, the bailee shall hold and deliver the goods according to the directions of the lessor, but the lessor is liable to the bailee for any ensuing charges or damages.

(c) A carrier who has issued a nonnegotiable bill of lading is not obliged to obey a notification to stop received from a person other than the consignor.

§2A-527. Lessor's Rights to Dispose of Goods.—

(1) After a default by a lessee under the lease contract of the type described in Section 2A-523(1) or 2A-523(3)(a) or after the lessor refuses to deliver or takes possession of goods (Section 2A-525 or 2A-526), or, if agreed, after other default by a lessee, the lessor may dispose of the goods concerned or the undelivered balance thereof by lease, sale, or otherwise.

(2) Except as otherwise provided with respect to damages liquidated in the lease agreement (Section 2A-504) or otherwise determined pursuant to agreement of the parties (Sections 1-102(3) and 2A-503), if the disposition is by lease agreement substantially similar to the original lease agreement and the new lease agreement is made in good faith and in a commercially reasonable manner, the lessor may recover from the lessee as damages (i) accrued and unpaid rent as of the date of the commencement of the term of the new lease agreement, (ii) the present value, as of the same date, of the total rent for the then remaining lease term of

the original lease agreement minus the present value, as of the same date, of the rent under the new lease agreement applicable to that period of the new lease term which is comparable to the then remaining term of the original lease agreement, and (iii) any incidental damages allowed under Section 2A-530, less expenses saved in consequence of the lessee's default.

(3) If the lessor's disposition is by lease agreement that for any reason does not qualify for treatment under subsection (2), or is by sale or otherwise, the lessor may recover from the lessee as if the lessor had elected not to dispose of the goods and Section 2A-528 governs.

(4) A subsequent buyer or lessee who buys or leases from the lessor in good faith for value as a result of a disposition under this section takes the goods free of the original lease contract and any rights of the original lessee even though the lessor fails to comply with one or more of the requirements of this Article.

(5) The lessor is not accountable to the lessee for any profit made on any disposition. A lessee who has rightfully rejected or justifiably revoked acceptance shall account to the lessor for any excess over the amount of the lessee's security interest (Section 2A-508(5)).

§2A-528. Lessor's Damages for Non-Acceptance, Failure to Pay, Repudiation, or Other Default.—

(1) Except as otherwise provided with respect to damages liquidated in the lease agreement (Section 2A-504) or otherwise determined pursuant to agreement of the parties (Sections 1-102(3) and 2A-503), if a lessor elects to retain the goods or a lessor elects to dispose of the goods and the disposition is by lease agreement that for any reason does not qualify for treatment under Section 2A-527(2), or is by sale or otherwise, the lessor may recover from the lessee as damages for a default of the type described in Section 2A523(1) or 2A-523(3)(a), or, if agreed, for other default of the lessee, (i) accrued and unpaid rent as of the date of default if the lessee has never taken possession of the goods, or, if the lessee has taken possession of the goods, as of the date the lessor repossesses the goods or an earlier date on which the lessee makes a tender of the goods to the lessor, (ii) the present value as of the date determined under clause (i) of the total rent for the then remaining lease term of the original lease agreement minus the present value as of the same date of the market rent at the place where the goods are located computed for the same lease term, and (iii) any incidental damages allowed under Section 2A-530, less expenses saved in consequence of the lessee's default.

(2) If the measure of damages provided in subsection (1) is inadequate to put a lessor in as good a position as performance would have, the measure of damages is the present value of the profit, including reasonable overhead, the lessor would have made from full performance by the lessee, together with any incidental damages allowed under Section 2A-530, due allowance for costs reasonably incurred and due credit for payments or proceeds of disposition.

§2A-529. Lessor's Action for the Rent.—

(1) After default by the lessee under the lease contract of the type described in Section 2A-523(1) or 2A-523(3)(a) or, if agreed, after other default by the lessee, if the lessor complies with subsection (2), the lessor may recover from the lessee as damages:

(a) for goods accepted by the lessee and not repossessed by or tendered to the lessor, and for conforming goods lost or damaged within a commercially reasonable time after risk of loss passes to the lessee (Section 2A-219), (i) accrued and unpaid rent as of the date of entry of judgment in favor of the lessor, (ii) the present value as of the same date of the rent for the then remaining lease term of the lease agreement, and (iii) any incidental damages allowed under Section 2A-530, less expenses saved in consequence of the lessee's default; and

(b) for goods identified to the lease contract if the lessor is unable after reasonable effort to dispose of them at a reasonable price or the circumstances reasonably indicate that effort will be unavailing, (i) accrued and unpaid rent as of the date of entry of judgment in favor of the lessor, (ii) the present value as of the same date of the rent for the then remaining lease term of the lease agreement, and (iii) any incidental damages allowed under Section 2A-530, less expenses saved in consequence of the lessee's default.

(2) Except as provided in subsection (3), the lessor shall hold for the lessee for the remaining lease term of the lease agreement any goods that have been identified to the lease contract and are in the lessor's control.

(3) The lessor may dispose of the goods at any time before collection of the judgment for damages obtained pursuant to subsection (1). If the disposition is before the end of the remaining lease term of the lease agreement, the lessor's recovery against the lessee for damages is governed by Section 2A-527 or Section 2A-528, and the lessor will cause an appropriate credit to be provided against a judgment for damages to the extent that the amount of the judgment exceeds the recovery available pursuant to Section 2A-527 or 2A-528.

(4) Payment of the judgment for damages obtained pursuant to subsection (1) entitles the lessee to the use and possession of the goods not then disposed of for the remaining lease term of and in accordance with lease agreement.

(5) After a lessee has wrongfully rejected or revoked acceptance of goods, has failed to pay rent then due, or has repudiated (Section 2A-402), a lessor who is held not entitled to rent under this section must nevertheless be awarded damages for non-acceptance under Sections 2A-527 and 2A-528.

§2A-530. Lessor's Incidental Damages.—Incidental damages to an aggrieved lessor include any commercially reasonable charges, expenses, or commissions incurred in stopping delivery, in the transportation, care and custody of goods after the lessee's default, in connection with return or disposition of the goods, or otherwise resulting from the default.

§2A-531. Standing to Sue Third Parties for Injury to Goods.—
(1) If a third party so deals with goods that have been identified to a lease contract as to cause actionable injury to a party to the lease contract (a) the lessor has a right of action against the third party, and (b) the lessee also has a right of action against the third party if the lessee:
   (i) has a security interest in the goods;
   (ii) has an insurable interest in the goods; or
   (iii) bears the risk of loss under the lease contract or has since the injury assumed that risk as against the lessor and the goods have been converted or destroyed.
(2) If at the time of the injury the party plaintiff did not bear the risk of loss as against the other party to the lease contract and there is no arrangement between them for disposition of the recovery, his [or her] suit or settlement, subject to his [or her] own interest, is as a fiduciary for the other party to the lease contract.
(3) Either party with the consent of the other may sue for the benefit of whom it may concern.

§2A-532. Lessor's Rights to Residual Interest.—In addition to any other recovery permitted by this Article or other law, the lessor may recover from the lessee an amount that will fully compensate the lessor for any loss of or damage to the lessor's residual interest in the goods caused by the default of the lessee.

Article 3: Negotiable Instruments (Revised 1990)

Part 1: General Provisions and Definitions

§3-101. Short Title.—This Article may be cited as Uniform Commercial Code—Negotiable Instruments.

§3-102. Subject Matter.—
(a) This Article applies to negotiable instruments. It does not apply to money, to payment orders governed by Article 4A, or to securities governed by Article 8.
(b) If there is conflict between this Article and Article 4 or 9, Articles 4 and 9 govern.
(c) Regulations of the Board of Governors of the Federal Reserve System and operating circulars of the Federal Reserve Banks supersede any inconsistent provision of this Article to the extent of the inconsistency.

Note: The previous version of Article 3, Commercial Paper, is found in the Instructor's Resource Guide. You may wish to photocopy it for your students' use.

§3-103. Definitions.—
(a) In this Article:
   (1) "Acceptor" means a drawee who has accepted a draft.
   (2) "Drawee" means a person ordered in a draft to make payment.
   (3) "Drawer" means a person who signs or is identified in a draft as a person ordering payment.
   (4) "Good faith" means honesty in fact and the observance of reasonable commercial standards of fair dealing.
   (5) "Maker" means a person who signs or is identified in a note as a person undertaking to pay.
   (6) "Order" means a written instruction to pay money signed by the person giving the instruction. The instruction may be addressed to any person, including the person giving the instruction, or to one or more persons jointly or in the alternative but not in succession. An authorization to pay is not an order unless the person authorized to pay is also instructed to pay.
   (7) "Ordinary care" in the case of a person engaged in business means observance of reasonable commercial standards, prevailing in the area in which the person is located, with respect to the business in which the person is engaged. In the case of a bank that takes an instrument for processing for collection or payment by automated means, reasonable commercial standards do not require the bank to examine the instrument if the failure to examine does not violate the bank's prescribed procedures and the bank's procedures do not vary unreasonably from general banking usage not disapproved by this Article or Article 4.
   (8) "Party" means a party to an instrument.
   (9) "Promise" means a written undertaking to pay money signed by the person undertaking to pay. An acknowledgment of an obligation by the obligor is not a promise unless the obligor also undertakes to pay the obligation.
   (10) "Prove" with respect to a fact means to meet the burden of establishing the fact (Section 1-201(8)).
   (11) "Remitter" means a person who purchases an instrument from its issuer if the instrument is payable to an identified person other than the purchaser.
(b) Other definitions applying to this Article and the sections in which they appear are:

"Acceptance"	Section 3-409
"Accommodated party"	Section 3-419
"Accommodation party"	Section 3-419
"Alteration"	Section 3-407
"Anomalous indorsement"	Section 3-205
"Blank indorsement"	Section 3-205

"Cashier's check"	Section 3-104
"Certificate of deposit"	Section 3-104
"Certified check"	Section 3-409
"Check"	Section 3-104
"Consideration"	Section 3-303
"Draft"	Section 3-104
"Holder in due course"	Section 3-302
"Incomplete instrument"	Section 3-115
"Indorsement"	Section 3-204
"Indorser"	Section 3-204
"Instrument"	Section 3-104
"Issue"	Section 3-105
"Issuer"	Section 3-105
"Negotiable instrument"	Section 3-104
"Negotiation"	Section 3-201
"Note"	Section 3-104
"Payable at a definite time"	Section 3-108
"Payable on demand"	Section 3-108
"Payable to bearer"	Section 3-109
"Payable to order"	Section 3-109
"Payment"	Section 3-602
"Person entitled to enforce"	Section 3-301
"Presentment"	Section 3-501
"Reacquisition"	Section 3-207
"Special indorsement"	Section 3-205
"Teller's check"	Section 3-104
"Transfer of instrument"	Section 3-203
"Traveler's check"	Section 3-104
"Value"	Section 3-303

(c) The following definitions in other Articles apply to this Article:

"Bank"	Section 4-105
"Banking day"	Section 4-104
"Clearinghouse"	Section 4-104
"Collecting bank"	Section 4-105
"Depositary bank"	Section 4-105
"Documentary draft"	Section 4-104
"Intermediary bank"	Section 4-105
"Item"	Section 4-104
"Payor bank"	Section 4-105
"Suspends payments"	Section 4-104

(d) In addition, Article 1 contains general definitions and principles of construction and interpretation applicable throughout this Article.

§3-104. Negotiable Instrument.—

(a) Except as provided in subsections (c) and (d), "negotiable instrument" means an unconditional promise or order to pay a fixed amount of money, with or without interest or other charges described in the promise or order, if it:

(1) is payable to bearer or to order at the time it is issued or first comes into possession of a holder;

(2) is payable on demand or at a definite time; and

(3) does not state any other undertaking or instruction by the person promising or ordering payment to do any act in addition to the payment of money, but the promise or order may contain (i) an undertaking or power to give, maintain, or protect collateral to secure payment, (ii) an authorization or power to the holder to confess judgment or realize on or dispose of collateral, or (iii) a waiver of the benefit of any law intended for the advantage or protection of an obligor.

(b) "Instrument" means a negotiable instrument.

(c) An order that meets all of the requirements of subsection (a), except paragraph (1), and otherwise falls within the definition of "check" in subsection (f) is a negotiable instrument and a check.

(d) A promise or order other than a check is not an instrument if, at the time it is issued or first comes into possession of a holder, it contains a conspicuous statement, however expressed, to the effect that the promise or order is not negotiable or is not an instrument governed by this Article.

(e) An instrument is a "note" if it is a promise and is a "draft" if it is an order. If an instrument falls within the definition of both "note" and "draft", a person entitled to enforce the instrument may treat it as either.

(f) "Check" means (i) a draft, other than a documentary draft, payable on demand and drawn on a bank or (ii) a cashier's check or teller's check. An instrument may be a check even though it is described on its face by another term, such as "money order".

(g) "Cashier's check" means a draft with respect to which the drawer and drawee are the same bank or branches of the same bank.

(h) "Teller's check" means a draft drawn by a bank (i) on another bank, or (ii) payable at or through a bank.

(i) "Traveler's check" means an instrument that (i) is payable on demand, (ii) is drawn on or payable at or through a bank, (iii) is designated by the term "traveler's check" or by a substantially similar term, and (iv) requires, as a condition to payment, a countersignature by a person whose specimen signature appears on the instrument.

(j) "Certificate of deposit" means an instrument containing an acknowledgment by a bank that a sum of money has been received by the bank and a promise by the bank to repay the sum of money. A certificate of deposit is a note of the bank.

§3-105. Issue of Instrument.—

(a) "Issue" means the first delivery of an instrument by the maker or drawer, whether to a holder or nonholder, for the purpose of giving rights on the instrument to any person.

(b) An unissued instrument, or an unissued incomplete instrument that is completed, is binding on the maker or drawer, but nonissuance is a defense. An instrument that is conditionally issued or is issued for a special purpose is binding on the maker or drawer, but failure of the condition or special purpose to be fulfilled is a defense.

(c) "Issuer" applies to issued and unissued instruments and means a maker or drawer of an instrument.

§3-106. Unconditional Promise or Order.—

(a) Except as provided in this section, for the purposes of Section 3-104(a), a promise or order is unconditional unless it states (i) an express condition to payment, (ii) that the promise or order is subject to or governed by another writing, or (iii) that rights or obligations with respect to the promise or order are stated in another writing. A reference to another writing does not of itself make the promise or order conditional.

(b) A promise or order is not made conditional (i) by a reference to another writing for a statement of rights with respect to collateral, prepayment, or acceleration, or (ii) because payment is limited to resort to a particular fund or source.

(c) If a promise or order requires, as a condition to payment, a countersignature by a person whose specimen signature appears on the promise or order, the condition does not make the promise or order conditional for the purposes of Section 3-104(a). If the person whose specimen signature appears on an instrument fails to countersign the instrument, the failure to countersign is a defense to the obligation of the issuer, but the failure does not prevent a transferee of the instrument from becoming a holder of the instrument.

(d) If a promise or order at the time it is issued or first comes into possession of a holder contains a statement, required by applicable statutory or administrative law, to the effect that the rights of a holder or transferee are subject to claims or defenses that the issuer could assert the original payee, the promise or order is not thereby made conditional for the purposes of Section 3-104(a); but if the promise or order is an instrument, there cannot be a holder in due course of the instrument.

§3-107. Instrument Payable in Foreign Money.—

Unless the instrument otherwise provides, an instrument that states the amount payable in foreign money may be paid in the foreign money or in an equivalent amount in dollars calculated by using the current bank-offered spot rate at the place of payment for the purchase of dollars on the day on which the instrument is paid.

§3-108. Payable on Demand or at Definite Time.—

(a) A promise or order is "payable on demand" if it (i) states that it is payable on demand or at sight, or otherwise indicates that it is payable at the will of the holder, or (ii) does not state any time of payment.

(b) A promise or order is "payable at a definite time" if it is payable on elapse of a definite period of time after sight or acceptance or at a fixed date or dates or at a time or times readily ascertainable at the time the promise or order is issued, subject to rights of (i) prepayment, (ii) acceleration, (iii) extension at the option of the holder, or (iv) extension to a further definite time at the option of the maker or acceptor or automatically upon or after a specified act or event.

(c) If an instrument, payable at a fixed date, is also payable upon demand made before the fixed date, the instrument is payable on demand until the fixed date and, if demand for payment is not made before that date, becomes payable at a definite time on the fixed date.

§3-109. Payable to Bearer or to Order.—

(a) A promise or order is payable to bearer if it:
   (1) states that it is payable to bearer or to the order of bearer or otherwise indicates that the person in possession of the promise or order is entitled to payment;
   (2) does not state a payee; or
   (3) states that it is payable to or to the order of cash or otherwise indicates that it is not payable to an identified person.

(b) A promise or order that is not payable to bearer is payable to order if it is payable (i) to the order of an identified person or (ii) to an identified person or order. A promise or order that is payable to order is payable to the identified person.

(c) An instrument payable to bearer may become payable to an identified person if it is specially indorsed pursuant to Section 3-205(a). An instrument payable to an identified person may become payable to bearer if it is indorsed in blank pursuant to Section 3-205(b).

§3-110. Identification of Person to Whom Instrument is Payable.—

(a) The person to whom an instrument is initially payable is determined by the intent of the person, whether or not authorized, signing as, or in the name or behalf of, the issuer of the instrument. The instrument is payable to the person intended by the signer even if that person is identified in the instrument by a name or other identification that is not that of the intended person. If more than one person signs in the name or behalf of the issuer of an instrument and all the signers do not intend the same person as payee, the instrument is payable to any person intended by one or more of the signers.

(b) If the signature of the issuer of an instrument is made by automated means, such as a check-writing machine, the payee of the instrument is determined by the intent of the person who supplied the name or identification of the payee, whether or not authorized to do so.

(c) A person to whom an instrument is payable may be identified in any way, including by name, identifying number, office, or account number. For the purpose of determining the holder of an instrument, the following rules apply:
   (1) If an instrument is payable to an account and the account is identified only by number, the instrument is payable to the person to whom the account is payable. If an instrument is payable to an account identified by number and by the name of a person, the instrument is payable to the

named person, whether or not that person is the owner of the account identified by number.

(2) If an instrument is payable to:
    (i) a trust, an estate, or a person described as trustee or representative of a trust or estate, the instrument is payable to the trustee, the representative, or a successor of either, whether or not the beneficiary or estate is also named;
    (ii) a person described as agent or similar representative of a named or identified person, the instrument is payable to the represented person, the representative, or a successor of the representative;
    (iii) a fund or organization that is not a legal entity, the instrument is payable to a representative of the members of the fund or organization; or
    (iv) an office or to a person described as holding an office, the instrument is payable to the named person, the incumbent of the office, or a successor to the incumbent.

(d) If an instrument is payable to two or more persons alternatively, it is payable to any of them and may be negotiated, discharged, or enforced by any or all of them in possession of the instrument. If an instrument is payable to two or more persons not alternatively, it is payable to all of them and may be negotiated, discharged, or enforced only by all of them. If an instrument payable to two or more persons is ambiguous as to whether it is payable to the persons alternatively, the instrument is payable to the persons alternatively.

§3-111. Place of Payment.—

Except as otherwise provided for items in Article 4, an instrument is payable at the place of payment stated in the instrument. If no place of payment is stated, an instrument is payable at the address of the drawee or maker stated in the instrument. If no address is stated, the place of payment is the place of business of the drawee or maker. If a drawee or maker has more than one place of business, the place of payment is any place of business of the drawee or maker chosen by the person entitled to enforce the instrument. If the drawee or maker has no place of business, the place of payment is the residence of the drawee or maker.

§3-112. Interest.—

(a) Unless otherwise provided in the instrument, (i) an instrument is not payable with interest, and (ii) interest on an interest-bearing instrument is payable from the date of the instrument.
(b) Interest may be stated in an instrument as a fixed or variable amount of money or it may be expressed as a fixed or variable rate or rates. The amount or rate of interest may be stated or described in the instrument in any manner and may require reference to information not contained in the instrument. If an instrument provides for interest, but the amount of interest payable cannot be ascertained from the description, interest is payable at the judgment rate in effect at the place of payment of the instrument and at the time interest first accrues.

§3-113. Date of Instrument.—

(a) An instrument may be antedated or postdated. The date stated determines the time of payment if the instrument is payable at a fixed period after date. Except as provided in Section 4-401(c), an instrument payable on demand is not payable before the date of the instrument.
(b) If an instrument is undated, its date is the date of its issue or, in the case of an unissued instrument, the date it first comes into possession of a holder.

§3-114. Contradictory Terms of Instrument.—

If an instrument contains contradictory terms, typewritten terms prevail over printed terms, handwritten terms prevail over both, and words prevail over numbers.

§3-115. Incomplete Instrument.—

(a) "Incomplete instrument" means a signed writing, whether or not issued by the signer, the contents of which show at the time of signing that it is incomplete but that the signer intended it to be completed by the addition of words or numbers.
(b) Subject to subsection (c), if an incomplete instrument is an instrument under Section 3-104, it may be enforced according to its terms if it is not completed, or according to its terms as augmented by completion. If an incomplete instrument is not an instrument under Section 3-104, but, after completion, the requirements of Section 3-104 are met, the instrument may be enforced according to its terms as augmented by completion.
(c) If words or numbers are added to an incomplete instrument without authority of the signer, there is an alteration of the incomplete instrument under Section 3-407.
(d) The burden of establishing that words or numbers were added to an incomplete instrument without authority of the signer is on the person asserting the lack of authority.

§3-116. Joint and Several Liability; Contribution.—

(a) Except as otherwise provided in the instrument, two or more persons who have the same liability on an instrument as makers, drawers, acceptors, indorsers who indorse as joint payees, or anomalous indorsers are jointly and severally liable in the capacity in which they sign.
(b) Except as provided in Section 3-419(e) or by agreement of the affected parties, a party having joint and several liability who pays the instrument is entitled to receive from any party having the same joint and several liability contribution in accordance with applicable law.

(c) Discharge of one party having joint and several liability by a person entitled to enforce the instrument does not affect the right under subsection (b) of a party having the same joint and several liability to receive contribution from the party discharged.

§3-117. Other Agreements Affecting Instrument.—

Subject to applicable law regarding exclusion of proof of contemporaneous or previous agreements, the obligation of a party to an instrument to pay the instrument may be modified, supplemented, or nullified by a separate agreement of the obligor and a person entitled to enforce the instrument, if the instrument is issued or the obligation is incurred in reliance on the agreement or as part of the same transaction giving rise to the agreement. To the extent an obligation is modified, supplemented, or nullified by an agreement under this section, the agreement is a defense to the obligation.

§3-118. Statute of Limitations.—

(a) Except as provided in subsection (e), an action to enforce the obligation of a party to pay a note payable at a definite time must be commenced within six years after the due date or dates stated in the note or, if a due date is accelerated, within six years after the accelerated due date.

(b) Except as provided in subsection (d) or (e), if demand for payment is made to the maker of a note payable on demand, an action to enforce the obligation of a party to pay the note must be commenced within six years after the demand. If no demand for payment is made to the maker, an action to enforce the note is barred if neither principal nor interest on the note has been paid for a continuous period of 10 years.

(c) Except as provided in subsection (d), an action to enforce the obligation of a party to an unaccepted draft to pay the draft must be commenced within three years after dishonor of the draft or 10 years after the date of the draft, whichever period expires first.

(d) An action to enforce the obligation of the acceptor of a certified check or the issuer of a teller's check, cashier's check, or traveler's check must be commenced within three years after demand for payment is made to the acceptor or issuer, as the case may be.

(e) An action to enforce the obligation of a party to a certificate of deposit to pay the instrument must be commenced within six years after demand for payment is made to the maker, but if the instrument states a due date and the maker is not required to pay before that date, the six-year period begins when a demand for payment is in effect and the due date has passed.

(f) An action to enforce the obligation of a party to pay an accepted draft, other than a certified check, must be commenced (i) within six years after the due date or dates stated in the draft or acceptance if the obligation of the acceptor is payable at a definite time, or (ii) within six years after the date of the acceptance if the obligation of the acceptor is payable on demand.

(g) Unless governed by other law regarding claims for indemnity or contribution, an action (i) for conversion of an instrument, for money had and received, or like action based on conversion, (ii) for breach of warranty, or (iii) to enforce an obligation, duty, or right arising under this Article and not governed by this section must be commenced within three years after the [cause of action] accrues.

§3-119. Notice of Right to Defend Action.—

In an action for breach of an obligation for which a third person is answerable over pursuant to this Article or Article 4, the defendant may give the third person written notice of the litigation, and the person notified may then give similar notice to any other person who is answerable over. If the notice states (i) that the person notified may come in and defend and (ii) that failure to do so will bind the person notified in an action later brought by the person giving the notice as to any determination of fact common to the two litigations, the person notified is so bound unless after reasonable receipt of the notice the person notified does come in and defend.

Part 2: Negotiation, Transfer, and Indorsement

§3-201. Negotiation.—

(a) "Negotiation" means a transfer of possession, whether voluntary or involuntary, of an instrument by a person other than the issuer to a person who thereby becomes its holder.

(b) Except for negotiation by a remitter, if an instrument is payable to an identified person, negotiation requires transfer of possession of the instrument and its indorsement by the holder. If an instrument is payable to bearer, it may be negotiated by transfer of possession alone.

§3-202. Negotiation Subject to Rescission.—

(a) Negotiation is effective even if obtained (i) from an infant, a corporation exceeding its powers, or a person without capacity, (ii) by fraud, duress, or mistake, or (iii) in breach of duty or as part of an illegal transaction.

(b) To the extent permitted by other law, negotiation may be rescinded or may be subject to other remedies, but those remedies may not be asserted against a subsequent holder in due course or a person paying the instrument in good faith and without knowledge of facts that are a basis for rescission or other remedy.

§3-203. Transfer of Instrument; Rights Acquired by Transfer.—

(a) An instrument is transferred when it is delivered by a person other than its issuer for the purpose of giving to the person receiving delivery the right to enforce the instrument.

(b) Transfer of an instrument, whether or not the transfer is a negotiation, vests in the transferee any right of the transferor to enforce the instrument, including any right as a holder in due course, but the transferee cannot acquire rights of a holder in due course by a transfer, directly or indirectly, from a holder in due course if the transferee engaged in fraud or illegality affecting the instrument.

(c) Unless otherwise agreed, if an instrument is transferred for value and the transferee does not become a holder because of lack of indorsement by the transferor, the transferee has a specially enforceable right to the unqualified indorsement of the transferor, but negotiation of the instrument does not occur until the indorsement is made.

(d) If a transferor purports to transfer less than the entire instrument, negotiation of the instrument does not occur. The transferee obtains no rights under this Article, and has only the rights of a partial assignee.

§3-204. Indorsement.—

(a) "Indorsement" means a signature, other than that of a signer as maker, drawer, or acceptor, that alone or accompanied by other words is made on an instrument for the purpose of (i) negotiating the instrument, (ii) restricting payment of the instrument, or (iii) incurring indorser's liability on the instrument, but regardless of the intent of the signer, a signature and its accompanying words is an indorsement unless the accompanying words, terms of the instrument, place of the signature, or other circumstances unambiguously indicate that the signature was made for a purpose other than indorsement. For the purpose of determining whether a signature is made on an instrument, a paper affixed to the instrument is a part of the instrument.

(b) "Indorser" means a person who makes an indorsement.

(c) For the purpose of determining whether the transferee of an instrument is a holder, an indorsement that transfers a security interest in the instrument is effective as an unqualified indorsement of the instrument.

(d) If an instrument is payable to a holder under a name that is not the name of the holder, indorsement may be made by the holder in the name stated in the instrument or in the holder's name or both, but signature in both names may be required by a person paying or taking the instrument for value or collection.

§3-205. Special Indorsement; Blank Indorsement; Anomalous Indorsement.—

(a) If an indorsement is made by the holder of an instrument, whether payable to an identified person or payable to bearer, and the indorsement identifies a person to whom it makes the instrument payable, it is a "special indorsement". When specially indorsed, an instrument becomes payable to the identified person and may be negotiated only by the indorsement of that person. The principles stated in Section 3-110 apply to special indorsements.

(b) If an indorsement is made by the holder of an instrument and it is not a special indorsement, it is a "blank indorsement". When indorsed in blank, an instrument becomes payable to bearer and may be negotiated by transfer of possession alone until specially indorsed.

(c) The holder may convert a blank indorsement that consists only of a signature into a special indorsement by writing, above the signature of the indorser, words identifying the person to whom the instrument is made payable.

(d) "Anomalous indorsement" means an indorsement made by a person who is not the holder of the instrument. An anomalous indorsement does not affect the manner in which the instrument may be negotiated.

§3-206. Restrictive Indorsement.—

(a) An indorsement limiting payment to a particular person or otherwise prohibiting further transfer or negotiation of the instrument is not effective to prevent further transfer or negotiation of the instrument.

(b) An indorsement stating a condition to the right of the indorsee to receive payment does not affect the right of the indorsee to enforce the instrument. A person paying the instrument or taking it for value or collection may disregard the condition, and the rights and liabilities of that person are not affected by whether the condition has been fulfilled.

(c) If an instrument bears an indorsement (i) described in Section 4-201(b), or (ii) in blank or to a particular bank using the words "for deposit", "for collection", or other words indicating a purpose of having the instrument collected by a bank for the indorser or for a particular account, the following rules apply:

(1) A person, other than a bank, who purchases the instrument when so indorsed converts the instrument unless the amount paid for the instrument is received by the indorser or applied consistently with the indorsement.

(2) A depositary bank that purchases the instrument or takes it for collection when so indorsed converts the instrument unless the amount paid by the bank with respect to the instrument is received by the indorser or applied consistently with the indorsement.

(3) A payor bank that is also the depositary bank or that takes the instrument for immediate payment over the counter from a person other than a collecting bank converts the instrument unless the proceeds of the instrument are received by the indorser or applied consistently with the indorsement.

(4) Except as otherwise provided in paragraph (3), a payor bank or intermediary bank may disregard the indorsement and is not liable if the proceeds of the instrument are not received by the indorser or applied consistently with the indorsement.

(d) Except for an indorsement covered by subsection (c), if an instrument bears an indorsement using words to the effect that payment is to be made to the indorsee as agent, trustee, or other fiduciary for the benefit of the indorser or another person, the following rules apply:

   (1) Unless there is notice of breach of fiduciary duty as provided in Section 3-307, a person who purchases the instrument from the indorsee or takes the instrument from the indorsee for collection or payment may pay the proceeds of payment or the value given for the instrument to the indorsee without regard to whether the indorsee violates a fiduciary duty to the indorser.

   (2) A subsequent transferee of the instrument or person who pays the instrument is neither given notice nor otherwise affected by the restriction in the indorsement unless the transferee or payor knows that the fiduciary dealt with the instrument or its proceeds in breach of fiduciary duty.

(e) The presence on an instrument of an indorsement to which this section applies does not prevent a purchaser of the instrument from becoming a holder in due course of the instrument unless the purchaser is a converter under subsection (c) or has notice or knowledge of breach of fiduciary duty as stated in subsection (d).

(f) In an action to enforce the obligation of a party to pay the instrument, the obligor has a defense if payment would violate an indorsement to which this section applies and the payment is not permitted by this section.

§3-207. Reacquisition.

§3-207. Reacquisition.—Reacquisition of an instrument occurs if it is transferred to a former holder, by negotiation or otherwise. A former holder who reacquires the instrument may cancel indorsements made after the reacquirer first became a holder of the instrument. If the cancellation causes the instrument to be payable to the reacquirer or to bearer, the reacquirer may negotiate the instrument. An indorser whose indorsement is canceled is discharged, and the discharge is effective against any subsequent holder.

Part 3: Enforcement of Instruments

§3-301. Person Entitled to Enforce Instrument.

§3-301. Person Entitled to Enforce Instrument.—"Person entitled to enforce" an instrument means (i) the holder of the instrument, (ii) a nonholder in possession of the instrument who has the rights of a holder, or (iii) a person not in possession of the instrument who is entitled to enforce the instrument pursuant to Section 3-309 or 3-418(d). A person may be a person entitled to enforce the instrument even though the person is not the owner of the instrument or is in wrongful possession of the instrument.

§3-302. Holder in Due Course.

§3-302. Holder in Due Course.—

(a) Subject to subsection (c) and Section 3106(d), "holder in due course" means the holder of an instrument if:

   (1) the instrument when issued or negotiated to the holder does not bear such apparent evidence of forgery or alteration or is not otherwise so irregular or incomplete as to call into question its authenticity; and

   (2) the holder took the instrument (i) for value, (ii) in good faith, (iii) without notice that the instrument is overdue or has been dishonored or that there is an uncured default with respect to payment of another instrument issued as part of the same series, (iv) without notice that the instrument contains an unauthorized signature or has been altered, (v) without notice of any claim to the instrument described in Section 3-306, and (vi) without notice that any party has a defense or claim in recoupment described in Section 3-305(a).

(b) Notice of discharge of a party, other than discharge in an insolvency proceeding, is not notice of a defense under subsection (a), but discharge is effective against a person who became a holder in due course with notice of the discharge. Public filing or recording of a document does not of itself constitute notice of a defense, claim in recoupment, or claim to the instrument.

(c) Except to the extent a transferor or predecessor in interest has rights as a holder in due course, a person does not acquire rights of a holder in due course of an instrument taken (i) by legal process or by purchase in an execution, bankruptcy, or creditor's sale or similar proceeding, (ii) by purchase as part of a bulk transaction not in ordinary course of business of the transferor, or (iii) as the successor in interest to an estate or other organization.

(d) If, under Section 3-303(a)(1), the promise of performance that is the consideration for an instrument has been partially performed, the holder may assert rights as a holder in due course of the instrument only to the fraction of the amount payable under the instrument equal to the value of the partial performance divided by the value of the promised performance.

(e) If (i) the person entitled to enforce an instrument has only a security interest in the instrument and (ii) the person obliged to pay the instrument has a defense, claim in recoupment, or claim to the instrument that may be asserted against the person who granted the security interest, the person entitled to enforce the instrument may assert rights as a holder in due course only to an amount payable under the instrument which, at the time of enforcement of the instrument, does not exceed the amount of the unpaid obligation secured.

(f) To be effective, notice must be received at a time and in a manner that gives a reasonable opportunity to act on it.

(g) This section is subject to any law limiting status as a holder in due course in particular classes of transactions.

§3-303. Value and Consideration.

§3-303. Value and Consideration.—

(a) An instrument is issued or transferred for value if:

   (1) the instrument is issued or transferred for a promise of performance, to the extent the promise has been performed;

(2) the transferee acquires a security interest or other lien in the instrument other than a lien obtained by judicial proceeding;

(3) the instrument is issued or transferred as payment of, or as security for, an antecedent claim against any person, whether or not the claim is due;

(4) the instrument is issued or transferred in exchange for a negotiable instrument; or

(5) the instrument is issued or transferred in exchange for the incurring of an irrevocable obligation to a third party by the person taking the instrument.

(b) "Consideration" means any consideration sufficient to support a simple contract. The drawer or maker of an instrument has a defense if the instrument is issued without consideration. If an instrument is issued for a promise of performance, the issuer has a defense to the extent performance of the promise is due and the promise has not been performed. If an instrument is issued for value as stated in subsection (a), the instrument is also issued for consideration.

§3-304. Overdue Instrument.—

(a) An instrument payable on demand becomes overdue at the earliest of the following times:

(1) on the day after the day demand for payment is duly made;

(2) if the instrument is a check, 90 days after its date; or

(3) if the instrument is not a check, when the instrument has been outstanding for a period of time after its date which is unreasonably long under the circumstances of the particular case in light of the nature of the instrument and usage of the trade.

(b) With respect to an instrument payable at a definite time the following rules apply:

(1) If the principal is payable in installments and a due date has not been accelerated, the instrument becomes overdue upon default under the instrument for nonpayment of an installment, and the instrument remains overdue until the default is cured.

(2) If the principal is not payable in installments and the due date has not been accelerated, the instrument becomes overdue on the day after the due date.

(3) If a due date with respect to principal has been accelerated, the instrument becomes overdue on the day after the accelerated due date.

(c) Unless the due date of principal has been accelerated, an instrument does not become overdue if there is default in payment of interest but no default in payment of principal.

§3-305. Defenses and Claims in Recoupment.—

(a) Except as stated in subsection (b), the right to enforce the obligation of a party to pay an instrument is subject to the following:

(1) a defense of the obligor based on (i) infancy of the obligor to the extent it is a defense to a simple contract, (ii) duress, lack of legal capacity, or illegality of the transaction which, under other law, nullifies the obligation of the obligor, (iii) fraud that induced the obligor to sign the instrument with neither knowledge nor reasonable opportunity to learn of its character or its essential terms, or (iv) discharge of the obligor in insolvency proceedings;

(2) a defense of the obligor stated in another section of this Article or a defense of the obligor that would be available if the person entitled to enforce the instrument were enforcing a right to payment under a simple contract; and

(3) a claim in recoupment of the obligor against the original payee of the instrument if the claim arose from the transaction that gave rise to the instrument; but the claim of the obligor may be asserted against a transferee of the instrument only to reduce the amount owing on the instrument at the time the action is brought.

(b) The right of a holder in due course to enforce the obligation of a party to pay the instrument is subject to defenses of the obligor stated in subsection (a)(1), but is not subject to defenses of the obligor stated in subsection (a)(2) or claims in recoupment stated in subsection (a)(3) against a person other than the holder.

(c) Except as stated in subsection (d), in an action to enforce the obligation of a party to pay the instrument, the obligor may not assert against the person entitled to enforce the instrument a defense, claim in recoupment, or claim to the instrument (Section 3-306) of another person, but the other person's claim to the instrument may be asserted by the obligor if the other person is joined in the action and personally asserts the claim against the person entitled to enforce the instrument. An obligor is not obliged to pay the instrument if the person seeking enforcement of the instrument does not have rights of a holder in due course and the obligor proves that the instrument is a lost or stolen instrument.

(d) In an action to enforce the obligation of an accommodation party to pay an instrument, the accommodation party may assert against the person entitled to enforce the instrument any defense or claim in recoupment under subsection (a) that the accommodated party could assert against the person entitled to enforce the instrument, except the defenses of discharge in insolvency proceedings, infancy, and lack of legal capacity.

§3-306. Claims to an Instrument.—A person taking an instrument, other than a person having rights of a holder in due course, is subject to a claim of a property or possessory right in the instrument or its proceeds, including a claim to rescind a negotiation and to recover the instrument or its proceeds. A person having rights of a holder in due course takes free of the claim to the instrument.

§3-307. Notice of Breach of Fiduciary Duty.—

(a) In this section:

    (1) "Fiduciary" means an agent, trustee, partner, corporate officer or director, or other representative owing a fiduciary duty with respect to an instrument.

    (2) "Represented person" means the principal, beneficiary, partnership, corporation, or other person to whom the duty stated in paragraph (1) is owed.

(b) If (i) an instrument is taken from a fiduciary for payment or collection or for value, (ii) the taker has knowledge of the fiduciary status of the fiduciary, and (iii) the represented person makes a claim to the instrument or its proceeds on the basis that the transaction of the fiduciary is a breach of fiduciary duty, the following rules apply:

    (1) Notice of breach of fiduciary duty by the fiduciary is notice of the claim of the represented person.

    (2) In the case of an instrument payable to the represented person or the fiduciary as such, the taker has notice of the breach of fiduciary duty if the instrument is (i) taken in payment of or as security for a debt known by the taker to be the personal debt of the fiduciary, (ii) taken in a transaction known by the taker to be for the personal benefit of the fiduciary, or (iii) deposited to an account other than an account of the fiduciary, as such, or an account of the represented person.

    (3) If an instrument is issued by the represented person or the fiduciary as such, and made payable to the fiduciary personally, the taker does not have notice of the breach of fiduciary duty unless the taker knows of the breach of fiduciary duty.

    (4) If an instrument is issued by the represented person or the fiduciary as such, to the taker as payee, the taker has notice of the breach of fiduciary duty if the instrument is (i) taken in payment of or as security for a debt known by the taker to be the personal debt of the fiduciary, (ii) taken in a transaction known by the taker to be for the personal benefit of the fiduciary, or (iii) deposited to an account other than an account of the fiduciary, as such, or an account of the represented person.

§3-308. Proof of Signatures and Status as Holder in Due Course.—

(a) In an action with respect to an instrument, the authenticity of, and authority to make, each signature on the instrument is admitted unless specifically denied in the pleadings. If the validity of a signature is denied in the pleadings, the burden of establishing validity is on the person claiming validity, but the signature is presumed to be authentic and authorized unless the action is to enforce the liability of the purported signer and the signer is dead or incompetent at the time of trial of the issue of validity of the signature. If an action to enforce the instrument is brought against a person as the undisclosed principal of a person who signed the instrument as a party to the instrument, the plaintiff has the burden of establishing that the defendant is liable on the instrument as a represented person under Section 3-402(a).

(b) If the validity of signatures is admitted or proved and there is compliance with subsection (a), a plaintiff producing the instrument is entitled to payment if the plaintiff proves entitlement to enforce the instrument under Section 3-301, unless the defendant proves a defense or claim in recoupment. If a defense or claim in recoupment is proved, the right to payment of the plaintiff is subject to the defense or claim, except to the extent the plaintiff proves that the plaintiff has rights of a holder in due course which are not subject to the defense or claim.

§3-309. Enforcement of Lost, Destroyed, or Stolen Instrument.—

(a) A person not in possession of an instrument is entitled to enforce the instrument if (i) the person was in possession of the instrument and entitled to enforce it when loss of possession occurred, (ii) the loss of possession was not the result of a transfer by the person or a lawful seizure, and (iii) the person cannot reasonably obtain possession of the instrument because the instrument was destroyed, its whereabouts cannot be determined, or it is in the wrongful possession of an unknown person or a person that cannot be found or is not amenable to service of process.

(b) A person seeking enforcement of an instrument under subsection (a) must prove the terms of the instrument and the person's right to enforce the instrument. If that proof is made, Section 3-308 applies to the case as if the person seeking enforcement had produced the instrument. The court may not enter judgment in favor of the person seeking enforcement unless it finds that the person required to pay the instrument is adequately protected against loss that might occur by reason of a claim by another person to enforce the instrument. Adequate protection may be provided by any reasonable means.

§3-310. Effect of Instrument on Obligation for Which Taken.—

(a) Unless otherwise agreed, if a certified check, cashier's check, or teller's check is taken for an obligation, the obligation is discharged to the same extent discharge would result if an amount of money equal to the amount of the instrument were taken in payment of the obligation. Discharge of the obligation does not affect any liability that the obligor may have as an indorser of the instrument.

(b) Unless otherwise agreed and except as provided in subsection (a), if a note or an uncertified check is taken for an obligation, the obligation is suspended to the same extent the obligation would be discharged if an amount of money equal to the amount of the instrument were taken, and the following rules apply:

(1) In the case of an uncertified check, suspension of the obligation continues until dishonor of the check or until it is paid or certified. Payment or certification of the check results in discharge of the obligation to the extent of the amount of the check.

(2) In the case of a note, suspension of the obligation continues until dishonor of the note or until it is paid. Payment of the note results in discharge of the obligation to the extent of the payment.

(3) Except as provided in paragraph (4), if the check or note is dishonored and the obligee of the obligation for which the instrument was taken is the person entitled to enforce the instrument, the obligee may enforce either the instrument or the obligation. In the case of an instrument of a third person which is negotiated to the obligee by the obligor, discharge of the obligor on the instrument also discharges the obligation.

(4) If the person entitled to enforce the instrument taken for an obligation is a person other than the obligee, the obligee may not enforce the obligation to the extent the obligation is suspended. If the obligee is the person entitled to enforce the instrument but no longer has possession of it because it was lost, stolen, or destroyed, the obligation may not be enforced to the extent of the amount payable on the instrument, and to that extent the obligee's rights against the obligor are limited to enforcement of the instrument.

(c) If an instrument other than one described in subsection (a) or (b) is taken for an obligation, the effect is (i) that stated in subsection (a) if the instrument is one on which a bank is liable as maker or acceptor, or (ii) that stated in subsection (b) in any other case.

§3-311. Accord and Satisfaction by Use of Instrument.—

(a) If a person against whom a claim is asserted proves that (i) that person in good faith tendered an instrument to the claimant as full satisfaction of the claim, (ii) the amount of the claim was unliquidated or subject to a bona fide dispute, and (iii) the claimant obtained payment of the instrument, the following subsections apply.

(b) Unless subsection (c) applies, the claim is discharged if the person against whom the claim is asserted proves that the instrument or an accompanying written communication contained a conspicuous statement to the effect that the instrument was tendered as full satisfaction of the claim.

(c) Subject to subsection (d), a claim is not discharged under subsection (b) if either of the following applies:

(1) The claimant, if an organization, proves that (i) within a reasonable time before the tender, the claimant sent a conspicuous statement to the person against whom the claim is asserted that communications concerning disputed debts, including an instrument tendered as full satisfaction of a debt, are to be sent to a designated person, office, or place, and (ii) the instrument or accompanying communication was not received by that designated person, office, or place.

(2) The claimant, whether or not an organization, proves that within 90 days after payment of the instrument, the claimant tendered repayment of the amount of the instrument to the person against whom the claim is asserted. This paragraph does not apply if the claimant is an organization that sent a statement complying with paragraph (1)(i).

(d) A claim is discharged if the person against whom the claim is asserted proves that within a reasonable time before collection of the instrument was initiated, the claimant, or an agent of the claimant having direct responsibility with respect to the disputed obligation, knew that the instrument was tendered in full satisfaction of the claim.

§3-312. Lost, Destroyed, or Stolen Cashier's Check, Teller's Check, or Certified Check.—

(a) In this section:

(1) "Check" means a cashier's check, teller's check, or certified check.

(2) "Claimant" means a person who claims the right to receive the amount of a cashier's check, teller's check, or certified check that was lost, destroyed, or stolen.

(3) "Declaration of loss" means a written statement, made under penalty of perjury, to the effect that (i) the declarer lost possession of a check, (ii) the declarer is the drawer or payee of the check, in the case of a certified check, or the remitter or payee of the check, in the case of a cashier's check or teller's check, (iii) the loss of possession was not the result of a transfer by the declarer or a lawful seizure, and (iv) the declarer cannot reasonably obtain possession of the check because the check was destroyed, its whereabouts cannot be determined, or it is in the wrongful possession of an unknown person or a person that cannot be found or is not amenable to service of process.

(4) "Obligated bank" means the issuer of a cashier's check or teller's check or the acceptor of a certified check.

(b) A claimant may assert a claim to the amount of a check by a communication to the obligated bank describing the check with reasonable certainty and requesting payment of the amount of the check, if (i) the claimant is the drawer or payee of a certified check or the remitter or payee of a cashier's check or teller's check, (ii) the communication contains or is accompanied by a declaration of loss of the claimant with respect to the check, (iii) the communication is received at a time and in a manner affording the bank a reasonable time to act on it before the check is paid, and (iv) the claimant provides reasonable identification if requested by the obligated bank. Delivery of a declaration of loss is a warranty of the truth of the statements made in the declaration. If a claim is asserted in compliance with this subsection, the following rules apply:

(1) The claim becomes enforceable at the later of (i) the time the claim is asserted, or (ii) the 90th day following the date of the check, in the case of a cashier's check or teller's check, or the 90th day following the date of the acceptance, in the case of a certified check.

(2) Until the claim becomes enforceable, it has no legal effect and the obligated bank may pay the check or, in the case of a teller's check, may permit the drawee to pay the check. Payment to a person entitled to enforce the check discharges all liability of the obligated bank with respect to the check.

(3) If the claim becomes enforceable before the check is presented for payment, the obligated bank is not obliged to pay the check.

(4) When the claim becomes enforceable, the obligated bank becomes obliged to pay the amount of the check to the claimant if payment of the check has not been made to a person entitled to enforce the check. Subject to Section 4-302(a)(1), payment to the claimant discharges all liability of the obligated bank with respect to the check.

(c) If the obligated bank pays the amount of a check to a claimant under subsection (b)(4) and the check is presented for payment by a person having rights of a holder in due course, the claimant is obliged to (i) refund the payment to the obligated bank if the check is paid, or (ii) pay the amount of the check to the person having rights of a holder in due course if the check is dishonored.

(d) If a claimant has the right to assert a claim under subsection (b) and is also a person entitled to enforce a cashier's check, teller's check, or certified check which is lost, destroyed, or stolen, the claimant may assert rights with respect to the check either under this section or Section 3-309.

Part 4: Liability of Parties

§3-401. Signature.—

(a) A person is not liable on an instrument unless (i) the person signed the instrument, or (ii) the person is represented by an agent or representative who signed the instrument and the signature is binding on the represented person under Section 3-402.

(b) A signature may be made (i) manually or by means of a device or machine, and (ii) by the use of any name, including a trade or assumed name, or by a word, mark, or symbol executed or adopted by a person with present intention to authenticate a writing.

§3-402. Signature by Representative.—

(a) If a person acting, or purporting to act, as a representative signs an instrument by signing either the name of the represented person or the name of the signer, the represented person is bound by the signature to the same extent the represented person would be bound if the signature were on a simple contract. If the represented person is bound, the signature of the representative is the "authorized signature of the represented person" and the represented person is liable on the instrument, whether or not identified in the instrument.

(b) If a representative signs the name of the representative to an instrument and the signature is an authorized signature of the represented person, the following rules apply:

(1) If the form of the signature shows unambiguously that the signature is made on behalf of the represented person who is identified in the instrument, the representative is not liable on the instrument.

(2) Subject to subsection (c), if (i) the form of the signature does not show unambiguously that the signature is made in a representative capacity or (ii) the represented person is not identified in the instrument, the representative is liable on the instrument to a holder in due course that took the instrument without notice that the representative was not intended to be liable on the instrument. With respect to any other person, the representative is liable on the instrument unless the representative proves that the original parties did not intend the representative to be liable on the instrument.

(c) If a representative signs the name of the representative as drawer of a check without indication of the representative status and the check is payable from an account of the represented person who is identified on the check, the signer is not liable on the check if the signature is an authorized signature of the represented person.

§3-403. Unauthorized Signature.—

(a) Unless otherwise provided in this Article or Article 4, an unauthorized signature is ineffective except as the signature of the unauthorized signer in favor of a person who in good faith pays the instrument or takes it for value. An unauthorized signature may be ratified for all purposes of this Article.

(b) If the signature of more than one person is required to constitute the authorized signature of an organization, the signature of the organization is unauthorized if one of the required signatures is lacking.

(c) The civil or criminal liability of a person who makes an unauthorized signature is not affected by any provision of this Article which makes the unauthorized signature effective for the purposes of this Article.

§3-404. Impostors; Fictitious Payees.—

(a) If an impostor, by use of the mails or otherwise, induces the issuer of an instrument to issue the instrument to the impostor, or to a person acting in concert with the impostor, by impersonating the payee of the instrument or a person authorized to act for the payee, an indorsement of the instrument by any person in the name of the payee is effective as the indorsement of the payee in favor of a person who, in good faith, pays the instrument or takes it for value or for collection.

(b) If (i) a person whose intent determines to whom an instrument is payable (Section 3-110(a) or (b)) does not intend the person identified as payee to have any interest in the instrument, or (ii) the person identified as payee of an instrument is a fictitious person, the following rules apply until the instrument is negotiated by special indorsement:

    (1) Any person in possession of the instrument is its holder.

    (2) An indorsement by any person in the name of the payee stated in the instrument is effective as the indorsement of the payee in favor of a person who, in good faith, pays the instrument or takes it for value or for collection.

(c) Under subsection (a) or (b), an indorsement is made in the name of a payee if (i) it is made in a name substantially similar to that of the payee or (ii) the instrument, whether or not indorsed, is deposited in a depositary bank to an account in a name substantially similar to that of the payee.

(d) With respect to an instrument to which subsection (a) or (b) applies, if a person paying the instrument or taking it for value or for collection fails to exercise ordinary care in paying or taking the instrument and that failure substantially contributes to loss resulting from payment of the instrument, the person bearing the loss may recover from the person failing to exercise ordinary care to the extent the failure to exercise ordinary care contributed to the loss.

§3-405. Employer's Responsibility for Fraudulent Indorsement by Employee.—

(a) In this section

    (1) "Employee" includes an independent contractor and employee of an independent contractor retained by the employer.

    (2) "Fraudulent indorsement" means (i) in the case of an instrument payable to the employer, a forged indorsement purporting to be that of the employer, or (ii) in the case of an instrument with respect to which the employer is the issuer, a forged indorsement purporting to be that of the person identified as payee.

    (3) "Responsibility" with respect to instruments means authority (i) to sign or indorse instruments on behalf of the employer, (ii) to process instruments received by the employer for bookkeeping purposes, for deposit to an account, or for other disposition, (iii) to prepare or process instruments for issue in the name of the employer, (iv) to supply information determining the names or addresses of payees of instruments to be issued in the name of the employer, (v) to control the disposition of instruments to be issued in the name of the employer, or (vi) to act otherwise with respect to instruments in a responsible capacity. "Responsibility" does not include authority that merely allows an employee to have access to instruments or blank or incomplete instrument forms that are being stored or transported or are part of incoming or outgoing mail, or similar access.

(b) For the purpose of determining the rights and liabilities of a person who, in good faith, pays an instrument or takes it for value or for collection, if an employer entrusted an employee with responsibility with respect to the instrument and the employee or a person acting in concert with the employee makes a fraudulent indorsement of the instrument, the indorsement is effective as the indorsement of the person to whom the instrument is payable if it is made in the name of that person. If the person paying the instrument or taking it for value or for collection fails to exercise ordinary care in paying or taking the instrument and that failure substantially contributes to loss resulting from the fraud, the person bearing the loss may recover from the person failing to exercise ordinary care to the extent the failure to exercise ordinary care contributed to the loss.

(c) Under subsection (b), an indorsement is made in the name of the person to whom an instrument is payable if (i) it is made in a name substantially similar to the name of that person or (ii) the instrument, whether or not indorsed, is deposited in a depositary bank to an account in a name substantially similar to the name of that person.

§3-406. Negligence Contributing to Forged Signature or Alteration of Instrument.—

(a) A person whose failure to exercise ordinary care substantially contributes to an alteration of an instrument or to the making of a forged signature on an instrument is precluded from asserting the alteration or the forgery against a person who, in good faith, pays the instrument or takes it for value or for collection.

(b) Under subsection (a), if the person asserting the preclusion fails to exercise ordinary care in paying or taking the instrument and that failure substantially contributes to loss, the loss is allocated between the person precluded and the person asserting the preclusion according to the extent to which the failure of each to exercise ordinary care contributed to the loss.

(c) Under subsection (a), the burden of proving failure to exercise ordinary care is on the person asserting the preclusion. Under subsection (b), the burden of proving failure to exercise ordinary care is on the person precluded.

§3-407. Alteration.—

(a) "Alteration" means (i) an unauthorized change in an instrument that purports to modify in any respect the obligation of a party, or (ii) an unauthorized addition of words or numbers or other change to an incomplete instrument relating to the obligation of a party.

(b) Except as provided in subsection (c), an alteration fraudulently made discharges a party whose obligation is affected by the alteration unless that party assents or is precluded from asserting the alteration. No other alteration discharges a party, and the instrument may be enforced according to its original terms.

(c) A payor bank or drawee paying a fraudulently altered instrument or a person taking it for value, in good faith and without notice of the alteration, may enforce rights with respect to the instrument (i) according to its original terms, or (ii) in the case of an incomplete instrument altered by unauthorized completion, according to its terms as completed.

§3-408. Drawee Not Liable on Unaccepted Draft.—A
check or other draft does not of itself operate as an assignment of funds in the hands of the drawee available for its payment, and the drawee is not liable on the instrument until the drawee accepts it.

§3-409. Acceptance of Draft; Certified Check.—

(a) "Acceptance" means the drawee's signed agreement to pay a draft as presented. It must be written on the draft and may consist of the drawee's signature alone. Acceptance may be made at any time and becomes effective when notification pursuant to instructions is given or the accepted draft is delivered for the purpose of giving rights on the acceptance to any person.

(b) A draft may be accepted although it has not been signed by the drawer, is otherwise incomplete, is overdue, or has been dishonored.

(c) If a draft is payable at a fixed period after sight and the acceptor fails to date the acceptance, the holder may complete the acceptance by supplying a date in good faith.

(d) "Certified check" means a check accepted by the bank on which it is drawn. Acceptance may be made as stated in subsection (a) or by a writing on the check which indicates that the check is certified. The drawee of a check has no obligation to certify the check, and refusal to certify is not dishonor of the check.

§3-410. Acceptance Varying Draft.—

(a) If the terms of a drawee's acceptance vary from the terms of the draft as presented, the holder may refuse the acceptance and treat the draft as dishonored. In that case, the drawee may cancel the acceptance.

(b) The terms of a draft are not varied by an acceptance to pay at a particular bank or place in the United States, unless the acceptance states that the draft is to be paid only at that bank or place.

(c) If the holder assents to an acceptance varying the terms of a draft, the obligation of each drawer and indorser that does not expressly assent to the acceptance is discharged.

§3-411. Refusal to Pay Cashier's Checks, Teller's Checks, and Certified Checks.—

(a) In this section, "obligated bank" means the acceptor of a certified check or the issuer of a cashier's check or teller's check bought from the issuer.

(b) If the obligated bank wrongfully (i) refuses to pay a cashier's check or certified check, (ii) stops payment of a teller's check, or (iii) refuses to pay a dishonored teller's check, the person asserting the right to enforce the check is entitled to compensation for expenses and loss of interest resulting from the nonpayment and may recover consequential damages if the obligated bank refuses to pay after receiving notice of particular circumstances giving rise to the damages.

(c) Expenses or consequential damages under subsection (b) are not recoverable if the refusal of the obligated bank to pay occurs because (i) the bank suspends payments, (ii) the obligated bank asserts a claim or defense of the bank that it has reasonable grounds to believe is available against the person entitled to enforce the instrument, (iii) the obligated bank has a reasonable doubt whether the person demanding payment is the person entitled to enforce the instrument, or (iv) payment is prohibited by law.

§3-412. Obligation of Issuer of Note or Cashier's Check.—

The issuer of a note or cashier's check or other draft drawn on the drawer is obliged to pay the instrument (i) according to its terms at the time it was issued or, if not issued, at the time it first came into possession of a holder, or (ii) if the issuer signed an incomplete instrument, according to its terms when completed, to the extent stated in Sections 3-115 and 3-407. The obligation is owed to a person entitled to enforce the instrument or to an indorser who paid the instrument under Section 3-415.

§3-413. Obligation of Acceptor.—

(a) The acceptor of a draft is obliged to pay the draft (i) according to its terms at the time it was accepted, even though the acceptance states that the draft is payable "as originally drawn" or equivalent terms, (ii) if the acceptance varies the terms of the draft, according to the terms of the draft as varied, or (iii) if the acceptance is of a draft that is an incomplete instrument, according to its terms when completed, to the extent stated in Sections 3-115 and 3-407. The obligation is owed to a person entitled to enforce the draft or to the drawer or an indorser who paid the draft under Section 3-414 or 3-415.

(b) If the certification of a check or other acceptance of a draft states the amount certified or accepted, the obligation of the acceptor is that amount. If (i) the certification or acceptance does not state an amount, (ii) the amount of the instrument is subsequently raised, and (iii) the instrument is then negotiated to a holder in due course, the obligation of the acceptor is the amount of the instrument at the time it was taken by the holder in due course.

§3-414. Obligation of Drawer.—

(a) This section does not apply to cashier's checks or other drafts drawn on the drawer.

(b) If an unaccepted draft is dishonored, the drawer is obliged to pay the draft (i) according to its terms at the time it was issued or, if not issued, at the time it first came into possession of a holder, or (ii) if the drawer signed an incomplete instrument, according to its terms when completed, to the extent stated in Sections 3-115 and 3-407. The obligation is owed to a person entitled to enforce the draft or to an indorser who paid the draft under Section 3-415.

(c) If a draft is accepted by a bank, the drawer is discharged, regardless of when or by whom acceptance was obtained.

(d) If a draft is accepted and the acceptor is not a bank, the obligation of the drawer to pay the draft if the draft is dishonored by the acceptor is the same as the obligation of an indorser under Section 3-415(a) and (c).

(e) If a draft states that it is drawn "without recourse" or otherwise disclaims liability of the drawer to pay the draft, the drawer is not liable under subsection (b) to pay the draft if the draft is not a check. A disclaimer of the liability stated in subsection (b) is not effective if the draft is a check.

(f) If (i) a check is not presented for payment or given to a depositary bank for collection within 30 days after its date, (ii) the drawee suspends payments after expiration of the 30-day period without paying the check, and (iii) because of the suspension of payments, the drawer is deprived of funds maintained with the drawee to cover payment of the check, the drawer to the extent deprived of funds may discharge its obligation to pay the check by assigning to the person entitled to enforce the check the rights of the drawer against the drawee with respect to the funds.

§3-415. Obligation of Indorser.—

(a) Subject to subsections (b), (c), and (d) and to Section 3-419(d), if an instrument is dishonored, an indorser is obliged to pay the amount due on the instrument (i) according to the terms of the instrument at the time it was indorsed, or (ii) if the indorser indorsed an incomplete instrument, according to its terms when completed, to the extent stated in Sections 3-115 and 3-407. The obligation of the indorser is owed to a person entitled to enforce the instrument or to a subsequent indorser who paid the instrument under this section.

(b) If an indorsement states that it is made "without recourse" or otherwise disclaims liability of the indorser, the indorser is not liable under subsection (a) to pay the instrument.

(c) If notice of dishonor of an instrument is required by Section 3-503 and notice of dishonor complying with that section is not given to an indorser, the liability of the indorser under subsection (a) is discharged.

(d) If a draft is accepted by a bank after an indorsement is made, the liability of the indorser under subsection (a) is discharged.

(e) If an indorser of a check is liable under subsection (a) and the check is not presented for payment, or given to a depositary bank for collection, within 30 days after the day the indorsement was made, the liability of the indorser under subsection (a) is discharged.

§3-416. Transfer Warranties.—

(a) A person who transfers an instrument for consideration warrants to the transferee and, if the transfer is by indorsement, to any subsequent transferee that:
    (1) the warrantor is a person entitled to enforce the instrument;
    (2) all signatures on the instrument are authentic and authorized;
    (3) the instrument has not been altered;
    (4) the instrument is not subject to a defense or claim in recoupment of any party which can be asserted against the warrantor; and
    (5) the warrantor has no knowledge of any insolvency proceeding commenced with respect to the maker or acceptor or, in the case of an unaccepted draft, the drawer.

(b) A person to whom the warranties under subsection (a) are made and who took the instrument in good faith may recover from the warrantor as damages for breach of warranty an amount equal to the loss suffered as a result of the breach, but not more than the amount of the instrument plus expenses and loss of interest incurred as a result of the breach.

(c) The warranties stated in subsection (a) cannot be disclaimed with respect to checks. Unless notice of a claim for breach of warranty is given to the warrantor within 30 days after the claimant has reason to know of the breach and the identity of the warrantor, the liability of the warrantor under subsection (b) is discharged to the extent of any loss caused by the delay in giving notice of the claim.

(d) A [cause of action] for breach of warranty under this section accrues when the claimant has reason to know of the breach.

§3-417. Presentment Warranties.—

(a) If an unaccepted draft is presented to the drawee for payment or acceptance and the drawee pays or accepts the draft, (i) the person obtaining payment or acceptance, at the time of presentment, and (ii) a previous transferor of the draft, at the time of transfer, warrant to the drawee making payment or accepting the draft in good faith that:

(1) the warrantor is, or was, at the time the warrantor transferred the draft, a person entitled to enforce the draft or authorized to obtain payment or acceptance of the draft on behalf of a person entitled to enforce the draft;

(2) the draft has not been altered; and

(3) the warrantor has no knowledge that the signature of the drawer of the draft is unauthorized.

(b) A drawee making payment may recover from any warrantor damages for breach of warranty equal to the amount paid by the drawee less the amount the drawee received or is entitled to receive from the drawer because of the payment. In addition, the drawee is entitled to compensation for expenses and loss of interest resulting from the breach. The right of the drawee to recover damages under this subsection is not affected by any failure of the drawee to exercise ordinary care in making payment. If the drawee accepts the draft, breach of warranty is a defense to the obligation of the acceptor. If the acceptor makes payment with respect to the draft, the acceptor is entitled to recover from any warrantor for breach of warranty the amounts stated in this subsection.

(c) If a drawee asserts a claim for breach of warranty under subsection (a) based on an unauthorized indorsement of the draft or an alteration of the draft, the warrantor may defend by proving that the indorsement is effective under Section 3-404 or 3-405 or the drawer is precluded under Section 3-406 or 4-406 from asserting against the drawee the unauthorized indorsement or alteration.

(d) If (i) a dishonored draft is presented for payment to the drawer or an indorser or (ii) any other instrument is presented for payment to a party obliged to pay the instrument, and (iii) payment is received, the following rules apply:

(1) The person obtaining payment and a prior transferor of the instrument warrant to the person making payment in good faith that the warrantor is, or was, at the time the warrantor transferred the instrument, a person entitled to enforce the instrument or authorized to obtain payment on behalf of a person entitled to enforce the instrument.

(2) The person making payment may recover from any warrantor for breach of warranty an amount equal to the amount paid plus expenses and loss of interest resulting from the breach.

(e) The warranties stated in subsections (a) and (d) cannot be disclaimed with respect to checks. Unless notice of a claim for breach of warranty is given to the warrantor within 30 days after the claimant has reason to know of the breach and the identity of the warrantor, the liability of the warrantor under subsection (b) or (d) is discharged to the extent of any loss caused by the delay in giving notice of the claim.

(f) A [cause of action] for breach of warranty under this section accrues when the claimant has reason to know of the breach.

§3-418. Payment or Acceptance by Mistake.—

(a) Except as provided in subsection (c), if the drawee of a draft pays or accepts the draft and the drawee acted on the mistaken belief that (i) payment of the draft had not been stopped pursuant to Section 4-403 or (ii) the signature of the drawer of the draft was authorized, the drawee may recover the amount of the draft from the person to whom or for whose benefit payment was made or, in the case of acceptance, may revoke the acceptance. Rights of the drawee under this subsection are not affected by failure of the drawee to exercise ordinary care in paying or accepting the draft.

(b) Except as provided in subsection (c), if an instrument has been paid or accepted by mistake and the case is not covered by subsection (a), the person paying or accepting may, to the extent permitted by the law governing mistake and restitution, (i) recover the payment from the person to whom or for whose benefit payment was made or (ii) in the case of acceptance, may revoke the acceptance.

(c) The remedies provided by subsection (a) or (b) may not be asserted against a person who took the instrument in good faith and for value or who in good faith changed position in reliance on the payment or acceptance. This subsection does not limit remedies provided by Section 3-417 or 4-407.

(d) Notwithstanding Section 4-215, if an instrument is paid or accepted by mistake and the payor or acceptor recovers payment or revokes acceptance under subsection (a) or (b), the instrument is deemed not to have been paid or accepted and is treated as dishonored, and the person from whom payment is recovered has rights as a person entitled to enforce the dishonored instrument.

§3-419. Instruments Signed for Accommodation.—

(a) If an instrument is issued for value given for the benefit of a party to the instrument ("accommodated party") and another party to the instrument ("An accommodation party") signs the instrument for the purpose of incurring liability on the instrument without being a direct beneficiary of the value given for the instrument, the instrument is signed by the accommodation party "for accommodation".

(b) An accommodation party may sign the instrument as maker, drawer, acceptor, or indorser and, subject to subsection (d), is obliged to pay the instrument in the capacity in which the accommodation party signs. The obligation of an accommodation party may be enforced notwithstanding any statute of frauds and whether or not the accommodation party receives consideration for the accommodation.

(c) A person signing an instrument is presumed to be an accommodation party and there is notice that the instrument is signed for accommodation if the signature is an anomalous indorsement or is accompanied by words indicating that the signer is acting as surety or guarantor with respect to the obligation of another party to the instrument. Except as provided in Section 3-605, the obligation of an accommodation party to pay the instrument is not affected by the fact that the person enforcing the obligation had notice when the instrument was taken by that person that the accommodation party signed the instrument for accommodation.

(d) If the signature of a party to an instrument is accompanied by words indicating unambiguously that the party is guaranteeing collection rather than payment of the obligation of another party to the instrument, the signer is obliged to pay the amount due on the instrument to a person entitled to enforce the instrument only if (i) execution of judgment against the other party has been returned unsatisfied, (ii) the other party is insolvent or in an insolvency proceeding, (iii) the other party cannot be served with process, or (iv) it is otherwise apparent that payment cannot be obtained from the other party.

(e) An accommodation party who pays the instrument is entitled to reimbursement from the accommodated party and is entitled to enforce the instrument against the accommodated party. An accommodated party who pays the instrument has no right of recourse against, and is not entitled to contribution from, an accommodation party.

§3-420. Conversion of Instrument.—

(a) The law applicable to conversion of personal property applies to instruments. An instrument is also converted if it is taken by transfer, other than a negotiation, from a person not entitled to enforce the instrument or a bank makes or obtains payment with respect to the instrument for a person not entitled to enforce the instrument or receive payment. An action for conversion of an instrument may not be brought by (i) the issuer or acceptor of the instrument or (ii) a payee or indorsee who did not receive delivery of the instrument either directly or through delivery to an agent or a co-payee.

(b) In an action under subsection (a), the measure of liability is presumed to be the amount payable on the instrument, but recovery may not exceed the amount of the plaintiff's interest in the instrument.

(c) A representative, other than a depositary bank, who has in good faith dealt with an instrument or its proceeds on behalf of one who was not the person entitled to enforce the instrument is not liable in conversion to that person beyond the amount of any proceeds that it has not paid out.

Part 5: Dishonor

§3-501. Presentment.—

(a) "Presentment" means a demand made by or on behalf of a person entitled to enforce an instrument (i) to pay the instrument made to the drawee or a party obliged to pay the instrument or, in the case of a note or accepted draft payable at a bank, to the bank, or (ii) to accept a draft made to the drawee.

(b) The following rules are subject to Article 4, agreement of the parties, and clearing-house rules and the like:

(1) Presentment may be made at the place of payment of the instrument and must be made at the place of payment if the instrument is payable at a bank in the United States; may be made by any commercially reasonable means, including an oral, written, or electronic communication; is effective when the demand for payment or acceptance is received by the person to whom presentment is made; and is effective if made to any one of two or more makers, acceptors, drawees, or other payors.

(2) Upon demand of the person to whom presentment is made, the person making presentment must (i) exhibit the instrument, (ii) give reasonable identification and, if presentment is made on behalf of another person, reasonable evidence of authority to do so, and (iii) sign a receipt on the instrument for any payment made or surrender the instrument if full payment is made.

(3) Without dishonoring the instrument, the party to whom presentment is made may (i) return the instrument for lack of a necessary indorsement, or (ii) refuse payment or acceptance for failure of the presentment to comply with the terms of the instrument, an agreement of the parties, or other applicable law or rule.

(4) The party to whom presentment is made may treat presentment as occurring on the next business day after the day of presentment if the party to whom presentment is made has established a cut-off hour not earlier than 2 p.m for the receipt and processing of instruments presented for payment or acceptance and presentment is made after the cut-off hour.

§3-502. Dishonor.—

(a) Dishonor of a note is governed by the following rules:

(1) If the note is payable on demand, the note is dishonored if presentment is duly made to the maker and the note is not paid on the day of presentment.

(2) If the note is not payable on demand and is payable at or through a bank or the terms of the note require presentment, the note is dishonored if presentment is duly made and the note is not paid on the day it becomes payable or the day of presentment, whichever is later.

(3) If the note is not payable on demand and paragraph (2) does not apply, the note is dishonored if it is not paid on the day it becomes payable.

(b) Dishonor of an unaccepted draft other than a documentary draft is governed by the following rules:

  (1) If a check is duly presented for payment to the payor bank otherwise than for immediate payment over the counter, the check is dishonored if the payor bank makes timely return of the check or sends timely notice of dishonor or nonpayment under Section 4-301 or 4-302, or becomes accountable for the amount of the check under Section 4-302.

  (2) If a draft is payable on demand and paragraph (1) does not apply, the draft is dishonored if presentment for payment is duly made to the drawee and the draft is not paid on the day of presentment.

  (3) If a draft is payable on a date stated in the draft, the draft is dishonored if (i) presentment for payment is duly made to the drawee and payment is not made on the day the draft becomes payable or the day of presentment, whichever is later, or (ii) presentment for acceptance is duly made before the day the draft becomes payable and the draft is not accepted on the day of presentment.

  (4) If a draft is payable on elapse of a period of time after sight or acceptance, the draft is dishonored if presentment for acceptance is duly made and the draft is not accepted on the day of presentment.

(c) Dishonor of an unaccepted documentary draft occurs according to the rules stated in subsection (b)(2), (3), and (4), except that payment or acceptance may be delayed without dishonor until no later than the close of the third business day of the drawee following the day on which payment or acceptance is required by those paragraphs.

(d) Dishonor of an accepted draft is governed by the following rules:

  (1) If the draft is payable on demand, the draft is dishonored if presentment for payment is duly made to the acceptor and the draft is not paid on the day of presentment.

  (2) If the draft is not payable on demand, the draft is dishonored if presentment for payment is duly made to the acceptor and payment is not made on the day it becomes payable or the day of presentment, whichever is later.

(e) In any case in which presentment is otherwise required for dishonor under this section and presentment is excused under Section 3-504, dishonor occurs without presentment if the instrument is not duly accepted or paid.

(f) If a draft is dishonored because timely acceptance of the draft was not made and the person entitled to demand acceptance consents to a late acceptance, from the time of acceptance the draft is treated as never having been dishonored.

§3-503. Notice of Dishonor.—

(a) The obligation of an indorser stated in Section 3-415(a) and the obligation of a drawer stated in Section 3-414(d) may not be enforced unless (i) the indorser or drawer is given notice of dishonor of the instrument complying with this section or (ii) notice of dishonor is excused under Section 3-504(b).

(b) Notice of dishonor may be given by any person; may be given by any commercially reasonable means, including an oral, written, or electronic communication; and is sufficient if it reasonably identifies the instrument and indicates that the instrument has been dishonored or has not been paid or accepted. Return of an instrument given to a bank for collection is sufficient notice of dishonor.

(c) Subject to Section 3-504(c), with respect to an instrument taken for collection by a collecting bank, notice of dishonor must be given (i) by the bank before midnight of the next banking day following the banking day on which the bank receives notice of dishonor of the instrument, or (ii) by any other person within 30 days following the day on which the person receives notice of dishonor. With respect to any other instrument, notice of dishonor must be given within 30 days following the day on which dishonor occurs.

§3-504. Excused Presentment and Notice of Dishonor.—

(a) Presentment for payment or acceptance of an instrument is excused if (i) the person entitled to present the instrument cannot with reasonable diligence make presentment, (ii) the maker or acceptor has repudiated an obligation to pay the instrument or is dead or in insolvency proceedings, (iii) by the terms of the instrument presentment is not necessary to enforce the obligation of indorsers or the drawer, (iv) the drawer or indorser whose obligation is being enforced has waived presentment or otherwise has no reason to expect or right to require that the instrument be paid or accepted, or (v) the drawer instructed the drawee not to pay or accept the draft or the drawee was not obligated to the drawer to pay the draft.

(b) Notice of dishonor is excused if (i) by the terms of the instrument notice of dishonor is not necessary to enforce the obligation of a party to pay the instrument, or (ii) the party whose obligation is being enforced waived notice of dishonor. A waiver of presentment is also a waiver of notice of dishonor.

(c) Delay in giving notice of dishonor is excused if the delay was caused by circumstances beyond the control of the person giving the notice and the person giving the notice exercised reasonable diligence after the cause of the delay ceased to operate.

§3-505. Evidence of Dishonor.—

(a) The following are admissible as evidence and create a presumption of dishonor and of any notice of dishonor stated:

  (1) a document regular in form as provided in subsection (b) which purports to be a protest;

(2) a purported stamp or writing of the drawee, payor bank, or presenting bank on or accompanying the instrument stating that acceptance or payment has been refused unless reasons for the refusal are stated and the reasons are not consistent with dishonor;

(3) a book or record of the drawee, payor bank, or collecting bank, kept in the usual course of business which shows dishonor, even if there is no evidence of who made the entry.

(b) A protest is a certificate of dishonor made by a United States consul or vice consul, or a notary public or other person authorized to administer oaths by the law of the place where dishonor occurs. It may be made upon information satisfactory to that person. The protest must identify the instrument and certify either that presentment has been made or, if not made, the reason why it was not made, and that the instrument has been dishonored by nonacceptance or nonpayment. The protest may also certify that notice of dishonor has been given to some or all parties.

Part 6: Discharge and Payment

§3-601. Discharge and Effect of Discharge.—

(a) The obligation of a party to pay the instrument is discharged as stated in this Article or by an act or agreement with the party which would discharge an obligation to pay money under a simple contract.

(b) Discharge of the obligation of a party is not effective against a person acquiring rights of a holder in due course of the instrument without notice of the discharge.

§3-602. Payment.—

(a) Subject to subsection (b), an instrument is paid to the extent payment is made (i) by or on behalf of a party obliged to pay the instrument, and (ii) to a person entitled to enforce the instrument. To the extent of the payment, the obligation of the party obliged to pay the instrument is discharged even though payment is made with knowledge of a claim to the instrument under Section 3-306 by another person.

(b) The obligation of a party to pay the instrument is not discharged under subsection (a) if:

(1) a claim to the instrument under Section 3-306 is enforceable against the party receiving payment and (i) payment is made with knowledge by the payor that payment is prohibited by injunction or similar process of a court of competent jurisdiction, or (ii) in the case of an instrument other than a cashier's check, teller's check, or certified check, the party making payment accepted, from the person having a claim to the instrument, indemnity against loss resulting from refusal to pay the person entitled to enforce the instrument; or

(2) the person making payment knows that the instrument is a stolen instrument and pays a person it knows is in wrongful possession of the instrument.

§3-603. Tender of Payment.—

(a) If tender of payment of an obligation to pay an instrument is made to a person entitled to enforce the instrument, the effect of tender is governed by principles of law applicable to tender of payment under a simple contract.

(b) If tender of payment of an obligation to pay an instrument is made to a person entitled to enforce the instrument and the tender is refused, ...

§3-604. Discharge by Cancellation or Renunciation.—

(a) A person entitled to enforce an instrument, with or without consideration, may discharge the obligation of a party to pay the instrument (i) by an intentional voluntary act, such as surrender of the instrument to the party, destruction, mutilation, or cancellation of the instrument, cancellation or striking out of the party's signature, or the addition of words to the instrument indicating discharge, or (ii) by agreeing not to sue or otherwise renouncing rights against the party by a signed writing.

(b) Cancellation or striking out of an indorsement pursuant to subsection (a) does not affect the status and rights of a party derived from the indorsement.

§3-605. Discharge of Indorsers and Accommodation Parties.—

(a) In this section, the term "indorser" includes a drawer having the obligation described in Section 3-414(d).

(b) Discharge, under Section 3-604, of the obligation of a party to pay an instrument does not discharge the obligation of an indorser or accommodation party having a right of recourse against the discharged party.

(c) If a person entitled to enforce an instrument agrees, with or without consideration, to an extension of the due date of the obligation of a party to pay the instrument, the extension discharges an indorser or accommodation party having a right of recourse against the party whose obligation is extended to the extent the indorser or accommodation party proves that the extension caused loss to the indorser or accommodation party with respect to the right of recourse.

(d) If a person entitled to enforce an instrument agrees, with or without consideration, to a material modification of the obligation of a party other than an extension of the due date, the modification discharges the obligation of an indorser or accommodation party having a right of recourse against the person whose obligation is modified to the extent the modification causes loss to the indorser or accommodation party with respect to the right of recourse. The loss suffered by the indorser or accommodation party as a result of the modification is equal to the amount of the right of recourse unless the person enforcing the instrument proves that no loss was caused by the modification or that the loss caused by the modification was an amount less than the amount of the right of recourse.

(e) If the obligation of a party to pay an instrument is secured by an interest in collateral and a person entitled to enforce the instrument impairs the value of the interest in collateral, the obligation of an indorser or accommodation party having a right of recourse against the obligor is discharged to the extent of the impairment. The value of an interest in collateral is impaired to the extent (i) the value of the interest is reduced to an amount less than the amount of the right of recourse of the party asserting discharge, or (ii) the reduction in value of the interest causes an increase in the amount by which the amount of the right of recourse exceeds the value of the interest. The burden of proving impairment is on the party asserting discharge.

(f) If the obligation of a party is secured by an interest in collateral not provided by an accommodation party and a person entitled to enforce the instrument impairs the value of the interest in collateral, the obligation of any party who is jointly and severally liable with respect to the secured obligation is discharged to the extent the impairment causes the party asserting discharge to pay more than that party would have been obliged to pay, taking into account rights of contribution, if impairment had not occurred. If the party asserting discharge is an accommodation party not entitled to discharge under subsection (e), the party is deemed to have a right to contribution based on joint and several liability rather than a right to reimbursement. The burden of proving impairment is on the party asserting discharge.

(g) Under subsection (e) or (f), impairing value of an interest in collateral includes (i) failure to obtain or maintain perfection or recordation of the interest in collateral, (ii) release of collateral without substitution of collateral of equal value, (iii) failure to perform a duty to preserve the value of collateral owed, under Article 9 or other law, to a debtor or surety or other person secondarily liable, or (iv) failure to comply with applicable law in disposing of collateral.

(h) An accommodation party is not discharged under subsection (c), (d), or (e) unless the person entitled to enforce the instrument knows of the accommodation or has notice under Section 3-419(c) that the instrument was signed for accommodation.

(i) A party is not discharged under this section if (i) the party asserting discharge consents to the event or conduct that is the basis of the discharge, or (ii) the instrument or a separate agreement of the party provides for waiver of discharge under this section either specifically or by general language indicating that parties waive defenses based on suretyship or impairment of collateral.

Glossary

abandoned In contract law, the condition that exists when a minor has left home and given up all rights to parental support.

abandoned property Property that has been discarded by the owner without the intent to reclaim ownership of it. Courts require clear and convincing evidence of both the desertion by the owner and the owner's intent never to return.

abandonment of contractual obligations The situation that exists when a party to a contract stops performance once it has begun.

abuse of process The use of a legal procedure for a purpose other than that for which it is legitimately intended.

acceleration A provision in a mortgage agreement that allows the mortgage to demand the entire balance due when the mortgagor misses a single installment payment.

acceptance A promise or act on the part of an offeree indicating a willingness to be bound by the terms and conditions contained in an offer. Also, the acknowledgment of the drawee that binds the drawee to the terms of a draft.

acceptor A drawee of a draft who has promised to honor the draft as presented by signing it on its face.

accommodation party A person who signs an instrument in any capacity for the purpose of lending his or her name to another party to the instrument. That person then assumes the same liability as the marker.

accord The implied or expressed acceptance of less than what the creditor billed the debtor.

accord and satisfaction An agreement (accord) whereby a creditor accepts as full payment an amount that is less than the amount due.

accounting A statement detailing the financial transactions of a business and the status of its assets.

acknowledgment The official recognition by a notary public that another's signature was made by that party's free will. The acknowledgment is accomplished when the notary has signed the document and added the official seal to it.

active data Data in a computer system that is actually being used at the present time.

active fraud A false statement made or an action actually taken by one party with the intent to deceive a second party and thus lead that second party into a deceptively based agreement.

actual damages A sum of money equal to the real financial loss suffered by an injured party. Also called *compensatory damages.*

actual eviction An eviction in which the tenant is physically deprived of the leasehold.

actual malice The legal test used by the courts to determine defamation against a public official or a public figure. The actual malice test requires the public official or public figure to prove not only that the statement was false, but also that it was made with the knowledge that it was false or with a reckless disregard for its truth or falsity.

adhesion contract A contract drawn by one party that must be accepted as is on a take-it-or-leave-it basis.

administrative law That body of law, including decrees and legal decisions, generated by administrative agencies.

administrator (male); administratrix (female) A person appointed by the court to do the work of an executor if none is named in a will or if the executor either refuses to perform or is incapable of performing the duties.

ADR contract clause A clause that specifies that the parties to the agreement have promised to use an alternative dispute resolution technique when a disagreement arises rather than litigating the issue.

adversarial system The system on which the American legal process is built. An orderly and aggressive way to settle disputes in which attorneys for each side attempt to persuade a judge or jury of the veracity of his or her case.

adverse opinion An auditor's opinion that states that deviations from generally accepted accounting principles are so serious that an unqualified opinion is impossible and a qualified opinion is not justified.

adverse possession Title to real property obtained by taking actual possession of the property openly, notoriously, exclusively, under a claim of right, and continuously for a period of time set by state statute.

affirmance See *ratification.*

affirmative defense A set of circumstances that indicates that a defendant should not be held liable, even if the plaintiff proves all of the facts in a complaint.

agency A legal agreement between two persons, whereby one is designated the agent of the other.

agency coupled with an interest An irrevocable agency agreement in which the agent is given an interest in the subject matter of the agency. Also called *irrevocable agency.*

agent A person authorized to act on behalf of another and subject to the other's control in dealing with third parties.

aggregate theory A theory in partnership law which holds that a partnership is actually a conglomeration of the partners rather than a separate legal person with its own legal identity.

agreements in restraint of trade Agreements that remove competition, deny to the public the services it would otherwise have, or result in higher prices and hardship.

algorithm A series of mathematical steps that, if followed properly, will reach a desired goal.

alien corporation A corporation that although incorporated in a foreign country, does business in the United States.

alternative dispute resolution (ADR) A process that occurs whenever individuals attempt to resolve a disagreement by stepping outside the usual adversarial system and applying creative settlement techniques, many of which have fact finding and the discovery of truth as their goal.

allonge A strip of paper attached to a negotiable instrument for the writing of indorsements.

American Law Institute (ALI) test A test under which a criminal defendant will be judged not guilty by reason of insanity is "as a result of mental disease or defect he lacks substantial capacity either to appreciate the criminality of his conduct or to conform his conduct to the requirements of the law."

annual percentage rate (APR) The true rate of interest on a loan.

annuity A guaranteed retirement income.

anomalous indorsement An indorsement made by an accommodation party.

answer A defendant's official response to a complaint.

anticipatory breach A breach that occurs when a party to a contract either expresses or clearly implies an intention not to perform the contract even before being required to act. Also called *constructive breach.*

apparent authority An accountability doctrine whereby a principal, by virtue of words or actions, leads a third party to believe that an agent has authority but no such authority was intended. Also called *ostensible authority.*

appeal bond The payment of a set sum of money into a protected account to secure the payment of that money to the plaintiff should the defendant be defeated.

appellate jurisdiction The power of a court to review a case for errors.

arbitration The process by which an outside party settles a dispute between two other parties.

arbitrator The third party in the arbitration procedure whose job is to settle the dispute.

arraignment A formal court proceeding, during which the defendant, after hearing the indictment or information read, pleads either guilty or not guilty.

arson The willful or malicious act of causing the burning of another's property.

articles of incorporation A written application to a state for permission to incorporate.

articles of organization The written application to the state for permission to form a limited liability company.

articles of partnership A written agreement that establishes a partnership.

assault An attempt to commit a battery.

asset acquisition The purchase of all the property of a corporation by another corporation.

assign To transfer property by sale, mortgage, pledge, or otherwise.

assignee A person to whom an assignment is made.

assignment The transfer of a contract right from one person to another.

assignor A person who assigns rights or delegates duties under an assignment.

associative corporativism The process of doing business as a self-governing business association, that is, as a corporation. Also known as *corporativism.*

assume the mortgage An agreement whereby the buyer of real property already mortgaged agrees to pay the mortgage.

ATM card A card used together with a personal identification number (PIN) to gain access to an automatic teller machine.

attachment The act of taking a person's property and bringing it into the custody of law.

auction with reserve An auction at which the auctioneer has the right to withdraw goods and not sell them if acceptable bids are not made.

auction without reserve An auction at which the auctioneer cannot withdraw goods unless no bid is made within a reasonable time.

audit An examination of the financial records of an organization to determine whether those records are a fair representation of the actual financial health of the institution.

auditor The accountant who examines the financial records of an organization to determine whether those records are a fair representation of the actual financial health of the institution.

authenticate (*a*) to sign; or (*b*) with the intent to sign a record, otherwise to execute or adopt an electronic symbol, sound, message, or process referring to, attached to, included in, or logically associated or linked with, that record.

automatic stay A self-operating postponement of collection proceedings against a debtor who has filed a petition for bankruptcy.

automatic suspension A court order that stops a debtor's creditors from making any further moves to collect the money that the debtor owes them.

back-up data Data associated with a computer system that has been duplicated for safekeeping at another location.

bailee The person to whom personal property is transferred under a contract of bailment.

bailment The transfer of possession and control of personal property to another with the intent that the same property will be returned later.

bailment by necessity Arises when a customer must give up possession of property for the benefit of both parties; for example, when one purchases a suit or dress and is required to give up possession of one's own property while being fitted.

bailment for the sole benefit of the bailee A bailment in which the bailee receives all the benefits of the transaction.

bailment for the sole benefit of the bailor A bailment in which the bailor receives all the transaction.

bailor The person who transfers personal property under a contract of bailment.

bait-and-switch scheme An illegal promotional practice in which a seller attracts consumers by promoting a product (bait) that he or she does not intend to sell and then directs the consumers' attention to a higher-priced product (switch).

balloon payment A large final payment on a mortgage that has relatively low fixed payments during the life of the mortgage.

balloon-payment mortgage A mortgage that has relatively low fixed payments during the life of the mortgage followed by one large final (balloon) payment.

bank draft A check drawn by one bank on another bank in which it has funds on deposit in favor of a third person, the payee. Also called *teller's check*.

bankruptcy The legal process by which the assets of a debtor are sold to pay off creditors so that the debtor can make a fresh start financially.

bankruptcy trustee A person appointed by the court who is charged with the responsibility of liquidating the assets of the debtor for the benefit of all interested parties.

bargain-and-sale deed A deed that transfers title to real property but contains no warranties. This type of deed is not valid without consideration.

bargained-for exchange In reference to agreements, when a promise is made in exchange for another promise, in exchange for an act, or in exchange for a forbearance to act.

bargaining unit Employees joined together for the purpose of collective bargaining.

battered spouse syndrome A defense to criminal liability available to defendants if they can prove that they believed the only way to escape death or severe bodily injury was to use force against their tormentors.

battery The unlawful touching of another person.

bearer A person who is in possession of a negotiable instrument that is payable to the "bearer" or "cash" or that has been indorsed in blank.

bearer paper An instrument payable to bearer or cash that may be negotiated by delivery only.

beneficiary A third party receiving benefits from a contract made between two other parties. Also, the person named in an insurance policy to receive benefits paid by the insurer in event of a claim.

bequest Personal property left in a will. Also called *legacy*.

best evidence rule The legal rule that holds that the courts generally accept into evidence only the original of a writing, not a copy.

bilateral contract A contract in which both parties make promises.

bilateral mistake In contract law, a mistake made by both parties to a contract. Bilateral mistake allows rescission by either party. Also called *mutual mistake*.

bill of exchange See *draft*.

bill of lading A document evidencing the receipt of goods for shipment and issued by a person engaged in the business of transporting or forwarding goods.

bill of sale A written statement evidencing the transfer of personal property from one person to another.

binder An oral or a written memorandum of an agreement for insurance intended to provide temporary insurance coverage until the policy is formally accepted.

binding precedent A previous cause that a particular court must follow.

blank indorsement An indorsement made by a signature alone, with no particular indorsee, written on a negotiable instrument.

blue laws State statutes and local ordinances that regulate the making and performing of contracts on Sunday.

bodily injury liability insurance A type of automobile insurance that covers the risk of bodily injury or death to pedestrians and to the occupants of other cars arising from the negligent operation of the insured's motor vehicle.

bond A certificate of indebtedness that obligates a government or corporation to pay the bondholder a fixed rate of interest on the principal at regular intervals and to pay the principal on a stated maturity date. Also, a promise by the executor or administrator (and the sureties, if any) of a will to pay the amount of the bond to the probate court if the duties of the position are not faithfully performed.

borrowed servant A servant loaned to another master.

bot A type of cyberagent that searches cyberspace for the lowest price in a contract, sifts through the net for the best accommodations, hunts cyberspace for the most economical plan, or spontaneously responds to a bidding process. Also known as *robot, shopping bot, cyberbot,* and *e-bot.*

boycott A concerted refusal to have dealings with someone to force the acceptance of certain conditions.

breach of contract The failure of one of the parties to a contract to do what was previously agreed upon.

bribery The act of offering, giving, receiving, or soliciting something of value to influence official action or the discharge of a public duty.

bulk transfer Any transfer of a major party of the materials, supplies, merchandise, or other inventory of an enterprise that is not in the ordinary course of the transferor's business.

burglary The break-in of a dwelling or building for the purpose of carrying out a felony.

business compulsion See *economic duress.*

business judgment rule The rule that a corporate manager's decisions will not be interfered with by a court as long as the decision was made with due care, is in good faith, is lawful, and is in the best interest of the corporation.

business system Until recently business systems were considered unpatentable because they were not a "process, machine, or composition of matter." Recently, however, some computerized business systems have been patented if they consist of some nonobvious, new, and useful feature not known or understood before the invention of this system.

buyer in the ordinary course of business A person who in good faith and without knowledge that the sale is in violation of ownership rights or security interests of a third party buys goods in ordinary course from a person in the business of selling goods of that kind, not including a pawnbroker.

Buyer's Guide A window sticker that is required by the Federal Trade Commission Act to be placed in the window of each used car offered for sale by a used car dealer. The sticker discloses the warranties that are made with the sale of the car and other consumer protection information.

bylaws Rules that guide a corporation's day-to-day internal affairs. Also known as regulations.

c.f. Cost and freight. Terms instructing a carrier to collect the cost of goods shipped and freight charges.

c.i.f. Cost, insurance, and freight. Terms instructing a carrier to collect the cost of goods shipped, insurance, and freight charges.

Can Spam Act A federal law designed to reduce the use of unsolicited email, commonly known as spam, on the Internet.

c.o.d. Cash on delivery. Instructs a carrier to retain goods until he or she has collected the costs of the goods.

capacity In contract law, the legal ability to enter into a contractual relationship.

capital The money and property that a business needs to operate.

capital contribution The sum contributed by a business partner as a permanent investment in the business. It is then considered to be the property of the partnership.

carrier A business that undertakes to transport persons, goods, or both.

case in chief The collection of evidence that will prove a plaintiff's version of case to a jury.

cash dividend Dividend paid to shareholders in the form of cash.

cashier's check A check drawn by a bank upon its own funds.

certificate of authority A document that grants a foreign corporation permission to do business within another state.

certificate of deposit (CD) An acknowledgment by a bank of the receipt of money and a promise to pay the money back on the due date, usually with interest.

certificate of incorporation A corporation's official authorization to do business in a state. Also called *charter* or *corporate charter.*

certification authority (CA) It is the job of the CA to provide businesses with digital signatures and to make certain that those signatures are kept current.

certified check A check that has been marked, or certified, by the bank on which it was drawn, guaranteeing payment to the holder.

certified public accountant (CPA) An accountant who has met certain age, character, education, experience, and testing requirements.

chattels Property that has substance and that can be touched.

check A draft drawn on a bank and payable on demand.

Check 21 Act A law that makes check clearing much quicker by the use of a *substitute check* in place of the original check for electronic check processing.

chemical abuse The use of drugs or alcohol to such an extent that a person's judgment is impaired or his or her physical body is harmed.

chemical dependency The state a person reaches when she or he can no longer function normally without regularly consuming drugs or alcohol.

chose in action Evidence of the right to property but not the property itself.

class-action lawsuit A lawsuit that is brought by one or more plaintiffs on behalf of a class of persons.

click-on acceptance A method acceptance used in Internet contracts in which a party manifests acceptance by clicking on an icon on the computer screen that states that he or she agrees to the terms of the contract. Also called *click-on agreement.*

close corporation A corporation whose shares of stock and managerial control are closely held be fewer than 50 shareholders (often members of the same family) or by one person.

close-end credit Credit that is extended only for a specific amount of money, such as to buy a car or other expensive item.

closed shop A place of employment in which the employer, by agreement, hires only union members in good standing.

code A compilation of all the statutes of a particular state or of the federal government.

Code of Professional Ethics A set of rules established by the American Institute of Certified Public Accountants that outlines rules that govern the ethical conduct of accountants.

codicil A formal document used to supplement or change an existing will.

coinsurance An insurance policy provision under which the insurer and the insured share costs, after the deductible is met, according to a specific formula.

collateral The property that is subject to a security interest.

collecting bank Any bank handling an item for collection except the payor bank.

collective bargaining A good faith meeting between representatives of employees and employers to discuss the terms and conditions of employment.

collective bargaining agreement A contract negotiated by an employer and a labor union that covers all issues related to employment.

collision insurance A type of automobile insurance that protects the insured against any loss arising from damage to the insured's automobile caused by accidental collision with another object or with any part of the roadbed.

.com lawsuit See *domain name dispute.*

comaker A person obligated, along with at least one other person, as a payor on a promissory note.

commerce Trade among the several states or between any foreign country and any state or territory.

Commerce Clause The clause in the U.S. Constitution that gives the federal government the power to regulate business.

commercial impracticability A doctrine under which the courts may excuse the performance of one party to a contract because an unforeseen and very severe hardship has arisen that would place an enormous amount of hardship on that party.

commercial unit A single whole for the purpose of sale, the division of which impairs its character or value on the market, such as a set of furniture.

commingled Mixed together, as in goods stored at a warehouse.

common carrier A company that transports goods or persons for compensation and offers its facilities to the general public without discrimination. Compare *contract carrier.*

common law The body of recorded decisions that courts refer to and rely upon when making later legal decisions.

common stock The most usual type of corporate stock. It carries with it all the risks of the business and does not guarantee its holder the right to profits.

community property Property that is acquired by the personal effects of either spouse during marriage and which, by law, belongs to both spouses equally.

comparative negligence A form of contributory negligence that requires the court to assign damages according to the degree of fault of each party.

compassion A respect for others and their rights. Compassionate people are sympathetic to the suffering of others and are understanding of their shortcomings.

compensatory damages See *actual damages.*

complaint A legal document filed by a plaintiff to begin a lawsuit. The complaint sets forth the names of the parties, the facts in the case, and the relief sought by the plaintiff.

complete performance In contract law, the situation that exists when both parties to a contract have fully accomplished every term, condition, and promise to which they agreed.

complex adaptive system A network of interacting conditions that reinforce one another, while, at the same time adjusting to changes from agents both inside and outside of the system.

comprehensive coverage A type of automobile insurance that provides protection against loss when the insured's car is damaged or destroyed by fire, lightning, flood, hail, windstorm, riot, vandalism, or theft.

computer firmware Computer software that is written to be used with only one type or brand of computer.

computer hardware The actual device known as a computer and its components, including the keyboard, screen, disk drive, and the printer.

computer information Information in a form directly capable of being processed or used by, or obtained from or through, a computer.

computer package The combination of the computer hardware and the computer software when sold together.

computer program The instructions that tell the computer hardware what to do and when to do it.

computer software The card, tape, disk, or silicon chip that contains the computer program.

concealment In insurance, the intentional withholding of a fact that would be of material importance to the insurer's decision to issue a policy. See also *passive fraud.*

condemnation See *eminent domain.*

condition concurrent A condition in a contract that requires both parties to perform at the same time.

condition precedent In contract law, an act or promise that must take place or be fulfilled before the other party is obligated to perform his or her part of the agreement.

condition subsequent A condition in a contract in which the parties agree that the contract will be terminated depending on a prescribed event occurring or not occurring.

conditional indorsement An indorsement that makes the rights of the indorsee subject to the happening of a certain event or condition.

confidential relationship A relationship of trust and dependence between persons in a continued relationship, as between doctor and patient or between parent and child.

confirmation In bankruptcy law, the official approval of a reorganization plan.

conforming goods Goods that are in accordance with the obligations under the contract.

conglomerate expansion The joining of two companies that were not in competition with one another either because they dealt in different products or services or because they operated in different geographical areas.

consent order Under the Federal Trade Commission Act, an order under which a company agrees to stop a disputed practice without necessarily admitting that the practice violated the law.

consequential damages Losses that do not flow directly and immediately from an act but only from some of the consequences or results of the act.

consideration In contract law, the mutual promise to exchange benefits and sacrifices between parties.

consignee One to whom goods are entrusted under a *consignment contract* for the purpose of selling them.

consignment contract A type of mutual benefit bailment in which the *consignor* entrusts goods to the *consignee* for the purpose of selling them.

consignor One who entrusts goods under a *consignment contract* to a *consignee* for the purpose of selling them.

consolidation The joining of two corporations.

conspiracy The crime that occurs when people get together with others to talk about, plan, or agree to the commission of a crime.

constitution The basic law of a nation or state.

constitutional law That body of law that involves a constitution and its interpretation.

constructive discharge Discriminatory action whereby an employee is demoted to a job with less pay, authority, or poorer working conditions than the job that person previously held, or is subjected to supervisory harassment.

constructive eviction An eviction that occurs by the act of the landlord depriving the tenant of something of a substantial nature that was called for under the lease.

consumer Someone who buys or leases real estate, goods, or services for personal, family, or household purposes.

consumer goods Goods normally used for personal, family, or household purposes.

continuity of existence doctrine A concept promoted by the Revised Uniform Partnership Act which permits a partnership to continue to operate as an entity even after individual partners are no longer associated with it.

contract An agreement based on mutual promises between two or more competent parties to do or to refrain from doing some particular thing that is neither illegal nor impossible. The agreement results in an obligation or a duty that can be enforced in a court of law.

contract carrier A company that transports goods or persons for compensation only for those people with whom it desires to do business. Compare *common carrier.*

contract of record A special type of formal contract usually confirmed by a court with an accompanying judgment issued in favor of one of the parties.

contract for sale Either a present sale of goods or a contract to sell goods at a future time.

contributory negligence A legal defense that involves the failure of an injured party to be careful enough to ensure personal safety.

contributory copyright infringement A violation of copyright law in which one party provides a way for a second party to violate the copyright protection granted to the third party even though the first party never violates the copyright himself or herself.

controlled company A corporation that has more than half its voting power concentrated in one person or a small group of persons, who always vote together.

Convention on Contracts for the International Sale of Goods (CISG) A United Nations treaty designed to govern commercial transactions between parties whose places of business are in different countries.

conventional mortgage A mortgage that involves no government backing by either insurance or guarantee.

conversion The wrongful exercise of dominion and control over another's personal property.

conveyance in trust A trust in which the settlor conveys away the legal title to a trustee to hold for the benefit of either the settlor or another as beneficiary.

Cooling-off Rule A Federal Trade Commission rule under which sales of consumer goods or services over $25 made away from the seller's regular place of business may be canceled within three business days after the sale occurs.

copyright A right granted to an author, composer, photographer, or artist to exclusively publish and sell an artistic or literary work for the life of the author plus 70 years.

corporate democracy See *shareholder democracy.*

corporation A legal entity (or a legal person) created by either a state or federal statute authorizing individuals to operate an enterprise.

corporation by estoppel The doctrine by which parties who have benefited by dealing with a business as though it were a corporation—although in law it is not—cannot deny its existence as a corporation. Similarly, individuals who have acted as if they were a corporation would not be able to deny that the corporation existed.

cost-benefit thinking A system of thought that focuses on the consequences to one person or institution and then weighs the cost against the benefits of performing the action under scrutiny.

cost of repair rule The principle that states that an architect or contractor may have to reimburse a client for any extra money spent by the client to correct an error initially made by the architect or contractor.

cost-plus contract A contract in which the price is determined by the cost of labor and materials plus an agreed percentage markup.

cotenancy The quality or state of more than one owner of a single property.

cotenants Two or more persons who own real property together.

counteroffer A response to an offer in which the terms and conditions of the original offer are changed.

cover Buying similar goods from someone else when a seller breaches a contract.

creditor beneficiary A third party to whom one or both contracting parties owe a continuing debt of obligation arising from a contract.

crime An offense against the public at large punishable by the official governing body of a nation or state.

cross appeal An appeal filed by a party that has prevailed at trial.

cross-examination The questioning of witnesses by an opposing attorney.

cumulative voting A system of voting for corporate directors that is designed to benefit minority shareholders by allowing shareholders to multiply their voting shares by the number of directors to be elected.

cure The correction of a defect in goods that caused the goods to be rejected by a buyer.

current market price contract An agreement in which the prices are determined with reference to the market price of the goods on a specified date.

curtesy Under common law, the right that a widower had, if children of the marriage were born alive, to a life estate in all real property owned by the wife during the marriage.

cyberagent (AKA electronic agent and e-agent) A computer program that acts without human intervention to begin an activity, to answer cybermessages, to deliver or accept cybermail, or to enter cybercontracts.

cybercontract A contract involving the sale or licensing of information in a digital format.

cybercrime Any criminal act that includes a computer.

cyberdefamation The communication of false and destructive information about an individual through the use of a computer or other electronic device.

cyberdiscovery A search for evidence using a computer. Also called *cyberspace discovery*.

cyberevidence Any and all types of computer generated-data.

cyberextortion Gaining access to the computer records of a business or other institution and, in the process uncovering the illegal, unethical, or negligent conduct of that organization and using that information to commit extortion. Also called *cyberblackmail*.

cybergerm warfare Using viruses to attack a computer system.

cyberinvasion of privacy The unwelcome intrusion into private matters initiated or maintained by a computer.

cyberjurisdiction The authority of a court to hear a case based on Internet-related transactions.

cyberlaw A single law or a series of laws that deals exclusively with some aspect of computers and their attendant elements, such as their hardware and software.

cyberpirate Someone who registers a trademark or trademarks as a domain name with little or no intention of actually using the domain name in the hope that the actual holders of the trademark will buy the domain name for enormous sums.

cyberprincipal A principal who places authority in the hands of a cyberagent.

cyberspoiler See *cyberpirate*.

cyberspoofing Falsely adopting the identity of another computer user or creating a false identity on a computer website to commit fraud.

cyberspyware (AKA cybersnoopware) A program which, once it is installed in a computer, can keep a record of the keyboarding patterns established by the computer user.

cybersquatter See *cyberpirate*.

cyberstalking Targeting an individual for exploitation using that person's computer connections.

cyberterrorism Using a computer to disrupt or destroy one of the critical elements of the nation's electronic infrastructure.

cybertort The invasion, distortion, theft, falsification, misuse, destruction or financial exploitation of information stored in a computer.

cybertrespass Gaining access to a computer with the intent to commit a crime.

cybervandalism Attacking a computer system so that a website is completely destroyed or paralyzed.

damage cap A limit on the amount of money that juries can award in certain types of tort law cases.

damages Money recovered by a party in a court action to compensate that party for injury or loss.

data mining Searching for and placing together two or more pieces of public information to create information that the victim considers private.

database The compilation of information in a form that can be understood and used by a computer.

debit card A card used to electronically subtract money from a bank account to pay for goods or services.

de facto **corporation** A corporation defectively incorporated in good faith that exists in fact although not in law.

de jure **corporation** A corporation whose existence is the result of incorporators having fully or substantially complied with the relevant corporation statutes.

debtor-in-possession A debtor who continues to operate his or her business after filing for bankruptcy.

declaration of trust A trust in which the settlor holds the legal title to the property as trustee for the benefit of some other person (the beneficiary) to whom the settlor now conveys the equitable title.

deductible An amount of any loss that is to be paid by the insured.

deed of trust A formal written instrument that transfers legal ownership of real property to a third party while the mortgagor remains on the property. The third party holds certain rights to that property as security for the mortgagor's creditors.

defamation The intentional tort that occurs when false statement is communicated to others that harms a person's good name or reputation.

default statute A statute used to fill in the gaps when the parties to an agreement have failed to consider some matter in their agreement.

defective agreement An apparent contract in which mutual assent has been destroyed thus rendering the alleged contract void.

defective condition A condition that makes a product unreasonably dangerous to the consumer, the user, or property. See *product liability*.

defendant The person against whom a lawsuit is brought and from whom recovery is sought.

defense of others A defense to criminal liability to defendants if they can show they used force to rescue another person who is the victim of an apparent attack. The rescuer must have good reason to believe the victim was in danger of severe bodily injury or death.

del credere agent (del·KREH·de·reh) A factor who guarantees the credit of a third party to a principal and guarantees the solvency of the purchaser and the performance of the contract.

delegation The transfer of a contractual duty.

demand note A promissory note that is payable whenever the payee demands payment.

demurrage charge A fee charged by a carrier for the storage of goods still remaining in its possession beyond the time allowed for unloading by the cosignee.

demurrer A motion for dismissal of a case on the grounds that a plaintiff has failed to state a claim for which relief can be granted.

depositary bank The first bank to which an item is transferred for collection; the depositary bank may also be the payor bank.

deposition An oral question-and-answer session conducted under oath during which an attorney questions parties or witnesses from the opposition in a lawsuit.

derivative suit A lawsuit brought by shareholders on behalf of the corporation.

descriptive theory A system of ethical thought that describes the values at work within a social system.

design patent A patent granted to someone who invents a new, original, and ornamental design for an article of manufacture.

destination contract A contract under which the seller is required to deliver goods to a place of destination. The title and risk of loss remain with the seller until the goods reach the place of destination.

detriment In contract law, doing (or promising to do) something that one has a legal right not to do, giving up (or promising to give up) something that one has a legal right to keep, or refraining from doing (or promising not to do) something that one has a legal right to do.

devise Real property that is left in a will. In states that have adopted the Uniform Probate Code, the term refers to both real and personal property.

devisee One who receives the real property under a will. In states that have adopted the Uniform Probate Code, the term refers to a person who receives a gift of either real or personal property under a will.

digital information contract A contract involving the sale or licensing of information in a digital format.

digital signature An encoded message that appears at the end of a contract created online.

direct examination The questioning of witnesses by the lawyer who has called them.

disability Any physical or mental impairment that substantially limits one or more of the major life activities.

disaffirm In contract law, to indicate by a statement or act an intent not to live up to the terms of the contract.

disclaimer In employment law, a statement that regardless of provisions or policies in an employment handbook and regardless of oral promises to the contrary, an employment-at-will situation still exists between an employer and its employees. Also, a statement declaring that an auditor has decided not to give any opinion on a firm's financial records.

disclaimer of general partner status A document filed with the appropriate state office when a limited partner has been incorrectly named as a general partner.

disclosed principal The person known by a third party to be the principal of an agent.

discounting System by which a bank will buy an instrument at a price below its face amount with the aim of ultimately collecting the face amount.

discovery The process by which parties to a civil suit search for information relevant to the case.

dishonor To refuse to accept or pay a negotiable instrument when it is presented.

disparagement Any false statement made to others that questions the legal ownership or raises doubts as to the quality of merchandise.

disparate impact A type of discrimination which an employer's policy seems neutral on the surface, but has an unequal or unfair impact on members of one or more of the protected classes.

disparate treatment Intentional discrimination against an individual or group belonging to a protected class. The protected classes are sex, race, color, religion, and national origin.

Dispute Settlement Board (DSB) See *Dispute Settlement Understanding.*

Dispute Settlement Understanding (DSU) A series of measures administered by an international Dispute Settlement Board that are designed to improve the way trading quarrels are handled.

disputed amount Consideration on which parties to a contract never agree.

dissociation A process authorized under the Revised Uniform Partnership Act which takes place whenever a partner is no longer associated with the running of the partnership firm.

dissolution of a partnership A change in the relation of partners caused by any partner ceasing to be associated in the carrying on of the business.

diversity cases Federal lawsuits that are between persons from different states, between citizens of the United States and a foreign government, or between citizens of the United States and citizens of a foreign nation. Diversity cases must involve an amount over $50,000.

dividends Net profits, or surplus, set aside for shareholders.

document of title A paper that serves as evidence that the person holding the paper has title to the goods mentioned in the document.

domain name The Internet address of a business, institution, or individual.

domain name dispute Arises when an individual or organization has registered a domain name that is actually the protected trademark of a business or institution.

domestic bill of exchange A draft that is drawn and payable in the United States.

domestic corporation A corporation created by or organized under the laws of the state where it is operating.

domestic violence statute State laws that outlaw physical violence directed at any family member.

dominant tenement The property to which the right or privilege of an easement attaches.

donee One to whom a gift is given.

donee beneficiary A third party who provides no consideration for the benefits received and who owes the contracting parties no legal duty.

donor One who gives a gift.

double indemnity An optional provision in life insurance policies that provides that the insurer will pay double the amount due to a beneficiary if the insured dies from accidental causes.

dower By common law, the vested rights of the wife to a one-third lifetime interest in the real property owned by her spouse. Compare *curtesy.*

draft A written order by which the party creating it orders another party to pay money to a third party. Also called *bill of exchange.*

drawee The party named in a draft who is ordered to pay the money to the payee.

drawer The party who draws a draft, that is, the party who orders that the money be paid.

drug trafficking The unauthorized manufacture or distribution of any controlled substance or the possession of such a substance with the intention of manufacturing or distributing it illegally.

dummy corporation A corporation that is set up as a mere instrumentality of a parent corporation. Also called *corporate shell* and *empty shell.*

dunning letter A letter representing payment for goods.

durable power of attorney A document that authorizes an agent to act on another's behalf, with the power either surviving incapacity or becoming effective upon incapacity.

duress An action by one party that forces another party to do what need not be done otherwise.

duty An obligation placed on individuals because of the law.

duty of due diligence A duty that says that corporate managers when acting on behalf of the corporation must act (1) in good faith; (2) using the same level of care that an ordinary prudent person would use in a comparable situation, and (3) in the reasonable belief that the best interests of the corporation are being met.

early neutral evaluation (ENE) A process similar to that of a settlement hearing which may result in a final decision or be used to help shape the final decision.

E-911 location identifier system An electronic chip located in a mobile phone that sends out a signal that is designed to ensure that EMS personnel can locate people who are unable or unwilling to reveal their location when making an emergency call.

easement The right to use the land of another for a particular purpose.

easement by prescription An easement that is obtained by passing over another's property without permission openly and continuously for a period of time set by state statute (20 years in many states).

e-check (sometimes called *electronic check conversion*), A system in which funds are electronically transferred from a customer's checking account, eliminating the need to process a paper check.

E-Commerce Involves transacting business by any one of several types of electronic communication from debit card purchases to buying and selling goods on the Internet.

economic compensatory damages Damages that are directly quantifiable including damages awarded for lost wages, medical expenses, and expenses incurred in the repair or replacement of property.

economic duress Threats of a business nature that force another party without real consent to enter a commercial agreement. Also called *business compulsion.*

E-Consumer Someone who buys something on the Internet.

ejectment The common law name given to the lawsuit brought by a landlord to have a tenant evicted from the premises.

elective share See *forced share.*

electronic data interchange (EDI) An electronic process used to negotiate contracts.

electronic fund transfer (EFT) A method of banking that uses computers and electronic technology as a substitute for checks and other banking methods.

emancipated In contract law, the condition that exists when minors are no longer under the control of their parents and are responsible for their contracts.

embedded niche Levels of influence within a complex adaptive system.

embezzlement The act of wrongfully taking property entrusted into one's care.

eminent domain The right of federal, state, and local governments, or other public bodies, to take private lands, with compensation to their owners, for public use. Also called *condemnation.*

emotional duress Acts or threats that create emotional distress which lead a person into a contract against his or her will.

employment-at-will A doctrine followed by most jurisdictions in the United States that says an employer can dismiss an employee at any time for any reason.

endowment insurance Insurance protection that combines life insurance and investment so that if the insured outlives the time-period of the policy, the face value is paid to the beneficiary.

end user A purchaser who is not involved in the production or assembly of the product.

entity theory A theory in partnership law which holds that a partnership is actually a separate legal person with its own legal identity.

entrapment A defense to criminal liability that claims that a previously law-abiding citizen was induced to commit a crime by a law enforcement officer.

equal dignities rule The legal rule that provides that when a party appoints an agent to negotiate an agreement that must be in writing, the appointment of the agent must also be in writing.

equipment Goods that are used or bought for use primarily in business.

equitable estoppel See *part performance.*

equity financing The issuing and selling of shares of stock to raise capital.

equity of redemption A mortgagor's right to pay off the mortgage in full, including interest.

escheat To revert to the state; to become property of.

E-Sign Act A federal statute, officially known as the Electronic Signatures in Global and National Commerce Act, which states that if the parties to a contract have voluntarily agreed to transact business electronically, then the electronic contract that results will be just as legally acceptable as a paper contract.

espionage The gathering or transmitting of information pertaining to the national defense of a nation for the political or military use of any foreign nation.

estate in fee simple An estate in which the owner owns the land for life with the right to use it or dispose of it freely.

estoppel A legal bar to denying acts, statements, or promises that are relevant and material to the validity of an insurance contract.

ethical relativism A system of ethical thought that says there is no objective or absolute standard of right and wrong.

ethics Rules of conduct that transcend legal rules, telling people how to act when the law does not.

euro Europe's common currency.

European Central Bank (ECB) The bank was established by provisions within the Maastricht Treaty and is the central hub of the European System of Central Banks.

European System of Central Banks (ESCB) A system of banks including the European Central Bank and the National Central Banks.

European Union (EU) A group of countries in Europe that have joined together to formulate a common European economic policy, minimize trade barriers, and introduce a common currency with the goal of making the EU a major global competitor.

eviction An act of the landlord that deprives the tenant of the enjoyment of the premises.

exculpatory agreement A clause that says one of the parties to a contract, generally the one who wrote the contract, is not liable for any economic loss or physical injury, even if that party caused the loss or injury.

exculpatory clause A clause in a contract that releases a party from liability for his or her wrongful acts. These clauses are not favored by law.

executed contract A contract whose terms have been completely and satisfactorily carried out by both parties.

executor (male); executrix (female) The party named in a will to carry out the terms of the will.

executory contract A contract that has not yet been fully performed by the parties.

exempt property Property of a decedent that passes to the surviving spouse or children and is beyond the reach of creditors.

express authority An agent's authority that the principal voluntarily and specifically sets forth as oral or written instructions in an agency agreement.

express contract A contract in which both parties accept mutual obligations through either oral discussion or written communication.

express warranty An oral or written statement, promise, or other representation about the quality of a product.

extant data Data that is difficult to retrieve because it is hidden within a computer system.

extortion The act of taking another's property with consent when such consent is coerced by threat to injure a victim's person, property, or reputation.

f.a.s vessel Free alongside vessel. Indicates that the seller must deliver goods, at the seller's own risk, alongside the vessel or at a dock designated by the buyer.

f.o.b. Free on board.

f.o.b. the place of destination Terms indicating that goods will be delivered free to the place of destination.

f.o.b. the place of shipment Terms indicating that goods will be delivered free to the place of shipment.

factor A special agent who is employed to sell merchandise consigned for that purpose.

failure of consideration A personal defense that may be used by a maker or drawer of a negotiable instrument when the party with whom the maker dealt breaches the contract by not furnishing the agreed consideration.

fair use An exception to the copyright protection rights granted to copyright holders that permits individuals to reproduce items for purposes of criticism, comment, news reporting, teaching, scholarship, and research.

fairness The ability to treat people with justice and equality.

fairness rule The rule that requires managers to be fair to the corporation when they personally benefit from their business decisions.

false imprisonment An intentional tort involving the unjustified confinement or detention of a person.

family allowance An amount of money taken from a decedent's estate and given to the family to meet its immediate needs while the estate is being probated.

family farmer Under Chapter 12 of the Bankruptcy Code, a farmer who receives more than half the total income from the farm. In addition, to qualify as a family farmer, 80 percent of the farmer's debt must result from the farm expenses.

farm products Crops, livestock, or supplies used or produced in farming operations.

featherbedding Requiring an employer, usually by a union, to keep unneeded employees, to pay employees for not working, or to assign more employees to a given job than are needed.

federal question A matter that involves the U.S. Constitution, a federal statute or statutes, or a treaty; handled by federal district courts.

felony A crime punishable by death or by imprisonment in a federal or state prison for a term exceeding one year.

fiduciary A person who acts in a position of trust or confidence.

fiduciary relationship A relationship based on trust such as exists between an attorney and a client, a guardian and a ward, a trustee and a beneficiary, or a director and a corporation.

field warehousing The practice of using goods that are stored in a warehouse as security for a loan.

finance charge The actual cost of a loan in dollars and cents.

firm offer A rule that no consideration is necessary when a merchant agrees in writing to hold an offer open for the sale of goods.

fixture An article of personal property physically attached to real property in such a way that an interest arises in it under real estate law.

flexible-rate mortgage A mortgage that has a rate of interest that changes according to fluctuations in the index to which it is tied. Also called *variable-rate mortgage.*

floater policy A policy that insures property that cannot be covered by specific insurance because the property is constantly changing in either value or location.

floating lien A provision, placed by the creditor, in a security agreement that a security interest of the creditor also applies to goods the debtor acquires at a later time.

forbearance The act of refraining from doing (or promising not to do) something that a person has a legal right to do.

forced share The portion of a decedent's estate assured to the family by state statute.

foreclosure The right of a mortgagee to apply to a court to have property sold when the mortgagor defaults or fails to perform some agreement in the mortgage.

foreign corporation A corporation created by or organized under the laws of a state other than the one in which it is operating.

foreign draft See *international bill of exchange.*

forgery The false making or alteration of a writing with the intent to defraud.

formal contract Under common law, a contract that is written; signed, witnessed, and placed under the seal of the parties; and delivered.

formalist theory A theory of legal interpretation under which the court will look to see if certain elements (offer, acceptance, mutual assent, consideration,

capacity, and legality) exist before concluding whether or not the parties in a lawsuit have actually entered a legally binding contract.

forum shopping The process of locating a jurisdiction that has a friendly track record for the type of lawsuit that is about to be filed.

fraud A wrongful statement, action, or concealment pertinent to the subject matter of a contract knowingly made to damage the other party.

fraudulent conveyance A transfer of property with the intent to defraud creditors.

friendly suitor See *white knight.*

frustration-of-purpose doctrine In contract law, the doctrine that releases a party from a contractual obligation when performing the obligations would be thoroughly impractical and senseless.

full warranty A warranty under which a defective product will be repaired or replaced without charge within a reasonable time after a complaint has been made about it.

fungible goods Goods of which any unit is, by nature or usage of trade, the equivalent of any like unit; wheat, flour, sugar, and liquids of various kinds are examples.

future goods Goods that are not yet in existence or under the control of people; they include fish in the sea, minerals in the ground, goods not yet manufactured, and commodities futures.

general agent A person who is given broad authority to act on behalf of the principal in conducting the bulk of the principal's business activities on a daily basis.

General Agreement on Tariffs and Trade (GATT) A nonstatic agreement among the principal trading countries to reduce or eliminate tariffs and to promote free trade on a global basis.

General Assembly The member nations of the United Nations.

general consent Consent that arises automatically when a patient enters a hospital for routine tests and procedures needed for diagnosis and treatment.

general jurisdiction The power of a court to hear any type of case.

general partner A partner who takes an active part in running a business and has unlimited liability for the firm's debts.

general release A document expressing the intent of a creditor to release a debtor from obligations to an existing and valid debt.

general warranty deed A deed that contains express warranties under which a grantor guarantees property to be free of encumbrances created by the grantor or by others who had title previously. Also called *full convenant* and *warranty deed.*

generally accepted accounting principles (GAAP) Rules established by the Financial Accounting Standards Board (FASB) that outline the procedures that accountants use in accumulating financial data and in preparing financial statements.

generally accepted auditing standards (GAAS) Standards set up by the Auditing Standards Board of the American Institute of Certified Public Accountants (AICPA) that measure the quality of the performance of the auditing procedures.

Geneva Conventions International meetings that attempted to deal with many of the contemporary complications brought on by the nature of warfare in the twentieth century.

gift *in causa mortis* (in·KAWS·ah·MORE·tes) A gift given during one's lifetime in contemplation of death from a known cause.

gift *inter vivos* (IN·ter·VY·vose) A gift between the living. For an exchange to be valid, the donor must intend to make a gift, the gift must be delivered to the donee, and the donee must accept it.

good faith Honesty in fact and observance of reasonable commercial standards of fair dealings in the trade.

goods All things (other than money, stocks, and bonds) that are movable.

goodwill The expected continuance of public patronage of a business.

government control A theory of corporate control based on the belief that because corporate decision making impacts upon more individuals and groups than just shareholders and managers, those decisions should be made by a group of corporate outsiders, usually government officials. Also called *state control*.

graduated-payment mortgage A mortgage that has a fixed interest rate during the life of the mortgage; however, the monthly payments made by the mortgagor increase over the term of the loan.

grantee A person to whom title to real property is transferred in a deed.

grantor A person who transfers title to real property in a deed.

gratuitous bailment A bailment for the sole benefit of either the bailor or the bailee, in which the other party receives no consideration for benefits bestowed.

greenmail A strategy used to shake off a bidder's hostile suit by offering to buy, at significantly higher cost, the portion of stock already owned by the bidder who is trying to take over the company.

grievance procedure A procedure that allows employees to appeal any decision an employer makes that employees feel violates just cause.

gross negligence Very great negligence.

guaranteed insurability An optional provision in an insurance contract that allows the insured to pay an extra premium initially in exchange for a guaranteed option to buy more insurance at certain specified times later on with no questions asked and no medical examination required.

guaranty of payment A promise to pay another's bills or to settle wrongful acts if that party does not settle them personally.

health care proxy A written statement authorizing an agent to make health care decisions for another in the event of incapacity.

heir One who inherits property either under a will or through someone's dying without a will.

holder A person who is in possession of a negotiable instrument that is issued or indorsed to that person's order or to bearer.

holder in due course A holder who has taken a negotiable instrument for value, in good faith, without notice that it is overdue or has been dishonored and without notice of any defenses against it or claim to it.

holder in due course rule A rule adopted by the FTC that states that holders of consumer credit contracts who are holders in due course are subject to all claims and defenses that the buyer could use against the seller, including personal defenses.

home equity loan A line of credit made available to homeowners based on the value of the property over and above any existing mortgages.

homeowner's policy A type of insurance that gives protection for all types of losses and liabilities related to home ownership. Items covered include losses from fire, windstorm, burglary, vandalism, and injuries suffered by others while on the property.

homestead exemption A provision in the Bankruptcy Code that allows debtors to exclude a statutory amount of equity in the debtor's place of residence and in property used as a burial ground when filing for bankruptcy.

homicide The killing of one human being by another.

honesty A character trait of a person who is open and truthful in his or her dealings with other people.

horizontal expansion The joining of companies involved in the same business.

hostile bidder See *unfriendly suitor.*

hot-cargo contract An agreement whereby an employer voluntarily agrees with a union not to handle, use, or deal in nonunion-produced goods for another employer.

identified goods Specific goods that are selected as the subject matter of a contract.

identity theft Using a computer to steal confidential information to clean out a person's bank account, to run up credit card debt, to divert cash transfers, and to disrupt the financial and personal life of the victim.

illusory promise A promise that does not obligate the promisor to anything.

implied authority The authority of an agent to perform acts that are necessary or customary to carry out expressly authorized duties.

implied contract A contract created by the actions or gestures of the parties involved in the transaction.

implied covenant An implied promise in any employment relationship that the employer and the employee will be fair with one another.

implied warranty A warranty that is imposed by law rather than by statements, descriptions, or samples given by the seller.

implied-in-fact contract A contract implied by direct or indirect acts of the parties.

implied-in-law contract A remedy imposed by a court in a situation in which the parties did not create a written, oral, or implied-in-fact agreement but one party has unfairly benefited at the innocent expense of another. Also called *quasi-contract.*

in pari delicto (in pah·ree de·LIK·toh) In equal fault. A contract relationship when both parties to an illegal agreement are equally wrong, in the knowledge of the operation and effect of their contract.

inactive data Data in a computer system that is not being used at the present time but that can be easily retrieved.

incidental beneficiary A third party for whose benefit a contract was not made but who would substantially benefit if the agreement were performed according to its terms and conditions.

incidental damages Damages awarded for losses indirectly, but closely, attributed to a breach to cover any expenses paid out by an innocent party to prevent further loss.

incorporators The people who actually sign the articles of incorporation to start a corporation.

indemnification Payment for loss or damage suffered.

indemnify To compensate for loss or damage or insure against future loss or damage.

independent contractor One who contracts to do a job and who retains complete control over the methods employed to obtain completion.

independent directors Directors who have no family members employed by the corporation, who are not themselves employed by the corporation, or, if they were once employed by the corporation, have not been on staff for at least three years.

independent director control A theory of corporate control that states that the best way to make certain that corporate decisions are made in the best interests of the corporation is to make sure that the decision makers themselves are not affected by the decisions.

indictment A set of formal charges against a defendant issued by a grand jury.

individual justice Justice that is meted out to the people on a case-by-case basis.

indorsee A person to whom a draft, note, or other negotiable instrument is transferred by indorsement.

indorsement in full See *special indorsement.*

indorser A person who indorses a negotiable instrument.

infliction of emotional distress The intentional tort that allows those injured emotionally by the wrongful acts of others to recover damages even without the accompanying physical injury.

informal contract An oral or written contract that is not under a seal or is not a contract of record. Also called *simple contract.*

information A set of formal charges against a defendant drawn up and issued by the prosecutor or district attorney.

informed consent Written consent given by patients for diagnostic tests or treatments that will involve danger or pain after being told about the procedure and the risks involved.

injunction A court order preventing someone from performing a particular act or commanding the defendant to do some positive act to alleviate a problem.

inland marine insurance An insurance contract that covers goods that are moved by land carriers such as rail, truck, and airplane.

innkeeper An operator of a hotel, motel, or inn that holds itself out to the public as being ready to accommodate travelers, strangers, and transient guests.

inside information Material, nonpublic, factual data that can be used to buy or sell securities at a profit.

insider trading Using inside information to either cheat the corporation or take unfair advantage of corporate outsiders.

insider trading rule A rule of corporate governance which states that when managers possess important inside information they are obligated to reveal that information before trading on it themselves.

insolvent Inability of a business entity to pay its debts as they become due in the usual course of business.

installment note A promissory note in which the principal together with interest on the unpaid balance is payable in installments at specified times.

insurable interest The financial interest that a policyholder has in the person or property that is insured.

insurance A contract whereby one party pays premiums to another party who undertakes to pay compensation for losses resulting from risks or perils specified in the contract.

insured A party that is protected by an insurer against losses caused by the risks specified in an insurance policy.

insurer A party that accepts the risk of loss in return for a premium (payment of money) and agrees to compensate the insured against a specified loss.

integrity The quality of having the courage to do what is right regardless of personal consequences.

intellectual property An original work fixed in a tangible medium of expression.

intended beneficiary A third party in whose favor a contract is made.

interference with a contract The international tort that results when a person, out of ill will, entices a contractual party into breaking the contract.

interlocking directorates In antitrust law, a situation that occurs when individuals serve as two corporations that are competitors.

intermediary bank Any bank to which an item is transferred in the course of collection except the depositary or payor bank.

international bill of exchange A draft that is drawn in one country but is payable in another. Also called *foreign draft.*

International Court of Justice (ICJ) One of the principal vehicles for the establishment of international law and justice.

International Law Commission A thirty-four-member panel of judges who seek to codify international law in as objective a manner as possible.

international terrorism Acts transcending national boundaries that violate a state's criminal laws and are intended to intimidate that country's civilians or influence the policy or conduct of the government.

interrogatories Written questions to be answered in writing under oath by the opposite party in a lawsuit.

interstate commerce Business activities that touch more than one state.

interstate shipment A shipment that goes beyond the borders of the state in which it originated.

intestacy The quality or state of one who dies without having prepared a valid will.

intestate Having died without leaving a valid will. Compare *testate*.

intrastate commerce Business activities that have no out-of-state connections.

intrastate shipment A shipment that is entirely within a single state.

invasion of privacy The intentional tort that occurs when one person unreasonably denies another person the right to be left alone.

inventory Goods held for sale or lease, or raw materials used or consumed in a business.

invitation to trade An announcement published for the purpose of creating interest and attracting a response by many people.

involuntary bailment A bailment arising from the leaving of personal property in the possession of a bailee through an act of God, accident, or other uncontrolled phenomenon.

irresistible impulse test Under this rule, criminal defendants are judged not guilty by reason of insanity if, at the time of the action in question, they suffered from a mental disease that either prevented them from knowing right from wrong or compelled them to commit the criminal act.

irrevocable offer A rule that no consideration is necessary when a merchant agrees in writing to hold an offer open for the sale of goods. Also called *firm offer*.

issue Descendants (children, grandchildren, great-grandchildren).

issuer Either a maker or a drawer of an instrument.

joint tenants Two or more persons who own property where the right of any deceased owner is automatically transferred to other surviving owners.

joint tenants with the right of survivorship See *joint tenants*.

judicial review The process by which a court determines the constitutionality of various legislative statutes, administrative regulations, and executive actions.

junk science The distorted, exaggerated, misapplied, or misrepresented use of scientific evidence.

junior mortgage A mortgage subject to a prior mortgage.

juris-economic system The interaction of the legal system and the economic system so as to become, in effect, a single system.

jurisdiction The authority of a court to hear and decide cases.

just cause A criterion under the just war theory which states that to be morally permissible a war must be waged only for honorable motives.

Just War Theory A theory for determining when a war can be considered legally and morally correct.

kidnapping The unlawful abduction of an individual against that individual's will.

knowledge In criminal law, the awareness that a particular result will probably occur.

labor union An organization that acts on behalf of all employees in negotiations with the employer regarding terms of their employment.

laches The equitable doctrine that a delay or failure to assert a right or claim at the proper time, which causes a disadvantage to the adverse party, is a bar to recovery.

lack of consideration A personal defense that may be used by a maker or drawer of a negotiable instrument when no consideration existed in the underlying contract for which the instrument was issued.

landlord A person who owns real property and who rents or leases it to someone else. Also called *lessor*.

larceny The act of taking and carrying away the personal property of another without the right to do so.

larceny by false pretenses The taking of someone's money or property by intentionally deceiving that person.

last resort A criterion under the just war theory which states that a war must be waged only as a final course of action.

law A set of rules created by the governing body of a society to maintain harmony, stability, and justice in that society.

law merchant In England, the commercial law developed by merchants who needed a set of rules to govern their business transactions.

lease A contract granting the use of certain real property to another for a specified period in return for the payment of rent.

leasehold estate The creation of an ownership interest in the tenant. An interest in real estate that is held under a lease. Also called *tenancy*.

legal tender Money that may be offered legally in satisfaction of a debt and that must be accepted by a creditor when offered.

legatee One who receives personal property in a will.

lessee See *tenant*.

lessor See *landlord*.

liability The legal responsibility of an individual for his or her actions.

liable Legally responsible.

libel Any false statement that harms another person's good name or reputation made in a permanent form, such as movies, writing, and videotape, and communicated to others.

license A grant of permission to do a particular thing, to exercise a certain privilege, to carry on a particular business, or to pursue a certain occupation; an agreement that gives no property right or interest in land but merely allows the licensee to do certain acts that would otherwise be a trespass; a privilege granted by a state or city upon payment of a fee, which is not a contract and may be revoked for cause, conferring authority to perform a designated task, such as operating a motor vehicle.

licensing agreement An agreement in which one party is given permission from another party to do a particular thing in exchange for consideration.

lien A claim that one has against the property of another.

life estate An estate in which the owner owns real property for his or her life or for the life of another.

life insurance An insurance contract that provides monetary compensation for losses suffered by another's death.

limited defense See *personal defense.*

limited liability Status that specifies that an individual's liability will not go beyond his or her original investment.

limited liability company (LLC) A business organization that borrows elements from a partnership and a corporation. LLCs may come into existence only through following the steps laid out in the state code.

limited partner A partner who does not take part in the management of a firm and whose liability does not extend beyond his or her investment.

limited partnership A partnership formed by two or more persons having one or more general partners and one or more limited partners.

limited-payment life insurance Insurance that provides that the payment will stop after a stated length of time—usually ten, twenty, or thirty years.

limited warranty A warranty that does not meet all of the requirements of a full warranty.

lingering apparent authority Apparent authority that stays with an agent if the principal has terminated the agent but has failed to give proper notice to third parties entitled to such notice.

liquidated damages Damages agreed to by the parties to a contract in the event of a breach.

liquidation The conversion of property into cash.

litigant A person involved in litigation.

living trust A trust that comes into existence while the person who establishes it is alive. Also called *inter vivos trust.*

living will A document in which individuals can indicate their desire not to be kept alive by artificial means if there is not hope for recovery.

local option The practice in a state of eliminating uniform statewide laws regulating Sunday activities and allowing the local counties, cities, towns, and villages to adopt their own special Sunday ordinances.

locus sigilli The place of the seal. The abbreviation L.S. is often used in place of the seal itself on formal written contracts.

lodger A person who has the use of property without actual or exclusive possession of it.

M'Naghten Rule The oldest test for insanity whereby a criminal defendant is declared not guilty by reason of insanity if, at the time of the criminal act, he or she suffered from a mental disease that prevented him or her from understanding the nature of the act and that the act was wrong.

Maastricht Treaty The outcome of a conference held in Maastricht, the Netherlands. The objectives of the treaty were to create a general European economic policy as well as a foreign policy acceptable to all member states.

majority A term used to describe persons who have reached the legal age of adulthood.

maker A person obligated as the payor on a promissory note. See also *comaker.*

malicious prosecution Bringing false criminal charges against an innocent victim.

malpractice Occurs when a professional—accountant, health care professional, and attorney—fails to meet his or her duty of care.

managerial control A theory of corporate management that favors insulating managers from shareholders by limiting the shareholders' power to vote and by making it difficult for the shareholder to sue managers.

master An outdated term signifying an individual who has the right to control the physical conduct of a servant or employee.

material fact An essential or important fact; a fact of substance.

med-arb A form of ADR that combines the best aspects of both mediation and arbitration. The parties first submit to a mediation session. If the matter cannot be settled, it moves to an arbitration hearing.

mediation The process by which an outside party attempts to help two other parties settle their differences.

mediator The third party in mediation whose job is to convince the contending parties to adjust or settle their dispute.

Medicaid A healthcare plan for low-income people that is administered by state governments but funded by both state and federal funds.

medical payments insurance A type of automobile insurance that pays for medical (and sometimes funeral) expenses resulting from bodily injuries to anyone occupying the policyholder's car at the time of an accident.

Medicare A federally funded health insurance program for people 65 and over who are eligible for Social Security.

memorandum A written agreement containing the terms of an agreement, an identification of the subject matter of the agreement, the consideration promised, the names and identities of the parties to the agreement, and the signature of the party charged to the agreement.

merchant A person who deals in goods of the kind sold in the ordinary course of business or who otherwise claims to have knowledge or skills peculiar to those goods.

merger The acquisition of one corporation by another.

midnight deadline The deadline by which banks must settle or return checks, or be responsible for paying them. If the payor bank is not the depository bank, it must settle for an item by midnight of the banking day of receipt. If the payor bank is also the depository bank, the deadline is midnight of the next banking day following the banking day on which it receives the relevant item.

minimum contacts The doctrine of minimum contacts identifies the fewest number of contacts that will permit a court to exercise personal jurisdiction over an out-of-state defendant.

minority A term used to describe persons who have not reached the legal age of adulthood.

mirror image rule In contract law, the rule that an acceptance must duplicate the terms in the offer.

misdemeanor A crime less serious than a felony that is generally punishable by a prison sentence of not more than one year.

misrepresentation A false statement innocently made by one party to a contract with no intent to deceive. Also, in insurance, giving false answers to questions in an insurance application that materially affect the risk undertaken by the insurer.

misuse of legal procedure Bringing legal action without probable cause and with malice.

money order A type of draft that may be purchased from banks, post offices, telegraph companies, and express companies as a substitute for a check.

monopoly The exclusive control of a market by a business enterprise.

morals Values that govern society's attitude toward right and wrong.

mortgage A transfer of an interest in property for the purpose of creating a security for a debt.

mortgagee The party who lends money and takes back a mortgage as security for the loan.

mortgagor The party who borrows money and gives a mortgage to the lender or mortgagee as security for the loan.

most favored nation principle A principle that states that the World Trade Organization Nations must apply the same privileges, advantages, and benefits to all other member nations in relation to similar imports.

mutual assent In contract law, the state of mind that exists between an offeror and an offeree once a valid offer has been accepted and once the parties know what the terms are and have agreed to be bound by them. Also known as "a meeting of the minds."

mutual-benefit bailment A bailment in which both the bailor and the bailee receive some benefit.

mutual mistake See *bilateral mistake.*

mutual recession A condition in which both parties to a contract agree to rescind the contract and return to the other any consideration already received or pay for any services or materials already rendered.

mutuum (MYOO·choo·um) A loan of goods with the intention that the goods may be used and later replaced with an equal amount of different goods.

National Central Banks (NCB) Part of the European System of Central Banks, the NCBs are located within the member nations of the EU.

national standard A rule that allows a court to judge a health care provider's degree of care by determining how the same procedure is performed on a national basis.

national treatment principle A principle that states that the World Trade Organization Nations must apply the same standards to imports that they apply to domestic goods.

natural law theory A system of ethical thought that sees an unbreakable link joining the law and morality.

navigable airspace The space above 1,000 feet over populated areas and above 500 feet over water and unpopulated areas.

necessaries Goods and services that are essential to a minor's health and welfare.

negligence The failure to use that amount of care that a reasonably prudent person would have used under the same circumstances and conditions.

negligent credentialing Occurs if a hospital has retained a physician that the governing body of the hospital knew or should have known was incompetent.

negligent hiring The proprietor's liability for the hiring of an incompetent contractor who consequently harms an innocent third party while performing the hired-for work.

negligent retention The failure of a proprietor to dismiss an incompetent contractor after the proprietor has learned of the contractor's incompetence.

negotiable instrument A written document that is signed by the maker or drawer and that contains an unconditional promise or order to pay a certain sum of money on delivery or at a definite time to the bearer or to order.

negotiated rule making Occurs when an agency which is about to create a new rule or revise existing rules enters into a cooperative process by which all parties affected by the rule have a chance to shape the final form that the rule will take.

negotiation The transfer of a negotiable instrument in such form that the transferee becomes a holder.

next of kin Those who are most nearly related by blood.

no-fault insurance A type of automobile insurance that allows drivers to collect damages and medical expenses from their own insurance carriers regardless of who is at fault in an accident.

nominal damages Token damages awarded to parties who have experienced an injury to their legal rights but no actual loss.

nonconforming goods Goods that are not the same as those called for under a contract or that are in some ways defective.

nonconforming uses Uses of land permitted to continue even though newly enacted zoning laws no longer permit similar uses.

nondelegable duty A duty that the proprietor cannot delegate, or pass off, to another party.

nondisclosure See *passive fraud.*

nondisclosure agreement An agreement that requires employees to promise that, should they leave their employment with their present employer, that they will not reveal any confidential trade secrets that they may learn at their current job.

noneconomic compensatory damages Damages that result from injuries that are intangible and, therefore, not directly quantifiable. Examples include damages resulting from pain and suffering, mental anguish, and loss of companionship.

note A written promise by one party to pay money to another party. Also called *promissory note.*

novation The substitution, by mutual agreement, of another party for one of the original parties to a contract.

object code A computer program after it has been translated by the computer into a language that only the computer can comprehend.

obligee In contract law, the party to whom another party owes an obligation.

obligor In contract law, the party who is obligated to deliver on a promise or to undertake some act.

ocean marine insurance A type of insurance that covers ships at sea.

offer In contract law, a proposal made by one party to another indicating a willingness to enter into a contract.

offeree In contract law, the person to whom an offer is made.

offeror In contract law, the person who makes the offer.

open-end credit Credit that can be increased by the debtor, up to a limit set by the creditor, by continuing to purchase goods on credit.

open-price terms A contract for the sale of goods that is established even though the price is not settled.

operating agreement An agreement containing various rights, provisions, and powers that aid in establishing the bylaws of an LLC.

option In contract law, the giving of consideration to support an offeror's promise to hold an offer open for a stated or reasonable length of time. Also called *option contract.*

order bill of lading A negotiable bill of lading.

order for relief In bankruptcy law, a court's command that the liquidation begin.

order paper A negotiable instrument that is payable to someone's order.

ordinary life insurance See *straight life insurance.*

ordinary negligence Failure to use that amount of care that a reasonable person would use under the same circumstance.

original jurisdiction The authority of a court to hear a case when it is first brought to court.

ostensible authority Occurs when a hospital leads a patient to believe that a physician with staff privileges is an employee of the hospital.

output contract An agreement in which a seller agrees to sell "all the goods we manufacture" or "all the crops we produce" to a particular buyer. See also *requirements contract.*

outside party See *third party.*

overdraft A payment by a bank on behalf of a customer for more than the customer has on deposit.

paper data Data in a computer system that has been printed out in a hard copy for storage or filing in a conventional way.

par value The value that is placed on the shares of stock at incorporation.

parol evidence rule The rule that states that evidence of oral statements made before signing a written agreement is usually not admissible in court to change or to contradict the terms of a written agreement.

part performance An exception to the rule that contracts for the sale of land must be in writing. It applies when a person relies on an owner's oral promise to sell real estate and then makes improvements on the property or changes his or her position in an important way. Also called *equitable estoppel.*

partially disclosed principal A person, in a transaction conducted by an agent, whose existence is known to the third party but whose specific identify is unknown.

partnership An association of two or more persons to carry on a business for profit.

partnership at will A partnership in which any partner may leave without liability.

partnership by estoppel A partnership that occurs when someone says or does something that leads a third party to reasonably believe that a partnership exists.

passenger A person who enters the premises of a carrier with the intention of buying a ticket for a trip. One continues to be a passenger as long as the trip continues.

passive fraud A failure to reveal some material fact about the subject matter of a contract that one party is obligated to reveal to the other party and that intentionally deceives that second party leading him or her into a damaging contract. Also called *concealment* and *nondisclosure.*

past consideration A promise to give another something of value in return for goods or services rendered and delivered in the past.

patent A grant from the government that gives an inventor the exclusive right to make, use, and sell an invention for a period set by Congress.

patent infringement Any unauthorized making, using, or selling of a patent invention during the term of the patent.

pawn See *pledge.*

payee The party named in a note or draft to whom payment is to be made.

payor bank A bank by which an item is payable as drawn or accepted. It includes a drawee bank.

peer-to-peer networking Connections among personal computers joined to the same interconnected network. Also called *P2P networking.*

per se violation In antitrust law, a restraint of trade practice so serious that it is prohibited whether or not it actually harms anyone.

perfected The state of a security interest when the secured party has done everything that the law requires to give the secured party greater rights to the goods than others have.

performance In contact law, the situation that exists when the parties to a contract have done what they had agreed to do.

periodic tenancy A leasehold estate, or tenancy, that continues for successive periods until one of the parties terminates it by giving notice to the other party.

personal defense In negotiable-instruments law, a defense that can be used against a holder but not against a holder in due course of a negotiable instrument. Also called *limited defense.*

personal jurisdiction A court's authority over the parties to a lawsuit.

personal property Everything that can be owned other than real estate.

personal representative Executors and administrators of wills in states that have adopted the Uniform Probate Code.

persuasive precedent A previous case that a court is free to follow or to ignore.

phishing A cyberspoofing method that involves sending out phony e-mails that solicit buyers and, in the process, obtain credit card information, account numbers, passwords, and the like.

phonecam A mobile phone which can transmit video and record digital photographs.

physical duress Violence or the threat of violence against an individual or that person's family, household, or property that is so serious that it forces a person into a contract against his or her will.

picketing The placement of persons for observation, patrol, and demonstration at the site of employment as part of employee pressure on an employer to meet a demand.

pierce the corporate veil The doctrine holding shareholders of a corporation personally liable when they have used the corporation as a facade to defraud or commit some other misdeed.

plaintiff The person who begins a lawsuit by filing a complaint in the appropriate trial court of general jurisdiction.

plant patent A patent granted to someone who invents or discovers and asexually reproduces any distinct and new variety of plant.

pledge The giving up of personal property as security for performance of an act or repayment of a debt.

pledgee A person to whom property is given as security for a loan.

pledgor A person who gives property to another as security for a loan.

police power A state's authority to restrict private rights in order to promote and maintain public health, safety, welfare, and morals.

policy The contract of insurance.

pooling agreement An agreement made by shareholders whereby they promise to vote the same way on a particular issue. Also called *shareholder agreements* and *voting agreements.*

power of attorney An instrument in writing by which one person, as principal, appoints another as agent and confers the authority to perform certain specified acts on behalf of the principal.

precedent A model case that a court can follow when facing a similar situation.

preemptive right A shareholder's right to purchase a proportionate share of every new offering of stock by the corporation.

preemptive war A conflict waged when one nation attacks a sovereign nation in order to stop that nation from engaging in activities that the attacking nation has decided are against its national interests. Also called *preventive war.*

preexisting duty An obligation that a party is already bound to by law or by some other agreement. The party may not use this as consideration in a new contract.

preferred stock A class of stock that carries with it the right to receive payment of dividends and/or the distribution of assets on the dissolution of the corporation before other classes of stock receive their payments.

preliminary hearing A court procedure during which the judge decides whether probable cause exists to continue holding a defendant for a crime.

premium The consideration paid by the insured to the insurer for insurance protection.

prescriptive theory A system of ethical thought that describes how to come up with the values at work within a social system.

presenting bank Any bank presenting an item except a payor bank.

presentment A demand for acceptance or payment of a negotiable instrument made upon the maker, acceptor, or drawee by or on behalf of the holder of the instrument.

prima facie **evidence** (PRY·mah FAY·shee) Evidence that is legally sufficient to prove a fact in the absence of evidence to the contrary.

primary committee In bankruptcy law, a committee of creditors set up to work with a debtor in drawing up a reorganization plan.

principal A person who authorizes an agent to act on her or his behalf and subject to her or his control.

principal objective The main goal that the parties to a contract hoped to meet by entering the contract in the first place.

principle of honorable surrender A criterion under a modern version of the just war theory which requires a victor to accept the surrender of the enemy and to treat the defeated combatants with dignity and respect.

principle of repentance A criterion under a modern version of the just war theory which calls for a genuine expression of remorse for the death and destruction caused by war.

principle of restoration A criterion under a modern version of the just war theory which requires a victor in a conflict to act responsibly in rebuilding the defeated nation's physical environment, economy, and governmental structure.

private carriers Companies, not in the transportation business, that operate their own trucks and other vehicles to transport their own goods.

private civil trial Trials run according to the same rules of procedure and evidence as trials run under the official auspices of the court. In a private trial, the parties can hold the trial when and where they choose and they can choose the judge. Lengthy civil cases are well-suited to this approach.

private corporation A corporation formed by private persons to accomplish a task best undertaken by an entity that can raise large amounts of capital quickly or that can grant the protection of limited liability.

private information Reports on personal matters, family matters, sexual habits, employment records, medical data, and financial records. Also called *private-private* information.

private warehouser A warehouser whose warehouse is not for general public use.

privity In contract law, the relationship that exists between two parties to a contract giving each a recognized interest in the subject matter of the contract so that they are bound to that contract.

probability of success A criterion under the just war theory which states that a war must be waged only when there is a reasonable chance of success.

probate To settle the estate of a decedent under the supervision of a court.

product liability A law that imposes liability on the manufacturer and the seller of a product produced and sold in a defective condition.

professional An individual who can perform a highly specialized task because of special abilities, education, experience, and knowledge.

promisee In the making of a contract, the party to whom a promise is made.

promisor In the making of a contract, the party who makes a promise.

promissory estoppel The legal doctrine that restricts an offeror from revoking an offer, under certain conditions, even though consideration has not been promised to bind the agreement. To be effective, promissory estoppel requires that the offeror know, or be presumed to know, that the offeree might otherwise make a definite and decided change of position in contemplation of promises contained in the offer.

promoters The people who do the day-to-day work involved in creating a corporation.

property damage liability insurance A type of automobile insurance that provides protection when other people bring claims or lawsuits against the insured for damaging property such as a car, a fence, or a tree.

proportionality A criterion under the just war theory which states that the good advanced by the war must exceed the negative consequences of entering the conflict.

proprietor An owner, as of a business. The party for which an independent contractor works.

prosecutor An attorney that represents the government in a criminal procedure.

prospectus A document published by a corporation explaining, in simplified fashion for potential investors, the details of a stock issuance and the business making the offer.

protest A certificate of dishonor that states that a draft was presented for acceptance or payment and was dishonored.

provisional Not final.

proximate cause In tort law, the connection between the unreasonable conduct and the resulting harm. Proximate cause is determined by asking whether the harm that resulted from the conduct was foreseeable at the time of the original negligent act.

proxy The authority given to one shareholder to cast another shareholder's votes.

proxy contest A struggle between two factions in a corporation, usually management and a group of dissident shareholders, to obtain the votes of the other shareholders.

proxy solicitation The process by which one shareholder asks another for his or her voting right.

public accountant (PA) An accountant who works for a variety of clients but who is not certified.

Public Company Accounting Oversight Board A regulatory agency that is charged with the task of making certain that correct, unbiased, and comprehensive data finds its way to potential investors, so that they can make informed decisions about investment opportunities.

public corporation A corporation created by the federal, state, or local government for governmental purposes. Also, a large private corporation that generally sells its stock to the public at large.

public offer An offer made through the public media but intended for only one person whose identity or address is unknown to the offeror.

public policy The general legal principle that says no one should be allowed to do anything that tends to injure the public at large.

public-private information The association of two or more pieces of public information to create information that the victim considers private.

public warehouser A warehouser who owns a warehouse where any member of the public who is willing to pay the regular charge may store goods.

pump and dump scheme A scheme designed to lure unsuspecting investors into the trap of investing in what is essentially an empty shell, that is, a poorly financed corporation that appears to be more valuable than it really is.

punitive damages Damages in excess of actual losses suffered by the plaintiff awarded as a measure of punishment for the defendant's wrongful acts. Also called *exemplary damages.*

purchase money security interest A security interest that arises when someone lends money to a consumer and then takes a security interest in the goods that the consumer buys.

purpose In criminal law, the intent to cause the result that does, in fact, occur.

qualified indorsement An indorsement in which words, such as "without recourse," have been added to the signature to limit the liability of the indorser.

qualified opinion An opinion issued by an auditor saying that, as of a given date, the books of a firm represent its financial health; however, the auditor may qualify the opinion either because the firm is facing some uncertainty that might affect the company in the future, or because the firm has deviated from generally accepted accounting principles (GAAP) in some minor way.

quasi-contract See *implied-in-law contract.*

quasi-public corporation A corporation that is privately organized for profit but also provides a service upon which the public is dependent.

quid pro quo sexual harassment A supervisor's unwelcome advancement or suggestion to a subordinate to trade sexual favors for preferential treatment.

quiet enjoyment The right of a tenant to the undisturbed possession of the property that he or she is renting.

quitclaim deed A deed that transfers to the buyer only the interest that the seller may have in a property and that contains no warranties.

racial profiling The act of targeting a person for criminal investigation primarily because of racial or ethnic characteristics.

radio frequency identity device A tiny electronic tracking chip that can be implanted in any physical object from clothing to canned goods.

rational ethics A system of ethical thought that uses reason as the basis for making ethical judgments.

ratification The principal's approval of an unauthorized act performed by an agent or by one who has no authority to act as an agent. Also, an approval of a contract made by a minor after reaching maturity.

real defense In negotiable-instruments law, any defense that can be used against everyone, including holders in due course. Also called *absolute defense* and *universal defense.*

real property The ground and everything permanently attached to it including land, buildings, and growing trees and shrubs; the air space above the land is also included.

reasonable accommodation The quality of accommodation that allows a disabled worker to accomplish essential functions in the workplace without imposing undue hardship on the employer.

reasonable care The degree of care that a reasonably prudent person would have used under the same circumstances and conditions.

reasonable time In contract law, the time that may fairly, properly, and conveniently be required to do the task that is to be done, with regard to attending circumstances.

rebuttable presumption A disputable presumption that a defending party has the right to attack.

rebuttal The presentation of evidence to discredit the evidence by the opposition and to reestablish the credibility of his or her own evidence.

recklessness In criminal law, a perverse disregard for a known risk of a negative result.

Registered Limited Liability Partnership (RLLP or LLP) A general partnership in which partners are not jointly or severally liable for partnership liabilities caused by the act or omission of another partner or employee unless the partner had supervision over the other partner or employee.

registration statement A statement required by the Securities and Exchange Commission to indicate details about a business selling securities.

reg-neg See *negotiated rule making.*

regulatory justice A fair and balanced interpretation of the law that evolves from and is consistent with previous law.

rejection The express or implied refusal by an offeree to accept an offer.

release In contract law, a promise made by one party agreeing to sue a second party.

remainder estate A future interest in property when title is to pass to someone other than the grantor or grantor's heirs at the expiration of a life estate.

remitting bank Any payor or intermediary bank remitting for an item.

renter's insurance An insurance policy that protects tenants against loss of personal property, against liability for a visitor's personal injury, and against liability for negligent destruction of the rented premises.

renunciation A legal act by which a person abandons a right acquired, but without transferring it to another.

reorganization In bankruptcy law, a plan created by a qualified debtor that alters his or her repayment schedule and allows the debtor to stay in business.

request for admission A request made to secure a statement from a party that a particular fact is true or that a document or set of documents is genuine.

request for real evidence A discovery device that asks the opposing party in a lawsuit to produce papers, records, accounts, correspondence, photographs, or other tangible evidence.

requirements contract An agreement in which one party agrees to purchase all of his or her requirements of a particular product from another party. See also *output contract*.

rescission A remedy in contract law that returns both parties to a contract back to their original positions before the contract was entered into.

reserve funds Earnings from a business that are held in reserve.

respondeat superior (re·SPOND·ee·yat se·PEER·ee·or) The legal doctrine that imposes liability on the employers and makes them pay for torts committed by their employees within the scope of the employer's business. Literally translated it means "Let the master respond."

restraint of trade A limitation on the full exercise of doing business with others.

restrictive covenant A promise by an employee in an employment contract not to work for anyone else in the same field of employment for a specified time period within a particular geographical area.

restrictive indorsement An indorsement in which words have been added to the signature of the indorser that specify the purpose of the indorsement or the use to be made of the commercial paper, such as "for deposit only."

reverse mortgage A type of loan that allows home owners, over the age of 62, to convert some of the equity in their home into cash while retaining ownership of their home.

reversion estate A future interest in property when title is to return to the grantor or grantor's heirs upon expiration of a life estate.

revocation The calling back of an offer by the offeror.

revolving charge account A charge account with an outstanding balance at all times.

right intention A criterion under the just war theory which states that a war must be waged only if the combatant has the correct objective.

right of way See *easement.*

right-to-work laws State laws that prohibit labor-management agreements requiring union membership as a condition of getting or keeping a job.

riparian owners People who own land along the bank of a river or stream. They have certain rights and duties with respect to the water that flows over, under, and beside their land.

robbery The act of taking personal property from the possession of another against that person's will and under threat to do great bodily harm or damage.

role model ethics A system of ethical thought that examines people and their patterns of behavior in order to uncover examples of the proper way to act.

rule of contemporary ownership The rule that holds that shareholders must own stock at the time of the injury and at the time of the lawsuit if they wish to begin a derivative suit.

rule-of-reason standard In antitrust law, a doctrine that holds that a court should stop certain practices only if they are an unreasonable restriction of competition.

sale A contract in which ownership of goods is transferred by the seller to the buyer for a price.

sale on approval A conditional sale that becomes absolute only if the buyer approves or is satisfied with the article being sold.

sale or return A sale in which the buyer takes title to goods with the right to revest title in the seller after a specified period or reasonable time.

sales puffery Persuasive words or exaggerated arguments made by salespeople to induce customers to buy their product. As long as such comments are reserved to opinion and do not misstate facts, they are not actionable as fraud, even if they turn out to be grossly in error. Also called *puffery.*

salvage A reward given to persons who voluntarily assist a sinking ship to recover its cargo from peril or loss.

salvor A person who salvages. The law of salvage gives the salvor the right to compensation for assisting a foundering vessel.

satisfaction The agreed-to settlement as contained in an accord.

satisfactory performance In contract law, the situation that exists when either personal taste or objective standards determine the contracting parties have performed their contractual duties according to the agreement.

science court A proposed court that would act as a forum for disputes involving scientific and technological controversies.

scope of authority The range of acts done while performing agency duties. Also called *scope of employment.*

scope of employment See *scope of authority.*

S corporation A corporation in which shareholders have agreed to have the profits (or losses) of the corporation taxed directly to them rather than to the corporation.

screen display The audiovisual configuration that appears on the screen of the computer monitor.

seal A mark or impression placed on a written contract indicating that the instrument was executed and accepted in a formal manner.

second level domain (SLD) name Indicates the actual name, trade name, or other identifying mark of the institution, organization, or business using the domain name.

second mortgage See *junior mortgage.*

secondary boycott Conspiracy in which a union places pressure on a neutral customer or supplier with whom the union has no dispute in order to cause the neutral entity to cease doing business with the employer with whom the union has a dispute.

Secretariat The administrative bureaucracy of the United Nations.

Secretary General of the United Nations The chief administrator of the United Nations.

secret partner A partner whose identity and existence are not known outside of the firm but who can participate in the management of the firm.

secured loan A loan in which creditors have something of value, usually called collateral, from which they can be paid if the debtor does not pay.

secured party A lender or seller who holds a security interest.

security In secured transactions, the assurance that a creditor will be paid back for any money loaned or credit extended to a debtor. In corporate law, a money investment that expects a return solely because of another person's efforts.

security agreement A written agreement that creates a security interest.

Security Council The United Nations body that deals with international crises.

security interest A creditor's right to use collateral to recover a debt.

self-defense A defense to criminal liability available to defendants if they can demonstrate (1) that they did not start the altercation, (2) that they had good reason to believe they were in danger of death or severe bodily injury, and (3) that they used only enough force to repel the attack.

servant An outdated term signifying a person employed to perform services in the affairs of another and who, with respect to the physical conduct in the performance of the service, is subject to the other's right to control.

service of process The act of giving the summons and the complaint to a defendant.

servient tenement The property through which an easement is created or through which it extends.

settlement week An ADR technique where the court clears its docket of all business except settlement hearings.

severalty The quality or state of sole ownership of a single property.

sexual harassment A type of sexual discrimination.

shareholder democracy A theory of corporate management that favors making management more responsive to shareholders by giving shareholders greater voting power and by making it easier for shareholders to sue managers.

shareholder of record A person to whom stock has been transferred and whose name has been entered on the corporate books as the owner of that stock. Shareholders of record are entitled to vote, receive dividends, and enjoy all other privileges of being a shareholder.

shareholder proposal A suggestion submitted by a shareholder about a broad company policy or procedure.

shareholders Persons who own units of ownership interest called shares of stock in a corporation. Also called *stockholders.*

shelter provision A provision whereby a holder who receives an instrument from a holder in due course acquires the rights of the holder in due course even though he or she does not qualify as a holder in due course.

shipment contract A contract under which a seller turns goods over to a carrier for delivery to a buyer. Both the title and risk of loss pass to the buyer when the goods are given to the carrier.

shoplifting The act of stealing goods from a store.

sight draft A draft that is payable as soon as it is presented to the drawee for payment.

silent partner A partner who does not participate in the day-to-day business of the firm.

similar locality rule The rule that allows a court to judge a health care provider's degree of care by determining how the same procedure is performed at another hospital located in a similar locality.

Single European Act (SEA) A law that contains hundreds of directives designed to diminish the effects of trade obstacles among the nations of the EC.

situational ethics A system of ethical thought that argues that each of us can judge a person's ethical decisions only by initially placing ourselves in that person's position.

slander Any false statement that harms a person's good name or reputation made in a temporary form, such as speech, and communicated to others.

slight negligence The failure to use that degree of care that persons of extraordinary prudence and foresight are accustomed to use.

software contract A contract involving the sale or licensing of information in a digital format.

sole proprietorship A business formed by the sole proprietor. It is the easiest business organization to form.

source code A set of instructions that tells the computer what to do or how to perform a particular task.

source code escrow agreement An agreement in which the computer source code is deposited with a third party. Once the agreement is made, the code can be released only by following precisely outlined procedures, and usually only if both the buyer and seller agree to the release.

sovereign immunity The somewhat discredited doctrine preventing a lawsuit against government authority without the government's consent.

spam Unsolicited email.

special agent A person who is authorized to conduct only a particular transaction or to perform only a specified act for a principal.

special indorsement An indorsement made by first writing on the back of a negotiable instrument an order to pay a specified person and then signing the instrument. Also called *indorsement in full*.

special interest group control A corporate control theory that is based on the fact that because corporate decision making impacts special interest groups, those groups should participate in that decision-making process.

special jurisdiction The power of a court to hear only certain kinds of cases.

special warranty deed A deed containing express warranties under which the grantor guarantees that no defects arose in the title during the time that he or she owned the property.

specific performance A decree from a court ordering a contracting party to carry out the promises made in a contract.

speculative damages Damage computed on losses that have not actually been suffered and that cannot be proved; they are based entirely on an expectation of losses that might be suffered from a breach; the courts do not allow speculative damages.

staff privileges When a hospital grants physicians, who are not employed by the hospital, the privilege to treat their patients at that hospital.

stale check A check that is presented for payment more than six months after its date.

standard construction rule A theory of legal interpretation under which the court will determine the principal objective of the parties in the making of the contract.

state control A theory of corporate management that is based on the belief that because corporate decision making impacts upon more individuals and groups than just the shareholders and the managers, those corporate decisions should be made by an impartial group of corporate outsiders, usually government officials.

statute A law passed by a legislature.

Statute of Frauds A law requiring certain contracts to be in writing to be enforceable.

statute of repose An absolute time limit for bringing a cause of action regardless of when the cause of action accrues, such as a certain number of years after a defective product has been sold to an injured customer.

statutes of limitations State laws that restrict the time within which a party is allowed to bring legal action against another.

statutory agent An individual who is designated to receive service of process when a lawsuit is filed against a corporation.

stock acquisition The purchase of enough of the voting stock of a corporation to allow the buyer to control the corporation. Also called *takeover*.

stock certificate Written evidence of ownership of a unit of interest in a corporation.

stock dividends Dividends paid to shareholders in the form of shares of capital stock.

stoppage in transit A right of the seller, upon learning that the buyer is insolvent, to have the delivery of goods stopped before they reach their destination.

straight bill of lading A bill of lading that does not contain words of negotiability.

straight life insurance Insurance that requires the payment of premiums throughout the life of the insured and pays the beneficiary the face value of the policy upon the insured's death.

strict liability The doctrine under which people may be liable for injuries to others whether or not they have been negligent or committed an international tort. Also called *absolute liability*.

strike A stoppage of work by employees as a means of enforcing a demand made on their employers.

subject matter jurisdiction The power of a court to hear a particular type of case.

subject to the mortgage An agreement whereby the seller of real property that is already mortgaged agrees to continue paying the mortgage payments.

subjective ethics An ethical theory that holds that there are no objective or absolute standards of right and wrong.

sublease A lease given by a lessee to a third person conveying the same interest for a shorter term than the period for which the lessee is holding it. Also called *underlease*.

subordinate To place in a lower order.

subordinated mortgage A mortgage that is reduced in priority to a person holding a second mortgage.

subordination agreement An agreement made by holders of first mortgages to allow their mortgage to be reduced in priority to a person holding a second mortgage.

subrogation The right of one party to substitute itself for another party.

substantial performance In contract law, the situation that results when a party to a contract, in good faith, executes all the promised terms and conditions of the contract with the exception of minor details that do not affect the real intent of their agreement.

substantial similarity test A test to determine whether a work has violated a copyrighted work's integrity by determining whether the two are so like one another that an ordinary reasonable observer would have no recourse other than to conclude that the second was copied from the first.

substitute check A paper reproduction of both sides of an original check that can be processed electronically.

substitute transportation insurance Insurance that reimburses the insured up to specific limits for transportation costs while a car is undergoing covered repairs.

sui generis A law unto itself. An area of the law that has developed its own independent self-contained rules.

suitor A corporation or individual who offers to purchase the voting stock of a corporation with the objective of taking over the corporation.

summary judgment motion A motion that asks a court for an immediate judgment for the party filing the motion because both parties agree on the facts in the case and because under law the party who introduced the motion is entitled to a favorable judgment.

summary jury trial A shortened version of a trial conducted in less than a day before a jury. The jury's verdict is advisory only.

surebuttal A reply to the defendant's rebuttal.

surety One who stands behind executors or administrators and becomes responsible for their wrongdoing.

surplus Funds that remain after a partnership has been dissolved and all other debts and prior obligations have been settled.

survival statute A state law that allows a lawsuit to be brought even if both the plaintiff and the defendant are deceased.

takeover bid In corporate law, the offer to buy the voting stock of a corporation.

target In corporate law, a corporation that is the object of a takeover bid.

tariff based principle A principle that states that the only way that World Trade Organization Nations can regulate the imports of other nations is through tariffs.

teller's check See *bank draft.*

tenancy An interest in real estate that is held under a lease. Also called *leasehold estate.*

tenancy at sufferance A leasehold estate, or tenancy, that arises when a tenant wrongfully remains in possession of the premise after his or her tenancy has expired.

tenancy at will A leasehold estate, or tenancy, that continues for as long as both parties desire.

tenancy by entirety Ownership by husband and wife, considered by the law as one, with full ownership surviving to the living spouse on the death of the other.

tenancy for years A leasehold estate, or tenancy, for a fixed period of time.

tenancy from year to year See *periodic tenancy.*

tenancy in partnership Ownership in which each person has an interest in partnership property and is co-owner of such property.

tenant A person to whom real property is rented or leased. Also called *lessee.*

tenants in common Owners of an undivided interest in property, with each owner's rights going to his or her heirs upon death rather than to the surviving cotenants.

tender To offer to turn goods over to a buyer.

tender of delivery An offer by the seller of goods to turn the goods over to the buyer.

tender of payment An offer by the buyer of goods to turn the money over to the seller.

tender of performance An offer to do what one has agreed to do under the terms of a contract.

term partnership A partnership that is set up to run for a set time period or in order to accomplish a task of some sort.

termination by waiver The situation that exists when a party to a contract with the right to complain of the other party's unsatisfactory performance or nonperformance fails to complain.

term insurance Insurance that is issued for a particular period, usually five or ten years.

testamentary trust A trust that is created by a will.

testate Having made a valid will. Compare *intestate.*

testator (male); testatrix (female) A person who makes a will.

third party In contract law, a person who may, in some way, be affected by a contract but who is not one of the contracting parties. Also called *outside party.*

time draft A draft that is not payable until the lapse of a particular time period stated on the draft.

title The right of ownership to goods. Also, a subdivision of a code containing all the statutes that deal with a particular area of law.

top level domain (TLD) name The portion of the domain name that identifies the addressee's zone, for example, .com, .org, .edu.

tort A private wrong that injures another person's physical well-being, property, or reputation.

tortfeasor A person who commits a tort.

tortious bailee Any party unlawfully in possession of another's personal property.

towing and labor insurance Insurance that reimburses up to specified limits for towing and labor charges whenever a car breaks down, whether or not an accident is involved.

trade acceptance A draft used by a seller of goods to receive payment and also to extend credit. It is often used in combination with a bill of lading.

trade fixtures Items of personal property brought upon the land by a tenant that are necessary to carry on the trade or business to which the premises will be devoted. Contrary to the general rule, trade fixtures remain the personal property of the tenant and are removable at the expiration of the terms of occupancy.

trademark Any word, name, symbol, or device adopted and used by a manufacturer or merchant to identify goods and distinguish them from those manufactured or sold by others.

trade secrets A plan, process, or device that is used in a business and is known only to employees who need to know the secret to carry out their jobs.

transactions in computer information A contract whose subject matter entails the acquisition, development, or distribution of computer information.

transient A person who accepts the service of a hotel or other public accommodation without any obligation to remain a specified length of time.

traveler's check A draft purchased from a bank or express company and signed by the purchaser at the time of cashing as a precaution against forgery.

treason The levying of war against the United States, or the giving of aid and comfort to the nation's enemies.

trust A legal device by which property is held by one person for the benefit of another.

trustee A person who is entrusted with the management and control of another's property or the rights associated with that property.

tying agreement In antitrust law, an illegal practice that occurs when one party refuses to sell a given product unless the buyer also purchases another product tied to the first product.

unconscionable Ridiculously inadequate.

unconscionable contract A contract that is so one-sided that it is oppressive and gives unfair advantage to one of the parties.

underinsured-motorist insurance Insurance that provides protection against the risk of being injured by an underinsured motorist.

underlease See *sublease.*

undisclosed principal A person, in a transaction conducted by an agent, whose existence and identity are unknown to the third party.

undisputed amount An amount upon which the parties to a contract have mutually agreed.

undue hardship The amount of inconvenience beyond that which is required of an employer who seeks to provide reasonable accommodation for a disabled worker.

undue influence The use of excessive pressure by the dominant member of a confidential relationship to convince the weaker party to enter a contract that greatly benefits the dominant party.

unenforceable contract A contract that cannot be upheld by a court because of some rule of law.

unfair labor practices Improper employment practices by either an employer or a union.

unfriendly suitor A suitor of a corporation who intends to change management and shake up the corporation after its takeover.

Uniform Commercial Code (UCC) A unified set of statutes designated to govern almost all commercial transactions.

Uniform Computer Information Transactions Act A statute that establishes standards for digital information contracts.

Uniform Electronic Transactions Act (UETA) A model code that declares that if the parties to a contract have voluntarily agreed to transact business electronically, then the electronic contract that results will be just as legally acceptable as a paper contract.

Uniform Facsimile Signatures of Public Officials Act A law that allows use of facsimile signatures of public officials when certain requirements are followed.

Uniform Power of Attorney Act A unified set of statutes designed to govern all aspects of the durable power of attorney agency relationship.

unilateral contract An agreement in which one party makes a promise to do something in return for an act of some sort.

unilateral mistake In contract law, a mistake made by only one of the contracting parties. Unilateral mistake does not offer sufficient grounds for recession or renegotiation.

unimpaired class In bankruptcy law, a group of creditors whose collection rights are not impaired by a reorganization plan.

uninsured-motorist insurance A type of automobile insurance that provides protection against the risk of being injured by a motorist who does not have insurance.

union shop A place of employment where nonunion workers may be employed for a trial period of not more than 30 days, after which the nonunion workers must join the union or be discharged.

United Nations Commission on International Trade (UNCITRAL) A fraternity of thirty-six countries that seeks to cultivate the organization and integration of international law in relation to international trade.

United States Code (USC) A compilation of all the statutes passed by Congress.

universal defense See *real defense.*

universal life insurance A form of straight life insurance that allows the policy owner flexibility in choosing and changing terms of the policy.

unlawful detainer A legal proceeding that provides landlords with a quick method of evicting a tenant. Also called *summary process, summary ejectment, forcible entry and detainer,* and *dispossessory warrant proceedings.*

unqualified opinion An opinion issued by an auditor that indicates that the financial records of a firm are an accurate reflection of the firm's financial status.

unsecured loan A loan in which creditors have nothing of value that they can repossess and sell in order to recover the money owed to them by the debtor.

Uruguay Round Agreements (URA) The eighth round of GATT talks, lasting from 1986 to 1993, out of which the World Trade Organization and the Dispute Settlement Understanding were created.

usage of trade Any method of dealing that is commonly used in the particular field.

Used Car Rule A rule established by the Federal Trade Commission requiring used car dealers to place a sticker, called a *Buyer's Guide,* in the window of each used car they offer for sale. The sticker provides consumer protection information.

usury The practice of charging more than the amount of interest allowed by law.

utilitarianism A system of ethical thought that focuses on the consequences of an action.

utility patent A patent granted to someone who invents or discovers any new and useful process, machine, article of manufacture, or composition of matter, or any new and useful improvement thereof.

utility thinking A system of thought that focuses the consequences to one person or institution and then weighs the cost against the benefits of performing the action under scrutiny.

uttering The crime of offering a forged instrument to another person, knowing it to be forged.

valid contract A contract that is legally binding and fully enforceable by the court.

values A standard for determining what things hold central importance.

vandalism The act of willfully or maliciously causing damage to property.

variable-rate mortgage See *flexible-rate mortgage.*

variance An exemption that permits a use that differs from those allowed under the existing zoning law.

verdict A finding of fact by the jury in a court case; the jury's decision.

vertical expansion The joining of two companies that were in a customer-supplier relationship.

vicarious liability The concept of laying responsibility or blame upon one person for the actions of another.

video conference A conference that uses a televised connection to permit any number of people at widely diverse locations to discuss the details of a case.

void contract A contract that has no legal effect whatsoever.

void title No title at all.

voidable contract A contract that may be voided or canceled by one of the parties.

voidable title Title that may be voided if one of the parties elects to do so.

voting trust An agreement among shareholders to transfer their voting rights to a trustee.

waiver The voluntary surrender of some right, claim, or privilege.

waiver of premium An optional provision in an insurance contract that excuses the insured from paying premiums if the insured becomes disabled.

warehouse A building or structure in which any goods, but particularly wares or merchandise, are stored.

warehouse receipt A receipt issued by a person engaged in the business of storing goods for hire.

warehouser A person engaged in the business of storing goods for hire.

warehouser's lien The right of a warehouser to retain possession of goods stored in the warehouse until the satisfaction of the charges imposed on them.

warranty A promise, statement, or other representation that an item has certain qualities; also, an insured's promise to abide by restrictions, especially those written into an insurance policy. Also, an obligation imposed by law that an item will have certain qualities. Warranties made by means of a statement or other affirmation of fact are called *express warranties;* those imposed by law are *implied warranties.*

warranty of fitness for a particular purpose An implied warranty that goods will be fit for a particular purpose. This warranty is given by the seller to the buyer of goods whenever the seller has reason to know of any particular purpose for which the goods are needed and the buyer relies on the seller's skill and judgment to select the goods.

warranty of habitability The landlord warrants that the premises are fit for human habitation.

warranty of merchantability An implied warranty that goods are fit for the ordinary purpose for which such goods are used. Unless excluded, this warranty is always given by a merchant who sells goods in the ordinary course of business.

warranty of title A warranty given by a seller to a buyer of goods that states that the title being conveyed is good and that the transfer is rightful.

waste Substantial damage to premises which significantly decreases the value of the property.

Web conference A conference that is carried out on-line via the Internet using personal computers to permit any number of people at widely diverse locations to discuss the details of a case.

white knight A post-offer technique where a target company invites another suitor to outbid a hostile bidder. The second suitor agrees that it will retain the existing management.

whole life insurance See *straight life insurance.*

widow's allowance See *family allowance.*

will A legal document, not valid until the testator's death, expressing the testator's intent in distribution of all real and personal property.

will theory A theory of legal interpretation under which the court will look to see if the parties to a contact have freely assumed the obligations and benefits due them under the contract.

worker's compensation Worker protection provided for by state statutes that compensates covered workers or their dependents for injury, disease, or death that occurs on the job or as a result of it.

World Trade Organization (WTO) A corporate nucleus for the management of international trade relationships.

writ of certiorari An order from the U.S. Supreme Court to a lower court to deliver the records of a case to the Supreme Court for review.

writ of execution A court order directing the sheriff of a county to sell the property of a losing defendant to satisfy the judgment against that defendant.

writ of replevin A court order requiring a defendant to turn goods over to a plaintiff because the plaintiff has the right to immediate possession of the goods.

wrongful civil proceedings Filing a false civil lawsuit.

wrongful death statute A law that allows third parties affected by a death to bring a lawsuit only if the death is caused by the negligence or intentional conduct of the defendant.

wrongful discharge Exceptions to employment-at-will that give employees legal ground for lawsuits against employers who have dismissed them unfairly.

yellow-dog contract An agreement whereby an employer requires, as a condition of employment, that an employee promises not to join a union.

zoning law A local regulation or ordinance that restricts certain areas to specific uses; for example, areas zoned for residential, commercial, agricultural, industrial, or other uses.

Photo Credits

Case Index

Subject Index